A COMMENTARY
ON THE BOOK OF

JOB

E. DHORME

Membre de l'Institut
Emeritus Professor at the Ecole des Hautes
Etudes, Sorbonne, and the College de France

TRANSLATED BY
HAROLD KNIGHT

With a Prefatory Note by
H. H. ROWLEY

With a Preface by
FRANCIS I. ANDERSEN

THOMAS NELSON PUBLISHERS
Nashville • Camden • New York

Preface copyright © 1984
Thomas Nelson, Inc., Publishers

Published in Nashville, Tennessee, by Thomas
Nelson, Inc., Publishers and distributed in Canada
by Lawson Falle, Ltd., Cambridge, Ontario.

Printed in the United States of America.

This translation was first published 1967
© Thomas Nelson and Sons, Ltd. 1967

Library of Congress Cataloging in Publication

ISBN 0-8407-5421-3

PREFACE

When H. H. Rowley fostered the English translation of Edouard Dhorme's commentary on the book of *Job,* he reported an opinion that it was 'the finest commentary on any book of the Bible in any language' (p. I). No praise could be higher than that. Doubtless there could be other nominations for this prize, for we all have our favorites. But at that level of excellence there is room for several 'best' books, and comparison is pointless. Advances in biblical research since the French original was published in 1926 have dated this work. But it is not obsolete. Let us say rather that it has become a classic.

Two notable discoveries in particular have thrown Job studies into new perspectives—the Ras Shamra tablets and the Dead Sea Scrolls. The first set of documents come from a time when the writing of the Old Testament was in its beginning; the second set after it was finished. The Canaanite myths from Ugarit provide background for the language and literature in *Job;* the Qumran manuscripts—including an actual Targum of Job, to our great surprise!—throw light on the text in its later transmission and translation. Yet even in these two matters of philology and text-criticism, Dhorme's work remains indispensable for the serious student.

Of course, Dhorme has to be supplemented, sometimes revised, in the light of these later revelations. Some great commentaries on *Job* have been produced since Dhorme's—those of Tur Sinai, Pope, Fohrer, Rowley, and Gordis come to mind. How very much different these are among themselves! The greatness of the book of *Job* demands attention from many perspectives, but until someone does some of the tasks as comprehensively as Dhorme did for his day, we shall need his tome on our workbench. His shrewd grammatical observations are ignored by too many subsequent workers. His textual notes remain unsurpassed

I

for thoroughness and clarity. This is seen in his patient, detailed review of the versions and most in his full reportage of variant readings.

Topics in the study of Job

The study of a book such as Job proceeds on three distinct levels: (a) Close-up inspection attends to the minute details of the text, the grammar, and the meanings of individual words; (b) An overview attempts to perceive the organization of the book as a whole and to grasp its total meaning; (c) In between the minute and large questions the scholar must attend to the texture of the literary composition, using the chief tools of form-criticism and poetic analysis. The two parts of Dhorme's commentary manage the first and last of these three admirably.

Organization

The long section on 'Teaching' (chapter 8) reviews and sum-marizes the *content* and themes. The section on 'Composition' (chapter 7) analyzes the structure of the complete work. Here the major components of the book—Prologue, Dialogue, and Epi-logue—are recognized, along with the speeches of Elihu, the speeches of Yahweh in the whirlwind, and the poem of wisdom.

How are all these parts connected? Dhorme worked through the usual issues, listing all the diversity which points to multiple origins for the material. He arrived at the conclusion, on artistic and thematic grounds, that the major parts have a common ori-gin (p. lxxxv). He concludes similarly that the Yahweh speeches (chapters 38-41), to which he links the poem on wisdom (chapter 28) 'reveal a common origin with the poetic dialogue and the Prologue' (p. xcvi). His insight is worth quoting: 'Variety in unity will always be one of the conditions of beauty' (p. xcvi).

The speeches of Elihu are more problematical, as most scholars know. Dhorme's analysis of the numerous differences between chapters 32-37 and the rest of the book results in the judgment that here we have 'an author working on an already completed book.' Dhorme does not favor the view that the Elihu speeches are integral to the original work of a single author, nor that they represent a later revision made by the original author. But he condemns ('one of the masterpieces of brutal vivisection' [p. cx])

theories at the other extreme which find these chapters incoherent, intrusive, or disruptive. He affirms this revisor as 'a
new inspired writer' who supplements and completes the work.

Comparative literature

The backdrop for research on *Job* has been enormously expanded since Dhorme's time by the recovery of more literature
from the Ancient Near East. The affinity of Hebrew with
Ugaritic in Northwest Semitic is recognized by all specialists, but
the extent to which evidence from old North Canaanite can be
used to clarify *Job* has been vigorously debated. The most generous (some would say extravagant) use of such material was made
by Mitchell Dahood, and it is much regretted that his untimely
death prevented him from completing a major work on *Job*. See
the summary of characteristic observations in Anton C. M.
Blommerde, *Northwest Semitic Grammar and Job,* Biblica et Orien-
talia—N. 22 (Rome: Pontifical Biblical Institute, 1969).
Pope's notable contribution to the Anchor Bible represents
temperate use of Ugaritic evidence by a fully qualified specialist.
At the other extreme the tribute to be drawn from Ugaritic has
been downplayed by some scholars. Robert Gordis is wary, to say
the least. Instead of working upstream from the biblical tradition
to more ancient sources he prefers to look for clues downstream
in rabbinic materials (p. xviii).
Dhorme was thoroughly conversant with the literature of the
Ancient Near East, yet he made surprisingly little use of this
knowledge in his commentary on *Job*. His chapter on this topic is
less than one page (cx-cxi). However, comparative literature has
much to offer the student of *Job*. The book belongs in the setting
of ancient 'wisdom' thought. See Chapters IV and V of R. Gordis, *The Book of God and Man* (Chicago: University of Chicago
Press, 1965) and Section IV of the Introduction to my commentary on *Job* in *The Tyndale Old Testament Series*.
At what point can the most substantial entrance to the book be
achieved? What outside materials offer most help to philology?
Do we look at Ugarit or in the Talmud? The problem is compli-
cated. Many of the words used in the book of *Job* are very per-
sistent. Their careers may be traced from earliest attestation
through biblical usage down into ensuing commentaries. Some-

times their behavior is almost protean, and all along the way it
can be truthfully said, 'This is the meaning.' Such a mercurial
word does not lose its old meaning when it acquires a new one.
An old denotation may remain as connotation. And a genuine
potential in its artistic use may generate new associations, not
consciously intended by the author but quite legitimate for later
readers. In all this flux there is no such thing as *the* meaning, fixed
and definitive. *Job* is living literature.

Artistic texture

In between the lower levels of close work on language, grammar, style, and the higher levels of overall organization of the
complete book, there lies an intermediate zone of literary composition. This largely uncharted region of artistic presentation is
overlooked by Dhorme. Here we study the identity and structure
of compositional units larger than a verse or even a strophe. In *Job*
these are the individual speeches of one or more chapters. These
too have both fine texture and overall design, and the student
needs to acquire skill in observing from two perspectives—a
close-up inspection for the fine weaving of verbal threads; a dis-
tancing perception for the holistic, strategic placement of individual threads at various points in the entire fabric.

The systematic study of literary texture can bring another dimension to this task. Dhorme dismissed some previous work on
strophic structure with disdain—'this little game' (p. clxxxvii)—
but the problem is still real and awaits solution.

Dhorme's study of meter (chapter 11) does not advance a firm
theory. He echoes 'the melancholy admission of Budde'
(p. clxxxvi), admission of a failure to find 'the laws of Hebrew
versification.' The search for regularity becomes a vice when the
text is smashed or hammered into neater shape. Perception of 'a
certain licence' is a virtue in Dhorme, because it respects the text;
but it can also be an excuse for abandoning the search for the
system within which poetic licence represents legitimate variation.

The grammar of Job

Dhorme's commentary is essentially verse by verse. This
means that the larger connections which bind the verses into

longer units (speeches) are hardly explored. Yet even within such small units, much work remains to be done in syntax.

It is an almost universal approach among Old Testament scholars to learn their Hebrew from texts in standard literary prose. Indeed the grammars imply that the language of the Old Testament is uniform throughout. But as soon as we come to poetry we discover that it is quite different from the 'correct' Hebrew we learned. The innumerable differences between Hebrew prose and Hebrew poetry have been attributed to 'poetic licence,' or else the poetic texts have been judged 'corrupt' and corrected to the norms of prose.

It is not just a matter of special poetic diction. There is plenty of that, of course. More important, but less noticed, is the use of different grammar. Here the differences between poetry and prose are so substantial and systematic that one should recognize two distinct dialects.

It has long been known that archaic Hebrew poetry uses certain 'particles' sparingly, notably the article *ha-*, the relative pronoun *'ăšer,* and *nota accusativo, 'et/'ōt.* What has not been appreciated is the fact that this feature prevails in *all* lyric poetry (cult and wisdom) right down until the sixth century. There is a striking change during (perhaps not until after) the Exile. Deutero-Isaiah still follows this tradition; but Psalm 137 shows the new trend. [D. N. Freedman, 'The Structure of Psalm 137,' pp. 303-321 in *Pottery, Poetry, and Prophecy: Studies in Early Hebrew Poetry* (Winona Lake: Eisenbrauns, 1980). Originally in *Near Eastern Studies* in Honor of William Foxwell Albright (1971).]

Psalms, Job, Proverbs, Lamentations, and some portions of prophecy line up against the rest of the Hebrew Bible in having low frequencies for these 'prose particles.' In normal prose the count can be over 30 percent of words. It is usually 15 percent or over. In most poetry it is less than 5 percent of all tokens. In *Job* there are thirty-nine chapters containing poetic speeches. In thirty-seven of these fewer than 1.25 percent of vocabulary tokens are 'prose particles.' Twenty-nine chapters have lower than 1 percent. These particles, ubiquitous in standard Hebrew prose, are hardly used at all in this poetry. The two exceptions are chapter 28 (2.59 percent) and chapter 3 (5.05 percent). By contrast, these particles contribute 9.16 percent to the narrative portions of *Job.*

The significance of these statistical facts has yet to be appreciated. It is no longer possible to assume that Hebrew poets used the language of prose, but simply left out these three words, 'stripped bare of the definite article or the relative pronoun' (Gordis, p. 32). We must ask more carefully if they avoided constructions in which these particles would have to be used. If so, by what alternative devices did they show that a noun was definite, that a clause was relative, that something was an object? Furthermore, other words, notably prepositions and conjunctions, are rarer in poetry than in prose. In *Job* the contrast in the use of conjunctions between Yahweh speeches (9.7 percent) and narrative (19.5 percent) is astonishing. Except for the dialogue in the prose narrative, the use of prepositions overall is lower than average. One has only to think of the enormous amount of grammatical work which is normally done by such words to realize that completely different grammatical questions have to be addressed to texts which manage with a lower quota of them. An early pioneer in asking such questions is Dhorme. His treatment of each poetic unit as a single line consisting of two hemistichs (= a bicolon) can greatly assist us.

In most cases the legacy of Lowth is still with us. In his classic analysis he viewed each line (= hemistich or colon) of poetry as a 'sentence.' A bicolon consists of two sentences which say the same thing twice. It was assumed that each statement was grammatically complete. Often, of course, the second hemistich was seen to be incomplete. 'Incomplete synonymous parallelism' is one of the well-known categories. It was usually considered enough to say 'ellipsis'; something in the first hemistich was 'understood' in the second. In recent years there has been more awareness that an item in one hemistich may operate simultaneously in two hemistichs—i.e., a 'double duty' item. There is reluctance, however, to recognize such a function as retroactive (something in the second colon has to be 'understood' in the first; which is thus left in suspense until the second line completes it). Even so, such explanations have been invoked *ad hoc,* as a last resort, to solve an otherwise insoluble problem. In the eyes of many scholars, such results seem to be contrived and unconvincing. This is partly because they are still felt to be grammatically abnormal. A systematic theoretical treatment is urgently needed, as is demonstrated by the following examples.

1. In Job 4:6; 10:8; 19:23 Dhorme recognized *wĕ-,* ('and') 'within the proposition instead of remaining at the head' (p. 45). The dual example in Job 19:23 is particularly striking. Fohrer and Gordis pass over the phenomenon without remark. Their translations imply the removal of 'and' from within the colon to its beginning (an old solution, but too heavy-handed). Others have rewritten these lines extensively, thereby mutilating the verbal art. The text *as it is,* is grammatically irreproachable so long as post-positive 'and' is not ruled out of the language by the prescription of modern grammarians.

In Job 10:8 the postponement of the verb brings 'you dissolved me' into opposition with 'they [your hands] made me.' Dhorme's defence of this text and of its grammar is exemplary, and it raises a grave methodological issue. Much modern criticism is not working out the grammar and prosody from the text—that would be scientific—but rewriting the text out of a grammar and a metrical theory like a teacher correcting a schoolboy's exercise. Dhorme's instinct for retaining the text and his willingness to let grammar be descriptive (not prescriptive) can now be supported by observations on the artistry of the bicolon.

2. The new holistic approach is revolutionary in another particular. The old assumption was that parallels were synonyms (sometimes antonyms). When synonyms were not found, texts were corrected to improve the parallelism, or new meanings were invented to secure parallelism.

When the bicolon is viewed as a single (grammatical-semantic) construction, matching items in the two colons often turn out to be complementary. Two nouns in contiguous colons may be attributive, or coordinated (sometimes hendiadys), or even (perish the thought!) a discontinuous construct phrase. We have to study the grammar across neighboring colons, not just within single colons. Thus Dhorme appreciated the fact that in Job 19:25, 'The adjective ['aḥărōn] . . . is therefore an epithet which qualifies the go'ēl' (p. 283).

In a verse such as Job 11:7 it is obvious that the two parts of the dual name of God, 'ĕlôᵃh šadday, are spread over the two colons.

That is routine. But the other two parallels, *ḥēqer* 'depth' and *taklît* 'limit,' are both governed by the delayed double-duty preposition *'ad*. This settles the grammar of *ḥeqer*. The word is not instrumental ('Canst thou *by searching* find out God?'; AV). It is not construct ('the deep things of God'; RSV and many others). The preposition is often simply ignored. It is best to translate, 'Can you find God Shadday *unto* ultimate depth?'

A seemingly unimportant grammatical discussion has settled an important theological point. It is not that God cannot be found at all. Rather is it impossible to know everything about God. So the question becomes one about the legitimate limits within which humans are capable of exploring God. This point is crucial to the debate; for Job is strenuously pressing beyond the limits set by his friends, who are alarmed to see him venturing into fresh, and to them dangerous, territory.

3. The most spectacular trick played by Hebrew poets is to make grammatical constructions operate over quite a distance in the text. Double-duty items are only one aspect of this. They might sometimes receive their second application, not in a contiguous line, but in one at considerable remove. Some scholars, perceiving such long-range connections, have 'solved' the problem by shunting the related lines together. This is usually a mistake; it loses more than it gains.

For example, Dhorme correctly saw the affinity between Job 3:11 and 3:16, recognizing that the one *lāmmâ*, 'Why?' governs all four lines. But he needlessly moved verse 16 next to verse 11 (cf. NEB). Gordis (p. 36) rightly recognized the chiastic structure of verses 11-16, and left them as is; but he did not follow through by making verse 16 a double question. The insight of Dhorme (but not his error) and the insight of Gordis (but not his error) must now be combined to gain a full solution.

4. More serious is Gordis' argument that *wĕ-* in *wĕ'egwā'* (3:11) and *wĕ'ešqôṭ* (3:13) is 'a weakened pronunciation of the wāw-consecutive' (pp. 36, 37). Dhorme is on firmer ground—'these two verbs are again real aorists' (p. 32).

It is remarkable that the 'imperfect' as such is never used in narrative portions of the book; it reaches over 13 percent of tokens in Zophar's speeches. In contrast its sequential use is prominent in narrative (13.44 percent), as one would expect, but very sparse in the speeches. The sequential 'perfect' is hardly used anywhere, and even the use of 'perfect' for past tense is rare—rarest in Joban narrative! The 'imperfect' (preterite in many instances) is over 10 percent of tokens in most speeches; the perfect (mainly stative) is under five percent in most speeches.

Dhorme's instinct concerning the verbal tense was sound. It is another case where forcing poetry into the grammar of prose (as Gordis does with the verbs in Job 3:11-13) is unfortunate and unnecessary. Until our bearings on such problems are more secure, it will always be wise to go back and see what Dhorme said.

FRANCIS I. ANDERSEN
June 20, 1984

PREFATORY NOTE

Dhorme's commentary on the Book of Job is one of the great Biblical commentaries. I once heard it described in a lecture as the finest commentary on any Book of the Bible in any language. Certainly it deserves a very high place in any list of important commentaries. Yet it has long been out of print in the original French edition, and is difficult of access. For this reason it has been presented in an English dress, which will make its riches available to readers who would not use the French, as well as to those who are unable to obtain the original edition. The author was asked if he wished to make changes in the text, but in view of his advanced age he felt unable to make an extensive revision and preferred to leave it as it was. No account is therefore taken of work which has appeared since the commentary was written. On all the major problems raised by the Book of Job the author's judgment will be valued by every reader, as it has long been valued by scholars who have used the original work, and his massive learning is apparent on every page.

Dr Harold Knight is responsible for the basic translation of the work into English. I have harmonised the rendering of the translation of the Book of Job in one place with that found elsewhere (especially in cited passages in the Introduction), and have corrected slips, either in the original or in the translation, where I have noted them. In addition I have been responsible for all the Greek and oriental words used in the volume.

H. H. ROWLEY

CONTENTS

SYMBOLS AND ABBREVIATIONS

Ital. in translation of text indicates emendation of MT.
[ ] Omission of words from MT.

Contra. Against the view of.

א   Codex Sinaiticus (cf. pp. ccivf.).
א$^{c \cdot a}$, etc. Correctors of א (cf. ibid.).
A.   Codex Alexandrinus (cf. p. cciv).
B.   Codex Vaticanus (cf. p. cciv).
C.   Codex Ephraemi rescriptus (cf. p. ccv).
G.   Septuagint (cf. pp. cxcviff.); G(A), etc., see A, etc.
MT. Massoretic text (cf. pp. cxcff.).

Ald.   Aldine edition of Septuagint (cf. p. ccvi).
Aq.   Aquila's version (cf. pp. ccxiif.).
Arab.   Arabic version in Walton's Polyglot (cf. p. ccxix).
Arab. Baud.   Arabic version ed. by Baudissin (cf. pp. ccxif.).
Aug.   St Augustine (cf. p. ccxxii).
Bod.   Bodleian MS (cf. p. cci).
Cod. 23, etc.   MSS of Septuagint (cf. p. ccv).
Chrys.   St John Chrysostom (cf. pp. ccxif.).
Compl.   Complutensian Polyglot (cf. p. ccvi).
Eth.   Ethiopic version (cf. p. ccxi).
Gall.   MS Sangallensis (cf. p. ccvii).
Jerome.   Jerome's Latin version from Septuagint (cf. pp. ccviff.).
Memph.   Memphitic or Bohairic Coptic version (cf. pp. ccxf.).
Olympiod. Olympiodorus.
Sah.   Sahidic Coptic version (cf. pp. ccixf.).
Sam.   Samaritan Pentateuch.
Sangall.   = Gall. (q.v.).
Symm.   Symmachus' version (cf. p. ccxiii).
Syr.   Peshitta Syriac version (cf. pp. ccxviff.).
Syro-hex.   Syro-hexaplar version (cf. pp. ccviiif.).
Targ.   Targum (cf. pp. ccxviiif.).
Theod.   Theodotion's version (cf. p. ccxiii).
Tur.   MS Turonensis (cf. p. cci).
Vulg. Vulgate version (cf. pp. ccxivff.).

AHW.   Fried. Delitzsch, *Assyrisches Handwörterbuch* (1894-6).
Choix de textes   Dhorme, *Choix de textes religieux assyro-babyloniens* (1907).
CIS. Corpus inscriptionum semiticarum.
ÉRS.   Lagrange, *Études sur les religions sémitiques* (2nd ed., 1905).
Field.   *Origenis Hexaplorum quae supersunt* (2 vols., 1875).
Gesenius-Buhl.   *Hebräisches und aramäisches Handwörterbuch über das A.T.*
   (17th ed., 1921).
Gesenius-Kautzsch. *Hebräische Grammatik* (28th ed., 1910; English trans.
   by A. E. Cowley, 1910).

H. P. Holmes and Parsons, *Vetus Testamentum Graecum cum variis lectionibus* (5 vols., 1798-1827).

L'emploi métaphorique. Dhorme, *L'Emploi métaphorique des noms de parties du corps en hébreu et en akkadien* (1923).

MDVG. *Mitteilungen der vorderasiatischen Gesellschaft.*

OLZ. *Orientalistische Literaturzeitung.*

P.G. Migne, *Patrologia Graeca.*

P.L. Migne, *Patrologia Latina.*

RA. *Revue d'Assyriologie et d'Archéologie orientale.*

RB. *Revue Biblique.*

WZKM. *Wiener Zeitschrift für die Kunde des Morgenlandes.*

ZA. *Zeitschrift für Assyriologie.*

ZATW. *Zeitschrift für die alttestamentliche Wissenschaft.*

ZDMG. *Zeitschrift der deutschen morgenländischen Gesellschaft.*

Note. It is to be observed that the exegetical comment on each verse is preceded by a short *apparatus criticus,* on which the conclusions presented in the section of the Introduction on 'Text and Versions' are based.

BIBLIOGRAPHY [1]

Arnheim, *Das Buch Hiob* (1836).
Avronin and Rabinovitz, *Job, Commentaire en Hébreu* (Jaffa, n.d.).
Ball, *The Book of Job* (1922).
Baethgen, *Hiob* (1898).
Beer, *Der Text des Buches Hiob* (1897); also edition of M.T. in Kittel, *Biblia Hebraica*.
Bible [traduite du texte original par les membres] *du rabbinat français*, vol. II, pp. 399ff. (1899).
Bickell, *Carmina V.T. Metrice* (1882).
    Das Buch Job (1894).
Bigot, Article 'Job (Livre de)' in *Dictionnaire de théologie catholique*, fasc. lxv-lxvi, cols. 1458ff. (1925).
Bochart, *Hierozoicon, sive Historia Animalium S. Scripturae* (1663).
Budde, *Beiträge zur Kritik des Buches Hiob* (1876).
    Das Buch Hiob (1st ed., 1896; 2nd ed., 1913).
Buttenwieser, *The Book of Job* (1922).
Calmet, *Commentaire littéral sur le livre de Job* (1722).
Cheyne, Article 'Job (Book of)' in *Encyclopaedia Biblica*, vol. II, cols. 2464ff. (1901).
Crampon, *La Sainte Bible*, large ed., vol. III, pp. 404ff. (1901).
Davidson and Lanchester, *The Book of Job* (1918).
Davison, Article 'Job (Book of)' in Hastings' *Dictionary of the Bible*, vol. II, pp. 660ff. (1899).
Delitzsch (Franz) and Wetzstein, *Das Buch Hiob* (2nd ed., 1876).
Delitzsch (Friedrich), *Das Buch Hiob* (1902).
Dillmann, *Hiob* (4th ed., 1891).
Driver and Gray, *The Book of Job* (1921).
Duhm, *Das Buch Hiob* (1897).
Ehrlich, *Randglossen zur hebräischen Bibel*, Hiob (1918).
Ewald, *Das Buch Iob* (1836).
Giesebrecht, *Der Wendepunkt des Buches Hiob* (1879).
Graetz, *Emendationes in V.T. Libros* (1892).
Gray, *see* Driver.
Grill, *Zur Kritik der Komposition des Buches Hiob* (1890).
Grimme, 'Metrisch-kritische Emendationen zum Buche Hiob', in *Theologische Quartalschrift*, **80** and **81** (1898-9).
Hengstenberg, *Das Buch Hiob erläutert* (1870, 1875).
Hirsch and Wright, *A Commentary on the Book of Job* (1905).
Hirzel, *Hiob* (1874).
Hitzig, *Das Buch Hiob* (1874).
Hoffmann, *Hiob* (1891).
Hontheim, *Das Buch Hiob* (1904).
Houbigant, *Notae Criticae in V.T. Libros* (1777).
Kautzsch, *Das sogenannte Volksbuch von Hiob* (1900).

---

[1] Only modern authors are listed here. A chapter of the Introduction is devoted to older authors, including Patristic writers (cf. pp. ccxxiff.).

Kleinert, 'Das spezifisch Hebräische im Buche Job', in *Theologische Studien und Kritiken* (1886).

Klostermann, Article 'Hiob', in *Realencyklopädie für protestantische Theologie und Kirche*, 3rd ed., vol. VIII, pp. 97ff. (1900).

Knabenbauer, *Commentarius in Librum Job* (in Cornely's *Cursus S. Script.*, 1886).

Königsberger, *Hiobstudien* (1896).

Köster, *Das Buch Hiob und der Prediger* (1831).

Lanchester, *see* Davidson.

Landersdorfer, *Eine babylonische Quelle für das Buch Job?* (1911).

Laue, *Die Composition des Buches Hiob* (1896).

Le Hir, *Le Livre de Job* (1873).

Ley, 'Die Abfassungszeit des Buches Job', in *Theologische Studien und Kritiken* (1898).

Loisy, *Le Livre de Job* (1892).

Marshall, *The Book of Job* (1904).

Merx, *Das Gedicht von Hiob* (1871).

Michaelis, *Adnotationes in Hagiographos* (1720).

Olshausen, *Hiob* (1852).

Peake, *Job* (Century Bible, 1905).

Perles, *Analekten zur Textkritik des A.T.* (1895; 2nd series, 1922).

Posselt, *Der Verfasser der Elihureden* (1909).

Prat, Article 'Job (Livre de)' in *Dictionnaire de la Bible*, vol. III, cols. 1560ff. (1903).

Rabinovitz, *see* Avronin.

Renan, *Le Livre de Job* (5th ed., 1894).

Ricciotti, *Il libro di Giobbe* (1924).

Richter, *Erläuterungen zu dunklen Stellen im Buche Hiob* (1912).

Rosenmüller, *Scholia in Job* (1824).

Schlottmann, *Das Buch Hiob* (1851).

Schnurrer, *Animadversiones ad quaedam loca Iobi* (1781-2).

Schultens, *Liber Iobi* (1737).

Segond, *La Sainte Bible*.

Seyring, *Die Abhängigkeit der Sprüche Salomos Kap. i-ix von Hiob* (1889).

Siegfried, *The Book of Job* (in Haupt's Bible, 1893).

Stickel, *Das Buch Hiob* (1842).

Strahan, *The Book of Job* (1913).

Studer, *Das Buch Hiob* (1881).

Stuhlmann, *Hiob* (1804).

Thilo, *Das Buch Hiob* (1925).

Torczyner, *Das Buch Hiob* (1920).

Umbreit, *Das Buch Hiob* (1832).

Vetter, *Die Metrik des Buches Iob* (1897).

Voigt, *Einige Stellen des Buches Hiob* (1895).

Volz, *Hiob und Weisheit* (1921).

Wetzstein, *see* Delitzsch (Franz).

Wright (W.A.), *see* Hirsch.

Wright (G.H.B.), *The Book of Job* (1883).

INTRODUCTION

CHAPTER ONE

THE NAME OF THE BOOK AND ITS PLACE IN THE CANON

The Book of Job receives its title from the name of the principal character around whom the narrative revolves: אִיּוֹב (MT), ᾿Ιώβ (G), Job (Vulg.), ܐܺܝܽܘܒ (Syr.), أَيُّوب (Arab.). Similarly the Books of Joshua, Samuel, Jonah, Ruth, Esther, Daniel, Ezra, and Nehemiah took their title from the name of the hero or heroine whose deeds and words they related.

The inclusion of the Book of Job in the Canon of the Old Testament has never been the subject of any difficulty.[1] But the various traditions have shown discrepancies with regard to its proper position in the sacred collection. It figures of course among the *kethûbîm* or Hagiographa. But where precisely?

The oldest testimony of Jewish tradition about the order of the *kethûbîm* is furnished by the Babylonian Talmud. In the treatise *Baba Bathra* (14b) we find after the Prophets the series of the *kethûbîm* listed as follows: 'The order of the *kethûbîm* is: Ruth, and the Book of Psalms and Job and Proverbs, Ecclesiastes, the Song of Songs, and Lamentations, Daniel and the roll (*megillath*) of Esther, Ezra and Chronicles.' It will be noticed that this text does not yet group into a single series the five rolls (*megillôth*), Ruth, Ecclesiastes, the Song of Songs, Lamentations, Esther. On the other hand, the Psalms, Job, and Proverbs are juxtaposed and will continue to be so, as belonging to a tripartite whole. The Massoretes will give this group of poetic books a special system of accentuation, called, after the initial letters of the books themselves, sometimes אֱמֶת (אִיוב, משלי, תהלים), sometimes תָּאם (the order given in the Babylonian Talmud, as above).

---

[1] Theodore of Mopsuestia, however, according to the Second Council of Constantinople, denied the inspiration of the Book of Job (in P.G. LXVI, cols. 697f.). The allegations of Theodore are refuted by the Abbé Grandvaux in his edition of the commentary of Le Hir on the Book of Job (p. 110).

This passage of the *Baba Bathra* giving the list of the *kᵉthûbîm* contains further, in the form of question and answer, certain observations about the order adopted.[1] A belief which seems to have been fairly widespread was that Job lived in the time of Moses. Why then does the Book of Job not stand at the head of the *kᵉthûbîm*? Answer: 'We do not begin with a calamity!' To the further objection: 'But Ruth also describes a calamity', the answer is: 'That is a calamity which has a good result, as it is put by Rabbi Jochanan: "Why was she called Ruth? Because from her sprang David who refreshed [2] the Holy One, blessed be His name, with songs and praise."'[3] It is clear that the position of the Book of Ruth at the head of the Hagiographa was regarded as an anomaly. While the order Ruth, Psalms, Job, Proverbs, is maintained by nine of the principal MSS,[4] Jewish tradition attests other lists. Thus the Leningrad manuscript of 1009 begins the *kᵉthûbîm* with the following series: Chronicles, Psalms, Job, Proverbs, Ruth.[5] This is the order that is recognised by the Massoretic compilation עדת דבורים ('*Adath dᵉbôrîm*) dating from 1207. It is to be found also in some other manuscripts.[6]

According to Elias Levita (sixteenth century) two groups of manuscripts may be distinguished [7]: those of the *Sephardim*, who, faithful to the Massoretes, follow the order Chronicles, Psalms, Job, Proverbs, Ruth; those of the *Ashkenazim*, who maintain the order Psalms, Proverbs, Job, the five *mᵉgillôth* (including Ruth), Daniel, Ezra, Chronicles. The Psalms, followed by Job and Proverbs, open the *kᵉthûbîm* in the MS Or. 2201 (of A.D. 1246).

The first five editions of the Hebrew Bible begin the Hagiographa with Psalms, Proverbs, Job. Thus it is the order of the *Ashkenazim* which in the end was adopted. It should be observed that in this arrangement the Psalms follow the prophetic books immediately,

---

[1] The text is studied by Strack in 'Kanon des AT's' (*Realencyklopädie*, 3rd ed., IX, p. 745).

[2] On the verb used, cf. J. Levy, *Neuhebr. und chald. Wörterbuch*, II, p. 433 A, s.v. רוה, רוי.

[3] The observation of Rabbi Jochanan with regard to the name of Ruth is found again in another passage of the Babylonian Talmud (Treatise Berachoth, 7b).

[4] On these MSS and the order of the *kᵉthûbîm*, cf. Ginsburg, *Introduction to the Hebrew Bible*, pp. 6ff. As for the rest of the Hagiographa, these nine MSS are classified into three groups (ibid.).

[5] Ginsburg, op. cit., pp. 6f.

[6] Ibid., and Strack, op. cit. p. 756.

[7] Same references as in the two preceding notes.

a fact which recalls the order of the sacred books suggested by Lk 24:44, πάντα τὰ γεγραμμένα ἐν τῷ νόμῳ Μωυσέως καὶ προφήταις καὶ ψαλμοῖς.

The general conclusion which may be drawn from the facts set out above is that the three books—Psalms, Job, Proverbs—form an indivisible group in which the Psalms always stand first, while the positions of Job and Proverbs are interchangeable. In the earliest nomenclature known to us it is not this group which opens the list of the Hagiographa but the Book of Ruth. In that case our group occupies second place. When Chronicles figure at the head of the Hagiographa, this group comes next, and it is the Book of Ruth which follows it. The only exception to be found is the MS Arund. Orient. 16, which begins with Chronicles and Ruth and continues with the group Psalms, Job, Proverbs.[1]

The principle discernible behind the earliest arrangement seems to be of a historical nature. The Book of Ruth which narrated the story of David's ancestress must clearly come before the Psalms of that monarch. And of course the Psalms of David must precede the Proverbs of Solomon. The proper position of Job was a matter of perplexity, and we have seen how *Baba Bathra* discussed this point. The fact is, as we shall see farther on, that there was no agreement about the date of the hero, while the poetic form of the book, and the arguments and theories which it contained, all helped to place it in the same category as the Psalms and Proverbs.

If we now pass to the order followed in the Greek Bible we note considerable divergences, not only as regards the Hebrew Bible but also between the various Christian traditions.

The great uncials are not agreed as to the position to be assigned to the Book of Job (᾿Ιώβ). In G (B) it stands between the Song of Songs and the Wisdom of Solomon [2]; in G (א) at the end of the Old Testament and even after Ecclesiasticus; between the Psalms (and Odes) and Proverbs in G (A) and, probably, in the Codex Basilianus Venetus.[3]

Among ecclesiastical lists, the earliest, that of Melito of Sardis, preserved by Eusebius,[4] places the Book of Job between the Song of Songs and the Prophets (Isaiah, Jeremiah, the Twelve, Daniel,

---

[1] Ginsburg, op. cit., pp. 6f.

[2] Order adopted by Swete, whose text follows G(B) in *The O.T. in Greek*.

[3] In any case before Proverbs: Swete, *Introduction to the O.T. in Greek*, p. 202.

[4] *Hist. eccl.* IV, xxvi, 14 (ed. Schwartz-Mommsen, p. 388).

Ezekiel), Ezra concluding the series. Origen gives the Alexandrian
grouping, for his list belongs to his commentary on Psalm 1, which
was written at Alexandria.[1] Here Job figures after Ezekiel, the last
of the prophets, and is followed simply by Esther and Maccabees.
Athanasius, like Melito, places Job between the Song of Songs and
the Prophets, but begins the series of Prophets by the Twelve.[2]
St Cyril of Jerusalem mentions after 'the historical books' five
books which he calls στιχηρά ('in verse'): Job, Psalms, Proverbs,
Ecclesiastes, the Song of Songs.[3] It is interesting to note here the
recurrence of the Jewish grouping (Job, Psalms, Proverbs) but with
Job placed first, according to the exigences of a certain chronology
reflected in the passage of the *Baba Bathra* which we have quoted.
The description πέντε στιχήρεις, closely related to the τὰ δὲ στιχηρὰ
τύγχανει πέντε of St Cyril, was analogous to the designation of the
books of Moses by the term πεντάτευχος.[4] It recurs in one of the
catalogues of St Epiphanius,[5] who places these five writings in
verse immediately after the Pentateuch and in the same order
as that of Cyril. But elsewhere [6] the same Doctor will mention
the Book of Job between Joshua (which follows the Pentateuch)
and Judges (followed by Ruth), or again after Ruth (which follows
the Pentateuch, Joshua, and Judges) and before the four other
στιχήρεις (Psalms, Proverbs, Ecclesiastes, Song of Songs). St
Gregory of Nazianzus places the five βίβλοι στιχηραί,[7] that is, Job,
David (Psalms), and the three writings of Solomon (Ecclesiastes,
Song of Songs, Proverbs), after the 'historical books'.[8] The Apostolic
Canons [9] place the series Job, Psalms, the three books of Solomon
(Proverbs, Ecclesiastes, Song of Songs), after Maccabees and before
the Prophets.

In the *Prologus Galeatus* [10] St Jerome returns to the arrangement

---

[1] Eusebius, *Hist. eccl.* VI, xxv, 2. Origen claims to give the canon καθ'
'Εβραίους (ed. Schwartz-Mommsen, pp. 573f.).

[2] *Ep. fest.* 39, (P.G. XXVI, col. 1437).

[3] *Catech.* IV, 35 (P.G. XXXIII, col. 499).

[4] St John of Damascus divides the books of the O.T. into four Penta-
teuchs followed by two separate books (*De fide orthod.* IV, 17, in P.G. XCIV,
col. 1180).

[5] *De mens. et pond.* 4 (P.G. XLIII, col. 244).

[6] Ibid., 23 (P.G. XLIII, cols. 277ff.) and *Haer.* I, i, 5 (P.G. XLI, col. 213).

[7] *Carm.* I, xii, 5ff. (P.G. XXXVII, cols. 472ff.).

[8] Same designation as with St Cyril of Jerusalem.

[9] Canon LXXXIV.

[10] At the head of the translation of the Books of Samuel and Kings
(P.L. XXVIII, cols. 547ff.).

of the sacred books which is characteristic of the Hebrew tradition. After the five books of Moses and the eight prophetic books (Joshua, Judges, and Ruth, Samuel, Kings, Isaiah, Jeremiah, Ezekiel, the Twelve) he enumerates the nine Ἁγιόγραφα in the following order: Job, Psalms, Proverbs, Ecclesiastes, Song of Songs, Daniel, Chronicles, Ezra, Esther. It will be noticed that the order of the first five of these, with the Book of Job standing first, is exactly the same as that of St Cyril of Jerusalem and St Epiphanius in one of his lists (see above). It recurs too in Rufinus.[1] On the other hand, St Hilary [2] cites the book of Job at the close of the series, after Ezekiel (the last of the Prophets) and before Esther, an arrangement which recalls that of Origen (see above). St Augustine includes Job among the historical books, after the Paralipomena (Chronicles) and before Tobit, Esther, Judith, Maccabees, Ezra.[3] The councils of Hippo (393) and of Carthage (397) likewise place Job after the Paralipomena, but here it is followed by the Psalter and the five books of Solomon.[4] The letter of Innocent I to Exuperius [5] concludes the list of O.T. books with the *historiae* given in the following order: Job, Tobit, Esther, Judith, Maccabees, Ezra, and the Paralipomena. The decree attributed to Gelasius [6] also puts the *historiae* at the end of the list: Job, Tobit, Esther, Judith, Maccabees. If we add Ezra between Judith and Maccabees, we get the order of Cassiodorus.[7] The canon known under the name of Mommsen [8] and the list furnished by the Codex Claromontanus,[9] which give the number of verses contained in the O.T., are not agreed as to the place to be assigned to Job in the series. The former places Job after Maccabees and before Tobit, Esther, Judith, the Psalms, Solomon, the Prophets. The latter concludes its catalogue with Maccabees, Judith, Ezra, Esther, Job, Tobit. The Latin Church is no more than the Greek Church in agreement as to the place which befits the Book of Job.

The Syriac Bible places the Book of Job between the Pentateuch and Joshua, in such a way as to connect the hero of the narrative

---

[1] *Comm. in symb.* 37 (P.L. XXI, col. 374).
[2] *Prolog. in libr. Psalm.* (P.L. IX, col. 241).
[3] *De doctr. Christiana*, II, 13 (P.L. XXXIV, col. 41).
[4] *Enchiridion* of Denzinger (ed. 1900), no. 49.
[5] Ibid., no. 59.
[6] P.L. LIX, col. 168.
[7] *De inst. div. litt.* 14 (P.L. LXX, col. 1125).
[8] In Zahn, *Geschichte des N.T. Kanons*, II, pp. 143ff.
[9] Ibid., p. 157ff.

with the patriarchal age and Moses. The catalogue of Ebedjesu
(fourteenth century) puts Job at the end of the sapiential books,
but before the Prophets,[1] an arrangement which recalls that of
Melito and of Athanasius (see above).

We have seen that among the Jews the Book of Job was classed
with the *kᵉthûbîm* in a tripartite group sometimes found in the form
Psalms, Job, Proverbs, at other times in the form Psalms, Proverbs,
Job. The order Psalms, Job, Proverbs, recurs in one of the great
uncials of the Septuagint, the Alexandrinus. Yet another order,
Job, Psalms, Proverbs, no doubt chronologically based, was certainly current in Palestine, since it is attested by St Cyril of Jerusalem, St Epiphanius (in two of his lists), St Jerome, and Rufinus.
This order figures in the Apostolic Canons. Origen and St Hilary
are agreed on the arrangement Ezekiel, Job, Esther. St Hilary
mentions next Tobit and Judith as being annexed to the preceding
books by those who wished to obtain twenty-four books, i.e. the
number of letters in the Greek alphabet. Thus there emerges an
order Job, Esther, Tobit, Judith which will be replaced by the order
Job, Tobit, Esther, Judith (the names of the men preceding those
of the women) in the lists of St Augustine, Innocent I, Gelasius,
Cassiodorus, and the so-called Canon of Mommsen. This is the order
typical of the Latin Fathers. But the Vulgate of course maintains
the order fixed by St Jerome and finally sanctioned by the Council
of Trent.

[1] Assemani, *Bibl. Or.* III, 5ff.; Swete, *Introduction to the O.T. in Greek*,
p. 208.

CHAPTER TWO

ANALYSIS OF THE BOOK OF JOB

The hesitation shown by the various traditions with regard to the due place of the Book of Job in the Canon evidently springs from the subject treated and the way in which it is treated.

The subject is the story of a man who is 'perfect and upright, fearing Elohim and turning away from evil', and hence, according to the ideas of the time, happy in the midst of his family and his goods. We have here the picture of a veritable patriarch surrounded by his kin, exercising even priestly functions, since he offers burnt offerings in order to expiate the sins which his sons might have committed in the course of their daily feasts.

As the result of an intervention by Satan, who has secured from Yahweh permission to test the virtue of this upright man, misfortunes rain down, one after the other, striking first his property, then his family, and finally his body. In spite of all these trials, Job perseveres in his submission to God. His own wife is unable to shake his resignation.

Job is scraping himself among the ashes when the three protagonists of the drama arrive on the scene: Eliphaz the Temanite, Bildad the Shuhite, and Zophar the Naamathite. They are to be the interlocutors in the subsequent discussions.

Up to this point, events have been narrated in prose. When Job begins to voice his lament before his friends, however, he expresses himself in poetry. And the three interlocutors also will speak in poetry.

Thus we have three cycles of poetic discourses, each of the friends speaking in turn three times, and each time calling forth a reply from Job. In the present form of the book, the third cycle is incomplete, but we shall see that this section, in which the final replies of Bildad and Zophar have become mixed with the penultimate speech of Job, may still be restored to its essential and original purport.[1]

After the tenth and last speech of Job, some conclusion is ex-

---

[1] See below, pp. xlv ff.

pected. At this point however a new personage named Elihu intervenes to take up the glove which the three friends have dropped. He is introduced to us in a short prose introduction and then begins to speak in verse as did Job and his friends. He expresses himself in a whole series of monologues, at the same time being careful to address himself to Job and the earlier interlocutors in order to draw attention to his theories.

Elihu now fades out and Yahweh Himself enters on the scene. From 'the heart of the tempest' He speaks in the sublime accents of a poetry which far surpasses the strophes of the other characters. Every one is reduced to silence. Job alone stammers out a few words of humility and repentance 'on dust and ashes'.

The prose narrative resumes in an epilogue which shows how virtue is rewarded. The equilibrium between moral and material values is firmly restored. Job recovers his former prosperity two-fold. He will die in the bosom of his children and grandchildren. All's well that ends well!

This simple sketch enables us clearly to discern the component parts of the book: a prose Prologue (1-2), a lengthy exchange of poetic discourses between Job and his friends (3-31), a series of poetic monologues by Elihu preceded by a small prose introduction (32-7), the discourses of Yahweh in poetry, with a few comments on the part of Job (38-42:6), and the Epilogue in prose (42:7-17). It is clear that by far the longest section and the one which forms the real heart of the work is the discussion of 3-31 in which Job engages his friends. This discussion is moreover interpolated in a historical narrative apart from which it is unintelligible to the reader. Furthermore, it is extended first by the speeches of Elihu and then by those of Yahweh. Hence there is reason to study carefully what we might term the prose framework and the various poetic passages inserted into it. This study will facilitate for us an understanding of the composition of the book as a whole.

CHAPTER THREE

THE PROSE NARRATIVE

JOB AND HIS FAMILY. — If we leave out of account the brief introduction to the speeches of Elihu,[1] and the terse formulae introducing the comments of the various speakers in the debate,
the prose narrative is reduced to a Prologue (1-2) and an Epilogue
(42:7-17).

It is Job who is the hero of the story. He is not an Israelite, and
for this reason the author feels no need to give his genealogy, any
more than that of his three friends. It is this which has led to one of
the opinions quoted by the Babylonian Talmud,[2] namely, that Job
was merely a parable, a *māshāl*, and never existed: 'Job did not
exist and was not created, he was only a parable' (איוב לא היה ולא
נברא אלא משל היה). Such a radical theory has left some traces in the
Bereshith Rabba (§ 57) and in the affirmations of Maimonides (*Guide*,
III, 22) concerning the fiction which lies at the basis of the Book of
Job.[3] Attempts have accordingly been made to find in אִיוֹב, a
symbolic name meaning 'he who attacks' or 'he who repents'.[4]
The Talmud already puns on the name איוב, the opposite of אוֹיֵב
'enemy'.[5]

The name Job is in fact found outside Israel in the el-Amarna
letters, where it assumes the form *A-ia-ab*. It is a question of a king
of *Pi-ḫi-lim*,[6] which is Pella (Faḥil). He was a vassal of the Pharaoh.
His name was known only through an allusion in a letter.[7] We now
have a missive addressed by him to the king of Egypt.[8] Of course

---

[1] This little passage in prose (32:1-6a) has been given the poetic accentuation peculiar to the books of the Psalms, Job, and Proverbs (system
אמת or תאם; cf. above, p. vii).

[2] *Baba Bathra*, 15a.

[3] Wiernikowski, *Das Buch Hiob nach der Auffassung des Talmud und
Midrasch*, I, p. 28, n. 2 and n. 3.

[4] Cf. Comm. on 1:1.

[5] Allusion to 13:24. *Baba Bathra*, 16a; *Nidda*, 52a.

[6] *RB*, 1924, p. 9.

[7] Knudtzon, *el-Amarna*, no. 256 (p. 817).

[8] Thureau-Dangin, *Rev. d'assyriologie*, **19**, pp. 95f.

we have not here the Biblical character. But the name is the same, and it belongs to the West Semitic group of names, as is testified to by the uninflected form *A-ia-ab*. The transformation of *Aiâb* into *Ayôb* and finally into *'Iyôb* is paralleled by the changes of *qattâl* into *qittôl* known to grammarians.[1]

Not only is the name Job now known to us outside the borders of Israel but the Bible itself bears witness to a tradition woven around the figure of this hero. The second part of Ezk 14 (from v. 12) takes the case in which Yahweh punishes a country whether by famine, wild beasts, war, or pestilence.[2] In the midst of the land are found 'these three men' [3] whose presence will avail to save only themselves.[4] They are, Noah, Daniel, and Job. The prophet alludes to Daniel as the type of the wise man in the oracle against the King of Tyre (Ezk 28:3). Here he appears along with Noah and Job as the type of the righteous man, for these three will be saved by their righteousness בצדקתם (Ezk 14:14, 20). In the time of Ezekiel the personality of our hero had its character well defined. In the poetic part of the book it is precisely of his righteousness that Job speaks: 'I have held fast my righteousness (בצדקתי) and will not let it go' (27:6). Thus he belongs to the category of the righteous and on this score ranks with Noah. The prose Prologue says simply that Job is 'perfect and upright', but in the poetic part Job applies to himself the epithet צדיק תמים 'righteous and perfect man' (12:4; cf. Comm.), which is that which Genesis applies to Noah (Gn 6:9). Again it is in this light that Job appears in Sir 49:9, which makes allusion to the passage in Ezekiel: 'Ezekiel beheld a vision and there was revealed to him the various kinds of chariots, and he mentioned also Job the

---

[1]   Gesenius-Kautzsch, § 84e, 24.

[2]   The four scourges are summed up in v. 21. There is a striking resemblance to the Babylonian story of the Flood. The scourges which, instead of the Flood, might have struck humanity, are: a lion, a leopard, a famine, a plague (*Choix de textes*, p. 119). Cf. also Jer 27: 8-9 and 2 S 24: 13.

[3]   The description שלשת האנשים האלה 'these three men' is that by which the introduction to the speeches of Elihu designates the three friends of Job (32: 1, 5).

[4]   The case is different from that of Abraham, interceding in favour of Sodom and Gomorrah. God would pardon the accursed towns if only ten righteous were found therein (Gn 18: 23-33). In Jer 5: 1 God shows Himself prepared to forgive Jerusalem if a single righteous man can be found there. On the other hand, in Jer 15: 1 even if Moses and Samuel interceded for the people God would not reply. There follows the enumeration of the scourges which threaten the people; sword, famine, captivity; then, to tear to pieces the corpses, dogs, birds, wild beasts (cf. above).

prince, who practised the ways of righteousness.'[1] The Epistle of James insists rather on the patience [2] of Job: 'You have heard of the patience (ὑπομονήν) of Job and have seen the end which the Lord granted him (τὸ τέλος Κυρίου)' (Ja 5:11).

Tradition has not been able to resign itself to ignorance as to the ancestors of Job and the position of this righteous man in the genealogies. The Septuagint has at the end of the Book of Job (42:17) an appendix intended to supply details lacking in the Hebrew text. This appendix is a translation 'of the Syriac book',[3] i.e. an Aramaic text. Theodotion and the versions derived from the Septuagint also have this appendix,[4] which the version of Jerome and the Syro-hexaplar version mark with an obelus to indicate its absence from the Hebrew text. The Arabic version, which derives from the Peshitta, has this addition, but not preceded by any indication as to its origin. The point of departure is simply the identification of 'Ιώβ (אִיּוֹב) with 'Ιωβάβ (יוֹבָב) of Gn 36:33ff. This is stated formally in Job 42:17d: 'Ιωβάβ ὁ καλούμενος 'Ιώβ.[5]

We translate here the passage of the Septuagint which supplies us with information as to what was said concerning the person of Job. 'It appears from the Syriac book that he (Job) lived in the land of Uṣ, on the confines of Idumaea and Arabia. Previously his name was Jobab. After taking an Arab woman to wife he gave birth to a son whose name was Ennon ('Εννών). His father was Zerah

---

[1] The Greek version had interpreted אִיּוֹב by אִיב, ἐχθρῶν, ἐχθροῦ. Already in 1858 Geiger had recognised that the original must have borne the name of Job (cf. Renan, *Le Livre de Job*, 5th ed., p. xxix). Hypothesis brilliantly confirmed by the discovery of the Hebrew text.

[2] It is from the same point of view that the Vulgate compares the situation of Tobit with that of Job: *ut posteris daretur exemplum patientiae ejus, sicut et sancti Job* (To 2:12). A further allusion to the Book of Job in the Vulg. of To 2:15. These allusions are not found either in the Greek texts or in the ancient Latin.

[3] Cf. Comm. on 42:17.

[4] The Greek text in the ed. of Swete, at the end of the Book of Job. V. 17, thus excessively enlarged, is divided by the letters of the alphabet.

[5] Conversely, we have the equivalence of Jobab with Job in the margin of the cursive k (HP 58) and the anonymous chronicle edited by Lagarde: cf. the large edition of the Cambridge Septuagint (Gn 36: 33). It should be noted that the equivalence Jobab-Job is much easier in Greek than in Hebrew or Aramaic. The two latter languages maintain the full value of the initial consonants א (אִיּוֹב) and י (יוֹבָב), while in both cases Greek transcribes the initial letters ιωβ. Hence it is probably a Greek tradition which later passed into the 'Syriac book' of Job 42: 17. The apocryphal writing known as the *Testament of Job* also identifies Job and Jobab.

(Ζάρε, A Ζάρεθ), descended from Esau, and his mother was Bosorras (Βοσόρρας, A Βοσσόρας), so that he was the fifth from Abraham.' There then follows the list of the ancient kings of Edom on the lines of Gn 36:31-5. 'And these are the kings which reigned in Edom, a country which he too governed.' This passage adds nothing to the text of Genesis. Finally come the names and the titles of the three friends who visited Job. They are described in the same terms as in Job 2:11, but it is added that Eliphaz was 'of the sons of Esau' (τῶν 'Ησαῦ υἱῶν). Codex Alexandrinus adds that Teman (Θαιμάν), the son of Eliphaz, was the chief of Idumaea.[1]

Thus it was as a result of a confusion between Job and Jobab that the genealogy of our hero was forged, and that he came to be classed among the chiefs of Esau. Although the addition of the Septuagint was indeed utilised by Aristeas the historian,[2] it did not easily establish a position in the Greek Bible, since we learn from Olympiodorus [3] that some scholars rejected the conclusion of the Greek text, from γέγραπται δέ (cf. Comm. on 42:17), as not being τῆς ἱερᾶς Γραφῆς. St Jerome protests against the conclusions drawn from this appendix, on the grounds that the words it contains are not found in the Hebrew books: *in hebraeis voluminibus non habentur*.[4]

Tradition was no more able to remain silent on the subject of Job's wife than on his ancestors; her intervention, moreover, is intimated in the prose Prologue (2:9-10). The Targum on 2:9 calls her Dinah (דִּינָה). Her identification as the daughter of Jacob had as its consequence the dating of the story of Job in the period of the great patriarch.[5] The reason for the identification is simply an

---

[1] Then the same MS repeats the indications of the opening of the appendix with regard to the country of Job. But, instead of 'on the confines of Idumaea and Arabia', it has ἐπὶ τῶν ὁρίων τοῦ Εὐφρατοῦ 'on the borders of the Euphrates'. After the mention of Zareth, father of Jobab, it adds further: ἐξ ἀνατολῶν ἡλίου 'of the East', which is inspired by 1:3.

[2] Cited by Eusebius in *Praep. evang.* IX, 25 (P.G. XXI, col. 728). The confusion which, in Aristeas, gives βασσάρας (= βασσόρας) as the wife of Esau and thus makes of Esau the father of Job does not necessarily rest on a wrong quotation of Alexander Polyhistor but might come from a wrong understanding of the appendix of the Septuagint (contra Freudenthal, who thinks that Aristeas is the source of the appendix): cf. Schürer, *Geschichte des jüd. Volkes*, 3rd ed., III, pp. 356f.

[3] *In beat. Job*, XLII, ii (P.G. XCIII, col. 460).

[4] *Quaest. in Genesim*, XXXI, 20 (P.L. XXIII, col. 971).

[5] According to R. Abba (Jerusalem Talmud, *Sota*, V, 5, trans. Schwab,

association [1] of the word נְבָלוֹת in Job 2:10 with נְבָלָה in Gn 34:7. The apocryphal *Testament of Job* gives Job's wife the name of Sitis.[2] This same document places a whole speech [3] in her mouth. The Septuagint provides the basis for this amplification, for it contains a lengthy addition, Greek in origin,[4] to 2:9. It was evidently felt that the few words given to Job's wife in 2:9 were inadequate. Hence the following speech: 'For how long will you exercise patience, saying: "See, I will persevere a little longer, waiting and hoping for my redemption"? For consider, the memory of you has vanished from the earth, your sons and your daughters are no more, those who were the pains and the travail of my womb, and for whom I exhausted myself in vain. As for you, there you sit, your body rotting amid worms, and spending the nights in the open air. While I, wandering about a slave, roaming [5] restlessly hither and thither, from house to house, await the hour of sunset that I may rest from my weariness and from the sorrows which now press upon me.' Then follows the translation of the Hebrew: 'Curse God and die!'

Legend was more restrained on the subject of Job's children. Sons and daughters had perished in one of the catastrophes of the Prologue. As for the three daughters who came to cheer the hearth of the righteous man after his trials, there was no need to invent their names since these have been preserved in the Epilogue. It was felt to be sufficient, in the *Testament of Job*, to picture them at the bedside of their dying father, and to attribute to them symbolic words and actions.[6] The name of one of them 'horn of cosmetic paint' had been translated in the Septuagint as 'horn of Amalthea' (Ἀμαλθείας κέρας). This mythological allusion shocked Theodore

VII, p. 289). Cf. *Genesis rabba*, XIX, 12 and LVII, 4 (Wiernikowski, op. cit., p. 26, n. 2).

[1] Treatise *Sota*, V, 5.

[2] Cf. M. R. James, *Old Testament Legends*, p. 93. French translation of the *Testament of Job* (following the Greek text ed. by Cardinal Mai) in the *Dictionnaire des Apocryphes* of Migne, II, cols. 403ff. Cf. *Dictionnaire de la Bible*, III, col. 1578.

[3] Ibid.

[4] A certain number of Greek words betray a vocabulary quite different from that of the Septuagint translation. In particular the words λάτρις, μόχθος, αἴθριος, διανυκτερεύειν, πλανῆτις, εἰς τὸ κενόν; cf. Gray, *Job* (Introduction, p. lxxiii, n. 2).

[5] According to Codex Alexandrinus.

[6] M. R. James, op. cit., pp. 100ff. Migne, *Dict. des Apocryphes*, II, cols. 417ff.

of Mopsuestia, who, according to one of the Councils of Constantinople, protested against the notion that the saintly Job should have been capable of giving such a name to one of his daughters.[1]

Finally, it was thought necessary to give Job a brother who was called either Nachor or Nereus, according as Jewish or Greek nomenclature prevailed.[2]

THE PERIOD OF JOB.—We have seen that the restraint of the Bible on the subject of Job and his family did not satisfy tradition. What is certain is that the 'righteous and perfect man', the man who was 'perfect and upright', did not belong to the lineage of Israel and could not even be fitted into the great genealogical patterns which comprehended the whole history of humanity. Is it possible at least to determine the epoch in which he lived? Again it is in the prose narrative and not in the later legendary accretions that we must seek an answer.

We should, moreover, be sadly disappointed if we sought information on the subject from Jewish tradition. The Jerusalem Talmud handles the matter *ex professo* in the Treatise *Sota* V, 5 (trans. Schwab, VII, pp. 288f.), and the opinions of succeeding rabbis variously locate Job in the period of Abraham, of Jacob, of the twelve chiefs of the tribes, of the entry into Egypt, of the Judges, of the Queen of Sheba, of the Babylonians, of Ahasuerus, of the return from exile; so that eventually Rabbi Simon ben Laqish adopted the thesis that the figure of Job was purely parabolic.[3] Such a clash of opinions sprang from exegetic subtleties and artificial associations.

What seems clear, however, is that the period which the sacred author had in mind was that of the patriarchs. The resemblance is striking between the description of the wealth of Job as given in 1:3 and that of the prosperity of Isaac in Gn 26:13-14. Job belongs to the class of great cattle owners. To show how the blessing of Yahweh multiplies the herds of the righteous, Satan uses the same terms as does Jacob in referring to the abundant increase in the cattle of Laban.[4] As in the time of the patriarchs, it is the father of the family who offers sacrifices for his kin (1:5) and any one may sacrifice victims (42:8). The content of the sacrifice, seven bulls

---

[1] P.G. LXVI, col. 697.
[2] *Testament of Job*, in the works quoted above.
[3] Above. Cf. Wiernikowski, op. cit., p. 28, n. 2.
[4] Compare 1:10 with Gn 30:29-30.

and seven rams (42:8), is exactly the same as in the case of the sacrifices offered on the high place by Balak and Balaam (Nu 23:1ff.). It is the cult of nomads. Like Abraham in the episode of Abimelech (Gn 20:7), Job himself intercedes for his friends (42:8). The currency is the *kesîṭāh* (קְשִׂיטָה) (42:11), just as in the time of Jacob (Gn 33:19; Jos 24:32). After the restoration of his fortunes Job lived for a hundred and forty years, which enabled him to see his sons' sons up to the fourth generation (42:16). The patriarch Joseph lived for only a hundred and ten years, and saw his sons' sons only up to the third generation (Gn 50:23). We should notice that the generation forms roughly the same unit in both cases: rather more than thirty-six years for Joseph, thirty-five for Job. Finally the death of Job is described (42:17) in exactly the same terms as are used for the deaths of Abraham (Gn 25:8; cf. Samaritan and the Septuagint) and of Isaac (Gn 35:29). Everything reveals as the context of Job's story the period and the atmosphere in which are unfolded the vicissitudes in the lives of the great ancestors, Abraham, Isaac, and Jacob. But the essential difference is that Job does not belong to the same race. He is not a descendant of Abraham and he does not live in the land of Canaan. We shall now attempt to discover in what country the inspired author situates his hero.

THE COUNTRY OF JOB.—As we showed in a former essay,[1] there are two conflicting traditions with regard to the situation of Job's country, which the Bible calls the 'land of Uṣ'. The one locates this country in the Hauran or Trachonitis, the other in Idumaea or Arabia, more precisely along the frontier between the two. In short, with reference to Palestine, the land of Uṣ is to be sought towards the northeast or towards the south. In favour of which are we to decide?

The geographical name עוּץ is well transcribed in Targ., Syr., Arab. In the Septuagint it is translated as Αὐσῖτις, Αὐσεῖτις, which represents a Hellenisation of the Hebrew word,[2] while in the Vulgate it is rendered *Hus*. As the name of a country עוּץ recurs in Jer 25:20, where are mentioned 'all the kings of the land of עוּץ' (the name עוּץ preceded by the article); it appears too in La 4:21, where the 'daughter of Edom' is described as dwelling in the 'land of עוּץ', בארץ עוץ as in Job 1:1. By an error of haplography the Septuagint

---

[1] *RB*, 1911, pp. 102ff.
[2] In 32:2, the Septuagint adds τῆς Αὐσείτιδος χώρας after רם.

omits to mention all the kings of the land of Uṣ of Jer 25:20. It is interesting to see that the Vulgate translates by *terrae Ausitidis*, parallel to the Septuagint's rendering of Job 1:1 as ἐν χώρᾳ τῇ Αὐσίτιδι. In La 4:21 Vulg. returns to its translation *in terra Hus* (Job 1:1), but the Septuagint fails to translates עוץ, which is however faithfully rendered by Targ. and Syr.

The text of La 4:21 is categorical with regard to the location of the land of Uṣ. Since the daughter of Edom dwells there, it is evidently a question of a country identifiable with Idumaea or including it. This country figures in the enumeration of Jer 25:19ff., where the peoples of the south are mentioned. In fact it is after 'Pharaoh, King of Egypt' and before 'all the kings of the land of the Philistines' that we find 'all the kings of the land of Uṣ'. Coming to the Philistine coast, the prophet mentions the four big towns (Ashkelon, Gaza, Ekron, Ashdod), then returns to the south with Edom, and passes to the east with Moab and Ammon (Jer 25:20-1). Only at the close of his enumeration does he arrive in Phoenicia (Jer 25:22), to go south again immediately towards Arabia and the desert (23-4).

Thus the Biblical texts suggest the south, around Idumaea. One of the characters in Genesis who bears the name עוץ is presented as the son of Dishan (Gn 36:28), who is classed among the 'sons of Seir, who are chiefs of the Horites (21) in the land of Edom'. The name שֵׂעִיר denotes a quite considerable district, called in the el-Amarna letters *Mâtât Šeri* ('the regions of Seir').[1] It is a question of the whole stretch of land which extends from the south of the Dead Sea to the Elanitic Gulf. This is indeed the country of the Horites [2] or Troglodytes (Gn 14:6) who were supplanted by the descendants of Esau or Edom (Gn 32:4; Dt 2:4-8, 12; Jg 5:4). The relation between Uṣ and Seir confirms the relation between the land of Uṣ and that of Edom in La 4:21. Let us note further that the sequence 'all the kings of the land of Uṣ' and 'all the kings of the Philistines' of Jer 25:20-1 has a complement in Sir 50:26, 'the inhabitants of Seir and the Philistines'.

Hence we are constantly brought back to Edom as the location of the land of Uṣ. And the appendix of the Septuagint to which

---

[1] *RB*, 1908, p. 517.
[2] From the word חוֹר 'hole' has been formed the word חֹרִי. It is interesting to note that in the poetic part of Job (30:6) allusion is made to those who live by the side of the torrents, 'in the holes of the earth and the rocks'.

allusion was made above [1] in fact locates the country of Job 'on the borders of Idumaea and Arabia'. We find the same indication in the itinerary of Etheria: *in terra Ausitidi, in finibus Idumeae et Arabiae*.[2] The Αἰσίται of Ptolemy,[3] whose name is perhaps a relic of Αὐσίται ('dwellers in Ausitis'), are a tribe of Arabia. Let us notice again that the Arabic name of Esau is عيص or عيصو, and that there is a correlation with עוץ and עיץ. According to St John Chrysostom [4] the dunghill of Job was shown in Arabia. The commentary of Isho'dad (on Job 1:1) localises the land of Uṣ in Arabia.

In Gn 22:21 we find mentioned another personage of the name of עוץ described as the first born of the sons of Nahor. His brother is בּוּז. In ch. 25 of Jeremiah, quoted above, the town of בּוּז is mentioned after דְּדָן and תֵּימָא, with which it forms a group (Jer 25:23). The town of Dedan is the oasis of el-'Ela,[5] that of Tema the oasis of the same name. Hence it is in the region northnorthwest of the Arabian peninsula that the town of Buz is situated, and thus we are near the borders of Arabia and Idumaea. Now, it so happens that Assyrian inscriptions know a land of Bâzu adjacent to the Jauf in the south, thus bringing us into the area of Buz.[6] It is quite likely therefore that the localities of Buz and Bâzu are the same. All the more as adjacent to the district of Bâzu is that of Ḥazu,[7] in which we may recognise the Biblical name חֲזוֹ, who ranks among the sons of Nahor in the list of Gn 22:22, which opens with עוץ and בּוּז. Hence it would seem that the areas of Uṣ and Buz form a link between the Aramaean, Edomite, and Arabic regions. And it is interesting to note that the Nabataeans, who later occupied these areas, represent a mixture of the two great civilisations, those of Syria and Arabia.

The text which has been of most influence in suggesting Syria and especially the Hauran [8] as the land of Uṣ is Gn 10:23, where the name עוץ is attributed to the first born of Aram. No doubt the

---

[1] P. xvii.
[2] Ed. Geyer, p. 56.
[3] *Geogr.* V, xix, 2.
[4] On Job 2:8.
[5] Jaussen and Savignac, *RB*, 1910, pp. 525ff.
[6] *RB*, 1911, pp. 208f.
[7] Ibid.
[8] Especially since Wetzstein (cf. Budde, *Das Buch Hiob*, 2nd ed., pp. xviii f.).

brothers of this personage, namely חוּל, גֶּתֶר, and מַשׁ, would suggest rather, according to geographic equivalences,[1] northern Mesopotamia. But a legend, the echo of which persists in Josephus,[2] had it that Οὔσης or Οὔσος son of Aram was the founder of Damascus[3] and Trachonitis. Thus Jewish tradition and subsequently Byzantine and Arabic tradition sought the land of Uṣ in the Hauran. The country of Job and his cult were localised around Nawâ and Sheikh-Miskîn on the high road which cuts diagonally across Trachonitis.[4] The name Δεννάβα (Hebrew דִּנְהָבָה), found in the appendix of the Septuagint (Job 42:17d), caused the city of Job to be identified with Dhuneibeh, between Sheikh-Miskîn and Ezraʿ. Thus in the very passage in which she locates the land of Ausitis ʿon the borders of Idumaea and Arabia' Etheria identifies the town of Job with Carneas and Dennaba (Dhuneibeh): *Carneas autem dicitur nunc civitas Job quae ante dicta est Dennaba in terra Ausitidi, in finibus Idumeae et Arabiae.*[5] Let us note then that we have here a first location at Carneas, which is Καρνάειμ or Ἀσταρὼθ Καρνάειμ (Tell-Aštara south of Nawâ), found in the *Onomasticon.*[6] Hence by a series of confusions the traditions concerning Job were firmly centred in Trachonitis. Here was found the Deir-Ayûb ʿhouse (or monastery) of Job'. A stele of Ramses II, unearthed at Sheikh-Saʿad, to the south of Nawâ, became the ʿpillar of Job' in Arabic tradition. But a Deir-Ayûb and a Bir-Ayûb are found in Palestine in the vicinity of ʿAmwâs.[7] Another ʿwell of Job' is the famous Bir-Ayûb in the valley of Kidron near the village of Siloam.[8] A certain Tannûr-Ayûb or ʿJob's kiln' is a hot spring between Capernaum and eṭ-Ṭabgha, near the Lake of Tiberias. Thus the memory of the holy man was carried hither and thither. We cannot legiti-

---

[1] Identifications of חוּל with Ḫulia of the cuneiform texts and of מַשׁ with the Μάσιον ὄρος; cf. *RB*, 1911, pp. 102ff.

[2] *Ant. Jud.* I, vi, 4 (ed. Niese, I, 145).

[3] Whence the identification of עוּץ (of Gn 10: 23) with al-Ghauṭah, al-Ghûṭah, the name of the plain surrounding Damascus (Bochart, *Phaleg*, ed. 1707, col. 80).

[4] *RB*, 1911, pp. 103f. For the Arabic legends see Guy Le Strange, *Palestine under the Moslems*, pp. 515f.

[5] Ed. Geyer, p. 56.

[6] *RB*, 1911, p. 103.

[7] There is also a ʿspring of Job' to the north of Beit-ʿUr and another to the northeast of Ḥalḥul, on the Hebron road.

[8] On the legends relative to the well of Job, cf. Guy Le Strange, op. cit., pp. 220ff.

mately argue from tradition in order to adopt a different location from that which is suggested by the O.T. texts.

The presence of the 'sons of the east' among the Amalekites and Midianites (Jg 6:3, 33; 7:12; 8:10) enables us to understand why Job, who dwells in the land of Uṣ on the borders of Edom and Arabia, should be considered as one of the sons of the east.[1]

Nearby is found the country of שְׁבָא, which is the starting point of the Sabaean raids (1:15). Here it is not a question of the great kingdom in southern Arabia which became famous through the Queen of Sheba but of a territory connected with the oasis of Tema (6:19) and with Dedan (el-'Ela), the very two towns whose associations with Uṣ and Buz we have noted.[2] Cuneiform inscriptions are in agreement with the Bible [3] in linking together Sheba' (שְׁבָא), and Tema (תֵּמָא). Perhaps, as Glaser has suggested, the memory of Sheba has persisted in the wâdi-eš-Šabâ of the territory of Medina.[4]

The nomad tribes called *Kaldu*, well known in cuneiform texts,[5] are distinct from the Sabaeans as belonging to an Aramaean group rather than to the Arabian group. They make incursions into the desert borders, and under the description of כַּשְׂדִּים 'Chaldaeans' they also attack the land of Job.[6] We shall see below how the habitat of Job's friends also invites us to locate the land of Uṣ in the south, in the region bordering both on Edom and western Arabia. But we know already that the land of Buz to which Elihu the Buzite belongs (32:2) is to be situated between el-Jauf and Tema.[7]

THE FRIENDS OF JOB.—Before following the dramatic development of Job's story, we may now consider the three friends who are the interlocutors in the poetic section, and who reappear in the Epilogue. They are mentioned in an unvarying order: Eliphaz the Temanite, Bildad the Shuhite, and Zophar the Naamathite. The Septuagint has made of them three kings, and, in order to pass from the less known to the better known, has reversed the conso-

---

[1] Cf. Comm. on 1:3.
[2] Above, p. xxiii.
[3] Cf. Comm. on 1:15.
[4] Ibid.
[5] *RB*, 1910, pp. 384ff.
[6] Cf. Comm. on 1:17.
[7] Above, p. xxiii.

nants of Naamah and succeeded in making Zophar a king of the Minaeans.[1]

According to Gn 36:4ff., the name Eliphaz is Idumaean; this need not surprise us, since Teman figures among the sheikhs who sprang from Eliphaz (Gn 36:11, 15) and belongs, as we shall see, to the country of Edom. In the various contexts where the city of Teman is met with, it always represents one of the chief localities in Idumaea (Jer 49:7; Ezk 25:13; Am 1:12ff.; Ob 8, 9). The reputation for wisdom which the Edomites (Ob 8, 9) and especially the Temanites (Jer 42:7; Bar 3:22-3) enjoyed no doubt had something to do with the choice of Eliphaz as the first of Job's interlocutors.

The name of the town locates it in the south, since תֵּימָן (from ומן) signifies the region to the right, when facing eastwards, i.e. south.[2] A text of Pliny juxtaposes Nabataeans and Thimanaeans, i.e. the inhabitants of Teman: *Nabataeis Thimaneos junxerunt veteres.*[3] Likewise the note of Eusebius in the *Onomasticon* [4] suggests the land of the Nabataeans: καὶ εἰς ἔτι νῦν κώμη ἐστὶ Θαιμάν, ἀπέχουσα Πέτρων ἀμφὶ τὰ ιε' [5] σημεῖα, ἐν ᾗ καὶ ἐγκάθηται στρατιωτικόν. Two principal identifications have been suggested for Teman. The note of Eusebius which situates this town in the Gebalene, ἐν τῇ Γεβαλιτικῇ, has suggested that there survives a memory of Teman in *Tawâneh,* a locality situated in the region called el-Jibâl (Jebalene) which lies to the eastsoutheast of eṭ-Ṭafileh, right in the heart of Idumaea.[6] But the distance between this place and Petra is three times that given by the *Onomasticon* for the distance between Petra and Teman.[7] Furthermore, according to the Table of Peutinger, it is Thornia which occupied the site of Tawâneh, a locality which is the same as the Θοάνα of Ptolemy.[8]

It has been proposed to identify the Θαιμάν of the *Onomasticon* with Odroḥ, which is roughly three hours' distance to the east of Petra.[9] The distance would fit well, and it is known that there was

---

1   Cf. Comm. on 2:11.
2   Cf. the designation of southern Arabia by the term Yaman, Yemen, 'right', 'south'.
3   *Hist. nat.* VI, xxxii, 14.
4   Ed. Klostermann, p. 96; ed. Lagarde, p. 264.
5   St Jerome has 5 miles instead of 15.
6   Musil, *Arabia Petraea,* II, Edom, I, p. 158.
7   Brünnow and Domaszewski, *Die Prov. Arabia,* I, p. 89.
8   Ibid.
9   *RB,* 1898, p. 447.

formerly a Roman camp at Odroḥ,[1] which agrees with the datum of the *Onomasticon*. It is more likely, however, that Odroḥ is the ʾΑδροῦ of Ptolemy [2] and the ʾΑδρόων of the edict of Beersheba.[3]

According to Gn 36:34, the Edomite חֻשָׁם was of the land of the Temanites. The name Husham is identified by Clermont-Ganneau with el-Ḥesma (الحسمى), the immense plateau stretching from Tebuk in the south to the route of Maʿan-ʿAqabah in the north. This is the region which, following the various indications noted above, would best suit the land of Teman, though we should locate it as near as possible to Petra in the west, in order to satisfy the data of the *Onomasticon*. In this way we remain close to the land of Uṣ, the country of Job, and the land of Buz, that of Elihu.[4]

The other two friends of Job are Bildad of Shuaḥ and Zophar of Naʿamah.[5] Formerly Fried. Delitzsch had suggested that in שׁוּחַ we should see the land of Suḫu which is frequently attested in cuneiform texts. But in his commentary on Job this Assyriologist felt compelled to give up the identification (p. 139). We know in fact that the land of Suḫu was situated on the Euphrates and that its principal town was Anat, now known as ʿAnah.[6] Now, in Gn 25:2-3 the elder brother of שׁוּחַ has sons called Dedan and Sheva, which are names suggesting once more the regions of Idumaea and Arabia.[7] It is here that we should look for the country of Shuaḥ, as distinct from the Suḫu of Assyrian inscriptions.

The country of Zophar is Naʿamah, which we would situate in the area of Jebel-el-Naʿâmeh [8] or J. Naʿam,[9] about 60 kilometres to the east of Tebuk (turning slightly southwards). Such an identification would harmonise better with the other localities than that of Wetzstein, who places Naʿamah at en-Noʿemeh to the northeast of Deraʿah.

PRELIMINARIES OF THE DRAMA.—In the previous pages we have been endeavouring to shed light on the scant information given us

---

[1]   Ibid.
[2]   *Geogr.* V, 16.
[3]   *RB*, 1906, pp. 417ff.
[4]   Above, pp. xxii f.
[5]   On the names of Bildad and Zophar, cf. Comm. on 2:11.
[6]   *RB*, 1924, p. 107.
[7]   Above, pp. xxiii, xxv. Note that the text of the Septuagint has Teman as well as Dedan and Sheva.
[8]   Huber, *Journal d'un voy. en Arabie*, I, p. 342.
[9]   Jaussen and Savignac, *Miss. arch. en Arabie*, I, p. 64.

in the Prologue and Epilogue about Job, his family, his country, his friends, and his times. The picture with which we have been confronted is that of a man 'perfect and upright, fearing God and eschewing evil' (1:1), living as a wealthy shepherd surrounded by his family, in the area of country which extends between Idumaea and Arabia. Exercising priestly functions like the head of any family in the days of the patriarchs, he conjures away by his sacrifices every threat of evil, and seeks to cleanse his family from every fault, no matter how secret. Yahweh is proud of His servant.

Then suddenly we are carried aloft into the courts of heaven. The angels, who are described as the sons of Elohim,[1] present themselves before Yahweh. Each of them has a mission to fulfil and comes to give an account of his work. Among them has slipped a personage called the Satan, that is to say, the chief prosecutor.[2] He too roams the earth and carries out a mission which he defines in terms similar to those used to depict the goings and comings of the heavenly messengers.[3] His special rôle is to accuse human beings before God (Zec 3:1-2). In post-exilic theology he appears as the seducer of men, and this is why in 1 Ch 21:1 he replaces the Yahweh of 2 S 24:1 in the function of prompting David to number Israel.

A discussion now takes place between Yahweh and Satan on the subject of the hero of the story. Yahweh boasts of the perfection and uprightness of Job, whose virtue is peerless. Satan sneers: 'It is for nothing that Job fears Elohim?' No, not quite for nothing. Yahweh well rewards him for his piety, blessing his person, his family, and his goods. Satan, the public prosecutor, throws down a real challenge. One blow struck at the wealth and prosperity of Job and the whole edifice of his virtue will crumble: 'He will curse Thee to Thy face!' Yahweh makes a suitable reply, accepting the challenge and commissioning Satan to carry out the test to which the holy man is about to be submitted. The health and the life of Job must, however, be spared.

Naturally patristic tradition has interpreted this scene, in which the whole destiny of Job is at stake, as a parable. St John Chrysostom interprets it as κατὰ σχηματισμὸν τὸν λόγον, and St Thomas Aquinas adds the further explanation: *Hoc symbolice et sub aenigmate*

---

[1] Comm. on 1:6.
[2] Ibid.
[3] Cf. 1:6-7 and Zec 1:10-11; 3:1-2; 6:5, 7.

proponitur, secundum consuetudinem Sacrae Scripturae, quae res spirituales sub figuris rerum corporalium describit.

THE DRAMA.—We can easily foresee the repercussions on earth of the scene which has just taken place in heaven. Misfortunes are about to strike at Job. In a series of short sharp episodes, the drama is developed. At the instigation of Satan, who remains always in the background, the Sabaeans first advance to attack.[1] Raids on oxen and asses, massacre of servants. Three times the recital of the catastrophe is followed without intermission by the recital of a yet greater catastrophe (1:16, 17, 18). St Thomas Aquinas well brings out the underlying psychology (on 1:17): *Hac autem adversitate nuntiata, statim altera nuntiatur, ne, si quod intervallum fieret, intus ad cor suum rediret et se ad patientiam praepararet, et sic sequentia facilius sustineret.* Satan wishes to break down the resistance of his adversary before the latter has time to recover his self-possession.

So that the reader may be kept informed of the stages of the action, a witness, the traditional sole survivor (Gn 14:13; Ezk 24:26f.), arrives each time to announce the news to Job (1:15, 16, 17, 19) at the moment when the previous one has just finished telling his tale. Fr. Prat says justly: 'There is also, and we should not fail to recognise it, in the recital of these misfortunes striking the holy man in swift succession, an element of artificial technique, which we cannot take literally.'[2]

The second catastrophe is brought about by the 'fire of Elohim', i.e. lightning and thunderbolts,[3] which strike the sheep and destroy them together with their shepherds. Not men only but also the elements become the auxiliaries of Satan. The fire of heaven was especially dreadful and dreaded. For was it not the instrument of divine vengeance? Again St Thomas Aquinas recognises the psychological significance of this second act of the drama: *ut ejus menti imprimeret quod non solum ab hominibus, sed etiam a Deo persecutionem pateretur.*

After the oxen, the asses, and the sheep, what will there remain to the great proprietor who was half landed, half nomadic? He had been assessed as having 500 yoke of oxen, 500 she-asses, 7,000 sheep, and 3,000 camels (1:3). Now it is the turn of the camels, the last companions of the nomad, to be the victims of the third

[1] Above, p. xxv.
[2] *Dictionnaire de la Bible*, III, col. 1562.
[3] Comm. on 1: 16.

catastrophe. A new raid, executed with decisive vigour by the Chaldaeans, puts the servants to the sword and carries off the camels. Men are once again the accomplices of Satan. But only for a time, for the fourth raid and the last trial was produced like the second by the unleashing of the elements.

Now it is a great wind blowing from the desert under the impact of which the house crashes where the seven sons and three daughters of Job are gathered for their daily feast. Not one escapes. Herds, flocks, and family, Satan has dealt with them all.

What will be the attitude of Job in the face of these evils which, in the space of a few minutes, are announced without giving him time to recover? His suffering is violent and he manifests it by rending his garments, shaving his head and prostrating himself on the ground (1:20). Meanwhile Satan lurks, waiting for the blasphemy which, as he hopes, will issue from the lips of his victim. But what a contrast! It is a phrase of resignation which Job utters: 'Naked I came out of my mother's womb, and naked shall I return; Yahweh gave and Yahweh has taken away! Blessed be the name of Yahweh!' Job expresses his mind in the Psalmist's terms: 'Blessed be the name of the Lord from this time forth and for evermore!' (Ps 113:2). The author does not hesitate to place the divine Tetragrammaton on the lips of the righteous man. And he emphasises his conduct: 'In all this Job did not sin or charge God with folly.'

We return to heaven where Yahweh holds a second plenary session of His court, parallel in every respect to the first. God triumphs. He points out to Satan the uselessness of his attacks on Job: 'He still clings to his perfection, and it is without reason that thou didst stir me against him to ruin him!' Satan however does not admit defeat: 'Skin for skin!' The trial has only skimmed the surface of the life of this servant of God. The blows should have been delivered against his bones and his flesh. Yahweh agrees to this supreme test. Satan is permitted to attack Job's body, though he must spare his life.

A terrible disease consisting of foul ulcers, which were considered one of the divine scourges (Dt 28:35; Rev 16:2), attacks the body of Job from head to foot. This is too much! His wife now allies herself with Satan and exhorts her husband to curse Elohim before dying. But Job remains immovable: 'If we accept good from Elohim, shall we not also accept evil?' This time it is the name Elohim which Job utters, as also his wife had done (2:9-10). The judgment of the author is expressed in the same terms as before: 'In all this Job did not sin with his lips.'

Seated among the ashes and armed with a potsherd to scrape himself in an attempt to relieve the itchings of his skin, Job presents us with the picture of the righteous man from whom every worldly good has been snatched. Death alone could put an end to his sufferings. But as yet we are only in the prelude to the story. Three new protagonists appear on the scene, and, as in the dramas of Aeschylus, their only rôle is to listen to the sufferer and to reason with or against him. They are the three friends and neighbours of Job. We already know whence they have come.[1] At the sight of Job, whom they have difficulty in recognising, they give vent to their grief. Then for seven days and nights they sit silent.

It is Job himself who first breaks the gloomy silence by his brilliant malediction of the day of his birth. The prose Prologue is now finished. The dialogues that are to be engaged in consist of pure poetry. The poetic part of the work now begins.

THE CONCLUSION.—After the poem which includes, besides the speeches of Job and his friends, those of Elihu and finally those of Yahweh, the story ends with the prose Epilogue (42:7-17). Satan is no longer present, neither is Job's wife. It is Eliphaz of Teman and his two companions who are reproached by Yahweh Himself. They were not able to speak, as did Job, what was right. The latter, faithful to his functions as patriarch and religious leader, intercedes for the three guilty parties and secures their forgiveness after they have offered an expiatory sacrifice.

And now Job recovers twofold all that he had lost: sheep, oxen, and asses. Relatives and friends of former days find their way once more to his house. He will enjoy prosperity to the end of his days Instead of seven sons, he will rejoice in fourteen. And three daughters with charming names will replace those who perished.

Finally Job dies old and full of days, after seeing his sons and his sons' sons up to the fourth generation.

Thus did also the patriarchs Abraham (Gn 25:8), Isaac (Gn 35:29), and Joseph (Gn 50:23).

THE RELATION BETWEEN THE PROLOGUE AND THE EPILOGUE.— The story of the righteous Job may be divided into three phases: before, during, and after his trials. One and the same narrator is

---

[1] Above, pp. **xxv** ff.

responsible for the whole book. Above the drama stands Yahweh in sovereign control. He it is who holds in His hands all its threads, and moves the actors. When He speaks of Job He uses the expression: 'My servant', both in the Prologue (1:8; 2:3) and in the Epilogue (42:7, 8). When He bids Eliphaz offer a burnt offering He uses the same terms as we find in the Prologue.[1] Job is depicted everywhere with the same features, everywhere he is the patriarch who is to live long, surrounded by his children and grandchildren, rejoicing in the abundance of his flocks and herds.[2] Just as he intervened to atone for the possible sins of his sons (1:5), so he becomes an intermediary with Yahweh on behalf of his friends (42:8). The latter are the same both in the Prologue and the Epilogue. They were presented to us in 2:11, and we find them again, with the names and their countries of origin, in 42:9. At their head stands always Eliphaz of Teman (42:7). Elihu is mentioned neither in the Prologue nor the Epilogue.

Buttenwieser [3] proposed to isolate v. 11 in the Epilogue and to see in it 'the real and original end' of the story, while the section 42:10, 12-17 would be a later addition.[4] V. 11 would alone be in harmony with 42:7-9 and with the Prologue. It would mark the change of attitude brought about in the friends of Job by the observations of Yahweh.

This argument is hardly conclusive. In 42:7-9 it is a question of the three friends who have been present on the scene since the Prologue (2:11) and who have debated keenly with Job in the poem. It is they who needed special forgiveness, for, says Yahweh, 'you have not spoken the truth concerning me as has my servant Job' (42:8). At v. 9 they disappear from the scene. God has spared them out of consideration for Job.

Those who enter at v. 11 are all the brothers, sisters, and former acquaintances. Their intervention is described in the same terms as that of the three friends in 2:11, in order to emphasise that a new episode is being introduced. The consolations brought by these latecomers are retrospective, as is emphasised by the expression: 'all his acquaintances of yore'. Their behaviour has been in accordance with the melancholy observations of Ovid:

[1] Cf. Comm. on 42:8.
[2] Cf. Comm. on 42:11, 12, 13, 16, 17.
[3] We were not able to obtain the work of this author (*The Book of Job*) until after the completion of our Commentary.
[4] Op. cit., pp. 67ff.

Donec eris felix multos numerabis amicos,
Tempora si fuerint nubila, solus eris.

They vanished with good fortune, they return with its restoration, and this is what validates v. 10b: 'and Yahweh doubled all that had belonged to Job.' This restoration of fortune is the cause of the return of the friends.[1] They no longer hesitate to come and eat in his house the bread of prosperity. If they bring gifts it is not to succour distress, but to conform to oriental custom so well characterised in the Gospels: 'For to him who has more will be given; and from him who has not, even what he has will be taken away.'[2] Hence there is no reason whatever to seek in the feast and the gifts symbols of reconciliation.[3]

The sequence of events in the Prologue and the Epilogue is developed according to the strictest logic. First the description of the hero, showing in particular his wealth and his virtue. The problem is posed by Satan's rejoinder to Yahweh's boast of the perfection of His servant: 'Is it for nothing that Job fears Elohim?' There is only one means of proving that in fact the moral life of Job is disinterested: to plunge him into distress.

And who is capable of persecuting a righteous man? Not God Himself; for He permits evil, but does not directly initiate it. Hence it is Satan, the ancient enemy of mankind, who will perform the nefarious deeds.

The trial must not immediately proceed to extremes. The malicious action of Satan will stop short at the person of Job. There follows the description of the first series of catastrophes which

---

[1] Thus we cannot accept the hypothesis of Budde, who finds in v. 10b a gloss or addition. If the clause seems an anticipation of v. 12, it is because it must introduce v. 11. Duhm would make of v. 10b a reflection by a reader, who would thus have strengthened the efficacy of the intercession for the neighbour. But the expression 'all that belonged to Job' does not belong to a reader; it is characteristic of the author of the Prologue (1: 10, 12).

[2] 'If the form is paradoxical, the truth of the saying is manifest, especially in the usages of the East. It is to the rich that one makes gifts; from those who have nothing (usage has confirmed this paradoxical expression), one takes away even their last farthing' (Lagrange, on Mk 4: 25).

[3] Whatever Buttenwieser thinks, who bases himself on Gn 31: 46, 54, where it is not a question of a visit to a friend, but of a meeting between Laban and Jacob, of a feast of reconciliation and a pact of alliance. If one eats bread with some one it is not necessarily because one should be reconciled with him. It is easy to see that the story of the Book of Job stresses merely the end of the isolation to which Job had been reduced by his misfortune. Cf. 6: 15-21; 12: 4-5; 19: 13-20.

deprive the hero of his wealth and his children. Then comes a pause in which Job blesses God instead of cursing Him.

Second phase: Job is afflicted in his flesh and bones. The foul sores disfigure and isolate the patient. Job is no longer face to face with his affliction in solitude. His wife attempts to elicit from him a cry of malediction. But it is the note of resignation which we find on Job's lips. Satan suffers a new check.

Neither Satan nor Job's wife reappear. Their part in the action is finished. The former has been the agent of the evils which have crushed Job. The latter has proved herself an instigator of evil. Both of them have fixed the terms of the problem. Must virtue and good fortune necessarily be correlated? Is suffering the corollary of sin? Must God be incriminated when an innocent man is assailed by misfortune?

The debate on these points will be developed with all desirable amplitude in the poem. It will take the form of a dialogue. Hence Job's interlocutors must be brought on to the scene to confront their unhappy friend. The Prologue terminates with the introduction of the new scene. But in concluding it foreshadows the opening of the poem: 'After this Job opened his mouth and cursed his day' (3:1).

The Epilogue begins with a turn of phrase similar to that with which the Prologue concluded: 'And after Yahweh had spoken these words to Job, Yahweh said to Eliphaz of Teman.' A direct intervention of Yahweh has taken place. The Prologue gave no hint of it, but it was necessary in order to bring to a satisfactory conclusion the debate between Job and his friends. The thesis of the latter, which was the common belief of the time, namely that virtue and happiness, sin and distress, are strict moral equivalents, was condemned by Yahweh, who took the part of His servant, Job, supporting the latter's thesis that virtue is compatible with suffering.

The story might have ended at this point. But the reader is impatient to know the sequel. All will end well for every one. The friends are forgiven, thanks to the intercession of Job. As for the hero, he will enjoy the reward of his virtue, which in its fullness overflows his own life and goes out to save his neighbours. It must not be forgotten that, if God permits the righteous to suffer misfortune, it is a temporary affair and justified as a means of testing their worth. Hence goods of all kinds, wealth and family, return to Job and exceed his former degree of prosperity.

Unless we are going to deprive the writer of all personality, it cannot be said that there is anything superfluous in this narrative. But it must be recognised, and here we are anticipating the problem of the literary composition, that neither the Prologue nor the Epilogue is self-sufficient, that what they absolutely require is that which forms the heart of the book, namely the discussion between the friends. And further, if we consider 42:7 as a whole and as forming a unity with the rest of the narrative, then the speeches of Yahweh are likewise presupposed by the story in prose. On the other hand, this story contains not a word of Elihu, who appears and disappears as though in parentheses during the course of chs. 32-7. These very simple points should be remembered as throwing light on the conclusions which we shall have to draw in the study which follows. For the sake of greater clearness and so as to distinguish the sections of the book properly, we shall describe as 'poetic dialogue' the chapters containing the controversy between Job and his friends (12-31), to which the 'speeches of Elihu' (32-7) and the 'speeches of Yahweh' (38-41) form a sequel.

CHAPTER FOUR

THE POETIC DIALOGUE [1]

JOB'S LAMENT (3).—Ch. 3 is devoted to Job's lament. This poem, one of the most superb not only in the Bible but in the whole literature of the world, forms a whole which may be isolated from the rest of the poetic section. Job curses the day of his birth and the night of his conception (3:3-10). Why was he not an abortion or still-born (3:11-12, 16)! Then he would have enjoyed the peace of death (3:13-15) the calm of Sheol (3:17-19). What is the use of life if it consists but in suffering and in longing for death? (3:20-3). Such a lament with its anguished questions is drawn forth by the sad condition in which Job finds himself: a condition of tears, dread, agitation (3:24-6).

In fact the problem of suffering has not yet been posed. The unhappy man notes simply that it would be better for him to be dead than alive. But the exaggeration of the terms in which he expresses his feelings becomes, as it were, the spark which kindles the discussion. The latter begins with the intervention of the first of the friends, Eliphaz of Teman, who condemns Job's attitude in the face of suffering and suggests the remedy for his ills: recourse to God.

FIRST CYCLE OF DISCUSSIONS (4-14).—Eliphaz has been struck by the tone in which Job expressed himself and cannot refrain from making some reply (4:2). He begins on a note of irony. Job has been accustomed to teach others and to exhort them when they were in trouble; but now that he suffers himself he is like every one else, depressed and terrified (4:3-5). What is the reason for this anomaly? It must be that, if traditional ethics are to be believed, the piety and the perfection of Job are apparent only, for trouble is the indication of moral evil: in this world there is the closest connection

---

[1] The analysis of the entire poetic dialogue is intended to bring out clearly the sequence of ideas and the principal motifs which recur over and over again in the clash of opposing theories. This analysis must precede the study of the composition of the book. It is above all indispensable to an appreciation of the third cycle of speeches.

between sin and punishment (4:6-11). There is nothing surprising in this. In a dream, Eliphaz has been favoured by an apparition (4:12-16) which has disclosed to him the truth that in the presence of Eloah no man can consider himself righteous, for God finds error in the angels, and with much more reason then in frail and foolish man (4:17-21; 5:2). If sometimes the doctrine of the connection between moral and physical evil seems to be contradicted, it is the result of fallacious appearances: a closer observation of the matter suggests that it is man who, through his iniquity, is the real cause of his troubles (5:2-7). The best course is to turn, not to the angels [1] but to God Himself (5:1-8), as does Eliphaz. For God is the author of the overwhelming changes in nature and society (5:9-16). If Job has been afflicted, it is only a salutary chastening (5:17-18), the final result of which will be his deliverance from all scourges (5:19-23) and his unchequered prosperity until he attains a happy death (5:24-6). Such are the affirmations which Eliphaz uses to counter the complaint of his friend (5:27).

Thus we have here the thesis of a traditionalist theologian: there is no man without sin, and there is no sin that goes unpunished; but punishment is a chastisement which God sends to recall man to the good and thus to happiness. It is unnecessary to become despairing and to long for death, as Job has done.

Job's reply is contained in chs. 6-7. The unhappy man begins by justifying his complaint. Its cause is the extremity of his evil (6:2-3), which springs directly from God (6:4). Why should they be astonished if he groans (6:5-7)? Then comes a new invocation of death (6:8-10), for life is no longer worth living (6:11-13). It is impossible to rely on his friends; they are deceivers (6:15-21) and evasive (6:22-3). Job invites them to reply not by platitudes, like Eliphaz, but by reference to precise facts: it is for them to prove that the sufferings of Job are the punishment for some real sin, rather than to reprove words which are carried away by the wind and to speculate in the void (6:24-7). Even the words of Job are righteous (6:28-30). If he is in distress, it is because he is subjected to the common lot of man; his state is like that of the soldier and the hireling (7:1-2). Day and night he suffers, and his path leads inevitably towards death (7:6-8), towards the land from which there is no return (7:9-10). It is impossible to keep silence (7:11). And Job addresses himself directly to God, who, as

[1] Cf. Comm. on 5:1 (after 5:7).

he has said in 6:4, is the author of his ills. Why should he be persecuted day and night (7:12-14) in such a way as to make him long for death (7:15)? Does man who is so transient a being deserve that God should thus pursue him relentlessly (7:16-19)? Even if he is a sinner, why not exercise a little patience towards him? Life is so slight a thing (7:20-1)!

There is the most striking contrast between the dry, professorial, arrogant tone in which Eliphaz affirms his thesis, and the very personal accents, imbued with pathos, in which Job makes his reply. It is not a question of discovering whether misfortune is the effect of sin; it is a question of noting facts: Job is unhappy beyond all expression, he has no longer any basis of security on earth, he feels the approach of death. Surely God might leave him in peace and refrain from tormenting him. Even were he guilty, Job has ceased to be an object worthy of divine chastisement, since he has one foot in the grave, and already can hardly be said to exist any more.

Thus Job has challenged God. Bildad the Shuhite takes up the challenge. Job's tone is insufferable (8:2). God cannot help being just (8:3). To the guilty is apportioned punishment (8:4), while he who turns to God is recompensed with the recovery of prosperity (8:5-7). We still have here the assertion of the equivalence between moral evil and misfortune on which Eliphaz insisted. To the arguments of the first speaker Bildad adds the testimony of the ancients (8:8-10), a fact which shows that he is the exponent of tradition. This testimony is categorical: those who forget God and involve themselves in evil are punished, and the guilty even perish (8:11-19). God takes into account the righteousness or iniquity of every one (8:20). Job has only to follow the advice of his friends, and he will soon smile again, while his enemies, who will then be the wicked, will be doomed to destruction (8:21-2).

The argument runs in a circle. But Bildad has linked his thesis firmly with the orthodox doctrine of Israel which was transmitted from father to son.

Job is well aware of all this, and he affirms it at the beginning of his reply (9:2). However, he reverts to a previous point and alludes first of all to the question which the nocturnal vision put to Eliphaz (4:17), 'How can a man be just before God?' (9:2). There can be no question of considering in parallel two beings so different as man and God. Man does not even merit a reply if he presumes to debate with God (9:3). To such an extent does the Creator surpass all creatures! It is Job's turn now to strike up a doxology (9:4-13) which is wider in scope than that of Eliphaz (5:8-16). It almost seems as though he affects to pass over Bildad's head in order to give a direct answer to the first speaker. Job cannot possibly cherish the pretension of wrestling with this God whose might he knows so well, and before whom he can but humble himself even when he is convinced of his rightness (9:14-16). Nothing escapes the glance of this supreme Judge who pursues Job so inexorably that the latter can no longer reason about his own case (9:17-21). He ends by exclaiming that the righteous and the wicked are treated in the same way by this God who laughs at the despair of the innocent and allows injustice to prevail (9:22-4). The undertone of lament suddenly bursts forth with a vehemence mingled with gentleness: the days of man flee away, with never a moment of true joy (9:25-7); for, whether innocent or guilty, Job expects a harsh judgment (9:28-31), since there is no appeal and no arbiter when God judges man (9:32-5). He might just as well stake all (10:1) and bluntly challenge Eloah (10:2). Why does He attempt chicanery with His creature and pass His time spying on him as would a man with eyes of flesh (10:2-7)? Yet humanity is God's favourite work, which He has fashioned with marvellous and loving care (10:8-12). And all this to end in making of this living statue which has issued from His hands the object of an unceasing persecution, as though it were an enemy or game (10:13-17). Job then returns to his two chief ideas: What is the use of life (10:18-19; cf. 3:11ff., etc.)? Why cannot God leave in peace a being who has only a short time to live (10:20-2; cf. 7:16-21)?

The task of refuting Job now devolves on the last speaker, Zophar of Na'amah (11). He is wearied by Job's inexhaustible babble and his pretension to be in possession of the truth (11:2-4). It is a question of a divine mystery: God alone could disclose the secret fault which has caused Job his suffering (11:5-6). It is an untenable paradox to attempt to discuss the infinite perfection of God, which eludes all human valuation and is not confined by laws (11:7-10)! Now, it is this God who can sway the hearts of men and teach them wisdom (11:11-12). There is only one thing for Job to do, namely, to take the course recommended by Eliphaz and Bildad: to be converted and to turn to God and thus recover happiness (11:13-19; cf. 5:8ff.; 8:21ff.). The speech, like that of Bildad (8:22), concludes with a contrast between the fate of the wicked (11:20) and that of the righteous man whose blessedness has been described (11:15-19).

Job now concludes the first cycle of discussions, and that is why his exordium embraces the three friends:

> Truly you are the people,
> And with you wisdom will die! (12: 2)

The irony is all the more striking because Job feels that he knows as much about the matter as his friends (12:3), especially as it is a question of truths universally known (12:3b), even to the animals (12:7-8), and all the more then to those who have understanding (12:11) and have lived long (12:12). A parenthesis (12:4-6), which however is conceived in the style of the poem,[1] seems to separate v. 3 from its natural sequel in v. 7. But it is difficult to see into what other place it might fit. This passage, in which Job's mind returns to the thought of the abandonment in which the unhappy righteous man finds himself, by contrast with the ease and security of the wicked, may be a sort of aside, suggested by the reflection in v. 3: 'But I too have a heart like you!' Vv. 9-10, which should be linked with v. 13 (cf. Comm. on 12:8), make the point that the whole world is aware of the divine activity. This gives rise to a new doxology (12:13-25), exalting the action of God which causes revolutions in society as well as in the world of nature. On this subject Job knows as much as Eliphaz (vv. 9-16); he is no whit inferior to any of his friends (13:1-2).

Silence therefore! Job addresses himself to God, not to inventors of lies or worthless quacks (13:3-4). These have only to be silent and listen (13:5-6); they have no business to come forward as though they were the advocates of God (13:7-12). Job is not afraid to lift up his voice; he is ready for anything; he must confront God (13:13-16). It is a regular lawsuit that he demands, and he only wishes that the machinery of divine justice did not exceed his strength (13:17-21), so that the case might follow its normal course (13:22). What he required to know from his friends (6:24ff.) he now demands of God:

> How many are my iniquities and sins?
> Make me to know my transgression and my sin! (13: 23)

Job has no reason to cause God so much preoccupation, and he is not worthy of the persecution pursued against him (13:24-7). For, after all, he is only a man. And man, born of a woman and of few

---

[1] Note especially the divine names in vv. 4 and 6.

days, does not deserve the attention of God (14:1-6). This idea recurs often with Job (7:16-21; 10:20-2). It deserves the amplification which is given it in the comparison with a tree, which even if cut down can bud again and reproduce itself, whereas man remains forever cut off from the land of the living (14:7-12). For it is not for a season only but for ever that he is shut up in Sheol (14:13-20), forgetting earth and its doings (14:21-2).

Even when reduced to this bare analysis, the first cycle of talks does not fail to make a profound impression, for in it the positions of the opposing parties are clearly defined. Impelled by his overwhelming personal grief, Job curses life and invokes death. He knows no other cause of his suffering but a persecution which has its source in God. Such a persecution seems to him inexplicable, for he is a just man. Moreover, it seems to him unworthy of God, for man is so small, so ephemeral, that there is no reason for God to pursue him so bitterly. As for the friends, they are deceivers. Besides, it is not with them, but with God Himself, that Job wishes to discuss his affair. There must be advocates between the client and his judge. It will be noticed that every speech of Job is skilfully calculated to produce a very precise effect by means of the repetition, under different forms, of a particular gamut of emotions and ideas, which eliminate any uncertainty as to the state of his soul.

The same art informs the distribution among the three friends of the orthodox theories. The basis of all that they affirm is the connection between sin and misfortune. Since Job is unfortunate, he is guilty. There is only one thing for him to do, namely to be converted and thus to re-enter the category of the good whose lot is so different from that of the wicked.

Job and his friends are agreed as to the transcendence, the omnipotence, and the omniscience of God. They are divided only in their opinions as to the application of His righteousness, the former disclosing, on the basis of his personal experience, the disconcerting aspect of this application, the latter insisting on adjusting the operations of divine justice to the norm of human justice.

At the close of the first cycle, each remains firmly fixed in his position, Job standing alone against the three.

SECOND CYCLE OF DISCUSSIONS (15-21).—With the return of Eliphaz on to the scene, the discussion becomes more aggressive (15). Eliphaz begins by reproaching Job not only with inconsistency and futility but also with the impiety and craftiness of his speeches (15:2-5), which will only serve to condemn him (15:6). Job boasts of understanding wisdom and seems to lay claim to a monopoly of it (15:7-10). Eliphaz makes a direct allusion to the words of Job in 12:3, 9, 12; 13:1-2, etc.[1] He accuses him further of being angry and even of attacking God (15:11-13). In fact, in the first cycle Job seemed to criticise as unworthy of God the ruthlessness with which He watches man's conduct,[2] and he cast on God the responsibility for his ills.[3] Eliphaz now repeats the syllogism which he heard in the dream recounted in 4:17-19 (15:14-16), and the conclusion of which is that every man is amenable to God's judgment. Next he invokes tradition (15:17-19), pure doctrine such as has not been contaminated by the admixture of alien elements. Like Bildad, he appeals to the sages of former times (cf. 8:8-10). He expounds the traditional thesis with rigorous logic; the wicked cannot be happy. He is pursued by remorse, fear, anguish (15:20-4). There can be no other cause for his evils but his attitude towards God (15:25-6) or his neighbour (15:27-8). The wicked man is like a tree which withers and loses its branches, which does not mature and has no shoots (15:29-34). It is crime which is the origin of misfortune (15:35-6). This imagery recalls the first speech of Eliphaz (4:8; 5:6-7).

Job repeats that he is being told nothing new (16:2), and he asks to be left in peace (16:3). He too could be lavish in consolations if the rôles were reversed (16:4-5). But alas! it is he who is the victim, and his distress is inescapable (16:6). He sees none but enemies and persecutors around him (16:7-10). It is God who has exposed him to these blows and has undertaken to torment him (16:11-14). Hence he shows every sign of the most extreme and frightful misery. He insists upon his tears (16:15-16). But he is innocent (16:17) and will not have the cry of his blood stifled (16:18). In the heavens some one pleads for him, it is God Himself (16:19-20); but this God is both judge and litigant (16:21). Job then returns to his favourite themes: the shortness of life and the imminence of death (16:22-17:1), his desertion by his friends (17:2-5), and the scorn of the indifferent and vulgar (17:6). He is worn away by grief (17:7). Instead of simply remaining astonished at what may happen to

[1] Cf. Comm. on 15:9-10.
[2] Above, p. xxxviii.
[3] Above, p. xxxvii.

the righteous man (17:8-9), the friends have wished to interpret his sufferings, and there they have erred (17:10). The close reflects the tone of the whole: vexations night and day (17:11-12), no hope except in death and the tomb (17:13-16). Job likes to conclude his speeches with the evocation of Sheol (7:24; 10:21-2; 14:19-22).

Bildad too becomes more aggressive: he resents being called an animal (18:2-4). He reinforces the thesis of Eliphaz about the misfortunes which are reserved for the wicked man: symbolic darkness (18:5-6), snares (18:7-10), terrors (18:11-12), repulsive diseases and death (18:13-15), after death complete oblivion for lack of progeny to perpetuate his name (18:16-21).

Job does not consider himself beaten. He resents the insults heaped upon him (19:2-5). The cause of his ills does not lie in some sin which he has committed, as his interlocutors suppose. God is the author of everything. Job now depicts with fiercest vehemence the way in which God assails his life (19:6-12). After God, it is his family, friends, kinsfolk, servants, who forget and despise him (19:13-16). He has become repulsive and horrible to his wife and sons (19:17), the young insult him (19:18), his intimate friends have conceived a loathing for him (19:19). His very body is rotting away (19:20). Crushed and wearied, Job turns to his three companions and longs that they at least should have pity on him:

> Have pity on me, have pity on me, O you my friends!
> For the hand of Eloah has smitten me. (19: 21)

Why should they make common cause with the God who persecutes him (19:20)? And suddenly the tone of his discourse becomes exalted. He appeals to posterity (19:23-4). He feels strongly that his innocence will clearly emerge on the last day, and that God Himself, standing on the earth, will undertake the final vindication of His servant (19:25-7). His friends will then have to fear this ultimate judgment, if they continue to persecute him with their insinuations (19:28-9).

Zophar intervenes. He is moved with indignation by what he hears (20:2-3). And without delay he resumes for his own part the thesis of Eliphaz and Bildad: the wicked man is doomed to misfortune here below; even if he seems fortunate, his happiness lasts only for a time (20:4-5). There follows the classic comparison with the tree (20:6). The wicked man vanishes like a dream; he fades away at the climax of his prosperity (20:7-11). The evil thing which he has savoured becomes a source of misfortune; the food which he has relished is transformed into a poison which kills him (20:12-16). There is a detailed description of the ills apportioned to the wicked: loss of ill-gotten gains (20:17-21), divine wrath striking down the terrified criminal (20:22-5), disappearance of his family and his house (20:26-8). On the day of judgment to which Job alluded (19:25-9) the wicked man is condemned by heaven and earth (20:27-9).

Once more Job craves attention (21:2-3). If he is impatient, it is because he has not to complain of men but of God (21:4). The affirmations which his friends have just made are contradicted by many horrifying facts (21:5-6). Happiness, and not misfortune, is meted out to the wicked: a prosperous life, in the bosom of numerous progeny and a family which dwells free from fear (21:7-9), cattle which multiply abundantly, and children who dance to music (21:10-12), a happy death (21:13).

And these are the very people who boasted of having no dealings with the Almighty (21:14-15)! Contrary to the prevalent opinion, God does not punish them (21:16-18). To say that He punishes their sons is to speak of an ineffective punishment (21:19-21). Why should men wish to dictate to God what He is to do (21:22)? Death strikes right and left without taking any account of the condition of individuals (21:23-6). Isolated catastrophes cannot be urged (21:27-8)! As is well known to the much travelled, the wicked often escapes in the day of disaster and has no fear (21:29-31). Even his death is peaceful and his obsequies are carried out with pomp (21:32-3). The contention of the friends is absolutely false (21:34).

In this second cycle of discussions the rigour of the logic is more marked than anywhere else in the poetic section. The two theses which clash are presented with an energy and a skill which far surpass the normal reasoning of orientals. The position of the debaters has not changed: the wicked is punished with misfortune (thesis of the three friends), the wicked is just as happy as any one else (thesis of Job).

THIRD CYCLE OF DISCUSSIONS (22-31).—It is again Eliphaz who reopens the debate, and this time, without preliminaries, he announces a theory which is momentous in its consequences. Virtue must be productive of effects. Such is the meaning of all ancient tradition in Israel. The usefulness of virtue cannot be maintained with reference to God but only with reference to man, who alone profits by his good deeds (22:2-3). Now, if man gains advantages from virtue, he must be punished if he commits evil; whence the need for divine judgment (22:4-5). If Job is judged, it is because he is guilty. There follows a list of the crimes which Job might have committed, and all of which come under the heading of things forbidden by current ethics (22:6-9), as can be seen if we compare the passage with Ex 22:25-6; Is 58:7; Ezk 18:7; Ex 22:21; Dt 24:17; Is 1:17; Mt 25:42-3. Then comes the application to Job of the theories sketched in the previous cycle about the fate of the wicked (22:10-11; cf. 18:8-11, 5-6; 21:17; 20:28). Eliphaz next attacks the theory of Job with regard to God's lack of concern about human affairs (cf. ch. 21), though he clothes this theory in a form which is rather that of a whole school (22:12-16; cf. Is 29:15; Ps 73:11). He exhorts Job not to follow the path which was trodden by those who were the victims of great catastrophes (22:15-16) because they repudiated the activity of God in the world (22:17) and forgot His benefits (22:18). Such punishments are the triumph of divine righteousness, and the pious man cannot but applaud them (22:19-20). A conclusion, always the same, follows: return to God by humble conversion (22:21-3), which will restore peace and happiness (22:24-8). God loves those who humble and cleanse themselves (22:29-30).

Job cannot remain silent (23:2). It is with God that he would wish to discuss his case (23:3-7), but God hides Himself (23:8-9). For God knows the innocence of His servant (23:10-12). But the sovereign Lord does as He pleases (23:13-15), and this is the mystery which terrifies Job and wrings cries of pain from him (23:15-17). The problem moreover goes far beyond Job's own case. In fact, God allows the world to drift and permits evil to reign as master (24:1). Property is violated, widows and orphans are robbed, the poor are oppressed, the peasants are exploited and reduced to the most squalid misery, while their exploiters are sated with luxury (24:2-11). If from the country we pass to the town, we are faced with the same scenes of disorder and crime: murder, adultery, theft, plunder, the triumph of those who roam at night and fear the light of day (24:12-17).

The remainder of Job's speech (24:18-24) is certainly surprising. It has reached us in a bad state, though the sense can be restored

with the help of the versions.[1] In the first place, there is an alternation of the singular and plural which is quite inexplicable in the
present context (24:18). Now, it is precisely with this v. 18 that
there begins the description of the punishments which strike the
sinner: malediction, descent into Sheol, oblivion after death (24:
18-20). The crimes of the wicked are the cause of their misfortunes
(24:21-2). Their prosperity was apparent only and it fades away like
the plant that is torn up or which withers (24:23-4). It is God who
has executed the punishment (24:22-3).

Such is the meaning which may be elicited from this very difficult
passage, of which the *Bible du rabbinat français* declares that 'it is
somewhat lacking in clarity and its sequence of ideas leaves something to be desired'. We are here confronted by the very thesis of
Job's friends, as it has been expounded by Eliphaz (15:20-36),
Bildad (18:5-21), and Zophar (20:4-28), principally in the second
cycle of discussions. There is the same logical argument, the same
imagery. It is question here of a passage which has been accidentally
torn out of its original context.[2] Note that the accursed domain
(24:18) recalls the malediction of Eliphaz against the dwelling of
the fool (5:3ff.) and the isolation where the wicked dwell in the
midst of ruins (15:28). With what speech of Job's friends can we
connect 24:18-24? The preceding analyses have revealed no lacuna
into which it would fit. But we shall see that there was a speech
of Zophar (27:13-23) which has been assigned to Job at the cost
of many singularities. In fact our passage forms the link between
27:13, the opening of Zophar's speech, and 27:14.[3] The mysterious
alternation of the singular and plural in 24:18 thus becomes quite
natural.[4] The punishment and death of the guilty precede the ills
of those who survive him (27:14-17).[5]

[1] See our translation and Commentary between 27:13 and 27:14.

[2] Another hypothesis, that of an interpolation intended to modify the
impression produced by the speech of Job, cannot be maintained. Such
interpolations would only be justified if occurring through all the speeches
of Job. The bad state of the text bears witness to its age. Peake merely
states the hypothesis mentioned above, and he admits that the passage may
come from the speech of one of the friends (Peake, *Job*, p. 228, n. 18).

[3] Fr. Hontheim placed 24:18-20 between 27:13 and 27:14. It is the
whole passage 24:18-24 which we shall intercalate here.

[4] Cf. Comm. on 24:18 (after 27:13).

[5] Marshall considered 24:18-21 as a speech of Bildad, which obliged him
to put in the mouth of Zophar (contrary to the data of the text) the passages
25:2-6; 26:5-14. Hoffmann and Ley attribute to Bildad 24:18-20, which
they place between 25 and 27:13-23. Laue also is inclined to attribute 24:18,

24:25 remains, of course, as the conclusion of Job's speech. This verse is well in harmony with the general style of interjections or interrogations of the sufferer (cf. Comm.).

Following the order observed in the first two cycles, it is now Bildad's turn to speak. It is he, in fact, who appears in ch. 25. He does not directly address the interlocutors any more than does Eliphaz or Job in this third cycle. Without introduction he begins a doxology without even mentioning the name of God, who is simply 'He' (25:2-3). Whilst Eliphaz (5:8-18), Zophar (11:5-12), and Job on two occasions (9:2-13; 12:9-25), have devoted a few strophes to the exaltation of the divine glories, Bildad has neglected to do so, and it is this omission which the poet now makes good.[1]

He inserts into this doxology the classic syllogism about the impossibility of man's being pure in the eyes of God, which Eliphaz had twice affirmed (4:17-19; 15:14-16). Bildad changes the term of the comparison, which is no longer the angels or the saints, but the moon and the stars (25:4-6). We now expect a conclusion. Bildad suddenly stops. Had he uttered something especially inadmissible, we should understand that Job suddenly interrupts him (26). But this is not the case. Bildad expresses himself within the framework of the customary platitudes. Job's interruption—if in fact it is an interruption—is introduced by a whole strophe (26:2-4), which implies that a long speech must be interrupted by an ironic comment. In fact, however, it is only a few verses about God and man. And what is even more puzzling, Job interrupts only to continue the doxology (26:5-14) at the very point where Bildad has left off. What we lacked in order to complete the speech of Bildad we now find on the lips of Job. If we place 26:5-14 after

---

21, 24, to Bildad. On these various theories, see Peake, op. cit., p. 228 and p. 232; Regnier, *RB*, 1924, pp. 187f. Various selections among all the verses of ch. 24, with the purpose of recomposing from them short poems, are proposed by Merx, Bickell, and Duhm, who furnish only arguments drawn from the poetic *form*, whether it be a question of metre or strophe. As 24:18-20 is one of the most difficult passages, merely from the point of view of the text itself, G. B. Gray can easily show the subjective character of these reconstructions, which, furthermore, are not mutually consistent (*The Book of Job*, p. 205). We cannot follow the methods of recomposition of Torczyner (*Das Buch Hiob*, pp. 172ff.) and Buttenwieser (*The Book of Job*, pp. 52ff., 253, etc.), who pick up a verse or part of a verse here and there in order to scatter it about the rest of the speeches. The Book of Job thus becomes a puzzle which each critic re-fashions as he pleases.

[1] This observation does not favour those who, like Marshall, would attribute ch. 25 to Zophar (cf. preceding note).

25:6, Bildad, like Eliphaz, recovers his third speech. The doxology began with the heavenly beings (25:2-3) and continued with the terrestrial beings (25:4-6). We expect the infernal beings, the Manes, and that is what we find in 26:5-6. Then comes some reference to the activity of God in the creation and organisation of the world (26:7-10), as also in extraordinary phenomena (26:11-13), to conclude with the impossibility of understanding the divine mysteries (26:14), which brings us to a kind of agnosticism, preached by Zophar (11:5-10) and Eliphaz (15:7-8). Hence it seems to us indisputable that the speech of Bildad, begun in 25:2-6, continues in 26:5-14.[1]

If we restore to Bildad the section 26:5-14, the result will be that Job's speech, 26:1-4, will be continued by 27:2ff., and that the formula of introduction, 27:1, becomes unnecessary. Now, we believe that there is a close connection between 26:4 and 27:2-3, which contains an allusion to the spirit that is man.[2] Let us see now whether Job's speech develops according to a logical sequence.

First, the irony of the unhappy man who has been given only Platonic consolations (26:2-3): Bildad has been speaking in the air (26:4). This is such a comment as we expect from Job, after he has listened to a speech in which there has been no allusion to the evils he is suffering, and which has consisted merely of general speculative ideas. With a new burst of energy, and despite the apparent injustices of God, Job refuses to remain silent, but insists on speaking in the name of the truth (26:2-4). He will not give way to the sophisms which aim at making him pass as guilty because he is

---

[1] The various reconstructions of Bildad's speech are enumerated by Gray (op. cit., p. xl) and by Regnier (*RB*, 1924, pp. 186ff.): ch. 25+28 (Stuhlmann); 25+26: 5-14 (Elzas, Cheyne, in his first position, Reuss, Siegfried); 26: 2-4+ 25: 2-6+26: 5-14 (Duhm); 25: 2-3+26: 5-14 (Peake); 15: 17-19+25: 4-6 (Hontheim); 25+24: 13-25 (Hoffmann; see above, as regards ch. 24); 25+ 24: 18-20+27: 13-23 (Ley; cf. ibid.); 24: 18-21 (Marshall). Bickell changed his system between 1882 (25+27: 8-10, in *Carmina V.T. Metrice*) and 1894 (25: 2-3 and 26: 12, 13, 14c+25: 4-6, in *Das Buch Hiob nach Anleitung*, etc.). Our own system, which we had reached as a result of a simple study of the text, is in fact the same as that of Elzas and a few others (see above). We suppose simply that a page of the MS or one column, on which was written 26: 5-14, has been intercalated accidentally after 26: 1-4, whereas it should have been placed after 25: 1-16. The arrangement of the present text has been supported by Budde and defended by Regnier (op. cit.). In reply to the article of the latter I have expounded my point of view in *RB*, 1924, pp. 351ff. Father Ricciotti, whose commentary *Il libro di Giobbe* reached me too late for use, supports the traditional order (pp. 187ff.).

[2] Cf. Comm. on 27: 3.

unfortunate; he will not renounce his innocence (27:5-6). It is not against himself but against his enemy that divine vengeance would exert itself; Job is not the wicked one whom God refuses to hear: quite the contrary (27:7-10)! Of this Job is keenly aware. His conscience is above the insinuations of his friends, and the problem still remains untouched; why then continue a debate which has no issue (27:11-12)?

The last verse, 'If you all have observed this, why then do you do uselessly a vain thing?' (27:12), is one of those incisive traits by which Job is accustomed to terminate his replies (cf. 21:34).

At 27:13 there is an abrupt change. We have here a verse of Zophar repeated almost literally (20:39):

> This is the portion of the wicked man, as decreed by God,
> And the lot which tyrants receive from Shaddai. (27: 13)

The verse announces a descriptive passage, for it cannot be, as in 20:29, the conclusion of a speech. If we leave it in the mouth of Job, it is clear that—according to all his previous utterances and especially 21 [1]—the description will stress the good fortune of the wicked, contrary to the thesis of the friends, who insist that the wicked are unfortunate and that the good man must be prosperous. But it is this very contention of the friends which Job now supports: the sons of the wicked are given over to the sword, to famine, pestilence, and ruin (27:14), and it is the good man who enjoys their wealth (27:17). The guilty man perishes, he dies in the midst of his riches (27:18-19), or, if he lives, it is to be the victim of terror and contempt (27:20-3). Thus we are back again in the doctrines of Eliphaz (15:20-36), Bildad (18:11-21), and Zophar (20:4-29). Thus we have here a passage like that of 24:18-24, which too was found to be out of place on the lips of Job, as we have seen above.[2] Now, 24:18-24 ought to have belonged to the speech of a friend; but it is impossible to transfer it to one of the previous chapters since all the speeches are complete. Eliphaz has made his third speech, which is complete (22). As for Bildad, we have been able to recover the text of his third speech by adding to ch. 25 the passage 26:5-14, which had got accidentally astray from its original context. Hence there remains 24:18-24 and 27:13-23—sections which belong to a friend of Job other than Eliphaz and Bildad. They can only be

---

[1] We have pointed out in detail in *RB*, 1924, pp. 344ff., the opposition between the remarks of Job in 21 and those which are attributed to him here.
[2] Pp. xlvi ff.

the utterance of Zophar, who for the moment has disappeared from the scene. If the passages 24:18-24 and 27:13-23 can be welded together so as to form one whole, there can be no doubt that such a speech will be that of the third friend.

The quite natural introduction is found in 27:13, which is certainly from Zophar, since it is the repetition of his last conclusion (20:29). But instead of the fate of the wicked and tyrants, declared in 27:13, it is the fate of their sons and survivors which the following passage (27:14-17) depicts, and this is exposed to the irony of Job in 21:19-21: it is not in his sons but in himself that man should be punished.[1] Now, this punishment which overtakes the wicked and tyrants, we have found in 24:18-24, and since this passage must be combined with 27:13-23 to form the final speech of Zophar, the obvious course is to interpolate it between 27:13 and 27:14. By an unhoped-for chance, 24:18, which contains the alternation of singular and plural, becomes thus explained in the most normal way, the singular הוּא 'he' referring to the 'wicked man' and the plural suffix of חֶלְקָתָם 'their domain' referring to the tyrants of 27:13. The page or column which contained 24:18-24 was torn from its original context and became affixed to the place which it now occupies and where as we have seen it has no justification.[2]

---

[1] Cf. RB, 1924, p. 349.

[2] As early as 1780 Kennicott claimed for Zophar the passage 27: 13-23, but he considered ch. 28 as a reply to Zophar, whereas Stuhlmann, connecting ch. 28 with ch. 25 (cf. above) began at 27: 11 the speech of Zophar (Regnier, RB, 1924, pp. 186f.). For Graetz and Hoffmann it is 27: 7-28: 28 which contains the speech of Zophar. Bickell thinks the speech of Zophar includes 27: 7-10, 14ff. This also is the opinion of Duhm, Peake, and (with a query) Gray. The general tendency is to restore to Zophar part of ch. 27. It will be observed that certain critics, such as Studer, Bernstein, Wellhausen, Kuenen, Siegfried, dispute the authenticity of 27: 7-10, 14-23. Dillmann considers that the passage 27: 13-23 has been revised and watered down (Hiob, 4th ed., p. 247). It is clear that the delicate point is always 27: 13-23. Our own explanation has the advantage of avoiding the wholesale changes in the text recommended by Volz. It should be noted that Buttenwieser, always so bold, transfers the whole pericope 27: 13-23 to a position after 22: 16, in the speech of Eliphaz. The account of the various systems figures in the article of Regnier which we have already cited (RB, 1924, pp. 186ff.). The author attempts to maintain the traditional order, and his analysis is interesting as showing the last effort of those who wish to retain, at any and every cost, in the speech of Job the very doctrine which Job has most hotly contested. One feels that everywhere the text has to be subjected to explanations so subtle that they become disconcerting. And above all the irony which it is desired to impute to Job is in no wise apparent (cf. RB, 1924, p. 348). Budde, who also maintains the traditional order, transfers

The result of this accident has been the disappearance of the little formula which introduced the speech of Zophar and which we restore in front of 27:13. If it is felt that Zophar begins *ex abrupto*, it will be noticed that the same is true of Eliphaz (22:2) and Bildad (25:2) in this third cycle.

Ch. 28 does not belong to the discussion. It is a magnificent poem on wisdom, in the style of Pr 8:22-31. Here it is not a question of evil but of the intrinsic nature of wisdom and the mystery of knowledge. Man knows where to find silver, gold, iron, copper (28:1-2); he searches the rocks and the earth, he digs mines, he finds precious stones far from any living creature; nothing escapes him (28:3-11). And in a melancholy tone the author adds this refrain which will reappear a little further on, scarcely modified:

> But whence comes Wisdom?
> And where is the place of understanding? (28: 12)

Vainly is it sought for on the earth and in the deep (28:13-14). In the market where are displayed gold, silver, precious stones, coral, crystal, topaz, and every kind of treasure, it is not be found, and cannot be bought (28:15-19):

> Whence then comes Wisdom?
> And where is the place of understanding? (28: 20)

Inaccessible to the living, perhaps it is in the realms of death that a trace of it may be found (28:21-2). God alone has seen it and known it, in the time when He organised the structure of the universe (28:23-7). A verse was added later (28:28) to bring to a practical conclusion this fine metaphysical flight.[1] The poem has been inserted in the Book of Job in order to express a general judgment on the previous discussions. The author may very well be the same as he who wrote the poetic debate.[2] He wished to show that wisdom is not to be found as the end of human seeking and that God alone, who possesses it, can impart it to man's understanding.

v. 7 to a place after v. 10 and eliminates vv. 21-2. The very disagreement between critics is a proof of the difficulty of the problem. We have thought it best to adhere to a solution which is both simple and easily admissible: a material error in the pagination. To conclude we shall note that by the distribution suggested by the text the last speech of Bildad (25: 2-6+ 26: 5-14) counts 15 verses, that of Job (26: 2-4+27: 2-12) 14 verses, that of Zophar (27: 13+24: 18-24+27: 14-23) 18 verses. Thus there is a certain proportion between these speeches, chiefly between that of Bildad and that of Job.

[1]   Cf. Comm. on 28: 28.
[2]   Below, p. xcvii.

The reader has a breathing space after the discussions which have not been interrupted since ch. 4. The pause here is deliberate before the long speech of Job which is to conclude the poetic dialogue.

Job's lament in ch. 3 had opened the fire. The last word in the debate will naturally remain with the hero of the story and of the poem. Job now rises above the dialogue. He no longer takes account of the interlocutors; he speaks for posterity and for God.[1]

First of all he takes a long retrospective glance at that past felicity the remembrance of which is so bitter to the heart of the sorrowing:

> Who will make me once more as I was in the months
> now gone,
> In the days when Eloah made me secure? (29: 2)

He evokes a past of happiness, family life, opulence, esteem, power, prestige, personal influence (29:3-10, 21-5). Praises were added to congratulations, for his fortune was compatible with largesse towards the poor, the orphan, the widow (29:12-13) and with righteous conduct towards all (29:14). Those who were unfortunate through their birth or the wrongs of society found in Job a ready support, a father, a defender (29:15-17). Everything predicted a happy old age, an eternal springtime of prosperity and glory (29: 18-20).

What a contrast with his present situation! Scorn from urchins of low degree, whose fathers died of hunger, were tramps and pariahs (30:1-8). It is these wretches who now insult Job, spit in his face, freed as they are from every sort of constraint (30:9-11). In terms reminiscent of his previous speeches (16:7ff.), Job describes the assaults of which he is the victim (30:12-15), and then returns to his grief by day and by night (30:16-17). From his present persecutors he turns to the original author of his ills, exactly as in 16:11ff. and 19:6ff. It is God who persecutes him, strikes him down, sports with him to the point of death (30:18-23)!

Why? Job has done nothing but what is praiseworthy. Not only has he practised justice, but also charity (30:24-5). Hence he had every right to expect happiness (30:26). Alas! what has come is misfortune, parching want, cries of pain, the anguish of disease, sighs and tears (30:27-31).

And Job has avoided even the occasion of sin (31:1). What an

---

1 An accident similar to that which has resulted in the misplacing of 24: 24-8 and 26: 5-14 (cf. above) has occurred in ch. 29, where the passage 11-20 must be replaced after 21-5.

enigma! Either God does not treat the wicked man according to his works (31:2-3), or else he pays no attention to His servant (31:4). Otherwise He would know that Job is righteous and blameless (31:5-6).

Job will affirm his innocence solemnly so that no one should be ignorant of it.[1] A negative confession, such as was placed on the lips of the dead before Osiris. No sin of desire or of action (31:7-8). No adultery (31:9-12). No injustice towards manservant or maidservant (31:13-15). No resistance to the beseeching of the poor, the widow, the orphan (31:16-18). Job has clothed the naked (31:19-20), has respected the defenceless orphan (31:21-2). The fear of God has guided his steps, and it is not in gold that he has placed his trust (31:23-5). Above all, he has not given himself to the cult of the stars or denied his God (31:26-8). He has spared even his enemies (31:29-30). He has been a model of hospitality, not only for his kinsmen, but for the wayfarer and the sufferer (31:31-2). He has respected the goods of others and has not seized land (31:38-40). He is not ashamed of his conduct, he has nothing to hide (31:33-4). On the contrary, he demands the widest publicity, and, proud of his part, he presents himself before the Almighty, armed with the indictment which his friends wished to draw up against him but which should constitue his crowning glory (31:35-7).

On this declaration of innocence and this appeal to the supreme tribunal the admirable peroration of Job ends. All the insinuations of his friends are reduced to nought. He is unhappy beyond all expression, but his distress is not the punishment of a sin, for Job has remained true to himself, faithful to God, just and kindly to his neighbour. Misfortune is one thing, innocence is another. The theories of Job's friends denied this antinomy; they did not explain it. Job affirms it, but does not explain it either. The problem of the relation between moral good and good fortune, moral evil and misfortune, has not yet been solved. We still await a solution. Will it be given us in the speeches of Elihu?

---

[1] A short passage, 31:38-40, has been the victim of an accident to the text. Its natural position is after v. 32.

CHAPTER FIVE

THE SPEECHES OF ELIHU
(cf. pp. xcviiiff.)

From ch. 32 a new person appears on the scene. Nothing has prepared us for his intervention. A short prose prologue explains why he has so far remained silent (32:1-5). But since he was not introduced to us in the narrative which opens the book, we were not concerned with his attitude. His genealogy, country, and family are given, whilst for the three friends of Job it was felt to be sufficient to give their country. Elihu is a young man and has listened patiently while old age speaks. But his impetuosity can no longer be restrained, and he will speak so much that neither Job nor his three friends will have an opportunity of saying a word. The speeches of Elihu will be monologues. The formula of introduction repeats the name of his father and country: Elihu, the son of Barachel the Buzite, is to speak.

We are given a long exordium, to explain how Elihu has been waiting for these old men to display their wisdom (32:6-7), and how his expectation has been disappointed, for it is the spirit in man and not the age which renders him wise and intelligent (32:8-13). Elihu will take care not to follow the method of the aged, since it has resulted only in their confusion, and Job has reduced them to silence (32:14-15). Elihu has done his duty by listening; he will now do it by talking (32:16-17). Furthermore, he can no longer remain silent; too many ideas crowd upon his brain (32:18-20). He will have no regard for any one whomsoever (32:21-2).

He begins by directly apostrophising Job, with whom he proposes to enter on a discussion (33:1-5). There is nothing to fear since the argument is between two men, not between a man and God (33:6, 4, 7).

Elihu then sums up the contention of Job: I am innocent and yet God persecutes me (33:8-11)! Such is the position which Job has clung to throughout the debate. Further, Job has complained because God does not answer him (33:12-13). It is this second complaint which will first be dealt with. The former will be the object of ch. 34.

God does speak, and it is for man to hear Him when He does (33:14). Sometimes it is in dreams and apparitions (33:15-16), so that man may be delivered from pride and death (33:17-18); sometimes by pain and illness which are the gates of death (33:19-22). It is an angel who plays the part of intermediary between God and the sufferer, and of intercessor with God on behalf of the sufferer (33:23-4), to save him. The effect of this intervention is healing, return to grace, joy, salvation (33:25-8). The action of God, in these various aspects, has as its aim and effect to save man from death (33:29-30).

After this first theory, Elihu demands the attention of Job and even invites him to speak (33:31-3). But it is now Job who adopts the rôle of listener in silence. Elihu turns to the friends and proposes to them a serious examination of what Job has said (34:2-4). The first point to be attacked (33:8-11) has as its corollary the injustice of God, since God is persecuting an innocent man (34:5-6). This is an impious and untenable thesis (34:7-8), since it is tantamount to saying that there is no advantage in serving God (34:9).

This is precisely the opposite of the truth. God is supremely righteous. He renders to each according to his works; it is impossible for Him to act unjustly (34:10-12). And, in fact, it is God to whom the world belongs, it is He who must govern it, He who is above kings, noblemen, princes, and the rich; how could He exercise justice if He were not Himself just (34:13-20)?

God is supremely righteous. Besides, He knows all things, nothing escapes Him (34:21, 22, 25). He has no need to make investigations or appointments (34:23-4); He chastises as He pleases those who have become estranged from Him and have oppressed their neighbour (34:26-8). He intervenes in the life of societies as in that of individuals, for His justice is independent of all (34:29-30). The passage which follows, and of which the text is corrupt, seems to confront Job with a case of conscience and to throw on him the onus of a reply, so that his ignorance may be exposed to all (34:31-3). Elihu triumphs (34:34-5). But he wishes to pursue his examination and silence Job, for he cannot suffer that he does not admit his fault and speaks against God (34:36-7).

The concatenation of ideas in ch. 35 is somewhat difficult to grasp, and it will be necessary to make constant reference to the Commentary on each verse. This is how we think it possible to understand the thought of Elihu.

A new grievance against Job is his having claimed that his fault was of no consequence to God (35:2-3; cf. 7:20). Doubtless, replies Elihu, God is too exalted for us to be able to reach Him either in bad fortune or good, by our faults or by our righteousness (35:4-7). But there is man, and it is our brother man who is either profited or harmed by our conduct (35:8).

Job had complained of the excess of violence and of the fact that God paid no attention to the cries of the oppressed (24:12). Elihu takes up this idea, of which he is reminded at this point by his observation that man harms his fellow-man (35:9). If God fails to intervene, it is because the unfortunate utter vain cries without turning directly to God, the Creator and Governor of all things (35:10-13). Still more justifiably will God refrain from replying if man refers to Him by remarks such as Job has uttered and which have been heard by all (35:14-16).

Once again Elihu calls for attention. He insists on his veracity and his knowledge (36:2-4). This time it is a long dogmatic and historic exposition to which he subjects Job. God is great and righteous, rendering to each man according to his works (36:5-7). He takes an example drawn from the history of Judah. Kings have been placed on the throne by God, but the only result is that they become proud (36:7). They are then punished with captivity and affliction (36:8). God reveals to them their sin (36:9, 10). The guilty man is faced with the alternative either of being converted and thus attaining salvation (36:11), or else of refusing to hearken and that means death without more ado (36:12). Some remain insensible in the face of misfortune; only death can punish them (36:13-14). In brief, misfortune is an instrument in the hands of God to save the guilty (36:15). Job may therefore hope that his misfortunes will result not in his ruin but in his happiness and glory (36:16-17).[1] In that case he should be careful to avoid a further lapse (36:18-21).

And now Elihu abandons his harsh reasonings on the case of Job. He rises to a more exalted plane, and soars on the wings of doxology. He will make the sublimity of God apparent (36:22). God is above all things: man can only sing His praises and contemplate His works (36:23-5). God is not to be measured by time (36:26). He is

---

[1] Vv. 19-20 are alien to the context (cf. Comm.).

the author of all meteoric phenomena: rain, storm, snow, showers, cold, ice, lightning, and thunderbolts. These phenomena are described, with more or less detail, but with a somewhat high-flown poetic style, in 36:27-37:13. Elihu draws Job's attention more especially to certain extraordinary facts such as the lightning, the balancing of the clouds, the heat (37:14-18). He interrupts the flow of his eloquence in order to declare that there is no more to be said in the presence of these wonders (37:19-20). But suddenly, as though a storm had occurred during his speech, he stresses the action of the wind which has just swept the clouds away (37:21-2). The conclusion is that God is not within our reach: He is Eloah, Shaddai, the Almighty, by reason of His power and righteousness; He must be feared and reverenced; He has no accounts to render us (37:22-4).

The striking feature of this long monologue of Elihu is that it is conceived with a subtlety to which the three friends of Job had not accustomed us. The latter had confined themselves to the essential points of the thesis: the relation between virtue and happiness, as between sin and misfortune. Elihu tries to discover the meaning of sorrow and trial; he explains the various ways in which the divine justice may manifest itself; he shows how in societies this justice, which is sometimes so little apparent, does in fact operate, and he concludes with an exalted treatise on the action of God in the world of nature. He envisages the case of Job only to a very secondary degree, although quite often he addresses the hero, even by his name. His thesis is the summing up a of whole body of theological teaching the sources of which it will be easy for us to recognise.[1]

[1] See below, pp. xcviiiff.

CHAPTER SIX

THE SPEECHES OF YAHWEH
(cf. pp. lxxxvff.)

The poetic section of the Book of Job does not end with the speeches of Elihu. The Lord Himself 'out of the heart of the tempest' finally speaks. He addresses Job directly, paying no attention either to Elihu or even to the three friends. Job is shaken by the speeches of Yahweh. He can only stammer forth a few words of apology and repentance (40:3-5; 41:1-3, 5). The only reproach which he feels on his conscience is that of having spoken lightly about things which he did not understand. The words of Yahweh have no other aim but to show how vain and futile it is to presume to speak about the nature of God and His works. God alone knows these marvels and He alone can give voice to them. A sense of sublimity governs these verses from beginning to end and puts them among the most admired examples of inspired poetry.

Yahweh then apostrophises Job and subjects him to an interrogation (38:2-3). By skilful questions, He shows Job that the mysteries of nature elude his understanding. Where was Job when God laid the foundations of the earth, constructed it, and brought it into existence (38:4-7)? Who enclosed the sea, swathed it like an infant, and broke the pride of its waves (38:8-11)? Who brings forth the dawn and the morning light whose function is to banish the night and the power of darkness (38:12-15)? And who can reach the depths of the abyss and Sheol (38:16-18)? Light and darkness, snow, hail, mist, the sirocco, rainstorms, thunderbolts, the rain that waters the desert places, dew, ice, hoarfrost, all these are phenomena of day and night, of the months and seasons, which are depicted in succession in a few words to show how their origin and their causes escape man's perception (38:19-30). Then comes reference to the constellations, whose structure and course and influences are inaccessible to us (38:31-3). Finally Yahweh speaks of storms and especially rain, which is heralded by the cock and falls on the earth from the sky according to a skilful design (38:34-8).

After these common and yet inexplicable phenomena, Yahweh describes the animals in their range and variety, and especially those whose life and reproduction conform to laws which escape us: the lioness and the raven, those hunters which satisfy their young with the venison they have caught (38:39-41), the antelopes and the hinds which at specific times crouch and bring forth their off-spring, the latter fleeing away into the desert (39:1-4); the wild ass roaming freely far from towns (39:5-8); the buffalo which refuses to be tamed (39:9-12); the ostrich above all which appears stupid yet mocks at the horse and its rider (39:13-18); the horse whose exultant strength and warlike snorting and ferocity are described in terms which have become classic (39:19-25); and the monarchs of the air, the hawk and the eagle, dwelling on rocky crags whence they spy out the prey for their young which suck up blood (39:26-30).

At this point Yahweh breaks off, for the ceaseless stream of sublime utterances crushes Job, who at the interpellation of Yahweh can find only one word to reply, namely that he has nothing to say (40:1-5).

The speech is resumed with accents of divine irony, Yahweh asking Job to give evidence of his power, his glory, his anger, his mastery, and thus to prove that he is capable of doing without God (40:7-14). Job makes no reply.

To bring the stupefaction of the hearer to its height, Yahweh resumes His description of wild beasts, now choosing the most extraordinary specimens. First the hippopotamus, whose amphibious ways, proverbial strength, and overlordship of the other animals make of him a creature apart, both formidable and amusing (40:15-24). Then the crocodile, with its terrible name, Leviathan, which cannot be approached without alarm or danger (40:25-32; 41:2, 1, 3). Of extraordinary strength, it is armed with a solid, inviolable protective covering, it spits out fire through the nostrils and mouth, it is compact and invulnerable, both within and without, it mocks at every weapon. It leaves traces of its passage on land and water; it is a creature unparalleled and fearless, the king of all ferocious beasts (41:4-26).

The last blow has been struck. Job confesses that he has been speaking out of ignorance. Now he knows what to believe; he is plunged in repentance (42:1-3, 5).

It may be said of the speeches of Yahweh, as of those of Elihu, that they form a perfectly distinct whole, by comparison with the rest of the poetic book. They consist of monologues in which the author has surpassed himself and is able to give free rein to his imagination no longer trammelled by the exigencies of the debate. They give us a series of pictures which progressively unfold before our gaze the wonders of the world, beginning with land, sea, atmosphere, skies, proceeding through the world of living creatures both quadrupeds and birds, to finish with those two monstrous beings, Behemoth and Leviathan, which seem to elude all classification and were felt to form a group apart in the fauna of the Nile, as is confirmed by texts and monuments.

Let us remember that the prose Epilogue is linked with the speeches of Yahweh by 42:7a: 'And after Yahweh had spoken these words to Job.'

CHAPTER SEVEN

THE COMPOSITION OF THE BOOK OF JOB

In the previous pages we have been satisfied to follow the course of development taken by the book of Job, in order to discern clearly the sequence of facts and ideas in each of its component parts: the prose book, the poetic colloquy, the speeches of Elihu, and those of Yahweh. Here there were four elements, the first of which, the prose book, was subdivisible into a Prologue and Epilogue, within the framework of which are fitted, as by successive stages, the three great unities of the poetic work. And it is this whole which forms our present Book of Job.

The question now before us is to discover how these various elements have been merged into a whole which begins with the eulogy of Job and ends with the death of the hero. Tradition has not named the author of this sacred book. We know of course that a certain passage of the Babylonian Talmud attributes its composition to Moses,[1] and this idea has been adopted by some Greek and Latin authors.[2] But the sequel to the Talmudic passage gives the varying opinions of the rabbis on the age in which Job lived, and since the period is sometimes placed well after the time of Moses [3] it is clear that the attribution of the work to Moses represents only an isolated opinion.

If our analysis of the four great sections which compose the book has been carefully followed, it will be appreciated that the problem before us is not that of discovering whether stories or poems existing separately have been compiled to form a whole. The work of compilation presupposes the existence of isolated elements which, more or less skilfully, are juxtaposed to form a whole, and of this nature is the *Diatessaron* of Tatian. In such cases each part may have an independent end and existence, separate from the rest of the work. The art of the compiler consists in making of these scattered members an organic whole and infusing into them a

---

[1] *Baba Bathra*, 14b.
[2] Cf. Cornely, *Introductio specialis*, II, pp. 48f.
[3] Above, p. xx.

unified life. But such is not the aspect in which the Book of Job offers itself to our consideration. Each part of it was written in view of the totality. No part existed separately. The development of the composition is purely internal and intrinsic. It is not comparable to the snowball which as it rolls gathers more snow to itself. It is comparable rather to the plant which grows in virtue of its own internal life and is nourished by the same sap until the time of its complete blossoming. How could we understand the speeches of Elihu apart from the framework of the Book of Job? Where could we situate the magnificent pictures drawn by Yahweh, after the speeches of Elihu, except where we find them, as a conclusion to the poetic book? Can the discussion between Job and his friends dispense with the Prologue and Epilogue? It would no longer have any meaning. Hence what is important for us to know is not the particular origin of each part but rather the moment of its appearance, the stage which it represents in the dramatic development of the theme, the point to which it leads us in our progress to the solution. Excessive dissection would deprive of all life a work which from one end to the other is controlled by a few governing ideas. We must retain as a basis for our investigation the fact that each part possesses an apparent unity, a unity which, apart from certain inevitable and very minimal adventitious elements, implies a single author.[1] Hence it is fundamentally a question of deciding to what extent the author of one of the parts is at the same time the author of another or several other parts, or whether the work, taken up to a certain point by one author, has then been continued or completed by one or by several other authors. In short, the question of unity does not arise in regard to each part, but in regard to the whole, and it has been variously resolved. In order to give to this exposition all desirable clarity, we shall first of all determine the characteristics of the prose narrative as contrasted with those of the poem, then we shall try to understand the relation between this prose part and the essential section of the poem, namely the great dialogue which goes from ch. 3 to ch. 31 inclusive. This dialogue is in fact welded with the Prologue, and we shall have to see whether the link is an artificial one or whether it is integral to the original theme. Next, leaving aside the speeches of Elihu, which are directly connected with neither the Prologue nor the Epilogue, we

---

[1] An observation which will have been made by all those who have followed the preceding analyses.

shall study the function fulfilled by the speeches of Yahweh which are welded with the Epilogue. Lastly we shall consider the speeches of Elihu.

A. Characteristics of the Prose Narrative and those of the Poem

There is no need for us to return to the subject matter itself of the two parts which we have in view. This work has been done separately for the prose narrative [1] and for each constituent element in the poem.[2] What we wish to examine rather are the formal, somewhat external, features which divide into two distinct categories the Prologue and Epilogue on the one hand and the rest of the work on the other.

1. *Poetry and Prose.* The first of these features consists in the language adopted. Whereas the Prologue and Epilogue are written in prose, the rest of the work, apart from the formulae of introduction to each speech and the short notice preceding the intervention of Elihu, is composed in poetry.[3] The characters hold their colloquy in verse, Elihu recites his monologues in verse, and it is in verse that Yahweh expresses Himself on the theme of the marvels of nature. We shall see farther on what are the characteristic features of this Hebrew poetry, whose rhythms are equally well adapted to teaching and exposition on the one hand, and on the other to the vehemence of passion and the ardour of thought. The Massoretes were not wrong in using for this book the special system of accentuation which they adopted for Psalms and Proverbs.[4]

This mixture of prose and poetry is found also in other books of the Bible, for example, in the historical books where sometimes in the course of a narrative one of the personages or indeed several 'sing' a poem which tradition has consecrated. Similarly in the prophetic books the poetic oracles are introduced and commented on in a prose preface. The titles of the Psalms, when not simply consisting in the attribution of a Psalm to a certain author, contain at times an allusion in prose to the circumstances in which the particular Psalm was written. To the same prose style belong the

---

[1] Above, pp. xv ff.

[2] Above, pp. xxvi ff.

[3] St Jerome insists on this distinction in the Book of Job between the prose portions and what he calls 'hexameters' (*Praef. in lib. Job*, P.L. XXVIII, col. 1081).

[4] Above, p. vii.

superscriptions of Proverbs in chs. 30-1. As for the Book of Ecclesiastes, M. Podechard has been able to write that 'it is a question
whether Ecclesiastes is written in prose or verse' (p. 135), and that,
if the greater part of the book was written in prose, 'and even in a
rather poor prose' (p. 137), certain passages have a poetic form
(p. 141), in particular that of the classic *māshāl* (p. 139). Ecclesiasticus is entirely in poetry, the prose prologue coming from the
translator. As for the Book of Wisdom, it too is written in a poetic
style the laws of which are akin to those of formal Hebrew poetry.

The special feature of the Book of Job, however, is that the prose
and the poetic sections remain distinct, prose being reserved for the
narrative part and poetry for the colloquy or monologues.[1] Prose
is used only to furnish a framework for the whole poem. The situation
is different in the prophetic books, such as those of Isaiah or
Jeremiah, where prose is used to build up the collection of oracles,
to string together passages of varying origin and style. In the Book
of Job everything turns upon one episode: the misfortune which
strikes the hero. This misfortune is only the pretext for the greater
part of the book, which is in verse; it furnishes the theme of the
poetic dialogue. The author had only to make us acquainted with
this situation of calamity and the circumstances which make it
quite exceptional. And likewise the Epilogue, which gives us the
conclusion of the adventure, hardly permitted the amplitude of
treatment which characterises the dialogue where the theme is
debated. Thus it is easily understandable that prose was sufficient
for such accessory narrations. The monument which the author
aims at creating is the poem. The Prologue and Epilogue are no more
than its entrance and exit. Such considerations suffice to show that
the mere difference of prose and poetry could not be used as a basic
principle of discrimination. Such a difference of style is controlled
by the subject matter itself and is deliberately intended by the
author. The reader finds quite natural the transition from prose to
poetry when he ascends from the Prologue to the lament of Job,

---

[1] Gray rightly cites as an analogy, in oriental literature, the *maqâmat* of
Hariri, the narrative part of which is in prose, while the speeches are in verse
(*The Book of Job*, p. xxiii). In the fine dialogue between the god Nebo and
King Ashurbanipal, short prose notes introduce the speakers (recto, lines
13, 19, 23: verso, line 1): see the translation of Jensen, in *Keilinschr. Biblio-
tek*, VI, 2, pp. 136ff. The dialogue between the master and the slave (*RB*,
1921, pp. 624f.), as also the dialogue between the two friends (*RB*, 1923,
pp. 7ff.) are wholly in verse, without introduction or conclusion in prose.

quite natural also the return from poetry to prose when he descends from the exalted speeches of Yahweh to the Epilogue.[1]

This distinction between the language of the poetic book and the prose portions brings about also, as is natural, a great diversity in the means of expression employed. Poetry permits a wealth of rhetorical turns of phrase, special rhythms, imagery, which would not be suitable in the more pedestrian style of prose. Prose narration aims solely at truth and simplicity. The effect is produced by the facts themselves rather than the way in which they are presented. The poetry of the Book of Job belongs to several categories: it is sometimes elegiac, sometimes didactic, sometimes lyric or epic. Vivacity of style, emphasis of thought or hyperbolic expression, audacity of images, impetuosity or flexibility of the rhythms—these are all qualities required by the aesthetics proper to poetry. It is not only the style but the whole cast of sentiments and ideas which normally change when the voice or the pen abandons one mode to take up another. Here again we shall not find any compelling reason to attribute the poem to a different author from him who is responsible for the narrative portions. One and the same man can tell a story when necessary and sing when necessary.

2. *The Divine Names.* This is the place in which to consider the question of the divine names, the choice of which seems to have been dictated by a different principle in the prose as distinct from the poetic parts. This principle of differentiation generally heads the list of those features by means of which the two books are distinguished.[2] In fact it is remarkable that not only in the poetic dialogue (3-31) but also in the speeches of Elihu (32-7) and in those of

[1]   These reflections refute the hypotheses of Richard Simon, who placed on the same footing the narrative prose parts of the prophecies, the titles of the Psalms, and the Prologue of Job: 'A fact which will be the more easily recognised, on account of the diversity of the style, in regard to the first two chapters of Job, which have been placed at the head of this poem in the form of an argument or prologue.' There must be an essential difference between the presentation of the personages and the speeches which they utter. The text of Richard Simon is to be found in his *Hist. critique du Vieux Testament*, Book I, ch. IV (p. 33 of the 1680 ed.).

[2]   Note carefully that the question of the use of the divine names is adduced in support of a distinction between the author of the prose book and the author of the verse book. Other arguments are invoked for the attribution of a different origin to the poetic dialogue (which forms the very basis and essence of the verse book) and the Prologue or Epilogue. We shall examine these arguments in the section concerned with the 'relation between the prose narratives and the poetic dialogue'.

Yahweh (38-42) we find the rigorous application of a principle which seems to have been less absolutely applied in the prose narrative.

The principle is the following. Job and his interlocutors, whether Eliphaz and his two companions or even Elihu, not being Israelites, are forbidden to utter the sacrosanct name יהוה Yahweh. The poem scrupulously observes this law. A sole exception (12:9), due to a reminiscence,[1] only confirms the rule.

It was natural too that the name of Yahweh should not have been found on the lips of Yahweh Himself.

The divine names used in the poetic book are אֵל 'God', אֱלוֹהַ 'Eloah', אֱלֹהִים 'Elohim', שַׁדַּי 'Shaddai'.[2]

It should be noted further that the use of these names obeys certain laws or rather certain habits of speech typical of the various characters. The least frequent is Elohim, which is never accompanied by the article. It is found in isolation, i.e. not in parallelism with other divine names, in the poem on Wisdom (28:23), in a speech of Elihu (34:9), and in the stereotyped expression 'the sons of Elohim' which occurs in the speech of Yahweh (38:7). In the poetic dialogue (3-31) it is uttered only twice, once by Eliphaz (5:8) and once by Zophar (20:29). On both occasions it is in parallelism with אֵל 'God'. It should be noted that in the repetition of 20:29, at the beginning of the last speech of Zophar (27:13),[3] the name Shaddai is substituted for that of Elohim. One feels that the name Elohim is avoided in the poem, and especially in the poetic dialogue, where it plays only the part of a synonym, to be at once withdrawn as though the author had a scruple about allowing it to be repeated.

On the other hand, the other divine names occur frequently in the poem. Let us except, however, the speech uttered by Yahweh Himself. It is quite a matter of course that Yahweh should speak of Himself in the first person, just as Job, in his stammerings at the end, addresses Him in the second person. The name אֵל occurs in a short subordinate clause (38:41) and also when it is a question of such phrases as 'the arm of God' (40:9) or the 'works of God'

---

[1] Cf. Comm. on 12:9. The mention of Adonai, written in full, in 28:28 is due to the fact that the poem of Wisdom (28) has been given a conclusion of a practical kind (cf. Comm.).

[2] In order to give effectively the impression of the original, we have had to be satisfied with transcribing the names other than אֵל which represents the generic term 'God'.

[3] See above for the arrangement of ch. 27 (p. xlix).

(40:19) which are common expressions like 'the sons of Elohim' (38:7). As for Eloah, it figures only in 39:7 and in the apostrophe, 40:2, where it is parallel with Shaddai, which is found only in this connection in the speeches of Yahweh.

Let us now pass to the poetic dialogue (3-31). Statistics have been drawn up of the use of the three names אֵל, אֱלוֹהַ, and שַׁדַּי. The number of times that they recur either in the dialogue or the speeches of Elihu has been counted.[1] But what has not sufficiently been discerned is the skill with which—and herein lies a proof of unity—the poet has distributed these three names in the various speeches and above all in the poetic dialogue. The most striking examples are found towards the end of it, in ch. 27, where Job speaks for the last time against his friends, before delivering his last great apologia (29-31). In the following quotation the divine names are in italics, so as to bring out their sequence. Here is first 27:2-4.

> By *God* who has set aside my right,
> And by *Shaddai* who has embittered my soul!
> So long as my spirit remains inviolate within me,
> And the breath of *Eloah* is in my nostrils,
> My lips shall not speak any falsehood,
> Nor my tongue utter a lie.

Here we see the succession of the three names אֵל, שַׁדַּי, and אֱלוֹהַ, the three synonyms of the name of God.

Here now is 27:8-11.

> For what is the hope of the godless when he prays,[2]
> When he lifts up his soul[3] to *Eloah*?
> Does *God* hear his cry
> When calamity seizes him?
> Is his delight in *Shaddai*?
> Does he call upon *Eloah* at all times?
> I teach you the ways of *God*,
> What is in the mind of *Shaddai* I do not conceal.

Twice we have the alternation of the three terms אלוה, אל, and שדי. Hence it is a plainly perceptible device of the poet to have recourse in this way to the three divine names in order to vary his style and to avoid the repetition of one name. In this second series it is the name Eloah which stands first, while Shaddai comes last. Now, it is the name Eloah which occurs in Job's lament (3:4, 23), where

---

[1]　See especially the Table drawn up by Gray in *The Book of Job*, p. xxxv.
[2]　Read יִפְגַּע, which has become יבצע (cf. Comm.).
[3]　Read יִשָּׂא לֶאֱלוֹהַ, which has become ישל אלוה (cf. Comm.).

there is no other divine name, and it is the name Shaddai which will conclude the speeches of Job (31:35).

Of the three terms אל, אלוה, and שדי, the two former are more easily interchangeable, for it was fairly obvious to make the name אל and its plural אלהים derivatives of אלוה. For this reason the parallelism of אל and אלוה will be somewhat rare. Apart from 27:2-4; 8-11, where, as we have seen, the poet wished to give the series of three terms, אל in parallelism with אלוה is found only once. This occurs in a phrase of Job (12:6) which is very difficult to explain in its present context. We have pointed out [1] that the name Elohim occurred only twice in the poetic dialogue as a parallel to אל (5:8; 20:29). There was some hesitation in making parallel with El those names which were derived from it, Eloah and Elohim.

Hence the poet prefers to pair together Shaddai and Eloah or El (which we have translated 'God'). Thus Shaddai is made parallel with Eloah in the speeches of Eliphaz (5:17; 22:26), of Job (6:4; 21:19-20; 29:4-5; 31:2) and of Zophar (11:7). Bildad never uses the name Eloah and hence cannot make it parallel with Shaddai. But it is he who begins the parallelism of El and Shaddai (8:3, 5), and this association will be continued by Job (13:3; 21:14-15; 23:16), Eliphaz (15:25; 22:2-3, 17), and probably Zophar (27:13, which in the present text is in Job's speech).

These observations involve another, namely, that the name Shaddai hardly ever appears without the association of El or Eloah. It is found in isolation only in a passage of Eliphaz (22:23, 25) and a verse of Job (24:1).

The really independent divine names which can be used interchangeably are therefore El and Eloah. But here again it is remarkable that the name Eloah was never placed on the lips of Bildad. Apart from the cases of parallelism which we have cited (with El or Shaddai), it is also found three times in Eliphaz (4:9, 17; 15:8), twice in Zophar (11:5, 6), but fourteen times [2] in Job (6:8-9; 9:13; 10:2, 12:4; 16:20, 21; 19:6, 21, 26; 21:9; 24:12; 29:2; 31:6).

As for El, if we likewise eliminate the cases of parallelism noted above, it is found four times in Bildad (8:13-20; 18:21; 25:4), nine times in Job (9:2; 13:7, 8; 16:11; 19:22; 21:22; 31:14, 23, 28), four times in Eliphaz (15:4, 11, 13; 22:13), never in Zophar. Just

---

[1] Above, p. lxvi.

[2] We could say fifteen, if in truth, as we suppose to be the case, it is 'Eloah' which occurred in 12: 9.

as the author had refrained from placing Eloah on the lips of Bildad, so he gives El only once or twice to Zophar, and then by reason of parallelism (20:29; 27:13). And it should be observed that 20:29 is the conclusion of a speech containing the very rare Elohim, while 27:13 is a prefatory note which we attribute to Zophar only for lack of a better solution.[1]

These facts betray the author's intention of not using indifferently such or such divine names. The choice which he imposes on the speakers is dictated not only by the desire to vary his style but also by concern to assign quite deliberately to their use a particular name. If Job and Eliphaz have resort sometimes to one, sometimes to another of the three divine names used in the poem, Bildad and Zophar have certain restrictions imposed on them. In fact the name which all the characters may use, the term common to the four speakers and forbidden to none, is Shaddai,[2] pronounced eleven times by Job (6:4; 13:3; 21:15, 20; 23:16; 24:1; 27:2, 10; 29:5; 31:2, 35), seven times by Eliphaz (5:17; 15:25; 22:3, 17, 23, 25, 26), twice by Bildad (8:3, 5), and probably twice by Zophar (11:7; 27:13).

If now we pass to consider the speeches of Elihu, we notice the same phenomena as in the poetic colloquy in regard to the use of the divine names. We have already noted [3] that the name Elohim appeared only once (34:9). As for Shaddai, it is, as we should expect, made parallel to another divine name, either El (33:6; 34:10, 12; 35:13), or more rarely Eloah (37:22-3). It occurs in isolation only in 32:8. Leaving aside 34:31, where the divine name should probably be corrected,[4] the cases in which El is used without a parallel divine name are 32:13; 33:4, 14, 29; 34:5, 23, 37; 35:2; 36:5, 22, 26; 37:5, 10, 14. Those in which Eloah figures alone are 33:12, 26; 35:10; 36:2; 37:15.

Thus Elihu shows a marked predilection for El, and when he uses Shaddai it is generally as a parallel term to El or Eloah. The tendencies of the poetic dialogue in regard to the use of the divine names are manifested equally in the speeches of Elihu. We noted at the beginning of our investigation that these features were also

---

[1]   Above, p. xlix.
[2]   We leave out of account 6:14, which seems to be a later gloss (cf. Comm.).
[3]   Above, p. lxvi.
[4]   Cf. Comm.

present in the discourses of Yahweh (although less apparent, since God has rarely occasion to cite a divine name).

Hence the entire poetic book excludes the name Yahweh, accepts only very rarely and as if reluctantly that of Elohim, uses in the main only the three names El, Eloah, Shaddai, and subjects its uses of these names to certain laws, the most obvious of which is the parallelism of Shaddai with one or other of the two other names.

Now, a first fact to which attention has long been drawn is that these three names of the poem appear not once in the Prologue, Epilogue, or introduction to the speeches of Elihu (32:1-6).

On the other hand, the name Yahweh, excluded from the whole of the poem, is found at every stage of the narrative in the Prologue and Epilogue, as also in the prose formulae which announce the speeches of Yahweh. From 1:6 we feel that Yahweh is the transcendent being who holds in His hands all the threads of the drama. He is the protagonist who speaks with Satan in the Prologue, with Job in the speeches of Yahweh, and with Job's friends in the Epilogue. It is He who authorises the testing of Job, that experience from which the whole discussion is to arise, and it is He who puts an end to it, after giving His critical observations on the attitude of the characters in the drama. Actor, witness, and judge, it is not surprising that His name is found in the whole course of the narrative. Since the author was telling a story similar to all the other stories of the Old Testament, he had no scruples in referring throughout to Yahweh, considered as the supreme cause of events. He felt that there was absolutely no need to vary the style of his prose narration by substituting for Yahweh one of the three divine names used in the poem.

But there is one case, it would seem, where the author should have abstained from using the divine Tetragrammaton, namely, where this name is uttered by Job in 1:21, 'Naked I came out of my mother's womb, and naked shall I return. Yahweh has given and Yahweh has taken away! Blessed be the name of Yahweh!' This is one of the facts that have long been stressed in the thesis that separates the composition of the poem from the prose book. Duhm, who accepts the anteriority of the prose book,[1] writes as

---

[1] We shall return below to this theory and to the various opinions concerning what a certain type of German exegesis calls the *Volksbuch* or 'popular book'.

follows [1]: 'The author of the popular book, like the earliest narrator in the Pentateuch, the Yahwist, quite ingenuously (*ganz unbefangen*) puts the name Yahweh in the mouth of Job, whilst the poet (more recent) never does so, but remains constantly faithful to the idea that Job and his friends, because they are Edomites and Arabs, do not know this name of God.'

Hence a distinction has been made between a poet who is self-consistent in forbidding Job and his friends to utter the name Yahweh and a prose narrator who does not hesitate to leave this name on the lips of Job. To some critics the argument has seemed decisive, but it is not used by Budde, who, while accepting the idea of a *Volksbuch* distinct from the poem, claims that the presence of the name Yahweh in Job's benediction (1:21) is probably due to later changes in the text and that the name originally employed was that of Elohim.[2] According to Dillmann, the author had conveyed in the word of Job (1:21) a loftiness of conscience which might well have seemed ideal to any Israelite, and he had succeeded in expressing this note of sublimity in a fine sentence; hence the hero was given the licence to pronounce the sacrosanct name.[3]

But what should be noted above all is that in the prose narrative the passage in question (1:21) has all the features of an exception to be explained (exactly as in 12:9 in the poem); it does not flow from a general principle which can become the basis of an argument. In fact one may say that the author, who used the name Yahweh in the prose narrative itself, obeys the same scruples as the poet when it is a question of making his characters refer to God. It is Elohim, and not Yahweh, which is uttered by Yahweh Himself (1:8; 2:3), by Job (1:5; 2:10), by the messenger (1:16), by Job's wife (2:9), by Satan (1:9). And when one remembers the art with which the poet in his poem has made use of the three divine names El, Eloah, Shaddai, to the exclusion of Yahweh and almost of Elohim, one cannot but find in this procedure a fixed plan, that of reserving to the characters who speak in prose the use of the name Elohim, while the other three names are to belong to the speakers in verse. This surely is a very clear indication of the common origin from which the prose narrative and the poetic book alike

---

[1] *Das Buch Hiob*, Einleitung, p. vii.
[2] *Das Buch Hiob*, 2nd ed., commentary on 1:21 (p. 6) and Einleitung (p. xx).
[3] *Hiob*, 4th ed., p. 14.

stem. The only exception is 1:21. The reasons given above in explanation of it do not seem to us conclusive. What involved here the use of the name Yahweh was in the first place the formula *Sit nomen Domini benedictum*, which was part of ordinary eulogies, as is to be seen from Ps 113:2, where the words are found verbatim. Now, what Satan dared to say to Yahweh was that Job would 'curse Him to His face' (1:11). Instead of cursing Job blesses, and naturally it is Yahweh whom he must bless. Hence the exception to the common rule, an exception which also involves that of the preceding phrase: 'Yahweh has given and Yahweh has taken away.' For if the name to be blessed is that of Yahweh, this is done not only from the motive of giving the lie to Satan, but also from the recognition that it is Yahweh and none other who grants or takes away blessings and thus has the right to our gratitude or resignation.

Far from exploiting the use of the divine names in order to sever the prose narrative from the poetic book, we ought to see that the art of selecting these names, both in the prose and the poetic parts, suggests one head and one hand.

We shall have an opportunity of discussing the other arguments adduced in favour of this severance in the study on which we are now about to embark concerning the essential relation between the prose narration and the poetic dialogue.

B. THE POETIC DIALOGUE (3-31) AND ITS PROSE FRAMEWORK (1-2; 42:7-17)

After setting aside the poem on Wisdom (28), we were able to find three cycles of discussions between Job and his friends, discussions introduced by Job's lament (3) and terminated by his apologia (29-31). The question now before us is to decide to what extent the poetic dialogue comes from the same hand as the prose narrative.[1] We have already eliminated two arguments of a general nature, which, by the very fact that they severed the poem from the prose framework, would have entailed the consequence of a dual composition.[2] We must now examine the special reasons which have led some authors to make of the poetic dialogue (3-31) a substantially different work, both as to origin and development, from the narrative which now frames it (1-2; 42:7-17).

[1] We have seen (pp. xxxiff.) that the Prologue and Epilogue formed a unity.
[2] It is a question of arguments drawn from the use of a different language (poetry and prose) and from the method of using the divine names.

It is curious to observe, as Karl Kautzsch [1] has done, that the same arguments have been used to support two diametrically opposed theories, the one claiming the earliest date for the poetic dialogue, to which the prose story was added later,[2] the other recognising in the prose account the early substratum of the work to which a more recent writer would have joined the poetic colloquy. It is this second theory which has become most fashionable, and which is still held by some critics. But it has been used in various ways. Sometimes it has been thought that the poet had simply drawn upon that tradition which is reflected in Ezk 14:14, and in which he found the sources for an introduction to his dialogue.[3] Or again it has been maintained that a first author composed a story to which a dialogue was annexed; this story became the basis for the Prologue and Epilogue, while the dialogue was replaced by the present poem.[4] About 1895 L. Laue saw in the hypothesis of a popular story 'which the author presumably placed at the beginning of his poem, either by verbal borrowing or a free reproduction' the means of explaining the discrepancies between the prose narration and the poetic dialogue.[5]

Meanwhile Wellhausen, in a review of Dillmann's commentary dating from 1871, and Vernes, in an article in the *Revue de l'Histoire des Religions* (1880),[6] with the support of Bickell,[7] gave the hypothesis a precise shape. They felt that the traditional story which served as a point of departure for the poet consisted in the Prologue and Epilogue as we now have them. What remained was to find the word which would successfully launch the theory. Budde sup-

---

[1] *Das sogenannte Volksbuch von Hiob*, pp. 4, 15.

[2] We have cited above the opinion of Richard Simon. The main champions of the theory which places the poetic dialogue before the prose narrative were, in the eighteenth century, Schultens (1737) and Hasse (1789), in the nineteenth, Stuhlmann (1804), de Wette (1807), Bernstein (1813), von Cölln (1836), Knobel (1842). This theory, brilliantly disputed by Heiligstedt (1846), who, however, makes concessions in regard to Satan (cf. below), has been gradually supplanted by the theory of the old popular narrative. For the history of these hypotheses, see K. Kautzsch, op. cit., pp. 3ff.

[3] This seems to have been the first idea of Cheyne, as described in Kautzsch, op. cit., pp. 12f. It should be noted that Cheyne separated the question of the Prologue from that of the Epilogue. He did not admit the authenticity of the Epilogue.

[4] Cf. G. Hoffmann, *Hiob*, p. 22.

[5] *Die Komposition des Buches Hiob*, p. 123.

[6] Quotations in Kautzsch, op. cit., p. 14, Budde, *Das Buch Hiob*, 2nd ed., p. xiii, n. 3.

[7] *Das Buch Job* (1894), p. 7.

plied it in the first edition of his commentary (1896); thus the
Prologue and the Epilogue became the *Volksbuch*, that is, the popular book. The latter existed before the poem and was an independent
composition. The poet borrowed merely its framework. He was not
hampered by it, and his poetic verve could find plenty of scope.
In 1897 Duhm began the introduction to his commentary by a
paragraph entitled *Das Volksbuch* in which he discussed this work
as if it were an independent composition and claimed to assess its
value: 'It was written at a time when the activity of the great
prophets and the misfortunes of Israel and Judah had not yet
modified the spiritual and especially religious attitudes of the people;
when sacrifice was still held to be efficacious and the technical
expiatory sacrifices of the Torah were not yet known; when it was
not yet realised that sacrifice could only be offered to Yahweh in
one place and by specially chosen priests; when the Sabaeans were
not the industrious traders, or the Chaldaeans the great power
which they subsequently became after the capture of Babylon;
a time when it was still possible with all simplicity of mind to associate Edomite legends with the religion of Yahweh' (p. viii).
Such considerations would take us back to pre-Deuteronomic times,
and evidently, in the opinion of the author, prior to the reform of
Josiah. According to this theory the poetic book was substituted for
a dialogue between Job and his friends, as also for speeches by
Yahweh which formed part of it. Fried. Delitzsch in 1902 sought to
emphasise the distinction between the prose and poetic parts by
an extremely vague linguistic argument: 'The prose narrative is
written in fine and pure Hebrew, whilst the language of the poem
is deeply penetrated with Aramaisms.' [1] English exegetes such as
Barton [2] and Strahan [3] were content to rally in support of the
theory of the *Volksbuch*. Professor Volz of Tübingen thus determined the stages in the development of this book: 'The historical
material was not perhaps Israelite in origin, but emanated from the
Edomites or the sedentary tribes in the neighbourhood of Damascus;
the name of the hero, Job, might well support this hypothesis. A

---

[1]   *Das Buch Hiob*, p. 13. The presence of the Aramaic קִבֵּל in 2:10 (cf.
Comm.) is a direct blow at the allegation of Fried. Delitzsch. It is interesting
to see how this Aramaism had proved awkward for the theory of Duhm
concerning the age of the prose narrative by comparison with the poem;
cf. Kautzsch, op. cit., pp. 26f.

[2]   Quoted by Buttenwieser, in *The Book of Job*, p. 20, n. 1.

[3]   *The Book of Job*, p. 23.

highly gifted Israelite writer then seized on the subject of which he had been informed by oral tradition and lent it its present artistic and incomparably beautiful form.' [1] Volz then seeks to show how a later poet in his turn takes up the 'old legend and the splendid narrative' in order to sing the praises of the man who suffers, but without following the earlier narrative too closely.[2]

The theory the development of which we have just been following has been adopted and expounded in manuals such as the *Introduction à l'Ancien Testament* of Lucien Gautier, in which one may read [3] about 'the genesis of the poem of Job'. First there is said to have been 'a kind of popular story' which included a prologue, a central nucleus, and an epilogue. 'This story inspired a great poet with the theme of a masterpiece. Leaving as they were, in the form of prologue and epilogue, the beginning and the end of the work, he seized upon the central part and transformed it into a series of speeches, animated by a powerful current of inspiration, and dealing with the gravest problems.'

The same author well summed up the reasoning of those who thought that two stages should be traced in the work, the composition of the prose narrative, and that of the poetic dialogue: 'If the author of the poem was also that of the story as a whole, if the data of the prologue and epilogue were his creation, it is difficult to see why the most perfect harmony should not prevail from one end of the work to the other. On the other hand, if the poet took the opportunity offered by an already well-known narrative to adapt to it and graft on to it, as it were, the development of his poetic thought, then it is easier to understand why there is manifest an incongruity between the old element and the new.' [4] Indeed, if the theory has found some adherents, the reason is that critics thought they could recognise a certain number of antinomies between the prose narration and the poetic dialogue.[5]

The moment has come for us to examine these antinomies.

---

[1]   *Hiob und Weisheit*, 2nd ed. (1921), p. 2.
[2]   Ibid., p. 16.
[3]   2nd ed. (1914), II, pp. 98f.
[4]   Ibid., p. 101.
[5]   This is what struck M. Hackspill when, in a review of the work of K. Kautzsch, quoted above, he wrote: 'Another reason why we believe the Prologue and the Epilogue not be to due to the author of the poem lies in the difference in tendency and of problem which is to be observed in the two parts, and this difference remains, in spite of all that K. says' (*RB*, 1902, p. 451).

There is no need for us to speak now of the contrast between the prose and the poetry, since we have seen that this argument has no validity. The use of the divine names, as we have also noted, would rather tend to demonstrate a unity of composition than a duality, since the same tendency is clearly at work in both the prose story and the poem.[1]

What then are the proofs urged to show that either the poetic dialogue, anterior to the prose narration, was subsequently endowed with a prologue and epilogue, or, on the other hand, that the old popular story was later adorned with the poetic dialogue, whether the latter were an innovation pure and simple, or were substituted for an already existing dialogue?

Arguments drawn from the rôle and character of Satan have been various and conflicting. Hasse (1789), who urged the priority of the poetic dialogue, thought there was a very marked contrast between the figure of Satan in the Prologue and the theory of angels in the dialogue.[2] This contrast seemed so strong that one of those who refute Hasse *per longum et latum*, Heiligstedt (1847), feels obliged to throw overboard, as resulting from a late interpolation, the references to Satan in the Prologue (1:6-12; 2:1-7a).[3] The reasons which influenced Heiligstedt are as follows. The poem would dissuade us from investigating the causes of the divine decisions, an attitude which is not justified if we are already aware of the circumstance which gave rise to the trial of Job. In the matter of the wager between God and Satan it is the latter who would have shown the better foresight with regard to Job's attitude, 'his audacious revolt'. The allusions to Satan are extraneous and can be eliminated without difficulty, provided that in 2:7b we add יהוה as the subject of ויך 'and he struck', so as to see God as the author of Job's ills, which is the idea of the poem. It is urged that there is a similar case in I Ch 21:1, which substitutes Satan for the Yahweh of 2 S 24:1 as the author of the blindness which comes upon David. A final argument is extrinsic, for it is drawn from the date of the poem, which is fixed as pre-exilic, a hypothesis which would exclude the personage of Satan, a post-exilic development.[4] Duhm, who is one of the cham-

---

[1]   Above, pp. lxvff.
[2]   K. Kautzsch, *Das sogenannte Volksbuch von Hiob*, p. 5.
[3]   Ibid., p. 10.
[4]   König seems inclined to a similar theory, for the presence of Satan in the Prologue is due, in his opinion, to some revision of the original text (*Theologie des A.T.*, 3rd and 4th eds., 1923, p. 230).

pions of the theory that the prose narrative precedes the poetic dialogue in date, expresses thus the discrepancy arising from the introduction of Satan: 'In the popular book, it is the suspicions of Satan which are the cause of Job's cruel trial; in the work of the poet, there is no room for such an intermediary agency.'

We have confined ourselves to giving the three aspects assumed by the opinions relative to Satan: either the whole Prologue has been added to the poetic dialogue, or it is the allusions to Satan which have been added to the Prologue, or finally it is the poetic dialogue which has been annexed to the Prologue containing the passages relative to Satan.

If we were certain in advance of the date of composition of the Book of Job, and of the date at which the ideas regarding Satan made their appearance in Holy Scripture, we could immediately advance arguments concerning the greater or lesser importance of the part which Satan plays in determining the dates of such and such sections of the work. But this is not the case. To maintain that the poem is earlier or later, because Satan figures in the Prologue, to claim that a certain passage must have been added because it alludes to Satan, is to presuppose that the problem is solved and to anticipate the study of the date at which the composition was completed. The sole relevant point is to discover whether—yes or no—the presence and function of Satan are compatible with the remainder of the Prologue and with the poetic dialogue.

Now, what we suggest is that if this character did not exist it would be necessary to invent it in order to give to the story all its savour. The culminating point is the vision of a righteous man suffering a cruel trial despite his innocence, and the whole story converges on the spectacle of Job scraping his sores on his dunghill.

Such is the paradox which, with fine audacity, the poet wishes to bring before us. The poem takes its point of departure in Job's lament, and this lament is motivated by the fact of sufferings which he does not deserve. How have these sufferings come to be inflicted on him? It would be truly repugnant to us to have to admit that God has sported with His servant out of pure caprice, that He simply wished to use him as a subject of experiment, and to show, *in anima vili*, that the theory of the relation between moral good and prosperity was contradicted by a particular individual case. For Job to be struck, an instigator was needed, and such a mysterious being could not have been found on earth. But he is to be found in the host of heaven, among the sons of Elohim, i.e. in the ranks of those angels who serve the purposes of the Most High. It is amid this heavenly court that there appears the spirit who obtains from Yahweh the authorisation to ruin Ahab (1 K 22:19ff.). Under the name of Satan, this spirit eventually becomes the agitator who incites to evil (1 Ch 21:1). Ready for any kind of work, he roams the world, and seeks opportunities of doing harm. In particular he likes to point out the weaknesses of humanity and to constitute himself, as his name suggests, the legal adversary and the official prosecutor of mankind before God's tribunal (Zec 3:1ff.). Here then was to be found ready for use the agent who would have no hesitation in striking the righteous man! This is his function, his pleasure, for he does not believe in man's righteousness. Doubtless he cannot have failed to come across Job, who is 'perfect and upright, fearing Elohim and turning away from evil'. Moreover, Yahweh Himself draws his attention to this man of exemplary virtue (1:8). Satan however is not impressed. This virtue is merely an ordinary business arrangement, a clever deal. Yahweh cannot admit this depreciation of His servant; and thus the drama is engaged. By a series of trials Satan will attempt to force Job into such a position that he curses Yahweh. All this explains clearly the logic of those ills which gradually bring Job, tortured by foul sores, to the *mazbaleh* on which his friends find him.

The rôle of Satan in the Prologue is of capital importance. To eliminate it is to mutilate most lamentably a narrative of which the graduated effects produce an admirable climax. It is not a question of an ordinary calamity. Job is tormented by a special being who is quick to take advantage of the successive permissions which are granted him. Satan is the torturer who prolongs the agony of his victim, the tormentor who has undertaken to wring from the sufferer the shriek of blasphemy for which he waits. Far from being in the nature of an episode, the part of Satan is vital to enable us to understand how God can have allowed to be martyred thus the man whom He calls His servant and whose virtues He extols.

But can the personage of Satan, so necessary to the Prologue, be made compatible with the requirements of the dialogue? We have cited Duhm's contention that the dialogue does not presuppose the suspicions of Satan as the primary cause of Job's trials. We should note, however, that the characters taking part in the dialogue do not know and must not know the immediate author of Job's sufferings. Who can know what has taken place, in the heavenly court, between Yahweh and Satan? The wager has not been divulged. Has not Duhm himself (who, as opposed to Heiligstedt and others, considers the whole of the Prologue to be a unity) remarked that Job not only in the dialogue but also in the Prologue regards God as the original cause of the calamities which have struck him (1:21; 2:10)?

To say with Heiligstedt that the poem dissuades us from seeking the cause of the divine decisions and that this is inadmissible if we already know the part played by Satan in the Prologue, is to substitute the reader for the protagonists. We know how Job has been reduced to the most agonising distress, but his friends do not know, just as he himself does not know, and it is for this reason that the discussion can be indefinitely prolonged. All are confronted by one outstanding fact: Job overwhelmed by evils. We know by what secret agency this fact has come to be, and our knowledge does not lessen our interest in the argument which the fact occasions. The author has taken us into his confidence. Hence we shall not be shaken by the protestations of Job and the sophistry of his friends. In this way we can enjoy at our leisure the exaltation of thought, the vehemence of feeling, the beauty and the appropriateness of the style. Moreover, we do not know the end, and until we have read the Epilogue we cannot know whether Job, driven to despair, will not eventually justify Satan and prove that it is not for nothing that he had served God. Finally, it is of no avail to say that Satan showed better foresight than God into the reactions of Job. The poetic dialogue springs from the prose narrative and then develops with all the liberty characteristic of poetry. The fact that Job's protestations seem to be excessive is only natural, as we shall see below. But what Satan had predicted was a cry of defiance hurled in the face of Yahweh (1:11; 2:5). And we know, even before finishing the reading of the Prologue, that in this Satan has been mistaken (1:21; 2:10). Now, the poem contains nothing which can persuade us that the malediction foreseen by Satan has been expressed.

Thus, after the Prologue, Satan can disappear from the scene, as can also Job's wife. The part they play is finished. There must remain on the stage only the three interlocutors, who will not make their exit until the close of the poetic dialogue.

A further objection to the unity of the Prologue and dialogue is drawn from the alleged difference of Job's attitude in the two parts. It is again Duhm who stresses this point: 'In the popular book, Job submits to the blows of misfortune with patience and wisdom, at its conclusion (42:7, 8) he is praised for having spoken of God what is right; in the poem, Job—and he himself confesses as much—is anything but patient, he hurls the most exacerbated invectives against God and subjects the divine government of the world to the fiercest criticism; in short, he himself allows that he has not spoken rightly of God (42:6).'

We must certainly take account of the force of this objection. The poet referred to is the author not only of the poetic dialogue but also of the speeches of Yahweh, since 42:1-6 gives the conclusion to these speeches. The prose narrative is not only the Prologue but also the Epilogue, since 42:7-8 opens the final section of this prose narrative. The question then is how the Job of the poetic dialogue can on the one hand be reconciled with the Job of the Prologue and Epilogue, on the other with him who makes a final reply to the remarks of Yahweh.

It is certain that in the Prologue Job is given only testimonials of satisfaction (1:22; 2:10), and that in the Epilogue he is openly praised by Yahweh (42:7-8). Is his attitude in the dialogue so blameworthy as to contradict these praises? If he is the type of the righteous man in the prose account, we have noted too, and precisely in seeking to establish the traditional characteristics of the hero,[1] that in the dialogue he presents himself as righteous and perfect (12:4; cf. Comm.) and that he declares himself to have held fast to his righteousness, without being willing to deviate from it (27:6). In all the speeches of Job one can perceive the profound consciousness of his innocence. In order that the debate may assume its full value, this innocent man must suffer, and suffer beyond measure. It is no artificial suffering but a true distress of body and soul which wrings from him the sublime and agonised cries of ch. 3. And these cries of pain are met with the cold consolations of the friends who are content to confront the righteous man in his agony with the theory of the misfortunes of the wicked and the happiness of the innocent. It is this which enrages Job. He can only proclaim with ever increasing vehemence how undeserved are his misfortunes. He does not know why he has been thus smitten. And of course he inquires of God the reason of his ills. He does so with all the bitter-

---

[1] Above, pp. xvf.

ness and angry passion of a crushed heart. His pathetic appeals are indeed a far cry from the formulae of gentle and serene resignation which he had used in the Prologue (1:21; 2:10). But the action has progressed. For seven days the sufferer was silent in the presence of his friends. It is this suppressed grief which finally bursts forth when Job opens his mouth and curses his day (3:1). How could the debate proceed in the poetic colloquy, in three cycles of discussions which include ten speeches of Job, three of Eliphaz, three of Bildad, three of Zophar, if the hero only repeated his *fiat!* of the Prologue? Even in moments when he indulges all the bitterness of his soul, Job turns to God and invokes His righteousness, His mercy, His pity. If sometimes he passes due bounds, it is in an attempt to make clear to his friends the violent paroxysm which his grief has reached and how utterly inexplicable it is. It is indeed they, with their frigid phrases, their malicious insinuations, their monotonous and tiresome repetitions, who throw oil on the fire. And the approbation of Yahweh in the Epilogue emphasises the difference: the three friends have not spoken the truth as has Job (42:7). The aim of the author is to put forward a new theory, that the cause of misfortune is not necessarily sin. It is indeed for this reason that the Prologue has shown that the ills of Job are not due to his faults, for he is the very type of the blameless and upright man. The contention of Job remains the same throughout the dialogue. It is the thesis of his friends, who cling faithfully to commonly received notions which must be proved wrong. And if Job manifests repentance (40:3-5; 42:1-6), it is not because he has declared his innocence so emphatically but because he has discussed too vehemently questions which surpassed the scope of his mind. He has dared to speak of God before having seen and heard Him. In that, both he and his friends have been presumptuous. The speeches of Yahweh have the effect of showing that man should not seek to fathom divine mysteries. It is for his ignorance that Job is criticised, and it is on that score that he is accused (38:1-2; 40:1-2; 42:1-5).

Whatever Duhm may say, the attitude of the three friends does not differ in the prose story and the poem. If they are condemned and need rehabilitation in the Epilogue, it is precisely because throughout the dialogue they have maintained an outmoded theory, contradictory to the ideas of the Prologue and to those which the author intimates through the words of Job: the theory that misfortune flows from sin, happiness from virtue. The other

reflections of Duhm on the contrast between the theories of the
dialogue and those of the prose narrative are of only subordinate
interest, for after all we have to do with a debate between Job and
his friends. The poet from time to time broadens the horizon of one
or the other speaker. He may put into the mouth of Eliphaz and
the two others some very true ideas, just as he may make Job
express some very exaggerated or debatable ideas. But what must
be grasped is the *Leitmotif* of the poem as a whole, and this leading
theme is the same as that which moulds the prose story: misfortune
is not necessarily the fruit of sin.

As for the inconsistent details which critics have tried to find,
they are of a triviality which can be neglected in serious criticism.
Thus Job speaks of the sons of his loins as still alive (19:17),
whereas they are in fact dead [1] according to the Prologue (1:18-19).
It is forgotten however that Bildad makes a clear allusion to the
death of Job's sons (8:4) and deduces from it a consequence in
support of his theory. Job himself evokes the memory of the time
when his boys were still around him (29:5), which implies that they
are no longer so. It is clear that in 19:17 it is parallelism which,
careless of the Prologue, has suggested 'the sons of my loins' as
corresponding to 'my wife'.

Renan, who will not be suspected of distrust of criticism, has
concluded as follows a rapid sketch of the anomalies alleged to be
found in the Book of Job: 'One circumstance, however, should
inspire in us a certain reserve when it is a question of inductions
of this nature. The Hebrews and the orientals in general had very
different ideas about composition from our own. Their works never
had that perfectly definite outline to which we are accustomed,
and we must be careful not to see interpolations or revisions wherever we find a lack of consistency which surprises us.' [2] It is the
greatest mistake to imagine the inspired writer first tracing, either
in his head or with his calamus, a rigid plan that was to be the
guiding thread of the whole work. We are not here faced by a
dialogue of Plato, or a speech of Cicero, or a passage from St Thomas
Aquinas. In the Holy Scriptures composition is not governed by the
laws of Western logic. What we must remember is the fact that
each section generates the next, though with a greater or lesser

---

[1] This is an objection already made by Hasse (K. Kautzsch, op. cit.,
p. 5).

[2] *Le Livre de Job*, 5th ed., p. xliv.

degree of immediate influence. The thought rebounds rather like a stone ricocheting on the surface of the water and whose points of fall are not at equal distance from each other.

If we wish to know how one and the same mind could conceive and compose on the theme of the traditional Job the prose narrative and the poetic dialogue, it is enough for us to imagine the setting of ch. 2. The four protagonists are face to face. The first to speak, and whose lamentation is foreshadowed (3:1), is Job. What is the reason for the curses which he utters? It is that he is unhappy. What are his misfortunes and their cause? What were their first effects and what was the first attitude of the hero when faced by his wretchedness and disease? If he is a sinner there is nothing to be said, and he is wrong to groan so much! But no! He is a righteous man, the very symbol of the righteous, and he is recognised as such by Yahweh Himself. Hence a problem arises, and the three friends have a subject for debate. Here is a concrete, tangible, moving case, providing a point of departure for poetry. The poetry can soar aloft independently, upborne on its own wings, and carrying the speakers away into the most exalted regions of speculation. Job will take care not to let it get lost in the clouds. Again and again he will bring it back to the subject of his own personal fate, and he is indeed still the same person as in the Prologue. As for the Epilogue, we shall see later that it is welded to the speeches of Yahweh, which are an integral part of the original book. For the moment we are content to show that the pretexts alleged for dissociating the prose narrative from the poetic dialogue have scarcely any objective value. Supposing the prose narrative to have existed separately, it is clear that it would require a dialogue to complete it. Supposing the dialogue to have existed separately, it is not less clear that it would need a framework.[1] Well, we have both, the picture and its frame, and in both we recognise the same hand. Hence it is unnecessary to try to separate them by violent means. If one of the two elements had been composed to complete the other and render it more intelligible, why imagine that the redactor would have been so unskilful as to leave in the work those anomalies which it is said to contain?

Let us add that the language used both in the prose and the poem, far from being, as Fried. Delitzsch [2] claimed, indication of diversity

---

[1]   This argument is well brought out by P. Cornely (op. cit., pp. 56f.).
[2]   Above, p. lxxiv.

of origin, would suggest rather certain constant features. K. Kautzsch has collected a whole series of words, forms, expressions, which classify the vocabulary and grammar of the two parts in the same category.[1] Thus the use of תָּם 'perfect' instead of תָּמִים [2] is characteristic both of the prose (1:1) and the poem (8:20; 9:20-2). Similarly the abstract תֻּמָּה 'perfection' [3] which is found in the Prologue (2:3, 9) and the poem (27:5; 31:6), but outside the Book of Job appears only in Pr 11:3. The adverb חִנָּם 'gratuitously' (1:9) is found with the shade of meaning 'without good reason' [4] both in the Prologue (2:3) and the dialogue (9:17; 22:6). It is likewise interesting to note that the locution וְאוּלָם 'and yet', 'however', [5] which appears only nine times outside the Book of Job, is found in the Prologue (1:11) and several times in the dialogue (11:5; 12:7; 13:4; 14:8).[6] As for אוּלָם alone, it is found only in the Prologue (2:5) and the dialogue (5:8; 13:3). Characteristic again is the use of נגע 'strike' with בּ before its complement,[7] both in the Prologue (1:11, 19) and in the dialogue (5:19, 19:21) Let us note too עַל־פְּנֵי and אֶל־פְּנֵי 'in the face of' in the sense of 'with effrontery', [8] in the Prologue (1:11; 2:5) and the dialogue (6:28; 13:15; 21:31). The very typical formula זֶה...וְזֶה to mean 'the former ... the latter', 'the one ... the other',[9] figures several times in the Prologue (1:16, 17, 18) and once in the dialogue (21:23-5). The alternation of gender in the case of רוּחַ 'wind', 'spirit' can be seen in the Prologue (1:19) and in the dialogue (4:15). The expression 'come forth from the womb' is common to the prose (1:21) and the poetry (3:11; 38:29). The construction of the *hiph'il* of חזק with בּ before the name of the thing to which one holds fast is found in the Prologue (2:3, 9) and the dialogue (8:15, 20; 27:6). Note too the use of the *pi'el* of בלע to mean 'ruin', 'remove', etc., in the Prologue (2:3) and the dialogue (8:18; 10:8). The plural of רֵעַ for 'the friends' of Job appears in

---

[1] Op. cit., pp. 24ff. and pp. 40ff.
[2] Cf. Comm. on 1: 1. The presence of תמים in 12: 4 is due to a reminiscence of Gn 6: 9.
[3] Cf. Comm. on 2: 3.
[4] Cf. Comm. on 1: 9.
[5] Cf. Comm. on 1: 11.
[6] It is also found once in Elihu (33: 1).
[7] Cf. Comm. on 1: 11.
[8] Cf. Comm. on 1: 11.
[9] Cf. Comm. on 1: 16.

the prose (2:11; 42:7) and in the dialogue (19:21). The noun הַכְּאֵב 'pain' of the Prologue (2:13) has its complement in כְּאֵבִי 'my pain' of the dialogue (16:6), while in the speeches of Elihu we find מַכְאוֹב 'pain' (33:19). In the Epilogue we have to note the use of בְּעַד in the sense of 'on behalf of' (42:8), found also in the dialogue (6:22). The noun נְבָלָה 'disgrace' (42:8), is both in the style of the Prologue (2:10) and the dialogue (30:8). The participle יֹדֵעַ to mean 'an acquaintance' is found in the Epilogue (42:11) and the dialogue (19:13), on both occasions together with the mention of brothers. The antithesis רֵאשִׁית 'first condition' and אַחֲרִית 'last condition' characterises both the Epilogue (42:12) and the dialogue (8:7). As for the Aramaisms which are said to be the typical feature of the poem, in contrast with the prose parts, we have already alluded to the Aramaic verb קבל in the *pi*'*el* in the prose Prologue (2:10), a fact which is sufficient to invalidate the conclusion which critics would draw from the Aramaising tendency of the poem.

The total picture presented by these facts, the examination of the various theories which have been put forward about the origin of the poem and its prose framework, the right understanding of the bond which links not only by thought but also by style the Prologue, the dialogue, and the Epilogue, all these factors serve to bring out the fact that these three component parts have a common origin and that they are not the work of two or three different authors. We must now study another section which is very closely linked with the dialogue and the Epilogue: the speeches of Yahweh.

C. The Speeches of Yahweh (38-42) and the Poem of Wisdom (28)

With ch. 31, according to the text itself, 'the words of Job are ended' (31:40), and, in the nature of the case, we have the conclusion of the poetic dialogue which was opened by the hero's lament and closed by his own apologia. The discussion has been taken to its extreme limit, since each of the friends has had the opportunity of expounding, three times over, his explanation of the problem presented by the misfortunes and the lamentations of Job. After it all, he remains firm in his position and will dispute no further. The analysis of his final speech has enabled us to recognise,[1] after the

---

[1] Above, p. liii.

description of his present misery succeeding to his past felicity, a sublime protestation of innocence and an appeal to the supreme tribunal (31:35-7).

> Would that someone would listen to me!
> Behold! here is my signature! Let Shaddai answer me!
> As for the indictment which my adversary has drawn up,
> Shall I not wear it on my shoulder,
> Shall I not bind it as crowns about my head?
> My steps in life will I recount unto him,
> Like a chief will I present myself before him!

Thus Job demands judgment. He does not fear it. He will present himself with head erect before Shaddai. It is to this judgment that, if we are to believe the straightforward interpretation of the text,[1] he has made allusion in 19:25-9.

> As for me, I know that my Vindicator lives,
> And that, as the Last, He will arise on the earth,
> And that behind my skin I shall stand up,[2]
> And from my flesh I shall see Eloah,
> Whom I myself shall see
> And whom my own eyes will behold, and none other!
> My reins grow faint within me!
> If you say: 'How shall we pursue him,
> And what grounds for proceeding against him can we find?'[3]
> Fear for yourselves the sword,
> When wrath is kindled against wrong,[4]
> So that you will know that there is a judgment!

Job has not appealed to God as judge only, but also as witness and arbiter (16:19-21). He has already repudiated the intervention of his friends (13:3-12) and has declared that he will have dealings with God alone (13:15-27). In this respect, moreover, he is following up to a certain point the example of Eliphaz (5:8ff.) and the advice of Bildad (8:5ff.). Has not Zophar himself expressed the desire to hear God (11:5-6)?

> But oh! that Eloah might speak,
> And open His lips to you
> And reveal to you the secrets of wisdom
> (For they are hard to understand)!
> You would then know that Eloah demands from you an
>   account of your sin![5]

---

[1] Cf. Comm. on 19:25ff.
[2] Cf. Comm. on 19:26.
[3] Cf. Comm. on 19:28.
[4] Cf. Comm. on 19:29.
[5] Cf. Comm. on 11:6.

Thus God is introduced into the case; it is He who must resolve the dispute. Moreover, He alone knows the situation of Job. The friends have given all the explanations which accepted ethics afford. Job has shown that these explanations are inadequate and false. And now Yahweh Himself speaks (38:1), to give Job an answer! The speeches of Elihu have been an interlude. Yahweh will comment on the words of Job (38:2; 40:2) and his three interlocutors (42:7-8). Elihu will not be mentioned. The Epilogue will be directly connected with the speeches of Yahweh: 'And after Yahweh had spoken these words to Job' (42:7). It is in fact between Job and Yahweh that the last conversation has taken place. Job has stammered a few words (40:3-5; 42:1-6). He must apologise for the excessive vehemence of his tone and for having discussed subjects too exalted for him.[1] He deserves the final eulogy on the substance of what he had said, while his friends, who have not spoken another word, incur criticism (42:7-8).

It does not appear possible to dispute the logical connection between the speeches of Yahweh and both the poem and the Epilogue. We have seen that the divine appearance was as it were an answer to an appeal arising more or less openly from all the discussions of Job and his friends. Yahweh appears in the tempest. That is perfectly natural (38:1; 40:6); it is in the tempest that theophanies occur.[2] This detail is not an allusion to the storm described by Elihu (36:29-37:5, 11-13), for the storm has passed when Elihu finished speaking.[3] Job is not mistaken. What happens as a result of his adjurations is the intervention which he has invoked (42:5):

> I had heard of Thee by hearsay,
> But now my eye has seen Thee!

In our analysis of the speeches of Yahweh we noted [4] that their essential aim was to make clear to man in general and to Job in particular the uselessness of discussions about problems which surpass the range of human understanding. This idea has already been expressed by Zophar, precisely in order to urge God to express Himself (11:7-9):

---

[1] Cf. above, p. lviii.
[2] Cf. the passages of the Prophets and the Psalms, quoted in the Comm. on 38: 1; Nah 1: 3; Zec 9: 14; Ezk 1: 4; Ps 50: 3.
[3] Cf. Comm. on 37: 21 and 38: 1.
[4] Above, p. lviii.

Can you discover the nature of Eloah?
Can you plumb the perfection of Shaddai?
It is higher than the heavens: what will you do?
Deeper than Sheol: what can you know?
Longer than the earth is its dimension,
Full broader than the sea!

The works of God are mysterious, unfathomable, even paradoxical. This was one of the affirmations found on the lips of all whenever it was a question of giving voice to the traditional doxologies culminating in a confession of incomprehension: Eliphaz (5:8-16), Job (9:4-10; 12:9-25), Bildad (25:2-6; 26:5-14). The first encounter between Eliphaz and Job was on common ground, the impenetrability of the wonders performed by God (5:9 compared with 9:10).

This is in fact the point of departure for Yahweh's speeches. But instead of confining Himself to vague and colourless affirmations, He enters into detail and, by a series of purposeful descriptions, He calls attention to the miracles of His power and providence. How do His speeches follow on from those of Job and his friends?

It is this question, which, answered as it has been in conflicting ways, has cast suspicion on the speeches of Yahweh and has led some critics to deny that they formed part of the original book. Studer, whose theory overturns all the parts of the Book of Job, thinks that the speeches of Yahweh were added only at the third and fifth editions (first 38-9 and then 40-2) of the total work.[1] Vernes also distinguished a certain number of strata the last of which was that which included the speeches of Yahweh; first the Prologue and Epilogue, then the poetic dialogue (excluding 19:25-9; 27:7-23; 28, all of which are later additions), finally the speeches of Elihu and those of Yahweh.[2] Through the variations in the

---

[1] He thought that the Book of Job passed through the following stages of evolution. First, a basis, called 'words of Job' (31:40), including the speeches 3:3-27:6 and ch. 31, to which chs. 29-30 served as introduction(!). An editor, to cut short all dispute about the doctrine of retribution, added ch. 28 (poem on Wisdom). A second editor, ignoring this ch. 28, eliminated, in his own way, all discussion of the burning issue by adding part of the speeches of Yahweh (38-9). A third proposes the monologues of Elihu (32-7) as less strange than those of Yahweh. A fourth invents the Prologue (1-2). A fifth adds the end of the speeches of Yahweh and the Epilogue (40-2), then intercalates 27:7-23 in a speech of Job. Note that often the revisers seem unaware of the work of each other. There is a good outline of the theory of Studer in Dillmann, *Hiob*, 4th ed., pp. xxvif.

[2] *Rev. de l'hist. des religions*, 1880, pp. 232.

thought of Cheyne [1] it is possible to discern his anxiety to make of the speeches of Yahweh a section added as a link between the poetic dialogue and the Epilogue. The author of the speeches is supposed to have belonged to the same school as the author of the poem on Wisdom (28), but this is believed to have been later than the speeches.[2] Cheyne thinks too that the speeches of Yahweh contain a number of interpolations: 39:13-18 (the ostrich), 40:15-24 (Behemoth), 41:1-24 (except perhaps v. 12). Volz credits a reader of Job's lament, who was both 'a man of intelligence' and a 'pious poet', with the idea of introducing Yahweh in order thus to give some idea of the abyss which yawns between man and God and correct the impression produced by the hero, who was too much inclined to place himself on a footing of equality with his Creator.[3]

One of those who have thrown a most interesting light on the problem is certainly van Hoonacker in his study 'Une question touchant la composition du livre de Job'.[4] He prudently formulates only by way of hypothesis a theory which might be described as that of the three editions of the Book of Job. The first edition would have included 'the discussion between Job and his friends, preceded by the Prologue'. The second, due to an 'author who was concerned above all to refute the impatient arguments of which Job had become guilty', adds the speeches of Elihu. A third edition, parallel and not consecutive to the second, adds the theophany, the questioning, the repentance and the reward of Job, i.e. the speeches of Yahweh and the Epilogue.[5] The present book stems from an amalgamation of the second and third editions.[6] The most original point in van Hoonacker's thesis is that much of the speeches of Yahweh figured in the original book, without being attributed to God.[7] Unfortunately demonstration has been touched on only very lightly.[8] It leaves us remarkably perplexed. The attempt to explain otherwise than as being the words of God those passages where

---

[1] In *Job and Solomon* (1887), pp. 66f. and in the article 'Job' (book) in his *Encyclopaedia Biblica* (II, 1901, cols. 2480ff.).

[2] This seems to result from the comparison between 28:26b and 38:25b.

[3] *Hiob und Weisheit*, 2nd ed., pp. 79f.

[4] *RB*, 1903, pp. 161ff.

[5] Ibid., pp. 188f.

[6] Ibid., p. 166.

[7] Ibid., p. 178.

[8] Ibid., p. 188.

Yahweh speaks in the first person [1] is doomed to failure.[2] To say
that 'the details of certain descriptions in the last section of our
book express rather the author's admiration of the works of God
than the Creator's exaltation of His own power' [3] is to forget that
the author becomes enraptured with his own poetry, that he is
speaking in Hebrew, and that his tone rises in proportion as the
theme grows lofty. The remarks on 38:28ff. have a disconcerting
subtlety. Why could not God, with transcendent irony, say to Job:

> Has the rain a father?
> Or who has begotten the drops of dew?
> From whose womb has the ice emerged,
> And the hoar frost of heaven, who has given it birth?
> The waters are frozen hard as stone,
> And the face of the deep becomes a solid mass! [4]

The explanation given of 38:8 is contradicted by the rest of the
passage.[5] The parts in which Yahweh cites the divine names are
explicable in the same way as the many texts of prophecy where the
Lord cites one or other of His names.[6] We have noted that these
parts are very rare in the speeches of Yahweh, since the use of the
first person made it unnecessary to have resort to them.[7] Our study
of the three cycles of speeches in the poetic dialogue [8] has enabled
us to find the complements of the last speech of Bildad (25) and
the last of Zophar (27:12, etc.), without any need to derive them
from the speeches of Yahweh. With even more reason we will
refrain from seeking in the poetic dialogue passages supposed to
have been added in order to compensate for the parts transferred
to the speeches of Yahweh! An author must have had a very genius

---

[1] Ibid., pp. 18off.

[2] It will be sufficient to see how the author attempts to explain 38:23
with the help of the Septuagint. The Greek version tries to avoid anthropomorphisms. It is clear that 38:23 alludes to the extraordinary phenomena
of which God makes use in the day of battle (cf. Comm.). The change from
the 1st to the 3rd person in 39:6 is purely arbitrary. We are in agreement
with van Hoonacker in cutting out the parenthesis of 40:15 (cf. Comm.).
But that does not in any way detract from the character of the passage.
It is God who, like an exhibitor of prodigious animals, draws attention to
Behemoth!

[3] RB, 1903, p. 183.

[4] Our Commentary sufficiently justifies those points where we translate
differently from van Hoonacker.

[5] It is by isolating 38:8 from vv. 9-11 that van Hoonacker can argue
from the verb וִיסֶךְ that we should read מִי סָךְ (cf. Comm.).

[6] For example, Is 1:4, 20; 3:17; 8:7, etc.

[7] Above, pp. lxvif.

[8] Above, pp. xlivff.

for decomposition thus to remove what was in its right place and substitute for it any sort of padding. Let us leave to Yahweh what belongs to Yahweh and to Job's interlocutors what is suitable to them.

We now return to the question which has caused certain critics to doubt that the speeches of Yahweh followed the poetic dialogue in the original work: how are these speeches to be connected with the discussion between Job and his friends? To us the answer does not seem to be in doubt. The thesis of Job was essentially negative. To the friends asserting and trying to prove the necessary nexus between misfortune and wickedness Job replied by referring to facts, and above all to his own example, which suggested that misfortune did not afflict the wicked only, but could also afflict the good. Such is the antinomy which no one can resolve. Why insist that the speeches of Yahweh should give the final solution? We already possess the solution in part in the Prologue, which has shown us that it was a *test* which God imposed on the righteous man, in order to counter the allegations of Satan. This premise is completed by the Epilogue. The test is only *temporary*; it must be followed by an increase, a redoubling, of good fortune, if the righteous man has persevered in the way of righteousness. But this temporary test is a *mystery* for man, because its origin is the divine counsel which is beyond our comprehension. For this reason the discussion between Job and his friends is vain. This is what Yahweh proposes to make them understand. Job was right to insist that the arguments adduced by the partisans of the accepted theory were of little value, but he was wrong to discuss a mystery beyond his knowledge. This mystery is not the only one. In the catechism the child is taught that 'it is not strange that there should be mysteries in religion since every moment we find mysteries in nature'. This is just what God Himself demonstrates in those sublime apostrophes where the most fantastic and curious phenomena pass before us, in a series of striking descriptions each of which is terminated by a question. Who has done this? Who has contrived that? Are you capable of doing the same? Are you capable of understanding even? And as for those extraordinary beings which live around you, who has endowed them with the qualities which disconcert you? And so on. This is the voice of God. We are the less surprised to hear it because—as we carefully noted at the beginning of this study—the voice of God has been invoked by the hero himself even more than

by his friends. And when God has thus pushed the problem back
to the heavens, He is of course in a position to blame Job for having
(38:2; 40:2), as Job himself will recognise (40:3-5; 42:1-6), spoken
of matters which are beyond his understanding. He will agree,
however, that the rejection with which Job confronted his friends
was better than all their speculations (42:7). The author of the book
of Job did not say to himself, after the discussion of the dialogue,
that he would immediately furnish a philosophical solution. It was
incumbent on him to make God intervene. He did so. But he did
not lower this God to the rank of a jouster picking up the glove
where it had been thrown down. He left God in the tempest,
uttering His divine discourses from the depths of His immensity.
Here lies hidden the solution to sorrow which Job had sought so
anxiously.

> Dans vos cieux, au delà de la sphère des nues,
> Au fond de cet azur immobile et dormant,
> Peut-être faites-vous des choses inconnues
> Où la douleur de l'homme entre comme élément.[1]

This is why the majority of critics have recognised the authenticity
of Yahweh's speeches.[2]

Nevertheless objections have been raised to some of the descriptions contained in these speeches. Thus it is maintained that the
ostrich of 39:13-18 has been brought in as an afterthought, and
critics have insisted on the fact that the passage is lacking in the
Septuagint.[3] But textual difficulties are not as such an indication
of lateness of composition, and, as in other cases,[4] it is such difficulties which have appeared insurmountable to the Greek translator. The introduction of the ostrich, after the wild ass (39:5-8)
and the wild ox (39:9-12), is perfectly natural, since the author's
intention is to describe these steeds of the desert which refuse to
be tamed. And it is to be noted that the last verse ends with this
simple phrase 'she laughs at the horse and his rider', which is the
connecting link to the author's admirable evocation of 'the noblest

[1] Victor Hugo, A Villequier (Les Contemplations, Aujourd'hui).
[2] The unity thus formed by the Prologue, the poetic dialogue, the
speeches of Yahweh, and the Epilogue, is well brought out by Grill, in a
dissertation Zur Kritik der Komposition des Buches Hiob (1890), pp. 59ff.
[3] Dillmann himself is inclined towards the hypothesis, put forward by
Bickell and Hatch, that the lacuna in the Septuagint might betray a late
interpolation: cf. Hiob, 4th ed., p. 334.
[4] On the value of the Septuagint for recovering the original state of the
text, cf. below, pp. cxcviff.

conquest that man has ever made', the horse, which is the very type of the steed that retains its wild impetuosity despite human domestication and training. Hence let us leave the ostrich passage where it is and take care not to eliminate it or transfer it elsewhere.[1]

Similarly attempts have been made to remove from Yahweh's discourse the descriptions of Behemoth (the hippopotamus, 40:15-24) and of Leviathan (the crocodile, 40:25-41:26), on the grounds that these descriptions exceed the others in length, lack the interrogative turn of phrase so characteristic of the previous passages, are devoid of that divine accent recognisable in other speeches of Yahweh, become prolix in describing the physical aspect rather than the temperament or the habits of the animal, and finally are concerned with two exotic Egyptian animals, rather than the Palestinian animals which make up the gallery as a whole.[2] Duhm, having already deleted the passage about the ostrich (39:13-18) for rather unconvincing reasons,[3] now brings forward

---

[1] Wright would place it after v. 30, after the hawk and the eagle (!).

[2] These objections are fully set out by Dillmann (op. cit., pp. 342f.) and Gray (*The Book of Job*, pp. 351f.). It is following Eichhorn and de Wette, in their Introductions, and Ewald, in his different works, that critics have decided in a negative sense the question of the authenticity of these two descriptions. The first step in this course had been taken by Stuhlmann and Bernstein, who simply eliminated 41: 4-26 as an addition to the first description of the crocodile. The history of the exegesis of these passages, together with the arguments of the partisans and the opponents of authenticity, is outlined by Simson, in *Zur Kritik des Buches Hiob*, pp. 20ff. Budde regards 41: 4-26 (cf. Stuhlmann and Bernstein) as a development of a description of the crocodile which included only 40: 25-41: 3. Following Bunsen, Hoffmann, Hontheim, he places 40: 25 and the rest of the description after 39: 18, the passage 39: 13-18 having been transferred to a place after 39: 30 (hypothesis of Wright, above). Cf. Budde, *Das Buch Hiob*, 2nd ed., p. 250 and pp. 262f.

[3] The lacuna of the Septuagint which has been stressed by Hatch and Bickell proves nothing (cf. above). The form of the description deviates, so it is maintained, from that adopted in the case of the other animals. An author, however, obviously has the right to vary his style, as we shall have occasion to note in regard to the depiction of Behemoth and Leviathan. The designation of God by the 3rd person (39: 17) is not without parallel (38: 41; 40: 2, 9, 19), and we have mentioned the case of prophecies placed in the mouth of Yahweh. What Duhm calls the awkwardness (*Ungeschicktheit*) with which 39: 18 introduces the horse is a proof of the authenticity of the passage, for this verse is the link which joins the description of the ostrich to that of the horse. The difficulties of 39: 13 ought to have dispensed Duhm from finding in this opening, which exegetes have difficulty in restoring to its original state (cf. Comm.), a *manirierte Ausdrucksweise*, i.e., if we understand it rightly, an affected manner of expressing one's self. Cf. Duhm, *Das Buch Hiob*, p. 190.

arguments of an aesthetic kind to those desirous of removing Behemoth and Leviathan: 'On the basis of a very superficial understanding of 40:8-14, the two poems seek to show the powerlessness of man and they do so by means of long, turgid descriptions, which in their exaggerations are most unconvincing, the two quatrains from the poet who wrote about the wild ass having far more value than these twenty-one quatrains which in fact deceived the later Jews to such an extent that they made mythical monsters of the two animals of the Nile. If even now some commentators follow the Jews in this respect, it is at least an indirect indication that such poems are without the naturalness and sense of reality which characterise the poet of Job.' [1] With this verdict put forth by the Basel critic we might contrast the opinion of the late L. Gautier when he was a professor at Geneva: 'This passage,[2] most brilliant and composed with great artistic skill, deserves to be ranked very high from the literary point of view. Hence it is by no means unworthy of the great writer to whom we owe the Book of Job, and there would be no difficulty in attributing its composition to him: what is debatable matter is whether it stands in its correct place in the poem and should serve as a peroration to the second speech of Yahweh.' [3]

This confrontation of the contrasting impressions of two equally independent critics shows quite clearly the little value possessed by arguments drawn from the nature of the artistic composition. In our translation of the two poems we have endeavoured to preserve the colour and the force of the thought and imagery. Those who read these verses in the original will feel even better the boldness of the imagination at work, the rhythm and the vigour of the style, the expressive and ever-recurrent hyperboles, all that oriental brilliance and glow which is so typical of the inspired writer to whom we owe the laments of Job and the descriptions which give colour not only to the recriminations of the sufferer but also to the rebukes of his friends. Not one verse should be cut out. The resumption of the description of the crocodile in 41:4-26 is managed by means of the most skilful transition. The interrogations which follow each other in 40:24 (cf. Comm.), 25, 26, 27, 28, 29, 30, 31, 32; 41:2 (cf. Comm.), 3, are thoroughly in the style of the speeches of

---

[1] Duhm, op. cit., pp. 195f.
[2] That is, the description of the hippopotamus and the crocodile in 40:10-41:25.
[3] *Introduction à l'A.T.*, 2nd ed., II, p. 113.

Yahweh. Is it not natural that God, who intervenes precisely in order to unfold the incomprehensible marvels of nature, should proceed in an ascending scale? After the animals whose instinct, nature, manners, and habits have about them an element of mystery, here finally are two monsters whose whole being is disconcerting! These two monsters live on the banks of the Nile and figure together in Egyptian art.[1] They belong almost to the sphere of myth and legend, and they are given typical names: Behemoth and Leviathan! They offer themselves quite naturally as the crown and climax of these descriptions of animals. They are fantastic and exotic, but all the more interesting for that reason. And when Yahweh brings to a culminating point His description of the crocodile (41:25-6),

> On earth there is not his like,
> He who was created intrepid!
> He gazes at every proud creature,
> He is king over all wild beasts!,

Job at this point can but stammer out his apologies for his ignorance, which stands in sharpest contrast to the almighty power of the Creator (42:1-5). The object of the intervening passage (40:1-14) is to give the reader a moment's pause for breath before he is transported to the heights where he will remain dumbfounded by the extraordinary spectacle which God has reserved for the conclusion. We should not be offended by the Egyptian character of the two monsters, for there is a Palestinian reminiscence in the mention of the Jordan (40:23). Quite apart from the allusion to the mines of Sinai in ch. 28 (see below), the mention of the lotus plant (40:21-2) has surely a parallel in that of the papyrus plant by Bildad (8:11). The skiffs of reed, of which Job speaks (9:26), are of the same provenance as the vessels of papyrus in Is 18:2, that is, Egypt. Had not the name of the Nile become a sort of common noun denoting a canal, or channel, or trench (28:10)? In 38:36 we believe that we have recognised the Egyptian name 'ibis', and this verse does not belong to those descriptions which the critics desire to remove. Thus the exotic character of 40:15-41:26 furnishes no argument against the attribution of this passage to the author of Yahweh's speeches, who is the same as that of the prose narrative and the poetic dialogue.

We shall conclude this exposition by referring to certain indications derived both from the descriptions of Behemoth and Leviathan

[1] Cf. Comm. on 40:15.

and from other parts of the speeches of Yahweh, indications which
seem to us to reveal a common origin with the poetic dialogue and
the Prologue.

In the whole of the poetic book the use of the divine names con-
forms to the same laws. We have noted this already.[1] A characteristic feature of the poet's style consists in the fact that he sometimes
effects his parallelism by using an Aramaic word instead of the corresponding Hebrew term. This technique, which occurs in 16:19,
is found again in 39:5 and 40:18. The 'sons of Elohim' of the
Prologue is a phrase which recurs in a speech of Yahweh (38:7).
The constellations to which Job points (9:9) are again alluded to
in the interrogation which God addresses to him (38:31-2). The
eyelids of dawn are mentioned in Job's lament (3:9) and in the
description of the crocodile (41:10). In referring to the wild beast
Yahweh uses the same terms as Eliphaz (5:23; 39:15; 40:20); like
the latter, He mentions the lioness and the young lions (4:10-11;
38:39). We find the parallelism between iron and bronze on the
lips of Zophar (20:24) and in the description of the hippopotamus
(40:18) and the crocodile (41:19). One special term is used to
express majesty in 13:11; 31:23; 41:17. After the speeches of
Yahweh Job uses again the formula 'dust and ashes' which he had
used in the poetic dialogue (30:19; 42:6). His favourite expression
'come forth from the womb' (1:21; 3:11) is used also by Yahweh
(38:29). The idiom שׂחק ל׳ 'laugh at' occurs in the descriptions
of the wild ass (39:7), the ostrich (39:18), the horse (39:22), the
crocodile (41:21). It was found also on the lips of Eliphaz (5:22).

We do not feel it necessary to pursue this enumeration further.
We believe it is a sufficient reply to those who might be struck by
certain peculiar features in the descriptions which occur successively
in Yahweh's speeches. We have no right to confine an author to
one narrow framework of thought and language and to prevent him
from leaving it where he changes his theme or wishes to vary his
style. Variety in unity will always be one of the conditions of beauty.
We must also take account of the various moments when the inspired writer had leisure to pursue his work. There is no need to
suppose that the whole book emerged in one single outburst. When
the author takes up his calamus again he feels a new inspiration,
and while remaining the same as to the basis of his ideas and
language he allows himself to be transported by an afflatus which

---

[1] Above, pp. lxvff.

raises him to heights which the discussion between Job and his friends could not reach.

It seems to us that it is at this moment that he composes not only the speeches of Yahweh but also the magnificent poem on Wisdom (28) which we have analysed above and whose function as providing a pause and moment of rest, after the poetic dialogue, we have noted.[1] What causes us to think that it springs from the same moment and inspiration as the conclusion of the work (38-42) is not only the subject treated, Wisdom and Intelligence in themselves, which are an essential part of those mysteries which man cannot reach and which God alone can know,[2] but also many details of style and atmosphere. The description starts with a contemplation of the mines of Sinai (28:1-11) and thus gains that Egyptian flavour which has been noted in the speeches of Yahweh, especially the pictures given of the hippopotamus and the crocodile. Gradually we come to the deep and the sea (28:14), which will recur together in 33:16. There is a verbatim recurrence of 28:26b in 38:25b, while 38:10a is inspired by 33:26a. The passage on creation (28:24-6) is amplified in ch. 38. One of the typical phrases, 'under the whole heavens' (28:24), recurs in the description of the crocodile (41:3). It is in this description, and nowhere else, that we find once more the expression בְּנֵי־שָׁחַץ 'sons of pride' which occurs in 28:8 to denote wild beasts.

Hence we may conclude that Yahweh's speeches, to which the Epilogue is welded, were written (perhaps after a certain lapse of time) by the author who composed the Prologue and the poetic dialogue.[3] These speeches form a perfect unity, and there is no serious ground for eliminating the descriptions of the ostrich, the hippopotamus, and the crocodile. To the same vein of inspiration belongs ch. 28, which was intercalated in the poetic colloquy as a kind of calm meditation, after the discussion of Job and his friends and before the final apologia of the hero. If the speeches of Yahweh show the uselessness of debates and disputes about the ultimate divine mysteries, the poem on Wisdom shows the powerlessness of man's effort to penetrate secrets which neither the earth nor the sea

---

[1] Above, p. li.

[2] The two terms חכמה and בינה, in parallelism in 38: 12, 20, 28, are again found together in 38: 36.

[3] There is no need for us to deal with the fantasies of Fullerton in 'The Original Conclusion to the Book of Job' (*ZATW*, 1924, pp. 116ff.). The author tries to prove, by means of far-fetched ideas worthy of the Talmud,

nor even the Underworld is able to disclose to us. In both cases [1] it would be necessary to be able to pierce to the very origins of things in order to find wisdom and attain the solution which Job's friends were incapable of supplying.

D. THE SPEECHES OF ELIHU (32-7) (cf. pp. livff.)

A close study of the component parts of the Book of Job has shown with quite sufficient evidence that its various constituent elements are complementary to each other. The Prologue requires the poetic dialogue, the latter the speeches of Yahweh, while the speeches of Yahweh are rounded off by the Epilogue. The poem on Wisdom was inserted into the poetic dialogue at the time when the composition of the final part, including the speeches of Yahweh and the Epilogue, was being completed. We have been able to detect two phases in the composition, but two phases which proceed from the same initial impulse and are directed to a single end. It was the same author who after finishing the Prologue and the 'speeches of Job' took up his calamus once more to write down the words of Yahweh and complete his work by the addition of the Epilogue, while at the same time slipping into the already completed part his poem on Wisdom as though to proclaim that the same hand had composed the whole work. The links between the various parts are contrived with an air of naturalness. The end of the Prologue (2:11-13) brings forward the interlocutors who will take part in the great debate, and in 3:1 foreshadows even the *Leitmotif* of Job's lament. The appeals to God's judgment which are scattered through-

that a double meaning was deliberately intended by the inspired writer. It is in the following that we find the clearest of Fullerton's ideas: 'Thus Prologue, Speeches of Jahweh, and Confessions share the peculiarity of having a double sense run through them. The *pious reader* would see in the Prologue the suggestion that suffering came from God and would be content with that, i.e. with a purely religious or, better, theological explanation. The *thinker* would see that this is no real explanation.... The *pious reader* would see in the Jahweh speeches a rebuke of Job's temerity in criticising God. The *thinker* would see in them the thesis of the inexplicability of the universe as a whole, of which the inexplicability of suffering is only an acute example. The *pious reader* would see in the Confession of Job a retraction of his former criticisms in view of the divine rebuke. The *thinker* would see in it the confession *of the author* that he had no further light to give upon this ultimately insoluble problem and the indication that *this was the end of the book*' (pp. 131f.). This machiavellianism belongs rather to the critic than to the author of the Book of Job.

[1] Cf. 28:23-7 and 38:4-11.

out the dialogue find their answer in the speeches of Yahweh. Since it was Job who spoke last, it is he who will be directly addressed (38:1; 40:1, 6), and who will stammer out a few words to prevent the speeches of Yahweh from being a mere uninterrupted monologue (40:3-5; 42:1-5). It is when God has finished speaking His wonderful poetic words (42:7) that a short account gives us the conclusion of a story which has kept us in breathless suspense from the start of the Prologue.

It is in this well-knit and logically conceived structure that we encounter the speeches of Elihu (32-7). This personage was not introduced in the Prologue.[1] Hence it was necessary to introduce him separately, and that is why we find a prefatory note before his speeches (32:1-6). Whereas the three protagonists, the 'three friends' of Job, were each of them distinguished by a single epithet indicating his place of origin, for Elihu we are given in addition the name of his father and family. His intervention needs so much explanation that four times the little preamble repeats that 'his wrath was kindled' (32:2, 3, 5). This is appreciably different from the sober and limpid tone of the Prologue. Budde, in order to remove this indication of a late addition, combines 31:40b with 32:1 and constructs the phrase: 'The words of Job were ended and these three men ceased to answer Job because he was righteous in his own eyes.' Thus we see what becomes of the little clause: 'The words of Job are ended'! At least one might have had simply 'ceased to answer him' and not 'ceased to answer Job'. And the silence of the three men, not now of the three friends, would be due to the fact that Job is righteous in his own eyes. But Job has been righteous in his own eyes from the very start of the debate![2] Hoffmann lightened the text by eliminating 32:2-5, but then Elihu is not introduced, and we do not know why a new interlocutor emerges. Let us recognise simply that in the little prose passage 32:1-5 there occurs a change of method and technique.

The need to justify the appearance of a new character on the stage is again very obvious in the long speech in which Elihu, addressing first Job's friends (32:6-22) and then Job himself

---

[1]　In the article of van Hoonacker which we have cited with regard to the speeches of Yahweh, the learned professor mentions a few of the reasons which lead him to think that the original edition did not include the speeches of Elihu (*RB*, 1903, pp. 162ff.), and these reasons seem to him to be 'decisive' (p. 161).

[2]　Cf. Comm. on 32: 1.

(33:1-8), merely repeats that he has been patient up to the present, but that at last he insists on speaking despite his youth.[1]

The oddest thing of all is that the long monologues of Elihu fall on empty air. He stops short in 37:24. Yahweh disregards Elihu's intervention to address Job (38:1). There is not a word of comment on him in the Epilogue, where the interlocutors are awarded their final marks (42:7ff.). Yahweh, Job, the three friends, these are the *dramatis personae* at the close, and we have known them from the beginning. Elihu is passed over in silence, but it is not for want of having made his views known.

The most striking feature about Elihu's speeches is the mode of discussion adopted. If the reader will refer to our analysis of the poetic dialogue,[2] he will easily note that each speaker expounds his point of view and doctrine without really troubling to confute previous arguments. The refutation arises of itself from the essence of the debate. It is not the *responsio ad primum, secundum, tertium*, which is characteristic of scholastic disputation. The speaker does not attack immediately what has just been said. Thus Job's reply [3] in ch. 9 is directed at Eliphaz, the first speaker (4-5), while ignoring the arguments of Bildad (8). We feel that the book is being built up, bit by bit, in proportion as the discussion advances. The opponents in the debate are familiar with each other's positions, but they do not attack in detail such or such a point. The theses as a whole clash and confront each other, but the speakers do not come to grips in particulars. We have here the tone of conversation, where each interlocutor follows his own ideas rather than troubles to reply to his opponent. There is no attempt to attack any particular mode of expression, or to sum up such or such a theory. For such a purpose it would be necessary to study minutely and calmly the arguments of one's adversary, bringing out and countering their weak points. Such are not the tactics of Job's friends. Their discussion in fact is not speculative at all but severely practical. Its aim is to restore Job to a state of mind which is in conformity to religious tradition: recognition of one's faults, return to God, conversion.

---

[1] What a contrast with the incisive phrases by which Job and his friends often enter into their subject! One might say that this contrast is intended by the author. But the long preamble of Elihu looks singularly like an explanation of his intervention. Its prolixity is such that authors such as Nichols and Torczyner (below, p. cx) have not hesitated to divide ch. 32: 6-22 into two parts. We shall see that this division is not justified.

[2] Above, pp. **xxxviff.**   [3] Above, pp. **xxxviiiff.**

Now read over again the speeches of Elihu! He attacks Job directly, addressing him by his name (32:13; 33:1, 31; 34:5, 7, 35, 36; 35:16; 37:14), which none of the friends have done. One has the very definite impression that Elihu has the whole debate under review, both the assertions of Job and those of his friends. That is why he can criticise every one and play the part of arbiter among the theories in conflict; sometimes he has Job in view (33:1ff., 31ff.; 34:16, 33; 35:2ff.; 36:2ff.; 37:14ff.), at other times his friends or the wise (32:6-22; 34:2ff., 34ff.), or Job and the friends at the same time (35:4). Thus one feels that the Book of Job is already in existence, that it is in the hands of a reader who can single out, from among the words which Job utters, certain assertions liable to criticism. The friends of Job have given no adequate reply to these assertions. As for the speeches of Yahweh, they lift the debate on to a height where there is no place for the criticism of particular ideas. It is Job's words in their totality which are called in question (38:2; 40:2). In short, we are faced by the following situation. Job has posed his case of conscience. His friends have tried to solve it by traditional theories. Job has proved that these theories are outworn. Yahweh shows that both Job and his friends are powerless to understand and explain the mystery. If we wished to reduce all this to scholastic formulae we would say that the title of the matter in dispute has been formulated by Job's friends: there exists a necessary relation between misfortune and moral evil. Job expounds the *videtur quod non*, and the friends reply by a series of *sed contra*. Then Yahweh formulates the *respondeo dicendum*. There now remains a final operation. It is the reply to objections, the *ad primum, secundum*, etc.

This complementary rôle has been assigned to Elihu. He no longer has to expound a thesis. But he has to take up certain of Job's assertions in a more detailed manner. He has before him all the matter relative to the dispute; he has simply to dispose of some of the more shocking and dangerous complaints. This is what he proposes to do by refuting some of the excesses in Job's mode of expressing himself. He will cite them sometimes verbally, sometimes in their essential import, to show clearly that if he has remained a silent participant in the debate it was so as to be able to draw up his final charge. He will take care to point out that he is a being of clay like Job himself and that consequently he may intervene even though Yahweh has already spoken, for Job will not be afraid of him as of the Lord.[1] Similarly he noted that the older men were not able to reduce Job to *quia* (32:6-13). He considers their method wrong, so he will adopt a different one (32:14-17). His procedure emerges very clearly in 33:8-11.

> You have done nothing but talk in my ears,
> And I have heard the sound of the words:
> 'I am pure, without transgression,
> I am clean, there is no fault in me!
> But see, He finds pretexts against me,[2]
> He regards me as His enemy,
> He puts my feet in the stocks,
> And watches all my steps!'

Verbal quotations of 13:24 (cf. 19:11) and of 13:27; quotation of the purport of 11:4. The thesis of Job is well summed up. Elihu will prove that Job is not correct (33:12ff.). His refutation gives occasion for a short dissertation on the salutary function of divine visitations, even though they cause suffering to him who is their object.

The examination of Job's remarks continues. Here is a new series of more or less verbal quotations (34:5-9).

> Since Job has said: 'I am righteous,
> But God has set aside my right,
> Concerning my right He speaks falsely,[3]
> My wound is incurable although I am innocent!'

Here again it is the basis of Job's speech which is condemned, and in particular 27:3 is verbally challenged. The corollary of Job's allegations is that

> It is no profit to man
> To make Elohim his delight. (34: 9)

This *responsio ad secundum* occasions a digression on the divine government of the world. And Elihu appears to apologise for not confining himself to this theme, but he will not allow to pass without a reply certain statements of Job which seem to him worthy of wicked men (34:36).

Hence he brings forward a new accusation which is based on a phrase of Job in 7:20.[4]

> When you say: 'What does it matter to Thee?
> What do I to Thee if I sin?' (35: 3)

---

[1] Cf. Comm. on 33: 6, 4, 7.
[2] Cf. Comm. on 33: 10.
[3] Cf. Comm. on 34: 6.
[4] Cf. Comm. on 35: 3.

This *responsio ad tertium* likewise involves a short digression on the varying attitudes of men when they suffer under the blows of fate.

Finally Elihu abandons his close following of the text. He expounds his ideas on the deity, his knowledge becomes far-reaching, he makes himself out to be 'perfect in knowledge', he shows how God deals with men in order to save them, and how He is revealed in nature. One might suppose that in chs. 36-7 he tries to complete the description of the wonders of the world of nature which have furnished the theme of Yahweh's speeches.[1] Hence he stresses the phenomena of rain and storm (36:27-37:5), of ice and snow (37:6-10), to return to those of the lightnings and thunderbolts (37:11-15) and the play of the clouds (37:16-22), which are the handiwork of God and staggering to men (37:22-4).

Not only does the intervention of Elihu appear episodic but everything in his speeches suggests the continuation of a work, the resumption of a theme which had already been completed by the first author. If there are cases where a clear distinction appears between a work in the process of formation and a work already complete, it is here. If so, however, will there not be manifest a difference in the language of the two authors?

The argument from style must be presented with the greatest caution. Critics have contrasted the style of Elihu—pompous and bombastic, stilted and prolix—with the style of Job, his friends, and Yahweh, a style which is on the contrary concise, vigorous, and unaffected. But it may surely be answered that the character of the person speaking dictates the nature of his style. The same author may well have given to the young Elihu a style different from that of the older speakers. Otherwise we should be condemning to monotony the most skilful and subtle artist.

It is clear that the use of the divine names as we have defined it above [2] proves nothing either for or against the attribution of the speeches of Elihu to the first author. The convention is so closely followed in the whole of the poetic book that the second author would have been guilty of the greatest clumsiness had he not obeyed it. For Elihu is no more an Israelite than Job and his friends. No more than they can he use the name Yahweh. Like them he must

---

[1] This explanation is more acceptable than that which would attempt to see here a Psalm on the tempest interpolated later in the speeches of Elihu (below, p. cx).

[2] Pp. lxvff.

ring the changes on the three other names of the deity. The preference for El which to Gray [1] seems an argument has already been
shown by Bildad.[2] It is neither in the style nor in the nomenclature
of the deity that we shall find the decisive characteristics of the
second author.

We are on more solid ground in studying the words which form
part of current vocabulary and often suggest, according to the
inclination which an author shows for certain of them, at what date
or in what environment the writing has been composed.

The pronoun of the first person may be expressed either by אֲנִי
or by אָנֹכִי, and critics have not failed to use this criterion for the
purpose of tracing in the composition of the historical books [3] a
variety of hands. Whereas the poetic book makes a free use of both
these forms, Elihu confines himself to אֲנִי, except in 33:31, which
is a literal citation of 21:3a, and in 33:9b, where the form אָנֹכִי
occurs only as a parallel to אֲנִי.[4] Now, it is a fact that in Biblical
literature there is a marked tendency to eliminate אָנֹכִי in favour of
אֲנִי in proportion as we reach later stages of development.[5] Here
then we have a material index suggesting a later date for the
speeches of Elihu by contrast with the poetic dialogue.

We shall not dwell on the use of prepositions, whether alone or
with suffixes. The statistics drawn up by Gray [6] should in our
opinion be handled with caution, not as attesting the predominance
of particular forms in the various component parts of Job, but as
possessing demonstrative value. The speeches of Elihu occupy too
small a place in comparison with the rest of the poetic dialogue for
it to be possible to base arguments on the greater or lesser degree
of frequency with which particles are used.

What is characteristic and truly demonstrative is the use of
certain words in preference to others to express the same object
or idea or psychological phenomenon, the recourse to one form in
preference to another to denote the same state of mind.

For example, Elihu uses דַּע 'knowledge' (32:6, 10, 17; 36:3;

---

[1] Driver-Gray, *The Book of Job*, p. xliii.
[2] Above, pp. lxviiif.
[3] Driver, *Introd. to the Literature of the O.T.*, 9th ed., pp. 134f.
[4] The statistics of Gray (op. cit., pp. xliii f.) are instructive in this respect.
The poetic dialogue uses אֲנִי fifteen times, אָנֹכִי eleven times. The speeches of
Elihu use אֲנִי nine times and אָנֹכִי only twice (by necessity).
[5] Cf. Giesebrecht, *ZATW*, **1** (1881), p. 256.
[6] Op. cit., p. xlv.

37:16). This word is not found in the rest of the book, where דַעַת is always used (13:2; 15:2; 21:14, 22; 38:2; 42:3). Instead of the *pi'el* (6:11; 14:14; 29:21, 23; 30:26), it is the *hiph'il* of יחל which is used in the sense of 'wait' (32:11, 16). In 33:9 the unusual term חַף takes the place of בַּר 'pure' (11:4). The *pi'el* of צדק (33:32) is substituted for the *hiph'il* (27:5) in the sense of 'justify'. Instead of מְתֵי 'men of . . .', which we find in use by Job and his friends (11:11; 19:19; 22:15; 31:31), Elihu says אַנְשֵׁי (34:8, 10, 34, 36). Instead of the verb רצץ 'to break' (20:19), Elihu does not hesitate to use the Aramaic רעע (34:24), just as he uses the Aramaic מַעְבָּד 'deed' (34:25) as synonym for the Hebrew מַעֲשֶׂה. One whole hemistich of Elihu (36:2a) is composed of Aramaic words.[1] A fondness for the verb פעל instead of עשׂה is yet another distinctive mark of the style of Elihu[2]. Again, the Aramaic בחר (36:21) instead of the Hebrew בחן; שַׂגִּיא (36:26; 37:23) meaning 'great'[3]; לְמַכְבִּיר (36:31) instead of לָרֹב 'in abundance'; perhaps עַלְעוֹלָה 'tempest' (36:33, cf. Comm.) rather than סְעָרָה; הוא in the sense of 'fall' (37:6); מִפְלָאוֹת instead of נפלאות 'wonders' (37:16); בָּהִיר 'obscure' (37:21).

Thus everything suggests a new stage in the composition of the Book of Job. The way in which Elihu is introduced, his total disappearance without trace, the secondary character of his intervention, the aim and method of his arguments, the highly personal colour and Aramaic tendency of his language—all these are indications of an author working on an already completed book and bringing in a new character whose mission is to confute some exaggerations in the language of the chief speaker.[4] For the rest of the work, we have noticed two successive stages, first the Prologue and the poetic dialogue, then the speeches of Yahweh, the poem on Wisdom, and the Epilogue. The third stage is that in which a new inspired writer, not content to recopy or redictate the original work, completes it and gives it the final form which is that of our canonical book.[5]

---

[1] Cf. Comm. on 36: 2.
[2] Cf. Comm. on 36: 3.
[3] Cf. Comm. on 37: 23.
[4] And not to 'correct' the first author, as is maintained by Loisy (*Le Livre de Job*, pp. 43f.).
[5] Hoffmann well defines the character of this work when he declares that the speeches of Elihu are a supplement rather than an interpolation.

The thesis that the speeches of Elihu were a later addition has met with the greatest favour among critics. Already in 1891 Dillmann drew up an impressive list of adherents from Eichhorn to Cheyne.[1] Let us note only the names of Ewald, Hirzel, Franz Delitzsch, Nöldeke, Merx, Reuss, Bickell, Hoffmann. Since then the list has constantly grown. Not only Dillmann but also Klostermann, König, Siegfried, Duhm, Fried. Delitzsch, Gray, Peake, Strahan,[2] Ball, Buttenwieser, and others also, are all partisans of the theory that a Book of Job was completed by the speeches of Elihu. Some exegetes, such as Bunsen, Kamphausem, Sellin, J. Herrmann,[3] were of the opinion that the addition might have been effected by the original author in order to forestall any ill interpretation of his work. Renan, who felt it 'certain that the speeches of Elihu were interpolated',[4] did not exclude the hypothesis of a rewriting by the first author: 'Who knows if the author himself, taking up his work after a long interval of time, and at a date when he had lost his verve and his particular style, did not think he was perfecting his poem by adding this section which in reality disfigures it?' [5] But it seems more likely that if the complement were the work of the hand which so admirably co-ordinated the Prologue, the dialogue, the speeches of Yahweh, and the Epilogue, the grafting on of the Elihu episode would have been solidly effected, and it would have been impossible to remove [6] chs. 32-7 without its being noticed.

It should not however be thought that there do not remain some who think that these chapters belong essentially to the original redaction of the work. To face the list of adversaries, Dillmann drew up a list of names which is in fact considerable, from Schärer (1818) and Rosenmüller (1824) to Budde, and including Umbreit, Stickell, Schlottmann, Keil, etc. To this list should be added Catholic authors, generally not mentioned, such as Knabenbauer in his commentary, Cornely in his *Introduction to the O.T.*, Gietmann and

[1] *Hiob*, 4th ed., pp. 277f. Cf. Budde, *Das Buch Hiob*, 2nd ed., pp. xxiv ff.
[2] The complementary character of the speeches of Elihu is well brought out in the *Introductions to the O.T.* by Lucien Gautier, Driver, Baudissin.
[3] Quoted by Budde, op. cit., p. xxv.
[4] *Le Livre de Job*, 5th ed., p. lvi.
[5] Ibid., p. lvii. Loisy refutes this hypothesis of Renan in *Le Livre de Job*, p. 42.
[6] Note the remark of Le Hir: 'One must admit that the drama would appear perfect even if this speech were cut out' (*Le Livre de Job*, p. 366).

Welte,[1] Hontheim,[2] and above all Posselt in a monograph,[3] Prat in Vigouroux' *Dictionary of the Bible*.[4]

It is especially Budde who, supported by Cornill [5] and Wilde-boer,[6] has taken up the cudgels in favour of the original presence of the Elihu section in the first redaction. Ever since 1876, when he published his *Beiträge zur Kritik des Buches Hiob*,[7] the learned commentator has not ceased to maintain his position, chiefly in his commentary which appeared in 1896 and was revised in 1913. Let us note at once that he does not hesitate to sacrifice the little prose prologue (32:2-5) and to create an artificial link between the notice 31:40b and 32:1, 6, as we have seen above.[8] This arbitrary proceeding, which produces the queerest impression on the reader, since we can no longer see where Elihu appears from, cannot fail to be disquieting. If we continue to examine the thesis, we notice that certain passages which, moreover, are not those omitted by the Septuagint are thrown overboard like so much ballast which is too heavy for the original book. Thus disappear: 32:11-17; 33:4, 33; 34:9, 10a, 25, 26-8, 29c; 35:4, 13-14, 17, 25-6, 29-30; 37:15-16. Budde's operation is like that of a chemist who in order to introduce a foreign body into a certain combination begins by dissociating from it whatever might prevent its assimilation. But if it is a question of true amalgamation it should not be necessary to effect this prior dissociation.

An argument of internal criticism which Budde is fond of bringing forward is that 'the speeches of Elihu achieve a complete and genuine expression of the author's thought',[9] or again that 'they embody in essence the final solution of the poet'. [10]

But it is surprising that the poet should not have found among Job's interlocutors a more prepossessing and attractive mouthpiece than the young and hot-headed Elihu, whose monologues sometimes

[1]   Quoted by Hontheim, *Das Buch Hiob*, p. 20, n. 1.
[2]   Op. cit. (in *Biblische Studien*, IX, **1**, 1904), pp. 20ff.
[3]   *Der Verfasser der Elihu-Reden*, in *Biblische Studien*, XIV, **3** (1909).
[4]   Same thesis in the *Bible* of Crampon (Introduction to the Book of Job).
[5]   In *Einleitung in das A.T.* (2nd ed., 1892), pp. 231ff.
[6]   In *Literatur des A.T.* (1895). The arguments of Wildeboer and Cornill have been passed through the crucible of criticism in the dissertation of Laue, *Die Composition des Buches Hiob*, pp. 103ff.
[7]   The arguments adduced by Budde have been taken up and developed by Bölicke, in *Die Elihu-Reden* (1897), pp. 6ff.
[8]   P. xcix.
[9]   *Das Buch Hiob*, 2nd ed., p. xlvi.
[10]   Ibid., p. xlviii.

show a presumption which makes even their finest passage painful reading. Furthermore, and this is a point of capital importance, how can we suppose that neither the speeches of Yahweh nor the Epilogue should have made the slightest reference to this solution which the author himself is alleged to have extolled? Finally, we have noted that the words of Elihu do not contain the exposition of a thesis but rather furnish replies to some of the remarks of Job, partial replies accompanied by pious digressions and attempts at explanation. The great reply, not only to Job, but also to his friends, lies in the speech of Yahweh. If it is Elihu who expounds the author's thesis, why is it that Job, who is constantly rebuked by Elihu, should receive the praises of the Epilogue?

Budde claims that the link between the speeches of Elihu and the rest of the book leaves nothing to be desired. He quotes 17:9; 18:2-3; 30:1ff. to show that Job and his friends carry on their discussions before an audience.[1]

We have not disputed that the speakers, and especially Job's friends, speak with an audience in view. This moreover is implied by the little prologue to Elihu's speeches and his entry on the stage. The author of this section did not seek anywhere except among the witnesses of the debate one who should argue about some of the remarks made. But we have seen that the method of presentation, both in the prose and poetic parts, differed appreciably from that which characterises the Prologue and the poetic dialogue. Nor should we forget that if the absence of Elihu in the Prologue might be justified it is the absence of any judgment about him in the Epilogue and especially the direct connection of Yahweh's speeches with those of Job which contain the most decisive implications. The explanations offered by Posselt [2] do not overcome the difficulty. This author inquires: 'What ought God to have said about Elihu?' Simply that, if Job had spoken better than his three friends (40:7), the refutations of Elihu were valueless. Or, on the other hand, had Elihu been right as against Job, and so against the others, it is he who should have received the palm of victory and should have interceded for all!

Posselt has the good sense to show [3] that the description of a storm (37:1ff.) in the speeches of Elihu, had it really been a pre-

[1] Ibid., p. xxvi.
[2] Op. cit., pp. 52ff.
[3] Ibid., p. 56.

paration for the theophany,[1] might have been the work of a second author who would thus have grafted his poem on to the original. Besides, we must recognise that this description is not directly connected with the theophany.[2] Posselt does recognise this, contrary to Budde, Hitzig, and Hontheim, who try to find an allusion to this theophany in 37:22 (cf. our Comm.).

The arguments relative to style and vocabulary are reversed by Budde, who brings out the harmony between the language of Elihu and that of the rest of the poem.[3] It is clear that the second author, who would be thoroughly acquainted with the work of the first, and would be writing in his wake, must have many features of style in common with him. We have noticed this in particular with regard to the use of the divine names.[4] But the characteristic differences which we have pointed out are only all the more striking. What we look for is not a new idiom, but simply a few features, a few indications, enabling us to recognise that the same language has been spoken or written by two distinct authors. Posselt, who dwells complacently on the statistics of Budde, admits that proof from affinity of language concerns only the 'possibility' of a single author, and that a mathematical exactitude should not be demanded.[5] Proof from vocabulary is adduced only at the end, and then as a confirmation rather than a reason. It enables us to infer the homogeneity of the Prologue and Epilogue,[6] of these and the poetic dialogue,[7] of the poetic dialogue and Yahweh's speeches[8]; but our inference had already been suggested by the study of these various parts and their function in the total structure. Such a study, applied to the speeches of Elihu, suggests rather a note of heterogeneity in relation to the rest of the book, and thus a new author. At this point linguistic verification supervenes and confirms the separation. It goes without saying that one cannot, nor should one, attempt to give apodeictic value to these arguments. It is always a question of the more or less likely.

It is obvious that our method is far removed from that which

---

[1] We have seen that this was not the case (above, p. lxxxiv).
[2] Ibid.
[3] Bölicke stresses this point in *Die Elihu-Reden*, pp. 41ff.
[4] Above, pp. lxixf.
[5] Op. cit., p. 83.
[6] Pp. lxxxiv f.
[7] Pp. lxxxiii f.
[8] Pp. xcvi f.

consists in detaching from the speeches of Elihu and their preamble single verses or whole passages in order to make the whole thing more easily assignable to the original author. This strategy of Budde is doomed to irretrievable failure, for it has every appearance of being a mere shift. Still less shall we follow the path of Nichols [1] and Barton,[2] who dissolve the speeches of Elihu into a series of themes successively interpolated. Whereas every one now is agreed that the lacunae of the Septuagint are of no significance for the appreciation of the original text,[3] we are asked by these critics to accept the Greek in order to see in 36:26-28a, 29-32; 37:2-4, 6b, 11, 12a, b, 13 a Psalm about the storm supposed to have been inter-calated in a speech.[4] This speech itself is supposed to be the final result of a process of compilation in which 34:1; 32:11-16; 34:2-27; 35:15-16; 34:34ff. are said to come from the hand of a 'second sage' addressing not Job but the wise. We are here faced by one of the masterpieces of brutal vivisection from which literary criticism has so cruelly suffered since the appearance of 'rainbow' Bibles. Instead of seeking to discern the poetic bond between ideas, critics of this type prefer to classify them in little pre-arranged compart-ments. We are reminded of a florist who might take from the bunch the flowers which compose it in order to arrange them according to genera and families. There is no need to refute in detail such theories, which, despite their novelty, could impress only those who require conformity to the most prosaic laws of association of ideas in a literary *genre* which permits the most varied movements and the loftiest flights of poetic imagination.

E. FOREIGN INFLUENCES

Not once, in our study of the composition of the Book of Job, have we had to have recourse to the hypothesis of extraneous influences. Much has been made of the Babylonian poem *Ludlul*

---

[1] *American Journal of Semitic Languages*, **27**, p. 97.
[2] *Journal of Biblical Literature*, **30**, p. 68.
[3] Below, pp. cxcixff.
[4] Account of the system of Nichols (approved by Barton) in the com-mentary of Budde (2nd ed.), pp. xxvi, 213, 234, and in the commentary of Driver-Gray, p. xlviii. It should be noted that Torczyner proposes to see in ch. 32 the remains of a double preamble, of which one would have been addressed to the friends (32: 6, 11-14) and the other (32: 7-10, 15ff.) to Job himself—the same technique of dichotomy as with Nichols, but reaching different conclusions. Always the concern for an impeccable sequence in ideas!

bêl nimêqi, 'I will Praise the Lord of Wisdom', the greater part of which we have translated under the title 'The Righteous Sufferer' in our *Choix de textes religieux assyro-babyloniens*.[1] The works of Jastrow, Landersdorfer, Zimmern, Landsberger, and Langdon [2] have made it possible to reconstruct the poem of which 'The Righteous Sufferer' is only the central part. A comparison between the theme of this poem and that of the Book of Job proves conclusively that the latter is independent of the Babylonian work. Certain similarities in the description of undeserved suffering may have been deceptive. But the poem *Ludlul bêl nimêqi* describes, first and foremost, the salvation which the god of Babylon grants to his servants in distress. It far more resembles certain Psalms in which, after depicting his wretchedness, the Psalmist sings his liberation and triumph.[3] On the other hand, we have thought that we were able to detect some resemblances between a Babylonian poem in dialogue form [4] and the poem of the Book of Job.[5] But these concern only external and scattered features. They may arise merely from the fact that the problem of evil was present also to the mind of the Mesopotamian poet. Nowhere is there to be noted a direct influence on the Book of Job.[5]

[1] Pp. 372ff.
[2] *RB*, 1925, p. 311.
[3] *RB*, 1925, p. 312.
[4] Contrary to the opinion of Ebeling.
[5] Cf. our article 'Ecclésiaste ou Job' in *RB*, 1923, pp. 1ff.

CHAPTER EIGHT

THE TEACHING OF THE BOOK OF JOB

We have now analysed the Book of Job and tried to understand the various stages in its composition. In order to appreciate the place which it should occupy in the literature of the Old Testament, it is necessary to sum up the teaching which it embodies and to consider to what stage in the religious evolution of Israel it properly belongs.

METHOD OF EXPOSITION. — Logic would seem to require us to approach this study, as is in fact generally done by commentators, by exploring the precise aim which the author or authors of the work were pursuing. This method is however fallacious. We have noted [1] that the oriental mode of composition, and especially that of the Semites, was not governed by our Western habits. The author does not begin by tracing a rigid plan to which he proposes to subject the movement of his ideas.[2] The Book develops rather in virtue of an interior movement, just as every living creature possesses what St Thomas calls so aptly the *motus ab intrinseco*. Thus each step towards the final goal depends on the preceding one without its being necessary that from the start the inspired writer should restrict his genius to a route whose smallest windings would be known in advance.

But there exist certain general outlines which guide the author and at the same time serve to identify his mind and purpose. His thought is the thought of a man who has lived in a particular environment and has imbibed an already existing doctrine. In certain respects he has accepted this doctrine as it stands, while in others he has questioned it and confronted it with the facts. Above all, he has expounded or criticised it within an appropriate frame-

[1] Above, pp. lxif. and pp. xcvf.
[2] To be convinced of this, it is enough to recall the 'intentions' that have been assigned to the author. A recapitulation of these intentions, as expounded in German exegesis, is given by Thilo, in his little book *Das Buch Hiob* (1925), p. 106. Job goes through all the categories of symbol and allegory, including the inevitable figure of the suffering people, in virtue of the *national-typische* exegesis.

work and according to a technique which is all his own. This is what we must discover and grasp if we wish to have a precise idea of the teaching which the Book of Job gives us.

THE LITERARY GENRE.—We have already said that the literary *genre* was ambiguous,[1] since the prose narrative belonged properly to historical books while the poetic speeches are to be classified among wisdom writings. Nowhere else in one and the same Biblical book do we find such a marked opposition between the narrative and didactic portions.[2]

This original feature is further emphasised if we consider the mode of exposition adopted in the speeches, that is, the dialogue form, whose advantages for discussion were so well understood by the Greeks and Romans. A few examples from Assyrian-Babylonian literature [3] prove that the dialogue form was known in the ancient Semitic world. They are none the less rare, and in the O.T. something of a remarkable novelty, for the few phrases in dialogue of the Song of Songs (1:7, 8-11, 15, 16; 2:10-14; 4, etc.) have the colour and tone of a lyrical duet, not of a poetic dialogue. They remind us of Theocritus rather than of Plato, Cicero, Lucian.

The Hagiographa do not discuss. They expound doctrine, at times under certain disconcerting aspects, as in Ecclesiastes [4]; but they do not introduce various personages to propound in turn their theories with regard to a given problem. The teaching of the Book of Job has to be sought for amid the clash of conflicting opinions. The Prologue and the Epilogue reveal not only the point of view of the original author but the generality of ideas shared by the various speakers. In the poetic dialogue we shall be able to discern certain unchallengeable and unchallenged views apart from the question at issue.

THE FRAMEWORK OF THE TEACHING.—One of the chief concerns of the author is to situate the theatre of discussion outside Israel and to select as his protagonists persons whom the chosen people would consider as heathen. The horizon of the work is similar to that in Ecclesiastes, where the author 'in speaking of God, does not adopt the specifically Israelite point of view, but rather a universa-

---

[1]   Above, pp. xiiif.
[2]   Above, pp. lxiiif.
[3]   Above, p. lxiv, n. 1.
[4]   Cf. Podechard, *L'Ecclésiaste*, pp. 196ff.

list point of view'.[1] Like Qoheleth, the author of the Book of
Job 'does not take into account the ideas and hopes proper to his
own nation; he is concerned about the relations of man in general
with God, or rather about the dealings of Providence with universal
man'.[2] Yet Qoheleth is presented as King of Israel, specifically like
the wise King Solomon.[3] The characters of the Book of Job are
Arabs or Edomites.[4] They represent essentially not the wisdom
current among the descendants of Abraham, Isaac, and Jacob, but,
as we might say, the wisdom of the nations, that which was not
refused recognition as the property of certain privileged beings,
whether 'Orientals', 'Egyptians',[5] or Edomites. Furthermore, the
period envisaged [6] is prior to the classical codification of the theology, ethics, jurisprudence, and cult in Israel. It is the era of the
nomadic patriarchs.

We shall note, however, certain transgressions of the rule to
remain outside Israel and the Law. Certain indications suggest that
Job's friends and Job himself generally argue according to the principles of Jewish tradition, and in the light of a conscience which
has been moulded by the discipline of Israel.[7]

GOD AND THE HEAVENLY BEINGS.—We have given lengthy
treatment to the question of the use of the divine names.[8] Job and
his friends, since they are not Israelites, will refrain from uttering
the name Yahweh, and only very rarely do they refer to Elohim.
Their God is of course the deity of the patriarchal period, namely
El-Shaddai, which may be analysed into a common element, El
'God', and a specific element, 'Shaddai'. The famous passage in

---

[1] Podechard, op. cit., p. 174.
[2] Ibid.
[3] According to Ec 1: 12-2 (cf. Podechard, op. cit., pp. 126f.).
[4] Above, pp. xxiff., xxvff. To the various facts that we have pointed
out in connection with Eliphaz of Teman (p. xxvi) it is suitable to add that
the name Eloah, so infrequent in the Bible outside the Book of Job (cf.
Comm. on 3: 4) is used to designate the God who comes from Teman (Hab
3: 3). The name is found on the lips of Agur (Pr 30: 5), whose language has
an Edomite look about it, as has been demonstrated by Ben-Yehuda in
'The Edomite Language' (*The Journal of the Palestine Oriental Society*, **1**,
1921, pp. 113ff.).
[5] 1 K 4: 30.
[6] Above, pp. xxf.
[7] Contrary to the opinion of Renan, according to whom 'not one allusion
is made to Mosaic customs, nor to the special beliefs of the Jews' (*Le Livre
de Job*, 5th ed., p. xvi).
[8] Above, pp. lxvff.

Ex 6:2-3 leaves no doubt as to the basic identity of Yahweh-Elohim-El-Shaddai: 'And Elohim spoke to Moses and said to him: "I am Yahweh and I appeared to Abraham, Isaac, and Jacob [1] as El-Shaddai; but by my name, Yahweh, I was not known to them."' Sometimes Yahweh (Gn 17:1) and sometimes Elohim (Gn 35:11) assumes the title El-Shaddai. The name Shaddai by itself, already placed in the mouth of Jacob (Gn 49:25), can be parallel to El (Nu 24:4, 16), or to Yahweh (Ru 1:21; Is 13:6; Jl 1:15), or to עֶלְיוֹן 'the Most High' (Ps 91:1). Instead of the two names El and Shaddai, the speakers may also use Eloah, and they will do so all the more readily since this name, which was very rare in Israel because supplanted by the plural Elohim, has a certain Edomite ring about it [2] which well suits Job and his friends.

Thus these names designate one and the same God, whose attributes are universal. A considerable part of the poetic dialogue is devoted to doxologies which would by no means be out of place on the lips of an Israelite. That of Eliphaz (5:8-18) stresses the wonders of which God is the author both in the world of nature and in that of society. The antitheses familiar in Canticles, the Psalms, and the Prophets recur here more or less literally, as is easily proved by glancing through the Commentary.[3] Job too extols the glory of God in the style of the Prophets and Psalms,[4] whether he points to the startling works which God accomplishes in the world (9:4-13) or demonstrates the upheavals which God effects in society (12:13-25). Is it not a verse of the Psalms (107:40) which lends Job the language in which to describe how God covers with confusion the great and wise of the earth (12:21, 24)? Zophar has been taught in the same school, for in 11:7-9 he seems indeed to summarise Ps 139:7-12. When Bildad sings in his turn (25:1-6; 26:5-14) the glories of God, he is inspired by the Psalms [5] and the Proverbs,[6] not to mention Isaiah.[7]

It goes without saying that when Yahweh Himself undertakes

[1] Cf. Gn 28:3; 43:14; 48:3.
[2] Above, p. cxiv, n. 4.
[3] Let us point out the formal resemblances between 5:9 and Ps 145:3; Job 5:10 and Ps 147:8; Job 5:11 and 1 S 2:7; Job 5:14 and Is 59:10; Job 5:16 and Ps 107:42; Job 5:17 and Ps 94:12; Job 5:18 and Dt 32:39.
[4] Cf. 9:6 and Is 13:13; Job 9:8 and Am 4:13; Job 9:9 and Am 5:8; Job 12:13 and Is 11:2.
[5] Cf. 26:5ff. and Ps 104:2ff.
[6] Cf. 26:10 and Pr 8:27.
[7] Cf. 26:12-13 and Is 51:9, 15; 27:1.

to describe His works He speaks with the language and in the spirit of traditional theology. A comparison between 38:4-7 (cf. 28:24-7) and Pr 8:22-31, which allude to the creation of the world, is most instructive in this respect. Elihu again is faithful to tradition when he magnifies and extols the work of the Creator in meteors, in thunders and lightnings, in storm cloud and in the serenity of the azure sky (36:26-33; 37:1-22). A simple glance at the Commentary will show that if the expressions used vary with each personage the stock of ideas is the same as in the whole doxological literature of the Old Testament.

The entire Book of Job is dominated by the idea of this one God:

> He who does great and unfathomable things,
> Marvels without number! (5:9; 9:10; cf. 37:5)

Creator and sovereign Lord of all things, He possesses all the qualities necessary for the conservation and government of the world:

> With Him are wisdom and power,
> Counsel and understanding are His! (12:13; cf. Is 11:2; 36:5)

We do not propose by a series of quotations to multiply allusions to the power and wisdom of God and His activity in the world.[1] We would not go outside the theodicy common to the various writings of Biblical literature. But we must refer to one or two specific features which are important for the understanding of the problem which is to engage the minds of the speakers in this debate.

This God who, according to Job's favourite expression (3:4; 31:2, 28), 'from on high' surveys the deeds of humanity, has His dwelling in the heavens.

> If I go to the east, He is not there,
> And to the west, I perceive Him not;
> In the north I have sought Him [2] and have not seen Him,
> I return to the south [3] and again fail to find Him. (23:8-9)

Man cannot know the nature of this God, for it exceeds all dimensions.

---

[1] There is no need to dwell on the traces of popular mythology which have been noted in the Book of Job. They are part and parcel of its language rather than its ideas. On Leviathan, cf. 3:8; on Tannin, 7:12; on Rahab, 9:13 and 26:12; on Tehom-Tiamat, 3:8; on the fabulous constellations, 9:9; 38:31-2.

[2] Cf. Comm. on 33:9.

[3] Ibid.

> Can you discover the nature of Eloah?
> Can you plumb the perfection of Shaddai?
> It is higher than the heavens: what will you do?
> Deeper than Sheol: what can you know?
> Longer than the earth is its dimension,
> Full broader than the sea! (11:7-9)

On the heights where He dwells He is surrounded by a court, composed of the 'sons of Elohim' (1:6; 38:7), who are His angels and servants,[1] His heavenly messengers. They are ranked high above men and can serve as intermediaries between the latter and God (5:1; cf. Elihu in 33:23-4), but they are not infallible: God can find faults in them (4:17-19; 5:2, 1, 8; 15:14-16), as He finds also even in the heavens and the stars (15:14-16; 25:4-6).

Among these mysterious beings is to be found the roamer and wanderer whose rôle it is to tempt humanity and accuse it before God. Whereas in an earlier period it was any angel (Nu 22:22, 32) or a malicious spirit (Jg 9:23) who could cause man difficulties, under the control of Yahweh, now in more recent writings [2] it is Satan or the Satan, i.e. the supreme Accuser, the denouncer, the prosecutor, to whom is assigned this function. In the Book of Job his business is to deny the disinterested nature of virtue, and to set in motion the various trials which are to make of Job a subject for experiment.

Whether by Himself or through His agents, God accomplishes all that He wills. His action is evident in the sphere of miracles on which the doxologies insist. It eludes all control:

> If He plunders, who can prevent Him,
> Who will say to Him: what are you doing? (9:12)

This outburst of Job on the divine caprice is not contradicted by his friends. Zophar will exclaim:

> If He passes by and keeps a matter secret,
> Or if He divulges it, who is to prevent Him? (11:10)

Yes, God does whatever He wills:

> What His soul has desired He will perform,
> For He accomplishes His decree. (23:13-14)

---

[1] Those whom the English call *attendants*: cf. *L'Emploi métaphorique*, p. 63.

[2] Cf. 1 K 22:20-1 (spirit) and Zec 3:1-2 (Satan): 2 S 24:1 (Yahweh) and 1 Ch 21:1 (Satan). See our Comm. on 1:6, on the sons of God and on Satan.

Thus we must say that in the last analysis all flows from Him, sorrow as well as joy, wounds as well as their healing,[1] riches as well as poverty.[2] Job formulates with precision the attitude of oriental resignation when he exclaims: 'Yahweh gave and Yahweh has taken away! Blessed be the name of Yahweh!' (1:21), or when he asks his wife (a foolish woman!) the following question: 'If we accept good from Elohim, shall we not also accept evil?' The high priest Eli was actuated by the same feeling when he said very simply: 'It is the Lord! Let Him do whatever seems good in His eyes!' (1 S 3:18).

The activity of God in nature and society is such that sometimes the divine name need not be mentioned. No ambiguity is possible. The author of what exists is 'He', as we see from Bildad's doxology (25:1-6; 26:5-14), where God is named only incidentally (25:4), after His glory has already been extolled. Often in the speeches of Job God is by implication the subject of sentences describing the blows received by the sufferer (20:23ff.; 30:18ff.). Again it is God of whom Job speaks as the Author of life:

> Why does He give light to one who is in misery,
> And life to those whose soul is bitter? (3:20)

MAN.—Life is in fact one of the most mysterious gifts which God has granted to man. It is the source of all other good, but also, when evil comes, of all other ills. Job's lament in ch. 3 is nothing but one long protest against life and an invocation of nothingness, or death. Life springs from God as does also the light which it enables man to enjoy (3:4-5, 20). Is it not God who with His own hands moulds, fashions, and organises the embryo in the womb of a mother (10:8-12)? The Psalmist has no less admiration than Job for this wonderful and incomprehensible work of the development of the foetus [3] which caused the mother of the Maccabees to say: 'I do not know how you have appeared in my bosom!' [4] And if she adds: 'It is not I who have made you the gift of spirit and life', she only continues the tradition of the Book of Job.[5]

For the spirit of life, as at the dawn of creation, can flow only from God, 'who holds in His hand the soul of every living thing,

---

[1] 5:18.
[2] 22:18.
[3] Ps 139:13-16.
[4] 2 Mac 7:22.
[5] Cf. *L'Emploi métaphorique*, pp. 5f.

and the spirit of all mortal flesh' (12:10). It is He who endows man
with this living spirit (10:12). Elihu goes so far as to say that his
life flows from the breath or spirit of God (33:4). He does not forget
that, if he is moulded of clay like Job (33:6; cf. 10:9 and 4:19) it
is God who breathes into his nostrils, as once into those of Adam,
the breath of life. If this living breath fails, then death supervenes.

> If He takes back [1] to Himself his breath,
> And withdraws from him his spirit,
> Then all flesh perishes together,
> And man returns to the dust. (34: 14-15)

God is the author of death, as He is the author of life; it is He alone
who can withdraw the gift which He has granted us (6:8-9; 34:
14-15). The idea of suicide [2] does not even occur to Job when he
curses the day of his birth and the night of his conception in the
womb (3). And yet death can be regarded as a good thing, under
the crushing excess of present sorrow (3:11-12, 16, 21, 22; 6:8-9;
10:18-19). Death brings rest (3:13, 17, 18) which contrasts with the
agitations and troubles of this life (3:20-6).[3] Death restores equality
between the various classes of society (3:14-15, 19).[4] Ch. 14, in
very sombre colours, plays upon the theme that man who dies
returns no more, visits the earth no more, but remains for ever in
the tomb (especially 14:7-12, 18-22).

An absolute separation divides the living from the dead (14:21-2).
The latter descend to a land from which there is no return, a realm
of dust and darkness, called Sheol.[5] A canal or a deep well, to which
we believe that we have detected allusions in the speeches of
Elihu,[6] gives access to this subterranean region. Here in these
infernal abodes throng the Rephaim (26:5) trembling before the
supreme master whose eye surveys all.

> The Shades tremble beneath the earth,
> The waters and their inhabitants become terrified.[7]

[1] Cf. Comm. on 34: 14.
[2] The Mosaic law does not envisage the case of suicide, instances of
which moreover are very rare among the Jews: cf. Lesêtre, article 'Suicide',
in the *Dict. de la Bible*, V, cols. 1879f.
[3] Death is compared to a sleep: cf. Comm. on 3: 13.
[4] Cf. Comm. on 3: 14.
[5] Cf. Comm. on 7: 9. On the resemblances between the conception of
Sheol in Israel and in Babylonia, cf. 'Le Séjour des morts chez les Babylo-
niens et chez les Hébreux' (*RB*, 1907, pp. 60ff.).
[6] Cf. Comm. on 33: 18.
[7] Cf. Comm. on 26: 5-6.

> Sheol is naked before Him,
> And Abaddon unveiled! (26: 5-6)

The association of ideas between death, the tomb, Sheol, Abaddon, is thrown into clear relief in the various passages where Abaddon, which is derived from the root אבד 'to perish', is made parallel with death (28:22), the tomb (Ps 88:12), Sheol (Job 26:6; Pr 28:20).

The perspective of death, the tomb, Sheol, constantly darkens with its shadow the speeches of Job. These speeches have been described as the Song of Songs of pessimism.[1] It is not only over his own ills that the hero laments but also over the sad condition in which man dwells on the earth. Between the moment of his birth and that of his death, what is man?

> Man, born of a woman,
> Living but a few days, and consumed with care,
> Springs up and withers like a flower,
> And flees like a shadow with no continuing stay,
> He wears away like a thing that rots,
> Like a moth-eaten garment. (14: 1-2; 13: 28)

In truth, there is no reason to be concerned about such a frail being.

> What is man that Thou dost set so much store by him
> And dost concentrate Thy attention upon him,
> That Thou shouldst inspect him every morning,
> And every moment scrutinise him? (7: 17-18)

Man is like a soldier, a mercenary who waits for one thing only, the end of his day's duties.

> Is not man's life on earth a term of military service?
> And are not his days like the days of a mercenary?
> Like a slave who longs for the shade,
> And a hireling who hopes for his pay! (7: 1-2)

Life is brief and rapid, flowing relentlessly towards death:

> My days have been swifter than the weaver's shuttle,
> And have come to an end for lack of thread;
> Remember that my life is but a passing breath,
> That my eye will never again see happiness! (7: 6-7)
> . . . .
> My days have been swifter than a runner,
> They have sped by without seeing happiness,
> They have glided away like vessels of reed,
> As an eagle which swoops down on its food. (9: 25-6)

This melancholy evaluation of human life is further darkened when

---

[1] Fried. Delitzsch, in *Das Buch Hiob.*

Job looks around him. As soon as he became the victim of misfortune, he was abandoned by his own (42:11). What is more pathetic than the following picture?

> My brothers He has put far from me,
> And acquaintances only turn away from me,
> My kinsmen and my familiar friends have disappeared,
> They have forgotten me, the guests I entertained!
> And my very maidservants treat me as a stranger,
> I am an alien in their eyes;
> I call my manservant, and he answers not,
> Even though with my own mouth I implore him.
> My breath has become repulsive to my wife,
> And I have become fetid to the sons of my bowels! (19: 13-17)

As for the friends,[1] Job depicts them in the following terms:

> My brothers have been as treacherous as a torrent,
> Like the bed of torrents which flow away:
> They were covered with ice,
> The snow was piled above them;
> As soon as the snows melt, they are dried up,
> As soon as it is hot, they leave the bed dry. (6: 15-17)

They are 'fabricators of lies' and 'worthless quacks', for whom silence alone would be becoming (13:4ff.). Every one knows the famous apostrophe:

> Have pity on me, have pity on me, O you my friends!
> For the hand of Eloah has smitten me.
> Why do you persecute me as does God,
> And why are you never sated with my flesh? (19: 21-2)

It would be necessary to quote the whole of ch. 24 to give some idea of the pessimism of Job with regard to the state of society, the distress of the poor and downtrodden, the crimes which everywhere are committed. Elihu too stresses the upheavals which occur in social situations, and the revolutions which overthrow the great (34:18ff.; 36:7ff.).

GOD AND MAN.—If only man could be at peace with God! But no! We know already that God who finds faults in the heavens, the planets, the angels, *a fortiori* discovers the weaknesses of mortals (4:17-19; 15:14-16; 25:4-6). And far from leaving man to his wretchedness, God holds him under a rigorous vigilance from which no action escapes (7:12, 17-20; 10:3-7, 13-15; 13:25-7) and which

---

[1] The name of 'brothers' must not be allowed to deceive us (cf. 6: 21ff.).

is hindered by no obstacle (22:12ff.). It is Elihu who best expresses this divine watchfulness [1]:

> For His eyes watch the ways of man,
> And He sees all his steps:
> There is no darkness and no depth of shade,
> In which evil-doers can hide from Him! (34: 21-2)

And this vigilance extends to nations as well as individuals (34:25-30).

Its object, moreover, is not merely to catch man at fault. Sometimes it is a vigilant anxiety on man's behalf, the effects of which Job recognises (10:12; 29:2-5). For God desires, above all, man's amendment; the corrections He inflicts are a salutary lesson (5:17), upon which Elihu does not shrink from dwelling at length (33:19ff.). Dreams are one of the ways in which God enlightens and corrects men (4:12-16; 7:13-15; 33:15-18).

The relations between God and man are governed and regulated by justice. God appears above all as a judge, as the author and upholder of what is right and equitable (9:14-16; 10:13-15; 37:23). He carries the balances in which the actions of men are weighed (31:6). There is no arbiter above Him (9:32-4). If need be, He plays the part of witness (16:19ff.) and vindicator (19:23ff.). He has no need to carry out investigations, for His verdicts are infallible and irrevocable, as Elihu declares (34:23-8). The very fact that He is the supreme Judge means that He is Himself absolute righteousness (8:3). Again it is Elihu who most effectively draws this conclusion:

> Do you really think that one who hates justice would govern,
> And will you condemn the supremely righteous One?
> He who says [2] to a king: Worthless man!
> And to nobles: You wicked ones! (34: 17-18)

It is true that Job is somewhat hesitant on this point, and his invectives are here somewhat bitter at times; for example, when he says that God is evasive (9:14-16), that He smites without cause (9:17-19), and that He exterminates indifferently the righteous and the wicked (9:22). He insinuates that God does not take account of his innocence:

> If I wash myself with snow
> And cleanse my hands with lye,

---

[1] Cf. Am 9: 2-3; Ps 139: 11-12.
[2] Cf. Comm. on 34: 18.

> Then Thou plungest me into filth [1]
> And my very garments abhor me! (9: 30-1)

He also complains that God abandons him to unrighteousness
(16:11-18) and refuses to do him justice (19:6-12; 27:2-3). But
these are outbursts which spring from the delirium brought on by
persecution, and which Elihu severely criticises (34:5ff.). Basically,
Job unwaveringly appeals to God's judgment (10:2-7; 13:3, 15-24;
16:18-21; 23:3ff.). He has every confidence in the ultimate manifestation of divine justice:

> As for me, I know that my Vindicator lives,
> And that, as the Last, He will arise on the earth,
> And that behind my skin I shall stand up, [2]
> And from my flesh I shall see Eloah,
> Whom I myself shall see,
> And whom my eyes will behold, and none other;
> My reins grow faint within me! (19: 25-7)

It is on a note of appeal to God that he concludes his long pleadings:

> Would that some one would listen to me!
> Behold! here is my signature! Let Shaddai answer me!
> As for the indictment which my adversary has drawn up,
> Shall I not wear it on my shoulder,
> Shall I not bind it as a crown about my head?
> My steps in life will I recount unto him,
> Like a chief will I present myself before him! (31: 35-7)

Thus Job is thoroughly in agreement with Eliphaz, who also lays
his cause in the hand of Elohim (5:8).

DUTY AND VIRTUE.—It is quite natural that man should have
certain duties to fulfil towards this one God, the Creator and
Preserver of the universe, the Author of life and death, the Witness
and Judge of man's actions, that man should entertain towards
Him certain sentiments and have recourse to certain acts of piety.

The feeling which controls all others in man's relation to God is
that of respectful fear. Here again we find concepts familiar to the
O.T. as a whole. Job is a man who fears God (1:1, 8; 2:3). This fear
of God, which is wisdom (28:28), expresses so well the very essence
of religion that the word יִרְאָה 'fear' by itself can imply piety or the
practice of religious duties (4:6; 15:4). To indicate the virtues of
Job, Satan will say simply: 'Is it for nothing that Job fears Elohim?'

---

[1] Cf. Comm. on 9: 31.
[2] Cf. Comm. on 19: 26.

(1:9). A corollary of this fear is the eschewing of evil.[1] To fear God and eschew evil are two correlative ideas, as is seen clearly from 1:1, 8; 2:3; 28:28; Pr 3:7, 16; 16:6.

In daily life this fear of God produces visible effects. It obliges man to follow a path which God Himself traces out:

> My foot has held fast to His step,
> I have kept His way and have not turned aside;
> I have not departed from the precept of His lips,
> And the words of His mouth have I hidden in my bosom.[2]
> (23: 11-12)

It is the practice of these precepts of Yahweh that enables man to become 'perfect' in himself and 'righteous' by relation to others.[3] Perfection of ways (4:6; 22:3) consists in walking as in God's sight, without turning aside to the right or the left (31:7-8; cf. 23:11). Righteousness is the concomitant of this perfection (26:5-6), but it controls in particular a man's relations with his neighbours (29:14; 31:13). It involves not only refraining from actual wrongdoing, the details of which we shall see when we come to consider the question of sin. It dictates also positive duties towards the poor and the oppressed. Such righteousness which grows into charity could hardly be more beautifully described than in these words of Job:

> For I delivered the poor man who cried,
> The orphan and him who had no helper.[4]
> The blessing of the wretched arose to me,
> And I made the widow's heart rejoice.
> I put on righteousness and it clothed me,
> My just dealing was as a mantle and a tiara [5];
> I was eyes to the blind,
> And feet was I to the lame;
> I was a father to the needy
> And I investigated the cause of the stranger;
> I broke the fangs of the wicked,
> And made him drop his prey from his teeth.[6] (29: 12-17)

Compassion is part of a man's duties towards the unfortunate (30:25).

---

[1] Cf. Comm. on 1:1 and 28:28.
[2] Cf. Comm. on 23:12. Compare Ps 119:11.
[3] Cf. Comm. on 1:1; 4:6; 8:20, etc.
[4] Cf. Ps 72:12.
[5] Cf. Is 59:17; Ps 132:9, 16, 18.
[6] Cf. Ps 58:7; Pr 30:14.

> Did I not weep with him for whom life was harsh,
> Was not my soul grieved for the needy? [1]

We ought also to cite the magnificent passage in which Job extols his charity towards the poor, the widows, the orphans, the oppressed (31:16-21) the passer-by, and the stranger (31:31-2).[2] Even enemies have a right to pity.[3]

> Did I rejoice in the misfortune which overtook my enemy,
> And did I exult because evil had struck him?
> I did not even allow my palate to sin,
> By asking for his life with a curse! (31: 29-30)

It is understandable that on such a lofty plane of ethics the usurpation of others' good—that sin against the earth (31:38-40)—cannot be tolerated, and that evil desire itself should be banished from man's heart (31:1).

Righteousness, which regulates the relations of man with his neighbour, is likewise necessary in man's relations with God. It is through prayer that these relations are directly set up, and their efficacy is thus described by Bildad:

> If now you will have recourse to God,
> And will make supplication to Shaddai,
> [If you are pure and upright,]
> From this moment He will watch over you,
> And will restore your abode of righteousness;
> Your former condition will have been but a little thing,
> So far will it be surpassed by your new state! (8: 5-7)

Prayer, if it is to be effective, requires purity of heart and righteousness, as Zophar affirms:

> As for you, if you have a faithful heart,
> And if you stretch out your hands towards Him,
> If you put away the iniquity which is in your hand,[4]
> And if you let not evil dwell in your tents,
> Then you will lift up your face without blemish,
> You will be securely established and you will not fear!
> (11: 13-15)

Job agrees that there is this connection between the efficacy of prayer and the virtue of the one who prays:

> For what is the hope of the godless when he prays,
> When he lifts up his soul to Eloah? [5]

[1] Cf. Ro 12: 15-16; 1 P 3: 8.
[2] Cf. Is 58: 7; Ezk 18: 7.
[3] Cf. Pr 24: 17.
[4] Cf. Comm. on 11: 14.
[5] Cf. Comm. on 27: 8. Compare Ps 86: 3-4.

> Does God hear his cry
> When calamity seizes him?
> Is his delight in Shaddai?
> Does he call upon Eloah at all times? (27: 8-10)

Elihu is careful to explain that the cry of human distress, if it is to achieve any result, must be addressed to the true God (35:9-13).

To prayer are of course added vows (22:26-7) and sacrifices (1:5; 42:8). Prayers and sacrifices may be offered on behalf of one's neighbour (1:5; 42:8, 10).

The righteous form a special group, as in Israel in the time of certain Psalms. They are the 'perfect',[1] the 'upright' יְשָׁרִים,[2] the 'innocent' נְקִיִּים,[3] the 'righteous' צַדִּיקִים,[4] those whose hands are pure.[5] In short, as we have seen above,[6] those who fear God and eschew evil.

SIN AND VICE.—With this category are contrasted 'those who forget God' (8:13) and who refuse His direction (21:14-16) and protection (22:15-18). Their actions are denoted by three almost synonymous terms: חַטָּאָה 'sin', עָוֹן 'fault', פֶּשַׁע 'transgression'.[7] Their habit of sinning, contrasting with the uprightness of righteous men, is called sometimes אָוֶן 'iniquity',[8] sometimes עָוֶל or עַוְלָה 'unrighteousness'.[9] They are the 'men of iniquity' (22:15), the 'workers of iniquity' (31:3; 34:8), the 'unrighteous'.[10] There arises a natural equivalence between עָוֶל 'unrighteousness' and רֶשַׁע 'wickedness'.[11] The wicked, רְשָׁעִים, are the opponents of the righteous and of righteousness (8:22; 10:3; 16:11). They are essentially malefactors, מְרֵעִים (8:20), those who do evil, רַע, by contrast with the perfect who eschew evil (1:1, etc.; 8:20). Among them one rather disreputable type of character—obviously one of the most detested in Israel—is especially stigmatised, namely, the חָנֵף, who is first the profane or pagan type, secondly the man who has sur-

---

1 Various nouns from the root תמם; cf. Comm. on 1: 1, 8; 2: 3; 4: 6; 8: 20.
2 Cf. Comm. on 1: 1.
3 Cf. Comm. on 4: 7.
4 Cf. Comm. on 12: 4; 17: 9; 22: 19.
5 Cf. Comm. on 17: 9.
6 Pp. cxxiii f.
7 Cf. Comm. on 13: 23; 14: 16-17.
8 Cf. Comm. on 4: 8.
9 Cf. Comm. on 16: 11.
10 Ibid.
11 Cf. Comm. on 27: 7.

rendered himself to the heathen world, the apostate, the renegade, or more vaguely the godless, finally the hypocrite.[1]

If to do good is wisdom (28:28), it is clear that to do evil will be folly. Sin is stupidity (1:22; 2:10), the sinner is senseless, an imbecile (5:2, 3).

Some acquaintance with the Psalms and Proverbs is enough to enable us to recognise in these ideas about sin the commonplaces of hagiographical literature. But it is above all in details that we shall note the application of the principles of the Law.

Sin may at times be purely interior (1:5; 31:1, 7). But out of the abundance of the heart the mouth speaks. The speech of man betrays his sin:

> Since your iniquity inspires the words of your mouth,
> Since you adopt the language of the crafty,
> It is your mouth which condemns you, and not I,
> And your own lips which testify against you! (15: 5-6)

The transgressions of the tongue may be directed against God (1:22; 2:10). Most often however it attacks one's neighbour by lying and deceit and treachery (6:29-30; 27:4; 31:5). Instead of חָכְמָה, which is true wisdom, man then has resort to עָרְמָה, which is human prudence, often craftiness or duplicity.[2]

It is chiefly in the field of action that the sinner, the wicked man, the godless, is to be recognised. Eliphaz when he invents Job's examination of conscience bases his suggestions on the teaching of the Law and the Prophets,[3] in order to catalogue his faults.

> The fact is that for no reason you took pledges from
>   your brothers,
> And tore their garments from the naked.
> You gave no water to the thirsty,
> And to the hungry you refused bread!
> And the man of brute force got the land!
> And the favourite was settled in it!
> You sent away widows empty-handed,
> And the arms of the orphans you crushed![4] (22: 6-9)

Job denounces the crimes which are committed in the world. He begins with the violation of property, the removal of landmarks (24:2), which is severely forbidden in Dt 19:14; 27:17; Hos 5:10;

---

[1] Cf. Comm. on 8: 13.
[2] Cf. 5: 12-13; 15: 5.
[3] Ex 22: 25-6; Is 58: 7; Ezk 18: 7; Ex 22: 21; Dt 24: 17; Is 1: 17.
[4] Cf. Comm. on 22: 9.

Pr 27:28, etc. He continues with theft, especially such as harms the orphan and widow (24:3). This again is one of the most odious of crimes in the Law.[1] He emphasises the exploitation of slaves and labourers (24:9 and 24:4-11), then comes to murder (24:12). Next we have the classic series (Ex 20:13; Jer 7:9; Hos 4:2): assassination (24:4), adultery (24:15), robbery (24:14c and 16; cf. Comm.). In his negative confession, Job returns to the question of adultery (31:9-12), injustice towards inferiors (31:13-15), harshness towards the poor, especially the widow and orphan (31:16-18, 21). It is the language of the Psalms [2] which we find echoed in his condemnation of putting trust and seeking honour in riches (31:24-5). The proscription of idolatry, especially in the form of a cult of the stars (31:26-8), is part of the stock of ideas characteristic of the Law (Dt 4:19; 2 K 21:3ff.) and of the Prophets (Jer 8:1-2; Is 45:8).

THE THESIS OF RETRIBUTION.—Thus the world is divided into two categories of men: the good and the evil, those who fear God and those who scorn Him, those who fulfil His laws and those who transgress them. Enthroned above this visible world in His dwelling in the heavens, the sovereign Judge watches the conflict of good and bad. His principal attribute is justice. It is understandable that He must intervene to reward the good by happiness and to punish the wicked by misfortune: κακοὺς κακῶς ἀπολέσει αυτούς (Mt 21:41). The doctrine of retribution is one of those requirements of the human mind which God cannot fail to satisfy without appearing unjust. Between human deeds and their reward or punishment there is a connection which God has willed.

The N.T. stresses this connection but defers to the Last Judgment the work of divine justice which is to restore the equilibrium broken by evil. The message of Ps 62 (Vulg. 61):13, 'For Thou wilt requite man according to his work', is interpreted by Our Lord in the framework of eschatology: καὶ τότε ἀποδώσει ἑκάστῳ κατὰ τὴν πρᾶξιν αὐτοῦ (Mt 16:27), as also by St Paul: ἐν ἡμέρᾳ ὀργῆς καὶ ἀποκαλύψεως δικαιοκρισίας τοῦ θεοῦ, ὃς ἀποδώσει ἑκάστῳ κατὰ τὰ ἔργα αὐτοῦ (Ro 2:6; cf. 1 Co 3:8).

In the Old Testament the horizon is less extended. Through the whole of its literature, historical, prophetical, moral, parenetic,

---

[1] Cf. Comm. on 22:9.
[2] Cf. especially Ps 49:7-8.

we feel the insistence on immediate justice,[1] the demand that happiness shall be meted out to the good and that the wicked shall be punished. We shall not dwell on the application of this postulate to the history of Israel. It is well known that this history, from the time of the establishment of the Jews in the land of Canaan, proceeds according to a 'pragmatism of four terms: sin, punishment, penitence, deliverance'.[2] Families and nations are worthy of Yahweh's mercy or deserving of His wrath, according as they obey or disobey His laws.[3] Even before the elaboration of legal codes, one feels that to render evil for evil is not merely a reflection of the law of retaliation but a principle rooted in the very government of the world. The sin of the first man and the lastingness of his punishment, the difference between the treatment of Noah and of sinning humanity at the time of the Flood, the story of Sodom and Gomorrah, of Joseph's brothers (Gn 44:16), all these are great pictures which emphasise the same point: good is rewarded, evil is punished. The whole history of Israel is governed by the balance existing between man's conduct towards God and God's conduct towards man.[4] The formula is played out chiefly between Yahweh and His people. The Prophets address themselves principally to the nation and only in certain rare cases is the principle applied to individuals.[5] It is not so much man as the Israelite or the Judaean to whom the anathema and the promises are addressed.

Gradually, however, and especially after the catastrophes which overtook and ruined Samaria and Jerusalem in turn, the individual emerges from the race.[6] Collectivity remains of interest, but it has lost its central place. The individual feels inclined to treat the affairs of his conscience directly with God. The Prophets and the Psalmists recognise that in the Jewish nation as elsewhere not all incur the

---

[1] They have not the patience to wait for another life. The Fathers of the Church have insisted on the ignorance of the Jews concerning retribution in the beyond: quotations in Podechard, *L'Ecclésiaste*, p. 179, n. 1.

[2] Lagrange, *Le Livre des Juges*, p. xxv. Cf. our Comm., *Les Livres de Samuel*, p. 69.

[3] Ex 20: 4-7, 12; 23: 20-33; 34: 6-7; Lv 26: 3ff.; Dt 5: 9-10, 28-33, etc.

[4] See the monograph of Balla, 'Das Problem des Leides in der israelitisch-jüdischen Religion' (*Eucharistērion* dedicated to Gunkel, 1923, I, pp. 214ff.).

[5] Ibid., p. 228.

[6] Of course, it is a question of a very easily explicable tendency, not a fact everywhere observed. König shows that a religion of individualism did not succeed one of nationalism (*Theol. des A.T.*, 3rd and 4th eds., pp. 103ff.). The matter is set out with much moderation by Löhr in his *Sozialismus and Individualismus im A.T.* (1906).

same responsibility. As we have seen above, there are the righteous and sinners in Israel, as in the rest of the world. Would it be just that the same fate should attend both? The famous proverb:

> The fathers have eaten soup grapes
> And the children's teeth are set on edge

is contradicted both by Jeremiah and Ezekiel in their clear formulation of the doctrine of individual responsibility (Jer 31:29-30; Ezk 18:2ff.). And Job will emphasise why it is that it is the guilty father and not his sons who should be punished:

> Does Eloah store up his iniquity for his sons?
> Let Him punish the man himself, that he may learn!
> Let his own eyes see his calamity,[1]
> And let him drink of the wrath of Shaddai! (21: 19-20)

If the guilty individual becomes thus detached from his family, still more can his link with the community be loosened. In the story of Korah, Dathan, and Abiram, the individual (אִישׁ) is clearly distinguished from the community (עֵדָה): 'Shall one man sin and wilt Thou be angry with the whole congregation?' (Nu 16:22). David discriminates between himself and his family, and on the other hand, the people: 'I have sinned and have done wickedly! But these sheep what have they done? Let Thy hand, I pray Thee, be against me and against my father's house!' (2 S 24:17).

Hence it is the individual who will be rewarded or punished, here and now, according to his conduct. Man's deeds are no longer considered only in their connection with God and neighbour but also as a cause followed by an effect, good or bad, according to whether they are good or bad.[2] Good engenders good, evil evil: to act well is to be happy; to do ill is to bring on one's self misfortune. The equation is thus expressed in Pr 11:31,

> If the righteous is requited on earth,
> How much more the wicked and the sinner!

This connection between moral good and happiness, moral evil and misfortune, is sometimes depicted by means of imagery taken from country life.

> Sow for yourselves righteousness (צְדָקָה),
> Reap the fruit of the steadfast love.

---

[1] Cf. Comm. on 21: 20.
[2] Cf. Is 3: 10-11.

.......You have plowed iniquity (רֶשַׁע),
You have reaped injustice (עַוְלָה). (Hos 10: 12-13)
He who sows injustice (עַוְלָה) will reap iniquity (אָוֶן). (Pr 22: 8)

This is one of the first observations of Eliphaz:

As I have seen, those who cultivate iniquity (אָוֶן)
And who sow trouble (עָמָל) reap the same. (Job 4: 8; cf. 5: 6)

The words און, עולה, עמל, become ambiguous, for they can be applied
now to evil itself, now to the result of evil, namely, trouble and
misfortune.[1] Thus men are divided into two categories, the חֹרְשֵׁי טוֹב
'who cultivate good' and the חֹרְשֵׁי רָע 'who cultivate evil' (Pr 14:22).

Another no less expressive image may be used to mark this relation of cause and effect between moral evil and concrete misfortune: 'Conceive mischief (עָמָל) and bring forth iniquity (אָוֶן)'
(Is 59:4). Here we have the same ambiguous terms as in the passages previously quoted. In Ps 7:15 we have the same idea and
image: 'The wicked man conceives evil (אָוֶן), and is pregnant with
mischief (עָמָל) and brings forth lies (שֶׁקֶר).' Eliphaz resorts to the
same figures of speech: 'It is man who engenders trouble' (5:7;
cf. Comm.); 'they conceive trouble and bring forth iniquity' (15:35).

Nowhere has the antithesis between the effects of virtue and those
of vice been emphasised so much as in the Book of Proverbs. It
would be necessary to quote the whole of chs. 10-13, which abound
in affirmations, definitions, and comparisons, whose object is always
the same: evil is punished, good is rewarded, the wicked man is
unhappy, the good man is happy. Here too we find aphorisms easy
to memorise and tersely expressing popular ethics:

Fear Yahweh and turn away from evil:
It will be healing to your flesh
And refreshment to your bones. (Pr 3: 7-8)

We have seen in particular [2] that the fear of God and the avoidance
of evil summed up the positive and negative precepts of the natural
law. The contrast between the lot of the righteous (צַדִּיקִים) and that

---

[1] In Assyrian, the word *šêrtu* denotes the anger of the god, then the
cause of this anger, namely sin, finally the punishment due to sin. On the
connection between sin and punishment, cf. our study *La Religion assyro-
babylonienne*, pp. 234ff.
[2] See above, pp. cxxiii f.

of the wicked (רְשָׁעִים), those two categories which divide the world,[1] is brought out in these terms:

> The path of the righteous is like the light of dawn,
> Which shines brighter and brighter until full day.
> The way of the wicked is like deep darkness;
> They do not know over what they stumble. (Pr 4: 18-19)

This was the general feeling:

> When it goes well with the righteous, the city rejoices;
> And when the wicked perish there are shouts of gladness.
> By the blessing of the upright a city is exalted,
> But it is overthrown by the mouth of the wicked. (Pr 11: 10-11)

The Psalms unceasingly bring out this contrast, which is also an antagonism, between the good and the wicked. Ps 1 brings into parallelism the 'way of the righteous' and the 'way of the wicked' (Ps 1:6; cf. Pr 4:18-19), in order to stress the felicity of the former and the instability of the latter. The alphabetic Psalm 37 is wholly composed on this theme. If the wicked man seems to be fortunate, it is but an insecure and transient appearance; there is no stable happiness except in virtue. The richest colours of oriental poetry serve to enhance the description of the happiness of the righteous by contrast with the misfortunes of the wicked in Ps 92, which ends on this beautiful image:

> The righteous (צַדִּיק) flourish like the palm tree,
> And grow like a cedar in Lebanon.
> They are planted in the house of Yahweh,
> They flourish in the courts of our God.
> They still bring forth fruit in old age,
> They are ever full of sap and green.

The alphabetic Psalm 34 is not afraid to point out the practical advantages of virtue:

> What man is there who desires life,
> And covets many days that he may enjoy good?
> Keep your tongue from evil,
> And your lips from speaking deceit;
> Depart from evil and do good,
> Seek peace and pursue it. (Ps 34: 13-15 [EV 12-14])

Individual as well as social morality has thus a tendency to become utilitarian. Virtue is a condition of happiness, sin a source of misfortune. These ideas, traditional in the Semitic world,[2] have been

---

[1] Cf. above, p. cxxvi.
[2] *La Religion assyro-babylonienne*, pp. 234ff.

most cogently expressed in the O.T. They lend colour to its idea of Wisdom, the חָכְמָה whose beauty and rarity are exalted in ch. 28 of the Book of Job. If the author of this poem, who, in our opinion,[1] is the same as that of the rest of the book (with the exception of the speeches of Elihu) lingers in a mystical contemplation of Wisdom at the moment of creation, a moralist has brought out its pragmatic side: 'And He said to man: Behold now, the fear of Adonai that is Wisdom, and the avoidance of evil that is understanding' (28:28). It is under this double aspect, fear of God and avoidance of evil, that Wisdom becomes a practical, advantageous virtue useful to one's self and to others. When Wisdom cries in the streets and at the crossroads, it appeals to the self-interest of those who listen (Pr 1:20ff.). It tells them that those who despise the good 'will eat the fruit [2] of their ways' (Pr 1:31), whilst he who listens to Wisdom 'will dwell secure and be at ease, without dread of evil' (Pr 1:33). We must further cite the description of Pr 3:13-18, which embodies a truly practical idea of Wisdom:

> Happy is the man who finds wisdom,
> And the man who gets understanding,
> For the gain from it is better than gain from silver,
> And its profit better than gold.[3]
> She is more precious than pearls
> And nothing you can desire can compare with her.[4]
> Length of days is in her right hand,
> In her left are riches and honour.
> Her ways are ways of pleasantness,
> And all her paths are peace.
> She is a tree of life to those who lay hold of her,
> Those who hold her fast are called happy.

Let us pause on this vision of Wisdom, bearing long life in the right hand, riches and glory in the left. We are still in the same circle of ideas. Two ways are open to man, that of virtue and happiness, that of sin and misfortune.

If however man has taken the wrong road, one recourse remains open to him: to be converted! Conversion, return to God, is the means of recovering lost happiness. It was one of the links in the chain which bound Yahweh to His people.[5] The Prophets' appeals

---

[1]   Cf. above, p. xcvii.
[2]   Cf. Is 3:10, 'for they will eat the fruit of their deeds'.
[3]   Cf. Job 28:15-17, 19.
[4]   Cf. Job 28:18.
[5]   See above, p. cxxix.

for penitence are made in the light of a double perspective: conversion restores happiness, while persistence in evil increases misfortunes (Is 1:18-20; 4:2-6; 44:22; 45:22; 58, etc.; Jer 3:14ff.; 4:1ff., 18:8ff.; Ezk 33:10, 11; Hos 14:2ff.; Jl 2:12ff.; Zec 1:3ff.). The close relation between conversion and the restoration of former happiness is very precisely expressed in Solomon's long prayer on the day of the dedication of the Temple: the consequences of sin, namely, defeat, drought, famine, are annulled by a return to God (1 K 8:33ff.). Even exile and captivity are only temporary, if the people turn again in an act of penitence towards the country, the city, and the Temple of their fathers and their God (2 K 8:46ff.). The equation of the nation's sin and its punishment has as a corollary that between conversion and the recovery of lost happiness.

This divine mathematics applies with equal force to individuals. It is Ezekiel who formulates it best in that ch. 18 which we have cited to show the individualising of sin.[1] The text is the more interesting as the same principles are applied to both conversion and perversion: 'If a wicked man (הָרָשָׁע) turns away from all his sin which he has committed and keeps all my statutes and does what is lawful and right, he shall surely live, he shall not die. None of the transgressions which he has committed shall be remembered against him; for the righteousness which he has done he shall live. Have I any pleasure in the death of the wicked, says the Lord God, and not rather that he should turn from his way and live? But when a righteous man (צַדִּיק) turns away from his righteousness and commits iniquity and does the same abominable things that the wicked man does, shall he live? None of the righteous deeds which he has done shall be remembered; for the treachery of which he is guilty and the sin which he has committed, he shall die' (Ezk 18:21-4). The whole of the end of this chapter consists of an exhortation to return to God and thus to regain life. The same ideas are vehemently repeated in Ezk 33:10-11, 12-19.

It was appropriate to make this little recapitulation of the theories in circulation in Israel,[2] for it is these theories which form the basis

---

[1] See above, p. cxxx.
[2] Father Knabenbauer makes a good appraisal of these theories and their connection with the Book of Job when he writes: *Dum enim in veteris foederis institutione et mosaicae legis promulgatione temporalis praecipue mercedis et poenae ratio habeatur, libri nostri est, hanc doctrinam suis circumscribere limitibus, eam perpolire et supplere ea, quae ei desint* (Commentary, p. 9).

of the speeches of Job's friends; and since they express traditional ethics, it is clear how unwise it would be to accept the strange declaration of Renan to the effect that 'the stock of ideas in the Book of Job has nothing specially Hebraic about it'.[1] On the contrary, the really typical feature of this book is precisely that it passes through the crucible of a critical and penetrating mind orthodox, accepted ideas. Job will firmly deny the truth of all short-sighted explanations. His friends seek to apply normal solutions to his exceptional case. Job refuses to be content with the currency of orthodox ideas. We are at a stage of development when thinkers have subjected to the verification of experience a religious philosophy which is far too *à priori*. The debate between Job and his friends represents the clash between observations based on daily experience and a tradition satisfied with outmoded aphorisms.

For Job's interlocutors claim indeed to represent tradition. Doubtless Eliphaz bases his arguments on observations common to Job and himself (4:7-8; 5:3ff., 27), on a night vision (4:12ff.), but the conclusions which he draws are those consecrated by tradition, those which old men have accepted from the lips of their fathers and have transmitted to their children. It is a question of pure and sound doctrine, uncontaminated by foreign infiltrations.

> What do you know that we do not know?
> What do you understand that is not understood by us?
> Among us also is found the gray-haired and the aged,
> More advanced in years than your father!
> I will explain to you, listen!
> And what I have seen, I will tell,
> What wise men declare,
> Hiding nothing, according to the tradition of their fathers,
> They to whom alone the land was given,
> And no stranger passed among them! (15: 9-10, 17-19)

It is clear that we have here the insistence on the tradition of the Holy Land, 'the land'.[2] It is sufficient to recall the words of Joel: 'So you shall know that I am the Lord your God, who dwell in Zion, my holy mountain, And Jerusalem shall be holy and strangers shall never again pass through it' (Jl 4:17). Likewise Bildad calls to witness previous generations:

> For inquire of the previous generations,
> And pay heed to the experience of their fathers,

[1]   Op. cit., p. xvii.
[2]   Cf. Comm. on 15: 19.

> Since we are but of yesterday and have no knowledge,
> Since our days on earth are a shadow,
> Is it not they who will instruct you and speak to you,
> And who will bring forth words from their heart? (8: 8-10)

In these lines there is an echo of Dt 32:7,

> Remember the days of old,
> Consider the years of many generations;
> Ask your father and he will show you;
> Your elders and they will tell you.

The image of the shadow which passes away is equally part and parcel of tradition (Ps 144:4; 1 Ch 29:15).

Job becomes ironic about this claim to embody ancient wisdom:

> Truly you are the people,
> And with you wisdom will die!

He insists that these truths, so learnedly set forth by his friends, are banalities which even the animals could teach. Ch. 12 is a satire attacking those moralists who think that they alone are the inheritors of sound doctrine. Job knows quite as much as all of them (12:3; 13:1-2). Yet he admits that old men have quite exceptional wisdom:

> Is it not among the old that wisdom is found,
> And in great age that understanding resides? (12: 12)

As for esoteric teaching, which has not been touched by foreign influence, he recks not of it. It is better not to allow one's self to have thoughts put into one's mind by ready-made theories (21:27-8), to address one's self boldly to those who have travelled much, for 'whoever has seen much may well have learned much':

> Have you not questioned those who travel the roads,
> And have you not understood their marks? (21: 29)

This appeal to the accounts and inscriptions of travellers is a deliberate novelty. Thus the door is opened to a wider and more universal understanding of the truths of tradition. The fact is that Wisdom and Understanding, as ch. 28 sings, are not the monopoly of any individual or nation. They elude the gaze of mortal beings. They are reserved to God. Yahweh's speeches will show that tradition cannot illuminate those mysteries which are more important for human life. If Job himself, who is approved by God (42:7), confesses that he has spoken of matters which are beyond the scope of his understanding and of which he is ignorant (42:1-6), how much more will his friends be charged with error (42:7ff.), although they are justified in claiming the authority of the aged and the wise! [1]

Their doctrine, moreover, is that which we have found everywhere characteristic of Israelite theology: retribution here below, strict equation between deeds and their reward or punishment. It is this narrow interpretation of divine justice which is served up over and over again by Eliphaz, Bildad, and Zophar. Job's protests against these outdated arguments arouse the susceptibilities of Elihu who comes to the rescue as though to take up the challenge which has been defiantly hurled at tradition. [2]

A glance at the ideas of Job's friends shows to what an extent they are keen supporters of the doctrine of earthly retribution. The double equation, virtue brings good fortune, sin misfortune, is the basis of all their arguments intended to demonstrate to Job that he is guilty and must be converted. Were he innocent, he would have nothing to fear:

> Is not your piety the ground of your confidence,
> And the perfection of your ways your hope?
> Call to mind, now! What innocent man ever perished,
> Or where were the upright cut off? (4:6-7)

Eliphaz has here chosen his words very carefully. We recognise the piety which means fear of God (יִרְאָה), the perfection of one's ways, uprightness, all the virtues which have been attributed to Job, 'perfect and upright, fearing Elohim and turning away from evil' (1:1, etc.). Eliphaz is only applying to Job well-known principles, [3] e.g. that of Pr 13:6a, 'Righteousness (צְדָקָה) guards him whose way is upright (תָּם־דָּרֶךְ)'.

This tendency to make of ethics a matter of self-interested bargaining, to buy happiness by virtue, is turned into derision by Satan: 'Is it for nothing that Job fears Elohim? Hast Thou not put a hedge around him and his house and all that he has on every side? Thou hast blessed the work of his hands, and his cattle have increased in the land!' (1:9f.). Satan is quite familiar with the prevalent theories. He is convinced that the equation between virtue and good fortune is so deeply anchored in the soul of believers

---

[1]   The long preamble of Elihu (32: 6-16) is a critique of the theory which claims wisdom for the ancients. But it is not because they are old, but because they represent a higher stage in tradition, that the aged are guarantors of sound doctrine.

[2]   See above, pp. cf.   [3]   See above, pp. cxxixff.

that if prosperity should fail a complete change of attitude is only to be expected (1:11; 2:4-5). The wife of Job thoroughly agrees with this point of view, since she fails to see how the sufferer can hold fast to his integrity (2:9) after he has been struck down by misfortune.

Without going quite so far, Eliphaz is equally a preacher of utilitarian morals, and his remarks are especially exposed to the irony of Satan. His thesis is very simple. Virtue must yield something. It cannot be profitable to God, so it must be profitable to man.

> Is it to God that a man is useful?
> It is rather to himself that a wise man is useful!
> Is it of any advantage to Shaddai that you should be righteous,
> And is it any gain to Him if you perfect your ways? (22: 2-3)

'If you are wise you are wise for yourself', said the author of Proverbs (9:12). One of Elihu's complaints against Job runs as follows:

> For he has said: 'It is no profit to man
> To make Elohim his delight!' (34: 9)

Job did not speak these words, but he insinuated, by his reflections on the prosperity of the wicked and the distress of the pious,[1] that the equations postulated by traditional ethics did not in actual fact rigorously apply. And if we are to believe Elihu, as the other speakers, this is tantamount to casting doubt on the supreme justice of God (34:10ff.).

Job himself had not altogether escaped common presuppositions. After depicting in admirable terms [2] the perfection of his piety, he added:

> And I said to myself: 'I shall die in a ripe old age,[3]
> And my days will be as many as the sand;
> My root is accessible to the waters,
> And the dew lies all night on my branches;
> My glory will always be fresh within me,
> And my bow ever new in my hand!' (29: 18-20)

We recognise here the reasoning which lies at the basis of the doctrine of retribution.[4] The righteous man is entitled to hope for happiness. But Job has been given the lie formally by reality:

[1] Cf. Comm. on 34: 9.
[2] See above, p. cxxiv.
[3] Cf. Comm. on 29: 18.
[4] See above, pp. cxxviiiff.

> It was happiness that I hoped for but it was misfortune
> which came,
> I expected light and darkness came! (30: 26)

This reversal of values is all the more terrible in that it makes the righteous man undergo the fate of the villain. For if prosperity is the reward of virtue, misfortune, according to the traditional thesis, is the penalty of vice.[1] On this point again the friends of Job fall in line with accepted morality. They are even more explicit about the latter equation, since the problem with which they are faced is not that of a wicked man who is prosperous but of an upright man who is unfortunate. The principle to be applied is as follows: misfortune implies a fault, a sin, a crime. In a few words, inspired by the Prophets, Psalms, and Proverbs,[2] Eliphaz defines the theory:

> As I have seen, those who cultivate iniquity
> And who sow trouble, reap the same!
> Under the breath of Eloah they perish,
> And at the blast of His nostril they fade away;
> The roar of the lion and the voice of the leopard,
> And the teeth of the young lions are broken;
> The lion perishes for lack of prey
> And the whelps of the lioness are scattered! (4: 8-11)

These wild beasts whom God reduces to helplessness and death are the classic representation of the wicked who attack the pious (Ps 58:7; 91:13; cf. Is 5:29). Disgust at the prosperity of the wicked is such that the sight of 'a fool taking root' provokes a curse on his dwelling (5:3-5). Tradition has already supplied us with the metaphor of the generation of misfortune[3] by the evil-doer (5:7; 15:35). A long description by Eliphaz (15:20-2) sets forth the terrors which torment the wicked man or the tyrant during his lifetime. His conduct is the sole cause:

> Because he stretched forth his hand against God,
> And hurled defiance at Shaddai,
> He ran against Him with neck outstretched,
> With the mass of his thick-bossed bucklers! (15: 25-6)

Such is the theory which Eliphaz brings forward to explain the situation of Job:

> Is it because of your piety that He corrects you,
> And goes to judgment with you?

[1]   See above, pp. cxxxf.
[2]   See above, p. cxxxi.
[3]   See above, ibid.

> Is it not rather because your wickedness is great,
> And because there is no limit to your sins? (22: 4-5)

There follows a detailed account of the faults which Job may have committed,[1] resulting in this conclusion:

> That is why around you there are snares,
> And sudden fear terrifies you! (22: 10)

Bildad is no less positive than Eliphaz. It is by the equation of sin and punishment that he explains the death of Job's sons (8:4) as a consequence of divine justice (8:3). If Eliphaz cursed the 'fool taking root' (5:3), Bildad compares those who forget God to the papyrus and reed which wither away for want of water (8:11-12). They have nothing solid to which they can cling (8:13-15). If the righteous man is a well-planted tree by the waterside producing its fruit in due season (Ps 1), the wicked man is uprooted and cast on the ground where he rots away (8:16-19). The light of the wicked man (i.e. his prosperity) is quickly quenched (18:5-6). And, following Eliphaz, Bildad recurs to the torments which punish the criminal during his lifetime: snares beneath his feet (18:7-10), remorse and fear (18:11-12), sickness and death (18:13ff.) deprivation of offspring (18:17-19). He is like the tree whose roots dry up and whose branches wither (18:16).

Zophar also exploits the traditional vein. If Job is in distress, it must be that he is guilty. God Himself would attest this if He deigned to speak (11:5-6; cf. Comm.). In three hemistichs, Zophar describes the fate which awaits the impious:

> But the eyes of the wicked languish,
> And every refuge fails them;
> And their hope is to give up the ghost! (11: 20)

Let not Job be deceived by appearances:

> Do you know that from oldest time
> Since man was placed on the earth,
> The elation of the wicked is fleeting,
> And the joy of the godless lasts but a moment? (20: 4-5)

The whole of ch. 20 should be re-read. By means of the most poetic imagery, Zophar insists that the prosperity of the sinner is but transient. God cannot tolerate it (23:23-8). The whole of nature rebels against it:

---

[1] See above, p. cxxvii.

> The heavens reveal his sin,
> And the earth rises up against him:
> Such is the lot of the wicked which Elohim has appointed,
> And such the portion which he receives from God! (20: 27, 29)

The last speech of Zophar (27:13; 24:18-24; 27:14-13) [1] begins with this last verse which summarises the whole thesis of Job's friends. God decrees for the wicked the just punishment of their sins. The detail of their penalties matters little. If necessary God has recourse to extraordinary means,[2] such as the fire (15:34; 20:26; 22:20) which consumed Korah's company (Nu 16:35; 26:10), or the water (20:28; 22:11) which engulfed sinners at the time of the Flood.

Elihu joins in the chorus with the others (34:21-8; 36:7-8, 13-14) to extol the justice of God which is manifested in the punishment of the wicked.

The corollary of the theories thus adopted by Job's friends is that conversion becomes the necessary and sufficient condition for the restoration of lost happiness.[3] Ch. 33 of Ezekiel imposes on the preacher the duty of warning the sinner so that he may be converted and thus not perish. Job's interlocutors will not fail to exhort him to return to God, holding out to him the promise of happiness. It is sufficient to have resort to prayer, the sovereign remedy against sin:

> If now you will have recourse to God,
> And will make supplication to Shaddai,
> From this moment He will watch over you,
> And will restore your abode of righteousness.
> Your former condition will have been but a little thing,
> So greatly will it be surpassed by your new state! (8: 5-7)

We have cited this text in connection with the efficacy of prayer.[4] The rest of the chapter shows clearly that Bildad suggests to Job this means of dispelling all ambiguity and ranging himself afresh in the category of the righteous. On this condition

> Your mouth will again [5] be filled with laughter,
> And your lips with gladness;
> Those who hate you will be clothed with shame,
> And the tent of the wicked will be no more! (8: 21-2)

[1] Cf. above, p. 1.
[2] Cf. Gn 38: 7, 'But Er, Judah's first-born, was wicked in the sight of Yahweh and Yahweh slew him.' The same fate overtakes Onan (Gn 38: 10).
[3] See above, pp. cxxxiiif.
[4] See above, p. cxxv.
[5] Cf. Comm. on 8: 21.

Zophar is even more explicit when he insists that before betaking himself to prayer Job should put away the iniquity which is in his hand, and should not allow unrighteousness to dwell in his tent (11:13-14). Conversion followed by prayer, such is always the procedure recommended. The result is infallible:

> Then you will lift up your face without blemish,
> You will be securely established and you will not fear!
> For you will forget your sorrow,
> As waters that have flowed away will you remember it!
> And more glorious than noonday will life emerge for you,
> Darkness will be as the morning, etc. (11:15ff.)

Eliphaz gives advice worthy of a banker:

> Reconcile yourself with Him, then, and make your peace:
> By this means your yield will be good! (22:21)

Conversion becomes a sort of profitable investment:

> If you return to Shaddai and humble yourself,[1]
> If you remove unrighteousness from your tent,
> Then you will esteem gold as though it were dust,
> And Ophir as the stones of the torrent beds;[2]
> For Shaddai Himself will be your ingots,
> And heaps of silver for you! (22:23-5)

Thus God does not punish merely for the sake of punishing. In depriving the godless man of prosperity, He is instigating him to change his ways and be reconciled to Himself. Thus the self-interest which induces man to practise virtue assumes a new aspect: it is a question of turning to God. Divine punishment becomes salutary. It is not merely justice but pity which supervenes. Eliphaz exclaims:

> Happy is the man whom Eloah corrects,
> And who does not despise the teaching of Shaddai! (5:17)

This is but the echo of the Psalmist:

> Blessed is the man whom Thou dost chasten, O Lord,
> And whom Thou dost teach out of Thy law! (Ps 94:12)

Is not the correction inflicted by God similar to the punishment which a father gives the child whom he loves (Pr 3:11-12)? If Job is able to take advantage of the experience of misfortune, he will become once again the man who is blessed, shielded from famine,

---

[1] Cf. Comm. on 22:23.
[2] Cf. Comm. on 22:24.

the sword, slander, pillage, wild beasts, stones (5:19-23), he whose
dwelling is sheltered from evil (5:24), who numbers a large posterity, and whose shoots 'are like the grass of the earth' (5:25).
A happy death will follow a happy life:

> You will come to the grave in a ripe old age,
> As a shock of grain rises in due time! (5:26)

Such is the fruit of conversion!

Elihu is fully aware of this divine operation which God effects
through suffering and the consequence of which is the salvation
of the sinner. He shows complacently how, to save man from death
(33:18, 22, 24, 28, 30), God uses not only revelation (33:15-18) but
also sorrow (33:19-22). The conversion which results from this
treatment restores life and joy to the heart of the sinner (33:25-8).
Even kings who have been cast into chains for having offended
God can be delivered by a salutary repentance (36:7-11). This is
why Job should not despair of regaining his former felicity (36:
15ff.).

The theory of retribution in this life, a theory which is based on
the justice of God rendering to each man according to his works,
lies at the very heart of Jewish ethics. Job's friends only follow
tradition when they argue on these lines about his situation,
whether it be to explain his ills by his sins or to exhort him to regain
happiness by conversion and prayer. But Job from personal experience considers that the theory has lost its validity. When he
reasoned according to orthodox ideas, he was the victim of a painful illusion (29:18-20; 30:26). What should he do? Declare simply
that the theory has not the force assigned to it. To the arguments
based on too simple an idea of divine justice must be opposed the
facts of daily observation.

THE ANTITHESIS.—We have just seen how Job, to his own cost,
has had melancholy experience of the common error. He hoped
for happiness since he was accustomed to practise virtue, 'but it
was misfortune which came' (30:26). The contrast between his
expectation (29:18-20) and the sad reality (30:1ff.) is a flat contradiction to the whole system of morals based on the equation of
moral good and material happiness. Even before hearing Job's
lament (3), we realise that the converse order, namely that happiness
is the condition of moral good, that is to say, that virtue proposes
happiness as its object, is not verifiable in every case. Satan had

claimed that Job practised this utilitarian ethic. He was greatly mistaken, since Job persevered in the right way despite the loss of his cattle, his family, and his health, and in spite of the sinister suggestions of his wife. Job, the blameless and righteous man, fearing God and turning away from evil, expresses in the name of the author a double protest against the equation of moral good and material happiness: it is false to assert that good fortune inevitably follows the achievement of moral good; it is equally false to say that material happiness should be the objective of virtue. Hence Job's friends are wrong. All their descriptions, comparisons, and exhortations fail to convince in face of one fact: Job is unfortunate although he is innocent. And their promises of a renewal of happiness are in a double sense fallacious, since such promises are not guaranteed by experience, and must remain ineffective in view of the fact that Job, as shown by the Prologue, does not consider that material good is a necessary condition and concomitant of virtue. The two orders, virtue and material happiness, are not mutually involved in human life, since the evils which afflict the latter belong essentially to the nature of man [1] and are not necessarily the result of his conduct.

Job's declarations of innocence are his reply to the traditional arguments (6:10; 9:17; 13:16; 16:17; 27:2-10). We have quoted most of the passages in which he enumerates his virtues and makes a reckoning of the state of his conscience.[2] His friends reproach him for an apologia of this kind which contradicts their thesis (11:4). Elihu is visibly irritated by this pretension on the part of an unfortunate man to affirm his innocence (33:9ff.). But Job appeals to God who tries the reins and the heart:

> Hast Thou eyes of flesh?
> Seest Thou as a man sees?
> Are Thy days as the days of a man?
> Thy years as the days of a mortal being?
> That Thou dost seek out my fault
> And inquire into my sin,
> Although Thou knowest that I am not guilty,
> And there is none to deliver from Thy hand! (10: 4-7)

The conscience of Job goes beyond the horizon which limits his friends. The earth and the heavens plead for him (16:18-21).

---

[1] See above, pp. cxixff.
[2] See above, pp. cxxivf.

He is not afraid to define his conduct in the face of God.[1] Nothing can make him relax his claim:

> Far be it from me to admit that you are right;
> Until I die, I will not renounce my integrity;
> I have held fast to my righteousness and will not let it go;
> My heart is not ashamed [2] of my days. (27: 5-6)

When the friends of Job have exhausted all the resources of their dialectic, when they have tried to prove that misfortune presupposes moral evil, and that in consequence, if Job is in distress, he must be guilty, the latter has the audacity to describe his ills once more, opposing them to his felicity in former days (29-30), and in contrast drawing the picture of his virtues, his righteousness, and his charity, his piety and morality (31). It is on this diptych that the discussion ends. The antinomy has remained the same right to the end of the debate. The traditional thesis, far from resolving it, has only aggravated it.

For if the justice of God requires that good should receive its reward and evil its punishment here and now in this world, the case of Job would tend to prove that this justice does not exist at all. It is this which explains the violence and bitterness of tone in which Job complains of God's dealings with him. For argument's sake, he adopts the point of view of his interlocutors. Your idea of justice, see to what it leads us!

> Know then that it is Eloah who has done me wrong,
> And who has encompassed me with His net!
> If I cry 'Violence'!, I receive no reply,
> In vain do I cry for help; there is no judgment!
> He has blocked up my way so that I cannot get through,
> And upon my paths He has set darkness! (19: 6-8)

Before his final apologia, Job exclaims:

> By God who has set aside my right,
> And by Shaddai who has embittered my soul! (27: 2)

No, virtue does not create an absolute right to happiness. Job proves it in painful experience. He can only attribute his ills to the agency of God who treats him as He pleases (6:4; 7:12ff.). There is no serious pretext for these tortures:

> He who crushes me for a hair,[3]
> And multiplies my wounds for no reason! (9: 17)

---

[1] See above, p. cxxiii.
[2] Cf. Comm. on 27: 6.
[3] Cf. Comm. on 9: 17.

It seems almost as if God takes delight in blackening His servant:

> If I wash myself with snow
> And cleanse my hands with lye,
> Then Thou plungest me into filth,[1]
> And my very garments abhor me! (9: 30-1)

Job's fear turns into a frenzied obsession with persecution; he thinks that God aims relentlessly at his ruin (10:13-17; 16:11ff.). He cries out to God:

> Am I the sea or the dragon
> That Thou shouldst erect a barrier against me? (7: 12)

And to his friends:

> Have pity on me, have pity on me, O you my friends!
> For the hand of Eloah has smitten me.
> Why do you persecute me, as does God,
> And why are you never sated with my flesh? (19: 21-2)

Job has a deep feeling for the truth. If he is the victim of poverty, sickness, and indescribable sorrows, it is because God from the height of heaven has consented to the trial and given Satan the right to test Job. It is true that God has forbidden Satan to touch Job's life itself. God wills that the experiment should last for a time only. Job has a certain presentiment of the way in which the adventure will finish (19:23ff.). But the sufferings which he endures are the present overwhelming fact, the actuating motive of his apostrophes or invectives. What matter if in the Epilogue all is put right again! Job suffering in spite of his innocence constitutes a proof that distress is not caused by sin alone, nor is it an implication that the sufferer needs to be converted, for, to be converted, one must have sinned.

If Job is struck by God, it is then solely because God has willed to treat thus one whom He has called His servant (1:8). The O.T. knows a symbolic personage who was likewise a target for the blows of the divine hand. This is the 'servant' of Yahweh.[2] He is the elect one, the righteous one, the apostle (Is 42:1-4), he who is to be the light and the salvation not of Israel only, but of the nations of the whole world (Is 49:1-6). Like Job, he is a victim of injustice and violence, of insult and outrage (Is 50:4-9). But the meaning of his

---

[1] Cf. Comm. on 9: 31.
[2] On this whole question, cf. Condamin, 'Le Serviteur de Iahvé', in *Le Livre d'Isaïe*, pp. 325ff.

pain does not elude us. He is the expiatory offering. If he suffers and if he dies, it is because of the iniquities of others.[1] He is laden with the sins of the world. Let the reader study again Is 53 and interpret it in the light of the Christian Gospel! He will without difficulty recognise the radical difference between Job and the servant of Yahweh. The cause of the sufferings and the ignominies to which the latter is exposed is sin, as the traditional doctrine suggests, but not individual sin, since it is a just man who is in question. The servant of Yahweh is substituted for the race, the nation, the world, to undergo the sufferings merited by the sins of the world, the nation, the race:

> Verily he has borne our griefs
> And carried our sorrows,
> Yet we esteemed him stricken,
> Smitten by God and afflicted.
> But he was wounded for our transgressions,
> He was bruised for our iniquities,
> Upon him was the chastisement that made us whole,
> And with his stripes we are healed.
> All we like sheep have gone astray
> We have turned every one to his own way;
> And Yahweh has laid on him
> The iniquity of us all. (Is 53: 4-6)

V. 10 of this same chapter gives the true meaning and appraisement of this suffering. The servant of Yahweh has given his life as אָשָׁם, that is, as an expiatory offering. Divine justice exercises its effects on an innocent life, but always in punishment of sin. In the case of Job it is not for his own sin or for that of others that the righteous man suffers. He suffers because God has willed it so. The contrast between these two righteous sufferers shows clearly to what an extent the Book of Job is anxious to dissociate completely the question of sin and that of misfortune, just as it dissociates virtue from the pursuit of material good. Hence we must not be surprised if, as far as the problem of evil is concerned, Job rebels against prevailing theories. His personal situation has opened his eyes. Looking out on the world, he has noted that more often than not evil goes unpunished, whereas some imagine chastisement and misfortune to be connected with moral evil, as effects to their cause. To the assertions of his friends he replies by voicing his personal and reasoned convictions. The divine will is not concerned to se-

---

[1] An idea parallel to that which makes the sin of Jonah the cause of the storm which threatens the crew with death. Evil, like good, is contagious.

parate, in this world, the just from the unjust, when a catastrophe occurs. We know from the Christian Gospel that it is on the Last Day that this precise discrimination will be made between the wheat and the tares, the sheep and the goats, the good and the wicked. For the moment Job observes a fact:

> That is why I have said: 'It is all one!
> He destroys both the blameless and the wicked!'
> If a scourge brings sudden death,
> He mocks at the despair of the innocent!
> If a land has been delivered into the hand of a wicked man,
> He covers the face of its judges!
> If it is not He, who then is it? (9: 22-4)

No discrimination is made among the inhabitants when a land is struck by misfortune or oppressed by injustice. It must have required long days of reflection to dare to conclude that all was not for the best in the best of all possible worlds:

> Turn towards me and be appalled,
> And put your hands on your mouths;
> For, when I think of it, I am terrified,
> And my flesh feels a shudder. (21: 5-6)

What produces this shudder of dismay? Job does not hesitate to declare it:

> Why do the wicked continue to live,
> Grow old, and even increase in power? (21: 7)

The whole of what follows is an admirable description of the prosperity of the wicked:

> Their posterity are firmly established in their presence,
> And their offspring abide [1] before their eyes
> Their houses are secure, without fear,
> And no rod of Eloah is upon them!
> Their bull breeds without fail,
> Their heifer brings to birth without abortion.
> They let their boys frolic like sheep,
> And their children delight in the dance,
> They sing to the tambourine and the lyre,
> And they disport themselves to the sound of the pipe.
> (21: 8-12)

This is a far cry from the ethics of Job's friends! [2] Will God avenge Himself when they die?

---

[1] Cf. Comm. on 21: 8.
[2] See above, pp. cxxixff.

> They end their days in prosperity,
> And in peace they go down to Sheol! (21: 13, cf. Comm.).

Yet it is these wicked men who defied God and claimed that there was nothing to be gained from the practice of virtue! God seems to justify them. Unfathomable mystery!

> Now they said to God: 'Go away from us!
> We do not wish to know Thy ways!
> What is Shaddai that we should serve Him,
> And what profit should we gain by imploring Him?'
> (21: 14-15)

Job protests energetically against the trite metaphors or allegories of popular ethics which stress the troubles of the wicked:

> How often is the lamp of the wicked extinguished? [1]
> How often are they struck down by misfortune?
> How often does He destroy evildoers in His wrath?
> And are they as straw before the wind,
> Like the chaff which a whirlwind has swept away? [2]
> (21: 17-18)

The assertion that the sons would pay for their fathers was, as we have seen,[3] a subterfuge which Job rejected (21:19-21). Death strikes indiscriminately, right and left:

> One dies in his full maturity,
> When he is entirely happy and at ease,
> When his sides are full of fat [4]
> And the marrow of his bones quite fresh.
> And another dies with bitterness in his soul,
> Without having tasted of happiness;
> Together they lie down in the dust,
> And the worms cover them! (21: 23-6)

These positive observations are confirmed, as we have seen [5] by the testimony of travellers (21:27-9). Often it is the guilty who escapes vengeance:

> [Their testimony is] that in the day of calamity the
>   wicked man is spared,
> In the day of wrath he is merry! [6]
> Who denounces his conduct to his face,
> And who punishes him for what he has done? (21: 30-31)

[1] Pr 13: 9; 24: 20 are alluded to (cf. Comm.).
[2] Ps 1: 4 is alluded to (cf. Comm.).
[3] See above, p. cxxx.
[4] Cf. Comm. on 21: 24.
[5] See above, p. cxxxvi.
[6] Cf. Comm. on 21: 30.

Far from honours being refused him, they are granted him to the very end [1]:

> And when to the grave he is carried,
> On a mound he keeps watch;
> Sweet to him are the clods of the torrent bed!
> Behind him all move in procession,
> And before him a numberless throng! (21: 32-3)

This is enough to silence the supporters of the theory of retribution in this life (21:34). Nothing can prevail against a fact. Evil reigns in the world. It is met with everywhere. And in truth in vain do we seek the hand of God which should exterminate it. Before enumerating the crimes which deface the countryside and the towns (24:2ff.), Job exclaims:

> Why have times been hidden from Shaddai,
> And why have those who know Him not seen His days?

We are always brought up against the mystery. The replies of Yahweh to the invocations of Job (38-42) will legitimate the mystery and show that it is inevitable. Man is everywhere frustrated by the enigma of the world. His limited intelligence can do no other than submit, as Job will do (42:1-5). It is not the homilies of Elihu, which have the stamp of popular moral notions, that can succeed in rehabilitating principles whose lack of validity Job has so eloquently demonstrated.[2]

Christianity alone will be able to give the final solution.[3] But this solution is already foreshadowed in the Book of Wisdom. One should complete the speeches of Job or his friends by those admirable promises which create 'a hope full of immortality' in the heart of the righteous (Wis 3:1ff.). To the picture of the distresses of the righteous and the good fortune of the wicked [4] we should

---

[1] Cf. the picture of the happiness of the hypocrite as described by Glaucon in Book II of Plato's *Republic*.

[2] To claim, as some authors have done, and especially Budde, that the speeches of Elihu embody the solution extolled by the inspired author, is in truth to misunderstand the whole meaning of the Book of Job.

[3] See above, p. cxxviii.

[4] It is not to be forgotten that Glaucon, in Book II of Plato's *Republic*, describes admirably the contrast between the treatment meted out to the ideally virtuous and that reserved for the wicked hypocrite. Every kind of misfortune, including flagellation and crucifixion, is the lot of the virtuous, while the hypocrite receives every good. But Glaucon notes that rewards and honours go to the appearances of virtue, not to virtue itself. His thesis is based on the social utility of virtue, and this evidently depends on the

oppose the wonderful description of the final vindication of good
over evil, which vividly portrays the confrontation of the persecuted
with their persecutors on the Day of Judgment, the latter recognising the wisdom of the former and their own folly, the former
secure in their triumph and standing erect before their torturers
(Wis 5). The author of 2 Mac will see 'a pious and holy thought'
in the belief that a fine reward awaits those who have fallen asleep
in piety (2 Mac 12:45). The evolution of Israel has carried us from
immediate to future retribution. The Book of Job marks an important stage on this road. It shows how the supreme justice of
God which must one day be manifested (as Job is aware, 19:25ff.)
is not subject to the narrow laws of the human mind; how virtue
can live on without being inevitably accompanied by prosperity;
how misfortune can be met with even in the life of the innocent
man; how the archaic equation between moral good and happiness,
moral evil and misfortune, needs to be revised if it is to continue
to exert a salutary influence on consciences. The Epilogue in itself
is sufficient to show that the author does not dispute the truth of
retribution. But the latter rests like all else on the inscrutable
mystery of the divine will. The trial of Job began when God permitted it, and ends when God so determines. It was not the consequence of sin and it is not conversion which causes it to cease.
God alone knows the motives of His own decrees. Man cannot
subject them to the demands of human logic or morals. He can but
adore in silence the mystery of the divine government of the world.
The sovereign Judge will exercise His justice. But when and how?
Those who have tried to explain it all in too mechanical a way have
been on the wrong track. God Himself suggests that they be more
circumspect in the face of problems whose ultimate solution will
be truly evident only in the light of final revelation.

idea which the citizens form of such or such an individual. They think him
just or unjust, and this is what suggests their attitude with regard to him.

CHAPTER NINE

THE BOOK OF JOB IN THE OLD TESTAMENT

METHOD TO BE ADOPTED.—The study which we have just made of the doctrine of the Book of Job has revealed clearly the part played by tradition and that played by innovation in giving the book its full originality. The normal principles of religion and morals, based on a very exalted idea of God as He is in Himself and as He is in His relations with humanity, lead to conclusions which seem incontestable to the majority of the people and which are defended in the first place by Job's interlocutors, his three friends, and later by the youthful Elihu. Job, the mouthpiece of the author, does not hesitate to attack these conclusions, which may be summed up in two fundamental theses: the righteous prosper, and the wicked are overtaken by calamity. Not only does he prove by his own example that virtue and misfortune can meet in one person; he steadily presses home an anomaly which strikes any observer, namely that happiness is often the lot of the wicked. It is especially in ch. 21 [1] that this happiness is described at length in contrast to the misfortunes of the good, of whom Job is the living symbol. There is no distinction between the way in which the just and the unjust are treated (9:22-4).

Two figures, that of the suffering righteous man and that of the prosperous godless man, exactly as in Book II of Plato's *Republic*, strikingly illustrate all the speeches of Job. This is a reaction against the habit of constantly contrasting the good fortune of the pious observer of the Law with the misfortune of the scorners of the divine precepts. To situate the Book of Job in the literature of the O.T. as a whole means in the first place to try to discover whether we are here confronted by an isolated phenomenon or whether it is a question of a contrary current some manifestations of which it might be possible to trace. Such a study will enable us to see by what influences, direct or indirect, the thesis of our inspired author may have been moulded. In literature as in history, causes produce their effects either by their positive action, or negatively, by pro-

[1] Cf. above, pp. cxlviiif.

voking a reaction. Our task then will consist essentially in inserting the Book of Job into its appropriate place in that long series of literary productions which mark the course of development undergone by religious ideas in Israel.

The time has gone by when Voltaire could mock by insisting on the Arabic character of the original work, of which the Hebrew version was supposed to be only a translation.[1] Renan was equally mistaken when he allowed himself to be influenced by the conventions imposed on the characters and claimed to be able to distinguish their ideas from the Mosaic Law or the usages of the Jews.[2] The Book of Job is a thoroughly Israelite work in spite of its setting in Arabia or Edom.[3] We shall see that the problem which it discusses has been dealt with by other sacred writers. The theories which it disputes we shall find again sometimes couched in the same terms, appearing through the most severely Israelite tradition. Part of our task has already been accomplished. It was that which consisted in recognising the influence of the Law and the Prophets on the religious or moral ideas of Job and his friends. There is no difficulty in admitting—and on this point all exegetes are agreed— that the Book of Job reflects the ideas, and sometimes the very expressions, of the chief historical or prophetic books of the O.T.[4] The important point, however, is to discover the characteristic signs and special features which enable one to trace the immediate influences to which the author was subject. The nature of the problem debated is in itself a mark of the age. The manner of considering previous solutions is another such mark. The comparison of the work with other works which had the same object will be one of the best means of deciding its chronological position. We shall have to proceed with the greatest caution, for similar phenomena have sometimes been interpreted in diametrically opposed senses. It will also be good to consider whether a veiled allusion to some historical fact or some idea peculiar to a certain period may not help to corroborate the first conclusions. We will leave to a special chapter[5] those deductions which may be made from language itself and the importance of which can escape no one's attention.

[1]   Article 'Job' in the *Dictionnaire philosophique*.
[2]   See above, p. cxiv, n. 7.
[3]   See above, pp. cxivff.
[4]   See above, pp. cxvff.
[5]   See below, pp. clxxvff.

THE PROBLEM OF EVIL.—We have suggested that two figures dominate the whole of the discussion: the suffering righteous man, and the happy godless man. These are two aspects of one and the same problem: the problem of evil. Now, this problem had often engaged the attention of Israelite thinkers. The origin of the ills which afflict humanity caused various theories to be offered in explanation, from that of collective responsibility to that of individual responsibility.[1] Just as good, which at first was envisaged as profiting the whole community,[2] was eventually attributed solely to the individual who practised it,[3] so evil, at first considered as exercising harmful effects on the whole community, is later limited in its action to the guilty party.[4] The theory which finally prevails is that the individual receives his deserts: happiness for the good, misfortune for the wicked.[5] It is at this stage that, in the thought of some rare minds, there takes place a reaction against this automatic release of happiness by virtue and of misfortune by sin.

THE RIGHTEOUS SUFFERER (in Isaiah).—One of the chief causes of this reaction was the spectacle of the righteous man suffering. In order to define clearly Job's attitude towards his own sufferings, we contrasted his idea on the subject with that which is expressed in the fine poems of the second part of Isaiah.[6] The difference between these two types, the one prophetical and the other hagiographical, is very apparent. The former suffers as a result of sin. It is not of course his own individual sin, but the sin of the race or the people. None the less, the righteous man in Isaiah is an expiatory victim. The righteous man in the Book of Job, Job himself, suffers from a cause which is wrapped in mystery. He in no way expiates a personal or collective guilt. Whereas the Servant of Yahweh, as depicted in Isaiah 42:1-4; 49:1-6; 50:4-9; 52:13 - 53:12, furnishes an additional proof of the strict connection between sin and suffering, the servant of God, Job, constitutes a proof that the connection escapes us and that God alone knows the ultimate reason for the good and evil that come to us. Isaiah's Servant of Yahweh has already extricated current ethics from too narrow a conception

---

[1] See above, pp. cxxviiif.
[2] The story of the righteous who could have saved Sodom (Gn 18: 22ff.).
[3] See above, pp. cxxxf.
[4] See above, pp. cxxixf.
[5] See above, p. cxxxi.
[6] See above, pp. cxlvif.

of the retribution due to sin, since this retribution may fall on the shoulders of an innocent man, in accordance with the principle which Caiaphas affirms without understanding the extent of its implications: συμφέρει ὑμῖν ἵνα εἷς ἄνθρωπος ἀποθάνῃ ὑπὲρ τοῦ λαοῦ καὶ μὴ ὅλον τὸ ἔθνος ἀπόληται (Jn 11:50; cf. 18:14). This is the old theory of the substitution for the guilty party of a victim in which the 'sin is incarnate so that it may be destroyed along with it.[1] Job is not struck by virtue of any sanction. Divine justice, manifest in the case of the Servant of Yahweh, is hidden from us in the case of Job as it is understood by the protagonists of the drama, who are unaware of the happenings in the Prologue and the issue in the Epilogue. A further step has been taken in the development towards the dissociation of physical from moral evil. We are speaking from the logical point of view, for chronologically it is difficult to decide which of these two portrayals precedes the other.

The designation 'my servant' by which Yahweh introduces Job (1:8; 2:3; 42:7, 8) and the righteous sufferer (Is 42:1; 49:3; 52:13; 53:11) is also applied, in the Bible, to Abraham, Moses, Caleb, Joshua, etc.[2] There is nothing singular about it. There are common features in the descriptions given of the ills from which both servants of God suffer. Job exclaims:

> They have opened wide their mouth against me,
> Insolently they have struck my cheeks,
> They mass themselves together against me! (16: 10)

> They have held me in abhorrence, they have remained aloof
>   from me,
> And they have not spared to spit in my face! (30: 10)

The Servant of Yahweh:

> I gave my back to the smiters
> And my cheeks to those who pulled out the beard;
> I hid not my face from shame and spitting. (Is 50: 6)

If there has been influence, in which direction has it worked? The same question might be asked with regard to the points of similarity between Is 50:8 and Job 13:19; Is 50:9 and Job 13:28; Is 53:9 and Job 16:17. Merely by looking at the two sets of des-

---

[1] Among the Babylonians and Assyrians this idea reached a high degree of expression. It would be interesting to compare the texts which I have quoted in *La Religion assyro-babylonienne*, pp. 272ff., with the rituals of Lv 4-7 for sacrifices for guilt.

[2] Condamin, *Le Livre d'Isaïe*, p. 331.

criptions it is impossible to conclude that there has been mutual influence. Nevertheless, both have a similar, though not identical object. In one a righteous man suffers; hence suffering is compatible with virtue. In Isaiah suffering is expiatory. It restores the balance, since the guilt of the community is atoned for by the suffering of Yahweh's servant. Job's interlocutors, especially Eliphaz and Elihu,[1] also attribute to suffering a certain expiatory value. It is corrective, restoring the balance and leading to conversion.[2] But here it is the individual who atones for his own misdeeds. Job contests this interpretation of suffering, which, he suggests, is due to the mysterious and inscrutable dealings of God. The face of the righteous man here resembles that which Isaiah sketches only in its marks of suffering. The suffering of Yahweh's servant has a well-defined purpose. The suffering of Job is presented to us only in its connection with the good pleasure of God. Chronologically speaking, it is not necessary to suppose that these two ideas should have followed each other or should have belonged to the same line of development. They may have developed on parallel lines. Can a righteous man suffer? Yes, to expiate the sins of the people, and this is the situation of Yahweh's servant. Because God has so willed it, and this is the situation of Job.

Budde [3] recognises the difficulty of coming to a decision when, while admitting the interdependence of Job and Second Isaiah, he hesitates between the thesis of Kuenen on the priority of Isaiah [4] and that of Cheyne on the priority of Job.[5]

Apart from the passages concerning the righteous sufferer, chs. 40-66 of Isaiah offer some further analogies [6] to the Book of Job. There is a striking similarity between the reasoning imputed to the Israelites in Is 40:26-7 and that which Eliphaz imputes to Job in 22:12-14.[7] The comparison [8] which is applied to man in general by Job (14:2) we find applied to the people in Is 40:6-8. The formula used by Job [9] to describe God's hostility towards him

[1] See above, pp. cxliif.
[2] See above, p. cxliii.
[3] *Das Buch Hiob*, 2nd ed., p. lii.
[4] *Theol. Tijdschr.* 7, 1873, pp. 540f. This is also the thesis of Peake and Strahan.
[5] *Job and Solomon* (1887), p. 84. This is also the thesis of Dillmann.
[6] We refer to formal resemblances, of course, not to simple coincidences of words or expressions.
[7] Cf. Comm. on 22:12.
[8] Cf. Comm. on 14:2.   [9] Cf. Comm. on 30:21.

(30:21) resembles that suggesting God's hostility to the people in Is 63:10. The metaphor implying the relation of cause and effect between moral evil and misfortune found in the speeches of Eliphaz (5:7; 15:35) is the same as in Is 59:4. But we have seen [1] that it is part of the common stock of tradition.

In our opinion, the most significant passages are those in the doxologies. We have seen in 8:20-2 and 9:8-10 a technique which consists in combining a number of features borrowed from various authors to make of them the elements of a single strophe.[2] Now, in 9:8, Job says of God: 'He alone stretches out the heavens, and walks on the waves of the sea.' It is Yahweh who in Is 44:24 exclaims: 'I am the Lord who made all things and who stretched out the heavens alone.' The very words of Yahweh, forming part of a coherent speech, have been borrowed by the author of the Book of Job to compose his mosaic. Similarly, the resemblance between Is 51:9-10, where we have a sublime apostrophe to the arm of Yahweh, and Job 26:12-13, in which can be detected also the influence of Jer 10:12; 31:25, seems to us to be due to a doxological borrowing on the part of the Book of Job.[3] We might then infer that in the previous cases, especially when the same ideas or images are applied on the one hand to the nation and on the other to the individual, it is the texts of Second Isaiah which are prior to the parallel ones in the Book of Job. It is typical of the order of things in Biblical literature that the social group precede the isolated individual.[4]

Hence we should be inclined to conclude that in the portrait of the righteous sufferer it is the Book of Isaiah which has the priority. The more personal and vehement character of the laments of Job very easily led to the accumulation of traits among which reminiscences may have slipped in. It is very natural to suppose that in order to express his grief a man should draw from his memory typical formulae whose suggestiveness would enhance the description of his personal sufferings.

THE PROSPEROUS WICKED MAN (in Jeremiah).—We must now seek in the Book of Jeremiah some account of the prosperity of the wicked, parallel to that which has been the pivot of Job's objections

---

[1]   See above, p. cxxxv.
[2]   Cf. Comm. on 9:8.
[3]   Cf. Comm. on 26:12-13.
[4]   See above, p. cxxix.

to the thesis of his friends.[1] The famous passage is Jer 12:1-3, which we translate:

> Thou art too righteous, O Yahweh,
> For me to complain of Thee,[2]
> I invoke Thee only with regard to Thy judgments:
> Why does the way·of the wicked succeed?
> Why are all treacherous men secure?
> Thou hast planted them and they have even struck root;
> They flourish and have even borne fruit;
> Thou art near to their lips
> And far from their reins!
> Now, Thou, Yahweh, dost know me,
> Thou seest me and dost search closely my heart!
> Tear them up like sheep for the slaughter,
> And mark them for the day of butchery! (12: 1-3)

It is impossible not to see a striking analogy between these lines and those of Job in 21:7ff. about the prosperity of the wicked.[3] In both contexts it is a question of the רְשָׁעִים.[4] The same transition, by means of the adverb גַּם 'further', 'and even', is found in both Jer 12:2 and Job 21:7b. Both descriptions begin with the same interrogative מַדּוּעַ 'why?'[5] If there are cases where influence is clearly perceptible, it is certainly here. But the question is which of the two has exerted influence. Here too opinions are divided. Dillmann argues for the priority of Job, while admitting that most critics from Kamphausen and Wellhausen are rather inclined to make Job the borrower.[6] One cannot, in fact, escape the impression that Job's long description is the elaboration in poetic terms of a given theme. Jeremiah describes the happiness of the wicked in four hemistichs, and immediately (12:2b) declares their guilt: 'Thou art near to their lips and far from their reins!' Then comes the demand for their punishment: 'Tear them up like sheep for the slaughter, and mark them for the day of butchery!' Job begins by referring to the disconcerting character of what he is about to declare (21:5-6). After formulating the question (21:7), he begins a detailed description of the prosperity of the wicked. Jeremiah

---

[1] See above, pp. cxliiiff.
[2] On the meaning of רִיב with אֶל before the complement, cf. our Comm. on 33:13.
[3] See above, p. cxlviii.
[4] Above, p. cxxvi.
[5] Note the difference from Hab 1:13.
[6] *Hiob*, 4th ed. (1891), p. xxxiii.

confined himself to the classical image of the well-planted tree [1]
which has taken root and bears fruit. The posterity of the wicked,
his scions and family, these are the fruit which it bears, and it is
Job who describes it (21:8-9). As a term of comparison for the
victim led to the slaughter, Jeremiah naturally makes use of the
traditional image: כְּצֹאן 'like sheep'. We find כַּצֹּאן 'like the sheep'
in the mouth of Job (21:11), but it is in order to symbolise the
children of the wicked disporting themselves. And it is only after
a whole long descriptive passage (21:8-13) that reference is made
to the guilt of the wicked. Jeremiah had said that Yahweh was
'near to their lips'. Job says that even their lips do not wish to be
near to God:

> Now they said to God: 'Go away from us!
> We do not wish to know Thy ways!
> What is Shaddai that we should serve Him,
> And what profit should we gain by imploring Him?'
>
> (21: 14-15)

And when Job adds: 'Is not the counsel of the wicked far from
Him?', it is again a reminiscence of Jeremiah who said that 'Yahweh
was far from their reins'.

JOB AND JEREMIAH.—There is yet another passage of Jeremiah
which has raised the question of a connection with Job. It is Jer
20:14-18, which must be translated again as follows: 'Cursed be
the day on which I was born! Let not the day when my mother
bore me be blessed! Cursed be the man who brought the good news
to my father, saying: "A male child has been born to you", thus
delighting his heart! Let this man be like the cities which Yahweh
pitilessly overthrew! Let him hear a cry in the morning and an
uproar at noon! He who did not slay me in the womb, so that my
mother would have been my grave and her womb have perpetually
borne me! Why did I come forth from the womb to see trouble and
affliction and to end my days in shame?' We have not ventured to
divide our translation into hemistichs, since the first part of the
passage is hardly rhythmic.[2] If this passage is compared with Job's
malediction (3:3ff.), a certain number of points will be noted which
recall the technique of amplification by which we felt that Jer 12:1-3
was turned into Job 21:7ff. The theme is a malediction of the writer's
birth:

---

[1] See above, p. cxxxii.
[2] Notice the accumulation of relative pronouns (אֲשֶׁר) in vv. 14-16.

> Cursed be the day on which I was born! (Jeremiah)
> May the day perish in which I was born! (Job)

In translation the difference seems to lie only in a change of the main verb. But the Hebrew gives the impression that Job has ingeniously lightened the text of Jeremiah, by eliminating the relative אֲשֶׁר and substituting for the perfect *puʻal* יֻלַּדְתִּי the imperfect *niphʻal* אִוָּלֵד. To achieve parallelism, Jer 20:14 replaces the words by their usual equivalents: 'when my mother bore me'='on which I was born'; 'let it not be blessed'='cursed'.[1] But Job deepens and adds a sinister touch to the malediction. The night of conception corresponds to the day of birth. It is no longer a man who speaks but the night itself:

> And the night which said: 'A male child has been
>   conceived!'

The Aramaic גֶּבֶר has replaced the בֵּן זָכָר of Jer 20:15. The fact is all the more significant since the expression 'a male child' is very understandable at the moment of birth, whereas if used, as in Job 3:3, of the moment when the child has merely been conceived, it is an anticipation. In admirable logical sequence, Job then develops first the malediction of the day (3:4-5) followed by that of the night (3:6+9, 7-8, 10). It is only after this double couplet that he can exclaim, almost in Jeremiah's own words:

> Why did I not die on coming forth from the womb,
> And why did I not expire when I came forth from the belly?
>   (3:11)

The series of interrogatives, suggested by a single verse in Jer 20:18, is prolonged with many reverberations in the development of Job's lament (3:11, 12, 16, 20). The judgment of Cornill,[2] Budde, Duhm, and many others, that Job was the imitator, seems to us irresistible. This fact does not in any way diminish the poetic value of the passage, whatever Rosenmüller and Knabenbauer[3] may think. To

---

[1] The malediction is reduced to its simplest expression in Jer 15:10, 'Alas for me, my mother, that you gave me birth!'

[2] *Einleitung in das A.T.*, 2nd ed., p. 236. Cf. Lucien Gautier, *Introduction à l'A.T.*, 2nd ed., II, p. 118.

[3] Knabenbauer, p. 15, quotes at length Rosenmüller: *Jobeidos tamen auctorem ab alio quidpiam mutuatum esse, quo suum opus exornaret, quis exspectabit a tali poeta*, etc.? The fact is that the poet has extracted pure gold from the gangue still surrounding it in the rough style of the prophet of Anathoth.

say, with Renan,[1] that 'the flabbiness, the heaviness, the lack of vibrancy and parallelism, which characterise the passage of Jeremiah, betray the change which had taken place in the language and poetry of the nation at the period when this prophet was writing, that is to say, in the second half of the seventh century', is to imply a development in reverse and to forget that a writer such as Jeremiah would never have wished to render clumsy the concise, nervous, staccato style of the great poet who wrote Job's lament. We will not go so far as to assert, with Duhm,[2] that the imitation is rather cold and less impressive than the explosions of grief which burst from the heart of Jeremiah. The fact is that this imitation is not 'slavish'.[3] Inspired by the malediction launched by the Prophet, the author of Job at once soars on his own wings and circles the mountain peaks of the purest poetry. The clumsier phrases are lightened and surge upwards. The hesitating style becomes firm and vigorous. The metrical form compresses the ideas and words in order to fit them into the general rhythm. As for supposing that Jeremiah's passage is an interpolation [4] inspired by Job, this is to raise a question which the most radical criticism considers out of place: 'On the other hand, no reader will feel Jer 20:14-18 to be inauthentic (unecht). It is an explosion of furious despair which no one could have invented to place in the mouth of the Prophet.' [5] For Jer 20:14-18 as for Jer 12:1-3, the priority of the Prophet as compared with the hagiographer seems then the most probable conclusion.

Again, in Job 10:18-19, we find a few reminiscences of Jer 20:14-18. We should note in particular the transformation of Jer 20:17, 'He who did not slay me in the womb so that my mother would have been my grave and her womb have perpetually borne me',

---

[1] *Le Livre de Job*, 5th ed., pp. xxxvf.

[2] *Das Buch Hiob*, p. 17.

[3] It is clear how puerile is the argument of Dillmann (p. xxxiii), who claims that the author could not possibly have begun his work by a plagiarism.

[4] Dillmann, p. xxxiii, following Stade.

[5] Duhm, *Das Buch Jeremia*, p. 166. The matter has been studied by Ley in 'Die Abfassungszeit des Buches Hiob' (in *Theol. Stud. und Kritiken*, 1898), p. 48. He thinks that the passage of Jeremiah at most should be transferred to follow v. 6 of this chapter. According to Father Condamin, who lists the various attempts at transposition, vv. 14-18 were perhaps the 3rd strophe of the original poem which later was replaced by the strophe 11-13 (*Le Livre de Jérémie*, p. 165). The malediction 14-18 would in fact be better placed after v. 10.

into Job 10:18-19, 'Why then didst Thou bring me forth from the womb?... I should have been carried from the womb to the grave.'

We will not dwell on the resemblances between Jer 15:18 and Job 6:15; Jer 49:19 and Job 9:19; Jer 17:1 and Job 19:24. But it seems impossible not to recognise that in Jer 15:16-18 we have as it were a first sketch of the diptych which will embrace the entire book of Job: on the one side, the innocence of the unfortunate man, on the other, the mysterious sufferings by which he is overwhelmed.

Let us now return to the problem of evil. We have seen that for Jeremiah as for Job the serious question was why God permits the prosperity of the wicked. The prophet Habakkuk feels the same anguish: 'Thou art of purer eyes than to behold evil and canst not look on wrong! Why dost Thou look on faithless men and art silent when the wicked swallows up the man more righteous than he?' (1:13). Divine justice should not tolerate the triumph of wickedness over innocence.[1] This is the period when Jeremiah is still active, and the problem of evil is becoming most urgent. Jerusalem and Judaea are passing through their sharpest crisis, a situation which turns men's minds to reflect on the reason for these scourges. The persecution to which Jeremiah is exposed gives immediate reality to the agonised question of Habakkuk. One feels that the two prophets are living in the same atmosphere. As we have seen, the words of Jeremiah seem to have directly influenced the Book of Job. This however is not true of the text of Habakkuk; we cannot know whether it influenced subsequent literature in any way.

JOB AND THE PSALMS.—It is in Ps 73,[2] which opens the group of Psalms [3] attributed to Asaph (73-83), that we find once more the paradox of the happiness of the wicked, described in a way which recalls both Jeremiah and Job. This Psalm begins by an affirmation which in itself contains a reply to the anguish of the thinker:

> Truly he is good to the upright, our God,[4]
> To the pure in heart, is Elohim!

This assertion is the result of a series of reflections aroused by the

---

[1] See above, p. cxlviii.
[2] On this Psalm, cf. Podechard, *RB*, 1923, pp. 238ff.
[3] One should add Ps 50, also attributed to Asaph.
[4] Parallelism seems to require the punctuation לְיָשָׁר אֵל (cf. ed. Kittel), instead of לְיִשְׂרָאֵל; cf. Podechard, *RB*, 1923, p. 241.

scandal and indignation which the spectacle of the prosperity of the wicked provokes:

> As for me, my feet had almost stumbled,
> A trifle, and my steps would have slipped,
> For I grew indignant [1] at the arrogant,
> When I saw the prosperity of the wicked!

There follows a description of this prosperity (Ps 73:4-5), which makes a more intense impression as a result of their proud insolence and boastfulness (6-9). And yet they scoff at God, saying:

> How should God know?
> And is there knowledge in the Most High? (11)

In spite of everything, they continue to increase in strength (12), to the scandal of the weak:

> In vain then have I cleansed my heart
> And washed my hands in innocence,
> For I am smitten every day,
> And my punishment begins anew every morning! (13-14)

And the Psalmist begins to ponder this anomaly:

> When I meditated in order to understand this:
> It was painful to my eyes,
> Until I entered the sanctuary of God,
> Until I realised what was their end! (16-17)

The solution discovered is that of traditional ethics: the happiness of the wicked lasts for a time only; punishment will soon come, while the righteous will remain in peace near to his God (18-28). The concern of the Psalmist is to prevent the righteous from being overcome with anger when they see the triumph of wickedness. Ps 37 ceaselessly recurs to this theme (1, 7, 8), which is found again in Pr 24:19. Remain calm in the face of this apparent injustice! He laughs best who laughs last! It is also the doctrine of Ps 49, which is earlier in date than Ps 73.[2] We have seen *per longum et latum* that the theory was in harmony with current ethics and was shared by Job's friends.[3]

A comparison of Ps 73 with the account in Jeremiah [4] and in Job [5] shows in all three cases the same movement of ideas: observation

---

[1] On this meaning, cf. our Comm. on Job 17:8.
[2] Podechard, *RB*, 1923, pp. 250ff.
[3] See above, pp. cxxixff.
[4] See above, pp. clviif.
[5] See above, pp. clviiif.

of the prosperity of the wicked, allusion to their fault, which is that they elude all sense of the reality of God. But Jeremiah ends by invoking their punishment, the Psalm predicts and describes that punishment. Job remains uncertain. He is aware of the classical theory and knows that his friends will appeal to it:

> Yes, I know your thoughts,
> And the ideas which you imagine about me.
> You say to yourselves: 'Where is the house of the nobleman,
> And where is the tent in which the wicked dwelt?' (21: 27-8)

But he has made other inquiries about the end of the wicked. He has inquired of travellers (21:29). We have already seen [1] that their ideas were no longer in accord with too summary an idea of divine justice. In particular, the descriptions of Ps 37 would be more suitable in the mouth of Job's friends than in his own.[2]

Ley has rightly drawn attention to some instances where the Book of Job certainly borrows from the Psalms.[3] Ps 107, whose descriptions are so interesting because they show God coming to the rescue of His servants in their difficulties,[4] is quoted in the speech of Eliphaz (5:16) and in the doxology of Job (12:21, 24). This is the more significant because the post-exilic origin of the Psalm seems beyond doubt (cf. vv. 1-3). The resemblance between Job 7:10b and Ps 103:16b suggests equally a borrowing or reminiscence on the part of Job.[5] The exclamation of Ps 8:5; 144:3 is repeated in a pejorative sense in Job 7:17. And in fact Job 7:16 is directly based on Ps 144:4.[6] In connection with the doxologies [7] we have cited a whole series of contacts between the formulae of the Psalms and those of the Book of Job. And similarly we have recognised the style of the Psalms in the precepts of the moral law,[8] as in the expression of the idea of retribution.[9] To draw up a list

---

[1] See above, pp. cxxxvif.

[2] Cf. Comm. on Job 4: 7, 8; 8: 13; 11: 17.

[3] Op. cit., p. 60f.

[4] Cf. Comm. on relevant texts.

[5] On the other hand it seems that Job 19: 20a does not reproduce Ps 102: 6b (contre Ley); cf. Comm. on 19: 20.

[6] Cf. Comm. on Job 7: 16. When Job exclaims: 'Leave me alone, for my days are but a breath' he assumes as known the phrase of Ps 144: 4, 'Man is like a breath.' The word for breath is the same in both cases (הֶבֶל). And when Bildad replies: 'since our days on earth are a shadow' (8: 9) he reproduces the end of Ps 144: 4, 'his days are as a shadow which passes away'.

[7] Cf. above, p. cxv, n. 3.

[8] Cf. above, pp. cxlixf.

[9] Cf. above, p. cxxxii.

of similar or parallel passages would be an interminable task. Even when there is no direct influence, one feels a similarity of atmosphere or of religious and moral concerns.

The most remarkable instance is that in which Job directly quotes a passage from the Psalms. In the remarkable ch. 21 where he describes the prosperity of the wicked,[1] he asks his audience, in regard to the wicked, רְשָׁעִים (21:17),

> How often are they as straw before the wind,
> Like the chaff which a whirlwind has swept away? (21: 18)

How is it possible not to think of Ps 1:3,

> The wicked are not so,
> But they are as the chaff which the wind drives away!

Especially if one observes that the 'counsel of the wicked' (Ps 1:1) figures in the same terms in this same chapter of Job (21:16).

JOB AND PROVERBS. — It happens that the verse preceding the one which we have quoted from ch. 21 of Job is itself a reminiscence. Proverbs declares that 'the lamp of the wicked goes out' (13:9; 24:20). It is a way of saying that their prosperity does not endure.[2] Bildad has already taken up this thought, but with amplifications:

> Yes, the light of the wicked goes out,
> And his flame of fire ceases to shine.
> The light in his tent grows dim,
> And his lamp is put out above him. (18: 5-6)

Job goes back to the actual text of Proverbs:

> How often is the lamp of the wicked put out? (21: 17)

The words are the same. Proverbs said: נֵר רְשָׁעִים יִדְעָךְ. Job merely adds the interrogative כַּמָּה to the sacred formula.

We have already seen how many are the resemblances between the style of Proverbs and that of Job.[3] It is curious to note that the hesitancy we have met with concerning the relation between Job and Isaiah or Jeremiah recurs in regard to the relation between Job and Proverbs.[4] Some few critics, such as Ewald, Franz Delitzsch,

---

[1] Cf. above, pp. cxlviiif.
[2] Cf. Comm. on Job 20: 26; 21: 17.
[3] Above, pp. cxxxff.
[4] See Budde's Introduction (*Das Buch Hiob*, 2nd ed., p. liii) for the positions of the various critics.

and Dillmann, argue for the priority of Job. In particular chs. 1-9 of Proverbs have been envisaged as subsequent to Job in the monographs of Seyring[1] and Strack.[2] But the way in which the problem of good and evil is treated in the two works reveals in Job a development, we might even say a reaction,[3] and hence suggests its later composition.[4] Like the Psalms, the Proverbs lend arguments to Job's friends. This must never be forgotten in regard to the question of literary dependence. It is not a matter of chance that Eliphaz in v. 17 expresses himself in the terms of Pr 3:11-12, although he replaces Yahweh by the names Eloah and Shaddai. The allusion in Job 15:7 to Pr 8:25 is in itself sufficiently obvious.[5] One point in the doxology of Bildad (26:10) is borrowed from the description in Pr 8:27. Again, Pr 8 is cited in Job 38:10-11 (=Pr 8:39). In particular the fine poem on Wisdom (Job 28) seems to reflect the direct influence of Pr 8, where Wisdom itself defines and describes itself,[6] as also of Pr 3, where the praise of Wisdom is sung with masterly skill.[7] Let us observe further that Job 26:8 and 38:5 answer the questions of Agur in Pr 30:4, and that the image of Job 29:17 is inspired by that of Agur in Pr 30:14.

ALLUSIONS TO THE EXILE.—Taking these comparisons as a whole, they seem to require the priority of the Book of Proverbs.[8] It is well known however that for Proverbs as for Psalms it is impossible to fix an assured date. Such collections have been compiled from writings composed at various periods. Nevertheless, the nature of the problems dealt with in those parts which have been used by Job consistently suggests a date around the time of the exile, or even later.[9]

Now, there exists in Job a passage which can only be an allusion to the captivity. It is among Job's speeches that we find it.

---

[1] *Die Abhängigkeit der Sprüche Salomos Kap. I-IX von Hiob* (1889).

[2] 'Die Priorität des Buches Hiob' (1896; *Theol. Studien und Kritiken*).

[3] We have seen this in respect of Pr 13:9; 24:20.

[4] Above, pp. cxliiiff.

[5] Cf. Comm. on Job 15:7. Wildeboer rightly stresses the fact that Job 15:7 presupposes on the part of the reader an acquaintance with Pr 8:25, which stands in the latest part of the book of Proverbs (*Die Literatur des A.T.*, 1895, p. 387).

[6] Compare Job 28:15-19 and Pr 8:10-11; Job 28:23-7 and Pr 8:22-31.

[7] Compare Job 28:15-19 and Pr 3:14-15; Job 28:23-7 and Pr 3:19-20.

[8] The same conclusion is reached by Hitzig, Merx, Kuenen, Cheyne, Bickell, Budde, Duhm, Davidson, etc. The reasons are methodically expounded in Ley (op. cit., pp. 35ff.), who sees that Job, both as regards doctrine and method, marks an advance on Proverbs.

[9] Above, pp. cxxixf.

> He causes the counsellors to go bare-footed,
> And the judges He makes mad;
> He has loosened the bond [1] of kings,
> And has bound a girdle around their loins.
> He makes the priests to walk bare-footed,
> And potentates He overthrows! (12: 17-19)

This passage gains all its colour and relevance if compared with the speeches of Elihu in 36:7-12, where we see kings at first enthroned by God, then cast into chains, finally delivered after their conversion. Elihu is probably thinking of the story of Manasseh (2 Ch 33:10-13). Job confines himself to depicting in broad outline the sorry spectacle of counsellors [2] and priests led away to Babylon behind Jehoiachin or Zedekiah (2 K 24-5). The comparison between 2 K 25:7 and Job 12:18; 36:8 shows clearly that the events narrated in the Book of Kings are reflected in the descriptions of Job and Elihu. Moreover, the rôle of Cyrus will be to 'ungird the loins of kings' (Is 45:1).

JOB AND ZECHARIAH.—A further important stage in fixing the date of Job is the mention of Satan in the Prologue,[3] where the noun שָׂטָן is preceded by the article, as in Zec 3:1f. It is still a question of the adversary in chief, and not yet of Satan quite simply, as we find in 1 Ch 21:1, where שָׂטָן is no longer preceded by the article. This suggests the period intermediate between the Books of Kings, which know only the Spirit as the instigator of evil,[4] and the Books of Chronicles which invest the Spirit of evil with its definitive personality by calling it Satan. And it is just at this time that the prophecies of Zec 1-8 appear, the earliest dating from about 520 B.C.[5] The presence of הַשָּׂטָן in these prophecies and in Job is not the only point of contact between the two literary creations. We have referred to a number of similar expressions in the Prologue of Job (1:6-7; cf. Comm.) and Zec 1:10-11; 3:1-2; 4:10; 6:5-7. If we compare these texts we shall have no doubt of the priority of the prophet, who uses a style appropriate to each of the scenes he describes, whereas Satan in Job relies on stereotyped phrases. Thus the *terminus a quo* for the composition of Job would be after the captivity, around the close of the sixth century.

---

[1] Cf. Comm. on 12:18.
[2] The mention of kings and counsellors is characteristic. It is found in Job 3:14 and Ez 7:28; 8:25.
[3] Cf. Comm. on 1:6. [4] Above, p. cxvii.
[5] Cf. van Hoonacker, *Les Douze petits prophètes*, pp. 545 and 577.

JOB AND MALACHI.—Is it possible to find a *terminus ad quem?*
We think so. The concern with the problem of evil which we have
met in Jeremiah, Habakkuk, the Psalms, and especially Job,[1]
increased at the time of the exile. We have seen how the sight of the
prosperous wicked caused scandal among pious Israelites. Job had
insisted with sincere energy on the paradox of good fortune accompanying the wicked man to the very grave.[2] One of the chief
reasons for the intervention of Elihu was precisely that he might
protest against this alleged discrepancy between man's conduct and
his destiny. Certain allusions of Malachi likewise have in view Job's
assertions. Consider carefully Mal 2:17:

> You have wearied the Lord with your words.
> Yet you say: 'How have we wearied Him?'
> By saying: 'Everyone who does evil
> Is good in the sight of the Lord
> And He delights in them.'
> Or by asking, 'Where is the God of justice?'

Is this not an echo of the recriminations of Job?[3] The impression
is still stronger in Mal 3:13-15:

> Your words have been stout against me, says the Lord.
> Yet you say: 'How have we spoken against Thee?'
> You have said: 'It is vain to serve God.
> What is the good of our keeping His charge
> Or of walking as in mourning
> Before the Lord of Hosts?
> Henceforth we deem the arrogant blessed;
> Evildoers not only prosper
> But when they put God to the test they escape.'

Again we recognise here the method and complaints of Elihu,[4] and
above all we see that the speech of Job on the prosperity of the
wicked despite their conduct towards God furnishes the theme from
which false conclusions are drawn by those whom Yahweh chal-
lenges through His prophet. The interesting thing is that they are
not unbelievers but the pious. 'Thus[5] those who fear Yahweh speak
to each other' (Mal 3:16). This is the case of Job, who is essentially
'one who fears Elohim' (1:1; cf. Comm.). The prophet adds: 'and
Yahweh heeded and heard them'. These are precisely the terms
used by Elihu in addressing Job (33:31).

[1] Above, pp. cxliiif.
[2] Above, p. cxlix.
[3] Above, pp. cxlvf.
[4] Above, p. cii.
[5] Correct אַ to הֵן (cf. van Hoonacker).

DATE AND AUTHOR.—The prophecies of Malachi date from about the middle of the fifth century.[1] Thus it is between 500 (date suggested by the influence of Zechariah on Job) and 450 (date suggested by the influence of Job on Malachi) that the book was probably composed. The speeches of Elihu reveal the same state of mind as that of Malachi. It is very understandable that at the date when the prophet was delivering his oracles the second author of Job should have taken in hand a re-edition of the whole work and added the speeches of Elihu. The interval between the writing of the first part (Prologue, poetic dialogue, speeches of Yahweh, Epilogue) and the addition of the second (Elihu) must have been quite short. This would explain why the differences of style between the two parts are rather an indication of two authors than of two epochs.[2] In our study of the language of Job, we shall see that this date is singularly well confirmed by vocabulary and grammar.

After the investigation which we have just carried out to elucidate the relation of Job to O.T. literature, it would be idle to enlarge on the theories which have been proposed concerning the origin of our book. Jewish tradition (*Baba Bathra* 15a) attributed its composition to Moses, and in the nineteenth century there were authors like Ebrard and Rawlinson who maintained the same paradox.[3] Very soon critics began to advance the date to the time of Solomon. This had already been the opinion of St Gregory of Nazianzus, and it too enjoyed a certain fashion.[4] Among modern critics one of the most favourably received dates has been the seventh century B.C.[5] To aesthetic considerations have been added those of literary dependence interpreted in a sense opposite to that which we thought most probable.[6] Dillmann, who first decided in favour of the period of King Manasseh (early seventh century), later [7] decided in favour of the days of Jehoiakim or Zedekiah (early sixth century). It is interesting to note that Duhm gives his verdict for the 'first half

[1]   Cf. van Hoonacker, op. cit., p. 699.
[2]   Above, pp. ciiif.
[3]   Cf. Davison, art. 'Book of Job' in Hastings' *Dictionary of the Bible* (II, p. 669). The worthy Calmet ends a list of authors who have assigned the authorship to Moses by saying: *et alii innumeri* (Comm., p. v, n. e).
[4]   Cf. Calmet, op. cit., pp. 4f.; Knabenbauer, p. 14; Budde, p. l.
[5]   Ewald, Nöldeke, Merx, Reuss, etc. (cf. Budde, p. l).
[6]   Above, pp. clviff.
[7]   4th ed. of his Commentary, p. xxxiv. He quotes for this date Matthes, Kosters, Kuenen, and some others.

of the fifth century'—the conclusion we thought most suitable in
view of the comparison of this book with the other books of the
O.T. The arguments of Budde [1] and Peake [2] in support of as late a
date as 400 B.C. are based on the presumption that the practices
required by the so-called Priestly Code were not known earlier.
Buttenwieser arrives at the same conclusion [3] by considerations
relative to eschatology which are by no means convincing.[4] Kuenen
claimed that 400 was the latest possible date for the composition
of Job. However, some critics have tried to advance the date still
further. O. Holtzmann postulates the period of the Ptolemies [5] and
asserts that the author was influenced by Plato.

One of the main arguments of Holtzmann is that the Jews had no
inclination towards philosophy before their contact with Hellenism.
But Job is not a philosophical treatise. It is the result of a whole
line of development in theodicy whose strictly Israelite character
we have seen.[6] The author has imprinted a strongly personal mark
on the mode of the discussion. But just as we have recognised traditional ideas in the arguments of Job's friends,[7] we have also noted
that the thoughts and objections of Job were not an isolated phenomenon in O.T. literature.[8]

To claim that the dialogue form betrays a Platonic influence is to
forget that the Semites of the Tigris and Euphrates were quite
familiar with this dialectical technique.[9] One can hardly say even
of Ecclesiastes, where traces of Hellenism have most, and most
justifiably, been sought, that 'it reveals direct and immediate contact with the works of Greek philosophers'.[10]

---

[1] 2nd ed. of his Commentary, pp. liiiff.
[2] *Job*, p. 40.
[3] *The Book of Job*, pp. 75ff.
[4] For example, when he says that the emphatic denial of the resurrection
(Job 7: 9-10; 14: 10-12, 14) shows that such a hope had penetrated and was
gaining ground among the Jews (p. 76). Job does not speak of resurrection.
He asserts that the dead no more return, but he is aware of survival in Sheol
(3: 13-19; 14: 13-15, 22). The arguments of Buttenwieser assume gratuitously
that Isaiah's apocalypse (24-7) was written *in all probability* in the days of
Artaxerxes Ochus (348-340 B.C.) or after the battle of Gaza (312 B.C.).
We should also have to suppose that belief in a Hereafter could not have
arisen before 400 (p. 78). We distrust these arguments based on the genesis
of religious ideas in Israel.
[5] Stade, *Geschichte des Volkes Israel*, II, pp. 351f.
[6] See above, pp. cxxxviii ff.
[7] See above, pp. cxxxv f.
[8] Above, pp. cliv ff.
[9] Above, p. cxiii.   [10] Podechard, *L'Ecclésiaste*, p. 109.

It should be added that Greek ideas may have been known in the
Jewish world, by way of Syria and Egypt, even before the conquests
of Alexander.[1] It is certain that speculation about Wisdom, considered as a guide in morals and a principle of knowledge, received
a new vitality from the day when the Israelites, whether willingly
or by force, became intermingled with their neighbours through the
vicissitudes of political events.

Now, the Book of Job is precisely on the crossing of the ways.
The author knew Idumaea and Arabia,[2] he had seen the procession
of those long convoys which carried both merchandise and ideas
through the desert,[3] he had made inquiries of travellers,[4] and he
had travelled himself. His knowledge of Egypt seems to us indisputable. If he needs a poetical term to denote 'canals', he hits upon
יְאֹרִים 'Niles' (28:10). If he wishes to describe ephemeral flora, his
memory recalls the papyrus and reed (8:11-12). He knows too
'the vessels of reed' (9:26) like the papyrus canoes used by the
Egyptians.[5] In some sacred lake or on the banks of the river he has
watched the crocodile, to which he could give no other name than
Leviathan (40:25ff.). He knows that in art as in literature the inevitable companion of this Egyptian animal is the hippopotamus,
which he calls Behemoth (40:15ff.). That is why he describes them
both [6] after depicting the animals of the desert and, among them,
the ostrich (39:13ff.), which lives in Arabia and Edom. On the road
which has led him to Egypt and has brought him back again, his
gaze has rested admiringly on those mines of Sinai where the
Pharaohs, from time immemorial, had required from the bowels of
the earth gold, silver, copper, turquoise (28). He has met the
fishermen on the shores of the Red Sea and has seen how they
collected coral or extracted pearls (28:18). One might imagine in
fact that he wrote the second part of his work, the speeches of
Yahweh and the poem on Wisdom (28), on his return from one of
these journeys and with his mind filled with the memory of the
marvels he has seen.

Let us observe incidentally that he was thoroughly at home in the

[1]   Ibid.
[2]   Above, pp. cxiiif.
[3]   Cf. Comm. on 6: 18-19.
[4]   Above, p. cxxxvi.
[5]   Cf. Comm. on 9: 26.
[6]   We believe that the ibis was designated by its Egyptian name in
38: 36 (cf. Comm.).

land of the Pharaohs. It was especially in the fifth century B.C.
that the Jewish communities, and especially that of Elephantine,
flourished under the dominion of the Achaemenians. Aramaic
papyri, among which is to be found a fragment of the book *The
Wisdom of Ahiqar*, are a proof of the intellectual activity of these
exiles. There were not only Jewish mercenaries, settled by Psamme-
ticus, and to whom we like to think there is an allusion in Job
7:1-2; 14:14; there were also all those who with Jeremiah and
Baruch had taken refuge in Egypt to escape the Chaldaeans (Jer
43:5-7; 44). Aramaic was their normal language. The author of
our book and his supplementer were led by the very force of
things to besprinkle their Hebrew with a certain number of
Aramaisms.[1]

INFLUENCE OF THE BOOK OF JOB.—In order to situate the Book
of Job in the context of the Bible, it remains for us to try to discover
the influence it may have had on other literary works. But the very
special nature of this piece of literature, the mode of exposition
adopted, the clash of ideas on various subjects, did not facilitate
any sort of immediate influence.

In Lamentations we find certain notes similar to those in which
Job bewails his distress. Thus it would be interesting to compare
La 3:7-9 and Job 3:23; La 3:12 and Job 16:12-13; La 3:14 and
Job 30:9. It seems as if this ch. 3 of Lamentations which borrows
here there and everywhere in order to complete its acrostics is based
almost directly on the laments of Job. The other comparisons which
we have been able to make yielded some similar images, which
however do not appear to be borrowings.

The author of Ecclesiastes has perhaps taken from Job certain
touches on the necessity of leaving everything at the moment of
death,[2] the abortion which is preferable to a birth,[3] the unconscious-
ness of those who go down to Sheol,[4] the origin and the end of
things.[5] But these two authors are so deeply original that they can
have the same ideas and imagery without the Book of Job having
any direct influence on Ecclesiastes.[6] The resemblance of Job 9:12

---

[1] Below, pp. clxxvif.
[2] Compare Job 1:21 and Ec 5:14.
[3] Compare Job 3:16 and Ec 6:4-5.
[4] Compare Job 14:21-2 and Ec 9:5-6.
[5] Compare Job 38:24 and Ec 11:5; Job 34:14 and Ec 12:7.
[6] Since the date of Ecclesiastes is probably 2nd half of 3rd century
(Podechard, p. 122), there is no question of Ec influencing Job.

to Ec 8:4 (and also Dn 4:32) is due to the proverbial character of the idea expressed.

Ecclesiasticus is fond of taking advantage of earlier works.[1] Hence we are not surprised to find there some borrowings from Job. Here again we need only refer to the really typical instances.[2] It is clear that Job 1:21 is explained in Sir 40:1. Job's lament (3:1, 3; 10:19) is reflected in Sir 23:19,[3] where beneath the Greek we recognise the corresponding Hebrew words. The very characteristic expression 'lash of the tongue' (Job 5:21) is found in Greek (Sir 26:9) and in Hebrew (Sir 51:2) in Ecclesiasticus. The terms of Sir 8:9 are closely akin to those of Job 8:8. It is from Job 8:12 that Sir 40:16 borrows its exoticism. Sir 9:5 gives the reason of Job 31:1. The phrase 'one in a thousand' of Job 9:3; 33:23 is found again only in Ec 7:28 and Sir 6:6. Job 9:5 is reflected in Sir 39:28. The dimensions indicated in Sir 1:3 recall Job 11:8. Other passages again suggest Job's influence on Ecclesiasticus: e.g. Sir 9:13 (Job 18:8-9); Sir 49:1 (Job 20:12); Sir 51:10 (Job 30:3; 38:27); Sir 13:7 (Job 33:29); Sir 16:15 (Job 34:11); Sir 43:24 (Job 42:5). Finally we would refer to the similarities in vocabulary between Job 13:4 and Sir 51:5; Job 14:1 and Sir 10:18 (22); Job 17:7 and Sir 31:19; Job 18:5 and Sir 8:10; 45:19; Job 21:23 and Sir 41:1; Job 24:15 and Sir 23:25; Job 34:21 and Sir 23:19 (28); Job 38:37 and Sir 42:8.

The Book of Baruch clearly quotes, in regard to Wisdom under all its forms, Job 28:12-13, 23 and 38:35.[4] It should be noted that Baruch is in agreement with the Septuagint in preserving the right text at a place where MT is wrong.[5]

It seems that Tobit 4:16 is based on Is 58:7 rather than on Job 31:17-19 (cf. Comm.).

The Book of Wisdom offers some formulae which bear a resemblance to those of Job, although it is not possible to prove direct borrowing. Cf. Job 4:19 and Wis 9:15; Job 28:15 and Wis 7:8-9; Job 29:9 and Wis 8:12; Job 38:17 and Wis 16:13.

---

[1] Cf. Schechter-Taylor, *The Wisdom of Ben Sira*, pp. 12ff., and Touzard, *RB*, 1900, pp. 60f.

[2] When the original Hebrew exists, we use Peters, *Hebr. Text des Buches Ecclesiasticus* (1902). For the Greek, Swete, *The O.T. in Gr.*, II, pp. 644ff. (2nd ed.). Cf. our Comm. on Job in justification of the parallels.

[3] Between vv. 14 and 15 in Swete, p. 690.

[4] Cf. Comm. The quotations from Job are found in Bar 3:15, 20, 23, 31, 32, 33, 35.

[5] Cf. Comm. on Job 28:13.

In the N.T. 1 Co 3:19 has been noted as a citation from Job 5:13 (according to the Septuagint).[1] But the Greek of St Paul is not by any means a reproduction of that of the Septuagint.[2] The terms of Mt 12:45 and Lk 11:26 are based on Job 8:7 (cf. Comm.); 42:12 (according to the Septuagint). The ideas of the Book of Job on charity (22:6-7; 31:19) are found in almost the same terms in Mt 25:42-3, 35-6, 37-8. Let us mention further the analogy of style between Job 14:1 and Mt 11:11; Lk 7:28; Job 18:20 and Mt 8:11; Job 34:11 and Mt 16:27; Job 39:30 and Mt 24:28; Lk 17:37; Job 40:30 and Lk 5:10. Two texts from St John's Gospel (8:46, 56) closely resemble Job 24:1, 25.

The scene of Acts 22:23 recalls Job 2:12.

As well as the passage of the Epistles already quoted, there are perhaps similarities of terminology between Job 1:21 and 1 Ti 6:7; Job 4:3 and He 12:12; Job 4:8 and Gal 6:7f.; Job 4:9 and 2 Th 2:8; Job 4:19 and 2 Co 5:1 (2 P 1:13f.); Job 8:7 and 2 P 2:20; Job 11:8 and Eph 3:18.

We believe that we have observed a certain analogy between the phraseology of Job 2:7 and Rev 16:2; Job 3:21 and Rev 9:6; Job 31:35 and Rev 7:1ff.

[1] Swete, *Introd. to the O.T. in Greek*, p. 384.
[2] Cf. Comm. on Job 5:13.

THE LANGUAGE OF THE BOOK OF JOB

We should take as the basis of this study the oldest parts of the Book of Job: the prose narrative, the poetic dialogue, and the speeches of Yahweh.[1] We have already noted that the style of Elihu was distinct from that of the rest of the work and had a more pronounced Aramaic colour.[2]

The language of the Book of Job, thus reduced to its essential elements, reveals a strong literary personality. The author has his own vocabulary, grammar, and special technique of expression. He copies hardly at all and imitates only rarely.

A list of the words which are found only in Job has been drawn up by Fried. Delitzsch.[3] They can be classified into a number of categories which bear witness to the author's fondness for neologisms or uncommon words.

For example, he has recourse to the feminine form which corresponds to the *nomen unitatis* of the Arabs נהרה (3:4), עננה (3:5), חילה (6:10), דאבה (41:14). Sometimes the masculine will be substituted for the feminine which is usual elsewhere: נחוש (6:12). The form alone distinguishes שעפים (4:13; 20:2) from the same word in the Psalms (cf. Comm. on 4:13).

Most of the terms peculiar to the Book of Job are to be explained by reference to Hebraic or Semitic common roots: תהלה (4:18), סלד (6:10), חתת (6:21), נדדים (7:4), גוש or גיש (7:5), מחנק (7:15), מפגע (7:20), מסת (9:23), רקבון (13:28; 41:19), ניד (16:5), התלים (17:2), תפת (common noun 17:6), מלכדת (18:10), שיא (15:31; 20:6), צהר (24:11), בלימה (26:7), הליך (29:6), שחר (30:30), באשה (31:40), התלה (38:9), אגל (38:28), משכות (38:31), ירוק (39:8), רנים (39:9), רעמה (39:19), נחר (39:20), and נחיר (41:12), אבר (39:26), חברים (40:30), חדוד (41:22).

---

[1] See above, p. xcviii.
[2] See above, pp. civf.
[3] *Das Buch Hiob*, pp. 125ff. We have left out of account those words which are due to distortions of the text. Our list is moreover independent of that of Delitzsch.

Sometimes a transformation of the root explains the new word: כלה (5:26), נתס (30:13), יזרבו (6:17), מעדנות (38:31).

The unusual term is sometimes borrowed from other branches of the Semitic family of languages. Thus Assyrian, Arabic, and Aramaic possess the equivalents of גֶּלֶד (16:15) and of מֹחַ (21:24). Assyrian and Arabic explain אֵבֶה (9:26), שְׂכוֹת (40:31), and the verb זקק of 28:1; 36:27. Aramaic and Arabic enable us to recognise the verbs גרד (2:8), נהק (6:5; 30:7), רפף (26:11), the nouns גְּבִינָה (10:10), זְכוּכִית (28:17), עֲטִישָׁה (41:10). Through Assyrian we can analyse the terms מֶזַּח (12:21), גָּבִישׁ (28:18), מִשְׁטָר (38:33), בּוּל (40:20), תּוֹתָח (41:21). Aramaic, the influence of which we have already detected,[1] explains a certain number of words: נתע (4:10), טוּשׁ (9:26), אחוה (13:17), סד (13:27; 33:11), רזם (15:12), חב (31:33), ערוד (39:5), שָׂרִיר (40:16), דוץ (41:14). The Arabic language also supplies keys to the understanding of terms peculiar to Job: כידור (15:24), הכר (19:3), בצר (22:24, 25), הדך (40:12), מטיל (40:18), צאלים (40:21), צלצל (40:31), כידוד (41:11), מסע (41:18), שריה (41:18). The terms שכוי and טחות of 38:36 are perhaps of Egyptian origin.

If the author of the Book of Job does not hesitate to introduce into his vocabulary words of foreign origin or of new formation, we shall not be surprised to find, apart from the *hapax legomena*, a certain number of roots, verbs, nouns, whole expressions even, which betray the infiltration of other Semitic tongues. Here we shall simply give the references which will enable the reader to find in the Commentary the words in question and their etymology.[2]

Explanations by Assyrian, Aramaic, Arabic: 2:7; 8:16; 14:5. By Assyrian and Arabic: 14:19; 20:2; 28:9; 31:3; 40:22; 41:12. By Arabic and Aramaic: 8:12; 16:15.

By Assyrian or Babylonian[3]: 1:10, 15; 3:5, 8, 14; 6:4, 21; 12:21; 15:26, 32; 16:22; 17:11; 18:2, 17; 19:17, 23; 20:7, 23, 25, 28; 21:17, 21; 26:9, 15, 18; 28:15, 16; 30:3, 25; 31:26; 33:6, 9, 18, 19; 34:3, 13, 17; 36:8, 16, 17, 32; 37:1; 38:5, 6, 23, 33; 39:8, 9, 10, 13, 23; 40:20, 23.

---

[1] See above, p. lxxxv. On the Aramaisms of Elihu, see pp. civf.

[2] This list completes the preceding one. It is here a question not of special terms but of words and expressions in general.

[3] We normally use the term 'Akkadian', which denotes the Assyro-Babylonian language.

By Aramaic [1]: 3:25; 4:20; 5:22; 6:5,6,16; 8:2, 13; 11:7; 12:5;
14:6, 10; 15:17, 24; 16:2; 17:1; 18:5; 20:16; 21:7, 10, 12; 22:16;
24:24; 28:1, 8, 16; 30:3, 6; 31:9; 38:30.

By Arabic: 6:3, 10; 10:8, 17; 11:6; 14:20; 15:23; 16:6, 16;
17:8, 13; 18:8; 19:20; 20:18; 21:32; 26:13; 28:26; 29:4; 30:4, 6,
17, 22; 31:31; 33:21; 34:19; 36:10, 18; 37:2, 6, 9, 11, 20; 38:25;
39:1, 3, 4, 21.[2]

These phenomena are to be explained by the affinity between
the various Semitic languages. A certain Hebrew word belongs to
a root which has disappeared from the domain of Hebrew itself but
still persists in all other domains. It is not then necessary to assume
a direct borrowing. Furthermore, the scantiness of our documen-
tation explains the disappearance of a certain number of words or
expressions which were known in popular or literary speech but
which have not been established in the Bible. Thus the *hapax
legomena* are often due to the chances of the written tradition of the
Bible. A word which is found only very rarely in Holy Scripture
may have been perpetuated in current speech.

The truly significant facts are those whose only explanation lies
in the definite influence of a foreign language. From this point of
view, it has long been noted that the author of the Book of Job was
often subject to Aramaic influences.

A study of the vocabulary reveals the fact that sometimes an
Aramaic word has been chosen to supply, in the parallelism, the
equivalent of the Hebrew word. We have already drawn attention
to this fact in our discussion of the speeches of Yahweh.[3] To the
Hebrew עֵד 'witness' corresponds the Aramaic שָׂהֵד (16:19); to the
Hebrew פֶּרֶא 'onager' the Aramaic עָרוֹד (39:5); to the Hebrew
עֶצֶם 'bone' the Aramaic גֶּרֶם (40:18). The case is typical. The poet
quite naturally uses Hebrew. When he seeks a synonym, it is
Aramaic which supplies him with one. Note that Aramaic always
comes second.

Another significant procedure of the author is to use Aramaic
rather than the current Hebrew word, either to vary the style or
because Aramaic has become so deeply rooted in his mother-tongue.

---

[1]   As regards the Aramaisms in the speeches of Elihu, cf. above,
pp. civf.
[2]   The many Arabic etymologies of 40-1 are noted in the list of the *hapax
legomena* above.
[3]   See above, p. xcvi.

Thus 'to come' is in Hebrew בוֹא but אתה in Aramaic. In the Book of Job we find that בוֹא sometimes takes the place of אתה, for example in order to avoid the repetition of the word בוֹא in 3:25, or for the sake of the rhythm in 16:22 (cf. 37:22, Elihu). The Aramaic מְלַל replaces the Hebrew דִּבֶּר 'to say' in 8:2 (cf. 33:3, Elihu). Its derivative מִלָּה 'word' is quite characteristic of the Book of Job, in which it appears 34 times.[1] Note that its plural[2] sometimes assumes the Hebraic form מִלִּים (10 times), sometimes the Aramaic form מִלִּין (13 times). Very symptomatic again is the substitution of כָּפָן (Aramaic) for רָעָב 'famine' in 5:22; 30:3; of חִוָּה (Aramaic) for הִגִּיד 'to explain' in 15:17 (cf. 32:6, 10, 17; 36:2, Elihu); of כֵּפִים (Aramaic) for סְלָעִים 'rocks' (30:6).

Sometimes it is one of the consonants of the root which is to be explained by an Aramaic pronunciation: thus דעך 'to become extinguished' instead of זעך.[3]

Aramaic makes its influence felt even in regard to grammar. We have mentioned the plural מִלִּין alongside מִלִּים. Again, we find אַחֲרִין in 31:10. The reflexive is expressed by נַפְשִׁי 'my soul' (an Aramaism) in 4:21. It is above all the use of הֵן 'if', instead of אִם, which betrays the habit of using Aramaic (4:18; 9:11, 12; 12:14, 15; 13:15, etc.). It appears that in poetry either conjunction is used indifferently.

We have here confined ourselves to pointing out the most characteristic features. They suffice to situate the language of the Book of Job in that period when Aramaic was penetrating into Israel to a very considerable extent, that is, in the post-exilic period.[4] The exile in Chaldaea and the return to the mother-country had the effect of bringing the Jews into unceasing contact with populations for whom Aramaic formed a bond with other Semites. Under

---

[1] Cf. E. Kautzsch, *Die Aramaismen im A.T.*, I, p. 61.
[2] Cf. Comm. on 4:2.
[3] Cf. Comm. on 17:1.
[4] Cf. E. Kautzsch, op. cit., p. 6. We do not at all deny the inter-penetration of the Syrians of Damascus and the Hebrews, especially those of the Northern Kingdom, well before the exile. But Aramaic, even in the time of Hezekiah, was still understood only by a tiny minority, as may be seen from the dialogue in which the envoys of the King of Judah ask the Assyrian general to speak 'in Aramaic' and not 'in the Jews' language' so that his words should be understood only by the initiated and not by the people (2 Kg 18:26).

the hegemony of the Persians, as the papyrus records testify, Aramaic became the language of commerce and of international exchanges.[1] The Jewish colonies in Egypt used this idiom, and we have seen that the author of the Book of Job had probably visited his compatriots in the valley of the Nile.[2] His language confirms the conclusions we have reached with regard to his date and personality.

[1] See Cowley, *Aramaic Papyri*, pp. xvff.
[2] See above, p. clxxii.

CHAPTER ELEVEN

METRES AND STROPHES

The question of rhythm in Hebrew literature is one of those which periodically arouse debate. A mere glance at the bibliography relative to the subject as it is outlined for example in the *Introduction to the Old Testament* of the late J. Nikel [1] will show clearly enough the predilection with which the problem has been studied among scholars. The works of Lowth,[2] Herder,[3] Ley,[4] Bickell,[5] Budde,[6] Zenner,[7] Müller,[8] Sievers,[9] G. B. Gray [10]—not to speak of the French critics Le Hir,[11] Condamin,[12] Touzard,[13] Podechard [14]—have failed to create agreement among scholars.

The question is so delicate that a whole school of philologists, following Scaliger, has been found to contest the very existence of rhythm, properly speaking, among the Hebrews.[15] Nevertheless the distinction between prose and poetry is immediately apparent to any one who reads Hebrew texts. The Massoretic accentuation, which adopts a special system for those books which have a lyrical character, namely the Psalms, Proverbs, and Job,[16] was in conformity with Hebrew tradition. It was possible to make a clear dis-

[1] *Grundriss der Einleitung in das A.T.* (1924), pp. 250ff.
[2] *De Sacra Poesi Hebraeorum* (1753).
[3] *Vom Geist der hebr. Poesie* (1782).
[4] In a number of articles, but especially in *Grundzüge des Rythmus* (1875) and *ZATW*, 1892, p. 215 (cf. Podechard, *RB*, 1918, p. 58).
[5] Chiefly in his *Carmina V.T. Metrice* (1882).
[6] *ZATW*, 1882, pp. 47ff.
[7] *Die Chorgesänge im B. der Psalmen* (1896).
[8] Chiefly on the strophic system, in various works (1896, 1904, 1907-8): cf. Condamin, *Le Livre de Jérémie*, p. xxxviii, n. 2.
[9] *Metrische Studien* (1901).
[10] *The Forms of Hebrew Poetry* (1915).
[11] *Du Rythme chez les Hébreux*, published from the manuscript of the author, with notes, by Grandvaux, in *Le Livre de Job* (1873), pp. 54ff.
[12] In several articles of the *Revue Biblique* (1899-1904, 1908-10), in the Preface to Isaiah and in that to Jeremiah (pp. xxxviiff.).
[13] *Dictionnaire de la Bible*, III, cols. 487ff.
[14] In his *Notes sur les Psaumes* (*RB*, 1918 onwards; cf. especially *RB*, 1918, pp. 59ff.
[15] Le Hir, op. cit., pp. 87ff.
[16] See above, p. vii.

tinction between prose which was intended to be read and poetry which was intended to be sung. To the latter was reserved a special nomenclature which leaves no doubt as to the prosodic character of certain passages or books of the Bible.[1] The name of נְגִינוֹת 'musical signs' found alongside that of טְעָמִים 'tastes', to designate the accents, is proof that certain passages were recognised to be rhythmic or to have the character of psalmody.

We do not propose to treat *in extenso* the question of Hebrew prosody, for we must confine ourselves to the Book of Job. But at once a question arises which requires to be first resolved: in what does the metric unit consist?

In our translation the poetic verses have been divided into small short lines which correspond to the 'hemistichs' referred to in our Commentary. This arrangement is the one followed by Ginsburg in his edition of the Hebrew text. It in no way solves the problem posed, but it permits us easily to follow the balancing of the thought between the two hemistichs.

If critics were agreed as to the meaning of their terms, a great step would have been taken towards agreement. But, as will be realised from the reflections of Podechard,[2] such terms as verses, stichs, distichs, tristichs, hemistichs, etc., assume different shades of meaning in the context of each theory. What divides the authors who have written about metrics into two camps is that some take as the basis of the rhythmical scheme what we call the hemistich, that is (in general), the half-verse, while others take as their basis the verse itself composed of two hemistichs (in general).[3] Hence it arises that the 'stich', that is, what we might describe *grosso modo* as the half-verse or member of the parallelism, is identified by some with the 'line', by others with the one half (sometimes one third) of the complete line, which in that case will be a distich (composed of two stichs) or tristich (composed of three stichs).

The reasoning of those authors who identify the line of poetry with the double or the triple stich (that is, the Biblical verse) is derided by Podechard,[4] who, applying it to French verse, points

---

[1] Cf. Parisot, 'Musique des Hébreux', in *Dictionnaire de la Bible*, IV, cols. 1347ff.

[2] *RB*, 1918, pp. 59ff.

[3] On the partisans of the one or the other theory, cf. Podechard, loc. cit., pp. 59ff.

[4] Ibid., pp. 61f.

out that it would lead to the conclusion that a line of poetry must be constituted by a 'symmetrical pair' of lines. The fact is that the supporters of the distich or tristich theory of the line of poetry [1] have insisted too much on the need for symmetry or parallelism in Hebrew poetry. But we do not think Podechard is right when he claims that for the authors whom he is attacking the exigencies of rhyme in French poetry correspond to those of the stich in Hebrew poetry, which would lead to absurdity. There is no parity between the two things. If we want an example of a line of verse which constitutes a unit and yet is composed of a double element, we should look for it in the Latin pentameter. When we write:

Tempora si fuerint | nubila solus eris

we are writing one line only. But this one line includes two essential and inseparable elements. It is certainly a 'distich' [2] and neither stich is a line in itself. Note especially that the caesura is necessary. The rhythm is divided in the middle of the line, and yet the two halves belong together.

In Hebrew we find much the same system of versification. The law of parallelism, although it has not the strictness that is sometimes imputed to it, demands that a second member should balance and complete the first. The members of the parallel together form the line of poetry. They are separated by a caesura, normally indicated by the *athnah* accent ('rest'), whose function corresponds to the cadence preceding the resnmption of the last two dactyls in the pentameter. If we wish to retain only one of these two members as the unit of the metrical system, then we cannot explain the elegiac verse, that of the *qinah* ('lamentation'),[3] the structure of which has long been correctly defined by Budde as consisting of a longer member followed by a shorter one.[4]

Origen, in a text to which Vetter has drawn attention,[5] notes that the Greek translators transformed the Hebrew stich into two stichs: ἰστέον τοίνυν ὅτι οἱ Ἕλληνες οἱ ἑρμηνεύσαντες πεποιήκασι τὸν παρ' Ἑβραίοις στίχον ἐν τοιούτοις δύο.[6] Hence the Jewish tradition,

---

[1] In particular, Condamin and König, quoted ibid., pp. 6of.

[2] Taking the word in the restricted sense usually given to it.

[3] Cf. Condamin, *Le Livre de Jérémie*, p. xxxvii, n. 7.

[4] *ZATW*, 1882, pp. 1ff.; 1883, pp. 299ff.; 1891, pp. 234ff.; 1892, pp. 261ff.

[5] Scholion on Psalm 119 (=118): 1, in the *Analecta Sacra* of Pitra (II, 341); cf. Vetter, *Die Metrik des Buches Job* (1897), p. 2.

[6] This is what explains the difference between the count of the stichometries and the number of verses in the Hebrew Bible; see below, p. cxcix.

which no doubt he is taking as a basis, recognised one line of poetry where the Septuagint counted two stichs. There was nothing repugnant about the combining of two elements for the formation of the metrical unit.

The objection that has been made to the system is that it results in the composition of 'lines that are excessively long and irregular' [1] in cases where a third stich is added to the first two. Here, however, a distinction must be made. The ancient poets did not trouble to confine their poetic flight within the limits of a particular rigid form. If their thought needed a complement, they did not hesitate to add a half-line or stich. But these are exceptional cases. Their system gave rise to a phenomenon similar to that which splits the French alexandrine into two lines of six syllables each, a possibility that brings about combinations of one alexandrine followed by a half-alexandrine:

> Et, rose, elle a vécu ce que vivent les roses,
> L'espace d'un matin.

Thus are to be explained the cases in which the Hebrew line seems to be formed of three hemistichs.[2] The lament of Job, in particular, includes four tristichs (3:4, 5, 6, 9) which originally succeeded each other.[3] The remarkable feature is that the last two hemistichs form a verse or line of poetry which amplifies the first hemistich (half-line):

> Let that day be darkness:
> Let not Eloah from on high regard it, And let not light
> shine upon it!
> May gloom and darkness pollute it:
> May a cloud rest upon it, may fogs terrify it!
> That night, let darkness seize!
> Let it not be added to the days of the year, Or enter
> into the reckoning of the months!
> May the stars of its dawn be dimmed:
> May it hope for light, and find none! And may it not
> see the eyelids of the dawn! (3: 4, 5, 6, 9)

In other cases, it is the first two hemistichs which form the line of poetry and which are echoed in a final half-line:

---

[1] Touzard, *Dictionnaire de la Bible*, III, col. 490: cf. Podechard, *RB*, 1918, pp. 6of.

[2] Catalogue in Gray, Introduction to *The Book of Job* (Driver-Gray), p. lxxvii.

[3] Cf. Comm. on 3: 6 and 3: 9.

> For the arrows of Shaddai are in me, It is their poison
> which my spirit drinks;
> The terrors of Eloah are marshalled against me! (6: 4)

> If a land has been delivered into the hand of a wicked man,
> Then He covers the faces of its judges!
> If it is not He, who then is it? (9: 24)

This phenomenon is very easily explained if we take into account the flexibility of the Semitic genius. The poet begins his line by a hemistich and continues it by a second. But this second hemistich suggests a third which forms the climax of his thought. Let us designate the three hemistichs by A, B, C. As the first line we have had A+B. Then B+C forms a second. But it is unnecessary to repeat B which already figures in succession to A.[1] The result is that we have neither a single line including A+B+C nor two separate lines which would be A+B and B+C but a line and a half, just as we have an alexandrine and a half when the poet writes:

> Mais elle était du monde où les plus belles choses
> Ont le pire destin.

The very rhythm of Semitic poetry demands repetition, an echo. Metrical speech has its origin in song, and song is essentially a social phenomenon. It is necessary to have been present at the processions of the Neby Mousa in Jerusalem, at the rhythmic dances, accompanied by singing, of the Bedouins of Sinai or the fellahin of Palestine, to appreciate how rhythm became irresistible for the Semites. The master of the music strikes up a tune. The chorus repeats it, beating out its rhythm with their hands or by means of the tomtom. Often however the chorus acclaims the *motif* by a single repeated refrain as in Psalm 136, where *kî le'ôlam ḥasdo* stresses each new outburst of the Psalmist. The line of poetry results from the combined action of the singer and the chorus which surrounds him. The caesura marks the pause intervening between the musical phrase and its echo. Among the Babylonians we find similar phenomena. In a hymn to Ishtar [2] the words *usuma šamê* [3] complete the line in the case of lines 9, 10, 11:

---

[1] In the Babylonian poem of the *Descent of Ishtar into Hell* (*Choix de textes*, p. 326) we see the 2nd hemistich (B) explicitly repeated: *pêtû mê | pitâ bâbka | pitâ bâbkama | lurûba anâku* (recto 14-15).

[2] *Choix de textes*, pp. 366ff.

[3] These are the five syllables which are brought out so well by the tomtom.

ardatum Ištar | usuma šamê
ša šukutti šubî šaknat | usuma šamê
talimti Šamaš | usuma šamê [1]

Shall we maintain that *usuma šamê* constitutes in itself a line of verse? Is it not rather the complement of the poetic line, like the second hemistich in the verses of Ps 136? When prosody becomes more individual, it retains from its origins the traces of this doubling of the phrase, of the theme with twin motifs, of which the parallelism of members forms only one aspect.

If the line is thus divided into two hemistichs, each hemistich includes a certain number of tone-syllables. By the very nature of things, a balance is established, except in the case of the elegiac or broken line,[2] between the two parts of the verse. Just as the pentameter requires two feet and a half before the caesura and two feet and a half after it, so the Hebrew line of verse will have in general the same number of accents before and after the caesura. As is the case with the alexandrine, the line is divided into two series of syllables; but these syllables in the Hebrew line are not counted. They are grouped around a few stresses, which naturally stand out as such. It is of course these disjunctive stressed syllables which, by the creation of secondary caesuras,[3] impart to the line its characteristic beat. But often the Massoretes did not feel it essential to have recourse to this technique and were pleased to group into one whole, by means of conjunctive accents, the words of each hemistich.[4] It seems that the essential feature of the verse, rather as in the case of the Latin pentameter, is always the medial caesura. The effect of the latter is to divide the words into groups which are often equal. The normal verse or metrical unit is that

---

[1] The same phenomenon is found in the prayer to the god of fire (*Choix de textes*, p. 370, 1-2), where the first two lines have the same second hemistich *ša ina mâti šaqû*.

[2] See above, p. clxxxii.

[3] Vetter has studied in the Book of Job all the modalities of the caesura. He distinguishes between the main caesura (that in the middle of the verse) and the secondary ones (within each hemistich). His very copious statistics result in the following formula: 'Each verse of the Book of Job contains, when a distich (=2 hemistichs), one main and two secondary caesuras. If a tristich (=3 hemistichs) it counts 5 caesuras, two main and three secondary' (op. cit., pp. 17f.). We, however, think that the tristich verse does not exist. It is a question of one verse or line accompanied by a further hemistich or half-line.

[4] Vetter estimates at 652 the number of hemistichs in which only conjunctive accents are found (op. cit., p. 15).

which contains two hemistichs each of which has three words.[1]

To take this analysis further would be to engage in a discussion, which would be out of place here, on the poetic forms of the Old Testament as a whole.[2] Moreover, we have had the opportunity of expressing our views on this subject in various reviews in the *Revue Biblique*.[3] Father Knabenbauer, in his commentary on the Psalms, had no hesitation in associating himself with the reservations which Father Lagrange and we ourselves have formulated with regard to too great a strictness in the determination of metrical structure.[4] As regards the Book of Job, we can only note the melancholy admission of Budde [5]: 'For the verse of the Book of Job, there is no inviolably fixed structure; at least I must again and always admit that after I have specially concerned myself with this question for almost forty years my understanding of the laws of Hebrew versification does not go far enough to permit me to impose strict rules on the verse which employs it and to use such rules as a criterion for the reconstruction of the text.' [6] If we bear in mind that the verse was originally sung, we shall appreciate that a certain licence was granted to the poet and that, according to circumstances, he was able to lengthen or shorten the normal metre, without however totally disregarding it.

We must approach the strophic system with the same caution as we have felt in regard to the metric system. As early as 1831 Kosters, one of the pioneers in the investigation of the Hebrew strophic system, attempted to arrange Ecclesiastes and the Book of Job in strophes.[1] But it was especially with Merx that the arrangement in

---

[1] According to Ley, quoted by Budde (*Das Buch Hiob*, 2nd ed., p. vii, n. 2), there are 800 verses out of 1,000 which have this feature.

[2] Cf. Grimme, 'Abriss der hebr. Metrik', in *ZDMG*, 1896-7; Sievers, op. cit.; Rothstein, *Grundzüge des hebräischen Rythmus* (1909); Zapletal, *De Poesi Hebraeorum* (1911). For the Psalms very complete bibliography may be found in the Commentary of Knabenbauer (1912), pp. 5ff. After comparing the systems of Grimme, Duhm, and Baethgen, so different from one another, the learned exegete concludes: *Vestigia terrent* (p. 6).

[3] *RB*, 1908, pp. 145f. (Sievers); 1909, pp. 467ff. (Rothstein, Zapletal, König); 1914, p. 304 (Schlögl, Zorell, Euringer), etc.

[4] '*De cantico Ex. 15 adnotat Lagrange*: "As for the metre of each verse, it is the more difficult to determine because the verses do not seem equal" (*RB*, 1899, p. 534); *et de elegia Davidis in mortem Saul et Jonathan similiter monet Dhorme*: "just as much as we must stress the rhythm of the ideas, so must we distrust too severe laws of metre"' (loc. cit., 1908, p. 63).

[5] *Das Buch Hiob* (2nd ed.), p. vii.

[6] What a contrast to the audacity of Bickell, who arranges all the verses of the Book of Job in heptasyllables!

groups of verses began to become common.[2] Each chapter is headed by a 'schema' which enables the reader to see at a glance what principle of division has been adopted. Thus the scheme of ch. 2 is 2 || 666 / 444 / 666 || 2, of chs. 4-5 888 / 77 / 88888, etc. A perusal enables us to register the conclusion that the work consists in cataloguing phenomena rather than in explaining them. The same observation will occur to the mind of any unprejudiced reader when he studies the pages in which Father Hontheim [3] has endeavoured to apply to the Book of Job the principles of Father Zenner.[4] Statistics and synoptic Tables become ever more numerous, but basic and guiding principles do not stand out clearly. The author distinguishes 21 kinds of strophe (p. 292). The lament of Job contains an initial *Vorstrophe*, followed by an initial *Gegenstrophe*, then a *Zwischenstrophe*, followed by the 1st and the 2nd half of the 2nd *Vorstrophe*, the counterpart of which are the 1st and the 2nd half of the 2nd *Gegenstrophe*. The multiplicity of combinations to which this little game leads forms an undeniable proof of the artificial character of the classification adopted.

There are two questions to be distinguished: the existence of strophes and the combination of the strophes with each other.[5] It is certain that groups of verses can be constituted by the style of the passage or its sequence of ideas. The law of parallelism which governs not only two individual hemistichs but often also two or three verses can easily lead to the formation of categories of 4 or 6 hemistichs, sometimes 5 or 7, which present the appearance of a classic strophe.[6] These are successful combinations which every exegete has noticed. For example, if we take 3:3,

> May the day perish in which I was born
> And the night which said: 'A male child has been conceived!'

we then obtain 6 hemistichs (4-5) for the malediction of the day, 6 others (6 and 9; cf. Comm.) for the first malediction of the night, 6 others again (7-8, 10) for the second malediction of the night. And each strophe begins with the typical word: that day... that

---

[1] *Das Buch Hiob und der Prediger Salomos nach ihrer strophischen Anordnung*: cf. Budde, op. cit., p. viii, n. 2.
[2] *Das Gedicht von Hiob* (1871).
[3] *Das Buch Hiob* (1904).
[4] *Chorgesänge im Buche der Psalmen* (1896).
[5] *RB*, 1924, p. 411ff.
[6] *RB*, 1923, p. 447, and 1924, p. 412.

night... yes, that night.... Unfortunately we have here an exceptional case. Furthermore, we have to put aside the first verse before beginning the strophic arrangement.

The repetitions of words on which arguments are based for the division into strophes are too often deceptive, as we have pointed out in a reply to Father Condamin in the *Revue Biblique*.[1] We drew attention to the poem of Elihu (33:15-30), in which the words which illustrate the main idea recur at irregular intervals (vv. 18, 22, 24, 28, 30) with slight variations. The poet does not feel the need to give to his strophes (if, in fact, there are strophes) that uniformity and regularity which it is wished to exact from them by analogy with the techniques of Greek and Latin poets. This point has been well understood by D. H. Müller in his studies on *Komposition und Strophenbau*.[2] If he succeeds in dividing ch. 4 of Job into strophes of 10 and 11 hemistichs, in ch. 6 he finds the series 7, 6, 7, 6, 14, 14, 6. A comparison with the division of Merx[3] makes quite clear the subjectivity of these arrangements.[4] With all the more reason we must object to the artifices thanks to which ingenious exegetes such as Bickell and Duhm have transformed into quatrains the whole of the poetic part of the Book of Job. The number of verses which have to be sacrificed to the theory[5] is sufficient to expose its artificial and illusory character. Basically the classification which would be most akin to the verses and hemistichs of Hebrew poetry would be that resting on *laisses* or *couplets* of unequal length, such as we find in the *Chansons de Geste*.[6] In the uncertainty in which we most often are, through lack of the regular use of assonance, in the consequent impossibility of determining the conclusion of one series of hemistichs, and the start of the next, we have given up our original arrangement, which classified into strophes or periods of equal length the verses of the Book of Job. In the course of our

---

[1] *RB*, 1924, p. 413.

[2] In his *Biblische Studien*, III (1907), pp. 79ff.

[3] See above, p. clxxxvii.

[4] It is sufficient to re-read the chapter of D. H. Müller, 'Zur Geschichte und Kritik meiner Strophentheorie' (op. cit., pp. 88ff.), in order to realise the difficulty of bringing into agreement the builders of strophes. Since König (1900), Sievers (1901), Cobb (1905), who are refuted by Müller, many others have arisen to dispute the laws of the *responsio*, as of the *concatenatio* and *inclusio*.

[5] It is easy to realise this by glancing at the many quotations of Bickell which are scattered throughout the translation of Loisy.

[6] *RB*, 1924, pp. 417f.

work, we were compelled, again and again, to modify the arrangement which we had earlier adopted. As in the case of Penelope's
web, we undid during the night what we had done during the day.
That is why we have resigned ourselves to inscribing the hemistichs
the one beneath the other, in Hebrew fashion, without attempting
to compel them to fit into too rigid a framework.

As for the primitive phenomena of alliteration, assonance, and
rhyme, such techniques belong to the most rudimentary and natural
devices of poetry. In 6:16, 25, it seemed to us that alliteration,
together with assonance, had brought about a change of consonant
in יִתְעַלֶּם and נִמְרְצוּ.[1] Often an effect of the law of parallelism is to
produce rhymes between the hemistichs or the verses.[2] Very
remarkable is the long example [3] of 10:8-18, where the rhymes in
nî and in *î* continue at first for 10 hemistichs (8-12) and then for
12 hemistichs (14-18). Only v. 13 is excluded. Rhyme is found in
other passages also,[4] and even counter-rhyme, which rhymes the
first word of the 2nd hemistich with the last word of the 1st.
More or less consciously, the poet feels himself led to multiply
certain sounds which express the same movements of feeling or the
same ideas. Throughout the O.T. we meet such elementary manifestations of the instinct for prosody, which elude all rigorous
classification.

[1] Cf. Comm. on 6: 16, 25.
[2] For example in Assyrian and Babylonian poetry.
[3] Quoted by Vigouroux in the article 'Poésie hébraïque' of the *Dictionnaire
de la Bible*, V, col. 479.
[4] Cf. Vetter, op. cit., pp. 14f.

CHAPTER TWELVE

TEXT AND VERSIONS

1. THE MASSORETIC TEXT

STATE OF THE TEXT.—All those who have been concerned with
the Hebrew text of the Book of Job have encountered certain
difficulties which can only be attributed to the corrupt state of the
text. Even the translation of the Bible 'by the members of the
group of French Rabbis' [1] admits that some passages are ambiguous,
obscure, and almost impossible to interpret. And yet this translation
is based on the work of the masters of Jewish exegesis, in particular
of Rashi and Ibn Ezra. Already in the eighteenth century, Houbigant, pursuing the path opened up by Louis and Jean Cappel, did
not hesitate to recognise textual errors and to propose corrections,
some of which have been adopted by modern critics. [2] The excellent
work of Georg Beer, entitled *Der Text des Buches Hiob* [3] does not
scorn to use hypotheses put forward by the learned Oratorian.

Merx has merely systematised procedures that were already
known, conceding to the Septuagint and above all to the Peshitta
an exaggerated value. This confidence in the versions is made worse
by a confidence no less great in metric and strophic systems, the
application of which in the sphere of textual criticism produces the
most regrettable results. Merx however did maintain a certain degree
of caution in the use of metre and strophe. But Bickell was unable to
restrain himself in this direction. For him the Massoretic text became
a subject of experiment and was made to conform to all the requirements of a preconceived system. The differences between what are
known as Bickell 1 and Bickell 2, in the characterisation of his first [4]

---

[1]   Under the direction of Zadoc Kahn.
[2]   Budde is mistaken when he imagines that the textual criticism of the
Book of Job was inaugurated by Merx (1871): *Das Buch Hiob* (2nd ed.),
p. lvi.
[3]   Marburg, 1897.
[4]   *Carmina V.T. Metrice* (1882) and *Dichtungen der Hebräer*, II (1882).
It is this first edition which influenced Loisy's *Le Livre de Job*: 'The boldest
and at the same time the most fruitful attempt which has yet been made
for the correction of the Massoretic text of Job seems to be that of a Catholic

and second[1] editions of the Book of Job, constitute a decisive proof of the weakness of the system and of the unwisdom of using it for the correction of the Hebrew text.[2]

In reality it is not the poetic framework, the more or less regular disposition of the lines, which can best serve to restore for us the original text. Prosody was the same for authors and readers, for writers and copyists. Had it possessed the rigour which Bickell and others[3] impute to it, it would have been a vigilant guardian of the original readings: rhythm imposed itself on the ear, lines with precisely numbered syllables engrave themselves more easily than free and flexible prose on the memory of those who read, especially when, as is the case with the Semites, it is a question of reading aloud or in fact chanting. The prosody which it is proposed to use for the restoration of the text would in truth have prevented the latter from becoming subject to the process of corruption. It may well suggest the line of demarcation between verses and hemistichs, but in the body of a sentence it cannot substitute one word for another. It is by other means that we shall attempt to rectify the text in those cases where it is evidently corrupt.

If the Septuagint, which represents the oldest version of the Hebrew, were a faithful reflection of the original text, it would be enough to compare it with the Massoretic text and to modify the latter by that which the Greek version presupposes. We shall see that unfortunately however, as far as the Book of Job is concerned, the Alexandrian version is one of the most imperfect. Not only does it abound in errors which we shall catalogue[4] but it represents a text which has been shortened at pleasure,[5] as if the translator was in a hurry to finish. Quite often it is an explanation *ad usum Graecorum* rather than a literal interpretation of the Hebrew.

This does not mean to say that the Septuagint is devoid of value

---

exegete, Dr. G. Bickell, who was well prepared for this work by his studies on the ryhthm of Hebrew poetry' (p. 6). Loisy refers to his own appreciation of Bickell in his *Histoire critique du texte et des versions de la Bible*. The few reservations with regard to Bickell's system (pp. 202ff.) would certainly have been emphasised if Loisy had foreseen the palinode of Bickell's 2nd edition.

[1] Prepared in 'Kritische Bearbeitung des Jobdialogs' (*WZKM*, 1892-4) and published in a German translation in *Das Buch Job* (1894).

[2] In spite of the efforts of Ley, Ball, Duhm (cf. *RB*, 1923, pp. 446f.).

[3] In particular Sievers: cf. *RB*, 1908, pp. 145f.

[4] See below, pp. cxcviif.

[5] See below, pp. cciif.

for textual criticism. We shall often have the fortune to find
beneath its Greek attire the original Hebrew which will enable us
to reconstruct the original reading. The other Greek versions, those
of Aquila, of Symmachus, and of Theodotion, the Vulgate or Latin
version, and the Syriac version, the Peshitta, and also the Aramaic
interpretation of the Targum, although they are based on a text
which is perceptibly the same as the Massoretic text, do not fail
however to furnish here and there some improvement of the latter.
A glance at the notes placed beneath our translation and at the
short critical apparatus with which we have prefaced the Commentary on each verse will suffice to prove how precious has been the
help furnished us by the ancient translations. Sometimes it is the
case, however, that conjecture alone can enlighten us as to the
original state of a notoriously corrupt passage. Often we have felt
compelled to set out a whole string of hypotheses, none of which
seemed satisfactory. The most convincing, of course, are those which
can best explain how the corruption has come about, and which
remain most closely in contact with the Massoretic text. Far be it
from us to yield to the attractions of arbitrary corrections [1] which
swiftly lead to an avalanche.

MASSORETIC TEXT.—Hebrew tradition itself recognised that the
last word was not said with the work of the Massoretes. The divergences between the Oriental schools (Babylonian) and the Western
(Palestinian) had been noted [2] both in the case of distinct readings
(14:15; 19:24; 21:14; 22:17; 32:11; 39:15) where one or the other
version [3] contained a *qerê* and a *kethîb* (2:7; 5:5; 6:21; 10:17;
17:10; 22:24; 23:8, 13; 24:4; 26:12; 27:15; 30:13; 31:7; 34:14;
37:19; 40:22; 41:2; 41:4). The number of texts in which variations
between *qerê* and *kethîb* are concerned is 54.[4] Other hesitations are
seen in the divergences of vocalisation or accentuation between
Ben-Asher and Ben-Naphtali.[5]

The Massoretes were well aware of sources of errors. In 7 instances
they have used the indication *paseq*, either to avoid haplography
(7:20; 27:13; 40:9) or to prevent possible confusion between

---

[1] Such as one finds in Georg Richter, *Erläuterungen zu dunkeln Stellen
im Buche Hiob* (cf. *RB*, 1914, pp. 127ff.); Torczyner, *Das Buch Hiob* (1920);
Ball, *The Book of Job* (cf. *RB*, 1923, pp. 446ff.).

[2] Cf. S. Baer, *Liber Jobi*, pp. 56ff.

[3] Especially the Western.

[4] Cf. the list of Baer, op. cit., pp. 69ff. and p. 72.

[5] Ibid., pp. 59ff.

parallel passages (27:9 and 35:13; 38:1 and 40:9). Anomalies have been catalogued and scrupulously respected.[1] Those passages where similarity might create confusion have been carefully juxtaposed to draw attention to the matter.[2]

Before this work the object of which was to mummify the text, certain modifications had taken place which it will not be useless to point out.[3] Some of these were made deliberately with the object of removing what might shock the ears of the pious. Tradition preserved the memory of 'scribal corrections' (תקון סופרים),[4] two of which are found in the Book of Job: a change of suffix in 7:20 and a replacement of אלהים by איוב in 32:3. Sometimes a conjecture (סביר) rectifies the text (9:24).

More often than not these deliberate changes have become firmly established and it is only by comparison with the versions or by conjecture [5] that we are able to surmise what the original text was. Four times in the Prologue (1:5, 10; 2:5, 9), the association of the divine name with an obnoxious term has been avoided by a modification of the verb. Or else it is the substitution of a suffix or a pronoun for another one which does away with the offensive expression (9:19; 34:6).

The scribes' respect for the canonical books of Scripture did not permit the multiplication of these changes which were due to theological scruple. Hence most of the variations of the text are to be ascribed to accidents, such as are unavoidable in every oral or manuscript tradition. We may classify them under a certain number of headings.[6]

TRANSPOSITIONS.—Sometimes it is a whole passage which as a result of a mistake in the arrangement of pages or columns has been transferred to a context where it is no longer in place. We have noted this phenomenon in 24:18-24; 26:1-4; 29:21-5; 31:33-7.[7] Or else it is a verse which has been misplaced: 3:9, 16; 5:1; 12:11,

---

[1]   Ibid., p. 64 and p. 71.

[2]   Ibid., p. 66.

[3]   The justification of corrections will be found in the Commentary. We choose only the most characteristic cases.

[4]   Cf. Ginsburg, *Intro. to the Hebrew Bible*, pp. 347ff.

[5]   For details see Commentary.

[6]   It will be easy to recognise, in the verses quoted, with what words the reference is concerned.

[7]   Nothing authorises the game played by Torczyner and Buttenwieser in regard to the verses of the Book of Job which are scattered in every direction to satisfy the logic of these exegetes.

12; 13:28; 20:10, 28; 24:9, 13; 34:23, 24; 36:29, 30. Again, a hemistich may have lost its original position: 4:21a; 9:35b; 14:14a; 24:14c; 33:26a. More usual is the transposition of isolated words: 9:24; 24:5, 19; 29:5-6, 21; 30:12; 33:17, 19-20; 34:20, 23, 26-7, 31; 36:5; 38:10; 39:10; 40:22. Or there may be a simple transposition of letters in one word or from one word to another: 10:20; 13:15; 14:19; 18:7; 19:26, 28; 20:19; 24:21; 27:6; 30:11; 33:10; 34:29; 40:19, 14; 41:5.

WRONG DIVISIONS.—It has occasionally happened that before the words were carefully separated from each other the consonants of the text have been wrongly distributed, and this has caused strange associations in the elements composing a sentence. We think we can draw attention to a few of these accidents: 6:13; 9:19; 11:6; 12:8; 24:14; 27:8; 28:4; 30:17; 31:23; 34:31; 35:3; 36:33; 37:13; 38:11; 41:4, 17.

Sometimes it is as between one clause and another that a wrong division has been made. One or two words are then joined to the proposition preceding or following the one to which they ought logically to belong: 15:23-4, 31-2; 26:5.

MATRES LECTIONIS.—The character of the *matres lectionis* (consonants doing duty as vowels) caused them for a long time to be neglected by the scribes.[1] There was for long hesitation between the one or the other of these consonants, and the result has been somewhat regrettable confusion, especially as regards the ׳ and the ׳ which mark pronominal suffixes. Hence transformations of the 1st to the 3rd person (6:21) and above all of the 3rd to the 1st (14:3; 19:28; 23:14; 41:3). At other times it is the א which has been interchanged with ׳ or ׳ (6:21; 10:8; 11:11; 23:9; 27:19; 30:24; 41:3).

OMISSIONS.—These are usually a question of either haplography or homoeoteleuton. Sometimes it is a word which has vanished from the text: 7:4; 16:5, 20; 18:3; 20:25; 24:2; 26:5; 30:3, 20; 33:22, 24; 37:12; 38:8; 40:24. Or a letter may have fallen out of a word: 5:5; 6:7, 13; 8:14; 11:8; 15:30, 31; 16:20, 21; 17:4, 16; 18:12; 21:8, 16; 22:11, 18, 30; 23:6, 7, 9, 10; 24:12; 28:12; 29:18; 30:8, 24; 32:14; 34:6, 23, 25; 35:3, 10, 15; 36:8, 13, 33; 37:4, 7; 38:14, 27; 41:2, 21.

---

[1] Cf. Ginsburg, op. cit., pp. 137ff.

ADDITIONS.—These are sometimes a matter of dittography or explanatory glosses. Sometimes it is a word, rarely several words, which have the effect of overloading the phrase: 12:7, 24; 13:14; 15:30; 19:20; 20:26; 22:29; 23:13, 17; 24:1; 34:14; 36:16, 17; 37:6; 39:1, 10; 40:15; 42:3, 4. Sometimes it is a letter which has by mischance slipped into a word: 8:19; 14:6, 12; 15:32; 17:12; 24:2, 16; 25:5; 26:9, 13; 27:13; 30:18; 33:7, 24, 25; 34:32; 39:30; 41:3, 6, 7, 12.

CHANGES OF CONSONANTS.—It is possible that the resemblance between certain consonants has brought about the substitution of the one for the other.[1] The confusion of ד and ר is classic: 10:8; 19:20; 36:30; 38:24. That between ב and כ is no less frequent: 20:18; 21:12, 13; 22:24; 28:27; 29:25; 34:36. We may note a few cases where ה and ת have been mistaken for each other: 8:3; 11:14; 17:2. Interchange of נ and מ: 12:23; 21:24; 22:17, 20; and of ד and ע: 28:13; 36:7. The passage from one consonant to another may have been caused by a mistake in hearing: thus in permutations between ב and פ: 14:18; 26:8; 28:11; between כ and ח: 16:4; between ד and ז: 36:31; between ו and צ: 30:13; between ת and ד: 15:31.

VOCALISATION.—It was especially in regard to vocalisation that the hesitations of the Massoretes were most clearly to be seen, as is easy to note if we compare the *qerê* and the *kethîb*. Hence it is no matter of surprise if sometimes it is found necessary to modify this vocalisation in order to discover the meaning of the original text. On an average, mistakes are hardly two per chapter, as can be realised from the following list: 1:18; 3:5, 6; 5:5, 7, 15; 6:18; 8:21; 9:15, 17, 19, 31; 10:17; 11:2, 17, 18; 12:18; 14:12; 15:23, 24; 16:7, 8, 9; 17:3, 6, 7, 16; 18:13; 19:11; 20:18, 22, 23, 25, 28; 21:13, 24; 22:21, 24; 24:9, 11, 13, 18, 22, 23, 24; 26:9, 10; 28:11; 29:3, 25; 30:13; 31:18, 32, 34; 32:4, 19; 33:3, 16; 34:13, 18, 37; 36:18, 21, 27, 32; 37:6, 10, 23; 39:13, 21; 40:2, 19; 41:10.

RESULTS.—The statistics listed above are not alarming. It must first be remembered that amendments to the text are hypothetical in character and hence do not warrant the inference of any absolute conclusion. But above all it will not be forgotten that the Book of

[1] We indicate the confusions which have been produced in both directions, for example from the *resh* to the *daleth* and from the *daleth* to the *resh*.

Job contains 1,069 verses.[1] It will easily be appreciated that in a work of this extent errors in copying or writing down may seem numerous, although by comparison with the size of the book they are not really frequent. It would therefore be quite unjustifiable to yield to that 'strong suspicion' which according to Budde [2] seems to prevail among modern critics in regard to the Massoretic text of the Book of Job.

2. THE SEPTUAGINT

DATE.—The date of the Greek version of the Book of Job can be roughly determined, at least as regards the *terminus ad quem*, owing to the use of this translation by the historian Aristeas. We have seen that Aristeas knew the appendix peculiar to the Septuagint.[3] Now, this author is already cited by Alexander Polyhistor (80-40 B.C.), whose work is the source of Eusebius.[4] Hence we know quite certainly that the text of the Septuagint was in circulation about the year 100 B.C. If we had here a faithful and literal translation of the type of that of Aquila, we should find in it an incomparable witness for the reconstruction of the pre-Massoretic text.

CHARACTER.—Unfortunately this is not so. As has been recognised with considerable perspicacity,[5] the author of this version of the Book of Job was an Alexandrian Hellenist writing for a wide circle of readers and not for the purposes of the Synagogue. We find in his translation sacrifices to Graecism (4:2; 31:31; 38:12) which introduce into the sacred text the mention of Hades (33:22) and the Horn of Amalthea (42:14) which made Theodore of Mopsuestia so indignant.[6]

More often than not, instead of a literal translation, we encounter a paraphrase or explanation (1:22; 2:2, 11, 12; 3:16; 5:18; 6:5-7, 9, 16, 18, 21, 22-3; 7:9, 20; 8:21, 22; 9:21, 23; 10:14, 22; 11:2, 18; 12:24; 14:17; 16:6, 7, 9; 17:15; 18:2, 4, 14, 19; 20:15, 18; 21:17; 22:25, 27; 23:7, 19; 24:6, 23, 24; 26:2; 27:3, 6, 7, 10, 13, 14; 28:24; 29:6, 22, 23; 30:19, 23, 25, 30; 31:14, 16, 27, 35; 32:21;

---

[1] Ginsburg, op. cit., p. 102.
[2] *Das Buch Hiob*, 2nd ed., p. lvi.
[3] Above, p. xviii.
[4] *Praep. evang.*, IX, 25 (P.G. XXI, col. 728).
[5] Cf. Swete, *An Introduction to the O.T. in Greek*, p. 256.
[6] P.G. LXVI, cols. 697f. Cf. above, pp. xixf.

33:25; 34:12, 27; 37:7, 15, 21, 22; 38:30, 36, 41; 39:26; 41:17; 42:3, 9) or a vague translation (3:6, 9, 23, 24; 4:14, 20; 5:1, 10; 6:4, 6, 15; 28:1-2; 38:18-19; 40:21-2; 41:10).

Harmonisation plays its part in the manner of interpreting certain verses: 32:1; 35:4, 11; 37:24; 42:10-11.

Theological speculation or theological scruples make their influence felt in the translations given of certain words or turns of phrase: 1:6, 16; 2:1, 3, 5, 9; 5:1, 5; 10:3, 13; 13:3; 14:14; 20:29; 21:14, 15; 23:8; 24:4; 38:7; 40:8. In certain passages the concern is chiefly to avoid anthropomorphism: 4:9; 10:16-17; 13:8, 23; 14:3, 13; 20:15; 21:20; 22:26; 23:12; 26:13; 31:6, 15; 34:21; 36:2; 42:7.

The translator also takes a certain liberty in the use or the suppression of metaphors and comparisons: 3:9; 6:16, 18; 13:27; 17:14; 20:21; 28:2; 40:18.

LICENCE.—We should also note the passages where a common noun takes the place of a proper noun (1:15, 17; 3:8; 9:13; 26:12), where concrete and abstract terms are interchanged (8:14; 15:21; 24:10, 13; 27:4; 28:4; 31:5), where there is interchange between singular and plural (16:13-14; 18:5, 8; 19:20, 22; 21:14; 22:7; 29:15; 32:10), between various persons of the pronoun or verb (16:15; 17:6; 23:2, 4; 29:7; 34:37; 36:23; 37:1, 15; 38:12, 20, 23; 41:2), between various parts of the body, or between words of different meaning (16:15, 16; 21:5; 22:10; 27:4, 16; 29:13; 35:13; 40:6, 17).

More serious are those cases in which the negative is suppressed (9:13; 10:2; 13:20; 31:31; 35:13) or added (9:21; 10:18; 11:4; 20:24; 21:2, 3, 22; 36:4).

ERRORS.—An incorrect reading or a failure to understand the Hebrew text occasions wrong meanings and confusions which are regrettable: 3:3, 14; 4:19; 5:6; 6:4, 7, 10, 13, 17, 18, 19, 20; 6:26, 29; 7:3, 5, 21; 8:6, 18, 20; 9:14, 27, 29; 11:3, 6, 10, 15, 17; 12:18; 13:9, 12, 13, 15; 14:2; 15:11; 17:1, 2, 7; 18:7; 19:3, 7, 17, 18, 25, 27; 20:2, 6, 7, 25, 26, 28; 21:8, 10, 11, 22; 22:21; 23:2, 17; 24:6, 11, 12, 13; 26:13; 29:5, 7, 11, 18; 30:13, 14, 21, 24; 31:8, 10, 11, 12, 19, 21, 23, 30, 31, 37; 32:13, 19, 22; 33:4, 12-13, 17, 23-4, 27; 34:17-18, 20; 35:10; 36:3, 10, 12-13, 15, 17-18, 22; 37:15, 16, 20, 22, 23; 38:2, 14, 17, 24; 39:10; 40:11, 20, 31; 41:1.

Other errors are due to changes in the vocalisation which was

traditional and which was later fixed by the Massoretes: 4:5, 17;
5:22, 24, 27; 6:25, 29; 8:21; 9:19, 31, 33; 10:8; 12:25; 13:16;
18:12, 13; 25:2.

Sometimes it is a question of words whose position has been
inverted with the effect of creating new meanings: 2:11; 7:1, 13;
8:17; 9:35; 11:17, 20; 15:33; 19:16; 22:8; 30:23. The anticipation
of a word in a preceding phrase is also an element of confusion:
19:3, 23; 24:11; 24:18; 32:19.

Wrong divisions in the clauses are also not uncommon: 3:5, 9,
22-3; 6:17; 7:5; 8:2; 10:2; 13:8; 20:25; 22:12, 25; 23:10-11;
28:24-5; 31:9, 26, 38-9; 31:37-32:1; 32:13-14; 34:12-13, 17-18;
36:3-5; 37:22-3; 39:21-2.

REDUNDANCIES.—The translation is often overloaded with
doublets, repetitions, redundancies: 1:1, 3, 4, 5; 2:3; 3:17; 4:12;
5:9, 26; 7:5; 9:3, 10; 10:4; 13:22; 19:13; 21:22; 22:17; 23:14-15;
24:10, 13, 20-1; 27:18; 30:8; 33:5-6, 23; 34:19; 37:20; 38:1;
39:19-20, 21; 42:6, 10, 12. Dittography in 13:7.

Sometimes we find long additions to the text. In addition to those
which we have studied above [1] and which are veritable *midrash*,
there are others which are quite appreciable (1:5, 21, 22; 2:8, 10;
7:2; 38:1). To this category belong the many passages which have
been added [2] on the basis of some other context of the Book of
Job or some other book of the Old Testament: 4:21; 5:21; 7:16;
9:7, 33; 10:13; 11:3, 9, 10, 12, 16, 20; 13:2; 14:5; 15:15, 35;
16:16; 17:1; 18:19; 19:4; 20:24; 22:2, 28; 24:14, 19, 20; 25:4;
30:4, 26; 31:29, 34; 32:17; 33:5, 23; 33:31-3; 34:13, 23, 24;
36:5, 15, 17, 28; 40:19; 41:25. These are reminiscences which
have crept into such or such a manuscript, sometimes in the course
of the translation itself.

Certain slight additions are aimed at making the text more lucid
or flowing: 1:1, 8, 13, 14, 16, 17, 19, 20; 2:6, 10, 11; 4:16; 5:4, 8,
15, 20, 27; 6:15, 21; 7:16, 19; 8:12, 19; 9:22, 32; 11:19; 12:17, 19;
13:6, 10, 12, 15, 16, 25; 15:22, 28, 33; 16:18; 20:5; 23:6; 29:12;
31:26; 32:2; 33:5; 34:15; 38:17; 40:29, 32; 42:5, 10.

OMISSIONS.—In the section which follows we shall study those
suppressions which have appreciably shortened the original text
of the Septuagint by comparison with the Hebrew text. It is a

---

[1] Pp. xviiff.
[2] Sometimes in a single MS (see Comm.).

question of hemistichs, verses, whole passages, which have thus disappeared from the Greek version.

For the moment, let us note a certain tendency to shorten the text in the interpretation: 6:28; 12:5; 13:23; 18:11b-12a; 19:17, 26; 21:7, 27; 28:4, 13, 25; 29:8, 14; 30:2-6; 31:33, 36; 32:16-17; 33:8-9; 34:2, 22; 38:37; 39:23; 40:12, 14.

Hence arise a few slight omissions, which are sometimes noticeable side by side with redundancies and contribute to lend to the interpretation quite a different aspect from that of the original: 1:3, 5, 15, 18; 2:3, 11, 13; 3:5; 5:11, 15, 26; 6:14, 17; 7:15-16; 8:17; 9:16, 22, 25, 26; 10:5, 15; 11:4, 5; 12:10, 21, 24; 13:1, 13, 20; 14:12, 21-2; 15:21; 18:3; 19:3, 4-5, 9, 15, 19; 21:8, 10, 19; 22:12, 17; 23:7, 11; 24:1; 27:5, 18; 30:17, 30; 31:10; 32:14; 33:1, 14; 34:14; 35:11; 39:20, 22; 40:5, 15.

THE LACUNAE OF THE SEPTUAGINT. — Any one who compared the present text of the Greek version with the Massoretic text would hardly notice any difference between the length of the former and that of the latter. We have seen [1] that the Hebrew text consists of 1,069 verses. The great Greek MSS number 2,153 'stichs' (Vaticanus), 2,126 (Sinaiticus), 2,021 (Alexandrinus).[2] If we reckon each verse as consisting of two stichs on an average, we see that the discrepancy is not considerable. Yet the original text of the Septuagint was appreciably shorter. We know this from Origen, who says categorically [3]: πάλιν τε αὖ πλεῖστά τε ὅσα διὰ μέσου ὅλου τοῦ Ἰὼβ παρ' Ἑβραίοις μὲν κεῖται, παρ' ἡμῖν δὲ οὐχί, καὶ πολλάκις μὲν ἔπη τέσσαρα ἢ τρία· ἔσθ' ὅτε δὲ καὶ δεκατέσσερα καὶ δεκαεννέα καὶ δεκαέξ.[4] The testimony of St Jerome is no less explicit. These are the terms in which he offered to Paula and Eustochium his translation of the Septuagint not in accordance with the curtailed text but in accordance with the edition as revised and augmented by Origen: *ac beatum Job qui adhuc apud Latinos jacebat in stercore,*

---

[1]   Above, p. cxcvi.
[2]   Swete, *The O.T. in Greek*, II, at the end of Ἰώβ.
[3]   Letter to Julius Africanus, par. 4.
[4]   The last word is doubtful. Various corrections have been proposed: ἐννέα καὶ ἕξ (Nestle, Swete, *Intro. to the O.T. in Greek*); καὶ ἑξῆς (Klostermann, *Realencyklopädie*, 3rd ed., VIII, p. 100). The anomaly is removed in the Latin translation of Martianay which it may be useful to quote: *rursum plurima per medium totum Jobum apud Hebraeos posita reperiuntur; non item apud nos. Et saepe quidem quatuor vel tres versus, interdum et quatuordecim, et sedecim, et novemdecim* (P.L. XXIX, col. 60).

et vermibus scatebat errorum, integrum, immaculatumque gaudete.[1]
The same Doctor declares, in his Preface to the translation of Job
on the basis of the Hebrew: *coeterum, apud Latinos, ante eam
translationem, quam sub asteriscis et obelis nuper edidimus,*[2] *septin-
genti ferme aut octingenti versus desunt*: *ut decurtatus et laceratus
corrosusque liber, foeditatem sui publice legentibus praebeat.*[3]

Origen filled the gaps in the original text by having recourse to
the version of Theodotion. The asterisks placed before certain
stichs enabled the reader to identify passages where the translation
was no longer that of the Septuagint. The ancient stichometric
catalogues took this fact into account. Thus in the catalogue attributed to Nicephorus and in the so-called Canon of Mommsen,
the Book of Job included only 1,800 stichs, in the Latin MSS used
by Martianay and Thomasius only 1,700 stichs, in the *Catal. Claromontanus* only 1,600 stichs.[4] A few Greek MSS [5] confirm the number
1,600. Let us note especially the valuable indication of Cod. 161
(Holmes-Parsons) which counts 1,600 stichs without the asterisks,
but 2,200 with the asterisks. The number 2,200 is near that given
by the great uncials which offered the total text. Thus the number
of stichs absent from the original Greek version was estimated at
about 600. St Jerome is exaggerating in counting 700 or 800.

Thus the text of the Septuagint is an amalgam of the first Greek
translation and that of Theodotion. Origen was careful to indicate,
following his usual procedure, the additions to the original text.
In most cases the asterisks have been omitted by the copyists.
The contribution of Theodotion would be difficult to assess were it
not that, fortunately, two Greek MSS and two MSS of the first
version of Jerome, and especially the famous Syro-hexaplar, had
preserved the diacritical signs. To these positive witnesses is
added a negative one, namely the Sahidic version, the characteristic
of which is to omit the passages due to Theodotion.

The two Greek MSS are the Colbertinus [6] and the Cod. 248

---

[1]   Preface addressed to Paula and Eustochium (P.L. XXIX, cols. 61f.).
[2]   Allusion to the first translation which Jerome had made in accord with
the complete Greek text (above).
[3]   P.L. XXVIII, col. 1080.
[4]   See the list drawn up by Zahn in *Geschichte des N.T. Kanons*, II, i,
pp. 394-5.
[5]   Klostermann, loc. cit., p. 101.
[6]   On this MS (no. 1952), cf. Field, *Origenis Hexaplorum quae Supersunt*,
II, p. i.

(Holmes-Parsons = Rome, Vat. Gr. 346),[1] which contain not only
the asterisks and the obeli but also the attribution of stichs to
hexaplar authors. In regard to the Latin version, the two MSS with
obeli and asterisks are that of Oxford (Bodleian 2426) and that of
Tours (Turonensis 18) edited by P. de Lagarde.[2] The Syro-hexaplar
is known from the magnificent edition of Mgr Ceriani in facsimile.[3]
Besides the diacritic signs, it marks the attributions to Theodotion.
Finally, the Sahidic version has been edited in masterly fashion by
Father Ciasca.[4] We shall return to these MSS and texts when we
come to deal with the Greek manuscripts,[5] the version of Jerome,[6]
and the Coptic versions.[7] It is solely as witnesses to the lacunae in
the Septuagint that we are using them at the moment.

If there prevailed perfect agreement between these various testimonies, it would be easy for us to assess what is lacking to the
Septuagint and to draw up a list of the passages omitted. But this
is not the case. For example, one of the most accurate of the MSS,
the Syro-hexaplar, has the asterisk instead of the obelus in 2:10;
forgets the asterisk in 15:26b-27; 21:21-23; 24:15a; 34:11b;
37:21b; places the asterisk wrongly in 22:20b; 23:9b. The recension
of Jerome uses the asterisk wrongly in 2:13; 3:6; 5:22; 7:11; 10:1;
14:5; 18:10a; 22:28b; 34:26-7; 41:8b. It omits it where we should
expect it in 31:4; 37:21b.

A collation of the witnesses, however, enables us to arrive at a
positive result and to establish with almost complete certainty the
additions to the text of the Septuagint. But a new difficulty arises
when we compare the passages thus determined with those which
are lacking in the Sahidic version.

It had been supposed, and this was the thesis of Ciasca, followed
by Bickell, that this Sahidic version, lacking the passages added by
Origen on the basis of Theodotion, represented the original text of
the Septuagint.[8] But the fact is that certain passages, which, in
accordance with the witnesses as a whole and even according to style,

---

[1]   Cf. ibid., p. 2.
[2]   *Mittheilungen*, II, pp. 193ff.
[3]   Below, p. ccviii.
[4]   Below, p. ccx.
[5]   Below, pp. cciiiff.
[6]   Below, pp. ccviff.
[7]   Below, pp. ccixff.
[8]   The fact that this version contains the notorious additions of the Septuagint in 2:9 and 42:17 proves that the text used by the Sahidic translator was already a Greek text far removed from the Hebrew.

would appear to belong to Theodotion, nevertheless have a place in the Sahidic version. Thus 9:15b of the Septuagint certainly comes from Theodotion, as is attested by the Greek, Latin, and Syriac traditions.[1] But it is found in the Sahidic version (9:14). The latter again contains 17:16b; 20:3-4a; 25:6b, which likewise belong to Theodotion.[2] Hence we cannot do otherwise than associate ourselves with the reservations of Burkitt [3] as regards the pre-hexaplar character of the Sahidic version. The fact which seems to us undeniable is that the Coptic translator has deliberately omitted the stichs marked by asterisk. In a few cases his perspicacity has failed him.

If we combine the data of the Sahidic version with those of the Syro-hexaplar, the two Greek MSS, and the two Latin MSS, we can gain a clear and exact idea of the lacunae of the Septuagint. Our statistics, which are independent of those of Ciasca [4] and of Gray,[5] yield the following results: 1:15b; 2:1 (in part); 3:2, 16 (in part); 5:23a; 7:8; 9:15b, 24 (in part); 10:4a; 11:5b; 12:3b, c, 4, 8b-9, 18b, 21a, 23; 13:19b, 20b; 14:12c, 18-19; 15:10, 26b-27; 16:3b, 8, 10a, 21b; 17:3b-5a, 10 (in part), 12; 18:9a, 10, 15-16, 17b, 18b; 19:24a, 28b; 20:2b-4a, 9, 11-13, 14b, 20b, 21a, 23a, 25 (in part); 21:15, 19b, 21, 23, 28-33; 22:3b, 13-16, 20, 24, 29-30; 23:9, 15; 24:4b, 5 (in part), 8a, 14c-18a, 25b; 26:5-11, 14a; 27:19b, 21-3; 28:3b-4, 5-9a, 14-19, 21b-22a, 26b-27a; 29:10-11a, 13a, 19-20, 24b-25; 30:2-4a, 7a, 11-13, 16a, 18b, 20b, 22b, 26b-27a; 31:1-4, 18, 23b-24a, 27a, 35a; 32:4b, 5, 11b-12, 15-16; 33:2, 8a, 19b, 20b, 28-9, 31b-33; 34:3-4, 6b-7, 11b, 18b, 23a, 25b, 28-33; 35:7b-10a, 12a, 15-16; 36:5b-9, 10b-11, 13, 16, 19b, 20, 21b-22a; 37:1-5a, 6b, 7a, 10a, 11-12a, 13, 17 (in part), 18, 21b; 38:26-7, 32; 39:1a, 2b-3a, 3b-4, 6b, 8, 13-18, 28b, 29b; 40:1-2a, 23b-24, 25b; 41:4, 8a, 9, 15b, 18b, 21a, 24 (in part); 42:8b, 16b, 17.

Such are the passages which were omitted in the Septuagint and later added by Origen following Theodotion. A mere glance at the list is sufficient to show that the lacunae are not on the same proportion throughout the whole of the Book of Job. If, as has been roughly estimated,[6] they are in the proportion of 4% as far as

---

[1] For critical notes, see Commentary on the texts quoted.
[2] Vocabulary confirms the attribution made by the MSS or versions of hexaplar origin.
[3] *Encyclopaedia Biblica*, IV, cols. 5027f.
[4] Op. cit., pp. 23ff.   [5] *The Book of Job* (Driver-Gray), pp. lxxiv f.
[6] Gray, op. cit., p. lxxv.

ch. 15, they reach 16% in 15-21; 25% in 22-31, 35% in the speeches of Elihu (32-7), while in the speeches of Yahweh and the Epilogue (38-42) the proportion is 16%. It seems as if the translator has curtailed his text more and more. He has omitted the passages he felt to be unnecessary and shortened those which were too long. He has evaded some difficulties, and one feels that his fatigue increases as he progresses.

What must above all be noted is that the verses or hemistichs which are absent from the Greek version have nothing which differentiates them from the context where they are embedded in the Hebrew. They differ by no peculiarity in the use of the divine names. Not only are these passages not out of place in the Hebrew but their omission entails a disturbance of the sense and rhythm. Gray quite rightly cites as examples: 10:4a; 20:14b; 31:27a; 33:8a; 34:6b, 11b, 18b; 39:6b.

No critic now accepts the hypothesis advanced by Hatch [1] in 1889 according to which the Septuagint version was produced on the basis of an original Hebrew text, of which the present text is only an amplification. Bickell attempts to exploit this thesis in the interests of his strophic theory. He has done so only at the cost of innumerable inconsistencies. The French translation of Loisy generally prints in italics those passages which were lacking in the Septuagint. It is enough to compare them with the context to realise that they are not duplicates and are indispensable. Let us remember that in 1862 Bickell in a study specially devoted to the Greek version of the Book of Job [2] made the following judgment on this version: *Interpretem ea quae in ejus versione deficiunt non ideo omisisse quia in suo textu hebraico, e quo vertit, non haberentur, sed e solo ipsius arbitrio et licentia ejecisse, probatione omnino non egere videtur, praesertim cum perspexerimus, qua libertate etiam in iis quos retinuit, versibus usus sit, et quomodo sententiarum nexus et cohaerentia per has omissiones interrumpatur et deleatur.* [3] At this time 'metric' was not yet rife.

MANUSCRIPTS.—We have seen that the MSS of the Septuagint do not represent a pre-hexaplar text. Their value is none the less very great for the determination of the oldest Greek version. The

---

[1] *Essays on Biblical Greek*, pp. 215ff.
[2] *De indole ac ratione versionis Alexandrinae in interpretando libro Jobi.*
[3] Quotation from Budde, p. lviii.

work of Origen consisted in filling gaps rather than in touching up what existed before him.

But manuscript tradition inevitably entails errors in the text to be copied. Before making use of the version, it is well sometimes to ask one's self whether the Greek itself is not defective. We may point out a few instances where the copyist is wrong: 3:5, 17, 18, 19; 4:6, 12, 16; 7:13, 15, 16; 9:3, 16, 33; 11:12, 13; 12:11; 14:14; 16:10; 17:12; 19:20; 20:7, 10, 18, 19, 23, 25; 21:16, 22, 23, 28; 22:8, 15, 22; 23:4, 5, 17; 24:5, 7, 11, 17, 21, 22; 26:5, 11, 12; 27:12; 28:10; 29:1; 30:1, 4, 21, 28, 31; 31:10, 24; 34:3, 17; 36:16, 31, 30, 33; 38:30; 39:22; 40:22.

Such errors are fairly rare. Often they are found only in an isolated MS.[1] Generally, it is quite easy, thanks to the Hebrew, to recognise what was the Greek word in the original translation.

Among the uncials, it is the Vaticanus (B) which has been least tampered with. It has a certain number of readings peculiar to itself: 2:4; 3:4; 7:11; 9:19; 12:23; 19:24; 24:21; 31:22; 36:30, 31; 37:14; 38:30. A few mistakes by omission: 7:11; 19:24; 27:15; 30:4; 33:33; 35:3; 40:32; 41:1; 42:16. A note in the margin of 20:18 has its source in Origen (cf. Comm.).

The Alexandrinus (A) contains a text which has often been adjusted to the Hebrew. This is why this MS has many readings not found elsewhere.[2] A fact worthy of note is that the corrections of the Sinaiticus frequently coincide with the readings of the Alexandrinus: 1:17; 2:8, 9; 3:18, 19, 21; 7:6; 24:21; 31:17; 35:3; 39:13, 22; 40:22. Variants quoted in the margin of the Syro-hexaplar or of the Colbertinus sometimes represent readings of the Alexandrinus (5:5; 8:10, 21). Many additions [3] more or less considerable and of diverse provenance swell the recension which this MS offers us: 1:6, 21, 22; 2:11; 3:23 (following Theodotion); 5:17, 21; 11:8; 19:29; 21:26; 27:18; 32:11; 33:31b, etc.

The Sinaiticus (‫א‬) has been the object of three revisions which are designated respectively by ‫א‬[c.a], ‫א‬[c.b], ‫א‬[c.c].[4] We have seen above that in several instances the corrections coincided with the readings of the Alexandrinus. One of these readings is quoted in the margin

---

[1] For details, see Commentary.
[2] It is impossible to catalogue all these readings. Those which are of some interest will be found in the Commentary.
[3] Same remark as above.
[4] Cf. Swete, *Intro. to the O.T. in Greek*, p. 131.

of the Sinaiticus (21:26). In general, it is Theodotion who supplies the corrections adopted (26:5; 32:20; 37:17; 38:21).

The Codex Ephraemi rescriptus (C) [1] is often found to be in agreement with the Alexandrinus as against the other uncials (22:8, 14; 27:2, 9; 29:21; 31:22; 32:7; 34:2). It has a few slight omissions (32:17; 35:1).

Among the cursives, we have already cited the Colbertinus and the Codex 248,[2] which are so precious for the recognition of the contribution of Theodotion as regards the additions to the Greek version. The marginal notes of these two MSS are of the very highest importance for the reconstitution of the text of the Hexapla.[3]

We will content ourselves with referring the reader to the Commentary for the use of the other MSS [4]:

Cod. 23 (33:23, 31; 34:3; 35:11).

Cod. 68 (9:7).

Cod. 106 (19:15; 27:15).

Cod. 137 (7:18; 24:25; 30:7, 11-13); cf. Field, vol. ii, p. 2.

Cod. 138 (7:18); cf. ibid.

Cod. 161 (2:5, 8, 9; 4:21; 6:15; 30:4); cf. ibid.

Cod. 249 (2:13; 5:23, 24; 7:8; 19:15; 24:1; 34:2, 26; 35:3; 37:20; 40:15); cf. ibid.

Cod. 250 (6:15); cf. ibid.

Cod. 252 (1:17; 5:18; 18:9, 10; 19:17; 22:2; 34:26); cf. ibid.

Cod. 253 (3:5; 30:4; 35:11).

Cod. 254 (5:17; 9:7; 21:14).

Cod. 255 (1:21; 2:9, 13; 16:8; 19:12; 29:10-11; 30:11-13; 31:17); cf. ibid.

Cod. 256 (3:5); cf. ibid.

Cod. 258 (2:7, 13); cf. ibid.

Cod. 264 (19:15).

MS 36 of the treasury of Sainte-Croix in the library of the Orthodox Patriarchate in Jerusalem has been the object of a special study by Mgr Tisserant in the *Revue Biblique* [5] and of Professor Rahlfs in the *Mitteilungen des Septuaginta-Unternehmens*.[6] Fol-

---

[1]   This MS contains only part of the Book of Job; cf. Swete, op. cit., p. 128.

[2]   Above, pp. ccf.

[3]   Field, op. cit., II, pp. 1f.

[4]   We follow the numbering of Holmes-Parsons.

[5]   1912, pp. 481ff.; 1919, pp. 89ff.

[6]   Cf. *RB*, 1919, p. 500 n. 1 and n. 2. The work of Professor Rahlfs was done on the basis of a collation made by Dr M. Flashar (cf. ibid.).

lowing Field,[1] we have also been able to cite Cod. regius unus (2:5, 11; 3:3; 7:18).

Let us draw attention to a few interesting quotations from the polygots: Complutensis (2:8; 3:5, 24; 4:21; 11:6; 24:11; 30:4, 28; 31:24; 32:16; 35:3, 15; 37:17; 38:30; 40:22); Aldine (3:5; 5:23; 31:24; 37:17).

3. VERSIONS DERIVED FROM THE SEPTUAGINT

A. *The Recension of Jerome*

We have seen in what energetic terms St Jerome expressed himself with regard to the ancient Latin version which was made on the basis of the Septuagint.[2] Hence it is no matter for surprise if the great Doctor began his revision of the Bible by a new recension of the version. His work consisted chiefly in replacing in the text the many hemistichs or verses which the Septuagint had omitted: *ita ego in lingua nostra (audacter loquor) feci eum habere quae amiserat.*[3] Origen had already completed this task of reconstitution with the help of Theodotion. St Jerome followed the example of the famous exegete and borrowed from him the diacritic signs: *rogo ut ubicumque praecedentes virgulas videritis, sciatis ea quae subjecta sunt in hebraeis voluminibus non haberi. Porro ubi stellae imago fulserit ex Hebraeo in nostro sermone addita.*[4] To this work of critical discernment were added the numerous corrections necessitated by the bad state of the text: *necnon et illa quae habere videbamur, et ita corrupta erant, ut sensum legentibus tollerent, orantibus vobis, magno labore correxi: magis utile quid ex otio meo Christi ecclesiis venturum ratus quam ex aliorum negotio.*[5] It was between the years 389 and 392 that this work took shape.[6]

The suggestions contained in the recension of Jerome are useful primarily for the reconstruction of the Septuagint of Origen, as also for the discrimination between the original Greek and the later additions.

[1] Cf. op. cit., p. 1.
[2] See above, pp. cxcixf.
[3] Preface to Paula and Eustochium (P.L. XXIX, col. 62). Jerome did not retranslate the text of the ancient Latin version so that his version can serve as a testimony to the first translation of the Septuagint into Latin; cf. Sabatier, *Bibliorum Sacrorum Latinae Versiones Antiquae* (1751), I, p. 828.
[4] Ibid.
[5] Ibid. The last phrase is inspired by Sallust, *Jugurtha*, IV.
[6] Cf. Cavallera, *S. Jérôme*, I, ii, p. 157.

Three MSS have come down to us. We have already mentioned the Bodleian and the Turonensis,[1] which have preserved the diacritic signs. The Sangallensis 11, edited by C. P. Caspari,[2] has not maintained these signs. As regards the respective value of these three witnesses, we must, above all, refer the reader to the erudite studies of Beer.[3] From the point of view of information about the Syro-hexaplar, the most appreciable of them is the Turonensis, which shows itself to be the most scrupulously conservative.[4] But even the Turonensis does not reach the faithfulness of the Syro-hexaplar.[5] As for the discrepancies between the three MSS, it is enough to draw attention to them in the Commentary (1:6, 19; 3:4, 22, 24; 4:10; 5:4, 11, 16, 17, 18, 21; 7:6, 13, 14; 11:1, 6, 12; 14:8, 12; 18:7; 20:19; 21:14; 23:3; 27:23; 28:10; 30:1; 36:20; 38:16).

Even apart from the passages added on the basis of Theodotion, it is easy to recognise hexaplar influences, especially the influence of Symmachus, in those places where the Latin version deviates from that of the Septuagint: 2:11, 13; 3:2, 5, 18, 23, 25; 4:6, 18; 5:4, 10; 6:28; 7:8; 9:13, 16, 22, 26, 29, 35; 10:1, 5; 11:10, 20; 12:10; 13:4; 15:5, 8, 9, 10, 16; 16:10; 17:10; 18:5; 19:12, 24, 29; 21:12, 19, 21; 22:2, 6,; 23:3, 4; 26:11; 27:18; 28:21; 30:1, 4, 15, 29, 30; 32:11-17; 34:2, 10, 11, 22, 23; 35:11; 36:31; 37:3, 4, 9, 10, 12, 13, 21; 38:25, 32, 37; 39:19, 23; 40:15, 16; 41:13, 15, 18; 42:8.

There will also be noticed a tendency to restore the version to closer accord with the Hebrew text: 1:6, 16, 18; 2:1, 2, 11, 13; 3:2, 10; 11:4; 12:11; 13:6, 25; 14:5, 9, 21; 15:15; 17:10; 20:13; 22:8, 15; 23:3, 4, 11; 24:1, 5, 7; 31:19, 21, 24; 32:20, 21; 34:8; 35:3; 36:33; 37:11; 42:11, 16.

The Greek text to which the recension of St Jerome is attached is that of the Hexapla. In case of conflict between the uncials the following is the position of the Latin text:

With the Alexandrinus: 1:12; 2:12; 3:2, 3, 17; 4:3; 5:24, 26, 27; 6:7, 23, 25; 7:13; 9:7; 11:13; 12:2, 14; 13:5; 15:7; 17:2, 12; 20:26; 22:19; 23:6; 27:3; 31:29; 34:26; 38:38; 39:12.

---

[1] See above, p. cci.
[2] *Das Buch Hiob* (1: 1-38: 16) in *Hieronymus's Übersetzung aus der alexandrinischen Version nach St. Gallener Handschrift saec. VIII* (Christiania, 1893).
[3] 'Textkritische Studien zum Buche Job,' in *ZATW*, 1896, pp. 297ff.; 1897, pp. 97ff.; 1898, pp. 257ff.
[4] *ZATW*, 1898, p. 283.
[5] Ibid., p. 284.

With the Alexandrinus and the Sinaiticus: 3:18, 19; 7:20; 22:14, 22; 23:5; 33:8; 38:30.

With the Alexandrinus and the Cod. Ephraemi rescriptus: 27:2, 9, 23; 30:1; 31:22.

With the Alexandrinus, the Sinaiticus, and the Cod. Ephraemi rescriptus: 27:14; 34:37; 37:14.

With the Sinaiticus: 26:5; 30:21; 32:20; 33:21.

With the Sinaiticus and the Cod. Ephraemi rescriptus: 24:21; 27:15.

With the Sinaiticus and the Vaticanus: 2:8.

With the Vaticanus: 2:9; 3:4; 9:19; 22:8; 26:12.

With the Cod. Ephraemi rescriptus: 28:10; 38:14.

Finally, let us note a few repetitions (2:11; 21:11; 24:2; 32:17), omissions (14:8; 16:10; 24:17; 31:13), errors in the Latin (4:10; 5:4, 11, 16, 17, 18, 21; 6:13, 25; 7:13; 11:6, 12; 14:8; 15:20, 32; 16:6, 10; 18:7; 28:18, 25; 36:20; 37:6).

B. *The Syro-hexaplar*

We have already had occasion to cite this version in the matter of determining the additions to the Septuagint.[1] A mere glance at the magnificent facsimile edition of the Codex syro-hexaplaris ambrosianus of Mgr Ceriani [2] is sufficient to make known the play of obeli and asterisks, the citations of Aquila, of Symmachus and Theodotion, the scholia of every kind which furnish proof of the precision and erudition of Origen.[3] It is well known that the Syro-hexaplar version was made in A.D. 616-17 at Alexandria by Paul, Bishop of Tella. It will not be superfluous to note the salient features of this document, so precious for the reconstruction of the Hexapla of Origen.[4]

As far as the use of obeli and asterisks is concerned, the Syro-hexaplar is infinitely more reliable than the MSS of the recension of Jerome.[5] However, let us draw attention to a few cases where the obeli have been omitted (1:7, 18; 2:2; 5:20; 7:2; 15:22; 19:4) or wrongly placed (1:19; 2:3; 9:17). The asterisks figure sometimes in the body of the text, sometimes in the marginal readings. They

---

[1] Above, p. ccii.
[2] Tome VII of the *Monum. Sacra et Profana* (1874).
[3] Cf. Field, *Origenis Hexaplorum quae Supersunt*, II, p. 3.
[4] Our statistics draw attention only to the most interesting cases.
[5] See above, p. ccvii.

have been omitted in 15:26b-27; 20:21-3; 24:15a; 34:11b; 37:21b; wrongly placed in 20:6; 22:20b; 23:9b. The asterisk is put for the obelus in 2:10.

Besides the citations of hexaplar authors, which have been very carefully collected by Field, we find in the margin of the Syro-hexaplar allusions to the copy of Origen (6:4; 31:19), to 'the others' (Greek translators) (3:4), to a copy which has the same text as the Alexandrinus (8:10), to Origen (20:18), to the 'three' (Greek translators) (12:24; 33:10).

In the margins again we find a certain number of Greek words which take us back to the original (1:1; 2:7; 6:4; 8:9, 11; 9:25, 31; 10:5; 14:8; 20:18; 21:18, 22; 36:30); a few returns to the Hebrew text (1:6, 17, 18; 2:9; 7:15; 11:4; 31:19, 21; 32:8; 42:15).

Among the variants cited in the margin, we should carefully note the readings of the Alexandrinus: 1:12, 13; 5:5; 7:11, 15; 8:10, 12; 9:33; 11:8; 19:26; 20:2, 18, 26; 21:14, 18, 22, 23; 22:8; 23:6; 25:4; 32:11; 33:31; 35:3, 11; 40:16.

In case of conflict between the uncials, the Syro-hexaplar is in agreement:

With the Vaticanus: 3:4, 19, 21; 6:10; 7:10; 22:8, 22; 26:11; 30:1.

With the Alexandrinus: 3:2, 23; 5:26, 27; 6:7; 9:7; 13:5; 14:20; 15:22; 17:2, 12; 21:8; 22:14, 19; 23:5; 27:3; 31:7, 29; 34:17, 26; 38:38.

With the Sinaiticus: 30:21; 32:20; 38:21.

With the Vaticanus and the Sinaiticus: 1:13; 2:8; 3:17; 14:6; 28:10.

With the Alexandrinus and the Sinaiticus: 2:9d; 7:20; 9:16; 24:17; 30:4; 32:3; 33:8; 36:31; 38:30.

With the Sinaiticus and the Cod. Ephraemi rescriptus: 24:14; 27:16; 34:37; 37:14.

C. *The Sahidic Coptic Version*

We have attempted to define the value of this version, the characteristic of which is that it offers the short recension of the Septuagint.[1] We thought it possible to affirm that this recension had been obtained not by the use of a pre-hexaplar text but by the curtailment of the stichs marked with asterisk.[2] The ancient sticho-

---

[1] See above, pp. ccif.
[2] See above, p. ccii.

metric systems carefully distinguished between the two sorts of stichs, those with and those without asterisk.[1] Hence it was easy for a translator to confine his task to those passages of the Septuagint proper, leaving aside the ones which arose from Theodotion.

The Sahidic version has been edited by Ciasca, on the basis of the MSS (chiefly Z. 24 and Z. 25) of the Borgia collection.[2] A lacuna in the MSS deprives us of chs. 39:10- 40:13 .

In case of conflict between the uncials, the Sahidic version is in agreement:

With the Vaticanus: 3:4, 19; 7:11; 22:22; 23:5; 28:10; 34:26.

With the Alexandrinus: 1:6, 12; 2:8, 10, 12; 3:23; 4:3; 5:13, 26, 27; 6:7; 9:3, 7, 23; 11:16; 13:5; 14:15; 18:6; 20:15; 21:5, 8; 22:19; 23:17; 27:3; 31:7; 32:2, 20; 33:17; 34:17; 36:18; 40:16.

With the Sinaiticus: 20:4; 30:21.

With the Vaticanus and the Sinaiticus: 1:13; 3:17.

With the Alexandrinus and the Sinaiticus: 2:9d; 3:21; 7:20; 30:4; 32:3; 33:6, 8.

With the Alexandrinus and the Cod. Ephraemi rescriptus: 26:12; 27:2, 9; 30:1; 31:22; 34:2.

Let us note a few transpositions (9:14; 28:20) and omissions (1:7, 8, 15; 2:3; 3:13; 5:23; 6:15; 7:11; 15:19; 16:15; 19:16; 30:17; 33:15c-16a).

D. *The Bohairic Coptic Version*

In the work in which he published the Sahidic Coptic version, Ciasca gave the interesting readings of the Bohairic version, which he designates by the name Memphitic.[3] A first edition of the Bohairic version had been published by Tattam [4] in 1846, on the basis of a manuscript of the Patriarchal library of Cairo, which was collated with two MSS from private libraries. A new edition was prepared by M. E. Porcher,[5] who was able to utilise, besides the work of Tattam, a Cairo manuscript collated with a manuscript

---

[1] See above, p. cci.

[2] *Sacrorum Bibliorum Fragmenta Copto-sahidica* (Rome, 1889), II. On the MSS, ibid., pp. xviiif. Cf. Vaschalde, *RB*, 1920, pp. 95f. In 1912 Dieu published a few things complementary to the edition of Ciasca: cf. *RB*, 1913, p. 624.

[3] Whence our abbreviation **Memph**.

[4] *The Ancient Coptic version of the Book of Job the Just.*

[5] *Le Livre de Job, version bohaïrique*, in *Patrologia Orientalis*, XVIII, 2 (1924).

from the British Museum. The editor has added to his text a French translation and critical notes. He points out that Cod. 160 (Holmes-Parsons) is the Greek manuscript whose text has the closest affinity with the Bohairic version. We have had occasion to quote a few instances where this version is akin to some manuscript tradition (1:6, 20; 2:2, 12; 5:22; 6:7; 7:11; 9:6; 21:8; 22:8; 23:2, 5; 24:21; 26:11; 27:23; 29:20; 31:17; 32:20; 34:2; 35:3; 36:28; 42:15).

E. *The Ethiopic Version*

It is likewise in the *Patrologia Orientalis* that appeared the critical edition of the Ethiopic version of the Book of Job.[1] The author of this edition, F. M. Esteves Pereira, mentions 23 MSS of the Ethiopic translation and takes as the basis of his text a manuscript from the Bibliothèque Nationale, another from the Bodleian at Oxford, and a third from the collection of d'Abbadie.

Pereira thinks that the author of the Ethiopic translation of the Book of Job, based on the Septuagint, is none other than the translator of the Book of Ecclesiastes.[2]

We have thought it proper to cite this translation in those cases where it was affiliated to a fairly sharply characterised manuscript tradition: 1:6, 12, 13; 2:7, 8, 9d, 12; 3:1, 4, 17, 21, 24; 4:4, 7; 5:13, 23; 6:7; 7:20; 9:7; 12:11; 14:20; 19:8, 16; 22:8; 23:17; 24:21; 27:15, 23; 32:2, 11; 42:16.

F. *The Arabic Version Based on the Septuagint*

In 1870 Graf Baudissin edited[3] with a truly remarkable precision, an Arabic manuscript brought from Egypt by Tischendorf in 1853 which later came into the possession of the British Museum (1856), where it was catalogued as Add. 26,166. This manuscript, probably dating from the ninth century, contained an Arabic version of the Book of Job (1:8-3, 18; 6:26-28:21), based on the Septuagint and especially the hexaplar text.[4] A reminiscence of Mt 10:30 in Job 14:5[5] proves that the author was a Christian.

---

[1] *Le Livre de Job, version éthiopienne*, in *Patrologia Orientalis*, II, 5 (1905).
[2] Ibid., p. 573.
[3] *Translationis Antiquae Arabicae Libri Jobi quae Supersunt* (Leipzig, 1870). From the name of the editor, we have designated the MS by the abbreviation Arab. Baud.
[4] Cf. ibid., pp. 116ff.
[5] Cf. ibid., p. 56, n. 2.

Its Egyptian origin explains the points of contact with the Alexandrinus (1:12, 20, 21, 22; 2:8, 10, 12; 7:6, 11, 20; 9:7, 35; 19:20; 23:17; 26:11; 27:2, 3, 9). A characteristic feature is the mention of the *mazbaleh* in 2:8. Mistakes in the reading of the Greek explain 15:31, 35; 19:26; 27:12. A few omissions: 2:11; 9:5; 16:10. Slight additions: 1:14, 15.

4. GREEK VERSIONS OTHER THAN THE SEPTUAGINT

The love of truth professed by Origen led him to seek, by every possible means, to restore the Septuagint translation to harmony with the original Hebrew.

A long time ago attention was drawn to an authority quoted by Origen under the name of ὁ ʽΕβραῖος 'the Hebrew'. Field has proved that it is not a question of a version to be identified with τὸ ʽΕβραϊκόν, nor of Aquila, nor of corrections based on the Hebrew and induced into the Hexapla in the light of the commentaries of the Fathers, principally St Jerome.[1] He sees in 'the Hebrew' *Hebraeum quemdam, cujus nomen deperditum est, sive Judaeum, sive Christianum, utriusque linguae doctum, qui certos Veteris Testamenti libros (in primis Genesim, Jobum et Ezechielem) e sermone nativo in Graecum transtulerit.*[2] One might equally well see in this personage the Hebrew teacher frequently mentioned in the work of Origen and from whom the Alexandrian Doctor liked to draw information of the first order.[3]

It is he who interprets as an euphemism the benediction of 2:5. He is a supporter of the strictest literalism (2:8; 13:20; 14:9), a feature which brings him close to Symmachus (3:3) and sometimes to the Vulgate (3:7). Yet he regards 'the hair of my flesh' (4:15) as meaning 'the hair of my head'.

The versions whose influence was chiefly exercised on Origen and St Jerome in their effort to return to the *hebraica veritas* are Aquila, Symmachus, and Theodotion.

A. *Aquila*

The tendency of Aquila to reproduce Hebrew words appears in 26:5; 30:4; 37:9; 40:30. He is in agreement with the Massoretic text to avoid obnoxious expressions in 1:5; 2:5; he favours the

---

[1] *Origenis Hexaplorum quae Supersunt*, I, p. lxxvff.
[2] Ibid., p. lxxvii.
[3] Cf. Bardy, *RB*, 1925, pp. 221ff.

word or the meaning chosen by the Targum (3:5; 4:11). His influence is discernible in the Greek translation of 5:26 and in the Latin translation (of Jerome and the Vulgate) of 7:8, 21. He generally adopts the *qerê* reading (13:15; 37:12). His interpretations are at times contaminated by a wrong reading (11:9; 12:2) or by a wrong vocalisation (16:8; 28:4, 6).

Let us note the agreement of Aquila with the Septuagint (and the Peshitta) against the Massoretic text in 4:16; 33:16. His interpretation is sometimes reflected in the Peshitta (6:29; 40:12), or in the group formed by the Vulgate, the Targum, and the Peshitta (33:16).

B. *Symmachus*

The version of Symmachus contains a few prolixities and redundancies (6:5; 8:17; 16:4; 25:3), even a double translation (20:4). At times it springs from a vocalisation which differs from the Massoretic (16:8; 17:5; 24:25; 28:4, 6). When there is a variety of interpretations, it is often in harmony with the Targum (4:16; 32:19; 33:29; 35:9, 15; 36:20, 33; 37:10), sometimes with the Septuagint (29:4; 32:1; 38:31) or with the Peshitta (16:9; 20:4). It prefers the *kethîb* to the *qerê* in 14:5; 19:29; 37:12.

C. *Theodotion*

The importance of the work of Theodotion in the recasting of the Greek text emerges from the fact that this translation was chosen by Origen for the purpose of filling the gaps in the Septuagint.[1]

Still more markedly than in the work of Aquila, we find in Theodotion the tendency to preserve the Hebrew word in the Greek version: 7:11; 28:18; 30:4; 37:9, 12; 38:32; 39:6, 13. In some cases he chooses the *kethîb* (19:29; 33:28), in others the *qerê* (30:22; 33:19). He sometimes translates אל 'God' by ὁ ἰσχυρός (22:13), and avoids anthropomorphism (22:14). His interpretations are often in accord with those of the Targum (26:9; 34:30; 36:7) and of the Vulgate and Peshitta (12:23; 18:9; 20:9, 12; 33:29; 35:15). There are a few mistakes in reading (8:2, 18; 12:23; 35:16; 36:16) or in vocalisation (17:5; 18:15; 19:24; 22:24; 24:19; 28:4; 30:20; 36:4; 37:2). The Greek transmission is not free from errors (22:15; 31:2, 24; 38:32).

[1] See above, p. cc.

5. THE VULGATE

There was no long interval of time between the work accomplished by St Jerome on the Septuagint version [1] and his direct translation of the original Hebrew.[2] If the need for recourse to the original made itself felt, it was above all for the Book of Job. The Greek text was not merely incomplete.[3] It was also very often defective and reproduced the Hebrew only imperfectly.[4] The labours of Origen had consisted in a vigorous attempt to put things right. But one does not put a new patch on an old garment. St Jerome realised that it was necessary to begin the translation of the Hebrew text again from the original.[5] So he shook off the yoke of the Septuagint and declared in his Preface to this new Latin version which was to become the Vulgate: *Haec autem translatio nullum de veteribus sequitur interpretem, sed ex ipso hebraico, arabicoque sermone, et interdum syro, nunc verba, nunc sensus, nunc simul utrumque resonabit.*[6]

On examining his translation closely, we see that St Jerome did not free himself completely from the Hexapla. Whether he is directly influenced by the one or the other of the hexaplar authors, or whether he follows the same tradition in interpretation, we can frequently recognise remarkable analogies between the Vulgate and the versions of Aquila, Symmachus, and Theodotion. We shall content ourselves with drawing attention to the passages where these analogies are striking.

Vulgate and Aquila: 1:1; 4:6; 5:3, 7, 24; 7:8, 12, 15; 9:4; 10:10; 11:7; 16:8; 21:12, 21; 26:7; 37:3; 39:9, 13; 41:7, 10, 14.

Vulgate and Symmachus: 1:3; 4:2, 13, 18, 19; 6:5; 7:8, 11, 20, 21, 22; 8:20; 9:21; 10:12; 11:10, 12; 12:17, 24; 13:20; 14:11; 15:12; 16:2, 8; 18:17; 19:8; 20:11, 20; 21:11, 27; 22:3, 16; 23:3; 24:4, 12, 25; 26:12; 28:3, 18, 22; 30:1, 2, 4; 31:1; 32:19; 33:3, 29; 36:11, 25, 26, 29, 32; 37:12, 13; 38:31, 35; 40:8; 41:20; 42:3.

Vulgate and Theodotion: 13:2; 20:9, 12, 14; 21:31; 22:30; 26:5, 6; 27:21; 28:7, 14, 18; 31:3; 33:19; 36:9; 38:32; 39:16, 19; 42:10, 11.

---

[1] See above, pp. ccviff.
[2] Cf. Cavallera, *S. Jérôme*, I, ii, p. 157.
[3] See above, pp. cxcviiiff.
[4] See above, pp. cxcviif.
[5] A comparison between the ancient Latin version and the Vulgate shows clearly the need for this work. The two texts are compared in Sabatier, op. cit., I, pp. 832ff.
[6] P.L. XXVIII, cols. 1080f.

It appears that it was Symmachus who was most highly valued by St Jerome, who has given the following appreciation of the work of the three translators: *Quamobrem Aquila et Symmachus et Theodotion incitati, diversum paene opus in eodem opere prodiderunt; alio nitente verbum de verbo exprimere, alio sensum potius sequi, tertio non multum a veteribus discrepare.*[1] In his Commentary on Am 3:11, St Jerome observes with approval that Symmachus adheres above all to the meaning: *non solet verborum* κακοζηλίαν *sed intelligentiae ordinem sequi.*[2]

The Vulgate is in agreement with the Massoretic text in those places where obnoxious expressions have been avoided (1:5, 11; 2:5). In 9:63 it seems that a similar scruple has influenced the translation.

Very often harmony between the Vulgate and the Septuagint will be noticed: 2:10; 3:12, 13; 6:16, 19, 24, 26, 27, 30; 7:1, 21; 8:5, 7; 10:2; 11:10; 12:2; 13:25; 14:17; 15:13, 34; 16:9; 18:18; 19:9, 19; 20:8, 22; 21:17; 22:25; 23:7, 10, 12; 24:7; 26:2-3; 28:11; 29:9, 17; 30:11, 14, 15, 19, 28; 31:26, 28, 31, 32; 33:21; 35:14; 38:3; 41:14.

The resemblances between the interpretation of the Vulgate and that of the Targums may stem from a common exegetical tradition: 4:18; 5:5; 6:10; 11:11; 12:5, 18; 17:16; 18:15; 20:7; 23:7, 13; 24:23; 26:13; 27:8; 28:10, 17; 29:10; 31:10, 35; 33:30; 35:14; 36:14, 33; 40:17.

Let us mention further the analogies with the Peshitta, which also may be explained by a common tradition: 3:5, 7; 6:16, 25; 7:2; 8:18; 13:13; 14:15; 15:2, 24; 16:12; 17:4, 10; 18:3, 8; 20:3, 10, 23, 28; 21:23; 22:12, 30; 23:9, 14; 24:9, 20; 28:4; 30:11, 24, 28; 31:18; 33:14, 17, 32; 40:15.

The style of St Jerome in his rendering of the Book of Job is extremely smooth-flowing. We notice even a tendency to paraphrase or explanation: 3:21, 24, 25; 4:15; 5:10; 6:2, 5, 10, 28, 29; 7:6; 9:12, 13, 20, 28, 32; 10:22; 11:6, 12, 17; 12:3, 4, 16, 23, 24; 13:4, 12; 14:2, 9, 15, 16; 15:2, 3, 11, 12, 21; 16:9; 17:1, 3, 5, 7, 16; 18:4, 11, 14, 15; 19:6, 18, 25; 20:2, 18, 20, 24; 21:19, 25, 29, 33, 34; 22:2, 11, 17, 24; 23:7, 10, 13; 24:6, 12; 26:8, 12; 27:21; 28:1, 4, 5, 16; 30:2, 3, 5, 8, 13, 14, 24; 31:14, 21, 23; 33:17, 24;

[1] Preface to the translation of the *Chronicle* of Eusebius (P.L. XXVII, col. 35).
[2] P.L. XXV, col. 1019.

34:19, 35, 37; 35:3, 13, 15; 36:17, 22, 27, 28; 37:10, 13, 15, 19, 21; 38:12, 26, 27, 37; 39:3; 40:5, 24; 41:7, 15. The fact is that, in St Jerome's own words: *Obliquus enim etiam apud Hebraeos totus liber fertur et lubricus, et quod graece rhetores vocant ἐσχηματισμένος, dumque aliud loquitur, aliud agit; ut si velis anguillam aut muraenulam strictis tenere manibus, quanto fortius presseris, tanto citius elabitur.*[1]

Latinisms are not uncommon: 6:7; 14:1, 3; 16:12, 17; 19:21, 24; 20:5; 21:3, 23; 23:8; 24:17; 25:4; 36:4, 16; 37:16-17, 20, 24; 38:4; 39:1, 25; 40:32.

A few copyist's errors have slipped into the transmission of the Latin: 7:2; 8:16; 16:15; 17:9; 19:24; 30:12.

To be noted are cases of double translation (32:2; 36:13; 41:25), of slight additions (1:12; 2:5; 4:2, 5; 5:15; 8:6; 11:17; 15:22; 16:6, 7; 17:16; 22:14; 23:2, 6; 24:2, 5; 31:2; 24:12; 35:8; 36:13), of curtailments or omissions (3:7; 6:2, 21, 26; 10:15; 12:23; 13:4; 19:19; 24:1, 5; 32:5; 37:6; 38:40; 39:12), of fusions of two hemistichs into a single clause (6:7, 14, 16; 20:14; 27:6, 11; 36:5; 41:18, 23), of transpositions (11:11; 27:18; 38:21).

Sometimes the original has been read wrongly (6:15, 25; 11:3; 13:9; 19:27; 24:5, 9; 30:5, 17; 34:32; 41:22) or the sentence wrongly divided (12:9; 13:13; 19:25; 22:24, 25; 26:2; 33:7; 39:28).

These unavoidable accidents cannot cause us to disregard the value of this version. When we compare the Vulgate with the Septuagint or the Peshitta,[2] we are compelled to admit the inestimable superiority of the genius of St Jerome, whose concern to safeguard the *hebraica veritas* was reconciled with the demands of his taste in Latin.

6. The Peshitta

The Syriac translation of the Book of Job has been the object of a study by Eberhard Baumann to which it would be difficult to add anything whatsoever.[3] In order to show to what an extent this version may be useful for the correction of the Hebrew text, the author, with consummate erudition, deals in turn with the Syriac text itself,[4] the features of the translation,[5] the divergencies

---

[1] Preface (P.L. XXVIII, col. 1081).
[2] See below.
[3] 'Die Verwendbarkeit der Pešita zum Buche Ijob für die Textkritik' in *ZATW*, 1898-1900.
[4] *ZATW*, 1898, pp. 311ff.; 1899, pp. 15ff.
[5] *ZATW*, 1899, pp. 50ff.

between it and the Massoretic text,[1] and the points of contact between it and the other versions.[2] We can simply refer to this work for the criticism of the Peshitta. However, since our statistics are independent of those of Baumann, it will not perhaps be superfluous to draw attention to what seems to us to be worthy of notice. We have made use of the edition of Walton's Polyglot and of the admirable facsimile reproduction of the Codex Ambrosianus which we owe to the careful work of Mgr Ceriani.[3]

In connection with the Vulgate [4] we have pointed out those passages where the Latin version and the Syriac version were in accord.

The cases where the Peshitta is in agreement with the Septuagint might be explained by a direct influence of the Greek on the Syriac version: 5:3; 6:4, 19, 21; 7:15; 9:19, 33; 10:20; 12:14; 13:18, 28; 14:5; 16:5, 9; 17:16; 18:3; 19:23; 22:3, 17; 23:2; 24:20; 27:15, 18, 19; 29:12; 31:23; 34:36, 37; 37:19, 24; 38:7.

The resemblance between the Aramaic and the Syriac languages is often the reason for the agreement between the Peshitta and the Targum: 6:12, 22; 26:5, 9, 10; 28:16; 29:16, 17; 33:27; 34:6, 17; 38:3, 31; 40:7; 41:17; 42:10.

The Syriac translation is not distinguished for its faithfulness to the Hebrew. It is especially in the divisions between clauses, even between verse and verse, that we note some regrettable anomalies: 9:5; 13:13; 15:16; 16:10; 17:5; 19:24, 26-7; 20:15; 21:17; 22:3-4, 15-16, 21; 23:11-12; 24:11-12, 15, 22, 23; 27:20-1; 28:4, 5-6, 17-18; 30:5-6, 7-8, 17-18, 25; 31:26-7; 32:15-16; 34:5, 25-6, 31-2; 35:12-13; 36:18-19, 24-5; 38:8-9, 17-19, 28-9; 39:27-8; 41:5-7, 15-16, 25-6.

Incorrect readings and defective vocalisations are fairly frequent: 5:5; 6:7, 13, 17, 19; 7:5; 9:27, 35; 11:3, 6, 11, 12, 15; 12:4, 12; 15:4, 27; 16:3, 7; 18:13, 19; 19:13; 20:5, 7, 9, 22, 23, 25; 21:10; 22:2, 11; 23:16; 24:1, 13, 21, 22; 26:7; 27:11; 28:13, 26; 29:7, 22; 30:2, 15, 23; 31:8, 10, 11, 20, 28, 30, 34; 32:4, 9, 12, 18, 19, 22; 34:5-6, 24; 35:15; 36:5, 27, 28; 37:14; 38:8, 20; 39:20, 22, 29; 40:2, 24, 26, 31; 41:1, 12, 20, 24.

Let us note further a certain number of passages where there

---

[1] *ZATW*, 1899, pp. 71, 288ff.; 1900, pp. 177ff., 264ff.
[2] *ZATW*, 1900, pp. 284ff.
[3] *Translatio Syra Pescitto Veteris Testamenti* (Milan, 1876).
[4] See above, p. ccxv.

occur repetitions and double translations (2:10; 4:21; 11:3; 12:16, 25; 13:2; 15:26; 17:9, 15; 19:16; 20:12; 24:6, 11, 24; 29:18; 31:23, 24; 33:9, 15, 20, 21, 26; 34:5, 18; 36:13, 20), slight additions (1:12, 13; 2:6, 11; 3:6; 4:16, 20; 6:22; 9:33; 15:6; 19:16; 21:15; 23:6; 24:20; 27:19; 31:14, 34; 33:5, 9; 34:10), implicit quotations (9:18; 28:19), and theological adaptations (1:6; 37:7).

At other times we find transpositions (2:5; 10:11; 12:19; 16:22; 31:35; 32:3; 38:36), or omissions (1:13, 15, 21; 3:7; 6:2, 15; 7:13; 8:16; 10:6; 11:15, 20; 12:11; 13:10, 15; 14:6; 15:28; 21:8; 22:26; 23:3; 24:2, 5, 14; 27:5, 17; 29:6, 25; 30:3-4, 12, 16; 34:20; 37:4, 23; 38:25; 40:8, 18, 20; 41:21, 22, 23, 24), or compressions (6:14; 23:13; 27:3; 29:5; 33:18; 35:5; 37:6-7; 39:3-4; 40:11-12, 16).

Sometimes the translation is based on the meaning of the Aramaic root: 6:2, 9; 8:17; 9:27, 29; 20:27; 23:2, 10; 24:10; 29:4, 19; 32:6; 35:14; 36:32; 38:22.

The MS transmission has caused a few errors in the Syriac: 4:12; 6:4; 7:6, 17; 13:26; 15:28; 21:30; 26:11; 31:26, 39; 37:17, 19.

7. THE TARGUM

The Targum of the Book of Job seems to be by the same author as that of the Psalms and to have been written before the year A.D. 476.[1]

It is more often a commentary than a translation.[2] Theological and mythological explanations, and above all allusions to the history of Israel, abound in it: 1:6, 15; 2:9, 11; 3:3, 5, 17, 18, 19, 26; 4:4, 6, 8, 10, 18, 19, 21; 5:2, 4, 7, 10, 13, 15, 17, 20, 21, 22, 23, 24; 6:10, 17, 20; 7:12; 9:5; 11:10, 18; 12:6; 13:11, 24; 14:11, 17; 15:15, 20, 21; 17:6; 18:12, 13; 20:26, 27, 28; 21:22; 24:1, 15; 25:2; 26:13; 27:11; 28:5, 6, 13, 22, 27; 31:33; 32:2, 8; 33:28; 34:20; 35:8, 10; 36:20, 28, 32; 37:12; 38:1, 7, 13, 17, 18, 22, 36, 37.

Paraphrase sometimes takes the place of translation: 1:21; 2:4, 10; 3:6, 7; 5:11, 20; 6:7, 9; 8:10; 9:25; 10:22; 19:29; 22:25; 23:3; 25:6; 26:7; 30:2, 3, 4; 33:23; 34:24; 36:10; 37:13; 38:10, 16.

What is of particular interest to note are those cases where the Targum, obeying a theological scruple, tries to avoid every kind

---

[1] Cf. Nestle, *Realencyklopädie* (3rd ed.), III, p. 110, ll. 31ff.

[2] We have drawn up our statistics independently of the dissertation of Adolphe Weiss, *De Libri Job Paraphrasi Chaldaica* (1873).

of anthropomorphism or any expression concerning God that is deemed too realistic. Thus instead of 'Yahweh' simply, the writer says 'the word (מימר) of Yahweh' (1:21; 42:9, 10, 12). Similarly Shaddai becomes 'the word of Shaddai' (29:5), and Elohim 'the word of Yahweh' (2:9). Instead of 'Thou' the writer says 'Thy word' (1:10, 11) and instead of 'I', 'My word' (2:3). The use of מימרי 'my word' to mean 'I' will become common in speaking not only of God but also of men. It is thus that בי 'in me' becomes במימרי 'in my word', i.e. 'in my person' (7:8; 19:18; 27:3). We have explained this periphrasis in the Commentary on 20:29. It is not a negligible factor for the study of the terminology concerning the Logos. It is 'the word' of God which replaces His breath in 4:9 and 33:4. The *shekinah* [1] will be substituted for the 'face' of God in 34:29.

The Targum is inclined to expand rather than shorten the text. We find in it double translations (3:10; 24:19-20; 31:7; 34:9) and even a triple interpretation (36:33). Additions are not uncommon (1:7, 11, 12, 13; 2:2, 5, 6, 7; 3:3, 16; 4:16, 20; 5:5; 9:11; 14:12; 18:15; 22:14; 23:6; 26:8; 29:23, 25; 31:2; 32:22; 33:17, 20; 36:24; 41:8).

We have mentioned the agreements between the Targum and the Vulgate [2] and between the Targum and the Peshitta.[3]

8. ARABIC VERSIONS

Among the versions derived from the Septuagint we have cited an Arabic version made on the model of the Greek.[4]

The one published in Walton's Polyglot is derived from the Peshitta.[5] A late document,[6] it offers but little interest for the text of the Syriac version. It contains a doxological formula (from Ps 113:2) in 1:21. Note that the addition taken from 'the Syriac book' [7] which is found at the end of the Septuagint has also been translated in the Arabic version.

It was Saʿadia Gaon Ben-Joseph, the Fayoumite († A.D. 942),

[1] On this hypostasis, cf. *RB*, 1924, pp. 449f.
[2] See above, p. ccxv.
[3] See above, p. ccxv.
[4] See above, pp. ccxif.
[5] It is this which we denote by Arab. as distinct from Arab. Baud. (above, p. ccxi, n. 3).
[6] Cf. Nestle, *Realencyklopädie* (3rd ed.), III, p. 94.
[7] Cf. above, pp. xvii f.

who assumed the task of translating the Hebrew Bible direct into Arabic.[1] His very literal interpretation is useful for the understanding of the text. The Arabic is transcribed in Hebrew characters without vowels. The divine names are rendered by Allah. Satan is interpreted by 'the adversary of Job' (1:6). In 27:18, Sa'adia is in agreement with the Septuagint and Vulgate in seeing in כעש a sort of abbreviation of כעכביש 'like the spider's web'. Sa'adia's Arabic interpretation of the Hebrew would make the subject of an interesting study.[2]

[1] Cf. Nestle, *Realencyklopädie* (3rd ed.), III, p. 92.
[2] The most convenient edition is that published under the direction of H. Derenbourg and Mayer Lambert (Paris, Leroux). The text is accompanied by a French translation. The 5th volume contains the Book of Job. The text and notes (in Hebrew) are edited by W. Bacher. French translation by J. and H. Derenbourg.

CHAPTER THIRTEEN

THE EXEGESIS OF THE BOOK OF JOB

Among the Greek Fathers, it is possible that St Clement of Alexandria wrote on the Book of Job, if we are to judge from a fragment of the *catena* of Nicetas.[1] Origen's exegetical work on Job has largely disappeared.[2] What has remained of it has been collected, in accord with the *catenae*, in the *Selecta in Job*[3] and the *Enarrationes in Job*[4] of Migne's *Patrologia Graeca*.[5] More often than not it is impossible to know whether it is a question of scholia of the learned Alexandrian or simply of extracts from his other works.[6] The attribution to Origen is sometimes debateable. Huet has proved that the Commentary on Job, preserved in a Latin translation, which formerly was numbered among the works of Origen, was in fact by an anonymous writer.[7]

St Athanasius did not write a commentary on Job, but a few passages relative to this text have been extracted from his works by the authors of *catenae* and then collected in the *Patrologia* under the title *Excerpta in Job*.[8] Eusebius of Emesa preached on Job, as is attested by the fragments which Mai has edited.[9] The *catena* of Nicetas offers a few remnants of the exegetical work of Didymus the Blind on Job.[10]

To St John Chrysostom are attributed a certain number of exegetical fragments in the *catena* of Nicetas.[11] These fragments often belong to homilies. They are of the greatest interest, because they

---

[1] P.G. IX, cols. 739ff.
[2] On Origen's method of exposition, cf. Batiffol, *Anc. litt. chrétiennes, La Littérature grecque*, p. 170.
[3] P.G. XII, cols. 1029ff.
[4] P.G. XVII, cols. 57ff.
[5] According to the works of de la Rue, Gallandi, Mai.
[6] Bardenhewer, *Patrologie*, p. 155.
[7] P.G. XVII, cols. 371ff.
[8] P.G. XXVII, cols. 1343ff.
[9] P.G. LXXXVI, cols. 331ff. On Eusebius of Emesa, cf. Batiffol, op. cit., p. 278.
[10] P.G. XXXIX, cols. 1119ff. On the Origenist mode of exegesis of Didymus the Blind, cf. Bardenhewer, op. cit., p. 292.
[11] P.G. LXIV, cols. 503ff.

seem indeed to confirm the authenticity of a Commentary of St John Chrysostom on Job which exists in the Biblioteca Laurenziana in Florence, and which has formed the object of an erudite study by L. Dieu.[1] An allusion to the theory of Theodore of Mopsuestia on the Book of Job is to be found in the Acts of the Fifth Oecumenical Council.[2] The *catena* of Nicetas has preserved a certain number of scholia of Olympiodorus of Alexandria.[3] This author quite often quotes the Hexapla (5:12; 13:20, 22; 14:6; 20:16).

Among the Latins, St Hilary of Poitiers composed a treatise on Job which was quoted by St Jerome.[4] Only two fragments of it remain.[5] The ancient Latin version was utilised by St Ambrose in his four books *De interpellatione Job et David*.[6] The revision of this old Latin version [7] and the translation of the Vulgate [8] are what remains to us of the work of St Jerome on Job. The *Expositio interlinearis libri Job* which is reckoned among his works [9] is not authentic.[10] It is to his disciple Philip the Deacon that is due the *Commentarii in librum Job*.[11] The marginal notes of St Augustine entitled *Adnotationum in Job liber unus* [12] make use of Jerome's version of the Septuagint without taking into account the diacritic signs.[13] On the other hand, it is the version which follows the Hebrew that is cited in a commentary attributed by Father Vaccari to Julian of Aeclanum, the antagonist of St Augustine.[14] A few interpretations of difficult passages in the Book of Job are to be found, in the form of questions and answers, in the Instructions of Eucherius of Lyons.[15] The great work of St Gregory the Great was his *Expositio in librum Job, sive Moralium libri XXXV*.[16] All the resources of historical, typical, and moral interpretation were exploited by

1 'Le Commentaire de S. Jean Chrysostome sur Job', in *Revue d'Histoire Ecclésiastique*, **13** (1912), pp. 604ff.

2 Above, pp. xixf.

3 P.G. XCIII, cols. 13ff.

4 Bardenhewer, op. cit., p. 379.

5 P.L. X, cols. 723f.

6 P.L. XIV, cols. 793ff.

7 Above, pp. ccvif.

8 Above, pp. ccxivf.

9 P.L. XXIII, cols. 1401ff.

10 Bardenhewer, op. cit., p. 433.

11 P.L. XXVI, cols. 618ff.; cf. LIII, col. 1011.

12 P.L. XXXIV, cols. 825ff.

13 P.L. XXIX, col. 61, at top of column.

14 Cf. *RB*, 1915, p. 595, and 1922, p. 140.

15 P.L. L, cols. 782f.

16 P.L. LXXV, cols. 500ff.

the indefatigable pontiff. St Gregory is in general the inspiration
of the *glossa ordinaria* on Job[1] attributed to Walafrid Strabo,
but probably the work of Rabanus Maurus. A summary of the work
of St Gregory was drawn up by St Odo, Abbot of Cluny.[2] The
Expositio in Job of St Bruno,[3] the *Super Job Commentarius*[4] of
Rupert of Deutz, the *Compendium in Job* of Pierre de Blois,[5] are
likewise under the influence of the *Moralium*. With the *Commentarii
in Job* of Beatus Albertus Magnus[6] and the *Expositio in librum
Sancti Job* of St Thomas Aquinas,[7] we return to the most praiseworthy concern for the literal exact meaning. As regards Catholic
exegesis from the time of the Angelic Doctor onwards, it will be
enough to refer the reader to the very complete bibliography of
Fr Knabenbauer.[8]

Among the Syrians, St Ephraem had written an elucidation of
Job, of which there remains a fragment in an Armenian *catena*.[9]
The version on which the work rests must have been the Peshitta,
in agreement with the normal custom of the Oriental Doctor.[10]
A discourse on Job had been composed by one of the disciples of
St Ephraem, Mar Aba.[11] Further, there survive a few fragments of an
explanation of Job by John of Lycopolis.[12] Other commentators of
Job are Hannana of Adiabene and the Patriarch Elisha (sixth
century). A long poem on Job[13] featured among the poetic works
of Jacob of Sarug. Let us mention further, at the end of the
seventh century, the scholia on Job by Jacob of Edessa[14] and, in
the middle of the ninth century, the work of Isho'dad, Bishop of
Hedatta.[15]

Jewish exegesis of the Book of Job has followed in the steps of

[1] P.L. CXIII, cols. 747ff.
[2] P.L. CXXXIII, cols. 105ff.
[3] P.L. CLXIV, cols. 551ff.
[4] P.L. CLXVIII, cols. 963ff.
[5] P.L. CCVII, cols. 795ff.
[6] Excellent edition by Melchior Weiss, based on five MSS (Fribourg, 1904).
[7] Bibliography in *Angelicum*, **2**, 2 (1925), p. 170.
[8] *Commentarius in Librum Job*, pp. 22ff.
[9] Baumstark, *Geschichte der syrischen Literatur*, p. 38.
[10] R. Duval, *La Littérature syriaque*, p. 75.
[11] Ibid., p. 76.
[12] Baumstark, op. cit., p. 90.
[13] Ibid., p. 152.
[14] Ibid., p. 250.
[15] Edition with German translation, by J. Schieblitz: *Išodadh's Kom-
mentar zum Buche Hiob*, I Teil (1907), in *Beihefte zur ZATW*, XI.

the Talmud and the Midrash, the interpretations of which are not
without interest.[1] Rashi at the end of the ninth century is of the
first order in giving the exact meaning and citing parallel passages.
Sometimes his commentary contains Old French words transcribed
in Hebrew. In the Jewish manual editions of the O.T.[2] he is generally
to be found placed after the Targum and is followed by two anonymous compilations, called *Meṣudat Ṣion* and *Meṣudat David*.
Ibn-Ezra in the eleventh century represents rather the exegesis of
the Spanish Jews, an exegesis which also is concerned with the exact
and literal meaning. The Provençal Ralbag (R. Levi Ben-Gershom)
continued the French tradition in the fourteenth century, while
R. Samuel Ben-Nissim the Younger continued the Spanish tradition.[3] Jewish studies of the exegesis of Job up to the fourteenth
century have been used by the anonymous commentary of the
library of the University of Cambridge.[4]

[1] Cf. *Das Buch Hiob nach der Auffassung des Talmud und Midrasch*,
I (1902), by Isaak Wiernikowski.
[2] Chiefly in those of Warsaw.
[3] Cf. W. Bacher, *Rev. des Études juives*, **21** (1890), pp. 118ff., and the
correction, ibid., **22** (1891), pp. 135f.
[4] *A Commentary on the Book of Job, from a Hebrew Manuscript in the
University Library, Cambridge*, ed. by William Aldis Wright (London, 1905).

THE BOOK OF JOB

TEXT AND COMMENTARY

CHAPTER 1

1   There was in the land of Uṣ a man of the name of Job. This

Chapters 1-2 Prologue in prose. History: see Introduction, pp. xvff. Literary criticism: see Introduction, pp. lxiiiff. Composition: see Introduction, pp. lxxiiff.

1: **1** After ἄνθρωπος G (B, **א**) adds τις (Jerome *quidam*), marked by an obelus in Syro-hex. The words ἐν γῇ Οὑς, a translation of בארץ־עוץ in Aq. and Theod., become ἐγγύους in the margin of Syro-hex. For תם וישר G has ἀληθινός, ἄμεμπτος, δίκαιος (A puts ἀληθινός at the end). In Syro-hex. ἄμεμπτος is marked by an obelus; cf. 2: 3. The adjective תם is translated ἁπλοῦς in Aq. and Theod. (cf. Vulg. *simplex*). G renders מרע by ἀπὸ παντὸς πονηροῦ πράγματος. In Syro-hex., obelus before πράγματος. No obelus in Jerome *ab omni re mala*; cf. v. 8 and 2: 3.

The opening phrase איש היה, instead of the current formula ויהי איש, shows that the story is not connected with any previous narrative. It is by a similar idiom that Nathan begins his parable in 2 S 12: 1, 'There were two men in a certain city . . . .' Again, compare Est 2: 5, 'Now there was a Jew in Susa, the capital, and his name was Mordecai . . . .' On the question of Job's country and his friends, cf. Intro., pp. xxiff. The expression איוב שמו takes the place of the normal ושמו איוב. Similarly we find בקע משקלו 'a half shekel its weight' with the meaning 'of the weight of a half shekel', in Gn 24: 22. Attempts have been made to derive the name איוב from a root appropriate to the story

narrated about Job. Some suggest the root איב 'to be hostile' and see in איוב a form analogous to ילוד 'new-born', and thus arrive at the meaning 'hated', 'persecuted'. Job, it is thus suggested, is a man who is the target of the persecutions of God or Satan. It is thus that the word is explained in the *Thesaurus* of Gesenius (I, p. 81), who quotes further גבור as a parallel form. But גבור 'strong', 'brave', 'warlike' has rather an active than a passive meaning. The form *qittôl* derived from *qittâl* or *qattâl* designates those people who are accustomed to perform a specific action (Gesenius-Kautzsch, § 84 e). It is by way of exception that ילוד has a passive sense, and it is probable that the original form was *yullôd* (Barth, cited ibid.). The meaning of איוב would in that case be 'enemy', 'one who nourishes hatred'. Merx, who modifies this meaning to that of 'aggressor', wishes to see nevertheless in איוב a symbolic name. It must be admitted, however, that such a symbolic name would have been extremely ill chosen, for after all it is not as an aggressor that the personality of Job has remained in the memory of mankind! Arabic exegetes have preferred to seek in איוב a connection with the Arabic root اوب 'to return', 'to be converted' whence *'awwâb*

man was perfect and upright, fearing Elohim and turning away from evil.

2   There were born to him seven sons and three daughters.

'*resipiscens*', 'he who turns again', an epithet applied to David and Job in the Koran (Sura 38). But it is clear that the Arabs punned on the words *Ayûb* (Job) and *'awwâb*. Here too the symbol would have been in bad taste. Job is not the type of the repentant man. He is the type of the righteous man who suffers despite his righteousness, of the man who is overwhelmed by undeserved afflictions. Outside the Bible his name recurs in A-ia-ab (for Ayâb, whence אִיּוֹב, אִיּוֹב) found in the letters of el-Amarna (Knudtzon, no. 256, 6, 13; Thureau-Dangin, *RA*, **19**, pp. 95f.). Let us notice that this *Aiâb* is a king of the town wrongly read as *Bi-ḫi-ši*, which should be read as *Pi-ḫi-lim*, identical with Fâhil, Pella (*RB*, 1924, p. 9). The virtue of Job is well expressed by the phrase תם וישר 'perfect and upright' (v. 8; 2 : 3). The adjective תָּם, which recurs in 8 : 20 and three times in 9 : 20-2, has yielded to the word תָּמִים (12 : 4; 36 : 4; 37 : 16), which is frequently found. Outside Job, תָּם is found only in Gn 25 : 27; Ps 44 : 5; Pr 29 : 10. It is by a mistake that it appears in Ps 37 : 37, where the versions have the abstract words תֹּם 'perfection' and יֹשֶׁר 'uprightness', demanded by such verbs as שמר 'observe' and ראה 'contemplate'. The plural seems to exist in Ex 26 : 24; 36 : 29. But it is תֹּמִים (for תְּאֹמִים) which these two texts should have (Gesenius-Buhl, p. 880 A, s.v.). Feminine is תַּמָּתִי 'my perfect lady' (Ca 5 : 2; 6 : 9). The root תמם has the meaning of 'complete', 'finished', 'perfect' (31 : 40; cf. 4 : 6; 22 : 3). Its exact meaning is that a thing or a person is intrinsically perfect, whilst the root ישר 'to

be upright, just' suggests rather perfection in relation to others. The two ideas are complementary. There is parallelism between תֹּם 'perfection' and יֹשֶׁר 'uprightness' in Ps 37 : 37 (cf. sup.); the expression תֹּם־וָיֹשֶׁר 'perfection and uprightness' occurs in Ps 25 : 21. What follows, 'fearing Elohim and turning away from evil' (v. 8; 2 : 3) likewise expresses two correlative ideas, for the 'fear of Adonai is wisdom and to depart from evil is understanding' (28 : 28). Cf. Pr 3 : 7, 'Be not wise in your own eyes: fear Yahweh and turn away from evil'; Pr 14 : 16, 'A wise man fears (God) and turns away from evil.' The fear of God in itself turns man away from evil: 'and by the fear of the Lord a man avoids evil' (Pr. 16 : 6). Job is the perfect man. He will carry his anxiety to avoid evil so far as to remove from his house whatever, remotely or at hand, voluntarily or involuntarily, might bring disgrace (v. 5).

2 The consecutive *waw* establishes a close connection between the perfection of Job and the number of his children, for 'the heritage which Yahweh gives consists of sons, His recompense is the fruit of the womb' (Ps 127 : 3). He who fears God and walks in His ways beholds his sons as olive plants around his table (Ps 128 : 3). Sons, much more appreciated than daughters by orientals, exceed his daughters in the proportion of seven to three. In 42 : 13 the number of Job's sons will be doubled (cf. Comm.), while that of his daughters remains the same. Fecundity such as indicates the blessing of God should include 'seven sons' (1 S 2 : 5; Ru 4 : 15). The proportion seven to three is found again in the seven

3   His cattle consisted of seven thousand sheep and three thousand camels, five hundred yoke of oxen and five hundred she-

thousand sheep and the three thousand camels (v. 3). Compare the 700 wives and 300 concubines of Solomon (1 K 11: 3).

3   For אתונות G has ὄνοι θήλειαι νομάδες. Obelus before θήλειαι in Syrohex. A double translation of ועבדה רבה מאד is found in G: καὶ ὑπηρεσία πολλὴ σφόδρα καὶ ἔργα μεγάλα ἦν αὐτῷ ἐπὶ τῆς γῆς. The translation καὶ ὑπηρεσία πολλὴ σφόδρα was marked by an obelus, according to Chrysostom. It figures however in Sah. and has no obelus in Jerome, nor in Syro-hex. For עבדה, Aq. has δουλεία but Symm. οἰκετία (cf. Vulg. *familia*). G omits כל before בני and translates בני־קדם by τῶν ἀφ’ ἡλίου ἀνατολῶν (cf. G in Is 9: 11).

Generally camels and asses are not included among the animals grouped under the name of מקנה 'possessions', 'herds', 'flocks' (cf. Gk κτῆνος). However Ex 9: 3 enumerates thus the animals composing the 'cattle which are in the field'—horses, asses, camels, oxen, and sheep. The number 10 obtained by adding 7 thousand and 3 thousand occurs again if we add 500 yoke of oxen and 500 she-asses. Camels were regarded as constituting the chief wealth of the nomad. Bochart cites an interesting passage from Aristotle affirming that Arabs possess sometimes as many as 3,000 camels (precisely our figure): κέκτηνται δ'ἔνιοι τῶν ἄνω καμήλους καὶ τρισχιλίας (*De anim. hist.*, IX, 50,5). The she-ass is more valuable than the ass because of its milk and fecundity. עבדה is found again only in Gn 26: 14, where, after 'flocks of sheep and herds of oxen', wealth included עבדה רבה as here. Now, in the parallel passage Gn 12: 16, the wealth of Abraham includes 'sheep

and oxen and asses, and menservants and maidservants, and she-asses and camels'. A comparison of our verse with Gn 26: 14 and Gn 12: 16 shows clearly that עבדה replaces עבדים ושפחות 'menservants and maidservants'. It is an abstract term like פקדה 'magistracy' (Is 60: 17). Hence there is no reason to dispute the meaning 'domestic personnel', Latin *famulatus* (contra Ehrlich, who translates *Arbeitsvieh*) for עבדה. Sa'adia interprets by means of עבידא, i.e. the Arabic عبيد plural of عبد 'servant', 'slave'. What follows, 'and this man was the greatest of all the sons of the east', takes גדול in the sense of great by means of wealth. We have quoted Gn 26: 14 in connection with wealth of cattle and servants. This verse is preceded by the following: 'And the man grew great, and went on increasing until he became very great' (Gn 26: 13). Thus three times the verb גדל 'to be great', 'to become great', is used with the meaning of 'to be and become rich'. בני־קדם 'sons of the east', a general term for orientals. In Gn 29: 1 the 'land of the sons of the east' denotes the regions to the east of the Euphrates. For the inhabitants of Palestine the designation includes the countries situated east of the Jordan and the Dead Sea. The sons of the east are contrasted, geographically, with the Philistines of the west (Is 11: 14). The same term is applied in particular to the nomadic Arabs (Jer 49: 28; Ezk 25: 4, 10) who make common cause with the Midianites and the Amalekites (Jg 6: 3,33; 7: 12; 8 :10). The wisdom of the sons of the east is made parallel to that of the Egyptians (1 K 4: 30).

asses; in addition he had many servants. And this man was the greatest of all the children of the east.

4   Now, his sons were accustomed to go and hold a feast in the house of each, on his day, and they would send invitations to their three sisters to eat and drink with them.

5   As soon as the feast days were finished, Job used to send for

5   וְקִלְלוּ (cf. G, Targ., Syr.); MT: וברכו (cf. v. 11).

4 After בניו G adds πρὸς ἀλλήλους. The word בית is omitted by G καθ' ἑκάστην ἡμέραν and by Aq. ἕκαστος τὴν ἑαυτοῦ ἡμέραν.

Perfect tense of habit in v. 4 and the second part of v. 5; cf. 1 S 1: 3. The sons of Job are seven. They hold a feast 'in the house of each, on his day', i.e. every day of the week (cf. v. 13). The three sisters are present at all the meetings. The numeral שלשת before a feminine seems irregular. The construction, however, recurs in Gn 7: 13; 1 S 10: 3. The verb קרא 'cry', with לְ" before the complement, in the meaning of 'cry to . . .' (17: 4), 'call' (19: 16), 'invite' (1 K 1: 19, 25, 26).

5 G adds περὶ αὐτῶν after והעלה but has simply αὐτῶν for כלם (cf. v. 3). The addition which G makes after כלם, καὶ μόσχον ἕνα περὶ ἁμαρτίας περὶ (A ὑπὲρ) τῶν ψυχῶν αὐτῶν (Sah., Eth., Jerome *et vitulum unum pro peccato animarum ipsarum*), is a gloss on the previous phrase and imputes to the children of Job a fault which is hypothetical only. This addition is marked by an obelus in Syro-hex. and Jerome. For ברכו, Targ. ארגיזו 'they have irritated' (trans. of קללו; cf. Levy, *Chald. Wörterbuch*, p. 405), Syr. ܐܠܗܐ 'they have offended', G κακὰ ἐνενόησαν (Jerome *et maledixerint*), but Aq. ηὐλόγησαν, Vulg. *et benedixerint*; cf. 5: 11; 2: 5, 9.

Ehrlich rightly protests against those who make of יְמֵי the subject of הָקִיפוּ. The verb נקף, whence comes

the *hiph'il* הקיפו, has exactly the same meaning as קוף which is the root of תקופה 'a cycle of time', 'the revolution of a period', 'a season'. The *hiph'il* means to 'complete a cycle' and the subject is contained in the characters mentioned in v. 5: 'as soon as they had completed the days of their feast'. וַיְקַדְּשֵׁם is translated as 'and he sanctified them', or 'he purified them'. Duhm argues at length about the type of purification involved. Now, as is shown by B. Jacob (*ZATW*, 1912, p. 278), the verb קָדַשׁ, in this context and others like it (Ex 19: 10, 14; Jl 1: 14; 2: 15; 4: 9; Lv 25: 10), means 'to convoke to a solemn feast', or, as is proposed by Ehrlich, 'to give warning that a solemn feast is being prepared'. Cf. the use of קַדֵּשׁ in Jer 22: 7. Job sends to summon his sons to a sacrifice which he will perform in their name. We are outside the borders of Israel. The father of the family is the high priest. His rectitude is such that he fears even the shadow of a fault which might sully the good name of his family. In the heat of wine, the young men may have forgotten the commandments of God. The verb בֵּרְכוּ is a euphemism to prevent contact between the divine name and a verb expressing affront. We think it evident that the verb was קִלְלוּ; cf. Targ, and 1 S 3: 13, where the juxtaposition of the verb קלל with the divine name has been avoided by the writing of להם in-them; then he would rise early in the morning, and offer burnt sacrifices according to their number, for Job said to himself: 'Perhaps my sons have sinned and have *cursed* Elohim in their hearts!' Thus did Job always.

6   There was a day when the sons of Elohim came to present themselves before Yahweh, and Satan also came among them.

stead of אלהים. The meaning 'curse Elohim' is further elucidated by בִּלְבָבָם 'in their heart', for the verb קִלֵּל. mean originally 'treat lightly and contemptuously'. At the end of the verse, כָּל־הַיָּמִים 'every day' implies 'always'.

6 Targ. identifies the day with 'the day of judgment at the beginning of the year' (cf. 2: 1). Syro-hex. places an obelus before the αὕτη of G ἡ ἡμέρα αὕτη, which translates היום. For ויבא, G has καὶ ἰδοὺ ἦλθον, but G (A) omits ἰδού (Sah., Eth.), which is marked by an obelus in Syro-hex. G renders בני־האלהים by οἱ ἄγγελοι τοῦ θεοῦ (Sah., Syro-hex., Eth.). In Jerome (Gall.) and Aug. we find *angeli Dei*, but *angeli* alone in Bod. and Tur. Syro-hex. quotes in the margin the translation 'sons', instead of 'angels'. Targ. translates כתי מלאכיא 'hosts of angels' (cf. 2: 1; 38: 7). The word גם, omitted in G, is rendered *equidem* in Jerome (Bod., and Tur.), *etiam* in Gall. For השטן, Targ. and Syr. have סטנא, Vulg. *Satan*, G ὁ διάβολος. At the end, G (A) adds περιελθὼν τὴν γῆν καὶ ἐμπεριπατήσας τὴν ὑπ' οὐρανόν in accordance with v. 7. This addition is found also in Sah. and Memph. The introductory phrase וַיְהִי הַיּוֹם (v. 13; 2: 1; 1 S 1: 4; 14: 1; 2 K 4: 8, 11, 18) means 'there came a day when', or simply 'one day when . . .' (cf. our Comm. on 1 S 1: 4). The succeeding phrase is regularly introduced by *waw* consecutive and the imperfect. The 'sons of Elohim' are identified with the angels by Septuagint and Targum, whilst the

Vulgate and the Peshitta retain 'the sons of God'. In truth, here as in 38: 7, it is the angels who are meant. Their title 'sons of Elohim' contrasts them with the sons of man (Gn 11: 5ff.) and the daughters of man (Gn 6: 1-4). From their union with the latter were born the giants (Gn 6: 4). The sons of God, set in parallelism with the stars of the morning (38: 7), dwell in the heavens (Ps 89: 7) and form the 'hosts of heaven' who hold themselves in readiness to obey Yahweh (1 K 22: 19 ff.). The scene is the same as that in 1 K 22: 19ff., where among the sons of God, i.e. the angels who serve Yahweh, is found the spirit who is to lead Ahab to ruin. The expression התיצב על־יהוה 'present themselves before the Lord' implies the attitude of the servant before his master (cf. Zec 6: 5). Cf. עמד עליו in 1 K 22: 19. Among the sons of God Satan has insinuated himself. The noun שָׂטָן is preceded by the article as in Zec 3: 1ff. He is essentially the adversary at law, the accuser (ibid.); cf. below Comm. on 30: 12 and the use of שָׂטָן in Ps 109: 6. After becoming a proper noun it is written without the article, and the figure comes to represent the instigator of evil; cf. 1 Ch 21: 1, where it replaces Yahweh who is found in the parallel passage of 2 S 24: 1. Our story gives him a very well defined personality. Not only will he challenge the virtue of Job, but he will be given the task of inflicting calamities on Job. St Thomas Aquinas shows well how the scene should be interpreted: *Hoc symbolice et sub aenigmate proponitur,*

7　　And Yahweh said to Satan: 'Whence comest thou?' And Satan
answered Yahweh and said: 'From roaming the earth and
walking up and down in it!'

8　　And Yahweh said to Satan: 'Hast thou considered my servant
Job? There is no one like him on the earth; he is a perfect and
upright man, fearing Elohim and turning away from evil!'

9　　And Satan answered Yahweh and said: 'Is it for nothing that
Job fears Elohim?

secundum consuetudinem Sacrae Scripturae, quae res spirituales sub figuris rerum corporalium describit. St John Chrysostom interpreted: κατὰ σχηματισμὸν τὸν λόγον (cf. Knabenbauer).

7 Sah. omits τῷ Κυρίῳ, which renders את־יהוה in G. The reading τὴν ὑπ' οὐρανόν, which in G normally paraphrases הארץ, is marked with an obelus in Syro-hex. Sah. gives simply 'the earth'. After הארץ Targ. adds 'in order to examine the works of men' (cf. 2:2). At the end G (and its derived versions) adds πάρειμι, which is not marked by an obelus in Jerome and Syro-hex.

Yahweh addresses Satan in a familiar tone and the latter gives an account of his doings on the earth. Duhm thinks that the question 'Whence comest thou?' seems to imply a certain ignorance on the part of Yahweh. But Ehrlich retorts by referring to Ex 4:2 where the question 'What have you in your hand?' is intended to give occasion merely to some speech by the interlocutor. The verb שוט (written defectively in 2:2) means to 'go hither and thither', 'to roam' (Nu 11:8, 2 S 24:2). The second verb is התהלך 'to walk up and down', with ב'' before the name of the place (2:2; 38:16). Satan's reply recalls Zec 1:10-11, where the horses symbolise 'those whom Yahweh has sent to roam the earth', להתהלך בארץ (cf. Zec 4:10). Again, in Zec 6:7 the horses are sent off to 'patrol the earth'. Satan, who has travelled over the length and breadth of the earth, must have met the hero of the story. We are about to enter into the action of the drama.

8 For אל־השטן, G has simply αὐτῷ; cf. Vulg. *ad eum*. G renders מרע by ἀπὸ παντὸς πονηροῦ πράγματος (cf. v. 1). Sah. omits πράγματος, as does Jerome, who writes *ab omni malo*. Obelus before παντός and πράγματος in Syro-hex.

Use of שים with the complement לב to imply 'to give one's heart' to a thing, to turn one's attention to it. Cf. the use of שית with לב in 7:17. On these expressions and others like them which suggest that the heart is the seat of attention and of other intellectual activities, see *L'Emploi métaphorique*, pp. 122ff. The object of attention is introduced by על (Hag 1:5, 7) or by אל (2:3; 7:17). The locution 'my servant Job' is characteristic of the Prologue and Epilogue (2:3 and 42:7, 8). The conjunction כי introduces a clause which is a second complement of the verb and whose object is to explain the first complement 'my servant Job'. The construction is the same as that in Gn 1:4, where the verb 'and he saw' has as its first complement 'the light' and as its second, explanatory of the first, 'that it was good'. Yahweh then repeats the praise given in v. 1.

9 Syro-hex. places an obelus before ἐναντίον, which in G translates את. G's reading τὸν Κύριον for אלהים is a proof of the liberty taken by this version in its translation of the divine names. The author has care-

10 Hast Thou not put a hedge around him and his house and all that he has on every side? Thou hast blessed the work of his hands, and his cattle have increased in the land.

11 But do Thou only put forth Thy hand and strike all that he has! He will certainly *curse* Thee to Thy face!'

11 יְקַלְלֶךָ (Targ., Syr.); MT: יברכך (cf. v. 5).

fully avoided placing יהוה on the lips of Satan, who, moreover, merely repeats the stereotyped expression of vv. 1 and 8.

'Is it for nothing that Job fears Elohim?' The whole essence of Satan's irony is expressed in this question. God scatters lavishly His good gifts as the reward of virtue, and man acts from motives of self-interest. If he does good, good fortune follows; if he does ill, he is punished by misfortune. Hence he has no merit in fearing God and avoiding evil. For Satan, the problem set in the Book of Job is solved by asserting that self-interest dictates man's moral conduct. The trials of Job are intended to prove that it is indeed for nothing that the hero of the story is 'perfect and upright'. Use of the adverb חִנָּם in the etymological sense (cf. *gratis* from *gratia*), from חֵן (root חנן). From the meaning of 'gratuitous' is derived that of 'irrationally', 'without justification' (2: 3; 9: 17; 22: 6); cf. gratuitous (arbitrary) hypothesis, or affirmation.

10 There was a certain hesitation between the *kethîb* את and the *qerê* אַתָּה, the latter having finally prevailed by logic (cf. Ginsburg). Targ. softens אתה 'thou' into מימרך 'thy word' (cf. v. 11; 7: 8; 19: 18; 27: 3; 42: 9, 10, and Comm. on 20: 29). G πολλὰ ἐποίησας harmonises פרץ with the other verbs.

The verb שׂוך recurs only in Hos 2: 8, where it is parallel with גדר 'enclose by a hedge'. The noun מְשׂוּכָה, derived from שׂכך (twin root with שׂוך),

is made parallel with גָּדֵר 'wall' in Is 5: 3. In the form מְסוּכָה we find the same noun parallel with חֵדֶק 'thorn bush' in Mic 7: 4. In the form מְשׂכָה it occurs again in מְשׂכַת חָדֶק 'hedge of thorns' in Pr 15: 19. These facts show that the roots שׂוך, סכך, שׂכך, סוך have similar meanings. The original idea is 'to surround with thorns', as with a wall for the purposes of protection. The Arabic *šawk* 'thorn' belongs to the same root as שׂוך, while שֹׂכּות 'thorns', 'shafts' (40: 31) belongs to the root שׂכך. The verb יָשׂוך, with בְּעַד before its complement, has a similar meaning to גדר, which is followed by בעד in La 3: 7. Moreover we shall see that the verb סוך (equivalent root to שׂוך) is also followed by בעד in 3: 23 to signify 'enclose', 'shut in'. The meaning of 'protection' is retained here. The phrase מִסָּבִיב 'on every side' corresponds to the Assyrian *ana siḫirti* 'all around', meaning 'as a whole'. 'The work of his hands', like the Assyrian *epšit qâtâ* 'work of the hands', suggests what one does and undertakes. Cf. Dt 2: 7, 'for Yahweh thy God has blessed thee in all the work of thy (Sam., G, Syr., Vulg.) hands'. In 14: 15; 34: 19, it is the result of the work, man made by the hands of God. The verb פרץ 'overflow' marks the superlative degree of רבה 'to be numerous' (Ex 1: 12). It is the symbol for a superabundance of cattle (Gn 30: 30).

11 Targ. renders ידך by מחת ידך

12   And Yahweh said to Satan: 'All that he has is in thy power;
      only upon himself do not stretch forth thy hand.' And Satan
      left the presence of Yahweh.

13   And there came a day when his sons and his daughters were
      eating and drinking wine in their eldest brother's house.

'the blow of thy hand'. For יברכך,
Targ. ירגזנך, Syr. ܠܘܣܝ (cf. v. 5),
reading יְקַלְלָךְ. G εὐλογήσει is explained by Olympiodorus as a correction of βλασφημήσει. Similarly
Vulg. *benedixerit* is equivalent to
maledixerit for St Thomas Aquinas.
Targ. renders על־פניך by
באנפי מימרך 'in face of thy word' (cf. v.
10).

The formula וְאוּלָם 'and yet', 'but'
(Gn 48: 19) is frequent in Job as a
means of introducing a phrase which
expresses an idea contrary to what
precedes (11: 5; 12: 7; 13: 4; 14: 18;
33: 1). The verb שלח, with יד as a
complement, means to 'stretch out
the hand' in order to strike (Ex
3: 20; 9: 15, etc.). In 28: 9 the object which is struck is preceded by
the preposition ב״ which is placed
here before the complement of נגע
'touch', 'strike' (v. 19; 5: 19; 19: 21).
If this complement is preceded by
אל (2: 5) or by עד (4: 5) then the
verb נגע means 'touch', 'reach' rather
than hit violently. The formula
אם־לא 'if . . . not' is elliptical. It
implies the curse 'May God do so to
me and more also'; cf. 1 S 3: 17;
14: 44; 20: 13, etc. Cf. the use of אם
in 6: 28. Thus אם־לא becomes a
mode of absolute affirmation, 'most
certainly' (1 K 20: 23; Is 5: 9). St
Thomas explains very well that before *nisi* (אם־לא) we should add *ma-
lum mihi accidat*. The expression
על־פניך 'to thy face' means to say
'impudently'. Same meaning in
על־פניכם 'before your face' (6: 28),
על־פניך 'before his face' (21: 31).
These parallels do not authorise for
על־פניו the meaning of 'immediately' supposed by Ehrlich (on Dt

7: 10). We have אֶל instead of עַל in
2: 5 (cf. v. 8 and 42: 7); 13: 15.

12 The versions add a verb before
בידך: G δίδωμι (A δέδωκα), Vulg.
sunt, Targ. מסיר 'delivered to', Syr.
ܡܥܠܡ 'abandoned to'. Syro-hex.
marks δίδωμι with an obelus. G renders אל־ידך by μὴ ἅψῃ (Jerome *noli
tangere*). For מעם־פני יהוה G has
simply παρὰ τοῦ Κυρίου, but G (A) ἀπὸ
προσώπου Κυρίου (Jerome *a facie
Domini*; Sah., Eth., Arab. Baud.).
Syro-hex. has ܡܢ in the text but
ܡܢ ܦܢܝܘܣܦ (ἀπὸ προσώπου) in the
margin. Targ. adds בהרמנא 'with
permission' (הרמנא from ἁρμονία)
after the translation of ויצא, to show
that Satan leaves by divine authorisation.

The contention of Satan is that
Job's virtue depends on a self-interested calculation (v. 9): *do ut des!* God
who has emphasised the perfection of
His servant cannot allow him to be
thus depreciated. One test is possible,
that which Satan has suggested:
that of withdrawing the properties
which Job possesses. A beginning
will be made with כָּל־אֲשֶׁר־לוֹ 'all
that is his' (v. 10). The goods of Job
are in your hand, i.e. at your disposal; you can do with them as you
please. For the moment the person
of Job will be respected; the trial
must be progressive. Hardly has
Satan received the necessary authorisation when he hastens to put the
plan into execution.

13 For ויהי היום, Targ. has 'and it
was the beginning of the days of the
week'. G οἱ υἱοὶ Ἰὼβ καὶ αἱ θυγατέρες
αὐτοῦ and Syr. 'the sons and the
daughters of Job' make explicit the

14   And there came a messenger to Job and said: 'The oxen were plowing and the she-asses feeding beside them;

15   Then the Sabaeans made an incursion and took them and put the servants to the sword; and I alone am escaped to tell thee!'

suffixes of בניו ובנתיו. For אכלים ושתים יין G (B, א) has simply ἔπινον οἶνον (Sah., Syro-hex.) but G (A) ἤσθιον καὶ ἔπινον οἶνον. The words ἤσθιον καί, marked with an asterisk, are translated in Jerome and in the margin of Syro-hex. The word יין is not translated in Syr. (= v. 4). Note that οἶνον is omitted in Eth. and Arab. Baud.

The beginning וַיְהִי הַיּוֹם as in v. 6. Since the feast takes place in the house of the eldest brother, it must be the beginning of the week. This is how the Targum understood the matter. Wine is drunk as on feast days. The word יין will recur in v. 18. Its omission in Syr. (cf. Eth. and Arab. Baud.) is not a sufficient reason for eliminating it, since it is supported by G, Vulg. Targ. (cf. Beer in ed. Kittel). The author stresses the character of the banquet in order to make more vivid the contrast with the catastrophe which is to follow.

14   For וּמַלְאָךְ, G has καὶ ἰδοὺ ἄγγελος (cf. v. 6). Syro-hex. puts an obelus before ἰδού. After καὶ εἶπεν (וַיֹּאמֶר) G adds αὐτῷ, marked with an obelus in Syro-hex. For הבקר G has τὰ ζεύγη τῶν βοῶν. After 'yoke of oxen', Arab. Baud. adds 'have just died'. The same version introduces the camels of v. 3.

The verb בָּא is in the perfect, it is not a participle. To vary the style of his narrative, the author resorts to a new turn of phrase, instead of וַיָּבֹא which would normally be expected. The collective noun בָּקָר, like גָּמָל 'camel' and פֶּרֶא 'wild ass', is used indifferently as masculine and feminine (cf. Ex 21: 37 and Gn 33: 13).

The verb היה with the present participle marks the continuity of the action. It is like our English construction 'to be' with present participle. Cf. הָיוּ מְלַקְטִים 'used to pick up' (Jg 1: 7). Masc. suffix in יְדֵיהֶם, despite the gender of הבקר in this verse (cf. 39: 3; 42: 15; cited in Gesenius-Kautzsch § 135o). The expression עַל־יְדֵי 'beside' (Nu 34: 3; Jg 11: 26) is to be compared with the Assyrian idû, idâ, which often means 'beside' (cf. L'Emploi métaphorique, p. 139). The messenger dwells on the calm which prevailed at the moment. It was a time exactly right for a raid.

15   G connects שְׁבָא with שָׁבָה 'to take captive'. Hence οἱ αἰχμαλωτεύοντες (Sah., Eth., Syro-hex.); Jerome and Aug. hostes. In Syr. ‫ܠ‬ 'the bands'. Vulg. et irruerunt Sabaei recognises the proper noun. By identification of שבא with the precious stone שְׁבוּ, Targ. renders שבא by זמרגד 'emerald' in 6: 19, which permits it to see here, on account of the fem. תפל, 'Lilith queen of emerald'. Arab. Baud. places already here by anticipation the 'violent wind' of v. 19. Sah. omits the καὶ τοὺς παῖδας ἀπέκτειναν ἐν μαχαίραις of G. This passage is present in Syrohex. and Jerome. It is not marked by an asterisk. Instead of ἐν μαχαίραις (B, א, Syro-hex., Eth., Arab. Baud., Jerome gladiis), G (A) has more literally ἐν στόματι μαχαίρας. Syr. has simply ‫ܒܚܪܒܐ‬ 'by the sword'.

The name of the town שְׁבָא is used to denote its inhabitants, the Sabaeans (cf. Vulg.). The verb is feminine because the noun is used as the name of a place. Many examples in Ge-

16   As he was yet speaking, another arrived and said: 'The fire of
     Elohim has fallen from heaven; it has burnt the sheep and the

senius-Kautzsch, § 122i (cf. 1 S
17: 21; 2 S 8: 2, etc.). In 6: 19 שְׁבָא
is parallel with תֵּמָא. Now, in the
annals of Tiglath-pileser III the
town of Saba' is mentioned after
Tema (RB, 1910, p. 196). In Is
21: 13ff. and Jer 25: 23, תֵּימָא is
connected with דְּדָן, while in Gn
10: 7 (at the end) and 25: 3 it is שְׁבָא
which is grouped with דְדן. The
locality of Tema is known to us: it
is the oasis of Tema to the N.E. of
Medaïn-Ṣaleḥ, in the territory of
Medina. The name has remained the
same through the ages. As for Dedan, it is in the oasis of el-'Ela that
it should be sought, according to the
discovery of Jaussen and Savignac
(RB, 1910, p. 525). Thus the field is
fairly well circumscribed for the
localisation of Saba' in a zone crossed
by a line from el-'Ela to Teimâ.
Glaser suggests that we should see a
reminiscence of Sheba in the name
Wâdî-eš-Šabâ which Bekrî discovers
in the territory of Medina (RB, 1910,
p. 530). In any case we are on the
southern border of the land of Uṣ
(cf. Intro., pp. xxiif.). Thus it is understandable how the Sabaeans suddenly attack the servants of Job.
The verb נפל 'fall' is used in the
sense of 'make irruption'. The edge
of the sword is described as פִּי־חֶרֶב
'mouth of the sword', because the
sword devours its victim (Dt 32: 42;
2 S 2: 26); cf. L'Emploi métaphorique,
p. 86. The consecutive imperfect
with the cohortative ending will
occur again in the following vv. and
in 30: 26. The pleonasms רַק־אֲנִי
and לְבַדִּי which recur in vv. 16, 17,
19, stress the emotion of the messenger. The survivor has the mission
of telling the story of the catastrophe
(Gn 14: 13; Ezk 24: 26ff.).

16   For וזה G and its derived ver-

sions have ἕτερος ἄγγελος. Obelus before ἄγγελος in Syro-hex. After וַיֹּאמֶר
G adds πρὸς 'Ιώβ, marked with an
obelus in Syro-hex. G (A) puts πρὸς
'Ιώβ after ἄγγελος and αὐτῷ after εἶπεν.
For אֵשׁ אֱלֹהִים G has simply πῦρ,
but Jerome ignis Dei, with asterisk
before Dei. Instead of בַּנְּעָרִים, supported by vv. 15, 17, G has τοὺς
ποιμένας and Syr. ܟ݁ܢܰܘܳܬ݂ܳܐ reading
רֹעִים, which was perhaps a
variant.

The nominal phrase עוֹד זֶה מְדַבֵּר is
followed by a verbal one beginning
with waw, to indicate the simulta-
neity of the two actions (Gesenius-
Kautzsch §§ 116u and 164a). The
first phrase is as it were suspended;
cf. Vulg. illo adhuc loquente at v. 17.
The pronoun זה...וזה 'this . . . that',
'one . . . another', as in 21: 23, 25.
St Thomas brings out the psychology of the story: Hac autem adversitate nuntiata, statim altera nuntiatur,
ne, si quod intervallum fieret, intus
ad cor suum rediret, et se ad patientiam
praepararet, et sic sequentia facilius
sustineret. 'The fire of God' is the
same thing as the lightning. Same
expression, with מִן־הַשָּׁמַיִם as here,
in 2 K 1 : 10, 12, 14. Elsewhere it is
'the fire of Yahweh' which we find
with the verb נפל 'fall' (1 K 18: 38)
or with בער 'burn' (Nu 11: 1). In
Gn 19: 24 the fire comes 'from
Yahweh, from heaven'. The fire
consumes (15: 34; 20: 26; 22: 20),
as in the episodes of Korah and his
companions (Nu 16: 35; 26: 10),
and the soldiers sent against Elijah
(2 K 1: 10, 12, 14). The first blow
came from nomads, the second comes
from heaven and might put Job on
the wrong scent as to the origin of
his ills: ut ejus menti imprimeret quod
non solum ab hominibus, sed etiam
a Deo persecutionem pateretur (St
Thomas).

servants and has devoured them; and I alone am escaped to
tell thee!'

17 While he was yet speaking, another arrived and said: 'The
Chaldaeans have formed three companies, have made a raid
upon the camels, have taken them and have put the servants
to the sword; and I alone am escaped to tell thee!'

18 While he was *yet* speaking, another arrived and said: 'Thy
sons and thy daughters were eating and drinking wine in their
eldest brother's house;

18 Read עַד. MT: עַד.

17 The introductory phrase is rendered in G as in v. 16. Obelus marks in Syro-hex. as before. The proper noun כַּשְׂדִּים is retained by Targ. in the form כַּסְדָּאֵי; Syr. has ܟܠܕܝܐ, Aq. Χαλδαῖοι, and Vulg. *Chaldaei*. G and its derived versions have the common noun ἱππεῖς (cf. the translation of שְׁבָא in v. 15); but Syrohex. quotes in the margin the reading of Aq. After שָׂמוּ G adds ἡμῖν. For רָאשִׁים G (B) has κεφαλάς, G (A, א^{c.a}) ἀρχάς. A margin of Cod. 252 has τάγματα, which recurs in Sah. For לְפִי־חֶרֶב G (ἐν) μαχαίραις (cf. v. 15).

The Chaldaeans here represent the nomadic *Kaldu* met with in the history of the Babylonians and Assyrians. They dwell around the Persian Gulf and along the borders of Arab countries (cf. *RB*, 1910, pp. 384ff.). They form part of the ethnic group of the Aramaeans (ibid.). The plural כַּשְׂדִּים is used, for it is no longer a matter of the name of a town as is the case with שְׁבָא in v. 15. The eponym כֶּשֶׂד (from *Kasd* or *Kald*) is a nephew of Abraham and uncle of Aram (Gn 22: 22). This group forms the transition between the Terahites of the city of Ur (Chaldaeans) and the Aramaeans properly so-called, the *Arimu* who are neighbours of the Kaldu in cuneiform inscriptions (*RB*, 1910, p. 384). The Sabaeans of v. 15 denote rather

Arabic plunderers, whereas the Chaldaeans are Aramaean plunderers. The former came up from the south, the latter spring from the east and north. The word רֹאשׁ 'head' is the technical term to designate a group of combatants (*L'Emploi métaphorique*, p. 31). The tripartite division is classical (Jg 7: 16, 20; 1 S 11: 11; 13: 17f.). The use of פָּשַׁט 'hurl themselves' with עַל־ as in Jg 9: 33, 41. After the oxen, she-asses, and smaller cattle, it is the turn of the camels. The whole wealth of the nomad disappears in one stroke after another. The end as in vv. 15-16.

18 At the beginning, read עַד (cf. vv. 16, 17) with 18 MSS and the versions. Syro-hex. forgets to put the obelus before ἄγγελος, which is added by G (cf. vv. 16-17) but it does place itbefor e τῷ 'Ιώβ. The word יַיִן is not rendered in G or in Syr. (cf. v. 13). It should be noted that Jerome has *vinum* without asterisk and that Syro-hex. cites ܚܡܪܐ 'wine' in the margin (following Aq.).

The story reverts to the scene sketched in v. 13. All the events take place on the same day and at about the same time. Satan began by attacking the wealth of Job, 'all that is his' (v. 10). He will now attack Job's family, 'his house' (ibid.). The moment of the feast is well chosen for it ensures that doom overtakes all the children (v. 4).

19   And behold a great wind came from the direction of the desert,
     and struck the four corners of the house; it fell on the young
     people and they died; and I alone am escaped to tell thee!'

20   Then Job rose up and rent his mantle. He shaved his head, fell
     to the ground and prostrated himself.

19 G adds the subject of יפל, namely ἡ οἰκία. The text of Jerome,
*domus super pueros tuos et mortui
sunt*, does not figure in Bod. and Tur.
but is restored in Gall. For הנערים G
has τὰ παιδία σου. It is by mistake
that Syro-hex. marks with an obelus
the words corresponding to τοῦ ἀπαγ-
γεῖλαί σοι.

The meaning of מֵעֵבֶר is simply
'from the direction of', the word עבר
suggesting the zone which the wind
cuts across. The desert wind is
known as רוח מדבר (Jer 13:24). It
blows in whirlwind gusts and can
thus strike the four corners of the
house at the same time. The word
רוּחַ is used first in the feminine and
then in the masculine as subject of
יגע (cf. 4:15; 41:8). The verb נגע
takes ב״ before the complement (cf.
v. 11). The author includes all the
young people in the term הַנְּעָרִים
which up to now has denoted the
servants (cf. Latin *pueri*). The end
is always the same.

20 Syro-hex. marks with an obelus
οὕτως, which G puts at the beginning
of the verse. After οὕτως G (A) adds
ἀκούσας, and is followed by Arab.
Baud. For את־ראשׁ G has τὴν κόμην
τῆς κεφαλῆς, G (A, אᶜˑᵃ) adds αὐτοῦ
which recurs in the derived versions.
Later G (A) adds καὶ κατεπάσατο . . .
αὐτοῦ as in 2:12. At the close G
(A, אᶜˑᵃ) and Memph. add τῷ Κυρίῳ.
The opening וַיָּקָם 'and he rose up'
suggests the rapidity of the movements which are to follow; cf. 2 S
13:31. The first sign of sorrow is the
rending of the garments (2:12). Cf.
the action of Jacob (Gn 37:34),
Joshua (7:6), Ezra (9:3, 5), Mor-

decai (Est 4:1). It was customary to
tear garments in mourning (Lagrange, *ÉRS*, pp. 320ff.). The Sabines
tore their clothes when about to
fight (Livy, I, 13), Caesar tore his
clothes after passing the Rubicon
(Suetonius, *Div. Jul.*, 33). It is his
מְעִיל which Job rends. The word
denotes the mantle which eminent
persons wore above the tunic, e.g.
Saul (1 S 24:5, 12), Jonathan (1 S
18:4), the princes of the sea (Ezk
26:16). Another mark of sorrow was
the shaving of the head (Lagrange,
op. cit., p. 322). The custom is referred to again, with the verb גזז as
here, in Jer 7:29; Mic 1:16. Fried.
Delitzsch quotes quite rightly the
passage of Sargon (*Annals*, 204)
which says that Merodach-baladan
II 'threw himself on the ground,
tore his garments, and took the
razor'. The word *naglabu* 'razor' of
this passage reappears as a symbol
of the mourning inflicted by Sargon
on the king Ursâ of Urarṭu (Thureau-Dangin, *Huitième campagne de
Sargon*, pp. 74 ff.). Bochart heaps up
quotations from the classics relative
to the same customs. Thus in the
Iliad (XXIII, 45ff.) Achilles swears
that he will not again wash until he
has placed on the pyre the corpse
of Patroclus, has raised up for him a
tomb, and has shaved off his hair,
κείρασθαί τε κόμην. Eustathius, in his
commentary on this text of Homer,
points out the frequency of the custom among the ancients. He remarks (on *Iliad* XXIV, 165) that in
Greek tragedy Priam was always
represented with his head shaven as
a sign of his many afflictions. Hence
the typical expression πριαμωθῆναι
as a synonym of ξυρηθῆναι. Job pros-

21   And he said: 'Naked I came out of my mother's womb and

trates himself as a mark of adoration.

21 Syro-hex. marks with an obelus the pronoun אוֹ which replaces the αὐτός of G at the beginning of the words of Job. Syr. omits שָׁמָּה. G translates by ἐχεῖ, Vulg. by *illuc*, but Targ. clarifies by means of לבית קבורתא 'in the sepulchre'. The first two occurrences of יהוה are rendered by מימרא דיי 'word of Yahweh' in Targ. (cf. vv. 10-11). After לקח G and its derived versions add ὡς τῷ Κυρίῳ ἔδοξεν οὕτως ἐγένετο. This addition is marked by an obelus in Syro-hex. and accompanied by the remark οὐ κεῖται ἐν τῷ Ἑβραικῷ in Colb. and Cod. 253. The text of Jerome, *sicut Domino placuit ita factum est*, has been adopted by the Vulgate and the Latin fathers (cf. Sabatier). Let us note that the phrase, which appears neither in Targ. nor in Syr., would break the rhythm of the MT. At the end G (A) adds εἰς τοὺς αἰῶνας, adopted by Arab. Baud. Cf. the addition, 'from now and for evermore', in Arab. (after Ps 113: 2).

The reading יצתי is a defective writing for יָצָאתִי; cf. מלתי for מלאתי (32 : 18), צמתי for צמאתי (Jg 4 : 19), מצתי for מצאתי (Nu 11 : 11). Our passage inspires Sir 40: 1, 'from the day when he leaves the womb of his mother unto the day when he returns to the mother of all'. Of course it is not a question of a return to the maternal womb, since man 'cannot enter a second time into his mother's womb and be born again' (Jn 3: 4). But man, once dead, enters the matrix of the earth. It is from the ground that man was taken and it is thither that he must return (Gn 3: 19). It is in the bowels of the earth that the body of man has been formed (Ps 39: 13, 15; cf. *RB*, 1920, p. 468). Hence the earth is the 'mother of us all' (Sir 40: 1). The many allusions to the earth-mother in Greek and Latin authors have been collected by Dietrich in his study on *Mutter Erde* (*Archiv für Religionswissenschaft*, **8**, 1905, pp. 31ff.). Very striking are the quotations from Euripides: ἄπαντα τίκτει χθὼν πάλιν τε λαμβάνει, from Menander: γῆ πάντα τίκτει καὶ πάλιν κομίζεται, from Ennius: *terra gentes omnes peperit et resumit denuo* (ibid., p. 35). Caesar's interpreters explain to him a dream by reference to the double meaning of the word mother: *mater quam subjectam sibi vidisset non alia esset quam terra, quae omnium parens haberetur* (Suetonius, *Div. Jul.*, 7). For Virgil the earth is *omniparens* (cf. μητέρα πάντων of Sir 40: 1). In his Testament, Villon leaves his body '*à nostre grand mère la terre . . . . De terre vint, en terre tourne!*' In Shakespeare, Timon of Athens' apostrophe to the earth (IV, 3) might also be quoted: 'Common mother, thou, Whose womb unmeasurable and infinite breast Teems and feeds all', etc. Thus Job resigns himself to the common law: man leaves the womb of his mother naked and returns naked to the bosom of the earth. Cf. Ec 5: 14, 'As he came from his mother's womb he shall go again, naked as he came, and shall take nothing for his toil which he may carry away in his hand.' Similarly in 1 Ti 6: 7, 'For we brought nothing into the world and can take nothing out.' Another reason for resignation is that all comes from God, good as well as evil: 'Yahweh gave and Yahweh has taken away!' It is the very formula of oriental resignation. The only course is to allow the sovereign Ruler of the world to act as He wills: 'It is Yahweh: let Him do what seems good in His eyes' (1 S 3: 18). The final benediction is to be found verbally in Ps 113: 2, with the termination מעתה ועד־עולם, *ex hoc nunc et usque in saeculum*, which has

naked shall I return; Yahweh gave and Yahweh has taken
away! Blessed be the name of Yahweh!'
22   In all this Job did not sin or charge God with folly.

been so adopted by Arab. and is
shortened in G (A), Arab. Baud.
Satan, who was expecting to hear
a malediction (v. 11), is faced by the
contrary result.

22 G develops בכל־זאת as follows:
ἐν τούτοις πᾶσιν τοῖς συμβεβηκόσιν αὐτῷ. Syro-hex. and Jerome mark with
an obelus τοῖς σ. α. After איוב G adds
ἐναντίον τοῦ Κυρίου, marked with an
obelus by Jerome and Syro-hex.
After Κυρίου G (A) adds οὐδὲ ἐν τοῖς
χείλεσιν αὐτοῦ, which leaves traces in
Arab. Baud. This addition, like the
Vulg. *labiis suis*, comes from 2: 10.
For תפלה G has ἀφροσύνην, Vulg.
stultum quid, Targ. מלי מחטי 'sinful
words'. The locution נתן תפלה is
rendered by ἠφρονεύσατο in Symm.,
by ܣ݂ܟ݂ܠ in Syr. ('blasphemed').

We have here the author's judgment on Job's conduct. The expression בְּכָל־זֹאת 'in all that' is
ambiguous. G implies that it is a
question of all the circumstances
which have just been narrated. This
is also the opinion of Schlottmann,
Hitzig, and Duhm. But in 2: 10 the
complement 'by his lips' proves that
the author has in view the sin of the
spoken word, and that consequently
'in all that' is an allusion to what
immediately precedes, i.e. to the
words of Job. Moreover, Satan has
spoken about the possibility of bringing a curse to the lips of the holy
man. His failure is evident. The
meaning of the word תִּפְלָה has been
much discussed. Beer would like to

substitute for it עולה or נבלה. Ehrlich proposes to point it תָּפְלָה, giving
to the word the meaning of 'protestation' rather than 'prayer'. Tradition however very strongly affirms
תְּפִלָּה. G here translates תפלה by
ἀφροσύνην and uses this same word
for תָּפֵל in La 2: 14. Likewise, Vulg.
here translates תפלה as *stultum* and
תפל as *stulta* in La 2: 14. The reading
of Symm. ἠφρονεύσατο has as its pendant ἀφροσύνην, which renders תפלה
in Jer 23: 13. Hence for the ancient
translators there is a close connection
between תְּפִלָה and תָּפֵל, the common idea being that of stupidity or
folly. In modern Hebrew the word
תפלה has retained the sense of
extravagance or madness. It is easy
to understand how the root תפל 'to
be tasteless' (6: 6) has acquired the
meaning of 'to be foolish'. The development may be compared with that
by which the Latin *fatuus* came to
mean both 'insipid' and 'foolish'. It
should be noted that in French 'fade'
and 'fat' both derive from Latin
fatuus. The expression נתן תפלה ל״
is explained by נתן כבוד ל״ 'glorify'
(1 S 6: 5; Jer 13:16; Pr 26: 8). What
is in question is an external manifestation, especially in the form of
words, as is seen in 2: 10 where 'he
sinned not' has as its complement
'with his lips'. Hence 'and he did not
charge God with folly'. Note that
the presence of תפלה in 24: 12 is
probably due to an error in punctuation (cf. Comm.).

CHAPTER 2

1   Again there was a day when the sons of Elohim came to present
     themselves before Yahweh, and Satan came also among them
     to present himself before Yahweh.

2   And Yahweh said to Satan: 'Whence comest thou?' And
     Satan answered Yahweh and said: 'From roaming the earth
     and walking up and down on it!'

3   And Yahweh said to Satan: 'Hast thou considered my servant

2: 1 Targ. referred the day of 1: 6
to the 'day of judgment at the beginning of the year'. This time it is
the 'day of the great judgment, the
day of the remission of sins'. In both
cases the angels are 'in judgment before Yahweh'. Syro-hex. marks with
an obelus the words ὡς and αὔτη
which G incorporates in its translation of ויהי היום. The versions remain faithful to their interpretation
בני האלהים in 1: 6, with the exception of Jerome *filii Dei* instead of
angeli Dei (1: 6, following G). The
end להתיצב על־יהוה was not translated in G. The present text παραστῆ-
ναι ἐναντίον τοῦ Κυρίου, absent from
Sah., and marked with an asterisk in
Jerome and Syro-hex., comes from
Aq. and Theod. (cf. Colb.).

The verse repeats 1: 6 verbatim,
but adds להתיצב על־יהוה, which has
been omitted in G from a desire for
uniformity. Cf. Comm. on 1: 6.

2   For ויען ויאמר G has τότε εἶπεν ὁ
διάβολος ἐνώπιον τοῦ Κυρίου. Colb.
cites καὶ εἶπεν after Κυρίου, and this
reading is also found in Arab. Baud.
and Jerome *et dixit* (with an asterisk), suggested by 1: 7. Syro-hex.
does not mark with an obelus (cf.
1: 7) τὴν ὑπ' οὐρανόν, which translates the ארץ of G. As in 1: 7, Targ.
adds 'to examine the works of men'
after בארץ. G explains בה by τὴν

σύμπασαν. G (A) has γῆν, which is
followed by Memph. At the end G
adds πάρειμι (cf. 1: 7), marked by an
obelus in Syro-hex.

Question and answer as in 1: 7.
But we have אי מזה instead of מאין
and the defective משט for משוט.

3   For אל־השטן G (B, א) πρὸς τὸν
διάβολον, but G (A) πρὸς τὸν Σατανᾶν
repeated by Syro-hex., and marked
with an obelus. Sah. simply 'to him'
equivalent to the αὐτῷ of 1: 8. G and
its derived versions retain only the
προσέσχες of the locution προσέσχες
τῇ διανοίᾳ σου, which rendered השמת
לבך in 1: 8. For תם וישר G (B, א) has
ἄκακος, ἀληθινός, ἄμεμπτος (Sah.,
Eth., Syro-hex.), G (A) ἄμεμπτος
δίκαιος ἀληθινός (cf. 1: 1). Thus G
(B, א) has a double translation of תם,
whereas G (A) has a double translation of ישר. Arab. Baud. 'just and
blameless' omits ἄκακος, Jerome *innocens verax* omits ἄμεμπτος of G (B,
א). For מרע G has ἀπὸ παντὸς κακοῦ.
Obelus before παντός in Syro-hex.
The suffix of תסיתני becomes מימרי
'my word' in Targ. (cf. 1: 10, 11, 21).
G σὺ δὲ εἶπας τὰ ὑπάρχοντα αὐτοῦ διὰ
κενῆς ἀπολέσαι softens the final
phrase ותסיתני···חנם. Syro-hex. puts
in the margin the reading of Aq.,
which brings us back to the MT:
καὶ ἀνέσεισάς με ἐπ' αὐτῷ τοῦ κατα-
ποντίσαι αὐτὸν δωρεάν.

Job? There is no one like him on the earth; he is a perfect and upright man, fearing Elohim and turning away from evil. He still clings to his perfection, and it is without reason that thou didst stir me against him to ruin him.'

4   Satan answered Yahweh: 'Skin for skin! All that a man has he will give for his life.

Yahweh is triumphant. He repeats the praises of 1:8. The trial has only served to throw into greater relief the virtue of Job. Hence the formula וְעֹדֶנּוּ 'and he still' in spite of all that has happened to him. The *hiph'il* of חזק has the meaning of 'strengthen' or 'consolidate'. With בְּ preceding the object of this verb, the latter implies the 'hand': strengthen one's hand on something, i.e. seize and hold it firmly (Gn 21:18). Hence the elliptic expression הֶחֱזִיק בְּ means simply 'seize' (8:20) or 'hook on to' (8:15), and when the object is an abstraction 'cleave to' (27:6; Pr 3:18). It is the latter meaning which we find here and in v. 9. Outside the Book of Job (2:3, 9; 27:5; 31:6) the abstract תֻּמָּה 'perfection' appears only in Pr 2:3. On the meaning of the root, cf. 1:1. The *hiph'il* of סות with בְּ before the complement, means 'to stir up' some one against a person (1 S 26:19; Jer 43:3). On the evolution of the root, cf. 36:16. The verb בלע 'swallow' (7:19) assumes in the *pi'el* the meaning of engulf or destroy. Hence 'take away' (8:18) and 'destroy', 'ruin' (10:8). The adverb חִנָּם 'without cause' (1:9) at the end of the sentence is so placed so as not to separate תְּסִיתֵנִי from its immediate complement introduced by לְ.

4   For כָּל־אֲשֶׁר G (B) has ὅσα, but G (A, א) πάντα ὅσα (Sah., Syro-hex., Jerome, Eth., Arab. Baud.). Instead of עוֹר בְּעַד־עוֹר, literally rendered in the versions, Targ. has אברא אמטול אברא 'member for member'; cf. Rashi אבר בפני אבר.

There has been much discussion on the proverb 'skin for skin'. An old opinion, mentioned by Calmet and taken up by Duhm, interpreted the skin as the skin of an animal used for bartering. In this case the meaning of the proverb would be one gives the worth of a skin to receive the equivalent. Schultens thinks we should translate as *cutis super cute*: we remove one skin but there remains another. Merx further elaborates this to obtain the German idea, *das Hemd sitzt näher als der Rock*: 'the shirt is nearer than the coat' (cf. Budde, Hontheim). Olshausen couples together the skin of man and the skin of God; as long as you do not touch his skin, he will not touch yours! Others contrast the skin, considered as the life of animals and children, with the skin of Job. He sacrifices the life of others to save his own: *carnem alienam pro carne sua* (St Thomas). This is the meaning adopted by St Ephrem and preferred by Rosenmüller, who quotes Ex 21:23: נֶפֶשׁ תַּחַת נֶפֶשׁ 'life for life'. According to the Targum, Olympiodorus, Isho'dad, Albertus Magnus, the expression means that one is prepared to sacrifice one member that is less important to save another that is more important (cf. Rashi, above). This explanation is near to the true one. For it should be noted that in the following phrase Satan says, 'All that a man has he will give for his life.' And further on (v. 5) he asks God to afflict Job in his bones and flesh. The bones and the flesh, suggesting the inmost being of man (*L'Emploi métaphorique*, pp. 9f.), are contrasted with the skin which is

5   But put forth Thy hand now and touch his bone and flesh
and he will certainly *curse* Thee to Thy face.'

6   And Yahweh said to Satan: 'Behold, he is in thy power!
Only spare his life.'

7   Then Satan went forth from the presence of Yahweh and

5   יְקַלְּלֶ‍ךָ (Targ., Syr.); MT: יברכך.

external and superficial. 'Skin for
skin', i.e. the wound has been but a
scratch, God has only lightly touched the sufferer. Can one be surprised if the result has been negligible? And thus the expression is the
opposite of 'life for life'. Had the
wound been deep, had God attacked
the flesh and bones of Job, the reaction of the latter would have been
different.

5 For ידך, Targ. מחת ידך (cf. 1:11).
Syr. inverts the words עצמו and
בשרו Targ. renders אל־פניך by 'in
face of your word' (cf. v. 3). Syr. and
Targ. replace יברך by the same verbs
as in 1:5, 11. But G and its derived
versions: εὐλογήσει. Similarly Aq.
and Vulg. *benedicat*. In Cod. regius
unus and Cod. 161 (Field), we have
the interpretation of ὁ Ἑβραῖος:
βλασφημήσει. Very true remark in the
margin of Cod. 161: τὸ εὐλογήσει ἀντὶ
τοῦ ὑβρίσει.

The opening as in 1:11 (cf. Comm.).
The verb נגע, not this time with ״ב
but with ־אל, in the sense of 'touch';
cf. 1:11. The bones and the flesh
symbolise the whole man: his physical and also his social being (*L'Emploi métaphorique*, p. 10). Note the
use of ־אֶל instead of ־עַל (1:11)
before פָּנֶיךָ. Read of course יְקַלְּלֶ‍ךָ
(Targ. and Syr.); cf. 1:5, 11. This
time it will not be a question of 'skin
for skin' (v. 4). When God has afflicted the bones and flesh, Job will
revolt and blaspheme. Such is
Satan's thesis.

6 As in 1:12, the versions add a
verb before בידך. The verb used is

the same except in G (παραδίδωμι
instead of δίδωμι).

Yahweh accepts the challenge.
Satan must not continue to doubt the
perfection of Job. It is not only
כל־אשר־לו 'all that is his', but the
person of Job himself (הנו 'here he
is') who is now to be delivered up to
the blows of Satan. It is clear that
the bones and the flesh symbolise the
individual in his person by contrast
with his external wealth; cf. vv. 4-5.
The restriction is effected by אַךְ
instead of the רק of 1:12. The verb
שְׁמֹר 'safeguard' (10:12) expresses
the idea of respecting the life of some
one. Yahweh limits the action of
Satan. *Non enim totaliter Deus servos
suos voluntati Satan exponit, sed secundum mensuram convenientem* (St
Thomas).

7 G renders מאת פני by a simple
preposition ἀπό (B, **א**), παρά (A); cf.
Sah. and Syro-hex. But Eth. and
Arab. Baud. 'from before', Jerome
a facie (with asterisk). Syro-hex.
quotes in the margin προσώπου. After
יהוה Targ. adds 'with permission'
(cf. 1:12). For שחין Targ. שיחנא, Syr.
ܫܘܚܢܐ, G ἕλκει (variant ἐλέφαντι in
the margin of Colb. and Cod. 258),
Vulg. *ulcere*. The *kethîb* עַד in G and
Vulg., the *qerê* וְעַד in Targ. and Syr.

As in 1:12, the opening has מֵאֵת
instead of מעם. The *hiph'il* of נכה
'strike' with ״ב before the name of
the disease (Gn 19:11; Nu 14:12;
1 S 5:6). In the curses of Dt the
formula יככה יהוה בשחין רע introduces מכף רגלך ועד קדקדך at the
end of the verse. In v. 27 of the same

afflicted Job with a virulent ulcer from the sole of the foot
to the crown of his head.

8   So he took a potsherd with which to scrape himself and sat
among the ashes.

chapter, the first of the diseases
mentioned is שְׁחִין מִצְרַיִם, which has
been identified with leprosy, because
the ancients considered elephantia-
sis as a disease peculiar to Egypt
(Pliny, *Nat. hist.* XXVI, 7ff.; Lucretius, VI, 1105ff.). But leprosy has
other names, and the Bible does not
consider it as coming specifically
from Egypt. It is known that leprosy begins with a שְׁחִין (Lv
13: 18ff.) and that the שְׁחִין may be
accompanied by sores (Ex 9: 9). The
root שׁחן (in Arabic, Assyrian, Aramaic) means 'to be inflamed, hot'.
Hence it is a question of an inflam-
mation of the skin which causes sores
and boils. This is so, for example,
as regards the Nile button, which we
think to be the שְׁחִין מִצְרַיִם, and
which shows all the symptoms of
ulcers. Hence, with the versions we
may recognise in the word שְׁחִין an
ulcer. It is interesting to note that
the Syriac ܫܘܚܢܐ, which corresponds
to the OT שְׁחִין, is the term used to
render the ἕλκος 'ulcer' of Lk 16:
20ff. Still more striking is the translation of ἕλκος κακόν (Rev 16: 2) by
ܫܘܚܢܐ ܒܝܫܐ, which in our text is
precisely the expression used by Syr.
to render שְׁחִין רָע and by Syro-hex.
to translate ἕλκει πονηρῷ (G). Hence
Syriac and Greek tradition are in
complete agreement in recognising
שְׁחִין רָע as a malignant ulcer. It is
going too far to insist that it connotes leprosy (Barhebraeus, Ish-
o'dad, etc.). The symptoms of
leprosy, which both ancients and
moderns have sometimes seen in the
description which Job gives us of his
ills, can indicate equally well an ulcer
of an infectious nature. The expression מִכַּף רַגְלוֹ עַד קָדְקֳדוֹ (cf. Dt
28: 35) is more precise than the

מִכַּף־רֶגֶל וְעַד־רֹאשׁ of Is 1: 6 (*L'Emploi métaphorique*, p. 20).

8   G (A) adds 'Ιώβ as the subject of
ἔλαβεν (Eth., Arab. Baud.). The expletive לוֹ, not translated in G, is
rendered by ἑαυτῷ in Codd. 161, 248,
Compl. (Field). Jerome gives *sibi*,
marked by an asterisk. For לְהִתְגָּרֵד
בּוֹ G (B, א) has ἵνα τὸν ἰχῶρα ξύῃ (Syro-hex., Jerome *ut raderet saniem*,
cf. Vulg. *saniem radebat*), G (A) ἵνα
ἀποξέῃ τὸν ἰχῶρα αὐτοῦ (Sah., Eth.,
Arab. Baud.). The word αὐτοῦ is
cited in the margin of Syro-hex.
(with asterisk) and attributed to
Theod. The true meaning of לְהִתְגָּרֵד
בּוֹ is found in κνᾶσθαι ἐν αὐτῷ, which
is the interpretation of ὁ Ἑβραῖος
cited by Apollinaris of Laodicea
(Field). G (A, א^{c.a}) adds αὐτός as
subject of ἐκάθητο. Hence Jerome
ipse (with asterisk). Syro-hex. quotes the word in the margin and attributes it to Aq. and Theod. Instead of rendering הָאֵפֶר by 'ashes'
as do the other versions, G and its
derived versions have τῆς κοπρίας,
which enables Arab. Baud. to translate by 'and he was seated on the
mazbaleh' (cf. inf.). At the close G
adds ἔξω τῆς πόλεως, marked by an
obelus in Syro-hex. The obelus is
forgotten in Jerome before *extra
civitatem*. A note of Colb. gives the
reason for the addition: lepers were
not to remain in towns (cf. Lv
13: 64).

   The *dativus ethicus* לוֹ after וַיִּקַּח,
like the Latin *sibi*, indicating that the
subject is also the end of the action
(cf. Gesenius-Kautzsch, § 119s). The
word חֶרֶשׂ denotes the potsherd
(41: 22; Is 30: 14). Modern Hebrew
has maintained for the verb גרד the
sense of 'scrape', confirmed by Sy-

9   Then his wife said to him: 'Do you still hold fast your integrity? *Curse* Elohim and die!'

9 קַלֵּל (Syr.); MT: ברך.

riac and Arabic. The *hapax* הִתְגָּרֵד
thus means 'scrape himself' rather
than 'scrape the pus' (G, Vulg.). The
phrase introduced by וְהוּא with the
present participle is connected with
what precedes (Gn 18: 1, 8, 16, 22;
Jg 13: 9). Of course, הָאֵפֶר 'ashes'
and not 'dust', which will be expressed by עפר in v. 12. In 30: 19;
42: 6 (cf. Sir 40: 3) we have עָפָר
וָאֵפֶר 'dust and ashes'. Job sits on
this heap of dust, ashes, dirt, which
is found at the entrance of small
towns in Palestine and is called the
mazbaleh, 'dunghill' (cf. Arab. Baud.
following G). 'The basis of the
mound is the ash which is removed
from baking ovens, and which with
time becomes a mass of fine dust.
When a city is captured, destroyed,
burnt, it is the natural refuge of the
inhabitants. There, one can sit on
the dust (Is 47: 1) or on the ashes
(Jon 3: 6), roll in the ashes (Jer
6: 26; Mic 1: 10), put ashes on the
head (Jos 7: 6), or do both at the
same time (Ezk 27: 30)' (Lagrange,
ÉRS, pp. 325ff.); cf. Comm. on v. 12.
It is to be noted that the interpretation of G ἐπὶ τῆς κοπρίας recalls the
Homeric description of old Priam
weeping over the death of Hector
and rolling in the dung: κυλινδόμενος
κατὰ κόπρον (*Iliad*, XXII, 414). John
Chrysostom points out that pilgrims
came from the ends of the earth to
Arabia in order to visit the dunghill
of Job: ἀπὸ τῶν περάτων τῆς γῆς εἰς
Ἀραβίαν τρέχοντες, ἵνα τὴν κοπρίαν
ἐκείνην ἴδωσι κ.τ.λ.

9 Before וַתֹּאמֶר G has χρόνου δὲ
πολλοῦ προβεβηκότος, marked with an
obelus in Syro-hex., Colb., Cod. 255.
The obelus is forgotten in Jerome.
The wife of Job is called Dinah דִּינָה
in Targ. After אשתו a whole midrash

has been included in G. According to
Origen (*Epist. ad Africanum*, 3 (*PG*,
XI, col. 55)), the addition begins at
μέχρι τίνος and goes down to μὲ νῦν
συνέχουσιν, the translation of MT
starting again at ἀλλὰ εἰπόν. But
μέχρι τίνος καρτερήσεις may come
from עָדֶךְ מַחֲזִיק, and it is with the
word λέγων that the interpolated
text begins. This is why Jerome and
Syro-hex. mark with an obelus the
passage from λέγων to ἀλλὰ εἰπόν.
On the nature of this tradition of G,
cf. Intro., pp. xviiif. The versions
derived from G reproduce its text in
entirety. At v. 9d (ed. Swete), the
word περιερχομένη of G (A, א°·ᵃ)
recurs in Sah., Syro-hex., Eth.,
Arab. Baud. It is omitted in G (B)
and Jerome. The suffix μοῦ after
μοχθῶν is not reproduced in G (A,
א), Jerome, Arab. Baud. The translation of the MT reappears in ἀλλὰ
εἰπόν τι ῥῆμα εἰς Κύριον. It is clear that
εἰπόν τι ῥῆμα interprets ברך, which
is quoted in the margin of Syro-hex.
Another translation, εὐλόγησον, is
quoted in Colb., while Codd. 161 and
248 show the right interpretation
κατάρασαι (cf. v. 5). Syr. adheres
faithfully to its own translation as
in 1: 5, 11; 2: 5; but Targ. בריך
adheres to MT. For אלהים Targ. has
'the word of Yahweh' (cf. v. 4).

The Church Fathers emphasised
the rôle of the wife in the temptation.
She acts as intermediary between
Satan and Job, as she was between
the serpent and Adam. St Thomas
thinks that the devil spared her, *ut
per eam viri justi mentem pulsaret,
qui per feminam primum hominem
dejecerat*. The phrase ... עֹדְךָ is
interrogative, the ה being omitted
on account of the initial guttural
(Gn 19: 12; Ex 9: 17). The locution
מַחֲזִיק בְּתֻמָּתֶךְ is a repetition of the

10   And he said to her: 'As one of the foolish women you speak!
      If we accept good from Elohim, shall we not also accept evil?'
      In all this Job did not sin with his lips.

11   Now, three friends of Job heard of all this evil which had be-
      fallen him and they came each one from his own country.

words of Yahweh in v. 3. The sharp
reply which Job's wife gets in v. 10
excludes the translation of בָּרֵךְ
אֱלֹהִים as 'bless Elohim' (Targ. and
Vulg.). As has been understood by
Syr. and some Greek interpreters
(cf. sup.), the word ברך is a theological euphemism which we have
found in the whole of the narrative
(v. 5 and 1:5, 11). Hence we shall
continue to read קַלֵּל as before:
'Curse Elohim and die!' It is not
necessary to see death as a consequence of the suggested cursing. It
is simply a matter of succession in
time: Curse God before dying! Resignation is not the virtue of Job's
wife. She is prepared to accept good
but not evil at the hand of God
(v. 10).

10 Syro-hex. and Jerome mark
with an obelus the word ἐμβλέψας,
which G adds to MT. For כדבר G
has simply ὥσπερ, Vulg. quasi. Targ.
paraphrases הנבלות as 'women who
disgrace themselves in the house of
their fathers'. G renders גם by εἰ
(cf. Vulg. si). For מאת אלהים G has
ἐκ χειρὸς Κυρίου, Vulg. de manu Dei.
Syro-hex. omits the word ὑποίσομεν,
translation of the second נקבל in G.
The words τοῖς συμβεβηκόσιν αὐτῷ,
added by G, are marked with an
obelus in Jerome and Syro-hex. (cf.
1:22). After χείλεσιν G (B, א) omits
αὐτοῦ which figures in G (A), Sah.,
Syro-hex., Arab. Baud., and (with
asterisk) in Jerome suis. At the
close, Syr. repeats the formula ולא
נתן of 1:22; Targ. makes a gloss on
MT by adding, 'But there were
ulterior motives behind his words.'
G adds ἐναντίον τοῦ Θεοῦ as in 1:22.

The asterisk, instead of the obelus,
is wrongly placed in Syro-hex. (cf.
Field, II, *Auctarium*, p. 5).

With כדבר אחת הנבלות compare
כאחד הנבלים in 2 S 13:13. Etymologically, the נָבָל is the man who is
branded (cf. Comm. on 42:8),
whether because of his lack of intelligence, whence the meaning 'mad'
(Pr 17:21), or whether because of
his lack of moral sense, whence the
meaning 'wicked', 'impious' (Is 32:
5ff.). The נְבָלוֹת are foolish women,
who have neither brain nor moral
principles. The adverb גם brings into
relation the first and second clauses.
It has almost the meaning of 'just
as', 'since'. The best way of translating it is that of G and Vulg. *si*
(cf. Is 49:15). The *pi'el* of קבל is a
late Aramaism, and is synonymous
with לקח in the sense of 'receive',
'accept'. The Arabic *qabala* has the
same meaning. The interrogative
sense of the second clause is sufficiently indicated by the *waw* of ואת
(cf. Ex 8:22; 1 S 20:9; 29:20, etc.).
Job has accepted the loss of his
fortune and children. He also accepts
illness, for evil as well as good comes
from the Lord. The conclusion as in
1:22, but with the complement
בשפתיו 'by his lips', which makes it
possible not to repeat the last proposition ולא־נתן ···.

11 For רעי איוב G and its derived
versions have οἱ τρεῖς φίλοι αὐτοῦ. G
fails to translate הזאת, which is
restored as ταῦτα (following Theod.)
in Colb. and Cod. regius unus (with
asterisk). The word figures with
asterisk in Jerome and in the margin
of Syro-hex. (attributed to Theod.).
Targ. adds a note as to how the

They were Eliphaz the Temanite, Bildad the Shuhite, and
Zophar the Na'amathite. So they agreed together to come to
pity and console him.

friends of Job guessed his misfortunes: withered trees, bread changed
into flesh, wine changed into blood.
G (B, **א**) renders **מקום** by χώρας, as
do also the derived versions; G (A)
πόλεως is quoted in the margin of
Syro-hex. After **ממקמו** G adds πρὸς
αὐτόν, marked by an obelus in Syro-
hex. Also in Syr. we find 'towards
him', which, before **ויבאו**, anticipates the translation of **ויועדו**. G (A)
places after πρὸς αὐτόν a first translation of the end of the verse: τοῦ
παρακαλέσαι κ.τ.λ. Another addition
in Targ. states: 'and for that they
were delivered from the place assigned to them in Gehenna.' The names
of the friends and their countries
are exactly given in Targ., Syr., and
Vulg. But G wishes to make them
kings. Thus **התימני** becomes ὁ Θαιμανῶν βασιλεύς. Syro-hex. marks
βασιλεύς with an obelus. For **השוחי**
G has ὁ Σαυχαίων τύραννος. Obelus
stands before τύραννος in Syro-hex.
Finally **הנעמתי** is rendered ὁ Μει-
ναίων βασιλεύς. Obelus stands before
βασιλεύς in Syro-hex. Double reading
in Jerome: *Namathites Mineorum rex*
with asterisk before *Namathites* and
obelus before *Mineorum rex*. The
reading *Namathites* comes from Sym.
Ναμαθίτης. G freely translates **ויועדו**
יחדו בא καὶ παρεγένοντο πρὸς αὐτὸν
ὁμοθυμαδόν. The terms of the last
phrase are inverted in G to become τοῦ
παρακαλέσαι καὶ ἐπισκέψασθαι αὐτόν.
Order is restored in Jerome: *ut visitarent et consolarentur*. The word **לנוד**
is likewise interpreted as *visitarent*
in the Vulg. The names of Job's
friends are omitted in Arab. Baud.

V. 11 introduces the personages
who will be Job's interlocutors. Massoretic pointing places the accent on
the penultimate of **בָּאָה** and treats
the verb as a perfect. In this case
the article is considered as playing

the part of the relative **אשׁר** (cf. 1
Ch 26: 28; 2 Ch 29: 36; Ezr 10: 14;
cited in Gesenius-Kautzsch, § 138i).
G τὰ ἐπελθόντα implies that the accent
is on the last syllable and the word is
feminine participle. We have the
choice between the two; the meaning
remains the same. The expression
כָּל־הָרָעָה will recur in 42: 11. On
the countries of Teman, Shuah, and
Na'amah, cf. Intro., pp. xxvif. The
name Eliphaz is Edomite according
to Gn 36: 4ff. Teman figures among
the sheikhs who sprang from Eliphaz. The name Bildad cannot be
explained from the Babylonian element Bel—a hypothesis of Halévy
and of Nöldeke (*ZDMG*, **42**, p. 479)
—for it is a question of an Arabic
or Edomite person. The form is
derived from the root *qitlal* found
in Arabic words like *šimlâl* 'agile',
šimṭâṭ 'troop' or 'band'. We would
connect Bildad with *balad* 'town',
'region' so as to give the meaning
of 'townsman' or 'native' (cf. *baladî*).
As for Zophar, this comes from the
form *qawtal*, like the Arabic *jawzal*,
Hebrew **גּוֹזָל** ('young dove'). The
root is the same as that of **צִפּוֹר** and
the meaning 'little bird'. It is by
identification with a known kingdom
that the Septuagint made Zophar
a king of the Minaeans (cf. Intro.,
pp. xxvf.). The meaning of **יועדו** is
well settled by Am 3: 3, 'Can two
walk together unless they be agreed?'
Same use of the *niph'al* to mean
'agree'. The verb **נוד** with **ל//** before
its complement means 'condole' (Is
51: 19; Jer 15: 5; 16: 5, etc.) and
not 'visit' (contra G, Vulg.). Originally it is a matter of shaking the
head at some one; cf. Comm. on
16: 5. We again find the verbs **נוד**
and **נחם** in 42: 11. There it is a case
of retrospective consolation.

12   They lifted their eyes from afar and did not recognise him.
      Then they raised their voices and wept; they tore each one
      his garment and sprinkled dust on their heads [ ].

13   Then they sat down on the ground with him, seven days and

12   Omit השמימה (variant; cf. G).

12 G paraphrases וישׂאו את־עיניהם by ἰδόντες δὲ αὐτόν and וישׂאו קולם by καὶ βοήσαντες φωνῇ μεγάλῃ. G (B, א) omits על־ראשׁיהם השמימה, but G (A) ἐπὶ τὰς κεφαλὰς αὐτῶν (Sah., Memph., Eth., Arab. Baud. mistakenly). The reading of G (A) suggests to Jerome the translation *super caput suum in coelum*, with an asterisk before *in coelum*. The text of Syro-hex. follows G (B, א), but in the margin is a translation of the MT according to Theod. (with asterisk). A reading found in several copies is cited by Polychronius: καὶ ἀναβλέψαντες εἰς οὐρανόν, which is an explanation of השמימה based on Dt 4:19.

Job is outside the city on the *mazbaleh* (v. 8). His friends descry him from afar and fail to recognise him: *quantum mutatus ab illo*! Sickness and misfortune have disfigured their friend, like Yahweh's servant in Is 53:3ff. The *hiph'il* of נכר with the negative: 4:16; 7:10; 24:13. Like Job, his friends are wearing the mantle of the sheikhs, the *me'il* (1:20). Like him, they tear it. Instead of shaving their heads they defile them with dust. Garments are rent and the head is covered with ashes or dust as a mark of extreme grief (Jos 7:6; 2 S 13:9); cf. Comm. on v. 8. The Benjamite who brings bad tidings to the high priest Eli comes before him with rent garments and dust on his head (1 S 4:12). Before putting on sackcloth, dust was thrown on the head (Ezk 27:30; La 2:10). The custom is not necessarily connected with funeral rites (Lagrange, *ÉRS*, pp. 325ff.). It seems that the idea is to disfigure one's self or make one's self earthy.

The former idea is stressed in certain classical texts, for example in the *Iliad* (XVIII, 23ff.):

ἀμφοτέρῃσι δὲ χερσὶν ἑλὼν κόνιν αἰθαλόεσσαν
χεύατο κακκεφαλῆς χαρίεν δ᾽ ᾔσχυνε πρόσωπον

and in Catullus (LXIV, 224) *canitiem terra atque infuso pulvere foedans*. הַשָּׁמָיְמָה is generally interpreted as though it were a question of casting dust towards the sky and then catching it on the head: 'and they threw dust towards heaven so as to receive it back again on their heads' (Renan). But the throwing of dust towards the sky is another rite totally different from the one described here (cf. Ac 22:23). On the other hand we find the verb זרק with the complement השמימה in Ex 9:8, 10. Here it is a question of casting heavenwards ash from the oven. What seems to us probable is that the words על־ראשׁיהם and השמימה are two variants of the original text. In the one Job's friends scatter dust on their heads; in the other, they throw dust towards the sky. The two complements were later juxtaposed, thus occasioning the oddity of the phrasing: they sprinkled dust on their heads towards heaven.

13 G omits לארץ. The Hebrew reading is mentioned in Polychronius, Cod. Orat., Cod. 249 εἰς τὴν γῆν. Jerome places an asterisk before *in terra*. G has the translation of ושׁבעת לילות, but Syro-hex. puts an asterisk before these words and notes that they are not found in the copies of Origen. There may have been an haplography in the Greek text. G (B) does not translate אליו דבר but G

seven nights; and no one spoke a word to him, for they saw
that his suffering was very great.

(A, C) has πρὸς αὐτὸν λόγον. These
words are cited (with asterisk) in
the margin of Syro-hex. and attributed to Symm. and Theod. (similarly in Codd. 255, 258). They recur,
preceded by asterisk, in Jerome *ad
eum verbum*. The complement אליו
is omitted in Syr. For כי־מאד··· G
gives τὴν πληγὴν δεινὴν οὖσαν καὶ με-
γάλην σφόδρα. Syro-hex. marks δεινήν
with obelus, while Jerome places
asterisk (mistakenly for the obelus)
before *et magnum dolorem valde*.

V. 13 closes the scene with an impressive picture. Job's friends, instead of lavishing vain consolations
on him, keep silence with him; *recens
enim dolor consolationes rejicit* (Pliny,
Epist., V, xvi, 11). St John Chrysostom and St Thomas dwell on the
psychology of this passage. Grief in
its intensity is always silent. The
four men remain seated on the *mazbaleh*. The verb ישׁב joined with
לָאָרֶץ as in Is 3: 26; 47: 1. Cf. especially La 2: 10 where 'the old men of
the daughter of Zion sit on the
ground silent and have sprinkled
dust on their heads'. Seven days and
seven nights form a time period
sacred to mourning (Gn 50: 10;
1 S 31: 13; Sir 22: 12). The form of
the participle דֹּבֵר is borrowed from
the *qal*. It is found fairly frequently,
whereas other moods have recourse
to the *pi'el*. The word כָּאַב reappears
in 21: 6 and, outside Job, in Is
17: 11, 65: 14; Jer 15: 18; Ps 39: 3.

CHAPTER 3

1   After that, Job opened his mouth and cursed his day.

2   And Job spoke and said:

3   May the day perish in which I was born;
       And the night which said: 'A male child has been conceived!'

Chapters 3-31   The poetic dialogue: see Introduction, pp. xxxviff. and lxxiiff.
Chapter 3   Job's complaint: see Introduction, p. xxxvi.

3:1   Instead of κατηράσατο, which translates יקלל in G, a variant ἐλοιδόρησεν is cited by Colb. For יומו, Syr. 'the day on which he was born' (Arab., Eth., Isho'dad).

The transitional phrase אחרי־כן 'after that' is in classical style (Gn 15:14; 23:19; 25:26, etc.). The phrase פתח...את־פיהו 'he opened his mouth' draws our attention to what is to follow (cf. 33:2). Job curses his day, i.e. the day of his birth (cf. v. 3 and Jer 20:14). There is no reason to postulate for 'his day' the meaning of his destiny or his star (contra Ehrlich). The context is sufficiently clear in itself (cf. Syr.). The interpretation is clearly formulated in Sir 23:19—καὶ τὴν ἡμέραν τοῦ τοκετοῦ σου μὴ καθαράσῃ (cf. below, Comm. on v. 3).

2   G has simply λέγων for the whole verse; cf. Vulg. et locutus est; Arab. 'and he said'. But Syr. and Targ. are in agreement with MT, the text of which is restored by G (A) καὶ ἀποκρίθη Ἰὼβ λέγων. The reading of G (A) is given in the margin of Syrohex. and attributed to Aq. and Theod. There is an asterisk before the respondens Job of Jerome.

V. 2 gives the type of the formulae which introduce the various speeches (4:1; 6:1; 8:1; etc.).

3   After ἐγεννήθην, which translates אולד, G (A) adds ἐν αὐτῇ, repeated in Jerome with asterisk, in eo. After the first hemistich, Targ. adds 'and the angel appointed to watch over conception'. With the exception of Targ., which copies MT, the versions interpret אמר impersonally: 'it is said', adding 'in which' after הלילה. Instead of הרה, the ἰδού of G seems to be a confusion with הרי, which in post-Biblical Hebrew corresponds to הנה 'behold'. In Cod. regius unus the translation of MT (ἐχύθη) is noted in accordance with Symm. and ὁ Ἑβραῖος.

The accent is transferred to the first syllable in יאבד and הרה, to the penultimate in אולד, so as to avoid collision with the accented syllables which immediately follow (the monosyllables יום and בו, first syllable of גבר). The expression יום אולד בו 'the day in which I was born' corresponds to יום הִוָּלְדוֹ 'day of his birth' in Hos 2:5; Ec 7:1. The imperfect is used as a true aorist (Fried. Delitzsch); cf. 15:7. In v. 6 Job requests that the night of his conception may not be numbered among the days of the year and the reckoning of the months. Hence he does indeed mean his birthday. It is a fatal day which should be erased from the calendar. Cf. Ovid (Trist., III, 13):

Ecce supervacuus—quid enim fuit utile gigni?—

Ad sua natalis tempora noster adest.

4   Let that day be darkness:
     Let not Eloah from on high regard it,
     And let not the light shine upon it!

Complementary to the day of birth stands the night of conception: *dies partui et nox conceptui debetur secundum congruentiam* (Albertus Magnus). The night is presented as a being which may be gloomy (v. 7), may hope (v. 9), may close the womb (v. 10). It is cursed for the share it has had in his conception. The only logical translation is 'the night which said' (cf. Targ.), the relative אֲשֶׁר being understood. In Ps 19: 3f. the personified night also speaks. An interpretation such as 'the night in which it was said' meets the difficulty that we do not know who can have said: 'A male child has been conceived!' But the night knows what is taking place in it, and since it has not closed the doors of the womb, it has allowed the conception to be effected. The expressions used in Jer 20: 14ff. are less strong, and there it is not the conception but the birth itself which is announced by some messenger. The reasons adduced by Beer, Budde, and Duhm, etc., for replacing הָרָה by הָרָה or הִנֵּה 'behold', following G, ignore the logic of the poet. Job has just cursed the day of his birth, a theme announced already in v. 1. Complementarily he must curse the night as corresponding to the day. This evidently will be the night of conception, as Albertus Magnus, quoted above, has well suggested. Let us note that in Ps 51: 7, we have a parallelism between חוֹלָלְתִּי 'I was brought forth' and יֶחֱמַתְנִי אִמִּי 'my mother conceived me'. Job does not say 'I was conceived', but 'a male child has been conceived', for he is not yet himself at the moment of conception, he is only the embryo which will become גֶּבֶר 'a male' or בֶּן זָכָר 'a male son' (Jer 20: 15). Our verse is much more concise and

vigorous than Jer 20: 14-15. The phrase יוֹם אוּלַד בּוֹ removes the superfluities of הַיּוֹם אֲשֶׁר יֻלַּדְתִּי בּוֹ (Jer 20: 14). The tautological 'may the day when my mother gave me birth not be blessed' (Jer 20: 14) is eliminated. The poet does not hesitate to refer the malediction to the night which was a witness and an accomplice of the conception, whereas Jer 20: 15 reproaches the 'man who announced the good news to my father, saying, "a male child has been born to you", and thus filled him with joy!' The themes of the day of birth and the night of conception will be developed in turn. There is an allusion to our verse in Sir 23: 19 (14): καὶ θελήσεις εἰ μὴ ἐγεννήθης καὶ τὴν ἡμέραν τοῦ τοκετοῦ σου μὴ καθαράσῃ '[lest] you should wish not to have been born and should curse the day of your birth' (cf. v. 1).

4   The reading 'that day' is supported by G (A, C, אᶜ·ᵇ) ἡ ἡμέρα ἐκείνη (Eth., Jerome, Bod. *dies illa*), Symm., Theod., Vulg., Syr., Targ. But G (B) has ἡ νὺξ ἐκείνη, which recurs in Sah., Syro-hex., Arab. Baud., Jerome, Tur., Gall. *nox illa.* The margin of Syro-hex. has a note: 'the others: the day'. On the correct reading, cf. inf. G μηδὲ ἔλθοι (which interprets וְאַל־תּוֹפַע) is translated *nec inveniat eam* in Jerome, Bod., Tur., *nec veniat in eam* in Jerome, Gall., and Aug.

Bickell and Beer, relying on G (B), eliminate v. 4a, whilst Duhm replaces הַיּוֹם by הַלַּיְלָה and transfers to this place יְקַו לָאוֹר וָאַיִן of v. 9 in order to obtain a first line. The concern to conclude with tetrastichs results with Bickell and Duhm in diametrically opposed hypotheses. The reading of G (B) cannot be allowed to supersede the other witnesses. It may be

5   May gloom and darkness pollute it:
     May a cloud rest upon it,
     May *fogs* terrify it!

5   כִּמְרִירֵי. MT: כַּמְרִירֵי ;כִּמְרִירֵי 5

explained as a repetition of ἡ νὺξ
ἐκείνη which figures in the previous
hemistich. With no change in the
text, we may translate simply: 'that
day, may it be darkness!' This is the
negation of the *fiat lux* of Genesis.
To God alone belongs the privilege
of declaring this *fiat*. That is why
the poet immediately adds: 'Let not
Eloah from on high regard it!' The
verb דרש 'seek' (10: 6; 39: 8),
whence 'to address' someone (v. 8),
'to be concerned about . . .' (here;
cf. Dt 11: 12; Jer 30: 14, 17). The
word אֱלוֹהַּ is found forty times in the
Book of Job as a personal name of
God. Elsewhere, with the same
meaning, in Dt 32: 15; Hab. 3: 3;
Ps 50; 22; 139: 19; Pr 30: 5 (Gesenius-Buhl, s.v.). The name יהוה must
not occur on the lips of Job and his
friends: cf. Intro., p. lxvi). The
expression מִמַּעַל 'from on high' is
specially applicable to God and
forms a real apposition (cf. 31: 2,
28). It is contrasted with מִתַּחַת in
18: 16. The *hiph'il* of יפע has the
causative sense 'make to shine' only
in 38: 15. Its normal meaning is
'shine' (10: 22), whence 'smile' (10:
3). The *hapax* נְהָרָה stems from the
root נהר 'gleam' (Is 60: 5; Ps 34: 6),
related to נור. Cf. the Aramaic
נהורא 'light' in Dn 2: 22 and the
Arabic *nahâr* 'day'.

5 The various meanings of גאל are
found in the versions. 'Claim', 'redeem': G and its derived versions
have ἐκλάβοι δὲ αὐτήν, Theod. ἀγ-
χιστευσάτω, Symm. ἀντιποιήσαιτο.
'Pollute' (cf. געל): Targ. טנוף,
Aq. μολύναι αὐτήν. 'Darken': Vulg.
obscurent eum, Syr. and Arab. 'may

it be overshadowed!' The versions
are unanimous in translating צלמות
by 'the shadow of death'. G renders
תשכן by ἐπέλθοι (cf. the translation
of תופע in v. 4). The word כמרירי
has been connected with the root
מרר, the כ being treated as a
preposition by Targ. 'like the bitternesses of day', and by Aq., whose
reading καὶ ἐκθαμβήσαισαν αὐτὴν ὡς
πικραμμοὶ ἡμέρας has influenced
Jerome *et conturbent eam quasi amaritudines diei* (with asterisk). Vulg.
amaritudine and Syr. ܡܪܝܪܘܬܐ
neglect the כ and also connect
מרירי with מרר. G isolates the
word יום to join it to הלילה of v. 6.
Its reading καταραθείη before ἡ ἡμέρα
does not come from מרירי, from the
root ארר (Beer), but is a corruption
of καὶ ταραχθείη (maintained in Cod.
256, Ald., Compl.), which harmonises
with the καὶ ἐκθαμβήσαισαν αὐτήν of
Aq. The transition between the two
is furnished by the καταραχθείη of
Colb. and Cod. 253. Hence G
renders יבעתהו, but omits כמרירי.
Targ. sees in the last hemistich an
allusion to the sorrow of Jeremiah
before the ruins of the temple, and
to that of Jonah cast into the sea.

As is correctly observed by Ehrlich,
the interpretation of גאל as 'redeem',
'deliver', with the implication of
'claim', is too artificial. The real
meaning is that of 'pollute' (Targ.
and Aq.; cf. Syr. and Vulg.). Rashi
interprets it thus and justifiably
quotes Mal 1: 7,12. The root גאל is
related to געל 'to show repugnance
for'. The pointing צַלְמָוֶת 'shadow of
death' is due to a failure to recognise
the root צלם 'to be dark', Arabic
ظلم, Assyrian *ṣalmu* 'black'. Everywhere we should read צַלְמוּת, an

6   That night let darkness seize!
Let it not *be added* to the days of the year,
Or enter into the reckoning of the months!

9   May the stars of its dawn be dimmed!

6 יֵחַד (Symm., Vulg., Targ., Syr.); MT: יִחַדְּ.

6-9 Transfer v. 9 to stand between v. 6 and v. 7 (cf. Comm.).

abstraction whose form ends in *ût* (Assyrian *ûtu*). The shadow of death would have referred specially to Sheol. But, with the exception of 10: 21, 22; 38: 17, the word צלמות is used to denote darkness in general. Some arguments adduced by Nöldeke (*ZATW*, 1897, pp. 183ff.) in favour of the MT pointing are refuted by Driver (Comm. on this verse). The *hapax* עֲנָנָה 'cloud' is the *nomen unitatis* of עָנָן; cf. נהרה in v. 4. The verb שָׁכַן 'alight', 'settle on', with עַל before the name of the place, is used in speaking of the cloud which rested on the tabernacle (Ex 40: 35; Nu 9: 17). There is no reason to replace יבעתהו by יתעבהו 'may it be made odious!' (contra Beer). On the *pi'el* of בעת, cf. 7: 14. We have seen how the versions have deduced from כמרירי the word מריר 'bitterness'. Rosenmüller also translates by *amara diei* and compares with the יום מר of Am 8: 10. Hitzig corrects to כמרידי 'like the rebels', and compares the מרדי אור of 24: 13. But the particle כ" is troublesome, whatever hypothesis we adopt. Bochart already recognised that כמרירי was a single word stemming from the root כמר 'to be black', which exists not only in Syriac but also in Assyrian *kamâru* 'to overshadow', 'darken'. The form is analogous to סַגְרִיר, שָׁפְרִיר, חַכְלִיל. The pointing of כ with a *hireq* is due to the fact that the Massoretes and the versions saw in כ a particle denoting comparison. The normal reading would be

כַּמְרִירֵי. Its government by יום gives the meaning 'blacknesses of the day', that is the mists which overshadow the daylight, namely the fogs. The idea suggested is that of an extraordinarily thick fog which makes day like night; such was the darkness which overcast Egypt (Ex 10: 21-23). Le Hir and Renan see in this an allusion to eclipses. Duhm detaches v. 5c to join it with v. 6, but he eliminates הלילה ההוא, whilst Bickell and Beer omit altogether v. 5c. Both proposals rest on G, without questioning the value of its readings (cf. sup.).

6 The text of G comes from a combination of יום (v. 5) with הלילה. We may not take advantage of this to replace הלילה by היום (Hontheim) or to suppress הלילה ההוא (Duhm). Instead of ἀπενέγκαιτο αὐτήν, which renders יקחהו in G, there exists a variant cited in Colb. ἀνατείλαι ἐπ' αὐτήν and mentioned in the margin of Syro-hex. It is by mistake that Jerome places an asterisk before *suscipiant tenebrae*. Because of בימי, Syr. adds 'that day' as the subject of יחד. The verb יחד is translated as יתיחד in Targ., ܐܣܬܒ 'be counted' in Syr., *computetur* in Vulg., συναφθείη in Symm. G has very vaguely εἴη. Targ. interprets ימי by יומין טבין 'good days', 'festival days', and ירחים by רישי ירחיא 'new moons'.

After the malediction of the day comes that of the night. The verb לקח means 'to seize' something and hold it firmly. Darkness seizes the fatal night and will not let it go. And

> May it hope for light and find none!
> And may it not see the eyelids of the dawn!

in this way the night will not be added to the days of the year, nor enter into the reckoning of the months. To be so included, it would have to be followed by day, but this event will not occur (cf. v. 9). The pointing יַחַדְּ is meant to imply that the verb is connected with חדה 'rejoice'. But the versions have properly realised that the verb was יֵחַד 'to be combined, added' (cf. sup.), and their reading יֵחַדְ (jussive imperfect) is confirmed by Gn 49:6, where we have a parallelism between the verb בוא ב״ and the verb יחד ב״ exactly as here. The apparent contradiction between the night and the 'days' has seemed surprising to certain moderns, who have wished to replace or suppress 'that night' (cf. sup.). But for the Hebrews the night is included in the day, which extends from one evening to the next (Gn 1). The idea of v. 6 is interrupted by vv. 7, 8. But it continues admirably in v. 9, which is composed of three hemistichs, like vv. 4, 5, 6. The words הנה הלילה ההוא of v. 7 suggest that a second malediction of the night is in question (cf. the beginning of our v. 6). Hence if we continue v. 6 by v. 9 we obtain the following result which cannot be fortuitous: a strophe of 6 hemistichs (6 and 9) for the first malediction of the night, and a strophe of 6 hemistichs for the second (7, 8, and 10). If we bear in mind that the malediction of the day was also a strophe of 6 hemistichs (4 and 5), we shall not hesitate to transfer v. 9 so that it stands before v. 7. Note also that the three strophes thus obtained all begin by the characteristic words: היום ההוא (v. 4), הלילה ההוא (v. 6), הנה הלילה ההוא (v. 7).

7-8 After v. 9. Cf. Comm. on v. 6.

9 The translation of G τῆς νυκτὸς ἐκείνης for נשף shows how unwise it is to correct the MT in this whole passage by G. In Targ. the word נשף is determined by שיריה 'of its song', which is perhaps a corruption of שפריה (cf. Syr. ܚܨܦܪܗ) 'its dawn'. Vulg. *caligine ejus*, because נשף has the further meaning of 'twilight'. A bad arrangement in G results in ὑπομεῖναι καὶ εἰς φωτισμὸν μὴ ἔλθοι. καὶ should be replaced after φωτισμόν to restore the MT. The eyelids of the dawn, literally translated in Targ., become the 'rays of dawn' (Syr.), ἑωσφόρον ἀνατέλλοντα (G), *ortum surgentis aurorae* (Vulg.).

V. 9 continues the curse of v. 6. The cursed night must not be allowed to see the light of day. The word נֶשֶׁף means sometimes 'twilight' (7:4; 24:15; Pr 7:9, etc.), sometimes the daybreak or dawn (Ps 119:147). According to the context, what is meant here are the morning stars. They will not appear to announce the coming of day: may the stars of dawn be dimmed! Compare the morning stars in 38:7. The following phrase is still more expressive: may it hope for light and find none! The verb is the pi'el of קוה with ל״ before the complement (6:19). The concise formula וָאַיִן 'and none', is meant to depict hope frustrated. In v. 21 we have ואיננו in a similar sense. Cf. 7:8, 21; 23:8; 24:24; 27:19. V. 9b recalls Is 59:11b. It is needless to change יִרְאֶה into יֵרָא (Bickell, Beer), for the imperfect is often used for the jussives in the verbs ל״ה (Gesenius-Kautzsch, § 109a note). The eyelids of the dawn are the first rays of daylight. Schultens says that the Arabs in ancient times regarded the rays of the sun as its eyelids. In 41:10, we find again the 'eyelids of dawn' with which the

7   Yes, may that night be full of gloom!
        May no joy penetrate it!
8   May it be execrated by those who curse the day,

crocodile's eyes are compared (see the text of Horapollon, cited in loc.). Sophocles speaks of the eyelids of a golden day: χρυσέας ἀμέρας βλέφαρον (*Antigone*, 103).

7 The word הנה is omitted in Vulg. and Syr. For גלמוד Targ. צערא 'sorrow' (cf. 15: 34), G ὀδύνη (B, א), ὀδυνηρά (A, C). In Symm., ἔκβλητος. Severian quotes ὁ Ἑβραῖος: μεμονωμένη (cf. Vulg. *solitaria*). But Syr. ܡܟܠܐ 'barren'; cf. ἄκαρπος for גלמוד in Aq., Theod., and Symm. (15: 34). The word רננה is doubly translated in εὐφροσύνη μηδὲ χαρμονή G. The words μηδὲ χαρμονή are marked with the obelus in Jerome and Syro-hex. According to Targ., רננה is the cry of the wood grouse.

Second malediction against the night. The word הנה 'behold!' is used to draw attention to the repetition הלילה ההוא (v. 6). The meanings 'lonely' and 'gloomy' (cf. sup.) for גַּלְמוּד are derived from 'barren', the latter being maintained in Syr. and the hexaplar authors (15: 34). In Is 49: 21 there is parallelism between גלמודה and שכולה 'she who is childless'. The גלמודה in the Talmud is she who must remain in isolation and have no relations with her husband. Among the Semites the field is often compared to a woman. Thus Rib-Addi of Byblos writes to the Pharoah: 'My field is like a woman who has no husband, because it is not sown' (*RB*, 1909, p. 370). This is why גלמוד 'barren' can be applied to a field that is not sown and eventually comes to denote an unproductive soil. In Arabic *julmûd* is the stony rocky field (in which the seed cast by the sower cannot take root). Barrenness results in sadness. This word גלמוד has the meaning of barren in 15: 34 and of 'gloomy' in

30: 3. The word רְנֶנָה (20: 5) reappears only in Ps 63: 4; 100: 2.

8 G considers the subject of יקבהו ἀλλὰ καταράσαιτο αὐτὴν ὁ καταρώμενος τὴν ἡμέραν ἐκείνην as a singular, which leads to ὁ μέλλων for העתידים. The translation of יום by τὴν ἡμέραν ἐκείνην distorts the idea contained in the text, an idea which has been well understood by the other versions. Syro-hex. quotes in the margin the hexaplar readings which bring us back to the MT. The word לויתן, simply transcribed in Aq., Symm., Syr., and Vulg., is translated τὸ μέγα κῆτος in G, and interpreted as אליותהון 'their complaint' in Targ.

The verb form יְקְּבֻהוּ comes from קבב 'execrate', 'curse' (5: 3) and not נקב 'pierce', 'perforate' (contra Rosenmüller). To change יום into יָם 'sea', as Schmidt, Gunkel, and Beer suggest, would result in a meaning diametrically opposite to the one expected and expressed. It is the supporters, not the cursers, of the sea, who are the enemies of the day (9: 13). As regards 'those who curse the day', Calmet already quotes a number of varying traditions: either 'those who languish in wearisome days' or 'those who curse the day of their birth', or again 'those who are praised for their lamentation over the dead, and are professional mourners in funeral rites', or finally 'those peoples who aim arrows at the sun which annoys them by its intense heat'. Modern commentators prefer to see in 'those who curse the day' witches, weavers of spells, magicians, who are able, by their words or magic practices, to make days auspicious or inauspicious (Rosenmüller, Knabenbauer, Duhm, etc.). Others propose to identify these

By those who are prepared to arouse Leviathan!

utterers of curses with those whose business it was to bring about eclipses. This would confirm the parallelism of the two members of the sentence, Leviathan being the monster who devoured the moon (Hitzig, Dillmann, Budde). It seems to us simpler and more logical to explain this expression 'those who curse the day' by v. 1 in which Job curses his day. In fact the beginning of the imprecation 'may the day perish on which I was born!' has a parallel in Jer 20: 14: 'Accursed be the day when I was born!' The word used for 'accursed' is precisely אָרוּר, and we have here אֹרְרֵי־יוֹם. Hence those who curse the day are those who curse the day of their birth. Among the Arabs, curses are like daily bread. One curses not only the father or mother of a man, his house or his religion, but also the day on which some untoward event took place. Then the formula begins: 'Cursed be the day when . . . .' It is a question of all those unhappy ones for whom to be alive is an evil, of which the original cause is the fact of their birth (cf. vv. 11 ff.). We do not see any need to season with mythology this first hemistich as is done by Gunkel and his colleagues. The natural translation of the 2nd hemistich is certainly 'those who are prepared to arouse Leviathan'. The word עָתִיד means 'prepared', 'ready', as in 15: 24; Est 3: 14. By poetic licence the לְ before the complement is omitted; cf. 4: 2 (with יכל); 9: 18 (with נתן). The po'lel of עוּר in its meaning of 'awaken' is used in Is 14: 9 to express the awakening of the shades in Sheol. Leviathan may thus denote a monstrous beast who is sleeping and whose awakening would have extraordinary consequences. In 40: 25ff. and Ps 74: 14 the name of Leviathan has been applied to the crocodile, and it is with good reason that in 41: 2 the poet

uses the verb עוּר (in the *hiph'il* according to the *kethîb*) to suggest the idea of 'awakening' the crocodile. Leviathan is a sea monster which God created to amuse Himself with לְשַׂחֶק־בּוֹ (Ps 104: 26). In 40: 29 the same expression שׂחק ב״ is found in connection with the crocodile: 'Will you play with him as with the sparrow?' Finally, in Is 27: 1 three sea monsters are distinguished: Leviathan as a fleeing serpent, Leviathan as a winding serpent, and the Tannîn which is in the sea. We shall find again the Tannîn as a personification of the sea in 7: 12. Another monster symbolising the sea is the Rahab of 9: 13 and 26: 12. It should be noted that in the Babylonian poem of the creation, the monsters which surround Tiamat at the time of the combat between the god of creation and the forces of chaos are first and foremost five species of serpents (*Choix de textes*, pp. 15ff. and passim). Among these serpents figures the *bašmu*, which is a sea serpent (*Cuneiform Texts*, XIV, 13, No. 91010, end of verso). Leviathan, which is one of the enemies of God (Is 27: 1), belongs to a species of the monsters of chaos and to the category of sea serpents (Ps 104: 26). The features common to Babylonian and Hebrew traditions are forcibly brought out, though with some exaggeration, in the work of Gunkel, *Schöpfung und Chaos*, passim. The main fact which must be retained is that in the origin of things there existed תְּהוֹם, which corresponds to the Assyrian Tiamat, whose name is but a personified form of *tiâmtu*, *tâmtu*, 'the sea'. To the sea serpents surrounding Tiamat correspond Leviathan, Tannîn, and Rahab, which eventually become personifications of the rebellious sea. The monstrous character of Leviathan makes it possible to have recourse to this name to describe the crocodile, whose

10   For it did not seal the doors of the womb in which I lay,
      And did not hide anguish from mine eyes!

11   Why did I not die on coming forth from the womb,
      And why did I not expire when I came forth from the belly?

dimensions are detailed in fantastic fashion in 40: 25ff. The ancients did not make a very clear distinction between reptiles and saurians, since furthermore the category of reptiles is divisible into four types, one of which includes ophidia and another saurians. Leviathan, the monster of chaos, has been conquered by God (Is 27: 1), like the Tannîn (Job 7: 12) and Rahab (9: 13; 26: 12); 'the helpers of Rahab' (9: 13) are beaten, just as the helpers of Tiamat were defeated in the struggle which marked the origin of things (*Choix de textes*, pp. 53, 107ff.). They are prisoners in Sheol. But they can be aroused (cf. Is 14: 9). This would mean the return to chaos and the end of the world. Such is exactly what those who curse the day desire, those for whom life is nothing but a series of evils. They would like to annihilate the existing order and to plunge into catastrophe. Instead of using the banal expression 'those who desire the end of the world', it was customary to say, like a proverb, 'those who are prepared to awaken Leviathan!' This is the meaning which appears to us the most probable. Following Targ. (cf. sup.), a whole Rabbinic tradition has developed on the passage. An attempt has been made to connect לויתן with לויה 'lamentation' and to translate 'those who are ready to arouse their mourning' (cf. English AV). This is the interpretation of the Talmud (cf. Jerusalem Talmud, *Mo'ed qaṭan*, 8od). But לויה has the meaning of 'company' rather than 'lamentation'. Besides, the suffix of לויתן would be difficult to understand after העתידים. It would be necessary to have לויתם.

9 After v. 6.

10   The versions have well understood that the subject is still 'that night'. The word בטני is explained as γαστρὸς μητρός μου in G. Obelus before μητρός μου in Syro-hex. Syr. has 'the uterus of my mother'. Vulg. *ventris qui portavit me*. Twofold interpretation in Targ.: 'the organs of my doors' and 'the doors of my belly'. G ἀπήλλαξεν is an interpretation of יסתר in the light of the preposition מן of מעיני 'hide from', 'remove from'. Jerome *abscondisset* is a return to MT.

This last verse of the malediction gives the reason for all that precedes. The night in question should have closed the womb of the mother to prevent her from conceiving. To open the womb is to allow conception to take place (Gn 29: 31ff.); to close it is to make conception impossible (1 S 1: 5). The word עמל has as its basic meaning heavy work, fatigue, hence sorrow, suffering; cf. the Latin *labor*. The night is personified as in v. 3 and v. 9. Notice that בטני has an objective suffix: 'the womb in which I lay'. The negation not repeated in the 2nd hemistich (Gesenius-Kautzsch, § 152z).

11   For מרחם, G and its derivatives have ἐν κοιλίᾳ, Vulg. *in vulva*, but Syr. and Targ. have on the other hand the preposition מן, supported by Jer 20: 17. It is needless to change to ברחם as Merx suggests. For ואגוע, G has καὶ οὐκ εὐθὺς ἀπωλόμην. Jerome puts the obelus before *protinus* (εὐθύς). Cf. Vulg. *non statim perii*.

The expression מרחם means 'on emerging from the womb' (Jer 1: 5; 20: 17; Ps 22: 2; 58: 4). The 2nd hemistich clarifies the meaning of the 1st. Parallelism between רחם and בטן 'belly' (31: 15; Ps 22: 2; 58: 4), between מות and גוע 'expire', 'perish'

12   Why did two knees welcome me,
        And why were there two breasts for me to suck?

12-16   Transfer v. 16 to precede v. 13 (cf. Comm.).

(10: 18; 14: 10). The negative question למה לא 'why not?' governs both אמות and אגוע. Note that these two verbs are again real aorists; cf. אולד in v. 3 and אהיה in v. 16. We have seen that v. 3 resembled Jer 20: 14f. V. 11 is similar to Jer 20: 17. Job has cursed the night in which he was conceived. But, since the doors of the maternal womb were not closed, he might at least have been an abortion or have died at the moment of birth! He begins with the second wish: 'Why did I not die at the moment of birth and why did I not expire when I came forth from the womb?' The verb יצאתי is in the perfect to mark the priority of the action in relation to אגוע. In 10: 18f.: 'Why then didst Thou bring me forth from the womb? I should have died and no eye would have seen me: I should have been as though I had not been, I should have been carried from the womb to the grave!' This passage which makes allusion to abortion shows that v. 16, which violently separates the strophe 13-15 from its logical conclusion (17-19), belonged originally to the context of v. 11. Reiske, followed by Beer and Duhm, proposed to transfer v. 16 to follow v. 11. But the presence of לא before the אהיה of v. 16 suggests that the understood word is simply the מדוע of v. 12 and not the למה לא of v. 11. Hence we shall place v. 16 after v. 12, which restores the proper sequence to the whole passage. With vv. 11-16 compare the idea expressed by Theognis (Croiset, *Hist. de la littér. grecque*, II, pp. 152f.): 'The best thing for man is not to be born, never to see the rays of the sun; once he is born, his best course is to pass without delay through the gates of Hades and to remain hence-forth lying under a heavy pile of earth.'

12   G renders מדוע and ומה by the equivalent expression ἵνα τί δέ. The MT is copied by Targ. and Syr., which retain the conjunction כי omitted by G ἵνα τί δὲ μαστοὺς ἐθή-λασα and Vulg. *cur lactatus uberibus?* After μαστοὺς G (A) adds μητρός μου.

Let us take care not to eliminate this verse on the pretext that it implies no longer God but men as the possible cause of a premature death (contra Duhm). V. 12 joins admirably with v. 11. Job was conceived and did not die at birth (v. 11). He might at least have died from lack of care and nursing: 'Why did two knees receive me?' The meaning of קִדֵּם 'to go to meet', 'to welcome' is confirmed by Sir 15: 2 where the verb is parallel to קִבֵּל (cf. 2: 10) and is used of a mother welcoming her child. Most critics see here an allusion to the father or grandfather receiving the child at birth (Gn 50: 23). This would imply a sign of adoption as with the Romans, among whom the father had the right to recognise or to cast off the newly born (cf. Rosenmüller, Duhm, etc.). Stade claims it is the women who receive the new born babe on their knees, as with the Bedouin (*ZATW*, 1886, p. 153). The meaning of the expression is much simpler. It is the mother's knees which welcome the child to give it suck. A text of Ashurbanipal gives direct support to this: 'You were weak, Ashurbanipal, you who sat on the knees of the goddess, queen of Nineveh; of the four teats which were placed near to your mouth, you sucked two and you hid your face in the two others' (Streck, *Assurbanipal*, p. 348). The inter-

16   Or why was I not like a hidden untimely birth,
     As infants which have never seen the light?

rogative מה with the sense of 'why' (*quare*) as in 7:21. Note the use of כי 'so that' after the interrogation (6:11; 7:17; 15:14). Literally: Why two breasts for me to suck? In the text of Ashurbanipal which we have just quoted, the verb which expresses the action of 'sucking' the breast is *enêqu*, which is the equivalent of ינק 'to suck' (20:16). It is after v. 12 that we put v. 16, which is at present torn from its original context; cf. Comm. on v. 11 and v. 16.

13-15   After v. 16.

16   G paraphrases טמון by ἐκπορευόμενον ἐκ μήτρας μητρός. Obelus before ἐκ μήτρας μητρός in Jerome and Syro-hex. After טמון Targ. adds במעינא 'in the womb'. In the margin of Syro-hex. are quoted the readings of Symm. κατορυγέν, of Aq., and of Theod. κεκρυμμένον (cf. Field). In order to connect v. 16 with v. 15, Syr. omits או and translates the כ of כנפל by 'with'. G does not render לא אהיה. For עללים Syr. ܚܒܠܐ 'foetus', Targ. טליא 'infants', G νήπιοι, Theod. ἔμβρυον, Vulg. *qui concepti*. In Targ. 'light' is determined by אוריתא 'of doctrine'.

V. 16 has been displaced from its original context (cf. Comm. on v. 11). It is evident that the description of the inhabitants of Sheol (13-15) has as a natural sequence the attitude of these inhabitants (17-19). The adverb שָׁם of v. 17 cannot be related to v. 16, but suits the context in which are gathered the personages described in the strophe 13-15. Modern critics who wish to leave v. 16 in its place suggest certain corrections: replacement of אהיה by היה (Hitzig, Beer, Hontheim) 'or like the abortive thing which has not existed'; suppression of לא (Wright,

Budde) 'I would be like the hidden untimely birth'. All difficulties disappear if we place v. 16 after v. 12. The formula לא אהיה is governed by the interrogative מדוע or מה of v. 12, the imperfect אהיה having the meaning of an aorist (cf. v. 3 and v. 11): 'Or why was I not like a hidden untimely birth?' There is a gradation in the expression of his desires: death at birth or the period of sucking the breast, abortion in the maternal womb. The verb נפל 'to fall' is used, like the Arabic *saqaṭa* 'fall', to signify 'fall from the mother's womb', 'come into the world' (Is 26:18). The noun נֵפֶל is the abortive thing which falls from the womb before the time is ripe (Ps 58:9; Ec 6:3). In Aramaic נפלא means abortion. The epithet טמון 'hidden' is appropriate to abortion, for 'it comes in vain and goes into darkness and in darkness its name is covered; moreover it has not even seen the sun or known anything' (Ec 6:4-5, Podechard's rendering). Thus it is clear that those who have not seen the light, as mentioned in our second hemistich, are the abortive. Cf. Ps 58:8b: 'like the untimely birth that never sees the sun'. The term עֹלְלִים 'nurslings' is a general designation for children and infants in general. Here it is applied to the abortive. The relative אשר is omitted before לא ראו (cf. v. 3 compared with Jer 20:14). Let us note that in Ec 6:6 the allusion to the abortive is followed by the question: 'Do not all go to the one place?' This place can be no other than Sheol. And it is just the description of Sheol which begins at v. 13. Sheol is essentially the abode in which one sees not the light (*RB*, 1907, p. 66); cf. Comm. on 7:9. The words 'have never seen the light' form a natural transition between the strophe 11, 12, 16 and the

13   For now I should be lying in peace,
     I should be sleeping and should be at rest!

14   With kings and counsellors of the land,
     Those who build for themselves in desert places;

strophe 13-15. Thus it is clear that everything suggests the transference of v. 16 to its natural position before vv. 13-15.

13   For the first hemistich, G has νῦν ἂν κοιμηθεὶς ἡσύχασα; cf. Vulg. *nunc enim dormiens silerem.* This 1st hemistich is omitted in Sah.

The opening phrase כִּי־עַתָּה has its original sense 'for now', but it gives to the perfect שָׁכַבְתִּי the meaning of the conditional (Ex 9: 15; cf. Gesenius-Kautzsch § 106p). The verb שָׁכַב 'to be lying down, asleep' alludes to those who lie in the tomb (Ps 88: 6) or in the dust (7: 21; 20: 11; 21: 26). Death is a sleep (14: 12). This very fact makes it a state of rest: וָאֶשְׁקוֹט 'I should be in peace'. In v. 26 we have וְלֹא־שָׁקַטְתִּי 'and I am not in peace'. The verb יָשֵׁן, like the verb שָׁכַב, represents the sleep of death (Ps 13: 4). The adverb אָז 'then' corresponds to the copula which precedes אֶשְׁקוֹט in the first hemistich. There are other cases in which אָז takes the place of the copula, for example in Ps 96: 12. The impersonal יָנוּחַ לִי 'it would be rest for me', as in Is 23: 12; Neh 9: 28. We have simply נַחְתִּי in v. 26. The rest of death evokes the idea of the tomb, for the tomb is truly the dwelling where man is in peace. Very interesting in this respect is the inscription on the stones of the tomb of Sennacherib: *ekal ṣalâli kimaḫ tapšuḫti šubat dârâti ša Sinaḫêrib šar kiššati šar Aššur*, 'Palace of sleep, tomb of repose, eternal abode of Sennacherib, King of the world, King of Assur' (Messerschmidt, *Keilschrifttexte aus Assur historischen Inhalts*, I, p. 49, No. 47). The tomb moreover is but the transition between the land of the living and the 'great land' where the dead are

gathered (7: 9). V. 14 begins the description of those who have already descended thither.

14   G (A) καὶ βουλευτῶν restores the copula of וְיֹעֲצֵי omitted by G and its derived versions. By confusing חֲרָבוֹת with חֳרָבוֹת (from חֶרֶב) G renders the second hemistich as οἳ ἠγαυριῶντο ἐπὶ ξίφεσιν. The word חרבות is translated ܚܪ̈ܒܐ 'ruins' (Syr.), ἐρείπια 'ruins' (Symm.), צדיין 'deserts' (Targ.), *solitudines* (Vulg.).

Death levels all conditions. Sheol is the meeting place of all men. First kings, then counsellors of the land, next princes. The series is found again in Ezr 7: 28; 8: 25. Fried. Delitzsch rightly connects with the יֹעֲצֵי אֶרֶץ the *bêlê ṭêmi mâti* 'masters of counsel in the land' among the Assyrians. Writers were fond of putting in Sheol personages of distinction: 'In the house of dust into which I entered myself, dwell the exorcists and the prophets, the anointed of the high gods, etc.' (*Choix de textes*, p. 215). The chiefs of the earth and the kings of the nations rise up from Sheol in Is 14: 9. Ezekiel describes the assembly of the heroes of all lands in Sheol (32: 21ff.). It is clear, from what precedes and from vv. 17-19, that the description must be an allusion to the state of the great ones of the earth after their death. The word חרבות should be interpreted in this context of ideas. Those who give to חרבות the meaning of 'ruins' (cf. Symm. and Syr.) see here an echo of the renown which kings gained for themselves by rebuilding ruins. And it is certain that the verb בנה with חרבות as a complement sometimes means 'raise up ruins', 're-build monuments that were des-

15   Or with princes who have gold
      And fill their houses with silver!

troyed' (Is 61: 4, cf. 68: 12). Similarly the *niph'al* of בנה with חרבות
as subject implies the restoration of
ruins (Ezk 36: 10, 33). But the
phrase הבנים...למו 'who build for
themselves' implies rather that it is
a question of a monument which
kings raise specifically for themselves, just as נבנה־לנו 'let us build
for ourselves' in Gn 11: 4 announces
the building of the tower of Babel.
It would be too easy a solution to
substitute for the difficult term
חרבות a banal word like רחבות
'public monuments' (Böttcher),
ארמנות 'palaces' (Olshausen), היכלות
'palaces', 'temples' (Beer). Still less
shall we change חרבות למו into
קברות עולם 'tombs of eternity'
(Cheyne, in *Exposit. Times*, **10**, 380).
The conjecture of Michaelis, who sees
in חרבות an equivalent of חרמות
with the meaning *adyta* or *mausolea*
(cf. Renan *mausolea*) would be a
very attractive hypothesis if the
root חרם did not exist in Hebrew
with the significance 'to be sacred,
inaccessible, inviolable'. The Arabic
harâm 'pyramid' (Ewald) is to be set
aside because of the first guttural,
which would be equivalent to ה and
not to ח. Schultens has suggested
that we should compare with the
Arabic *miḥrâb*, which is the niche
looking towards Mecca in the mos-
ques. But the etymology of this
word is uncertain and we cannot
infer from it that חרבות has the
meaning of royal dwellings such as
Schultens postulated. Now, the root
חרב 'to be devastated, in ruins', has
acquired as a parallel meaning that
of 'to be deserted, solitary'. Thus in
Is 48: 21 the word חֲרָבוֹת 'ruins' has
clearly the sense of 'desert' or
'steppe' (Condamin). In Syriac it is
this meaning which is predominant
in the derivatives of the root חרב.
In Assyrian *ḫuribtu* and *ḫurbatu*

simply mean 'desert'. We should
note that the tombs of the Pharoahs,
whether the pyramids or the royal
necropolis of Thebes, were built in
the desert. The Vulgate seems to us
to have wished to stress this idea of
solitary tombs by translating as *qui
aedificant sibi solitudines*.

15 G (A) replaces ἤ of the opening
by καί. This reading is isolated. For
זהב להם, G and its derived versions
have ὧν πολὺς ὁ χρυσός. Targ. renders
by קורטוריהון בתיהם 'their treasures'.
The relative אשר is omitted before
זהב (cf. v. 3 and v. 16). 'The princes
who have gold' are those whose
tombs were famous because of the
treasures contained in them. Thus
Tut-ankh-Amon has become famous
in modern times because of the
riches amassed in his tomb. It is well
known that there were in Egypt
veritable corporations of searchers of
tombs and riflers of corpses. The
golden masks of the mummies and
the other precious objects which
were piled up near the dead were an
attraction for robbers. Was not one
of the halls exhibiting funerary monuments called 'the house of gold'
(Erman, *La Religion égyptienne*,
translated by Vidal, p. 193)? It was
solely from fear of plunder that
Agbar, the priest of Nêrab, declared
that no object of silver or bronze had
been placed near his body (Lagrange,
ÉRS, p. 501). An unpublished Assyrian inscription says that a prince
who was burying his father 'had
first of all shown before Shamash
the gold and silver objects, the whole
furnishings of the tomb, the lordly
attire which he loved, and then had
placed all in the tomb with the king
his father' (Meissner, *Babylonien und
Assyrien*, I, pp. 427f.). Thus is clarified the 2nd hemistich 'who fill their
houses with silver'. The house is the

17   There the wicked cease all agitation
      And the weary are at rest.
18   Likewise the prisoners are in peace:
      They hear no more the voice of the taskmaster.

sepulchre as in Is 14: 18. We quoted in connection with v. 13 the interesting expressions comparing the tomb of Sennacherib with a palace of sleep and an eternal dwelling. This last formula recalls the ἀΐδίους οἴκους 'eternal houses' which, according to Diodorus Siculus (I, 51), denoted tombs among the Egyptians. One of the names for a tomb is, in fact, *pr-n-ḏt* 'house of eternity' in hieroglyphic texts (Erman, *Ägypt. Handwörterbuch*, p. 53). Among the Nabataeans it is בית מקברין 'house of the buried' (*RB*, 1897, p. 234). Hence we may consider their houses as representing the sepulchres of princes.

16 After v. 12.

17 All the versions support the reading רשעים. It is arbitrary to change the word into רעשים (Beer). For חדלו G has ἐξέκαυσαν (Sah., Syro-hex., Eth.), but G (A) ἔπαυσαν. Jerome and Aug. *deposuerunt* prove that the original reading was ἐξέπαυσαν = חדלו. G translates רגז by θυμὸν ὀργῆς, Jerome simply *furorem*. In the margin of Colb. and Syrohex. is given the hexaplar reading ἰσχύι instead of σώματι which translates כח in G. According to Syr., the יגיעי כח are those who have wearied themselves in their life. Targ. sees in רגז the restless torments of Gehenna and admits that the wicked 'who have done penance' escape the torment. The יגיעי כח are for it those who have wearied themselves in the practice of the law. The רְשָׁעִים are the wicked, and in particular those who torment others (15: 20; 27: 13). The verb חדל is used with the accusative (instead of the intransitive use) as in Is 1: 16

and 1 S 2: 5 (see our Comm.). Outside Job the abstract רֹגֶז recurs in Is 14: 3 as the antithesis of repose, in Hab 3: 2 and Sir 5: 6 with the meaning of anger. Here, as in v. 26 and Is 14: 3, there is a contrast between the peace of death or of sleep and the agitation of the living, the pain of the sick. The etymological sense of the verb רגז is 'to be agitated, excited', etc. Derivatively, רֹגֶז will imply the distress of man (14: 1), the nervousness of the horse (39: 24), the rumbling of thunder (37: 2). The wicked remain calm in Sheol, and, as a consequence of that fact, the unhappy victims of their vexations will be able to rest. Notice the parallelism between the perfect חדלו and the imperfect ינוחו (Is 5: 12b; Pr 1: 22, etc.). The word יָגִיעַ in the sense of יָגֵעַ 'wearied', 'exhausted' recurs only in Sir 37: 12. The complement כֹּה is added to confirm that it is a question of physical exhaustion; cf. שִׂגִיא־כֹּה (37: 23), אַמִּיץ כֹּה (9: 4).

18 G omits שַׁאֲנַנּוּ and renders אסירים by οἱ αἰώνιοι (B, א*, Sah., Syro-hex.) or δι' αἰῶνος (A, אc·ᵃ, Jerome *in aeternam*). The word αἰώνιοι was an epithet coming from a word which later disappeared; cf. Vulg. *et quondam vincti*. In Aq. and Theod. שַׁאֲנַנּוּ is rendered by εὐθήνησαν (which has become εὐθύνησαν in Colb.), and has passed (with asterisk) into Jerome and Syro-hex. For נגש G has φορολόγου (φωρολόγου in A, א). Jerome *exactoris* is inspired by Symm. ἐπαναγκαστοῦ. Targ. continues its fantasies: the prisoners are the children shut up in schools, the נגש is the master who teaches.

19   Small and great, there is no difference there,
     And the servant is freed from his master!
20   Why does He give light to one who is in misery,
     And life to those whose soul is bitter?

The adverb יַחַד implies that the prisoners form a group with those previously enumerated. They have the same fate; cf. 21:26. The verb שָׁאַן (pa'lel of שָׁאַן) recurs only in Jer 30:10; 46:27; 48:11, and Pr 1:33. In the texts of Jeremiah it implies, as here, the rest of the free man as contrasted with the harsh tasks imposed on prisoners. The latter were under the domination of the נֹגֵשׂ 'oppressor', who fulfilled the rôle of an inspector (Ex 3:7; 5:14, etc.). Armed with his rod (Is 9:3), he walked around among the workers to inspect their work (Zec 9:8). What a deliverance no longer to hear his voice! Similarly, the ass when freed 'hears not the vociferations of its driver' (39:7, where the word chosen for 'driver' is pricisely נֹגֵשׂ). In Sheol there are no more masters and slaves (v. 19). Seneca emphasised the liberation which death brings to the slave: *Haec servitutem invito domino remittit, haec captivorum catenas levat, haec e carcere educit quo exire imperium impotens vetuerat* (De consolatione, XX, 2). After enumerating the sufferings to which are exposed those condemned to hard labour, Diodorus Siculus concludes: αἱρετώτερος γὰρ αὐτοῖς ὁ θάνατός ἐστι τοῦ ζῆν (V, 38).

19 The versions attribute to הוּא the sense of the verb 'to be'. G rendered חָפְשִׁי 'free' by οὐ δεδοικώς 'unafraid' (A, אᶜ·ᵇ). Jerome, (Bod. and Gall.) *non metuens*. The negative has disappeared from G (B) δεδοικώς (Sah., Syro-hex., Eth.). In the margin of Syro-hex. is given the interpretation of Aq. and Symm. ἐλεύθερος. Instead of considering

אדנים as a plural of majesty, Theod., quoted by Syro-hex., translates אדניו by ἀπὸ τῶν κυρίων ἑαυτοῦ. In Targ. identifications are again made: the small man is Jacob, the great Abraham, the servant Isaac.

Bickell sacrifices v. 19 to the exigencies of his metrical system. The pronoun הוּא has here the meaning of the Latin *idem* 'the same thing'; compare אֲנִי־הוּא 'I am the same' in Is 41:4; 43:10, 13; 46:4; 48:12; אַתָּה הוּא 'thou art the same' in Ps 102:28. Repetition of the adverb שָׁם 'there', in Sheol; cf. v. 17. Great and small are made equal by death. This is the constant theme of the scoffs of Lucian in the *Dialogues of the Dead*. Seneca observes that death 'levels all things', *exaequat omnia* (loc. cit., XX, 18). Albertus Magnus completes the Vulg. *ibi sunt* by *aequales et pariter quiescentes*. Of course אדניו is a plural of majesty 'his master' (cf. Pr 25:13; 27:18; 30:10, etc.). The word חָפְשִׁי reappears in 39:5, whereas 39:7 is based on v. 18 (cf. sup.).

20 The versions interpret יתן as a passive, whence the correction יֻתַּן proposed by Beer. But it is obvious that the implied subject is God. The passive construction characteristic of the versions has arisen as a result of a theological scruple. For לעמל G τοῖς ἐν πικρίᾳ (Sah., Syrohex., Eth., Jerome *eis qui in amaritudine sunt*). G (A) adds ψυχῆς by anticipation of מרי נפש. The translation of מרי נפש in G is somewhat colourless: ταῖς ἐν ὀδύναις ψυχαῖς.

In the strophe 11, 12, 16 we had a first series of questions. Job himself was immediately in question. Here the inquiry embraces a much vaster

21   To those who wait for death and it comes not,
      And who dig in search of it more than for hidden treasures,
22   Who rejoice to the point of jubilation,
      And are exultant because they have found a tomb.

horizon. Why should the unhappy in general have been afflicted with life? It is Yahweh who makes alive and slays (1 S 2: 6). The subject of יתן is simply God, the author of all good and evil (2: 10). Sorrow and misfortune were called עָמָל (v. 10), and here the wretched one is called עָמֵל. In 20: 22 the two words have been confused. Parallelism between light and life: to see the light is to enter the world (cf. v. 16); to banish some one from light is to relegate him to the other world (18: 18). Cf. the use of the word 'light' in 33: 28, 30; 38: 15. The bitter soul is the one which has not tasted of happiness (21: 25), those who are bitter of soul are those whose soul is penetrated with bitterness (I S 1: 10; Pr 31: 6). With the phrase מָרֵי נֶפֶשׁ compare יגיעי כח of v. 17.

21 G and Vulg. add a verb to explain ואיננו: καὶ οὐ τυγχάνουσιν (G), *et non venit* (Vulg.). The suffix of יחפרהו is omitted in G (B) and Syrohex., but is restored as αὐτόν in G (A, אᶜ·ᵃ), Sah., Jerome *eam*, Eth. For ממטמונים, G ὥσπερ θησαυρούς (A θησαυρόν, Jerome *thesaurum*). In Vulg. the 2nd hemistich becomes *quasi effodientes thesaurum*.

The verb חכה in the *pi'el*, with ל" before its complement, is deliberately chosen. It is the verb used to mean 'wait for' Yahweh (Is 8: 17; 64: 3; Ps 30: 20, etc.). Death is the supreme hope to which the wretched cling. The 1st hemistich is in the same style as the יקו לאור ואין of v. 9. We find it again paraphrased thus in Rev 9: 6, Ζητήσουσιν οἱ ἄνθρωποι τὸν θάνατον καὶ μὴ εὑρήσουσιν αὐτόν. The verb חפר can have the meaning of 'to be on the watch' (39: 29) or

'to dig', 'to excavate', (39: 21). But, as it is a question of treasures, it is obvious that the second meaning is the one suitable to the context. In Ex 7: 24 we have חפר 'dig' with the accusative of the thing that is being sought for. To replace the comparative מן of ממַטְמוֹנִים by כ", like G, Syr., and Vulg. (Beer, Duhm), is to weaken the MT, which is here supported by Targ. The unhappy ones dig the soil to find death, more than others to find hidden treasures. It is in the earth that treasures were hidden (Mt 13: 44). What is alluded to is essentially מטמון 'hidden'; cf. the verb טמן in v. 16. The participial clause of the 1st hemistich is continued by the consecutive imperfect (Gesenius-Kautzsch, § 116x). We have noted the converse in 2: 8.

22 Targ. renders אלי־גיל literally by לדיצה 'with joy', while Syr. 'and who gather themselves together' seems to interpret אלי־גל as 'in a heap'. The verse is summed up by G in the words περιχαρεῖς δὲ ἐγένοντο ἐὰν κατατύχωσιν (A adds θανάτου) and by Vulg. *gaudentque vehementer cum invenerint sepulcrum*. The word קבר is implied in θάνατος of G in v. 23 and it is thence that G (A) derives the complement θανάτου. The words ἐὰν κατατύχωσιν, omitted in Jerome (Bod. and Tur.), are restored in Gall. *si impetrent*.

Parallelism between the participial phrase and the imperfect (cf. v. 21). The allusion is to the diggers who have just been mentioned. Out of concern for parallelism, Houbigant, followed by certain moderns, suggested replacing גיל by גַּל and giving to the word the sense of funerary mound. This slight correction at

23   To a man whose path is hidden
     And whom Eloah has hedged in!
24   For my sighing comes like my bread,
     And my groanings flow forth as water.

first appears attractive enough, for the funerary mound was originally a גל, a heap of stones. Such is the appearance of the tombs of the Bedouin in the desert. But they are not found by digging. And, above all, in Hos 9:1 we have the very typical formula אל־תשמה ישראל אל־גיל 'rejoice not, O Israel, with exultation' (van Hoonacker's rendering). Literally, אל־גיל means 'to the point of jubilation', the preposition אל having the meaning of עד 'to the extent of', as in 40:23 and Gn 6:16. Here the poetic אלי is used instead of אל (cf. 5:26; 15:22; 29:10). The verb שיש recurs in 39:21. We have already quoted this ch. 39 in connection with vv. 18, 19, and 21.

23 Targ. adds at the beginning 'all these bitternesses . . .'. Instead of the 1st hemistich, G has θάνατος (with the addition of γὰρ in A, Sah., and Syro-hex.), ἀνδρὶ ἀνάπαυσις (B ἀνάπαυμα). The word θάνατος comes from קבר of v. 22 (cf. A in v. 22), and ἀνάπαυσις can only be a vague paraphrase of אשר דרכו נסתרה. After ἀνάπαυσις G (A) adds οὗ ἧδος ἀπεκρύβη, which comes from Theod. οὗ ἡ ὁδὸς ἀπεκρύβη ἀπ' αὐτοῦ, a reading cited (with asterisk) in Colb. and (without asterisk) in Jerome cujus via abscondita est. The word יסך is interpreted in the meaning of 'protect' by Targ. and Syr. In G συνέκλεισεν; in Symm. ἀπέφραξεν. Vulg. paraphrases the 2nd hemistich as et circumdedit eum Deus tenebris.

After speaking of the wretched in general, Job returns to speak of his individual case. He is the man 'whose path is hidden and whom Eloah has hedged in'. The meaning

cannot be in doubt if we bear in mind 19:8, where Job will say: 'He has barred my path so that I cannot pass and my ways He has covered with darkness.' In this text the verb גדר 'to bar' has a meaning similar to the hiph'il of סוך 'surround with a hedge', 'close in' (38:8); on the connection between גדר and שוך or סוך cf. 1:10. It should be noted that שוך is used with בעד before its complement in 1:10, and that we have בעד before the complement of גדר in La 3:7. If גדר בעד means 'wall in' (La 3:7), הסיך בעד will mean 'enclose' (with thorns, a hedge, etc.); cf. 1:10. When man is hedged in by God, he can no longer see his way clearly. That is why we are told on the one hand that his path is obscure, on the other that God has covered his ways with darkness (19:8). The double thought expressed in our verse is developed in La 3:1-3 and 7-9. It is a question of some one (גֶּבֶר as here) whom God leads 'in darkness and not in light'; hence he can no longer recognise his path. This personage is shut in with no means of escape: 'He has walled me about so that I cannot escape . . . he has blocked my ways with hewn stones.' The description given in our v. 23 is not therefore of general application, but concerns a specific individual, namely the speaker, exactly as in La 3. Job applies to himself the reflections made in vv. 20-2 about humanity in general.

24 The versions give to לפני the meaning of 'before'. Vulg. paraphrases: antequam comedo suspiro. The suffix of לחמי has vanished from G (B, א) but is reflected in the μοι of G (A, C), Sah., and Eth. The

25　　For if I fear a thing, it happens to me,
　　　And what I apprehend befalls me.

MT is copied by Aq. ὅτι εἰς πρόσωπον
ἄρτου μου στεναγμός μου ἐλεύσεται.
The word *adest*, which in Jerome
(Gall.) and Aug. corresponds to the
ἥκει of G, has become *ad Dominum*
in Bod. and Tur. The 2nd hemistich
is paraphrased in G as δακρύω δὲ ἐγὼ
συνεχόμενος φόβῳ. The word φόβῳ
anticipates v. 25. A reading of Aq.,
to which attention is called in the
margin of Syro-hex., and which is
mentioned in Compl., brings us back
to the MT: καὶ χυθήσεται ὡς ὕδατα
βρυχήματά μου. The margin of Syro-
hex. also quotes a reading of Theod.
which again brings us back to
MT.

The conjunction כִּי, as in v. 25,
justifies v. 23, where Job complains
of being constricted by God within his
misfortune. The correction of לִפְנֵי to
כְּפִי (Budde) or to לְפִי (Beer) has no
kind of support in the versions. If we
give to לִפְנֵי the meaning of 'before',
we are obliged to paraphrase as 'before eating my bread'. Still less is
it possible to translate: 'My sighing
comes in the presence of my bread.'
Le Hir shows most convincingly that
the parallelism with כמים and the
use of the verb תבא compel us to
give to לִפְנֵי the meaning of 'in the
manner of'. Now, in 4: 19 and 1 S
1: 16, the locution לִפְנֵי certainly
means 'like'. The connecting idea is
'in the manner of', for פָּנִים 'face'
eventually came to signify 'manner'
(*L'Emploi métaphorique*, p. 66). The
formula of Ps 42: 4 הָיְתָה־לִּי דִמְעָתִי
לֶחֶם 'my tears have been as bread
for me' proves that here it is indeed
a question of a comparison of his
sighing to bread. The very vivid
term שְׁאָגָה denotes the roaring of the
lion (4: 10). It is also used to denote
the cries of those in distress (Ps
22: 2; 32: 3). Continuity is achieved

by the comparison 'like water'.
Duhm removes v. 24, which he
thinks is a marginal gloss on vv.
25-6. Decidedly, we should have to
give up the attempt to distinguish
what is poetry from what is not, if
this beautiful verse had to be ascribed to a commentator.

25 The copula of וַיֶּאֱתָיֵנִי is omitted
in G, Symm., Syr., and Vulg., which
interpret as 'the fear which I feared
befalls me'. The MT is literally
reproduced in Targ., Aq., and Theod.
For פָּחַדְתִּי G (B) has ἐφρόντισα
(Sah., Syro-hex.), G (A) εὐλαβούμην,
G (אᶜ·ᵃ) ἐφοβούμην (as in Symm.);
cf. Jerome *verebar*.

The expression פַּחַד פָּחַדְתִּי *timorem
timui* as in Dt 28: 67; Ps 14: 5; 53: 6.
The construction of the 1st hemistich is exactly the same as in 29: 11.
The use of the perfect shows that the
first action is completed when the
second takes place. The word פַּחַד
'fear' (13: 11; 21: 9; 22: 10, etc.)
sometimes suggests the effects of
fear, e.g. trembling (4: 14). The verb
אתה is Aramaic and is the equivalent
of the Hebrew בוא. The final *yod* (cf.
Arabic أَق) recurs in יאתיו of 16: 22
and 30: 14. The suffix is in the accusative as in יבואנו (5: 21) and
תבואנו (20: 22). The verb יגר 'to
be afraid' is used with the accusative
as here (9: 28; Ps 119: 39), or else
with מפני before the object of the
fear (Dt 9: 19; 28: 60). When the
verb בוא has as its subject a misfortune which befalls some one, the
complement of the person is sometimes in the accusative (20: 22),
sometimes preceded by a preposition: either עַל (2: 11) or אֶל
(4: 5), or simply לְ as here. Parallelism between the Aramaic אתה
and the Hebrew בוא as in Pr 1:
27.

26   I am neither quiet nor in peace,
      I cannot rest; but agitation comes upon me.

26 G εἰρήνευσα bases its translation of שלותי on the sense of שלם. The readings of Aq. εὐπάθησα and of Theod. εὐθήνησα are quoted in the margin of Syro-hex. The interrogative construction *nonne* adopted by the Vulg. necessitates the use of paraphrases: *Nonne dissimulavi? Nonne silui? Nonne quievi? Et venit super me indignatio.* In Targ. each verb is considered to be an allusion to Job's attitude after each of the catastrophes mentioned in the prose narrative.

The verb שלה 'to be quiet' is the only one of the ל"ה type which retains in the qal the original *waw*; cf. the adjective שָׁלֵו 'quiet' and the abstract noun שַׁלְוָה 'tranquillity'. The verb שקט implies rather physical rest (cf. v. 13), whilst שלה refers to the rest of the mind in the security which good fortune brings. As for נוח, it implies rest in every sense. The opposite of rest is agitation. The word רֹגֶז of v. 17 is well chosen to express the anxieties or turbulent emotions which prevent Job from resting or being happy. V. 26 closes Job's lament and sums up the hero's state of mind.

CHAPTER 4

1   Then Eliphaz the Temanite spoke and said:
2   Shall we *address* you? You are dejected!
      But who could refrain from speaking?

Chapters 4-14 First cycle of speeches: see Introduction, pp. xxxviff.
Chapters 4-5 First speech of Eliphaz: see Introduction, pp. xxxviff.

2 נָשָׂא (Aq., Symm., Theod., Vulg.); MT: נִסָּה.

4: **1** The verb ענה 'to speak' (3: 2), and not 'answer' as the versions interpret. Here we have the typical formula of introduction which prefaces the speeches of Job and his friends.

2 G μὴ πολλάκις is a Hellenism (cf. 31: 31) which cannot be used to amend the text. What follows, σοὶ λελάληται ἐν κόπῳ, is a vague interpretation of נסה···תלאה. The readings of Aq. μήτι ἐπαροῦμεν λαλῆσαι, of Symm. ἐὰν ἀναλάβωμεν λόγον, of Theod. εἰ ληψόμεθα λαλῆσαι, quoted in Syro-hex., interpret נסה in the sense of נָשָׂא (cf. inf.). Compare Vulg. *si coeperimus loqui tibi.* In Targ. it is a question of the trial that Job has had to undergo. Instead of יעצר G reads וערץ, whence ἰσχὺν δέ (cf. Is 10: 33). Syro-hex. marks with an obelus the suffix σοῦ, which G adds after ῥημάτων (מלין). Vulg. renders במלין by *conceptum sermonem.*

The 2nd hemistich is clear: 'But who could refrain from speaking?' Cf. עצרו במלים 'they restrained their words' in 29: 9 and יעצר במים 'He holds back the waters' (12: 15). Outside the Book of Job, where it occurs 34 times, the word מלה is found only in 2 S 23: 2; Ps 19: 5; 139: 4; Pr 23: 9. The Aramaic plural מלין is used 13 times in Job, the Hebrew plural מלים 10 times. On the omission of ל before the complement of יוכל, cf. 3: 8. Most commentators have considered the interrogative as a conditional clause: 'If we address a few words to you, perhaps you will have difficulty in understanding them' (Le Hir); 'If we break silence, we shall perhaps distress you' (Renan). But the interpretation of the interrogative ה as implying a simple hypothesis has but a fragile support in Pr 23: 5. It is a formal interrogation which opens the other speeches of Eliphaz (15: 2; 22: 2). Some exegetes have attempted to make תִּלְאֶה the verb governed by the interrogation: 'Will you be weary (impatient) if one tries to speak to you?' (Dillmann, etc.). Others suppose the relative אשר to be understood before תלאה: 'to you who are dejected' (Duhm). We think, however, that the verb תלאה contains a reply, in the form of an objection, to the opening question. The 2nd hemistich in its turn answers this objection. The difficulty lies in the word נִסָּה, which can only be the *pi'el* 3rd person m. sing. of נסה, with the meaning of 'try'. Literally, one should translate: 'Has one tried speech with you?' But we note that in Ps 4: 7 the writing נְסָה conceals the verb נָשָׂא and that here

42

3   Consider now, you have been accustomed to teach many,
     And to strengthen the weak hands;
4   Your words would uphold the tottering,
     And you strengthened the knees that gave way!

even the hexaplar authors, like the Vulgate, are unanimous in reading נָשָׂא, the sound of which is the same as נָסָה. We have here an error in audition. The verb נָשָׂא 'raise' is quite intelligible with the complement דָּבָר מָשָׁל 'word'; cf. נשא משל 'utter a parable, a speech' (27: 1), נשא זמרה 'utter a Psalm' (Ps 81: 3), and the current phrase נשא קִינָה 'to give voice to lamentation'. Thus the meaning of the first hemistich becomes clear: 'Shall we address you? You are dejected!', implying that it is not the seasonable moment to speak to you (2: 13). The verb לָאָה 'to be tired, exhausted', both in a physical and moral sense. Hence the meaning of 'dejected', here as in v. 5. The *hiph'il* has the meaning of 'exhaust' (16: 7). Hence Eliphaz ought to be silent in face of such sorrow. But he feels he must speak; a wave of thoughts springs to his mind and he must give it free course.

3   G stands alone in reading הֵן as εἰ γάρ instead of הִנֵּה. For רְפוֹת. G has ἀσθενοῦς, but G (A) ἀσθενούντων, followed by Sah. and Jerome *infirmium*.

The opening הִנֵּה 'consider now' leads to a series of observations expressed by a perfect of habit (1: 4), continued in a series of imperfects. The exact meaning of the verb יסר in the *pi'el* is 'to correct', whether by words, whence 'teach', or by chastisement, whence 'punish'. The double meaning of 'teach' and 'punish' is found also in מוּסָר 'lesson' (5: 17; 20: 3), 'warning'

(36: 10), but also 'punishment' (Is 53: 5, etc.). Compare the meanings of הוֹכִיחַ (5: 17). Plural רַבִּים 'numerous' (11: 19; 38: 21). Elsewhere 'great' (35: 9), 'old' (32: 9). The feminine plural רָפוֹת qualifies the dual יָדַיִם, just as כִּרְעוֹת qualifies בִּרְכַּיִם in v. 4. The hands are the seat of strength. 'Weak hands' symbolise collapse (2 S 2: 7; 4: 1). It is 'as a result of the weakness of the hands', מרפיון ידים, that the fathers no longer have the courage to look on their sons (Jer 47: 3). We find both כשלון ברכים and רפיון ידים 'tottering of the knees' (cf. v. 4) in Sir 25: 23. The expressions of v. 3b and v. 4b recur in Is 35: 3: 'Strengthen the weak hands and confirm the feeble knees!' Cf. He 12: 12.

4   Targ. clarifies כושל and כרעות by referring to a lapse into sin. The MT sing. for כושל is retained in Targ. and Aq., but rendered by a plural in G, Symm., Theod., Syr., and Vulg. *vacillantes*. G paraphrases יקימון מליך by ἐξανέστησας ῥήμασιν. The suffix σοῦ of ῥήμασι is added in Sah. and Eth. MT is copied by Aq. and Theod. ἐξανέστησαν ῥήματά σου.

The verb כשל is used specifically of knees which give way (Is 35: 3; Ps 109: 24). What is meant is a man who is about to fall. The *hiph'il* הקים means not only 'raise up' (16: 12) but also 'set upright again', 'uphold' (Ps 89: 44). In Is 35: 3 the epithet qualifying בִּרְכַּיִם is כֹּשְׁלוֹת, for which is here substituted כרעות 'giving way'. The meaning of כרע is 'bend', 'collapse' (31: 10; 39: 3). Job was the sage who by his advice used to prevent others from being

5   But now that the same thing happens to you, you are dejected;
    Now that the blow strikes you, you are terrified!
6   Is not your piety the ground of your confidence,
    And the perfection of your ways your hope?

crushed by the weight of misfortune. It is easy to exhort others by kind words. But when one is one's self afflicted, it is more difficult to preserve one's serenity. Calmet quotes Terence: *Facile omnes, quum valemus, recta consilia aegrotis damus; tu si hic sis, aliter sentias* (*Andria*, II, i, 9f.).

5 G νῦν δὲ ἥκει ἐπὶ σὲ πόνος reads תִּלְאָה, instead of ותלא. Vulg. adds the subject of תבוא: *venit super te plaga*. Instead of ἐσπούδασας, which translates תבהל in G, a reading quoted in Cod. 248 gives ἐθορυβήθης (cf. Vulg. *conturbatus es*).

The expression כִּי־עַתָּה has the sense of 'now that' (7:21); compare כי גם, which means 'even though' in Ec 4:14. (cf. Podechard). The feminine impersonals תָּבוֹא and תִּגַּע have a neuter sense. The understood subject is 'that', i.e. what is suggested by vv. 3-4 (cf. Ezk 12:25). The *waw* consecutive in וַתֵּלֶא and וַתִּבָּהֵל implies that Job's state of mind is a consequence of the events summed up by תבוא עדיך and תגע אליך. On the verb לאה, of which ותלא is the apocopated form, cf. v. 2. The verb נגע, with עד before the complement, means 'touch', '*attingere*', 'strike' (Is 16:8); cf. 1:11. Eliphaz uses a very vivid term תבהל 'you are terrified' (21:6; 23:15). The *niph'al* נבהל characterises the emotion aroused by the coming of misfortune (Jg 20:41). Job will speak of the terrors which assail him and will use the word בלהות (same root as נבהל, metathesis of בהל into בלה) in 30:15.

6 For כסלתך G has ἐστιν ἐν ἀφροσύνῃ (Jerome *stultus est*). The word

תקותך is rendered ἡ ἐλπίς σου (G), סברך 'your hope' (Targ. and Syr.), but ἡ ὑπομονή σου in Aq. (cf. Vulg. *patientia tua*). For ותם G has καὶ ἡ κακία, a corruption of ἡ ἀκακία (cf. ἄκακος and ἀκακία in 2:3). We find *et simplicitas* in Jerome, under the influence of Aq. καὶ ἡ ἁπλότης (cf. 1:1, etc.).

Calmet and, after him, Rosenmüller have given long enumerations of the various ways in which this verse has been interpreted. The cause of these divergences is the ambiguous כִּסְלָה, which is susceptible of a double meaning: 'foolishness' and 'hope', 'confidence'. On these meanings, cf. the Comm. on 9:9. The masculine כֶּסֶל is found in the Book of Job with the meaning of 'confidence' (8:14; 31:24), and as a parallel it has the word מִבְטָח 'security' (ibid.). It is clear that כִּסְלָתֶךָ, which, in virtue of antithetic parallelism, has as a parallel תִּקְוָתְךָ 'your hope', is used here in the sense of 'confidence'. It is characteristic of the speeches of Eliphaz that the word יִרְאָה 'fear' assumes the meaning of 'fear of God', 'piety' (15:4; 22:4). In Assyrian, the word *palḫu* 'one who fears' is used to indicate the fear of God, and so implies 'pious', 'religious'. In 1:1 Job has been described as a blameless and upright man, fearing God and avoiding evil. That is why, in the 2nd hemistich, his fear of God is paralleled by the perfection of his ways. With the expression 'the perfection of your ways' (תם דרכיך) cf. 'the perfection of the way' (תם דרך) in Pr 13:6. The perfect way is described as דרך תמים (Ps 101:6, etc.). The construction of the second

7 Call to mind, now! What innocent man ever perished?
   And where were the upright cut off?
8 As I have seen, those who cultivate iniquity
   And who sow trouble reap the same!

hemistich is characteristic. The copula *waw* with the words which it governs has been included within the proposition instead of remaining at the head. This construction is intended to place emphasis on the key word (10: 8; 19: 23). In 2 S 15: 34 we find a similar inversion: עבד אביך ואני מאז 'and I was formerly the servant of your master'. Hence it would be very unwise to transfer תקותך to the end of the verse (Hupfeld, Merx), or to place the ו of ותם in front of תקותך (Dillmann, Budde, etc.). The irony of Eliphaz is perceptible in every word. It will become even more biting in the following verses.

7 Instead of the τίς καθαρὸς ὤν of G (B, א, C) for מי הוא נקי G (A) has ὅτι οὐδεὶς καθαρὸς ὤν, followed by Eth. To the adjective נקי 'innocent' Targ. adds 'like Abraham', and to ישרים 'righteous' it adds 'like Isaac and Jacob' (cf. 3: 19). For נכחדו G has ὁλόριζοι ἀπώλοντο (Jerome *radicitus interierunt*).

The idea of the verse is repeated in Sir 2: 10ff., where זְכָר־נָא is developed into ἐμβλέψατε εἰς ἀρχαίας γενεὰς καὶ ἴδετε. We shall again meet זכרנא at the beginning of the verse in 10: 9. The interrogative מי הוא 'who indeed?' is more energetic than the simple מי (cf. 13: 19; 17: 3). The thesis of Eliphaz and his friends is well summed up by St Thomas: *opinionem . . . quod adversitates hujus mundi non adveniant alicui nisi in poenam peccati et e contrario prosperitates pro merito justitiae.* This is exactly the ethic of the Babylonians and Assyrians as it is disclosed in magical or religious texts (*La Religion assyro-babylonienne*, p. 235). The same prejudice is found in the com-

ment of the Maltese on the subject of the viper clinging to the hand of St Paul (Ac 28: 4). Our Lord rejects this doctrine in connection with the man born blind (Jn 9: 1 ff.). Similarly in Lk 13: 4 in regard to the victims of the catastrophe of Siloam. Ps 37 develops fully the thesis of the relation between moral good and good fortune and between moral evil and misfortune. Even if appearances suggest that good fortune comes at times to the wicked and misfortune to the righteous, this is only a false and transient illusion. The last word remains with God, who on this earth rewards the just and punishes the wicked. The author of the Psalm also appeals to his personal experience: 'I have been young and now am old, yet I have never seen the righteous forsaken' (Ps 37: 25; cf. Sir 2: 10f.). Thus the ideas of Eliphaz are current coin. The experience of the centuries shows that happiness is ascribed to the just, adversity to the wicked. The precise object of the speeches of Job will be to protest against these equations between the conduct of man and his retribution here below. Note that איפה is spelt thus in the interrogative sense 'when?' (38: 4), but that we have אפוא (9: 24) or אפו, peculiar to Job (17: 15; 19: 6, 23; 24: 25), in the enclitic sense. The parallelism between נקי and ישרים will recur in the mouth of Job (17: 8). The *niph'al* נכחד means etymologically 'to be hidden' (cf. the *pi'el* in 6: 10; 15: 18; 27: 11), whence 'to be effaced, destroyed, extirpated, annihilated' (15: 28; 22: 20).

8 The observations of Eliphaz are

9   Under the breath of Eloah they perish,
     And at the blast of His nostril they fade away;

applied by Targ. to the generation of the Flood. G renders אָוֶן by a plural τὰ ἄτοπα (Jerome *pessima*). For חרשׁי Targ. עבדי, Vulg. *qui operantur*, according to the meaning of the noun חָרָשׁ 'artisan'; but the meaning 'cultivate' for the verb חרשׁ is confirmed by זרעי and יקצרהו. G connects עמל with יקצרהו, whence ὀδύνας θεριοῦσιν ἑαυτοῖς (A ἐν αὐτοῖς).

In v. 7 Eliphaz appealed to Job's own experience. Now he brings forward his own personal experience: as I have seen! He likes to put himself on the stage (v. 12 and 5: 3). One wonders why Duhm would prefer the second person to רָאִיתִי confirmed by 5: 3 and Ps 37: 25. It is true that this author jettisons vv. 8-11, which have the defect of not answering to his ideas on the style of Eliphaz. A simple reading of the text is sufficient to show how the ideas of Job's friend are logically connected. It would be making the sentence curiously heavy to connect חרשׁי אָוֶן with ראיתי in order to translate 'each time I have seen people ploughing iniquity' (contra Umbreit, Franz Delitzsch). In reality זרעי עמל חרשׁי אָוֶן forms with the subject of יקצרהו. The clause כאשׁר ראיתי is subordinate, like זכר־נא in v. 7. The verbs חרשׁ 'plough', 'cultivate', זרע 'sow', קצר 'reap', mark very clearly the successive actions of the sinner. The words אָוֶן and עמל are in parallelism as in 5: 6 and 15: 35. The first is chosen deliberately, for it denotes physical evil, pain, and moral evil, iniquity. The sinner cultivates and sows moral evil, he reaps physical evil, punishment; there is a similar image in 5: 6. Cf. Hos 10: 13, 'You have ploughed iniquity, you have reaped injustice, you have eaten the fruit of lies', where the verbs חרשׁ

and קצר are used as here. The previous verse, 'Sow to yourselves righteousness, and reap mercy', employs the verbs זרע and קצר. Cf. Pr 22: 8, 'He who sows unrighteousness (עולה), reaps iniquity (אָוֶן)'. In Pr 14: 22 there is a contrast between the חרשׁי רע 'who cultivate evil' and the חרשׁי טוב 'who cultivate good'. The same metaphors are found in Gal 6: 7ff. Notice that Job has complained that sorrow, עָמָל as here, had not been spared him (3: 10). The comment of Eliphaz is insulting; Job is assumed to be the cause of his own misfortune.

9   Instead of מנשׁמת 'by the breath', G has ἀπὸ προστάγματος and Targ. מן מימר 'by the word', in order to avoid anthropomorphism.

Vv. 9-11 propose to explain how misfortune is the consequence of sin. The mediating agent is the divine anger manifested by the same symptoms as among human beings. Sin provokes God and He avenges Himself. We find the same thought among the Assyrians and Babylonians (*La Religion assyro-babylonienne*, pp. 232f.). The preposition מן is used to introduce the cause of the action expressed by the verb (7: 14). The breath of Eloah נשׁמת אלוה (cf. 37: 10) suffices to destroy the wicked. In Is 30: 33 the נשׁמת יהוה kindles the fire which is to consume the enemy. To the breath of God corresponds 'the blast of His nostril'. This is the very metaphor used to express the anger which exerts its effects on the enemies of Yahweh (Ex 15: 7f.). In 2 S 22: 16 the two expressions merge into a single one מנשׁמת רוח אפו. Under the breath of the divine wrath, the wicked perish as the plant withered by the east wind (Hos 13: 15; Ezk

10   The roar of the lion and the voice of the leopard,
      And the teeth of the young lions are broken;
11   The lion perishes for lack of prey
      And the whelps of the lioness are scattered.

17: 10; 19: 12). Cf. 2 Th 2: 8: ἀνελεῖ τῷ πνεύματι τοῦ στόματος αὐτοῦ. Parallelism between אבד and כלה (11: 20).

10 Targ. again sees symbols in the terms used (cf. 7-8): the 1st Targ. seeks allusion to Esau, Edom, Ishmael, the 2nd to Ishmael and the sons of Lot. The word שחל, transcribed שחלא in Targ., is interpreted as lioness in the other versions. Syr. inverts the order of the words שחל and כפירים: voice of the young lion and teeth of the lionesses. G renders ושני כפירים by γαυρίαμα δὲ δρακόντων; cf. 38: 39. Jerome had *et gaudium* (cf. Aug. and Gall.) for γαυρίαμα δέ, but *gaudium* has become *gladius* in Bod. and Tur.

Duhm and Fried. Delitzsch repeat an opinion already expressed by Dillmann, according to which the sentence breaks off after the 1st hemistich: roaring of the lion and voice of the roaring! .... the teeth of the young lions are broken! That is, hardly have you heard the roaring when the teeth of the young lion are broken. This construction could only be acceptable if we had 'its teeth' or the 'teeth of the lion' in the 2nd hemistich. It is clear that the three subjects of נתעו are 'the roaring of the lion', 'the voice of the leopard', 'the teeth of the young lions'. By syllepsis, the verb has been chosen solely to suit the last subject. In fact, the *hapax* נתע is the Aramaic form of נתץ (19: 10). Now, in Ps 58: 7 this verb נתץ has as its complement precisely מלתעות כפירים 'the fangs of the young lions'. After speaking of the roaring and the voice, the poet mentions the teeth, and chooses the characteristic verb, 'are broken'. A similar mode of expression is

found in Ex 20: 18, where the Israelites *see* the thunder, the flames, the *sound* of the trumpet, and the smoking mountain. Renan forgets the ו before קול in paraphrasing the 1st hemistich as 'the roaring of the lion is stifled'. Note the use of שְׁאָגָה 'roaring' of 3: 24 in a literal sense: the roaring of the lion. The word אַרְיֵה is the generic term for lion, whilst שַׁחַל (10: 16; 28: 8) denotes a species which outside the Book of Job is mentioned only in Hos 5: 14; 13: 7; Ps 91: 13, and Pr 26: 13. Parallelism between אריה = אֲרִי and שחל in Pr 26: 13. Elsewhere the parallel of שחל is כְּפִיר 'young lion' (Hos 5: 14; Ps 91: 13) or נָמֵר 'panther' (Hos 13: 7). Here שחל figures along with the lion itself and the young lions. In v. 11 we find the lion, as the king of beasts, and the lioness. These observations compel us to recognise in שחל an animal of the lion species, but also (following Hos 13: 7) suggesting the idea of the panther. We consider the reference is to the leopard, the name of which is compounded precisely of *leo* 'lion' and *pardus*, Gk. πάρδος, 'panther' or 'leopard'. Bochart would like to see here a reference to the black lion of the Arabs (*Hieroz.*, I, col. 717), but the etymology he proposes (verb שחר 'to be black') is very debatable. Lions are the symbols of the impious or wicked who attack and devour the righteous (cf. Ps 17: 12; 34: 11; Pr 28: 15, etc.). Vv. 10-11 merely develop the idea contained in v. 9. There is no reason to suppress them (contra Duhm, Merx, Siegfried).

11 To vary the terms, G renders

12   Now, to me a word was spoken in secret,
     And my ear caught something of the message;

לַיִשׁ by μυρμηκολέων 'ant-lion', Vulg.
by *tigris*. The word μυρμηκολέων does
not appear elsewhere in G. 1st Targ.
gives לֵישׁ in its Aramaic form לֵיתָא,
and Aq. chooses the Gk. λῖς, a poetic name for the lion. In 2nd Targ.
and Syr. the word is assimilated to
אריה in v. 10. In Symm. we have
simply λέων. It is mistakenly that
Field considers لِبؤ, attributed to
Symm. in the margin of Syro-hex.,
as an equivalent of βοράν in G. The
quotation of Symm. refers to the
verb (אבד أبِض). Hence we may, with
Montfaucon, consider the reading
ἀνύποστατος λέων ἀπόλλυται in Symm.
as a translation of the 1st hemistich.
For יתפרדו G has ἔλιπον ἀλλήλους.

The word לַיִשׁ, which corresponds to
the Assyr. *nêšu*, the Arabic لِيث, the
Aramaic לֵיתָא, denotes the lion as
the king of beasts (Pr 30: 30). Outside our verse and Pr 30: 30, לֵישׁ is
found only in Is 30: 6, where it is
linked with the לָבִיא 'lioness' of our
2nd hemistich. The present participle אֹבֵד, parallel to an imperfect,
expresses a universal truth (Gesenius-Kautzsch, § 116n). The מִן of
מִבְּלִי has a causative sense (cf. v. 9),
whence the word מבלי takes on the
meaning of 'for lack of', exactly as
in 24: 7. We shall meet again the
word מבלי with the verb אבד in v.
20. The word טֶרֶף indicates the prey
of the lioness (לביא) in 38: 39.
Bochart has long since proved that
לביא was the lioness (*Hieroz.*, I, col.
719). The text of Ezk 19: 2, where
לְבִיָּא is an artificial pointing, leaves
no doubt about this. We have seen
that in Is 30: 6 it is the companion
of the לֵישׁ, as here. Further, it is
coupled with the whelps in 38: 39
and in Is 5: 29. Fried. Delitzsch

thinks that the 'sons of the lion' is
simply a way of saying the 'lion', according to the use of בֵּן 'son' in certain compound terms, and of *mâr* 'son'
in certain Assyrian expressions. But
it should be observed that בני לביא
corresponds to כפירים in v. 10,
whereas לישׁ represents both אריה
and שָׁחַל. We should therefore allow
to בני לביא its ordinary meaning,
'the whelps of the lioness'. The meaning of יתפרדו 'are scattered' is
admirably confirmed by Ps 91: 10,
'For lo, Thine enemies perish and
all evil doers are scattered'; parallelism between אבד and התפרד. It
is carrying too far the concern for
synonymity to give to אבד its etymological meaning 'to go astray'
(Ehrlich), or conversely to postulate
for התפרד the meaning of 'disinte-
grate', 'burst' (Fried. Delitzsch). In
reality the 2nd hemistich marks the
consequence of the first. The lion
being dead, the whelps are scattered.
Compare the scattering of the
sheep for lack of a shepherd (Ezk
34: 5f.; Zec 13: 7; Mt 26: 31; Mk
14: 27).

12   The text of G offers special difficulties. A pointing אֱלַי instead of
אֵלַי has introduced the phrase εἰ δέ
τι ῥῆμα at the beginning. We then
find ἀληθινὸν ἐγεγόνει ἐν λόγοις σου,
but ἀληθινόν is due to a dittography
of the alpha of ῥῆμα. Schleusner recognised that the original text was
λήθιον 'secret'. Thus restored, the
translation of G for יֻגַּב comes materially close to Symm. ἐλαλήθη λα-
θραίως ὡς ἐν κλοπῇ (Vulg. *dictum est
verbum absconditum et quasi furtive*).
The rest of G οὐδὲν ἄν σοι τούτων κα-
κὸν ἀπήντησεν (A οὐδὲν ἂν τούτων κακῶν συνήντησέν μοι) enables us to
recognise שמץ מנה in οὐδὲν . . . . κακόν (or κακῶν) and a paraphrase of

13   In the nightmares accompanying visions of the night,
     When a heavy sleep falls upon men,

תקח אזני in συνήντησέν μοι (A). The
MT being obviously distorted in this
translation, there was juxtaposed a
new translation of the 2nd hemistich
πότερον οὐ δέξεταί μου τὸ οὖς ἐξαίσια
παρ' αὐτοῦ; Syro-hex. and Jerome
marked with an obelus the first
translation οὐθὲν . . . .ἀπήντησεν. The
interesting word יגנב is interpreted
'has been spoken with reserve'
(בנטיר) in Targ. Cf. G, Symm., and
Vulg. above. Syr. has ‏ܐܠ ܣܒ‎, which
seems to be a mistake for ‏ܐܠ ܓܒ‎ =
יגנב (Rosenmüller). For שמץ Targ.
has קצת 'a part', Syr. 'a little', but
Symm. ψιθυρισμόν, Vulg. venas su-
surri.
   In v. 8 Eliphaz brought forward the
testimony of his personal experience.
He supported his statements on the
ground of common observation such
as Job himself might have made
(v. 7). He is now proposing to allude
to a private vision, a terrifying
dream. It is needless to ask whether
he really experienced this vision or
whether he imagines it for the purposes of his argument: Eliphaz vel
vere vel ficte loquitur (St Thomas). At
the opening אלי 'to me', not to any
one else. We should leave דָּבָר with
its general sense of a 'word', for
there is nothing to suggest that we
have here a revelation such as the
prophets describe by the phrase
דבר יהוה, as Duhm claims. The imperfect יגֻנַּב in the sense of the aorist
(3: 3, 11, 16). The pu'al of גנב means
'to be stolen' and derivatively 'to be
done or said stealthily'; compare
Latin fur, furtim, etc. The hithpa'el
is found in 2 S 19: 4, to express
'enter stealthily'. The verb לקח with
אזן as subject, as in Jer 9: 19, where
the complement is 'word' (דבר).
The real sense of שמץ is 'a little',

'something' (cf. Targ. and Syr.). This
sense recurs in Sir 10: 10 and 18: 32.
Qimchi interprets as קצת דבר 'a
small thing' and we find precisely
שמץ דבר in 26: 14. Rashi is in agreement with rabbinic tradition in
interpreting שמץ by מקצת 'a little',
'something'. A similar meaning suits
שִׁמְצָה in Ex 32: 25, where we would
translate by 'idolatry', a meaning
derived from 'little', 'what is futile',
just as we have אֱלִיל 'nothing' and
'idol'. Far from being original, the
meaning 'murmur' (cf. Symm. and
Vulg.) is rather derivative from
'small voice', 'weakly spoken word',
etc.; cf. דממה וקול in v. 16. The
form מִנְהוּ is for מֶנְהוּ = מִמֶּנּוּ) by analogy with מֶנִּי for מִנִּי in pause (21: 16;
30: 10). The form מִנְהוּ is not found
elsewhere. In consequence of the
mysterious character of the com-
munication made to him, Eliphaz
has only been able to grasp a fragment.

13   For בשעפים Targ. במחשבתא
'in thought', G φόβος, Syr. ‏ܒܫܠܝܐ‎
'in rest', Aq. ἐν παραλλαγαῖς, Symm.
ἐν ἐκπλήξει (cf. Vulg. in horrore). The
preposition מן before מחזינות is rendered by ב" in Syr. and by the genitive in the Vulg. (visionis nocturnae).
But we have מן in Targ. and ἀπό in
Aq. and Symm. G καὶ ἠχώ is too isolated to permit the change of מ into
ו postulated by Bickell. Literalism
is not the characteristic of G, which
renders תרדמה by φόβος (cf. δεινὸς
φόβος in 33: 15) exactly as שעפים.
For תרדמה Targ. has שנתא 'sleep',
Vulg. sopor, Syr. 'deep sleep'.
   Eliphaz makes clear the exact moment of his vision. Compare, in
Racine's Athalie, the opening line of
Athalie's dream: 'C'était pendant
l'horreur d'une profonde nuit.' The

14   A trembling came over me—and a shudder!—
     Which made all my bones to shake.
15   Then a breath passes over my face,
     Making the hair of my flesh to stand on end.

word שְׂעִפִּים recurs only in 20: 2, but we have שַׂרְעַפִּים, by dissimilation, in Ps 94: 19 and 139: 23. The original idea of the root is 'what is most deep seated in the heart'. In Arabic *šaghifa* 'to be passionately smitten', *šaghafa* 'to touch the *šaghaf*', i.e. the inner part of the heart. The שְׂעִפִּים are the fixed ideas, preoccupations (Ps 94: 19), intimate thoughts (Ps 139: 23), reflections (Job 20: 2); here nightmares, such as are occasioned by dreams, which are truly 'night visions'. The preposition מִן is causative, as in v. 9. The 2nd hemistich, suggested by לילה, describes the moment when the dream occurs. The תַּרְדֵּמָה is a kind of lethargic sleep often induced by God: the sleep of Adam (Gn 2: 21), of Abraham (Gn 15: 12), of an army (1 S 26: 12). The verb נפל 'fall', here as in Gn 15: 12 and 1 S 26: 12, clearly shows that this torpor is inevitable. In Pr 19: 15 it is idleness which causes to fall (תפיל) the *tardêmah*. Elihu will almost quote this v. 13 in 33: 15.

14   The versions have rightly interpreted קראני as though it were קָרָנִי. G translates רב by μεγάλως, but Targ. and Syr. 'multitude', Vulg. *omnia*, remain faithful to the MT. The rendering of G διέσεισεν cannot be accepted as against Targ., Syr., and Vulg., which support the MT הפחיד. The change to החיל (Beer, following Ps 29: 8) does not take into account the imprecise nature of the translations of G.

The words פַּחַד 'trembling' (cf. 3: 25) and רְעָדָה 'shudder' strengthen each other as two synonyms. In Ps 55: 6

we find יראה ורעד יבא בי 'fear and trembling come upon me'. Note the analogy between the two texts: יִרְאָה instead of its synonym פחד, רַעַד instead of the *nomen unitatis* רעדה, the formula יָבֹא בִי 'come upon me' instead of קראני. The verb קרא is a parallel form to קרה *accidere*. It is met with in a number of Biblical texts (Gn 42: 4, 38; 49: 1, etc.; cf. Gesenius-Buhl, s.v. II קרא). The preposition לִקְרָאת is compounded of לְ and the construct infinitive of this verb. The subject of קְרָאַנִי is פחד. The second subject ורעדה has been rejected and placed at the end of the hemistich; cf. ותם in v. 6. The abstract רב 'multitude', 'abundance' (32: 8) in the sense of 'plenitude', 'totality'. The verb הִפְחִיד has as its subject פחד (whence the singular), but does not exclude ורעדה, which has been grafted on to פחד in the 1st hemistich.

15   Vulg. translates the 1st hemistich: *et cum spiritus me praesente transiret*. The other versions are more literal. For רוח Targ. has זיקא 'hurricane'. Under the influence of considerations of parallelism, Targ. translates שערת by עלעולא 'storm' (cf. 36: 33); confusion with שְׂעָרָה which equals סערה. G τρίχες καὶ σάρκες evades the translation 'the hair of my flesh'. Syr. and Vulg. *pili carnis meae* follow faithfully MT. Note that ὁ Ἑβραῖος, cited in Colb., renders שערת בשרי by αἱ τρίχες τῆς κεφαλῆς μου.

Exegetes are divided as to the meaning of רוּחַ 'a breath' (Renan), or 'a spirit' (Le Hir). Duhm claims that

16   A figure stands before me ...
      And I cannot recognise its appearance;
      An image is before my eyes,
      And I hear a whispered voice:

the masculine יַחֲלֹף would favour the translation 'a spirit'. But it should be observed that in 41:8 as well as in Ex 10:13; Ec 1:6; 3:19, the word רוּח 'wind', 'breath' is treated as a masculine. Further, in Is 21:1 the verb חלף 'pass by', 'blow across' has as its subject the hurricanes of the south. It is some breath of wind which makes the hair to rise. With Rashi, we consider רוּח as the subject of תְּסַמֵּר, since רוּח 'wind' can assume both genders. 'The hair of my flesh' is the complement and not the subject of תסמר, which dispenses with the need to transform the *pi'el* into a *qal* (contra Beer, Budde, after Ps 119:120). The poet has chosen בָּשָׂר in preference to ראֹשׁ because of עַצְמוֹתַי 'my bones' in v. 14. Do we not say in English 'to have goose-flesh'? The authority of Targ. cannot be accepted as against that of the other versions so as to change שֹׂעַרַת into שְׂעָרָה, which equals סערה 'whirlwind', 'tempest' (contra Merx). Still more arbitrary is the reading שַׂעֲרָה 'shudder' (Beer). Compare the Assyrian phrase: the spectre 'which makes the hair of my body to rise and of my skull to stand on end' (Thureau-Dangin, *Revue d'Assyrio-logie*, **18**, p. 187).

16 For יעמד G ἀνέστην, Aq. ἔστην, Syr. ܩܡܬ 'I stood up', have read אעמד. But Targ. יקום, Symm. ἔστη τις, Vulg. *stetit quidam* agree with MT. On the basis of G ἴδον, Merx and Siegfried propose to replace מראהו by אראה. In that case we should have the verb אכיר without a complement. Perhaps the ἴδον of G is but a corruption, through iotacism, of

εἶδος (Symm.). The negation is repeated by G before תמונה: καὶ οὐκ ἦν μορφή. Syr. places the negative before מראהו and omits תמונה. Hence we cannot appeal to both Syr. and G in order to restore ואין before תמונה (contra Merx, Bickell, Sieg-fried). G αὖραν καὶ φωνήν confirms the construction דממה וקול. Targ. adds the complement סוגעין after קול. At the end, Syr. adds 'which said', while Targ. adds 'it cried and said'.

After יַעֲמֹד it would seem that a word has disappeared. There was perhaps a subject such as the אלהים of the medium's vision in 1 S 28:13. The verb הכיר with negative as in 2:12; 7:10; 24:13. Eliphaz does not recognise the appearance of the figure standing before him. When Gudea speaks of the mysterious being which appears to him in a dream, he adds: 'I could not recog-nise him' (Cyl. A, IV, 21). The word תְּמוּנָה denotes strictly speaking the image of an object or an individual (cf. Dt 4:12, 15, 16, etc.). The root is the same as for מִין 'species' (*spe-cies*). The verb דמם means origi-nally 'remain silent' (29:21; 31:34), whence 'cease' (30:27) (cf. French *coi* from *quietus*). In Ps 107:29, the noun דְּמָמָה certainly means the calm which succeeds the storm: si-lence and peace. The word דממה is here coupled with קוֹל to make clear that it is a question of a slight, whispered sound (cf. 1 Kg 19:12). Here most commentators see in דממה וקול a hendiadys 'murmur and voice' to express 'murmuring voice', etc. But the construction קוֹל דממה of 1 Kg 19:12 proves that the

17 'Is a mortal man righteous in the presence of Eloah,
   Is a human being pure in face of his Maker?
18 If He does not trust His servants,
   And imputes madness to His angels,

word דממה in our text has simply been detached from its context to be thrown into relief. In fact, it is וקול which should open the hemistich. We have here a further instance of the relegation of the copula (with its accompanying word) to the interior of the clause (cf. v. 6). The most objective translation of the last hemistich is therefore simply: 'And I hear a whispered voice.'

17 Targ. and Syr. faithfully copy MT. G renders מאלוה by ἐναντίον τοῦ Κυρίου, Vulg. by *Dei comparatione*. G ἀπὸ τῶν ἔργων αὐτοῦ considers עשהו as coming from the passive participle of עשה, which results in nonsense.

In modern speech we have no equivalent to גֶּבֶר, ἀνήρ, *vir*, as contrasted with איש or אֱנוֹשׁ, ἄνθρωπος, *homo*. Hence we can only translate roughly. There are two ways of interpreting מֵאֱלוֹהַ יִצְדָּק: either 'Is he more just than Eloah?', or 'Is he just in the presence of Eloah?' The former translation seems the more literal. But, as Codurc pointed out, the remark being cited by Knabenbauer: *nemo enim tam delirus, tam vesanus fuit qui hominem plus quam Deum justum esse vel suspicatus sit*! There is no need of revelation to arrive at so evident a conclusion. Moreover, vv. 18ff. aim at showing that before God nothing and no one can claim either justice or purity. It has never occurred to Job to compare his perfection with that of God. Let us note that, in 9:2 and 25:4, which reflect our text, it is the preposition עִם which is used instead of מִן, so as to dispel all ambiguity (cf. Comm. on 9:2). In Nu 32:22 the phrase והייתם נקים

מיהוה ומישראל cannot be otherwise translated than as 'and you will be innocent before Yahweh and before Israel'. Similarly in Jer 51:5 the expression מקדוש ישראל means 'before the Holy One of Israel' (so Condamin). We shall again meet מאלהים 'before Elohim' after צדק נפשו 'to be justified' in 32:2. These observations prove that the translation 'in the presence of Eloah' and 'in face of his Maker' are not at all arbitrary. In fact it is the only plausible translation in the context. Instead of יְטָהַר, it is the synonymous יִזְכֶּה which will be chosen as a parallel to יצדק in 15:14; 25:4. The righteousness of man is opposed to man's sin in 35:6-7. These obvious truths known at all times are expressed by imperfects (Gesenius-Kautzsch, § 107f.); cf. vv. 8-9.

18 G translates הן by εἰ as it does הנה in v. 3, while the other versions render by 'behold': הא (Targ. and Syr.), ὅρα (Symm.), *ecce* (Vulg.). For לא יאמין Symm. has ἀβεβαιότης, Vulg. *non sunt stabiles*. Targ. identifies 'His servants' with the prophets. Instead of translating ἐπενόησεν (G), Jerome *reperit* (cf. Vulg.) follows rather Symm. εὑρήσει. The *hapax* תהלה is rendered σκολιόντι in G (Jerome *pravum quid*), ܠܬܡܗܐ 'astonishment' in Syr., *pravitatem* in Vulg. (cf. Jerome). But Symm. ματαιότητα connects it with הלל 'to be mad'; cf. Theod. ματαιοῦται, which translates מתהולל (read as מתהולל), in 15:20. Targ. עילא equals עולא 'iniquity'.

The particle הֵן is an equivalent of the Arabic *'in* and the Aramaic אִין 'if': 9:11, 12; 12:14, 15; 13:15, etc.

19   How much more so to dwellers in houses of clay,
      Whose foundation is in the dust!
      They are crushed like a moth.

It is sometimes an abbreviation of הִנֵּה 'behold' (8: 19, 20; 13: 1, etc.). According to parallelism the servants of God are the angels. We have seen that the 'sons of God', who are angels, 'come before Him' in the attitude of servants (1: 6; 2: 1). In Ps 104: 4 'His angels' are made parallel to 'those who serve Him' (מְשָׁרְתָיו). After the temptation, the angels approach Jesus with offers of service (Mt 4: 11). In 15: 15 'His angels' are replaced by 'His saints', the context being the same. The verb הֶאֱמִין with ב″ before the complement, to mean 'trust in' (15: 15, 31; 39: 12). The *hapax* תָּהֳלָה has shocked some commentators. Ehrlich points it as תְּהִלָּה 'praise' and repeats the negative of the 1st hemistich: 'and He finds no cause for praise in His angels'. Hupfeld, followed by Merx and some others, proposed תִּפְלָה as in 1: 22, a correction which seems supported by 24: 12, where we have יָשִׂים תפלה. But it is unnecessary if תהלה has a meaning similar to תפלה 'insanity', 'madness'. Now, the Hebrew tradition is firm as to the etymology of תהלה (cf. Rashi and Ibn Ezra), which belongs to the root הלל 'to be mad', 'to go beyond all bounds', whence הוֹלֵלוֹת 'follies', a word peculiar to Ecclesiastes (cf. Podechard on Ec 1: 17). The forms תֵּבֵל 'blemish' (from בלל) and תֶּמֶס 'fusion' (from מסס) enable us to assume a word תֹּהֶל (from הלל) of which תָּהֳלָה is the feminine. Those who wish to explain the word in the light of Arabic are not agreed as to the root, some having recourse to *wahila* 'to go astray' (Schnurrer) or to the Ethiopic תהל, which has the same

meaning (Dillmann), others to *tahil* 'to be fetid' (Rosenmüller), others again to *thahlal* 'vain' (Hottinger, Schultens). But all these roots have disappeared from Hebrew, and it would be necessary to concede that תהלה is a foreign word. Now, the word itself is not found in Arabic, and it is only by a series of approximations that a root can be found for it in that language. It is far better to keep to the traditional etymology. The verb שִׂים with ב″ before the complement of the person to imply 'impute', 'attribute' something to some one (1 S 22: 15).

19   While Syr. simply transcribes אף and G renders by δέ, Targ. כל דכן, Symm. πόσῳ μᾶλλον, and Vulg. *quanto magis* have well understood the meaning of this adverb. Targ. sees in the dwellers in houses of clay 'the wicked in sepulchres of clay'. The 2nd hemistich is ill understood by G: ἐξ ὧν (A οὗ) καὶ αὐτοὶ ἐκ τοῦ αὐτοῦ πηλοῦ ἐσμεν (Jerome *de quibus et nos ex eodem luto sumus*). Symm. ὧν γήινος ὁ θεμέλιος is reflected in the Vulg. *qui terrenum habent fundamentum*. G ἔπαισεν αὐτούς indirectly confirms יְדַכְּאוּם, which Targ., Syr., and Vulg. *consumentur* render by a plural passive. Targ. and Syr. translate לִפְנֵי by קדם, but G σητὸς τρόπον and Vulg. *velut a tinea* have better understood the meaning of לִפְנֵי־עָשׁ. Saadia confuses עש with the constellation עש (9: 9) or עיש (38: 32).

At the beginning the complete phrase should be אַף־כִּי (9: 14; 25: 6). Those who inhabit houses of clay are human beings. The body of man was made of clay חֹמֶר (10: 9; 33: 6; Is 64: 7). The body is a house of clay; cf. the expression γεῶδες

20   Between morning and evening they are reduced to dust,
     For lack of a *saviour* they perish for ever,

20   מוֹשִׁיעַ (cf. G); MT: מֵשִׂים.

σκῆνος parallel to φθαρτὸν σῶμα in
Wis 9:15. St Clement of Alexandria
(*Strom.*, V, xiv, 94) tells us that Plato
used to describe the body as γήϊνον
σκῆνος. In 2 Co 5:1 the body is ἡ
ἐπίγειος ἡμῶν οἰκία τοῦ σκήνους and in
2 P 1:13ff. simply σκήνωμα. The
following clause, 'whose foundation
is in the dust', is attributed sometimes to the inhabitants, sometimes
to the dwellings. But even in 22:16,
which is cited in support of the former opinion (Budde), 'their foundation' refers to the house of the
wicked (cf. Comm.). Here the presence of the word בתי in the 1st
hemistich prevents any confusion. A
house is founded either on rock or on
sand (Mt 7:26). The solidity of the
building depends on the foundations.
Now, the house of clay, which is
man's body, rests on the dust, for
man is dust and to dust must return
(Gn 3:19; Ps 103:14). Since God
finds defects in the angels, who are
superior beings, sons of God (1:6),
how much more will He find defects
in frail creatures who dwell in a body
of clay and whose foundation and
support is but the dust! It is evident
that the reasoning is conducted with
scholastic rigour. The final hemistich
is added to the strophe to depict
again the wretched state of man.
The plural יְדָכְּאוּ implies as its subject 'those who crush' and thus
serves as the equivalent of the impersonal 'one': 6:2; 7:3, etc. The
formula 'one crushes them' is equivalent to 'they are crushed', as in
Aramaic. This is what explains the
passive of Syr., Vulg., Targ. To replace the *pi'el* by a *pu'al* after eliminating the 3rd person pl. suffix
would be to substitute a commonplace form for a rare form of expression. Reiske read the *pu'al* and

transferred the *mem* of the suffix to a
place before לְפְנֵי so as to translate
'more quickly than a moth'. But we
have already met לְפְנֵי in the sense
of 'like' (3:24), and it is this meaning
which suits best here (G, Vulg., Ibn
Ezra, etc.). The simplest interpretation of the final hemistich is in
fact 'they are crushed like a moth'.
This frees us from the necessity to
have resort to the subtleties of modern commentators who, alleging
that the moth is an agent which
devours, translate 'as by a moth'
(Hitzig, following 13:28; Is 51:8;
cf. Rashi). Herz proposes to change
עָשׁ into עֹשֶׂם and to translate 'from
before their Maker' (!). Fried. Delitzsch would translate עָשׁ by 'building of reeds' following the Assyrian
ašašu 'nest of reeds' (cf. 27:18). But
the phrase 'like a moth' suits much
better the verb 'crush'. When the
text presents itself to us with normal
and simple meaning, it is unnecessary to complicate it.

20   For יֻכַּתּוּ G has οὐκέτι εἰσίν, a
vague translation. The words מִבְּלִי
מֵשִׂים are translated in the Vulg. *quia
nullus intellegit* 'for lack of some one
to remedy their plight' (Targ. with
the word ארכא 'remedy'; cf. Rosenmüller), 'so that inhabitants remain
for ever without a place' (Syr., which
transfers שׁכני from v. 19 and connects לנצח with מֵשִׂים). G παρὰ τὸ μὴ
δύνασθαι αὐτοὺς ἑαυτοῖς βοηθῆσαι ἀπώλοντο read מוֹשִׁיעַ instead of מֵשִׂים.
This is indeed the correct reading
(cf. inf.).

The expression 'from morning to
evening' does not mean 'always'
(contra Umbreit and others), but
the time between a morning and an
evening. Compare 'from day to night

21   [ ] They die and it is not of wisdom,

21 Transfer 4: 21a to follow 5: 5b; transfer 5: 1 to follow 5: 7 (cf.
Comm.).

Thou dost bring me to an end' (Vulg. *de mane usque ad vesperam finies me*) in the song of Hezekiah (Is 38: 12, 13). The contrast between man flourishing in the morning and withered up in the evening is poetically rendered in Ps 90: 5-6. Conversely, 'he who in the evening was alive, is dead in the morning' (*Choix de textes*, pp. 374-5, l. 39). The *hoph'al* of כתת has the meaning of 'to be pounded, pulverised, reduced to ashes' (Jer 46: 5; Mic 1: 7). The form יֻכַּתּוּ is Aramaic in type (Gesenius-Kautzsch, § 67y). It is easy to see that 'between morning and evening they are reduced to dust' is the parallel member to 'they are crushed like a moth' of v. 19. The consequence of this state of things is that 'they perish for ever'. Cf. לנצח יאבד 'he perishes for ever' in 20: 7 and לנצח ויהלך 'and for ever he passes away' (14: 20) (cf. Comm.). The difficulty lies in מִבְּלִי מֵשִׂים. It is proposed to find in משׂים the *hiph'il* participle of שׂום and to understand as the implied complement לֵב (1: 8; 2: 3), whence 'without any one paying attention' (Le Hir), 'without any one noticing it' (Renan), 'without any one regarding it' (*Bible du rabbinat français*), etc. It must be admitted that the ellipsis is rather too violent. Further, the use of the *hiph'il* instead of *qal* has but a precarious support in Ezk 14: 8, where we should read *qal*, and in Ezk 21: 21, where השׂימי is a dittograph. The examples sought in the Book of Job itself in illustration of the elliptic construction are all the result of textual corruption. It is ישׂמע and not ישׂים which was the original of 23: 6; 24: 12 (cf. Comm.). In 34: 23 the verb ישׂים had an explicit complement, namely מועד,

which has become עוד by haplography (cf. Comm.). Parallelism invites us to read ישׂמעו instead of ישׂימו in Is 41: 20, the final example adduced (same error as below, 23: 6; 24: 12). On the other hand the use of מבלי with the present participle is very much in the tradition of Hebrew poetic style (Jer 2: 15; 9: 10, 11; Ezk 14: 15; Zeph 3: 6; La 1: 4). Hence we shall hesitate to replace משׂים by שָׂם, in spite of the phrase בלי־שׂם in 30: 8 (contra Herz, *ZATW*, 1900, p. 160). Ehrlich suggests משׁיב and interprets מבלי משׁיב 'without any one bringing him back' as 'irrevocably', which obliges him to suppress לנצח and to regard it as a gloss (!). The true solution consists in restoring the original text מוֹשִׁיעַ, which has been maintained in G. Even Ginsburg accepts this correction which was suggested by Merx and Graetz. The מושׁיע is 'he who helps, rescues' (cf. 26: 2). It is through 'lack of a saviour', i.e. because no one can prevent their ruin (v. 19), that men perish for ever. Cf. the construction of אבד with מבלי in v. 11.

21 G ἐνεφύσησεν γὰρ αὐτοῖς καὶ ἐξηράνθησαν (A ἐτελεύτησαν) does not correspond to v. 21a. The text translated comes from Is 40: 24b, where וגם־נשׁף בהם ויבשׁו is rendered ἔπνευσεν (Aq. ἐφύσησεν) ἐπ’ αὐτοὺς καὶ ἐξηράνθησαν. It is impossible to recover in the Hebrew of our verse the basis of G (contra Beer, Ball). We have here a gloss which, at first inscribed in the margin, eventually supplanted the text. Ehrlich is wrong in thinking that he can find in G some support for the reading נָטַע 'planted' instead of נסע. A variant of G, mentioned

in Compl., Codd. 161, 248, translated יתרם by τὸ ὑπόλειμμα αὐτῶν (Cod. 161 omits αὐτῶν), in the light of יֶתֶר 'remainder'; cf. Vulg. *qui autem reliqui fuerint auferentur ex eis.* Double translation of יתרם in Syr., ܘܡܘܬܪܢܐ 'their advantage' and ܘܡܟܬܪܢ 'their remnant' (cf. Beer). Targ. paraphrases: 'Is it not by their lack of righteousness that they have been deprived of all support?' For ולא בחכמה G παρὰ τὸ μὴ ἔχειν αὐτοὺς σοφίαν; cf. v. 20b.

The word יֶתֶר being capable of the meanings 'what remains' and 'rope' (cf. 30: 11), the 1st hemistich has been the object of diverse interpretations, as may be seen by the variety of the French translations: 'All that they left disappears with them' (Le Hir); 'Their tent cord is cut' (Renan; cf. Loisy, Crampon); 'The thread of their life is cut' (Segond); 'Ah! the thread which supported them is broken' (*Bible du rabbinat français*). The prevailing opinion seems to be the one which sees in יִתְרָם 'their cord', the cord of their tent. It is supposed that life is compared to a tent whose cord is broken by death. It must be confessed that the comparison is not very convincing. Further, the tent cord is denoted by הֶבֶל or מֵיתָר and the meaning of the verb נסע is not 'cut' or 'break' but 'tear up', 'uproot', 'decamp' (cf. 19: 10). It is נתק which would be used in the sense of breaking a thread. The same objection applies to the translation of יתרם by the 'thread of their life', a translation which claims the support of Ec 12: 6, where is mentioned the 'silver cord' חבל הכסף. It is well known that this silver cord is the little chain on which was hung the lamp symbolising life (cf. Podechard on Ec 12: 6). The original text had the verb נתק (ibid.). Likewise the symbol would be too implicit, for after all 'their cord' is not usually

understood to mean the cord of the lamp which symbolises life. Neither is it clear whether 'their cord' implies the thread of life. In Is 38: 12 life is compared successively to a tent and a thread, but the comparisons are perfectly explicit and leave no room for ambiguity. This is why we hesitate to accept, in spite of its plausibility, the hypothesis of Olshausen, supported by Hitzig and Siegfried, which suggests the reading of יְתֵדָם 'their tent-peg' instead of יתרם. Such a correction would however receive solid support from Is 33: 20, where the verb נסע has as its complement 'its tent-pegs' (יתדתיו). But none of the versions knew the reading יתדם. Besides, mortals have been assimilated to 'houses of clay' (v. 19), not to tents. Now, it happens that in 22: 20 the word יתרם recurs, and has in the text a clearly defined sense: 'what remains over', 'superfluity'. This word יֶתֶר (from יתר 'to be in excess'), when accompanied by a suffix has the meaning; 'surplus', 'excess', 'remainder' (Ex 23: 11, Is 44: 19; Ps 17: 14). Thus 22: 20 may be translated: 'Has not their wealth been destroyed, and has not a fire consumed what was left over?' (cf. Comm.). The wealth of a man comprises what is necessary and what he has saved, the excess, which is called יִתְרָה (Is 15: 7; Jer 48: 36), Assyrian *atartu*. In the light of these analogies the 1st hemistich cannot be translated otherwise than as: 'Has not their superfluous wealth been snatched away from them?' The preposition ב״ after a verb connoting removal, instead of מִן, recurs in 20: 20. Fried. Delizsch rightly compares the Assyrian *ina*, which means 'in' and 'from', *in* and *ex*, according to the character of the verb. It is easy to see that the 1st hemistich belonged to a context similar to 22: 20, where the theme is the punishment of the wicked. If we withdraw it from the present con-

5:2   For it is vexation which kills a senseless man,
      And anger brings death to a fool!'

text, we note that v. 21b, 'they die and it is not of wisdom', furnishes the parallel member to v. 20b, 'for lack of a saviour they perish for ever'. We shall see that our v. 21a furnishes exactly the parallel member to v. 5c (cf. Comm.). After the verb מות the cause of death is preceded by the preposition ״ב; cf. 'die of thirst', מות בצמא (Jg 15:18; Is 50:2). It is not wisdom which causes the death of men. Now, ch. 5 begins with a verse which stood originally before v. 8. V. 2 of this chapter forms the natural sequence to our v. 21 and gives the true causes of death: grief and anger. This is precisely the malady from which Job is suffering (6:2). Cf. Comm. on 5:1 after v. 7.

5:1   After v. 7.

5:2   Targ. interprets כעש as the anger of the Lord, and קנאה as the jealousy of creatures. Syr. forgets to vary the style and renders by one and the same verb, ܩܛܠ 'kill', the verbs יהרג and תמית, and by one and the same noun, ܫܛܝܐ 'madman', the nouns אויל and פתה. For פתה Symm. has νήπιον, Vulg. parvulum, the meaning of פֶּתִי.

The כי of the opening, inexplicable in the present context, introduces a natural sequence to 4:21b. It is not of wisdom that men die! What kills

them is vexation and indignation. At bottom they reveal their stupidity by taking things too much to heart, so much so that they die as a result. Such is the clearest meaning assignable to this verse, which looks very much like a proverb. The two hemistichs balance each other, word for word. There is parallelism between אֱוִיל 'a senseless man' (cf. v. 3) and פְתָה 'one who is easily led astray', 'a fool' (cf. פתה in 31:9, 27), as in Sir 31:7. The preposition ״ל before the direct complement is an Aramaism (cf. v. 7). Elsewhere we have the verb הרג with ״ל before the object in 2 S 3:30. The words כַּעַשׂ (for כעס 6:2; 10:17; 17:7) and קִנְאָה correspond with each other as the hiph'il of כעס and the hiph'il of קנא in Dt 32:16, where these two causative verbs mean 'vex' and 'irritate'. They are almost synonymous. But כעס connotes rather the irritation we feel internally when we are annoyed, while קנאה is the indignation which is manifested outwardly. Such emotions and passions kill man. As Pascal observes: 'It is not necessary that the whole universe should arm itself for the purpose of crushing man.' In Pr 27:3, which we shall cite à propos of 6:3, we find mentioned כעס אויל 'the vexation of the madman'. The short description of vv. 3-7 is introduced by the word אויל.

CHAPTER 5

3   I myself have seen the fool taking root,
     And at once I have cursed his dwelling!

4   May his sons be far removed from all safety!
     May they be crushed at the gate with no one to deliver them!

1-3   V. 1 follows v. 7 (cf. Comm.). — V. 2 stands after 4: 21.

5: **3** G ἐβρώθη and Syr. ﺍﺣﺐ 'per-ishing' have read the 3rd person instead of the 1st אקוב. Aq. καὶ κατη-ρασάμην τὴν εὐπρέπειαν αὐτῶν brings us back to MT; cf. Vulg. *et maledixi pulchritudinem ejus*. The real meaning of נוהו, 'his dwelling', not 'his beauty' (Aq. and Vulg.), is maintained in G αὐτῶν ἡ δίαιτα, Targ. מדוריה, Syr. ﺳﻮﻩ؟.

The word אֱוִיל 'fool' in v. 2 draws the attention of Eliphaz back once more to his general thesis, namely that the fool, who is the same as the impious man (cf. 2: 10), cannot be happy on earth (4: 8-11). Eliphaz compares him to a tree which strikes deep into the earth its strong roots: 'I myself have seen the fool taking root!' Eliphaz is fond of putting himself on the stage: 'I myself have seen!' Cf. 4: 8, 12. The idea of prosperity is effectively expressed by the analogy with the tree which roots itself in the earth. Same use of השריש in Is 27: 6; Ps 80: 10. Duhm is shocked by the declaration of the 1st hemistich and will not accept the idea that the impious man strike roots. Hence his reading מְשֹׁרָשׁ 'uprooted', renewed by Hoffmann. This is making the text say the contrary of what it affirms and of what the versions have seen in it. The instability of good fortune itself requires that the good fortune should have existed once. What is the effect on Eliphaz of the sight which presents itself to him? 'And at once I cursed his dwelling!' The verb קבב as in 3: 8; the noun נָוֶה 'dwelling' (5: 24; 18: 15), rather than 'beauty', in the light of what follows. Supposing that the 2nd hemistich must picture the catastrophe itself, אקוב has been changed to וְרָקֵב (Merx, Bickell, Siegfried) or to וַיִּרְקַב (Duhm, Ehrlich), following G ἐβρώθη. It must be pointed out, however, that βιβρώσκω is never used to render רקב 'to rot'. And what would be the meaning of: 'His dwelling suddenly rotted'? The rotting of wood is not a sudden catastrophe. Other corrections have been suggested: וַיַּעֲבֹר 'and passes away' (Wright); וַיּוּקַב 'and is cursed' (Cheyne); וַיִּפָּקֵד 'and is empty' (Budde), etc. In this uncertainty the wisest course is to accept the text as it stands, especially as v. 4 may well contain the malediction which is indicated here. Eliphaz shows how abnormal seems to him the prosperity of the fool. He cannot refrain from solemnly cursing it. In doing so, he acts according to the prejudices of current ethics.

4 G rightly translates the verbs in the optative mood. G οἱ υἱοὶ αὐτῶν

58

5　What they *have reaped*, the hungry eat
　And carry away to *hiding places*;

5 קָצְרוּ (G); MT: קצירו. — מַצְפָּנִים; MT: מצנים. — Transfer 4:21a to precede 5:5c. — וְשָׁאֲפוּ צְמֵאִים (Aq., Symm., Vulg.; cf. Syr.); MT: ושאף צמים.

(for בניו) is corrected into οἱ υἱοὶ αὐτοῦ in א. Targ. gives an eschatological ring to the verse by translating שער as referring to the gate of Gehenna and adding לעלמא דאתי 'in the age to come', placing it after the translation of מישע. G renders ידכאו by κολαβρισθείησαν, but Jerome *conterantur* reflects Aq. ἐπιτριβήσονται (cf. Vulg. *conterentur*). The translations of Aq., Theod., and Symm. are quoted in the margin of Syro-hex. For בשער G has ἐπὶ θύραις ἡσσόνων. Obelus before ἡσσόνων in Syro-hex. The word *infirmorum* which translated ἡσσόνων in Jerome (Gall.) becomes *impiorum* in Bod. and Tur.

The fondness of Eliphaz for a personal tone encourages us to recognise in v. 4 the malediction announced in v. 3 (cf. G). This is the interpretation of Rashi, who adds: 'This is the malediction with which I have cursed him.' The witness does not directly curse the fool. The father must be injured through the son (Is 14:21). For the same reason Noah did not curse Ham, but his eldest son Canaan (Gn 9:24-5). 'May his sons be far removed from all safety!' —a formula which is easily understood if we compare it with Is 59:11b, 'We look for justice, but there is none! For salvation, but it is far from us!' As is abundantly shown by Is 59:12 and by our 2nd hemistich, it is a question of help in the matter of justice, in a court of law, of legal aid. The word יֵשַׁע (in Is וְישׁוּעָה) signifies 'help' and 'deliverance' (v. 11); cf. the verb הושיע in 4:20 (Comm.). 'May they be crushed at the gate!', i.e. in the Agora, in the Forum, the public place situated at the entrance gate

of the town. It is there that judgments were made (29:7; 31:21; Dt 25:7; Is 29:21, etc.). Cf. Pr 22:22, 'Do not crush the afflicted at the gate!' The form יְדֻכְּאוּ is a *niph'al* of the *pi'el* (cf. Comm. on 34:25-6). The close ואין מציל 'and no one to deliver them!' is a stereotyped formula (Is 5:29; Ps 7:3; 50:22, etc.). It is amplified in 10:7.

5 G ἃ γὰρ ἐκεῖνοι συνήγαγον (Jerome *quae enim illi congregaverunt*) reads קָצְרוּ and not קצירו. Instead of συνήγαγον G (A) has ἐθέρισαν, a variant cited in the margin of Syro-hex. We find ܢܣܒ in Syr. (reading קצר for קצירו). G interprets רעב as δίκαιοι, an allusion to the righteous who suffer from hunger, the poor. The 2nd hemistich is rendered αὐτοὶ δὲ ἐκ κακῶν οὐκ ἐξαίρετοι ἔσονται (A ἐξερεθήσονται) in G (pointing אֵל instead of אֶל and reading מְצָרִים for מצנים). Syr. 'and to thirst' replaces מצנים by some derivative or other of צמא. Targ. adds 'warriors' פולמוסין (πολέμιος) as the subject of יקחהו and interprets, מצנים in the light of צנה 'shield', whence במאני זינא 'with armour'. Cf. Vulg. *et ipsum rapiet armatus* and the translation of אל־מצנים by πρὸς ἐνόπλων in Aq. and Symm. G renders by ἐκσιφωνισθείη the expression שאף צמים. Targ. interprets צמים by ליסטיסין (from λῃστής). But Aq. διψῶντες, Symm. διψῶν, Vulg. *sitientes*, connect צמים with צמא (cf. 18:9). Similarly Syr. ܨܗܝܐ 'thirst'.

The MT אשר קצירו 'whose harvest' brings us back to the fool of v. 3. But from v. 4 we are concerned with

4:21a Has not their excess of wealth been snatched from them?

5:5c   And *have not those who are athirst* swallowed up their fortune?

the sons who are referred to by the suffix of חֵילָם. The pointing קָצְרוּ, attested by G, enables us to translate 'what they have reaped'; cf. the verb קצר in 4: 8. The sons of the fool, who have been condemned in a court of law, have no longer their property at their own disposal: 'what they have reaped, the hungry eat'. The hungry are those to whom the wicked rich have refused bread (22: 7). The word מִצִּנִּים seems to contain the preposition מִן and the noun צִנִּים 'thorns' of Pr 22: 5. Nevertheless extraordinary ingenuity is required to translate 'which he will carry off from the enclosed field' (Le Hir), or 'breaks down his hedge and robs him' (Renan), 'who come and snatch away his goods even to the thorny enclosure' (Segond). The preposition אֶל after לקח must indicate the place to which a thing is carried (2 K 2: 20). Hence we cannot see in מצנים a word meaning 'baskets', a plural of מָצֵן fabricated by Fried. Delitzsch from the root צנן (whence the Aramaic צִנָּא 'basket'). One carries *in* baskets but not *towards* baskets. An excellent conjecture is that of Winckler, who, in the light of Ob 6, reads מַצְפֻּנִים instead of מצנים. The meaning 'granaries', 'storehouses' which Winckler suggests for this term (*Altor. Forschungen*, III, pp. 235f.), is less close to the etymology of צפן 'hide' than 'hiding places'. We shall therefore translate the 2nd hemistich: 'And carry away to hiding places'. It is impossible to regard צמים as connoting the net or snare which is supposed to swallow up their fortune. Le Hir translates: 'with a click of the trap his riches will be lost'. But then the text ceases to be respected. We should note that in

20: 15 we find 'the fortune which he has swallowed he vomits up again', the word חַיִל being the complement of בלע 'swallow'. Hence there is no reason why we should not see in חֵילָם 'their fortune' the complement of שָׁאַף 'suck up', 'engulf'. It is unnecessary to substitute for חילם the word חלבם 'their milk' (Hoffmann, Beer) or חמרם 'their wine' (Cheyne). There remains the word צמים. We see in it a defective writing of צְמֵאִים 'those who are athirst, lust eagerly' attested by Aq., Symm., Vulg., and indirectly by Syr. (cf. sup.). The singular שָׁאַף has been introduced as a result of the transformation of צמאים into צמים. We should restore וְשָׁאֲפוּ. Thus the 3rd hemistich means 'and those who are athirst have swallowed up their fortune'. The presence of the perfect tense is indeed surprising, and one might be inclined to have recourse to the *kethîb* of the Orientals, which is ישאף instead of ושאף. But we are lacking a parallel member to v. 5c. In 4: 21, however, we had a hemistich torn from its context: 'Has not their excess of wealth been snatched from them?' The word יתרם corresponds to חילם. In combining 4: 21a with our 3rd hemistich, we get the result: 'Has not their excess of wealth been snatched from them? And have not those who are athirst swallowed up their fortune?' This verse is modelled exactly on the pattern of 22: 20, 'Has not their substance been destroyed? And has not a fire swallowed up their excess of wealth?' Hence we cannot hesitate to situate in this context 4: 21a. Note that Bickell and Duhm, in order to avoid all difficulty, eliminated v. 5b. It is surely better to reconstitute the text, of which we

6   For evil does not spring up from the soil,
     And trouble does not grow out of the ground,
7   But it is man himself who *engenders* trouble,
     As the sons of the lightning soar aloft in their flight.

7   יוֹלִד; MT: יוּלָד. — Transfer v. 1 to precede v. 8 (cf. Comm.).

possess the elements, than to mutilate it arbitrarily.

6 The versions differ as to the meaning of אָוֶן: G κόπος, Symm. ὀδύνη, Targ. and Syr. 'lie', Vulg. *sine causa*. For מאדמה G ἐξ ὀρέων (Jerome *de montibus*) reads perhaps מהרים.

The thesis of Eliphaz establishes a nexus between moral and physical evil, the latter being the punishment of the former. The connection between אָוֶן and עָמָל is brought out in 4: 8 and 15: 35. The author of the first is likewise the author of the second. Misfortune does not grow of itself like the grass in the field. It is a harvest which presupposes cultivation and sowing (4: 8). The word עָפָר, made parallel to אֲדָמָה (cf. 14: 8), conveys not only the idea of dust, but the soil and the ground in general. In 8: 19b we have וּמֵעָפָר אַחֵר יִצְמָחוּ 'and others sprout from the ground'. We see therefore that there is perfect equivalence between מעפר and מאדמה.

7 The word יולד is pointed as יֻלָד by the Massoretes, whilst G γεννᾶται, Vulg. *nascitur*, Targ. and Syr. אתילד, seem to read יֻלָד. For בְּנֵי־רֶשֶׁף 1st Targ. בני מזיקי 'sons of the demons', 2nd Targ. 'the sparks which shoot from coals of fire', but the other versions see here the name of a bird: νεοσσοὶ δὲ γυπὸς (G), υἱοὶ πτηνοῦ (Aq.), τὰ τέκνα τῶν πετεινῶν (Symm.), ܚܒ ܕܟܦܐ (Syr.), *avis* (Vulg.).

We have seen in v. 6 that trouble does not grow out of the ground.

The 2nd hemistich went on to specify that עָמָל does not sprout from אֲדָמָה. It is evident that our 1st hemistich is going to give the affirmative parallel since it repeats the word עמל and contrasts אָדָם with אדמה. The presence of ל before עמל has induced the pointing of MT and of the versions which have taken יולד as a passive. In reality ל״ is simply the sign of the accusative, as often in Aramaic (cf. v. 2). We should point as יוֹלִד, which enables us to translate 'it is man who engenders trouble'. Cf. the use of הוליד in Is 59: 4. The antithesis between this statement and that of v. 6b is thus clearly apparent. The thesis of Eliphaz develops: man, he suggests, by his own fault, is the author of his ills. The translations: *homo nascitur ad laborem* (Vulg.); 'in such a way that man is born to sorrow' (Le Hir); 'but man is born for trouble' (Renan), do not bring out the logical connection between v. 6 and v. 7. A simple change in the pointing produces perfect sense. The *hiph'il* of the 2nd hemistich (יַגְבִּיהוּ) confirms the *hiph'il* יולד. The expression יגביהו עוף, literally 'raise their flight' in the sense 'fly high', 'soar aloft'; cf. הַמַּגְבִּיהִי לָשֶׁבֶת 'He who sits on high' in Ps 113: 11. We have the *hiph'il* הגביה without the complement עוף in 39: 27, יגביה נשר 'the eagle soars on high'. This text shows that the subject of יגביהו עוף must be the name of a bird. It is thus that the text has been understood by G, Aq., Symm., Vulg. (cf. sup.). Hence the בְּנֵי־רֶשֶׁף are not the 'sons

1   Call now! is there any one who will answer you?
     And to which of the saints will you turn?

of the flame' as is generally understood, for the 'sparks' suggested by this metaphor have not the capacity to raise their flight. Le Hir and Renan saw in the בני־רשף the sons of thunder, but they were careful to point out that it was a question of the birds of the heavens (Le Hir), or birds of prey (Renan). The ancients also saw here an allusion to animate beings, whence the 'sons of demons' (Targ.) or else 'angels and spirits' (Rashi, cf. Schlottmann, Hoffmann). Hitzig seeks in רשף a metathesis of the Arabic šaraf 'honour', 'nobility' to conclude that the eagle is meant (cf. German *Adler* from *adel*). That the allusion is to some bird is proved not only by the context and the versions (cf. sup.) but also by the translation of רשף by עוף in the Targum of Onqelos (Dt 32:24) and the use of רשף in Sir 43:17 (πετεινά, Vulg. *avis*). This is how we would explain the various meanings of the word. First, רשף is 'the lightning': in this sense, the plural רשפים is parallel to ברד 'hail' in Ps 78:48; the sing. רשף is parallel to דבר 'the plague' in Hab 3:5 (the thunderbolt being considered as a scourge); the רשפי־אש are 'fiery lightnings' in Ca 8:6. Metaphorically used, the רשפי־קשת 'lightnings of the bow' are arrows (Ps 76:4), just as the arrows of God are lightnings (Hab 3:11). The Phoenician god Resheph is once called רשף חץ 'Resheph of the arrow' (Lagrange, *ÉRS*, p. 456, n. 2), which permits the identification of him with the god of the lightning, and at the same time facilitates the assimilation to Apollo ἑκατηβελέτης 'who hurls his thunderbolts afar'. The bird associated with thunder and lightning was the eagle, and Pliny is only echoing popular tradition when he says: *negant un-*

quam solam hanc alitem fulmine exanimatam, ideo armigeram Jovis consuetudo judicavit. The bird בן־רשף 'son of the lightning' will therefore be the eagle. Thus the analogy of our 2nd hemistich with 39:27 becomes still more striking. The *waw* which precedes בני־רשף is the *waw* of comparison (12:11; 14:12). Man creates his own misfortunes just as the eagle soars aloft in the air by its own innate power. After expounding his general thesis Eliphaz will pass on to a doxology which is introduced by v. 8. The word אולם, which should introduce an opposition (cf. Comm. on v. 8), does not connect v. 8 with v. 7, but rather with v. 1, which, as we have seen, separated 5:2 from 4:21 and should be transferred to a place before v. 8.

1 G renders מי by τινα 'some one', Vulg. *aliquem*. For קדשים G ἀγγέλων ἁγίων. Obelus before ἀγγέλων in Syro-hex. The verb תפנה is translated too freely by G ὄψη.

Instead of suppressing this v. 1, we have thought it preferable to restore it to its proper place, i.e. before v. 8 which contrasts the attitude of Eliphaz with that of Job. It looks as if the latter has made some gesture of impatience or has uttered some invocation. His friend addresses him ironically: 'Call then, is there any one to answer you?' We have here the same movement as in the speech of Job (6:29). Appeals are vain if they are not addressed to God. Eliphaz has already declared that God does not trust His angels and charges them with folly (4:18). Now, if we compare 4:18 with 15:15 it becomes clear that it is the angels who are meant here by the 'saints' (cf. Zec 14:5; Dn 8:13). This is why Eliphaz exclaims: 'To which of the saints will you turn?' He has tried

8   As for me, I invoke God,
      And it is before Elohim that I lay my cause.
9   He who does great and unfathomable things,
      Marvels without number!
10   He who pours rain on the face of the earth,
      And sends waters over the countryside.

to prove that neither angels nor men escape the scrutinising glance of God. Hence, instead of complaining bitterly, Job would do better to recognise that he is guilty and that his only hope lies in his Creator. God who brings about these evils in order to correct man (v. 17) is at the same time He who can mend the evil and re-establish Job in his original state (18-26). Eliphaz has long realised this, and in v. 8 he points to himself as an example.

8 In order to differentiate אלהים from אל, G places Κύριον after τὸν πάντων δεσπότην, which is replaced by τὸν παντοκράτορα in G (A). The versions translate דברתי by 'my word': Targ. and Syr. מלתי, Vulg. *eloquium meum*: G fusing דברתי with אשים: ἐπικαλέσομαι.

The adverb אולם (1:11; 2:5) brings forward a contrast. It is possible that Job might feel an impulse to address one of the angels (5:1). It would be taking trouble uselessly! Equally absurd to have resort to men who are only weak and malicious. Eliphaz once more puts himself on the stage (cf. v. 3). He says, I am not one of those who put their trust either in angels or men. It is God Himself whom I invoke. The phrase 'But I commune with Shaddai' (13:3), which is modelled on our 1st hemistich, proves that we cannot give to these verbs a conditional sense as is generally done. Eliphaz is simply contrasting his conduct with that of others; he acts in conformity with his declared principles. His appeal to God becomes the occasion of a long doxology. Verb

דרש with אל־ before the complement to connote 'address one's self to' (cf. 8:19; 40:10, and also Job 3:4). The feminine דִּבְרָה does not mean simply 'word', but 'cause' (cf. the French *causer* in the sense of 'speak'), whence the expression עַל־דִּבְרַת 'because of', 'with regard to' (cf. Podechard on Ec 3:18). Note the use of שִׂים 'to put' in the sense of 'expound' a cause, 'lay before' in law.

9 G renders ואין חקר by καὶ ἀνεξιχνίαστα (Jerome *et investigabilia*), cf. Vulg. *et inscrutabilia*. For נפלאות G has ἔνδοξά τε καὶ ἐξαίσια. Syro-hex. marks with an obelus καὶ ἐξαίσια. By mistake the obelus follows (instead of preceding) *et ingentia* in Jerome (Tur.).

The verse reappears in 9:10 with but slight modifications. It is usual for doxologies to begin with participles (9:10ff.; 12:17ff.). They are drawn up in the style of the Psalms. The expressions אֵין חֵקֶר 'no investigation' is used to signify 'unfathomable' (Ps 145:3; Is 40:28). On the root חקר cf. v. 27. The circumstantial style as in ואין מציל v. 4. Compare ולא חקר in 36:26, parallel to ולא נדע 'which we do not know'; it determines גדלות in 37:5. These formulas are stereotyped. The parallelism between נפלאות and גדלות reappears in 37:5. With עד־אין מספר (9:10; Ps 40:13) compare the Assyrian *ana lâ manî* 'not to be counted' or *ana lâ mîni* 'having no number', to imply 'innumerable' or 'incalculable'.

10 G has simply ἐπὶ τὴν γῆν for

11   In order to exalt the lowly on high,
     And to raise the afflicted to safety,

עַל־פְּנֵי אֶרֶץ. The reading of Aq.
ἐπὶ πρόσωπον τ.γ., quoted in the
margin of Syro-hex., has influenced
Jerome *super faciem terrae*. Targ.
considers that the allusion is to 'the
land of Israel'. Vulg. paraphrases
the 2nd hemistich: *et arrigat aquis
universa*. G vaguely translates
חוּצוֹת by τὴν ὑπ᾽ οὐρανόν (cf. 1:7).

Duhm would cut out this verse on
the pretext that it is out of place
in the context and that the participle נֹתֵן is preceded by the article. It
should be noticed, however, that the
article is clearly necessary as a result
of the distance of the word אֵל or
אֱלֹהִים (v. 8). Among divine marvels
in the created universe, the rain
which falls from heaven and the
springs which gush from the ground
are the ones most appreciated by
orientals. These two phenomena are
the very type of the great things
which God accomplishes for humanity. First, 'He who pours rain on
the face of the earth'; rain is a gift,
hence the use of the verb נתן. God
is the Maker of the clouds and the
rain, and by that very fact He fertilises the soil (Ps 147:8). In Jer
14:22 it is neither the idols nor the
heavens which 'give' the rain, but
Yahweh alone. Corresponding to the
rain is the spring of water, 'and He
who sends waters over the countryside'. It is God who makes the spring
to become the torrent (Ps 104:10
with מְשַׁלֵּחַ instead of שֹׁלֵחַ). The
word חוּץ is parallel to אֶרֶץ in 18:17.
We find אֶרֶץ וְחוּצוֹת in Pr 8:26.
The meaning of 'countryside' for
חוּצוֹת is clearly attested in Ps 144:
13. Literally חוּץ connotes 'what is
without', namely the region *extra
muros*, i.e. the countryside.

11   Targ. explains שְׁפָלִים as 'those
who are humiliated by hunger' and

קֹדְרִים as 'those who are sullied by
poverty'. For שְׁפָלִים G ταπεινούς,
whence Jerome *infimos* (Gall.), which
has become *infirmos* in Bod. and
Tur. For קֹדְרִים G has ἀπολωλότας,
Jerome *perditos* (Gall.) which has
become *impeditos* in Bod. and Tur.
Instead of שֻׂגְּבוּ, G ἐξεγείροντα harmonises with the 1st hemistich. Similarly Vulg. *erigit*. The word יֵשַׁע,
omitted in G, is restored, following
Symm. ἐν σωτηρία, in Colb. and the
margin of Syro-hex. In Jerome we
find *in salutem* (with asterisk).

After the praise of the wonders of
God in the world of nature, we have
that of His action in the social field.
The revolutions in human life manifest the finger of God. Cf. 1 S 2:8,
'He raises up the poor from the dust
and He lifts the needy from the ash
heap.' The שְׁפָלִים 'those who are
down' represent the lowly and the
despised, vile in their own eyes and
in the eyes of others (2 S 6:22). It is
usual to oppose the שָׁפָל to the גָּבֹהַּ
'lifted up', 'proud', as in Ps 138:6.
Infinitive preceded by ל״י (a sort of
gerundive) in parallelism with a perfect, exactly as in 28:25. The clauses are subordinated to v. 12. There
is a deliberate contrast between
שְׁפָלִים 'who are down' and מָרוֹם
'height'. The participle קֹדֵר 'blackened', 'tanned' (30:28) is meant to
depict a person in sorrow or affliction
(Ps 35:14; 38:7, etc.). The custom
was to soil one's face and head in
great sorrow (cf. Comm. on 2:12).
The verb שָׂגַב 'to be very high',
whence 'to be inaccessible' (Dt
2:36). As a complement indicating
aim, it has יֵשַׁע 'safety' or 'help' (v.
4). The meaning of שֻׂגְּבוּ יֵשַׁע will
therefore be 'raise to safety' (cf.
גָּבְרוּ חַיִל in 21:7). This again is an
effect of the power of God (Ps 12:6).

12   He thwarts the designs of the crafty,
      So that their hands do not achieve what they had planned!
13   He ensnares the wise in their craftiness,
      And the counsel of the wily becomes foolishness;

Compare the ideas expressed in the Song of Hannah, especially 1 S 2:7b.

12 For מפר Targ. and Syr. 'making futile' (verb בטל), G διαλλάσσοντα, Aq. τὸν ἀκυροῦντα, Symm. διαλύσει, Theod. διασκεδάζοντα (according to the margin of Syro-hex. and Olympiodorus), cf. Vulg. *qui dissipat*. G πανούργων retains the ambiguity of ערומים 'skilful' or 'cunning'; Syr. sees here an allusion to the 'wise', but Vulg. the 'malicious' (pejorative), *malignorum*. The word תושיה is again capable of many meanings (cf. inf.). That of 'wisdom' is adopted by Syr. and Targ., 'the counsel of their wisdom', while G interprets by ἀληθές and Vulg. by *quod coeperant*. The *hiph'il* of פרר in the sense of 'break', 'crumble to pieces' to signify 'annihilate', with מחשבות 'thoughts', 'designs' as the complement (Pr 15:22). Cf. 15:4; 40:8. The ערומים are the crafty, those who use cunning to attain their ends (Gn 3:1). Later the word became synonymous with 'wisdom', 'prudence' (the wisdom of the serpent). In v. 13 the ערמה will convey the quality of those who are wise. God baffles the clever plans of those who think themselves astute. The abstract תושיה is a word characteristic of the Hebrew wisdom literature. The various texts in which it figures have been catalogued by Driver, who comes to the following conclusions: תושיה parallel to wisdom (26:3), to counsel (Pr 8:14, Is 28:29), to help (Job 6:13), to strength (12:16). We would explain these various meanings as follows. The word תושיה first of all denotes the foresight which plans ahead, and it is in this sense that it is used here: 'and their

hands do not achieve what they had planned'. God thwarts the schemes of the astute. By derivation תושיה will come to mean the faculty of foresight or prudence in general (12:6; 26:3), and, more broadly, intelligence (11:6). Finally, because to foresee means also to provide, תושיה will eventually convey the idea of help or assistance (6:13).

13 For בערמם G ἐν τῇ φρονήσει, but G (A) adds αὐτῶν (Sah., Eth.). The 1st hemistich is cited by St Paul (1 Co 3:19), ὁ δρασσόμενος τοὺς σοφοὺς ἐν τῇ πανουργίᾳ αὐτῶν, from a text different from that of G. With ἐν τῇ πανουργίᾳ cf. the translation ערומים in G v. 12. Targ. brings in the wise men and magicians of Pharaoh (cf. v. 12). For נמהרה Targ. אוחית עליהון 'rushes on them'. The other versions, in a spirit of harmonisation (cf. G and Vulg. for v. 11), replace the passive by an active: G ἐξέστησεν, Vulg. *dissipat*, Syr. ܡܗܦܟ. But Symm. παραχθήσεται brings us back to MT. The word נפתלים is perfectly translated by G as πολυπλόκων.

God uses the cunning of the wily to catch them in their own trap. The verb לכד 'ensnare' and, by extension, 'hold firmly', 'grasp' (cf. the derivative forms in 36:8; 38:30; 41:9). Instead of the snare it is the very craftiness of the wily which serves as an instrument for trapping the wise: 'He ensnares the wise in their wisdom.' Same idea and a similar image in Ps 7:16, where the wicked fall into the pit that they have dug (cf. Ps 57:7); similarly in Pr 26:27; 28:10. The form עָרְמָם is by euphony for עָרְמָתָ, as one has תְּבוּנָם for תְּבוּנָתָם (Hos 13:2). The

14   In broad daylight they encounter darkness,
      And at the height of noon they grope as in the night!
15   And He saves from their mouth the *ruined man*,
      And from the hand of the mighty, the needy!

15 מֶחָרֶב; MT: מֵחֶרֶב.

participle נִפְתָּל recurs in Pr 8:8,
where it is applied to words. Etymologically it implies 'twisted' (like
a thread פָּתִיל), then 'tortuous' (Pr
8:8), and here 'wily'. Cf. the use of
the *hithpa'el* in Ps 18:27. The *niph'al*
of מהר in the sense of 'to be hasty,
irresponsible'. The design of those
who have hatched intricate plots
comes to have no more value than
if it had been conceived in a hasty
manner. It is needless to postulate
new meanings such as 'fall to the
ground' (Hitzig) or 'to be diminished in scale, despised' (Fried.
Delitzsch, on the model of the Assyrian *mâru* 'child'!).

14 G συναντήσεται αὐτοῖς is a free
translation of יְפַגְּשׁוּ. Beer wanted to
read יְפַגֵּשׁ, but more recently (in
Kittel's *BH*) he suggests יְגַשְּׁשׁוּ. Syr.
renders חשֶׁךְ by 'as in darkness'.
The versions have correctly interpreted כַּלַּיְלָה by 'as in the night'.
The wise of this world, the astute,
think they see clearly into the web
of their affairs, and think out plans
intended to ensure success. But God
blinds them. 'In broad daylight,
they encounter darkness', like the
Syrians whom Elisha led to Samaria (2 K 6:18ff.). Notice the antithetic parallelism. The expression
כַּלַּיְלָה 'as in the night' is meant to
avoid the juxtaposition of the preposition "בְ with the particle "כְ
(cf. 29:2). The verb משֶׁשׁ characte-
ristically expresses groping about
in the darkness: 'and at the height
of noon they grope as in the night!'
This is the realisation of the pro-

phecy of Dt 28:29: 'and you shall
grope at noonday as the blind grope
in darkness'. The same images in Is
59:10, where the verb used is גשׁשׁ
instead of משׁשׁ. Job will take up the
idea of Eliphaz for his own purposes
(12:24-5).

15 Targ. continues to interpret as
though the reference were to the
exodus from Egypt. G omits מפיהם
and seems to read וִיגֹעַ (cf. 3:11)
for וִישַׁע, whence: ἀπόλοιντο δὲ ἐν
πολέμῳ. Targ., Syr., and Vulg. *a
gladio oris eorum* neglect the preposition of מפיהם. Vulg. adds a complement in the 1st hemistich (*egenum*).
G adds the verb ἐξέλθοι in the second.
The juxtaposition of מִפִּיהֶם with
מֶחָרֶב causes a grammatical difficulty. Rosenmüller in his commentary follows the interpretation of
Targ., Syr., and Vulg. *a gladio oris
eorum* 'from calumny' (Ps 57:5;
59:8; 64:4); but in his translation
he separates *ab ense* from *a faucibus*.
A few MSS of MT replace the difficult reading by the easier פִּיהֶם,
which is adopted by de Rossi and
Dillmann. Le Hir translates 'from
the sword of their tongue' and explains 'from the sword coming out of
their mouth, i.e. their tongue'.
Modern exegetes propose various
corrections: מַפִּיהֶם (equals מפאיהם)
'their murderers' (Hitzig); פִּיפִיּוֹת
'two-edged' (Ehrlich, cf. Ps 149:6).
Siegfried deletes מפיהם and substitutes עָנִי 'the poor' (Duhm),
while Budde hesitates between
מֶחַרְבָּם יָתָם and (suppressing מחרב)

16   Thus the poor man has hope,
     And injustice shuts her mouth.
17   Therefore, happy is the man whom Eloah corrects,
     And who does not despise the teaching of Shaddai!

מפיהם יָתָם 'he saves the orphan from their sword (or from their mouth)'. It should be noted that מפיהם 'from their mouth' corresponds very well with וּמִיַּד חָזָק 'from the hand of the mighty' of the 2nd hemistich (cf. the parallelism between חשך and וכלילה in v. 14). What is lacking is a parallel word to אֶבְיוֹן. Now, the violent, the wicked, the tyrants, are wild beasts (4: 10-11) who devour the poor (Pr 30: 14; Hab 3: 14). God snatches from their jaws their unfortunate victims, just as David snatched the sheep from the mouth of the lion or the bear (1 S 17: 35). It is the unfortunate, the distressed, or the poor, who are covered by the word מחרב. Cappel was right in pointing as מְחֻרָב hoph'al participle of חרב, whose meaning of 'ruined' may be as applicable to men as to things (Ewald, Fried. Delitzsch). The parallelism then becomes excellent and all difficulty disappears. The metaphor of the sword of the tongue (cf. sup.) may have caused the present Massoretic pointing the disadvantages of which we have seen. The phrase מיד חזק 'from the hand of the strong' as in Jer 31: 11. Strength resides in the hand or the arm; cf. the expressions יד חזקה 'strong hand' and זרוע חזקה 'strong arm' (L'Emploi métaphorique, p. 140). The cunning of the so-called wise does not enable them to realise their design, which is to seize the goods of the poor. They think they hold the latter at their mercy, but God intervenes and tears their victims from their grasp. The verb הושיע is used with its meaning of 'save' (cf. Comm. on 4: 20).

16   For לדל G ἀδυνάτῳ, Aq. ἀτόνῳ, Symm. πτωχῷ (cf. Vulg. egeno). The text of Jerome for the 1st hemistich was sit autem infirmo spes (Tur.). which became si autem infirmo pes (Bod.) and sit autem infirmus spes (Gall.). Targ. and Vulg. iniquitas retain the abstract עלתה, but Syr. 'the unrighteous man' and G ἀδίκου render by a concrete term. Jerome had et iniqui os obstruatur (Gall.), which became et iniquus obstruatur in Bod. and Tur.

V. 16 concludes the picture of the changes in fortune which has been drawn in the preceding verses. The weak is often the victim of the strong (v. 15). But he must not despair: 'thus the poor man has hope.' Thanks to the help which God sends, he escapes the oppressor. Then the wicked can no longer triumph with loud boasting, nor open wide his mouth to celebrate his victory (1 S 2: 1); on the contrary, 'injustice will shut her mouth'. The form עלתה, poetic for עַוְלָה, recurs in the kethîb of Ps 92: 16. The ending תָה, as in עִיפָתָה (10: 22), causes the contraction of the aw of the first syllable into ô, just as we find עֹלֹת in the plural (Ps 58: 3; 64: 7). On the meaning of the root עול cf. 16: 11. The 2nd hemistich recurs in Ps 107: 42, but with וְכָל־עַוְלָה instead of ועלתה. Verb קפץ 'shut' the mouth, as in Is 52: 15.

17   Targ. applies v. 17a to Abraham, and v. 17b to Israel (cf. v. 10). After אלוה G (A, אc·a), Cod. 254 adds ἐπὶ τῆς γῆς. For מוסר G νουθέτημα, Jerome correptionem (which has become correctionem in Bod.). For שדי, transcribed by Targ., we

18   For it is He who wounds and who binds up,
He strikes and His hands heal.

have Παντοκράτορος (G), *Domini*
(Vulg.), ‏ܚܣܝܢܐ‎ 'the Mighty' (Syr.);
cf. 6:4.

V. 17 forms the transition between
the consideration of the part which
God plays in human affairs (11-16),
and that of His dealings with the
righteous man (18-26). Trial is a
transitory experience. Its aim is to
make God's servant a worthier man.
It is a salutary correction: 'Therefore, happy is the man whom Eloah
corrects!' The opening הִנֵּה (4:3) to
link the statement with what precedes. The verb הוֹכִיחַ is a legal term
the real meaning of which is 'incri-
minate', whence 'criticise' (6:25, 26;
15:3; 32:12; 40:2) or 'discuss'
(13:15), and, as a consequence of
the debate, 'correct' (here and 13:
10; 22:4; 33:19). If the complement is preceded by the preposition
אֶל, then הוֹכִיחַ assumes the meaning
of 'make a charge against' (13:3); if
it is the preposition עַל, then we
have the meaning of 'reproach with'
(19:5). Hence for the noun תּוֹכַחַת,
so frequent in Proverbs (1:23, 25,
30; 3:11, etc.) the meaning 're-
crimination', 'reproach', 'remon-
strance' (13:6; 23:4). When it is a
question of assigning rights as between two parties, הֵכִיחַ means 'to
be the arbiter' (9:33; 16:24). Cf.
the various senses of the *pi'el* of יסר
in 4:3. It is precisely this *pi'el* of
יסר which we find, in parallelism
with the *pi'el* of למד, in a passage of
the Psalms similar to our 1st hemistich: 'Blessed is the man whom
Thou dost chasten, O Lord, and
whom Thou dost teach out of Thy
law' (Ps 94:12). Note that we have
מוּסָר, a derivative of יסר (cf. 4:3),
in our 2nd hemistich: 'And despise
not the teaching of Shaddai!' The
same idea, clothed in almost the same
terms, in Pr 3:11: 'My son, do not

despise the Lord's discipline or be
weary of His reproof!' Parallelism
between מוּסָר and תּוֹכַחַת. The
reason for the respect which should
be shown towards the reproofs of
God is that they testify to His love.
'For the Lord reproves, (יוֹכִיחַ, cf.
above) him whom He loves, as a
father the son in whom he delights'
(Pr 3:12). Thus Eliphaz can expound the theme of divine chastisement. The same thesis will be developed by Elihu (33:16ff.; 36:10).
We see here appearing for the first
time the name שַׁדַּי, which will be
found 31 times in the Book of Job.
Cf. Intro., pp. lxvff.

18 For יַכְאִיב G ἀλγεῖν ποιεῖ, Jerome *dolere facit* (Gall.), which becomes *dolorem facit* in Bod. and Tur.
G paraphrases יֶחְבָּשׁ by πάλιν ἀπο-
καθίστησιν. The readings of Aq. μοτώσει and of Symm. ἐπιδήσει are
grouped together in the margin of
Cod. 252: μοτώσει καὶ ἐπιδήσει. The
versions support the *qerê* יָדָיו (*kethîb*
יָדוֹ) confirmed by the plural תִּרְפֶּינָה.

Vv. 18-23 give the reasons which
justify acceptance of God's chastisement. It is the same hand which
wounds and which heals. At the beginning כִּי הוּא 'for He', i.e. the same
person; cf. the use of הוּא in 3:19.
The *hiph'il* of כאב in the sense of
causing a physical pain (cf. the *qal*
in 14:22). The reference is to a pain
caused by a wound, as is shown by
וְיֶחְבָּשׁ 'and He binds up, He tends'
(Is 30:26). Pointing יֶחְבָּשׁ instead
of יַחְבֹּשׁ because of the pause (Gesenius-Kautzsch, § 63d). Note the
writing of תִּרְפֶּינָה, from the verb
רפא, by analogy with the ל"ה
verbs (cf. תַּעֲשֶׂינָה in v. 12). The ideas
and the style of Eliphaz are inspired

19   In six calamities He will deliver you,
      And in seven no evil shall harm you:
20   In famine He will save you from death,
      And in war from the hands of the sword;

by Dt 32: 39, 'I kill and make alive;
I wound and I heal', as also by Hos
6: 1, 'For he tears and He heals us;
He has stricken and He will bind us
up.' Cf. the use of מחץ, חבש and
רפא in Is 30: 26.

19 G ἑξάκις ἐξ ἀναγκῶν translates
according to the sense. The other
versions confirm the reading בשש of
MT, which there is no reason to correct to מֵשֵׁשׁ (Beer, Duhm). For
בשבע the versions have used the
ordinal number 'in the seventh' but
Aq. and Theod. ἐν ἑπτά.

The figure of rhetoric used consists
in marking the arithmetical progression by adding a unit to a number which in itself would suffice to
express the thought; cf. Latin expressions such as *bis terque* (Cicero),
ter quaterque beati (Virgil). Numerous examples of this figure are in the
Bible (König, *Stilistik*, p. 163). The
series one-two in 40: 5; two-three in
33: 29. Characteristic examples of
the series three-four in Am 1: 3ff.
Juxtaposition of two-three and four-
five in Is 17: 6. For five-six, cf. 2 K
13: 19. The example which comes
closest to our text is Pr 6: 16,
'There are six things which the Lord
hates, and seven which are an abomination to Him.' The author of
Proverbs then enumerates the seven
abominable things. But in this case
the numbers have been chosen as
excluding all exceptions, and it
would be useless to look for a description of the seven calamities
in the following verses. Calmet justifiably protests against the pretension
of the rabbis to reach the number
seven. Use of צָרָה 'calamity' as in
27: 9. The *hiph'il* הציל (cf. v. 4) is

specially used to denote the idea of
deliverance from calamity (צָרָה as
here) in 1 S 26: 24; Ps 54: 9. On the
verb נגע with ב″ before its complement, cf. 1: 11.

20 Faithful to its technique, Targ.
situates in the history of Israel the
calamities mentioned. Here it sees
an allusion to the 'famine of Egypt'
and the 'war of Amalek'. At the
close of the 2nd hemistich G adds
λύσει σε, translated without obelus
in Syro-hex. and Jerome. The plural
ידי is faithfully given by Syr. but
replaced by the singular in G ἐκ
χειρός and in Vulg. *de manu*, whilst
Targ. interprets by מקטול 'from
murder', which corresponded to מחרב
in v. 15.

The perfect פָּדְךָ is used to emphasise the certainty of an affirmation
which is in effect a prophecy. The
first two scourges mentioned are
famine and war. The parallelism
between רָעָב 'famine' and יְדֵי־חָרֶב
'the hands of the sword' is found in
Jer 18: 21. The expression 'the hands
of the sword' recurs in Ps 63: 11.
The sword, an instrument of destruction, is sometimes described as
having a mouth with which it devours (Ex 17: 13; Nu 21: 24), sometimes as having hands with which it
strikes. It will be noticed that, in
Jer 14: 13, 15, the calamities are
placed in the reverse order: sword,
famine. The normal order of the
scourges is: famine, war, pestilence
(2 S 24: 13). For lack of a sword,
the tongue can be used as an instrument for smiting (Jer 18: 18).
The lash of the tongue thus readily
occurs to the mind, v. 21.

21   From the lash of the tongue you will be protected,
      And you will not fear devastation, when it comes;
22   At devastation and famine you will scoff,
      And you will not fear the beasts of the earth.

21 Targ. sees here an allusion to 'the tongue of Balaam' and the 'devastation wrought by the Midianites' (cf. v. 20). No more than in v. 19 is it necessary to change ‏ב׳‎ of ‏בשוט‎ into ‏מן‎ following G, Syr., and Vulg. *a flagello*, which translate in their idiom. For ‏תחבא‎ G has σὲ κρύψει. A gloss drawn from Ps 30 (Heb. 31): 21 is added in Colb. The close ‏כי משוד‎ ‏יבוא‎ is rendered in G ἀπὸ κακῶν ἐρχομένων. Jerome *neque timebis quae supervenient mala* (Gall.) becomes, by haplography, in Bod. and Tur. *neque supervenient tibi mala*. A second more literal translation is added by G (A) at the end of the 2nd hemistich: καὶ οὐ φοβηθήσῃ ἀπὸ ταλαιπωρίας ὅτι ἐλεύσεται ταλαιπωρία.

The scourge of the tongue suceeds that of the sword, just as we have ‏חרב ולשן‎ in the so-called inscription of Hadad, l. 9 (Lagrange, *ÉRS*, p. 493). Budde insists on an infinitive form for ‏שוט‎, while Hoffmann would like to replace ‏לשון‎ by ‏לושן‎ 'calumniator'. But the expression, 'the lash of the tongue' is firmly attested by μάστιξ γλώσσης of Sir 26: 9 and ‏שוט דבת לשון‎ of Sir 51: 2. We find a comparison between πληγὴ μάστιγος 'the lash of the whip' and πληγὴ γλώσσης 'the blow of the tongue' in Sir 28: 17 (= 21). In common parlance we say that malicious gossip is worse than blows. Backbiting sows discord and strife; that is why this scourge is mentioned immediately after war. The preposition ‏ב׳‎ before ‏שוט‎ has the meaning of ‏מן‎ postulated by the following verb (cf. 4: 21). The *niph'al* of ‏חבא‎ 'to be hidden', i.e. to be in a hiding place, hence protected, sheltered. Cf. Ps 31: 20, 'Thou holdest them safe under Thy shelter from the strife of tongues.' The 2nd hemistich offers us the same idea and expression as Pr 3: 25b, 'and of the ruin of the wicked when it comes'. The verb ‏בוא‎ to denote the coming of a misfortune; cf. 3: 26; 4: 5. It is rather a curious notion to want to substitute ‏שֵד‎ 'the demon' (Hoffmann) for ‏שד‎ 'devastation'. Note the homophony between the names of the two scourges ‏שוט‎ and ‏שד‎. In Pr 3: 25b we have ‏שאת‎.

22 Targ. continues its historical allusions: the devastation of Zion and famine in the wilderness, Og being likened to the wild beast. G ἀδίκων καὶ ἀνόμων καταγελάσῃ interprets the abstracts ‏שד‎ and ‏כפן‎ as though the text read ‏שדד‎ and ‏כפר‎ (Aramaic). For ‏ומחית הארץ‎ G has ἀπὸ δὲ θηρίων ἀγρίων, which G (A) brings nearer to MT by adding τῆς γῆς. The 2nd hemistich is absent from Memph. and marked by an asterisk in Jerome (Tur.).

This verse forms a link between v. 21 and v. 23. The word ‏שד‎ is repeated from v. 21, while the Aramaic ‏כָּפָן‎ 'famine' is substituted for the ‏רעב‎ of v. 20. Then the phrase ‏חַיַת הָאָרֶץ‎ anticipates ‏חית השדה‎ of v. 23, and ‏אַל־תִּירָא‎, a jussive form conveying prediction (Gesenius-Kautzsch, § 109e) is inspired by the phrase ‏לֹא־תִירָא‎ of v. 21. These observations have inclined some exegetes to suppress this v. 22 as artifical and inconsequential (cf. Budde, Duhm, Beer). But is not v. 23 an explanation of this v. 22? It is easy to see that v. 23a gives the reason for v. 22a, whilst v. 23b explains v. 22b. In such circumstances it seems to us preferable to retain v

23   For with the stones of the field you will have a pact,
      And the wild beast will dwell at peace with you.
24   And you will know assuredly that your tent is secure,
      And, when you inspect your dwelling, you will not be
      disappointed.

22. We may note that תִּשְׂחָק לְ״
'you will scoff at . . .' (39: 7, 18,
22; 41: 21) goes further in emphasis
than v. 21.

23 The 1st hemistich is lacking in
G (B, א), Sah., and Eth. It is marked
by an asterisk in Jerome and Syro-
hex. which adds in the margin: 'is
not found in the Octapla of Origen'.
The translation is restored in G (A),
Cod. 249, Ald., at the end of the
verse. The lacuna of G may arise
from a haplography resulting from
the resemblance between אבני השדה
and חית השדה. Targ. finds in the
stones of the field an allusion to the
tables of the law which were given
in the open country, and in the
animals of the field an allusion to
the Canaanites.

Knabenbauer lists a series of interpretations of the first hemistich. For
some exegetes the stones of the field
represent the boundaries which,
thanks to the pact, will no more be
violated. For others it is an allusion
to the custom of the Arabs who
would place stones in a field to threat-
en with death any one who might
cultivate it (Pineda). The opinion
of Sa and Calmet, who consider that
the 1st hemistich is an allusion to
Ps 91: 12, *ne forte offendas ad lapidem pedem tuum*, is repeated in the
Hebrew commentary of Avronin
and Rabinowitz. Rashi saw in the
stones of the field an allusion to
some species of beings, which inclined K. Kohler and Beer (*ZATW*,
1915, pp. 63f.) to read אדני instead of אבני. The 'lords of the field'
were thought of as the genii of the
countryside, *Erdmännlein*. However
attractive the hypothesis may be,
the testimony of Rashi is too isolated

to justify us in changing the text.
The reference to a pact suggests that
we should seek in the stones of the
field a reference to some kind of
scourge, for one makes a pact with
death (Is 28: 15)—an expression
signifying that one is protected from
its blows. In Hos 2: 18, 'And I will
make for them a covenant on that
day with the beasts of the field, the
birds of the air, and the creeping
things of the ground.' Now, the
stones of the field are a real scourge,
for they prevent fertility (Mt 13: 5).
And they are precisely one of the
means employed to devastate a
country that is hostile (2 K 3: 19,
25). To have a pact with the stones
of the field means to be assured that
they will not come and spoil the
ground, preventing it from being
fertile. But devastation may be
caused by another factor, namely,
the 'animal of the field', i.e. the wild
beast (39: 15; 40: 20). Cf. the Greek
ἄγριος 'wild' (from ἀγρός 'field').
In Ezk 14: 21 four scourges are enumerated: sword, famine, evil beasts,
and pestilence. The evil beast, חיה
רעה, which implies the wild beast, is
contrasted with the domestic animal,
בהמה, which is to be exterminated
just as much as man. The *hoph'al*
הָשְׁלְמָה is not found elsewhere. It
is indeed the passive form of the
hiph'il 'to make or have peace with
some one'. In Ps 91: 13 he who is
protected by God tramples under
foot harmful beasts.

24 For שלום G has εἰρηνεύσει, but
G (A) and Cod. 249 ἐν εἰρήνῃ, Jerome
in pace. For אהלך Targ. 'the house
of instruction', G σου ὁ οἶκος (but
Cod. 249 τὸ σκήνωμά σοῦ), G (A)
τὸ σπέρμα σου. It looks as if G (A

25   You will be certain also of a numerous posterity,
       And of offspring like the grass of the earth.

26   You will come to the grave in a ripe old age,
       As a shock of corn rises in due time!

and Cod. 249 are following a hexaplar translation, for they have for the 2nd hemistich καὶ ἐπισκοπὴ τῆς εὐπρεπείας σου καὶ οὐ μὴ ἁμαρτήσῃ (cf. εὐπρέπεια for נוה, Aq. in v. 3) instead of G: ἡ δὲ δίαιτα τῆς σκηνῆς σου οὐ μὴ ἁμάρτῃ. Note that the readings ἡ δὲ δίαιτα and καὶ ἐπισκοπή point וּפָקַדְתָּ instead of וּפָקַדְתָּ. Vulg. rendered נוהו by pulchritudini ejus in v. 3; here speciem tuam for נוך; cf. Aq. ὡραιότητά σου.

The verse opens with 'and you will know assuredly' to convey the idea of the complete security enjoyed by him who puts his trust in God. 'Your tent' is a poetic variant of 'your house', and reflects the taste of Eliphaz (22: 23). Use of שָׁלוֹם 'peace', 'safety', etc. as though it were an adjective (21: 9). Cf. Gn 43: 27: הֲשָׁלוֹם אֲבִיכֶם. 'Is your father in good health?' Same use of שָׁלוֹם in 1 S 25: 6; 2 S 20: 9. Hence 'and you will know assuredly that your tent is secure'; such a one can have no reason for anxiety. Use of the imperfect תֶּחֱטָא after the perfect פָּקַדְתָּ to indicate that the second action is consequent upon the first: 'and when you inspect your dwelling'. On נָוֶה 'dwelling', parallel to אֹהֶל 'tent', cf. v. 3. The verb חטא 'to sin' connotes etymologically 'to miss', not to hit the mark, exactly like the Greek ἁμαρτάνω and the Arabic ḥaṭi'a (in its derivative forms). This meaning recurs in Is 65: 20 (cf. Condamin), Pr 8: 36, where חֹטְאִי 'he who misses me' is contrasted with מֹצְאִי 'he who finds me' in v. 35. The hiph'il of חטא is used in the same sense in Jg 20: 16,

where it is a question of the slingers who 'do not miss' the hair which is their target. From the meaning of 'miss' is derived that of 'to be frustrated, disappointed'.

25   The verse has been well understood by the versions. For צֶאֱצָאֶיךָ Targ. 'the sons of your sons', G τὰ τέκνα σου, Vulg. progenies tua. For עֵשֶׂב G παμβόρτανον, Jerome omnie herba.

Parallelism between זַרְעֶךָ 'your seed, posterity' and צֶאֱצָאֶיךָ 'your shoots', exactly as in 21: 8 and Is 44: 3. Both metaphors are taken from plant life. There is no need to stress the high value for an oriental of a numerous posterity. The word צֶאֱצָאִים recurs in its literal meaning (31: 8) and in its metaphorical meaning (21: 8; 27: 14). Outside Job and Isaiah, it is found only in Sir 42: 20 (= 22), where likewise it means progeny; G τὰ τέκνα, Vulg. liberos. The comparison 'like the grass of the earth' to convey the picture of a great multitude recurs in Ps 72: 16.

26   G ἐλεύσῃ δὲ ἐν τάφῳ omits בכלה. Then ὥσπερ σῖτος ὥριμος κατὰ καιρὸν (together with αὐτοῦ in A, Sah., Jerome, Syro-hex.). θεριζόμενος is a first translation of 26b (cf. Beer). A second translation follows: ἢ ὥσπερ θιμωνιὰ ἅλωνος καθ' ὥραν συνκομισθεῖσα. The translation of גָּדִישׁ by θιμωνιά (Ald. θημώνια) in 21: 32 is due to Aq., that by σωρῷ (σωρῶν) is due to Theod. (contra Beer, who attributes to Aq. and Theod. the translation θιμωνιά). It is thus probable that the second translation of G, in our passage, comes from Aq. The words κατὰ καιρὸν αὐτοῦ θεριζό-

27   This then is what we have searched out; so it is!
Heed it and know it for yourself!

μενος and ἄλωνος are marked with obelus in Syro-hex. It is impossible to base one's self on G in order to change בכלח into כאביב לח (contra Herz, *ZATW*, 1900, p. 160). For בכלח Vulg. *in abundantia*, Targ. בשלימות שניך 'in the plenitude of your years', Syr. ܫܠܡܐܝܬ 'peacefully'.

The expression בְּכֶלַח is a *crux interpretum*. The Jewish tradition, represented by the Targum, Sa'adia (بهرم 'in decrepitude'), Qimchi (עת וזקנה), gives to כלח the meaning of fullness of years, extreme old age (cf. *Thesaurus* of Gesenius, I, p. 688 A). The addition of the numbers represented by the letters of בכלח (2, 20, 30, 8) provided certain rabbis with the figure 60, and this enabled them to consider the age of sixty years or so as the beginning of old age and to organise feasts in celebration of it (*Lexicon* of Buxtorf, s.v. כלח, p. 212). Various etymologies have been investigated. Castel postulated a Syriac word ܟܠܚ 'integrity', 'health', but mistakenly (Gesenius, loc. cit.). Others have had recourse to the Arabic كلح 'to look severe' (Schultens) or 'have pursed lips' (Michaelis), and كهل 'arrive at a ripe age' (Hitzig). The first root is too distant in meaning, the second in form, to enable us to conclude that 'old age' is the meaning. Modern exegetes have tried to emend the text. We have seen that Herz was on the wrong track in seeking in G a support for a reading כאביב לח 'like a new blade of corn' (see above). Merx reads בְּלֵחַ 'in vigour' (cf. Dt 34:7), Cheyne and Ball בְּלַחָך 'in your vigour', Beer בְּחֵלָך 'in your strength'. But parallelism guides us

in a way which brings us back to the Jewish tradition. In fact, the 2nd hemistich means 'as a shock of corn rises up in due time'. It is a question of the time of harvest. It is then that there rise up over the fields shocks, piles of sheaves, גָּדִישׁ (Ex 22:5; Jg 15:5), which should not be confused with its homonym גָּדִישׁ 'funeral mound' (Job 21:32). The emergence of the shock of corn corresponds to 'you will come to the grave' in the 1st hemistich, while the circumstance 'in due time' (cf. Ps 1:3) corresponds to בכלח. Now, we are familiar with the formula תקבר בשיבה טובה 'you shall be buried in a good old age' (Gn 15:15; cf. Gn 35:29; Jg 8:32). It is clear that בכלח means 'in old age', as contrasted with a premature death (22:16). Job will die 'old and full of days' (42:17), while the wicked man is snatched away in the height of his youth (20:11). Thus understood, the word כֶּלַח will be connected with the root כלה 'to be completed' (strengthening of the final guttural), and lastly with כלל 'to be whole, perfected'. It is as a result of a textual error that we have כלח in 30:2 (cf. Comm.).

27   G ἃ ἀκηκόαμεν points שְׁמָעֶנָּה so as to harmonise with חקרנוה. At the end G adds εἴ τι ἔπραξας, but we find simply τί ἐποίησας in G (A), Sah., Syro-hex., Jerome *quid egeris*. Conclusion of the entire speech of Eliphaz. Feminine זֹאת with the sense of a neutral (1:22; 2:10). The relative אשר is implicit in the feminine suffix of חֲקַרְנוּהָ. Cf. יום אולד בו 'the day on which I was born' (3:3). The verb חקר 'search out' (28:3), 'seek' (32:11), 'study' (29:16), 'examine', 'scan' (13:9; 28:27). Cf. the

noun חֵקֶר in v. 9. Eliphaz emphasises his pedagogic tone כֶּן־הִיא 'so
it is!' Several commentators prefer
the reading of G שְׁמַעֲנָה 'we have
heard it' to the MT שְׁמָעֶנָּה 'heed it!'
Ehrlich claims that if the MT is
correct, we should have וְאַתָּה before
שמענה. But we may have here the
case in which a copula is displaced
by poetic licence (cf. 4:6). The 2nd
hemistich will be translated simply:
'heed it and know it for yourself!'
Eliphaz wishes that the knowledge
he possesses should be heard by the
ear and assimilated by the mind of
his friend. The dative לְךָ strengthens
the imperative דַּע; cf. 2:8 and
12:11.

CHAPTER 6

1 Job spoke and said:
2 Ah! if only my grief could be weighed,
   And my misfortune too placed in the balances!

Chapters 6-7 Second speech of Job: see Introduction, pp. xxxviif.

6: 1 The verb ענה as in 4: 1, etc. The translation of Jerome is omitted in Bod.

2 Symm. ὡς εἴθε ἐσταθμίζετό μου ἡ ὀργή brings back to MT the free translation of G εἰ γάρ τις ἱστῶν στήσαι μου τὴν ὀργήν. Vulg. translates with prolixity כעשי as *peccata mea quibus iram merui*, and היתי as *calamitas quam patior*. The *kethîb* הַיָּתִי recurs in 30: 13 as the *kethîb* of the Westerns. It should be noted that Syr. 'and what happens to me' connects with the verb היה. Hence we may leave the *kethîb* הַיָּתִי instead of the *qerê* הַוָּתִי. In Targ. we have אתרגושתי 'my agitation' (cf. v. 30), in G τὰς δὲ ὀδύνας μου. Syr. omits ישאו, Vulg. ישאר־יחד.

Without making any direct reply to Eliphaz, Job undertakes to justify his lament. It is generally thought that the 2nd hemistich explains the 1st, as though Job proposed to place his grief (כַּעֲשִׂי) in one scale of the balances and his misfortune (הַיָּתִי) in the other. But in v. 3 we shall see that his grief is heavier than the sand of the seas. Hence it cannot be weighed, and this is precisely of what Job complains: 'Ah! if only my grief could be weighed and my misfortune too placed in the balances!' The conjunction לוּ is used, in contrast to אִם, to imply

unrealisable wishes, and it also serves as an interjection in the sense of the Latin *utinam* (Gesenius-Kautzsch, § 159, 3 and § 151, 2); cf. Gn 17: 18 with the imperfect as here. On כַּעַשׂ cf. 5: 2. The parallel word is הַיָּתִי (*kethîb*), which has the same meaning as הַוָּתִי (*qerê*); from the root הוה 'fall' (37: 6). In Pr 19: 13, the plural הֹוֹת takes the place of the כַּעַס of Pr 17: 28. If so, הוות denotes the 'misfortunes' which are the cause of כעס 'grief' or 'vexation'. The sense 'misfortune' also suits the plural הֹוֹת of Ps 57: 2 and 91: 3. It is easily derived from הוה 'to fall'; hence 'fall', 'accident', 'misfortune'. In 30: 13 the singular לְהַיָּתִי will mean 'for my misfortune'. The nexus between physical and moral evil, which has determined the various meanings of עמל and און (cf. Comm. on 4: 8 and 5: 6), also changes the meaning of the plural הוות into that of 'wickednesses', 'bad deeds', etc. Thus it comes about that in Ps 55: 11, 12 הוות בקרבה 'wicked deeds are within it' sums up ואון ועמל בקרבה 'iniquity and evil are within it'. Hence there will be no difficulty in rendering the plural in v. 30 הַוֹּת by 'evil things'. In order to avoid the repetition of the verb שקל the author uses נשא 'convey', 'place on', and to avoid a second *niph'al* a plural impersonal is used,

75

3   But because it is heavier than the sand of the seas,
     My words are but stammered out!

4   For the arrows of Shaddai are in me,
     It is their poison that my spirit drinks;
     The terrors of Eloah are marshalled against me!

יִשָּׂאוּ 'they place'; cf. ידכאום in
4:19. We shall have the verb שׁקל
with במאזני־צדק 'in the scales of
justice' in 31:6. The adverb יַחַד
'also', 'similarly' (3:18).

3 Vulg. does not translate כי־עתה.
For חול ימים G has ἄμμου παραλίας.
Vulg. paraphrases יכבד as *haec gra-
vior appareret*. For על־כן G has
ἀλλ' ὡς ἔοικεν, but Aq. ἐπὶ τούτῳ,
Symm. διὰ τοῦτο, Vulg. *unde*. The
verb לעו is connected with the root
לאה (4:2) by Targ. משׁתלהין
'exhausted', with לעע by Aq. κατε-
πόθησαν. Syr. ܡܠܐ 'hindered' interprets according to the sense. Similarly Symm. κατάπικροι, Theod.
ἔγκοποι, Vulg. *dolore sunt plena*.
Still more vague is G ἐστιν φαῦλα.
    The construction of the phrase is
the same as in 17:4; 20:19-21; 23:
14-15, where the cause is introduced
by כִּי 'because', and the consequence
by עַל־כֵּן 'that is why'. It is clear
that כִּי־עַתָּה 'now that' (4:5) has
no more value than the simple כִּי.
Heavier than the sand of the seas,
the grief of Job cannot be weighed
(v. 2). The subject of יִכְבָּד is כעשׂי
of v. 2, as is to be seen from Pr 27:3,
'A stone is heavy and sand is weighty,
but a fool's provocation (כעס) is
heavier than both.' The sand of the
seas (Jer 15:8) or of the sea (Is
10:22) symbolises what is immeas-
urable; cf. Gn 22:17; 32:13, etc.
Some confusion reigns in the dictionaries with regard to the verb לעו,
for which is postulated a root לעע,
different from לעע, לוע 'suck up'
(39:30). This root is supposed to lie

behind יָלַע of Pr 20:25. But it is
more likely that this יָלַע belongs to
another root attested by the Arabic
ولع 'to feel passion' and 'to lie',
whilst our verb לָעוּ comes from לעה,
connected with the Arabic لغو 'to
chatter'. Modern Hebrew has retained for לעה the meaning of 'to be
stammered out', as is seen from the
poetic texts cited by Ben-Yehuda
(*Thesaurus*, V, p. 2709). This sense
fits our text admirably. The idea
common to the root לעו (לעה) both
in Arabic and Hebrew is rashness in
speech, whence gossiping, babbling,
stuttering, stammering.

4 For חצי G, as normally, βέλη,
but Syro-hex. adds in the margin
the epithet 'burning' which might
come from Symm., following Ps
56:5 (Field). G renders שׁדי by Κυρίου; cf. 5:17. Colb. draws attention
to the fact that the Hebrew is σαδδαι,
to be interpreted as ἱκανός, and the
margin of Syro-hex. notes that Origen's copy has Κυρίου σαδδαι, 'which
is interpreted as ἱκανός'. Compl. has
retained the reading τοῦ ἱκανοῦ. For
עמדי G has ἐν τῷ σώματί μού ἐστιν,
Syr. 'in my flesh'. With the exception of Targ. the versions have made
of חמתם (interpreted as 'their anger') the subject of שׁתה. G insisted
that the complement of שׁתה should
be a liquid, whence μοῦ τὸ αἷμα for
רוחי. It is difficult to see how G gets
ὅταν ἄρξομαι λαλεῖν from בעותי אלוה
(cf. Beer). For יערכוני G κεντοῦσί με
(Jerome *stimulant me*), Syr. ܣܡܦܘܠܝ
'has terrified me', which is a corruption of ܣܡܦܘܠܝ; cf. Targ. יסדרו.
One cannot base either on G or Syr.

5   Does the wild ass bray when he is near to the grass?
     Does the ox low within sight of his fodder?

the correction of יערכוני into יַעֲכְרוּנִי,
as Beer proposes, along with Dillmann, Budde, etc. Vulg. *militant
contra me* is in agreement with MT,
Targ., and Syr. (corrected).

V. 4 explains why the grief of Job
exceeds all measure and why, in
consequence, his words are hasty
(vv. 2-3): 'For the arrows of Shaddai are in me.' The locution עִמָּדִי
'with me' often recurs in the Book
of Job with various shades of meaning (9:35; 10:12, 17; 13:19, 20,
etc.). It is found as a parallel to בִּי
'in me' in 28:14, and it is this
meaning which is best suited here.
The arrows pierce the flesh of the
sufferer. 'For Thy arrows have sunk
into me' cries the Psalmist (Ps
38:3). The arrows suggest the sick-
nesses or calamities which God
sends upon men. In 16:12-13 Job
compares himself with a target at
which God aims His shafts. It is
clear from 21:20 that the subject of
שָׁתָה is not חֲמָתָם, but rather רוּחִי.
In 21:20 the word חֵמָה has still its
meaning of anger: 'and let him drink
of the anger of Shaddai!' But here
חמה denotes a property of the arrow.
It is a question of the poison of serpents (in Assyrian *imtu*), known to
us from Ps 58:5; Dt 32:24, 33. The
people of the ancient world were
quite familiar with the custom of
coating with poison the sharp end of
arrows, as is still the practice with
certain primitive tribes. Virgil: *Un-
gere tela manu ferrumque armare
veneno* (*Aeneid*, IX, 773); Ovid: *Qui
mortis saevo geminent ut vulnere causas, Omnia vipereo spicula felle li-
nunt* (*Epistulae ex Ponto*, I, ii, 17f.).
The spirit drinks the poison of the
arrows, for the vital springs of life
are directly affected by the calamities which the poisoned arrows

symbolise. The word בְּעוּתַי recurs
only in Ps 88:17, where again the
allusion is to the terrors sent by God
('Thy terrors' parallel to 'Thy furies' חרוניך). The construction
יַעַרְכוּנִי 'are marshalled against me'
implies that ערך is an equivalent of
ערך מלחמה *aciem instruere*, and
regards the intransitive thus obtained as an active verb (cf. Gesenius-Kautzsch, § 117u). The 3rd
hemistich, 'the terrors of Eloah are
marshalled against me', is confirmed by an extract from a prayer of
Ashurbanipal, cited by Fried. Delitzsch: *duluḫḫû amât limuttim suddurûni kaian* 'trouble, malicious
words are constantly arrayed in
battle formation against me'. The
verb *sadâru* (in the permansive
pi'el) has the same meaning as ערך
(cf. סדר in Targ. and Syr.). Thus
there is a complete analogy between
suddurûni and יערכוני. It is now
obvious that it would be unwise to
change to יעכרוני (following G or
Syr.; cf. sup.), or even to יערקוני
'gnaw me' (Merx, Siegfried). As in
10:17, God attacks Job on every side.

5 G interprets this verse in a very
prolix way. The 1st hemistich τί γάρ;
μὴ διὰ κενῆς κεκράξεται ὄνος ἄγριος,
ἀλλ' ἢ τὰ σῖτα ζητῶν seems to arise
from a reading of שוא διὰ κενῆς for
דשא. Later the sense was completed
by the addition of ἀλλ' ἤ κ.τ.λ. Symm.
renders ינהק by στένει λιμῷ. For
עלי-דשא Symm. παρούσης χλόης,
Vulg. *cum habuerit herbam*. G renders
על-בלילו by ἐπὶ φάτνης ἔχων τὰ βρώ-
ματα; cf. Vulg. *cum ante praesepe
plenum steterit*. The word בלילו is
translated ܣܡܒܠܐ 'ripe hay' in Syr.,
אספסתיה 'its fodder' in Targ.

Job seeks to justify his complaint
by pointing to the immensity of his
sorrow. He makes use of a proverbial

6   What is tasteless, is it eaten without salt?
    Or is there any relish in the white of an egg?

saying: Does the wild ass bray when he is near to the grass? Does the ox low within sight of his fodder? When the animal is well fed, he no longer utters cries or manifests his hunger by braying and lowing. The verb נהק 'to bray' which is found also in Arabic and Aramaic, recurs only in 30: 7 where it refers to the unfortunate ones who, in the desert, utter cries like those of the wild ass. In 39: 5-8 we shall have the description of the wild ass, פֶּרֶא, a type of the undomesticated animal. Its despair, when it lacks food, is depicted in Jer 14: 6. The word דֶּשֶׁא is quite wittingly chosen, for it indicates the grass which grows wild on the surface of the soil (Gn 1: 11), and which serves as pasture for wild beasts. Contrasted with it is the בְּלִיל, which is the food of domestic animals, such as the ox and the ass (Is 30: 24). Apart from this text of Isaiah, the word בליל does not recur in the Bible. Its presence in 24: 6 is due to a mistake in pointing (cf. Comm.). The denominative בלל means to give fodder to animals (Jg 19: 21). In Assyrian, *ballu* is synonymous with *imrû* which is the technical term for fodder, the nourishment of beasts of burden. The verb געה, which exists in Aramaic, recurs only in 1 S 6: 12, where it has, as here, the sense of 'lowing'. The distress of domestic animals when deprived of their normal nourishment is described in Jl 1: 18.

6   G renders תפל by a vague word ἄρτος, as does Targ. תבשילא 'cooked food'. The sense is well secured by Symm. ἀνάρτυτον, Vulg. *insulsum*, Syr. פחמא 'insipid'. For מבלי־מלח Symm. τῷ μὴ ἔχειν ἅλα, Vulg. *quod non est sale conditum*. For אם־יש־טעם Vulg. *aut potest aliquis*

gustare? G renders בריר חלמות by ἐν ῥήμασιν κενοῖς, which has caused some critics to believe there was a reading דבר instead of ריר (Rosenmüller, Beer). It seems more likely that G interprets ריר חלמות by connecting the second word with the root חלם 'dream' (cf. inf.), i.e. the saliva of dreams, what one says while sleeping, empty words, baseless dreams. Vulg. *quod gustatum affert mortem* reads perhaps חלת מות 'cake of death' (Rosenmüller). Syr. repeats the MT which gives ܚܡܝܡܐ ܘܒܠܥܐ 'in the sap of the mallow', while Targ. בחלבון ביעתא וחלמונא interprets by 'in the white and yoke of the egg' (2nd Targ. ברירא דחלמונא); cf. inf.

On תָּפֵל 'insipid, tasteless', cf. Comm. on 1: 22. It is unnecessary to try to discover for it a new meaning, such as 'spittle' or 'sputum' (Schultens, Ilgen, after the Arabic *tufl*). The locution מִבְּלִי means simply 'without'. By the law of parallelism it is clear that ריר חַלָּמוּת must express the type of what is insipid. The word ריר recurs only in 1 S 21: 13, where it certainly means saliva (like the Aramaic רירא, the Arabic *rair* and *rail* 'slaver', 'slobber', the Assyrian *lêru*). Many hypotheses have been put forward on the subject of חלמות. Critics have tried to see in ריר חלמות 'the saliva of the healthy man' (from חלם 'to be healthy, robust'), the dribble of dreams (from חלם 'to dream'; cf. G) in the sense of uncontrolled babbling (Schultens), or of the saliva which is swallowed in sleep (Calmet, who quotes Is 29: 8). Cappel connected חלמות with the Arabic *halameh* 'end of the udder'. All these meanings are too

7   My soul has refused to touch it,
     My heart has been sickened by my bread.

7   ‏הָמָה כְּבֹדִי‎ ;MT: ‏הָמָה כדוי‎.

far-fetched for what we expect, namely a type of food which is characterised by a lack of savour. Some
authors see in ‏חלמות‎ the name of
a plant (cf. Syr.) identified at times
with the marsh mallow, at times
with the bugloss (cf. Dillmann,
Hontheim, Fried. Delitzsch who
translates by *ḥallamût-Schleim*). The
Arabic translation (which follows
Syr.) having 'in the saliva of the
purslane', it has been noted that the
Arabic name for purslane, *ḥamqâ'*,
belongs to the same root as *aḥmaq*
'idiot' and that the link between the
two meanings would no doubt be
that the purslane sheds its mucilage
as the idiot lets his saliva drip (cf.
Thesaurus of Gesenius, I, p. 480;
Driver, etc.). But would it occur
to an author to choose 'the saliva
of the purslane' as the type of what
is insipid? The interpretation of
2nd Targ. is in agreement with that
of the 1st in that it links ‏חלמות‎
with the Aramaic ‏חלמונא‎ 'egg-yolk'.
The word ‏ריר‎ 'saliva', 'slobber' can
be applied to glaireous substances
resembling spittle. This is the case
with the white of an egg. In fact
‏ריר חלמות‎ means the glair which
surrounds the yolk of an egg. A
distinction was made between
‏חלבון‎ 'the white' and ‏חלמון‎ 'the
yolk' of the egg; cf. 1st Targ. and
Levy, *Neuhebr. und chald. Wörterbuch*, p. 474, A. There could be no
better example chosen to convey
the idea of insipidity than the white
of an egg: is there any taste in the
white of an egg? Thus it has been
understood by Saadia. Like v. 5,
v. 6 forms a popular saying. Job
wishes to justify his complaint. In
v. 5 he stressed the point that the
animal does not complain when it
finds its fodder. For man, his food

must be well prepared and savoury,
otherwise he turns away from it in
disgust (v. 7).

7   G παύσασθαι reads ‏רגוע‎ instead
of ‏נגוע‎ (Drusius). For ‏נפשי‎ G (B, ‏א‎)
μοῦ ἡ ὀργή, but G (A) μοῦ ἡ ψυχή
(= MT) is followed by Sah., Syro-
hex., Jerome *anima mea*, Memph.,
Eth. The 2nd hemistich is translated 'or my combat groans like a
drunkard' in Syr., which links ‏הֵמָה‎
with the verb ‏המה‎ 'make a din',
reads ‏רוי‎ 'drunk' instead of ‏דוי‎, and
interprets ‏לחמי‎ as 'my combat',
from ‏נלחם‎ (cf. Beer). In the 1st
Targ. ‏כדוי לחמי‎ is interpreted by
‏היך דוותא לסעודתי‎ *sicut menstruata
ad prandium meum*. 2nd Targ. paraphrases as 'they make me faint [and
it is enough] for my meal'. Vulg. combines the two hemistichs in a single
sentence: *quae prius nolebat tangere
anima mea, nunc prae angustia cibi
mei sunt*. G sees in the 2nd hemistich the explanation of the 1st:
βρόμον γὰρ ὁρῶ τὰ σῖτά μου ὥσπερ
ὀσμὴν λέοντος (Jerome *foetidas enim
video escas meas sicut est odor leonis*).
Merx would elicit from the text
‏כריח שחל‎ instead of ‏כדוי לחמי‎, but
Bochart had already noted that
ὥσπερ ὀσμὴν λέοντος is a gloss intended to dissipate the ambiguity
between βρόμον 'smell' and βρόμος
'shudder' (*Hieroz.*, I, col. 745).
    Exegetes are very divided as to the
meaning of this verse. The 1st hemistich 'my soul has refused to
touch it' continues the idea contained in v. 6. The soul is the organ
of taste and appetite, as in the
Arabic *mâ fî nafs* 'I have no appetite'; cf. 33: 20. It is in the 2nd
hemistich that the difficulty begins.
Duhm gets rid of it by changing
‏לחמי‎ into ‏חלמון‎, to obtain, thanks

8   Oh, that my prayer might be realised,
     That Eloah might concede what I hope for,

to other conjectures, המה כדו חלמון
'it is now the yolk of an egg',
which is supposed to be a gloss on
חלמות of v. 6 (!). In accordance
with the meaning of דְּוָי 'sickness',
one translates כדוי לחמי 'like the
sickness of my food' i.e. my invalid
food; or else, stressing the meaning
'impure' which derives from that of
sickness (root דוה), 'like corrupt
bread' (Dillmann); 'a food which
disgusts me' (Le Hir); 'my bread
covered with defilement' (Crampon); 'a nourishment that I cannot
endure' (Loisy); 'that is my food,
however disgusting it may be' (Segond), etc. Fried. Delitzsch postulates a word כדי, supposed to mean
'spices', 'condiments', but this is
pure hypothesis. Others see in כדוי
an equivalent of כדי in the sense of
'like', whence the paraphrase 'what
my soul touched only with disgust
has become my daily bread' (Renan). Torczyner replaces המה by
אזהמה and proposes for the 2nd
hemistich: 'I have a horror of my
bread as of something disgusting',
following Is 30: 22 which he also
corrects. Making a comparison with
33: 20, Wright very ingeniously
conjectures that המה is a remnant
of וְהָמָה (cf. G βρόμον γὰρ ὁρῶ), but
he changes כדוי into בדאבה, which
is quite inadmissible (41: 14). Budde
retains זהמה and gives it as complement דוי or בדוי (instead of כדוי);
he translates דוי לחמי by meiner
unreinen Speise (cf. sup.). The difficulty remains as long as one retains
דוי לחמי. For this reason, McNeile,
quoted by Gray, proposes to read
חכי 'my palate' as the subject of
זהמה. A comparison with 33: 20
proves that the first word is indeed
זהמה and the last לחמי, but that
כדוי conceals the synonym of חיתי
or נפשי 'my soul'. This word, parallel

to נפשי of the 1st hemistich, is none
other than כְּבֵדִי. As well as the
sense of 'glory', the word כָּבוֹד has
the sense of 'heart', 'soul' which is
connected with כָּבֵד 'liver', Assyrian
kabittu and kabattu. The liver is the
the seat of the activities of the soul
(L'Emploi métaphorique, pp. 129f.).
If the Hebrew כָּבֵד has not followed
the Assyrian kabittu in the sense of
'heart', 'inner principle', etc., the
reason is that כבוד was substituted
for it in this sense. The parallelism
between כבודי and נפשי (Gn 49: 6;
Ps 7: 6), or between לבי and כבודי
(Ps 16: 9) leaves no doubt about the
use of this word in our verse. Hence
we shall have: וְהָמָה כְּבֵדִי לַחְמִי 'my
heart has been sickened by my
bread'. On the verb זהם cf. 33: 20.
The word כבוד with the meaning of
'heart', 'soul', etc., is feminine (Gn
49: 6). After declaring that insipid
food excites no appetite, Job applies
the proverb to himself. He cannot
touch what is set before him. He
has a horror of his bread and his
daily food. The words are symbolic.
In reality it is sorrow which is hateful
to him and which he repels with
groaning.

8   For תקותי G has τὴν ἐλπίδα μου,
Aq. ὑπομονήν (given in the margin
of Syro-hex.), Targ. and Syr. סברי
'my hope', Vulg. quod expecto.
     The optative מִי־יִתֵּן 'who will
grant?' followed by the imperfect
exactly as in 13: 5 and 14: 13. In
19: 23 we have the waw before the imperfect. Verb בוא with abstract subject (cf. 3: 25, 26; 4: 5, etc.) in the
sense of 'come to pass' or 'be realised',
'be fulfilled' (Pr 13: 12). The word
תִּקְוָתִי 'my hope' is deliberately
chosen by Job in reply to Eliphaz

9   And that Eloah would consent to crush me,
     That He would free His hand and cut me off!

10   And some consolation will still remain for me,
     And I will rejoice, in spite of pitiless fear,
     Because I shall not have concealed the ordinances of the Holy
     One.

(4: 6; 5: 16). There is no need to replace it by תאותי 'my desire' (Hupfeld, Merx, Duhm, Driver, following Pr 10: 24). We find תקוה as the complement of the verb נתן in Jer 29: 11. What is implied in תקותי is the object of my hope, what I hope for; cf. Vulg. *quod expecto*. Similarly שְׁאֶלָתִי is the object of my prayer, what I implore. V. 9 will show us what Job implores and hopes for: death! Thus we rejoin the theme of ch. 3.

9 G ἀρξάμενος, Vulg. *et qui coepit*, Targ. ושרי have interpreted יאל in the sense of 'begin', but Syr. ﻮﻧﺛﺑﻌﻬﻮ 'and that He would devise' is nearer to the real meaning. Syr. connects ידכני with the Aramaic דכא (זכה), whence the interpretation 'that He would clear me'. G εἰς τέλος δὲ μή με ἀνελέτω is a paraphrase which puns on the meaning of 'free His hand', of the 2nd hemistich. We cannot see in this, as does Beer, the result of a reading לאחרית instead of יתר ידו. Aq. and Symm. ἐπιβαλὼν τὴν χεῖρα bring us back to MT. The translation given by Targ., 'God has begun to make me poor, may He free His hand and make me rich!', is based on a metaphorical interpretation of ידכאני 'He crushes me' and on a play of words between the verb יבצעני and the noun בצע 'gain'.

The object of Job's hope and prayer is 'that Eloah would consent to crush me!' The verb הואיל 'begin', 'decide', 'consent' with *waw* before the dependent verb (Jos 7: 7; Jg 19: 6). The two verbs in the same

mood may be simply juxtaposed (v. 28; 2 K 5: 23). The verb דכא in the *pi'el* denotes 'crush', as in 4: 19 where it is used in the literal sense. It is used figuratively in 5: 4. The *hiph'il* of נתר means 'detach', 'untie', 'free' (Is 58: 6), and especially 'free' (Ps 105: 20; 146: 7). With the complement יָדוֹ 'his hand', it implies releasing the hand and giving it all its liberty of action. In the light of Is 38: 12 the verb יְבַצְּעֵנִי means 'He cuts me out of' the woof, an image which conveys that one is cut off from existence. Job longs for death, but it must come from the hand of God. The idea of suicide does not occur to his mind.

10 Vulg. *et haec mihi sit consolatio* is in agreement with Targ. 'and may this be my consolation!' as regards the interpretation of the 1st hemistich. But Aq. and Theod. καὶ ἔσται ἔτι παράκλησίς μου follow more closely MT. G εἴη δέ μου (A, Sah., Jerome, μοι) πόλις τάφος comes probably from a reading עיר instead of עוד (Drusius). As a result of this first mistake, G reads חִילָה 'his wall' for חִילָה 'suffering' and אחמל instead of יחמל: ἐφ' ἧς ἐπὶ τειχέων ἡλλόμην ἐπ' αὐτῆς οὐ φείσομαι. Targ. interprets אסלדה by אבוע 'I will rejoice', Syr. by ﺍﺛﻬﺛﻣﻼ 'I will be filled'. Then Targ. sees in חילה לא יחמל the wrath which does not forgive the wicked. Syr. connects חילה with חַיִל 'force'. The 2nd hemistich is paraphrased in the Vulg. *ut affligens me dolore non parcat*. For אמרי קדוש G (B) has ῥήματα ἅγια θεοῦ μου

11   What is my strength that I should linger,
     And my future that I should prolong my life?

(Sah., Syro-hex.) but G (A) ἁγίου instead of ἅγια; cf. Jerome *verba sancti Dei mei.*

The key of this passage is supplied us by Ps 119: 50, 'This is my comfort in my affliction, that Thy promise gives me life.' The 2nd hemistich of the verse begins with כִּי, the function of which is to introduce the explanation of נֶחָמָתִי 'my consolation'. It is clear that our 3rd hemistich, beginning with כי, explains נחמתי. The function of the 2nd hemistich is merely to strengthen the 1st. It is not necessary to replace עוֹד by זאת (Targ., Vulg.), for the adverb 'still' i.e. 'in spite of all that is happening to me' (cf. Ps 42: 6, 12) gives more emphasis to the phrase 'and some consolation will still remain for me'. The *pi'el* סָלֵד is a *hapax*, which is too easily got rid of by reading אעלסה (Driver-Gray) or אעלזה 'I will be jubilant' (Graetz). In quite different contexts G ἡλλόμην 'I jumped' and Targ. אבוע 'I will exult' are at one in attributing the meaning of 'jump for joy' to סלד. It should also be noted that the root סלד is akin to the Indo-European root *sal*, whence the Latin *salire* and the Greek ἅλλομαι 'jump', 'leap'. In post-Biblical Hebrew the verb סלד denotes the action of one who jumps backwards to avoid fire or some other dangerous substance, whence the sense of 'retreat'. The combination of these facts encourages us to retain the *hapax* אֲסַלְּדָה and to accept for it the meaning attested by G and Targ. 'I will leap', 'I will exult'. The *hapax* חִילָה is a *nomen unitatis*; cf. נהרה and עננה in 3: 4-5. Same meaning as חִיל (derived from חוּל 'writhe'), which expresses the contorsions of a woman in childbirth, or the shudders

aroused by fear (Ex 15: 14; Ps 48: 7). By extension it comes to denote the cause of this trembling, namely terror. The locution לֹא יַחְמֹל 'it has no pity' (16: 13; 27: 22) becomes a kind of epithet, 'ruthless', which enables us to join it to the preceding noun without concern for the matter of agreement. The 3rd hemistich is jettisoned by Siegfried and Duhm. We have seen that Ps 119: 50 invites us to retain it. The *pi'el* of כחד means 'to hide' a thought, a teaching (15: 18; 27: 11). In 22: 22 and 23: 12 we shall have an allusion to the words of God's mouth. Here they are denoted by the phrase 'the words of the Holy One'. The word קדוש is the very special attribute of the thrice holy God (Is 6: 3). It is used as a noun to designate God (Is 40: 25; Hab 3: 3; Sir 45: 6-7). It is only in the plural that it conveys the idea of the angels (5: 1; 15: 15). The sense of the 3rd hemistich is therefore 'because I shall not have hidden the ordinances of the Holy One'. The meanings 'contradict' (Le Hir), 'violate' (Renan), 'transgress' (Segond, Crampon), which are attributed to כחד, are not confirmed by the other texts in which this verb occurs. The words of God are the decrees of His providence, the decisions which He takes in His dealings with man. Cf. the use of the verb אמר in 9: 7 (Arabic *'amara*: 'order'). Job knows these divine decisions (10: 13; 27: 11). It is impossible for him to conceal them. And it is in this way that he will not have hidden the ordinances of the Holy One.

11   For קצי G has μοῦ ὁ χρόνος, less literal than τὸ τέλος μου (Aq.), *finis meus* (Vulg.). The expression אאריך

12   My strength, is it the strength of stones,
      And my flesh, is it of bronze?
13   *Is not* my power to help myself as nothing,
      And has not every resource been removed far from me?

13   הֲלֹא מֵאַיִן (cf. G); MT: האם אין.

נַפְשִׁי is capable of a literal meaning 'I prolong my life' (cf. inf.), such as is adopted by Targ. and Syr., or on the other hand, of a figurative meaning, 'I am long-suffering and patient', which is adopted by Aq. ὅτι μακροθυμήσω and Vulg. *ut patienter agam*. G makes of נַפְשִׁי the subject of the verb: ὅτι ἀνέχεταί μου ἡ ψυχή.

The 1st hemistich, 'What is my strength that I should linger?' offers a very clear meaning: Have I the strength to wait any longer? Job is impatient to finish with the business of living. He no longer has the courage to go on living, that is, to await the end of the story which should fill his being with joy. The sense of קִצִּי 'my end', 'the term of my life' is the same as in Ps 39:5 where קֵץ is in parallelism with מִדַּת יָמַי 'the measure of my days', the span that it remains for me to live through. It is 'my future' which is conveyed by this expression. Generally critics interpret כי אאריך נפשי as 'for me to gather patience', following the meaning of הַאֲרִיך רוּח. But, in the context, Job wishes to express the fact that he no longer has any taste for life. Now, the original sense of הַאֲרִיך 'make long' is secured in the expression הַאֲרִיך יָמָיו 'prolong his days'. On the other hand, it is rather רוּח than נֶפֶשׁ which is used, when it is a question of expressing the idea: 'to be long-suffering, patient', literally 'to have great sustaining power' (cf. Comm. on 21:4; Ec 7:8, Sir 5:11). The end of the hemistich is therefore most naturally translated 'that I should prolong my life' (Ehrlich).

12   The energy of the thought is weakened by Targ. and Syr., which place 'like' before 'the strength of stones'. Vulg. substitutes for the question the negation which it implies. For נְחוֹשׁ G χαλκεῖαι, Vulg. *aenea*, Targ. כנחשא, Syr ܘܝܣ 'of bronze'.

V. 12 confirms the idea expressed in v. 11. Job feels no more the courage necessary to drag out a dying life. To endure the ills of life, he would need a power of endurance which he has not: 'My strength, is it the strength of stones?' The stone is the symbol of firmness and resistance (41:16). Calmet very aptly quotes Homer: ἐπεὶ οὔ σφι λίθος χρὼς οὐδὲ σίδηρος (*Iliad*, IV, 510). Here it is bronze which is in parallelism with stone: 'My flesh, is it of bronze?' Cf. 'the wall of bronze' as a symbol of solidity (Jer 1:19; 15:20), 'the heavens of brass' parallel to 'the earth of iron' in the description of drought in Dt 28:23. The word נָחוּשׁ does not recur elsewhere. It is the masculine form of נְחוּשָׁה 'bronze' which is always parallel to iron in the Book of Job (20:24; 28:2; 40:18; 41:19). The ordinary word נְחשֶׁת is never used in Job. Rosenmüller illustrates the comparison in the 2nd hemistich by citing Theocritus; σὰρξ σιδηρείη (*Idylls*, XXII, 47). The question which Job puts here is so much the more incisive because in 7:5 he dwells on his decomposing flesh. Interrogative particle אם (cf. 17:13).

13   G ἡ οὐκ ἐπ' αὐτῷ ἐπεποίθειν reads

14 [ ]

14 His friend has scorned (מאס instead of למס) compassion and forsaken the fear of Shaddai. Gloss (cf. Comm.).

הֲלֹא (cf. 8:10; 10:10, 20), which belongs to the original text (cf. inf.), but omits אין and reads בו instead of בי. Syr. 'Behold his help is not within me' reads עזרתו instead of עזרתי. Targ. סיועי בי and Vulg. *auxilium mihi in me* support the MT. Note that Syr. ﻫﺎ 'behold' and Vulg. *ecce* render האם exactly as does Onqelos in Nu 17:28, the only text in which האם recurs. For תשיה, G βοήθεια, Vulg. *necessarii mei*, Targ. חוכמתא 'wisdom', Syr. 'his salvation' (cf. עזרתו instead of עזרתי). G ἀπ' ἐμοῦ ἄπεστιν, which translates נדחה ממני, is rendered *a me recessit* in Jerome, whence the bad reading *amercescit* in Gall.

Exegetes generally give to הַאִם the same meaning as הֲלֹא: 'Am I not deprived of all help?' (Renan); 'Am I not without resources?' (Segond, etc.). Le Hir rightly protested against this interpretation, for האם recurs only in Nu 17:28, where the translation 'is it not' is very suspect. But must we, with Le Hir, separate the elements ה and אם in order to make the question bear on v. 14 and then see in v. 13 a conditional clause? But in that case, v. 14 is the object of fanciful renderings, as we can observe by comparing the text of Le Hir with the Hebrew in these vv. 13-14. 'Ought I, when all support within myself fails and every resource is taken away from me, ought I to find a friend who is without pity for my ruin, and disloyal to the fear of the Lord?' Duhm suggests, with much probability, that we should split up האם אין into הָא מְאַיִן 'behold, as a thing of nought', the Aramaic הָא (cf. Syr.) corresponding to הֵן or הִנֵּה (Gn

47:23; Ezk 16:43). We find in Is 41:24 the phrase הֵן אַתֶּם מֵאַיִן 'Behold, you are of nothing!', which is to say, 'Behold, you are nought!' (cf. Condamin). It may justifiably be objected that הָא does not belong to the style of the Book of Job. But G read הֲלֹא (cf. sup.). Now, the consonant ל at the beginning of v. 14 is a disturbing factor unfamiliar to G. If we replace it here, we have as the opening: הֲלֹא מֵאַיִן. 'Is not my power to help myself as nothing?' The help which I might seek within myself is reduced to a thing of nought. Cf. עֶזְרָתִי in 31:21. The 2nd hemistich of course depends likewise on הלא: 'And has not every resource been removed far from me?' Job no longer finds anything within him to sustain him. The change from בי to בו (Merx, following G) does not yield a meaning suitable to the context. The meaning of תּוּשִׁיָּה (cf. Comm. on 5:12) frees us from the need to replace the word by תְּשׁוּעָה (contra Beer, Ball, who follow G and Syr.).

14 G ἀπείπατό με ἔλεος, ἐπισκοπὴ δὲ Κυρίου ὑπερεῖδέν με reads מָאַס (cf. 10:3; 19:18) instead of למס (some MSS למאס; cf. Baer), omits מרעהו, and reads perhaps רעות (Beer) or ראית (from ראה Ball) instead of יראת. Vulg. combines the two hemistichs into a single sentence: *qui tollit ab amico suo misericordiam, timorem domini derelinquit.* Cf. Syr. 'he who refuses peace to his friend, forsakes the fear of the Most High', and Targ. 'as for the man who has refused mercy to his friend, he forsakes the fear of Shaddai'.

15   My brothers have been as treacherous as a torrent,
Like the bed of torrents which flow away:

This verse is a *crux interpretum*. We have seen how Le Hir tried to combine it with v. 13 (cf. Comm.). Generally, critics have connected מָס from לָמָס with מסס 'flow' (7: 5; 9: 23) in the sense of 'melt', 'become liquefied' and to מָס has been given the meaning of 'to be discouraged', as in the expression לֵב נָמֵס 'a heart which melts', 'a heart in despair' (Nah 2: 11). This is what explains the translations: 'The unhappy man has a right to the pity of his friends, even if he forsakes the fear of the Almighty' (Renan; cf. Segond, Crampon); 'He who is consumed with grief should receive the sympathy of his friends, even though he has renounced the fear of God' (*Bible du rabbinat français*). But the versions did not suspect the possibility of this rather too subtle interpretation. For after all the 2nd hemistich is clear: 'and he forsakes the fear of Shaddai'. What we expect is a member parallel to v. 14b and not an indeterminable subject of יעזב. Hence we shall hesitate to adopt the opinion of Beer and Hontheim who simply change למס into לְמָשׁ: 'As for him who refuses to pity his friend, he forsakes the fear of the Almighty.' No more successful is the substitution of מֹנֵעַ for למס (Merx, Graetz), only to end in the same unvarying sentence: 'He who refuses to pity his neighbour forsakes the fear of Shaddai.' Duhm changes מרעהו חסד into מָנַע הֶחָסָד, and thus arrives at an interpretation which is very like the previous ones: 'He who refuses pity to the dismayed forsakes the fear of Shaddai.' Jewish exegesis has sometimes endeavoured to make of לָמָס a single word. The Talmud thought to find in it the Greek word λιμός (Levy,

Neuhebr. und chald. Wörterbuch, I, p. 513 B), giving to λιμός the meaning of 'hungry dog'. Some critics have connected למס with the Arabic *lamasa* which means 'to touch' but also, in the derivative forms, 'solicit', 'seek', 'crave', 'beg' (cf. Mandelkern, *Concordantiae*, s.v. מָס and Ben-Yehuda, *Thesaurus*, V, p. 2700). We then obtain: 'He craved pity of his companion, and he forsakes the fear of Shaddai', or else: 'He who craves pity of his companion forsakes the fear of Shaddai.' But it should be noted that חֶסֶד 'pity', 'mercy' is a parallel term to יראת שדי 'fear of Shaddai'. Cf. Hos 6: 6, where חסד corresponds to דעת אלהים 'knowledge of Elohim'. In the Psalms, we find that חסד 'mercy' is constantly used as the name of a virtue, just like the fear of God, truth, justice, etc. (Ps 18: 51; 25: 10; 32: 10, etc.). In the 1st hemistich there is a parallel verb to יעזב, and it is מָאַס which both explains the ancient versions and also the writing למאס attested by certain manuscripts (cf. sup.). G had not the ל before מאס, and in fact this consonant comes from v. 13, where we should read הלא instead of הא at the beginning (cf. Comm.). The subject of מאס 'he has despised' (5: 17) is מֵרֵעֵהוּ 'his companion' (Gn 26: 26; 2 S 3: 8). Hence we shall translate: 'His friend has scorned compassion and has forsaken the fear of Shaddai.' This comment was not included in the original text. It was inscribed in the margin in order to explain what is to follow, namely the attitude of Job's friends. V. 15 forms a sequence to v. 13.

15   For אחי בגדו, G οὐ προσεῖδόν με οἱ ἐγγύτατοί μου. The translation of

16   They were covered with ice,
      The snow was piled up above them;

אחי by ἀδελφοί μου is noted in Colb.
and Codd. 161, 248, 250. Sah. omits
οὐ . . . μου, which compels it to add
'I have become'. For בגדו Vulg.
praeterierunt me (cf. G), Targ. בוזי
'have plundered', Syr. ܘ ? 'have
lied'. G renders נחל by χειμάρρους
ἐκλείπον. For כאפיק נחלים, G ἢ ὥσπερ
κῦμα (A, Sah. κύματα), explained
as 'the foam of the sea' in the
margin of Syro-hex. (cf. 2 S 22: 16).
Syr. has simply ܐܠ ܘ̈ ܘܣ 'and
like brooks'. The translations of G
and Syr. are approximations which
do not justify us in replacing כאפיק
נחלים by כאפיקים (contra Beer, in
Kittel). For יעברו, G παρῆλθόν με (cf.
the personal pronouns added in v.
14). Vulg. *in convallibus* reads באפיק
instead of כאפיק.

Job finds now no support within
himself. He might turn to his kinsmen and friends. Alas! 'My brothers
have been as treacherous as a torrent, like the bed of torrents which
flow away!' The brothers include
all his kinsmen and intimate friends
(19: 13). The נַחַל 'torrent' is distinguished from the נָהָר 'river' by
reason of the intermittent flow of
its waters. Thus the torrent of
Egypt (נחל מצרים) which the Assyrians call *naḥal Muṣur* is described
as a 'place which has no river' (*Les
Pays bibliques*, p. 100, n. 6). The
brook whose waters fail is called
אכְזָב 'deceitful' (Jer 15: 18; Mic
1: 14), i.e. a brook whose 'waters
are not faithful'. 'Faithful' waters
are mentioned in Is 33: 16. The
comparison is made more luminous
in the 2nd hemistich: 'as the bed of
torrents which flow away'. The relative אשר is understood before
יעברו (3: 3). What is there more
disconcerting than to find a torrent
whose bed is dry when you expected

to find gushing water! The word
אָפִיק, which must not be confused
with its homonym of 12: 21, denotes strictly speaking the bed of a
river (Is 8: 7), then by derivation a
tube (cf. Job 40: 18), a tier or row
(cf. 41: 7).

16 The versions have failed to
understand that הקדרים referred
to נחלים of v. 15. G paraphrases the
whole verse, combining קרח and
שלג: οἵτινές με διευλαβοῦντο (A. εὐλα-
βοῦντο) νῦν ἐπιπεπτώκασίν μοι ὥσπερ
χιὼν ἢ κρύσταλλος πεπηγώς (Jerome
*qui me metuebant nunc irruerunt
super me sicut nix aut glacies con-
stricta*; cf. Syro-hex., Sah., Eth.).
Syr. 'those who are afraid' and Vulg.
qui timent are in agreement with G
in assigning to קדר the meaning of
'fear', whilst Targ. דשחימין 'which
are darkened' is faithful to the traditional sense. For יתעלם, the versions seem to have been inspired by
the Aramaic sense of עלם 'to be
strong' whence Targ. יתחייל 'is forti-
fied', Syr. 'is abundant', Vulg. *irruet*;
cf. G ἐπιπεκτώκασίν μοι (Jerome
irruerunt super me).

Targ., Syr., and Vulg. have understood this verse as a kind of proverb: *qui timent pruinam irruet
super eos nix* (Vulg.). But in that
case it is difficult to fit it into the
context. The older commentators
had already realised that הַקֹּדְרִים is
an epithet applying to נחלים and
that v. 16 continues the description
begun in v. 15. V. 17 describes the
melting of the snows and uses this
as a symbol of the small degree of
confidence that can be placed in
the brethren who resemble these torrents (v. 15). V. 16 should suggest
the reasons for having confidence.
קדר is generally translated 'to be
black, muddy': 'its waters are

17 As soon as the snows melt, they are dried up,
As soon as it is hot, they leave the bed dry.

blackened by the ice' (Le Hir); 'which rolls along muddied by the ice-floes' (Renan). But it is not the property of ice to dirty or muddy water. The real meaning of the expression הקדרים is given by Avronin and Rabinowitz, who see in this participle an equivalent of הַמְכֻסִּים 'those which are covered'. Just as כסה 'to cover' has sometimes the meaning of 'darken', so קדר 'to be dark, black' (5 : 11; 30 : 28) will also mean 'to be covered'. It should be observed that ice and snow constitute the reservoirs which feed torrents, unlike rivers and their tributaries which have sources; cf. 'the reservoirs of snow' (38 : 22), whence flow 'snow waters' (9 : 30). The 2nd hemistich will express an idea parallel with 'they were covered with ice'. We cannot translate יִתְעַלָּם by 'was hidden', for in that case the complement would be preceded by מִן, whereas we have עָלֵימוֹ. The versions have not hesitated to connect יתעלם with the Aramaic עלם 'to be strong', though they reveal differences in translation. An excellent suggestion of Torczyner is that we should see in יתעלם an equivalent of יתערם 'pile up' (cf. Ex 15 : 8). There is no need to correct the text, for the form יתעלם, chosen on account of the alliteration with עלימו, may well have coexisted with יתערם (cf. v. 25). The meaning thus obtained is excellent: 'the snow was piled up above them'. The interpretation of Yellin (*Journ. of the Palestine Oriental Society*, **1**, p. 11), who would connect יתעלם with עולם, to give it the sense of 'to be eternal', seems to us much less plausible. It is on mountain peaks and not on torrents that the snows may be described as eternal. And it is precisely the ephemeral character of the snow and ice,

of which the poet is here speaking, that will receive emphasis in v. 17.

17 G καθὼς τακεῖσα θέρμης γενομένης (Jerome *cum tabuerit in calore*) connects בחמו with the 1st hemistich and omits נצמתו. In Syr. we find 'at the time when the sun rises', as a result of reading יזרח for יזרבו. Targ. sees here an allusion to the Flood, whence its interpretation of בחמו by ברתחיה 'in his anger'. Vulg. translates יזרבו by *fuerint dissipati*. Walton's *Polyglot* renders by *dissipati sunt* the verb of Targ. אשתרבבו, which in fact means *creverunt* (Rosenmüller). G οὐκ ἐπεγνώσθη ὅπερ ἦν reads perhaps נודע for נדעכו. Instead of ὅπερ, we have ὅπου in Colb. (as a variant), Sah., Syrohex.

We must be careful not to suppress the *hapax* יֹזֹרֹבֹוֹ, as is done by Beer (בעת שרב 'in the time of the scorching wind') and Torczyner (בעת חרב 'in the time of drought'). The personal verb יזרבו plays the part of a genitive (2 Ch 20 : 22). Those who interpret זרב in the light of the Syriac, where the root has the meaning *coarctari* (cf. the Assyrian *zarâbu* 'press', 'urge') have recourse to a strange paraphrase: *tempore quo coarctati decrescunt* (Rosenmüller), or again 'hardly does it decrease' (Le Hir). A more widespread opinion is that which sees in זרב a secondary form of צרב (cf. זעק and צעק, etc.), the *niph'al* of which means 'to be burnt' (Ezk 21 : 3). In that case we find in the expression בעת יזרבו 'in the time when they are burnt' an allusion to the intense heats of summer: 'the time of drought' (Renan, Crampon); 'when the great heat comes' (Segond). But this idea is expressed rather by the formula בְּחֻמּוֹ 'when it is hot'. Budde protests against this

18   Caravans *deviate* from their route,
     They go forward in the trackless waste and get lost;
19   The caravans of Tema look out,
     The convoys of Sheba hope in them;

18 יְלָפְתוּ (Targ.); MT: יְלָפֵּתוּ.

translation of בחמו in which he sees a Germanism. It suffices to note that the suffix is a substitute for the word יום understood, and that the terse phrase 'in its heat' corresponds to בְּחֹם הַיּוֹם 'when the day is hot' (Gn 18:1; 1 S 11:11, etc.). The immediate effect of the heat is to melt the ice and the snow. Now, Qimchi had already connected יזרבו with the Arabic *mizrâb* 'canal', 'gutter', and R Samuel Ben-Nissim recognised the root זרב in the post-Biblical Hebrew מַרְזֵב (metathesis) 'gutter', 'drain', etc. (cf. 3rd Targ. in 38:25). The meaning of זרב thus becomes 'flow', in the *pi'el* 'cause to flow' and in the *pu'al* 'to have been made flowing', i.e. 'melt'. The subject is קרח 'the ice' and שלג 'the snow', two masculine nouns mentioned in v. 16. The verb צמת is used in the *niph'al* in the sense of being 'consumed', 'destroyed'. When it is a question of waters, 'dry up'. The parallel word נִדְעָכוּ means literally 'become extinguished', 'vanish' (cf. 18:5-6; 21:17), and by extension 'wither away' (Sir 40:16); cf. the Latin *extinguere aquam*.

18 G οὕτως κἀγὼ κατελείφθην ὑπὸ πάντων interprets the 1st hemistich metaphorically, as though the friends turned aside from the road where Job was to be found. Then ἀπωλόμην δὲ καὶ ἔξοικος ἐγενόμην seems to read מביתי instead of בתהו and אבד instead of יאבדו. Vulg. *involutae sunt semitae gressuum eorum* makes of דרכם the complement of ארחות. Similarly Syr. 'the paths of their routes' and Targ. אסרטי אורחיהון

'the lanes of their routes'. For יְלָפְתוּ Targ. מקלקלין 'destructive' reads יְלַפְּתוּ (cf. inf.).

This verse is an integral part of the description. There is no reason to cut it out, unless it be to submit to the strophic system of Bickell. We are surprised to find in Hitzig and Budde the recurrence of the old interpretation which assigns as the subject of ילפתו and יעלו the torrents of v. 17. Cappel had already noted that ארחות indicates 'caravans' as in v. 19 and Gn 37:25 (cf. Is 21:13). The sense naturally gives rise to a masculine suffix, for the men who compose the caravan are the real subject of ילפתו. With Targ. we read יְלָפְתוּ, which enables us to translate the first hemistich as: 'Caravans deviate from their route.' The caravans are looking for a spring of water and turn aside from the direct route. Unfortunately they are the victims of a mirage. The torrent on which they counted turns out to be dry. That is why 'they go forward in the trackless waste and get lost'. The word תהו 'empty' (26:7) denotes especially the pathless desert (12:24). The verb אבד retains its original sense 'wander', 'get lost', from which is derived that of *perire* 'perish' (3:3, etc.).

19 G θαιμανῶν and Syr. ܬܝܡܢܐ confuse תמא with תימן. For שבא Targ. has זמרגד 'emerald' (cf. 1:15). G ἴδετε and Vulg. *considerate* make of הביטו an imperative. For קוו־למו G has οἱ διορῶντες, but Syro-hex.

20   They are ashamed to have been so confident,
      When they arrive, they are confounded.
21   *Thus* have you been on this occasion for *me*:
      You are overcome by terror and are afraid!

21   כֵּן; MT: כִי. — לִי (G, Syr.); MT: לוֹ or לֹא.

adds αὐτοῖς (Theod. and Symm.) in the margin. G (A) αἰσχύνθηται, at the end, comes from בש of v. 20. Faithful to its translation of הביטו by an imperative, Vulg. renders קוו־למו by *expectate paulisper*.

On the town of Tema, here written תֵּמָא instead of תֵּימָא, and on שְׁבָא (1: 15), cf. Intro., p. xxiii. The verb הביט 'to look' with the shade of meaning 'look from afar', 'watch', 'spy' (36: 25; 39: 29). The pointing of אָרְחוֹת is exactly the same as in v. 18. We have אָרְחוֹת in the construct state in Is 21: 13, where it is a question of 'the caravans of the people of Dedan'. In Ps 68: 25 the plural הֲלִיכוֹת means 'processions', but here 'convoys'. The construction of קוה with לְ'' in 3: 9 justifies us in seeing in לָמוֹ not simply a reflexive dative like the Latin *sibi* (Ewald, Hitzig, etc.), but indeed the complement representing the נחלים of v. 15.

20   For בשו, G αἰσχύνην ὀφειλήσουσιν. The word *intuemini* which renders διορῶντες in v. 19 in Jerome has been linked with v. 20: *intuemini quia confusionem consequentur*. In accordance with the sense, בטח is considered as a plural in G, Syr., and Targ. (which adds 'in their idols'). But Vulg. *quia speravi* favours the singular. For עדיה Targ. לגבה 'up to then' corresponds to MT, whilst the Vulg. *usque ad me* reads עדי. G οἱ ἐπὶ πόλεσιν καὶ χρήμασιν πεποιθότες interprets ויחפרו in the light of 3: 20-1 and confuses עדיה with עריה (from עיר; cf. v. 10).

The verb בוש 'to be ashamed' is strengthened by חפר 'to be confounded' in Ps 35: 26; 40: 15. The proposition בשו is continued by וַיֶּחְפָּרוּ, whilst בָּאוּ עָדֶיהָ is parallel to כִּי־בָטַח and implies the conjunction כִי. The singular בטח in spite of the plural subject, because no ambiguity is possible. The agreement is made with the word 'each one' or 'one' (Gesenius-Kautzsch, § 145u). It is unnecessary to add בָּהּ (Duhm) after בטח. The feeling of shame is caused by the deception. In Ps 22: 6, בך בטחו ולא בושו, 'They trusted in Thee and they have not been confounded.' The feminine suffix of עָדֶיהָ is used to represent the plural נחלים regarded as a collective (39: 15). Conversely we have בהם to mean 'by that means' in 22: 21. On these exchanges of pronominal suffixes, cf. Gesenius-Kautzsch § 135p.

21   The word לוֹ, a Western reading, is considered as *qerê* (with לֹא as *kethîb*) by the Orientals. Targ. 'you have been as though you were not' has read לֹא. The paraphrase of G καὶ ὑμεῖς ἐπέβητέ μοι ἀνελεημόνως and that of Syr. 'and you too have been against me' have read לִי instead of לוֹ. Vulg. *nunc venistis* does not translate the לוֹ or לֹא. For חתת Targ. תברא 'the ruin', Syr. ܣܟ 'the disturbance'. G τὸ ἐμὸν τραῦμα and Vulg. *plagam meam* add the suffix.

Exegetes hesitate between לוֹ and לֹא. Those who read לוֹ understand 'you are like' as implicit, and regard

22   Have I said: 'Give me something!
      And from your fortune make gifts in my favour!

the suffix as representing 'the river', נחל, of v. 15. Rosenmüller protests with reason against this interpretation which is forced to add the essential word. He decides in favour of the reading לא and translates: *et vos in nihilum abitis*. The negative לא is then considered as a substantive, as in the case of the Greek τὸ μηδέν. Thus are explained various modern translations: 'Thus have you failed me' (Renan); 'thus you fail me at this hour' (Le Hir, Crampon). Segond returns to the interpretation of Targ.: 'Thus you are as though you were not.' But we know from 10: 19 that this translation presupposes quite a different formula. Böttcher and Dillmann propose לאין instead of לא: 'you have become as nothing'. There then remains the difficulty of כִּי־עַתָּה 'now that' or 'because now', which is with difficulty joined to the context. Houbigant very justly remarked that G and Syr. read לִי. He then proposed the slight correction of כי to כֵּן. Thus we obtain for the 1st hemistich an excellent meaning: 'Thus have you been for me on this occasion!' You are like the deceiving torrents. I had hoped to be able to find in you my consolation and I have been confounded. The hypothesis of Houbigant has met with the approbation of most commentators (cf. Ewald, Olshausen, Budde, Driver, Torczyner). It will be preferred to that of Ehrlich, which makes the 1st hemistich clumsy by the addition of לאכזב after לִי (for לוֹ). Notice the alliteration of תִּרְאוּ...תִּירָאוּ, the first verb coming from ראה, the second from ירא (cf. Zec 9: 5; Ps 40: 4). The word חֲתַת is a *hapax*. We find elsewhere חַת 'terror' (41:

25), חִתַּת construct state of חִתָּה (Gn 35: 5), חִתִּית (Ezk 26: 17; 32: 23ff.). The Assyrian is *ḫattu* 'terror'. The expression 'to see fright' is similar to 'to see hunger, misery', etc., to mean 'to be a victim of hunger, misery' (cf. Gesenius-Buhl, s.v. ראה 3, b).

22   Syr. adds 'to you' after אמרתי 'I have said'. G suppresses the direct speech and paraphrases: τί γάρ; μή τι ὑμᾶς ᾔτησα ἢ τῆς παρ' ὑμῶν ἰσχύος ἐπιδέομαι. It is evident that G attributes to כֹּח the normal meaning of 'force', but Targ. and Syr. render מכחכם by מן נכסיכון 'of your wealth', Vulg. *de substantia vestra*.

The meaning of הֲכִי is literally 'Is it because?' (Gn 27: 36; 29: 15; 2 S 9: 1). Here, it simply indicates the direct question. The imperative הָבוּ 'give' (from יהב) without a direct object, as in the הַב הַב 'give, give' of Pr 30: 15. Like its synonym חַיִל the word כֹּח 'force' is used in the sense of 'riches', 'fortune' (cf. Targ., Syr., Vulg.); Pr 5: 10. For the Semites it is riches which confer strength, prestige, honour (cf. 1: 3). The verb שׁחד 'give a שֹׁחַד' (15: 34), i.e. make gifts (mainly in order to corrupt an official) recurs in Ezk 16: 33 and Sir 35: 14. The pointing שַׁחֲדוּ retains the *ḥireq* instead of changing it to *pataḥ* on account of the strong guttural ח (Gesenius-Kautzsch, § 64a). At the end, בַּעֲדִי 'for me', 'in my favour'; cf. בעד in 2: 4 and בעדכם in 42: 8. Elsewhere בעד means 'behind' (1: 10; 3: 23; 9: 7).

23   And deliver me from the hand of an enemy,
     And from the hand of tyrants ransom me?'
24   Instruct me and I for my part will be silent;
     In what way I have erred, explain to me;
25   How sweet are honest words!
     But of what value is a criticism coming from you?

23 G continues to avoid direct speech: ὥστε σῶσαι κ.τ.λ. For מִיַּד צָר, G ἐξ ἐχθρῶν (Syro-hex., Jerome *ab inimicis*), Sah. 'from my enemies'. G (A) ἐκ χειρὸς κακῶν, Syr. 'from the hands of my enemies'. For עָרִיצִים, G δυναστῶν, (Sah., Syro-hex.), G (A) δυνάστου (Jerome *potentis*).

The poet here gives us the reasons for which Job might have urged his friends to make gifts: 'Deliver me from the hand of an enemy, and from the hand of tyrants ransom me!' The *pi'el* of מלט means 'deliver' some one who is oppressed by a stronger than himself (29: 12). In parallelism, פדה means 'ransom', 'free' (5: 20; 33: 28). Co-ordination of the imperfect with an imperative is the same as our use of a future to express a command (Gesenius-Kautzsch, § 107n). The עָרִיצִים from עָרַץ 'terrify' (13: 25) and 'to be terrified by' (31: 34) are the dreaded people who inspire fear, the tyrants (15: 20; 27: 13). The parallel word is רְשָׁעִים 'the wicked' (ibid.). Cf. Jer 15: 21 where we find almost verbally repeated the same idea as is expressed in our verse: 'and I will deliver you out of the hand of the wicked and redeem you from the grasp of the ruthless.' This furnishes a good example of variation in the expression of the same thought: verb הִצִּיל (from נצל) instead of מלט; noun רָעִים 'the evil', 'the wicked' instead of צָר; מִכַּף instead of the second מִיַּד.

24 For the 2nd hemistich G εἴ τι πεπλάνημαι φράσατέ μοι, Vulg. *et si quid forte ignoravi instruite me*.

'Instruct me and I for my part will be silent'; the *hiph'il* הוֹרָה 'teach', 'instruct' with a suffix as complement (8: 10; 12: 7,8; 27: 11), in the imperative singular הֹרֻנִי 'instruct me' (34: 32). Job is on the point of capitulation. Elsewhere it is he who begs his friends to be silent (13: 5, 13). Elihu will exclaim: 'Be silent and allow me to speak; . . . be silent and I will teach you wisdom' (33: 31, 33). As Albertus Magnus remarks, *sapientis est semper velle instrui*. In the 2nd hemistich the verb שָׁגָה has not merely the sense of 'exaggerating in words' (Duhm), but also that of 'wandering', 'getting lost', 'being mistaken' in whatever way (19: 4, and cf. *hiph'il* in 12: 16). The verb הֵבִין 'to make to understand, discern' with לְ before the complement of the person to connote 'explain' to some one (Dn 8: 16).

25 G paraphrases: ἀλλ' ὡς ἔοικεν φαῦλα ἀληθινοῦ ῥήματα. G (A) ἀνδρὸς ἀληθινοῦ (Jerome *veri hominis*). The word φαῦλα is translated *prava* in Jerome, but by corruption has become *parva* in Bod. and Aug. (who insists on *parva* in the commentary). For מַה־נִּמְרְצוּ, Targ מָה בְסִימִין 'how sweet!', Aq. τί ἐμοχθηρώθησαν 'in what way would be painful?', Syr. 'why do you repel'; cf. Vulg. *quare detraxistis?* Instead of יֹשֶׁר, G (ἀνδρὸς) ἀληθινοῦ, Aq. εὐθοῦς, Targ. תְּרִיצִין 'of the upright' have pointed יָשָׁר. G reads הכח instead of הוֹכֵחַ, which compels the following paraphrase of the 2nd hemistich: οὐ γὰρ

26   Do you aim at criticising mere words?
     But the speech of a despairing man is lost in the wind!

παρ' ὑμῶν ἰσχὺν αἰτοῦμαι (A adds
ῥῆμα οὐδὲ before ἰσχύν). Targ., Syr.,
and Vulg. *cum e vobis nullus sit* have
read מי instead of the second מה.
Syr. regards הוכח as a verb used in
the personal mode and links it by
the copula to יוכיח.

Exegetes are no less divided than
the versions on the meaning of the
1st hemistich. The verb נִמְרְצוּ is
sometimes connected with מרץ 'to
be ill' (Arabic مرض, Aramaic מרע),
with the consequence that the
meanings 'are distressing' (Hitzig)
or 'are irritated' (Dillmann) are
somehow wrested from the text;
sometimes it is connected with מרץ
'to be hard or strong' (in the light of
Mic 2:10; 1 K 2:8), whence the
meaning 'are strong' (Le Hir, Crampon), 'are efficacious' (Budde), 'are
persuasive' (Segond), etc. It should
be pointed out that the meaning attested for מרץ is 'to be ill', whence
the *hiph'il* yields the sense 'to make
ill', 'to torment' (16:3). The *niph'al*
participle is used in Mic 2:10 to
qualify חֶבֶל 'torment' (van Hoonacker) and 1 K 2:8 to qualify קללה
'malediction'. Now, it is well known
that the *niph'al* of an intransitive
verb is sometimes used with the
meaning of the *qal*: the *niph'al* of
חלה means 'to be languid, ill' exactly like the *qal*. And this very root
חלה, synonymous with מרץ, has
the sense of 'to be painful' in both
the *qal* and *niph'al*, when it is
applied to an abstract term: רעה
חולה 'grievous evil' (Ec 5:13, 16;
cf. Podechard). Hence we find חבל
נמרץ (Mic 2:10) translated as 'a
painful torment', and קללה נמרצת
(1 K 2:8) as 'a painful curse'. But
here it is not the verb מרץ which is
used. We have in Ps 119:103 the
exclamation מה־נמלצו לחכי אמרתיך
'How sweet are Thy words to my

taste!', the affinity of which with
our 1st hemistich can escape no
one's attention. Without its being
necessary to change נמרצו into
נמלצו (Graetz and Duhm), we note
that the root מלץ has become מרץ,
just as we had יתעלם for יתערם
(v. 16). Let us note further that the
choice of יתעלם was occasioned by
עלימו (v. 16); here the poet chooses
נמרצו because of the אמרי which
follows. The 1st hemistich is perfectly intelligible: 'How sweet are
honest words!' This is the meaning
which has been adopted by Targ.,
Rashi, Schultens, and a certain
number of modern exegetes. The
2nd hemistich introduces the corrective: 'but of what value is a criticism coming from you?' The infinitive becomes the subject of the
same verb used personally and is
thus the equivalent of a real noun
(cf. Gesenius-Kautzsch, § 113b). On
the meaning of הוכיח, cf. 5:17.

26   G οὐδὲ ὁ ἔλεγχος ὑμῶν ῥήμασίν με
(A τὰ ῥήματά μου) παύσει replaces
הלהוכח by אל הוכח and תחשבו by
תחשׁו (from חשה). Note that Jerome
*neque increpatio vestra silentium mihi
imponit* paraphrases ῥήμασίν με παύσει. Vulg. omits the interrogative:
*ad increpandum tantum eloquia con-
cinnatis.* In the 2nd hemistich, G
οὐδὲ γὰρ ὑμῶν φθέγμα ἀνέξομαι and
Vulg. *et in ventum verba profertis*
seem to confuse נואש with the verb
נשא 'carry'. Syr. 'and you meditate
against the spirit of my word'
points אמרי and interprets נואש
according to the meaning of תחשבו.
Targ. understands תחשבו as implicit, and renders רוח by קבלא
'darkness': 'and you liken to darkness the words of despair'.

The 1st hemistich is the natural
sequence of v. 25b: 'Do you aim at
criticising mere words?' Job has

27   Even over an orphan do you cast lots,
      And you treat your friend as a subject for speculation.

been wondering at what the reproaches of his friends, represented
by Eliphaz, were aimed. The sole
object of their reproach consists in
the words uttered by a despairing
man! The *niph'al* participle נוֹאָשׁ
'despairing' is sometimes placed in
the mouth of one who declares that
a case is desperate, that there is
nothing more to be done (Is 57: 10;
Jer 2: 25; 18: 12). The verb יָאַשׁ
recurs only in 1 S 27: 1 (*niph'al*)
and Ec 2: 20. The 2nd hemistich is
the antithesis of the 1st, exactly
as in v. 25. The natural sense is
certainly: 'But the speech of a despairing man is lost in the wind!'
Cf. the French expression *autant en
emporte le vent* 'it is all idle talk'.
The words of Job must be considered
as a light feathery thing which is
the sport of the winds; cf. the use
of רוח in 21: 18 and Ps 1: 4, לרוח
in Ezk 5: 2. Much less natural is
the interpretation which makes לרוח
dependent on תחשבו (Fried. Delitzsch, Ehrlich; cf. Targ.): 'Do you
consider as idle the words of a despairing man?' The parallelism with
מְלִים 'words' shows clearly that Job
is anxious to stress the futility of his
words. It is entirely arbitrary to
change לרוח into לדוח 'to pro-
scribe' (Hoffmann, who hesitates
between the roots of נדה, דחה, הדיח),
or to substitute להדיח for לדיח
(Beer), or finally to substitute לריב
'debate', 'discuss' (McNeile). There
is nothing to suggest that we should
see in לרוח a parallel word to להוכח.
The *waw* introduces an antithesis as
in v. 25.

27   For תפלו, G ἐπιπίπτετε, Vulg.
irruitis, as though we had the *qal*.
In Targ. the word אף is interpreted
in the sense of 'anger', which results
in 'you show anger to an orphan'.
Syr. 'you magnify yourselves' is a

paraphrase of תפילו. G ἐνάλλεσθε
seems to connect תכרו with כרר
'dance', 'jump', while Vulg. *sub-
vertere nitimini* has recourse to כרה
'dig a ditch', 'lay a trap', and Syr.
'you make sad' sees here the *hiph'il*
of כרא 'suffer', 'be sad' (Aramaic).
Targ. תחשלון 'you plan (against)'
perhaps takes כרה in the sense of
'speculate' (cf. inf.).
    The 1st hemistich has been the ob-
ject of many differing interpretations. The verb תַּפִּילוּ has no complement, and the word פנים 'the
face' has been added (Umbreit), or
a word meaning 'net' (Rosenmüller).
The first hypothesis would yield
the meaning 'even on an orphan you
lower (your countenance)', i.e. you
show an angry countenance. The
second results in the translations of
Le Hir and Crampon: 'Ah! you
spread the net to catch an orphan!'
But we have a good example of
הִפִּיל with the complement הַגּוֹרָל
'lots' in 1 S 14: 42. The presence of
the preposition עַל before the object
of the casting of lots confirms the
interpretation; cf. Ps 22: 19; Neh
10: 35. When a person is in question,
the lot falls on him to disclose that
he is guilty (Jon 1: 7). The true
meaning is then: even over an
orphan do you cast lots. The orphan
is the type of the weak and defenceless (22: 9; 24: 3; 29: 12; 31: 17,
21). The friends should have pity
on such a one. They amuse themselves by bringing to light his guilt
as in a game of dice. To replace
עֲלֵי תָם by עַל יתום 'on a blameless,
innocent one' (Bickell, Duhm, Beer)
is to forget that Job is not arguing
on the basis of his innocence (v. 26),
but is excusing his language by
pleading the extremity of his suffering. Such a reading was unknown
to the versions. The same authors

28　But now be so good as to turn towards me,
　　And I will not lie to your face!

29　Return then! there is no falsehood here!
　　Return! my righteousness is still intact!

29　וְשֻׁבוּ (cf. Comm.); *kethîb*: ושבי.

then correct תפילו to תָּפֹּלוּ in the light of G and Vulg. But these versions were puzzled by the *hiph'il* without complement and gratuitously understood *qal*. In order to save the parallelism, Duhm sees himself obliged to change תִּכְרוּ into תָּגֹרוּ 'you throw yourselves on', following G, which however is equally explicable by the תכרו of MT (cf. sup.). The verb כרה recurs in 40: 30 with על before its complement, to signify 'speculate' on a certain object (cf. Comm.). Job's friends look as if they are treating him as a commodity whose value either appreciates or depreciates. Not only have they marked him out by the drawing of lots, but they are ready to deliver him up to the highest bidder. The terseness of the verse does not prevent us from grasping the logical link which binds the two hemistichs: neither Job's state of inferiority nor the friendliness which his companions ought to feel with regard to him prevent them from treating him as an object of commercial dealings. It is needless to point תָּכֹרוּ 'you hasten, rush forward' (Beer, following G), or to connect the verb with כרה 'to feast' (Mercier). Rosenmüller and others have recourse to כרה 'dig (snares)' (cf. Vulg.). But in that case it is no longer possible to understand the preposition על before רֵיעֲכֶם. The best course is then to adhere to MT, which offers us a satisfactory meaning. We should note the form ריעכם in which the *yod* is *mater lectionis*; cf. שליו in 21: 23.

28　G reduces the 1st hemistich to νυνὶ δὲ εἰσβλέψας (Α ἐμβλέψας); so Sah., Eth., Syro-hex., Arab. Baud. A reading of Theod. σχολάσατέ μοι for פנו־בי is given (with asterisk) in the margin of Syro-hex., with the annotation: 'is not found in the Octapla of Origen' (cf. 5: 23). Now, this reading figures (with asterisk) in Jerome *vacate mihi*. The complement בי is omitted by Syr., which adds: 'I will speak' after פניכם. Targ. interprets האילו by שרו, which means: 'begin' and 'be so good as to'. Vulg. decides on the meaning 'begin', whence its 1st hemistich: *verumtamen quod coepistis implete*. The 2nd hemistich is paraphrased by Vulg. *praebete aurem et videte an mentiar*.

The opening ועתה is in the style of Job (30: 1, 9, 16). There is asyndeton of הֹאִילוּ and פְּנוּ; cf. v. 9. The verb פנה 'to turn towards' with ״ב before the complement (2 K 2: 11) to convey the meaning of a turning of the eyes towards some one so as to look at him. In 21: 5 we shall have פנו־אלי in the same sense. The expression על־פניכם is chosen because of the relation between the verb פנה and the word פנים 'face'. Cf. על־פניך in 1: 11 and אל־פניך in 2: 5. Use of the conjunction אִם to mark the negation as in the formulae of oaths (Ps 89: 36, etc.). We had אם־לא in 1: 11. Job draws attention to the sincerity of the speech which is to follow. The *pi'el* of כזב as in 34: 6.

29　G καθίσατε connects שבו with the root ישב. After the 1st hemistich

30 Is there any falsehood on my tongue?
Cannot my palate discern evil things?

G(A) adds ἐν κρίσει, which is found too in Syro-hex. preceded by the obelus. Aq. μὴ γίνησθε and Syr. 'do not be as the wicked' read תהיו instead of תהי. Targ. translates עולה by רשיעא 'the wicked man' (cf. Syr.). G καὶ πάλιν τῷ δικαίῳ συνέρχεσθε omits בה, reads צדיק for צדקי, and seems to have the *qerê* וְשֻׁבוּ instead of the *kethîb* וְשֻׁבִי. It is the *qerê* which is accepted by Syr. and Targ. Instead of צדקי, Syr. 'be innocent' seems to read צדקו. The whole verse is paraphrased in the Vulg. *Respondete obsecro absque contentione, et loquentes id quod justum est, judicate.*

In the 2nd hemistich, the emphasis is on the repetition of an action. It is clear that we should read וְשֻׁבוּ, which repeats שׁובו. Thus is it pointed by *qerê*, as by Targ., Syr., and probably G. It would be an unacceptable subtlety to read וְשֻׁבִי 'and do thou return', supposing that Job is addressing his tongue mentioned in v. 30 (Ehrlich). The verb שׁוב 're-turn' with the sense of repeating an action or recommencing it (7:7). The action, expressed in v. 28, is understood. The jussive with the negative אל conveys the sense of absolute certainty as in predictions; cf. v. 22. The 1st hemistich simply means: 'Return then! There is no falsehood here!' In v. 30 Job will make clear the exact meaning of עֻלָה 'perversion', 'injustice', 'wickedness' (cf. 16:11). He is alluding to wickedness in words, i.e. falsehood. The Massoretic accentuation makes the 2nd hemistich clumsy by linking עוֹד with וְשֻׁבוּ, which yields the sense 'and turn again once more'. On the other hand we obtain an excellent meaning by connecting עוֹד with what follows:

'My righteousness is *still* intact!' The feminine suffix in בָּה has a neuter meaning, exactly as in Gn 24:14, ובה אדע 'and may I know by that means'. Hence there is no need to change בה into בִּי in order to translate 'my righteousness is within me', as do Hitzig, Bickell, and some others. It is the inspection to which Job submits which will manifest his righteousness; *by that means*, it will be seen that he is righteous. Le Hir has the unhappy idea of proposing to see in the feminine suffix of בה an allusion to עולה, to reach the very strange meaning: Return and my righteousness will triumph even over your prejudices!

30 G οὐ γάρ ἐστιν and Vulg. *et non invenietis* give a negative construction to the question. For יבין, G μελετᾷ, Targ. יתבין 'understands', Syr. ⲙⲁⲙⲗⲗ 'saying' (interpreting חכי by 'my mouth'). Vulg. paraphrases: *nec in faucibus meis stultitia persona-bit.* For הוות, G σύνεσιν, Targ. רגושתא 'the tumult', Syr. ⲕⲟⲟⲥⲁ 'truth', Vulg. *stultitia.*

The opening הֲיֵשׁ 'is there?' (5:1); cf. אם־יֵשׁ in the second clause of v. 6. Job's friends may scrutinise his words (v. 29): 'is there any false-hood on my tongue?' Have I spoken things that are not strictly true? The tongue is the organ of speech, as the palate is the organ of taste: 'Cannot my palate discern evil things?' The tongue and the palate are associated in 29:10 (cf. 20:12-13) and 33:2. Instead of the normal verb טעם 'taste' which expresses the action of the palate (12:11; 34:3), the poet uses the verb בין 'discern', 'under-stand' on account of the comple-ment הַוּוֹת 'evil things' (cf. 6:2), which takes us into the moral sphere.

Job knows what is the ground of his confidence as regards the scope of his words. Before uttering them, he has judged their value, just as one savours food by the tongue and the palate (20: 12-13). V. 30 completes the first part of Job's speech. A new theme is heard in Ch. 7, in which Job gives expression to his conception of human life in general. In Ch. 6 he has confined himself to the theme of his personal grief.

CHAPTER 7

1 Is not man's life on earth a term of military service?
   And are not his days like the days of a mercenary?
2 Like a slave who longs for the shade,
   And a hireling who hopes for his pay!

7 : 1 For צבא, G πειρατήριον (Jerome *tentatio*), Targ. חילא 'army', Aq. στρατεία, Vulg *militia*. It seems that Syr. رحا 'time' should have been followed by a complement: term of military service. According to the sense, לאנוש is interpreted ὁ βίος ἀνθρώπου (G), *vita hominis* (Vulg.). Syro-hex. quotes ὁ βίος in the margin, but translates: يوسبز 'conduct', 'manners', in the text. G καὶ ὥσπερ μισθίου αὐθημερινοῦ (Jerome *et sicut quotidiani mercenarii*) reverses the order of the terms: וכימי שכיר.

Job proposes here to expound his conception of life, which is very different from that of Eliphaz. Misfortune and weariness are not man's work (5: 6ff.). They are on the contrary inherent in human nature. The word צָבָא 'army' means also the period of time which is spent in the army, term of military service (14: 14; Is 40: 2). Literally the 1st hemistich runs: 'Is there not a military service for man on the earth?' The life of man resembles that of the soldier (cf. G and Vulg.). Human existence is a perpetual round of hard labour, like the life of military camps! Rosenmüller cites Arrian: στρατεία τίς ἐστιν ὁ βίος ἑκάστου (*Epict.* III, 24), and Maximus of Tyre: στρατηγὸν μὲν τὸν θεὸν στρατιὰν δὲ τὴν ζωήν (*Serm.* 3). Following the ordinary usage in the Book of Job we should read עֲלֵי

with the *qerê*, before the tone syllable (6: 5; 8: 9; 9: 26, etc.; so Budde). The 2nd hemistich 'and his days (are they not) like the days of a mercenary?' explains and develops the meaning of the first comparison. The שָׂכִיר 'the man who is hired for wages' (14: 6) is not merely the worker by the day, but also the soldier who serves for money (2 S 10: 6; Jer 46: 21). Here as in v. 2 it is the idea of servitude and forced labour which receives emphasis. The poet has in mind all those whose state in life is one of servility and bondage. It is they to whom Job compares the character of human existence on this earth: no rest is possible until death comes to bring release (3: 13ff.). With the expression of the 2nd hemistich compare: 'Are Thy days as the days of man?' (10: 5).

2 After כעבד G adds δεδοικὼς τὸν κύριον αὐτοῦ, marked with an obelus in Syro-hex. G gives to ישאף the meaning of 'obtain': καὶ τετευχὼς σκιᾶς (Jerome *et consecutus umbram*). Instead of Vulg. *sicut servus* (i.e. כעבד), certain manuscripts have *sicut cervus*, whence the commentary of St Thomas: *inducit exemplum animalis desiderantis umbram*. For פעלו, G τὸν μισθὸν αὐτοῦ (Jerome *mercedem operis sui*) as in Jer 22: 13. This is the true meaning. It recurs in Targ. סטריה 'his recompense', while Syr. 'the end of his work' and

97

3   Thus have I inherited months of disillusionment,
     And nights of sorrow have been allotted to me!
4   If I lie down, I say: 'When comes *the morning*?'
     If I rise up, I say: '*How long* till evening?'
     And I am assailed by fancies until darkness falls.

4 Add יוֹם (G). — וּמָתַי (G), MT: וּמדד.

Vulg. *finem operis sui* paraphrase in the light of the meaning of יקוה 'he hopes'.

V. 2 forms the logical sequence to v. 1, and there is no reason to attach it directly to v. 3. The כֵּן 'thus', with which v. 3 opens, sums up the comparisons of vv. 1-2. The verb 'to be' is understood as in v. 1. Of course, יִשְׁאַף־צֵל and יקוה פעלו are relative clauses which emphasise the special point of the comparison (cf. 6: 15). The particle "כ 'like' neatly introduces these relative clauses which are not preceded by אשר (9: 26; 11: 16, cited in Gesenius-Kautzsch, § 155g). Note the use of שָׁאַף 'breathe in', 'suck in', 'swallow up' (5: 5) in the sense of 'long for' (36: 20). The slave while working longs for the shade and cool of eventide (Jer 6: 4), which will enable him to rest. As for the mercenary, he waits for the end of his day's work, the moment when he will receive his wages (Dt 24: 15; Mt 20: 8). The word פֹּעַל 'activity', 'work' here expresses the result of the work for the workman: his recompense (Jer 22: 13). Man is like the slave or the mercenary soldier. What cause for surprise if he sighs after the evening of life, i.e. death?

3 G ὑπέμεινα seems to have confused הנחלתי with הוחלתי (a mistake in audition). For שׁוא, Targ. דמגן 'of futility', G κενούς, Syr. ﻣـﻬـﺒـ 'vain', Vulg. *vacuos*. G renders עמל by ὀδυνῶν, Vulg. *laboriosas*. The more literal translations of Aq. and Theod. are cited in the margin of Syro-hex. The verb מנו is pointed מֻנּוּ by G δεδομέναι and Syr. ﻭﻟﻤﺒﺤ.

By analogy with הנחלתי, Vulg. translates *enumeravi*. But Targ., Aq., and Theod. 'they have counted' have the pointing of MT. Mistakenly Syr. puts a negative before מנו.

The adverb כֵּן 'thus', that is, like the soldier, the slave, the mercenary (cf. 6: 21 corrected). The *hoph'al* of נחל is not found elsewhere. Literally 'I have been made heir', that is, 'I have inherited'. The poet shows clearly that this sad condition is not of Job's own choosing. It is a legacy of his forefathers. The complement לִי 'for me': as my lot, my portion. The abstract שָׁוְא 'vanity' or 'illusion' and 'lie' is coupled with יַרְחֵי 'months' to mark the deceptive nature of mortal life. We find חיי שוא 'life of disillusionment' in Sir 30: 17, 'Death itself is preferable to a life of disillusionment and eternal rest to a lasting sorrow.' Sorrows of both day and night are the lot of humanity (Ec 2: 23). The months of disillusionment have their counterpart in 'the nights of sorrow'; cf. עָמָל in 3: 10. The perfect *pi'el* מִנּוּ is used without subject to convey the impersonal 'one'; cf. 4: 19; 6: 2. It is unnecessary to replace it by the *pu'al* מֻנּוּ, as has been proposed by Beer and Budde, following G and Syr. The *pi'el* of מנה 'to count' is much used in Aramaic and modern Hebrew in the sense of 'apportion', 'assign', 'determine', 'allocate'.

4 The mysterious מדד is connected with the root נדד 'flee' by Targ., and with מדד 'measure' by Syr. A different text is attested by G (cf. inf.). For נדדים, G ὀδυνῶν, Vulg.

5   My flesh has become covered with worms and dirty scabs,
      My skin has split and runs with pus;

doloribus, Targ. שׁנתא נדת 'elusive sleep', 'insomnia', Syr. 'I toss about' (from נדד). The ambiguous נשׁף is considered as 'the morning' by G, Targ., Syr.; but Vulg. translates it by *tenebras*.

וְאָמַרְתִּי should not be made dependent on the conjunction אִם. The main clause is introduced by the copulative *waw*, exactly as in Gn 38:9; Nu 21:9b; Jg 6:3 (cf. Gesenius-Kautzsch, § 112gg). Cf. 21:6. As it stands the 1st hemistich might be translated: 'If I lie down, I say to myself: when shall I arise?' But how are we to explain מדד? Exegetes have sought in מדד the *pi'el* of מדד 'measure'. R. Levi and Ibn Ezra then understand לבי 'my heart' to be implied: 'My heart measures the evening.' It is perhaps a similar idea which has influenced Vulg. *et rursum expectabo vesperam.* Contrary to the normal sense of מדד, the meaning 'to be lengthened, prolonged' has been postulated, whence 'the night is long' (Renan). By connecting מדד with נדד 'to flee', Rosenmüller obtains the result *quando erit recessus tenebrae?* Le Hir splits up מדד into מן נדד to translate 'and the night having passed'. Bickell saw in ומדד ערב a doublet of נדדים עדי. Torczyner eliminated these words as being foreign to the context; Ehrlich replaces ומדד by וְנָדַד 'and if the evening flees away', Gray by וּמִדֵּי 'and each time the evening comes'. This multiplicity of hypotheses, in the interpretation or correction of the text, would lead us to suppose that the original has not been faithfully preserved by the Massoretes. Now, the translation offered by G rests on a different text: ἐὰν κοιμηθῶ, λέγω Πότε ἡμέρα; ὡς δ' ἂν ἀναστῶ, πάλιν Πότε ἑσπέρα. The text of G resembles Dt 28:67,

but does not just copy this passage, which in G runs: τὸ πρωὶ ἐρεῖς Πῶς ἂν γένοιτο ἑσπέρα; καὶ τὸ ἑσπέρας ἐρεῖς Πῶς ἂν γένοιτο πρωί. The contrast in Dt 28:67 is between the morning and the evening, whereas here, in our verse, it is between the day and the evening. Moreover the words of MT are reproduced in G. It is sufficient to add יום after מתי and to replace ומדד by the intelligible וּמָתַי, in order to recognise the original of G. It is unnecessary to overload the text, as does Duhm, by adding ואם קמתי after [ו]אקום, which would be linked with מתי יום. The real motive behind this restoration is the concern to obtain four hemistichs. We have three hemistichs in v. 4. First of all: 'If I lie down, I say: When comes the morning?' Then: 'If I rise up I say: How long till evening?' נְדֻדִים is generally regarded as indicating the restless movements of the sick man on his bed of suffering, or else his sleepless tossings. The word is a *hapax* derived from נדד 'flee', 'wander', 'be restless'. To express agitation, Job has recourse to the word רֹגֶז (14:1) coming after the adjective 'satiated with' (שׂבַע). Since the point here is the restlessness which pursues Job in his waking hours as in his sleep, we recognise in נדדים the rambling fancies and wanderings of the mind. The word נֶשֶׁף signifies no longer the dawn (3:9) but the twilight (24:25).

5   G translates the 1st hemistich φύρεται δέ μου τὸ σῶμα ἐν σαπρίᾳ σκωλήκων and connects וגישׁ עפר with the 2nd. The words ἐν σαπρίᾳ σκωλήκων (Jerome *putredine vermium*) are a tautological translation of רמה, which denotes sometimes worms, sometimes rotting. Vulg.

simply *putredine*. Then G, from וגיש
עפר, has τήκω δὲ βώλακας γῆς ἀπὸ
ἰχῶρος ξύων (A and C ξέων), Jerome
infundo glebas terrae radiens saniem.
The reading τήκω δὲ is based on
ואמס (from מסס) for וימאס, ξύων or
ξέων reads גרע for רגע, and finally
ἀπὸ ἰχῶρος comes perhaps from ἀπὸ
χρωτός (Beer), which is supposed to
translate עורי. The word גִּיש (*kethîb*)
or גֻּש (*qerê*) is well rendered by
βώλακας (G), גרגשתא 'clod', 'glebe'
(Targ.), more vaguely by Vulg.
sordibus. A reading גשם has introduced ܓܫܡܝ 'my body' of Syr.
For רגע, Targ. רטט 'has trembled',
Syr. 'has contracted' (cf. Levy,
Chald. Wörterbuch, s.v. קפד), Vulg.
aruit. The verb ימאס is connected
with מסס 'flow' by G τήκω, Targ.
and Syr. אתמסי, while Vulg. *con-
tracta est* is an interpretation in the
light of the context.

Bochart explains very well 'my
flesh is covered with worms': *vermes
me undequaque obsident et vestis
instar ambiunt* (*Hieroz.*, II, col. 620).
The word רִמָּה 'worm' in the collective sense (17: 14; 21: 26; 24: 20) is
used chiefly to denote worms which
devour corpses; cf. Sir 7: 17; 10: 11.
In 25: 6 it becomes the symbol of
the nothingness of man. Apart from
these texts the word רמה recurs
only in Ex 16: 24, where it denotes
the worms which batten on rotting
food, and in Is 14: 11 'the worms' of
the grave. The disease of Job is a
malignant ulcer (2: 7f.) which causes the corruption and rotting of the
skin. It is well known that worms
came out of the body of Antiochus
Epiphanes (2 Mac 9: 9) and from
that of Herod Agrippa (Ac 12: 23).
Bochart cites numerous examples
drawn from classical literature (loc.
cit.). The Hebrew tradition about
the meaning of the *hapax* גִּיש, *qerê*
גֻּש, 'clod', 'glebe' is in agreement
with the translation of Targ. and G.
We find in the Talmud גֻּש עָפָר

The word עפר is necessary to specify the clod of earth, for in other
cases גוש means rather 'curd' (of
milk) (cf. Levy, *Neuhebr. und
chald. Wörterbuch*, I, pp. 315f.).
Hence there is no reason to cut out
עפר as do Beer and Duhm. These
clods of earth are of course the dirty
scabs which like a garment cover
the body of the sick man. Cf. Sir
40: 3, where לבוש עפר ואפר 'covered with dust and ashes' has a metaphorical sense (Peters). After the
symptoms of the flesh, those of the
skin. Ehrlich is surely wrong to eliminate the interesting עוֹרִי, parallel
to בְּשָׂרִי, in order to read עוד רגע
'yet a moment'. He thus gets rid of
the verb רגע which recurs in 26: 12.
In this text רגע is parallel to מחץ
'break', 'shatter', and has as its
complement הים 'the sea'. This act
of God, analogous to breaking, shat-
tering, is again expressed by the verb
רגע in Is 51: 15; Jer 31: 35. Now,
the text in Isaiah follows an allusion
to the crossing of the Red Sea
(51: 9ff.). One may therefore agree
that רגע expresses the divine action
on the sea when it is necessary to
cut a way through it. Elsewhere this
action is expressed by the verb בקע
'cleave' (Ex 14: 16; Is 63: 12; Ps
78: 13). Everything inclines us to
believe that רגע had also the sense
of cleaving a path through the sea
(26: 12; Is 51: 15; Jer 31: 35). The
root is related to נגע 'strike', which
explains the parallelism with מחץ
in 26: 12. Here the verb is used
intransitively, 'my skin splits', and
as a result, 'it flows with pus'. The
root מאס in the sense of מסס, in the
niph'al 'flow', 'drip' (cf. G, Targ.,
Syr.) recurs in Ps 58: 8 יִמָּאֲסוּ 'they
will flow away'; cf. 7: 16 and 42: 6.
Thus it is unnecessary to change the
text. We understand very well how
the skin splits and runs with pus.
On the other hand, if we give to רגע
the meaning of 'contract', 'coagu-

6   My days have been swifter than the weaver's shuttle,
     And have come to an end for lack of thread;
7   Remember that my life is but a passing breath,
     That my eye will never again see happiness.

late', in the light of Ethiopic, we no longer grasp the link between the two verbs. The order would be the opposite, in accordance with 10: 10.

6 For ימי, G ὁ δὲ βίος μου, Jerome *vita mea* (Gall. and Aug.; Bod. and Tur. omit *mea*). Under the heading οἱ λοιποί Colb. cites the reading of Aq., Symm., and Theod. αἱ ἡμέραι μου, which is also given in the margin of Syro-hex. In 9: 25, where G again renders ימי by ὁ δὲ βίος μου, Colb. again cites the hexaplar readings in the same way. G translates מני־ארג by λαλιᾶς (Syro-hex., Sah., Eth., Jerome *quam loquela*), but G (A, ℵ^c·a) translates δρόμεως (Arab. Baud.) according to 9: 25. Colb. and Syro-hex. quote δρόμεως as a variant. Vulg. explains: *dies mei velocius transierunt quam a texente tela succiditur*. For ארג, Targ. גרדית מחי 'fabric of the weaver'; Aq., Symm., and Theod. ὑφάσματος. Syr. ܡܥܝ ? comes doubtless from ܡܥܝ ? (cf. Targ.) 'web of threads'. G renders באפס תקוה by ἐν κενῇ ἐλπίδι, but Symm. μὴ οὔσης ἐλπίδος.

The 1st hemistich recurs in 9: 25, with רָץ 'runner' instead of אָרֶג; cf. G (A, ℵ^c·a) above. The verb קלל originally means 'to be light' (40: 4), then 'to be rapid' (2 S 1: 23; Jer 4: 13; Hab 1: 8). The term of comparison for speed is the runner (9: 25), the leopard (Hab 1: 8), the eagle (2 S 1: 23; Jer 4: 13). Here it is a question of an object used for weaving, אָרֶג, not of the weft itself. This object is the shuttle (Qimchi). It is in this sense that the word אָרֶג is used by R. Ben-Gershon (*Thesaurus* of Ben-Yehuda, s.v.). The

shuttle is in fact the instrument which runs through the meshes of the web. In the Song of Hezekiah the MT contains the words: קפדתי כארג חיי 'like a weaver have I rolled up my life' (Is 38: 12). Life is compared to a tissue which man himself weaves. A verse of R. Moses Ibn Ezra illustrates the comparison: 'Man in the world weaves like a weaver and certainly his days are the thread' (quotation in the *Thesaurus* of Ben-Yehuda, s.v. אורג, I, p. 117). This verse is of particular interest because the Jewish poet uses to denote 'thread' the word תִּקְוָה (from קוה, whence קַו 'thread'), which has this same sense in the episode of Rahab the harlot (Jos 2: 18, 21). Now, it is precisely this word תקוה which appears at the end of our verse. Among exegetes only Marshall, cited by Driver-Gray, has recognised it. The others are unanimous in interpreting באפס תקוה as 'without hope', which however does not fit the requirements of parallelism. To Driver-Gray's objection that one would expect rather מבלי, our answer in the first place will be that Targ. has not hesitated to render באפס by מדלית, which translates מבלי in 4: 11, and secondly that in Pr 26: 20 we find באפס עצים תכבה־אש 'for lack of wood the fire goes out'. We shall thus translate the 2nd hemistich: 'and have come to an end for lack of thread'. Life is indeed comparable to a piece of texture. The shuttle supplies the thread of the woof, but if the days of our life speed past faster than the shuttle, the thread is no longer in time to form the tissue.

7 Targ. היך רוחא 'like a breath'

8   The eye of him who beheld me will see me no more,
     Thine eyes will rest on me and I shall be gone!
9   A cloud is dispersed and vanishes,

weakens the force of the Hebrew expression. Syr. omits the negative of the 2nd hemistich.

Job is now addressing himself directly to God, as is clearly to be seen by vv. 11ff. It is God, in fact, who has breathed into man's nostrils the breath which makes of him a living soul (Gn 2:7). Hence Job can say to God: 'Remember that my life is but a passing breath.' Further allusion to the shortness of human life. In v. 16 we shall see that the days of Job are a mere breath. Cf. Ps 78:39, where, to excuse sinners, God 'remembers that they are but flesh, a wind (רוּחַ) that passes and comes not again'. Note again זכר 'remember' in 10:9. Use of שׁוּב with ל׳ before the infinitive complement to convey the idea that one begins something again. Negative before שׁוּב (1 K 13:17; Hos 11:9). The word טוֹב 'good' in the sense of 'happiness' (21:13; 36:11); we shall have טוֹבָה with the same meaning in 9:25. In the light of our observations (on 6:21) in connection with the verb ראה, the expression 'see happiness' means 'to be happy' (Ps 4:7; 34:13; Ec 3:13; and cf. the note of Podechard on Ec 2:1). The 2nd hemistich, according to parallelism and what follows, notes that man, after death, never again returns to earth to enjoy happiness. Thus it had been understood by Olympiodorus. And again, many Catholic authors cited by Knabenbauer understand it in this way. Rashi in claiming that Job denies the resurrection exceeds the implication of the expressions used. On the other hand, Duhm restricts the poet's horizon too much when he finds here the suggestion of a worsening of

Job's malady: 'as his illness assails him ever more fiercely'.

8   This verse, absent from Sah., marked with an asterisk in Jerome and Syro-hex., did not exist in G. The present text comes from Theod. (cf. Colb.). For לֹא־תְשׁוּרֵנִי, Theod. (in G) οὐ περιβλέψεταί με, but G (A) οὐκ ἀτενοῖ μοι (sic), which comes from οὐκ ἀτενιεῖ (variant quoted in Colb.), whence also οὐ κατανοεῖ of Cod. 249. For בִי, Targ. בְּמֵימְרִי 'on my word' (cf. 1:10). Theod. renders וְאֵינֶנִּי by καὶ οὐκ ἔτι εἰμί (A omits ἔτι), but Aq. (according to Cod. 252 and Syro-hex.) καὶ οὐχ ὑπάρχω; cf. Jerome *et non subsisto*, Vulg. *et non subsistam* (same translation in v. 21).

There is no reason to suppress this verse in spite of the lacuna in G (contra Bickell). V. 7b alluded to the impossibility of man's return to earth to enjoy happiness. Hence the vision of death and its consequences: 'The eye of him who beheld me will see me no more! Thine eyes will rest on me and I shall be gone!' The verb שׁוּר 'to behold' is one of the characteristic words in the Book of Job (17:15; 20:9; 24:15; 34:29; 35:5, 13, 14). Critics are fond of making 'eye' its subject. But a comparison of the 1st hemistich with 20:9 abundantly shows that Job has death in mind. Preposition בְּ after 'thine eyes' to introduce the person on whom the eyes rest their gaze (Dt 11:12; Ps 101:6). At the close וְאֵינֶנִּי 'and I will be gone', whence the uselessness of looking towards the place where he was (v. 21b; 20:7-9). Cf. Ps 39:14b; 'before I go hence and am no more' (וְאֵינֶנִּי). There is a similar use of וְאֵינֶנּוּ in 3:21; 23:8; 24:24; 27:19.

9   At the opening the versions add

So he who goes down to Sheol comes not up again,
10   He returns no more to his dwelling,
And the place where he was sees him not again.

'like' in order to make explicit the comparison. G paraphrases: ὥσπερ νέφος ἀποκαθαρθὲν ἀπ' οὐρανοῦ. Syro-hex. quotes the translation of Symm. καθάπερ ἀναλωθεῖσα νεφέλη ἀπαλλα-γήσεται. Instead of עָנָן, Targ. תננא 'the smoke', following Ps 37: 20. For שְׁאוֹל Syr. ܠܫܝܘܠ, Targ. לבי קבורתא 'to the tomb', G εἰς ᾅδην, Jerome and Vulg. *ad inferos*.

It is a pure whim to wish to change כָּלָה into עלה as is suggested by Beer in Kittel. The verb כלה 'cease' (v. 6) 'vanish' (4: 9) is used to convey the image of smoke being dispersed (Ps 37: 20). The cloud and the dew are the very symbols of what passes away (Hos 13: 3). In this text of Hosea the verb הלך 'fades away' characterises precisely the transience of the morning dew. Cf. הלך in 14: 20; 19: 10. The pointing וַיֵּלֶךְ is brought about by the pause (Gesenius-Kautzsch, § 69x). The cloud vanishes away and no more returns. Such is the situation of man who goes down to Sheol. The use of ירד and עלה is typical. For the Hebrews, as for the Babylonians, Sheol is situated beneath the earth: one goes down to it, one comes up from it (cf. 1 S 28: 11ff.). The Babylonians called it 'the land from which there is no return', 'the abode which he who enters never leaves'. The analogies between this conception of the underworld and that of the Hebrews are set out in *RB*, 1907, pp. 60ff. Without leaving the Book of Job we learn that Sheol is a land from which no traveller returns (10: 21), a deep abode (11: 8), and hidden (14: 13; 24: 19; 26: 6), where all is shadowed by dust (17: 16) and thick darkness (10: 21f.; 17: 13). It is the meeting place of all the living (30: 23), whatever may have been their rank in this life (3: 13-19). Just as the cloud vanishes, so the dead never come up again to this earth, 'so he who goes down to Sheol comes not up again'. And that is why his eye 'will never again begin to see happiness' (v. 7).

10   Well expressed in the versions. For לביתו, G εἰς τὸν ἴδιον οἶκον (Sah.), but Syro-hex. and Jerome *in domum suum* omit ἴδιον which is given in the margin of Syro-hex.

We have seen in v. 9 that the dead return not again to earth, except in the case of an extraordinary intervention such as is narrated in 1 S 28: 11ff. Hence 'he returns no more to his dwelling'. The verb הכיר 'recognise' (2: 12; 4: 16) in the sense of 'see again' (this represents a constant connection between 'see' and 'know' in Hebrew). Of course מְקוֹמוֹ 'his place' means 'the place in which he dwelt'. Cf. בטני 'the womb where I was' in 3: 10. A comparison with 8: 18 shows that what is meant is the dwelling of the dead man when he lived on earth, and not his family or country. The text of the 2nd hemistich is found integrally in Ps 103: 16, at the close of a description where the days of man (cf. v. 6) are likened to the flower of the field which fades away in the wind: 'for the wind passes over it and it is gone and its place knows it no more'. In the Psalm as in our text, the comparison bears on the transience of human life. Job is quoting a universally known truth. St John Chrysostom concludes that Job's resignation is so much the more admirable because he has no clearly defined belief in the resurrection (τῆς ἐκ νεκρῶν παλιγγενεσίας). St

11   Therefore I will not restrain my mouth,
        I will speak in the anguish of my spirit,
        I will complain in the bitterness of my soul:
12   Am I the sea or the dragon,
        That Thou shouldst erect a barrier against me?

Thomas Aquinas is nearer to the literal meaning: *manifestum est autem ex his quod Job hic resurrectionem quam fides asserit non negat, sed reditum ad vitam carnalem quam Judaei ponunt et alii quidam philosophi posuerunt.*

11 For גם, G ἀτὰρ οὖν, but G (A) τοιγαροῦν, the reading of Aq. and Theod. The word רוחי, omitted in G (B) ἐν ἀνάγκῃ ὤν, is added in the form τοῦ πνεύματός μου (Aq., Symm., Theod.) in G (A, אᶜ·ᵃ), Jerome *spiritus mei*, Syro-hex. (with asterisk), Memph., Eth., Arab. Baud. In the margin of Syro-hex. it is pointed out that these words do not occur in Origen's copy. Sah. is in agreement with G (B) about the omission. For the 3rd hemistich, G ἀνοίξω πικρίαν ψυχῆς μου συνεχόμενος (Syro-hex. has obelus before συνεχόμενος, Jerome asterisk instead of obelus), Jerome *aperiam amaritudinem animae meae coarctatus*. The reading of G (A) ἀνοίξω τὸ στόμα μου ἐν πικρίᾳ ψυχῆς συνεχόμενος brings us back to MT. It is followed by Memph. and Arab. Baud., quoted in the margin by Syro-hex. A shortened reading in Sah., which omits ἀνοίξω τὸ στόμα μου and συνεχόμενος. For אשיחה, Symm. διαλεχθήσομαι, Vulg. *confabulabor*.
In order to avoid the three hemistichs, Bickell, followed by Duhm and Beer, cuts out בצר רוחי אשיחה. The result of this is to remove the expressive אָשִׂיחָה and retain the colourless אֲדַבְּרָה. These authors quite wrongly regard בְּצַר as a variant of בְּמַר. The anguish of the spirit and the bitterness of the soul

(3: 20) are parallel, not synonymous. In 10: 1 we shall have the expression אעזבה···שׂיחי 'I will pour out my complaint', parallel to אדברה 'I will speak'. The two last hemistichs, 'I will speak in the anguish of my spirit' and 'I will complain in the bitterness of my soul' are excellent as regards parallelism; cf. 12: 10. The adverb גַּם 'therefore' to introduce a conclusion (Ps 52: 7). Use of חשׂך 'restrain', as in 16: 5 (cf. Comm.), has the sense of preventing the mouth from speaking. Job excuses himself in advance for his apostrophe to God. The extremity of his distress, the perspective of imminent death, all urge him to give free course to his sorrows.

12 For תנין, Syr. ܬܢܝܢܐ, G δράκων, Aq. κῆτος (quoted in Syro-hex., which has ܬܢܝܢܐ in the text), Vulg. *cetus*. The 1st Targum identifies תנין with the Pharaoh, the second with Leviathan.
Job addresses himself directly to God: 'Am I the sea or the dragon, that Thou shouldst erect a barrier against me?' The sea is the symbol of those tumultuous elements in the universe which God alone can overcome. Sometimes He assigns as its limit the sand of the sea shore (Jer 5: 22), at other times He erects bars and doors to restrict it to its proper domain (Job 38: 8ff.). Hence we may say that He has erected a barrier against it to prevent it from overflowing its bounds. To go no further than the Book of Job, we find the sea set in parallelism with Tehom, primordial abyss, corresponding to the Tiamat of the Babylonians (28: 14; 38: 16), or again

13   If I say: 'My bed will comfort me,
     My couch will share in my plaint!'

with Rahab (26: 12). In connection
with 3: 8 we have seen that the sea
serpents, those fabulous and dreaded
beings, were the auxiliaries of Tiamat, and we have recognised that,
among the Hebrews, the three chief
of these monsters were Leviathan,
Tannîn, and Rahab. It is Tannîn
that is mentioned here. For want of
an exact equivalent we translate it
by 'the dragon' (cf. G). In reality, it
is a serpent (Ex 7: 9, 10, 12), and a
venomous one (Dt 32: 33; Ps 91:
13). Its abode is the sea (Is 27: 1;
Ps 74: 13). The *tannînim* are aquatic
reptiles (Gn 1: 21), especially those
of the subterranean abysses (Ps
148: 7). One of these monsters gives
its name to the 'dragon's well'
עֵין הַתַּנִּין (Neh 2: 13). If we compare 26: 12 with Ps 74: 13, we see
that Tannîn and Rahab are synonymous in so far as they symbolise
the sea and especially the Red Sea,
which was parted by God when the
Hebrews crossed it. For this reason,
Tannîn had a special connection
with Egypt (Is 51: 9), and was used
to represent the Pharaoh (Ezk
29: 3; 32: 2); cf. 1st Targ. In Ezekiel the name is written תַּנִּים, as
though the poet had wished to make
it the plural of תָּן (plural of majesty
as for בְּהֵמוֹת 40: 15). It looks as if
there were a word תָּן meaning serpent. From such a word would be
derived תַּנִּין (root תנן), לִוְיָתָן. 'Leviathan', 'coiled serpent' (cf. Is
27: 1), נְחָשְׁתָּן 'bronze serpent'. Job
complains that God leaves him no
respite (vv. 16ff.). He is treated
as though he were one of these
monsters which require special
vigilance because they are always
menacing. God has erected a
barrier מִשְׁמָר against him, as is done

when towns are besieged (Jer 51:
12). Cf. the use of the verb שׁמר in
10: 14.

13 G εἶπα ὅτι inverts כִּי־אָמַרְתִּי,
but Jerome *quia dixi* (with asterisk).
Syr. omits עַרְשִׂי. For the 2nd hemistich, G ἀνοίσω δὲ πρὸς ἐμαυτὸν
ἰδίᾳ λόγον τῇ κοίτῃ μου. It is clear
that G reads אֶשָּׂא for יִשָּׂא; similarly
Syr. ܘܠ‍ܬܒܚܐ 'and I will be com-
forted', Vulg. *et relevabor*. The words
ἰδίᾳ λόγον are a corruption of διάλογον, which figures in G (A), or of
εἰς διάλογον (in accordance with
εἰς διαλογισμόν of Cod. 248). Note
that שִׂיחִי is rendered ἡ διαλογή μου
in Ps 104: 34, and that Jerome *con-
fabulationem* (Gall.) or *consolatio-
nem* (Bod., Tur., Aug.) presupposes
διάλογον. Syr. 'torments of my couch'
regards שִׂיחִי as a construct plural,
while Targ. בְּמִלַּי 'in my words' and
Vulg. *loquens mecum* give to שִׂיח
its original sense of 'word'; cf.
Theod. ἐν τῇ ἀδολεσχίᾳ μου and
Symm. (following Syro-hex.) διὰ τῆς
ἀδολεσχίας μου.

   In order to vary his style, the
author uses כִּי־אָמַרְתִּי in the sense of
אִם־אָמַרְתִּי, the conjunction אִם having been used in v. 4 in a similar
type of phrase; cf. כִּי תֵדַע 'if you
know it' (38: 5; Pr 30: 4). Parallelism between עֶרֶשׂ and מִשְׁכָּב as in
Ps 41: 4. 'My bed will comfort me.'
Sleep is the resource of the unhappy;
Job looks to sleep for the consolations which he does not find from
his friends. The preposition בְּ is
used before the complement of נשׂא
to convey a partitive sense, 'bear a
part', 'take one's share of' (Nu
11: 17). Cf. the use of בְּ in 21: 25
and 39: 17. The noun שִׂיחִי 'my
plaint', just as we had אָשִׂיחָה 'I will
complain' in v. 11.

14   Then Thou dost scare me with dreams,
      And by visions dost Thou terrify me,
15   And my soul would prefer strangling,
      Death rather than my *sufferings*!

15   מֵעַצְּבוֹתָי; MT: מעצמותי.

14 G (A) at the beginning adds
διὰ τί. For בחלמת, G ἐνυπνίοις may
come (by haplography) from ἐν
ἐνυπνίοις; cf. ἐν ὁράμασιν and Jerome
per somnia. For ἐν ὁράμασιν (i.e.
מחזינות), Jerome *per visionem*, corrected to *per visiones* (cf. Vulg.) in
Gall. The prepositions ב" and מן
are both rendered by ב" in Syr., by
per in Vulg., but Targ. faithfully
adheres to MT.

The opening *waw* introduces the
main clause; cf. ואמרתי in v. 4.
Notice the alternation of ב" with
מן to denote the instrument of causality. In 4:13 we had מֵחֶזְיֹנוֹת
'(coming) from visions'. There, as
here, it was a question of visions of
the night. Similarly in 20:8 and
33:15. The *pi'el* of חתת (cf. the noun
in 6:21) recurs only in Jer 51:56,
where the form is doubtful. Here
the meaning is clearly 'scare', 'star-
tle'. The verb תְּבַעֲתַנִּי recurs, but in
the 3rd person fem., in 9:34 and
13:21. Everywhere we find the
suffix *anni* in pause. It is a survival
of the original termination *anni*
which is quite normal in Assyrian.
The *pi'el* of בעת is one of the characteristic words in the Book of Job:
3:5; 9:34; 13:11, 21; 15:24; 18:
11; 33:7. Apart from these texts we
find it only in 1 S 16:14, 15; 2 S
22:5; Is 21:4; Ps 18:5. The meaning which is everywhere suitable
is 'terrify suddenly'. It is in vain
that Job has relied on sleep to alle-
viate his sorrows. He is haunted by
nightmares. Döderlein quotes Ovid
(*Epistulae ex Pont.*, I, 2):

At puto, cum requies medicinaque
          publica curae

*Somnus adest, solitis nox venit orba
          malis,*
Somnia me terrent.

Hitzig cites Plutarch (*De virt. et vit.*,
2):

ὅταν δὲ νυστάζοντά μ' ἡ λύπη λάβη
    ἀπόλλυμ' ὑπὸ τῶν ἐνυπνίων.

15 For the 1st hemistich, G ἀπαλ-
λάξεις ἀπὸ πνεύματός μου (A and
Jerome omit μου) τὴν ψυχήν (A ζωήν)
μου. G considers תבחר as the 2nd
person sing., as does also Syr. An
excellent conjecture of Bahrdt, cited
by Beer, recognises in πνεύματος a
substitute for πνίγματος = מחנק.
Syr. interprets מחנק by ܡܢ ܐܒܕܢ 'of
destruction'. The word is rendered
by שרנוקא 'strangulation' (Targ.),
ἀγχόνην 'hanging' (Aq.), cf. Vulg.
suspendium. G continues its phrase
by ἀπὸ δὲ θανάτου τὰ ὀστᾶ μου, but
Jerome *repuli* (with asterisk) and
Syro-hex. ܘܐܒܥܕ 'I have driven
away' (in the margin, with asterisk)
retain, at the close, מאסתי of v. 16,
omitted in G. On the other hand,
G (A) τὴν δὲ ψυχήν μου ἀπὸ τοῦ σώ-
ματός μου omits the word מות and
repeats נפשי. This reading is cited in
the margin of Syro-hex. Note that
Syr. 'and my bones of death' is in
agreement with G (B). In Vulg.
simply *et mortem ossa mea*. Only
Symm. καὶ θάνατον διὰ τῶν ὀστέων μου
and Targ. מותא מן קיום גרמי 'death
rather than the conservation of my
bones' adhere to MT.

Of the pointings מַחֲנָק and מַחֲנַק,
noted by Ginsburg, we should decide in favour of the first, for מחנק
is in the absolute. The subject of
תִּבְחַר is נַפְשִׁי 'my soul' (Aq., Vulg.,

16 I am pining away! I shall not live for ever.
Leave me alone, for my days are but a breath!

Targ.). The meaning of the *hapax* מחנק is not in doubt, according to the use of the verb חנק in the *pi'el* 'strangle' (Nah 2 : 13), in the *niph'al* 'strangle one's self' (2 S 17: 23). We find the same meaning of the root חנק in Arabic and Assyrian. The verb בחר 'to choose', followed by the preposition מן, to signify 'prefer to' (Ps 89: 11). The preference is the result of conscious choice and discernment: 'and my soul would prefer strangling'. This is the longing of the sick when oppressed by insomnia. The 2nd hemistich is generally interpreted by regarding 'my soul prefers' as understood. Job would prefer death rather than to see his bones crushed by the weight of his sufferings. This sense seems rather unnatural to Le Hir, who suggests the interpretation of 'with my bones' as 'with all the force of my being', whence the translation: 'I call for it (death) with my whole heart's desire.' Renan translates on the same lines: 'My bones have called for death' (cf. Crampon). But in that case we are obliged to add a verb which is not suggested by the context. To be logical we should have to say that the soul chose death with all the force of its bones! It is evident that מָוֶת 'death' corresponds to מחנק 'strangling' as the effect to the cause, and that the word עצמותי must denote the thing to which Job prefers strangling and death, since it is preceded by the preposition מן (cf. sup.). We think at once of the sufferings which make life utterly intolerable. Hence the slight correction of Reiske, עַצְּבוֹתָי 'my sufferings' (9: 28) for עצמותי 'my bones', is accepted by most modern commentators (Merx, Beer, Budde, Loisy, etc.). The meaning thus yielded is perfect.

There is no necessity to take the correction further by linking מאסתי of v. 16 with the end of v. 15 (cf. Jerome and Syro-hex.): 'I despise death because of my sorrows' (Merx, Siegfried, Duhm). The meaning would rather be: 'I despise death more than my sorrows.' Far from despising or rejecting death, Job calls aloud for it with all his being. Thus we shall be satisfied to read עצבותי while noting that the reading עצמותי has been brought about by the attraction of the preceding word מות.

16 G omits מאסתי (Sah., Eth., Arab. Baud.), which is added at the end of v. 15 in Jerome and Syro-hex. (cf. sup.). For מאסתי Targ. רחיקית ד'' 'I refuse', Syr. ܠ ܐܬܚܡܠ 'all is finished for me', Vulg. *desperavi*. After אחיה G adds ἵνα μακροθυμήσω, which comes from 6: 11 (cf. Aq. and Vulg. in loc.). The addition is marked by an obelus in Jerome and Syro-hex. For הבל, G κενός (A and א καινός), Targ. למא 'nothing', Vulg. *nihil*. Transcription in Syr. ܘܗܒܠ.

If we accept for מָאַסְתִּי the normal meaning 'I have despised, refused', we have to presuppose as complement either 'death' (v. 15) or 'my life' in accordance with 9: 21. But in that case we no longer see the link between this clause and the following one. The verb is used without a complement, and it is only by artificial dexterity that it can be joined to what follows in order to produce the translation: *aversor ut perpetuum vivam* (opinion quoted by Rosenmüller; cf. Targ.). In v. 5 we noted that there exists a verb מאס parallel to מסס, in the sense of 'flow', 'drip'. In 42: 6 we find it used in the *qal* to mean 'to be sunk (in repentance)'. L. de Dieu and

17   What is a man that Thou dost set so much store by him
     And dost concentrate Thine attention upon him?
18   That Thou shouldst inspect him every morning,

Cappel had already proposed to explain by means of this verb the מאסתי of our verse. Whence arise such translations as *tabesco* (Rosenmüller), 'I am growing weaker' (Le Hir), 'I am fading away' (Renan), 'I succumb' (Loisy). Such a French expression as *fondre à vue d'œil* 'melt visibly away', used in the sense of 'grow thin', authorises us to render מאסתי by 'I pine away'. The Vulg. *desperavi* is based on understanding מאס in the sense of מסס, and treats the verb as a metaphor (cf. Comm. on 6:14). What follows, 'I shall not live for ever', is ironical. Why does God take so much trouble to persecute a man whose life is so transient? It is needless to force the meaning of לְעוֹלָם

in aeternum to produce, in the light of modern Hebrew, a banal idea: 'I no longer live in any sense' (contra Jacob, *ZATW*, 1912, p. 283). Job is asking God to exercise patience: 'Leave me alone, for my days are but a breath!' Cf. 10:20: 'Are not the days of my life but a little thing? Withdraw from me ....' Verb חדל 'cease', with מן before the complement to imply 'leave' some one in peace (Ex 14:12; Is 2:22). In accordance with v. 7 we can accept the word הֶבֶל in its original sense of 'breath', from which are derived such meanings as 'vanity', 'nothingness' (9:29; 21:34; 27:12; 35:16). In Ps 144:4, 'Man is like a breath (הבל), his days are like a passing shadow.' The various shades of meaning of הבל, one of the words for which the author of Ecclesiastes has a peculiar predilection, are well defined by Podechard (on Ec 1:2).

17 Syr. ܠܘܩܒܠܘܗܝ 'that Thou

shouldst ruin him', according to Beer, is the result of a reading תקטלנו or תדגלנו. But it may possibly be a corruption of a derivative form of ܪܒ, a verb to which Syrohex. has recourse in order to translate G ἐμεγάλυνας = M.T. תגדלנו.

Job passes from his individual situation to the consideration of that of humanity in general. He is a man like other men, i.e. a creature of clay whose frailty and perishableness are notorious (4:9ff.). The exclamation מָה־אֱנוֹשׁ recurs in Ps 8:5, where the theme is an exaltation of the grandeur of man. Ps 144, which we quoted in connection with v. 16, contains a phrase similar to our v. 17: 'O Lord, what is man that Thou dost regard him, or the son of man that Thou dost think of him?' (Ps 144:3). In this passage the subordinate verbs are preceded by the consecutive *waw*, whereas in Ps 8:5 we have כִּי exactly as in our verse; cf. 3:12b. The *pi'el* of גדל generally has the meaning of 'extol', 'magnify'. The context here suggests that it is a question of magnifying in thought, appreciating, thinking highly of. The expression שִׁית לב 'set the heart on' is used in the sense of the Latin *animadvertere*, to convey 'lend attention', 'concentrate the thought on' (1 S 4:20; 2 S 13:20). Cf. שִׂים לב (1:8; 2:3, etc.). The heart is the seat of the intellectual faculties (8:10). Cf. *L'Emploi métaphorique*, p. 124.

18 For ותפקדנו, G ἢ ἐπισκοπὴν αὐτοῦ ποιήσῃ. Aq. καὶ ἐπισκέπτῃ αὐτόν (cited in Syro-hex.) restores us to the MT. We find three variants of Aq. for לבקרים: πρωίας (following Syrohex. and Cod. regius unus), εἰς

And every moment scrutinise him?

19   For how long wilt Thou refuse to avert from me Thy gaze?
Wilt Thou not leave me alone while I swallow my spittle?

πρωίας (following Cod. 248), ἕως πρωί (following Codd. 137, 138); cf. G ἕως τὸ πρωί. The expression לרגעים is rendered εἰς ἀνάπαυσιν in G, which is thinking of רגע 'be at rest'; but Aq. and Symm. (following Syro-hex.) ἐν τοῖς αἰφνιδίος, Vulg. *subito*, Targ. לשעתא 'at the moment', Syr. ܒܚܪܐ 'at the time'. The verb בחן, reproduced in Targ., is interpreted by בחר in Syr., the two roots having the same sense in Syriac.

We find again the parallelism between פקד 'visit' (5: 24) and בחן 'test', 'scrutinise' in Ps 17: 3, 'Thou triest my heart, Thou visitest me by night.' The exact shade of meaning in פקד is 'to visit with a view to inspection' (31: 14). Of course the result of the visit may be chastisement (35: 15). The many senses of פקד in Hebrew can all be reduced to the original basic idea of visit or inspection. As for בחן, which means specifically 'pass through the crucible' in order to discover the degree of purity of a metal, it is used metaphorically for 'examine carefully', 'inspect', etc. (23: 10), and in consequence 'discern' (12: 11; 34: 3). The expression לבקרים, generally used with the article לַבְּקָרִים, is the equivalent of לבקר לבקר (1 Ch 9: 27) in meaning 'each morning'. And similarly לרגעים will mean 'at every moment' (Is 27: 3; Ezk 26: 16; 32: 10). The double meaning of the root רגע 'move' and 'be at rest' is apparent in the derivative רֶגַע 'instant' (*momentum* from *movimentum*) and 'tranquillity', 'rest' (21: 13; cf. G sup.). In Ps 8: 3 God 'visits' man in order to exalt him, here in order to test him. It is God who

'tries', 'tests' (verb בחן) the reins and the heart (Ps 7: 10; cf. Ps 26: 2); it is His eyelids which scrutinise the sons of men (Ps 11: 4; cf Ps 139: 23). He passes them through the crucible like silver (Ps 26: 2; 66: 10). Everywhere the verb בחן; cf. 23: 10.

19   For כמה G ἕως τίνος, Jerome and Vulg. *usquequo*, Syr. ܟܡܐ 'for how long?', but Targ. כמה. It is unnecessary to change כמה to עד־מה (Bickell, Beer) or to כימה (Reiske, Hitzig); cf. inf. At the close, G adds ἐν ὀδύνῃ [Jerome *in dolore*], marked by obelus in Syro-hex.

The interrogative כַּמָּה 'how much?' (13: 23) 'how many times?' (21: 17) has also the meaning of 'how long?': כמה תראה 'how long wilt Thou look on?' (Ps 35: 17). Hence the slightly different shade of meaning suggested by 'until when?', adopted by G, Vulg., Syr. The verb שעה 'look' with מִן before the complement (Is 22: 4), to mean 'look away from' 'avert one's gaze'; cf. 14: 6. The eyes of God, like those of a severe inspector, scrutinise man's conduct. Job would like to avoid this unremitting examination: 'For how long wilt Thou refuse to avert from me Thy gaze?' The *hiph'il* of רפה to mean 'leave some one alone', release him (Ca 3: 4); cf. 27: 6. The form בְּלְעִי, infinitive with suffix, like בְּגְדוֹ in Ex 21: 8. 'Until I swallow my spittle', that is to say, giving me time to swallow my spittle. Schultens quotes the Arabic proverb *'abli'ni rîqî* 'cause me to swallow my spittle', to mean 'leave me a moment'. In 9: 18 Job will ask for time to take a breath.

20 If I sin, what do I do to Thee,
O Thou watcher of men?
Why hast Thou taken me for Thy target,
And why am I burdensome to *Thee*?

20 עָלֶיךָ (G); MT: עָלָי.

20 The first part of the verse is
literally reproduced in Targ. and
Vulg. *peccavi, quid faciam tibi, o
custos hominum*? G and Syr. render
חטאתי by 'if I have sinned' (cf. inf.).
The first לך omitted in G (Eth.,
Arab. Baud.) is restored as σοί in G
(A, ℵ), Sah., Syro-hex., Jerome *tibi*.
The word נצר is connected with יצר
in Syr. 'Creator of man'. G paraphrases: ὁ ἐπιστάμενος τὸν νοῦν τῶν
ἀνθρώπων. G renders למפגע לך by
κατεντευκτήν σου 'thy accuser'. Syr.
'let me come before Thee' (retaining
the verb פגע), Targ. למארע לך
'as an injury to Thee', Symm. (according to Syro-hex.) ἐναντιοῦσθαί
σοι, Vulg. *contrarium tibi*. Instead
of עלי (Targ., Syr., Vulg. *mihime-
tipsi*), which is one of the eighteen
tiqqunê sopherîm 'corrections of the
scribes', G ἐπὶ σοί has retained the
original reading עָלֶיךָ.

Those commentators who see a
single hemistich in חטאתי...האדם
find themselves embarrassed by its
length. Bickell suppresses the whole
phrase, Merx cuts out נֹצֵר הָאָדָם. It
should be noted that נצר האדם
'Watcher of men' is ironical and is
an allusion to v. 12: 'that Thou
shouldst erect a barrier against me'.
This apostrophe constitutes in itself a small hemistich, 'O Thou
watcher of men!', like יעמד, which
is thrown into relief in 4: 16. The
1st hemistich is made up of
חטאתי...לך. And in fact we have in
35: 6a the perfect replica of this
hemistich: אם־חטאת מה־תפעל־בו
'If you sin, what effect do you produce on Him?' The perfect חטאתי

is the hypothesis: 'Let us admit that
I have sinned!' The imperfect which
follows marks the conclusion to be
drawn in such a hypothesis: 'What
harm can it do to Thee?' God ought
not to be affected in any way by
the sins of men. In 22: 2-3 Eliphaz
will insist on the fact that virtue is
man's concern, not God's concern.
The interrogative לָמָה, with the
accent on the first syllable, does not
recur elsewhere. When the *dagesh*
is not placed in the *mêm*, the accent
is on the last syllable. We have לָמָה,
with the accent on the first syllable,
in 1 S 1: 8. Construction of שׂים
with לְ before the indirect object.
One could have the accusative
(38: 9; 39: 6) or the particle "כ
(41: 23). The *hapax* מִפְגָּע conveys
the idea of what is encountered,
what one hits, or strikes, i.e. the
target; cf. במפגיע in 36: 32. 'Why
hast Thou taken me for Thy target?'
is certainly in the style of Job, who
has been complaining of being
struck by the arrows of God (6: 4).
Cf. 16: 12c, 'and He has set me up
as His target', where the word used
for 'target' is מַטָּרָה 'what one
watches, aims at'. The natural
meaning of מַשָּׂא is 'load', 'burden'.
It should be carefully distinguished
from משׂא 'oracle' (cf. Condamin on
Jer 23: 33, p. 186). The scribes have
changed עָלֶיךָ (cf. G) into עָלָי 'on
me' so as to avoid the offensive expression 'to be burdensome to God'.
The sin of Job must be felt to have
repercussions on himself, and not
on God. Cf. 19: 4.

21 And why dost Thou not tolerate my transgression,
And overlook my fault?
Now that in the dust I lay me down,
In vain wilt Thou seek me, I shall be no more.

21 G οὐκ ἐποίησω .... λήθην καὶ καθαρισμόν paraphrases תשא and תעבר, connecting תשא with נשא for נשה 'forget'. Instead of אשכב G reads אשוב ἀπελεύσομαι. In the light of שחר 'dawn', ושחרתני is rendered ὀρθρίζων δέ in G, et si mane me quaesieris in Vulg. But Targ. and Syr. translate by the Aramaic בעי 'seek'; cf. Symm. (according to Syro-hex.) κἂν ζητήσῃς με. For ואינני Symm. οὐχ ὑπάρξω, Vulg. non subsistam (cf. v. 8).

Pointing מֶה, because of the distance between this word and the pause (Gesenius-Kautzsch, § 37f); elsewhere because of a guttural (26: 2; 31: 2). The neuter interrogative pronoun מָה sometimes assumes the sense of 'why', like the Greek τί, the Latin quid (cf. 3: 12). Verb נשא 'raise', 'carry' but also 'lift', 'endure'. With the object פֶּשַׁע 'transgression' (Gn 50: 17) or עָוֹן 'fault' (Ps 85: 3), it has rather the sense of 'tolerate' (cf. tolerare from tollere) than that of 'pardon' which is generally given it. Olympiodorus had very well understood that Job argues on the basis of the shortness of his days in his request that God

would leave him in peace, even accepting the hypothesis, dato non concesso, that he is guilty. The hiph'il of עבר has as its object עון in 2 S 24: 10, just as here, and in 2 S 12: 13 חטאתך 'your sin'. The literal translation 'allow to pass' is very intelligible in the sense of 'not take into account', 'forgive'. The explanation of Job's special request is introduced by כִּי־עַתָּה 'now that' (4: 5). Notice the use of לְעָפָר for the phrase עַל־עָפָר of 20: 11 and 21: 26, where we have the same expression 'lie down in the dust' for 'die'. Dust is one of the characteristics of Sheol (17: 16); cf. RB, 1907, pp. 70f. To lie down in the dust implies not only to be consigned to the earth, but also to go and rest in Sheol. The pi'el of שחר 'seek out' carefully (8: 5). Job regards himself as already dead. In vain will God seek him out; He will no more find him. What is well emphasised here is the complete disappearance brought about by death. At the close וְאֵינֶנִּי as in v. 8. Job's speeches often end with the vision of death, the tomb, Sheol (10: 21-2; 14: 20-2; 17: 13-16; 21: 32-3).

CHAPTER 8

1   Then Bildad the Shuhite spoke and said:

2   For how long will you articulate such opinions,
     And the words of your mouth be a great wind?

3   Does God pervert the right,
     And does Shaddai make the course of justice to *deviate*?

Chapter 8 First speech of Bildad: see Introduction, p. xxxviiif.
3 יְעַוֵּה (cf. G, Vulg., Targ.); MT: יעות.

8:1 G renders בלדד השוחי by Βαλδαδ ὁ Σαυχείτης, a more literal translation than in 2:11.

2 For כביר, G πολυρῆμον, Jerome *multiloquax*, replaced by *multiplex* in Bod. (cf. Vulg.). G has joined אמרי to כביר. It seems that Theod. βαρύτατον (cf. βαρύτερος in 15:10) reads כבד 'heavy', 'grave' for כביר.

Bildad interrupts Job with a cry of impatience: *videbatur enim ei quod nimis protraxisset sermonem* (St Thomas). His second speech (18:2) will begin with עַד־אָנָה, which is the usual form, instead of עַד־אָן. Job will reply by the introductory עד־אנה in 19:2. אָן for אנה recurs in 1 S 10:14. The meaning of עַד־אָן or עַד־אָנָה 'up to where?' is also 'for how long?'; cf. the Latin *usquequo* and *quousque*? The verb מִלֵּל 'utter', 'articulate', 'speak' (33:3; Gn 21:7; Ps 106:2; Sir 32:3) is Aramaic; cf. מִלָּה (4:2). Note the use of אֵלֶּה 'these things', 'such opinions', alluding to the preceding speech: 12:3c, 9; 16:2. The question is of course continued in the 2nd hemistich: 'and the words of your mouth be a great wind?' Outside Job (15:10; 31:25; 34:17,

24; 36:5), the word כַּבִּיר 'great' recurs only in Isaiah (16:4; 17:12; 28:2). This adjective combines the meanings of greatness and abundance; cf. the verb הַכְבִּיר in 35:16 and 36:31. It corresponds to the Arabic *kebîr* 'great' in its various meanings. The Assyrian verb *kabâru* has in particular the sense of 'to be thick' (Meissner, *MVAG*, 1913, 2, p. 53, n. 3). Although in the masculine, the word רוח represents the wind (cf. 1:19; 4:15). There is no point in interpreting it as 'spirit', as Hontheim would. In 16:3 Job will characterise the speeches of Eliphaz as דברי־רוח 'words of wind'. The word אֹמֶר 'utterance' often attracts the complement פֶּה 'of the mouth'. Job is being accused of speaking rashly and illogically. The criticism of Bildad is aimed at both form and substance.

3 Syr. and Symm. (μεταστρέψει . . . εἰς ἄδικον μεταστρέψεται) are in agreement with MT in reading twice יעות. But G ἀδικήσει . . . ταράξει, Vulg. *supplantat . . . subvertit*, Targ. יקלקל⋯יעקם postulate two different words. In 33:27 it is the *hiph'il* of עוה which Targ. renders as קלקל. On the other hand, יעות משפט is

4 If your sons have sinned against Him,
   He has delivered them up to the fruits of their transgression.

confirmed by 34: 12. It is therefore the second יעות which must be replaced by יְעַוֵּה (Duhm). For שַׁדַּי, G ὁ τὰ πάντα ποιήσας. G and Symm. render צדק by τὸ δίκαιον (Jerome and Vulg. *quod justum est*).

The question of Bildad poses clearly the problem: 'Does God pervert the right?' Job has unceasingly protested that he is innocent, and has rebelled against the persecutions to which God subjects him (7: 11ff.). His last cry doubtless included some kind of concession to divine justice, but still contained a bitter protest. Admitting that he may have sinned, he demands that God should leave him in peace, since he has but a few days more to live (7: 20f.). Bildad is certain that the sovereign Judge cannot act except according to the principles of right. Bildad's words will be repeated by Elihu (34: 12b). Judgment, מִשְׁפָּט, is not merely the action of judging, or the place where judgment is declared, but also 'what is just', the right (34: 4, 5). The verb עִוֵּת 'bend', 'make swerve from the norm', 'distort' is used in the sense of 'falsify balances' (Am 8: 5). When the object is the name of a person, it means to fail to recognise some one's rights, to oppress (19: 6). Read יְעַוֵּה (cf. sup.) instead of the second יעות. The etymological sense of עוה is 'to be bent'. The *hiph'il* has the sense of making a path deviate in Jer 3: 21. Hence the expression ישׁר העויתי 'I have distorted the right' (33: 27). The *pi'el* offers here a similar meaning יעוה־צדק 'does He make the course of justice to deviate?' The parallelism is perfect.

4 The suffix of ישׁלחם, omitted in G, is translated in Sah. For בְּיַד, Targ. בְּאַתַר 'to the place'. G ἀνομίας,

which renders פֶּשַׁע, is considered as a genitive singular by Sah., Syro-hex., Eth., while Jerome *iniquitates eorum* sees here an accusative plural. G (A) τὴν ἀνομίαν αὐτῶν.

Bickell arbitrarily eliminates this v. 4. The allusion to the Prologue is plain. Job himself admitted that his sons might have sinned (1: 5). For Bildad, punishment presupposes crime. Duhm, who would make the 2nd hemistich a conditional clause, finds himself obliged to change אם־אתה into ואתה in v. 5. Ehrlich sees the main clause only in v. 6c. But the most natural understanding of the whole construction would be to distinguish two hypotheses, one applying to Job's sons, the other to Job himself. The first hypothesis is answered by 4b. That chapter is closed. The introduction of the apodosis by the consecutive *waw* is a rare construction, but there does however exist a certain number of examples which have been collected by Driver (*Hebrew Tenses*, § 127γ). The construction is purposely chosen to allow ישׁלח to be rendered as a perfect. The expression שִׁלַּח בְּיַד corresponds to שִׁלַּח בְּ" in Ps 81: 13, where God delivers up His people to their evil inclinations. Here the sons of Job are delivered up into the hands of their sin, for sin carries in itself an inevitable consequence its own punishment (4: 7ff.). Bildad proposes to separate the cause of Job from that of his sons. Each is responsible for his own deeds. 'The soul that sins shall die; the son shall not suffer for the iniquity of the father, nor the father suffer for the iniquity of the son: the righteousness of the righteous shall be upon himself, and the wickedness of the wicked shall be upon himself' (Ezk 18: 20; cf. Dt 24: 16). In La 1: 14

5   If now you will have recourse to God,
     And will make supplication to Shaddai,
6   [   ] From this moment He will watch over you,
     And will restore your abode of righteousness;

6a 'If you are pure and upright'. Gloss (see Comm.).

sins are described as a yoke attached to the neck of the sinner.

5 Syr., Targ., and Vulg. are in favour of MT אִם־אַתָּה, as against G σὺ δέ, from which Beer and Duhm would extract וְאַתָּה. For תְּשַׁחֵר G ὄρθριζε, Jerome *consurge diluculo*, Vulg. *diluculo consurrexeris* (cf. 7:21). Similar idea in Targ. תקדם בצלו 'you make your prayer early'. G renders שַׁדַּי by παντοκράτορα.

The fate of Job's sons is settled. Bildad proposes to his friend that he should avoid the final catastrophe by addressing himself to God. Eliphaz likewise recommended seeking refuge in God (5:8). Instead of violent words, supplications would be more likely to soften the Almighty. The verb שָׁחַר 'seek', 'seek out' (7:21) is synonymous with דרש, which is used with אֶל before its complement in the sense of 'address', 'have recourse to' (5:8). Thus the phrase תְּשַׁחֵר אֶל־אֵל corresponds to אדרש אֶל־אֵל in 5:8. Parallelism between אֵל and שַׁדַּי as in v. 3. The verb הִתְחַנֵּן 'beseech', 'implore' means etymologically 'endeavour to conciliate some one'. With לְ (instead of אֶל) before its complement (9:15; 19:16). Cf. the Assyrian *ana Marduk utnen* 'I have implored Marduk' and similar expressions in which figures the *iphta'al* of *enênu* (חנן). The argument of Bildad is the same as that of Eliphaz. All is not lost for Job. It is open to him to mitigate the rigours of divine justice and to

recover his former prosperity (5:17ff.).

6 Syro-hex. (following Aq. and Theod.) and Jerome *es tu* re-establish the translation of אתה (omitted in G), while marking it with an asterisk. After *si mundus et rectus*, Vulg. adds *incesseris*. G δεήσεως ἐπακούσεται reads יֶעְתַּר instead of יָעִיר. There is no justification in appealing to G for the elimination of the 2nd hemistich, which was in fact the basis of G's translation (contra Merx, Siegfried, Duhm). For נות, Targ. יאית 'beauty', Theod. εὐπρέπειαν (cf. Aq. and Vulg. 5:3), but G δίαιταν (cf. 5:3), Syr. 'domicile', Vulg. *habitaculum*.

Modern exegetes have recognised that v. 6 contains one hemistich too many, and it has been proposed to cut out the second. But it should be noted that כִּי־עַתָּה, no longer 'now that' (4:5; 7:21) but 'from this very moment' (cf. 13:19), introduces the apodosis which counts two parallel hemistichs. The subject of יָעִיר and שִׁלַּם is God, mentioned in v. 5 under the names of אֵל and שַׁדַּי. Now, the 1st hemistich 'if you are pure and upright' introduces an element which is alien to the main theme, for it suggests that personal purity is a prerequisite of efficacious prayer. Bildad is repeating the counsel of Eliphaz (5:8), who recommended seeking the help of God, to whom it belongs to restore Job to his former state of life and even to a better situation. For the moment the personal inte-

7 Your former condition will have been but a little thing,
So greatly will it be surpassed by your new state!
8 For inquire of the previous generation,
And pay heed to the experience of their fathers,

grity of Job is not in question. The restriction 'if you are pure and upright' is intended to show that, without a real conversion of the one who prays, prayer must remain inefficacious. The *hiph'il* הֵעִיר means not merely 'waken', but also 'awaken' 'wake up' (Ps 35: 23). With על before the complement, it means 'watch over' some one. The *pi'el* שִׁלֵּם means to restore something to its original wholeness, to repair, or re-establish. It is the *hiph'il* which has the meaning of 'pacify' (Vulg. *pacatum reddet*); cf. the *hoph'al* in 5: 23. The construct נְוַת presupposes a feminine נָוָה corresponding to the masculine נָוֶה 'abode', 'dwelling' (5: 3). The expression נְוַת צֶדֶק 'abode of righteousness' has a parallel נְוֵה צֶדֶק applied to the Holy Land (Jer 31: 23), and even to God (Jer 50: 7). The suffix of צדקך removes all doubt: 'the abode of righteousness' is the place where you live as a righteous man. One wonders why Ehrlich wishes to change the natural meaning of the verse by replacing יעיר by יעיד 'he will testify', and נות by מנת 'portion'. Ball changes נות into the prosaic כמו 'like'. Note that Eliphaz has made allusion to the abode (נוה) of the fool (5: 3).

7 Targ. and Syr. translate very literally. G and Vulg. render ראשית and אחרית by neuter plurals τὰ μὲν πρῶτά σου, *priora tua* . . . τὰ δὲ ἔσχατά σου , *et novissima tua*. For ישׂגה מאד, G ἀμύθητα (Jerome *infinita*).

The words רֵאשִׁית and אַחֲרִית are contrasted as the beginning and the end, the past and the future; cf. *RB*, 1920, pp. 496f; 1922, p. 224. When applied to a person they express his former and his new condition. Hence it is that, in 42: 12, where God blesses the new state of Job more than the old, the words used are אחרית and ראשׁית. Judging by the way in which G translates, it seems evident to us that these terms are at the root of those New Testament texts in which the new state of a man is contrasted with his former state: καὶ γίνεται τὰ ἔσχατα τοῦ ἀνθρώπου ἐκείνου χείρονα τῶν πρώτων 'and the last state of that man is worse than the first' (Lk 11: 26; cf. Mt 12: 45; 2 P 2: 20). The use of the masculine היה, in spite of the feminine subject, is not unusual when the verb precedes the subject (Gesenius-Kautzsch, § 145o). Parallelism has likewise permitted the masculine form of the verb יִשְׂגֶּה. The noun מִצְעָר 'little thing', 'trifle' (Gn 19: 20), 'a mere nothing'. It is contrasted with ישׂגה מאד 'will be very considerable'. The verb שׂגה is merely a variant of שׂגא 'to grow' (v. 11). The *qal* is found again only in Ps 92: 13, 'The righteous flourish like the palm tree, and grow (יִשְׂגֶּה) like a cedar in Lebanon.' Thus there is a clear comparison between the two conditions of the man, aimed at showing how insignificant was the former state by contrast with the new which is possible.

8 The pointing of רִישׁוֹן invites us to read רִאשׁוֹן (*qerê*). Syr. renders by the plural the words דור רישׁון. The reading בונן instead of כונן, which is proposed by Olshausen and Ball (following Syr.), is

9   Since we are but of yesterday and have not knowledge,
     Since our days on earth are a shadow,

more commonplace than כונן, supported moreover by Targ. כן. G
ἐξιχνίασον δὲ κατὰ γένος πατέρων and
Vulg. *et diligenter investiga patrum
memoriam* omit the suffix of אבותם.
The words ἐξιχνίασον and *investiga*
correspond to חקר (cf. 5: 27), while
κατὰ γένος and *diligenter* paraphrase
כונן according to the idea of 'do
suitably, in due order'.

The כי of the opening brings the
confirmation of previous statements. Bildad is now appealing to
the experience of former generations.
However, it is not a question of the
remote past, but simply of the previous generations in the more recent
past (cf. ראשית in v. 7). The Hebrews were fond of having recourse
to the authority of the fathers, or of
an older generation. The 1st hemistich recalls Dt 4: 32: כי שאל־נא
לימים ראשנים 'for ask now of the
days that are past!' Cf. Dt 32: 7
with vv. 8-10. The *po'lel* כונן 'fix'
implies the object לב 'heart', 'mind',
'attention' (cf. 7: 17). We find כון
with ל'' before the indirect object,
to convey the idea 'think on', 'meditate', in Is 51: 13. The meaning is
similar here, 'pay heed to'. The
plural suffix, on account of the collective, is confirmed by 15: 18, and
there is no reason whatever to suppress it (contra Duhm, Ball), for
Bildad wishes to show that even
the previous generation derives its
teaching and wisdom from tradition.
Furthermore, we have a confirmation of אבותם in Sir 8: 9, 'the
tradition of the aged which they
have received from their fathers'.
The exact meaning of חקר is investigation, study (5: 9); here, the
object and result of such study. Cf.
the abstract לקח in 11: 4.

9 G χθιζοί and Vulg. *hesterni* are

not calculated to favour a reading
מתמול instead of תמול (contra
Olshausen). Targ. and Syr. weaken
the text by rendering צל as 'like a
shadow' (cf. 6: 12; 7: 7). Syro-hex.
marks with an obelus ἐστίν of G's
phrase σκιὰ γάρ ἐστιν. For ימינו, G
ἡμῶν . . . ὁ βίος, but Colb. quotes in
the margin the more literal translation αἱ ἡμέραι ἡμῶν, which is that
of the other Greek interpreters, οἱ
λοιποί. Syro-hex. puts in the margin
the Greek ὁ βίος.

Life is too short for man to be able
to acquire the experience he needs.
This is why he must assimilate the
teaching and wisdom of previous
generations. The adverb תמול fulfils
the function of a predicate, exactly
like the noun שלום in 5: 24. Hence
we may translate, 'for we are of
yesterday', without its being necessary to place מן before תמול.
Hebrew has preserved אתמול and
תמול, like the Assyrian *itimâli* and
timâli 'yesterday', i.e. *itti mâli*, עת מול
'the time before'. Alfred de Musset
speaks of '*vieillards nés d'hier*'. We
have not yet been able to acquire
knowledge since we are but of
yesterday; 'we have not knowledge'.
The verb ידע is used without a complement; cf. ידע 'one who knows',
'the scholar', in 34: 2. A long life
would perhaps permit one to become learned. But 'our days on
earth are but a shadow'. The formula עלי־ארץ was applied to man
in 7: 1. The shadow is the symbol of
ephemeral things: 'man flees away
like the shadow' (14: 2); 'his days
are as the shadow which passes
away' (Ps 144: 4). Job has been
comparing his life to a wind (7: 7)
and his days to a breath (7: 16).
The shadow is another symbol of
that which vanishes (17: 7). Our

10   Is it not they who will instruct you and speak to you,
      And who will bring forth words from their heart?
11   Does papyrus grow where there is no marsh?
      Does the reed flourish in a waterless land?

2nd hemistich recurs in 1 Ch 29: 15, but with כְּצֵל 'like the shadow' (cf. Targ. and Syr.) instead of כי צל. Compare the reflection of Ulysses in the *Ajax* of Sophocles (125f.): Ὁρῶ γὰρ ἡμᾶς οὐδὲν ὄντας, ἄλλο πλὴν εἴδωλ᾽, ὅσοιπερ ζῶμεν, ἢ κούφην σκιάν.

10 After σὲ διδάξουσιν (יורוך) G (A) adds ῥήματα. After καὶ ἀναγγελοῦσιν (יאמרו לך), G (A) adds σοὶ σύνεσιν σοφίας. These readings of G (A) are quoted in the margin of Syro-hex. as coming from another copy. Jerome has simply *tibi* after *et referent* (καὶ ἀναγγελοῦσιν). Note that G (A) repeats σὲ διδάξουσιν ῥήματα in the 2nd hemistich instead of the literal translation ἐξάξουσιν ῥήματα of G (B, א). For מלבם Targ. מרעותהון ומרעיונהון 'from their will and thought'. The suffix of לבם, omitted in G, is restored by Aq., Theod., and Symm., which are cited in Syro-hex.

Duhm would suppress the verse on the ground that it is 'too empty and barren even for a Bildad'. But the opening הֲלֹא־הֵם 'is it not they?', which recalls the old men of v. 8, fits in very well with the whole sequence of the thought, and the verb יורוּך is confirmed by 6: 24 (cf. 12: 7, 8). Some moderns desire to insert the copula before יאמרוּ, in accordance with G, Syr., Targ. It seems to us more logical to take יאמרו לך, 'they will speak to you', as an explanation added and juxtaposed to יורוך, 'Is it not they who will instruct you, who will speak to you?' The 2nd hemistich, 'and will find words from the depths of their understanding?', characterises very well the teaching of the elders. Their

words spring not merely from their lips (15: 13) but from the depths of their heart and understanding. It is the heart which is the organ of the intellectual faculties: memory, attention, intelligence (1: 8; 7: 17, Comm.), wisdom (9: 4; 12: 3; 34: 10). The comparison with 15: 13 favours the authenticity of the verse (contra Duhm).

11 For גמא, G πάπυρος, Jerome and Vulg. *scirpus*. Syr. confuses with אגם 'marsh' and renders בלא בצה by 'in a dry or thirsty land'. G translates בצה simply as ὕδατος; cf. Vulg. *humore*. In Targ. the word אחו is rendered by ערקא 'covert of reeds', which will translate בצה in 40: 21. For אחו, G βούτομον (Jerome *juncus*), transcribed in the margin of Syro-hex. We have ἕλος in Aq. and Symm., *carectum* in Vulg., while Theod. keeps the word ἄχι, which recurs in Gn 41: 2, 18; Is 19: 7; Sir 40: 16; and in G (A) at Gn 41: 3, 19. Syr. gives ܘ̈ܚܠ 'rush', 'papyrus'. So as not to repeat ὕδατος, G paraphrases בלא־מים as ἄνευ πότου.

The wisdom of the fathers is expressed by means of proverbs (Sir 39: 1-3). It is indeed a proverb which is enshrined in these two hemistichs, each word of which is securely based. The same interrogative construction as in 6: 5-6. The two names of plants are גמא and אחו. The former denotes the papyrus of Egypt, the stem of which is used for making skiffs (Ex 2: 3; Is 18: 2). This plant requires a very humid, marshy soil (Is 35: 7). It is probable that גמא stems from an Egyptian word from which is derived the Coptic ⲕⲁⲙ 'river bulrush'. It should be noted

12   It is still flowering, it is not yet gathered,
       And before any other plant, it withers away!

that גמא is rendered by πάπυρος in
G, and that in Ex 2:3 Aq. and
Symm. also translate it as πάπυρος.
Similarly, Theod. in Is 18:2 and
Vulg. *papyri* (genitive) in Is 18:2.
Saadia translates by the Arabic
bardiy, which is one of the names of
the papyrus. The parallel word to
גמא is אָחוּ which is found in Gn
41:2, 18, to denote the locality
where the fat kine feed. Whence the
translations of באחו by ἐν τῷ ἕλει
'in the marsh' (Aq. and Symm., as
here), *in locis palustribus* and *in
pastu paludis* (Vulg.), حمني 'in
the meadow' (Syr.). But Arab. and
Saadia render by *fi-l-qurṭ* 'in the
clover'. Onqelos באחוא and G ἐν τῷ
ἄχει content themselves with transcribing אחו as an exotic word (Gn
41:2-3, 18-19; cf. sup.). G renders
by τὸ ἄχει τὸ χλωρόν the Hebrew
ערות of Is 19:7. With regard to ἄχει
or ἄχι, Jerome makes this interesting
remark: *cumque ab eruditis quaererem
quid hic sermo significaret, audivi ab
Aegyptiis hoc nomine, lingua eorum,
omne quod in palude virens nascitur
appellari* (on Is 19:7 (Migne, *PL*,
XXIV, col. 252)). These indications, combined with the interpretations of the versions in our
text, prove that the Hebrew אחו
denotes both an aquatic plant and
also the marshy land in which it
grows, hence very probably 'the
rush' here and 'the plantation of
rushes' or the marshy soil in Gn
41:2, 18. The verb גאה 'to rise', of
waters (Ezk 47:5), 'to be exalted,
sublime' (Ex 15:1, 21), or 'to be
haughty, proud' (Job 10:16; Sir
10:9). In speaking of plants,
'become tall', 'grow', 'flourish'. Since
the verbs שׂגה and שׂגא vary only in
orthography, one may hesitate between the reading יִשְׂגֶּה, which was
that of Hillel, and יִשְׂגָּא, which is

that of Qimchi. We had יִשְׂגֶּה in v. 7,
but it is the spelling שׂגא which
recurs in the *hiph'il* in 12:23; 36:24.
Outside the Book of Job, we find the
qal יִשְׂגֶּה in Ps 92:13 (cf. v. 7) and
the *hiph'il* הִשְׂגִּיו in Ps 73:12. The
meanings of שׂגא are the same as
those of גאה. The word בִּצָּה recurs
only in 40:21, where it means as
here 'the marsh', and in Ezk 47:11,
where it represents 'the lagoon'. V.
13 will apply the proverb to the
impious man, whose lot is comparable with that of the papyrus and
bulrush which inevitably wither
away in a soil that is dried up.

12   For באבו, G ἐπὶ ῥίζης, Aq. ἐν ὥρα
αὐτοῦ, Vulg. *in flore*, Targ. בגיותיה
'in its height', Syr. חרבה 'in its
fruit'. G καὶ οὐ μή and Vulg. *nec* put
the copula before לא. But Targ. and
Syr. are in agreement with MT. G
πρὸ τοῦ πιεῖν πᾶσα βοτάνη οὐχὶ ξηραίνεται repeats the negative, but secures the sense by making the
phrase interrogative. The introduction of τοῦ πιεῖν suggests a special meaning. Instead of οὐχὶ ξηραίνεται, G (A) ἐὰν δὲ μὴ πίῃ ξηραίνεται
conveys the meaning demanded by
the context. The reading of G (A) is
cited in the margin of Syro-hex. The
versions agree as to the meaning of
לפני 'before': G πρό, Vulg. *ante*,
Targ. and Syr. קדם.
   The first clause begins with עוֹד, the
second with the copula, exactly as
in 1:16-18. The parenthetical לא
יִקָּטֵף is juxtaposed to the principal
clause to emphasise the meaning of
the latter. With excellent appositeness Driver cites Nu 11:33, where
טֶרֶם יִכָּרֵת 'it was not yet consumed'
is simply juxtaposed to 'while the
meat was yet (עוֹדֶנּוּ) between their

13   Such is the fate of all those who forget God,
      And the hope of the godless man thus perishes.

teeth'. The 1st hemistich should
therefore be translated: 'It is still
flowering, it is not yet gathered.'
The plant is still in the early stages
of its growth, it has not yet reached
maturity. The word אֵב 'flower'
occurs again only in Ca 6: 11, where
אִבֵּי הַנַּחַל means 'flowers of the
valley'. Since the absolute form of
the singular is not found, we might
hesitate between the pointings אָב
and אַב (cf. *Thesaurus* of Ben-
Yehuda, I, p. 7). In Arabic, *abb*
means 'meadow', 'pasture'. To the
same root as אב belongs the word
אָבִיב 'ear of corn'. In view of these
various meanings, we conclude that
אב means the plant which is still
in its early or blossoming stages,
whence the meanings just noted in
Hebrew and Arabic, whereas אביב
implies that it has reached the stage
of maturity. And we note that in
Aramaic, the root אבב has precisely
the meaning of 'to be ripe, mature'.
The word חָצִיר 'plant' will recur in
40: 15. Our verse is the inspiration
of Sir 40: 16, where the original
text, as attested by the ἄχει of G,
contained for certain the word אחו
of v. 11 (cf. Peters).

13 G τὰ ἔσχατα read אַחֲרִית (cf.
inf.) instead of ארחות. For חָנֵף, G
ἀσεβοῦς, Vulg. *hypocritae*, Targ.
דִּילָטוֹר (*delator*, cf. Krauss). Syr.
ﺳﻨﻔﺎ preserves the Aramaic equivalent.
    The comparison is introduced by
כֵּן, exactly as in 6: 21 (cf. Comm.) and
7: 3. Instead of אָרְחוֹת 'the paths',
we might be inclined to read אַחֲרִית
'end', 'fate' (v. 7) with G (cf. Ginsburg), if Pr 1: 19 did not formally

confirm the MT. The paths are the
tracks of fate, already marked out
by God and inevitably followed by
man; cf. the use of the word דֶּרֶךְ
in Is 40: 27; Jer 10: 23; Ps 37: 5.
'Those who forget God' recurs in
Ps 50: 22 where אֵל is replaced by
אֱלוֹהַּ. The 2nd hemistich figures in
Pr 10: 28, where however we find
רְשָׁעִים 'the wicked' instead of חָנֵף,
which is a favourite word in the
Book of Job (8: 13; 13: 16; 15: 34;
17: 8; 20: 5; 27: 8; 34: 30; 36: 13).
The original meaning of the root
חנף is 'to be profane or profaned',
as is clear from the use of the verb
חָנֵף in Is 24: 5; Jer 3: 1; Ps 106: 38.
This same verb in the *hiph'il* means
'to profane' (Nu 35: 33; Jer 3: 2, 9).
It is very understandable that
Syriac has deduced from this meaning that of 'pagan' or 'heathen'
for the noun ﺳﻨﻔﺎ. This meaning
was known in Aramaic, and it seems
that the causative of הנף in Dn
11: 32 means nothing else but 'to
make heathen'. In Is 10: 6 the גוי
חנף means 'the profane people', i.e.
a people which has renounced its
divine mission. Here the implication
of apostasy is added to that of
heathenism. Let us note that Syriac
uses the epithet ﺳﻨﻔﺎ to characterise Julian the Apostate. In our
verse the חָנֵף is in parallelism precisely with the אל שֹׁכְחֵי 'those who
forget God'. The חָנֵף is thus both a
renegade and an impious man. The
deeds of this godless man will inevitably be bad, in view of the nexus,
which, among the Semites, has always existed between religion and
morals. Thus the חנף will be included in the category of the wicked.
That is why, in Pr 10: 28, רשעים

14   He whose trust lies in a *bag*,
      Whose security is slender as the spider's house:

14   יַלְקוּט ;MT: יקוט.

'the wicked' play the same part as the חנף in our verse. In Job 20: 5 חנף will be in parallelism with רשעים; in 27: 8 it will close the enumeration begun with רשע 'the wicked man' and עול 'the evil doer'. In Is 33: 14, the חנפים are parallel with חטאים 'sinners'. Let us note further that in Sir 16: 6, עדת חנף 'the company of the godless' (cf. Job 15: 34) is replaced by עדת רשעים 'the company of the wicked' in parallelism with גוי חנף (Is 10: 6). Naturally the חנף will be contrasted with the innocent (13: 16; 17: 8) or with the חסיד 'pious', 'faithful' (Sir 41: 10-11). The meaning of hypocrite or flatterer which arose later for חָנֵף (cf. 36: 13) springs from the fact that the root חנף possessed, in addition to the meaning 'to be profane', the further meaning of 'to be deceitful, calumniatory'. This meaning appears in the phrase *ḥanpa ša iḥnupû ana muḥḥi-ia* 'the false accusation with which they have slandered me', found in an el-Amarna letter which was sent from Jerusalem (Knudtzon, No. 288, 7-8). It is possible that this meaning of חנף arises from a distortion of the root חלף 'change' 'substitute'. The slanderer, the hypocrite, the flatterer, falsify deeds and words, according to their requirements. Cf. Levy, *Neuhebr. und chald. Wörterbuch*, s.v. חנף, for the connection between חנף and חלף.

14 G renders כסלו by a concrete expression αὐτοῦ... ὁ οἶκος. Similarly, מבטחו is translated αὐτοῦ... ἡ σκηνή (G) and 'his house' (Syr.) under the influence of the 'house of the spider'. The word ἀράχνη (G) means not only 'the spider' but also

'the spider's web'. G (A) adds καὶ ἡ ὁδὸς αὐτοῦ after οἶκος; this is perhaps the surviving trace of a divergent translation. The word יקוט is interpreted as a verb by G ἀοίκητος .... ἔσται, Vulg. *non ei placebit*, Targ. תזוח 'is set aside', Syr. ܡܣܬܚܦ 'is broken'.

The 2nd hemistich, 'whose security is slender as the spider's house', offers no difficulty. In Arabic as in Hebrew, the spider's web is its house. It is of course a symbol of fragility, as in Is 59: 5, where the terms used are קורי עכביש 'spider's web'. To מִבְטָחוֹ 'his security' (18: 14; 31: 24) corresponds, in the 1st hemistich, כִּסְלוֹ 'his trust'. The same parallelism recurs in 31: 24. For the meaning of כָּסָל cf. 4: 6. It is evident that יקוט must correspond to בית עכביש, which seems to exclude translation by means of a verb. Nevertheless attempts have been made to relate יקוט to the Arabic *qaṭṭa* 'cut' (Rosenmüller), or to *qâḍa* 'break' (Hitzig and Dillmann). Qimchi and Rashi connect it with קט (Ezk 16: 47), which seems to be the Arabic *qaṭ* 'only', and so these authors assign to it the meaning of 'little'. Saadia translates, in the light of the parallelism, by חבל אלשמש, Arabic *ḥabl eš-šams* 'string of the sun', a name for gossamer. This translation which, unfortunately, has no support in the Semitic tongues, inspires Bickell with the suggestion חוט קיץ 'summer thread' for יקוט, and suggests to Budde קורי קיט 'summer threads' for אשר יקוט, both critics interpreting with the help of the German *Sommerfaden*, a name for gossamer. Beer proposes to replace יקוט by

15   He leans on his house and it does not hold,
      He lays hold of it, and it has no resisting power!
16   He is watered before the sun rises,
      And in the garden where he is rooted appear his suckers.

קורים or קוּרים (Is 59: 5), plurals of
קו or קוּר 'thread'. Ehrlich gives up
the search for the original word.
Torczyner changes אשר יקוט into
אש זקות, which he translates by *Feuer-
fünkchen*, 'a little fiery spark'. We
ourselves somewhat timidly suggest the reading יַלְקוּט, which denotes the shepherd's bag or scrip
(1 S 17: 40). An empty bag would
be the symbol of something un-
stable and futile.

15 G puts at the beginning the
conditional particle ἐάν. The versions, with the exception of the
Vulg., repeat the copula before
יחזיק. For יחזיק בו, G ἐπιλαβομένου
δὲ αὐτοῦ (Jerome *et cum coeperit*).

Budde suppresses v. 15 as being a
mere explanation of v. 14. But we
have here a real development of the
thought occasioned by the image of
the 'spider's house'. The confidence
of the evil doer is no more solid than
the spider's web. He cannot rest on
it. Since the web and the house are
equivalent, we can understand very
well the 1st hemistich, 'he leans on
his house and it does not hold!' Note
that in 24: 23 the verb נשען 'to be
supported' has as its complement
לבטח 'with security'; cf. מבטחו in
v. 14. The verbs עמד and קום indicate two aspects of a single action:
קום 'rise', 'stand up', עמד 'to be,
remain, standing'. This original
distinction is very well brought out
in 29: 8. Here קום becomes almost
synonymous with עמד, whose
meaning of 'to be standing' (4: 16;
30: 20) develops into that of 'remain', 'stay' (14: 2; 32: 16; 37: 14).
To remain where you are is to 'hold'
(neuter sense) and 'resist'. On החזיק
ב" cf. Comm. on 2: 3.

16 Targ. and Syr. preserve the
root רטב. The adjective is very well
translated ὑγρός . . . ἐστιν (G),
ἔνικμός ἐστιν (Aq.), *humectus videtur*
(Vulg.). For לפני, G ὑπό, but Targ.
and Syr. קדם 'before'. Vulg. *antequam*. By haplography, the 2nd
hemistich has fallen out of Syr.
Instead of על־גנתו 'on his garden',
G ἐκ σαπρίας αὐτοῦ (?). Vulg. *et in
orto suo* is a corruption of *et in horto
suo*.

The godless man is here compared
to a well-watered plant which produces shoots (cf. 5: 3; 15: 31ff.,
etc.). The root רטב 'to be moist,
watered' recurs in Aramaic, Arabic,
and Assyrian. It occurs only twice
in the Bible, and both times in Job:
we shall have the verb ירטבו 'they
are moist' in 24: 8. Here the adjective רָטֹב, whose form is *qatul* (like
the Assyrian *raṭubtu* in the feminine)
means specifically 'watered'. In
Assyrian *iṣṣu raṭbu* is the 'well-
watered tree', whether by nature
or by man. Hence our translation:
'he is watered before the sun rises';
cf. לפני in v. 12. The plant is bathed
in the freshness of the dew before
the sun rises. The 2nd hemistich,
'and in the garden where he is
rooted appear his suckers', has seemed curious to some moderns, who
have thought that 'his garden' meant
the garden of the godless man.
Hence the corrections of גנתו into
גנות 'the gardens' (Beer) or גגות 'the
roofs' (Budde). But גנתו 'his garden'
means simply 'the garden where he
is rooted'; cf. 7: 10. Verb יצא
'spring up out of the ground' (5: 6),
'germinate', 'grow' (14: 2). Cf. the
use of the *hiph'il* in Gn 1: 12; Is

17   Against a heap of stones are his roots intertwined,
     In a house of stones he *lives*!

17 יִחְיֶה (G); MT: יחזה.

61: 11, etc. The word יוֹנַקְתּוֹ, literally
'his nursling' (cf. ינק in 3: 12), conveys well the idea of the sucker
which is detached from the base of
the trunk; cf. 14: 7; 15: 30.

17 Syr. interprets גל in the sense
of the plural גַּלִּים 'waves' (38: 11).
The meaning of 'heap' is well understood by Targ. אִיגָר, G συναγωγὴν
λίθων, Vulg. *acervum petrarum*. The
word שָׁרָשָׁיו is omitted in G. For
יְסֻבְּכוּ G κοιμᾶται reads יִשְׁכַּב. For
וּבֵית אֲבָנִים, G ἐν δὲ μέσῳ χαλίκων,
Vulg. *et inter lapides*. Instead of
יחזה, G ζήσεται read יִחְיֶה. The 2nd
hemistich is arbitrarily paraphrased
in Symm. ἐπὶ πίονι γῇ φύεται.

Some commentators would see in
this verse a description of the punishment which overtakes the godless. It is supposed that the plant
encounters rocky soil and can no
longer live: *sed silicibus implicantur
radices ejus, fundum sentit petrosum*
(Rosenmüller). But this is not the
way in which the plant is to die.
In v. 18 it is uprooted from its place,
and it is thus that it disappears.
The natural sense of the 1st hemistich is 'against a heap of stones are
his roots intertwined', the preposition עַל marking the fact of contact between the roots and the
stones. The use of the *puʻal* of סבך
'intertwine' (Nah 1: 10) indicates
that the complement גל must denote
the object around which the roots
are twined, a fact which excludes
the interpretation of גל as 'source'
(Perles and Duhm, on the basis of
Ca 4: 12). The parallelism with בֵּית
אֲבָנִים is a further proof that גל is
the 'heap of stones' (Targ., G.,
Vulg.); cf. גלים in 15: 28. It is a

source of strengthening to the plant
to be able to knot its roots around
stones. In particular, the mandra-
gora cleaves with such vigour to
the rocky fragments around which
it grows that as a result it becomes
almost impossible to uproot. The
parallel to the heap of stones is the
בֵּית אֲבָנִים 'house of stones' mentioned in the 2nd hemistich. The גל
'heap' is formed by means of stones
(Gn 31: 46ff.), and the word אבנים
'stones' determines גל in Jos 7: 26;
8: 29; 2 S 18: 17. The house of
stones then represents the tumulus
to which the roots of the plant cling.
This forms a solid base of support,
by contrast with the 'houses of
clay' of 4: 19. It is not necessary to
give to בֵּין the meaning of 'between'
(Pr 8: 2; Ezk 1: 27; 41: 9), still less
to correct it by the substitution of
the preposition בֵּין 'between'
(Wright, Siegfried, etc.). The difficulty lies in יַחֲזֶה 'he sees' which is
made to mean 'he feels', 'he touches',
or even 'he chooses' (Ball). Ehrlich
considers יחזה as an impersonal
verb: 'people think they see a house
of stones' (cf. יחשב in 41: 24). But
it would be extraordinary for a
plant to produce this effect on those
who look at it. Various corrections
have been proposed by the moderns:
יָחֹז (from חזז not in use) 'he pierces',
or יֶחֱז (from אחז) 'he grasps, clutches
at' (Budde), or יַחֲזֵק 'holds on
(between)' (Wright). According to
the parallelism with עַל־גל, it would
seem that בֵּית אבנים should also be
a complement of place. Naturally
the preposition בְּ is omitted before בֵּית (cf. Gesenius-Kautzsch,
§ 118g). Instead of יחזה, G ζήσεται

18   If he is removed from his place,
     Then it will disown him, saying: 'I have never seen you!'
19   Behold him lie rotting on *a* path
     And from the soil others spring!

19   דָּרֶךְ; MT: דרכו.

offers the excellent reading יִחְיֶה 'he lives' (Graetz, Siegfried, Duhm). The 2nd hemistich depicts perfectly the plant growing in the midst of stones and gaining as a result only the greater robustness and solidity.

18 Syr. interprets בלע as 'uproot', while G ἐὰν καταπίῃ (in A αὐτόν is added), Vulg. *si absorbuerit eum*, Targ. אם יסלעמניה, are faithful to the etymological meaning 'swallow', 'absorb', 'devour'. Symm. and Theod. κυριεύσει read perhaps בעל for בלע. Syr. and Vulg. *et dicet* add a formula of introduction to the direct speech. G οὐχ ἑόρακας τοιαῦτα seems to read ראית כן instead of ראיתיך.
Description of the punishment which strikes the godless man. He will be torn up like the plant which was growing vigorously in the garden. Verb בלע in the *qal* 'swallow' (7:19; 20:15, 18), in the *pi'el* 'engulf', 'destroy', 'ruin' (2:3; 10:8), but here, because of the complement מִמְּקֹמוֹ 'from his place', simply 're-move' (cf. the French word *ôter* which comes probably from *haus-tare*, a derivative of *haurire* 'empty', 'absorb', 'engulf'). Of course מקמו 'his place' means 'the place where he is rooted'; cf. גנתו in v. 16. The subject of יְבַלְּעֶנּוּ is the impersonal 'one'. The godless man leaves neither trace nor memory. The verb כִּחֵשׁ 'disown' (cf. 31:28) has as subject מקמו. Compare 7:10b: 'and the place where he was sees him no more', a phrase which recurs in Ps 103:16. In Ps 37:36 (according to G) it is the passer-by who no longer

finds any trace of the wicked man in this context compared to a tree.

19 G ὅτι καταστροφὴ ἀσεβοῦς τοι-αύτη recalls the godless man of v. 13, where חנף was rendered by ἀσεβοῦς. The word καταστροφή paraphrases מְשׂושׂ דרך and does not presuppose a reading מְשׁוּבַת (contra Merx), for the meaning of משׁובת is 'defection', 'apostasy'. Targ. and Vulg. *haec est enim laetitia viae ejus* render the text very literally, leaving to משׂושׂ the meaning of 'joy'. Syr. כי 'he has examined' seems to read מִשֵּׁשׁ 'he has examined by touching' (Beer).
The 1st hemistich has been inter-preted as ironical: 'Such is the joy of his way!' (cf. Targ. and Vulg.). Commentators have paraphrased this to yield: 'That is where his joy ends' (Le Hir; cf. Crampon); 'That is what becomes of his good fortune' (Loisy); 'Such are the delights which his mode of life earns for him' (Segond). One cannot urge against such renderings that in this construction it would be preferable to use הוּא rather than זֶה (Beer, Ehrlich), for in 31:28 we find an example of הוא in the sense of 'this' or 'that'. But it is clear that the 2nd hemistich 'from the soil others spring' contrasts these 'others' with הֶן־הוּא 'behold him!'—an expression which must refer to a person or some object. The word מְשׂושׂ has been written thus because it has been regarded as the noun meaning 'joy' (root שׂושׂ). But it may have

20   No, God does not despise the perfect man,
Nor does He grasp the hand of evil doers!

21   Your mouth *will again be filled* with laughter,
And your lips with gladness;

21   עֹד יְמַלֶּה (cf. G, Syr., Vulg.); MT: עד־ימלה.

been written thus (מָשׁוֹשׁ) for מסוס, just as we find כעשׂ for כעס in 5:2, etc. Hence instead of connecting מָשׁוֹשׁ with a root שׁושׂ, we might derive it from סוס, from which stems סָס 'moth', in Assyrian *sâsu*, in Arabic *sûseh*. The Arabic verb *sâs* is denominative and means 'to be eaten by moths or worms, worm-eaten' or again 'to be decayed, rotting'. Thus we see how מְשׁוֹשׁ, a form analogous to מתם 'perfect', 'intact' (from תמם), can mean 'rotting'. We then read דְּרָךְ (in pause) for דרכו, the suffix of which springs from a mistaken interpretation of the 1st hemistich or simply from dittography. The word דרך plays the part of an accusative of place (cf. Gesenius-Kautzsch, § 118b, g). Hence we shall translate: 'Behold him lie rotting on a path.' The adjective אַחֵר 'other' is considered to be a collective, hence the plural יִצְמָחוּ, although the subject comes before the verb. The noun עָפָר, exactly as in 5:6, denotes the soil in which plants germinate. The godless man was compared to a vigorous plant which is suddenly torn up. The plant is thrown away by the roadside, while on the spot where it grew other plants will shoot up.

20   Vulg. renders תם by *simplicem* (cf. 1:1). G interprets יחזיק ביד in the sense of 'take by the hand', whence the 2nd hemistich πᾶν δὲ δῶρον ἀσεβοῦς οὐ δέξεται. With Symm. οὐδὲ ὀρέξει χεῖρα κακουργοῖς compare Vulg. *nec porriget manum malignis*.

Bildad returns to his opening thesis, namely that God is supremely just (v. 3). This divine justice is manifested in the protection which He grants to the good and refuses to the wicked. The verb מאס is no longer the same as in 7:5, 16. It is indeed here מאס 'despise', 'reject'. God does not reject the blameless man; on the contrary He is concerned for him and surrounds him with loving care. The negative sentence forms a kind of litotes. With the perfect man תָּם (1:1) are contrasted the מְרֵעִים, who are, properly speaking, 'the evil doers', plural of מֵרַע, *hiph'il* participle of רעע 'to be wicked'. The מרעים are frequently met with in the Psalms, where they constitute the band of persecutors of the just and the godfearing (22:17; 27:2; 64:3, etc.). The real meaning of החזיק ביד is 'grasp the hand' of some one (cf. Comm. on 2:3), to support or help the person.

21   G δὲ reads עֹד and not עַד (Targ., Syr., Vulg. *donec*). Instead of יְמַלֶּה Syr. and Vulg. *impleatur* read יִמָּלֵא, confirmed by Ps 126:2. G ἀληθινῶν . . . . στόμα interprets the suffix of פִּיךְ in accordance with v. 20. For תרועה G (B, א) ἐξομολογήσεως, but G (A) ἀγαλλιάσεως, quoted as a variant in Colb. Following the interpretation of פִּיךְ, G renders ושׂפתיך by τὰ δὲ χείλη αὐτῶν.
The reading עֹד instead of עַד, proposed by Houbigant (cf. G), has been generally accepted by exe-

22 Those who hate you will be clothed with shame,
    And the tent of the wicked will be no more!

getes. The text cannot be understood with עַד 'until', whereas the
adverb עֹד 'once again' is perfectly
in keeping with the context; cf.
1:18. Bildad borrows the 1st hemistich from Ps 126:2, where we find
אָז 'then' as the opening adverb.
Following this Psalm it is clear
that we must read יְמַלֶּה 'will be
filled' instead of יְמַלֵּה 'he will fill'.
The spelling with ה instead of א is
no more than a variation in orthography (Gesenius-Kautzsch, § 23e).
In 12:4, שְׂחוֹק 'laughter' is the
victim of the laughter or mockery.
Bildad has invited his friend to
turn to God who may restore him
to happiness and prosperity (5-7).
He has pointed out to his friend that
abiding joy is not found among the
wicked. He assumes that Job accepts his ideas, and promises him
felicity: 'Your mouth will again be
filled with laughter, and your lips
with gladness.' The word תְּרוּעָה
(33:26) expresses the shout of joy;
cf. the *hiph'il* of רוע (not used in
the *qal*) in 38:7. It will also be the
war cry (39:25).

22 G continues its universalisation
of the suffixes and renders שֹׂנְאֶיךָ by
οἱ δὲ ἐχθροὶ αὐτῶν (cf. v. 21). For
אֹהֶל, G δίαιτα and Aq. σκέπη are
rather vague. Vulg. renders אֵינֶנּוּ by
non subsistet (cf. 7:8, 21).
The style of the Psalms, which became apparent in the use of מְרֵעִים
in v. 20 and especially in the citation
of v. 21, is again evident in this
conclusion. First of all, the expression שֹׂנְאֶיךָ 'those who hate you',
i.e. your enemies, which corres-

ponds to שֹׂנְאַי 'my enemies' constantly used in the Psalms (9:14;
18:18; 21:9; 35:19, etc.). Note
that the allusion is in particular to
the enemies of the righteous man, a
fact which explains the parallelism
with רְשָׁעִים 'the wicked' (cf. Ps
34:22). We meet again the phrase
יִלְבְּשׁוּ־בֹשֶׁת 'may they be clothed
with shame' in Ps 35:26, and we
find אַלְבִּישׁ בֹּשֶׁת 'I will clothe with
shame' in Ps 132:18; cf. Ps 109:29.
Shame is envisaged as a garment
which clothes the enemies of the
righteous. There is a similar use of
לָבַשׁ in 7:5. 'The tent of the wicked'
is likewise a feature of the style of
the Psalms, where 'the tents of un-
godliness' are contrasted with 'the
tents of the righteous' (Ps 84:11
and Ps 118:15). Further, the nomadic setting in which the story
of Job moves explains the use of
'tent' or 'tents' to connote the
dwelling, the family (cf. Ps 52:7;
69:26). Sometimes it is the tent of
Job (5:24; 19:12; 22:23; 29:4;
31:31) or his tents (11:14). At
other times, as here, the tent of the
wicked (18:6, 14, 15) or their tents
(21:28), the tents of bribery (15:
34). We have אֵינֶנּוּ conveying in
itself the idea 'exists no more'.
Generally אֵינוֹ is joined by the
copula to the previous clause; cf.
וְאֵינֶנּוּ in 3:21; 23:8; 24:24; 27:19.
Similarly וְאֵינֶנּוּ (7:8, 21). Like the
speech of Eliphaz, that of Bildad
concludes with a promise of happiness for the godly, by contrast
with the punishment which sooner
or later will overtake the wicked.

CHAPTER 9

1 Then Job spoke and said:
2 In truth, I know that this is so;
And how can a man be just before God?
3 If he wishes to dispute with Him,
He will not answer him once in a thousand times.

Chapters 9-10. Third speech of Job: see Introduction, pp. xxxviiif.

9: 2 Vulg. and Syr. interpret וּמַה as a negative. But G πῶς γάρ and Targ. וּמַה faithfully reproduce the MT. Vulg. paraphrases עִם־אֵל by *compositus Deo*.

The adverb אָמְנָם 'in truth' is a characteristic word in the Book of Job (12: 2; 19: 4; 34: 12; 36: 4). Apart from this book, it is found only in 2 K 19: 17; Is 37: 18; Ru 3: 12. Elsewhere אֻמְנָם (Gn 18: 3; Nu 22: 37; 1 K 8: 27; Ps 58: 2; 2 Ch 6: 18). The next speech of Job will begin also with אָמְנָם (12: 2). The friends of the unhappy man have been dwelling on commonplace truths: 'In truth, I know that this is so!' Job knows as much about it all as his friends (13: 2). Instead of attacking Bildad directly, he recurs to points made by Eliphaz: 'And how can a man be just before God?' This is almost verbally the question put by the nocturnal apparition in 4: 17. Interrogative מָה before an intransitive with the sense of 'how?'; cf. מַה־נִּצְטַדָּק 'How shall we justify ourselves?' (Gn 44: 16). The preposition עִם 'with', 'before', 'in the presence of' dispels the ambiguity raised by מִן in 4: 17. The hemistich is repeated in 25: 4.

3 G has a double translation of

לֹא יַעֲנֶנּוּ: οὐ μὴ ὑπακούσῃ αὐτῷ (cf. vv. 14 and 16; 5: 1; 13: 22, etc.) and ἵνα μὴ ἀντείπῃ πρός (cf. 32: 1). According to Colb., the first translation is that of Symm. and Theod. In Syro-hex. the words οὐ μή are not given in the text, but are referred to in the margin as coming from Aq., Symm., and Theod. In Jerome, *non respondebit ei unum de mille*, by omission of ἵνα μὴ ἀντείπῃ πρός. Instead of χιλίων (= אֶלֶף), G (A) χειλέων, which passes into Sah. 'his lips'.

Duhm asserts that the subject of יַחְפֹּץ can be none other than God, and that, if man were the subject, we should rather have הוֹאִיל (Gn 18: 27). This assertion is contradicted by 13: 3, where Job, speaking in the 1st person, in a similar context, uses the expression אֶחְפָּץ. Verb חָפֵץ 'wish' (13: 3; 21: 14; 33: 32), 'make stiff, rigid' (40: 17). The root רִיב, which means 'dispute', 'contend', 'go to law', is fairly frequently used in the Book of Job. First it is the verb רִיב, the precise meaning of which is determined by the prepositions which introduce the complement: with עִם as here, 'contend', 'dispute with' (13: 19; 23: 6; 40: 2), with אֶל־ 'complain' (33: 13), with לְ'' 'plead on behalf of' (13: 8), with the accu-

4   He is wise in heart, and robust in strength;
     Who has resisted Him and remained safe?

5   He who moves mountains and they know not

sative 'quarrel with' (10: 2). The meaning of dispute in a court of law, litigation, is especially felt in the substantive רִיב, whether it be in the singular (29: 16; 31: 13, 35) or the plural (13: 6). The complement עִמּוֹ refers to עִם־אֵל of v. 2 and confirms that the subject of יַחְפֹּץ is indeed man and not God. Most commentators are of the opinion that it is man once more who is the subject of לֹא יַעֲנֶנּוּ 'he will not answer him'. The meaning is supposed to be that man would be incapable once in a thousand times of answering the questions or the accusations of God. But it seems to us that 33: 13-14, where we see clearly that God does not reply to the sophisms of man, would imply that the proposition 'he does not reply once in a thousand times' refers to God. The idea is a very natural one. God refuses to appear at the bar in answer to so wretched an adversary as man; cf. vv. 33-5. The poetic preposition מִנִּי for מִן is regularly used in the Book of Job and the Psalms. We have met it already in 6: 16 and 7: 6. Apart from these two books it appears only in the Song of Deborah (Jg 5: 14), in Is 46: 3, and Mic 7: 12. The expression אַחַת מִנִּי־אָלֶף means literally 'one thing among a thousand'; cf. 33: 23 'one among a thousand'; Ec 7: 28; Sir 6: 5(6).

4   G renders לבב by διανοίᾳ, and כח by καὶ μέγας. The verb הקשה, retained in Targ. and Syr., is translated σκληρὸς γενόμενος (G), resistit (Vulg.). For ישלם (same root in Targ. and Syr.), G ὑπέμεινεν, Symm. διετέλεσεν, but Aq. εἰρήνευσεν, Vulg. pacem habuit.

It would be much too subtle to consider 'wise in heart and robust in strength' as attributes of the man who proposes to rebel against God. The doxology which begins at v. 5 is anticipated in our 1st hemistich. Moreover, the epithets applied to God are intended to give justification to the 2nd part of the verse: 'Who has resisted Him and remained safe?' God possesses both wisdom and strength. Hence any struggle with Him would be foredoomed to failure. Thus the 1st hemistich is a kind of casus pendens referring to the suffix of אֵלָיו. The heart is the seat of wisdom (cf. 8: 10). The חֲכַם־לֵב 'wise in heart' will be mentioned in 37: 24. The form לֵבָב as in 12: 3; 34: 10, 34. Just as חָכָם calls for the complement לֵב or לֵבָב 'the heart', so the root אמץ 'to be sturdy, strong, robust' (4: 4) attracts the word כֹּחַ 'strength'; cf. v. 19 and מאַמִּיצֵי־כֹחַ (36: 19). V. 19 well confirms the attribution of the terms in the 1st hemistich to God. The hiph'il of קשה 'to be hard' is generally used with the complement עֹרֶף 'nape of the neck', in the sense of 'stiffen the neck', and so 'oppose', 'resist' (L'Emploi métaphorique, p. 93). The complement is understood. In 30: 25 the adjective קשֶׁה 'hard' will be used to describe the harshness of fate. With the 2nd hemistich cf. 41: 3 (corrected): 'who has confronted Him and remained safe?' The verb שָׁלֵם means 'to be safe, intact', etc., as in 41: 3; cf. שָׁלוֹם in 5: 24 and שָׁלֵם in 8: 6.

5   G παλαιῶν gives to עתק the

The One who has overturned them in His anger!
6   He who shakes the earth from its foundations,
     So that its pillars quiver!

meaning of 'to be old'. The copula ולא omitted in G (B), Sah., reappears in G (א, A), Syro-hex., Jerome, Eth. The translation of καὶ οὐκ οἴδασιν is absent from Arab. Baud. For ידעו, Syr. ו ידעו, whence the correction of ידעו to יָדַע adopted by Bickell, Beer, Duhm. Targ. sees in הרים 'kings who are strong as mountains'. The relative אשר is considered by Targ. as a conjunction: 'and they do not know that...'. Vulg. *et nescierunt hi quos subvertit* relates אשר to the suffix of הפכם.

As in 5: 10 the doxology begins with the article. Job proposes to show that he knows as much theology as any one else, and that, just as well as Eliphaz (5: 9ff.) and Bildad (8: 3ff.), he is able to extol the perfections of God. The verb עתק 'to be moved, transported' (14: 18; 18: 4), originally 'move forward' or 'pass' (cf. the Assyrian *etêqu* 'pass' in Thureau-Dangin, *Huitième campagne de Sargon*, p. 5, n. 11), whence 'advance in age' (cf. G and 21: 7). The *hiph'il* means 'move', 'transport', though sometimes it has the same meaning as the *qal* (32: 15). The change from יָדְעוּ to ידע (cf. sup.) would oblige us to translate ולא ידע by 'without effort or difficulty', as of a thing of which one is hardly aware. But it is better to retain ידעו, which offers an excellent meaning, 'and they do not know it', or rather, 'they do not know *Him*', the complement being supplied by the 2nd hemistich. The latter is generally regarded as a parallel member to the 1st hemistich: 'He overturns them in His anger' (Le Hir; cf. Crampon, Segond, etc.). But the presence of the perfect הָפַכָם favours the interpre-

tation of Dillmann, who sees in this 2nd hemistich a relative clause. However, we do not think that אֲשֶׁר should be made an equivalent of כִּי (cf. Targ.). In reality, it means 'He who' and constitutes the subject of the relative clause at the same time as forming the object of the main clause. Hence: 'they know not the One who has overturned them in His anger'. The verb הפך 'turn over' something, hence 'knock over, upside down' (34: 25) and 'overturn' (12: 15; 28: 9); in the *niph'al* 'to be turned up' (28: 5) and 'turn upon, against' (19: 19; 30: 15), 'to be changed' (20: 14), 'turn into', 'become' (30: 21; 41: 20); in the *hithpa'el* 'become' (38: 14), and 'turn round and round', 'whirl' (37: 12). Of course בְּאַפּוֹ 'in His anger' and not here 'by His nostril' (4: 9). The mountains are convulsed or tremble under the impact of the divine anger or majesty (Ps 18: 8ff.; 46: 3-4; 97: 4-5; 114: 4-6, etc.).

6   G renders ארץ by τὴν ὑπ' οὐρανόν (1: 6, 7), but Jerome simply *orbem*. For ממקומה, G ἐκ θεμελίων (cf. 18: 4), Syr. 'from its roots'. Memph. omits the 2nd hemistich. G renders יתפלצון by σαλεύονται, but οἱ λοιποί have περιτραπήσονται (in Field).

God is the author of earthquakes. It is enough for Him to shake the supports on which the earth rests. These supports or pillars are mentioned in Ps 75: 4. The earth is the apex of an edifice whose construction is described in 38: 4-6. The columns of the earth should not be confused with those of the sky (26: 11), which are the mountains rooted in the ground (Pr 8: 25). Similar descriptions in Is 13: 13: 'Therefore

7   He who commands the sun and it rises not,
     And who places a seal on the stars!

I will make the heavens tremble
and the earth shall be shaken out of
its place.' Same use of the *hiph'il* of
רגז 'to be shaken' (cf. רֹגֶז in 3: 17,
26) to connote 'tremble', 'quiver'.
In 12: 6 הִרְגִּיז will mean 'provoke'.
The verb הִתְפַּלָּץ is a *hapax*. The
root פלץ has the meaning of 'to be
tossed, buffeted': in the *hithpa'el*
'to quiver'. The noun פַּלָּצוּת is the
'shudder' (21: 6) brought on by terror (Is 21: 4; Ezk 7: 18; Ps 55: 6).
It is interesting to draw attention
to the hypothesis of Seneca (*Quaes-
tiones naturales*, VI, 20) on the
subject of earthquakes: *Fortasse
aliqua pars terrae velut columnis
quibusdam ac pilis sustinetur, quibus
vitiatis ac recedentibus tremit pondus
impositum.*

7 The order of the hemistichs is
reversed in Eth. The versions are
unanimous in rendering חרס by
'sun'. After חרס, G (A) adds μὴ
ἀνατέλλειν (Sah.). For יחתם, Vulg.
claudit quasi sub signaculo. In Targ.
it is the clouds which serve as a
seal to the stars. At the close G (B)
adds κατὰ δὲ ἀγγέλων αὐτοῦ σκόλιόν
τι ἐπενόησεν from 4: 18b. This addition is not found in G (A), Sah.,
Syro-hex., Jerome, Arab. Baud., but
appears in G (אc·ᵃ), Codd. 68, 254.
    Verb אמר is used in the sense of
'command' as in Arabic; cf. 36: 10.
The nature of the order is shown
by what follows: 'and it shines not'.
The verb זרח, Aramaic דנח, is the
regular term for the sunrise; the
east is called מִזְרָח. The word חֶרֶס
is a poetic name for the sun, and
appears in proper names like Har-
heres 'mountain of Heres' (Jg 1: 35),
'ascent of Heres' (Jg 8: 13), and
Timnath-Heres (Jg 2: 9). The mountain of Heres is situated precisely

in the region of Beth-Shemesh,
'house of the sun', and perhaps
Heres was identified with this locality (cf. Lagrange, in loc.). Further, in Is 19: 18 we find עִיר הַחֶרֶס
(the reading חרס is preferable to
הרס), which has been translated
πόλις ἡλίου (Symm.), *civitas solis*
(Vulg.). This is certainly Heliopolis.
On the other hand, it seems that in
Jg 14: 18 הַחַרְסָה is a corruption of
הַחַדְרָה (cf. 15: 1); this is a hypothesis of Stade which has been
accepted by most moderns. Ought
we to see in Heres the name of
Horus, as Ball proposes? In Egyptian this name was written simply
Ḥr (Coptic ϧⲱⲣ). It might be supposed that the termination was
added by those who brought the
name (perhaps the Philistines) and
substituted it for Shemesh in proper
names. The phenomenon to which
allusion is made here is that of the
fading away of the light, whether
by the oncoming of a mysterious
darkness (Ex 10: 21-3), or by the
piling up of clouds (3: 5). Then
comes the darkening of the stars.
In eschatological visions, the sun,
the moon, and the stars are eclipsed
(Is 13: 10; Ezk 32: 7-8; Mk 13: 24-
25; Mt 24: 29-31; Lk 21: 25; cf.
Lagrange). It is interesting to note
that the disappearance of sidereal
light accompanies an earthquake
in Jl 2: 10; 3: 15-16, as also in Is
13: 10-13. The verb חָתַם 'seal'
(14: 17; 37: 7) with בעד before the
direct object as for verbs meaning
'close', 'wall up', etc. (1: 10; 3: 23).
The same construction is found in
37: 7, where we should read בעד
instead of ביד (cf. Comm.). The
presence of יַחְתָּם in 33: 16 is due to
textual corruption (cf. Comm.). The
noun חוֹתָם 'seal' is in 38: 14; 41: 7.

8   He alone stretches out the heavens,
        And walks on the waves of the sea.

Hence God places a seal on the stars, He holds them sealed down to prevent them from unveiling their light.

8   The copula of ודורך, omitted in G (B, א), Sah., is found in G (A), Syro-hex., Jerome. For על־במתי, G ὡς ἐπ' ἐδάφους, Vulg. *super fluctus*, Targ. על רום תקוף 'on the height of solidity', Syr. ܚܠ ܠܘܩܒܠ 'on strength'.

The verses 8-10 are cut out, as being an interpolation, by Beer, Duhm, Fried. Delitzsch, Torczyner. It is claimed that this description of the creative activity of God does not fit in to this context and would be better placed on the lips of Eliphaz (5: 9). It is argued, further, that the verses are a series of citations from other passages in Job or from the prophetic writings. It should be observed, however, that Job began his speech by saying that he knew as much about these high matters as his friends. He in fact describes the attributes of God in terms of current theology, and in v. 10 he concludes his strophe by repeating ironically the general affirmation of Eliphaz with a slight modification. The description he gives is not a mere string of quotations. The texts which inspire him are skilfully adapted to a new context. The technique of the author is the same as in 8: 20-2, where the citations from the Psalms are recast to form a strophe of six hemistichs. And here we have again three verses (each of two hemistichs), beginning with present participles unaccompanied by article, so as to differentiate this strophe from the previous one, each verse of which began with present participle together with article. V. 8a affirms of God

what Yahweh says of Himself in Is 44: 24, 'I stretch out the heavens, I alone!' The change from לְבַדִּי to לְבַדּוֹ enables the author to retain the phrase in the context of a new description. Compare the use of the participle נֹטֶה 'stretching out' in 26: 7. The verb נטה 'stretch' (15: 25; 26: 7; 38: 5), intransitive 'be extended', 'be lengthened' (15: 29). Since the root has also the meaning 'bend', 'bow', related meanings will be: 'turn aside' (31: 7), whence the *hiph'il* 'cause to deviate from' (36: 18), and the intransitive 'deviate' (23: 11). God stretches out the heavens like a tent or curtain (Is 40: 22; Ps 104: 2). There, on high, He walks above the clouds (Is 14: 14). But He does not confine Himself to those heights. He can 'lower' (another meaning of נטה) the heavens to reveal Himself (Ps 18: 10). Then He will be able to walk on the high places of the earth (Am 4: 13; Mic 1: 3). The expression 'tread the heights' of a country, or even of some one, eventually came to mean simply 'dominate it or him'. Our author, who is immediately inspired by Am 4: 13 or Mic 1: 3, replaces the 'heights of the earth' by the 'heights of the sea', i.e. the waves which rear themselves so that their crests become as mountain peaks. Cf. the image of Virgil: *praeruptus aquae mons* (*Aeneid*, I, 105). Thus all the poetic pregnancy of the expression is maintained, and it becomes clear that the imitation is not slavish. Under the influence of Is 14: 14, three MSS have substituted עָב 'the cloud' for יָם. On the pretext that ים cannot be parallel to שָׁמַיִם, Ehrlich proposes במתיהם 'their heights'. But all the versions confirm the MT. The writing בָּמֳתֵי

9   He creates the Bear, Orion,
      And the Pleiades and the Chambers of the South;

for בָּמוֹתֵי (*kethîb* in Mic 1: 3) recurs in Is 14: 14; Am 4: 13. The verb דָּרַךְ 'trample under foot' (22: 15; 24: 11) and the same meaning in the *hiph'il* (28: 8). With עַל־ before the complement, 'walk' (Dt 33: 29; 1 S 5: 5, etc.). Hence the derivative דֶּרֶךְ 'way'.

9   The order of the constellations is reversed in G and Syr., which have read כימה first (G πλειάδα, Syr. ܟܣܝܠ). For the translations, cf. inf.
Creation of the constellations. The alliterative effect of עֹשֶׂה עָשׁ suggests that the order of MT should be maintained (as in Targ. and Vulg.). The order of G and Syr. has been influenced by 38: 31-2 and Am 5: 8, where the enumeration begins with כִּימָה. The constellation עָשׁ is certainly the same as עַיִשׁ of 38: 32. Syr. renders עָשׁ and עַיִשׁ by the same word ܟܣܝܠܐ, which translates כֶּסֶל in 15: 27, and כְּסִיל in Am 5: 8. The Arabic translation renders ܟܣܝܠܐ by عيّوق 'the Goat'. According to Bar-Hebraeus, ܟܣܝܠܐ is Aldebaran, the eye of the Bull (cf. *Thesaurus* of Payne-Smith, II, p. 2866). It is clear that the Syriac tradition hesitates between Orion (כסיל, cf. inf.), the Goat, and Aldebaran. Targ. here transcribes by עָשׁ, but interprets עַיִשׁ by זגתא, 'the Hen' (38: 32). G here translates by ἕσπερον, which renders עַיִשׁ in Theod. (38: 32), but also כסיל in Theod. (Am 5: 8). Vulg. too will have *vesperum* in 38: 32, but here *arcturum*. Now, Arcturus will correspond to כסיל in 38: 31, and Ἀρκτοῦρος renders כסיל in G (here), כימה in Aq. (Am 5: 8, where Vulg. also

translates by *Arcturum*). The Greek translations and the Latin version are thus no more definite than Syr. and Targ. on the exact meaning of עָשׁ or עַיִשׁ. They hesitate between Vesper (the planet Venus) and Arcturus, though without reserving these equivalent terms to עָשׁ or עַיִשׁ. Saadia translates both times by *banât-na'š*, literally 'daughters of the coffin', which is the Arabic name for the stars composing the Great and Little Bears. It should be noted that each star of this group bears the name *ibn-na'š* 'son of the coffin'. And at once we remember 38: 32: 'And *'ayiš* with its children, can you guide them?' Ibn Ezra identifies עָשׁ, עַיִשׁ with 'the Bear, the Chariot, the seven stars', those seven stars being the *septem triones* (hence the French word *Septentrion* for north), i.e. the stars of the Great Bear. Let us now observe that here, as in 38: 31-2, the constellation עָשׁ or עַיִשׁ forms a group with כסיל, Orion (cf. inf.), and כימה, the Pleiades (cf. inf.). Now, in Homer, we have the series: Pleiades, Boötes, Bear (also called Wain), and Orion (*Odyssey*, V, 272-5); or else Pleiades, Hyades, Orion, and Bear (*Iliad*, XVIII, 486-9). In both passages the Bear is described as revolving while looking at Orion. If we remember that Boötes was linked with the Bear through Arcturus, 'the guardian of the Bear', we see that Homer's enumeration throws into relief the Pleiades, the Bear, and Orion, at the same time insisting on the connection between the two latter. This is an indirect proof of the assimilation of עָשׁ or עַיִשׁ to the Bear, whose little ones (38: 32) will be 'the little Bear'. The identification of כסיל with Orion offers no difficulty. By an error, which has its counterpart in the

10   He does mighty things, unfathomable,
      And marvels without number!

interpretation of עשׁ or עישׁ as
Arcturus (Vulg. here), or even of
כימה as Arcturus (Aq. and Vulg. in
Am 5:8), we find כסיל rendered
Ἀρκτοῦρον (G here), *Arcturi* (Vulg.
38:31). And similarly כסיל will have
as equivalent Ἕσπερον in Theod.
(Am 5:8), while Vesper corresponds
also to עשׁ (G here), עישׁ (Theod.
and Vulg. in 38:32). These divergences only bring out the more the
agreement on the interpretation of
כסיל as Orion in G (38:31), Aq.
(Am 5:8), Vulg. (here and Am 5:8).

The confusion of כסיל with ܚܙܘܐ
in Syr. (Am 5:8) again only emphasises the agreement which exists
between the translation by ܥܫܝܢܐ
'the Strong', (Syr. here and 38:31)
and Targum's interpretation by
נפלא 'the Giant' (here and 38:31),
or by כסילא, an Aramaic form of
כסיל 'the Big' or 'the Mad'. An
astronomical legend, collected in the
Chronicon Paschale (*PG*, XCII, col.
145) and in an anonymous chrono-
graph (*PG*, XCVII, col. 81), identified the constellation of Orion with
the giant Nimrod transported into
the heavens. We have shown elsewhere (*La Religion assyro-babylonienne*, pp. 90ff., and *Anniversary
Volume* of Hilprecht, pp. 365ff.) that
Orion was the Babylonian god Nin-
ib, god of the chase and war, whose
name should probably be read as
Ninurta, prototype of Nimrod.
Among the Arabs the constellation
is called *al-jabbâr* (cf. Syr.) 'the
Giant'. The meaning of כסיל is the
'fool', 'madman', especially from the
religious point of view; that is, the
'godless'. The root כסל 'to be heavy
and thick', whence כֶּסֶל 'loins and
kidneys' (15:27), develops meanings
such as 'to be coarse' or 'to be lum-
pish and clumsy', whence כָּסַל 'to
be stupid' (Jer 10:8), כְּסִיל 'stupid',

'mad', 'senseless', 'impious', כֶּסֶל
'craziness' and 'wild hope' or 'confidence' (Job 8:14; 31:24), כִּסְלָה
'folly' (Ps 85:9), and 'confidence'
(Job 4:6). The third constellation is
כימה, transcribed כימא in Targ. and
Syr. The transcription כימא will be
maintained by Syr. in 38:31 and
Am 5:8, whilst Targ. has כימה in
Am 5:8, כימתא in Job 38:31.
Translation by 'Pleiades' in G (here
and 38:31), Symm. (38:31 and Am
5:8), Theod. (Am 5:8), Vulg. (Job
38:31). On the other hand Vulg.
here interprets by 'Hyades', and in
Am 5:8 Aq. and Vulg. interpret by
Arcturus. The Arabic version and

Saadia translate by *thurayyâ*, ﺛُﺮَﻳَّﺎ
'Pleiades'. Thus it is clear that the
majority of the versions are in favour
of the meaning 'Pleiades'. The normally accepted etymology is that
which derives כימה from כום, Arabic
kûm 'herd of camels', and *kûmeh*
'heap of earth'. The Pleiades, it
seems, would thus be an accumulation of stars. In the light of 38:31
'will you bind the chains of the
Pleiades?', we would prefer to connect כימה with the Assyrian *kamû*
'bind', whence *kîmtu* 'family'. The
chambers 'of the south', which
should be compared with the expression הַחֶדֶר 'chamber' to mean
the south (37:9), form an austral
constellation not mentioned elsewhere. According to Schiaparelli
(*Die Astronomie im A.T.*, pp. 58ff.),
it is an allusion to a group of stars
at present scattered among Argo,
Centaur, and the Southern Cross.
The versions have been content to
translate MT, whilst Targ. paraphrases: 'the chambers of the planets towards the south'.

10 Vulg. varies its translation of
5:9: *incomprehensibilia* instead of

11   If He passes near me, I do not see Him;
     If he glides past, I perceive Him not.

12   If He plunders, who can prevent Him?
     Who will say to Him: What art Thou doing?

inscrutabilia and *quorum non est numerus* instead of *absque numero.* For ונפלאות, G ἔνδοξά τε καὶ ἐξαίσια (obelus before ἔνδοξά τε in Syrohex.), Aq. θαυμάσια (Vulg. *mirabilia*), Theod. ὑπερμεγέθη.

Job repeats with a touch of irony a whole verse of Eliphaz (5: 9). There are slight variants: עַד־אֵין repeated, whilst 5: 9 had וְאֵין in the 1st hemistich; copula before נִפְלָאוֹת.

11 Targ. adds בשׁמי מרומא 'in the heavens above' after 'if He passes near me'. For וְלֹא אָבִין לוֹ, G οὐδ' ὡς ἔγνων (Jerome *nec sic sciam*), Symm. οὐδὲ ἐννοήσω, Vulg. *non intelligam.*

The phrase אֶרְאֶהוּ יַחֲלֹף, postulated by some authors (according to Syr. and Vulg. *non videbo eum*), has against it G and Targ. The complement of אֶרְאֶה, easily guessed, has been added by Syr. and Vulg. At the opening, הֵן 'if' (4: 18), as in v. 12. 'If He passes near me, I do not see Him': God eludes man's vision. The verb רָאָה 'see' might also mean 'know', 'be acquainted with' (cf. Comm. on 7: 10). The parallelism with בִּין 'perceive' allows the original sense to be preserved. The verb בִּין with לְ before its complement to mean 'perceive' (14: 21; 23: 8), sometimes 'understand' (13: 1), as with the accusative (15: 9; 23: 5; 36: 29). The exact meaning of חלף is 'to follow after' (cf. חֲלִיפָה in 10: 17; 14: 14), whence the *hiph'il* 'cause one thing to succeed another', 'to be renewed' (14: 7; 29: 20) and 'change'. Hence 'pass' from one place to another (11: 10), or 'glide' into a place and simply 'glide past' (4: 15). The same root can mean 'cross', 'pierce' (20: 24). The close, from

וְלֹא, is verbally repeated in 23: 8.

12 יַחְתֹּף, G ἀπαλλάξῃ, Symm. ἀναρπάσει, Syr. ܠ 'tear': interpretation in the sense of חטף. Targ. retains יחתוף, but supposes the meaning to be 'remove man from this world'. Vulg. *si repente interroget* paraphrases in the light of the 2nd hemistich.

The root חתף recurs only in Pr 23: 28; Sir 15: 14; 32: 22; 50: 4. In the last text we have מחתף parallel to מצר, the preposition מן being prefixed to חֶתֶף and to צַר 'enemy'. In Pr 23: 28, the harlot prepares ambushes like a חֶתֶף and thus increases the number of בּוֹגְדִים 'traitors'. The parallelism of מחתף with רְשָׁעִים 'wicked' in Sir 32: 21-2 invites us to point מְחַתֵּף, *pi'el* participle, used in a sense similar to the *qal* participle חוֹתְפוֹ of Sir 15: 14. The comparison of these texts proves that חתף denotes a wicked deed committed by a man, in particular by trickery or treachery, against his fellow man. Now, the verb חטף which means 'snatch', 'remove by force' (Jg 21: 21) is, as it happens, used with אָרַב 'lay an ambush' in Ps 10: 9. It is this verb אָרַב which indicates the action of the חֶתֶף in Pr 23: 28. It is thus clear that the roots חתף and חטף have the same meaning, as was well understood by G, Symm., and probably Syr. Thus חוֹתְפוֹ will be 'his ravisher' (Sir 15: 4), חֶתֶף 'the brigand' (Pr 23: 28; Sir 50: 4), מְחַתֵּף 'the plunderer' (Sir 32: 22). The formula הֵן יַחְתֹּף therefore means: 'if He plunders'. On the supposition, *per impossibile*, that God behaves like a brigand, 'who will

13   Eloah does not restrain His anger;
      Under Him the helpers of Rahab lie crushed.
14   How much less, then, shall I answer Him,
      And choose words with which to speak to Him!

prevent Him?' The *hiph'il* of שׁוּב,
literally 'cause to return', here means
'prevent'. We find again מי ישׁיבנו
'who will prevent him?' in 11:10;
23:13. The 2nd hemistich: 'who
will say to Him: What art Thou
doing?' recurs with לו instead of
אליו in Ec 8:4, where it is a question
of an omnipotent king. Cf. Dn 4:35,
'And none can stay his hand or say
to him: What dost thou?' In Sir
36:8-10, in the midst of a prayer
to God: 'Who will say to you:
What dost thou?' Same construction
as here and as in Ec 8:4, with
לך instead of לו. St Thomas well
brings out the significance of these
terms which place God outside the
law: *non habet superiorum qui de
ejus factis judicare possit.*

13 G αὐτὸς γὰρ ἀπέστραπται ὀργήν
removes the negation, perhaps as a
result of theological scruple (Beer).
It is, however, restored in Symm. ὁ
Θεὸς οὗ ἀναπόστρεπτος ἡ ὀργή, Jerome *ipsius enim inavertibilis ira*; cf.
Vulg. *Deus cujus irae nemo resistere
potest.* The word רהב is interpreted
as an abstract 'mass', 'greatness' in
Targ. and Syr., ἀλαζονείᾳ (reading
רֹהַב) in Symm. But G κήτη τὰ ὑπ'
οὐρανόν and Vulg. *qui portant orbem*
have seen in 'the helpers of Rahab'
persons or animals.

V. 12 showed the boundless exercise
of the activity of God. This activity
has permanent effects. In v. 5 it was
the divine anger which caused the
convulsions of nature. God alone
could modify His decrees, but 'Eloah
does not restrain His anger'. The
hiph'il of שׁוּב 'to cause to turn back'
(cf. v. 12), to connote that an action
is interrupted or that a thing begun
is not allowed to continue to its full

development. The same verb is used
in Ps 78:38, but the idea expressed
is that of the divine pity: 'and often
He restrains His anger'. In Jer 18:20
and Pr 15:1 it is חֵמָה 'fury' which is
the complement of הֵשִׁיב. One proof
given of the abiding nature of this
anger is the fact that 'under Him the
helpers of Rahab lie crushed'. Verb
שׁחח means 'to be prostrate' or 'to
crouch' (38:40). In Pr 14:19 'the
evil bow down before the good';
here the enemies are prostrate *under*
the feet of God. They are His foot-
stool (cf. Ps 110:1). We see here the
appearance of the third monster,
Rahab, whose analogies with Leviathan (3:8) and with Tannîn (7:12)
we have already noted. It is a symbol
of the sea (26:12), in particular of
the Red Sea, like Tannîn in Ps 74:13
(cf. Comm. on 7:12 and Is 51:9).
Hence the use of Rahab as a symbol
of Egypt (Is 30:7; Ps 87:4). Originally it is the untamed sea (Ps 89:
10-11) which God subjugates at the
moment of creation. Thus Rahab is
akin to Tiamat (תהום), the adversary
of the demiurge, in Babylonian cos-
mology; cf. Comm. on 3:8. It should
be noted that the gods who march
with Tiamat against Marduk are
called *rêṣû-ša* 'her auxiliaries' (*Choix
de textes*, p. 52, l. 107). The 'helpers
of Rahab' supply the parallel to this
expression. The original meaning of
the root רהב is 'to be agitated,
excited' (Aramaic); sometimes by
fear, whence 'tremble', 'be afraid'
(Syriac and Arabic); at other times,
by anger, whence *ra'âbu* 'to be provoked' (Assyrian). The sea is essentially the element that is subject to
moods of fury. The name Rahab is
well chosen.

14 G ὑπακούσεται .... διακρινεῖ up-

15   I, who, though I am in the right, *receive no reply,*
       When I implore my Judge.

15   אֶעֱנֶה (G, Syr., Theod.); MT: אֶעֱנֶה.

sets the sense by replacing the 1st person by the 3rd. The end, עמו, omitted in G, is restored μετ' αὐτοῦ in Aq, and Theod., whence Jerome *secum* (with asterisk). Syro-hex. quotes, in the margin, 'with Him'. Sah. transfers to this context the 2nd hemistich of v. 15.

The verb ענה 'answer' figures in all three verses of the strophe 14-16, with the implication of answering an accusation in law. Job supposes that God is relentless in His anger, as is shown by the fate of Rahab's helpers (v. 13). What can he, a simple mortal man, effect when confronted by the divine majesty? Discussion is impossible. At the opening, אַף־כִּי (cf. אַף in 4: 19) 'how much less!' (15: 16; 25: 6). The verb אענו will be repeated in v. 32 where it is a question of a judicial contest between God and Job. The cohortative אֶבְחֲרָה marks the inner struggle which Job would have to make, if he wished to contend with God. The verb בחר 'choose' (7: 15) between several arguments. The choice indicated by בחר concerns the words which the accused would use in his reply to a legal charge before a tribunal. Literally, the meaning is: 'I will choose my words with Him', i.e. I will choose the words with which to speak to Him. In v. 3 Job stressed the impossibility for man to engage in a discussion with God.

15   G and Syr. omit the relative אשר. Syr. anticipates the negation לא before צדקתי. G εἰσακούσεταί μου, Theod. ἀποκριθήσεταί μου and Syr. ܐܠܗܐ point אֶעֱנֶה (*niph'al*). The 2nd hemistich of G τοῦ κρίματος αὐτοῦ

δεηθήσομαι, marked by an asterisk in Syro-hex. and Jerome, comes from Theod. (cf. Colb.). This 2nd hemistich figures at the end of v. 14 in Sah.

The MT לֹא אֶעֱנֶה 'I do not answer' duplicates the אענו of v. 14. Even Ginsburg admits that the *niph'al* אֶעֱנֶה 'I am not answered' (G., Theod., Syr.) is preferable to the *qal*. And, in fact, in v. 3 we have been told that God does not answer once in a thousand times to the objurgations of His opponents. Cf. the *niph'al* of ענה in 11: 2 and 19: 7. V. 16 will accept for argument's sake that God replies, but it will be an incredible thing. The verb צדק 'to be righteous' (4: 17; 9: 2, 20; 10: 15, 15: 14; 22: 3; 34: 5; 35: 7) has equally the sense of 'to be in the right' in a debate or lawsuit (11: 2; 13: 18; 33: 12; 40: 8). It is the latter meaning which is best suited here: 'I who, though I am in the right, receive no reply!' God refuses to recognise the right which is based on the arguments of man. The verb התחנן is used, as in Bildad's speech (8: 5). The participle מְשֹׁפֵט is of interest as representing a *pâ'el* form (Arabic 3rd form), of which there remain but very few examples except in verbs ע״ע and ע״ו. Cf. מְלוֹשְׁנִי 'my calumniator' (*kethîb*, Ps 101: 5). The comparison with 8: 5 shows that למשפטי must indeed be a concrete noun and that one cannot point לְמִשְׁפָּטִי 'in my judgment' (contra Hitzig, Hoffmann). Note that the clause 'I implore my Judge' is simply juxtaposed to the preceding one, and indicates concomitance which we render as 'when I implore'.

16   If I call and He answers me,
      I will not believe that He is listening to my voice!
17   He who crushes me for a *hair*,
      And multiplies my wounds for no reason,

17 בְּשַׂעֲרָה (Targ., Syr.); MT: בִּשְׂעָרָה.

16 G (B) καὶ μὴ ὑπακούσῃ suggests to Duhm וְלֹא יַעֲנֵנִי instead of וְיַעֲנֵנִי. But μή is not found in G (A, **א**), Syro-hex. We should like to see in it a corruption of μέ. The reading καί με ὑπακούσῃ would faithfully reproduce by Targ., confirmed by Syr., Vulg. For קוֹלִי, G simply μοῦ, but Theod. τῆς φωνῆς μου, whence *vocem meam* in Jerome. The reading of Theod. is cited in Syro-hex. (with asterisk).

The connection between קרא 'cry', 'call' and ענה 'reply' (13:22 and 19:16) should be observed. Notice that 19:16 also contains אתחנן of v. 15. The comparison of the two texts shows clearly that 'if I call' repeats the idea expressed by 'I implore' in v. 15. What is in question is an appeal to God. Job supposes that God replies. This would be such an extraordinary hypothesis (v. 3) that he would hardly be able to believe his ears: 'I shall not believe that He is listening to my voice.' The *hiph'il* הֶאֱזִין, denominative of אֹזֶן 'ear', means 'lend ear' (32:11; 33:1; 34:2, 16; 37:14). Verb הֶאֱמִין means 'trust', 'have confidence in' (4:18), in the sense of 'believe' (29:24; 39:12).

17 Instead of אֲשֶׁר, G μή, considered as interrogative in Eth. and Arab. Baud. (cf. pointing of Swete). For בִשְׂעָרָה, G γνόφῳ (A ἐν γνόφῳ), Vulg. *in turbine*, Symm. διὰ καταιγίδος. But Targ. and Syr. point שַׂעֲרָה 'hair' (cf. inf.). Syr. renders יְשׁוּפֵנִי by 'He has struck me with violence', less literal than G μὲ ἐκτρίψῃ, Vulg.

conteret me, Targ. מדקדק עמי 'He crushes (in His dealing) with me', i.e. 'He behaves with the utmost severity in His dealings with me'. G renders וְהִרְבָּה by πολλὰ δὲ ... πεποίηκεν, misunderstood by Syro-hex., which puts the obelus before πεποίηκεν.

Le Hir had already protested against the connection of יְשׁוּפֵנִי with the root שׁאף (5:5; 7:2), which has caused certain exegetes to translate the 1st hemistich as 'who snatches me in a tempest' (cf. Ewald, Dillmann, Budde, Duhm). The verb שׁוּף, as is to be seen from Targ., G, and Vulg., has the meaning of 'crush' or 'pound', 'bruise', exactly as in Gn 3:15, הוּא יְשׁוּפְךָ רֹאשׁ 'he will bruise thy head'. The root שׁוּף, parallel to שׁפף, has retained in Aramaic the sense of 'pound', 'crush', 'grind', while in Assyrian *šâpu* has rather the meaning of 'trample', whence the noun *šêpu* 'foot' (Streck, in *Babyloniaca*, **2**, p. 218, n. 1). The double meaning of the Arabic شوف 'polish' (by rubbing) and 'see', 'look at' might give us the clue to the pun in Gn 3:15, where the clause corresponding to 'he will bruise thy head' is וְאַתָּה תְּשׁוּפֶנּוּ עָקֵב 'thou shalt take aim at his heel'. Hence it is not necessary, in the latter case, to have resort to a kinship between שׁוּף and שׁאף, in the sense of 'aspire to', 'seek to', 'aim at'. The verb שׁוּף recurs in Ps 139:11, where it has as subject חֹשֶׁךְ 'darkness'. It is generally proposed that we should replace יְשׁוּפֵנִי by יְשׂוּכֵנִי 'darkness will cover me'. But leaving the text as it is and giving to שׁוּף the second meaning

18 He does not let me get my breath,
So much does He make me to drink bitterness!

19 As for strength, *He* is the strong;
As for judgment, who can summon *Him*?

19 הַנֵּהוּ; MT: הנה ו. — יוֹעִידֶנּוּ (G, Syr.); MT: יועידני.

attested by Gn 3:15, we should naturally translate Ps 139:11 as 'And I have said: even the darkness sees me and the night is light for me.' Thus it becomes clear that שׁוף contains two distinct meanings: 'crush' and 'see'. Now, in 6:9 Job said: 'Oh! That Eloah would consent to crush me, that He would free His hand and cut me off!' The verb ידכאני 'let Him crush me!' had as its parallel יבצעני 'let Him cut me off!' Here we have in the 2nd hemistich 'and who multiplies my wounds'. It is clear that the parallel verb, namely ישופני, will be used in its former meaning 'He crushes me'. The difficulty which has caused exegetes to hesitate is the association with בשׂערה, interpreted as 'in a tempest' (cf. G, Symm., Vulg.). It is true we find שְׂעָרָה 'tempest' in Nah 1:3. But the Book of Job writes סְעָרָה (38:1; 40:6), and it is the normal writing in other Biblical texts. It should be noted that the word בשׂערה corresponds to חִנָּם 'for no reason' (2:3). But Targ. and Syr. have pointed בְּשַׂעֲרָה and have recognised here the word שַׂעֲרָה 'hair' (4:15). In Jg 20:16 we find אֶל־הַשַּׂעֲרָה 'to a hair's breadth'. All in all, it seems to us logical to render בְּשַׂעֲרָה (Targ., Syr.) as 'for the worth of a hair', i.e. a trifle. This supplies a good parallel to the phrase 'for no reason' in the 2nd hemistich. It is the hypothesis suggested by Ehrlich. The *hiph'il* of רבה in the sense of 'multiply', 'increase', followed by direct object

(10:17; 29:18; 34:37; 40:27).

18 Syr. ܐܬܬܢܝܚ and Vulg. *requiescere* give to השׁב the meaning of 'to rest'. G ἀναπνεῦσαι interprets more literally השׁב רוחי. At the end, Syr. adds 'and He has made me to drink absinth', coming from La 3:15.

In 7:19 Job said to God: 'Will you not leave me time enough for me to swallow my saliva?' Here he begs to be allowed to breathe. The verb נתן 'to give', in the sense of 'permit', 'allow' generally with ל'' before the infinitive complement (31:30) but sometimes without ל'' as here (Nu 20:21; 21:23). On the omission of ל'' cf. 3:8; 4:2. The *hiph'il* השׁיב 'to bring back' (cf. v. 12) with רוּחִי 'my breath' (4:9) to mean *re-spirare*, 'breathe'. The 2nd hemistich explains the 1st. The word מַמְרֹרִים with the *dagesh dirimens*, to preserve the second *mem*, is a *hapax* which it has been attempted to replace by בַּמְּרֹרִים (following La 3:15; cf. Löhr and Beer). But it is more logical to assume that La 3:15 desired to substitute for the difficult reading a more natural and current one. The word מְרֹר (the plural of which is מררים in La 3:15) will be used in the feminine plural 'bitter things' (not in the masculine) in 13:26. The *qal* שׂבע 'to be sated' had no preposition before its complement in 7:4. The *hiph'il* הִשְׂבִּיעַ not only 'satiate', 'cloy', but also 'to cause to drink' (38:27).

19 G (B) ἰσχύει (Jerome *potest*) comes from ἰσχύι (A, א, Sah., Syro-

20   Though I am just, my mouth condemns me,
      And though I am blameless, it declares me wicked.

hex., Eth., Arab. Baud.), which translates לכח; cf. Symm. ἐν τῇ ἰσχύι. Instead of יועידני (Targ., Vulg.), G τίς οὖν κρίματι αὐτοῦ ἀντιστήσεται and Syr. ܢܙܕܡܢܝܗܝ 'will go before him' have certainly read יועידנו.

It is clear that לְכֹחַ 'as for strength' corresponds to the לְמִשְׁפָּט 'as for judgment' of the 2nd hemistich, and should be read as a heading. There remains אַמִּיץ הִנֵּה, which Le Hir interprets 'it is He the strong!' Schnurrer realised very rightly that the *waw* of ואם should be linked with הנה so as to read: הִנֵּהוּ (cf. *kethib* of Jer 18:3). Hence 'As for strength, He is the strong.' Cf. אמיץ כח 'robust in strength' of v. 4. Job is stressing the disproportion between man and God. How could he contend in justice with God the possessor of supreme power? And who would be so rash as to summon God to appear before a tribunal? The verb יעד, used in the *niph'al* in the sense of 'agree' (2:11), in the *hiph'il* assumes a juridical implication, 'summon', 'cite' before a court of law. Those who leave it as יועידני 'who will summon me?' are obliged to add: 'he will say' (cf. Le Hir, etc.). But Ginsburg himself recognises that the original reading was יועידנו (G, Syr.). It is likely that the substitution of the 1st person for the 3rd is due to a theological scruple, just as the 1st was substituted for the 2nd in 7:20. Moreover, in the only two texts where we have the *hiph'il* of יעד (Jer 49:19; 50:44), the reading is מִי יועִדֵנִי 'who will summon me?' the reminiscence of which may have influenced the MT here.

20 Vulg. paraphrases אם־אצדק *si*

justificare me voluero, and תם אני *si innocentem ostendero*. For ירשיעני, G ἀσεβήσει, Jerome *impia loquetur.* G renders יעקשני by σκολιὸς ἀποβήσομαι, Jerome *pravus inveniar.* A hexaplar reading, probably Aq. (cf. Field), had καὶ ἐστρέβλωσέ με; cf. Arab. Baud. عوجني 'he has made me crooked'.

The verb צדק, in its normal sense 'to be just', is opposed to הרשיע 'declare a verdict of guilty', 'condemn' (10:2; 15:6; 32:3; 34:17; 40:8). In 34:12 the *hiph'il* of רשע means 'do wrong', 'be evil'. Following Olshausen, a certain number of exegetes replace פִּי by פִּיו 'his mouth' (Merx, Hoffmann, Siegfried, etc.). It is supposed that it is God's mouth which condemns Job; in consequence of a theological scruple (cf. 7:20), 'His mouth' is thought to have been replaced by 'my mouth'. But no trace of the reading פיו has remained in the versions. In 23:12, where we have פיו 'his mouth' applied to God, the text has not been modified. The apparent injustice imputed to God is more clearly formulated in v. 22, where however the text has not been changed. Finally, in 15:6 Eliphaz will say to Job: ירשיעך פיך 'Thy mouth condemns thee.' All these facts taken together argue in favour of the MT: 'Though I am just, my mouth condemns me.' Job is incapable of perceiving whether there is good or bad in himself: 'I do not know myself' (v. 21). The expression: תָּם אָנִי 'Am I blameless?' is used in the sense of 'though I am blameless', parallel to אם־אצדק. From the root עקשׁ 'to be twisted, tortuous' we find the *pi'el* 'twist', 'bend' (Mic 3:9) and 'pervert' (Jer 59:8; Pr 10:9). Here the pointing hesitates between the *pi'el* and the

21   Am I perfect? I do not know myself!
      I despise my life!
22   That is why I have said: 'It is all one!
      He destroys both the blameless and the wicked!'
23   If a scourge brings sudden death,
      He mocks at the despair of the innocent!

hiph'il. Parallelism suggests the adoption of the *hiph'il* 'declare wicked'. The softening to *shewa* of the vowel *î* of the *hiph'il* is not without further examples (Gesenius-Kautzsch, § 53n).

21   G corrects the 1st hemistich by rendering תם as its opposite: εἴτε γὰρ ἠσέβησα. For תם אני, Symm. κᾶν ἀναίτιος ὦ, Vulg. *etiamsi simplex fuero* (cf. 1:1 for *simplex*). The end is paraphrased in G πλὴν ἀφαιρεῖταί μου ἡ ζωή.

Job has just formulated a hypothesis: 'If I am perfect!' But how is he to know this? The only objective interpretation of לֹא אֵדַע נַפְשִׁי 'I do not know my soul' is 'I do not know myself.' The complement נפשי 'my soul' has the value of a reflexive pronoun 'myself'; cf. Gesenius-Buhl, s.v., no. 5. Job does not know himself and so cannot affirm his innocence. Thus תם אני is equivalent to an interrogative: 'Am I perfect?' He no longer knows on what he can rely, and so his last cry is one of dejection and despair: 'I despise my life!' Further on he will say that his soul is disgusted with life (10:1). In this state of mind, he can give free rein to his indignation about the injustices which are rampant in the world, and which imply that the same treatment is meted out to the righteous and the guilty. We leave the last hemistich in all its laconic terseness. Duhm prosaically prolongs it by attaching to v. 21 the אַחַת־הִיא of v. 22.

22   Syr. literally translates אַחַת־הִיא

'one single thing'; Targ. 'it is one sole measure'; Vulg. fuses with the following clause: *unum est quod locutus sum.* G does not translate, but Symm. ἕν ἐστιν is quoted (with asterisk) in Syro-hex., and is introduced (with asterisk) in Jerome *unum est.* G adds ὀργή (read as ὀργῇ in Syro-hex.) as the subject of מכלה, and interprets תם ורשע by μέγαν καὶ δυνάστην.

It is clear that אַחַת־הִיא 'it is all one, one and the same thing' expresses the idea of undiscriminating equality of treatment—an idea to which v. 20 had alluded and to which the 2nd hemistich of v. 22 also refers emphatically. The numeral adjective 'one' (אחד) sometimes means 'the same' (31:15; Gn 40:5; 41:11), just as we say in English 'it amounts to one and the same thing'. The feminine pronoun היא is used in a neuter sense: 'this', 'that', 'it' (5:27; 31:11). By a bold stroke of inversion the poet has placed על־כן אמרתי 'that is why I have said' after 'it is all one', which is Job's own exclamation. The rest can be understood of itself: 'He destroys both the blameless and the wicked.' The *pi'el* of כלה 'to be finished', 'to vanish' (4:9; 7:9) assumes the meaning of 'to complete' (36:11), whence 'to terminate', 'to destroy'. Hence the blameless man and the wicked share the same fate.

23   For the 1st hemistich, G ὅτι φαῦλοι ἐν θανάτῳ ἐξαισίῳ, completed by ἀπολοῦνται in G (A), Sah., Syrohex. (obelus), simply *erunt* in Jerome. The paraphrase of G inter-

24   If a land has been delivered into the hand of a wicked man,
      Then He covers the faces of its judges!
      If it is not *He*, who then is it?

24 Transpose אפוא and הוא (*sebîr*).

prets שׁוֹט by φαῦλοι to effect an antithesis with δίκαιοι, which becomes
the subject of the verb in the 2nd
hemistich ἀλλὰ δίκαιοι καταγελῶνται.
The difficult word מסת is omitted.
Vulg. *si flagellat* takes שׁוֹט as a verb,
Syr. reads שׁוֹטוֹ 'his scourge', Targ.
translates ברוגז 'in anger'. Vulg. *et
non de poenis innocentum rideat* corrects the meaning of the 2nd hemistich by adding a negation. Syr.
interprets מסת by 'folly', but Targ.
מתמסמסין 'dismayed' well recognises the root מסס.

The aim of vv. 23-4 is to show that
God does not discriminate between
the innocent and the guilty: 'If a
scourge brings sudden death, He
mocks at the despair of the innocent!' The word שׁוֹט means 'whip'
(5: 21) and 'scourge' (Latin *flagellum*). The *hiph'il* of מות is used as
in 5: 2. Job takes the opposite line
of the theory expounded by Eliphaz
in 5: 19ff., and he seems to allude
especially to 5: 22: 'At devastation
and famine you will scoff'. It is God
who mocks at the despair of the
innocent. The *hapax* מַסַּת does not
come from מַסָּה 'temptation' (root
נסה) but derives from מסס 'flow'
(cf. 7: 5), which is used in the *niph'al*
in speaking of the heart which
'melts' in anguish or dismay; cf. מאס
in 7: 5, 16. It is despair which is
expressed by this metaphor: the
heart loses its solidity, support, and
confidence. The innocent, נְקִיִּם, are
deliberately chosen to refute the
argument of Eliphaz, who said
(4: 7): 'Call to mind, now: what innocent man ever perished?' The
verb לעג 'mock', 'laugh at' with ל"
before the complement (22: 19).
In the latter text (Eliphaz), it is the

innocent (נקי) who mock at the
wicked.

24 G omits אָרֶץ, which is restored
in Aq. and Theod. (quoted by Syro-
hex.), Jerome *terra* (with asterisk).
From פְּנֵי, the text, absent from Sah.,
marked by an asterisk in Colb.,
Jerome, and Syro-hex., did not
figure in G. The present translation
comes from Theod. Instead of אֵפוֹ,
Syr. points אַפּוֹ 'his anger'.

The 1st hemistich expresses a new
hypothesis. The word אָרֶץ does not
here mean the earth in general, but
a particular country. The evil judges
are a local menace. God not only
does not spare the innocent at the
time of public calamity, but He goes
further in that He permits these innocent to become the victims of the
wicked. We are acquainted with the
רָשָׁע, who is especially the oppressor
of others (3: 17) and who corresponds to the tyrant of 6: 23. It is the
special business of the judges to
compel such criminals to make
restitution and thus to re-establish
and vindicate justice. But God 'veils
their faces'. Job traces back to their
original cause the actions of men. St
Thomas explains that this divine
causality is reducible to mere permission: *ex sapientia Dei permittentis*.
The 'judges of the country', שׁוֹפְטֵי
אָרֶץ, are mentioned in Ps 2: 10;
148: 11. They form a category of
high dignitaries like the 'counsellors
of the land' in 3: 14. The last line,
'If it is not He, who then is it?', is
shorter than the others. It is a
broken-off sentence, and consequently all the more striking. The
sebîr of the scribes, who transpose
אָפוֹא and הוּא, puts in order a text

25 And my days have been swifter than a runner,
  They have sped by without seeing happiness,
26 They have glided away like vessels of reed,
  As an eagle which swoops down on its food.
27 If I say: 'I will forget my complaint,
  I will change my look and be cheerful',

which perhaps seemed too harsh to the first copyists. On the writing אפוא, cf. 4: 7. After these general considerations, Job returns to the examination of his individual case.

25 G translates וימי by ὁ δὲ βίος μου. The word βίος is cited in the margin of Syro-hex. G omits טובה, which is restored, with asterisk, in Syro-hex. and Jerome *bonitatem*. We have ἀγαθόν in Symm. and Theod. Instead of 'runner', Targ. sees here 'the shadow of a bird which flies past'.

Job returns to the theme of the rapidity with which life passes away (7: 6). It is not now the weaver's shuttle, but the 'runner' who serves as the term of comparison. The 2nd hemistich is very like 7: 7b, where we have טוב instead of טובה after the verb ראה. It is not the eyes now, but the days which do not see happiness. Life passes away so swiftly that the happy moments are swallowed up without trace. Juxtaposition of לא־ראו and of ברחו, to mark the concomitance; compare ידעתי and יגרתי in v. 28.

26 The word אבה has baffled translators: ἴχνος ὁδοῦ (G), σπευδούσαις (Symm., cited in the margin of Syrohex.), 'which bear precious things' (Targ.), *poma portantes* (Vulg.). Syr. connects it with איבה 'hostility'. The word חלפו, omitted by G, is rendered ἀπῆλθον in Symm. (cf. *abierunt* of Jerome).

A new comparison, this time drawn from the rapid passage of skiffs. We had an allusion to the papyrus and reed in 8: 11. The word used for 'papyrus' was גמא. Now, in Is 18: 2 there are mentioned the כלי־גמא 'skiffs of papyrus' in which speedy messengers sail. Pliny tells us that the Egyptians used papyrus for the construction of their vessels: *ex ipso quidem papyro navigia texunt* (*Naturalis historia*, XIII, 22). The Assyrian *abu* (and *apu*) 'bed of reeds' and the Arabic *abâ'* 'rush', 'reed' permit us to interpret the *hapax* אבה as 'reed'. The verb חלף (cf. v. 11) is used as in 4: 15. Preposition עם 'with' to mean 'like' (Ps 73: 5; 106: 6, etc.). The final comparison is taken from the phenomenon of the eagle's flight. Of course we must add אשר before the verb (cf. 7: 2). It is when it swoops down on its prey that the king of birds gives the impression of crushing, lightning speed. The *hapax* טוש is explained by the Aramaic טוס, which means 'soar', 'hover in flight'. Post-Biblical Hebrew uses טוס (*Thesaurus* of Ben-Yehuda, IV, p. 1800). Here the exact connotation is 'pounce, while in flight' on prey. The word אכל 'food' will again be used for that on which the eagle feeds in 39: 29. Prey properly speaking would be denoted by the term טרף (4: 11).

27 Syr. connects אמרי with the root מרר. For אשכחה שיחי, G ἐπιλήσομαι λαλῶν, Vulg. *nequaquam ita loquar*. The translation of Theod. ἀδολεσχίας for שיחי is cited in the margin of Syro-hex. The words אעזבה פני are rendered by συνκύψας τῷ προσώπῳ (G), *commuto faciem meam* (Vulg.). The meaning of אבליגה is ill understood by G στενάξω and

28   Then I dread all my sufferings,
     For I know that Thou dost not hold me blameless.
29   If I am guilty.
     Why weary myself in vain ?
30   If I wash myself with snow
     And cleanse my hands with lye,

Vulg. *dolore torqueor*. It looks as if Syr. has read אבליגה twice and replaced פני by רני (Beer), whence: 'if I forget my care or my words, I feel calmer'.

Job has complained of not seeing happiness. He has not a moment's respite. Even when he would like to feel a little cheerful, he remains a prey to fears and terrors (v. 28). At the beginning, אִם אָמְרִי 'if my saying is such', that is to say, 'if I say'. The infinitive with suffix is treated as a clause. In 7:13 we had simply כִּי־אָמַרְתִּי. The verb שָׁכַח 'forget' is used as in 11:16, where it is a question of forgetting sorrow. Job had hoped that, at least during the night time, his troubles might be alleviated (7:13). But the situation is quite otherwise. Literally אֶעֶזְבָה פָנַי 'I will leave my face', that is to say, 'I will abandon the look which I have had up to the present', 'I will change the expression of my countenance'. The verb הבליג corresponds to the Arabic *balija* 'to shine' and 'to be merry'. On the connection between a shining, bright countenance and cheerfulness, cf. *L'Emploi métaphorique*, pp. 52ff. We shall meet הבליג again in 10:20 (cf. Ps 39:14).

28 G σείομαι πᾶσιν τοῖς μέλεσιν reads עצמתי instead of עצבתי. But יגר means 'fear' and not 'tremble', which would be required by the reading 'my bones'. Vulg. translates עצבתי by *opera mea* and paraphrases לא תנקני by *non parceres delinquenti*. The verb יגר is used as in 3:25. We have restored עצבתי 'my sufferings' (instead of עצמתי 'my bones') in

7:15. It may be seen that here G has done the opposite. The verb יָדַעְתִּי, in the same tense as יָגֹרְתִּי, expresses concomitant action, and may be rendered by a participle (cf. v. 25b). What causes the fears of Job is his realisation that God does not treat him as an innocent man, does not clear him of all blame; cf. the *pi'el* of נקה in 10:14 (denominative from נקי 'innocent').

29 The versions, with the exception of Targ., understand the first clause as a hypothesis. G διὰ τί οὐκ ἀπέθανον and Syr. 'why do you cause me to perish?' connect איגע with גוע. Jerrome *quare non sum mortuus, sed laboro* juxtaposes to the reading of G that of Aq. κοπιῶ.

The opening clause אָנֹכִי אֶרְשָׁע is of the same type as ארץ נתנה of v. 24. It is the opposite hypothesis to that of v. 20: 'if I am just . . . if I am perfect'. If I am guilty, it is useless to try to exculpate myself: 'Why weary myself in vain?' God will always find some blemish (30-1). On the word הֶבֶל, used as an adverb, cf. 7:16. The verb יגע 'tire one's self' (cf. יגיע in 3:17) is well chosen to denote an effort which is the more painful because foredoomed to failure. There is no reason to see in this v. 29 a prosaic gloss on v. 30, as Duhm asserts without giving any proof of his assertion.

30 The *kethîb* בְּמוֹ (poetic for בְּ) is followed by G χιόνι, the *qerê* בְּמֵי 'with waters' is followed by Targ., Syr., Vulg. *aquis nivis*. The versions

31   Then Thou plungest me into *filth*,
     And my very garments abhor me!
32   The truth is that He is not a man like myself, that I might
        answer Him,
     That we might go to law together;

31   בְּשַׁחַת (G, Vulg.); MT: בַּשַּׁחַת.

interpret בר as 'purity', but Targ. אהלא 'with aloes'.

Snow waters (*qerê*) are not specially white. The *kethîb* 'with snow' is preferable. The expression is weakened if we read כמו (Merx, Ball), for 'like snow' is platitudinous. The parallelism with בְּבֹר shows that שֶׁלֶג indicates the substance with which one washes one's self. The *qal* of רחץ 'wash' in 29: 6. Outside Job (15: 15; 25: 5) the verb זכך occurs only in La 4: 7, where it conveys the sparkle and purity of snow. The adjective זַךְ 'pure' (in the gloss of 8: 6) is thoroughly in the style of the Book of Job (11: 4; 16: 17; 33: 9) and of that of Proverbs (16: 2; 20: 11; 21: 8). The noun בֹּר does not mean 'the purity' of the hands (22: 30), but the ingredient which is used for the purposes of washing or cleansing (Is 1: 25). It has the same meaning as בְּרִית which denotes the alkali, the soda, the soap made from the ashes of certain plants. More than two thousand years before our era, the art of mixing the ashes of plants such as salt-wort with oil to make soap was known in Chaldaea (cf. Thureau-Dangin, *Rev. d'assyriologie*, 7, p. 111).

31 Instead of בַּשַּׁחַת, G ἐν ῥύπῳ and Vulg. *sordibus* authorise the reading בְּשָׁחֹת (Hoffmann), which is preferable (cf. inf.). The word ἐβδελύξατο, which translates תעבו in G, is quoted in the margin of Syro-hex. The adverb אָז (3: 13) retains its

sense of 'then'. Those who adhere to the Massoretic pointing בַּשַּׁחַת add an epithet: in a (muddy) ditch (*Bible du rabbinat français*). The idea of filth is demanded by the context. If we read בְּשָׁחֹת (cf. sup.), we have the equivalent of בְּסָחוֹת 'in filth' (Is 5: 25). 'Then Thou plungest me into filth' occasions the admirable hyperbole of the 2nd hemistich. Job has just washed himself in snow. God, however, plunges him into a bath of filth. Hence when Job wishes to put on again his garments, the latter seem to abhor him. The verb תעב, in the *pi'el*, is used as in 19: 19; 30: 10. It shows a curious lack of taste to change שַׂלְמוֹתַי 'my garments' into שְׂלָמַי (Duhm) or מְשָׁלָמַי (Lagarde) 'my friends'. Dom Calmet struck the right note when he wrote: 'This way of speaking which endows clothes with feelings, such as those of horror and aversion from a sullied body, has about it something most striking, something which seizes the attention and gives the idea of terrible corruption.' Similar images will be found in the complaint of the leper of Victor Hugo (*La Fin de Satan, Ceux qui parlaient dans le bois*).

32 Vulg. gives a long paraphrase of the verse. G adds εἶ 'Thou art' before ἄνθρωπος (אִישׁ). The relative, understood before אַעֲנֶנּוּ, is expressed by G and Syr.

The 1st hemistich is made very

33   There is no arbiter between us,
      Who might place his hand on us both,
34   Who would take his rod from over me,
      So that his terror should not make me afraid.

clumsy if the phrase is regarded as a single whole, by putting אִישׁ כָּמוֹנִי in apposition to the suffix of אֶעֱנֶנּוּ. The relative אֲשֶׁר is understood after כמוני (cf. v. 33). The meaning is clearly: 'The truth is that He is not a man like myself, that I might answer Him.' The verb אענו used as in v. 14. With the 2nd hemistich compare 22:4. The expression בוא במשפט means 'to go to law' with some one (Ps 143:2). The judge or arbiter will figure in v. 33. It is pure whim to cut out אענו in order to add אתה 'thee' after אישׁ (contra Duhm). Job has been arguing on the supposition that he might be guilty. Every resource is vain if he tries to exculpate himself. If he seeks to cleanse himself, God makes him only the more unclean. Furthermore, to whom should he apply in order to insist on justice? He is not a man like myself! All juridical discussion, every appeal to courts of law is utterly out of the question. The word יַחְדָּו 'together' is used as in 2:11.

33 G εἴθε ἦν and Syr. ܐܠܘ ܦܘܐܠ point אָל (= לוּ) which is found in a few manuscripts. For ישׁת ידו, G (B, א) διακούων, which has become διακρίνων in G (A). The addition δυεῖν δέ μοι χρεία of G (A), quoted in the margin of Syro-hex., comes from 13:22. Syr. adds 'the mouth' after על.

In spite of the fondness of some modern exegetes for the reading אָל, the negative לֹא seems preferable. We have here the sequel to the thought expressed in v. 32. Job

cannot go to law with God, for 'there is no arbiter between us'. On הוכיח (with בין before the two parties in litigation), cf. 5:17; 16:21. Compare ויוכיחו בין שׁנינו 'that they may decide between us two!' in Gn 31:37. The relative is understood before יָשֵׁת (cf. v. 32). The judge places his hands on the two parties to show that he is taking them under his jurisdiction and exercising his authority over them both. The same expression is found in Ps 139:5, 'Thou dost beset me behind and before, and layest Thy hand upon me' (תשׁת עלי כפכה).

34 For יסר, G ἀπαλλαξάτο, but οἱ λοιποί ἀποστησάτο (in Colb.). The suffix of שׁבטו, omitted in G (B, א), is restored in G (A), Sah., Jerome (with asterisk), and in the margin of Syro-hex. (following Aq., Theod., and Symm.).

The subject of יָסַר is the arbiter of v. 33. It is he whose business it is to remove the rod which God uses in order to punish Job. The rod of Eloah is mentioned in 21:9. Compare the cry which Job flings at God in 13:21a, 'Remove Thy hand from over me!' The 2nd hemistich will be almost literally repeated in 13:21b. The copula ו establishes a relation of cause and effect between the 2nd and 1st hemistichs: 'so that His terror should not make me afraid!' Defective writing of אֵמָתוֹ for אֵימָתוֹ (39:20; 41:6). Our verse will be ironically echoed, as also 13:21, in the speech of Elihu (33:6-7). V. 35 serves both as a conclusion to vv. 32-4 and as introduction to 10:1-2. It would be better to make it the beginning of ch. 10 (cf. inf.).

35   35b Since it is not so, I with myself
      35a Will commune and will not fear Him.

35 Transpose the two hemistichs.

35 G καὶ οὐ μὴ φοβηθῶ ἀλλὰ λαλήσω
reverses the order of the verbs in the
1st hemistich. But Jerome *loquar et
non timeam eum* follows the order of
the MT, probably in accordance
with a hexaplar reading. For the 2nd
hemistich, G οὐ γάρ οὕτω συνεπίσταμαι
(Sah., Eth., Syro-hex.), G (A) adds
ἐμαυτῷ ἄδικον (Arab. Baud.). The
reading of Jerome *non enim nunc
sum mecum* reflects Symm. οὐ γάρ
εἰμι ἐγὼ ὁ αὐτὸς παρ' ἐμαυτῷ. Syr.
replaces עמדי by עמדו.

Those who read לֹא in v. 33 see here
the main clause and render the verbs
by conditional tenses: 'I would speak
and would not fear Him' (cf. 16: 4).
It has not been sufficiently noted
that אֲדַבְּרָה recurs at the end of
10: 1 and has as parallel אעזבה of
10: 1b. These cohortatives form part
of one and the same whole. The
verses 9: 35 and 10: 1 are in fact the
introduction to the אמר of 10: 2.

The 2nd hemistich has been interpreted in many ways: 'I am not such
(as you think)' (Ibn-Ezra), or ('that
I should fear)' (most of the moderns). Critics have tried to see in
עִמָּדִי 'with me', 'in me' the witness
of conscience: 'for my conscience
does not reproach me in that way'
(Le Hir), 'for I am aware of being
innocent' (Loisy). It is difficult to

extract from the text: 'otherwise I
am not in possession of myself'
(Segond, Crampon). The expression
לֹא־כֵן sometimes means 'unsuitable',
'unjust', 'unworthy' (cf. Is 16: 6;
Jer 23: 10; Pr. 15: 7), so Ehrlich
and Torczyner have suggested replacing אָנֹכִי by הוא 'He', i.e. God,
who would prove to be unjust 'towards me'. This is too bold a correction. Let us note that אנכי עמדי
'I with myself' could very well be
juxtaposed to אדברה 'I will speak
with myself'. And Qimchi had already pointed out that כִּי־לֹא־כֵן
has the effect of an intrusion which
interrupts the text. Again, in 9: 2 we
had כִּי־כֵן 'that it is so'. The natural
sense of כִּי־לֹא־כֵן will be: 'since it
is not so'. It forms a kind of *résumé*
of the negative observations of vv.
32-4. Now, if we transpose the two
hemistichs, we obtain a perfect
sense: 'Since it is not so, I with myself will commune and will not fear
Him.' Job has previously complained
that he could not meet God before a
tribunal. There was no arbiter between him and his adversary. There
remains to him the resource of com-
muning with his own spirit (9: 35),
of complaining in the bitterness of his
soul (10: 1), and finally of attacking
God in his inmost self (10: 2ff.).

CHAPTER 10

1   My soul is weary of my life!
     I will pour out to myself my complaint,
     And will speak in the bitterness of my soul!

2   I will say to Eloah: 'Do not condemn me!
     Make me to know why Thou dost dispute with me!'

3   Is it good for Thee to act with violence,

10: **1** G στένων, instead of בחיי, seems to have read נהי (Beer), but Jerome *in vita mea* is probably following a hexaplar reading which is closer to MT. G (B) ἐπ' αὐτόν stems from ἐπ' ἐμαυτόν preserved in G (A), Syro-hex., Sah., Jerome *contra me*. The word συνεχόμενος, added by G to the end of the verse, is marked by an obelus in Syro-hex., by an asterisk in Jerome.

The passage is inspired by 7: 11, 'Therefore I will not restrain my mouth, I will speak in the anguish of my spirit, I will complain in the bitterness of my soul!' The 1st hemistich, 'my soul is weary of my life!', is a kind of parenthesis to show that Job will now be able to speak without fear (9: 35). He does not fear retaliation. The verb נָקְטָה, which is pointed like a *qal* form, is originally a *niph'al* of קוט (Gesenius-Kautzsch, § 72dd). It is unnecessary to have recourse to the Assyrian *naqâtu* or *nakâdu* (whence *nakuttu* 'anguish') in order to translate as 'is in anguish' (Fried. Delitzsch). The meaning 'to be weary' better suits the context, and recalls the phrase 'I despise my life' of 9: 21. Compare, moreover, קצתי בחיי 'I am weary (קיץ form parallel to קיט) of my life' in Gn 27: 46. The verb עזב 'let go', 'let slip', to signify what one lets drop through the lips (20: 13). The change from עָלַי to

עליו 'against Him' (Merx, etc.) has but frail support in G (cf. sup.). Job is going to commune with himself. If he addresses himself to God (v. 2), it is not in the tone of one who laments, but of one who calls God to account. It should be noted that in 7: 11, after saying that he would not restrain his mouth and would speak in the bitterness of his soul, Job asks God an ironic question (7: 12).

2 G μή με ἀσεβεῖν δίδασκε connects הודיעני with the 1st hemistich. Aq. and Symm. take us back to the MT; cf. Vulg. *noli me condemnare*. The meaning of תריבני is completed by ὅυτως in G, and by *ita* in Vulg.

Job gives free rein to his complaint and bitterness. Since God does not come to court and there is no umpire, it is a whole series of objurgations which Job here addresses to his tormentor. The verbs הרשיע 'condemn' (9: 20) and ריב 'dispute', 'quarrel with' (9: 31) are deliberately chosen. They are juridical terms. Job stands confronted by the presence of God, like an accused whom a judge overwhelmingly condemns, without there being any possibility of appeal. In 13: 23 Job will repeat the imperative הֹודִיעֵנִי in an apostrophe to God. Irony bursts forth in vv. 3-6.

3 G corrects תעשק, in order to

146

> To despise the work of Thy hands,
> And to smile at the council of the wicked?

4   Hast Thou eyes of flesh?
    Seest Thou as man sees?

5   Are Thy days as the days of a man,
    Thy years as the days of a mortal being?

avoid a term which would be offensive to the deity. Hence it has ἐὰν ἀδικήσω (A ἀσεβήσω). This text cannot be used to authorise the replacement of תעשׁק by ארשׁע, as is proposed by Merx. G renders יגיע by ἔργα, but Jerome has *opus*.

In 7:7 the word טוֹב signified happiness. Here it means good in a more general sense: 'Is it good for Thee?', i.e. 'hast Thou any profit thereby?' Cf. 13:9 for the construction of the phrase. The verb עשׁק 'to be strong, violent' (cf. 40:23). The root יגע shows the same semantic development as עמל 'to exert great efforts in work' (3:10); that is, 'to tire one's self' in the performance of a piece of work (cf. 3:17). The noun יְגִיעַ will be 'trouble' (39:16) and 'work' (39:11), especially the work of the hands (Gn 31:42) and the result of that work, whether the work itself as here, or the recompense which rewards it (Ps 109:11; Hag 1:11). 'The council of the wicked' implies the assembly in which they meet (cf. 21:16 and Ps 1:1). By the very fact that God persecutes Job who is innocent, He favours the designs of such an assembly. The verb הופיע 'shine' with על before the complement (3:4) will recur as an impersonal verb in v. 22. Since the subject is the name of a person, the meaning here is 'to have a glowing countenance,', i.e. 'to be radiant', 'to smile' (*L'Emploi métaphorique*, p. 54). The picturesqueness of the expression suggests that those critics are not correct who wish to efface the last hemistich as a useless gloss (contra Bickell, Beer, Budde, Duhm, Gray).

4 G does not translate the 1st hemistich. The present text is in fact a double translation of the 2nd hemistich. The first translation is that of G. The second, absent from Sah., and marked with asterisk in Jerome and Syro-hex., comes from Theod. The force of the 1st hemistich is weakened in Syr. 'Are Thy eyes as eyes of flesh?' and in Targ. 'Hast Thou eyes like a son of flesh, like a man?'

The interrogative ה will require כי in the subordinate clause (v. 6), exactly as in v. 3. The expression 'Hast Thou eyes of flesh?' is immediately intelligible. The flesh is the sign of humanity; to have eyes of flesh means to have the outlook and vision of a man. Cf. Ps 57:5, where 'the flesh' is contrasted with God, as humanity with divinity. The 2nd hemistich is an elucidation of the 1st: 'Seest Thou as man sees?' The answer to this question is given in 1 S 16:7, 'The Lord sees not as man sees; man looks on the outward appearance, but the Lord looks on the heart' (*L'Emploi métaphorique*, pp. 49f.).

5 G paraphrases the 1st hemistich by ἢ ὁ βίος σου ἀνθρώπινός ἐστιν. The Greek ὁ βίος is cited in the margin of Syro-hex. The second כימי is not rendered in G. But the ὡς ἡμέραι of Aq. and Theod. is cited (with asterisk) in the margin of Syro-hex., while Jerome introduces *tamquam dies* into his text (with asterisk before *dies*).

A few critics reject this v. 5 on the ground that it separates v. 6 from v. 4 (Bickell, Loisy, Duhm). But it

> That Thou dost seek out my fault,
> And inquire into my sin,
>
> 7 Although Thou knowest that I am not guilty,
> And there is none to deliver from Thy hand!
>
> 8 Thy hands have fashioned me and created me,
> And *afterwards* Thou wilt destroy me utterly!

8 אַחַר (G); MT: יחד.

expresses a new idea. Job has spoken of the eyes of flesh and the characteristic way in which man sees things. Now his thought grasps a wider horizon: 'Are Thy days as the days of a man?', that is, Hast Thou the same mode of life as human beings who spend their time watching each other and defending themselves against each other? The expression כִּימֵי as in 7:1, where it is certainly a question of mode of life. Parallelism between אֱנוֹשׁ and גֶּבֶר is as in 4:17, where, as here, man was opposed to God.

6 G and Syr. render חטאתי by a plural. Syr. omits תדרוש.

Job returns to his idea of ch. 7. Man is so vile and wretched a being that there seems to be no solid reason why God should pursue him with investigations (7:17-19). Even if man has sinned, how can that fact affect God (7:20-1)? The ל״ before the complement of תְבַקֵּשׁ marks effort in search. The verb בָּקֵשׁ with the accusative will recur in 23:9 (cf. Comm.). The word עֲוֹנִי 'my fault' is parallel to פִּשְׁעִי 'my transgression' (7:21; 14:17), פְּשָׁעַי 'my transgressions' (31:33). The words עָוֹן 'fault', חַטָּאת 'sin', פֶּשַׁע 'transgression', will figure side by side in 13:23. They are almost synonymous, as is to be seen further from 14:16-17, where 'my sin', 'my transgression', 'my fault', follow

after each other in the same context. The verb דרשׁ, parallel to בקשׁ, has its proper meaning of 'seek out' or 'inquire into' (cf. 3:4 and 39:8).

7 For עַל־דַעְתָּך, G οἶδας γάρ, which has become οἶδα γάρ in G (A). The singular מִידְ is rendered by a plural in G and Syr.

To change מִיָּדְךָ into בִידִי 'in my hand' (Beer, Duhm), and to replace מַצִּיל by פֶּשַׁע 'transgression' (Beer) or מַעַל 'treachery' (Duhm), is an attempt to adapt the text to too rigid a parallelism. Preposition עַל has the sense of 'in spite of' (cf. 16:17 and 34:6); whence עַל־דַּעְתָּך means 'in spite of your knowledge', 'although you know'. In 9:29 Job cried out: 'If I am guilty!' It was a hypothesis, inspired by irony, intended to lead to the rest of the speech on the impossibility of his ever cleansing himself. God knows well that it was not true: 'Although Thou knowest that I am not guilty!' And even were he guilty, could he escape? The expression וְאֵין...מַצִּיל as in 5:4, 'And that there is none to deliver from Thy hand!' The fact is that man is the work of God (vv. 3 and 8ff.). He remains helpless in the hands of his Creator, who treats him as He pleases. Why should he be persecuted and harassed? It is an occupation unworthy of God (7:17ff.).

8 For יחד סביב, Aq. and Theod. ἅμα κύκλῳ, Vulg. *totum in circuitu.*

9   Remember that Thou hast made me as it were with clay,
     And wilt reduce me again to dust?
10   Hast Thou not poured me out like milk,
     And curdled me like cheese?

G μετὰ ταῦτα μεταβαλών read אַחַר for יחד, and perhaps סֹבֵב for סביב (cf. the *kethîb* סביב for סֹבֵב in 2 K 8:21).

Job is the handiwork of God (v. 3 and 14:15): 'Thy hands have fashioned and created me!' The root עצב, whence עֲצַבִּים 'idols', is probably related to the Arabic عضب 'cut out', 'hew'. God fashions man as a statue. It is difficult to attach a specific meaning to יחד סביב, which conveys the idea 'all around' or 'as a whole'. If the words are connected with the 1st hemistich, they are translated 'on every side' (Le Hir), 'wholly, in every part' (*Bible du rabbinat français*), 'wholly and completely' (Segond). But סָבִיב is in itself sufficient to express this meaning, and יחד is left aside. G has not invented μετὰ ταῦτα, which presupposes אַחַר 'afterwards', 'then'.

If we adopt this reading, to which most moderns give their approval, it becomes clear that the words אחר סביב belong to the 2nd hemistich, and that in consequence the verse becomes better balanced. Must the correction be taken further and סביב, following G, be replaced by derivatives of סבב 'turn', such as סֹבֵב (Loisy), תָּסוֹב (Franz Delitzsch) סַבּוֹתָ (Bickell), סָבוֹב (Duhm)? Or again should we replace סביב by תָּשׁוּב 'Thou wilt begin again' (Merx)? The reading of G is to be explained by a confusion similar to that which has become established in 2 K 8:21 (cf. sup.). On the other hand in 19:10 we find יִתְּצֵנִי סָבִיב. 'He demolishes me on every side', which encourages us to see in סביב

the adverb qualifying וַתְּבַלְּעֵנִי 'and Thou dost destroy me!' We have here another instance of the phenomenon we have already noted (4:6) of the transposition of the copula. Hence the translation of the 2nd hemistich will be: 'And afterwards Thou wilt destroy me utterly!' It is a good parallel to the 2nd hemistich of v. 9. On the *pi'el* of בלע cf. 2:3.

9 Syro-hex. quotes in the margin (with asterisk) the translation οὖν of Aq. and Theod. (for the particle נא omitted in G). The כ of כחמר is not rendered in G.

As in 7:7, Job addresses God with an imperative זְכֹר 'remember!' He repeats the verb עשה of v. 8. Men are dwellers in houses of clay (4:19). Elihu will exclaim: 'of clay have I been moulded' (33:6). The expression כַּחֹמֶר means 'as it were with clay', the preposition "ב being unacceptable after the "כ of comparison (cf. Gesenius-Kautzsch, § 118w). The 2nd hemistich implies that God is the Author of the law weighing on humanity: 'To dust shalt thou return' (Gn 3:19). Parallelism between חֹמֶר 'clay' and עָפָר 'dust' is as in 4:19; 30:19.

10 Syr. replaces הלא by the copula. For תתיכני, Targ. סנינתא יתי 'Thou hast purified me', G μὲ ἤμελξας, Aq. μὲ ἀπέσταξας, Vulg. *mulsisti me*. For תקפיאני, G ἐτύρωσάς με, but G (A) and Aq. ἔπηξάς με, cf. Vulg. *me coagulasti*.

Job here expresses his thoughts through the ideas of the ancients on the subject of the formation of the embryo. Cf. Ps 139:13-16. Calmet

11   With skin and flesh hast Thou clothed me,
      And with bones and sinews hast Thou woven me;
12   Then Thou didst grant me the favour of life,
      And Thy care preserved my breath!

quotes the testimony of Aristotle, Pliny, and Galen with regard to the way in which the seminal fluid is clotted to become the body of the foetus. God Himself presides over this mysterious operation, as will be formally asserted by the mother of the Maccabees (2 Mac 7: 22-3); cf. *L'Emploi métaphorique*, p. 6). The Koran, quoted by Hitzig, dwells on the same idea (Sura XL, 69). The *hiph'il* of נתך 'to flow' (3: 24) means 'to cause to flow', e.g. to make metals molten (Ezk 22: 20), and to 'liquefy' silver (2 K 22: 9; 2 Ch 34: 17). The 1st hemistich, 'Hast Thou not poured me out like milk?', prepares for the 2nd, 'and curdled me like cheese?' The verb קפא means strictly 'to coagulate'. The *hiph'il* recurs with the meaning of 'stiffen', 'congeal' in Sir 43: 20. For the author of Wisdom (7: 2) the foetus is παγεὶς ἐν αἵματι; cf. the translation of G (A) and Aq. (above) for תקפיאני. The word גְּבִנָה is a *hapax*, corresponding to the Aramaic גְּבִנָּא and the Arabic *jubn* 'cheese'. Note the use of imperfects as aorists (3: 3).

11 Syr. reverses the order of עצמות וגידים. For תשׂככני, G μὲ ἔνειρας, Targ. אשׁתיתני 'Thou hast woven me', Vulg. *compegisti me*.

Third phase in man's formation. St Thomas recognises in v. 10a *seminis resolutio*, in v. 10b *compactio massae corporeae in utero mulieris*, in v. 11 *distinctio organorum*. The clothes one wears are what is outwardly visible. The skin and the flesh form the exterior of man. The framework of the body consists of bones and sinews. The form תְּשׂכְכֵנִי is for תְּסֹכְכֵנִי, *po'el* of סכך, the *qal* of

which is used in Ps 139: 13, 'Thou didst knit me together in my mother's womb.' The bones and the sinews form the meshes of the texture.

12 For עשׂית, G ἔθου, Symm. παρέσχες μου (cf. Vulg. *tribuisti mihi*). G ἡ δὲ ἐπισκοπή σου and Vulg. *visitatio tua* interpret פְּקֻדָּה in the sense of 'visit', 'inspection'.

The common expression עשׂה חסד 'grant mercy', 'pardon' favours the MT, as against the change of עשׂית to שָׂת (Bickell and Duhm following G). Modern critics, dissatisfied with the juxtaposition חיים וחסד, suggest certain corrections: חֵן 'grace' instead of חיים (Beer), חלד 'life' instead of חסד (Duhm), elimination of חיים (Ehrlich). It is inadequate to explain 'life and mercy' by 'a grace which is life'. If so, the word to be determined would follow the determining word. But let us note that וחסד⋯עמדי means 'and Thou hast been merciful towards me' or 'Thou hast granted me grace'. The word חיים 'life' made prominent as a result of the shift of the copula (4: 6; cf. v. 8), specifies the nature of this grace. The translation of the 1st hemistich will then be: 'and Thou hast granted me the favour of life'. God has not been content merely to grant life to the work of His hands. He preserves that life. The verb שׁמר 'preserve', 'safeguard' as in 2: 6. The basis of life is the breath which God has inbreathed into the nostrils of man (Gn 2: 7), and which becomes both breathing (Job 9: 18) and spirit (6: 4; 7: 11). The verb פקד 'visit', 'inspect' (5: 24; 7: 18) can equally well mean 'guard', 'take

13 But this is what Thou hast hidden in Thy heart,
   I know that this is in Thy thought:
14 If I sin, Thou dost watch me,
   And of my fault Thou dost not acquit me!
15 If I am guilty, woe to me!
   And if I am just, I lift not up my head!
   I who am sated with ignominy and *steeped in* affliction,

15 וְרֹוֵה עָנִי; MT: וראה עניי.

care of' (Ps 8:5; 65:10; 80:15, etc.), whence פְּקֻדָּה 'vigilant care'.

13 G weakens צפנת into ἔχων and בלבבך into ἐν σεαυτῷ (A ἑαυτῷ). The reading ἐμαυτῷ, to which attention is drawn in Colb., figures in Sah. and Syro-hex. G replaces the 2nd hemistich by οἶδα ὅτι πάντα δύνασαι, which comes from 42:2a and introduces 42:2b ἀδυνατεῖ δέ σοι οὐθέν.

The pronouns אֵלֶּה 'these things' and זֹאת 'this thing' refer to what follows. In the previous description Job has been alluding to universally known facts. It is now the secret intention of God which is going to be revealed: 'But this is what Thou hast hidden in Thy heart.' The 2nd hemistich has a good parallel in 27:11, 'I will not hide what is with Shaddai', to mean: I will disclose what He thinks. Cf. the use of עִם in 23:14b and of אֵת in 12:3. Job is about to give information concerning the most intimate thought of God, what is hidden in God's heart.

14 Vulg. paraphrases the 1st hemistich: *si peccavi et ad horam pepercisti mihi*, a translation which compels an interrogative structure for the 2nd hemistich: *cur ab iniquitate mea mundum me esse non pateris?*

The *waw* of וּשְׁמַרְתָּנִי simply means that the action expressed by שמר accompanies that expressed by חטא;

cf. וּבָרָא 'Then He will create' after אִם רָחַץ in Is 4:4-5. Cf. the construction of 9:11 and 20b. Job is alluding to what has happened since his birth. Hence we have the perfects חָטָאתִי, רָשַׁעְתִּי, and צָדַקְתִּי (v. 15). The verb שמר is as it were an echo of שמרה in v. 12. But it is no longer a question of 'preserving'. It is now a question of 'mounting guard' (cf. משׁמר in 7:12) and of 'watching' (33:11). The word עֲוֹנִי 'my fault' is used here as in v. 6. The *pi'el* of נקה stands here as in 9:28. God is still described as the severe guardian whose concern is to catch man in sin (vv. 3-7; 7:17-20).

15 G renders לֹא אֶשָּׂא רֹאשִׁי by οὐ δύναμαι ἀνακύψαι (Jerome *non possum respirare*). Syro-hex. attributes to Theod. the reading of Aq. οὐκ ἀρῶ κεφαλήν. G omits וראה עניי; Vulg. omits ראה.

The verb רשע employed as in v. 7 and in 9:29. Job still turns in the same circle. Whether he is guilty or innocent, it makes no difference to God (9:22). The antithesis between רשע and צדק is well brought out in 9:20a where the righteous is treated just like the sinner. The exclamation אַלְלַי recurs only in Mic 7:1, where it is accompanied by לִי as here. 'If I am guilty, woe to me!', since God constantly watches my steps and is not disposed to clear me (v. 14). 'And if I am just, I

16   And *exhausted as I am,* Thou dost hunt me like a leopard,
      And dost not cease to glorify Thyself through me.

16 וָיִגַע ; MT: ויגאה.

lift not up my head', since God does
not discriminate between the just
and the unjust (9: 20-2). He who
lifts high his head is exultant and
proud, and is able to confront his
enemies (Jg 8: 28; Zec 2: 4; Ps
83: 3). In 11: 15 he who is at peace
with God 'lifts up his face'. Beer
and Duhm get rid of the 3rd hemistich simply by cutting it out. But it
is a difficult passage which certainly
has not the character of a gloss. It is
impossible to translate שְׂבַע קָלוֹן by
'weary Thyself then of humiliating
me !' (Loisy). In 14: 1 Job will say
of man that he is שְׂבַע־רֹגֶז 'consumed with restlessness'. It is clear
that שְׂבַע־קָלוֹן means here 'sated
with ignominy'. Then the usual
translation is 'and seeing my misery',
'and witness of my misery', etc. But
there does not exist an adjective רָאֶה
'seeing', 'witness of'. A hypothesis of
Geiger is almost irresistible, that is,
that we should read: רְוֵה 'watered
with' (Dt 29: 18; Is 58: 11; Jer
31: 12) instead of ראה. The final
yod of עֶנְיִי is due to dittography. Let
us read then וּרְוֵה עֹנִי 'and steeped in
affliction', which is parallel to 'sated
with ignominy'. V. 15c forms the
first part of the verse continued at
16a.

16 G ἀγρεύομαι γὰρ (A δὲ) ὥσπερ
λέων εἰς σφαγήν renders תְּצוּדֵנִי by a
passive, in order to avoid the anthropomorphism, and paraphrases ויגאה
by εἰς σφαγήν (?). Vulg. *et propter
superbiam quasi leaenam capies me*
also paraphrases ויגאה. Syr. ‫لو‬
‫فتللL‬ 'and if I raise myself' reads
וְאֶגְאֶה. Targ. וארים ידיה 'and He has

lifted His hand' does not differ from
MT. Vulg. *reversusque mirabiliter me
crucias* paraphrases the 2nd hemistich; cf. G πάλιν γὰρ μεταβαλὼν δει-
νῶς με ὀλέκεις.

Duhm again gets rid of v. 16a by
regarding it as a gloss coming from
ch. 16 (!). The presence of ויגאה 'and
He rises up' (cf. 8: 11) at the beginning of the verse is somewhat
disturbing. Sometimes exegetes consider the subject of this verb to be
רֹאשִׁי 'my head', of v. 15. But it
must be confessed that in this case
the construction would be rather
odd, and the subject too far from
the verb. Hence we shall not accept:
'and let it be raised but a moment'
(Le Hir), 'and if I dare to raise it'
(Segond), 'if I lift it erect' (*Bible du
rabbinat français*). Some exegetes
connect יגאה with what follows and
provide as its subject שַׁחַל (Merx),
whence 'like a springing lion' (Loisy).
In this case it would be necessary to
transfer יגאה to a position after שַׁחַל.
The simplest solution might perhaps
be to read ואגאה 'and if I exalt myself' (Ball) with Syr. (cf. sup.). But
we think the true solution should
take into account v. 15c also: 'sated
with ignominy and steeped in affliction'. The opening ויגאה must
conceal a third epithet which would
link the preceding ones with תְּצוּדֵנִי
'Thou dost hunt me'. We propose to
read וָיִגַע 'and exhausted' (cf. יָגֵעַ in
3: 17 and the verb יגע in 9: 27)
which, as a result of an error in audition, would have become וְיִגְאֶה. The
poet has been giving prominence to
the reasons which should awaken
pity for the victim. They are all
epithets which qualify the suffix of
תְּצוּדֵנִי. In accordance with the po-

17   Thou dost renew Thy *hostility* towards me,
      And dost increase Thy anger against me;
      Relief troops are flung in to struggle with me!

17   עֵדֶיךָ; MT: עֵדֶיךָ.

sition occupied by כַּשַּׁחַל, it is the
hunter who is compared to the
leopard. For the meaning of שַׁחַל
cf. 4: 10. God Himself compares
Himself to a leopard in Hos 5: 14;
13: 7. The objections of Ehrlich and
others who refuse to accept that צוּד
should apply to the wild beast in
search of its prey do not take into
account 38: 39 where Yahweh exclaims: 'Dost thou hunt (הַתָּצוּד) a
prey for the lioness?' The verb שׁוּב
'return' (6: 29), in the sense of 'begin again', 'repeat' (7: 7), is simply
juxtaposed to the verb it governs to
convey that an action is constantly
repeated or renewed (Gn 30: 31; Ps
85: 7, etc.). The construction with
the infinitive preceded by לְ״ is as
in 7: 7. The *hithpaʿel* of פלא is the
reflexive of the *niphʿal* 'to be extraordinary, wonderful'. The exact
sense will be: 'to make one's self admirable, glorious' and so 'render
one's self distinguished'. The ב״ instrumental of בִּי gives to the complement the meaning of 'through
me'. V. 16 is ironical.

17 G τὴν ἔτασίν μου corrects עדיך
to עדי, but G (A) returns to the MT,
replacing μοῦ by σοῦ. The text of G
by no means implies עלי נגעך (Beer),
or עלי נגעי (Hontheim). Note that
G again avoids the 2nd person (cf. v.
16) by its translation of ותרב כעשׁך
as ὀργῇ δὲ μεγάλῃ μοι ἐχρήσω. The
noun חליפות is rendered by a verb
in G ἐπήγαγες and Syr. 'Thou dost
cause to follow after'. Vulg. renders
וצבא by *militant*. In G πειρατήρια
(cf. 7: 1).
   The 1st hemistich may be translated: 'Thou dost bring forward

fresh witnesses against me.' But we
are not in the scene of a court of law.
Job is describing the violent attacks of which he is the object. The
2nd hemistich, 'and dost increase
Thy anger against me', marks the
active hostility which God manifests
towards him. Ehrlich realised quite
rightly that עֵדֶיךָ should be connected with the Arabic عدى 'to be an
enemy, antagonistic'. If we point
עֵדֶיךָ we obtain: 'Thou dost renew
Thy hostility towards me', which
forms excellent parallelism with the
2nd hemistich. The *hiphʿil* of רבה is
used as in 9: 17. With the form וְתֶרֶב
compare וְיֶרֶב in 34: 37. On the word
כַּעַשׂ cf. 5: 2. The complement עִמָּדִי
'with me', i.e. 'as regards me'. The
3rd hemistich is elliptical. The end
עִמִּי 'with me' implies the verb 'fight'
(נלחם which takes the preposition
עם before the person 'with' whom
one fights). The expression חֲלִיפוֹת
וְצָבָא 'reliefs and army' is a hendiadys, the writer juxtaposing and
co-ordinating two words, the second
of which is the complement of the
first. Here it is a question of 'reliefs
of the army', i.e. relieving troops
being flung in perpetually. The presence of צבא and of חליפה in 14: 14
shows that the two words are complementary to each other, and that
it would be unwise to suppress them,
whether by reading יצבא with the
kethib of the Orientals or by substituting for חליפות a verb (G, Syr.).
Job sees in concrete terms the hostility and the anger of God. He
pictures himself as surrounded by
fighting troops. Later he will speak

18   Why then didst Thou bring me forth from the womb?
      I should have died and no eye would have seen me;
19   I should have been as though I had not been,
      I should have been carried from the womb to the grave!
20   Are not *the days of my life* but a trifle?
      Withdraw from me that I might be a little cheerful,

20 יְמֵי חֶלְדִּי (G, Syr.); MT: ימי יחדל‎ (*kethîb*), ימי וחדל‎ (*qerê*).

of the hordes which God flings against him as against a besieged city (19: 12).

18 G adds a negative before אגוע‎ to make it dependent on the opening question. It is unnecessary to suppose ולא‎ (contra Beer).

V. 18 re-echoes the cry, imbued with bitterness, which Job uttered at the beginning of his speeches (3:11ff.). He has come to the conclusion that, whether innocent or guilty, man is destined to suffering. And, above all, he has personally experienced the severity of the divine wrath. God seems to have created him especially to spy upon and persecute him (3-7), to hunt him and make war upon him (15-17). It would have been far better to remain in the darkness of nothingness: 'Why then hast Thou made me to come forth from the womb?' The author is careful not to copy literally the first outbursts of his hero (3: 11). There is no reason whatever to eliminate vv. 18-19 as Merx wishes to do. The imperfects אָגְוַע‎ and תְּרָאֵנִי‎ are used to emphasise regret for something which did not happen (Gesenius-Kautzsch, § 107n). The verb גוע‎ 'die' is used as in 3: 11. 'And no eye would have seen me!', this is indeed how Job envisages disappearance into the darkness of death; cf. 7: 8, 21.

19 G repeats the negative question διὰ τί . . . . οὐκ. For אובל‎, G ἀπηλλάγην, Aq. and Theod. ἀπηνέχθην; cf. Vulg. *translatus*.

A development of the wish expressed in v. 18. The imperfects אֶהְיֶה‎ and אוּבַל‎ with the nuance of אגוע‎ and תראני‎ in v. 18. The 1st hemistich recalls the היו כלא היו‎ of Ob 16. In Jer 20: 17 the prophet complains that the womb of his mother did not become his grave. It should not be forgotten that it is God Himself who shaped the embryo in the maternal womb (9-12). Job returns to his first idea: 'Why does He give light to an unhappy one and life to those whose soul is bitter?' (3: 20). The whole passage is inspired by ch. 3.

20 Vulg. *finietur brevi* follows the *kethîb* יֶחְדָּל‎, whilst Targ. adopts the *qerê* וַחֲדָל‎. G (B) ὁ βίος τοῦ χρόνου μου is for ὁ χρόνος τοῦ βίου μου, which has been preserved in G (A), Sah., Syrohex., Jerome *tempus vitae meae*. In Syr. 'the days of my life'. The reading of G and of Syr. was יְמֵי חֶלְדִּי‎ (cf. inf.). The י of חלדי‎ linked to the word שית‎ has given rise to the *kethîb* יְשִׁית‎, later transformed into the *qerê* וְשִׁית‎.

The present text reads: 'Are not my days but a trifle? now cease and depart from me . . .' (*qerê*), or else: 'Will not my brief span of life come to an end? Now depart from me . . .' (*kethîb*). The hesitations of the Massoretes arise from the circumstance that the text has been slightly modified. With Bickell and most modern exegetes we shall not hesitate to read יְמֵי חֶלְדִּי‎, an early reading pre-

21   Before I depart, no more to return,
      To the land of darkness and shade,
22   A land of deep darkness [   ] and confusion,
      Where the light is as the darkness.

22   כמו אפל צלמות. 'As darkness, shade'. Gloss (cf. Comm.).

served in G and Syr. Hence: 'Are not
the days of my life but a trifle?' The
parallel text 7: 16, where the verb
חדל figures, has brought confusion
into the MT. As the first letter of
ישית belongs to the previous word,
we shall read שִׁית מִמֶּנִּי, which corresponds to the חדל ממני 'leave me
alone' of 7: 16. Some critics have
wished to replace שׁית by another
verb: שָׁבַת 'finish', 'cease' (Lagarde),
שָׁעָה 'look (away from me)' (Beer,
following 7: 19), or הֵשַׁע (from שעה,
Gray, in accordance with Ps 39: 14).
But the verb שבת is not used with a
person as complement; it means 'to
cease' to do a thing, and not 'to
leave' a person. It is certain that Ps
39: 13, 'Look away from me that I
may know gladness before I depart
and be no more', is exactly attuned
to the note struck by our passage.
But this very likeness to our verse
and to 7: 19 would have secured the
maintenance of the verb שעה, had
it been part of the original text. The
transitive verb שׁית 'put', 'place' does
indeed create a difficulty. Rashi
overcomes the difficulty by regarding a reflexive pronoun as
understood. The formula שׁית ממני
will mean: 'put Thyself far from me,
depart from me!' This explanation is
preferable to that which understands 'Thy hand' or 'Thy face'
after שׁית. The verb הבליג as in 7: 27
and Ps 39: 14. The thought of Job
will assume a more general character
in 14: 5-6. The repetition of מעט at
the end of the verse is intentional.
Since his days are a mere trifle, he
might enjoy a 'little' good cheer. It

is quite arbitrarily that Bickell and
Duhm propose to eliminate this
second מעט.

21   For ולא אשוב, G ὅθεν οὐκ ἀνα-
στρέψω. The word צלמות is rendered
by γνοφεράν.
   The terse formula 'before I depart
and be no more' of Ps 39: 14 is amplified in vv. 21-2. The clause וְלֹא
אָשׁוּב makes an intrusion which separates אֵלֵךְ from its complement
אֶל־אָרֶץ. Sheol is essentially the
land from which man no more returns, the land of darkness and the
shadow of death (cf. Comm. on
7: 9). Cf. the description of 7: 9-10.
The juxtaposition חֹשֶׁךְ וְצַלְמָוֶת stands
as in 3: 5.

22   In G we find a paraphrase
rather than a translation: εἰς γῆν
σκότους αἰωνίου, οὗ οὐκ ἔστιν φέγγος
οὐδὲ ὁρᾶν ζωὴν βροτῶν, as also in Vulg.
terram miseriae et tenebrarum, ubi
umbra mortis, et nullus ordo, sed sem-
piternus horror inhabitat. Nor is there
any more literalism in Syr. 'a land
which is as abandoned as darkness
and the shadows of death, and in it
there is no order of generations, and
it is desolate as darkness itself'.
Likewise Targ. 'a land whose eyelid
is as the darkness of the shadows
of death, and in which there is no
order that men might dwell there,
and it sheds gloom like thick darkness'.
   A certain number of commentators
suppress this v. 22, claiming that it
is composed of a series of glosses
intended as an amplification of v.

21; cf. Bickell, Loisy, Duhm, Beer. It should, however, be remembered that the writers of the ancient world liked to accumulate typical details in their description of the underworld (cf. the beginning of the account of Ishtar's descent into hell, in our *Choix de textes*, p. 326). It is possible that the text has become overloaded; but the presence of עֵיפָתָה, a poetic form of עֵיפָה (cf. Comm. on 5: 16), which recurs only in Am 4: 13, seems to us a guarantee of authenticity. The term is explained by the first כְּמוֹ־אֹפֶל, which duplicates כמו־אפל of the end of the verse. And similarly the צלמות of v. 21 is redundant here. It is a further synonym of עפתה and אפל. There remains 'land of deep darkness and confusion', which forms a hemistich parallel to v. 21b. The words לֹא־סְדָרִים 'no orders' convey the idea of disorder and confusion. The

hapax סֶדֶר is current in post-Biblical Hebrew to express 'order', 'arrangement'. As regards the similarity of meaning between the roots סדר and ערך, see Comm. on 6: 4. It is needless to postulate for סדרים the meaning 'rows of stars' (*Abû-l-walid*) or of 'gradations', 'fine distinctions' (Ehrlich). The impersonal וַתֹּפַע implies נהרה 'light' (3: 4c) or some such term as subject: 'the light shines there as though it were darkness', i.e. 'the light is as the darkness'. Cf. Mt 7: 23b: εἰ οὖν τὸ φῶς τὸ ἐν σοὶ σκότος ἐστίν, and the antitheses of Sophocles (*Ajax*, 394ff.): ᾿Ιὼ σκότος ἐμὸν φάος,
῎Ερεβος ὦ φαεννότατον, ὡς ἐμοί,
ἕλεσθ᾿ ἕλεσθέ μ᾿ οἰκήτορα,
ἕλεσθέ μ᾿.

Once more the conclusion of Job's speech consists in a vision of death or Sheol (7: 21; 14: 20-2; 17: 13-16; 21: 32-3).

1   Then Zophar the Naamathite spoke and said:
2   Shall not *this man of many* words be answered,
     Is it the verbose speaker who will be found to be right?
3   Will your chatter reduce men to silence,
     And will you mock without any one rebuking you?

Chapter 11. First speech of Zophar: see Introduction, pp. xxxixf.
2 רַב (G, Symm., Vulg., Targ.); MT: רֹב.

11:1 For הנעמתי, G ὁ Μειναῖος, but Jerome *Minaeus* is corrected to *Nimatites* in Gall. (cf. 2:11).

2 With the exception of Syr., the versions have pointed רַב instead of רֹב, whence G ὁ τὰ πολλὰ λέγων, Symm. ὁ πολύλαλος, Targ. דמסגי מליא, Vulg. *qui multa loquitur*. The omission of the interrogative in G results in the suppression of the negative לֹא. For אִישׁ שְׂפָתִים, G ὁ εὔλαλος, Vulg. *vir verbosus*. G paraphrases יצדק: οἴεται εἶναι δίκαιος. The *niph'al* of ענה requires as subject the name of a person; cf. אֵעָנֶה (9:15 corrected; 19:7). The parallelism with אִישׁ שְׂפָתַיִם is also in favour of the slight change from רֹב to רַב, which is supported by G, Symm., Targ., Vulg. The present pointing has been influenced by Pr 10:19 and Ec 5:2. The רַב דְּבָרִים 'one who abounds in words' is the man who talks ceaselessly. Job is once more being accused of verbiage (8:2). In the light of the context, 'the man of lips' is not merely one who speaks with superficial levity as contrasted with the man who speaks from the depths of the heart (8:10), but also he who uses his lips to utter and pour forth

streams of words, the wordy, loquacious man. As an organ of speech, the lips are in parallelism with the mouth (8:21; 15:6; 16:5) or with the tongue (27:4); cf. *L'Emploi métaphorique*, p. 88. On the verb צדק in the sense of being right, cf. 9:15.

3 Vulg. *tibi soli* interprets בדיך as if we had לבדך (cf. לבדו in 9:8). G εὐλογημένος γεννητὸς γυναικὸς ὀλιγόβιος reads ברוך instead of בדיך, and quotes 14:1. Syro-hex. puts an obelus before this translation. Syr. reads מֵתִים 'the dead' instead of מְתִים, and translates the 2nd hemistich twice. For ותלעג, G μὴ πολὺς ἐν ῥήμασιν γίνου, which is inspired by v. 2. The suffix of מכלם is added by the versions with the exception of Targ. It is needless to add it to the text (contra Bickell and Duhm).
     The interrogation continues in v. 3. The word בַּדֶּיךָ 'your chatter' (Is 16:6; Jer 48:30) is the subject of יַחֲרִישׁוּ. The *hiph'il* of חרשׁ 'be silent' is generally used in the sense of the *qal* (cf. 6:24; 13:5, 13, 19; 33:31, 33); but it also is used transitively in the sense of 'to silence' (41:4). Hence we can here accept it as being used in a causative way: 'Will your chatter reduce men to

4   Now, you say: 'Pure is my teaching,
     And I am clean in Thy eyes!'

5   But oh! that Eloah might speak,
     And open His lips to you

6   And reveal to you the secrets of wisdom

6   יִשְׁאָלְךָ; MT: יׁשה לך.

silence?' The verb לעג has been used
by Job in speaking of God (9: 23).
The *hiph'il* of כלם has the meaning
of 'cover with shame', 'insult' (19:
3); cf. כְּלִמָּה 'insult' in 20: 3. Here
simply 'blame' (Latin *blasphemare*
'insult'). With וְאֵין מַכְלִים cf. ואין
מַצִּיל of 5: 4. Defective writing
מַכְלִם as in יַפְרַח (14: 9), יַגְעַל (21:
10), etc.

4 G μὴ γάρ λέγε adds a negative.
The translation τοῖς ἔργοις does not
presuppose לכתי 'my conduct'
(Duhm, Beer) instead of לקחי. לכת
(from הלך) is never rendered by
ἔργα in G. The word הייתי, omitted
in G, is restored by Jerome *fui* and
appears in the margin of Syro-hex.
For בעיניך, G ἐναντίον αὐτοῦ.
    In order to obtain rigid strophes,
Duhm transfers v. 7 to precede v. 4
and cuts out v. 6c and v. 10. Bickell
cut out vv. 4, 6c, 7, 10: Siegfried vv.
6c, 7-9, 12. The arbitrary nature of
these changes is sufficiently shown
by the divergences which exist between their authors. The adjective
זַךְ 'pure' here qualifies an abstract
term as in 16: 17. The word לֶקַח
'teaching', 'doctrine' is literally what
is received through tradition; cf. the
Assyrian *iḫzu* 'knowledge', 'learning',
derived from *aḫazu* (אחז) 'to take'.
In Dt 32: 2 we have לִקְחִי 'my
teaching' parallel with אִמְרָתִי 'my
speech', and in Is 29: 24 לֶקַח is
parallel to בִּינָה 'discernment'. Apart
from these texts, the word occurs
only in the Book of Proverbs. The
adjective בַּר, parallel with זַךְ, signi-

fies what shines (Ca 6: 10), and by
derivation what is clean and pure,
spotless (cf. the Assyrian *barâru*, 'to
be sparkling'). We had the word בֹּר
to express what makes sparkling
and pure in 9: 30. The expression
בְּעֵינֶיךָ 'in Thy eyes' is what we
expect in the mouth of Job, who has
always addressed himself to God by
using the 2nd person. It is to weaken
it to no purpose to read בעיניו 'in
His eyes' (Merx, in accordance with
G) or בעיני 'in my eyes' (Siegfried,
Duhm).

5 G renders מי יתן by πῶς ἄν, אלוה
by ὁ Κύριος. The words ויפתח שפתי
were omitted in G, which joins עמך
(translated πρὸς σέ) to דבר. The 2nd
hemistich καὶ ἀνοίξει χείλη αὐτοῦ μετὰ
σοῦ, absent from Sah., marked by an
asterisk in Jerome and Syro-hex.,
has been added in accordance with
a hexaplar reading, probably that
of Theod.
    Job has addressed himself directly
to God. He has complained (9: 15-
16) that God does not answer him.
Now Zophar prays that such an
answer might come from above:
'But oh! that Eloah might speak!'
It is in the eyes of God (v. 4) that
Job claims to be pure. The expression וְאוּלָם as in 1: 11. The
formula מִי־יִתֵּן 'who will give?'
(6: 8) is not here constructed with
the imperfect, but with the infinitive
(Ex 16: 3; 2 S 19: 1). Parallelism
between the verb דבר and 'open the
lips' as in 32: 21.

6 G δύναμιν connects תעלמות with

(For they are hard to understand)!
You would then know that Eloah *demands from you an*
account of your sin!

עלם 'to be strong'; but Aq. ἀπορρή-
τους and Symm. ἀπορρήτου are reflected in Compl. ἀπόρρητα. For
כפלים, Targ. כופלא, G διπλοῦς,
Vulg. *multiplex*, while Syr. reads
קפלים. G renders לתושיה by τῶν κατὰ
σέ. For ודע, G καὶ τότε γνώσῃ, Jerome *et tunc scies*, which becomes
et tu nescies in Gall. The verb ישה is
connected with שוה by G ὅτι ἄξιασει.
Vulg. paraphrases the 3rd hemistich
et intelligeres quod multo minora exi-
garis ab eo quam meretur iniquitas tua.
    The 1st hemistich offers no diffi-
culty. We shall meet וְיַגֶּד־לָךְ again
in 12: 7. The verb הגיד used in the
sense of 'reveal', 'unveil', 'disclose'
what is hidden (26: 4; 33: 23; 36: 9).
The noun תַּעֲלֻמָה 'a hidden secret
matter' in 28: 11. The plural, used
here, recurs in Ps 44: 22 where it is
a question of the secrets of the heart.
Hence: 'and that He might reveal
to you the secrets of wisdom'. The
2nd hemistich is an interpolated
clause which separates the 1st hemistich from its natural sequence;
but it should not be suppressed,
for it presents certain difficulties
which preclude its interpretation
as an explanatory gloss. The difficult כִּפְלַיִם has been replaced by
כִּפְלָאִים 'like wonders' (Merx, Duhm,
etc.), or by פְּלָאִים 'wonders' (Beer,
Budde, Driver-Gray, etc.). But we
already know that the secrets of
God are wonderful and there is no
need of a special revelation to teach
us that. What is expected is a statement of the precise reason why God
alone can reveal these secrets. Now,
the word כֶּפֶל 'double', 'twofold'
(41: 5) is used in the dual in Is 40: 2
to express the idea of the 'double'
of what was deserved. This then is
the context which clarifies the mean-

ing of כפלים. Now, לְתוּשִׁיָּה means
'for the understanding', the word
תושיה denoting the faculty which
enables man to foresee and provide
(5: 12). The things which are 'twofold for the understanding' are ambiguous matters which may be interpreted in two ways. This is so as
regards the secrets of divine wisdom.
Man does not know what explanation he should adopt. That is why
the debate between Job and his
friends is indefinitely prolonged.
The 3rd hemistich is sacrificed by
Bickell, Duhm, and Beer. But here
too the difficulties of the text do not
favour the hypothesis of an interpolation. Let us note that the imperative וְדַע, instead of the jussive,
may be used to stress the certainty
of a consequence (Gesenius-
Kautzsch, § 110i). Cf. the use of
אַל־תִּירָא 'do not fear', to mean 'you
shall not fear', in 5: 22b. The construction of the *hiph'il* of נשה 'forget', with לְ״ before the first complement and מִן before the second, is
disquieting. In 39: 17 we have a
double accusative. Much good will
is required to translate: 'You would
then see that He has been indulgent
towards your crimes' (Le Hir,
Crampon), or 'You would then see
that He does not treat you according
to your iniquity' (Segond). Bickell
corrects יַשֶּׁה to יְשַׁוֶּה (following G)
whence Loisy: 'You would then
realise that God has punished you
proportionately to your fault.'
Budde observes that at least כַּעֲוֺנֶךָ
would be required. An excellent
conjecture of Ehrlich and Torczyner
solves the problem: we should read
יִשְׁאָלְךָ for ישה לך and compare the
Arabic *sa'ala 'an* 'question about'.
Here in a juridical sense: 'You

7   Can you discover the nature of Eloah!?
     Can you plumb the perfection of Shaddai?
8   It is *higher than* the heavens: what will you do?
     Deeper than Sheol: what can you know?

8 גְּבֹהָה מִשָּׁמַיִם (Vulg.); MT: גבהי שמים.

would then know that Eloah asks
from you an account of your fault.'
This is exactly the central issue.
Job will not understand that, if
he is punished, it is because he is
guilty.

7 For חקר, G ἴχνος, Aq. ἐξιχνιασμόν,
cf. Vulg. *vestigia*. The second תמצא
is rendered ἀφίκου in G, whence the
corrections תָּבֹא (Merx, Torczyner),
תֵּצֵא (Budde, Beer), תִּגַּע (Siegfried).
But the reading of G is explained
by the meaning of תמצא in this
context. Note that Vulg. renders
the first תמצא by *comprehendes*, the
second by *reperies*. For תכלית שדי
Vulg. *perfectum omnipotentem*.
The word חֵקֶר implies not merely
research and investigation (5:9;
9:10), but further the object of the
inquiry, i.e. what is hidden under
appearances, the basis (38:16), the
inward essence; cf. חקר נסתרות
'the nature of hidden things' (Sir
42:16). The verb מצא, used twice,
conveys two distinct ideas, and there
is no reason to correct the תִּמְצָא at
the end. The normal sense of the
Hebrew word is attached to the first
תמצא. The preposition עַד 'as far as'
before the complement lends to the
second תמצא the sense of the Aramaic מטא (equivalent of מצא)
'attain', 'reach'; cf. Dn 7:13, where
מטה (for מטא) takes עַד before its
complement. The abstract תַּכְלִית
from כלה 'to be complete, perfect'
sometimes means the end or limit
of a thing (26:10; 28:3), sometimes
perfection (Ps 139:22).

8 For גבהי שמים, G ὑψηλὸς ὁ οὐρανός,
Jerome *sublime est coelum*, but Tur.
sublimior est coelo (cf. Vulg. *excelsior
est coelo*). G (A) adds γῆ δὲ βαθεῖα
(cf. Sir 1:3), which is quoted in the
margin of Syro-hex. Instead of
תפעל, Syr. reads תדע. For משאול, G
τῶν ἐν ᾅδου. The margin of Syro-hex.
cites a reading of Aq. which is nearer
to the MT.
In order to secure an acceptable
meaning, Targ. places the preposition בְּ" before the word גבהי. Both
parallelism and the context suggest
a reading גְּבֹהָה מִשָּׁמַיִם, which in fact
is attested by the Vulg. It may be
that G has wrongly arranged the
text in such a way as to give גבהים
שמים. The meaning, however, is not
in doubt: 'It is higher than the
heavens.' The epithets relate to the
perfection of God which has been
mentioned in v. 7. It is inappre-
hensible by human thought. It lies
beyond all known dimensions:
height, depth, length, breadth. Now,
'who will ever pierce the height of
heaven, and the width of the earth,
and the abyss and wisdom?' (Sir
1:3). The terms of comparison
chosen are heaven, the earth, and
the abyss. In our text is added a
further one, namely Sheol, which
Sirach does not mention. St Paul
alludes to the four dimensions of the
unfathomable in speaking of the
vocation of the Gentiles: 'that you
may be able to comprehend with
all the saints what is the breadth and
length and height and depth' (Eph
3:18). With the expression 'higher
than the heavens' cf. גבהו ממך 'they
are higher than you', speaking of the

9   Longer than the earth is its dimension,
    Full broader than the sea!
10 If He passes by and keeps a matter secret,
    Or if He divulges it, who is to prevent Him?

clouds (35:5). The question מה
תפעל recalls מה אפעל in 7:20.
Sheol, which is situated under the
ground (*RB*, 1907, pp. 6off.), is the
symbol of depth (cf. Comm. on
7:9).

9 G renders מארץ מדה by μέτρου
(A μέτρων) γῆς, Jerome simply *a
spatio*. G (A) adds ἐπίστασαι after
γῆς. For רחבה מני־ים, G εὔρους θαλάσσης. A reading of Aq. cited in
Syro-hex. seems to have read רקיע
for ארכה and מדת 'hast thou measured' for מדה (cf. Field).

It becomes clear that the world is
divided into four big zones: heaven
and Sheol (v. 8), the earth and the
sea (v. 9). The Babylonians divided
the universe into four great realms,
each having its lord and master:
heaven, the earth, the sea, and the
underworld (cf. *La Religion assyro-
babylonienne*, pp. 57f.). The form
מִדָּה for מִדָּתָה is dictated by considerations of euphony; cf. עָרְמָם
in 5:13. The poetic מִנִּי instead of
מִן, is part of the vocabulary of Job
(cf. 6:16; 7:6; 9:3, 25, etc.), and
of the Psalms. Outside these two
books it is found only in the Song of
Deborah (Jg 5:14), Is 46:3, and
Mic 7:12. Breadth is chosen as the
characteristic dimension of the sea;
cf. רחב מים 'breadth, extent of the
waters' in 37:10. On the other hand,
breadth is the dimension of the
earth in Sir 1:3; cf. G (A) in v. 8.

10 G ἐὰν δὲ καταστρέψῃ τὰ πάντα
omits יחלף and seems to read יְמַגֵּר
(cf. Ezr 6:12) instead of יסגיר. G
does not translate the 2nd hemis-

tich, but reproduces 9:12. Vulg.
follows G for the 1st hemistich: *si
subverterit omnia vel in unum coarc-
taverit*. The words *vel in unum coarc-
taverit* interpret ויקהיל in the sense
of Symm., whose translation, quoted
in the margin of Syro-hex., is rendered *aut congregaverit* in Jerome
(with asterisk). Targ. interprets
יסגיר (in accordance with Dt 11:17)
as if it were a question of sealing the
heavens, while ויקהיל would be an
allusion to the convocation of an
army.

V. 10 should be understood in the
light of v. 11, where God is shown
as a God who knows the mind of
deceitful men. It is certain that the
structure and turn of the phrase are
the same as in 9:11-12 and 12:14.
Further, the words מִי and יְחֲלֹף
יְשִׁיבֶנּוּ are also to be found in 9:11-
12. Is that a reason for cutting out
v. 10, as do Bickell, Beer, and Duhm,
or, as Torczyner suggests, for seeing
in it only certain variations on 9:12
and 12:14? But if we do so, then v.
11 remains without any link with the
context. The words יַסְגִּיר and יַקְהִיל
are difficult. They could not have
been used as a gloss on easier texts.
It is to be mistaken about the
reading of G to wish to replace יְחֲלֹף
by יחתף (Graetz, Ehrlich), for G
translates neither of these two verbs.
It is certain that v. 10 is inspired by
9:11-12; but v. 11b, which is retained in the text, is also inspired
by 9:11 so far as the use of the verbs
ראה and בין is concerned (cf. inf.).
The opening 'if He passes by' is as
though one said 'if the whim occurred to Him to ...' (cf. 9:11b).
The close 'who is to prevent Him?'

11   For it is He who knows the mind of deceitful men,
He sees iniquity and observes *it* closely.

11   לוֹ (cf. Syr.); MT: לֹא.

(9: 12) qualifies both וַיַּסְגִּיר and וַיַּקְהִיל, which must clearly express two opposites in order to bring out the absolute freedom of God. The *hiph'il* of קָהַל is a denominative from קָהָל 'assembly' (30: 28) and generally means 'to convoke an assembly'. It is supposed that, in reference to God, it must be a question of God's summoning a court of justice. This meaning however is out of keeping with the context, which stresses God's omniscience (v. 11). Again, the verb סגר, in the *hiph'il*, means 'to keep confined', whatever be the object in question. The antithesis between הסגיר and הקהיל resides in the fact that the former verb denotes the confinement and concealment of an object, while the latter declares that it is publicly exposed: to keep secret and to divulge. Cf. 31: 34, where Job speaks of the attitude of a guilty man: 'because I dreaded the din of the capital, and the scorn of families terrified me, I remained quiet and did not go out of doors!' God, who sees everything, can, as He pleases, either keep a thing secret or divulge it. He has not to render account to any one. No one can prevent Him from doing what it seems good to Him to do.

11 G adds ἔργα before ἀνόμων which translates מְתֵי שָׁוא. Syr. points מָתֵי 'for He knows when it is time' (!). Vulg. *hominum vanitatem* reverses the order of the terms מתי שוא. Syr. omits לא. Targ. and Vulg. agree in adding an interrogative to the 2nd hemistich: 'Is it possible for Him to see a deceit and not to mark it?'

(Targ.); *et videns iniquitatem, nonne considerat*? (Vulg.).

'For it is He who knows the mind of deceitful men'. Nothing escapes the vigilant eye of God; even those who can deceive human beings cannot succeed in deceiving Him. Hence the possibility, for God, of acting as He pleases, whether by revealing at once what He has observed, or by reserving the disclosure until later (v. 10). The מְתֵי שָׁוא 'men of deceit' (cf. שׁוא in 7: 3) are made parallel to the נעלמים 'dissemblers' (Ps 26: 4) or to the אנשׁי זדון 'men of pride' (Sir 15: 7). We shall find the מתי־און 'men of iniquity' in 22: 15. It is precisely אָוֶן which figures in the 2nd hemistich: 'and He sees iniquity'.

ולא יתבונן is interpreted, sometimes by considering און as the subject: 'before it suspects Him' (Le Hir), sometimes in leaving God as the subject, while weakening the force of the verb: 'without even looking at it closely' (*Bible du rabbinat français*). In the light of 9: 11 it becomes clear that ירא and יתבונן have one and the same subject, the second action only reinforcing the first. The *hithpo'lel* of בין 'discern', 'perceive' (6: 30; 9: 11) means 'to reflect on' (23: 15) and 'consider', 'notice' (37: 14), 'attend to' (30: 20; 31: 1; 32: 12; 38: 18), whence finally 'understand' (26: 14). To judge by the present text, we should have to suppose that God does not notice iniquity, and does not pay attention to it. But observation is the result of looking, it implies concentration of the attention on a certain point. With Reuss and some moderns, we do not hesitate to read לוֹ (cf. Syr.) instead of לֹא. There is the same

12   Thus a stupid man becomes wise,
      Just as a wild ass's colt becomes a master ass!
13   As for you, if you have a faithful heart,

confusion between לא and לו in
6: 21 (cf. Comm.). Hence: 'He sees
iniquity and observes it closely.' Cf.
the parallelism between 'I see not'
and 'I perceive not' (לא־אבין לו) in
9: 11, where the complement of בין
is preceded by the preposition ל־,
as here the complement of התבונן
(a strengthened form of בין).

12 G ἄνθρωπος δὲ ἄλλως νήχεται
λόγοις seems to differ totally from
MT. The reading springs from a
corruption of the Greek text: ἄλλως
comes from ἄνους (= נבוב, Schleusner) and νήχεται from ἐνέχεται, which,
with λόγοις, translates ילבב (Lagarde). Then βροτὸς δὲ γεννητὸς γυ-
ναικός completes אדם by 14: 1 (cf.
11: 3), while ἴσα ὄνῳ ἐρημίτῃ interprets עיר פרא יולד. The word *natat*
which translated νήχεται in Jerome
(Gall.) has become *nutat* in Bod.,
Tur., Aug. For נבוב, Symm. διακενῆς,
Vulg. *vanus*, Targ. חריף 'penetrating'. Syr. 'pure' reads נבר (from
ברר) instead of נבוב (Beer). The
2nd hemistich is paraphrased in
Vulg. *et tamquam pullum onagri se
liberum natum putat*.

This verse has the ring of a proverb.
The word נָבוּב 'hollow' (Ex 27: 8;
38: 7; Jer 52: 21), linked to אִישׁ, has
been chosen to denote a stupid man,
because of its assonance with יִלָּבֵב.
The *niph'al* of לבב does not mean
lack of, but possession of, heart, i.e.
understanding (7: 17). The participle נָלְבָּב is very much used in post-
Biblical Hebrew to denote a man
cordatus, 'sensible,' 'intelligent' (*Thesaurus* of Ben-Yehuda, V, p. 2601).
The normal meaning of the 1st
hemistich will therefore be: 'and a
stupid man becomes wise'. The expression פֶּרֶא אָדָם is borrowed from

Gn 16: 12, where it is said of Ishmael that he will be 'a wild ass of a
man', i.e. a veritable wild ass, because 'his hand will be against all
and the hand of all against him'. The
apposition אָדָם in this expression,
as in others like it, implies that the
individual has all the qualities necessary to represent the species of
which he forms a part. From failure
to have noticed the kinship between
our text and Gn 16: 12, critics have
made of אָדָם the object of the
action designated by יִוָּלֵד; 'and the
stupid wild ass becomes a man'
(Le Hir); 'and, ceasing to be a wild
ass, is born into the dignity of humanity' (! *Bible du rabbinat français*). Others have modified the text.
Thus Merx changes עיר פרא into
ילוד אשה and פרא יער into יולד
'man born of a woman is a wild ass
of the forest' (!). Budde proposes
יֻלְמָד 'is tamed' instead of אדם יולד.
Note that עַיִר 'ass's colt' is in the
absolute state. The verb יִוָּלֵד 'is
born' means 'to acquire the nature
of' (*natura* from *natus*) and hence
'become' (Pr 17: 17). The point of
departure is עיר, the point of arrival
פרא אדם. Hence quite simply: 'and
an ass's colt becomes a master ass!'
This 2nd hemistich supplies a term
of comparison introduced by the
copula, exactly as in 5: 7. Hence the
meaning of the proverb is quite
clear: a stupid man acquires wisdom
just as a wild ass's colt becomes a
master ass. This metamorphosis
takes place as a result of the intervention of God which has been
mentioned in v. 11.

13 G καθαρὰν ἔθου paraphrases
הכינות. For פרשת, G ὑπτιάζεις (A

And if you stretch out your hands towards Him,

14   If *you* put away the iniquity which is in your hand
And if you let not evil dwell in your tents,

15   Then you will lift up your face without blemish,
You will be securely established and you will not fear!

14   תַּרְחִיקֵהוּ (Vulg.);   MT: הַרחיקהו.

ὑπτίασας), a word which does not appear elsewhere in G and in which we would be inclined to see a corruption of πετάζεις (Aq. ἐκπετάζεις). For כפיך, G χεῖρας, but G (A) adds σοῦ (Sah., Jerome), marked with asterisk in Syro-hex.

Zophar now returns to the individual case of Job and begins by אִם־אַתָּה, exactly as Bildad did in 8: 5. The *hiph'il* of כון with לֵב as complement recurs in Ps 78: 5. To fix the heart, is to make it faithful and constant; cf. the Assyrian *kun libbi* 'faithfulness of heart' (*L'Emploi métaphorique*, p. 120). The 2nd hemistich recommends the resource of prayer, as in the speech of Eliphaz (5: 8ff.) and of Bildad (8: 5ff.). It was usual to stretch out the hands for prayer (Ex 9: 29, 33) in a certain direction (1 K 8: 22, 38). Cf. the Assyrian expression *upnâ-šu-iptâ* 'he has opened his fists' to convey the idea of prayer (Streck, *Assurbanipal*, pp. 24-5). The hands must be pure from all evil, otherwise God turns away (Is 1: 15-16). This will be suggested by v. 14.

As it stands, the 1st hemistich would have to be translated: 'if there is iniquity in your hand, put it away', and the 2nd: 'do not allow injustice to dwell in your tents!' But these two imperatives separate the protasis (v. 13) from the apodosis (v. 15). We expect rather a clause parallel to v. 13, to stress that the hands must be pure. Now, we find in 22: 23b the formula תרחיק עולה מאהלך 'if you put away injustice from your tent', which suggests that we should read תַּרְחִיקֵהוּ with the Vulg. Thus we obtain: 'If you put away the iniquity which is in your hand'. Zophar has no doubt of the guilt of Job (v. 6). He recommends him to seek the help of God. But above all his hands must be pure. The word אָוֶן is used as in v. 11. The change from בְּיָדֶךָ to מִידְךָ 'from your hand' (Duhm) is not necessary. In the 2nd hemistich we have וְאַל 'and let not' to introduce a second conditional clause. Cf. the use of אַל in 2 K 6: 27 to mean *nisi*. It is not only necessary to depart from the evil which makes the hands unclean, but also not to allow unrighteousness to enter the dwelling of the one who prays. The word עַוְלָה has its vaguest sense (5: 16). The 'tent' of the wicked has been mentioned by Bildad (8: 22).

14 Vulg. *si iniquitatem quae est in manu tua abstuleris a te* read תַּרְחִיקֵהוּ, which is preferable to the הרחיקהו of MT. For בידך G and Syr. have the plural, but Targ. and Vulg. keep the singular. After הרחיקהו G adds ἀπὸ σοῦ, marked by obelus in Jerome and Syro-hex. G αὐλισθήτω, Aq., Symm., Theod. σκηνωσάτω, Targ. תשרי, Vulg. *manserit* point תִּשְׁכֹּן instead of תַּשְׁכֵּן. Finally the versions read the singular instead of the plural באהליך.

15 Syr. replaces 'your face' by 'your hands', following v. 13. The word ממום, omitted by Syr., is translated ὥσπερ ὕδωρ καθαρόν (= ממים) in G. It seems that G ἐκδύσῃ

16   For you will forget your sorrow,
As waters that have flowed away will you remember it!

17   And more glorious than noonday will life emerge for you,
Darkness will be as the morning.

17 תְּעֻפָה (Targ., Syr.); MT: תָּעֻפָה.

δὲ ῥύπον and Targ. 'you will be cleansed from evil' stem from an interpretation of מצק in the sense of 'melted down', 'purified in the crucible'.

The expression כִּי־אָז takes the place of כִּי־עַתָּה in 8: 6; 13: 19, and simply means 'from then on'. The promise 'you will lift up your face' is an allusion to Job's own words 'I lift not up my head' (10: 15). Job will no longer need to lower his eyes, like one who is covered with shame. Cf. the use of שְׂאֵת, infinitive of נשא, in opposition to 'let fall the countenance', 'look on the ground' (Gn 4: 7). The word מוּם, written מֵאוּם in 31: 7, denotes a spot, a stain, whether physical or moral. Here the two meanings interpenetrate each other. Preposition מִן has a privative sense 'without' (21: 9). The participle מֻצָק (*hoph'al* of יצק) means 'melted down' like the metal which is molten into a statue, hence 'hard', 'solid', 'firm'; cf. מוּצָק (37: 10, 18; 38: 38) and יָצוּק (28: 2; 29: 6; 41: 16). The end וְלֹא תִירָא is as in the speech of Eliphaz (5: 21b, cf. 5: 22b).

16 Syr. seems to read וְעַתָּה instead of כִּי־אַתָּה. For עָמָל, G τὸν κόπον, G (A) τῶν κόπων σου (Sah.). G renders כְּמִים by ὥσπερ κῦμα of 6: 15. The end καὶ οὐ πτοηθήσῃ does not come from תזכר, but from וְלֹא תִירָא of v. 15.

We retain כִּי־אַתָּה which offers an acceptable meaning: 'for you', etc. (cf. אִם־אַתָּה in v. 13). Syr. is a frail support for the correction of אתה

into עתה 'now' (Merx, Beer, Budde, etc.), which would be a duplication of אז in v. 15. The word עָמָל means 'pain', 'sorrow' as in 3: 10; 4: 8. Job was trying to forget his troubles in 9: 27 (verb שכח as here). The 2nd hemistich strengthens the 1st by the addition of a picturesque image. The relative is understood before עברו, exactly as in נחלים יעברו 'torrents which flow away' in 6: 15. This similarity ought to have warned Ehrlich against the correction of כמים into כימים 'like days'.

17 The order of the two hemistichs is reversed in G and its derived versions. G σοὶ ζωή does not necessarily presuppose חלדך. This is rather an interpretation than a translation. Vulg. adds *ad vesperam* to the 1st hemistich and paraphrases תעפה according to the meaning of the root עיף 'to be exhausted': *et cum te consumptum putaveris.* G ἡ δὲ εὐχή σου reads the more ordinary word תפלה instead of the rarer word תעפה. Targ. פעפועא דקבלא 'the gloom of darkness' and Syr. ܚܫܘܟܐ 'darkness' connect תעפה with עוף or עיף 'to be dark'.

This verse is conceived on the same pattern as Is 63: 10b: 'then shall your light rise in the darkness and your gloom be as the noonday'. Note that זרח 'rise', in reference to a star or planet, corresponds in Isaiah to יקום of our 1st hemistich. It is clear, judging by this parallel passage, that the 2nd hemistich means 'darkness will be as the morning'. The Massoretic pointing considers תָּעֻפָה as a verbal form (3rd person fem. sing.

18   Then you will dwell in safety, since there will be hope;
      And you *will be* protected, you will lie down securely,

19   You will stretch out at ease without being disturbed,
      And many will stroke your face!

18 וְחָפַרְתָּ; MT: וְחָפַרְתָּ.

of the cohortative) of עוּף, עיף
(10: 22). But if so, we are faced by
the difficulty arising from the juxtaposition of תעפה 'will be dark' and
of 'will be as the morning'. It is
doing violence to the text to interpret as 'when it is dark, it will be as
the morning'. The true solution
consists in pointing as תְּעֻפָה (a form
like תְּרוּמָה תְּבוּסָה, etc.) and in recognising in this substantive (with
Targ. and Syr.) an abstract derived
from עוּף = עיף (cf. 10: 22). The text
of Isaiah is sufficient to exclude the
interpretation of תעפה, read as
תָּעֹף, by 'zenith' (Fried. Delitzsch,
on the basis of תעף 'surpass'), or
the correction of תעפה into תִּפְלָה
'prayer' (Siegfried, following G). The
1st hemistich begins with וּמִצָּהֳרַיִם,
which, according to parallelism, will
be interpreted 'and more than noonday'. The subject of the sentence is
חֶלֶד 'life', 'existence' (10: 20). We
find a similar comparison in Ps 37: 6.
Since there is no ambiguity about
the life that is in question, it is needless to add a suffix to חלד. G cannot
be cited in favour of this addition
(cf. sup.). Ehrlich proposes חלך
'darkness', on the basis of the Arabic
ḥalika 'to be very black'. But the
root became חכל in Hebrew, as is
shown by the derivatives חכליל and
חכלילות.

18 G adds σοί after יש (cf. v. 17a).
The end ἐκ δὲ μερίμνης καὶ φροντίδος
ἀναφανεῖταί σοι εἰρήνη is not a translation but a free interpretation of
the 2nd hemistich. Syr. omits וחפרת

לבטח. Targ. interprets וחפרת in the
sense of digging a grave, and שכב
in the sense of the sleep of death,
whence: 'And you will prepare a
sepulchral abode, you will rest in
safety'. Cf. Vulg. *et defossus securus
dormies*.
    The verb בטח is used as in 6: 20.
The 1st hemistich, 'And you will
dwell in safety, since there will be
hope', is easily interpretable, but
not the 2nd, where the expression
וְחָפַרְתָּ offers a *crux interpretum*.
חפרת is connected with חפר 'to dig'
(3: 21; 39: 21), or 'to spy out' (39:
29), so as to yield the translation
'and you will look into the distance'
or else 'and you will make your inspection'. But this meaning does not
fit into the context 'You will lie
down securely', which is supported
by Hos 2: 20. Again, it is difficult
to obtain a meaning with חָפֵר 'to be
confounded' (6: 20). It is impossible
to reconstitute the text on the basis
of G (contra Duhm). To change
חפרת into חסית 'you will be sheltered' (Siegfried) is too hazardous.
The best solution seems to us to be
that of Ehrlich, who adduces the
Arabic ḥafara 'protect' and 'give
assistance'. It is sufficient to point
וְחָפַרְתָּ 'and you will be protected'.
God protects His own even during
their sleep.

19 For מחריד, G ὁ πολεμῶν σε, Syr.
'who wakens you'. G μεταβαλόμενοι,
which answers to nothing in the
text, is not translated in Jerome *et
rogabunt faciem tuam multi*.
    The verb רבץ is chosen to avoid the
repetition of שכב in v. 18. It is used

20   But the eyes of the wicked languish,
      And every refuge fails them;
      And their hope is to give up the ghost!

especially in speaking of animals. The 1st hemistich makes use of a current expression which conveys the idea of perfect security (Is 17: 2; Zeph 3: 13). This, however, is not a valid reason for rejecting it as do Duhm and Ehrlich. In Lv 26: 6 the verb שׁכב is used, instead of רבץ, before וְאֵין מַחֲרִיד. The phrase 'and no one who disturbs' or 'without any one disturbing you', is frequent in the Bible. The *hiph'il* participle after וְאֵין is used to form a verbal phrase similar to וְאֵין מַצִּיל (5: 4; 10: 7). The locution חִלָּה פָנִים 'to soften the countenance' is commonly used when it is a question of imploring the favours of God. But in regard to petitioning men, it implies simply seeking to sway them by caresses or flatteries (*L'Emploi métaphorique*, p. 59). Cf. Pr 19: 6 and Ps 45: 13. Plural רַבִּים 'many', 'a lot' (4: 3) is used, just as in Pr 19: 6 which we have just quoted.

20   The 1st hemistich is placed at the end in G. But order is restored in Jerome, who begins by *oculi autem impiorum tabescent*, preceded by asterisk. It must be noted that Jerome introduces in his text *animae* corresponding to נפשׁ which is not translated in G and reflecting a hexaplar reading (according to Syrohex.). One may wonder whether G had not omitted the 1st hemistich, which was then added later to the close of v. 20 in the light of the other Greek manuscripts. Syr. omits מפח. The doxology of G (A) παρ'

αὐτῷ γὰρ σοφία καὶ δύναμις figures with the obelus in Syro-hex. Merx and Bickell add to the text this evident gloss which comes from 12: 13.

Here we have again a contrast between the misfortune of the wicked and the happiness of the good, as at the close of Bildad's speech (8: 20-22). The verb כלה 'cease', 'disappear', 'fade away' (4: 9; 7: 9) often has 'the eyes' as its subject (Jer 14: 16; Ps 69: 4, etc.). It then signifies 'to be languishing' (17: 5), as with hunger or desire (Ps 119: 82, 123). The category of the wicked, רְשָׁעִים, is one to which Job (10: 3) and Bildad (8: 22) have already made allusion. The 2nd hemistich again is a commonplace of Hebrew poetry (Jer 25: 35; Am 2: 14; Ps 142: 5). Literally 'and the place of refuge vanishes for them', i.e. every refuge fails them. Note the parallelism between אבד and כלה in 4: 9. The form מִנְהֶם is quite exceptional. We had מִנְהוּ in 4: 12. The word מַפַּח derived from נפח 'to breathe' (whether breathing in or out), means here the breathing out of the soul in the last sigh. It is the meaning suggested by the use of the *hiph'il* הפיח with נפשׁ in 31: 39. By a weakening of the original meaning, the expression מפח נפשׁ came eventually to denote simply distress which is manifested by sighs (Sir 30: 12). In rabbinical literature, מפח נפשׁ will mean rather disgust, sadness (cf. the dictionaries of Levy, s.v. מפח). The word תִּקְוָתָם 'their hope' indicates the object of this hope; cf. תקותי in 6: 8.

CHAPTER 12

1 Then Job spoke and said:
2 Truly you are the people,
   And with you wisdom will die!
3 But I too have a heart like you [　]
   And to whom are such matters unknown?

Chapters 12-14 Fourth speech of Job: see Introduction, pp. xlf.
3 Omit 'I am not inferior to you' (= 13: 26).

12: 2 For עַם, G ἄνθρωποι. G (A) adds μόνοι, whence Jerome (Tur.) and Vulg. *soli homines*. In Targ., חבריא 'companions'. Aq. τελειώματα and Symm. τελειότης connect תמות with תמם, but Theod. ἀποθανεῖται agrees with MT and the other versions.

The adverb אָמְנָם 'in truth' (9: 2), followed by the conjunction כִּי, stands out in relief and has the value of a clause: 'it is true that . . .'. Cf. the beginning of the preceding discourse of Job (9: 2). The word עַם 'people' is corrected to הָעָם 'the people' (Duhm), ערמים 'the cunning' (Beer), עִמּוֹ 'with Him' (Ehrlich), etc. Torczyner sees in אַתֶּם עָם a fragment of אתכם ערמה 'with you is cunning, ingenuity'. It is obvious that the critics are not in agreement as to the word to be substituted. Now, the alliteration עָם וְעִמָּכֶם favours the MT, which is supported by the versions. The reason behind these corrections is the desire to obtain a strict parallelism with the 2nd hemistich. But the clause: 'and with you will die wisdom' can quite well be consequential on the 1st hemistich. If we translate literally 'it is true that you are the people', the

word עָם without article denoting the people preeminently, as contrasted with גּוֹיִם 'nations' (cf. v. 23), we understand that Job addresses his friends ironically as representatives of popular opinion. All the wisdom of the people is concentrated in them. If they die, wisdom dies with them. And v. 3 will make a sharp protest against this apparent concession. It is not right that Job should be excluded from the circle of the wise, since he has 'a heart', i.e. a mind, like his friends. He has already argued on the basis of his knowledge: 'In truth I know that it is so' (9: 2). This later affirmation initiated a speech on the divine perfections. A similar speech will be begun in v. 9. It is seeking an oversubtle meaning in עָם to translate the 1st hemistich by 'you alone are men' (Le Hir), or 'the human species, it is you' (Segond), or again 'you are the élite of the people' (König).

3 G omits from לֹא־נֹפֵל to the end. The similarity between the translations of כְּמוֹכֶם and כְּמוֹ־אֵלֶּה may have caused an error of homoeoteleuton. For נֹפֵל, Syr. ܟܪܐ 'little', Vulg. *inferior*, Targ. פרישׁ 'sepa-

4   A laughingstock to his friend am I,
     I, who invoke Eloah and whom He answers.
     He is a laughingstock, the righteous and perfect man!
5   For misfortune, derision (so think the fortunate ones!),
     A blow for those whose feet slip!

rated'. Syr. omits אין. The 3rd hemistich is paraphrased in Vulg. *quis enim haec quae nostis ignorat?*

The 2nd hemistich, borrowed verbally from 13:2, has been added as an explanation of the first: 'I too have a heart like you.' The heart is the seat of knowledge and wisdom; cf. לבב (9:4) and the *niph'al* of the verb in 11:12. It is the 3rd hemistich which is parallel to the 1st. The preposition את 'with' takes on the same meaning as עם in 10:13. Hence 'and with whom are there not (things) like these things?' The verses which follow are ironical. Instead of taking up the thesis of his friends, Job is going to refer to current and commonplace opinions, to facts which are every day observable. The method is exactly the same as in ch. 24, where the anomalies of social life will be carefully expounded. The pronoun אלה denotes what follows and not what precedes (cf. 10:13). Job replies to the arguments of his friends by pointing to facts which they can observe as well as any other human creature.

4 G passes from the first שחוק to the second, which causes a whole verse to disappear. Vulg. *sicut ego* eludes the difficulty presented by אהיה. Syr. ܣܘܣܐ 'and he' seems to have read יהיה. G and Targ. place the copula before תמים. Vulg. translates צדיק תמים by *justi simplicitas*.

Job is about to point out the facts which any one should have noted (v. 3). The presence of אהיה compels us to translate: 'A laughingstock to his friend am I, I who invoke Eloah

and whom He answers.' We see no necessity to read יהיה (Syr.), as proposed by Beer, who wrongly quotes G (cf. sup.). On the contrary, the 3rd hemistich, 'he is a laughingstock, the righteous and perfect man', in which the formula צדיק תמים merely repeats the epithets applied to Noah in Gn 6:9, suggests that Job first spoke in the 1st person. In fact, the righteousness of Noah and of Job are placed on the same plane (Ezk 14:14, 20); cf. Intro., p. xvi. The allusion to Gn 6:9 prevents us from transferring תמים to v. 5 (contra Duhm, who adds איש before צדיק). The juxtaposition of צדיק and תמים has a good parallel in צדיק כביר of 34:17b. The word שחוק 'laughter' (8:21) denotes also the object of laughter (Jer 20:7; La 3:14).

5 The verse is summed up in εἰς χρόνον γὰρ τακτὸν ἡτοίμαστο πεσεῖν ὑπὸ ἄλλων. It is clear that G omits לפיד בוז and replaces לעשות by לעתות 'in the times'. It seems that πεσεῖν ὑπὸ ἄλλων is an attempt, for whatever it may be worth, at the interpretation of למועדי רגל. Syr. boldly paraphrases: 'In order to remove error and iniquity, to make firm the foot that slips'. The two Targums and Vulg. *lampas* agree to give to לפיד the meaning of 'torch', 'firebrand'. Vulg. *ad tempus statutum* gives to מועדי the meaning of the substantive derived from יעד.

In spite of the efforts of Ehrlich, who refers to Is 7:4 'stumps of firebrands', it is impossible to obtain a satisfactory meaning by translating לפיד בוז as 'a torch of scorn'. Ibn Ezra had already noted that the ל

6   Peaceful are the tents of plunderers,
     And full of confidence are those who provoke God,
     The man who has Eloah in his hand!

of לְפִיד is an otiose letter and that the noun was really פִּיד 'misfortune' (30: 24; 31: 29; Pr 24: 22). The word בּוּז 'scorn', 'derision' recurs in v. 21 and in 31: 34. 'For misfortune, derision', such is the natural interpretation of the opening. The expression לְעַשְׁתּוּת שַׁאֲנָן may be translated literally as 'according to the ideas of the fortunate', i.e. so think the fortunate ones! Tradition varies on the pointing עַשְׁתּוּת or עַשְׁתוֹת (cf. Ginsburg). The former is preferable, for we have here the abstract noun derived from עָשַׁת 'to think', an Aramaic verb which figures in Jon 1: 6. Cf. the use of לְתוּשִׁיָּה in 11: 6. The juxtaposition of שַׁאֲנָן (sic, according to the versions) and of שָׁלֵיו in 21: 23 shows that the fortunate people in question are the same as those referred to in v. 6, which begins with יִשְׁלָיו. The true meaning of שַׁאֲנָן (cf. the verb in 3: 18) is 'easy in mind', 'carefree' (Is 32: 9, 11; Am 6: 1), whence is derived the sense of 'happy'. The 2nd hemistich corresponds to לְפִיד בּוּז, the expression לעשתות שאנן forming a kind of interpolation. The מֹעֲדֵי רָגֶל are those who are in misfortune or distress; cf. 4: 4. If למעדי רגל corresponds to לְפִיד, it is clear that נָכוֹן answers בוז, which renders probable the hypothesis of Schultens, taken up by Dillmann and others, according to which נכון is here a noun derived from נכה 'to strike', as חָזוֹן 'vision' is from חזה 'to see'. Hence the 2nd hemistich is to be translated: 'A blow for those whose feet slip!' Instead of supporting them and raising them up (4: 4), men give them a final blow to crush them completely. Those who

consider נכון as the niph'al participle of כון (15: 23; 18: 12; 21: 8) are obliged to have resort to various subterfuges in order to extract a meaning: 'Their contempt welcomes him whose foot slips' (Le Hir), 'For him whose foot slips contempt is reserved' (Segond), 'That is what is done for those whose foot slips' (Bible du rabbinat français), etc. We have tried to give to v. 5 a literal translation, without ignoring the difficulties. The corrections that have been proposed are far too radical. Duhm connects the תמים of v. 4 to v. 5, reads בָּז for בוז, לְעִתּוֹת (cf. G) for לעשתות, לְמוֹעֵד for למעדי, רַגְלוֹ for רגל. Ehrlich, who translates בוז לפיד, by 'a vile firebrand', replaces לעשתות שאנן by לא אש לשאנן 'without fire, for the carefree'. This firebrand becomes 'a target for kicks', as a result of changing מועדי into מוֹעֵד! Torczyner changes לפיד into למה, finds a גוזל 'brigand' in בוז ל'', etc. Bickell had already reconstituted a 1st hemistich to yield the result: 'the fortunate despise the times of the Almighty'. Such are the manifold ways in which ingenuity exercises itself. The safest method is to give as literal an explanation as possible to the text.

6 G connects the 1st hemistich with v. 5 and seems to confuse יִשְׁלָיו with the verb שָׁלַל (Beer), whence οἴκους τε αὐτοῦ ἐκπορθεῖσθαι ὑπὸ ἀνόμων. Targ., which introduced the sons of Esau into v. 5, now brings forward the sons of Ishmael, in accordance with the descriptions given. Vulg. renders יִשְׁלָיו as abundant. Syr. changes the meaning by interpreting יִשְׁלָיו as 'they will pass',

7   But ask now the beasts [   ]
     And the birds of the skies: they will instruct you;

7   Omit ותרך (from v. 8).

'they will move away', giving to this word a double subject אהלים and בטחות. G isolates בטחות from its context in order to compose a moral saw which forms the 1st hemistich of v. 6. The end ὡς οὐχὶ καὶ ἔτασις αὐτῶν ἔσται reads כאשר for לאשר and replaces the MT by an adaptation. Syr. translates: 'because God is not in their heart'. Vulg. reads בידם: *cum ipse dederit omnia in manus eorum.*

A comparison with 21:23 ought to have put critics on their guard against correcting ישְׁלָיו to שלום (contra Siegfried, Budde, Beer). The last radical has remained in ישליו as in יאתיני of 3:25. Cf. Ps 122:6, where אהביך should perhaps be read אהליך: 'May thy tents be in peace!' The ל״י of לשְׁדָדים indicates ownership. The tent is synonymous with habitation, abode (11:14; 15:34). The שׁדָד (15:21) is the brigand, he who spoils and devastates (cf. 5:21, 22). The *hiph'il* הרגיז 'move', 'shake' (9:6) here has the sense of 'irritate', 'provoke' on account of the meaning 'anger' which has become attached to רגֶז 'agitation' (3:17, 26). Those who provoke God are the wicked. The same connection between sin and divine anger as with the Babylonians (*La Religion assyro-babylonienne*, pp. 232f.). The plural בַּטְחות 'confidences' is used to suggest a supreme degree of arrogant confidence; cf. אשרי in 5:17. The 3rd hemistich is to be interpreted in the style of proverbial formulae: יש לאל ידם 'their hand serves as their God' (Mic 2:1), יש לאל ידי 'my hand serves me as God' (Gn 31:29), to signify that one has full power to do something;

cf. ואין לאל ידך 'and your hand will not be able to serve as God!' (Dt 28:32) to mean 'and you will not be able to do anything'. 'He who has Eloah in his hand' is the man who considers himself to be invested with the fullness of divine power and feels no need to have recourse to God (cf. v. 4b). Virgil's expression: *dextra mihi Deus* (*Aeneid*, X, 773) is thus commented on by Servius: *ut non alium sibi putet deum esse sacrilegus quam dextram et fortitudinem.* Siegfried makes the text banal by transferring the preposition of בְּיָדו to precede אֱלוֹהַ. Duhm invents a new meaning by changing לאשר to לאמר, הביא to הֲכִי, and ידו to ידי.

7   For בהמות, G τετράποδα, Vulg. *jumenta.* G σοι εἴπωσιν does not imply ותאמר (Beer) instead of ותרך, since G will translate תרך by φράσῃ in v. 8.
    The opening וְאוּלָם, as in 11:5. It is in error that Duhm requires the elimination of the adverb. Merx is better advised when he cuts out ותרך, which lengthens the 1st hemistich and evidently comes from v. 8. The בְּהֵמָה Arabic *bahîmeh* is the brute beast, the type of stupidity (18:3). The בהמות ארץ 'beasts of the earth' are paired with עוף השמים 'birds of the sky' in 35:11, where the author is trying to show man's superiority, thanks to his mental development. The plural of majesty בהמות will be used to symbolise the brute beast *par excellence*, namely the hippopotamus (40:15). The close ויגד לך repeats verbally the words of Zophar (11:6). The latter desired a divine revelation. Job refers him to the voices of nature.

8   Or the *reptiles* of the earth and they will teach you;
       The fishes of the sea, and they will tell you!

11   Does not the ear appreciate words,
       As the palate tastes food?

8   זֹחֲלֵי אֶרֶץ; MT: שִׂיח לארץ.

9-10   After v. 12.

8 Vv. 8b-9, absent from Sah., marked by an asterisk in Jerome and Syro-hex., did not exist in G. The present text comes from Theod. (cf. Syro-hex. and Colb.). For ותרך, G ἐάν σοι φράσῃ, Vulg. *et respondebit tibi*.

The 1st hemistich 'or speak to the earth and it will instruct you!' is not without difficulties. First, the verb שׂיח, in the Book of Job, has rather the sense of 'to complain'; cf. 7: 11, and the noun שׂיח (7: 13; 9: 27). V. 7 has referred to the beasts, to huge animals, then to the birds of the heavens, and our v. 8 will conclude with a reference to the fishes of the sea (cf. 11: 8-9). What we expect therefore in the 1st hemistich are specific animals connected with the ground. The following have been proposed: חית ארץ 'animals of the earth' (Ewald), שֶׁרֶץ־הָאָרֶץ 'reptiles of the earth' (Hitzig). The best correction is that of Duhm, who replaces שׂיח לארץ by זוֹחֲלֵי אֶרֶץ 'the crawling things of the earth' (Mic 7: 17), equivalent to the זוחלי עפר of Dt 32: 24. We can leave the feminine singular תְּרֶךָ, since the subject represents a collectivity of animals; cf. Jl 1: 20; Jer 12: 4 (Gesenius-Kautzsch, § 145k). The *hiph'il* of ירה is used as in 6: 24; 8: 10. In the latter text Bildad was advising Job to question (שׁאל) the previous generation. It was the older people who were to instruct him (יורוך). Job quotes these very words. The fishes of the sea close the series. We have the opposite order in Gn 1: 26: fishes of the sea, birds of the

heavens, brute beasts, creeping things. Note the transposition of the two elements which compose v. 8b: 'and they will tell you' before 'the fishes of the sea', which forms the parallel member to the reptiles of the ground. The voices of nature, to which Job has just appealed, can be heard and understood by man. This point is made by vv. 11-12, which, in their present position, interrupt the sequence of ideas, to quote the *Bible du rabbinat français*. It is obvious in fact that v. 13, which begins by עִמּוֹ 'with him', 'in him', has been violently torn away from v. 10. The suffix of עמו represents God, who is mentioned in vv. 9-10. The presence of the words חכמה 'wisdom' and תבונה 'understanding' in v. 13 has attracted vv. 11-12, in which also figure the words חכמה and תבונה.

9-10 Placed after v. 12.

11 Syr. omits הלא. G seems to translate אזן by νοῦς (cf. Sah. and Syro-hex.). But νοῦς is a corruption of οὖς (Aq., Theod., Symm., quoted in Syro-hex.), which appears in Jerome *auris*, Eth., Arab. Baud. The word לו, omitted in G, is restored in the margin of Syro-hex. and (with asterisk) in the text of Jerome *sibi*.

We have seen that vv. 11-12 have a natural and immediate link with v. 8. Everything speaks in the world of animate nature. Man has only to listen. It is enough to have an ear in order to understand and appreciate the truth: 'Does not the ear appreciate words, as the palate

12   Is it not among the old that wisdom is found,
      And in great age that understanding resides?
9   Who does not know, in the whole universe,
      That it is the hand of *Eloah* which has done this?

9 אֱלוֹהַּ, variant of יהוה.

tastes food?' This verse will be quoted, with slight variations, in 34: 3. As regards the verb בחן cf. 7: 18. The *waw* introduces the comparison as in 5: 7 and 11: 12. The palate is the organ of taste (6: 30). The double meaning of טעם 'to taste', both literally and figuratively, is reflected in the use of the noun טַעַם 'taste' for the appreciation of food (6: 6) and for that of ideas (below, v. 20). Dative לוֹ, with the meaning of a reflexive, just as we had לְךָ in 5: 27 and as we shall have לָהּ in 13: 1.

12 G paraphrases בישישים by ἐν πολλῷ χρόνῳ. After חכמה G (A) adds εὑρίσκεται, marked by an obelus in Syro-hex. For וארך ימים, G ἐν δὲ πολλῷ βίῳ, cf. Vulg. *et in multo tempore.* G (A) μακρῷ instead of πολλῷ; cf. Jerome *in longa vita.*

As regards corrections, Duhm proposes הכי שנים for בישישים. The word יָשִׁישׁ 'old', 'old man' is characteristic of Job (15: 10; 29: 8; 32: 6). It is used as an epithet in Sir 8: 6. We have זָקֵן וְיָשֵׁשׁ in 2 Ch 36: 17. It is among the old that one finds experience of life and wisdom; cf. Sir 25: 4-6(6-8). The older generation are depositaries of knowledge (8: 8-10). Eliphaz will also invoke the authority of the aged (15: 10). Elihu, who is a young man, will deride the old who are unable to solve a problem (32: 6-9). V. 12 is not an irrelevant insertion. Job has declared that the ear can appreciate words (v. 11). These words are primarily those of nature (vv. 7-8). But

if they are not sufficient, then it will be necessary to have recourse to the teaching of the aged, a further source of knowledge. Since old men possess wisdom, they can impart it to the inquirer. The word חָכְמָה was used ironically by Job in v. 2. In the Book of Proverbs its parallel is usually תְּבוּנָה. This word, strictly speaking, implies the faculty of discrimination or understanding; the verb בין occurs in 6: 30; 9: 11. The expression אֹרֶךְ יָמִים 'length of days', abstract for the concrete, is used as a synonym for old age (cf. Dt 30: 20; Ps 21: 5; 23: 6; La 5: 20). Cf. the use of the verb הֶאֱרִיךְ in 6: 11, before נַפְשִׁי 'my life'. The two hemistichs are governed by הֲלֹא of the opening of v. 11 (cf. 13: 12).

9 On the text of G, cf. v. 8. Vulg. *quis ignorat quod omnia haec manus Domini fecerit?* connects כָּל־אֵלֶּה with the 2nd hemistich.

V. 9 is essential to the rest of the chapter, for it alone contains the divine name which will serve as the point of departure for the doxology of v. 10, which is continued in vv. 13-25. Doubtless, v. 9b materially repeats Is 41: 20b, 'that the hand of Yahweh has done this'. But the author intends just that—to echo truths universally known and forming an integral part of current literature. To realise this, it is sufficient to note the modification in Is 66: 2, 'and all these things (וְכָל־אֵלֶּה; cf. our 1st hemistich) my hand has done them!' Cf. Ps 109: 27, 'and let them know that Thy hand (has done) this (זֹאת as here), that it is Thou, Yah-

10   He who holds in His hand the soul of every living thing,
      And the spirit of all mortal flesh!
13   With Him are wisdom and power,
      Counsel and understanding are His!

11-12 Before v. 9.

weh, who hast done it!' The text of
Is 66: 2 will again be quoted in Ac
7: 49. Hence we cannot argue from
the fact of the quotation in support
of the elimination of the 2nd hemistich. What is more disconcerting
is the presence of יהוה, contrary to
the use characteristic of the whole
of the poetic part of Job (cf. Intro.,
pp. lxvf.). Three MSS of Kennicott
and two of de Rossi have אֱלוֹהַ, to
which Ginsburg also draws attention.
Ibn Ezra also decided in favour of
אלוה. It is our belief that the original
text had אלוה as in the rest of the
chapter, but that the reminiscence
of Is 41: 20 was quite naturally
responsible for the introduction of
יהוה. The complement of יָדַע begins
at כִּי (cf. Is 41: 20). The expression
בְּכָל־אֵלֶּה will not therefore mean
'all these things', but rather 'among
all these beings', or more precisely
'in the whole universe', the words
כל־אלה assuming a meaning similar
to *haec omnia* in Cicero (cf. Ehrlich,
on Is 45: 7). The same meaning for
כל־אלה is found in Is 66: 2; Jer
14: 22. The pronoun זֹאת 'this' or
'that' according to context (1: 22;
2: 10; 5: 27; 10: 13) has a rather
indeterminate character. It means
the thing in question that we are
discussing! Everything is traced
back to the primal cause.

10 G renders אשר by εἰ μή and
does not translate בשר. But Aq.
κρέως is quoted in Colb. and Syro-
hex. In Jerome we find *carnis* preceded by asterisk.
    It is God who holds in His hand the
soul of all living creatures. When He

takes back the soul unto Himself, it
means death (34: 14-15). To be in
the hands of some one implies to be
in his possession or subject to his
discretion (cf. 1: 12; 2: 6). The
words רוּחַ and נֶפֶשׁ are almost synonymous. They denote both the basic
principle of life and the seat of consciousness. There is parallelism between רוחי and נפשי in 7: 11. The
composite entity, the human being,
includes נֶפֶשׁ and בָּשָׂר; cf. 13: 14
and 14: 22. The word אִישׁ, which
governs בָּשָׂר, is not superfluous. In
fact, כָּל־חַי 'every living thing'
comprises even the animals (28: 21).
The 2nd hemistich is restricted to
human beings. The formula כָּל־בָּשָׂר
would apply to 'all flesh in which is
the breath of life' (Gn 6: 17; 7: 15);
but 'all mortal flesh' designates exclusively the human body. Not only
is Eloah the Author of all that is,
but further it is He who has in His
control the principle and source of
all life. Hence it is to Him, as the
primal cause, that we must attribute
all that happens in this world (v. 9).

11-12 Before v. 9.

13 The versions faithfully reproduce MT.
    Duhm's theory of strophes obliges
him to cut out v. 13. Note the parallelism between עִמּוֹ 'with Him'
and לוֹ 'to Him', as phrases introducing the divine attributes. In Is
11: 2 the spirit of God is endowed
with the four attributes mentioned
here, except that בִּינָה takes the
place of תְּבוּנָה. In Is 36: 5 we find

14   If he destroys, men cannot rebuild,
        If he confines, men cannot open;
15   If He holds back the waters, they dry up;
        And if He releases them, they overwhelm the earth.
16   With Him are might and prudence;
        Both the one who goes astray and the one who misleads him
        are His:

again עֵצָה coupled with גְּבוּרָה. It is clear how arbitrary is the change of עצה to עֹצֶם or עָצְמָה 'strength' (Budde). With the old were found wisdom, חָכְמָה, and understanding, תְּבוּנָה (v. 12). God possesses in addition, and to a preeminent degree, counsel which enables Him to guide and control all things, and the might which permits Him to realise what He wills. The גבורה 'might', 'power' recurs in 26: 14, in speaking of God. Compare again Pr 8: 14, where תּוּשִׁיָּה, which we shall meet in v. 16, takes the place of חכמה.

14 G τίς οἰκοδομήσει and Syr. 'who can build?' somewhat soften the MT. It is needless to change ולא into ומי; cf. Vulg. *nemo est qui aedificet* and Targ. ולא יתבני. For על־אִישׁ, G κατὰ ἀνθρώπων, but G (A) κατὰ ἀνθρώπου, Jerome *circum hominem*. For the second ולא, G τίς. Obelus before *quis* in Jerome.

The Aramaic conjunction הֵן 'if', as in 4: 18; 9: 11-12. The verb הרס 'destroy' is opposed to בנה 'build', just as סגר 'close', 'shut in' is contrasted with פתח 'open'. The rhythm of the phrasing and the antitheses recall 9: 11-12 and 11: 10. The *niph'al* is used to denote possibility (6: 2, 6). The 1st hemistich is to be taken in a very general sense; it may be a question of destroying a building or of destroying man. The 2nd hemistich is more precise in its bearing: 'If He confines, men cannot open.' The antithesis between סגר and פתח invites us to retain for

פתח its obvious primary meaning rather than assume a meaning such as 'deliver'. The verb סגר is used with על before the complement of person, exactly as in Ex 14: 3. We have seen the *hiph'il* used without complement (11: 10). The *niph'al* of פתח, preceded by לא, will recur in 32: 19. With the 2nd hemistich cf. Is 22: 22, 'He will open and none shall shut; He will shut and none shall open.' The antithesis between סגר an פתח is found there as here.

15 G ξηραινεῖ τὴν γῆν and Vulg. *omnia siccabuntur* to avoid saying that the waters 'dry up'. One cannot base on G a reading וַיִּבֶשׁ (contra Duhm). The suffix of וישלחם is omitted in G.

The series of antitheses is continued. The verb עצר is used with ב'' before the complement (4: 2; 29: 19). The subject of יָבָשׁוּ is מַיִם; cf. 14: 11 and Gn 8: 7. The *qal* of שלח had מים as its complement in 5: 10, where the beneficent action of the waters was referred to. The *pi'el* has greater force; cf. וַיְשַׁלְּחֵם in 8: 4. The verb הפך means 'overturn', (9: 5; 28: 9). V. 14 alluded to local restricted actions. Drought and flood have a more universal character.

16 Syr. twice translates the 1st hemistich and omits the 2nd. For תוּשִׁיָּה, G ἰσχύς, Theod. σωτηρία (cf. G in 30: 22), but Syr. and Targ. חוכמתא, Vulg. *sapientia*. G changes the 2nd hemistich, in accordance with the requirements of the parallelism and on the model of v. 12:

17   He causes the counsellors to go barefooted,
     And the judges He makes mad,
18   He has loosened the *bond* of kings,
     And has bound a girdle around their loins.

18   מוֹסֵר (Targ., Vulg.); MT: מוּסַר.

αὐτῷ ἐπιστήμη καὶ σύνεσις. Vulg.
paraphrases לוֹ to *ipse novit* and
renders מַשְׁגֶּה by the passive: *eum qui
decipitur.*

   Note the parallelism between עִמּוֹ
and לוֹ (v. 13). 'Might', עֹז (26: 2;
41: 14), and 'prudence', תּוּשִׁיָּה (5: 10,
cf. Comm.), are juxtaposed. The
double meaning of תּוּשִׁיָּה is reflected
in the divergence of the versions (cf.
sup.). Nothing escapes the power or
wisdom of God: 'Both the one who
goes astray and the one who mis-
leads him are His.' The שֹׁגֵג 'he who
goes astray' is he who is unable to
guide his steps by his own efforts
(Ps 119: 67). The verbs שׁגג and שׁגה
belong to the same root originally
'wander', 'go astray'. There is no
reason whatever to replace שֹׁגֵג by
שֹׁגֶה, as Duhm suggests, reading then
וּמַשְׁגֵּהוּ. The MT is perfectly intelligible as it stands. The verb שׁגה
'wander' occurs in 6: 24; 19: 4. The
מַשְׁגֶּה is the one who leads astray (Pr
28: 10).

17 G (A) adds γῆς after βουλευτάς.
Duhm is anxious to read יוֹעֲצֵי אֶרֶץ
(which anticipates v. 24) and to
invent שָׂכַל to take the place of שׁוֹלָל.
The word שׁוֹלָל is rendered by αἰχ-
μαλώτους (G), λάφυρα (Aq.), but also
by εἰς ἀβουλίαν (Symm.); cf. Vulg.
in stultum finem.
   The counsellors form a class of in-
fluential personages (Ezr 4: 5). They
are ranked with the kings in Job
3: 14. Their fate is the same as that
of the priests in v. 19. God causes
them to go barefooted. The word

שׁוֹלָל, from שׁלל 'to strip', is the
characteristic term for the 'barefooted' (Mic 1: 8). Cf. the use of יָחֵף
in the same sense (Is 20: 2). In the
light of these texts and of 2 S 15: 30,
to go barefooted is the sign of extreme grief bordering on utter di-
straction. The verb יְהוֹלֵל as in Is
44: 25. On the root הלל 'to be mad',
cf. Comm. on 4: 18. God makes the
judges mad. The שֹׁפְטִים are, like the
יוֹעֲצִים, a class of notable men. After
the counsellors and the judges come
the kings and the priests (18-19). In
9: 24 God veiled the faces of the
judges.

18 G καθιζάνων (A καθίζων) βασιλεῖς
ἐπὶ θρόνους reads מוֹשִׁיב instead of
מוֹסֵר and does not translate פתח.
The 2nd hemistich, absent from Sah.
and marked with asterisk in Jerome
and Syro-hex., did not exist in G.
The present text comes from Theod.
(cf. Syro-hex.). But G (A) περιζων-
νύων αὐτοὺς comes from Symm. For
מוֹסֵר, Targ. שׁוֹשִׁילְתָּא 'a chain', Vulg.
balteum, pointing מוֹסֵר.
   It is obvious that מוּסַר 'correction',
'lesson' (5: 17) is due to an erroneous
pointing for מוֹסֵר 'bond', 'chain',
derived from אָסַר 'to bind', 'chain
up' (which figures in the 2nd hemistich). The right pointing is attested
by Targ. and Vulg. In the light of
39: 5b, which is written with severe
correctness like our 1st hemistich,
the only precise translation will be
'He has unbound the chain of kings',
i.e. not the chain which kings have

19   He makes the priests to walk barefooted,
     And potentates He overthrows;
20   He deprives of speech the truthful,
     And takes away the insight of the aged;

imposed on others (as the line is generally understood), but the chain which keeps them in bondage. God plays with the fate of kings. If they are captives, he may deliver them. If they are free, He may 'tie a girdle about their loins'. The change from אֵזוֹר to אָסוּר 'bond' (Duhm) would have the result that the verse would contain a third word from the root אסר. The loins are indeed the part of the body postulated by the word 'girdle'. The *pi'el* of פתח in the sense of 'untie', 'unbind' (30:11; 38:31; 39:5).

19   The versions are in agreement with MT in repeating the expressions of v. 17 in the 1st hemistich. G adds γῆς after δυνάστας which translates איתנים. It becomes clear how unwise it is to base one's self on G for the addition of ארץ to v. 17. For איתנים, G δυνάστας, Vulg. *optimates*. Instead of יסלף, Syr. ܡܡܟ reads ישפל 'He abases'.

The 1st hemistich is modelled on v. 17a. The presence of the 'priests' in the doxology shows that Job is formulating ideas common in Israel. The word כֹּהֵן does not appear elsewhere in the book. The original meaning of אֵיתָן is 'perpetual', 'unceasing' (33:19). It is the epithet specially applicable to the everflowing torrent (cf. van Hoonacker on Am 5:24). The idea of continuity developed into that of normal state of affairs (Ex 14:27) and of permanence (Gn 49:24), of age (Jer 5:15), and of stability (Nu 24:21). Applied as here to persons of rank in society, איתן designates one whose power or strength is not subject to fluctuations: namely, the potentate. The verb סלף is used, in the *pi'el*,

in the sense of the Latin *pervertere*. The exact connotation is suggested by the context: sometimes 'falsify' the word (Ex 23:8; Dt 16:19; Pr 22:12), sometimes 'make tortuous a path' (Pr 19:3), finally to 'plunge' into misfortune (Pr 21:12) or 'overthrow' (Pr 13:6). It is the last meaning which is suitable here: God overthrows those whose position seems unshakeable.

20   G renders the 2nd hemistich by σύνεσιν δὲ πρεσβυτέρων ἔγνω. MT יקח is more accurately translated by Aq. λήψεται and Symm. ἀφαιρῶν.

The verb הסיר requires the preposition מִן before the indirect object. The ל״ of לנאמנים serves therefore to express the genitive, as with לשדדים in v. 6. In v. 24 the direct object of מסיר will be followed by the genitive. The word שָׂפָה 'lip' is used in the sense of speech, uttered words (cf. 11:2). The meaning of נֶאֱמָן is not only 'steadfast', 'faithful' but also 'sincere', 'truthful'. Some Jewish commentators connect נאמן with the root נאם, whence נְאֻם 'utterance', 'oracle', and so translate 'eloquent', 'fluent in words'. It would be the only case in the Bible where נאמן would not belong to the root אמן. The verb לקח retains its original sense of 'take away', 'seize', 'snatch'. Cf. the expression יִקַּח־לֵב in Hos 4:11. The genitive זְקֵנִים replaces the poetic turn of phrase לנאמנים of the 1st hemistich. The construction is exactly like את־נפש בעליו יקח 'it takes away the life of its possessors' (Pr 1:19). The word טַעַם 'taste' is used metaphorically to convey the idea of insight, discernment; cf. the verb טעם, parallel to

21   He pours scorn on noblemen,
     And the belt of the strong He slackens!   22 [   ]

22 'He divests the deeps of their darkness, and makes light to break forth
in the shadowy place.' Out of its proper context (cf. Comm.).

בחן 'discern' (v. 11 and 34: 3).
Wisdom and understanding are the
special endowment of old age (v. 12).

21 The 1st hemistich, absent from
Sah., marked with asterisk in Jerome and Syro-hex., did not exist in
G. The present text comes from
Theod. (cf. Syro-hex.). G omits מזיח
in the 2nd hemistich. The word
אפיקים is interpreted as תקיפיא 'the
strong' (Targ. and Syr.), as ταπεινούς
(G), eos qui oppressi fuerant (Vulg.).

The 1st hemistich echoes Ps 107:
40a, while Ps 107: 40b will be repeated as the 2nd hemistich of v. 24.
Here the author proceeds by more or
less literal quotations. The verb שפך
has an abstract complement, as when
one pours out 'anger', 'fury', etc.
The word בוז is used as in v. 5. The
נדיבים from נדב 'to be noble', are
the noblemen (34: 18); cf. נדיב in
21: 28 and נדיבתי 'my honour' in
30: 15. It is a pure whim to change
מזיח אפיקים into מכת אבינים, so as
to read רפא and translate 'He heals
the wound of the poor' (Siegfried,
claiming to be in accord with G,
which has omitted מזיח). The hapax
מזיח replaces מזח 'belt' of Ps 109: 19.

In Assyrian mezaḥ is a synonym of
mêsirru (root אסר) 'belt', 'strap'. It
is obvious that אפיקים, parallel to
נדיבים 'noblemen', cannot mean the
bed of rivers (6: 15), nor tubes (40:
18), nor series, rows (41: 7). Targ.
and Syr. have quite rightly realised
that there must here be an adjective
meaning the same as the Aramaic
תקיף 'strong'. It is not necessary to
change אפיקים to תקיפים, as does
Beer, or to read אבירים 'the powerful'
with Duhm, for the Assyrian epêqu,
synonymous with danânu 'to be

strong', belongs to a root which occurs in התאפק 'to do violence to
one's self'. To this root belongs אפיק
'the strong' (Fried. Delitzsch). The
pi'el of רפה 'to be slack, loose' (cf.
4: 3) simply means 'to loosen'. It is
in the loins that strength resides;
to gird the loins is to gather strength
(cf. L'Emploi métaphorique, pp.
131f.). Cf. Is 45: 1, 'I ungird the
loins of kings', where the meaning
is the same as our 2nd hemistich.
On the other hand, in v. 18 the expression offered rather a different
meaning, for there it was a question
of the belt as a chain binding a
captive.

22 The versions are unanimous in
rendering צלמות by 'the shadow of
death'; cf. 3: 5; 10: 21, as regards
the word thus translated.

V. 22 alludes to the action of God in
the world of nature. The pi'el of גלה
in the sense of 'unveil', 'strip' (cf.
20: 27) and 'lift the veil' (41: 5).
Here the implication is 'divest' the
deeps of the darkness which envelops
them as with a garment. The deeps
are those of Sheol (cf. 11: 8), where
darkness reigns (10: 21). Note the
parallelism between חשך 'darkness'
and צלמות 'shadow' (3: 5; 10: 21).
With the 2nd hemistich cf. 28: 11b,
where the accusative אור replaces
לאור. We find הוציא with כאור in
Ps 37: 6, with לאור in Mic 7: 9. The
meaning is not doubtful. It is a
question of irradiating with sudden
flashes of light what is concealed in
the depths of earth and hell. This
verse has nothing in common with
the doxology in which it is here
placed. From v. 16 we have been
given an account of the action which

23   He makes nations great and exterminates them,
      He extends the boundaries of *peoples*, and He *cuts them off*;

23 לְעַמִּים (עם from v. 34); MT: לגוים. — וַיְמֲחֵם; MT: וינחם.

God effects in the domain of social
life, and this action will continue
to be described in v. 23, where the
peoples and their chiefs will be
brought to account, after the
counsellors, the judges, the kings
(vv. 17-18), the priests, the poten-
tates, the aged, and the noblemen
(vv. 19-21). Thus it is evident that
this v. 22, which happens to be cast
in the same mould as the doxological
formulae, belonged originally to
another context.

23 V. 23, absent from Sah., marked
with an asterisk in Jerome and Syro-
hex., did not exist in G. The present
text, preserved in G (A, ℵ), Eth.,
Arab. Baud., comes from Theod.
(cf. Syro-hex.). G (B) has retained
only the 2nd hemistich (which ends
with αὐτά like the 1st). Theod. πλα-
νῶν and Syr. مَهَحَل 'causing to
wander' point מֵשְׁגִיא instead of מַשְׂגִּיא.
Vulg. does not translate the second
לגוים and paraphrases: *et subversas
in integrum restituit*. The repetition
לגוים is attested in Theod. ἔθνη . . .
ἔθνη. But Targ. and Syr. have first
לעממיא, then לאומיא (Targ.), لِمحمَلا
(Syr.). The versions, with the exception of the Vulg. *in integrum
restituit*, connect ינחם נחה with נחה.
    Good textual tradition favours
מַשְׂגִּיא (Baer-Delitzsch, p. 41). On the
verb שׂנא or שׂגה, cf. 8:7. The meaning
of the 1st hemistich is: 'He makes
nations great and exterminates
them.' The *pi'el* of אבד is normally
used in the sense of 'destroy', 'exterminate' a nation or people (Dt 11:4;
Jer 12:17; Ps 9:6, etc.). The antithesis is deliberate, as it was in the
case of the kings (v. 18). Nothing is
to be gained by reading מֵשְׁגִיא for

מַשְׁגִיה 'causing to wander' (Theod.,
Syr.), which obliges us to give to
יאבד the meaning of 'lead astray', a
meaning contradicted by other contexts. The ל״ occurs before the
accusative as in Aramaic (5:2,7).
The 2nd hemistich also contains an
antithesis. The literal meaning of שׁטח
is 'extend', 'spread out'. God extends, enlarges peoples when He
widens their frontiers. According to
the parallelism, the last verb will
have a pejorative meaning, which is
no longer so if we point וַיַּנִּחֵם 'and He
establishes them' (Hitzig). Wright
and Gray, who accept this pointing,
postulate a meaning 'and He abandons them'; but the verb הֵנִּיחַ when
it has as its complement 'nations'
means 'leave in peace' (Jg 2:23;
3:1). Again, one cannot argue on
the basis of 2 K 18:11, to give to
וַיַּנְחֵם 'and He leads them' the meaning of 'deport', for it is clear, in
the light of 2 K 17:6 and the versions, that the word is to be pointed
וַיַּנִּחֵם 'and He established them'.
With Ball, we propose to read
וַיְמַחֵם 'and He cuts them off', an
excellent parallel to ויאבדם. The
repetition of לגוים is curious. In
accordance with the variant of Ken.
160 and the margins of four manuscripts (Beer), לגוים has been changed into לְאֻמִּים (cf. Targ. and Syr.).
But it should be noted that in v. 24
we find a word עם which is superfluous and which did not occur in
the text of G. As Duhm remarks, it
is probably a word transferred from
v. 23. Hence we shall read לְעַמִּים 'to
the peoples'; parallelism between
עמים and גוים (Is 2:4; 11:10; 14:6,

24   He robs of their understanding the leaders [   ] of the country,
      And makes them wander in trackless desert wastes;
25   They grope in darkness without light,
      And *they reel* to and fro like the drunkard.

24   Omit עם (cf. G).
25   וַיִּתְעוּ (G); MT: ויתעם.

etc.). After the accidental misplace-
ment of עם, it was felt to be enough
to repeat the word of the 1st hemistich.

24   G does not translate עם. Syro-
hex. draws attention in the margin
to the translation 'of the peoples',
given by the 'three', i.e. Aq., Symm.,
Theod. In Jerome we find *populi*,
preceded by asterisk. G (A) omits
the word γῆς. As in 6: 18, תהו is
rendered למא 'the void' (Targ.),
ܠܐܘܠ 'desert', 'solitary place' (Syr.).
G, which renders תהו by ἀόρατος in
Gn 1: 2, paraphrases בתהו לא־דרך
by ἐν ὁδῷ ᾗ οὐκ ᾔδεισαν. Vulg. paraphrases בתהו: *ut frustra incedant* and
translates לא־דרך by *per invium*;
cf. Symm. δι' ἀνοδίας.

The abnormal length of the 1st hemistich comes from the addition עם,
which did not exist in the original
text (cf. G) but has been borrowed
from v. 23. The common idioms
רַאשֵׁי־עָם and עַם־הָאָרֶץ favoured
the intrusion. The ראשי הארץ are
the 'leaders of the country'. Compare
the יועצי ארץ 'counsellors of the
land' (3: 14), the עתודי ארץ 'the
rulers of the land' (Is 14: 9). God
takes away from them their heart, i.e.
their understanding. The expression
מֵסִיר לֵב, just as we have מסיר
שפה in v. 24. The 2nd hemistich corresponds, word for word, to Ps 107:
40b, the 1st hemistich of which was
reproduced in v. 21a. The verb תעה
means 'to go astray', 'to reel hither
and thither' (v. 25; 38: 41). God
makes them wander aimlessly in

trackless desert wastes; cf. תֹהוּ in
6: 18. The words לֹא־דֶרֶךְ 'no path'
form an apposition, the negation
לֹא performing a function similar to
that of the privative alpha (cf.
Symm. and Vulg.). Cf. ארץ לא־איש
'no man's land' (38: 26), לֹא־כֹּחַ
'with no strength', 'enervated', and
לֹא־עֹז 'nerveless', 'powerless' (26: 2),
לֹא חכמה 'without wisdom', 'ignorant' (26: 3).

25   Double translation of the 1st
hemistich in Syr. For חשך ולא אור,
Vulg. *quasi in tenebris et non in luce*.
Instead of ויתעם, G πλανηθείησαν =
וַיִּתְעוּ (Is 19: 14c).

V. 25 describes the effects produced
by the intervention of God, who
leads the chiefs astray and deprives
them of their understanding. The
verb מֹשֵׁש in the *pi'el* 'to grope' as in
5: 14, where the word חֹשֶׁךְ occurred
in the 1st hemistich. The complement is sometimes in the accusative,
as here (Gn 31: 34, 37), sometimes
preceded by ב" (5: 14; Dt 28: 29).
The formula חֹשֶׁךְ וְלֹא־אוֹר 'darkness
and not light' is strongly supported
by Am 5: 18, 20; La 3: 2, and it
would be unwise to remove the copula as is done by Siegfried, Duhm,
and Budde. The expression וַיַּתְעֵם of
the 2nd hemistich is a reminiscence
of v. 24. What is here being described
is no longer the divine action itself
but its effects. The verb expected,
in the light of the comparison כַּשִּׁכּוֹר
(cf. Is 24: 20; Ps 107: 27) must be

parallel to יְמַשְׁשׁוּ. Instead of ויתעם,
it is וַיִּתָּעוּ (*niph'al* of תעה) which was
carried by the original text, as attested by G and confirmed by Is
19:14c (Bickell, Duhm, Gray). Compare also Is 28:7 where the verbs
שגה 'wander to and fro' and תעה
'stagger', 'reel' alternate in the
description of the disorder caused by
strong drink.

CHAPTER 13

1   Yes, all that my eye has seen,
    My ear has heard and understood;
2   What you know, I know also,
    I am not inferior to you!
3   But as for me, it is with Shaddai that I speak,
    And with God that I wish to dispute!

13 : 1 For כל, G ταῦτα, Syr. 'all those things', Vulg. *omnia haec.* G omits לה ותבן. Syro-hex. quotes Theod. καὶ συνῆκεν αὐτά. Vulg. renders לה by *singula.*

The הֶן־ of the opening as in 8 : 19, 20: 'Yes, my eye has seen all that!' Compare Job's opening in 9 : 2 and 12 : 2f. The word כל refers to all the truths that have just been expounded. Job is annoyed with his friends for repeating banalities to him. Use of עֵינִי 'my eye' with ראה is as in 7 : 7. For the Semites, to see is to know, and *vice versa* (cf. Comm. on 7 : 10). The second organ of knowledge is the ear (12 : 11; cf. 4 : 12). In 29 : 11 we shall again meet the two expressions 'the ear heard' and 'the eye saw' in the opposite order. The verb בין means 'discern', 'perceive', 'understand' (cf. 9 : 11). The complement לה of the end certainly seems to be a dative reflexive; cf. 5 : 27 and 12 : 11.

2 G καὶ οἶδα ὅσα καὶ ὑμεῖς ἐπίστασθε is less literal than Theod. (quoted in Syro-hex.) κατὰ ἐπιστήμην ὑμῶν οἶδα καὶ ἐγώ; cf. Vulg. *secundum scientiam vestram et ego novi.* For לא נפל, G καὶ οὐκ ἀσυνετώτερος, preceded by καί γε νεώτερος ὑμῶν in G (A). The addition of G(A) comes from 32 : 6. At the end of the verse, Syro-hex. ﬞ and Jerome *quidem ego*, preceded by asterisk. Following Syro-hex.,

Theod. renders לא נפל by καὶ οὐχ ἥσσων (cf. Vulg. *nec inferior*).

With כְּדַעְתְּכֶם cf. כמו־אלה of 12 : 3. Literally: 'like your knowledge, I know also', that is, 'my knowledge is equal to yours', or again, 'I know no whit less than you'. The expression גַּם־אָנִי, just as we had גם־לי (12 : 3), גם־אני (7 : 11). The 2nd hemistich, which had been anticipated in 12 : 3b, is here perfectly in place. The verb נפל 'fall' (4 : 13), used in the sense of 'become lower than some one' (cf. Est 6 : 13), 'be inferior to some one'.

3 G ἐὰν βούληται, instead of אחפץ, is a theological correction. Vulg. renders הוכח אל־אל *disputare cum Deo.*

The opening אולם אני recalls the turn of phrase used by Eliphaz in 5 : 8. Job knows as much about these high matters as his friends. His business lies not with them but with God. The verb חפץ is not used here with לי before its complement as was the case in 9 : 3, but with a simple accusative (21 : 14; 33 : 32). On the verb הוכיח cf. 5 : 17. Job wishes to engage in debate directly with God. This was his ulterior aim in spite of what he said in speaking of man in general: 'If he wishes to dispute with Him, He will not answer him once in a thousand times' (9 : 3).

4   As for you, you are fabricators of lies,
     Worthless quacks, all of you!
5   Oh that you would keep silence
     And thereby prove your wisdom!
6   Listen then to my charge
     And be attentive to the arguments of my lips!

4 G ὑμεῖς δέ does not necessarily exclude וְאוּלָם. Vulg. *prius vos ostendens* smoothes the transition from v. 3 to v. 4. For טֹפְלֵי־שָׁקֶר, G ἰατροὶ ἄδικοι, Symm. προστίθεσθε ψεύσματι, Vulg. *fabricatores mendacii*, Targ. מחברי שקר 'associating with falsehood'. In Syr. simply 'speaking lies'. Vulg. paraphrases רֹפְאֵי אֱלִל as *cultores perversorum dogmatum*. The word אֱלִל is transcribed אֱלִיל (Targ.), translated 'without anything' (Syr.). G interprets רֹפְאֵי אֱלִל by ἰαταὶ κακῶν, Symm. by ἰατροὶ ἐπίπλαστοί μου. For כֻּלְּכֶם (omitted in Vulg.), G πάντες, but Jerome *omnes vos*, the word *vos* coming from Aq. and Theod. (according to the margin of Syro-hex.).

The words וְאוּלָם אַתֶּם are in antithesis to אוּלָם אֲנִי of v. 3. The expression טֹפְלֵי־שָׁקֶר is explained by Ps 119: 69a: טָפְלוּ עָלַי שֶׁקֶר 'they have besmeared me with lies', i.e. 'they have imputed to me falsehoods'. The literal meaning of טפל is 'coat', 'smear', 'varnish'. Figuratively, it is to apply to an object something which conceals its nature (14: 17), or distorts it, as here and in Ps 119: 69. Finally, טפל will mean 'attribute', 'impute' what is not true, invent a lie or a calumny. This is the meaning which has prevailed in Assyrian, where *tašqirtu ṭapiltu* means 'a lie falsely imputed' or 'an invented calumny'. We may translate טֹפְלֵי־שָׁקֶר by 'inventors of lies', a meaning which is equally suitable to Sir 51: 5. Job's friends have attempted to give him remedies, but they have turned out to be 'worthless quacks', of no value as doctors. Compare רֹעִי הָאֱלִיל 'worthless shepherd' in Zec 11: 17. The defective writing אֱלִל occurs only here. In 16: 2 the 2nd hemistich is copied on the model of this one, the word כֻּלְּכֶם finishing the verse, and מְנַחֲמֵי עָמָל corresponding to רֹפְאֵי אֱלִל.

5 For מִי־יִתֵּן G has simply εἴη, Vulg. *atque utinam*. For וּתְהִי לָכֶם, Vulg. *ut putaremini*. G renders לְחָכְמָה by σοφία, but G (A) εἰς σοφίαν is followed by Sah., Syro-hex., Jerome *in sapientiam*.

The opening מִי־יִתֵּן as in 6: 8; 11: 5. The *hiph'il* הַחֲרִשׁ has not here the causative sense (11: 3) but its normal meaning 'keep silence'. The infinitive before the personal verb for emphasis (v. 10). The 2nd hemistich means literally 'and that it may be wisdom to you!' The use of וּתְהִי impersonally, the subject being the idea contained in the 1st hemistich. Same use of the feminine is found in 4: 6. Compare Pr 17: 28, 'Even a fool who keeps silent is considered wise.' The spoken word reveals stupidity, silence conceals it. Hirzel quotes the Latin proverb: *si tacuisses, philosophus mansisses*.

6 G omits נָא, which is restored as *ergo* in Jerome and as ܝ܌ (with asterisk) in Syro-hex. For תּוֹכַחְתִּי, G ἔλεγχον τοῦ στόματός μου. Obelus before τοῦ στόματός μου in Syro-hex.

On the abstract תּוֹכַחַת (from הוֹכִיחַ of v. 3), cf. 5: 17. The change from תּוֹכַחַת־פִּי to תּוֹכַחְתִּי, recommended by some moderns in accordance

7   Is it for God that you say false things,
     Is it for Him that you speak lies?
8   Are you on God's side?
     Is it His cause that you are pleading?
9   Would it be well for you were He to scrutinise you,
     Seeing that, as one trifles with a man, you trifle with Him?

with G, makes the 1st hemistich clumsy and occasions an awkward jingle of sounds. The root ריב 'dispute', 'quarrel' (9:3; 10:2) retains its force in רִבוֹת 'discussions'. Elsewhere the singular ריב will be the 'lawsuit' (29:16; 31:35). Parallelism between שְׁמַע 'listen' and הַקְשִׁיב 'be attentive' as in 33:31a.

7 The interrogatives of vv. 7-9 are omitted in Syr. By dittography, G πότερον οὐκ ἔναντι reads הלא לאל. G omits עוֹלָה. Vulg. paraphrases: *numquid Deus indiget vestro mendacio?*

Note the interrogative as in the speech of Bildad (8:3). The לְ of לְאֵל and of לוֹ means 'in favour of'; cf. v. 8b. The word עוְלָה 'perversity', 'injustice', but also 'falsehood' when it is a question of sins of the tongue (6:29-30). Cf. 27:4, where we have the parallelism between עַוְלָה and רְמִיָה 'fraud', 'deceit', 'lie'. The friends of Job have no further justification in speaking. They have no reason to intervene in the debate, unless they are willing to put their bad arguments to the service of God!

8 G avoids anthropomorphism by not attempting to render פָּנָיו, which is translated πρόσωπον αὐτοῦ in Symm. and Theod. The verb תִּשָּׂאוּן is rendered ὑποστελεῖσθε in G and Symm., λαμβάνετε in Theod. Note G ὑμεῖς δὲ αὐτοί, which omits לאל. At the close G (A) adds καλῶς γε λαλοῦντες in anticipation of הַטוֹב in v. 9.

The expression נשׂא פנים 'lift up the face' of some one means to favour one person to the detriment of

others, to respect persons (cf. *L'Emploi métaphorique*, p. 46, n. 4). Here, as in 32:21; 34:19, it is a question of taking sides with some one. In 42:8f. it will mean 'to show consideration for some one'. All these meanings derive from the idea of favour granted by a superior to an inferior by permitting him to lift up his face towards his patron. The לְ of לְאֵל as in v. 7. The verb ריב to mean 'plead some one's cause' (Jg 6:31).

9 Vulg. *aut placebit ei quem celare nihil potest* has read אֶת־כֹּל for אֶתְכֶם and interpreted כִּי in the sense of the relative: 'He who scrutinises all things'. We can make no guess as to how G has extracted εἰ γὰρ τὰ πάντα ποιοῦντες προστεθήσεσθε αὐτῷ (A ὁδῷ αὐτοῦ) from the 2nd hemistich. Aq. εἰ ὡς παραλογισμῷ ἐν ἀνθρώπῳ παραλογίζεσθε brings us back to the MT.

The formula הַטוֹב stands as in 10:3 followed by כִּי to introduce the subordinate clause. On the verb חקר 'scrutinise', 'examine', cf. 5:27. Job's friends, by attempting to intervene, would expose themselves to the formidable and searching scrutiny of the sovereign Judge. It would be better for them to remain quiet. Job has nothing more to lose (14-15), he will be bold enough to plead his cause himself, and does not want to have dealings with bad advocates who would be useless to God (7-8) and disastrous to himself (4). The infinitive and the imperfect *hiph'il* of תלל retain the ה as in יְהָתֵלּוּ of Jer 9:4 (cf. Gesenius-Kautzsch,

10   He will certainly chastise you,
      If secretly you show partiality.
11   Will not His majesty terrify you,
      And the fear He inspires fall upon you?
12   Are not your wise saws maxims of ashes?
      Do not your replies become replies of clay?

§ 53q). From this *hiph'il* is formed a verb התל used in the *pi'el* in the sense of 'mock', (1 K 18: 27) and from which is derived the noun הַתֻלִים 'mockery' (17: 2).

10 G adds at the beginning οὐθὲν ἧττον. Jerome puts *quia* (with asterisk) after *nihilominus*. Syro-hex. in the margin draws attention to ὅτι (with asterisk) and notes that the word has no place in Aq., Theod., Symm. The word בסתר is omitted in Syr. For תשׁאון G has θαυμάσεσθε, Symm. δυσωπηθήσεσθε. Instead of פנים we find פניו (as in v. 8) in Symm. πρόσωπον αὐτοῦ, Vulg. *faciem ejus*, Targ. and Syr. אפוהי.

The 1st hemistich is inspired by 6: 25b; but the verb הוכיח, with God as subject, assumes the meaning of 'chastise' (cf. 5: 17). The infinitive before finite verb, as in v. 5a. The 2nd hemistich is conceived on the pattern of v. 9b. The expression בַּסֵּתֶר 'furtively', 'secretly' suggests a guilty action (31: 27a). The formula נשׂא פנים generalises the instance provided for in v. 8a. The versions have harmonised with this v. 8a, whence 'His face' instead of 'the face'. It would be unwise to adopt this harmonising reading (contra Merx, Beer, Duhm, etc.).

11 For שׂאתו, G δεινὰ αὐτοῦ, Symm. ἡ κίνησις αὐτοῦ, Syr. 'his fear', Targ. 'when He rises to the throne of judgment', Vulg. *statim ut se commoverit*.

As is to be seen from the parallelism with פַּחַד 'fear', both here and in 31: 23, as also by the reference to

the effect produced in 41: 17 (where שֵׁתוֹ = שְׂאֵתוֹ), the word שְׂאֵת denotes an attribute which inspires fear. In Gn 49: 3 it is parallel to עֹז (written עָז) 'power'; in Hab 1: 7 it is paired with מִשְׁפָּט 'right', 'justice'. Now, it is a question of an infinitive from נשׂא 'carry', 'lift up', 'raise'. The meaning of 'elevation' or 'height' is perfectly suitable for מִשְּׂאֵתוֹ 'from His eminence' in Ps 62: 5. A person whose rank is exalted will possess the quality designated by שְׂאֵת, and this quality, in its fullness, evokes respect and fear. Thus, in speaking of God, שְׂאֵתוֹ will connote 'His majesty' (cf. 31: 23), and the same too even in speaking of an animal which arouses terror (41: 17). This meaning suits very well Hab 1: 7 (cf. van Hoonacker) and Gn 49: 3. As for פַּחְדּוֹ, meaning 'the fear which He inspires', cf. the use of the same word in 1 Ch 14: 17. Fear 'falls upon' some one (Ex 15: 16; Ps 105: 38, etc.), like everything which cannot be avoided (4: 13b). On בעת in the *pi'el*, cf. 7: 14.

12 G adds ἀποβήσεται δέ for the sake of clearness. Syr. translates זכרניכם by 'remember that' and attributes to משׁלי the sense of 'domination'. The other versions bring out the idea of comparison inherent in the word משׁלי: G ἴσα, Targ. מתיל 'is compared', Vulg. *comparabitur*. In the 2nd hemistich Targ. faithfully reflects the MT, though reading לגב for לגבי. Syr. interprets לגב in the sense of the Aramaic לגב 'by the side of' and gives to גביכם the

13   Refrain from speaking to me, and I in my turn will speak,
      Come what may!

meaning 'your dwellings'. G sums up
the 2nd hemistich by τὸ δὲ σῶμα
πήλινον, reading גף instead of גב.
Vulg. paraphrases *et redigentur in
lutum cervices vestrae*.

The verb זכר means not only 'to
remember' but also 'to impart what
one remembers', 'to mention'; cf.
the *niph'al* in 28:18. In Assyrian,
zakâru means 'to name' and 'to
speak'. The noun זִכָּרוֹן, whence
זִכְרֹנֵיכֶם, connotes not only memory,
but also its expression: the faculty of
remembering and what is remembered. In the plural it means the
memorabilia of the aged, i.e. wise
saws or maxims. Thus we have a
word equivalent to מְשָׁלִים 'proverbs'
or 'maxims'. Ashes, symbol of transience and fragility, is often coupled
with dust (Comm. on 2:8). Dust is
parallel to clay, חֹמֶר (4:19; 10:9).
That is why חֹמֶר here corresponds to
אֵפֶר. Exegetes are divided as to
the meaning of גַּבִּים, which is interpreted as 'ramparts' or 'defences'.
As the word גבים, which means
'back', and the Arabic ظهر 'back'
may be used in the sense of fortress
(Schultens), גביכם has been translated as 'your fortresses' (Le Hir,
Crampon), 'your defences' (Renan),
'your entrenchments' (Segond), etc.
Others, like Rashi, see in גביכם
'your lofty structures' (cf. גב in Ezk
16:24, 25, 39), from which is deduced 'your pretentious arguments'
(*Bible du rabbinat français*). Modern
critics have been fairly ready to
accept the hypothesis of Duhm,
who, basing himself on a comparison
with the use of גבי in 15:26, proposes for גביכם the meaning of 'your
shields' or 'bucklers' (Budde, Gray).
But in 15:26 גבי connotes the 'boss'
of the shield and not the shield itself.
Ehrlich writes quite a dissertation

on the root גבב 'pick up crumbs,
trifles' etc., to conclude with a
paraphrase whose artificiality is
apparent through the German verbiage: *zusammengeklaubten bröckeln-
den Lehmklümpchen gleicht das, was
gegen mich zusammenkramt*. It should
be noted that גביכם is parallel to an
abstract term 'your wise saws'. Beer
has suggested a comparison with the
Syriac ܣܘܥ and ܝܡܒܐ 'reply'.
The Arabic *jawâb* is a current term.
The mutual influence of the roots
ע״ע and ע״ו has given rise to גבב
by the side of גוב. The ל״ before
גַּבֵּי to express what one becomes, as
one uses the dative in Latin. Both
hemistichs are governed by the הלא
of the opening of v. 11 (cf. 12:12).

13 G omits ממני and אני, but Jerome adds *ego* (with asterisk). The
2nd hemistich is connected with
אדברה in Syr. 'I will say all that has
happened to me', and Vulg. *loquar
quodcumque mihi mens suggesserit*. G
καὶ ἀναπαύσωμαι θυμοῦ reads חמה
instead of מה.

The imperative הַחֲרִישׁוּ 'keep silence' (cf. v. 5) is followed by מִמֶּנִּי 'far
from me', as we have אל־תחרש
ממני 'be not silent far from me' (Ps
28:1), *ne sileas a me*! Silence spells
abstention from action with regard
to some one. This pregnant construction means 'abstain from speaking to me', and not 'turn away from
me in silence' (contra Gesenius-
Kautzsch, § 119ff). Job is fond of
the cohortative form אֲדַבְּרָה (7:11;
9:35; 10:1; 16:4, 6). The pronoun
מָה at the end of the 2nd hemistich
has the same implications as in ויהי
מה 'and let be what will be' of 2 S
18:22, 23. The verb is understood
after מה. The phrase certainly means
'and let come upon me what is to
come'. The verb עבר is used with

14   [   ] I carry away my flesh in my teeth,
      And my soul I expose in my hand!

15   If He slays me, I will not *tremble*,
      Provided I argue my case before Him!

16   This, moreover, will be salvation for me,
      For no godless man dare appear before Him!

14   Omit על־מה (cf. G).
15   אָחִיל; MT: איחל.

על before the complement of the person to express the advent of a misfortune (Nah 3:19). It is unnecessarily making the 2nd hemistich clumsy to attach to it על־מה of v. 14 (contra Bickell, Duhm). We shall see that על־מה springs from dittography.

14   G does not include על־מה. Vulg. renders אשא by *lacero*. G (A) adds μοῦ after ὀδοῦσιν and χερσίν (אַ, instead of χειρί B).

Job intends to speak, come what may. He realises that his words may have serious consequences, but he recks not of it (9:35-10:1). The opening על־מה 'why?' (10:2b) introduces an unexpected question. Job is fully determined to risk his life (v. 15). Since the text of G does not include על־מה, it seems clear that these words are a dittograph of עלי מה in v. 13. The 2nd hemistich is easy to understand, if it is compared with Jg 12:3; 1 S 19:5; 28:11, 'I put my soul in my hand', i.e. I dispose of it as of something that belongs to me, I risk my life! Cf. the use of בידו in 12:10. The 1st hemistich may be translated literally 'I carry away my flesh in my teeth!' Parallelism between בָּשָׂר and נֶפֶשׁ (12:10; 14:22), as between the body and soul. Job carries off his flesh in his teeth, as the wild beast makes off with its prey to devour it. Cf. 29:17b, 'and I tore the prey from between his teeth!'

15   G adds ὁ δυνάστης as the subject of יקטלני. The *qerê* לו is followed by

Aq., Vulg., Syr., while G ἐπεί points לו. G ἦ μὴν λαλήσω reads אדבר instead of דרכי. Syr. omits אוכיח.
Conjunction הֵן means 'if' (4:18; 12:14, 15). Outside Job (here and in 24:14), the verb קטל appears only in Ps 139:19. לא איחל is usually translated 'I have no more hope' or, 'I have lost all hope'. But this meaning does not fit in with 'if He slays me'. Job should express here the feeling he will experience if God kills him. By adopting the *qerê* לו Fried. Delitzsch and Hontheim translate '*ich warte darauf*', i.e. 'I am expecting this', but the suffix should refer to God. Basically, it is impossible to arrive at a logical sense with איחל. A very slight change, suggested by Graetz and Ehrlich, resolves the difficulty. We should read אָחִיל from חיל (cf. חילה in 6:10). 'If He slays me, I will not tremble'. Cf. 9:35, 'I will speak and I will not fear Him.' The restrictive אַךְ (2:6) means 'provided that'. The plural of דֶּרֶךְ has not the sense of 'actions', but simply 'affairs' (Is 58:13). The verb הוכיח means 'discuss', 'argue', 'debate' (cf. 5:17). Note the expression אֶל־פָּנָיו, as we have אל־פניך for על־פניך in 2:5 (cf. Comm. on 1:11). Job wishes to argue his case at all costs. Moreover, the very fact of his presenting himself before God's tribunal is a pledge of innocence (v. 16). His friends could not do as much (9-12).

16   The pronoun הוא is transcribed

17 Listen well to my word,
    And may my explanation reach your ears!
18 Behold now, I have drawn up my case,
    I know it is I who am right!

in Targ. and Syr., translated *ipse* in
Vulg. But G τοῦτο sees in it a neuter.
As in v. 12, G adds ἀποβήσεται. The
translation of G, for v. 16a, is quoted
in Ph 1: 19. For חנף, Syr. ܣܟܠܐ,
Targ. דילטור (cf. 8: 13), Vulg. *hypo-
critica*. G δόλος points חנף.

If we refer to God the pronoun הוא,
it becomes impossible to understand
the 2nd hemistich. The fact that a
godless man does not dare to appear
before God is not a reason why God
should be the salvation of Job. The
phrase is conceived on the pattern of
6: 10, where, after having wished
for death, Job announces a consolation. The pronoun is used in a
neuter sense (15: 9; 31: 28) and
explained by the כי of the 2nd hemistich. The adverb גם 'yet', instead
of the עוד of 6: 10, to express 'moreover', 'at least'. There is a double
dative in the first clause exactly as
in v. 5b. The abstract ישועה (30: 15)
means 'salvation' and 'means of
salvation', 'help', 'succour'; cf. ישע
(5: 4, 11). Cf. in the Song of Moses
(Ex 15: 2) 'and He has become my
salvation', ויהי־לי לישועה. The expression בוא לפני 'to come before
some one', to present one's self before,
as before a judge. On the word חנף,
cf. 8: 13. Thus Job is not a godless
man, since he dares to appear before
God.

17 G ἀκούσατε ἀκούσατε reads שמעו
instead of שמוע. G replaces אחותי by
אחוה, ἀναγγελῶ. The other versions
see a noun in אחותי. For באזניכם, G
ὑμῶν ἀκουόντων.
    The expression שמעו שמוע is in pro-
phetic style (Is 6: 9; 55: 2). Elihu
will repeat it in 37: 2. Job will echo
the 1st hemistich as an opening in

21: 2. There is parallelism between a
clause containing a verb and another
in which the verb is replaced by
בְּאָזְנֵיכֶם 'in your ears', exactly as in
15: 21, where באזניו 'in his ears'
corresponds to the verb of the 2nd
hemistich. This observation favours
the maintenance of the noun אַחֲוָתִי,
which some would change into אַחֲוָה
in accordance with G. To the Aramaic מִלָּתִי 'my word' there corresponds the Aramaic אחותי 'my explanation', a *hapax* with which one
may compare אחוית אחידן 'explanation of the riddles' in Dn 5: 12.
On the Aramaic verb חוא or חוה,
whence the noun אַחֲוָה, cf. 15: 17.

18 G ἐγγύς εἰμι seems to read
קרבתי for ערכתי. Syro-hex. quotes
Aq. ἔταξα and Theod. προσέθηκα.
Vulg. translates the 1st hemistich
si fuero judicatus. G and Syr. read
משפטי instead of משפט. For צדקתי,
G δίκαιος ἀναφανοῦμαι, Vulg. *justus
inveniar*.

The particle נָא has always been
used after an imperative (v. 6; and cf.
1: 11; 2: 5; 4: 7; 5: 1; 6: 29; 8: 8;
10: 9; 12: 7). It is apparent that the
demonstrative הִנֵּה has the value of
an imperative: 'behold now' for
'see here', 'see there!' The 1st
hemistich has excellent support in
23: 4a: אערכה לפניו משפט. Hence
it would be unwise to change משפט
into משפטי in accordance with G
and Syr., as is proposed by Beer and
Duhm. The verb ערך 'to put in
order', 'to arrange and classify' draws
its precise connotation from the
complement, expressed or understood. The meaning of 'marshal'
troops in battle array results in the
meaning of 'arrange in order' or 'to

19   Who will contend with me?
      I will at once be silent and expire.
20   Spare me only in two matters;
      Then I will not hide myself from before Thee.
21   Remove Thy hand from upon me,
      And may Thy terror not crush me!

be arrayed' (6: 4). If it is a question of setting forth words in order (32: 14), we infer the meaning of 'drawing up a case' (here and in 23: 4). If things are set side by side, then one compares them (28: 17). The noun מִשְׁפָּט 'judgment', 'justice' in the sense of 'judiciary cause', 'lawsuit', (Nu 27: 5; 2 S 15: 4). Thus Job has drawn up his case at law. He is not afraid (v. 15), for he is very conscious of his right and the validity of his plea: 'I know that it is I who am right!' Note the emphatic use of אֲנִי before אֶצְדָּק. Verb צדק means 'to be right' (9: 15; 11: 2).

19   The 2nd hemistich, absent from Sah., marked with asterisk in Jerome and Syro-hex. did not exist in G. The present text comes from Theod. (cf. Syro-hex. and Cod. 248).

The opening מִי־הוּא as in 4: 7a. The 1st hemistich echoes the cry of Yahweh's servant: מִי יָרִיב אִתִּי 'who will contend with me?' (Is 50: 8). The verb רִיב well conveys the idea of dispute or contestation in a court of justice (9: 3). Job is certain of success (v. 18). The formula כִּי־עַתָּה, coming after the postulation of a hypothesis (should any contestant with Job appear) means 'at once' (8: 6); cf. כִּי־אָז in 11: 15. Were any one capable of picking up the glove, I would only have to be silent and die. It is clear that עתה 'now' applies to the time suggested by the question: 'then, when that happened'.

20   G δυεῖν δέ μοι χρήσῃ omits אַךְ

and אל. Syro-hex. cites Aq., Theod., and Symm., which are more literal. With Symm. μόνα δὲ δύο μὴ ποιήσῃς ἐμοί compare Vulg. *duo tantum ne facias mihi.* The 2nd hemistich, absent from Sah., marked with asterisk in Jerome and Syro-hex., did not exist in G. The present text doubtless comes from Theod. A reading οὐκ ἐκκλινῶ for לֹא אֶסָּתֵר is attributed to ὁ Ἑβραῖος by Olympiodorus (cf. Colb.).

The adverb אַךְ 'only' (cf. v. 15b) introduces a restriction to the expression of Job's resolution. He wishes indeed to enter the lists with God; but it is necessary that God should not abuse His authority, for there is no arbiter who can dispel from Job's mind the fear which God arouses (9: 33-4). It is God alone who can condescend to place Himself on the same footing as Job. That is why the latter appeals to God directly: 'Spare me only in two matters!' Literally: 'Two things only do not do with regard to me!' The adverb אָז 'then', i.e. were the condition fulfilled, if God abstained from doing the two things which will be specified in v. 21. Cf. the use of כִּי־עַתָּה in v. 19. The *niph'al* of סתר (3: 23; 34: 22) is used with מִן before the name of the person from whom one hides (28: 21). Here מִפְּנֵי as in Gn 4: 14; Dt 7: 20. Job has spoken of presenting himself before God to discuss the matter (v. 15). He must be able to appear fearlessly.

21   The negative of Syr. before

22   Then call and I will answer,
      Or else I will speak and Thou shalt reply.
23   How many are my iniquities and sins?
      Make me to know my transgression and my sin!
24   Why dost Thou veil Thy face,
      And consider me Thy enemy?

הרחק causes a wrong meaning. G translates כפך by τὴν χεῖρα (Jerome *manum*), but G (A) adds σοῦ (Sah., Syro-hex., Eth., Arab. Baud.). Aq. and Theod. render הרחק by μάκρυνον: Vulg. *longe fac.*

V. 21 formulates the two requests referred to in v. 20. First: 'Remove Thy hand from upon me!' Cf. 9: 34a 'who removes his rod from over me'. The verb הרחיק 'remove', 'withdraw' (11: 14) is used in the sense of הסיר (9: 34); complement מֵעָלַי as in 9: 34, because the hand of God is heavy 'on' the sufferer. The form הַרְחַק on account of the pause (Gesenius-Kautzsch, § 29q). Then: 'May Thy terror not crush me!', which is modelled on 9: 34b. The verse will be cited ironically by Elihu, with slight changes, in 33: 7. On בעת cf. 7: 14.

22 Syr. and Vulg. *voca me* add the suffix after קרא. G ἢ λαλήσεις ἐγὼ δέ σοι δώσω ἀνταπόκρισιν makes of the 2nd hemistich a repetition of the 1st. Olympiodorus quotes οἱ λοιποί, i.e. the hexaplar authors, who render the MT λαλήσω καὶ ἀποκρίνῃ μοι.

Job demands judgment. He may be either the 'appellant' or the 'respondent'. Antithesis between קרא and ענה (9: 16; 19: 16). The antagonist is God: 'Then call and I will answer!' Second hypothesis: 'Or else I will speak and Thou shalt reply!' The *hiph'il* השיב 'bring back' a word, i.e. 'answer' (31: 14; 33: 5, 32). Note the use of the imperative in the sense of the future (5: 22; 11: 6).

23 G δίδαξόν με τίνες εἰσίν avoids the repetition of the same nouns in the 2nd hemistich.

In the 1st hemistich it is a question of the number of sins, in the 2nd of their nature. Duhm sees 'at the first glance' that the text is faulty, but hesitates between עוני ופשעי and לי עון ופשע (for לִי צָוֹנוֹת וְחַטָּאוֹת). Let us leave the text as it stands, while noting that the plurals in the 1st hemistich are introduced by כַּמָּה (cf. Gn 47: 8b, etc.): 'How many are my iniquities and sins?' On the relation between פשע, הטאה, עון, cf. 10: 6 (Comm.). Note the presence of the three words in 14: 16, 17. The singular in the 2nd hemistich is quite natural. Here it is no longer a question of counting, but of knowing what the faults are. Job uses the imperative הדיעני 'make me to know' as in 10: 2.

24 G ἀπ' ἐμοῦ κρύπτῃ avoids the anthropomorphism of פּניך. Targ. interprets פּניך by שכנתך 'Thy shekinah', 'Thy divinity'.

The face is veiled in order to avoid seeing a thing, for the face is considered essentially as the seat of vision (*L'Emploi métaphorique*, p. 46). When God veils His face, it is a sign of anger (Is 54: 8; Ps 27: 9) or of indifference (Ps 30: 8; 104: 29). In 34: 29 God hides His face in order to make Himself invisible. In 9: 24, where the reference was to the veiling of the faces of the judges, to prevent them from administering justice aright, the verb used was the *pi'el* of כסה. Job comes into the presence of God. If God veils His face, the reason is that He considers

25   Dost Thou wish to frighten a leaf whirled away by the wind,
     And pursue a dry straw?
26   That Thou mightest write against me bitter things,
     And impute to me the faults of my youth,
27   That Thou mightest put my feet in the stocks,

Job as His enemy. The 2nd hemistich will annoy Elihu, who will use it as a ground of complaint against Job (33: 10b). The verb חשב stands with ל״ before the object to which the complement is assimilated (cf. 19: 15; 35: 2; 41: 19, 24).

25 For נדף, G κινούμενον ὑπὸ ἀνέμου, Vulg. *quod vento rapitur*. Syr. 'dry leaf' in anticipation of יבש. Syrohex. quotes Symm. φύλλον ἐκπίπτον. In accordance with the 1st hemistich, G renders יבש by φερομένῳ ὑπὸ πνεύματος. Jerome omits ὑπὸ πνεύματος.

The expression עָלֶה נִדָּף 'leaf whirled away by the wind' recurs in Lv 26: 36. The verb ערץ is sometimes used in the sense of 'fear', 'dread' (31: 34), sometimes in that of 'make afraid', 'terrify' (Is 2: 19, 21). It is the second meaning which is the more suitable here, considering the parallelism with רדף 'to pursue'. The word קַשׁ 'wisp of straw' will recur in 41: 20, 21 as a symbol of what is slight, insignificant. Dry straw, קַשׁ יָבֵשׁ, occurs in Nah 1: 10. It is indeed useless to pursue a wisp of dry straw: it flies away of itself. And why frighten the leaf which drops and is blown away by the wind? Cf. the irony of David in addressing Saul: 'After whom has the king of Israel come out? After whom do you pursue? After a dead dog? After a flea?' (1 S 24: 15). Job considers it unworthy of God to show so much suspicion and dislike of his wretchedly poor person (cf. 10: 3-7).

26 For מררות Vulg. *amaritudines*, G κακά. In the light of Targ. מרירתא, it seems indeed that Syr. ܡܪ̈ܝܪܬܐ

comes from a corruption of ܡܪ̈ܝܪܬܐ. For ותורישני, Vulg. *et consumere me vis*. G omits the suffix of נערי.

Conjunction כי after the interrogative of v. 25 as in 7: 12. The verb כתב 'write down' a charge (31: 35), made specific by מְרֹרוֹת 'bitter things'. The feminine מְרֵרָה 'bitter thing' will be used to denote poison (20: 14) and the organ which secretes bile (20: 25). The *hiph'il* of ירש, in the sense of 'cause to possess', or 'make to inherit' governs a double accusative. With מִן before the indirect complement, it will mean 'dispossess', 'expel', 'cast out' (20: 15). God causes Job to possess the faults of his youth, that is to say, He imputes them to him. With עֲוֹנוֹת נְעוּרָי compare חטאות נעורי in Ps 25: 7, where the Psalmist asks God to forget 'the sins of his youth'. We find again נעורי 'my adolescence', 'my youth' in 31: 18. Elsewhere, without suffix, we have the singular נֹעַר 'youthfulness' (33: 25; 36: 14). Job may have erred in his youth. But the mature man is not responsible for those trifling sins. It would indicate rancour on the part of God to persecute Job on account of these youthful errors, supposing them to have existed.

27 For רגלי (1°), G, Aq., Symm., Theod., Vulg. read the singular. Syr. rightly realised that סד corresponded to the Aramaic סדא and סדנא 'block of wood'; cf. Symm. ὑπὸ ξύλον, Aq. ἐν ξυλοπέδῃ. G more vaguely ἐν κωλύματι, but G (A) ἐν κυκλώματι (as in 33: 11). In Targ. כד בשיע 'as in cement'. In Vulg. (here and in

And keep a watch on all my steps!
My footprints Thou dost examine!   28 [   ]

28 Transfer v. 28 to follow 14: 2 (cf. Comm.).

33: 11) *in nervo*. Metaphor in Theod. ἐν ταλαιπωρίᾳ. G renders כל־ארחתי by μοῦ πάντα τὰ ἔργα. For שרשי, Vulg. *vestigia*.

Note the poetic use of the jussive וְתָשֶׂם instead of the imperfect, as in 15: 33b. God holds Job as a prisoner. He puts his feet in the stocks. The word סַד appears only here and in 33: 11a which is copied from our 1st hemistich. The Syriac ܣܕܐ translates τὸ ξύλον in Ac 16: 24. As is clearly apparent from the sentence in Acts: καὶ τοὺς πόδας ἠσφαλίσατο αὐτῶν εἰς τὸ ξύλον, the Greek ξύλον, the Syriac ܣܕܐ, and the Hebrew סד mean the wooden instrument in which the feet of prisoners were bound. This has been well understood in our text by Syr., Symm., and Aq. (cf. sup.) as by G (B, ℵ, C) ἐν ξύλῳ in 33: 11. A variant, attributed to 'some other' (cf. Field) supplies the exact translation: ἐν ποδοκάκῃ; for ποδοκάκη denotes the wooden shackles in which the feet of prisoners are made fast. We may translate the Hebrew by 'in the stocks', for the Latin *cippus* (whence Fr. *cep*), which originally meant 'stake', 'post', 'tree-trunk' comes to mean in Vulgar Latin the wooden fetter designed to bind the feet of prisoners (Du Cange, s.v.). Examples of this type of torture are given in the *Dictionnaire* of Vigouroux (II, 431) and the *Dictionnaire des antiquités* (IV, 116f.). Fr. Savignac brought back from Jeddah a photograph in which are to be seen prisoners of war of the *Sherif* with their feet wedged into the notches of a huge beam fixed into the ground. A transversal iron bar keeps them immovable. The 2nd hemistich presupposes that the pris-

oner enjoys a moment's liberty. God, however, continues to keep him well in sight. The verb שמר is used as in 10: 14. The word ארח 'road', 'path' is used here in the sense of the way in which one walks: a step! Beer cuts out this 2nd hemistich as coming from 33: 11b. But it is the whole of 33: 11 which is inspired by our verse. The 3rd hemistich is only a clarification of the 2nd. How does God keep track of Job's steps? By noting his footprints. Note the juxtaposition of the two clauses (cf. 8: 10; 11: 18). The verb חקה has furnished the *pu'al* participle מְחֻקֶּה 'hollowed out', 'encrusted' (1 K 6: 35), or 'imprinted' (Ezk 8: 10), 'marked out' (Ezk 23: 13). Thus it will be seen that the root חקה is parallel to חקק 'engrave', 'carve out', of which the *hoph'al* will be used in 19: 23. The sense of the *hithpa'el* חקה will be inferred from the etymological meaning: to imprint a thing on one's mind, to fix an outline of it in the imagination, by dint of study. The complement introduced by על denotes the object on which this concentrated attention is exercised; cf. התבונן על (31: 1). The 'roots of the feet' imply the spot where the feet dig into the ground; cf. the roots of the mountains in 28: 9. It implies both the soles of the feet and (the sign for the thing signified) the trace which they leave on the ground. Duhm is not satisfied with this tristich. He cuts out רגלי (2nd) to retain שרשי 'my root' and seeks in תתחקה a gardening operation supposed to consist in making a groove around the root to prevent it from extending (!). He then brings in

14: 5c to connect v. 27c with v. 28, so as to see in this v. 28 the effect produced on the plant by the operation, namely rotting. All this ingenuity is expended to produce as result the image of a root eaten by worms like a garment! V. 28 which begins with וְהוּא 'and he' is difficult to link with the context. Le Hir has to translate 'and this man' in order to continue, while the *Bible du rabbinat français* interprets 'and all that against some one, etc.'. Renan omits והוא in order to obtain an apposition to 'around an unfortunate man' which he inserts into the text of v. 27. Segond 'when my body' returns to the idea of Rashi, 'this body which thou pursuest'. It is clear that והוא is part of a narrative the subject of which is either a person or a thing: compare הן־הוא in 8: 19. Beer (in Kittel) proposes to transfer v. 28 to a position after 14: 2 or 14: 3. Merx interpolates it after 14: 2a. Since 14: 2 makes a good and natural sequence to 14: 1, we shall place it after 14: 2. It forms the conclusion of the description of man's infirmity. The exclamation אף־על־זה of 14: 3 will follow on quite naturally after the picture drawn in 14: 1, 2-13: 28.

28   After 14: 2.

CHAPTER 14

1 Man, born of a woman,
   Living but few days, and consumed with restlessness,
2 Springs up and withers like a flower,
   And flees like a shadow with no continuing stay!

14: **1** G γάρ connects v. 1 with
13: 28. For קְצַר יָמִים, G ὀλιγόβιος,
Vulg. *brevi vivens tempore*. For רֹגֶז,
G ὀργῆς, Aq. κλονήσεως, Vulg. *multis
miseriis*.

After alluding to the dealings of God
with himself in particular, Job passes
on to a consideration of the condition
of man in general. Cf. 7: 1-2. Most
critics consider v. 1 to be an independent clause. But the verbs appear only in v. 2. We have in fact
here a threefold apposition to אָדָם
which opens the strophe. First,
יְלוּד אִשָּׁה 'born of a woman': *de
muliere quasi de re fragili* (St Thomas). The phrase is parallel to אֱנוֹשׁ
in 15: 14; 25: 4; Sir 10: 18 (22); cf.
γεννητοὶ γυναικῶν (Mt 11: 11; Lk 7:
28). The genitive אִשָּׁה after a passive
participle to denote the author of the
action (Gesenius-Kautzsch, § 116l).
Woman is characterised not only by
her frailty but also by her uncleanness (cf. v. 4), in consequence of the
seasons to which she is subjected
(Lv 15: 19ff.) or her times of childbirth (Lv 12: 2ff.). The second apposition is קְצַר יָמִים 'short of days',
that is, living but a few days. Life is
envisaged as a measure, which may
be either long (cf. 6: 11b) or short.
But for man it is always too short
(Gn 47: 9). Job has already emphasised the brevity of life (7: 6ff.;
9: 25-26). In 10: 20, 'Are not the
days of my life but a little thing?'
The third of man's infirmities con-

sists in his unremitting agitation,
under sway of his distresses and difficulties: 'and consumed with restlessness'. Cf. the use of the verb שָׂבַע
(7: 4) and of the adjective שָׂבַע
(construct שְׂבַע) in 10: 15. Note the
genitive abstract, as we had קָלוֹן
(10: 15). On the word רֹגֶז cf. 3: 17,
26. The Preacher dwells on the
sorrows which fill the 'days' of man
(Ec 2: 23).

2 Vulg. adds *qui* before *quasi flos*,
to effect a link with *repletur multis
miseriis* in v. 1. G ἐξέπεσε reads
וַיִּבֹּל for וַיִּמַּל. Syr. translates יִמַּל by
a double verb: 'it fades and withers'.
Vulg. paraphrases וְלֹא יַעֲמֹד *et num-
quam in eodem statu permanet*.

Nothing is so ephemeral as the
flower, nothing so fugitive as the
shadow. The two images are well
chosen to depict the shortness of
life. The word צִיץ 'flower' is precisely
the one used by the prophet Isaiah
to convey the thought of the people
which will not abide, just as the
flower fades at the breath of the
Lord (40: 6-8). In Ps 103: 15 both
the noun and the verb צִיץ are used
in the same type of image: 'As for
man, his days are like grass; he
flourishes like the flower of the field.'
Grass also serves to illustrate the
transiency of life (Ps 37: 2; 90: 5-6).
The verb יָצָא 'to go out' is here used
to show the plant springing up out
of the soil (5: 6; cf. 1 K 5: 13; Is

13:28   He wears away like a thing that rots,
         Like a moth-eaten garment!

3   And it is on such a creature that Thou dost open Thy eye,
         And it is *he* whom Thou bringest to judgment with Thee!

3   וְאֹתוֹ (G, Vulg., Syr.); MT: וְאֹתִי.

11: 1). Hence it is unnecessary to try to replace יצא by יָצִיץ (Wright) or יִצְמַח (Beer). Duhm, following G and Is 40: 7, proposes וַיִּבֹּל instead of וימל. But the translation given by G may have been influenced by the parallel passages. יִמַּל recurs, applied to branches (18: 16) and ears of corn (24: 24). The exact sense is 'wither', 'wilt', i.e. the flower drooping on its stalk (cf. 24: 24). Outside Job the word only recurs in Ps 37: 2, where it is applied to verdure which fades and where its parallel is נבל 'wither', 'wilt away'. The flight of man towards death is likened to the flight of the shadows which are so elusive and impermanent. The verb ברח 'flee' has already been used to express the swift passage of the days (9: 25b). Bildad affirmed that 'our days on earth are a shadow' (8: 9). In Ps 144: 4, 'Man is like a breath, his days are like a passing shadow.' The same image is to be found in Ec 6: 12. Calmet quotes Horace: *pulvis et umbra sumus* (*Odes*, IV, 7). The verb עמד means 'stay fixed', 'remain upright' (8: 15) and by that very fact 'stay', 'abide'. The shadow does not abide, it is ever in motion, and nothing less than a miracle is needed to make it go back (2 K 20: 10-11). It is here that we put 13: 28, lost and out of place at the end of the preceding chap. The opening וְהוּא refers quite naturally to man in general.

13: **28**   Syr. renders רקב by ܙܩܐ, which in Syriac means 'goatskin bottle', and it is this sense which is

reflected in G ἀσκῷ. But Targ. רקבובית, Symm. σηπεδόνι, Vulg. *putredo* are faithful to the true meaning of the Hebrew רקב.

The verb רקב denotes the rotting of wood (Is 40: 20). The noun רָקָב connotes the rotting of bones, caries, decay (Pr 12: 4; 14: 30); cf. Hab 3: 16. In Hos 5: 12 we have כָּעָשׁ 'like a moth', parallel to כָּרָקָב 'like dry rot'. This text ought to have warned against a change from רָקָב to רֹקֶב 'goatskin bottle' (Gesenius-Buhl, s.v. following G) in our text. Cf. the *hapax* רִקָּבוֹן 'rotten wood' in 41: 19. Man is compared to a thing that is rotten, that crumbles and wears away. The same thing is expressed by the verb בלה, which is applied to garments 'worn away' by decrepitude (Jos 9: 13; Neh 9: 21). Cf Sir 14: 17a, כל הבשר כבגד יבלה 'All flesh wears away like a garment.' Our 2nd hemistich clarifies the comparison. The same image is to be found in Ps 102: 27, 'and they all wear out like a garment' (verb בלה). Nearer still is Is 50: 9, 'Yes, they all wear out like a garment; the moth eats them up!' The word עָשׁ has been used in 4: 19, but to express what is crushed. Here the moth is an agent of slow destruction.

3   Vulg. *et dignum ducis super hujuscemodi aperire oculos tuos!* to give to the אַף of the opening its full value. G οὐχὶ καὶ τούτου λόγον ἐποιήσω interprets the 1st hemistich by reading פקחתי עיני and understanding 'not open the eye' in the sense of not

4   Who can extract the pure from the impure?
     No one!
5   Since his days are decreed,
     Since the number of his months is known to Thee,
     Since Thou hast fixed his limit which he will not exceed,

esteeming. The change from the 2nd person to the 1st eliminates the anthropomorphism. Instead of אתי (Targ. ואתי, Aq. καὶ ἐμέ) we have וְאֹתוֹ in G καὶ τοῦτον, Vulg. *eum* and Syr. ܠܗ (correct reading).

There is the same movement of ideas as in 7:17-19. The meaning of אַף־עַל־זֶה 'even on such a one!' is not at all doubtful in the light of the context. It is an exclamation of surprise. It spite of the misery of this creature, whose condition I have just described, Thou openest Thy eye to judge him! The verb פקח 'open' the eyes, especially after sleep (27:19). From the opening of the chapter it has been a question of man in general. Job does not appear on the scene until v. 13. The correct reading is וְאֹתוֹ (G, Vulg., Syr.), as even Ginsburg admits, and not ואתי of the MT which brings Job back prematurely. The *hiph'il* of בוא is used with במשפט, just as we have בוא במשפט 'to go to law' (9:32; Ps 143:2). Hence 'And it is he whom Thou bringest to judgment with Thee!' It is unworthy of God to bring a charge against man in this way, and to cavil at his faults (13:26-7).

4 For מִי־יִתֵּן טָהוֹר, G τίς γὰρ καθαρὸς ἔσται; Vulg. paraphrases מטמא *de immundo conceptum semine* and interprets לֹא אֶחָד (cf. Targ. אלולפן אלהא די הוא חד 'if it be not God'). G ἀλλ' οὐθείς is marked by obelus in Syro-hex., but there is only the word ἀλλ' which is missing in MT.

The two words טָהוֹר and טָמֵא are clearly antithetic, as the pure and impure (Lv 10:10; Ezk 22:26).

Sometimes טהור is applied to physical purity (28:19), sometimes to moral purity (17:9). Here, of course, it is used in the latter sense, although טמא 'impure' is an allusion to the impurities incurred by woman in childbirth (v. 1a). The verb טהר has been used in 4:17, 'Is a man pure before his Maker?' As regards the original impurity of man, cf. Ps 51:5, 'Behold, I was brought forth in iniquity and in sin did my mother conceive me!' Similarly here too Christian exegesis has seen an allusion to original sin. The exclamation מִי־יִתֵּן 'Who will give?' implies something impossible (31:31b):'Who can extract the pure from the impure?' Man is unable to attain purity, i.e. righteousness (parallelism between טהר and צדק in 4:17). He is sullied in his very origins. The 2nd hemistich is reduced to לֹא אֶחָד 'not one', 'nobody'. This is a studied effect. Merx cuts out לא אחד. Others consider the whole of v. 4 as intrusive (Bickell, Loisy, Beer, Gray). Duhm retains it though lengthening it by the addition of the hypothetical מחטאות 'without sins'. Note that the idea of the 1st hemistich is suggested by ילוד אשה of v. 1. The reply 'No one!' implies a rejection of the validity of the charge.

5 G ἐὰν καὶ μία ἡμέρα seems to read חַד יוֹם instead of חרוצים. For ימיו, G ὁ βίος αὐτοῦ ἐπὶ τῆς γῆς following 7:1. Jerome places an asterisk (instead of the obelus) in front of *super terram*. G παρ' αὐτοῦ reads אתו for אתך, but Jerome *apud te* (cf. Symm. παρὰ σοί). The *kethîb* חֻקּוֹ is followed by Symm. ὅρον αὐτοῦ, while Vulg. *terminos ejus* and Targ. גזירתוהי 'his

6   Turn away from him Thy glance, and *leave him alone*,
     Until, like a hireling, he finishes his day's work!

6 וְ־חֲדָל; MT: ויחדל.

laws' follow the *qerê* חֻקָּיו. G εἰς
χρόνον and Syr. 'a law' read חוק.
It is difficult to know whether G ἔθου,
Symm. ἔταξας, Vulg. *constituisti* have
read שַׁתָּ instead of עשׂית or whether
their translation has not been influenced by the expression used in
v. 13c.

V. 5 forms the protasis of a sentence whose apodosis will occur in
v. 6. The conjunction אִם 'if' expresses a hypothesis which is verifiable as true: seeing that, since. Thus
it is close to the meaning of כִּי; the
alternation of אִם and of כִּי is found
in 7: 4, 13. Man's days on earth are
in the hands of God. God has fixed
them in advance and they cannot be
exceeded. Since such is the situation,
God should leave His creature a
breathing space, to be at peace (v. 6).
We have the same sequence of ideas
in 10: 20-2. Verb חרץ 'determine',
'decree' (1 K 20: 40; Is 10: 22). If
we compare with the Greek χαράσσω,
we note that the meanings of חרץ
'sharpen' one's tongue (Ex 11: 7;
Jos 10: 21), 'cut', 'engrave' (New
Hebrew, Judaeo-Aramaic), 'flay'
(Arabic حرص), 'hollow out' (Assyr.
ḥarâṣu) are all reflected in the Greek
verb. Now, χαράσσω has given
χαρακτήρ 'engraving', 'inscription on
stone', etc. We feel that the meaning
'decree' for חרץ derives from the
custom of inscribing on tablets of
stone decrees or solemn commands,
e.g. the tables of the Law (Ex 24: 4;
31: 18; 34: 1, etc.). We find חקק
used in the same way, to connote
'engrave', 'sculpture', 'inscribe', 'or-
dain' (cf. 19: 23b), whence חק 'or-
dinance', 'law', and 'limit' imposed
on activity. It is this very word
which occurs in the 3rd hemistich.

In the Book of Job, חֹק is used in the
singular with the connotations of
'decision', 'decree' (23: 14), 'limit'
(28: 26; 38: 10). The *kethîb* חֻקָּו
maintains the correct text (cf.
Symm.), confirmed by the singular
of G and Syr. We have חק as the
complement of עשׂה in 28: 26, to
express the imposition of a limit.
It is the limit which a man's life may
not exceed. The 2nd hemistich serves
as a link: 'the number of his months
is with Thee', i.e. lies in Thy knowledge. Use of אִתָּךְ 'with Thee', 'in
Thy hands' exactly like אֵת־מִי in
12: 3c and עמך in 10: 13. God fore-
ordains the number of the days of
man, He foreknows the number of
his months, He fixes the limit which
human life may not overstep. Let
Him then be patient!

6   Syr. omits שעה מעליו. Under the
influence of 7: 19 and 10: 20, G (A)
reintroduces the 1st person: ἀπ'
ἐμοῦ, ἡσυχάσω εὐδοκήσω. Some MSS
(cf. Beer) have followed this reading,
which is quoted as a variant by
Olympiodorus. G (B, א) omits the
suffix of יומו (Syro-hex.). The suffix
is restored in Sah. and Jerome. The
close is paraphrased in Vulg. *donec
optata veniat sicut mercenarii dies ejus.*
The verb שעה with מֵעָלָיו, as we had
תשׁעה ממני in 7: 19. מעליו is chosen
here because the glance of God lies
heavy on man; cf. מעלי in 9: 34 and
13: 21. וְיֶחְדָּל is rendered 'and that
he may breathe' (Le Hir), 'that he
may rest a little' (Renan), etc. But
1 S 2: 5 may not be quoted to authorise for חדל in isolation the meaning
of 'rest', 'cease from work' (cf. our
Comm.). Moreover the 2nd hemistich
implies that man continues to work

7   For there is a hope for the tree:
    If it be cut down, it may still spring to life again,
    And its sprouting will not cease.

8   If its root grows old in the earth,
    And if in the soil the stump decays,

9   At the scent of water, it flourishes anew,
    And grows boughs like a young plant!

until the end of the day. A reading וְחָדָל, attested by one manuscript, is suggested by 7: 16b and Jer 40: 4 (Budde). This slight correction is accepted by Beer, Ehrlich, Gray. We thus obtain quite a satisfactory sense: 'Turn from him Thy glance, and leave him alone!' For the expressions, cf. 7: 19, 16b. The verb רצה 'take pleasure', 'delight in' (33: 26; 34: 9) corresponds to the Aramaic רעי. Another verb, רצה, Judaeo-Aramaic רצא, means 'pay', 'acquit a debt' (Lv 26: 34, 41, 43). It is this second verb which is used here: 'until, like a hireling, he finishes his day's work'. The day means the work due for the day. Cf. 7: 1-2 for the image of the hireling or mercenary.

7 Symm., Vulg., Syr. read the plural instead of the singular, יִנְקתו.

Man's condition is worse than that of the trees. The latter spring to life again of themselves. Man disappears wholly. The motive behind the comparison will be brought out in v. 10. The conjunction כי 'for' refers back to the ideas expressed in v. 5 with regard to the limit imposed on the days of human life. The same is not true in the vegetable world. Job repeats Zophar's expression יֵשׁ תִּקְוָה (11: 18). With the 1st hemistich cf. 5: 16, 'thus the poor man has hope' (same construction with תְהִי instead of יֵשׁ). The copula of וְעוֹד within the hemistich (4: 6; 10: 8, etc.). On the *hiph'il* of חלף cf. 9: 11. The word יִנְקתו as in 8: 16. The verb חדל (v. 6) 'to cease', 'to finish' in the sense of 'to be absent' (19: 14) or 'to

fail', 'to be missing'. The connotation 'to leave some one in peace' was introduced by the complements מִמֶּנּי (7: 16) and מֵעָלָיו understood (v. 6). V. 7 alludes to the branches which have been cut off. V. 8 will depict the root aging in the soil and the trunk apparently dead.

8 G ἐν γῇ is not translated in Jerome, but *iterum* before *radix ejus* (in Gall.) might come from *in terra*. G renders וּבֶעָפָר by ἐν δὲ πέτρᾳ. The Greek word στέλεχος (= גזע) of G is quoted in the margin of Syro-hex.

It is not only by the hand of man that the tree is cut down and dies. Nature in its turn contributes to its death: 'if its root grows old in the earth and if in the soil the stump decays'. The author is thinking of those parts of the tree which are buried in the soil: the roots and the base of the trunk. They are buried, they grow old, and it cannot be known whether they are alive or dead. The *hiph'il* of זקן 'to be old' is used to connote 'to grow old' (Pr 22: 6; Sir 8: 6). Note the parallelism between אֶרֶץ and עָפָר (39: 14); cf. עפר and אדמה (5: 6). The noun גֵּזַע from גזע or גדע 'cut', 'cut down' trees means the trunk (cf. *truncus*, and *truncare*); cf. Is 11: 1; 40: 24. Of course the death of the roots and the trunk is only apparent.

9 G renders קציר by θερισμόν, but a translation καρπόν is attributed to ὁ Ἑβραῖος by Polychronius (Field); cf. Jerome *fructum*. We have *comam* in Vulg., זאזא 'foliage' in Targ.,

10 But man dies, and remains lifeless,
Mortal man expires, and where is he?

11 The waters will have fled from the sea,
And a river will have dried up and drained away,

פ֫רֶא 'leaves' in Syr. G well translates נטע νεόφυτον. Vulg. paraphrases: *quasi cum primum plantatum est.*

'At the scent of water' is an admirable image suggesting as it does the approach, the slightest contact; cf. Jg 16: 9 בהריחו אש 'as soon as it smells the fire'. Dillmann would replace the *hiph'il* יַפְרִחַ by the *qal.* But we have had יחליף (v. 7), יזקין (v. 8). The *hiph'il* form furnishes a good parallel עָשָׂה קָצִיר in the 2nd hemistich. The same use of הפריח with the sense of 'flourish' is found in Ps 92: 14; Pr 14: 11. The word קציר 'branches', 'boughs' (18: 16; 29: 19) is the complement of עשה 'grow', 'produce', 'make', as פרי 'fruit' in Gn 1: 11, 12. The noun נֶטַע connotes the tree which has just been planted (נטע).

10 G ᾤχετο seems to read יהלך (cf. v. 20) for יחלש, while Vulg. *et nudatus* interprets יחלש in accordance with the Aramaic *'aph'el* 'unclothe'. Instead of ואיו, G οὐκέτι ἐστίν, Syr. 'and he is no more', read the banal ואיננו, which is preferred by Merx and Siegfried. Much more alive is the 'and where is he?' which is supported by Targ. and Vulg.

Contrast between plant life and human life. Note the parallelism between גֶּבֶר and אָדָם (16: 21; 33: 17) as between גבר and אנוש (4: 17; 10: 5). To the verb יָמוּת of the 1st hemistich corresponds יְגְוַע of the 2nd (3: 11). The root חלש means 'to be weak' in Aramaic and Syriac. The use of חַלָּשׁ 'the weak' or 'the infirm', by contrast to גִּבּוֹר 'the strong', 'the warlike' in Jl 4: 10, attests the same meaning in Hebrew.

In the transitive sense, the verb חלש means 'weaken', 'defeat' (Ex 17: 13), whence חֲלוּשָׁה 'defeat' (Ex 32: 18). In Modern Hebrew חלש means 'weaken', whence חַלָּשׁוּת 'weakness', 'swoon'. This meaning easily develops into that of 'to be unconscious, inanimate', and hence it is understandable that the verb can have been used after ימות 'he dies'. It is better in every way to retain the uncommon word than change it to יחלף 'he passes away' (contra Wright, Graetz). The correction cannot be authorised by G, which is based rather on the reading יהלך, in accordance with v. 20. The end: 'where is he?' gives a striking touch; cf. אַיּוֹ in 20: 7. One inevitably thinks of Lamennais' dead: *Ou sont-ils? Qui nous le dira?* Confronted by the corpse, we wonder whither has fled the life which animated it. It is vain to insist, as does Beer, that the reader must know where the dead man is (especially after ch. 3) and to use this argument to suggest changing the text in the light of G and Syr. (cf. sup.).

11 Symm. ὡς ἐκρεῖ ὕδατα .... and Vulg. *quomodo si recedant aquae* in order to clarify the comparison the second term of which will be supplied by v. 12. G χρόνῳ γὰρ σπανίζεται θάλασσα paraphrases the 1st hemistich. Targ. sees here an allusion to the Red Sea and the Jordan.

Some moderns cut out v. 11 on account of its resemblance to Is 19: 5 (Studer, Beer, Duhm). Ehrlich retains it only on condition that we return to the old exegesis of Jewish commentators who saw here a vain attempt to reanimate the dead man, as one might try to reanimate a tree,

12   What time man will remain laid low and will rise no more;
     Not until the *disappearance* of the heavens will they awake,
     And arise out of their sleep.

12   בְּלֹת (G, Aq., Symm., Theod., Vulg., Syr.); MT: בלתי.

an attempt which exhausts for this
purpose the seas and the rivers. But
in that case we should expect a verb
meaning to draw from or exhaust,
whereas v. 11 speaks simply of
a natural phenomenon. Without
having to force the sense of the verse,
we shall see that it fits in well enough
with the context. Its resemblance to Is
19: 5 is not a proof of inauthenticity.
In the first place, only the 2nd
hemistich is a copy of Is 19: 5b. The
1st hemistich of Isaiah has נִשְׁתּוּ instead of אזלו and מֵהַיָּם instead of
מִנִּי־יָם. We have had quotations
from Isaiah and the Psalms in 12:
13-25. They fitted perfectly into the
context. Now, in Is 19: 5 it is a
question of a punishment inflicted
on the Egyptians, of a drying up by
the evaporation of the Nile which is
termed both הַיָּם 'the sea' and נהר
'the river'. But in our text it is a
question of the rivers and seas in
general. The usual interpretation is
to see in the sea which dries up and
the river which drains away symbols
of man who dies for ever. Then the
waw of the opening of v. 12 is translated 'thus . . . in the same way . . .',
waw comparationis. But then one is
obliged to think of the sea as an
inland sea, i.e. a lake, if the image
is to have its full force, for if a river
may, as we might if need be suppose,
lose its waters, the same is not true
of the sea (cf. Le Hir, Renan, Segond, Crampon, etc.). We think the
verse has been badly understood. It
is indeed an allusion to the sea and
the rivers. But it is not a comparison.
What v. 12 will insist on is the indefinite prolongation of the sleep of
death. We are confronted in fact

with a formula analogous to the
words of Our Lord: 'Heaven and
earth will pass away, but my words
will not pass away.' The perfect and
the imperfects of v. 11 fulfil the
function of perfect anteriors. What
the author means is that, even if *per
impossibile* the sea and the rivers
came to be dry, the time needed for
such a phenomenon to be realised
would make no difference to the condition of the dead. And v. 12b stresses the point further, since the sleep
of death lasts until the 'disappearance of the heavens', i.e. until the
end of the world. It will easily be
observed that our interpretation preserves for each word its full and true
value, secures the logical nexus
between v. 11 and v. 12, and, in
brief, allows us to leave in its place
v. 11 while appreciating the hyperbole it contains. The verb אזל 'cease',
'fail' (Dt 32: 36; 1 S 9: 7) and
'vanish away', 'depart' (Pr 20: 14)
to convey that the waters vanish
from the sea. The verb יבש 'dry up',
speaking of waters (12: 15), expresses
the result of the action expressed by
חרב (Gn 8: 13).

12 The words ולא יקיצו omitted
in G, are restored in a singular form
καὶ οὐ μὴ ἐξεγέρθη in G (A). For
עד־בלתי, G ἕως ἂν . . . οὐ μὴ συν-
φανῇ, Aq. (according to Syro-hex.)
ἕως ἂν κατατριβῇ, Vulg. *donec atte-
ratur*, Theod. and Symm. ἕως πα-
λαιωθῇ, Syr. ܥܕ ܚܠܡ, have read
עַד־בְּלֹת. Only Targ. עד דלית שמיא
remains faithful to MT. The 3rd
hemistich, absent from Sah., marked
with asterisk in Jerome and Colb.,
did not exist in G. The present text

13 Oh! that Thou wouldst hide me in Sheol,
    And wouldst conceal me until Thine anger be spent!
    Then wouldst Thou appoint me a term when Thou mightest
        remember me again!

14 [ ] All the days of my service would I then wait,
    Until my release came.

14 Transfer v. 14a to follow v. 19.

comes from Theod., which has the singular ἐξυπνισθήσεται (Colb.) and not the plural ἐξυπνισθήσονται (G, Syro-hex.). Jerome oscillates between *suscitabitur* (Tur.) and *suscitabuntur* (Bod. and Gall.). Targ. introduces 'the wicked' as the subject of the last clause. Vulg. puts all the verbs in the singular. Targ. and Syr. have plurals like MT.

The 1st hemistich 'man will remain laid low and will rise not' brings before us the image of the inert corpse, lifeless until the end of the world. The verb שָׁכַב connotes 'to lie' in the bed, in the tomb, in Sheol (3: 13; 7: 21b). Note the contrast between שכב and קום (7: 4, cf. Comm.). The expression לֹא יָקוּם is developed in the last two hemistichs. In the light of those texts where the verb בלה 'waste away' (13: 28) and 'be consumed', 'fade away' alludes to the disappearance of the heavens and the earth (Is 51: 6; Ps 102: 27), it is clear that the infinitive בְּלֹת, attested by the versions (with the exception of Targ.), is preferable to the prosaic בִּלְתִּי, as is recognised by Geiger, Bickell, Beer, Duhm. Thus we obtain: 'until the disappearance of the heavens', i.e. until the end of the world. The formula is the parallel to v. 11 (cf. Comm.). The plurals יקיצו and יערו imply the double subject גבר and אדם of v. 10 to be a collective. Cf. Ps 41: 9b, 'He who is laid low will not be able to rise', in which the

words שכב and קום are used as in our 1st hemistich.

13 For בשאול, preserved in Syr., we have ἐν ᾅδη (G), *apud inferos* (Jerome), *in inferno* (Vulg.), בבית קבורתא (Targ.); cf. 7: 9b. G σοῦ ἡ ὀργή for אפך is corrected to μοῦ ἡ ὀργή in G (C), so as to avoid the anthropomorphism.

The idea of death (10-12) awakens that of the abode of the dead, Sheol (3: 11ff.). At least the time spent there offered some refuge from the wrath of God! This wrath would eventually be appeased, and then God would remember the one whom He had hidden in Sheol just as He remembered Noah after the Flood (Budde; cf. Gn 7: 24; 8: 1). The interrogative of desire מִי־יִתֵּן followed by the imperfect (6: 8; 13: 5). The *hiph'il* of צפן as in Ex 2: 3. Note the parallelism with הסתיר 'veil', 'conceal', used in 13: 24a. The verb שׁוּב 'turn back' in speaking of anger implies 'to be appeased' (Gn 27: 44; Is 5: 25, etc.). Cf. the use of השיב in 9: 13a. The construction עד־שׁוב is like עד־בלת (cf. Comm.) of v. 12. On the word חק 'term' 'limit', cf. v. 5. Job here returns to his individual case.

14 Aq. and Theod. μήτι restore the interrogative of היחיה omitted by G. On account of גבר in the 1st hemistich, Syr. replaces by the 3rd person the suffixes of צבאי and חליפתי, as also the verb איחל. For כל ימי צבאי, G συντελέσας ἡμέρας τοῦ

15   Thou wouldst call, and I would answer Thee,
      The work of Thy hands wouldst Thou claim;

βίου αὐτοῦ reads צבאו (cf. Syr.).
Vulg. interprets צבאי by *quibus
nunc milito*. For חליפתי, Targ.
חלופי חיי 'the transformations of my
life', Aq. and Theod. τὸ ἄλλαγμά μου,
Vulg. *immutatio mea*. Syr. interprets
by 'his old age'. G introduces a dogmatic meaning: ἕως πάλιν γένωμαι.
Cf. Symm. ἡ ἀνάφυσίς μου for
חליפתי (reading ἀνάφυσις and not
ἁγία φύσις; cf. Kreyssiger, quoted
by Field).

The 1st hemistich, 'if a man die,
shall he live again?', seems, at first
sight, a marginal gloss intercalated
here to show that the hypothesis of
Job is unrealisable. On this ground,
Ehrlich suppresses it. Duhm, by
reading ויחיה translates 'if a man
could die and live again!' and connects this hemistich with v. 13c.
This would be a wish expressed by
Job. The interpretation is forced.
The precative formula has hitherto
been מי יתן, and Job would rather
have used לו as an optative conjunction. Duhm cannot justify himself by reference to G, which translates simply יחיה and not ויחיה.
In any case the hemistich is not
parallel to 13c. Reiske transferred
it to a place after 12a, but we have
seen that this 12a was at once explained by 12b and 12c, in which
recurred the synonyms of ולא יקום.
The true position of v. 14a is at the
end of v. 19. We thus obtain a verse
19c-14a in which the word גֶּבֶר
answers אנוש (4:7; 10:5; cf. v. 10).
V. 20a in which figures לנצח 'for
ever' answers the interrogation of v.
14a. Thus it is v. 14b which continues
the strophe begun in v. 13. Job has
expressed the wish that Sheol might
be but a period of transition between
the season of divine wrath and the
day when God would again remember His servant. In that case he
would only have to wait patiently.

He would be in the position of the
soldier awaiting relief: 'All the days
of my service I would then wait
until my release came!' The word
צבא 'army', 'military service' has
been used to symbolise the time that
man spends on the earth (7:1).
Here it symbolises the time he
spends in Sheol, given the hypothesis of v. 13. The חֲלִיפָה is relief
(10:17). The verb אֲיַחֵל at the end
of the hemistich as in 6:11a. Note
the preposition עַד with the infinitive construct, exactly as in vv. 12-13.

15   G (A) adds μέ after καλέσεις
(similarly Sah.). Syr. and Vulg. also
add the 1st person suffix after תקרא.
G and Targ. read the plural instead
of the singular, מעשה. G μὴ ἀποποιοῦ
and Vulg. *porriges dexteram* freely
translate תכסף; we find also ἐπιπο-
θήσεις (Theod.), תגרגר 'Thou eagerly
desirest' (Targ.). Syr. 'I will think'
reads אכסף.

Job replies to the appeal of God,
who now remembers him (v. 13c). The
verbs קרא and ענה stand in the 1st
hemistich (cf. 9:16a; 12:4b; 13:
22a). With מַעֲשֵׂה יָדֶיךְ 'the work of
Thy hands', to denote Job, cf. the
use of מעשה ידיו in 34:19 and of
יגיע כפיך in 10:3b. Man is God's
special creative work. The verb כסף,
originally 'to turn pale', is used to
express the sentiment which causes
pallor of face, namely, passion, eager
desire, and it is thus that it comes to
mean 'desire ardently', 'covet',
whether in the *qal* (Ps 17:12), or the
niph'al (Gn 31:30; Ps 84:3). The
object of the desire is everywhere
preceded by the preposition לְ.
Because of the parallelism, the verb
כסף will assume the connotation of
the Latin *expetere* (cf. *Lexicon* of
Buxtorf, s.v.), not merely 'ardently
desire' but rather 'claim'. The hypo-

16   Whereas now Thou dost count my steps,
      Then Thou wouldst no more mark my sin;
17   Sealed in a bag would be my transgression,
      And Thou wouldst whiten my fault!

thesis of vv. 13-14 is continued. Hence the translation of imperfects by conditionals.

16 Syr. puts a negative before תספור in order to obtain two parallel clauses. Vulg. *sed parce peccatis meis* paraphrases the 2nd hemistich. G καὶ οὐ μὴ παρέλθῃ σε seems to have read תעבור עליך instead of תשמור על-.

The interpretation of this verse differs completely according as to whether we see in it the suggestion of a divine inquisition intended to torment Job (13: 26-7) or, on the contrary, an act of mercy towards the sufferer. On the first hypothesis, critics borrow from G the verb תעבור instead of תשמׁר, without taking into account the rest of G, which read also עליך, and thus the 2nd hemistich is translated: 'Thou dost not overlook my sin' (Ewald, Dillmann, Beer, Duhm, etc.). Then, v. 17 is regarded as describing the sins of Job as being carefully kept by God in a package stuck with glue (Dillmann). Duhm thinks that it is a question of documents drawn up by God indicting Job (13: 26) and supposedly kept in a bag sealed with wax. In this way such far-fetched subtleties are arrived at that it seems better to keep to the text, while noting that G has not understood the כי-עתה of the opening (simply δέ) and has harmonised the two hemistichs. We find the same phenomena in Syr., which has introduced לא before תספור, to conclude with a meaning diametrically opposed to that of G. It would hardly be wise to follow Syr., as is done by Merx and Siegfried. In point of fact, the 1st hemistich is subordinated to

the 2nd. This is how the verse may be understood. The verb שמר means not only 'to keep' but also 'to watch over' (10: 14; 13: 27) and 'take note', 'mark'. It is the latter sense which is called for by the preposition על before the complement; cf. the use of עלי with the expression שׁים משמר in 7: 12. The 2nd hemistich therefore means: 'Thou wouldst no more mark my sin.' God would cease to be the severe inquisitor who unremittingly seeks out Job's faults (10: 6) and who spies on the least of his movements to discover evil there (13: 27). The 1st hemistich contrasts the present conduct of God with that which He would adopt in the given hypothesis (vv. 13-15). At the moment, 'He counts the steps' of His servant. The same expressions are used in 31: 4, 37; 34: 21. Compare what Job says about the vigilance God exercises over man in this life (v. 3; 13: 26-7).

17 G ἐσφράγισας and Vulg. *signasti* harmonise חתם with the other verbs. For בצרור, Targ. בספר דכרניא 'in the book of memories'. The 2nd hemistich is paraphrased in G ἐπεσημήνω δὲ εἴ τι ἄκων παρέβην. The idea of applying a coating, a plaster, causes Vulg. to render ותטפל על by *sed curasti*. In Targ. ותטפל is translated ותחבו (cf. 13: 4). Syr. says vaguely: 'and remove my sins far from me'.

There is association of פְּשָׁעִי and עֲוֹנִי with חַטָּאתִי in v. 16; cf. 13: 23. God would cease to mark Job's sin. Better still, He would not even perceive it, for 'my transgression would be sealed in a bag'. There is no reason whatever to change the passive participle of חתם, which is

18   But a mountain *will finally fall*,
      And a rock will be removed from its place,
19   The waters will wear away the stones,
      A *violent rainstorm* will flood the soil of the earth.
      Meanwhile Thou dost cause man's hope to perish.

18   נָפוֹל יִפֹּל (Theod., Syr.); MT: נופל יבול.

19   סְחִיפָה; MT: ספיחיה. Transfer here v. 14a.

frequently used in the Bible. The bag, צְרוֹר, contained precious things (Gn 42: 35; Pr 7: 20; Ca 1: 13), in particular those which it was desired to conceal from others (1 S 25: 29: the bag of life). The verb טפל (13: 4) 'coat', 'paint over', 'whitewash' something, and also 'paint' the face. The text of Is 1: 18, 'though your sins are like scarlet, they shall be as white as snow; though they are red like crimson, they shall become like wool', elucidates the 2nd hemistich. To put a coating over a fault is to paint it over or whitewash it so as to obliterate its blackness.

18 Vv. 18-19, absent from Sah., marked with asterisk in Jerome and Syro-hex., did not exist in G. The present text comes from Theod. (cf. Colb. and Syro-hex.). Instead of יבל, which makes no sense, Theod. διαπεσεῖται and Syr. נפאל read יִפֹּל, from which Lagarde has well restored the original text as נָפוֹל יִפֹּל.

The hypothesis of a temporary abode in Sheol is not realised. Just as in v. 11 (cf. Comm.), Job will now depict phenomena in the world of nature which could not take place before an indefinite lapse of time, in order by this means to symbolise poetically the fate of man after death (v. 19c and 14a). The first word וְאוּלָם 'but', to oppose what follows to what has preceded (11: 5; 12: 7; 13: 4). With a slight correction, following Theod. and Syr. (cf. sup.) we shall translate

'But a mountain will finally fall', i.e. in the revolutions of time and change! And even, with the lapse of time, 'a rock will be removed from its place'; cf. the verb עתק (9: 5). In 18: 4c, the 2nd hemistich will be quoted, but with inversion of verb and subject.

19   On the text of G, cf. v. 18. For ספיחיה, Targ. כתהא (cf. Syr. כתא in Ceriani), Theod. ὕδατα ὕπτια, Symm. τὰ παραλελειμμένα, Vulg. *alluvione*. The word תקות is omitted by Vulg.

Another example of a natural change produced by slow interminable action: 'the waters will wear away the stone'. Cf. the Latin line: *gutta cavat lapidem, non vi, sed saepe cadendo*! This action of water on stone is expressed by the verb שׁחק 'pound', 'crush', 'pulverise' but also 'wear away' as a result of constant rubbing (Sir 6: 36). The versions did not read the suffix of סְפִיחֶיהָ. The word is parallel to מַיִם and forms the subject of תשׁטף. Budde very rightly recognised that one ought to read סְחִיפָה, which corresponds precisely to the Arabic *sahîfeh* 'rainstorm', 'torrential rain'. The root סחף, which recurs in the Assyrian *sahâpu* 'overturn', 'devastate', is used precisely in order to depict the action of rain which sweeps over and ravages all things: מְטַר סֹחֵף (Pr 28: 3). The disasters caused by hurricanes are indicated in Assyrian by the verb *sahâpu*. The verb שׁטף 'flood' is

14a   If a man die, shall he live again?
20   Thou dost attack him, and for ever he departs,
      His face changes and Thou dost despatch him!

found, with מים 'the waters' as subject and with סתר 'hiding place' as direct complement, in Is 28:17. The construction of our 2nd hemistich follows the same pattern: 'A violent rainstorm will flood the soil of the earth.' Use of עָפָר is as in v. 8 (cf. 5:6). The 3rd hemistich does not introduce a comparison, as is generally supposed, 'and thus'. The sequence of the ideas is the same as in vv. 11 and 12. During the whole time that would be required, on the given hypothesis, for the production of the phenomena which have just been alluded to, man remains without hope: 'Meanwhile Thou dost cause man's hope to perish.' Cf. the use of אבד with תקוה as subject in 8:13b. This hope would consist in the possibility of leaving Sheol to return to life (v. 13). Job then asks the supreme, the decisive question, which has been transferred to the beginning of v. 14, but which must be restored to its true context at this point (cf. Comm.): 'If a man die, shall he live again?' V. 20 will show that it is for ever that man disappears from the earth.

20   Vulg. *roborasti* treats תתקפהו as a *pi'el*. After αὐτῷ τὸ πρόσωπον, which renders פניו in G, we find the suffix σοῦ in G (A), Syro-hex., Eth.

The important word is לָנֶצַח, which, as is clearly apparent from 4:20b and 20:7a, specifically refers to the irremediable ruin of man. The verb הלך 'to go away' (7:9; 10:21) has the sense of 'vanish', 'perish' (Latin *perire*), like the Arabic *halaka*; cf. הלך in a Nabataean inscription (Jaussen et Savignac, *Mission en Arabie*, I, pp. 172-4). The form יְהַלָּךְ is poetic (16:6; 20:25). The

comparison with 4:20 and 20:7 proves that יהלך takes the place of יאבד and that it is to the latter verb that the complement לנצח refers. This is a further case of the poetic transposition of the copula (cf. 4:6; 10:8, etc.). Hence we must translate תתקפהו separately and in parallelism with תשלחהו of the close. We can therefore leave to תקף its meaning of 'attack' (15:24; Ec 4:12), derived from that of 'to be strong, violent'. The rest is ambiguous, for there is some hesitation about the attribution of מְשַׁנֶּה פָנָיו 'changing his face' which some refer to God who changes the face of man (cf. Le Hir, Renan, Segond, etc.), others to man whose face becomes changed under the impact of death. This latter interpretation is the only logical one, if we take into account Sir 12:18; 13:25, where the *pi'el* of שנא (= שנה), with פנים or פני as complement, denotes the change which comes over one's face under the influence of personal feeling. Thus משנה פני is a kind of *casus pendens*, referring to the suffixes of the verbs תתקפהו and תשלחהו as also to the subject of יהלך. It is man who, in dying, reveals a change of face. Cf. the use of פני after אעזבה in 9:27. The texts from Ecclesiasticus which we have quoted do not favour the idea that we should see in משנה פני a proverbial expression, 'the time in which one turns one's face', 'no time', 'suddenly', as postulated by Fried. Delitzsch and Hontheim. The dead man is an encumbering object which is got rid of: 'Thou dost despatch him' to Sheol or *ad patres*. The dead man no longer belongs to the earth, he is no further interested in anything which goes on there (vv. 21-2).

21   If his sons are honoured, he knows nothing of it,
      If they are despised, he does not perceive it;
22   His flesh is grieved only for himself,
      His soul laments only over himself!

21 Vulg. well brings out the contrast between יכבדו and יצערו: *sive nobiles fuerint . . . . sive ignobiles.* G πολλῶν δὲ γενομένων which gives to כבד the sense 'to be many' (like Syr. and Sa'adia) translates יצערו by ὀλίγοι γένωνται, although צער never means 'to be few'. G omits למו. Symm. περὶ αὐτῶν is quoted by Syro-hex. and translated *de eis* (with asterisk) in Jerome.

The dead man recks not what becomes of his own family. The antithesis between כבד and צער is clearly brought out in Jer 30: 19b, והכבדתים ולא יצערו 'I will honour them and they shall not be brought low.' The כָּבֵד is a man of weight, a notable. The צָעִיר is the small man, the weak, the insignificant. Parallelism between ידע 'to know' and בין 'to perceive', as between בין and ראה 'to see' (9: 11). Ignorance of what goes on on the earth is the result of death. Cf. Ec 9: 5ff., 'For the living know that they shall die, but the dead know nothing, and there is no further reward for them, for they are forever forgotten. Their love, as well as their hatred and jealousy, has already perished, and they will nevermore have any part in whatever takes place under the sun' (Podechard's translation).

22 G omits the two עליו. Vulg. paraphrases the first by *dum vivet.* Syro-hex. quotes Aq. and Theod. ἐπ' αὐτῷ, which has passed (with asterisk) into Jerome *super eum.* In the 2nd hemistich G (A) has ἐπ' αὐτῷ (Jerome *super eum* with asterisk) which renders עליו in Aq. and Theod.

This verse has been the object of many interpretations. Modern exegetes have wrested oversubtle meanings from it to their heart's content. Thus Dillmann sees here an allusion to the sufferings of the soul and body at the moment of their separation. His argument rests on the attribution of the first עָלָיו to the suffix of בְּשָׂרוֹ and of the second to the suffix of נַפְשׁוֹ, regarded simply as clarifications of the individual to whom the body and soul belong. The same basic interpretation underlies the translations of Budde, Duhm, Driver, Ball. However, the particle אַךְ (2: 6; 13: 15, 20) ought to connect with what precedes and introduce the restriction. Now, v. 21 says clearly that the dead man is no longer concerned about his sons. About what is he concerned? From what does he suffer? The verb כאב 'to suffer' (cf. 2: 13; 5: 18) has as subject בשרו 'his flesh' or 'his body', parallel to נפשו 'his soul' (cf. 13: 14). The body and soul figure as essential elements in the composite structure of the human being, but 'his soul' and 'his body' separately could mean 'himself'. Such phrases as 'his body suffers' and 'his soul is sad' are mere variants to describe the pains of one who is in Sheol. Now, the object of this suffering is evidently the suffix of עליו; cf. אבל עליו in Hos 10: 5. It is 'for himself' that the dead man grieves, not for anything dishonourable that might happen to his sons (v. 21b). Thus it becomes immediately clear that עליו applies to אך 'only for himself!', and not for others (cf. Le Hir, Renan, Knabenbauer, etc.). The sequence of ideas from v. 7 is now limpidly clear. The condition of mortal man is worse than that of the tree. Even though the tree may seem to die, it can live again (7-9). Man dies and vanishes from the land of the living for an indefinite period; his death lasts for a longer time than would be required for the sea to lose its waters and for a river to become dry (10-12). In vain does Job hope that Sheol might prove only a temporary hiding place where he might patiently wait for the cessation of God's anger (13-14) and the manifestation of God's favour (15-17). Even the fall of mountains, the displacement of rocks, the wearing away of stones by waters, the flooding of the earth by rains, are phenomena of less duration than man's death (18-20). The last two verses introduce a new point in the description, for they show that it is not merely the duration of death that is terrible, but also the state to which it reduces humanity (Ec 9: 2-6), namely, a state of insensibility to whatever is not personal suffering, utter oblivion of even the closest relatives (vv. 21-2). The speech concludes by a vision of death (7: 21; 10: 21-2; 17: 13-16; 21: 32-33).

CHAPTER 15

1   Then Eliphaz the Temanite spoke and said:

2   Does a wise man answer with windy knowledge
      And does he fill his belly with east wind,

3   Reproving with useless talk
      And words that cannot profit?

4   You go even so far as to break off piety,
      And do away with meditation before God!

Chapters 15-21. Second cycle of speeches: see Introduction, pp. xliff.
Chapter 15. Second speech of Eliphaz: see Introduction, pp. xlif.

15:2 Vulg. paraphrases דעת רוח: *quasi in ventum loquens*. Syr. joins רוח to חכם. Targ. interprets רוח by דדמי לזעפא 'which resembles a storm' and קדים by היך רוח קדומא 'as with east wind'. In accordance with the effects of the east wind, G translates קדים by πόνον. Because of its heat, Aq. and Theod. καύσωνος, Vulg. *ardore*, Syr. ܠܫܘܒܐ. Because of its violence, Symm. πνεύματος βιαίου.

Job has boasted of his own wisdom (12:3; 13:2). Eliphaz turns it into derision: 'Does a wise man answer with windy knowledge?' The words דַּעַת־רוּחַ describe the character of the reply (Pr 18:23). Windy knowledge is knowledge without consistency; cf. רוח in 7:7. Bildad has already reproached Job with uttering words which are but a great wind (8:2). And Job will describe the reply of Eliphaz as דברי־רוח 'words of wind' (16:3). The knowledge reflected in speech has its seat in the inner man, whether in the heart, or the belly (*L'Emploi métaphorique*, p. 134). Eliphaz traces the effect back to its cause: 'and does he fill his belly with east wind?' Compare רוח בטני 'wind of my belly' in 32:18.

The parallelism between רוּחַ and קָדִים recurs in Hos 12:2. The sirocco, an east wind קדים, is maleficent (Ezk 17:10; 19:12). Here, however, the word is chosen especially as being synonymous with רוּחַ, to denote something vain and frivolous.

3 G οἷς οὐ δεῖ translates לֹא יסכון more faithfully than Vulg. *eum qui non est aequalis tibi*. G omits בם, but Syro-hex. and Jerome introduce into their text (with asterisk) the ἐν αὐτοῖς of Aq. and Theod.

The infinitive הוֹכֵחַ, not preceded by the preposition לְ, plays the part of an explanatory adverb (cf. Gesenius-Kautzsch, § 113h) or a gerundive. On the meaning of הוֹכִיחַ, cf. 5:17. The verb סכן 'to be useful, profitable' is peculiar to the Book of Job (cf. 22:2; 35:3). In 34:9 it will mean 'to profit (some one)'. The *hiph'il* of יעל has the same connotations as סכן (cf. 35:3). The relative אשׁר is understood before לֹא יָסְכּון and לֹא יוֹעִיל.

4 For שִׂיחה, G ῥήματα τοιαῦτα, Targ. מלתא, Vulg. *preces*. Syr. inter-

208

5 Since your iniquity inspires the words of your mouth
And you adopt the language of the crafty,
6 It is your mouth which condemns you and not I,
And your own lips which testify against you!

prets the 2nd hemistich: 'and you multiply words before God'.

The adverb אַף 'even' does not qualify אַתָּה, but rather the whole clause; cf. אַף in 14: 22. The *hiph'il* of פרר with an abstract complement as in 5: 12. The word יִרְאָה 'fear' is used by itself to denote the fear of God, religion, piety (4: 6): 'you go even so far as to break off piety'. The 2nd hemistich is parallel to the 1st. It is obvious that שִׂיחָה לִפְנֵי־אֵל corresponds to יראה. The verb שִׂיחַ 'to complain' (7: 11), whence שִׂיחַ 'plaint' (7: 13; 9: 27), has also the meaning of 'reflect', 'meditate', especially in Ps 119. And it is in this Psalm that we find שִׂיחָה 'meditation' (v. 97 and v. 99). Hence it would seem logical to translate the closing phrase by 'meditation before God'. Thus the verb תִּגְרַע is parallel to תפר. The root גרע 'to pull down' has often the sense of 'diminish' or 'do away with', in contrast to הוֹסִיף 'increase' or 'add' (Dt 4: 2; 13: 1; Ec 3: 14). We shall again meet the verb גרע in v. 8 and 36: 7. The utterances of Job tend to dissuade the pious from recourse to God which his friends recommend.

5 G omits כִּי (but Jerome *quia*). Syro-hex. translates ὅτι in the margin (with asterisk). For יאלף עונך, G ἔνοχος εἶ (Jerome *reus es*). Syr. omits the suffix of עונך. G translates the 2nd hemistich as οὐδὲ διέκρινας ῥήματα δυναστῶν, but Jerome *et elegisti linguam malorum* follows rather Symm. καὶ ἐξελέξω γλῶσσαν πανούργων. Targ. renders ערומים by חכימא 'wise'.

The conjunction כִּי introduces the

clause which is subordinate to the clause of v. 6: the meaning is 'since'. Hence: 'since your fault inspires your mouth and you adopt the language of the cunning', it is for that reason that 'your mouth, and not I, condemns you . . .' (v. 6). The 1st hemistich is ambiguous, and one might hesitate between *docet iniquitatem tuam os tuum* (Rosenmüller, Hirzel, etc.) and *docuit enim iniquitas tua os tuum* (Vulg.). The second translation alone is acceptable, for the verb אָלַף has the meaning of 'teach', 'instruct' (33: 33; 35: 11), and not that of 'reveal', 'evince' which the first translation implies. It is only in v. 6 that the mouth will betray Job. Further, it is more natural to consider the first noun עֲוֹנֶךָ as the subject, and the second פִּיךָ as the complement.

It is certainly thus that Rashi interprets the verse, placing the accusative particle before פִּיךְ. The words of Job are inspired by his fault. Hence, instead of speaking the language of the חָכָם (v. 2), he speaks that of the עָרוּם 'cunning', 'crafty' (Gn 3: 1), i.e. of him whom God cannot tolerate and who has pleasure in deceiving (5: 12f). The verb בחר 'choose' words (9: 14) means to adopt a language. Job has decided to use the language of the crafty and astute. It suffices to hear him to condemn him.

6 The phrase יענו בך is excellently translated as יסהדון בך 'testify against you' (Targ., cf. Syr.), καταμαρτυρήσουσίν σου (G). Vulg. *respondebunt tibi* misunderstands בך. Syr. adds 'before me' at the end of the verse.

V. 6 is very closely joined to v. 5. It

7   Were you the first man born,
     And were you brought forth before the hills?
8   Do you hear the confidences of Eloah,

is as a result of strophic considerations that Bickell cuts it out and Duhm transposes it to precede v. 13. Note the juxtaposition of the three organs of speech: the mouth, the tongue, the lips. The 1st hemistich, 'It is your mouth which condemns you, and not I', is a direct hit at Job, who in 9: 20 said: 'my own mouth condemns me.' The words are the same. But Job saw in this condemnation something arbitrary, for it happened even though he were righteous. Eliphaz sees in it the result of words inspired by iniquity or cunning (v. 5). Compare the tactics of the high priest to secure the condemnation of Jesus (Mt 26: 59-65). It is the very words of the accused which bear witness against him: 'and your lips bear witness against you'. The verb ענה with "ב before the complement is part of juridical vocabulary: to bear witness against some one. Cf. Jer 14: 7, אם עונינו ענו בנו 'if our faults bear witness against us'; 2 S 1: 16, פיך ענה בך 'your mouth has borne witness against you'. Note that the subject שפתים 'the lips', although feminine, generally requires a verb in the masculine plural (Gesenius-Kautzsch § 145u).

7   G adds τί γάρ at the beginning. For חוללת, G ἐπάγης (Jerome concretus es) suggested by the mode of formation of the foetus (10: 10). Instead of G ἀνθρώπων for אדם, G (A) ἄνθρωπος (Jerome homo).

Eliphaz is criticising the pretentions of Job. Vv. 7-8 show how difficult it is to attain wisdom. This too had been demonstrated by the speech of Zophar (11: 7-9), where the nature of God was shown to transcend the four dimensions and to be by that very fact inaccessible. Here we have

an undisguised allusion to the discourse of Wisdom in Pr 8. In particular, Pr 8: 22-31 stresses with a luxurious display of poetry the preexistence of wisdom before all things: before the earth, the waters, the mountains, the heavens, etc. In v. 25 we find: 'Before the mountains were rooted (in the ground), before the hills, I was brought forth.' Our 2nd hemistich literally copies (changing the 1st to the 2nd person) the 2nd hemistich of this v. 25. Now, it is clear that Pr 8: 22-31 forms a whole into which this hemistich fits so much the more congruously because it corresponds to v. 25a. It is then the Book of Job which borrows, while introducing the proposition into another context. It is obvious how futile it would be to change גְּבָעוֹת into גבהים 'heights' for the sole purpose of bringing in the angels (contra Duhm). The 1st hemistich carries us back to the very origins of man, when he was still very close to Wisdom who with God elaborated and shaped the world of creation. The 2nd hemistich goes still farther back, to before creation! And v. 8 will take us in thought even to the innermost secret counsel of God. The writing ראישון leaves us the choice between רִישׁוֹן (8: 8) and רִאשׁוֹן which is more natural. The construction אָדָם תִּוָּלֵד exactly as in 11: 12b. Here the niph'al of ילד retains its proper literal meaning (parallelism with חולל), whereas, in 11: 12b, it had the meaning of assume the nature of some one, or become. The imperfect has the sense of the aorist (3: 3).

8   The double meaning of סוד

And have you a monopoly of wisdom?

9   What do you know that we do not know,
     What do you understand that is not understood by us?

10   Among us also is found the gray-haired and the aged,
     More advanced in years than your father!

'secret' and 'secret counsel' is apparent in the diversity of the translations: Targ. רז 'secret' (Syr. ראא), Aq. ἀπορρήτῳ, Symm. μυστηρίῳ, Theod. μυστήριον (cf. Jerome *arcana*), but G σύνταγμα, Vulg. *consilium*. For תגרע, G ἀφίχετο, which cannot yield וְתִגַּע (Merx, Siegfried), for ἀφιχνεῖσθαι in G never corresponds to גגע. Syr. ⲗⲗⲁⲕⲁ is isolated and lends only slight support to Beer's correction וְתִגְּלֶה.

The pointing הֲ instead of הַ occurs when the interrogative particle is followed by a syllable with *šewa*. In such a case the *dagesh* may be inserted (23:6) or omitted (22:13b) in the consonant which follows הֲ (Gesenius-Kautzsch, § 100l). The proper meaning of סוֹד is 'confidence'; cf. מְתֵי סוֹדִי 'my confidants', 'my intimate friends' (19:19) and בַּעַל סוֹד 'confidant' (Sir 6:6). There was then inferred the meaning 'secret' and that of 'secret counsel', whence סוֹד יהוה 'counsel of Yahweh' (Jer 23:18). The verb שׁמע with ב״ before the complement sometimes assumes the meaning of 'listen' (37:2), but it can also mean simply 'hear' (26:14). Here it is indeed a question of a confidence on the part of God which only Wisdom, presiding with God in the work of creation, could have seized through the intimacy of her communion with the Creator (Pr 8:30-1). This wisdom is sparingly imparted to human beings. Is it possible that Job claims to arrogate the whole of it to himself, i.e. to have a monopoly of it? The verb גרע (v. 4b) 'diminish', 'do away with' also means 'to claim for one's self' or, more literally, 'attract

to one's self'. This is clearly implied by the complement אֵלֶיךָ, whence the translation 'have a monopoly of'.

9 For וְלֹא־עִמָּנוּ הוּא, G has simply ὃ οὐ καὶ ἡμεῖς, but Jerome *quod non nobiscum est* (doubtless following a hexaplar reading).

No, Job has not a monopoly of wisdom: 'What do you know that we do not know?' Eliphaz makes common cause with his friends. He repeats ironically Job's questions (12:3c, 9), which had made it clear that he knew as much as they (12:3a; 13:1-2). Note the parallelism between ידע and בין (14:21). הוּא is used with a neuter implication 'this', 'that' (13:16). The expression עִמָּנוּ 'with us' means that one possesses a thing through knowledge of it (10:13b; cf. אֵת in 12:3c). There is parallelism between ידעתי 'I know' and עמדי 'with me' in Ps 50:11.

10 V. 10, absent from Sah., and marked with asterisk in Jerome and Syro-hex., did not exist in G. The present text comes from Theod. (cf. Syro-hex. and Cod. 248). Note כביר rendered by βαρύτερος (cf. 8:2), corrected to πρεσβύτερος in some variants (whence Jerome *antiquior*).

A new direct hit at Job, who has spoken about the wisdom of the aged (12:12; cf. Comm.). The verb שׂיב 'to have white hair' (1 S 12:2) yields the noun שֵׂיבָה 'white hair' (Job 41:24). The participle שָׂב recurs only in Sir 32:3 but it is used in Aramaic (Ezr 5:5, 9; 6:7, 8, 14). On יָשִׁישׁ cf. 12:12. The word כַּבִּיר

11   Is it too slight a matter for you to receive the consolations of
         God
         And a word spoken in gentleness?
12   Why is your heart enraged,
         And why do your eyes blink,

'great' (8: 2) is qualified by יָמִים 'in days' of the close; cf. ארך ימים in 12: 12b. It is always in going back to the preceding generations that one finds more and more of wisdom (8: 8-10). If Job scorns his friends, let him apply to the old!

11 G deviates decisively from MT: ὀλίγα ὧν ἡμάρτηκας μεμαστίγωσαι, μεγάλως ὑπερβαλλόντως λελάληκας. Döderlein, Merx, Ball attempt to find the substratum of G in the Hebrew words. It seems better to recognise that G invents a meaning by interpreting תנחומות in the sense of 'vengeances' (cf. נחם in the *niph'al* and *hithpa'el*) and by reading לא טעם 'tasteless' instead of לאט עם. In Syr. the words המעט and דבר are regarded as imperatives. Targ. adds 'he seems to speak' before עמך. Vulg. *numquid grande est ut consoletur te Deus? sed verba tua prava hoc prohibent* is a bold paraphrase, seemingly based on a reading of מאד for מעט and on an attribution of a pejorative sense to לאט.

The friends of Job have tried to console him (2: 11) by speaking to him of God and His behaviour towards men: Eliphaz (5: 17-27), Bildad (8: 5-8), and Zophar (11: 13-20). Here were truly 'consolations of God', for it was God who inspired them. Eliphaz appealed to an immediate revelation (4: 12ff.). Job, however, considers all that as a string of platitudes, and he will not fear to tell his interlocutors that they are 'miserable comforters' (16: 2b), and that they give him vain consolations (21: 34). The word תַּנְחֻמֹת recurs only in 21: 2, where Job asks his friends to be kind enough to give

him a hearing which should take the place of any further administration of comfort. With the formula הַמְעַט מִמְּךָ 'is it too slight a matter for you?' (Gesenius-Kautzsch, § 133c) compare המעט מכם 'is it too little for you?' (Is 7: 13). Just as דִּבֶּר 'to speak' often takes עִם 'with' to introduce the person addressed (Gn 31: 29), so the noun דָּבָר will sometimes have the same preposition before the person to whom the word is addressed. The expression לָאַט 'in gentleness' is used instead of לְאָט; the same meaning is found in 2 S 18: 5; Is 8: 6. An allusion to the mysterious word (4: 12) of which Eliphaz is but the echo. Ball mistakenly proposes to read לאט עמ'' in order to obtain as the 2nd hemistich: ודבר אל'' מעט ממך 'and is Eloah's word too little for thee?' There is no end to such fantasies.

12 G paraphrases יקחך by ἐτόλμησεν. Symm. and Theod. translate ἐπῆρέ σε (cf. Vulg. *te elevat*). The 2nd hemistich is paraphrased in Vulg. *et quasi magna cogitans attonitos habes oculos*. For ירזמון G ἐπήνεγκαν seems to read ירומון (adopted by Reiske, Hoffmann, Budde). But it is noticeable that Targ. and Syr. מרמזין recognise in רום the same verb as רמז.

The pronoun מָה is used in the sense of 'why?' (7: 21). The verb לקח implying 'to be unhinged by passion', 'to be carried away by passion beyond the bounds of good sense' (Pr 6: 25). 'Why is your heart enraged?', the heart being the seat of anger; cf. the Assyrian *libbâtu* 'fury'. Job is

13   When you turn against God your animosity,
      And allow such words to proceed from your mouth?
14   What is a man that he should be pure,
      And the child of a woman that he should be righteous?
15   If even His saints He does not trust,
      And if the heavens are not pure in His eyes,

being swept away by the disordered impulses of his heart, which of course are reflected in his eyes. The *hapax* ירזמון is preferable to the ירזמון of G, which falls in the category of stereotyped phrases. The verb רזם corresponds to the Aramaic רמז. We have here a case of metathesis similar to that which we noted (Comm. on 6: 17) in מזרב for מרזב (root זרב). Targ. and Syr. have made no mistake about it. The meaning of רמז in Aramaic, in Syriac, in New Hebrew, is 'to make signs'. In the case of the eyes, 'to blink', 'to wink'. As Driver remarks, the Aramaic רמז corresponds to the Greek διανεύω or νεύω. Now, we have in Sir 27: 22 διανεύων ὀφθαλμῷ, which was certainly based on an original רמז בעינו. Thus it becomes apparent that there is no reason to change ירזמון.

13 Vulg. *quid tumet contra Deum spiritus tuus?* makes of רוחך the subject of תשיב. G brings out clearly the meaning of רוחך: θυμόν. The suffix of פיך, omitted by G, is found in Sah., Jerome, Syro-hex. For מלין G ῥήματα τοιαῦτα, Vulg. *hujuscemodi sermones*.

The complement אל־אל 'to God' or 'against God' shows that one cannot give to השיב רוח the meaning of 'breathe' (9: 18). Ehrlich, on the pattern of Ec 12: 7, would interpret the 1st hemistich 'that you may give back your soul to God'. But the parallelism is then destroyed; the words which Job utters are not the last sighs of a dying soul, but manifestations of his state of mind. The word רוח 'breath', 'spirit' is sometimes used in the sense 'anger' (Jg

8: 3; Pr 16: 32), exactly like θυμός (cf. G) and *animus* 'animosity'. Hence we may translate: 'When you turn against God your animosity and allow such words to proceed from your mouth.' The words which are uttered by the mouth are contrasted with those which are drawn from the depths of the heart (8: 10). The man of the lips is the man of many words (11: 2). Duhm proposes מרי 'revolt' instead of מלין, but for no plausible motive and without any basis of support in the versions.

14 G τίς and Syr. ܡܢܘ read מי instead of מה. For יצדק, G ἐσόμενος δίκαιος, Vulg. *justus appareat*.

The strophe 14-16 repeats, with modifications of phrasing, the syllogism of Eliphaz, or rather of the mysterious being who appears to him in the vision of 4: 17-19. The opening מה־אנוש כי exactly reproduces 7: 17. The parallelism between זכה 'to be pure' and צדק 'to be righteous', between אנוש and ילוד אשה, will recur in 25: 4, which is based on this verse and on 9: 2. The formula ילוד אשה 'born of woman' is in apposition to אדם in 14: 1. Woman is the source of impurity (14: 4). The verb צדק 'to be righteous', but without any indication of the connection of this righteousness with God (4: 17; 9: 2b).

15 Symm. ἰδού and Vulg. *ecce* fail to recognise the subordination of v. 15 to v. 16. The suffix of קדשו, omitted by G, is restored in Sah. and Jerome (with asterisk). Symm. οὐδείς

16   How much less a being that is abominable and corrupt,
     Man, who drinks iniquity like water!
17   I will explain to you, listen!
     And what I have seen, I will tell,
18   What wise men declare,
     Hiding nothing, according to the tradition of their fathers,

ἄτρεπτος reads אמן instead of יאמין. At the close G (A) adds ἄστρα δὲ οὐκ ἄμεμπτα, which comes from 25: 5.

The 1st hemistich reproduces 4: 18a, but with בקדשו (read בִּקְדֹשָׁיו with qerê) 'in His saints' instead of בעבדיו 'in His servants'. The saints, like the servants, represent the angels (cf. 5: 1). The 2nd hemistich is repeated in 25: 5, but with 'the stars' instead of the heavens. Targ. identifies the heavens with 'the angels on high'. Rashi saw in the mention of the heavens an allusion to 'the host of heaven'. Duhm finds here an allusion to the inhabitants of the heavens. But Gray very aptly quotes Ex 24: 10, where the expression כעצם השמים לטהר 'like the very heaven for purity' proves that the heavens may here be taken as a symbol of perfect purity. Hence we leave to שָׁמַיִם its normal sense. For the verb זכך, instead of זכה of v. 14a, cf. 9: 30; 11: 4.

16 For אף כי, G ἔα δέ, but Symm. πόσῳ μᾶλλον (cf. Jerome quanto magis). The word אישׁ is connected with the 1st hemistich in Syr.

Here we have the conclusion of the argument a fortiori, exactly as in 4: 19, but with אף כִּי instead of אף. According to the phrasing of the preceding clause, אף כי means 'how much more' or 'how much less' (cf. 9: 14). The niph'al participle has sometimes the value of Latin participles in -andus, -endus, or of adjectives in -bilis (Gesenius-Kautzsch, § 116e). Hence for נתעב the meaning 'abominable' (Vulg. abominabilis): that which disgusts or horrifies one

(cf. the verb תעב in 9: 31). Apart from this verse, the niph'al נאלח 'to be corrupt' recurs only in Ps 14: 3; 53: 4, and always in a moral sense. The expression שתה כמים 'drink like water' will be repeated by Elihu (34: 7). Man commits evil (עַוְלָה 5: 16; 11: 14) with the same facility as he swallows a draught of water.

17 The versions are agreed in interpreting זה in the sense of the relative. Targ. maintains the copula of ואספרה.

Eliphaz is fond of arguing on the basis of his personal experience (4: 8, 12; 5: 3, etc.). The Aramaism חִוָּה (whence אַחֲוָה 'explanation', 13: 17) is characteristic of the Book of Job (32: 6, 10, 17; 36: 2). Outside this book, it is met with only in Daniel and Ps 19: 3; Sir 16: 25. The verb שׁמע, with לְ before the name of the person speaking, to mean 'listen' to some one (29: 21; 31: 35; 32: 10; 33: 31, 33). Use of the demonstrative זֶה in the sense of the relative (19: 19). The waw before אספרה is pleonastic, but it serves to connect the verb with the 1st hemistich. It may be retained, as it is by Targ. The pi'el of ספר as in 12: 8.

18 Vulg. omits אשר. G πατέρας αὐτῶν and Vulg. patres suos omit the preposition of מאבותם. The testimonies of Syr. are not in agreement about this preposition. It has a place in the Codex Ambrosianus (Ceriani). The two Targ. have it.

Like Bildad (8: 8), Eliphaz invokes tradition. Wise men do not possess their wisdom intrinsically; they hold

19   They to whom alone was given the land,
       And no stranger passed among them.

20   All the days of his life the wicked man is tormented,
       And throughout the years that are laid up for the tyrant

it from their fathers, and transmit it to their sons. Note the verb הגיד after the verb ספר and compare with 12:7-8. The words וְלֹא כִחֲדוּ 'and they do not hide' (cf. 6:10) strengthen יַגִּידוּ 'they declare'. In Is 3:9 we find the juxtaposition of לֹא כחדו and הגידו, which confirms the MT at this point, and does not allow us to make of אבותם the subject of כחדו (reading כחדום אבותם). This correction of Houbigant, which is accepted by Beer, has further against it Sir 8:9, where we are advised not to despise the teaching of the aged 'which they have heard from their fathers', מאבותם. It is clear that מֵאֲבוֹתָם refers to the teaching given by the wise and which comes 'from their fathers'. In v. 10 Eliphaz referred to old men more aged than Job's father.

19 Vulg. *quibus solis* makes a very effective link between vv. 18 and 19. The 1st hemistich, which exists in G, is omitted in Sah.

The relative אשר is understood at the opening: 'they to whom alone was given the land'. Compare ארץ נתנה in 9:24. The forefathers, guardians of pure tradition, are the first occupants of the land of Canaan. The author takes a strictly Israelite point of view. Doctrine could be preserved intact, so long as the nation lived without intermixture with foreign peoples. At that far-off time, 'no stranger passed among them'. The word זָר denotes one who is not an Israelite. The 2nd hemistich recalls Jl 4:17b, 'and Jerusalem shall be holy and strangers shall never again pass through it'. The prophet sees realised, on the day of Yahweh, what

the Book of Job implies had existed at the time of the settlement in the promised land.

20 Vulg. *cunctis diebus suis* reads ימיו and makes of רשע the subject of the sentence. For מתחולל, G ἐν φροντίδι (Jerome in *sollicitudine* becomes *in solitudine* in Bod. and Tur.), Aq. ἐν ὀδύνῃ, Targ. מתפס 'seized'. But Symm. ἀλαζονεύεται, Vulg. *superbit*, Syr. ܡܫܬܒܗܪ 'exalting himself', read מתהלל 'boasting', while Theod. ματαιοῦται reads מתהולל 'showing himself to be mad' (cf. 4:18). G ἔτη δὲ ἀριθμητὰ δεδομένα δυνάστῃ skilfully paraphrases the 2nd hemistich. For נצפנו, Symm. and Theod. κεκρυμμένος, Vulg. *incertus*, Targ. אתטישו 'are concealed', Syr. ܢܛܝܪ 'is kept'. 2nd Targ. sees here allusions to Esau and Ishmael.

Eliphaz expounds the theory of the ancients which coincides with his own and that of his friends, the theory, namely, that the wicked man meets his punishment on this earth. The wicked man, רָשָׁע, is in the main he who causes others to suffer (3:17). His parallel is the tyrant, עָרִיץ (6:23). The *hithpoʻlel* of חיל 'to tremble' (13:15) has the meaning of 'torment one's self'; Grotius interpreted מתחולל in the sense of the Greek ἑαυτοντιμωρούμενος. Compare the *hithpalpal* תתחלחל 'she shuddered' (Est 4:4). The literal translation 'all the days of the wicked man, he torments himself' offers no ambiguity. The meaning is obviously: 'All the days of his life, the wicked man is tormented.' Thus we enter straight into the heart of the subject. To change מתחולל into מתהולל 'shows himself mad' (Mar

21   Terrifying voices sound in his ears,
      In the midst of peace a brigand attacks him.

22   He does not expect to escape the dark,

golis, *ZATW*, **25**, 200; cf. Theod.
above) or into מתהלל 'boasts' (Beer;
cf. Symm., Vulg., Syr. above) is to
introduce into the context something
alien. It is not a question of describing the conduct of the wicked
man, for we know that he is foolish
and proud, but rather of showing
the torment to which he is a prey,
despite his apparent happiness. All
the rest of the passage is conceived
on these lines. Conscience is the
tormentor. The wicked have not a
day's peace. The versions regarded
the 2nd hemistich as being parallel,
word for word, with the 1st and they
interpreted it as a description of the
troubles of the tyrant, supposed to
be that his years are few, or that the
limit of his life is hidden from him.
But these truths are applicable to
all human beings whatsoever! Let
us note that מִסְפַּר שָׁנִים 'number of
years' does not mean 'fewness of
years' which would be expressed
rather by שְׁנֵי מספר or שְׁנוֹת מספר (cf.
16: 22; so Driver). Further, מספר
שנים corresponds to כָּל־יְמֵי and
עָרִיץ to רשע, so that the 2nd hemistich is only another way of expressing כל־ימי רשע 'all the days of
the wicked man'. If נצפן meant 'to
be hidden' we should have מִן before
the complement of the person (24:1).
On the contrary, צפן with לְ before the complement of the person
means 'to save, store up, reserve' for
some one (21: 19; Ps 31: 20; Ca.
7: 14, etc.). Hence the meaning is
the years which are reserved or saved
for the tyrant. Rashi discerned quite
rightly that it was necessary to
understand אשר before נִצְפָּנוּ. Thus,
'the number of years that are laid
up for the tyrant' is an exact parallel to 'all the days of the wicked

man'. The plural נצפנו because of the
collective 'number of years'. We do
not think it necessary to understand
הוא מתחולל after לעריץ. In fact,
the 2nd hemistich passes smoothly
into v. 21, the 1st hemistich of which
forms the reply of הוא מתחולל.

21   Targ. sees here the terrors 'in
Gehenna' (בגהנם) and contrasts the
fate of the righteous who are 'in
peace' (בשלום) with the lot of the
wicked. G omits קול and renders
פחדים by ὁ δὲ φόβος αὐτοῦ. For בשלום,
G ὅταν δοκῇ ἤδη εἰρηνεύειν, Vulg. *et
cum pax sit*. For שודד, G ἡ καταστροφή. The close is paraphrased in Vulg.
ille semper insidias suspicatur.
    The tyrant feels the pangs of re-
morse in his conscience. He is a prey
to imaginary terrors. The words
קוֹל־פְּחָדִים 'the voice of fears'
evoke the sounds which arouse fear,
the terrifying voices which buzz in
the ears of the guilty man. With
בְּאָזְנָיו cf. באזניכם in 13: 17. The expression בַּשָּׁלוֹם 'in peace', i.e. when
all is quiet, in the midst of peace! On
the word שׁוֹדֵד, cf. 12: 6. The verb
בוא with direct complement can
have the meaning of בוא על 'pounce
on', 'attack' (Gesenius-Kautzsch,
§ 118f). Compare תבאנו in 20: 22.
Just when peace everywhere prevails, the wicked man, victim of his
remorse, thinks that brigands are
about to attack him. In Pr 28: 1,
'The wicked flee when no one pursues.' Hitzig quotes Seneca (*Epist.*
XCVII, 14): *Hae malam mentem se-
cundae poenae premunt et sequuntur,
timere semper et expavescere, et se-
curitati diffidere.*

22   G μὴ πιστευέτω reads אֵל (v. 31)
instead of לא. Vulg. completes the

And he feels marked for the sword,

23   *He is thrown as food for the vulture,*
     He knows that his *misfortune* is imminent;

23   Point נֹדֵד הוּא לְלֶחֶם אַיֵּה, with G. — פִּידוֹ (cf. G); MT: בְּיָדוֹ.

1st hemistich by adding *ad lucem.*
For צפו, Symm. προεσκοπεύθη, Vulg.
circumspectans, Targ. אטימוס (=
ἕτοιμος), Syr. ﺳ 'he sees', recognise a derivative of צפה. G ἐντέ-
ταλται (A ἐντέτακται) connects with
צוה. G εἰς χεῖρας σιδήρου, for
אלי־חרב, is a reminiscence of
5:20. At the close, G (A) adds
καταπίπτει δὲ εἰς ἐξάληψιν, which recurs, preceded by obelus, in Syro-
hex. It is a distortion of v. 23a in G.

The reading אַל (G), instead of לֹא,
accepted by Merx, is an anticipation
of v. 31. The aim here is not to give
a warning to the wicked man but to
describe his states of mind. The
phrase לֹא יַאֲמִין 'he has no confidence' (v. 15, 4:18) or 'he does not
believe' (9:16), 'he does not expect'
(39:12). Same use of האמין in Ps
27:13, where the infinitive is preceded by ל''. The verb שׁוב, with מִן
before the misfortune that is
avoided, means not only 'return from'
but also 'escape from'; cf. the use
of the *hiph'il* in 33:30 and Ps 35:17.
Duhm gets rid of all difficulty by
replacing, without any support in
the versions, the phrase לא יאמין
שוב by לא יסור of v. 30 (!). Darkness
symbolises misfortune, in contrast to
light which represents happiness
(Ps 112:4, etc.). The 2nd hemistich
and v. 23a will give examples of the
misfortunes by which the wicked
man feels threatened. V. 23b returns
to the theme of the presentiments
which arise in his conscience. The
word צָפוּ has been changed into
צפון 'hidden', 'reserved' (cf. 20b) by
Ewald, Bickell, Perles, and others.
But it is wrong to base this correction

on G, which read a derivative of צוה
(cf. sup.). We can leave צָפוּ, passive
participle of צפה, which is well guaranteed by עָשׂוּ 'made' in 41:25. The
qerê צפוי restores the normal form.
The verb צפה 'see', 'observe', 'spy'
here denotes the result of the inspection, namely, choice. Ehrlich
very appropriately compares Est
2:9 הָרְאָיוֹת ל'' 'those who were
chosen, marked for,' from the verb
ראה 'to see'. Thus we obtain for the
2nd hemistich: 'and he feels marked
for the sword'. All that is the consequence of a conscience suffering the
pangs of remorse.

23   G κατατέτακται δὲ εἰς σῖτα γυψίν
vocalises אַיָּה (cf. 28:7), which is
preferable to אַיֵּה (cf. inf.) of the
MT and the other versions. Syr.
renders ללחם by ﺩﻭﺳﻌﺎ by
'to the threat of judgment'. G
connects יום חשך with v. 24 and
translates the 2nd hemistich οἶδεν δὲ
ἐν ἑαυτῷ ὅτι μένει εἰς πτῶμα (א πτῶ-
σιν), reading איד (18:12) or פיד
(31:29) instead of בידו (cf. inf.).

The 1st hemistich is usually interpreted: 'He wanders about for bread
where (he can find some)', and thus
the picture is evoked of the wicked
man reduced to mendicity, at least
in his imagination. But it is apparent
how awkward is the construction of
נדד 'flee', 'wander' with לְלֶחֶם 'for
bread'. Further, אַיֵּה 'where?' means
neither 'where he happens to be',
nor (as it is sometimes translated)
'hither and thither'. V. 22b alluded
to some form of violent death. The
wicked man feels destined to fall to

24   *The day of darkness terrifies him.*
     Distress and anguish assail him,
     Like a king quick to the attack!

23-24 Attach יוֹם־חֹשֶׁךְ to v. 24.
24 יְבַעֲתֻהוּ (G, Syr., Vulg.); MT: יְבַעֲתֻהוּ.

the power of the sword. V. 23a expresses a similar idea or some kind
of consequence. It is clear that G
εἰς σῖτα γυψίν has vocalised לְלֶחֶם אַיָּה
'as food for the vulture', the word
γύψ translating אַיָּה in 28: 7. This
reading (adopted by Merx, Duhm,
Beer) respects all the consonants of
the MT, whilst ללחם לאיה (Ball) or
לחם לאיה (Siegfried) makes a slight
modification. There remains the
word נדד, which it is proposed to
change into נֹעַד (from יעד) 'fixed',
'decreed' (Duhm, Beer), or to נֻתָּן
'handed over to' (Siegfried, Ball). If
we vocalise נֹדָד we obtain a *niph'al*
participle of ידד, a verb parallel to
ידה in the sense of 'throw'. Without
changing a single consonant of the
MT and taking G as our point of
departure, we shall translate the 1st
hemistich: 'He is thrown as food for
the vulture.' This is the consequence
of death by the sword. The corpse
remains exposed to the voracity of
birds of prey. The word אַיָּה denotes
a whole species of rapacious creatures mentioned among the unclean
animals (Lv 11: 14; Dt 14: 13). We
shall find that איה recurs in 28: 7 as
the name of a type of bird with
piercing glance. It is identified with
the Arabic *yâyâ* and *yûyû*, which is
the technical term for the goshawk.
But the onomatopoeic *yâyâ* well
suggests the cry of the vulture of
Palestine, when it swoops down with
fury on carrion. It would seem that
originally *yâyâ* and *ayâ* applied to
a whole category of vultures. It was
only later that these words were
reserved to denote the goshawk, a

sort of falcon. The 2nd hemistich has
been translated: 'and he sees the
evil day looming ahead' (Le Hir), 'he
knows that dark days are prepared
for him' (Renan), 'he knows that the
day of darkness awaits him' (Segond,
Crampon). But we have seen that
יוֹם־חֹשֶׁךְ was connected by G with
v. 24. Now, in Zeph 1: 15 the words
צַר וּמְצוּקָה of our v. 24 figure in the
formula יוֹם צָרָה וּמְצוּקָה as a parallel to יוֹם חֹשֶׁךְ וַאֲפֵלָה 'day of darkness and gloom'. It is clear, in the
light of this text and of G, that יוֹם
חֹשֶׁךְ supplies the parallel to צַר
וּמְצוּקָה of v. 24 and that the 2nd
hemistich stopped after בְּיָדוֹ. Moreover, there would be something
peculiar in saying that the day of
darkness is standing at his side or
that it is ready in his hand. The verb
יָדַע 'he knows' suggests that it is
still a question of the presentiments
of the guilty man. The word נָכוֹן
'ready' declares the imminence of a
misfortune. G εἰς πτῶμα suggests to
Beer לְאֵיד 'for misfortune' (cf. 18:
12) and to Ehrlich אֵידוֹ 'his misfortune'. The correct reading is that of
Wright, who, taking a hint from G
and keeping close to the MT, has
found פִּידוֹ (cf. 31: 29) concealed
beneath בְּיָדוֹ. The 2nd hemistich
thus becomes: 'he knows that misfortune is imminent'. The word פִּיד
has already figured in 12: 5. The
correction of Duhm, נֶכֶר 'misfortune' (31: 3) instead of נכון, loses
the support of G and introduces too
radical a change in the MT.

24 G ἡμέρα δὲ αὐτὸν σκοτινὴ στρο-

25   Because he stretched forth his hand against God,
     And hurled defiance at Shaddai;

βήσει maintains the correct text,
making of יוֹם־חֹשֶׁךְ in v. 23 the subject of יְבַעֲתֻהוּ (instead of the plural).
The 2nd hemistich is then ἀνάγκη δὲ
καὶ θλίψις αὐτὸν καθέξει, the words
צר וּמצוקה becoming the subject of
תתקפהו. Further, ὥσπερ στρατηγὸς
πρωτοστάτης πίπτων is a paraphrase
of 'like a king quick to attack'. Vulg.
and Syr. consider צר the subject of
יבעתהו (read in the singular, cf. G)
and מצוקה the subject of תתקפהו.
For לכידור (paraphrased in G),
Vulg. *ad proelium*. Syr. ܠܩܪܒܐ 'for
battle', Targ. לגלוגדקא 'for the
bier' (i.e. 'for death').
   As it stands, the verse would be
translated: 'Distress and anguish
terrify him, they assail him like a king
quick to the attack.' The verb בעת
as in 3:5; 7:14, etc. The word צר
'anguish' (7:11) and 'trouble' (36:16;
38:23) forms a phrase with מְצוּקָה 'anguish' (from צוק; cf. 32:18), exactly
as in Zeph 1:15. The verb תקף
'attack' (from Aramaic תקף, 'to be
strong') is used as in 14:20. On
עָתִיד 'ready', 'prompt', cf. 3:8. The
hapax כִּידוֹר (same form as קִיטוֹר
'smoke') is fixed by its use in post-
Biblical Hebrew (*Thesaurus* of Ben-
Yehuda, V, pp. 2339f.). The meaning
of 'attack', 'assault' is easily deduced
from the Arabic *kadara*, which, in
the 7th form, means 'swoop down'
on some one, like a bird on its prey;
cf. the Syriac ܟܘܕܪܐ 'vulture'. It
should be noted that 'like a king
quick to the attack' forms a complete hemistich. It consists of a
comparison illustrating the kind of
attack of which the wicked man is
the victim. The image appeared
extraordinary to Duhm and Ball,
who remove the hemistich as being
a gloss on v. 26 (Duhm) or v. 25
(Ball). But the presence of the *hapax*

כידור and of the word עתיד (3:8)
guarantees authenticity. We ought
not to restrict the ancients to the
limits of modern taste. In 41:14, for
instance, it will be said of the crocodile that 'terror leaps before him'.
We have seen (v. 23) that the words
יום חשך overloaded the end of v.
23b. G preserves the original distribution and makes of יום חשך the
subject of יְבָעֲתֻהוּ (in the singular; cf.
Syr. and Vulg.), with the result that
the 1st hemistich emerges as: 'the
day of darkness terrifies him'. The
2nd hemistich is then: 'distress and
anguish assail him'; the agreement
is with the nearest noun (König,
Syntax, § 349t). There is parallelism
between יום־חשך and צר ומצוקה suggested by Zeph 1:15. The day of
darkness is the day of the great,
final catastrophe, of general upheav-
al, the prospect of which troubles
the wicked man (cf. Am 5:18-20;
Jl 2:2; Zeph 1:15). We have had
darkness as synonymous with misfortune in v. 22a. Thus then v. 24
contains three hemistichs, the structure and composition of the whole
being excellently preserved in G. It
is the end of the description of the
dark fancies which haunt the mind
of the wicked man.

25   For יתגבר, G ἐτραχηλίασεν, Jerome *contumax fuit*, Vulg. *roboratus
est.*
   V. 25 gives the reasons for which
the wicked man is tortured by remorse. They are to be summed up
in the fact that he has rebelled
against God. Vv. 25-8 are eliminated
by Siegfried, Beer, Duhm, on the
ground that they separate v. 24
from its immediate context, which
is said to be v. 29. Duhm, however,
rescues v. 28c, which he transforms
to suit the needs of the cause he

26   He ran against Him with neck outstretched,
      With the mass of his thick-bossed bucklers!

espouses (cf. inf.). He thinks that the
description contained in vv. 25-28b
could only be suitable in connection
with a popular leader, such as
Jason and his successors, Aristo-
bulus, Alexander Jannaeus. It would
be out of place in reference to a
private individual. But Duhm forgets that the theme of discussion is
the wicked man in general, and especially the tyrant (v. 20). It is a
question of the adversary of God,
one of those violent men who count
only on the strength of their arms
(12:6). Job himself will depict the
'wicked' in the attitude they assume
in face of God (21:7, 14-15). The
expression נטה יד 'stretch forth the
hand', with the intention of striking
some one, generally takes על before
the name of the person aimed at.
But the prepositions על and אל are
easily interchangeable in poetry (cf.
v. 26 and 1:11). The *hithpaʻel* of גבר
means 'to behave like a champion'
(Is 42:13) or again, 'to play the
hero' (Sir 31:25). It is the latter
sense which is suggested here by
the context. In 36:9 it will mean
simply 'to become proud'.

26 Vv. 26b-27, absent from Sah.,
marked by asterisk in Jerome and
Colb., did not exist from G. The present text comes from Theod. (cf.
Colb.). Syro-hex. has forgotten the
asterisk. For בצואר G ὕβρει and
Targ. בתוקפא 'with might', according to the sense. Double translation in Syr. 'with neck high' (Vulg.
erecto collo) and 'with the nape of his
neck'. Syro-hex. cites the hexaplar
reading (Aq., Symm., Theod.) τρα-
χήλῳ which reproduces the MT. For
the 2nd hemistich, Theod. (in G)
ἐν πάχει νώτου ἀσπίδος αὐτοῦ (Jerome
in crassa cervice scuti sui); cf. Vulg.
et pingui cervice armatus est. The
words גבי מגניו are rendered αὐχένων

θυρεῶν αὐτοῦ in Aq. (Field, *Auctarium*, p. 7) cited by Syro-hex. In
Targ. the 2nd hemistich is interpreted as 'by the hardness of his
raised bucklers'; in Syr. 'by the
multitude of his serried rows of
bucklers'.

V. 26 continues the description of
the wicked man who rebels against
God: 'He hurled himself against
Him, with neck outstretched.' Use
of אל instead of על, as in v. 25. The
expression בְּצַוָּאר 'with the neck'
recurs in Ps 75:6, to describe the
attitude of one who raises or stretches his neck in the tension of a
great effort. Strength resides in the
neck (41:14) and the nape; cf.
L'Emploi métaphorique, p. 36, n. 1
and p. 93. It is unnecessary to change
בצואר into כגבור (Graetz) in order
to make of our 1st hemistich a mere
doublet of 16:14b. Ehrlich removes
all the forcefulness of the image by
reducing בצואר to כצר 'as against
an enemy'. The 2nd hemistich pictures the assailant at the head of an
army manoeuvring in the manner
of the ancient Romans when they
joined their bucklers to form a
testudo (cf. Hitzig). Thus the word
עָבִי will mean not so much the
thickness of each separate buckler
as the compact mass obtained by the
assembling of them. Note that in
41:7 the back of the crocodile is
compared to rows of bucklers. The
word גַּב 'back' originally means the
boss. It is in this sense that it is
used here. In Assyrian the root גבב
supplies *gababu* and *kababu* 'buckler'.
It is apparent that 'the boss of the
buckler' is a technical term which
denotes a buckler of bulging shape,
the thick embossment of which forms
a hump, in fact a buckler such as
was known to the Babylonian or
Assyrian soldiers (cf. Meissner, *Ba-*

27 Because his face was hidden in fat,
    His loins had become big with fat,
28 And he dwelt in destroyed cities,
    In houses no longer inhabited,
    Because they threaten to fall in ruins.

bylonien und Assyrien, I, pp. 96f.).
Thus we may translate 'with the
mass of his thick-bossed bucklers'.
Despite the subtlety of this interpretation, it is preferable to reconstituting too short a line בכובע ומגן
'with helmet and buckler' (Beer,
following Ezk 27: 10; 38: 5), or to an
improvisation such as 'with a warrior's helmet and buckler' (Ball), or
to declaring that the text is irretrievably corrupt (Ehrlich).

27 The text of G comes from
Theod. (cf. v. 26). Vulg. reads חלבו
instead of בחלבו, whence *operuit
faciem ejus crassitudo*. Very curious
is the reading of Syr., whose translation is based on כימה instead of
פימה and כסיל instead of סכל,
which has the effect of bringing in
the constellations of 9: 9, 'and he
has made the Pleiades on Orion'.
Vulg. paraphrases the 2nd hemistich: *et de lateribus ejus arvina de-
pendet*.

Here the author evokes a picture
of the godless man as a bloated
egoist who in his greed puts on
fat. It matters little to him that he
enjoys his prosperity at the cost of
devastating and making barren the
areas around him (v. 28) so long as
he can fatten himself like a pasha. A
whole category of extortioners or
tyrants is characterised by sleekness
and stoutness (Jer 5: 28; Ps 73: 7).
Fat obstructs the heart, i.e. the intelligence (Ps 119: 70). It is when
Israel becomes fat and sleek that it
abandons its God (Dt 32: 15). The
literal translation of the 1st hemistich is: 'for he has hidden his
face in his fat'. The use of עשׂה 'make'
is as in 14: 9, where the tree grows a
branch. The *hapax* פִּימָה is to be

explained by the Arabic *fa'ima* 'to
be fat', in reference to the camel's
neck. The word כֶּסֶל denotes the
lumbar region as the fleshy part
(*L'Emploi métaphorique*, pp. 132f.).
On the root כסל cf. 9: 9.

28 G regards ישכון as an optative
αὐλισθείη and introduces εἰσέλθοι before בתים. Syr. omits בתים. For לא
ישבו למו, G ἀοικήτους, Vulg. *desertis*.
The 3rd hemistich is thus translated
in G: ἃ δὲ ἐκεῖνοι ἡτοίμασιν, ἄλλοι
ἀποίσονται. Houbigant sees in this
translation a reading לזרים instead
of לגלים. Syr. ܠܡܙܒܠ is a corruption
of ܠܓܙܒܠ (which translated לגלים).

The tyrant has ravaged and reduced to barrenness the regions around
him in order that he may settle in the
room of others: 'and he dwelt in
destroyed cities'. The verb שׁכן with
the accusative (cf. 4: 19). On the
niph'al of כחד cf. 4: 7. We meet
here the words which are normal
with Eliphaz. The 2nd hemistich,
'houses no longer inhabited', shows
that the characteristic of the wicked
is to settle themselves in dwellings
which have been abandoned by their
owners (cf. Hab 1: 6b). The plural
יֵשְׁבוּ implies as subject היושבים
(understood) and thus serves to
render the indefinite 'one' (cf. 4: 19;
7: 3). The dative reflexive למו
(5: 27; 13: 1) can be very properly
used after the verb ישב (Gn 21: 16;
22: 5). It is unnecessary to change
into לעד 'for ever' or into לעולם
'for always' (contra Beer). The verb
עתד whence עתיד (v. 24; 3: 8) is
found only once in the *pi'el* 'prepare' (Pr 24: 27) and once in the
hithpa'el 'get ready', 'be ready'

29   He will not grow rich and his fortune will not last,
      Neither will *his shadow* lengthen itself on the ground,

29 צַלְמוֹ (cf. G); MT: מנלם.

(here). The plural of גַּל 'heap' (8: 17) suggests heaps of ruins. Cf. the use of לְגַלִּים in Jer 9: 10, 51: 37. The relative אֲשֶׁר plays the part of the conjunction כִּי 'because'. It is because the houses are on the point of falling down that they are inhabited no longer. In the midst of this solitude lives the wicked man spreading terror around him; cf. 24: 18. Duhm, who wishes to connect v. 28c with v. 29a, is obliged to change לגלים into אחרים ישאו and to read: הִתְעַתָּד 'what he has prepared for himself, others carry off!' He bases himself on G, which anticipates the punishment of the evildoer. One wonders how the easily intelligible text אחרים ישאו could have become לגלים. Besides, in that case an active sense has to be attributed to the hithpa'el.

29 G βάλη, Vulg. *mittet*, and Syr. ܢܫܕܐ vocalise יַטֶּה (hiph'il) instead of יֵטֶּה (qal). For מנלם (Targ. מנהון 'from among them'), G σκιάν, Vulg. *radicem suam*, Syr. ܡܠܐ 'words'.

   We return here to the theme of the punishment of the wicked which was first described as the torments of remorse (20-4). The 1st hemistich, 'he will not grow rich and his fortune will not last', envisages two possibilities: either the wicked man will not acquire wealth, or, if he does become rich, his fortune will be of short duration. The verb עשר 'to gain wealth' as in Hos 12: 9 and Sir 3: 17. Elsewhere it is the hiph'il which is used in the sense of 'become rich'. The verb קום 'to stand', with the connotation 'resist', 'hold' (cf. 8: 15) whence is deduced the

meaning 'to last'. The use of חַיִל 'fortune' is as in 5: 5c. In the 2nd hemistich, the *hapax* מנלם constitutes an almost insoluble difficulty. It is interpreted as 'his possessions' (Le Hir, Renan, etc.), as though it could be split up into מן לם 'what is theirs' (cf. Targ.), either by assuming a root נלה corresponding to כלה (Qimchi) or a root נאל as an equivalent of the Arabic *nâl* 'gift', 'present', etc. In any case the form is difficult, and various corrections have been suggested. Most modern exegetes vocalise יַטֶּה in the hiph'il (cf. G, Vulg., Syr.) and make of מנלם the complement of the verb. Then a word adapted to the context is sought: אצלים 'roots' (Wellhausen, cf. Vulg.), מלילם 'their ear of corn' (Hitzig), ממלם 'their fullness' (Böttcher), שבלים 'ears of corn' (Dillmann), etc. Let us note that the expression: 'it is not stretched out on the ground' suggests the idea of a tree which stretches out its branches or of shadows which are lengthened on the ground. In Ps 80: 9-11 we have the description of a vine tree which fills the earth and covers the mountains with its shade. This vine is later consumed by fire (v. 17). We shall have, in v. 30b, the picture of the flame devouring the sprouting shoots of the evildoer, who is likened to a tree (vv. 30b-33). Our 2nd hemistich anticipates this comparison. We are given the clue by G σκιάν. Instead of reading צְלָם 'their shadow' (Graetz) which introduces the plural suffix, we propose צַלְמוֹ which takes account of the *mêm*. The word צֵלֶם retains its etymological sense of 'shadow' (cf. צלמות 3: 5, etc.). Compare the use

30   [   ] A flame will parch his shoots
      And his *blossom* will be *swept away* by the wind.

30 Omit לא…חשך, a variant of v. 22a. — ויסער…פרחו (cf. G); MT: ויסור…פיו.

of the word צֵל 'shadow' with נטה (2 K 20: 10; Ps 109: 23). The formula לָאָרֶץ as in 2: 13.

30 From יונקתו, G τὸν βλαστὸν αὐτοῦ μαράναι ἄνεμος ἐκπέσοι δὲ αὐτοῦ τὸ ἄνθος: omission of שַׁלְהֶבֶת and reading of פִּרְחֹו (cf. inf.) instead of פיו. Targ. adds דאלהא 'of God' after פיו.

We have seen that the comparison with the tree began with v. 29b (following G). It continues in v. 30b. In 8: 16-18 the evildoer was likened to a tree. The author spoke of יונקתו (8: 16) 'his shoots'. The word recurs in 14: 7c, where it is a question of the tree, literally. Our description is interrupted by 30a, 'he does not escape from the darkness', which is simply a paraphrase of v. 22a. After saying that his shadow is not lengthened on the ground, because the tree is checked in its growth, the poet adds: 'a flame will parch his shoots'. The word שַׁלְהֶבֶת, a development of לְהַב (39: 23; 41: 13), recurs only in Ezk 21: 3, where it refers to fire in a forest; in Sir 51: 3, where it is a question of the torments of the unhappy; and in Ca 8: 6, where we should read שלהבת יה 'a flame of Jah', which symbolises the fires of love. The 3rd hemistich has been translated (in accordance with Targ. and Rashi): 'and he perishes by the blast of God' (Le Hir), 'he will disappear at the breath of God's mouth' (Renan), 'and God will slay him by the breath of His mouth' (Segond, Crampon). But it should be observed that יסור which occurs in the 1st hemistich has rather the meaning of 'depart', 'be removed' than vanish or perish. Furthermore, the breath of the mouth of God is

somewhat unexpected, as God has not been mentioned since v. 27; and, again, the breath of His mouth is His word, and not His anger, which is symbolised by the breath of His nostrils (4: 9). The reading of G, which continues the comparison with the tree, preserves the original text. In accordance with Is 5: 24; 18: 5, where ἄνθος corresponds to פֶּרַח 'flower', 'blossom', it becomes apparent that αὐτοῦ τὸ ἄνθος presupposes פִּרְחֹו instead of פיו. This correction, suggested by Beer in the Kittel edition, is preferable to צִיצֹו 'his flower' (Bickell), צִיץ (Siegfried), נצתו (Merx), all of which deviate from the MT. It is supported by G, which is by no means the case for פריו 'his fruit' (Reiske, Graetz, Duhm, etc.). G ἐκπέσοι is a vague term which does not translate יסור, but is inspired by v. 33b. In Hos 13: 3 we have the phrase כמץ יסער מגרן 'like the chaff that swirls from the threshing floor' (cf. van Hoonacker), the *po'el* יְסֹעֵר being a mistake for the *po'al* יְסֹעַ. It is this *po'al* which has given rise to the banal יסור. We read ויסער, a conjecture of Perles which has been taken up by Beer and Budde (who read the *niph'al*) and by Duhm (who well reads the *po'al*). The 3rd hemistich offers a completely satisfactory meaning: 'and his blossom will be swept away by the wind'. Cf. Is 40: 24, 'Scarcely are they planted, scarcely sown, scarcely has their stem taken root in the earth, when He blows upon them and they wither, and the tempest (סערה) carries them off like stubble' (cf. Condamin). We shall have the *pi'el* of שער (for סער) in 27: 21.

31 Let him not trust in his *stature*!
We know that it is vanity:

31 בְּשִׂיאוֹ; MT: בשו (qerê בַּשָּׁוְא). — גָדַע; MT: נתעה.

31 G μὴ πιστευέτω ὅτι ὑπομενεῖ is a paraphrase rather than a translation of the 1st hemistich. Vulg. *non credet frustra errore deceptus* reads the *qerê* בַּשָּׁוְא (instead of the *kethîb* בשו). Similarly Syr. 'and he believes not in the lie which leads astray' and Targ. 'he believes not in a son of man who errs in falsehood'. The 2nd hemistich is closely joined to the 1st by Vulg. *quod aliquo pretio redimendus sit* (paraphrase). Targ. translates תמורתו by פרוגיה 'his exchange', but Syr. ܡܰܘܥܺܝܬܶܗ 'his shoot', 'his growth'. G κενὰ γὰρ ἀποβήσεται αὐτῷ, (32) ἡ τομὴ αὐτοῦ stops v. 31 at תהיה and connects with v. 32 the following word. It has been generally thought that ἡ τομὴ αὐτοῦ (v. 32) represented תְּמוֹרָתוֹ 'his palm' (Houbigant, Reiske, Beer, Budde) coming from v. 30, or that it was a translation of גִּזְעוֹ 'his trunk' (Merx, Bickell, Duhm), which was supposed to have disappeared from the text. But in Ca 2:12, the word τομή translates זמיר. The word which G read is indisputably זְמוֹרָתוֹ 'his vine shoots' (cf. v. 32).

Perles has very justly observed that the letter א of תמלא in v. 32 (where we should certainly read תִּמָּל; cf. Comm.) figures originally in בשו which the *qerê* reads בַּשָּׁוְא. None the less, the 1st hemistich remains odd, especially because of the juxtaposition of נִתְעָה with 'let him not trust in lies!', and because of the repetition of שו in the 2nd hemistich. The difficulties offered by the present text may be measured from a comparison of the various translations: 'Let him not trust in the lie,

he will be caught by it. The lie will be his recompense' (Le Hir); 'Let him not hope for anything from evil.... The fool! Evil will be his recompense' (Renan); 'Let him not trust in evil; it is illusory; he will reap only evil from it' (Loisy); 'Let him hope for nothing from deceit! He is on the wrong track. Deception will be his reward' (*Bible du rabbinat français*); etc. Modern exegetes have changed the words נתעה בשו into בש ונתעה 'he is confounded and bewildered' (Merx); בבשת ונתעבה 'in shame and abomination' (Siegfried); בשוב בעשרתו 'in his wealth' (Beer); נטעה 'in the return of his plant' (Herz, *ZATW*, **20**, p. 162; Beer reads נטעו in the Kittel edition). Duhm retains the text, but sees in v. 31 a marginal reflection elucidating v. 35. One first fact to notice is that the word תמורתו, originally זְמוֹרָתוֹ, did not belong to v. 31 but began v. 32, as is evidenced by G. It is the parallel word to כפתו of v. 32b. Further, comparing with 20:6a, it seems to us undeniable that בשא of the 1st hemistich disguises בְּשִׂיאוֹ: 'let him not trust in his stature!' On the word שִׂיא cf. Comm. on 20:6. Instead of נתעה, which makes no sense, we read simply גָדַע, which enables us to translate the 2nd hemistich: 'We know that it is vanity!' The word שָׁוְא (7:3) has the same meaning as הֶבֶל (7:16), and thus the remark of Eliphaz belongs to the predominant theme of Ec (1:14; 2:1, 15, 19, etc.). The transformation of גדע into נתעה may be explained as an error of audition, the ה of the end having been at first a *mater lectionis*.

32 His *vine shoot* will be *withered* before its day,
    And his branch will not grow green again;
33 Like the vine, he will let fall his sour grapes,
    And like the olive tree, he will cast off his blossom!
34 For the company of the godless is barren,
    And fire devours the tents of bribery!

32 זְמוֹרָתוֹ (G); MT (in v. 31): תמורתו. — תְּמָל (G, Vulg. Syr.); MT תמלא.

32 G ἡ τομὴ αὐτοῦ preserves the original text, which was זְמוֹרָתוֹ 'his vine shoot' (Herz, *ZATW*, **20**, p. 162). It is the parallel word to כפתו (cf. v. 31). Targ. reads תְּמֻלָא with the MT, which obliges it to add 'his tomb' as subject. But G φθαρήσεται, Vulg. *peribit*, Syr. ‏ܬܡܠ‎ 'withers' certainly read תְּמָל. Vulg. *manus ejus* connects כפתו with כַּף 'hand'. For רעננה, G πυκάσῃ, whence Jerome *virebit*, which becomes *videbit* (Bod.) and *videbitur* (Tur.).

We have seen that v. 31 had been overloaded by תמורתו, a transformation of זְמוֹרָתוֹ which is part of our 1st hemistich (G): 'His vine shoot will be withered before its day.' A mere glance at the use of יִמָּל (14: 2; 18: 16; 24: 24) abundantly proves that the original text had תְּמָל (G, Syr., Vulg.), which became תמלא through the accidental transposition of the א of בשיאו (later becoming בשוא) in v. 31 (cf. Comm.). The expression בְּלֹא־יוֹמוֹ 'not in its day' corresponds to the Assyrian *ina lâ ûmi-šu* which conveys the idea of a premature death. Compare ולא עת 'and not in the time' (22: 16), בלא עתך 'not in your time' (Ec 7: 17), בל עתי 'not in my time' (Phoenician, *CIS*, I, 3, l. 3). The word כִּפָּה 'branch' is the equivalent of the Assyrian *kippatu* which denotes in particular the branch of the palm tree (cf. Is 9: 13; 19: 15). We find only here the *pa'lel* רענן 'grow green again', but the adjective רַעֲנָן 'green' is very much used.

33 The 1st hemistich is paraphrased in G τρυγηθείη δέ ὡς ὄμφαξ πρὸ ὥρας, and Vulg. *laedetur quasi vinea in primo flore botrus ejus*. G reverses זית and נצתו: ἐκπέσοι δὲ ὡς ἄνθος ἐλαίας.

The evildoer has been compared to a tree which withers (v. 32). Here he is likened to the vine tree which lets fall its unripe grapes and to the olive tree which casts off its blossom. The verb חמס 'to use violence' also means to violate nature, and, in regard to a plant, to cast off its fruits before their ripening. The parallelism with יַשְׁלֵךְ leaves no doubt that this is the correct meaning. The word בֹּסֶר denotes the grape which is in the process of ripening (Is 18: 5), the as yet unripe grapes of proverbial fame: 'the fathers have eaten sour grapes and the children's teeth are set on edge' (Jer 31: 29; Ezk 18: 2). The form *bisrô* is an attenuation of *busrô*. Poetic use of the jussive וְיַשְׁלֵךְ instead of the imperfect (13: 27a). Cf. the use of וישלך in 27: 22. The נִצָּה is generally the flower or blossom of the vine (Gn 40: 10; Is 18: 5); the plural is used for every kind of flower in Ca 2: 12. The evildoer is like the vine which can produce sour grapes but does not give them time to ripen, or like the olive tree which bears blossom without yielding any fruit.

34 G μαρτύριον connects עדת with

35   They conceive trouble and bring forth iniquity,
      But the belly prepares deceit!

עֵד 'witness'. For חנף, Syr. ܣܗܕܐ, G
ἀσεβοῦς, Aq. and Theod. ὑποκριτοῦ,
Vulg. *hypocritae*, Targ. דילטור (cf.
8: 13; 13: 16). G θάνατος seems to
replace גלמוד by כל מות. For שֹׁחַד,
G δωροδεκτῶν, Jerome *eorum qui
munera accipiunt* (Vulg. *eorum qui
munera libenter accipiunt*).

Vv. 34-5 form the conclusion of all
that tradition reports on the subject
of the fate of the wicked (vv. 20ff.).
The words עֲדַת חָנֵף denote 'the
company of the godless'. Compare
עדת מרעים 'the band of evildoers'
(Ps 22: 17) and עדת עריצים 'the
band of tyrants' (Ps 86: 14). When
the complement is a proper name or,
as here, a singular noun, the expression refers to the clique or
faction whom a leader has in tow.
Thus 'the company of Korah' (Nu
16: 5f; 11, etc.) or of Abiram (Ps
106: 17). On the word חנף cf. 8: 13,
where it is a question of the fate of
the evildoer. The noun גַּלְמוּד means
'sterile thing' (3: 7). The comparison
with vegetable species which cannot
reach maturity in itself foreshadowed
that barrenness would be the punishment overtaking the wicked.
What is implied is not merely lack
of offspring, but also in general
privation of the goods of this earth.
The 2nd hemistich points to divine
intervention: 'and a fire devours the
tents of bribery'. We have seen fire
consume the shoots in v. 30. It is
the fire of God which 'devoured' the
sheep and the servants of Job
(1: 16). On the meaning of אכל cf.
Comm. on 1: 16. We find the same
formula in 20: 26 and 22: 20. The
שֹׁחַד is the backshish so common in
oriental countries and their courts;
cf. Comm. on 6: 22, where the related
verb occurs. The tents where cor-
rupting gifts are received are indeed
'tents of backshish, of venality'. The

tent of course is a synonym of dwelling place (5: 24). Cf. the 'tent of the
wicked' which vanishes (8: 22). The
Prophets denounce the venality of
functionaries and judges who allow
themselves to be influenced by שֹׁחַד
(Is 1: 23; Mic 3: 11). The willingness to accept gifts of this kind is one
of the well known features of the
evildoer (Ps 26: 10).

35   Targ. and Syr. render הרה and
ילד by verbs in the plural. Vulg.
*concepit dolorem et peperit iniqui-
tatem* exactly as in Ps 7: 15b. G
renders הרה עמל by ἐν γαστρὶ δὲ
λήμψεται ὀδύνας and וילד און by
ἀποβήσεται δὲ αὐτῷ κενά, which is no
longer a translation but an interpretation of v. 31b, where G has
κενὰ γὰρ ἀποβήσεται αὐτῷ. For ובטנם,
G ἡ δὲ κοιλία αὐτοῦ, Vulg. *et uterus
ejus*, Targ. ורעיוני כרסהון 'and the
thoughts of their belly'. Instead of
תכין, G ὑποίσει read תכיל (Perles).

Eliphaz returns to his favourite
idea: it is man himself who is the
author of his own misfortune through
his sin. In 4: 8 he said: 'They who
cultivate iniquity and sow trouble
also reap them.' We had the words
עָמָל and אָוֶן as here. The metaphors
of tilling and sowing are found again
with the same implication in Hos
10: 12, 13; Pr 14: 22. Yet another
metaphor, but still with the same
words עמל and און, appeared in
5: 6-7, 'For evil does not spring up
from the soil, and trouble does not
grow out of the ground, but it is man
himself who engenders trouble, as
the sons of the lightning soar aloft
in their flight.' We have indicated
here the two phases in the emergence of evil: its conception and its
bringing forth. Cf. the relation between הרה and ילד in 3: 3. Infini-
tives are used in order to lend greater
vividness to the description, as in

Latin the historic infinitive (Hos 4: 2, etc.; cited in Gesenius-Kautzsch, § 113ff.). Cf. Is 59: 4, הרו עמל הוליד און 'they conceive evil and bring forth iniquity' (where the verbs are in the infinitive as in our text). It is obvious that בִּטְנָם 'their belly' denotes the womb which conceives and brings to birth (3: 10). The 2nd hemistich is parallel to the 1st. We can leave תָּכִין 'prepares' (38: 41), for it is an allusion to the process of formation in the womb. The reading תכיל 'contains' (following G) would be quite attractive if הכיל meant 'bear in the womb'. The word מִרְמָה is parallel to שׁוֹא 'lie' in 31: 5. We have seen that שׁוֹא also meant deceit (7: 3). It is in a similar sense that מרמה is used here. It is a question of self-deceit. Thus we shall interpret the word שֶׁקֶר 'lie' in Ps

7: 15, a passage absolutely parallel with our v. 35 and where we have the words און, עמל, שקר (instead of מרמה): 'Behold he is in travail with iniquity, he has conceived trouble, and brought forth falsehood.' The rest of the description shows the evildoer himself falling into the pit which he had prepared, receiving on his own head the blows which he had destined for others. Thus it turned out to be a piece of self-deception which he had been hatching in his breast and had brought to the light of day. It becomes apparent to what a large extent the friends of Job borrow sometimes from the Prophets, sometimes from the Psalms, in order to substantiate their arguments and give colour to their images. And Job will reply, as always, that there is nothing new here, that these are hackneyed themes (16: 2-3).

CHAPTER 16

1   Then Job spoke and said:
2   I have heard many such things!
        Miserable comforters are you all!
3   Will there be an end to words of wind?
        Or what agitates you that you make reply?

Chapters 16-17   Fifth speech of Job: see Introduction, pp. xliif.

16: **2** For כאלה רבות, G τοιαῦτα πολλά, Vulg. *frequenter talia*. Symm. renders מנחמי עמל by παρηγοροῦντες ἐπαχθεῖς; cf. Vulg. *consolatores onerosi*.

Once again Job stresses the banality of the theories put forward by his friends (12: 3, 9). The expression כָּאֵלֶּה, as we had כמו־אלה (12: 3), כל 'all (that)' (13: 1), in allusion to the preceding speeches. With כאלה רַבּוֹת compare כָּהֵנָּה רַבּוֹת 'many such things' (23: 14). The adjective רַב is found in the masculine plural רַבִּים 'numerous' (4: 3; 11: 19), and in the feminine plural רַבּוֹת 'many things', 'much' (23: 14; Is 42: 20). The 2nd hemistich 'miserable comforters are you all', literally 'comforters of trouble'; cf. עָמָל in 3: 10, etc. Eliphaz had spoken about divine consolations (15: 11). It was to comfort that his friends had come (2: 11). Already in 13: 4 Job has reproached them: 'you are fabricators of lies, worthless quacks, all of you!', with the same ending: כֻּלְּכֶם. In v. 3 Job will criticise directly the last speaker, i.e. Eliphaz.

3 The 2nd hemistich, absent from Sah., marked with asterisk in Jerome and Syro-hex., did not exist in G. The present text comes from Theod. (cf. Colb.). Syr. quite transforms the verse: 'Do not distress my mind by words, and if you speak, I shall not answer' (?). For או ימריצך, Vulg. *aut aliquid tibi molestum est*, Targ. או מה יבסמנך 'or what amuses you?' (reading ימליצך; cf. 6: 25).

'Will there be an end to words of wind?' recalls the invective of Bildad: 'How long will you articulate such opinions, and the words of your mouth be a great wind?' (8: 2). The word קֵץ 'end', which we have seen used in the sense of the span of life that still remains (6: 11), here retains its normal sense (22: 5; 28: 3). The phrase 'words of wind' is deliberately chosen, for Eliphaz has just blamed Job for replying with windy knowledge and filling his belly with east wind (15: 2). The 2nd hemistich is no less vehement: 'or what agitates you that you make reply?' The *hiph'il* of מרץ does not occur elsewhere. On the meaning of 'make ill', cf. Comm. on 6: 25. The itch to speak which tortures Eliphaz amounts to a real mental sickness. Transition from the 2nd person plural to the 2nd person singular is as in 21: 3. Job is now addressing the last speaker.

4   I also could speak as you do,
      If your soul were where my soul is:
      I would *multiply* words at your expense,
      And wag my head over you!

4 אַכְבִּירָה‎; MT: אחבירה‎.

4 Symm. εἴθε ὑμεῖς τοῖς ἐμοῖς ὑπέκεισθε πάθεσιν paraphrases the 2nd hemistich, which is faithfully rendered by the other versions. For אחבירה‎, Targ. אחבר‎. G ἐναλοῦμαι does not come from ארחיבה‎ (Lagarde, Merx), for the verb ἐνάλλεσθαι, which occurs only in Job, never translates הרחיב‎ (cf. 6:27; 16:11; 19:5). We have here an approximate translation, like the Vulg. *consolarer* or Syr. ܟܡܐܠ 'I would examine'.

The opening: גַּם אָנֹכִי‎ 'I also' as in the previous speeches of Job: גַּם־אֲנִי‎ (7:11; 13:2), גַּם־לִי‎ (12:3). The expression כָּכֶם‎ 'like you', instead of the כמוכם‎ of 12:3. The presence of לוּ‎ before the subordinate clause allows us to give to the cohortatives אֲדַבְּרָה‎, אַחְבִּירָה‎, אָנִיעָה‎ the meaning of the conditional. The conjunctive לוּ‎ 'if' (6:2), which is used to indicate the optative, introduces a condition that is incapable of fulfilment (Gesenius-Kautzsch, § 159l); cf. 6:2. Of course 'your soul' and 'my soul' simply mean 'you' and 'I' (cf. Comm. on 14:22). The same use of לוּ יֵשׁ‎ is found in Nu 22:29. Generally אחבירה‎ is connected with חבר‎ 'bind', so as to see here a reference to the continuity of words in logical discourse, whence the translations: 'I would set forth speeches against you' (Le Hir), 'I would arrange words against you' (Renan). Barth proposes to see here the Arabic root خبر, which, in the 2nd form, means 'adorn', 'brighten up', whence the interpretation: 'I would utter some fine phrases about you.' But the idea of creating beautiful language occurs in Arabic only when it is a question of writing poetry. As Gray points out, this is a late expression, a rather subtle and arbitary development of the original meaning. Ehrlich proposes the root خبر, which in the 2nd and 4th forms means: 'to give news, information'. The construction of the sentence as a whole (especially because of עֲלֵיכֶם‎) does not allow us to make use of this interpretation, which, in itself, would be quite attractive. Let us note that the 3rd and 4th hemistichs are strictly parallel. The verbs אחבירה‎ and אניעה‎ are parallel to each other; then we have the two occurrences of עליכם‎ 'over you' or 'about you', and finally the complements בְּמִלִּים‎ and בְּמוֹ רֹאשִׁי‎, both introduced by the preposition ב'' (poetic בְמוֹ‎) which is expletive (cf. Gesenius-Kautzsch, § 119q). Hence everything suggests that we should regard במלים‎ as the direct complement of אחבירה‎. An excellent hypothesis which we find in the Hebrew commentary of Avronin and Rabinowitz, postulates that we should read simply אַכְבִּירָה‎. It is well known that the sound of *kaph* aspirate (without *dagesh*) is close to that of *ḥêth*. Now, in 35:16 we have precisely מִלִּין יַכְבִּר‎ 'he multiplies words'. Hence the 3rd hemistich will mean: 'I would multiply words at your expense.' While talking to a person in distress, one shakes the head as a sign of compassion; cf. the meaning of נוד‎ (2:11). But it is often also a sign of contempt or mockery (Ps 22:8; Sir 12:18; Mt 27:39). It is interesting to note that

5   I would strengthen you with my mouth,
       And the movement of my lips *I would not restrain*!
6   But if I speak, my sorrow is not relieved,
       And if I cease from speaking, it departs not far from me.

5   לֹא אֶחְשֹׂךְ (G Syr.); MT: יַחְשֹׂךְ.

the verb הֵנִיד (from נוד), synonymous with הֵנִיעַ (from נוע) in the sense of 'shake', is used in Jer 18: 16 with the complement בְּרֹאשׁ for 'shake the head', the ב being expletive as here the בְמוֹ. The poetic בְּמוֹ (as in 9: 30) will recur in v. 5. Cf., for the idea, the *tu si hic sis, aliter sentias* of Terence (Comm. on 4: 4).

5   G εἴη δὲ ἰσχύς omits the suffix of אאמצכם, while Syr. 'with your words' repeats it after פי. For יַחְשֹׂךְ, Targ. יתמנע 'would be checked', Vulg. *quasi parcens vobis*. But G οὐ φείσομαι and Syr. سمحت لن ي على 'I would not restrain' have read לֹא אֶחְשֹׂךְ, which is what we expect (cf. inf.).

The *pi'el* of אמץ to mean 'strengthen', 'fortify' (4: 4). It was by words that Job was wont to support the tottering man and to strengthen the feeble knees (4: 4). It is easy to support others 'with the mouth'. נִיד is generally translated 'consolation', following the meaning of the verb נוד in 2: 11; 42: 11. But נוד, parallel with נוע (cf. v. 4), means originally 'to be agitated, disturbed'; cf. נֹד in the Comm. on 7: 4. The expression נִיד שְׂפָתַי is a simple parallel to בְּמוֹ־פִי 'with my mouth' and does not include the idea of consolation. Note that G κίνησιν and Vulg. *moverem* are in agreement with Targ. טלטול in recognising the true value of the *hapax* נִיד 'movement', 'agitation'. As it stands, the 2nd hemistich should be translated 'and the movement of my lips would assuage'. In this case a complement must be understood, such as 'your

grief' (cf. Dillmann). In Is 58: 1 the formula אל תחשׂך means 'do not restrain yourself' and has nothing in common with יַחְשֹׂךְ in our text. If we compare with 7: 11, where Job exclaims לֹא אֶחְשָׂךְ פִּי 'I will not restrain my mouth', it becomes apparent that G and Syr., which have read לֹא אֶחְשֹׂךְ instead of יַחְשֹׂךְ, have preserved the correct reading: 'and I would not restrain the movement of my lips'. It is needless to suppose that יַחְשֹׂךְ represents a remnant of יֶחֱזַק 'would strengthen' (Wright), אֲחַזֵּק 'I would strengthen' (Duhm), renderings which have no kind of support in the versions. We shall meet the verb חשׂך once more in v. 6.

6   Vulg. adds to the opening *sed quid agam?* a formula of transition. G renders לֹא יַחְשֹׂךְ by οὐκ ἀλγήσω (reading אֶחְשֹׂךְ?). Jerome *non dolebo*, which has become *non delebo* in Bod. and Tur. The words יַחְשֹׂךְ and אַחְדָּלָה are rendered by the verb פסק 'to cease' in Targ. The end, from מה, is freely paraphrased in G τί ἔλαττον τρωθήσομαι and Syr. 'who will comfort me?'. The word מה is well translated *non* in Vulg.

Job now returns to his ever-present sorrow. He has already spoken out in the anguish of his soul (7: 11, 10: 1). But it is a trifling comfort: 'if I speak, my sorrow is not relieved'. Note the use of the cohortative after the conjunction 'if' (Ps 139: 8-9); cf. the cohortative to express a hypothesis (19: 18). The verb חשׂך 're-strain', 'check', 'prevent' (v. 5; 7: 11) assumes in the *niph'al* the sense of

7   For now *the jealous man* has wearied me,

7   הַשָּׁמוֹת ;MT: הֲשִׁמּוֹתָ. — עֵדָתוֹ ;MT: עדתי'' .

'to be spared', 'to be preserved' (21: 30), or 'to be controlled', 'to be assuaged' as here. Job is the man of sorrows; cf. כְּאֵב in 2: 13. The verb חדל 'cease' takes its exact connotation from the context: cease speaking, be silent. The close is usually interpreted as a question: what departs from me? (i.e. what am I eased?). The construction would be rather odd. Now, in 1 K 12: 16 we find מַה־לָּנוּ חֵלֶק, which corresponds to אֵין־לָנוּ חֵלֶק 'we have no portion in' of 2 S 20: 1, the two clauses belonging to one and the same context. It is clear that מָה conveys exactly the nuance of the Arabic *mâ*, which, from being an interrogative pronoun: 'what?' has become a simple negation. If we apply this meaning to our hemistich, we obtain 'and if I cease from speaking it departs not far from me'. It is certainly thus that Vulg. *non recedet a me* has understood the hemistich. The subject of יַהֲלֹךְ is כְּאֵבִי 'my sorrow'. The form יַהֲלֹךְ as in 14: 20. Instead of מִנִּי 'from me', which replaces מִמֶּנִּי (6: 13; 7: 16; etc.), we shall have מֶנִּי in pause (21: 16; 30: 10).

7   Targ. is content to copy the MT. G μωρόν, σεσηπότα replaces הֲשִׁמּוֹת כָּל־עֵדָתִי. It is impossible to discover the reading which is the basis of such a translation. Syr. connects עֵדָתִי with עֵד 'witness' (cf. G in 15: 34), whence its translation, 'and he has observed all my testimonies', which seems to rest on the reading וישמר instead of הֲשִׁמּוֹת. Vulg. *nunc autem oppressit me dolor mens* borrows from v. 6 the subject of הֶלְאָנִי. The rest is paraphrased *et in nihilum redacti sunt artus mei*, the word עֵדָתִי being interpreted, in agreement with the rabbis, as meaning *compago mea*

'my corporeal structure' (cf. R. Levi, quoted by Rosenmüller).

Vv. 7-8 present numerous difficulties. The alternation of the 3rd person הֶלְאָנִי with the 2nd person הֲשִׁמּוֹתָ (from שׁמם) and תִּקְמְטֵנִי (in v. 8), then the return to the 3rd הָיָה and וַיָּקָם (in v. 8); the length of the 2nd hemistich of v. 8 after the very short hemistichs of v. 7; the strangeness of the meanings which result from a strict adherence to the MT—all these are indications of a defective text. The wild confusion of the images compels Renan to add a note to v. 9: 'The distressed mind of Job here confuses in a series of terrible images God and his own personal enemies, passing abruptly from the one idea to the other.' Would it not rather be the case that the confusion is in the text? First of all it is necessary to find a subject for הֶלְאָנִי 'he has wearied me' (cf. the verb לאה in 4: 2, 5). For some (cf. Vulg., Ibn Ezra, etc.) it is 'my sorrow', for others it is God (Dillmann, Loisy, Segond, Crampon, etc.) or Eliphaz (Merx). Renan thinks that an impersonal subject is implied, whence 'my strength is exhausted'. Hontheim suggests 'I have been made exhausted'. What follows is no less ambiguous: 'O God, Thou hast mown down all my kinsmen' (Le Hir, Crampon); 'Thou hast ravaged all my family' (Renan); 'Thou hast ravaged all my house' (Segond); 'Thou hast brought trouble to all my household' (*Bible du rabbinat français*). But God will not appear on the scene until v. 11. In vv. 8-9, it is some character who is playing a part. Job calls him 'my slanderer' (cf. Comm. on v. 8), 'my adversary' (v. 9). Further, כָּל־עֲדָתִי does not mean 'all my family', but rather 'all my company', in

All *his* company   8   take hold of me,
He has become a witness and has risen up against me,
My *slanderer* gives evidence against me!

8   כְּחָשִׁי (cf. Syr., Vulg.); MT: כַּחֲשִׁי.

| accordance with the meaning of עֵדָה in 15: 34; the expression sounds odd in the mouth of Job. One first conclusion is irresistible, namely that the balance is perfectly restored between the hemistichs of vv. 7 and 8 if we adopt the distribution of Bickell (cf. also the Beer-Kittel edition), which consists in connecting וַתִּקְמְטֵנִי of v. 8 to the end of v. 7. The 1st hemistich finishes at הַשִׁמּוֹת, the 2nd at ותקמטני, the 3rd at בִּי of v. 8. In order to extricate himself from the impossible השמות, Bickell proposes to read השמותי, whence the translation of Loisy: 'But God has exhausted my strength, I am broken down'. We have already protested against this anticipation of the rôle of God. On the other hand, the slight correction of Bickell כָּל־עֲדָתוֹ תְּקָמְטֵנִי 'all his company seize me' (cf. the meaning of קמט in 22: 16) maintains the sense of עדה and abundantly shows that the personage in question is disguised behind השמות. We propose simply to vocalise הַשַׁמּוֹת without changing the consonants of the MT, and then we find ourselves faced with a noun of the *qittôl* form, similar to שִׁכּוֹר 'drunkard' (12: 25). The root שמת is no other than the Arabic *šamita* 'to rejoice in the misfortunes of others', which is the technical term to convey what the Germans call *Schadenfreude*. The *šâmit* is he who rejoices in the evil that befalls others, the envious, the malicious, etc. This feeling was known to the ancient Semites, as can be seen from David's elegy over Saul and Jonathan (2 S 1: 20), La 1: 21. The Babylonians said *hâdûa* to mean 'he who rejoices at my expense', in other | words, 'my enemy', as we see from the text: 'He has heard it, my enemy, and the features of his countenance shone: the message of joy has been announced to him and his heart was flooded with light' (*Choix de textes*, pp. 378-9). The root שמת is postulated by Perles to explain the incomprehensible שַׁמּוֹת of Ezk 36: 3 (*Jewish Quart. Review*, 1911, p. 110). Thus then, the שַׁמּוֹת will be the 'envious man' or 'jealous man', the 'malicious one'. Job feels himself to be persecuted by an enemy: 'for now the jealous man has wearied me'. The adverb אַךְ before עַתָּה simply serves to strengthen the idea of the immediate present; cf. אַךְ הִנֵּה 'surely, behold now' in Gn 26: 9. The scene will continue to be described in v. 8 where we see the sufferer brought before the tribunal and still pursued by his enemy. Among other suggested corrections, we would draw attention to that of Budde, who reads אתה for עתה and הלאתני for הלאני 'Thou alone hast wearied me, thou hast destroyed all my household.' This is not free from the disadvantages we have noted above. Duhm reads השמני for השמות and רעתו for עדתי, which produces: 'But now, he has wearied me, all my wretchedness takes hold of me', thus bringing God on to the scene again! Ball goes further, by restoring אל 'God' after הלאני and replacing השם ויבל עורי by השמות כל־עדתי, whence: 'But now God has wearied me, He has ravaged and destroyed my skin' (!). It is to the Septuagint they go in order to seek support for such hypotheses!

8 V. 8, absent from Sah., marked with asterisk in Jerome and (as far |

9   His anger has found a prey and he has persecuted me,
     He has gnashed his teeth against me,
     My enemy flashes his piercing eyes upon me!

as τὸ ψεῦδός μου = כחשׁי inclusive) in Syro-hex., did not exist in G. According to Cod. 255 (*Auctarium* of Field) the present text comes from Theod. For ותקמטני, Targ. ונקפתי 'and Thou hast wounded me', Theod. καὶ ἐπελάβου μου, Aq. καὶ ἐρρυτίδωσάς με 'and Thou hast brought furrows to my brow' (quoted in Syro-hex., Field); cf. Vulg. *rugae meae*, which becomes the subject of *testimonium dicunt contra me* (a translation of לעד היה). Symm. κατέδησάς με ἀδιαλείπτως ἐν ζυγῷ vocalises לְעַד instead of לְעֵד. Syr. ܣܘܣܒܐܠ reads והקימני instead of ותקמטני. Aq. εἰσέτι vocalises לָעַד. The word כחשׁ is rendered by 'my lie' in Targ. כדבובי, Syr. ܟܕܒܐܠ, Theod. τὸ ψεῦδός μου, Aq. ἄρνησίς μου. But Symm. καταψευδόμενος, Vulg. *falsiloquus* see here the liar himself. Syr. reads בפני אענה, which gives the opposite meaning to that of בפני יענה in the MT.

Le Hir himself recognised that the verse began at לְעֵד, but he failed to find the true subject of היה and ויקם. This subject is הַשָּׂמוּת 'the envious man' of v. 7. The formula הָיָה לְעֵד 'to be as a witness' in the sense of 'become a witness' (Jer 42: 5; Mic 1: 2). Note the use of וַיָּקָם בִּי 'and he has risen up against me' when it is a question of a witness who gives evidence against the accused. Cf. Ps 27: 12 כי קמו־בי עדי־שׁקר 'for false witnesses have risen against me'. This parallel passage invites us to see in כחשׁי a false witness, and this is also suggested by the translations καταψευδόμενος (Symm.), *falsiloquus* (Vulg.). Now, there exists in Is 30: 9 a plural form כֶּחָשִׁים meaning 'liars'. With Fried.

Delitzsch we propose to read here כֶּחָשׁי 'my liar', that is, the one who tells lies about me in a court of justice, 'my slanderer'. This is the only way in which we can obtain a natural subject for בְּפָנַי יַעֲנֶה 'he gives evidence against me'. The expression ענה בפני is only a development of ענה ב" (15: 6). Those who retain כחשׁי translate by 'my leanness' (in accordance with the Aramaic and the meaning of the verb כחשׁ in Ps 109: 24), or by 'my lie' which is the ordinary meaning. Le Hir already protested against the former interpretation: 'for it is obvious, from the following verses, that Job is complaining about quite a different witness from that which he carries on his emaciated features'. The second explanation sees in 'my lie' the lie of which I am the victim (Schultens), or again the suffering which witnesses falsely against me (Dillmann, etc.). All these ingenious subtleties are unnecessary. The context shows clearly that here, as in vv. 7 and 9, we are concerned with some personage who is essentially Job's enemy. It is his adversary in the court of justice, the false witness, the persecutor to whom God abandons him (v. 11). Job is brought before a court of law, evidence is given against him, he is insulted in every possible way, he becomes the victim of his arch-enemy and the gang which the latter had in tow. The drama continues in v. 9.

9 For אפו טרף, Targ. and Syr. רוגזיה תבר 'his anger has torn' (Syr. adds a suffix: 'has torn me'), Vulg. *collegit furorem suum in me*, G simply ὀργῇ χρησάμενος. For וישׂטמני, Targ. 'and he has nourished spite against me', Vulg. *et comminans*

10   They have opened wide their mouth against me,
Insolently they have struck my cheeks,
They mass themselves together against me!

mihi. Syr. ܣܦܣܝܢ 'and he has torn me' reads וישמטני (cf. 2 K 9: 33) which, according to the sense of שמט in 2 K 9: 33, is probably the reading behind G κατέβαλέν με. After בשניו, G adds βέλη πειρατῶν (A πειρατηρίων) αὐτοῦ ἐπ' ἐμοὶ ἔπεσεν which does not belong to the context. G omits צרי. The phrase ילטש בעיניו לי is paraphrased in G ἀκίσιν ὀφθαλμῶν ἐνήλατο and Vulg. *terribilibus oculis me intuitus est*. The metaphor contained in ילטש is explained by Targ. 'like a sharpened knife'. The plural οἱ ἐναντίον μου (Symm.) and 'my adversaries' (Syr.) for צרי is an anticipation of v. 10.

V. 9 depicts the fury of Job's enemy under the guise of a ferocious beast which hurls itself on its prey. Duhm unceremoniously deletes vv. 9c-11 and points out that Siegfried deletes vv. 10-11. But v. 9c forms the natural sequence to the two preceding hemistichs. V. 10 continues the description of the tribunal scene; cf. Mt 27: 65-8. V. 11 traces all these vexations back to their original source. The expression אפו טרף is supported by Am 1: 11, where ויטרף לעד אפו means 'and his anger (parallel to עברתו 'his fury') has unceasingly found a prey'. Hence there is no reason to see in אפו 'his nose', 'his snout' (contra Ehrlich). We shall have טרף נפשו באפו 'he who tears himself in his anger' in 18: 4. The verb טרף denotes the action of the wild beast which finds a prey and treats it as such, i.e. tears and devours it; cf. טֶרֶף in 4: 11. The verb שטם, parallel to שטן, means not only 'hate', but also 'pursue', 'persecute'. In Ps 55: 4 we find באף ישטמוני 'they persecute me with anger', which would give preference to the MT over the readings of G and Syr.

The subject of וַיִּשְׂטְמֵנִי 'and he has persecuted me' is the same as that of the following verbs, with the result that אפו טרף forms a suspended phrase whose object is to elucidate the nature of the anger manifested by the persecutor. The verb חָרַק 'grind', 'gnash' generally governs the accusative. The /"ב before שִׁנָּיו is expletive as in במו ראשי and במלים of v. 4, בפיהם of v. 10. Of course צָרִי 'my adversary' corresponds to כְּחָשׁ 'my slanderer' of v. 8. There is no reason to read צדי 'my hunter' (Hoffmann) or to change the singular to the plural (Merx, following Symm. and Syr.). The verb לטש 'to make sharp' produces a very striking image: 'he sharpens his eyes upon me' i.e. he flashes towards me his sharp, piercing looks.

10   The 1st hemistich is omitted by G, Jerome, Sah., Syro-hex., Arab. Baud. The verse is badly divided up in Syr., which links בחרפה to the 1st hemistich and יחד to the 2nd. G ὀξεῖ interprets חרפה by the Aramaic חורפא 'point', 'sharp edge' of the sword. For לחיי, G εἰς τὰ γόνατα (Aug. *in genibus*), corruption of εἰς σιαγόνας attested by Jerome (Gall.) *in genis* (which has become *ingens* in Bod and Tur.) and by Syro-hex. 'on the jaw'; cf. Aq. and Symm. quoted in Syro-hex. G κατέδραμον interprets יתמלאון in the light of the complement עלי. The other versions add a complement to יתמלאון interpreted as 'they are filled': with fury (Syr.), with indignation (Targ.), *poenis meis* (Vulg.).

Job's enemy is not alone. He has a whole gang with him (v. 7). They mass and press around the accused like wild beasts around a prey: 'They

11   God abandons me to an *evil man*,
      And to the hands of the wicked He *casts* me:

11 עַוָּל (G, Vulg., Syr., Targ.); MT: עויל. — יִרְטֵנִי; MT: ירטני.

have opened wide their mouth
against me.' The verb פער is specially used to convey that the mouth
is widely opened, whether in the expectation of something desired (29:
23; Ps 119: 131), or to swallow up
(Is 5: 14). The ב" of בְּפִיהֶם is expletive (cf. v. 4 and v. 9). Compare
Ps 22: 14, where the enemies 'open
wide their mouth against me, like a
lion which tears and roars'. The expression בְּחֶרְפָּה 'as an insult' is
perfectly in harmony with the context (cf. 19: 5). The word לְחִי denotes both the jaw (40: 26) and the
cheeks. To strike the cheeks, to give
a slap in the face, is the supreme
outrage (Mic 4: 14; Ps 3: 8; La 3: 30).
Cf. the passion scene with the high
priest, immediately after the false
witnesses have just given their
evidence (Mt 27: 67-8). The hithpa'el
of מלא 'to be full' is used to convey
the idea of 'piling up', 'pressing together', and in the text is made even
more precise by יַחַד 'together'. Job
pictures himself surrounded by a
crowd of enemies who deride and
mock him; cf. 30: 9-14.

11   Syr. vocalises אֶל־אַל and interprets אל עויל by ܡܠܐܟܐ ܒܝܫܐ 'the
bad angel'. It is clear that Syr. read
עַוָּל and not עויל. Similarly G ἀδίκου,
Vulg. iniquum, Targ. מרי זדונא 'the
proud'. G εἰς χεῖρας ἀδίκου adds ידי
before עול (= עויל). For ירטני, G
ἔρριψέν με, Vulg. me tradidit, Targ.
ממרטט יתי 'he causes me to be stripped of my hair'. Syr. renders by
ܐܫܠܡܢܝ 'he has abandoned me',
which translated also יסגירני.
    It is God who permits the enemies
of Job to wreak their fury and ven-

geance on their victim: 'God abandons me to an evil man.' The hiph'il
of סגר (11: 10) is often used in the
sense of 'delivering up' into the
hands of some one. The indirect complement is introduced either by בְיד
'into the hand' (cf. the translation
of G) or simply by the prepositions
לְ" (Ps 78: 48, 50, 62, etc.) or אֶל
(Dt 23: 16). The word עויל which
recurs in 19: 18, 21: 11 (and nowhere else) has the meaning of
'urchin', 'boy', derived from עול 'to
give suck'. On the other hand, the
parallel word to רָשָׁע 'wicked man'
is עַוָּל in 27: 7. It is this latter word,
derived from עול 'to be evil, unrighteous', etc. (cf. עַוְלָה in 5: 16;
6: 29ff.; 11: 14; 15:16), which the
versions have read in our text (cf.
sup.). The intensive form, which is
used for the noun עַוָּל, distinguishes
the individual who makes a profes-
sion of unrighteousness. We shall
therefore read עַוָּל instead of עויל,
which will preserve the parallelism
with the 2nd hemistich: 'and to the
hands of the wicked He casts me'.
Job's friends have spoken of the
רְשָׁעִים 'wicked' and have described
their sinister end (8: 22; 11: 20).
But Job has on the contrary observed that misfortune does not
strike them and that God Himself
seemed to smile on and favour their
counsels (10: 3). God delivers Job
over to them as a prey. The verb
יִרְטֵנִי does not stem from רטה, as
seems to be implied by the Massoretic
vocalisation, but rather from ירט
(Nu 22: 32) which belongs to the
same root as the Arabic warraṭa
(2nd form) meaning 'throw', 'hurl',
'fling' into a ditch, whence warṭeh

12   I was in peace and He has shattered me,
      He has seized me by the nape of the neck and dashed me to
            pieces!
      He has set me up as His target:
13   Around me His arrows fly,
      Pitilessly He transfixes my reins,
      He pours out my gall on the ground,

'abyss', 'ditch', 'danger', etc. The normal form would be יִרְטֵנִי. It is probable that one of the yods has had the effect of changing עוֹל into עוֹיִל; cf. the same phenomenon for aleph in 15: 31-2.

12 For שָׁלֵו הָיִיתִי, Vulg. *ego ille quondam opulentus.* G renders ערפי by τῆς κόμης; cf. the Assyrian *aruppu* and the Arabic *'urf* 'mane'. G omits לו and renders למטרה by ὥσπερ σκόπον. For למטרה, Vulg. *quasi in signum*; cf. Syr. اسو سعا 'as a sign'.

The attack took Job by surprise: 'I was in peace and He has shattered me.' The expression שָׁלֵו הָיִיתִי 'I was in peace' (cf. the adjective שְׁלֵו in 21: 23 and the noun שַׁלְו in 20: 20) recalls the Aramaic שְׁלֵה הֲוֵית in Dn 4: 4, 'I, Nebuchadnezzar, was at ease in my house'. For the verb שָׁלֵו cf. 3: 26; 12: 6. The cases cited in the dictionary of Gesenius-Buhl in favour of a root פרר 'shake' can all be explained by פרר, *hiph'il* הֵפֵר 'break', 'dash to pieces' (5: 12; 15: 4). The *po'el* in Ps 74: 13 alludes to God 'breaking' the sea in order to make a way for the Hebrews or in order to reduce it to impotence. The *hithpo'el* in Is 24: 19 shows the earth shivering into splinters, rent asunder (cf. Condamin). The *pilpel* of פרר has as its parallel the *pilpel* of פצץ, which equally signifies 'break in pieces', as is to be clearly seen from the meaning of the *po'el* 'to smash up' (Jer 23: 29) and of the *hithpo'el* 'scatter in fragments' (Hab 3: 6). It

is God who now enters into a struggle with Job. He seizes him by the nape of the neck. On the exact meaning of עֹרֶף cf. *L'Emploi métaphorique*, p. 93. The verb אחז 'take' with the preposition בְּ" before the part of the body that is taken (18: 9; Ps 73: 23). Literally 'He has seized my nape', i.e. He has taken me by the nape of the neck. An enemy was normally seized by the nape of the neck: 'your hand is on the nape of your enemies' necks' (Gn 49: 8). The 3rd hemistich runs literally: 'and He has set me up as a target for Himself'. In 7: 20 Job said to God: 'Why hast Thou taken me for Thy target?' Instead of the *hapax* מפגע (7: 20) we have here מַטָּרָה (from נטר 'watch', 'aim at') the target at which arrows are aimed (1 S 20: 20; La 3: 12). The parallel member to the 3rd hemistich is v. 13a (cf. Comm.). In comparing with 6: 4 and 7: 20 it is apparent that it is God who is now pictured as the bowman, as He was formerly the hunter pursuing his prey (10: 16).

13 Vulg. renders יסבו by the singular: *circumdedit.* For רביו, G λόγχαις, Vulg. *lanceis suis*, Targ. גררוי and Syr. جسوسهـ 'His arrows'. G puts the verbs in the plural, from יפלח to the end of v. 14.

The image of the bowman continues. The word רַבָּיו is ambiguous. One may translate: 'His bowmen', following Jer 50: 29, or 'His arrows', with the versions. The root is רבב, which means 'shoot arrows' (Gn

14 He batters me down, breach upon breach,
   He dashes upon me like a mighty man of war!
15 I have sewed sackcloth on my skin,
   And dug my horn in the dust,

49: 23). As the bowman remains alone on the scene, the interpretation of the versions seems preferable. We shall therefore translate: 'Around me His arrows fly', which recalls the image of 6: 4. Job is the target (v. 12) against which God shoots His shafts. It becomes obvious that v. 13a is the parallel member to v. 12c. It is the reins or kidneys which will be pierced. Note the use of the *pi'el* of פלח, exactly as in Pr 7: 23, 'till an arrow pierces its liver'. It seems inevitable to draw a comparison between the description of vv. 12-13 and that of La 3: 12-13, where the theme is the afflictions which God sends: 'He has bent His bow and set me as a mark for His arrow, He has pierced my reins with the sons of His quiver.' The word כִּלְיוֹתָי 'my reins' will recur in 19: 27. For וְלֹא יַחְמֹל 'and He has no pity', cf. 6: 10. With the, 3rd hemistich, 'He pours out my gall on the ground', compare: 'my liver is poured out on the ground' (La 2: 11), where נִשְׁפַּךְ לָאָרֶץ corresponds to יִשְׁפֹּךְ לָאָרֶץ in our text. The *hapax* מְרֵרָה 'bile', 'gall' belongs to the same root as מְרֹרָה 'something bitter' (13: 26), poison (20: 14), liver (20: 25).

14 For ירץ, Aq. and Theod. (according to Syro-hex.) read the plural with G (cf. v. 13). But Symm., Vulg., Syr., Targ. have the singular with the MT. For כגבור Syr. quite wrongly 'as against a giant'.
The exact meaning of פָּרַץ, as of the Assyrian *parasu*, is 'to make a breach' in a wall. The word פֶּרֶץ 'breach' serves as specific complement. Cf. Gn 38: 29, 'what a breach

you have made for yourself!' The wall in which a breach is made is in the accusative (Is 5: 5; Ps 80: 13, etc.). The suffix of יִפְרְצֵנִי assimilates Job to the wall in which God makes breaches. The locution עַל־פְּנֵי 'above' is complementary to the Babylonian *ana pâni* 'above' (meaning 'in addition') in the el-Amarna letters (*RB*, 1921, p. 398). The 2nd hemistich recalls 15: 26a, where we had אֵלָיו instead of עָלָי. God runs against His adversary as though He were a mighty man of war. In Ps 19: 6 the sun rejoices 'like a warrior' to run his course.

15 G ἔραψαν (A ἔρριψαν) is contradicted by Vulg., Targ., Syr., which follow the MT תפרתי parallel to עללתי. Sah. omits βύρσης which translates גלדי in G. For עללתי, G ἐσβέσθη, Vulg. *operui*, Targ. and Syr. פלפלית 'I have sprinkled'. G τὸ σθένος μου, and Targ. איקרי 'my honour' interpret metaphorically קרני 'my horn', which Syr. translates 'my head' and Vulg. *carnem meam* (perhaps a corruption of *cornu meum*).
The attitude of Job in the face of his tribulations is now described. 'I have sewed sackcloth on my skin', i.e. the sackcloth I have put on my skin cleaves to it as though it were sewed on. Sackcloth is the garment of mourning (Lagrange, *ÉRS*, pp. 321f.). It was worn in times of extreme grief and placed directly on the flesh (1 K 21: 27). It was tied around the loins (Gn 37: 34; Jer 48: 37). The verb תפר 'to sew' recurs only in Gn 3: 7; Ec 3: 7; and, in the *pi'el*, in Ezk 13: 18. The noun גֶּלֶד 'skin', used here instead of the ordinary

16   My face is reddened with tears,
       And on my eyelids is darkness,
17   Although there is no violence in my hands,
       And my prayer is pure!

word עוֹר, is not found elsewhere. It corresponds to the Arabic *jild*, the Aramaic גִילְדָא, and the Assyrian *giladu*. The *po'el* עֹלַלְתִּי belongs to the root עלל, which, in Aramaic, means 'enter', 'go in', in the *'aph'el* 'bring in'; in Arabic غَلّ 'put in', 'thrust in'. The meaning of the 2nd hemistich is clear: 'and I have dug my horn in the dust'. This symbolises the extremity of moral depression, in antithesis to 'raise one's horn' which is the sign of pride and exaltation (*L'Emploi métaphorique*, p. 37). Siegfried makes the expression banal when he replaces עֹלַלְתִּי by נתתי 'I have put'.

16   Instead of פָּנַי 'my face', G ἡ γαστήρ μου, following La 1: 20; 2: 11. The *qerê* חמרמרו corrects the singular חמרמרה of the *kethîb*. For צלמות, G σκιά, but G (A) and Olympiod. add θανάτου, which is found also in Eth. and (with asterisk) in Syrohex. and Jerome.

The feminine singular with the masculine plural as subject when the latter is the name of a thing (Gesenius-Kautzsch, § 145k); cf. 2 S 10: 9, where פָּנִים is the subject of הָיְתָה. The root of חֳמַרְמְרָה (form *qetaltal*; cf. Gesenius-Kautzsch, § 55e) is the same as the Arabic حَمِرَ 'to be red'. It is found again in חֹמֶר 'clay', 'red earth', in חֲמוֹר 'ass (reddish brown)', חֵמָר 'asphalt' (whence the verb חמר of Ex 2: 3). The poetic preposition מִנִּי (cf. 9: 3 Comm.) is used to indicate the cause (4: 9, 13; 7: 14): 'my face is reddened with tears'. The 2nd hemistich: 'and on my eyelids is darkness!', meaning: 'darkness

covers my eyelids'. Cf. the propositions 13: 17b; 15: 21a. The word צלמות means 'darkness' and not 'shadow of death' (3: 5; 10: 21; 12: 22). The eyelids are mentioned to denote the eyes: the part for the whole (Ps 11: 4). The eyes sparkle under the influence of joy, just as they grow dark in sorrow, like the face (*L'Emploi métaphorique*, p. 76).

17   Vulg. makes explicit the link between v. 16 and v. 17: *haec passus sum*. G ἄδικον δὲ οὐδὲν ἦν diminishes the force of על.

There is no nexus between the ills from which Job is suffering and his conduct: 'although there is no violence in my hands'. The preposition על is used in the sense of עַל־אֲשֶׁר 'although'. Cf. Is 53: 9, עַל לֹא־חָמָס עָשָׂה 'although he had done no violence', in reference to the sufferings of the righteous servant. In 10: 7 we had עַל־דַּעְתְּךָ 'although Thou knowest'. God knows that Job is not guilty (10: 7). But the friends are determined to find in Job some fault (15: 4-6). Zophar advised him to get rid of the 'iniquity' which was in his hand (11: 14). Evil is symbolised by the idea of violence, regarded as a form of unrighteousness; cf. the verb חמס (15: 33) and the noun חָמָס (19: 7). In 31: 7 Job will say that there is no impurity in his hands. Prayer is pure when the hands are pure (11: 13-14). Thus, since there is no violence in the hands of Job, he may justly add: 'and although my prayer is pure'. Because they fail to grasp the relation between the purity of the hands and the purity of prayer, certain modern exegetes, such as Duhm and Beer, propose to change תְּפִלָּתִי 'my prayer' into some word

18   O earth, hide not my blood,
       And may there be no shelter for my cry!
19   Even now, my witness is in heaven,
       And he who testifies on my behalf dwells in the heights:

or other meaning 'my behaviour'. Duhm would transfer v. 17 to a position after v. 14 on the grounds that it is supposed to be better connected with v. 14 than with v. 16; this would need to be demonstrated. On the contrary, note the succession of the parts of the body: my skin, my horn, my face, my eyelids, my hands, my blood (15-18).

18 This verse is rendered word for word in Syr. and Targ. For דמי, G ἐφ' αἵματι τῆς σαρκός μου. The word מקום is literally translated τόπος (G), στάσις (Symm.), but Vulg. *locum latendi*.

Job is persecuted despite his innocence. Victim of the shafts which his persecutor lets fly at him (12-13), he sees his blood flow. The earth cries out for vengeance when it is soaked in the blood of the innocent (Gn 4: 10-11). Blood shed on the rock can still cry out, but if the earth covers with dust the blood that is spilt, then it will be silent (Ezk 24: 7). Job exclaims: 'O earth, hide not my blood!' Cf. Is 26: 21b, 'and the earth will disclose the blood shed upon her and will no more cover her slain'. In this passage of Isaiah as in that of Ezekiel, it is the *pi'el* of כסה which is used to mean 'cover', 'hide'. The 2nd hemistich must be interpreted in accordance with the meaning of the 1st, for the parallelism is strongly marked. The earth is only the interpreter of Job. It echoes his cry; cf. 31: 38, where אדמתי 'my earth' is the subject of תזעק (the verb זעק, whence זעקתי 'my cry'). Tradition hesitates between the two meanings of מקום: the place where one stops (cf. Symm.), and the place where one hides (cf.

Vulg.). Knabenbauer quotes ancient opinions which diverge into two streams according to the mode of their interpretation. In conformity with the parallelism, the word מקום is certainly the place to which one withdraws (18: 21), the secret place where one shelters and hides.

19 Syr. translates by plurals עדי and שהדי, but renders מרומים by a singular. For ושהדי, G ὁ δὲ συνίστωρ μου, Jerome and Vulg. *et conscius meus*.

The expression גם־עתה 'even at the present moment', or 'even now'. In spite of all that is happening to me, I shall not lose courage, for I have a witness in the heavens. Job has requested that the earth may not hide his blood, and that his appeal may ring out freely. For his prayer must reach the very heavens. The interjection הנה 'behold' before בשמים recalls הנה באהל 'behold in the tent', for 'it is in the tent' (Gn 18: 9) and הנה באמתחתי 'behold in my bag' for 'it is in my bag' (Gn 42: 28). This witness, which is none other than God Himself, is being contrasted with the false witness who accused Job in v. 8. The hostility of God is fraught with mystery, for the victim is conscious of his innocence and can call on God as a witness. The 2nd hemistich is simply a repetition of the 1st. The author has been satisfied to replace בשמים by במרומים 'in the heights' (25: 2; 31: 2), for nothing is higher than the heavens (11: 8). Instead of עדי 'my witness', he now has recourse to the Aramaic שהדי. Cf. Gn 31: 47, where to the word שהדותא 'testimony' of the Aramaean Laban corresponds the word עד

20   My *clamant word has reached* even Eloah,
      Before Him my eye has flowed with tears;

21   *Ah*! *if only* He were arbiter between a man and Eloah
      As *between* a man and his neighbour!

20   מָצָא רֵעִי (cf. G); MT: מליצי רֵעָי. — Restore לְפָנָיו (G) before עיני.

21   לוּ; MT: וּ. — וּבֵין MT: ובן.

'witness' (in גלעד, explained in v. 48) of the Hebrew Jacob. The technique of using as a parallel the Aramaic synonym, in order to avoid the repetition of the Hebrew word, is further apparent in 39: 5 and 40: 18.

20 For מליצי רעי, Targ. פרקליטי חברי 'my comforters, my companions', Syr. 'my brothers and my friends', Vulg. *verbosi amici mei*. G ἀφίκοιτό μου ἡ δέησις πρὸς Κύριον connects אל־אלוה with the 1st hemistich, and reads a different text for the first words. Then ἔναντι δὲ αὐτοῦ στάζοι μου ὁ ὀφθαλμός had לפניו which has disappeared by haplography (cf. inf.).

According to the meaning attached to מליץ 'interpreter' 'intercessor' (33: 23) or 'arrogant', 'derisive' (Ps 119: 15), the first words are translated either as 'there have I intercessors and friends' (Le Hir; cf. Targ. and Syr.), or more usually as 'my friends mock me' (Renan, cf. Segond, Crampon, etc.). In any event, the hemistich is too short, and the connection with the context is far from clear. The text read by G certainly had דָּלְפָה לְפָנָיו עֵינִי (cf. sup.), and it is at once understandable that לפני should have disappeared on account of the resemblance of its consonants with those of the preceding and following words. Hence with G we must connect אל־אלוה with the 1st hemistich, which as a result gains normal dimensions. But we cannot be satisfied to retranslate ἀφίκοιτό μου ἡ δέησις by תחנתי תבא (Siegfried), for then

it is impossible to see how the MT could have sprung from such banal readings. The word רעי read as רֵעַ may be interpreted as meaning 'my clamour': רֵעַ from the root רוע (Mic 4: 9; cf. Ex 32: 17). In 11: 7, G ἀφίκου rendered תמצא, which corresponded to the Aramaic תמטא 'you will arrive' (cf. Comm.). It is this same verb which has given rise to ἀφίκοιτο in our passage. The MT מליצי is a remnant of מָצָא. The *lamed* of מליצי comes from the beginning of v. 21 (cf. inf.). We shall therefore translate the 1st hemistich: 'my clamant word has reached even Eloah', which forms an excellent parallel to 'before Him my eye has flowed with tears' (restore לְפָנָיו with G before עֵינִי; cf. sup.). The verb דלף means 'drip', 'stream', 'flow' (Ec 10: 18), and is meant to convey the thought of tears falling drop by drop from the eyes. In Ps. 119: 28 we have דלפה נפשי 'my soul has streamed' (i.e. has shed tears).

21 The 2nd hemistich, absent from Sah., marked with asterisk in Jerome and Syro-hex., did not exist in G. The present text comes from Theod. (cf. Syro-hex.). For ויוכח, G εἴη δὲ ἔλεγχος, Vulg. *atque utinam sic judicaretur*. In Syr. the subject of יוכח becomes בן־אדם, which results in a new meaning for the whole verse: 'If indeed a man could blame God, as a man (blames) his neighbour!' It will be observed that Vulg. and Syr. are in agreement with Targ. אפשר ד'' 'if it were possible that . . .'

to translate וַיּוֹכַח, as if we had
לוֹ יוֹכַח. These three witnesses regard
the copula of the 2nd hemistich as a
waw of comparison: *quomodo* (Vulg.),
'as' (Syr.), וְהֵיךְ 'and as' (Targ.).

Already Bouillier and Dathe, cited
by Rosenmüller and followed by
most moderns, had pointed out that
וּבֶן־אָדָם of the 2nd hemistich is a bad
writing for וּבֵין אָדָם. Had it been a
question of בֶּן־אָדָם 'son of man'
parallel to גֶּבֶר, we should have had
וּלְבֶן־אָדָם. The word which corresponds to גֶּבֶר is אָדָם (14: 10; 33:
17). The locution בֵּין אָדָם לְרֵעֵהוּ is
good Hebrew (Gn 1: 6; Dn 11: 45).
We find בְּבֵן instead of כְּבֵין in Is
44: 4 (cf. Condamin). The 2nd hemistich therefore means: 'as between
a man and his neighbour', the *waw*
marking the comparison (Vulg.,
Targ., Syr.). The use of the verb
הוֹכִיחַ in 9: 33, where it is followed
by בֵּינֵינוּ 'between us', proves that
we should here give to the verb the
meaning of 'to be an arbiter'. The
natural sense of the 1st hemistich, as
it stands at present in the MT, will
therefore be: 'that he may be an
arbiter between man and God'.
Exegetes are agreed in seeing here
the object of Job's prayer (v. 20).
But we are thus brought up against
an anomaly. Job prays and weeps
before God who is his witness in
heaven (v. 19), in order that this
God may deign to act as arbiter between man and God. It is man in
general who is at issue rather than
Job the individual. Everything con-
curs to show that we are faced here
by a hypothesis or a desire, as was
perfectly well understood by Vulg.,
Syr., and Targ. By taking the *lamed*
from מֵלִיצִי (cf. v. 20), we read
לוֹ יוֹכַח: 'If, at least, He were arbiter'.
The preposition לְ'' indicates that
God would be an arbiter 'for', 'on behalf of' man, while the preposition
עִם introduces the personage 'with'
whom man is in conflict. The meaning is not in doubt: it is a question
of some one being an arbiter between
two parties engaged in litigation.
This idea is presented as an unrealisable hypothesis (cf. לוּ in v. 4),
since God would, were the hypothesis
realised, be both judge and litigating
party. On the other hand, it is natural that God should be arbiter
'between a man and his neighbour'.
The *waw* of comparison (5: 7; 11: 12;
12: 11) is quite expected at the beginning of the 2nd hemistich. The
heart's desire of Job was that he
might be able to debate with God as
before a tribunal (13: 3, 18-23). But
unfortunately 'He is not a man like
myself, that I might answer Him,
that we might go together to justice:
there is no arbiter between us'
(9: 32-3).

16:22 For few are the years that lie ahead,
And I shall go away by the road along which I shall not
return!
17:1 My spirit is broken, my days have faded out,
The grave is what I need!

22 Transfer to the beginning of Chapter 17.

16: **22** Syr. reads מספר שׁנות (cf. 15: 20b) and applies to man in general what Job says of himself. For שׁנות מספר, G ἔτη δὲ ἀριθμητά, Vulg. *breves anni*.

The allusion to the shortness of life and the approach of death fits well the style and outlook of Job. The expression שׁנות מִסְפָּר 'years of number', by contrast with 'years without number' (5: 9; 9: 10), means the years that can be counted because they are so few (cf. Vulg.). Cf. the expressions מתי מספר 'men small in number' (Gn 34: 30; Ps 105: 12, etc.) and אנשׁי מספר (Ezk 12: 16). The verb אתה 'to come' retains its etymological *yod* in יֶאֱתָיוּ (30: 14) as in יאתיני of 3: 25. The meaning 'come' assumes the slightly modified connotation 'to be ahead, in the future' exactly as in האתיות 'the things to come' (Is 41: 23; 45: 11). The road along which one does not return is that to Sheol; for 'he who goes down to Sheol comes not up again; he returns no more to his dwelling and the place where he was sees him not again' (7: 9-10). In 10: 21, 'before I depart, no more to return, to the land of darkness and shade'. Note the similarity of the terms of 10: 21a with those of our 2nd hemistich. Among the Babylonians, one goes to the infernal regions by 'the road which has no return', for the abode of the dead is the 'house which he who enters never leaves' (*Choix de textes*, p. 327). The expression closest to that used by Job is *uruḥ lâ târi* 'road with no return' occurring in a hymn to Tammuz (in Zimmern, *Sumer. Babyl. Tamuzlieder*, p. 204, no. I, l. 12). It is clear that our v. 22 begins the description which is continued in 17: 1. With the edition of Bomberg, we should end ch. 16 at v. 21 and begin ch. 17 with 16: 22.

17: **1** G paraphrases the whole verse: ὀλέκομαι πνεύματι φερόμενος δέομαι δὲ ταφῆς καὶ οὐ τυγχάνω. The last words come from 3: 21. For קברים לי, Vulg. *et solum mihi superest sepulchrum*, Targ. 'they are preparing tombs for me' (likewise Syr.).

Instead of two hemistichs, we have here a rhythm similar to that of the alexandrine with two caesuras, sometimes employed in French poetry: three short phrase members, simply juxtaposed. Those who would restore the normal caesura make the break after יְמַי and, changing the vocalisation of חבלה, translate: 'My spirit hath pledged my life' (Wright); 'My spirit is destroyed within me' (עמי for ימי) (Beer); or again, re-

242

2   Am I not an object of derision?
     And is it not in *bitterness* that my eye passes the nights?

2   וּבְתַמְרוּרִים (cf. Vulg., Syr.); MT: וּבהמרותם.

placing רוּחִי by רוּחוֹ, 'His animosity
has destroyed my days (Duhm).
Ball transforms ימי into מאמר:
'my spirit is too disordered for
speech'. It will be noted that G
lends no sort of support to these
corrections, any more than to the
changes of נזעכו to יזעקו 'clamour'
(Wright), נזעקו 'are called' (Beer),
נעזבו 'are left' (Duhm). Ever more
audacious, Ball changes נזעכו קברים
into נתעבו דברים 'words are abhorrent to me'. Now the MT is perfectly justified, and it is only the
matter of the rhythm which has
brought about these artificial corrections. The verb חבל 'to act badly'
(34: 31) means in the *pi'el* 'to
destroy', 'to ruin' (cf. the Assyrian
ḥabâlu). In regard to moral conduct,
it means to make some one lose his
head, as is to be seen from the Arabic
ḥabala and (2nd form) *ḥabbala* 'to
make mad'. This shade of meaning,
recommended in the dictionary of
Gesenius-Buhl, cannot apply to the
interpretation of the *pu'al* in our
passage, for the context shows clearly
that רוּחַ is not the spirit from the
point of view of mental faculties but
from the point of view of vitality
(10: 12; 12: 10). We shall translate:
'My spirit is broken', parallel to 'my
days have faded out'. The verb זעך
is the Hebraic form of the Aramaic
דעך 'to be extinguished' (18: 5-6;
21: 17). The *niph'al*, which is used
here, we met in 6: 17; with the
meaning of 'to become dried up'
(same image as the Latin *extinguere
aquam*). The days fade out when
one reaches the evening of life. Life
is light, death is darkness (cf. 3: 16,
20; 18: 18). The close, קברים לי
'tombs for me', is the natural sequel
to what precedes (cf. Vulg., Targ.,

Syr.). The plural is used to suggest
the place where graves are to be
found, the graveyard. The terseness
of the phrasing does not prevent us
from grasping its force and implications: the graveyard, that is what
now suits me, what I now need.

2   G λίσσομαι κάμνων καὶ τί ποιήσας
(ποιήσω in A., Jerome, and Syro-
hex.) completely diverges from the
MT. It would seem that G had one
hemistich only, but we give up the
attempt to find it in any traces of
the Hebrew text. Vulg. interprets
התלים as 'sins', whence for the 1st
hemistich *non peccavi*. For התלים,
Targ. מתלעבין 'mockers', Syr. ܡܣܒ
'falsehood'. Vulg. *et in amaritudini-
bus* and Syr. ܒܟܪܝܘܬܗܘܢ 'in their
bitterness' connect המרותם with
מרר 'to be bitter', whilst Targ.
בפרוגיהון 'in their retribution' connects with מור, whence תמורה 'recompense', 'retribution' (cf. 15: 31).
Syr. interprets עיני by 'my spirit',
in accordance with רוּחִי of v. 1.
     The sentence is conceived exactly
on the pattern of 30: 25 and 31: 36,
where אִם־לֹא has interrogative value
and governs two clauses. The same
use of אם לא is found in Jer 48: 27.
The *hapax* הַתֻלִים is a plural abstraction, similar to זְקֻנִים 'old age',
נְעֻרִים 'youth'. The root is התל
derived from תלל (cf. Comm. on
13: 9); the meaning 'mockery' is
confirmed by Jewish tradition (cf.
Thesaurus of Ben-Yehuda, III, p.
1231). The expression: עִמָּדִי 'with
me' to mean 'in respect to myself',
'aimed at me' (cf. 10: 21, 17; 13: 20):
'Is not mockery aimed at me?', i.e.
'am I not an object of derision?'

3   Lay then *my pledge* beside Thee.
     Who would be prepared to strike my hand?

3 עָרְבֵנִי (Syr.); MT: עָרְבֵנִי.

Job feels he cannot turn to his friends whose consolations are insincere and deceptive (6: 14; 12: 4-5; 6: 16-23). Not one of them could serve as his surety (3-5). From them he expects nothing but mockery, and that is why he will address himself to God. The word וּבְהַמְּרוֹתָם is vocalised as if הַמָּרוֹת (with *dagesh dirimens*) represented the *hiph'il* of מרה 'to be rebellious'. Those who preserve this vocalisation look for a derivative sense, 'quarrel' or 'insult'. In that case one is obliged to consider הֲתָלִים as a concrete (cf. Targ.), in order to translate: 'my eye watches at night amid their insults' (Le Hir), 'and would that my eye were no longer afflicted by their quarrels!' (Renan). The same difficulties attend the change of המרותם into מרמתם 'their trickery' (Budde). What is expected is a word parallel to התלים. With Duhm we read וּבְתַמְרוּרִים (cf. Vulg. and Syr.). The word תמרורים is a plural abstract qualifying מספד 'bitter complaint' (Jer 6: 26) and בכי 'bitter tears' (Jer 31: 15). It is in fact precisely the eye which is in question in our 2nd hemistich. The word לין means at first 'pass the night' (24: 7; 29: 19), then 'dwell', 'reside' (cf. 19: 4; 41: 14).

3 The pericope 3b-5a, absent from Sah., marked with asterisk in Jerome and Syro-hex. (except v. 4a by mistake), did not exist in G. The present text, very literally translated, comes from Theod. (cf. Colb. and Syro-hex.). For 3a, G ἔκλεψαν δέ μου τὰ ὑπάρχοντα ἀλλότριοι scarcely reflects the MT. The difficulty of fitting this text to the Hebrew words becomes apparent from the varied hypotheses of the critics. It is said to be a translation of 2b (Ball), of 3a (Beer), of 2b-3a (Duhm), of 5a (Dillmann). Without attempting to discover the basis of G, we note that v. 2 of G formed only a single hemistich (cf. sup.), hence no more than 2a. Since v. 3 of G is likewise reduced to a single hemistich, it is quite likely that this represents 2b. Now, the text of G begins again only at 5b, which opens with וְעֵינִי. And it so happens that 2b ends with עֵינִי. A mistake of homoeoteleuton thus explains the lacuna of G. For ערבני, Targ. עריב יתי 'pledge me', Syr. 'my pledge'. For יתקע, Theod. συνδεθήτω, Targ. יקים 'will swear', Syr. 'making peace'. V. 3 is paraphrased in Vulg. *libera me, Domine, et pone me juxta te et cujusvis manus pugnet contra me.*

Job addresses himself directly to God who is his witness (16: 19). The present text separates שִׂימָה נָּא from the rest of the sentence and vocalises עָרְבֵנִי as an accusative. Thus one is obliged to understand 'my earnest' after שׂימה and to see a pleonasm in ערבנו, so as to be able to translate: 'O God! be my pledge against Thyself! (Renan) or 'be to Thyself my pledge' (Segond, Crampon). The difficulty is surmounted if we regard ערבני as the noun עֵרָבוֹן (Gn 38: 17, 18, 20) with suffix (cf. Syr.). This reading, proposed by Reiske, is accepted by most moderns. We shall vocalise עָרְבֵנִי 'my pledge', 'my earnest' (Ehrlich). The phrase שׂים ערבון means 'to lay down a pledge, a guarantee', exactly like נתן ערבון in Gn 38: 18. The 1st hemistich will be translated: 'Lay then my pledge beside Thee'. This earnest of Job, the pledge which he offers to God, consists in his sufferings which are

4   Because Thou hast deprived their heart of understanding,
     Therefore *their hand* is not raised.
5   Such a man invites his friends to share with him,
     While the eyes of his sons languish with want!

4   תָּרוּם יָדָם; MT: תרומם.

as it were an anticipation of death. There is no other possible pledge, for none of his friends would be willing to stand as his guarantor: 'Who would be prepared to strike my hand?' The interrogative מִי־הוּא as in 4:7; 13:19. To strike the hand of a person is the gesture by which a wager is made; among the Hebrews it is essentially the action through which one solemnly becomes the guarantor of another (Pr 6:1; 17:18; 22:26). The phrase eventually came to mean 'to warrant', 'to be answerable for', which allows in our passage the use of the *niph'al* instead of the *qal*.

4 On the text of G, cf. v. 3. For תרומם, Theod. ὑψώσῃς αὐτούς, Targ. תרומם להום, vocalising תָּרֵם. Syr. 'they exalt themselves' and Vulg. *exaltabuntur* make of תרומם a *hithpa'el* in the plural. The negative is omitted in Syr., which connects לחלק of v. 5 with v. 4.

Job has just declared that no one can stand as guarantor for him. Naturally he is thinking of his friends. The latter have egregiously failed to understand his situation, because of their lack of discernment. The 1st hemistich, 'because Thou hast hidden their heart from understanding', a hypallage meaning 'because Thou hast hidden understanding from their heart', i.e. Thou hast deprived their heart of understanding. The understanding, שֶׂכֶל, has its seat in the heart, as have the other mental faculties; cf. Is 44:18, where the heart is the organ of the intellectual operation denoted by השכיל 'to understand'. The 2nd hemistich,

which begins: עַל־כֵּן 'that is why', expresses the consequence of the 1st (cf. Comm. on 6:3). As it stands, it is usually interpreted 'that is why Thou wilt not exalt them' (Dillmann, etc.), or 'hence Thou wilt not allow them to triumph' (Segond), or, more broadly, 'hence Thou wilt not allow them to score a triumph in this debate' (Renan). Some regard תרומם as a jussive (Ehrlich); cf. already Le Hir: 'permit them not to triumph'. These translations agree to add the 3rd person plural suffix after תרומם. Following Merx, a few moderns vocalise תָּרֵמֶם (following Theod. and Targ.). The meaning remains the same. But whatever meaning is assigned to the *hiph'il* or the *po'lel* of רום, one comes up against the obstacle that the action of God, mentioned in the 1st hemistich, is implied to produce an effect on God Himself, whereas we expect its effect to be exerted on the hearers of Job. We propose to read at the close תָּרוּם יָדָם, the letters יד having fallen by haplography between the two *mêms*. Hence we attain the result 'it is for that reason that their hand is not raised'. Job is explaining why it is that no one is prepared to strike his hand as his guarantor.

5 G τῇ μερίδι ἀναγγελεῖ κακίας comes from Theod. (cf. v. 3). It is apparent that Theod. reads רָעִים instead of רֵעִים. Similarly Symm. κακοῖς. The opening לחלק being linked with v. 4 (cf. sup.), Syr. reconstitutes a 1st hemistich as 'and friend rises against his friend'. Targ. renders יגיד by על אחוית 'on an in-

6   And I have been made *a byword* to the common folk,
      I am he in whose face they spit!

6   **לִמְשֹׁל** (versions, with the exception of Syr.); MT: **לִמְשֹׁל**.

dication'. Vulg. conveys very appropriately the general sense of the proverb: *praedam pollicetur sociis et oculi filiorum ejus deficient.* G fails to understand the 2nd hemistich: ὀφθαλμοὶ δὲ ἐφ᾽ υἱοῖς ἐτάκησαν.

Cordier, quoted by Knabenbauer, had already written: *vix duos auctores reperias inter quos de hujus loci aut conversione aut explicatione conveniat.* Now, it is to be noted that the 2nd hemistich offers no difficulty: 'and the eyes of his sons languish'. It is almost a repetition of 11:20a: **וְעֵינֵי רְשָׁעִים תִּכְלֶינָה** 'and the eyes of the wicked languish'. Again, it is clear that **רֵעִים**, 'the friends' of the 1st hemistich, are contrasted with the sons. At first sight one feels that it is a question of some one whose sons pine with want while he is busy entertaining others. It is this idea which has guided the interpretation of modern exegetes: 'friends are invited to share a feast' (Arnheim, Hirzel, Hitzig, etc.; cf. Vulg. *praedam pollicetur sociis*), 'his friends are invited to share his booty' (Segond). Budde arrives at the same meaning by vocalising **לַחֵלֶק**? 'friends are invited to share with him'. Ehrlich sees in the 1st hemistich the man who appoints his friends for a share of the inheritance and who forgets his destitute sons. According to Avronin and Rabinowitz it is the man who invites his friends to his table, while his sons suffer from hunger. It becomes apparent that the general idea is always to contrast the attitude towards friends with that towards sons. And this interpretation is more easily reconcilable with the text than that which proposes to see in the 2nd hemistich the punishment of him who behaves badly towards his friends. On the last

hypothesis it is necessary to suppose that the 1st hemistich must mean: 'one abandons one's friends to exploitation' (Dillmann, etc.), or else 'he who delivers up his friends as a prey' (Le Hir), 'the man who betrays his friends' (Renan), 'he allows his friends to perish' (Loisy). A third interpretation is that which assigns to **הִגִּיד** the meaning of 'inform against (Jer 20:10), so as to translate: 'he who betrays friends for booty', and then to see in the 2nd hemistich the punishment of such conduct (cf. Driver-Gray). Torczyner recomposes a 1st hemistich thus: **לַחֵלֶק יַגִּיעוּ זָרִים** 'to give a share in his property (Ps 109:11) to strangers'. But he transfers the whole to a place after 31:13. We are in fact confronted by a case of hypallage similar to that in v. 4: the preposition **לְ״** should govern **רֵעִים**, whilst **חֵלֶק** should represent the direct object. Thus the meaning becomes clear: 'like one who invites his friends to a share-out'. The suffix of **יַגִּיד** is implicit in the suffix of **בָּנָיו**.

The idea is that of a man who invites his friends to share his goods, while his family are dying of hunger. The proverb is being quoted in support of v. 4, in which Job declared that God had deprived his friends of understanding. Instead of busying themselves with the affairs of others, they would do better to be concerned about what is of immediate import to them. It is a sally similar to the *Medice, cura teipsum!* Note that the ostrich which abandons its eggs and forgets its little ones will be singled out for mention as lacking in wisdom and understanding. A similar idea constitutes the link between v. 4 and v. 5.

6 G ἔθου δέ με replaces the 3rd

7   And with grief my eye has grown dim,
     My limbs as the shadow *vanish away*!

7   כָּלִים MT: כֻּלָּם.

person by the 2nd. Instead of לִמְשֹׁל,
G θρύλημα, Vulg. *quasi in proverbium*,
and Targ. למתלין 'in proverbs' read
לִמְשֹׁל?; cf. παραβολήν in Aq., Symm.,
and Theod. The 2nd hemistich is
rendered vaguely γέλως δὲ αὐτοῖς
ἀπέβην (G), *et exemplum sum coram
eis* (Vulg.). Targ. interprets תפת in
the sense of Gehenna, while Syr.
translates תפת by ܠܘܥܣܐ 'veil'.

Job returns to his lament. From
16: 19 he has ceased to regard God
as the cause of his ills. On the contrary, he calls on God as a witness
(16: 19). Hence there is no reason to
follow Siegfried and Duhm, who, in
agreement with G, read ותציגני 'and
Thou hast put me' instead of
והציגני 'one has put me'. The impersonal construction is expressed
sometimes by the 3rd person plural
(4: 19; 7: 3; 15: 28), sometimes by
the 3rd person singular (Gesenius-
Kautzsch, § 144d). In the light of the
expressions נתן לְמָשָׁל 'to put as a
proverb, a laughingstock' (Jer 24: 9;
2 Ch 7: 20), הָיָה לְמָשָׁל 'to become the
byword, laughingstock' (Dt 28: 37;
1 K 9: 7), it is evident that the vocalisation of the versions (except Syr.),
viz. לִמְשֹׁל, is preferable to the לִמְשֹׁל
of the MT. Cf. again Ps 69: 12 'and
I have become for them a byword'
ואהי להם למשל. The plural עַמִּים,
complement of the construct state
משל, corresponds to the Latin *gentes*
(whence Fr. *gens*). The 1st hemistich,
'And I have been made a byword to
the common folk', echoes 30: 9, 'and
now I am their song and have become
their byword'. Now, v. 10 of ch. 30
runs: 'They have held me in horror,
they have avoided me, and have not
spared to spit in my face!' The com-

parison obliges us to interpret our
2nd hemistich as literally 'and a spit
in the face, that is what I am!',
hence, I am he in whose face they
spit. This interpretation, which is
that of the ancients, finds good support in Is 53: 3, where the servant
of Yahweh is described as he before
whom one veils his face, and where
the expression chosen is 'like one
who veils his face before him'. It is
the object of the action which is, as
here, the subject of the clause. The
poet in fact sees simultaneously the
unhappy man who is despised and
the action by which the contempt is
manifested. There is thus no reason
at all to consider the *hapax* תֹּפֶת
(from תוף 'spit') as representing the
proper name תפת (2 K 23: 10; Jer
7: 31-2; 19: 6, 11-14); cf. Targ.
This name is said to have become
the symbol of a 'scarecrow', and
an attempt has been made to find in
לפנים a meaning 'for people' (Jacob,
in *ZATW*, 1912, p. 286), or else it is
replaced by לבנים 'for the sons'
(Graetz, Ehrlich). Others read
לפניהם 'before them' (cf. Syr., Vulg.)
and, following Perles, propose וּמוֹפֵת
'and a prodigy, a monster'. This correction cannot be supported by
Vulg. *exemplum*, which merely produces a meaning parallel to the 1st
hemistich. It is the word משל which
Vulg. translates as *exemplum* in 2 Ch
7: 20. The comparison with 30: 9-10
robs these needless corrections of any
semblance of probability.

7 For תכה, G πεπώρωνται, Aq.,
Symm., Theod. ἠμαυρώθησαν. The
plural comes from a reading עֵינַי
'my eyes'; cf. G οἱ ὀφθαλμοί μου.
The other versions have the singular.
The 2nd hemistich is rendered

8   Upright men are stupefied at this,
     And the innocent man is vexed with the godless,

πεπολιόρκημαι μεγάλως ὑπὸ πάντων by G, which connects יִצְרִי with the verb צוּר and reads מֵעַל instead of כְּצֵל (Beer). Vulg. paraphrases the end *quasi in nihilum redacta sunt.* For יִצְרִי, Vulg. *membra mea*, Targ. קְלַסְתּוּרִי 'my forms'. Syr. ܘܚܫܐܬܝ 'my thoughts' vocalises וִיצָרַי.

The verb כָּהָה 'become faint', 'grow dim' expresses the condition of the eyes which have lost their sharpness of vision as a result of old age (Gn 27: 1; Dt 34: 7; 1 S 3: 2). But here it is grief which dims the sight. The use of כָּעַשׂ is as in 6: 2. Cf. Ps 6: 8 עָשְׁשָׁה מִכַּעַס עֵינִי 'my eye has grown dim through grief'. In 16: 16 Job said: 'and on my eyelids is darkness!' The word יְצָרִים, from which comes יִצְרִי, recurs only in Sir 31: 19, where יִצְרָיו is a marginal gloss to indicate the inner organs (cf. Peters, p. 118). Vulg. translates very properly 'and my members'. The relation between יְצוּר and יֵצֶר is well brought out by the translation of Targ. 'my forms'. Rashi explains the derivation by his interpretation: 'my members of which I am formed' (נוֹצָר). The verb יָצַר is used to convey the idea of man's creation by God (Gn 2: 8), while Babylonian uses *banû* 'to build', 'to construct' (*Choix de textes*, p. 66, 7; p. 86, 20f.). And it is from this very verb *banû* that is derived *binâti* 'members' (*L'Emploi métaphorique*, p. 137). It is thus apparent that the semantic development is the same in both languages. The members are the primal elements of which the body of man is made. The change to וִיצָרַי 'and my fancies' or 'my imaginations' (cf. Syr.), recommended by Budde, introduces an ambiguous term in the place of one which offers a very clear sense in the light of etymology and trad-

ition. The Massoretes would never have replaced by a *hapax* the more common word. As it stands, the 2nd hemistich would be translated: 'and my members are as the shadow, all of them!' The shadow in this case would be the symbol of emaciation: I am no more than a shadow! But the word צֵל 'shadow' is essentially the symbol of what vanishes with the passage of time (8: 9; 14: 2; Ps 102: 12; 109: 23; 144: 4; Ec 6: 12; 8: 13; 1 Ch 29: 15). We have seen in 7: 9 that the verb כלה denotes what passes away, what is dissipated like smoke, what disappears like the cloud, the dew. In 33: 21, this verb כלה has as its subject בְּשָׂרוֹ 'his flesh'. These facts support the hypothesis of Houbigant and Reiske, who recognise in כלם a participle stemming from the verb כלה. Hence we shall read כָּלִים (Ehrlich, on Dt 28: 32), which is the plural masculine participle of כלה. The form כְּלִים (Beer) is no longer in use.

8   G δίκαιος δὲ ἐπὶ παρανόμῳ ἐπαναστάιη is certainly the translation of the 2nd hemistich (cf. Sah., Syrohex., Jerome, Arab. Baud.). G (A) δικαίῳ γὰρ παράνομος ἐπανέστη tries to weld the 2nd hemistich to the 1st (cf. γάρ), and cannot be used to emend the text (contra Beer).

The opening 'upright men are stupefied at this' is very natural in the context. Cf. the use of the verb שמם in Is 52: 14 in connection with Yahweh's servant, the righteous sufferer: 'just as many were stupefied on account of you (שָׁמְמוּ עָלֶיךָ)'. Hence it would be unwise to change יָשֹׁמּוּ to יִשְׂמְחוּ 'they rejoice' (contra Ehrlich, Torczyner) on the basis of 31: 29, which would compel us to transfer v. 8 to a different context. The difficulty which has inclined

9   But the righteous man perseveres in his way,
      And the man with pure hands increases in energy!

certain exegetes to remove vv. 8-9 from Job's speech (cf. Duhm, Peake, Gray), to place them in the mouth of one of his friends (Duhm suggests after 18: 3), arises especially from the 2nd hemistich. It has been proposed to assign to יִתְעֹרָר exactly the same meaning as in 31: 29, where הִתְעֹרַרְתִּי is parallel to אֶשְׂמַח 'I rejoice' (whence the correction of Ehrlich and Torczyner, above) and means 'I have exulted'. But the natural meaning of the *hithpo'lel* of עוּר is 'to become agitated, stirred up' (Is 51: 17; 64: 6), and the preposition עַל before the complement introduces the one against whom the person in question becomes stirred. Now, we find, in Ps 37: 1, 7, 8; Ps 24: 19, a series of propositions whose governing *Leitmotif* is אַל־תִּתְחַר 'vex not yourself' against the wicked, the godless, etc. The aim is to warn the believer against the indignation he feels in his heart when he notices that the workers of iniquity prosper: 'Fret not yourself against evildoers, do not be vexed with the fomentors of evil . . . . Fret not against him who succeeds in his business, against the man who accomplishes his plans' (Ps 37: 1, 7); 'Fret not against evildoers, be not indignant against the wicked' (Pr 24: 19). It is this feeling of indignation experienced by the believer when he is confronted by the prosperity of the wicked which is the theme amply developed in Ps 73, where we note v. 3: 'For I grew indignant with the impious, when I saw the peace of the wicked.' We should note that the root עוּר corresponds to the Arabic غير, the precise meaning of which is 'to be imbued with jealousy, zeal' and which takes the preposition على or من before the object of this jealousy or zeal. The agitation denoted by יתערר is a form of zeal; it is the indignation provoked by the spectacle of the apparent injustice in the distribution of goods in this world. Note that יְשָׁרִים 'the upright' and נָקִי 'the innocent' are parallel terms in 4: 7, and that we have parallelism also between נקי and צדיקים 'the just' (replacing יְשָׁרִים) in 22: 19. This fact in itself argues against the hypothesis of Merx and Bickell, who wish to transpose נקי and חָנֵף. The word חנף 'godless', 'unbeliever', which is characteristic of Job (cf. 8: 13), takes the place of the various terms used to designate the wicked in Ps 37 and 73, as in Pr 24 (cf. sup.). We can unhesitatingly keep v. 8 where it is and translate the 2nd hemistich: 'the innocent man is vexed with the godless'. We shall have an ascending series: 'the upright' and 'the innocent' (v. 8), 'the righteous man' and 'the man with pure hands' (v. 9), leading up to Job's declaration that he does not find 'a wise man' among his companions (v. 10).

9   Syr. adds to the 1st hemistich: 'and he will remain steadfast', a new translation of יֹאחֵז. Vulg. *mundis manibus* doubtless springs from *mundus manibus*, a translation of טֹהַר יָדַיִם. For יָדַיִם, Syr., and Targ. 'his hands'. The vocalisation וּטְהָר is the earliest (cf. Baer, Ginsburg).

In v. 8 we noted that צדיקים 'the righteous' replaced יְשָׁרִים as a parallel term to נָקִי in 22: 19 (compared with our v. 8 and 4: 7). We shall have צָדִיק 'the righteous man' complementary to נקי in 27: 17. Thus it becomes apparent that v. 9 is well knit to v. 8. The צדיק is that righteous man so often mentioned in the Psalms as the very type of the rigor-

10　But you, turn, all of you, and come here now:
　　I shall not find a wise man among you!

ous observer of the law. He corresponds to the טְהָר־יָדַיִם 'pure as to the hands', i.e. 'the man with pure hands', for the hands are the instruments of action. In 11:14 Zophar suggested to Job that he should remove the iniquity which lay in his hand. We are still in the climate of ideas typical of Job's friends. The parallelism between צדיק and טהר־ידים moreover recalls the parallelism between the verbs צדק and טהר (4:17) in the first speech of Eliphaz. The 1st hemistich reminds us of 23:11, 'His step has my foot followed: I have kept His way and have not turned aside.' The righteous man perseveres in the same path, for his ways are perfect (4:6b). There is no reason for him to change his behaviour. The sight of the misfortune of the wicked only confirms him in his chosen attitude. Far from dismaying him, this sight serves only to strengthen him: 'and the man with pure hands increases in energy'. The abstract אֹמֶץ 'strength' in the sense of 'moral strength and energy'. It is not found elsewhere. Cf. the use of the *pi'el* of אמץ in 4:4; 16:5. The *hiph'il* of יסף, as in 42:10, to mean 'increase', 'intensify'. It can be seen that the attitude of the righteous man and of the man with pure hands is firmer than that of the upright and innocent, mentioned in v. 8 as being overcome by stupefaction and indignation. The righteous man presents us with the spectacle of an unshakable stoicism. We shall see in v. 10 that this does not apply to Job's friends.

10 Vulg. *igitur omnes vos* and Syr. 'but you, all of you' translate כלם according to the sense, whilst G οὐ μὴν δὲ ἀλλὰ πάντες and Targ. וברם כלהון are in agreement with the MT.

G ἐρείδετε interprets תשבו in the sense of 'return to', 'insist on', but Jerome *convertimini* (like Vulg.) translates ἐπιστράφητε, a reading of Theod. and Aq., quoted in Syro-hex. The words ובאו נא were omitted in G. The words καὶ δεῦτε δή (Jerome *et venite*), absent from Sah., marked with asterisk in Syro-hex., probably come from Theod.

The apostrophe contained in v. 10 recalls 6:29, where Job cried out to his friends: 'Return then ... and return!', after telling them: 'Turn towards me' (6:28). The opening וְאָלָם כֻּלָּם aims at an effect of assonance, which explains the vocalisation וְאָלָם instead of וְאוּלָם 'but, on the other hand' (1:11; 11:5; 12:7; 13:4; 14:18), and the choice of כֻּלָּם 'they all' (cf. v. 7) instead of כֻּלְּכֶם (13:4; 16:2; 27:12). Ambiguity is impossible, and we have a similar use of the vocative in the 3rd person plural in Mic 1:2 (1 K 22:28), שִׁמְעוּ עַמִּים כֻּלָּם 'listen, peoples, all of you!' Cf. again 18:4a. Those authors who find the 1st hemistich too long are not agreed as to how much should be removed: sometimes ובאו נא (Bickell), at other times כלם (Duhm, Grimme, Ball). But the words ואלם כלם are regarded as forming a single expression, which enables us to retain them despite the excrescence of the 1st hemistich. The verb תָּשֻׁבוּ is used exactly as in Pr 1:23, 'turn again!' It is an invitation typical of the pedagogue. Then 'and come here now!', a further invitation to a searching examination the conclusion of which is contained in :'I shall not find a wise man among you!' Truly, the friends have conspicuously failed to understand the situation (v. 4). Their attitude has nothing in com-

11   My days are gone, my projects have been shattered,
      The desires of my heart

mon with that of the righteous man
(v. 9), nor even that of the innocent
(v. 8). They have insisted on explaining all, instead of maintaining
a prudent reserve.

11 G αἱ ἡμέραι μου παρῆλθον ἐν
βρόμῳ places the *athnaḥ* under זמתי
and connects this word with the root
זהם (cf. 6: 7). G (A) replaces βρόμῳ
by δρόμῳ (7: 6; 9: 25). Syr. cuts out
the suffixes, which has the effect of
producing a general observation:
'they spend their days with vain
thoughts, ruining the hearts of the
peoples'. G ἐρράγη δὲ τὰ ἄρθρα τῆς
καρδίας μου connects מורשי with the
Aramaic מרשא 'rope', attested by
the Syriac مَرْشَא. Vulg. paraphrases
מורשי לבבי by *torquentes cor meum*,
while Targ. interprets by לוחי לבבי
'the tablets of my heart'.
    Ehrlich considers this verse to be
irredeemably corrupt. What critics
have above all found obnoxious is
the rhythm of the verse. They have
insisted on dividing into two roughly
equal hemistichs, and already the
Greek version had connected נתקו
with the 2nd hemistich. A great difficulty arises from the fact that זמֹּתי
can no longer be explained after
'my days are gone'. We should expect
a term of comparison as in phrases of
a similar type (7: 6; 9: 25). Hence
modern critics have changed זמתי,
but without reaching a hypothesis
which could rally opinion. Merx
read המיתי 'I have sighed'; Wright
מדותי 'my limits' (complement of
עברו; cf. Ps 39: 5); Beer a derivative
of זהם (following G) but without
hazarding a guess as to the form of
it; Budde למות 'my days have been
spent in dying'; Ball כמו־מץ or כמץ
'like straw'. Duhm begins by in-
verting זמתי נתקו, then he corrects
נתקו into מתקוה and זמותי into צמתו,

which enables him to reconstruct as
follows: 'my days have been spent
without hope, the desires of my heart
are destroyed'. These divergences
continue in the interpretation of the
2nd hemistich, for the word מורשי
is connected now with the root ירש
'possess', 'inherit', whence מורשי
לבבי 'this patrimony of my soul'
(Le Hir), now with ארש (Ps 21: 3),
Assyrian *erêšu* 'desire', whence מורשי
לבבי 'the desires of my heart' (Dillmann, Hoffmann, Duhm, etc.). On
account of the meaning of נתקו 'are
broken' (connected with the 2nd
hemistich) it has been attempted to
find in מורשי 'the cords, fibres' of
the heart (following G), and resort
has been had to the Syriac مَرْشَא
'cord' (Beer). Wright and Budde
prefer to change מורשי to מיתרי
'cords', Klostermann proposes מוסרי
'chains'. The idea of the cords or
fibres of the heart breaking would be
rather attractive. But it should be
noted that in the MT the expression
מוֹרָשֵׁי לְבָבִי has as its parallel זְמֹתַי.
We know, moreover, that the heart
is the seat of thought, of desire, of
mental and voluntary activity. Hence
we shall not hesitate to connect
מוֹרָשׁ with the root ארש (see above),
whence comes אֲרֶשֶׁת of Ps 21: 3.
Note that in this passage of the
Psalms the formula ארשת שפתיו
'desire of his lips' is paralleled by
תאות לבו 'desire of his heart'. The
root ארש is well documented by the
Akkadian *erêšu* 'desire', 'long for'
whence *erištu* 'heart's desire'. The
form מוֹרָשׁ similar to מוֹסָר coming
from אסר 'bind' (12: 18). The parallel
word is זְמוֹתָי, which does not mean
'my lewd acts' (cf. זמה in 31: 11)
but rather 'my plans', 'my projects',
according to the meaning of the root

12   Change the night into day:
      The light is *closer* than the dark.

12   מִנֵּי‎; MT: מִפְּנֵי‎.

זָמַם‎ 'meditate', 'plan', etc.; cf. זָמַת‎
אִוֶּלֶת חַטָּאת‎ 'the devising of folly is
[already] a sin' (Pr 24: 9). In 5: 12
we had the *hiph'il* of פרר‎ which
means 'crumble', 'dash', 'break', used
metaphorically with the complement
מַחְשְׁבוֹת‎ 'thoughts'. It is a similar
image that we meet here, with the
verb נתק‎ in the *niph'al* 'to be broken,
shattered, dashed in pieces' and 'to
be torn away' (18: 14). Thus we have
a series of short clauses (exactly as
in v. 1): 'My days are gone, my projects have been shattered, the desires
of my heart . . . .' The verse has two
caesuras, but the 3rd part remains
suspended. In reality it will be
completed by v. 12a, which will
introduce the verb of which מוֹרָשֵׁי‎
לְבָבִי‎ is the subject. Such is the explanation which has seemed to us
to be the most objective, after the
failure of so many attempts to correct the text.

12   V. 12, absent from Sah., did not
exist in G. The present text comes
from Theod. (cf. Colb.). Syro-hex.
marks with asterisk the 1st hemistich
and attributes it to Aq., Theod.
(similarly Colb.). The reading ἔθηκα
does not indicate an original אָשִׂים‎
instead of יָשִׂימוּ‎ (contra Merx), for it
comes from ἔθηκαν, which is attested
by G (A), Syro-hex., Jerome *posuerunt*. The verb יָשִׂימוּ‎ and the word
קָרוֹב‎ are rendered by the 2nd person
plural in Syr. Paraphrase of the 2nd
hemistich in Vulg. *et rursum post
tenebras spero lucem*. Theod. has a
very literal translation: φῶς ἐγγὺς
ἀπὸ προσώπου σκότους. Before מִפְּנֵי‎
Targ. adds מְסַלְּקִין‎ 'removing'.
The straightforward sense of the
1st hemistich is not in doubt: 'they
change the night into day'. Cf. the
use of שִׂים‎ in Is 5: 20, 'Woe to those

who call evil good and good evil,
who change (שָׂמִים‎) darkness into
light and light into darkness, who
change (שָׂמִים‎) bitter into sweet and
sweet into bitter.' On the basis of
this text, it has been proposed to
give to our passage a purely moral
significance, and to see in those who
change night into day an allusion to
the friends of Job, who, by their
theories, distort the facts: 'and they
claim that night is day' (Segond). As
the 2nd person is expected, Renan
translates (cf. Syr.): 'Of the night
you make the day' (similarly Crampon). Cf. *Bible du rabbinat français*:
'Of the night they wish to make the
day.' On the other hand, Merx and
Duhm read אָשִׂים‎ instead of יָשִׂימוּ‎:
'I change night into day.' But G, or
more precisely Theod., lends no
support to such a correction. The true
meaning was foreshadowed by Le
Hir: 'My nights are changed into day'
(through insomnia). Job has complained of being unable to sleep, in
consequence of the nightmares which
haunt him (7: 3-4, 13-15). This time
it is the sighs of his heart (v. 11)
which prevent him from enjoying
rest, and thus 'change his nights into
days'. He feels that his days are irrevocably passing and that his projects
will never be realised (v. 11); he
sighs on his couch, and cannot sleep.
The 2nd hemistich is a *crux interpretum*. If we understand it in accordance with the Arabic construction which consists in placing the
preposition of removal من after the
verb قرب 'to be near', we might if
need be translate 'and the light is
near to the face of darkness'. But it
is difficult to grasp the point of this
image. Hence the paraphrases: 'and
my days are almost as gloomy as the

13 Can I hope again? Sheol is my home!
    It is in darkness that I have spread my couch.

night' (Le Hir), 'Ah! how your day resembles the darkness!' (Renan), '[in vain do they say] light dawns when for me it is darkness' (Loisy), 'in face of the darkness, [you say that] light is near' (Crampon), 'they say light is nearer than darkness' (*Bible du rabbinat français*). Duhm eliminates קרוב and vocalises מִפָּנַי: 'the light itself is darkness before me'. But in that case we should need לְפָנַי (Gray). Likewise, if one reads בֹּקֶר for קרוב (cf. Beer in Kittel's edition): 'the light of the morning is darkness before me'. Budde by a *tour de force* rearranges the MT in the following way: אור קרובם פֶּן־יֶחְשָׁךְ 'may the light of their kinsman not grow dark!' Now, the 2nd hemistich, consonantly with the parallelism between יוֹם and אוֹר, לַיְלָה and חֹשֶׁךְ, must offer an appropriate sequel or counterpart to the 1st. The expression מִפְּנֵי חֹשֶׁךְ recurs in 23:17 and 37:19, where it means 'because of the darkness', 'on account of the darkness'. This meaning cannot be fitted to the context. But if instead of מפני we read מִנִּי, we obtain as the end of the verse מִנִּי־חֹשֶׁךְ, which is attested by 12:22; 15:22. Further, we find the expression קָרוֹב מִמֶּנִּי 'nearer than I' in Ruth 3:12. Thanks to the slight change which we suggest, the 2nd hemistich becomes limpidly clear: 'The light is closer than the dark.' The change from night to day, brought about by the longings which haunt the mind of the sufferer, has the result of bringing light instead of darkness. Cf. Ro 13:12, ἡ νὺξ προέκοψεν, ἡ δὲ ἡμέρα ἤγγικεν.

13 G and Vulg. are in agreement with the MT in isolating אם אקוה. Targ. 'if I await the tomb as my

house'; Syr. 'if I wait for Sheol'.

Duhm rightly protests against the clumsy interpretation of Dillmann, Budde, and others, who make the conjunction אם govern all the phrases of vv. 13-14, so that the main clause begins at v. 15: 'where then is my hope?' The result is that we have a series of truisms worthy of La Palisse. It is true that Dillmann sees here a proof of the ignorance of Job's friends. But this subject has been dropped for some time. The meaning is not in doubt if we compare with v. 16 (cf. Comm.), where Job wonders if his hope can go down with him to Sheol and the dust. The hero feels that he is near to the gates of death and no longer hopes for anything from this life. The אם of the clause אם־אֲקַוֶּה is interrogative: 'Can I hope again?' Certainly not! since 'Sheol is my home and it is in darkness that I have spread my couch'. Cf. the use of אם in 6:12. Like the tomb (3:15), Sheol is a veritable dwelling place. But we know also that it is the house of darkness (cf. 7:9f.; 10:21f.). That is why בַּחֹשֶׁךְ 'in darkness' is the parallel to שְׁאוֹל: 'It is in darkness that I have spread my couch!' Cf. Ps 139:8, where the *hiph'il* of יצע (whence יָצוּעַ) means 'make one's bed': 'and I make my bed (וְאַצִּיעָה) in Sheol'. We meet again יְצוּעִי 'my couch' in Ps 63:7 and עֶרֶשׂ יְצוּעִי 'the bed of my couch' in Ps 132:3. Everywhere the plural of יָצוּעַ; but in Gn 49:4 we have יְצוּעִי 'my couch'. The proper meaning of the root רפד is 'support', 'prop' (Ca 2:5) with cushions (cf. the Arabic *rifâdah* 'cushion'). From this meaning is derived that of placing and arranging the cushions, spread-

14   To the grave I have cried: 'Thou art my father!'
      To the worms: 'My mother and sisters!'
15   And where then is my hope?
      And my *happiness*, who sees it?

15   וְטוֹבָתִי (G); MT: ותקותי.

ing the mattress, which are the components of the bed. It is needless to
replace by רבדתי as Ehrlich proposes, following Pr 7:16. We shall
have יְרְפַּד in 41:22.

14 For שַׁחַת, G θάνατον, Aq. and
Theod. διαφθοράν (cf. Syro-hex.),
Syr. ‏سحال‎ 'corruption', Vulg. *put-
redini*. These are all metaphors implying that the meaning of שַׁחַת 'pit'
is tomb (cf. inf.). Targ. faithfully
translates שׁחתא.

On the pretext that שַׁחַת is feminine, some moderns cut out אָבִי אַתָּה
to arrive at the colourless: 'I have
called the grave my mother and the
worms my sister.' Budde goes even
further by saying that the description sister suffices for רִמָּה. Duhm
builds up a psychological explanation: 'Some one felt that, if the
mother was mentioned, the father
should be too, and so unhesitatingly
introduced אבי אתה, in spite of the
fact that שׁחת is feminine: a striking
proof of the lack of perception which
has marked the approach to this
text.' It is rather the critic himself
who gives proof of lack of perception,
for after all the direct apostrophe
'thou art my father!' is admirable in
expressive force and the cry 'my
mother and my sisters' addressed to
the worms as a collective is perfectly
congruous with the context. The
author did not concern himself with
the gender of שַׁחַת, which though
etymologically 'the pit' in fact conveys the image of the tomb (33:18,
22, 24, 30). The idea of the tomb introduces by association that of the

worms which gnaw the rotting flesh;
cf. רִמָּה in 7:5. Job feels himself
bound by the closest ties to the grave
and the worms. Cf. Pr 7:4, 'Say to
Wisdom: thou art my sister!'—a
direct address, as here. In 30:29 Job
will describe himself as the brother
of the jackals.

15 The versions understood the
anomaly arising from the repetition
of תקותי; that is why Targ. renders
the first תקותי by סברי 'my hope',
the second by מתינתי 'my expectation'; Syr. repeats סברי, but adds
'and my confidence' to determine
the first תקותי; in Vulg. we have at
first *praestolatio mea*, then *patientiam
meam*. G certainly read תקותי, μοῦ...
ἡ ἐλπίς as the first word; but, instead
of the second תקותי, τὰ ἀγαθά μου
presupposes טוֹבָתִי. G ὄψομαι paraphrases מי ישׁורנה.

The interrogative אַיֵּה as in 21:28;
35:10. The adverb אֵפוֹ plays an
enclitic rôle (cf. Comm. on 4:7). The
repetition of תִּקְוָתִי surprised the
versions, and quite rightly so. The
original text was וְטוֹבָתִי, as is proved
by G. Ch. 8:3 cannot be cited in
favour of the repetition of the same
word (cf. Comm.). The corrections
to ותאותי 'my wish' ('Wright), or
ותוחלתי 'my expectation' (Hitzig),
have not the support of G. In 9:25,
Job explains that his days have not
seen happiness (טוֹבָה). Still more,
others cannot perceive it: 'And my
happiness, who sees it?' The verb
שׁור is used as in 7:8. We have here
the reply to the question of v. 13

16   Will they go down to Sheol *by my side*?
      Shall we together *descend* into the dust?

16   הַבְּיָדִי (G); MT: בדי. — נֵחָת (G. Syr.); MT: נָחַת.

(cf. Comm.). Job has nothing more to hope for on earth. He feels himself already in Sheol. And it is impossible for his hope to descend there with him (v. 16).

16   The word בדי is rendered טנדו 'together' in Targ., the element דִי of בדי being regarded like the Greek word δύω (according to Levy, *Chald. Wörterbuch*, I, p. 2 A and p. 309 B). Syr. 'with power' vocalises בְּדִי, whilst Vulg. *in profundissimum infernum* paraphrases בדי שאל 'the (deep) parts of Sheol'. Vulg. adds *omnia mea* as the subject of תרדנה. Targ. interprets שאל as the tomb (cf. v. 13). The reading of G ἦ μετ' ἐμοῦ εἰς ᾅδην καταβήσονται is excellent. It does not stem from העמדי (Duhm, Beer, Gray) or עמי (Siegfried) but from הַבְּיָדִי instead of בדי (cf. inf.). The 2nd hemistich is marked by asterisk in Jerome and Syro-hex., but it exists in Sah. The lacuna implied by the asterisk springs from an error of homoeoteleuton, since the two hemistichs finish with καταβήσονται ... καταβησόμεθα. Syr. replaces אם by the copula. Targ. שרן 'they rest' and Vulg. *requies* connect נחת with נוח. But Syr. ܢܚܬܘܢ and G καταβησόμεθα have recognised the verb נחת 'to go down' (cf. inf.).

The verb תֵּרַדְנָה in the feminine plural shows quite plainly that there were two distinct substantives in v. 15. It is a question of the hope and happiness of Job. The usual interpretation of בַּדֵּי שְׁאָל is as though we had here the word בַּדִּים 'bars' in the sense of 'bolts' (Hos 11 : 6), and critics see here the figure of rhetoric which consists in using the part for the whole. Hence the current translation is 'the gates of Sheol' (cf. Le Hir, Renan, Crampon, Segond, etc.). It is surprising that the author did not have recourse to שַׁעֲרֵי שְׁאוֹל of Is 38 : 10. Furthermore, we are faced by the difficulty of explaining אִם of the 2nd hemistich. Now, G ἦ μετ' ἐμοῦ is most certainly the parallel to אִם־יַחַד 'is it that together?' The interrogative particle ה has fallen out by haplography after יְשׁוּרֻנָה. But בדי comes neither from עמדי (cf. sup.) nor from אתי (Ehrlich). The Hebrew expression בְּיַד corresponding to the Assyrian *ina idi* 'by the side of' (*L'Emploi métaphorique*, p. 104 and p. 139), it becomes evident that the original text preserved by G had הַבְּיָדִי 'is it that by my side?' For the vocalisation of the particle, cf. 23 : 6. Thus the 1st hemistich becomes perfectly intelligible. Hope and happiness do not follow the dying man. Note the formula ירד שאול 'to go down to Sheol', exactly as in 7 : 9. It is now possible to grasp the sense of אִם which introduces the second part of the question. The verb נחת is vocalised as though coming from נוח 'to rest' (cf. Targ. and Vulg.), and it is maintained only by some such paraphrase as: 'I shall find rest' (Le Hir), 'one finds rest' (Renan, Crampon). Now, each word of the 2nd hemistich corresponds to a word in the 1st: אִם־יַחַד is complementary to הבידי, עַל־עָפָר to שאל. We expect from נחת the equivalent of תרדנה. In Targ. and Syr. the verb תרדנה is rendered by the Aramaic נחת 'to go down'. It is as clear as daylight that it is this verb (which moreover recurs in 21: 13 with Sheol as complement) which was read by G καταβησόμεθα (cf. Syr.). We must vocalise נַחַת.

Sheol is essentially the house of dust. To lie down in the dust means to die (cf. 7: 21), exactly like to descend into the dust (Ps 22: 20). It is clear that the tomb and Sheol often become merged together in the mind of Job. His speech ends with the vision of death, just as in 7: 21; 10: 21-2; 14: 20-2; 21: 32-3.

1   Then Bildad the Shuhite spoke and said:
2   For how long will you put shackles on words?
       Give ear and then we will speak.

Chapter 18   Second speech of Bildad: see Introduction, p. xliii.
2   תָּזִינוּ; MT: תבינו.

18:2 G μέχρι τίνος οὐ παύσῃ is a free interpretation of the 1st hemistich. The use of the singular, instead of the plural, for תשׂימון and תבינו (ἐπίσχες) has necessitated the negation before παύσῃ, which translates תשׂים קנצי, the word קנצי being regarded as an equivalent of קץ 'end'. Vulg. *usque ad quem finem verba jactabitis* seems likewise to interpret קנצי by קץ. Targ. translates קנצי by הרפתקי 'accidents', Syr. by ܡܘܟܠܐ 'obstacle'. For ואחר G ἵνα καὶ αὐτοί reads perhaps ואנחנו.

The opening עַד־אָנָה 'for how long?' will be repeated by Job himself as an introductory formula in 19:2. In 8:2 Bildad began with עַד־אָן, which has the same meaning. It is clear that it would be unwise to eliminate this characteristic formula, as is done by Duhm and Beer (ed. Kittel). These authors then correct תְּשִׂימוּן קִנְצֵי into תשׂים קץ or תשׂם קץ 'put an end to words', which obliges them to replace תבינו by תבין. If G is cited in support of these corrections, is it not inconsistent to neglect עד־אנה, which exists in G μέχρι τίνος? In fact, G believed that Bildad was addressing Job, whereas he is addressing his friends (cf. v. 3). He has the same feeling as Elihu in 32:3. The word קנצי is generally connected with קץ 'end', the *nun* being regarded as arising from dissi-

milation (cf. *Thesaurus* of Gesenius, s.v. קנץ). A comparison is made with 16:3, הקץ לדברי־רוח 'will there be no end to words of wind?' In that case we should have to see in קנצי an equivalent of קָצֵי. But the plural of קץ is nowhere found. Some have had recourse to the Arabic *qanaṣa* 'to give chase', in order to assign to קנצי the meaning of 'traps', 'snares', as if it were a question of laying snares for words (Castell, Schultens, etc.). But it would be Job rather than Bildad who could be suitably made to say that the friends are seeking to find fault with the preceding speech. Fried. Delitzsch connects קנצי with the Assyrian *qinazu* to which he attributes the meaning of 'straps', 'thongs'. The word means specifically 'whip', 'horsewhip' (cf. Jensen, in *KB*, VI, I, p. 450) and hence cannot be adapted to the context. On the other hand, there exists a word *qinṣu* (read wrongly in the dictionaries as *kurṣu*) the meaning of which is 'fetters', 'bonds', 'shackles' (Zimmern, in Gesenius-Buhl, s.v. קנצי). Noting that the construct state can be used before the preposition ל׳׳ (Gesenius-Kautzsch, § 130a), we suggest as a translation 'How long will you put shackles on words' or 'How long will you prevent one from speaking?' Bildad is addressing the audience. He will not

3 Why should we be accounted as beasts?
Why should we be *likened to cattle* in your eyes?

3 כַּבַּעַר נִדְמִינוּ (cf. G for נדמינו); MT: נטמינו.

tolerate being prevented from speaking any longer. The 2nd hemistich is interpreted: 'Be so good as to consider, then we will speak' (Le Hir), 'Have understanding, then we will speak' (Segond, Crampon), etc. It is clear that תָּבִינוּ plays the part of an imperative or jussive (cf. 6: 23b; 17: 10a), as is suggested by what follows: 'and then we will speak'. It is an ill-judged rhetorical device to say to one's listeners: be intelligent! Nor can one properly translate: 'be so good as to consider!' for such is not the meaning of בין or הבין 'perceive', 'discern', 'understand'. The meaning of 'give heed' that is postulated for this passage is hardly confirmed by the use of בין and הבין in the Bible. We propose to read: תַּזִינוּ (similar form to אָזֵין of 32: 11), from the verb הַאֲזִין 'give ear' (9: 16). Thus we obtain a perfectly clear meaning: 'Give ear and then we will speak.' Instead of preventing him from speaking, the audience would do better to listen to what he has to say. Cf. 33: 1; 34: 2, 16; 37: 14.

3 G omits נחשבנו. The verb נטמינו is connected with טמא 'to be unclean' by Syr. ܐܬܛܡܐܠ and Vulg. *sorduimus*, with טמן, 'to hide' by Targ. טמענא. G σεσιωπήκαμεν read a form of דמם (cf. 29: 21; 30: 27). G and Syr. replace the plural suffix by the singular in בעיניכם, translating 'in thy eyes'.

The interrogation מַדּוּעַ 'why?' as in 3: 12. The *niph'al* of חשב with כ" before the object of comparison, to express 'to be considered as', 'to be accounted', cf. 41: 21. Job has declared that even beasts of burden,

בהמות, knew as much as his friends (12: 7). Ignorance is the characteristic of the brute beasts (Ps 73: 22). The cry of Bildad, 'Why should we be accounted as beasts?', is very understandable. בְּהֵמָה is used in a collective sense; cf. רִמָּה in 17: 14. The word נְטְמִינוּ is understood by some moderns also as stemming from טמא (cf. Syr. and Vulg.). But in that case we should have to translate: 'Why should we be unclean in your eyes?' Uncleanness is not the consequence of a beast-like stupidity. Jewish exegesis already sought for a different meaning by having resort to a root טמה, which would be parallel to אטם and טמם (Aramaic). The *niph'al* of טמה would mean 'to be stopped up, obstructed', in which case we should expect as subject 'the heart' or 'the ears', which are the organs of understanding. It is not the person himself who could be the subject. On the basis of G σεσιωπή-καμεν, Bickell and Beer read נִדְמִינוּ, assigning to this verb the meaning of 'to be reduced to silence'. The passage of Ps 49: 13, 21, which is quoted in favour of such a meaning, is not conclusive, since G renders נדמו both times by καὶ ὡμοιώθη αὐτοῖς. In fact, G certainly had here נדמינו, but the verb has been confused with דמם (cf. sup.). We recognise in נִדְמִינוּ the original reading, while keeping for the *niph'al* of דמה the sense of 'to be compared with, likened with', which forms an excellent parallel to נֶחְשַׁבְנוּ. What is lacking is the term of comparison. Klostermann extricates himself from the difficulty by cutting out נחשבנו and connecting נדמינו בעיניכם with the 1st hemistich, which thus becomes

4   O you, who tear yourself in your anger,
     Because of you, will a country be abandoned,
     Or a rock removed from its place?

5   Yes, the light of the wicked goes out,
     And his flame of fire ceases to shine.

excessively long, even if we replace בעיניכם by בעיניך 'in thy eyes'. Ehrlich interpolates כבקר 'like oxen' between נחשבנו and כבהמה, which thus passes into the 2nd hemistich. We have quoted Ps 73: 22, where בהמות denotes the brute beast (plural of majesty) used as a symbol of ignorance. The corresponding word was בַּעַר 'cattle', 'stupid beast', another image of ignorance and lack of understanding (Ps 92: 7; Pr 30: 2). Hence we restore כַּבַּעַר 'like cattle' before נדמינו. The word fell out by haplography after כבהמה. The 2nd hemistich, 'why should we be likened to cattle in your eyes?', answers perfectly to: 'Why should we be accounted as beasts?' The change from בעיניכם to בעיניך following G and Syr., is not necessary, since Bildad is addressing the audience.

4 Vulg. *qui perdis animam tuam in furore tuo* has well understood that the 1st hemistich was vocative. G κέχρηταί σοι ὀργή is an approximation (following 16: 9, where ὀργῇ χρησάμενος rendered אפו טרף). Instead of הלמענך, G ἐὰν σὺ ἀποθάνῃς, whence Merx הבמותך (?). For the 3rd hemistich, G ἢ καταστραφήσεται ὄρη (A ἡ γῆ) ἐκ θεμελίων; Duhm translates this back into Hebrew and replaces ממקומו by ממסודיו, without noticing that ἐκ θεμελίων translates ממקומה in 9: 6.

In order to evade the three hemistichs, Duhm places here the passage 17: 8-10a. We have seen that this pericope was perfectly intelligible in the mouth of Job. The opening proposition, 'he who tears his soul in his anger', is vocative. Driver with ex-

cellent appositeness quotes 2 K 9: 31, where הרג אדניו 'assassin of his master' is an apposition to the vocative, Zimri. We have the same phenomenon in the use of כֻּלָּם 'they all' to mean 'you all' in 17: 10. Bildad at first addressed himself to a group. He now turns to Job and apostrophises him as 'he who tears his soul in his anger'. Cf. the use of אפו טרף 'his anger has found a prey' in 16: 9. The direct complement clarifies the meaning of טרף: 'treat as a prey', 'tear'. Job has been attacking an adversary. He is here shown as his own enemy. His manifestations of anger will not avail to change what is established: 'because of you, will a country be abandoned?' The supreme catastrophe is the abandonment of a country by its own inhabitants: Lv 26: 43; Is 7: 16, where the *niph'al* of עזב occurs, as here. The 3rd hemistich, 'or a rock be removed from its place', is a repetition of 14: 18b, although the first two terms are inverted. Man cannot influence events by his anger, while the anger of God can overturn mountains (9: 5). It is with ironical intent that Bildad echoes the phrase of Job in 14: 18b. There is no reason whatever to use G for the purpose of obtaining greater variety. Furthermore, G does not presuppose any other text than the MT (contra Duhm); cf. sup.

5 To avoid the anomaly of the sing. suffix of אִשׁ after the plural רשעים, G renders the word אשׁ by αὐτῶν ἡ φλόξ. G (A) corrects αὐτῶν into αὐτοῦ. Vulg. replaces רשעים by the singular: *lux impii*. For יגה, G ἀποβήσεται (A ἀναβήσεται), but Jer-

6   The light in his tent grows dim,
     And his lamp is put out above him.

7   His vigorous steps become cramped,
     And his own counsel causes him to *stumble*.

7 וְתַכְשִׁילֵהוּ (cf. G); MT: וְתַשְׁלִיכֵהוּ.

ome *splendebit* (cf. Theod. λάμψει).

Bildad resumes the general theme of the misfortunes which overtake the wicked. He has already shown that their happiness is but an illusion (8: 11-19). The adverb גַּם 'yet' opposes the affirmation of Bildad to all that has been said by his friend. Cf. Ps 129: 2b, where גם means 'in spite of everything'. Bildad is supported by the wisdom of the nations. The first idea 'the light of the wicked goes out' is current coin. It recurs, expressed in the same terms (with the exception of נֵר instead of אוֹר), in Pr 13: 9; 24: 20. Light is not only the image of life (3: 20; 17: 1); it is also the symbol of happiness (11: 17). The verb דָּעַךְ, used in the *niph'al* in 6: 17, is the Aramaic form of זעך 'to be extinguished' which appears only in 17: 1. Outside 22: 28, the verb נגה 'shine', 'illuminate' recurs in the *qal* only in Is 9: 1. The word שָׁבִיב 'flame' is Aramaic (Dn 3: 22; 7: 9). The locution שביב אש 'flame of fire' reappears in Sir 8: 10; 45: 19. It is a kind of compound word, parallel to אוֹר. It should be translated: 'his flame of fire' and not, as is generally done, 'the flame of his hearth'. The change of number is not at all surprising. After having enunciated the principle, Bildad begins to apply it to a particular case.

6 G renders אור by τὸ φῶς αὐτοῦ and נרו by ὁ δὲ λύχνος. The suffix of אהלו, omitted in G, is restored in G (A), Sah.
Same images as in v. 5. Verb חשׁךְ 'to grow dark' as in 3: 9. The tent is pre-eminently the dwelling place:

5: 24; 12: 6; 15: 34. Bildad has already spoken about 'the tent of the wicked' (8: 22). The 2nd hemistich is skilfully composed with the help of v. 5a. Note the use of נֵרוֹ 'his lamp', instead of אוֹר; cf. Pr 13: 9; 24: 20, where 'the lamp of the wicked' replaced 'the light of the wicked' of v. 5a. The expression עָלָיו 'above him' corresponds to בְּאָהֳלוֹ 'in his tent'. The lamp was placed on a stand to give light to the whole house (Mt 5: 15). Cf. 29: 3, where the lamp is again above the head. The thesis of Bildad will be called in question by Job in 21: 17a, 'How often is the lamp of the wicked extinguished?'

7 G θηρεύσαισαν ἐλάχιστοι reads יצדו צערי (interchanging ד and ר) and connects יצדו with צוד. The word *infimi*, which renders ἐλάχιστοι in Jerome, becomes *infirmi* in Bod. and Tur. Note that Syr. ܢܨܝܕ also reads יצדו, but connects it with the verb צדא, צדה 'to be devastated'. Instead of וְתַשְׁלִיכֵהוּ, G σφάλαι δέ had וְתַכְשִׁילֵהוּ (cf. inf.).

A new metaphor here conveys the idea of the instability of the prosperity of the wicked. First, 'his vigorous steps become cramped'. For the form יֵצְרוּ, from צרר intransitive, cf. יֵצַר in 20: 22. The צַעֲדֵי אוֹנוֹ 'steps of his vigour' mean 'his vigorous steps'. The noun אוֹן 'strength', 'vigour', is synonymous with כֹּחַ (40: 16) and with חַיִל (20: 10, cf. Comm.). The happy man walks with big strides, the roads are not wide enough for him. When

8   He has been cast into a snare by his feet,
     And it is on a net that he walks,
9   A gin catches him by the heel,
     A trap grips him,

adversity comes, he walks with short steps. In Ps 18: 37, 'Thou dost widen my steps under me, and my ankles do not slip.' There is a connection between the idea of narrowing the steps and that of causing to stumble. It is brought out especially in Pr 4: 12, 'When you walk, your step will not be narrowed (לֹא יֵצַר); and if you run, you will not stumble (לֹא תִכָּשֵׁל).' The parallelism between צרר and כשל in this passage abundantly proves that G has preserved the correct reading וְתַכְשִׁילֵהוּ in the 2nd hemistich: 'and his own counsel causes him to stumble'. Following Barth and Dillmann this correction has been accepted by almost all moderns. The text as it stands would require a complement of place after וּתְשַׁלִּיכֵהוּ 'and precipitates him'.

8   G ἐμβέβληται δὲ ὁ πούς αὐτοῦ omits the ב'' of ברגליו and adopts the singular רגלו which becomes the subject of שלח. Same omission of ב'' in Syr. and Vulg., but these versions regard רגליו (read as רגלו in Syr.) as the direct complement of שלח: *immisit enim in rete pedes suos* (Vulg.). For שבכה Vulg. *maculis* 'meshes'. The preposition על before the complement of יתהלך favours the reading of the MT, and there is no reason to read יתגולל, as is proposed by Beer following G ἐλιχθείη, which is a free translation.
     Vv. 8-10 will describe the various traps which are laid to ensnare the wicked man. The כי of the opening connects this description with v. 7, where it was a question of a fettered gait. If the steps of the wicked man are impeded, and if he stumbles, the reason is that he feels himself to be

surrounded by snares. First it is the 'net', pre-eminently an instrument of capture: רֶשֶׁת from ירשׁ 'catch', 'seize'. One is caught in it by the feet (Ps 9: 16; 25: 15). If we compare the 1st hemistich with Jg 5: 15, where we find once more שֻׁלַּח בְּרַגְלָיו 'he has been cast by his feet', it becomes apparent that it is not necessary to change the Hebrew text. The divergence between G and Syr. and Vulg. proves that these versions have tried to render the meaning rather than the literal words. The *pi'el* of שלח expresses the action of dismissing, sending away, driving off (cf. 8: 4; 12: 15; 14: 20, etc.), but also that of casting into the fire שלח באש. The second device is the שְׂבָכָה, a term specifying the *opus reticulatum* (1 K 7: 17ff., etc.) or the lattice window (2 K 1: 2). The Arabic *šabaka* 'to be intertwined' supplies *šabakeh* 'net', *šubbâk* 'net', 'matting', 'grating', 'window', etc. It is thus apparent that Hebrew and Arabic are in agreement as regards the development of the root. Thus then שבכה is indeed the 'network' or 'netting' stretched over a pit. In Sir 9: 13 we have וְעַל־רֶשֶׁת תִּתְהַלָּךְ 'on a netting thou dost walk', which confirms the verb יִתְהַלָּךְ (contra Beer).

9   G ἔλθοισιν δὲ ἐπ' αὐτὸν παγίδες is a translation of the 2nd hemistich. 5: 9a was omitted because the eye of the scribe passed from יֹאחֵז to יֶחֱזַק. The text of G has been regarded as translating v. 9a, and the verse has been completed by a new translation of the 2nd hemistich borrowed from Theod. (cf. Cod. 252): κατισχύσει ἐπ' αὐτὸν διψῶντας, absent from Sah., marked with

10   In the ground is hidden the rope to ensnare him,
      And the trap to catch him lies on the path.
11   On all sides terrors frighten him,
      And dog his steps.

asterisk in Jerome and Syro-hex. The word צמים is connected with צמא (cf. 5: 5) by Theod. διψῶντας, Vulg. *sitis*, Syr. ܬܘܡܐ 'thirst', 'dryness'. In Targ. ביבריא 'cage' or ניבריא 'diggers' (?).

The expression אחז בעקב 'catch by the heel' as in the story of Jacob's birth (Gn 25: 26). There is no reason to add the suffix after עקב, since the complement of יאחז is the wicked man, as is vouched for by עליו of the 2nd hemistich. The word פח is specifically the snare of the fowler (Hos 9: 8; Ec 9: 12, etc.). But the plural פחים (22: 10) denotes the netting stretched on the earth. We find in Sir 9: 13, 'know that thou dost go forwards among nets (פחים)', followed by the parallel member, 'and that thou dost walk on a snare', which we cited in connection with v. 8. Hence we may translate פח by a 'gin', which is certainly the trap that catches by the heel. The parallel word is צמים, which is not found elsewhere, for the vocalisation of 5: 5 is defective (cf. Comm.). The root is צמם, from which comes צמה 'plait of hair'. What is indicated is a trap of some kind which has the form of trellis or lattice work. For lack of an exact equivalent we shall translate by 'trap'. The *hiph'il* of חזק, with על before the object of the action (Neh 10: 30), denotes 'cleave to', 'grip'.

10 V. 10, absent from Sah., marked with asterisk in Syro-hex. (contra Field), did not exist in G. By mistake, Jerome has the asterisk only before the 2nd hemistich. The present text comes from Theod. (Cod. 252). It should be noted that G (A)

ends with κύκλοθεν (= סביב of v. 11) and that this word likewise terminated v. 9a in G (A). Now, we have seen that v. 9a of G was the equivalent of v. 9b of the MT. It seems then that the omission of v. 10 in G arises from an error of homoeoteleuton.

A new series of traps. The rope, חבל, figures with the פח 'gin' and רשת 'net' (cf. 8-9) in the description of the various pitfalls which are laid along the path of the Psalmist (Ps 140: 6). The verb used to convey that these traps are hidden is טמן as here. This verb again denotes the action of concealing a gin (Jer 18: 22), a net (Ps 9: 16, etc.). It is obvious that חבלו 'his rope' means the rope destined to catch him: objective suffix. Similarly מלכדתו 'his trap' is the trap laid to ensnare him. The verb לכד (5: 13) means precisely 'to catch' animals in a trap, whether the device be the net of the fowler or the trap laid by the hunter. The *hapax* מלכדת connotes therefore a trap in general. It is on the path that will be trodden that the trap is laid or concealed (Ps 140: 6; 142: 4). The poetic נתיב 'path' (28: 7; 41: 24) is used instead of the feminine נתיבה, which is more frequently found (19: 8; 24: 13; 30: 13; 38: 26).

11 G fuses v. 11b with v. 12a to arrive at a single sentence: πολλοὶ δὲ περὶ πόδα αὐτοῦ ἔλθοισαν ἐν λιμῷ στενῷ. Vulg. translates the 2nd hemistich rather vaguely: *et involvent pedes ejus*.

Vv. 11-12 are inspired by the thesis of Eliphaz in 15: 20ff. We have here the description of the remorse which

12   He is hungry *amid* his wealth,
     And misfortune stands at his side.

12   בְּאֹנוֹ; MT: אֹנוֹ.

assails the conscience of the wicked
man. In the midst of his prosperity
he is attacked by sudden terrors.
The words of the 1st hemistich are
thoroughly characteristic of the
Book of Job. The *pi'el* of בעת as in
7: 14; 13: 11, 21; 15: 24 (cf. 3: 5).
The plural בַּלָּהוֹת 'terrors' recurs in
v. 14 and in 24: 17; 27: 20; 30: 15.
On the root בלה, which is interchangeable with בהל, cf. 4: 5. 'On
all sides terrors frighten him', referring to the fears and the anguish
of the guilty soul (15: 21). Like the
ancient furies, inexorably they pursue the criminal, 'and dog his steps'.
Budde lists six corrections intended
to get rid of the difficult וְהֶפִצָהוּ,
which shows that none is satisfactory. Now, in Ezk 34: 21 we find
the *hiph'il* of פוץ used with a direct
complement and connoting 'pursue',
'scatter', as is proved by the circumstantial complement אֶל־הַחוּצָה
'abroad'. Again, the locution, לְרַגְלָיו
'at his feet' is contrasted with לְפָנָיו
'before him' in Hab 3: 5, to convey
'at his heels', i.e. 'behind him'. Thus
לְרַגְלָיו will have the same sense as
בְּרַגְלָיו 'at his heels', 'behind him';
cf. the alternation of לְרַגְל and בְּרַגְלִי
in 1 S 25: 27, 42. The meaning thus
obtained is in harmony with the
rest of the description (cf. Le Hir,
Renan, Crampon, etc.). It is needless to linger over the hypothesis of
Ehrlich, who would see in the 2nd
hemistich a coarse meaning: 'and
they cause him to pour over his
feet', i.e. *dass er vor Schrecken in die
Hosen pisst*.

12 G ἔλθοισαν ἐν λιμῷ στενῷ (in v.
11) and Vulg. *attenuetur fame robur
ejus* have vocalised רָעֵב. Similarly
Syr. ﻛﻔﻦ 'hunger'. For אֹנוֹ, Syr.

'his sorrow' (from אָוֶן), 1st Targ.
'his first-born son' (following Gn
49: 3), 2nd Targ. באנינותיה 'in his
mourning' (= בְּאֹנוֹ; cf. inf.). Self-
consistent, 1st Targ. renders לְצַלְעוֹ
'at his rib' by 'to his wife' (following
Gn 2: 22), while Syr. translates 'to
his progeny'. G ἐξαίσιον is a paraphrase of לְצַלְעוֹ; cf. 20: 5.
  In accordance with the sequel of
the description, we must consider יְהִי
as having the meaning of the future;
cf. the use of the jussive יחזק in v. 9
and the examples of 13: 27a; 15:
33b. אֹנוֹ is connected with אָוֶן 'sin' or
'misfortune' to give the translation
'his iniquity yawns before him' (Le
Hir), or 'misfortune opens its greedy
mouth over him' (Renan). But the
literal meaning would be simply: his
sin (or his misfortune) will be a-
hungered. G and Vulg. have recognised in אֹנוֹ the word אוֹן 'force',
'vigour' of v. 7, but these versions
paraphrase the text. Similarly the
Bible du rabbinat français: 'his vigour weakens through hunger'. Ehrlich returns to the metaphorical
interpretation of 1st Targ., which is
no more than an exegetical subtlety.
Duhm replaces אֹנוֹ by אוֹן לוֹ to translate: 'misfortune is greedy to devour
him'. We have seen that Bildad is
inspired by the speech of Eliphaz
(15: 20ff.). The contrast between
the opulence of the wicked man and
his pessimistic forebodings was the
very basis of the passage. In particular, we found that 'in the midst of
peace, a brigand attacks him' (15:
21b). In our 1st hemistich there is a
marked contrast between אֹנוֹ 'his
force' (v. 7) or 'his fortune' (20: 10)
and יְהִי רָעֵב 'he will be hungry'. By
haplography the ״ב before אֹנוֹ has
fallen out. We propose to read בְּאֹנוֹ,

13   His skin is *eaten away by a disease,*
     The first-born of death devours his limbs.

13   יֵאָכֵל בְּדָיו (cf. G); MT: יֹאכַל בַּדֵּי.

which in fact was foreshadowed by
2nd Targ. (cf. sup). Hence the
meaning of the first clause is, quite
simply: 'he will become hungry amid
his wealth', corresponding to 15:
21b. The 2nd hemistich corresponds
to 15: 23b, 'he knows that his misfortune is imminent'. The word נָכוֹן
which we have rendered 'imminent'
retains here however its literal
meaning 'upright', thanks to the
complement, לְצַלְעוֹ 'by his side'.
The meaning cannot be in doubt:
'and misfortune stands at his side'.
This is indeed how ancient exegesis
understood the line. The word צֵלָע
'rib', 'side' is used exactly as the
Assyrian *ṣêlu* in the locutions 'beside', 'by the side of', etc. (*L'Emploi
métaphorique*, p. 103). Some modern
exegetes have thought it well to
connect צלעו with צֶלַע 'ruin', 'fall',
found in Ps 35: 15; 38: 18. But only
the German language can feel satisfied with phrases such as *und der
Untergang lauert auf sein Fallen*
(Budde), *und das Verderben bereit zu
seinem Sturz* (Duhm). The word אֵיד
'misfortune' will recur in 21: 17, 30,
where Job will undertake to demonstrate the falsity of Bildad's
affirmations.

13 G βρωθείησαν αὐτοῦ κλῶνες ποδῶν
and Syr. 'his cities will be swallowed
up by violence' are in agreement to
vocalise יֵאָכֵל (cf. inf.). The Greek
αὐτοῦ κλῶνες ποδῶν 'the fingers of his
feet' is a free interpretation of בדי
עורו 'the branches of his skin', since
the word κλῶν means literally
'branch', 'shoot'. It seems that Syr.
read ביד 'by the hand', 'by force',
instead of בדי, and עריו 'his cities'
(from עיר) instead of עורו. Vulg.

devoret pulchritudinem cutis ejus and
Targ. 'he will eat the byssus clothing
(בוצין) which covers his skin' have
preserved the Massoretic vocalisation, but Targ. connects בדי with
בד 'linen', 'linen garment', while
Vulg. interprets בדי 'branches',
'limbs' in the sense of beauty, just as
בדיו is rendered by G τὰ ὡραῖα αὐτοῦ
in the 2nd hemistich. This word
בדיו is translated *brachia illius* in
Vulg., בנוהי 'his sons' in Targ. Quite
a new meaning is obtained by Syr.
for the 2nd hemistich, after the
elimination of the second יאכל and
the transposition of מות: 'and his
first-born (is devoured) by the power
of death'. For בכור מות, G θάνατος,
but Theod. and Symm. πρώιμος
θάνατος (in Syro-hex.), whence Jerome *matura mors* (with asterisk
before *matura*). 1st Targ. translates
by 'the angel of death', 2nd Targ. by
שרוי מותא 'the first fruits of death',
while Vulg. *primogenita mors* considers בכור as qualifying מות.

As it stands, the verse seems to be
built on a tautology, and critics
have thought it possible to reduce it
to a single hemistich. Thus for
example Duhm resolutely cuts out
the 1st hemistich, on the pretext
that בַּדֵּי עוֹר 'limbs of the skin'
makes nonsense. The translation of
Renan revealed the corrupt state of
the present text: 'The limbs of his
body will be the prey . . . his limbs
will be the prey of the first-born of
death.' Le Hir reversed the order of
the terms in the 1st hemistich: 'the
skin of his limbs is devoured'. Our
first observation is that the meaning
of the 2nd hemistich is perfectly
clear: 'the first-born of death devours his limbs'. The בַּדִּים 'boughs',
'branches' are the limbs of the body
which are attached to the 'trunk' as

14   He is torn away from the tent where he dwelt in safety,
      And you may lead him away to the king of terrors!

the branches to the tree (*L'Emploi métaphorique*, p. 137). בַּדָּיו recurs with the same meaning in 41 : 4. The first-born of death is the most horrible of diseases. Among the Arabs, diseases are 'the daughters of death' (cf. Schultens). It is well known that for the Babylonians and Assyrians the god of the plague, Namtaru, is the *sukallu*, i.e. the vizier, of the queen of hell (*Choix de textes*, p. 333, n. 67). Now, as a general rule, the *sukallu* is the first-born, *bukru*, of the god who employs his services. This is the case, for example, with Mummu, first-born and delegate of Apsû (ibid., p. 8, n. 30). Hence we are led to identify the first-born of death with the demon of the plague, the Plague personified. If now we make a comparison with the 1st hemistich, we note that עוֹרוֹ 'his skin' corresponds to בַּדָּיו 'his limbs'. The repetition of יֹאכַל is avoided by the vocalisation יֵאָכֵל, which is attested by both G and Syr. There remains בדי, which must yield the equivalent of the first-born of death. If, with Wright, we vocalise בִּדְוָי 'by a disease' (cf. Ps 41 : 4), we shall be able to translate the 1st hemistich 'his skin is eaten away by a disease', which forms an excellent parallel to 'the first-born of death devours his limbs'. Here it is no longer a question merely of remorse and gloomy forebodings, but of misfortunes themselves attacking the wicked man, that is, disease and death (14-19).

14 G ἴασις interprets מבטחו 'his confidence', 'his hope', i.e. the hope of the sick man, namely healing. The 2nd hemistich is literally translated in Targ. But G σχοίη δὲ αὐτὸν ἀνάγκη αἰτίᾳ βασιλικῇ seems to make of בלהות, rendered ἀνάγκη, the sub-

ject of the sentence and to paraphrase לְמֶלֶךְ by αἰτίᾳ βασιλικῇ. Syr. regards לְמֶלֶךְ as a complement of בלהות 'the terrors of the king'; cf. Aq. τοῦ βασιλέως ἀνυπαρξία. Vulg. *et calcet super eum, quasi rex, interitus* sees in בלהית the subject of the verb and reads כְּמֶלֶךְ.

The 1st hemistich might be translated: 'his confidence is torn away from his tent'; cf. Le Hir 'all his supports are removed from his tent'. But this statement would no longer fit in with the context. It is cut out by Duhm. The description with which we are engaged has just made allusion to the wicked man being gnawed by disease and by the 'first-born of death'. Now, our verse ends with the 'king of terrors', and v. 15 will show that this impious man no longer dwells in his tent. It is the wicked man himself who is the subject of יִנָּתֵק; the word מִבְטַחוֹ is in apposition to אָהֳלוֹ, exactly as in Is 32 : 18 we find מבטחים in apposition to משכנות 'dwellings', to convey the idea of dwellings where one enjoys full security (Torczyner). This interpretation, which is the correct one (cf. Dillmann), was well known to ancient exegesis and is supported by the frequent locutions שכן לבטח, ישב לבטח 'to dwell safely'. The *niph'al* of נתק 'to break' (17 : 11), and hence 'to break away' (Jer 6 : 29), 'to go away from' (Jos 8 : 16), or, as here, 'to be torn away' from a place: 'he is torn away from his tent where he dwelt in safety'. The versions experienced difficulty in finding a subject for תַּצְעִדֵהוּ regarded as 3rd person feminine. According to Rashi and a few Jewish exegetes, the reference would be to the wife of the wicked man, but we find it impossible to agree with them when they wish to see in 'his tent' a me-

15   You may dwell in his tent which is no longer his,
      Brimstone has been scattered on his abode!

taphor for 'his wife'. Le Hir considered that the allusion was to
death. Unfortunately מָוֶת is masculine. Let us note that the same
difficulty presents itself in regard to
תִּשְׁכּוֹן of v. 15. Now, v. 15a contains
the expression מִבְּלִי־לוֹ, which must
be translated literally 'since it is no
longer his' (cf. Comm.). If we consider תשכון as 2nd person singular,
v. 15a will mean 'you may dwell in
his tent which is no longer his'. And
thus we shall recognise a 2nd person
in תצעדהו of our hemistich: 'and
you may lead him away to the king
of terrors!'. The *hiph'il* of צעד 'to
walk', is used to mean 'take', 'lead';
cf. הוליך from הלך. The king of
terrors is the *rex tremendus* of Virgil
(*Georgics*, IV, 469), i.e. the chief of
the infernal kingdom, the Nergal of
the Babylonians, the Moloch of the
Canaanites, that king to whom messengers are sent even in Sheol (Is
57: 9); cf. Lagrange, *ÉRS*, pp. 107ff.
Rashi identifies him with the prince
of the demons, שלטון השדים. It is
a question of the death of the wicked
man. His body, which has been eaten
away by disease, is being carried off
(v. 13).

15 Vv. 15-16, absent from Sah.,
marked with asterisk in Jerome and
Syro-hex., did not exist in G. The
present text comes from Theod. (cf.
Colb. and Syro-hex.). But it looks as
if v. 19c in G ἀλλ' ἐν τοῖς (A ἐντὸς)
αὐτοῦ ζήσονται ἕτεροι, which is not
based on the Hebrew in this text,
is only an interpretation of our 1st
hemistich (Beer). Cf. the translation
of Vulg. *habitent in tabernaculo illius
socii ejus qui non est*. Instead of
מבלי לו, Theod. ἐν νυκτὶ αὐτοῦ reads
בלילו. Targ. adds 'his wife' as the
subject of תשכון. For נוהו, Theod.
τὰ εὐπρεπῆ αὐτοῦ (cf. 5: 3, 24), Syr.
'his land'. The right meaning is

given in Vulg. *tabernaculo ejus* and
Targ מדוריה 'his abode'.
    It is forcing the grammatical con-
struction to make of מִבְּלִי־לוֹ a
neuter partitive, the subject of
תשכון, so as to translate 'the stranger will dwell in his tent' (Renan),
'none of his family dwell in his tent'
(Segond, Crampon). We have seen
in v. 14 that תִּשְׁכּוֹן was 2nd person
masculine: 'you may dwell in his
tent'. The exact meaning of מבלי־לו
would be, in Latin, *eo quod non est ei*,
or, in English, 'since it is no longer
his'. Cf. מבלי לבוש 'for lack of
clothing' (24: 7) and מבלי־טרף 'for
lack of prey' (4: 11). It is by a
weakening of the basic sense that
מבלי eventually came to denote
simply 'without' (6: 6). In מבלי־לו
critics have attempted to find the
remnant of a feminine subject for
תשכון, whence the changes to לילית
'Lilith' (Voigt, Beer) or to בליעל
which here would mean *Unheilbar-
keit* 'incurability' (Duhm). Such
corrections are unnecessary. The
2nd hemistich has been interpreted
as expressing a punishment sent by
heaven (Gn 19: 24; Dt 29: 22; Ps
11: 6). But the verb זרה means
'scatter', 'sprinkle', 'winnow'. In the
pu'al it means 'to be scattered,
disseminated' like the chaff of the
threshing-floor. Hence here it is a
question of sulphur or brimstone
sprinkled with the hand. Brimstone
was well known to the ancients
for its curative and disinfecting
properties (Pliny, *Nat. hist.* XXXV,
50). In the *Odyssey* (XXII, 481f.),
Ulysses demands sulphur for the
purpose of cleansing the room which
has been sullied by the corpses. Cf.
Ovid (*Ars amat.* II, 329-30): *Et
veniat quae lustret anus lectumque
locumque, Praeferat et tremula sulphur
et ova manu*. Hence Ehrlich seems
to us to be right when he recognises

16   Beneath, his roots wither away,
        And above, his branches fade;
17   His memory has disappeared from the earth,
        And he is now nameless in the wilderness.
18   He is driven from light into darkness,
        And banished from the world;

that here we have a reference to the disinfecting of the dwelling. The word נָוֶה 'dwelling' (5: 3) is parallel to אֹהֶל 'tent' as in 5: 24. The verb יֹזֹרֶה at the beginning of the sentence remains masculine, despite the gender of גָפְרִית, which is relegated to the end.

16   For קְצִירוֹ, Theod. θερισμὸς αὐτοῦ, Vulg. *messis ejus*, Syr. ܡܦܩܗ 'his harvest', but 2nd Targ. זאזיה 'his leafage'.

Bildad resumes the comparison of the godless man with a tree (8: 16-19). Job has contrasted the fate of man with that of the tree which, even after its death, can experience rebirth and put forth new branches (14: 7-9). But Eliphaz declared that, as far as the wicked man is concerned, 'a flame will parch his shoots and his blossoms will be swept away by the wind' (15: 30). Such is also the opinion of Bildad: 'Beneath, his roots wither away, and above, his branches fade.' The words are part of current vocabulary. Cf. Am 2: 9, where we find a contrast between פִּרְיוֹ מִמַּעַל 'his fruit above' and שָׁרָשָׁיו מִתָּחַת 'his roots below'. The verb מָלַל as in 14: 2; 15: 32. The noun קָצִיר as in 14: 9.

17   The 2nd hemistich, absent from Sah., marked with asterisk in Jerome and Syro-hex., did not exist in G. The present text comes from Theod. (cf. Colb. and Syro-hex.). Theod. καὶ ὑπάρχει reads וְלוֹ instead of וְלֹא. Symm. translates חוּץ by ἀγορᾶς (Vulg. *plateis*).

In order to avoid the repetition of 'his name', we retain for זִכְרוֹ the etymological meaning of 'his memory', although זֵכֶר, exactly like the Assyrian *zikru*, has become synonymous with שֵׁם 'name' used in the parallel clause. The verb אבד with מִן means 'disappear from' (11: 20). On the antithesis between אֶרֶץ 'the earth' and חוּץ 'the countryside', cf. Comm. on 5: 10. The word ארץ represents the inhabited or tilled earth, as opposed to חוּץ which is the uninhabited and uncultivated earth. For lack of an exact equivalent, we render חוּץ by 'the wilderness'. The name of the wicked man disappears from the world; cf. Ps 109: 15b. Albertus Magnus quotes the decree issued by the Roman senate ordering the effacement of the name of Domitian from public monuments.

18   The 2nd hemistich has disappeared from G. For יהדפהו, G ἀπώσειεν αὐτόν, Vulg. *expellet eum*, verb in the singular. Similarly for ינדהו, Vulg. *transferet eum*. But Targ. and Syr. are in accord with the MT.

Vv. 18-19 take up again the idea contained in 14-17: the death of the wicked man and the disappearance of his name from this earth. It might seem more logical to place v. 18 after v. 14, but in that case v. 15 would be separated from its natural context, which is v. 14b; note the use of the two verbs in the 2nd person. Bildad returns to his general theme. The verbs are put in the 3rd person plural as an equivalent to an

19   No lineage and no posterity will there be for him among his
        people,
     And no survivor in those places where he stayed!
20   They of the west have been stupefied by his fate,
     And they of the east have shuddered with awe.

impersonal construction ('one') (4:
19; 7: 3; 15: 28, etc.): he is driven
from light to darkness and banished
from the world. Cf. Pr 2: 22, 'and
the wicked are cut off from the land
and traitors are rooted out of it'. The
light and the dark are contrasted as
life and death, as the terrestrial and
infernal abodes. In 3: 20 light is the
symbol of life. In 17: 13 darkness is
the symbol of Sheol. The light of the
living is restored to him who is
snatched from the infernal regions
(33: 30). Duhm would replace the
plural verbs by singulars and make
'God' their subject. But God has
hardly any place in this speech of
Bildad. The vocalisation of G and of
Vulg. cannot outweigh that of the
MT, Targ., and Syr. The similarity
in meaning of the roots נדה, נוד, נדד
dispenses us from the necessity of
having recourse to the vocalisation
יָנַדְהוּ recommended by Lagarde and
Siegfried, or to the יְנַדְהוּ of Hoffmann. We have here the *hiph'il* of
נדד, of which the *hoph'al* will appear
in 20: 8.

19 G again omits לֹא נִין לוֹ, a phenomenon of haplography as in the
case of 18b. Syr. stresses the resemblance to v. 17 by rendering נין as
'name' and נכד as 'memory'. Instead of בעמו Syr. reads בעולם 'in
the world'. G ἐν τῇ ὑπ' οὐρανὸν ὁ οἶκος
αὐτοῦ interprets במגוריו in the sense
of the current expression בארץ
מגוריו (Ball), but regards מגוריו as
the subject of the clause. The 3rd
hemistich of G comes from v. 15a.
   The name of the wicked man
vanishes from the earth, for he has
no lineage, no posterity among his

people. The words נִין and נֶכֶד always
evoke each other by a phenomenon
of alliteration (Gn 21: 23; Is 14: 22;
Sir 47: 22). In Sir 41: 5 one hemistich begins with נין and the other
with נכד. Note that in this passage
נכד is connected with מגור, which
appears also in our 2nd hemistich.
The meaning of מָגוּר is above all
'domicile in foreign lands', as is
proved by the etymology (root גור
'to be a guest, a client') and also by
the common formula ארץ מגוריך
'country of your sojournings'. Even
in these places where the wicked
man has made only a temporary
stay, no one is able to perpetuate his
memory. The שָׂרִיד is specifically
the one who escapes, survives a
catastrophe (20: 21, 26; 27: 15).

20 G ἐπ' αὐτῷ does not arise from a
reading עלימו (Beer) instead of
עַל־יוֹמוֹ, but from עליו, which is a
haplography of עַל־יוֹ[מוֹ]. The versions understand אחרנים וקדמנים
as 'the last and the first'. For אחזו
שער, G ἔσχεν θαῦμα, Vulg. *invadet
horror*, Syr. 'their hair stands on
end', read אחז and see in שער the
subject of the verb. Targ. is in
accord with the MT.
   The preposition עַל makes of יוֹמוֹ
'his day' the complement of נָשַׁמּוּ.
The day of the wicked man is that on
which his fate is fulfilled, the day of
his ruin and death (cf. 1 S 26: 10;
Ob v. 12; Ps 137: 7). Hence we can
translate by 'his fate'. The *niph'al* of
שמם, to mean 'to be stupefied' (Jer
4: 9). Cf. the *qal* in 17: 8. Ancient
tradition saw in the אַחֲרֹנִים 'the
recent ones', 'the descendants', and

21 No more than that are the dwellings of the unrighteous,
   And such is the place of him who has not known God!

in the קַדְמֹנִים 'the first', 'the forefathers'. Renan still interprets as
'the men of the last days', and 'the
coming generations'. But it is a
question of the fate of the wicked
man. The קדמנים cannot be witnesses of it if they represent bygone
generations, neither can the אחרנים
if they represent generations yet to
come. It is obvious that what the
author must have in mind are the
contemporaries of the wicked man.
Schultens and most modern exegetes have rightly realised that it is
here a question of westerners and
easterners. The ancients orientated
themselves by turning their faces
towards the rising sun: the east was
what they had in front of them, קדם,
the west what they had behind them,
אחר. The world is divided between
easterners and westerners: πολλοὶ
ἀπὸ ἀνατολῶν καὶ δυσμῶν ἥξουσιν (Mt
8:11). Hence we shall translate
אחרנים as 'they of the west' and
קדמנים as 'they of the east'. Following G, Vulg., and Syr., it has been
proposed to read אָחַז instead of אחזו
so as to translate: 'a shudder seizes
the orientals' (Merx, Siegfried). But
we have the expression אחזו···פלצות
'to feel a shudder' in 21:6, and we
find in Assyrian the formula rašû
nakutta 'to be seized by, to experience, a fright'. The word שַׂעַר
'shudder', originally the hair which
stands on end (cf. 4:15), recurs
only in Ezk 27:35 and 32:10, both

times in connection with the verb
שׁמם. The effect produced by the
catastrophe in which the wicked
man perishes is especially felt by the
righteous who rejoice in the triumph
of justice (22:19ff.). V. 21 will
resemble the exclamation uttered
by the faithful believer when he
sees the ruins which cover the lavish
dwelling of the wicked man. This
will form the conclusion of Bildad's
speech.

21 G neglects אַךְ, which Vulg.
renders *ergo*. The versions preserve
the meaning of 'place' for מקום and
add the relative before לֹא־יִדע.

The adverb אַךְ 'only', 'nothing
but', governs אֵלֶּה (cf. 13:20a). We
have had the word עַוָּל in 16:11,
where it was parallel with רְשָׁעִים 'the
wicked'. We shall find precisely the
מִשְׁכְּנוֹת רְשָׁעִים 'dwellings of the
wicked' in 21:28. To the word
משכנות corresponds מָקוֹם 'place' in
which some one dwells (16:18). The
construct state, because the phrase
'he who does not know God' (relative
אשר understood) plays the part of a
real genitive (Gesenius-Kautzsch,
§ 130d). Note the use of זֶה at the
beginning of the clause as in 20:29a.
Note also the parallelism with אלה
(10:13). With the 2nd hemistich
we may compare 8:13a, 'Such is
the fate of all those who forget
God!'

CHAPTER 19

1 Then Job spoke and said:
2 For how long will you distress my soul,
 And crush me with words?
3 Ten times now you have insulted me
 And have not been ashamed to ill-treat me.

Chapter 19 Sixth speech of Job: see Introduction, p. xliii.

19: 2 G ἔγκοπον ποιήσετε reads תגיעון instead of תגיון (cf. Is 43: 23; Ec 1: 8). The other versions are in agreement with the MT; cf. Aq. ὀδυνᾶτε, Vulg. *affligitis*, Syr. مرهم, رهم 'you afflict', Targ. תקנטון 'you vex'. The Massoretic tradition hesitates between the vocalisation וּתְדַכְּאוּנֵנִי (kethîb) and וּתְדַכְּאוּנִי (qerê).

The opening עַד־אָנָה 'for how long?' is a direct hit at Bildad, who began his two speeches by this very formula (8: 2; 18: 2); but Job is here addressing all his friends, for which reason the verbs are in the plural. It is difficult to decide between the reading תְּגִיעוּן 'you tire' (from יגע) of G, which is adopted by Ball, and the reading תּוֹגְיוּן 'you afflict' (from יגה) of the MT and the other versions. However, it would seem that the MT would have kept the verb תגיעון, which is less uncommon than תגיון. Note that we have here the only case in which a ל"ה pre- serves in the *hiph'îl* the final *yod* of the original form (Gesenius- Kautzsch, § 75gg). The verb יגה, whence יָגוֹן and תּוּגָה 'affliction', 'sor- row', etc., is one of the favourite words of Lamentations (1: 4, 5, 12; 3: 32, 33). Outside this book it

reappears only in Zeph 3: 18, where the text is corrupt (cf. van Hoon- acker) and in Is 51: 23. The *pi'el* of דכא to express 'crush' as in 4: 19; 6: 9. Job is literally crushed 'by the words' of his friends, by their monot- onous rhetoric (cf. v. 3). Addition of the 1st person suffix to a verbal form terminated by the *nun epen- theticum*; cf. Hos 5: 15; Pr. 1: 28.

3 G γνῶτε μόνον ὅτι ὁ Κύριος ἐποίησέ με οὕτως anticipates the opening of v. 6 and reads זה עשה (ἐποίησέ με οὕτως) instead of זה עשר. The word פעמים is omitted in G, for the sequel καταλαλεῖτέ μου corresponds to תכלימוני. For תהכרו־לי, G ἐπίκεισθέ με, which renders עלי תחמסו in 21: 27, Vulg. *opprimentes me*, Targ. לי תשתמודעו 'you make yourselves known to me' (connects תהכרו with הכיר), Syr. ومصفتس اهؤهم لا 'how you afflict me' (connects תהכרו with the Aramaic כרא, כרה 'to suffer'). The expression זֶה עֶשֶׂר פְּעָמִים 'these ten times' like זֶה פַּעֲמַיִם 'these two times' in Gn 27: 36. The figure ten is used, like the figure seven, to convey the idea of a great number; cf. 1 S 1: 8 with Ru 4: 15. We find זה עשר פעמים 'behold, ten times', 'this is the tenth time' in Nu 14: 22. The verb הכלים, with suffix as complement,

4   But even were it true that I have erred,
     My error would remain my own concern!

retains its normal sense of 'outrage', כְּלִמָּה; cf. 'outrage', 'shame' (20: 3). In 11: 3 the meaning was rather 'to blame'. The 2nd hemistich juxtaposes two verbs the second of which is dependent on the first. The same construction, with imperatives, occurs in 6: 28a; with jussives in 10: 16b; perfect followed by the imperfect in 32: 22a. The verb בוש 'to be ashamed' as in 6: 20. Commentators are no less embarrassed than the versions about the translation of the *hapax* תַּהְכְּרוּ. The Massoretic vocalisation regards the ה as a guttural, whence the use of the *patah* instead of the *hireq* in the first syllable. Qimchi explained the verb הכר by reference to the Arabic verb *hakara* 'to be astonished', which however has too weak a sense. Rashi interprets by תתנכרו לי 'you dissemble with me', but without justifying this translation which rests on an assonance between תהכרו and תנכרו (cf. Targ., which connects it with הכיר, from נכר). Ewald quite rightly saw in הכר a cognate of the Arabic *hakara*, the exact meaning of which is 'ill-treat', 'oppress': this is the meaning which was surmised by G and the Vulg. Here it is a question of ill-treating some one in words (cf. v. 2b). The weak pronunciation of the soft ח (Arabic ح) has brought about the transformation of חכר into הכר; cf. the transformation of המס into חמס in 21: 27. Many changes have been suggested by modern exegetes, but none of these has won any consensus of opinion. Some seek in תהכרו a derivative of כרר, whence the vocalisation תָּהְכְּרוּ 'you return to the attack' (Ehrlich), תָּכְרוּ 'you hurl yourselves' (Beer). Others resolutely depart from the MT: תחרפו 'you insult' (Olshausen), תעכרו 'you

trouble' (Bickell), תנכרו 'you dissemble' (Graetz), תחברו (Merx), or תתחברו 'you league yourselves' (Siegfried), תוכחו 'you reproach' (Torczyner), etc. Since the root may be justified as a derivative of حكر, the best course is to adhere to the text.

4   For וְאַף, G ναὶ δέ, Vulg. *etsi*, Syr. אס 'and if'. The suffix of מְשׁוּגָתִי, omitted by negligence in G πλάνος, is restored in Sah. 'my error'. At the end, G has quite a gloss, λαλῆσαι ῥήματα κ.τ.λ., which arises from a reminiscence of 15: 3. This gloss is marked with obelus in Jerome and Syro-hex.

Job has consistently asserted his innocence. The verb שָׁגִיתִי 'I have erred' (6: 24; 12: 16) can only be admitted in a hypothetical clause. Now, the 2nd hemistich throws emphasis on אִתִּי 'with me' in opposition to the friends who will be addressed in v. 5. This 2nd hemistich may easily be rendered: 'with me alone dwells my error'. The verb לין as in 17: 2; *hapax* מְשׁוּגָה, derived from שׁוּג 'wander', 'err', of which the root is parallel to שׁגה and שׁגג (12: 16). Hence Job means that it is his business alone to be concerned about his error, if indeed he has erred. Everything becomes clear if we take the phrase וְאַף 'and even' as applying to the word אָמְנָם 'truly', 'it is true that . . .'. It is this meaning which was well understood and brought out in Syr. We shall translate: 'But even were it true that I have erred, my error would remain my own concern.' It is not your business to be concerned about it, and especially not to reproach me with it so as to exalt yourselves at my expense (v. 5).

5   Is it not true indeed that you treat me insolently,
     And reproach me with my disgrace?

6   Know then that it is Eloah who has done me wrong,
     And who has encompassed me with His net!

7   If I cry out 'Violence!', I receive no reply,
     In vain do I cry for help; there is no judgment!

5 Syr. 'and if you defame me' replaces חרפתי by a verb. G ὀνείδει omits the suffix of חרפתי (as of משוגתי in v. 4).

There is nothing strange in the repetition of the אָמְנָם of v. 4. Job emphasises his astonishment at the attitude of his friends. The particle אם is interrogative (6: 12; 17: 13): 'is it not true indeed . . . ?' The alliteration אִם־אָמְנָם should have warned Duhm against the elimination of אמנם. The *hiph'il* of גדל, with על before the complement of the person, means 'to assume a lofty attitude', 'to be insolent towards' some one (Ps 35: 26; 38: 17; 55: 13). The verb הוכיח 'to reproach' (cf. Comm. on 5: 17) is deliberately chosen to characterise the speeches of Job's friends, which in fact are more or less disguised reproaches. The pretext for such reproaches is the present situation of Job. He defines it with one word חֶרְפָּתִי 'my disgrace'. The noun חֶרְפָּה 'shame', 'outrage' (16: 10) denotes also the infamy attaching to a crime (1 S 25: 39; 2 S 13: 13). The interlocutors of Job infer the hidden cause from the apparent effect. In this they are wrong, as Job suggests in the sequel of his speech. It is God Himself who is the cause of the trials which have come upon His servant.

6 Vulg. paraphrases עותני by *non aequo judicio afflixerit me*. G renders מצוד by ὀχύρωμα 'fortress', in accordance with the meaning of מצודה. Vulg. *flagellis* interprets metaphorically. Syr. and Targ. are faithful to the MT.

The expression דְּעוּ־אֵפוֹ 'know then' is used to introduce a solemn affirmation, as in 2 K 10: 10. On the word אפו cf. 4: 7. The *pi'el* of עות 'to warp' justice (8: 3) is used with the direct complement of the person to mean 'do wrong' to some one (Ps 119: 78; La 3: 36). The verb is chosen deliberately, in reply to Bildad who used it in his first speech and precisely with reference to God: 'Does God distort the right?' Job observes that, so far as his own personal case is concerned, God seems to act unjustly towards him. Bildad has spoken at great length about the snares which are laid under the feet of the wicked man (18: 8-10). Job knows no others but those which God had laid for him. The double meaning of צוד 'to hunt' and 'to fish' implies for מָצוֹד (Ec 7: 26) and מְצוֹדָה (Ec 9: 12; Sir 9: 3) the meaning 'net', instrument of both the huntsman and fisherman. The *hiph'il* of נקף in 1: 5 meant 'to complete a cycle, a turn'. Here simply 'to make something turn' around some one. The 2nd hemistich would be literally translated, 'and He has caused His net to turn around me', that is, 'He has surrounded me with His net.' Cf. the use of the preposition על after the verb סבב 'to wheel around' in 16: 13.

7 Syr. rightly interprets הן as 'if'. The other versions render as 'Behold'. G γελῶ ὀνείδει καὶ οὐ λαλήσω reads אצחק instead of אצעק and

8   He has blocked my way so that I cannot get through,
     And upon my paths He has set darkness;
9   Of my glory He has stripped me,
     And the crown He has removed from my head!

vocalises אֶעֱנֶה instead of אֶעֱנֶה.
Vulg. *et non est qui judicet* paraphrases ואין משפט 'and no judgment'.
The particle הֵן 'if' (4: 18; 12: 14;
13: 15, etc.). The construction of
the 1st hemistich is the same as in
9: 11, where הן introduces the conditional clause and וְלֹא the main
clause. Cf. also 9: 15-16, where אִם
replaces הן and לֹא takes the place of
ולא. The word חָמָס 'violence' is
used as in 16: 17. The locution אֶצְעַק
חמס 'I cry violence' recalls אזעק חמס
of Jer 20: 8 and Hab 1: 2. Note that
in Hab 1: 2 we have the parallelism
between אזעק חמס and שׁוַּעְתִּי (*pi'el*
of שוע as in our 2nd hemistich). The
niph'al of ענה, exactly as in 11: 2.
He to whom one replies is then the
subject of the *niph'al*. Thus we have
had לֹא אֶעֱנֶה (according to the
original text) 'I am not replied to' to
express 'I receive no reply' (9: 15).
The same construction occurs in Pr
21: 13b, 'In vain does he cry out, he
is not replied to' (i.e. he receives no
answer). Job will say to God: 'I cry
out to Thee, and Thou dost not
answer me' (30: 20). He will use the
pi'el of שוע as in the 2nd hemistich.
The closing וְאֵין מִשְׁפָּט 'and no
judgment' recalls other cadences of
the hemistich (5: 4, 9; 11: 3, 19).
For משפט 'judgment' and 'justice'
cf. 8: 3. The idea expressed in this
verse occurs again in La 3: 8, 'In
vain do I cry and call (verbs זעק
and שוע), He closes His ear to my
prayer.' We shall find in v. 8 further
resemblances to La 3.

8   For ארחי גדר, G κύκλῳ περιῳκ-
οδόμημαι, Jerome *circumseptus sum*
(obelus by mistake before *circum-*

septus), cf. Vulg. *semitam meam cir-*
cumsepsit. For וְעַל־נְתִיבוֹתַי, G ἐπὶ
πρόσωπόν μου, but G (A) ἐπὶ δὲ ἀτρα-
πούς μου, a hexaplar reading which
is recorded as a variant in Colb.
The former reading is followed by
Sah., Syro-hex., Jerome, Eth., Arab.
Baud., all of which have 'on my
face'.

   On the verb גדר 'wall up', 'block',
'fence up', cf. Comm. on 1: 10 and
3: 23. The 1st hemistich, 'He has
blocked my way so that I cannot get
through', recalls 3: 23 where Job
compared himself to 'a man whose
path is hidden, and whom Eloah has
hedged in'. Equivalent expressions
are found in La 3: 7, 'He has walled
me in so that I cannot get out' (use
of the verb גדר with בעד before the
complement; cf. Comm. on 3: 23)
and La 3: 9, 'He has walled up my
paths with hewn stones.' In the
latter text we find the parallelism
between דרכי 'my ways' and נְתִיבֹתַי
'my paths' which is a feature of our
2nd hemistich, 'and upon my paths
He has set darkness'. Compare the
2nd hemistich of La 3: 2, 'He has
driven me on and caused me to walk
in darkness and not light.' Job finds
himself enclosed in a dark tunnel
from which there is no exit. It is
God who has made his soul waver
and grope blindly. The ills with
which he is overwhelmed are like
thick darkness traversed by no
gleam of light.

9   G omits the suffix of כבודי (cf.
v. 4 and v. 5), which is however
restored in G (A) τὴν δόξαν μου (Sah.,
Syro-hex., Jerome, Eth., but not in
Arab. Baud.). The genitive ראשי
is rendered ἀπὸ κεφαλῆς μου in G, *de*
capite meo in Vulg.

10   He strikes me down on every side and I perish,
      And He uproots my hope as if it were a tree,
11   He kindles against me His wrath,
      And counts me as *His adversary*.

11   כְּצָרוֹ (G, Vulg., Syr., Targ.); MT: כצריו.

The verb הפשיט 'strip', 'take off clothing' (22: 6) can have as its direct complement the garment that is removed, and as indirect complement the person who is stripped of his clothing: ועורם מעליהם הפשיטו 'they have flayed their skin from off them' (Mic 3: 3). The 1st hemistich, 'He has taken from upon me my glory', will mean: 'He has stripped me of my glory.' Glory is a garment as well as shame (8: 22a, cf. Comm.). In 29: 14 Job will say that he was clothed with righteousness. The garment is made parallel with the headgear; cf. the 'mantle and tiara' of 29: 14. Glory can be a crown: 'Thou crownest him with glory and honour' (Ps 8: 6). Not only has God stripped Job of his glory, He has also removed the crown from his head. Cf. La 5: 16, 'it has fallen, the crown of our head', עטרת ראשנו. Job has been reduced to a state of extreme humiliation, whereas formerly he could be proud of his righteousness and his integrity.

10   Syr. well interprets סביב as 'on all sides'. For ואלך, Vulg. *et pereo*; for כעץ, *quasi evulsae arbori*.
   In accordance with the meaning of נתץ 'demolish', Duhm would interpret יתצני as 'He demolishes my house', and see in וָאֵלַךְ 'and I go away' the consequence of the former fact. But in Ps 52: 7 we have גם־אל יתצך לנצח 'moreover God will break you down for ever'. It is the person himself who is compared to the building that is destroyed. In 16: 14 Job said: 'He batters me down, breach upon breach.' The adverb

סָבִיב as in 10: 8b and in 18: 11. On the meaning of הלך 'to perish', cf. Comm. on 14: 20. The *hiph'il* of נסע 'tear away', 'snatch' (4: 21) has the meaning of 'uproot', 'replant' a vine in Ps 80: 9. The 2nd hemistich, 'and He uproots my hope as if it were a tree', does not contradict 14: 7, 'for there is hope for the tree; if it be cut down, it may still spring to life again'. The tree in question still had roots (14: 8). Job has no more hope (17: 15-16).

11   G ὀργῇ ἐχρήσατο favours the Massoretic vocalisation וַיַּחַר (*hiph-'il*), instead of וַיִּחַר (*qal*), which is presupposed by Vulg. *iratus est*, Syr. and Targ. ותקף 'and is strong'. For כצריו the versions read כְּצָרוֹ *quasi hostem suum* (Vulg.), ὥσπερ ἐχθρόν (G), 'as an adversary' (Syr.), 'as His enemy' (Targ.).
   The 1st hemistich, 'he kindles against me His wrath', is perfectly intelligible. God is the subject both of יַחַר and of יַחְשְׁבֵנִי. It would be unwise to replace the *hiph'il* of חרה by the *qal* so as to make it equivalent to the ordinary idiom, 'His wrath is kindled', as is proposed by Duhm and Beer. G confirms the MT. On the other hand, the reading כְּצָרוֹ 'as His adversary' which is supported by the versions, is preferable to כְּצָרָיו 'as His adversaries' of the MT. The 2nd hemistich is an echo of the cry of Job in 13: 24, 'Why dost Thou veil Thy face and consider me Thy enemy?' The construction is slightly different, כצרו

12   His troops attack together,
     They cast up their road against me,
     And camp around my tent.
13   My brothers He has put far from me,
     And my acquaintances only turn away from me.

replacing לאויב. The verb חשב with
כ' before the term of comparison
as in 18: 3.

12 For גדודיו, G τὰ πειρατήρια αὐτοῦ
(Jerome *temptationes ejus*), Aq. πει-
ραταὶ αὐτοῦ, Vulg. *latrones ejus*. G
sums up the last two hemistichs by
ταῖς ὁδοῖς μου ἐκύκλωσαν ἐνκάθετοι.
But Jerome *et fecerunt per me viam
suam et circumdederunt tabernaculum
meum* brings us back to the MT
through the intermediary of Theod.
and Symm., who are quoted by
Syro-hex. In Jerome there is an
asterisk before *et fecerunt* and in
Syro-hex. before the words 'and
they have prepared'. In Cod. 255
there is obelus before G ἐνκάθετοι.
God regards Job as His enemy (v.
11). He is going to attack him as one
attacks a besieged town. Already in
16: 14 God was likened to the warrior who makes breach upon breach
in a wall. On the other hand, in
15: 25-6 it was the wicked man who
flung himself with all his army into
an attack on God. The word גְּדוּדָיו
'His companies', i.e. the troops
which God mobilises, will recur in
25: 3. Duhm would delete v. 12 on
the ground that the description
resembles 30: 12ff. A simple comparison with 30: 12ff., where it is a
question not of God but of Job's
enemies, proves that there has not
been mutual influence. The only
formal resemblance is ויסלו עלי
ארחות of 30: 12, which reminds us
of וַיָּסֹלּוּ עָלַי דַּרְכָּם in our verse. But
since the meaning of סלל is specifically 'to cast up', 'to embank' a
road, it is not surprising that the
complements are words denoting
'road', 'path'. The three phases of

the attack are very clearly marked
out: the troops gather together, they
make a way for themselves, they
invest the besieged town.

13 Instead of הרחיק ו', G ἀπέστη-
σαν reads הרחיקו, which is found
again in Aq. and Symm. (quoted in
Syro-hex.) and in Syr. ܘܐܪܚܩ. G has
a double translation of the 2nd
hemistich: first ἔγνωσαν ἀλλοτρίους
ἢ ἐμέ, which omits אך and reads
זרים, then φίλοι δέ μου ἀνελεήμονες
γεγόνασιν, which reads אכזרו and
omits ממני. Syr. transfers ממני to
v. 14 and renders אך־זרו by ܚܒܪܝ
'they have passed'. Targ. translates
אך־זרו ממני by 'they have become
as strangers to me'; cf. Vulg. *quasi
alieni recesserunt a me*.
The complaint of being deserted in
consequence of misfortune begins
with אַחַי 'my brothers'; cf. 6: 15ff.
Literally מֵעָלַי 'from beside me'; cf.
סר מעליו 'he turned away from him'
(Jg 16: 20), סר מעלי 'He has turned
away from me' (1 S 28: 15). Parallelism seems to favour the reading
הרחיקו (G, Aq., Symm., Syr.), but
v. 14 supports the MT (copula at the
2nd hemistich). The word which is
complementary to אחי is ידעי 'those
who know me', 'my acquaintances'.
We have the series 'all his brothers
and all his sisters and all his former
acquaintances' in 42: 11. This passage, where ידעיו 'those who know
him' plays the same part as ידעי,
should have warned Merx and
Budde against changing ידעי into
ידעו (following the first translation
of G). The reading אכזרו of the
second translation of G implies an
Aramaic verb in the *'aph'el* form,

14   My kinsmen and my familiar friends have disappeared,
      They have forgotten me,   (15)   the guests I entertained!
15   And my very maidservants treat me as a stranger,
      I am an alien in their eyes.

the meaning of which would be 'to be pitiless, cruel'; (cf. אכזר in 30: 21; 41: 2). But in that case we should need, as complement, לי 'with respect to me' and not ממני 'far from me'. Note, however, that Rashi reads אכזרו as one single word. The verb זור meaning 'to turn away from' can take מן before the name of the thing or person from which one turns aside (Ps 78: 30). The particle אַךְ 'nothing but' (18: 21) bears on the action or the state expressed by the verb or adjective. Thus in Dt 16: 15 והיית אך שמח 'and you will be nothing but joyous', that is: 'and you will only rejoice'. Hence we shall translate the 2nd hemistich: 'and my acquaintances only turn away from me'. This idea is expressed in similar terms in several passages of the Psalms (31: 12f.; 38: 12; 88: 9).

14   This too short verse is lengthened by Syr., which includes in the 1st hemistich ממני from v. 13. G translates חדלו by οὐ προσεποιή-σαντό με and מידעי by οἱ εἰδότες μου τὸ ὄνομα.

Manifestly, vv. 14-15 have lost their natural proportions, v. 14 being clearly too short, v. 15 too long. With most modern exegetes, we join גרי ביתי to v. 14, the *athnaḥ* having to be placed under וּמְיֻדָּעַי. The verb חדל without a complement, exactly as in 14: 7, means 'cease', 'fail', 'disappear'. Use of קְרוֹבַי 'my relations' is as in Ps 38: 12 'and my kinsfolk remain afar' (antithesis between קרוב 'near' and רחוק 'far'). The *pu'al* participle of ידע is used in the sense of the Latin *notus* 'known', 'familiar', 'intimate'. Compare the use of מידעי in Ps 88: 9,

'Thou hast put far from me my intimate friends.' The participle of גור has the same meaning as גֵּר, which denotes in particular the stranger who is looking for a refuge, the client, the guest (31: 32). With גרי ביתי 'the guests of my house', i.e. the guests I entertained, cf. גרת ביתה 'the guest in her house', 'her tenant' in Ex 3: 22. It is ruining a perfectly clear text to substitute מדעי 'of my acquaintance' (complement of חדלו) for the word מידעי, as Duhm proposes to do, on the pretext that the 'acquaintances' of v. 13 cannot possibly reappear here. The distinction between the terms used is however quite clear. The *qal* participle of ידע does not convey the same shade of meaning as the *pu'al* participle.

15   Targ. interprets אמהתי by לחינתי 'my concubines', the Hebrew word אָמָה, like the Assyrian *amtu*, meaning both 'servant' and 'concubine'. The words לזר תחשבני, omitted in G, are restored εἰς ἀλλότριον ἐλογίσαντό με in Codd. 106, 249, 261 (Field). This translation, preceded by an asterisk, is a feature of Syro-hex. and Jerome *quasi alienum reputaverunt me*. The lacuna in G is due to an error of haplography: jumping from ἀλλότριον to ἀλλογενῆς which translates נכרי. Targ. renders נכרי by בר עממין 'Gentile', 'pagan'. The feminine form תַּחְשְׁבֵנִי (Gesenius-Kautzsch, § 60a) proves clearly that גרי ביתי belonged to v. 14. The house naturally involves the idea of menservants and maidservants. The verb חשב with לְ as in 13: 24. Job begins with אמהתי 'my maidservants' and continues with 'my manservant' עַבְדִּי in v. 16; we shall have

16   I call my manservant, and he answers not,
      Even though with my own mouth I implore him.
17   My breath has become repulsive to my wife,
      And I have become fetid to the sons of my bowels.

the parallelism between עבדי 'my manservant' and אמתי 'my maidservant' in 31: 13. The זָר is a general term for foreigner, alien, one who does not belong to the nation (15: 19). The נָכְרִי is one from a strange land, the man of another race (cf. G and Targ.). Perhaps the nearest equivalent is 'barbarian' in its original sense. The use of הֵם instead of the feminine suffix הן (cf. 39: 3; 42: 15) is a phenomenon fairly frequently found (Gesenius-Kautzsch, § 135o). The idiom בְּעֵינֵיהֶם 'in their eyes' just as we have 'in Thy eyes' (11: 4), 'in your eyes' (18: 3).

16 G (A) θεράποντας δέ μου, instead of θεράποντά μου, is followed by Eth. For ולא יענה, Syr. 'and he has not answered'. Similarly G (A) adds the complement μοῦ which recurs in Sah., Eth., Arab. Baud. For במו־פי, Syr. 'with the words of my mouth'. The end אתחנן־לו is translated twice in Syr. It is the word פי which becomes the subject of אתחנן in G στόμα δέ μου ἐδέετο (A adds αὐτῷ).

Observe the relation between קרא 'call' and ענה 'answer' (9: 16; 13: 22). The servant must be ready to obey the slightest sign (Ps 123: 2). But here the rôles are reversed. The servant does not condescend to answer. Job is obliged to humiliate himself, to beseech in vain. The expression בְּמוֹ־פִי 'with my mouth', 'with my own mouth' as in 16: 5. The *hithpa'el* of חנן with לי'' before the complement (9: 15), with אל־ (8: 5), to mean 'implore'. Cf. the use of the noun תחנונים in 40: 27.

17 G καὶ ἱκέτευον τὴν γυναῖκά μου omits רוחי זרה and repeats אתחנן of

v. 16. Syr. 'I am a stranger' regards רוחי as the equivalent of נפשי 'my soul', 'myself'. Vulg. *halitum meum exhorruit uxor mea* conveys the correct sense. For וחנתי, G προσεκαλού-μην δὲ κολακεύων (obelus before *blandiens* in Jerome). Vulg. *et orabam*, Targ. and Syr. ואתחננית. It is apparent that the versions connect חנתי with חנן in the sense of התחנן of v. 16. Syr. renders בני by the singular. For לבני בטני, G υἱοὺς παλλακίδων μου, but Jerome *filios uteri mei* (asterisk before *uteri mei*); cf. the variant τῶν υἱῶν γαστρός μου in the margin of Cod. 252. In Symm. υἱοὺς παίδων μου.

The meaning of the 1st hemistich is certainly 'my breath has become repulsive to my wife'. The verb זָרָה does not stem from זור 'to turn aside', 'to be a stranger to' (v. 13 and v. 15), but from זיר, which has supplied the Assyrian *zâru, izîr*, the original meaning of which is 'to feel repugnance towards' (especially on the part of a wife towards her husband), then, more generally, 'hate', 'detest'; cf. Haupt, in *Zeitschr. für Assyriologie*, **30**, pp. 93f.). Here the verb is used in the intransitive sense, 'to be repugnant, repulsive to'. It is a rabbinical subtlety to assign to רוחי the meaning of 'my conjugal privacies' (contra Ehrlich). In 9: 18 we had the expression השב רוחי 'to take a breath again'. The idols are statues which have not a breath (רוח) in their mouths, i.e. which do not breathe (Ps 135: 17b). In the 2nd hemistich, it is clear that לִבְנֵי בִטְנִי 'to the sons of my belly' corresponds to לְאִשְׁתִּי 'to my wife'.

It is certainly a question of Job's sons. Since he is using hyperboles, the poet does not bother to reconcile

18   Even youngsters have shown scorn for me,
      When I get up, they scoff at me.

this allusion with the Prologue in which the death of the sons is narrated. It has been claimed that the correct interpretation of 'the sons of my belly' is the sons of the same maternal womb and that the translation should therefore be 'my uterine brothers' (Hitzig, Merx, Budde, etc.). But though one can say 'my womb' for 'my mother's womb' (3: 10) it is difficult to see how 'the sons of my body' should mean the sons of the same womb as myself. The brothers have been mentioned in v. 13. Still more fanciful is the explanation recommended by Wetzstein, Robertson Smith, Nestle (quoted by Budde), and which consists in assigning to בטני the meaning of 'my tribe', following the Arabic baṭn in certain contexts. In point of fact, the expression 'the sons of my belly' or 'the sons of my entrails' (thus is it translated by Targ.) corresponds to the Assyrian ṣit libbi 'what springs from the heart, from the inward parts'. The father as well as the mother uses the idiom mar ṣit libbi-ia 'the child sprung from my heart'. In Hebrew פרי בטן 'fruit of the womb' has become a generic term to designate children in general (see especially Dt 28: 53; Mic 6: 7; Ps 127: 3). God said to David: 'I will put on thy throne a fruit of thy belly' (Ps 132: 11). It becomes apparent how useless it is to try to distort the normal meaning of בני בטני. The difficult word is וְחַנֹּתִי.

The versions are unanimous in seeing here a verb from the root חנן 'to be gracious', but in the sense of 'ask grace', 'beseech' (cf. v. 16). It is certainly thus that the Massoretic vocalisation understands it (cf. וחנתי in Ex 33: 19), without prejudging the meaning. The translations of Le Hir 'I ask grace', Renan 'I have had to make requests', follow the inter-

pretation of the versions. Loisy translates: 'I am unwanted' (?). The qal of חנן never has the meaning of 'beg', which is reserved for the hithpaʿel. Houbigant and Rosenmüller had already recognised that here we have to do with a verb חנן, distinct from חנן, 'to be gracious' and of the same root as the Arabic خن, the tenth form of which means 'to have a foul smell'; cf. the Syriac ܣܢܐ 'rancid', 'fetid', 'evil-smelling'. The 2nd hemistich will be translated: 'and I am become fetid to the sons of my body'. Duhm claims that חנתי is undoubtedly a corruption of צחנתי (Jl 2: 20), whence his translation 'and my foul smell (is repulsive) to the sons of my belly'. But it is natural that a foul smell should be repulsive. That is not what Job means. The antitheses, begun in v. 13, are continued in this verse. The wife ought to take pleasure in being near her husband; she feels repulsion even for his breath. The sons ought to press close to their father; but they move away from him as though he were a centre of infection. Changes of וחנתי to וחנפתי 'and I am as an unbeliever' (Merx), ונתעבתי 'and I am disgusting' (Siegfried), are pure conjecture. Budde easily refutes the hypothesis of Houtsma who would read וחיתי 'and my life' or 'and my soul', in the sense of 'my person', 'myself', which would become the equivalent of רוחי similarly interpreted (cf. Syr.).

18 The word עוילים is read עולם by G εἰς τὸν αἰῶνα, עולים by Syr. ܟܡܠܐ 'the impious' (cf. 16: 11), אוילים by Symm. ἄφρονες and Vulg. stulti (cf. 5: 2, 3). On מימרי for בי in Targ., cf. 1: 10 and Comm. on 20: 29. Targ. is in accord with the MT in translating

19   All my confidants have conceived a horror of me,
     And those whom I loved have turned against me!
20   In my skin *my flesh has rotted away*,
     And I have gnawed my bone [ ] with my teeth.

20   בְּשָׂרִי רָקָב (G); MT: ובבשרי דבקה .— בְּשְׂנֵי; MT: בעור שני.

ינקיא 'the children'. For ואקומה
Vulg. *et cum ab eis recessissem*.

On the word עֲוִילִים 'children',
'youngsters', cf. Comm. on 16:11.
The verb מאס 'despise', 'scorn' is
used with ב″ before the person towards whom scorn is shown (Jg
9:38; Jer 4:30): 'even youngsters
have shown scorn for me'. What a
contrast with the situation of Job
at the height of his prosperity, when
both young and old were struck
with a feeling of reverential fear in
his presence (29:8). Cf. 30:1ff. The
antitheses still go on. The cohortative אָקוּמָה to express 'if I get up'
as we have אחדלה parallel to
אם־אדברה in 16:6. The verb דבר
with ב″ before the complement of
the person to mean 'rail against',
'scoff at' (Ps 50:20; 78:19). When
Job rises to leave the company (cf.
Vulg.) the youngsters begin to jeer
at his expense.

19   G and Vulg. omit כל. For מתי
סודי, G οἱ ἰδόντες με, Symm. οἱ συν-
όμιλοί μου, Vulg. *consiliarii mei*.
Singular, instead of the plural, in
the 2nd hemistich in Vulg. *et quem
maxime diligebam aversatus est me*.

There is nothing so distressing as
desertion by one's friends and relatives (13-14); but when the most
intimate bosom friends and confidants become enemies and detrac-
tors it spells the extremity of affliction. The Psalmist gives expression
to a similar complaint in Ps 55:14-
15. The verb תעב in the *pi'el*, as in
9:31, 'to have a horror of'. Cf. again
30:10. On מְתֵי סוֹדִי 'my confidants',
cf. 15:8. The pronoun זה takes the

place of the relative אֲשֶׁר (15:17)
and remains indeclinable (Gesenius-
Kautzsch, § 138h). The *niph'al* נהפך
'to turn' with ב″ before the person
'against' whom one turns (Sir 6:12);
cf. Comm. on 9:5.

20   G ἐν δέρματί μου ἐσάπησαν αἱ
σάρκες μου reads בשרי (for ובבשרי)
and רקבה (for דבקה). The word
עצמי is then connected with the 2nd
hemistich: τὰ δὲ ὀστᾶ μου ἐν ὀδοῦσιν
ἔχεται. G (A) ἐν ὀδύναις (instead of
ἐν ὀδοῦσιν) is followed by Arab.
Baud. The word ובבשרי is paraphrased *consumptis carnibus* in Vulg.,
which interprets the 2nd hemistich
as *et derelicta sunt tantummodo labia
circa dentes meos*. In Syr. it is עורי
and בשרי which become subjects of
דבקה. Symm. renders אתמלטה by
ἐξέτιλλον (cf. inf.).

This verse raises many difficulties.
The 1st hemistich is obviously too
long, for the bones cleave to the
skin (La 4:8), or to the flesh (Ps
102:6), but not to both at once, in
spite of the commentary of Le Hir,
who proposes to see in this phenomenon an 'effect of fever'. Again,
we find בְּעוֹרִי in the 1st hemistich
and בְּעוֹר in the 2nd. One solution,
rather favoured by modern critics
(cf. Budde) is that of Bickell, who
eliminates וּבְבְשָׂרִי and replaces בעור
(in the 2nd hemistich) by בשרי.
Thus we obtain 'my bone cleaves to
my skin, and I escape with my
flesh in my teeth' (cf. 13:14). But
it is precisely when there is no more
flesh that the bones cleave to the
skin; cf. Vulg. *consumptis carnibus*.
We note that the text of G divides

21   Have pity on me, have pity on me, O you my friends!
      For the hand of Eloah has smitten me.

the verse perfectly into two hemistichs and eliminates the second עוֹר,
reading בְּשָׂרִי at the end, instead of
בְּעוֹר שִׁנָּי. The MT, as regards the
1st hemistich, may have been influenced by the formulae of Ps
102: 6 and La 4: 8. We do not hesitate to adopt the reading which G
has not invented and, with Merx,
we propose to read: בְּעוֹרִי בְשָׂרִי רָקָב
'in my skin my flesh has rotted
away', which offers excellent sense.
It is unnecessary to read בשרי in the
plural, as Duhm suggests. As it
stands at present, the 2nd hemistich
is translated: 'I have skin only
around my teeth' (Le Hir), or more
literally, 'I have escaped with the
skin of my teeth' (Renan). It would
seem that we have here a popular
proverb, meaning: I have lost all.
'My gums' has been proposed for the
skin of my teeth (cf. Schultens,
Rosenmüller, etc.), which, however,
compels us to adopt a rather oversubtle interpretation: *nihil toto cor-
pore sanum aut integrum remansit,
praeter eam cutem, quae est circum
dentes, cutem gingivarum* (Rosenmüller). The difficulty of the text
as it stands is recognised even by
Ehrlich, who declares that it is 'in-
curably corrupt'. Merx reads
ואתמלטה בשני עצמי and translates:
'I escape, my bones in my teeth' (!).
Bickell and Duhm reduce the hemistich to two words ויתמלט שני
'and my teeth fall out'. Other conjectures will be found in Beer's study
on the text of Job (p. 120), as also
in the commentaries of Budde and
Gray. We cannot set them all forth
here. We have seen that G begins
the 2nd hemistich at עַצְמִי and does
not include the second עוֹר. The
clause thus becomes: עצמי וָאֶתְמַלְּטָה
בְּשִׁנָּי. The verb, together with the
copula, has passed into the body of

the clause (cf. 10: 8 and 14: 20),
which has brought about the wrong
division of the MT. In fact, עצמי is
the direct complement of אתמלטה,
while בשני 'with my teeth' expresses
the instrument of the action. The
hithpa'el takes an accusative as its
complement, when it enunciates an
action which the subject fulfils on
itself (cf. Gesenius-Kautzsch, § 54f).
Now, there is a root מלט parallel to
מרט 'rub', 'polish', 'furbish', 'make
smooth', with the meaning of 'to
shave' or 'to be smooth' in Arabic.
It is this root which Symm. recognised in its translation ἐξέτιλλον 'I
plucked out my hair'. The Arabic
maraṭa means at one and the same
time 'to pluck out the hair' and
'to eat', 'to chew', 'to nibble'. The
transition from the one meaning to
the other seems possible to us
through the intermediary of 'render
smooth, polished' by gnawing at, as
for example, a dog gnawing a bone.
The similarity between the roots
מלט and מרט is probably due to a
common origin; cf. יתעלם and יתערם
in the Comm. on 6: 16. Hence for
the 2nd hemistich we propose the
very clear meaning of 'and I have
gnawed my bone with my teeth'.
The singular 'my bone' which has a
collective sense has been used in
preference to the plural because of
the preceding 'my skin' and 'my
flesh'. Job has no longer any flesh.
His bones are visible under the skin,
he can gnaw them with his teeth.

21 G (A) replaces the first ἐλεήσατέ
με by ἐγγίσατέ με, but adds ἐλεήσατέ
με after ὦ φίλοι. For אתם רעי, Vulg.
saltem vos amici mei. For יד, Targ.
מחתא 'the blow', 'the wound', so as
to avoid the anthropomorphism.

What could be more vehement,
more piercing than the twofold cry:
Have pity on me, have pity on me!

22   Why do you persecute me as does God,
      And why are you never sated with my flesh?
23   Oh that my words might be written down!
      Oh that they might be engraved on brass,

Cf. Ps 123: 3a, 'Have mercy on us, Yahweh, have mercy on us!' Job here uses the word רֵעָי 'my friends', which did not occur in the enumeration of vv. 13-14 and which is specially suitable to his three companions (2: 11). It is God who is the author of Job's ills (cf. vv. 6ff.). The hand of God is the instrument of punishments and scourges (cf. Targ.). The Assyrian *qât ili* connotes a misfortune sent by a god (cf. *L'Emploi métaphorique*, pp. 144f.). The verb נגע with ״ב before the complement with the meaning 'strike' some one (1: 11, 19; 5: 19).

22 The versions have rightly read כְּמוֹ־אֵל 'like God', which must be preserved in the text (cf. inf.). G ἀπὸ δὲ σαρκῶν again replaces a singular by a plural (cf. v. 20).

The meaning is very clear. Job is persecuted by God (v. 21). Instead of helping him, his friends join in the chase with God: 'Why do you persecute me as does God?' It is a pure whim to read כמו־גאל 'like an avenger' (Neubauer) or כמו־איל 'like a stag' (Reiske, Perles, Beer). The verb רדף as in 13: 25, where Job addressed God. Use of שבע with מן is as in 31: 31, where 'to be sated with meat' is taken in the literal sense. Job compares his friends to carnivorous beasts pursuing their prey and devouring his flesh gluttonously. At the same time, however, 'to eat the flesh of some one' is to do him all possible harm (Ps 27: 2). Note that 'to eat the morsels' of some one, Aramaic אכל קרצי (Dn 3: 8; 6: 25), Assyrian *akâlu qarṣê*, means 'calumniate', 'slander'. It becomes apparent that the literal and the figurative

meanings are inextricably intermingled in the apostrophe of Job: 'and why are you never sated with my flesh?'

23 G and Syr. replace by the copula the second מי־יתן, which figures in Vulg. and Targ. At the close, G adds εἰς τὸν αἰῶνα, which corresponds to לעד of v. 24 (q. v.).

After appealing to his friends (21-2), Job makes his appeal to posterity. His heart's cry of distress ought to be fixed in writing: 'Oh that my words might be written down!' The optative formula מי־יתֵּן lit. 'who will grant?' with the copulative *waw* before the dependent imperfect (6: 8b; 11: 5b). The particle אֵפוֹ as in v. 6. Cf. Ps. 102: 19, 'May this be recorded for the generation to come!', where we have the same use of the *niph'al* of כתב. One wonders why Duhm modifies the text by making the caesura after וְיִכָּתְבוּן, while suppressing the second מי־יתן and reading בספרו 'in his book' instead of ספר. The book of God is hardly suggested by the context, since the sole point at issue is that of transmitting to posterity the words of Job. בַּסֵּפֶר 'in the book' is generally interpreted as meaning 'in writing' which is the normal sense of the idiom. But the verb חקק denotes the action of 'engraving', 'carving' (cf. Comm. on 13: 27; 14: 5). Here the *hoph'al* יֻחָקוּ (instead of יֻחַקּוּ) so as to avoid duplicating the emphatic form in pause (Gesenius-Kautzsch, § 20m). Consistently with the meaning of חקק and the expressions of v. 24, everything seems to suggest that we should recognise here, with Fried-

24   That with a tool of iron and lead
      They should remain engraved in the rock for ever!
25   As for me, I know that my Vindicator lives,
      And that, as the Last, He will arise on the earth,

länder (*JQR*, **15**, pp. 102f.) and
Perles (*Analekten*, Neue Folge, p.
70) the Assyrian word *siparru* 'copper', 'brass' which recurs in Is 30: 8,
'to engrave in brass', and Jg 5: 14,
where שבט ספר is a 'brass rod'.
Further example here of the displacement of the verb with copula
(cf. v. 20). V. 23b has as an exact
parallel v. 24b. Engraving is done
on brass or rock.

24   The 1st hemistich, absent from
Sah., marked with asterisk in Jerome and Syro-hex., did not exist in
G. The present text comes from
Theod. (cf. Syro-hex.). G εἰς τὸν
αἰῶνα in v. 23 comes from לעד. It
seems that, by an error of homoeoteleuton, the scribe passed from בעט
to לעד in the original translation.
The 2nd hemistich is lacking in G
(B), but it exists in G (א, A), Sah.,
Jerome, Syro-hex., Eth., Arab.
Baud. A reading of Theod. εἰς μαρτύριον, quoted in the margin of Syro-
hex., has passed into Jerome *in testimonium* (with asterisk). It is clear
that Theod. vocalised לָעֵד. Syr.
connects לעד with the 1st hemistich. Vulg., which translates ועפרת
by *et plumbi lamina*, renders לעד by
celte or *certe* (variants cited by Calmet and Knabenbauer). *Celte* is a
Low Latin word, which figures in an
inscription mentioned by du Cange
(s.v. *celtis*) and Calmet: *sed mall-
eolo et celte litteratus silex*. The meaning of *celtis* is 'bodkin', 'graver'.
But it has been established by Burkitt (*Journal of Theological Studies*,
17, pp. 589ff.) and Dom Amelli
(*Alcuni scritti*, 1917, pp. 28, 46) that
celte is an inner-Latin corruption,
and that the original reading was
certe.
The literal translation of the 1st

hemistich is simply 'with a graver
of iron and lead'. It is clear that
what is referred to here is the instrument with which engraving is
done on rock (2nd hemistich). The
explanation of Rashi, which has
passed into the dictionaries of Gesenius-Buhl (s.v. עפרת) and of
Vigouroux (s.v. 'Plomb') implies
that molten lead was poured into
the grooves of the engraved characters. But such a custom was unknown to antiquity. And with what
justification can we assign such a
meaning to the Hebrew phrase?
It seems that at least the preposition
ב would have been repeated before עֹפָרֶת. Those who claim that
what is alluded to here is the material on which one writes, the μολύβ-
δινοι χάρται of the Greeks, the *tabulae
plumbeae* of the Latins (cf. Vulg. *et
plumbi lamina*), ought to translate
ועפרת by 'on lead', which leads
Budde to change ועפרת into בעפרת
and to suggest a reading וצפרן or
בצפרן 'with a stylus point'. We
prefer to suppose that there was
known an alloy of iron and lead,
the lead serving the purpose of
colouring matter to enable the en-
graver to mark out his letter before
cutting into the stone. Note that
iron and lead stand side by side as
elements in an alloy in Ezk 22: 20.
The material on which engraving is
done is not lead but brass (v. 23)
and rock; for the inscription must
last for ever. There is no reason to
change לָעֵד to לְעֵד 'for a witness'
(Merx, Hoffmann, following Theod.).
In Is 30: 8 it seems that לָעֵד has
replaced לְעֵד, but we also have the
phrase עד־עולם 'for ever'.

25   For גאלי, G ὁ ἐκλύειν με μέλλων

(Jerome *qui me resoluturus est*), Theod. ὁ ἀγχιστεύς μου, Targ. פריקי and Syr. פרוקי 'my Redeemer', Vulg. *redemptor meus*. Then G ἀένáος ἐστιν (Jerome *aeternus est*) translates חי ואחרון (Schleusner), the word אחרון being understood in the sense of 'last times'; cf. Vulg. *et in novissimo die*, Syr. 'and at the last'. Targ. renders ואחרון simply 'and after that' and adds 'his redemption' as the subject of יקום. Vulg. *surrecturus sum* departs from the MT and the other versions; similarly *de terra* for על־עפר, instead of 'on earth' (G, Syr., Targ.). G, which has included ואחרון in the 1st hemistich, is obliged to connect the sequel to v. 26.

Job has asked that his words might be transmitted to posterity. The reason is that he is deeply conscious of his innocence and of the legitimacy of his protestations. He knows that some one is prepared to undertake his defence. He has already made allusion to the witness in the heavens (16: 19). Here it is a question of the one who will defend him in a court of justice: 'As for me, I know that my Vindicator lives!' The word גאל basically denotes the avenger of blood (2 S 14: 11), then the one who, on account of his kinship with the deceased, has the right of preemption in redeeming his property (Ru 4: 4-6) or of recovering what has been stolen from him (Nu 5: 8). Hence it is also he who redeems or delivers, the redeemer and the liberator. Quite naturally the *go'el* becomes the defender in justice, he who vindicates the rights of the oppressed (Pr 23: 10-11). It is in this rôle that God is often invoked in the Psalms as the *go'el* of the Psalmist or of his people. Thus Ps 19 ends with the exclamation: 'Yahweh, my rock and my Defender'. Cf. the use of the verb גאל in Ps 119: 154, 'Concern Thyself with my cause and defend me!' Thus it is the living God who is the Vindicator of Job. It has been proposed

to see in the אחרון of the 2nd hemistich a synonym of גאלי, and a comparison has been drawn with the meaning of the German *Hintermann*, he who takes upon himself the responsibility of another. A comparison is also made with the modern Hebrew אחראי 'responsible' (cf. Gesenius-Buhl, s.v. אחרון). Nowhere in the Bible does the root אחר or the word אחרון authorise such an inference. If this were the intended meaning, we should need the suffix of the 1st person after אחרון parallel to גאלי; cf. עדי and שהדי in 16: 19. The adjective אחרון is therefore an epithet which qualifies the *go'el*. The meaning of the word in our verse is completely clarified by the use of אחרון in Is 48: 12, where Yahweh says: 'I am the first and I am also the last', when this text is compared with Is 44: 6, 'Thus speaks Yahweh, the King of Israel and his Defender (גאלו), Yahweh of hosts: I am the first and I am the last.' It is clear that, in this second passage, it is God, in His rôle as *go'el*, who is the first and the last. Whatever events take place, it is He who will have the last word. The meaning of the 2nd hemistich is most certainly 'and that, as the Last, He will arise on the earth'. The verb קום means precisely 'to rise' in order to be a witness in a court of justice (16: 8), and it is used to describe God as rising up to mete out justice to the lowly of the earth (Ps 76: 10). The phrase על־עפר, just as in 41: 25, 'on earth'; cf. the word עפר in 5: 6; 8: 19; 14: 8. Job is expecting that God, as witness for the prisoner, will descend from the heavens (16: 19), in order to come and assume his defence on earth. Such is the natural interpretation of the text. Budde refutes *per longum et latum* those who wish to render על־עפר in this passage as 'on the grave' or 'on my grave'. Wherever עפר refers to Sheol or the tomb, the context

26   And that, behind my skin, *I shall stand up*,
       And from my flesh I shall see Eloah,

26 נְזְקָפְתִּי; MT: נקפו־זאת.

leaves no room for any ambiguity
(cf. Comm. on 7: 21 and 17: 16).

26 Each of the versions has adopted a different meaning for this
verse. G takes על־עפר יקום from v.
25 and translates: ἐπὶ γῆς ἀναστῆσαι
τὸ δέρμα μου τὸ ἀναντλοῦν ταῦτα, παρὰ
γὰρ Κυρίου ταῦτά μοι συνετελέσθη (Jerome *super terram resurget cutis mea*
quae haec patitur, a Domino enim mihi
haec contigerunt). G (A) μοῦ τὸ σῶμα,
instead of τὸ δέρμα μου, figures as a
variant in the margin of Syro-hex.
A reading σπέρμα, instead of σῶμα or
δέρμα, gives the reading 'my seed'
in Arab. Baud. It is apparent that G
omits אחר, reads ומשדי for ומבשרי,
אלה (ταῦτα) for אלוה. Vulg. *et*
rursum circumdabor pelle mea et in
carne mea videbo Deum meum translates מבשרי by *in carne mea* and
bears witness to the Christian belief
in the resurrection of the flesh. In
Syr. the words אחזה אלוה, interpreted 'if my eye sees God', are
relegated to v. 27. The sequel is
translated 'these things surround
both my skin and my flesh', the verb
נקפו being connected with הקיף (cf.
Vulg.). Finally, Targ. interprets נקפו
by 'that will be' and renders זאת by
אתפח (from נפח) 'will be swollen',
whence the translation 'and after
my skin has swollen, that will come
to pass, and from my flesh I shall
still see God'.

Much ink has been spilt over this
verse. A glance at the versions
shows that the difficulties did not
arise yesterday, and Knabenbauer
is right in saying: *versiculus brevis,*
septem constans voculis, at undequa-
que difficultatibus septus. First of all,
it is the word אַחַר, which can be an
adverb 'afterwards', a preposition
'after' or 'behind', or a conjunction

'after'. Then the verb נִקְּפוּ, which is
from נקף 'to be around', whence
הקיף 'to surround' (cf. Syr. and
Vulg.), or from נקף 'to strike down'
(Is 10: 34). Finally, מִבְּשָׂרִי is understood as 'from my flesh' or 'without
my flesh', which produces two contradictory meanings. The reader can
gain an idea of the extreme divergences in interpretation by comparing the translations of Le Hir
'that from this skeleton covered
with its skin, that from my flesh, I
shall see God', or of Crampon 'then
from this skeleton clad in its skin,
from my flesh, I shall see God', with
those of Renan 'when this skin will
have fallen into shreds, divested of
my flesh, I shall see God', or of
Segond, 'when my skin shall have
been destroyed, He will rise up;
when I no longer have any flesh, I
shall see God'. The commentaries of
Rosenmüller and Knabenbauer
quote the numerous opinions of the
ancients, all of which can be reduced, in the last analysis, to one or
other of those underlying the translations we have just mentioned. Let
us note that Calmet gave as the
literal meaning of the Hebrew 'and
after my flesh will have been pierced
(by worms, gnawed away by ulcers,
consumed by leprosy, worn out by
illness) and I shall see the Lord from
within my flesh'. Moderns have not
scrupled to correct the text, for it
seems indeed that the 1st hemistich
is hardly susceptible of a grammatical interpretation, whatever
meaning be adopted for נקפו. The
differences between the first and
second editions of Bickell (cf. Beer)
are sufficient to show that this critic
attached less importance to his own
hypotheses than did Loisy, who borrows from him 'my witness waits

27   Whom I myself shall see,
      And whom my own eyes will behold, and none other!
      My reins grow faint within me!

until all that is overpast'. Even by changing עורי to עדי 'my witness', one does not obtain such an interpretation. Duhm accepts the correction עדי and, by the process of amalgamating G with the MT, composes a verse consisting of the 1st hemistich and fragments of v. 25: 'and another will rise up as my witness, and he will raise his sign', reading ונקפו for זה אתו, וזקף for זאת, etc. Ball finds some means of bringing in 'the vengeances of God', for he reads נקמות אל (!) for נקפו זאת, while Ehrlich makes 'God' disappear by replacing אלוה by אלה 'these things' (cf. G). In the Kittel edition, Beer reconstitutes the text by replacing עורי by עדי 'my witness' and by extracting ומשהדי 'and my witness' from ומבשרי (on the basis of G ומשדי), which obliges him to make the further change of נקפו־זאת into נזקף אתי 'rises up by my side'. Faced by such a series of corrections, the list of which could be lengthened, we must seek the solid elements of the MT. Now, we observe that the 2nd hemistich, 'and from my flesh I shall see Eloah', is confirmed by v. 27 where Job dwells on the fact that his own eyes will see God. The preposition מן indicates clearly the view-point, the position from which one looks, or the thing through which one looks; cf. Ps 33:14 ממכון־שבתו השגיח 'from the place where He dwells He looks out' and Ca 2:9 משגיח מן־החלנות 'looking through the windows'. Now, the word בְּשָׂרִי 'my flesh' corresponds to עורִי 'my skin' of the 1st hemistich, as in 7:5. We have had עורי and בשרי in the 1st hemistich of v. 20. נקפו־זאת still remains the disturbing quantity. In accordance with the parallelism, these words are the

counterpart to 'I will see Eloah' of the 2nd hemistich. Hence what we expect is a verb in the 1st person singular. If we neglect the *matres lectionis* (*waw* and *aleph*), and if we suppose that the *zayin* has been accidentally displaced, we can read נִזְקַפְתִּי, which is the *niph'al* form of זקף 'stand erect', 'rise up', and of which the meaning will be 'I will stand erect, upright'. Now, in Ca 2:9 the well-beloved who is looking through the windows (cf. sup.) is precisely עמד אחר כתלנו 'standing up behind our wall', where we have the same use of the preposition אחר. In our passage: 'and, behind my skin, I shall stand up', as behind a curtain which I shall draw aside at a given moment, 'and through my flesh I shall see God', just as the well-beloved gazes through the windows. The expressions 'behind my skin' and 'through my flesh' show that it is Job in person who will be present at the ultimate drama.

27 G ἃ ἐγὼ ἐμαυτῷ συνεπίσταμαι as a result of reading אלה instead of אלוה of v. 26. Syr. 'if my eye sees God, it sees the light' combines with the last two words of v. 26 the whole of the first part of v. 27 (as far as the *athnaḥ*) and seems to read לאור instead of לא־זר. For ולא־זר, G καὶ οὐκ ἄλλος, Vulg. *et non alius*. G renders כלו כליתי by πάντα δέ μοι συντετέλεσται, which confuses כלו with כל 'all'. Vulg. *reposita est haec spes mea* reads כסלתי for כליתי.

Nothing justifies the changes of אֲשֶׁר אָנִי into אשרוני 'congratulate me' (a suggestion of Budde, referred to by Beer in the edition of Kittel), or אשריני 'happy am I' (Neubauer), or אשירה כי 'I will sing that' (Grimme). The text is perfectly

28   If you say: 'How shall we pursue him,
      And what grounds for proceeding against *him* can we find?'

28 בוֹ (G, Theod., Vulg., Targ.); MT: בִי.

clear and the versions confirm it. The 1st hemistich, 'whom I myself shall see', reinforces the affirmation of v. 26. The complement לִי 'for myself' refers to the subject, just as in English we say, in order to emphasise the subject pronoun, 'I shall see for myself' (where 'for myself' is properly a dative reflexive). Cf. נִגְזַרְנוּ לָנוּ 'we ourselves are clean cut off' (Ezk 37: 11). The 2nd hemistich, 'and whom my own eyes shall behold and none other', has been very well understood by G and Vulg. It is clear that the word זָר has not the meaning of 'enemy', but implies simply 'other', as in Pr 27: 2, where זָר 'a stranger' is opposed to פִיךָ 'your own mouth', and in Sir 40: 29, where שֻׁלְחַן זָר means 'the table of another'. Job means that he will see with his own eyes the vision of God. It is a needless distortion to give to וְלֹא־זָר the meaning of *non ut Deo contrarius*, referring to Job (Knabenbauer), or to suggest 'and not as an enemy', referring to God (Hitzig, Hontheim). With the expression 'whom my eyes shall behold' cf. עֵינִי רָאָתֶךָ 'my eye has seen Thee' in Job's last reply to God (42: 5). Our verse is a foreshadowing of the final theophany. Job with all his heart's yearning calls for the moment of his final justification: 'My reins grow faint within me!' The words כָּלוּ and כִלְיֹתַי attract each other by alliteration. The reins are, in Hebrew as in Assyrian, the seat of the emotions (*L'Emploi métaphorique*, p. 131), and this fact often occasions the parallelism of the reins and the heart (Jer 11: 20; 17: 10; 20: 12; Ps 7: 10, etc.). The verb כלה 'to grow faint', as in 11: 20; 17: 5. Just as the eyes languish with hunger,

the heart and the reins grow faint with desire. The expression בְּחֵיקִי 'in my breast' is the equivalent of 'within me'. Cf. the use of קרב in the idioms 'my heart within me' (Jer 23: 9, etc.) or 'his heart within him' (1 S 25: 37).

28 The 2nd hemistich, absent from Sah., marked with asterisk in Cod. 248 and Syro-hex., did not exist in G. The present text comes from Theod. (cf. Syro-hex.). In fact, G τί ἐροῦμεν ἔναντι αὐτοῦ seems to us to be a paraphrase of 'what root of words shall we find against him?' (בוֹ). G had therefore omitted נִרְדָף־לוֹ. It was believed that it was the 2nd hemistich which was lacking, and it was supplied from the text of Theod. Note that Theod. ἐν αὐτῷ read בוֹ and not בִי. Similarly Vulg. *contra eum* (cf. G) and Targ. בֵיהּ.

In accordance with the parallelism, the reading בוֹ, attested by the original translation of G, Theod., Vulg., and Targ. is preferable to the בִי of the MT. It has, moreover, penetrated a certain number of Hebrew manuscripts (cf. Ginsburg and Beer). It is clear that the 2nd hemistich corresponds to נִרְדָף־לוֹ and depends on the interrogative מַה. The conjunction כִּי is used in the sense of 'if'; cf. כִּי־אָמַרְתִי 'if I say' (7: 13). Here the imperfect, כִּי תֹאמְרוּ 'if you say', because it is a question of a future action. The interrogative מה is used adverbially sometimes in the sense of 'why?' (3: 12; 7: 21; 15: 12), sometimes in the sense of 'how?' (9: 2). The verb רדף governs the accusative (v. 22). The preposition of לוֹ is the Aramaic particle which

29   Fear for yourselves the sword,
      When wrath *is kindled against* wrong,
      So that you will know that there is a judgment!

29 בַּעֲוֺות תְּחַר ; MT: עונות חרב.

marks the accusative in 5: 2, 7 (cf. Comm.). Job's friends pursue him even to his last entrenchments. They wish to find in him 'a root of words', i.e. 'some pretext for a lawsuit'. The root means what serves as a basis for an accusation, a pretext enabling a complaint to arise and to develop. The word דָּבָר 'word' and 'thing' sometimes means a judicial cause, a case in law proceedings (Ex 18: 16; 24: 14; Is 29: 21). Cf. the meaning of דברה in 5: 8. The 2nd hemistich, 'And what grounds for proceeding against him can we find?', restores to מה its normal sense *'quid?'*. Job is reproaching his friends with their desire to judge and condemn him at any cost. Their arguments have no other purpose. The translations: 'and the right will be found to be on my side' (Renan), 'you who flatter yourselves that you have found me guilty' (Le Hir), 'and the justice of my cause will be recognised' (Segond, Crampon), are sufficient to show to what devices it is necessary to have resort if we wish to preserve the בי of the MT, as against the testimony of the versions.

29 For מפני־חרב, G ἀπὸ ἐπικαλύμματος, but Jerome *a gladio* (with asterisk). The 2nd hemistich is translated in G θυμὸς γὰρ ἐπ' ἀνόμους ἐπελεύσεται (cf. inf.). Vulg. *quoniam ultor iniquitatum gladius est* and Syr. 'because the sword is the fury (which avenges) sins' consider חמה as a construct state. Targ. paraphrases 'because, when God is provoked against iniquities, He sends those who slay with the sword'. Similarly the 3rd hemistich is para-

phrased in Targ. 'so that you may know that there is a true Judge and Lord of judgment'. Vulg. simply: *et scitote esse judicium*; cf. Syr. 'that you may know that there is a judgment'. But G καὶ τότε γνώσονται ποῦ ἔστιν αὐτῶν ἡ ὕλη connects שדין with שדי, translated ὑλώδης in 29: 5. The reading of Symm. and Theod. ὅτι ἔστι κρίσις, noted in Syro-hex., has influenced Jerome *quia est judicium* (with asterisk). G (A) adds a gloss to the text of G: ὅτι οὐδαμοῦ αὐτῶν ἡ ἰσχύς ἐστιν. It is apparent that the versions, with the exception of G, which makes a single word of שדין, support the *kethîb* שָׁדִין, as against the *qerê* שַׁדּוּן.

The verb גור 'to fear', sometimes with מן before the object of fear (41: 17), sometimes with מִפְּנֵי as here (Nu 22: 3; Dt 1: 17, etc.). The person for whom one fears is preceded by לְ (Hos 10: 5). Thus גורו לָכֶם will be translated 'fear for yourselves', the dative לכם marking a contrast with the לו and בו of v. 28. God is the Vindicator of Job (v. 25), He will be able to make His decisions respected. The sword of God is the instrument of His vengeance (Dt 32: 41f.; 34: 5-8) and of His anger (Zec 8: 7, etc.). It is also the symbol of authority (Ro 13: 4). The 2nd hemistich is a *crux interpretum*. By modifying as best they could the etymological meaning of חֵמָה 'burning heat', exegetes have arrived at such interpretations as 'the vengeances of the sword are fiery' (Le Hir), 'punishments by the sword are terrible' (Segond, cf. Crampon), or again 'for the anger of God will punish you by the sword' (Renan).

It becomes apparent that such interpretations assign to עֲווֹת חֶרֶב
'wrongs of the sword', the meaning
of 'punishments by the sword',
whence also 'vengeances of the
sword'. Le Hir mentions another
opinion which sees here an allusion
to sins worthy of the sword and
regards חמה as the fury which Job's
friends evince. This is the interpretation of Rashi. The difficulties
which it raises are sufficiently apparent from the translation of the
Bible du rabbinat français: 'for the
anger (which you show) is a crime
worthy of the sword'. Ball is right in
saying that the MT is 'ungrammat-
ical and untranslatable'. Following
G θυμὸς γὰρ ἐπ᾽ ἀνόμους ἐπελεύσεται,
the moderns have reconstituted a
text: כי חמת עונות תבא 'for fury
overtakes sins' (Merx), כי־חמה
בעולים תבא 'for fury is unleashed
against the ungodly' (Siegfried),
כי־חמה עולים תחרב 'for fury will
destroy the ungodly' (Duhm). Ball
is content to follow Duhm, while
suggesting תבער 'will consume' instead of תחרב. First let us note that
ἐπ᾽ ἀνόμους may come from the MT,
the word ἀνομία often being used
to translate עון in G (7: 21; 10: 6, 14,
etc.). The whole difficulty arises
from חרב. Now, if we transfer the
ב" to a place before עונות and if we
suppose a haplography of the last
letter of עונות, we obtain a perfectly
clear clause: כי־חמה בעוונות תחַר
'when wrath will be kindled against

wrongs'. The jussive form תְּחַר (from
חרה) instead of the imperfect (13:
27; 15: 33; 18: 9, etc.). It is of
course a question of the anger of
God, of which the sword is the instrument and the wrongdoing of
man the cause. We have made only
a slight modification in the MT.
There could be nothing more prosaic
than the meaning obtained by
Gesenius and Budde by their reading
המה (instead of חמה): 'such are the
pains of the sword!' The 3rd hemistich is deleted by Duhm as a
gloss which is betrayed by the use of
the relative שׁ. But Rashi had already pointed out the similarity of
שדין with עד שַׁקַּמְתִּי 'until I rose
up' from the Song of Deborah (Jg
5: 7). Fr. Lagrange notes quite
rightly that שׁ for אשר can no longer
be treated as a recent development,
since it is found in Assyrian, to say
nothing of the Phoenician אשׁ. Let
us add that the Babylonian relative
ša is used in the sense of the conjunction 'that' after *idû* (ידע) 'to
know' in one of the el-Amarna
letters (Knudtzon, no. 149, 82).
Hence we conclude that the translation should be 'with the result that
you will realise that there is a
judgment', a further allusion to the
ultimate drama proclaimed by vv.
25-7. We have seen that the *kethîb*
had the support of the versions.
Nothing can be obtained from the
qerê.

1   Then Zophar the Naamathite spoke and said:
2   This is why my thoughts bring me back:
     It is because of the sensation I feel within me,

Chapter 20   Second speech of Zophar: see Introduction, pp. xliiif.

20: 2 G οὐχ οὕτως ὑπελάμβανον ἀν-τερεῖν σε ταῦτα reads לֹא־כֵן instead of לָכֵן. This confusion recurs rather frequently in the historical books (Driver on 1 S 3: 14). G (A) has in addition σὲ εἶναι καί after ὑπελάμβανον. The reading of G (A) is cited in the margin of Syro-hex. It will be seen that G paraphrases the text. Similarly Vulg. *idcirco cogitationes meas variae succedunt sibi.* The verb יְשִׁיבוּנִי and the word חוּשִׁי are regarded as imperatives by Syr. The 2nd hemistich of G καὶ οὐχὶ συνίετε μᾶλλον ἢ καὶ ἐγώ is a translation of v. 4a read as הֲזֹאת יְדַעְתָּם מִנִּי (Bickell). The present text of G, in v. 3 and v. 4a, comes from Theod. (cf. inf.). Vulg. paraphrases the 2nd hemistich: *et mens in diversa rapitur.* For חוּשִׁי, Targ. רְגִישְׁתִּי 'my agitation'.

There is no reason to prefer לֹא־כֵן of G to לָכֵן of the MT, since G often confuses לָכֵן and לֹא־כֵן (cf. sup.). The ordinary meaning of לָכֵן is 'that is why' (32: 10; 34: 10; 37: 24), referring to what precedes. But at the beginning of a speech, it is an allusion to what follows. We translate 'This is why!' On שְׂעִפַּי 'my thoughts', cf. 4: 13. The *hiph'il* of שׁוּב retains here its etymological sense 'to cause to return', 'to bring back'. Zophar is about to explain the reason for his new intervention: 'This is why my thoughts bring me back.' Commentators have been em-

barrassed by חוּשִׁי בִי of the 2nd hemistich, for they have wished to see in חוּשׁ the infinitive of the verb חוּשׁ 'to hasten' (31: 5). Hence the translations: 'It is for that reason that they (the thoughts) agitate my breast' (Le Hir), 'to relieve my inner distress' (Renan), etc. Modern critics have modified the text. Fried. Delitzsch replaces חוּשִׁי by רַחֲשִׁי 'my agitation', while Beer takes the correction further by reading רָחַשׁ לִבִּי 'my heart has trembled' (cf. Ps 45: 2). The meaning of the root רָחַשׁ 'to be in a state of agitation or ebullition' (Podechard, *RB*, 1923, p. 30) would sufficiently favour this hypothesis if a change were necessary. But בַּעֲבוּר remains in that case difficult to explain. One is obliged to understand זֹאת or כֵּן in order to translate: 'and because of this, my heart has trembled'. Ball accepts לִבִּי instead of בִי, but he reads יֵחֹם instead of חוּשׁ and בְּקִרְבִּי instead of וּבַעֲבוּר: 'and within me my heart is hot'. What seems to us certain, in the light of the context, is that חוּשִׁי בִי must denote a mental phenomenon, similar to שְׂעִפַּי 'my thoughts', בִּינָתִי 'my understanding' (v. 3). In modern Hebrew the word חוּשׁ means 'sense' and derives from the verb חוּשׁ 'to feel', which corresponds to the Arabic حَسَّ 'to feel', whence حَاسَّة 'sense', and حِسّ 'sen-

3   When I hear a reproof which insults me,
     Then an impulse of my understanding prompts me to reply!

sation', 'feeling'. In Akkadian we have ḫasâsu 'to understand', 'to think', whence ḫasîsu 'intelligence', understanding', 'ear' (*L'Emploi métaphorique*, pp. 89f.), whilst in Aramaic it is חוש which means 'to think', 'to be preoccupied'. Thus it can be seen that the parallel roots חוש and חשש (חסס) evolve from the idea of sensation to that of thought. We can interpret חושי בי as 'my sensation within me', i.e. the sensation which I feel within me. The *waw* before בעבור becomes a sort of explanatory *waw*, the function of which is merely one of punctuation. The shock which Zophar has received is explained in v. 3, by the circumstantial clause. Cf. the juxtaposition of clauses in 19:16.

3   We have seen that G translated v. 4a in v. 2b. Vv. 2b-3 were therefore omitted. Further, the translation of v. 4a was no longer in its right place. The text has been restored by the introduction of the version of Theod. for vv. 3-4a. These three hemistichs are marked with asterisk in Jerome and (with the exception of ἀποκριθήσεταί μοι) in Syro-hex. The source is indicated in Colb. and Syro-hex. The translation of כלמתי by ἐντροπῆς μου confirms the attribution to Theod. (cf. Is 61:7; Ezk 16:63; 32:25). And yet the passage is found in Sah., except ἀπὸ τοῦ ἔτι of v. 4, these three words being likewise omitted in G (א). For the explanation of this curious fact, cf. Introduction, p. cc. Vulg. translates מוסר כלמתי by *doctrinam qua me arguis*. The word מבינתי is regarded as a genitive by Syr. and Vulg. *spiritus intelligentiae meae*. In Theod. ἐκ τῆς συνέσεως. The expression מוסר כְּלִמָּתִי means 'a reproof which insults me'. Cf. מוסר שלומנו 'a chastisement which

is our salvation' in Is 53:5. The second noun is in apposition, although the first is in the construct state (cf. Gesenius-Kautzsch, § 130e). This then is the reason why Zophar returns to the attack: he is obliged to listen to the speeches of Job, the aim of which is to cover him with confusion. For the meaning of כְּלִמָּה cf. הכלים in 19:3. The word מוסר (5:17) is often used as a complement of שמע 'to hear' in the Book of Proverbs (1:8; 4:1; 8:33; 19:27). The 2nd hemistich has been interpreted in many ways. A distinction has been drawn between the spirit, רוח, and the understanding, בינה, whence 'my indignation finds a reply in my wisdom' (Le Hir), 'but from the depth of my conscience the spirit answers me' (Renan), *mens mea ex vera intelligentia depromit responsum* (Knabenbauer), etc. According to Dillmann, the spirit draws upon the treasures of the understanding to furnish an answer. According to others, the expression מִבִּינָתִי indicates the cause, while רוח marks the effect: 'and to my understanding, he answers me with wind' (cf. Hitzig and Budde). Ehrlich finds in this 2nd hemistich a meaning which is still more difficult to justify: 'but he answers my logic even with nonsense'. The real meaning may be surmised, if we bear in mind that the 2nd hemistich is complementary to v. 2a and that the verb יַעֲנֵי is a *hiph'il*, corresponding to יְשִׁיבוּנִי. Zophar cannot refrain from replying. He is in the situation of Elihu who is urged by his inner promptings and feels himself obliged to speak (32:18). The faculty which prompts answers is the בִּינָה i.e. the understanding (28:12, 20, 28; 39:17, 26); cf. the verb בין in the Comm. on 9:11. It is from this under-

4   Do you know that from oldest time,
     Since man was placed on the earth,
5   The elation of the wicked is fleeting,
     And the joy of the godless lasts but a moment?

standing that arises the inspiration which urges Zophar. The preposition מִן marks the source. Hence we translate simply: 'an impulse of my understanding prompts me to reply'. It is a consequence flowing from the 1st hemistich. Zophar cannot leave without a reply the humiliating words which he has just heard. There is thus no need to alter the text so as to obtain a strict parallelism with the 1st hemistich, as does Duhm, who reads מבינה תענני 'and you answer me by wind without understanding'.

4   The translation of G begins at ἀφ᾽ οὗ ἐτέθη. The 1st hemistich, ill understood, is found in v. 2 (q.v.). The present text is from Theod. (cf. v. 3). For מני־עד, Theod. ἀπὸ τοῦ ἔτι, omitted in G (א) and Sah. (cf. v. 3). Double translation of the 2nd hemistich in Symm., the verb שׂים being treated at first as passive, then as active. Instead of ידעת, Symm. (according to Syro-hex.) Syr., and Vulg. scio read ידעתי. For שׂים, G ἐτέθη, Vulg. positus est, Targ. אשתוי, have well understood the passive meaning.

The relation between זאת and כי (from v. 5) excludes the interpretation of Budde, who connects זאת with what precedes and translates כי by 'No!' It is obvious that v. 5 which begins with 'namely that' only explains and amplifies the 'this'. The question 'do you know this?' has an excellent parallel in הזאת חשבת 'have you considered this?' of 35: 2, likewise followed by an explanatory clause beginning with כי (35: 3). Hence there is no reason to postulate הלא זאת (Rosenmüller), or הלא (Duhm), instead of הזאת.

The translation μὴ ταῦτα of Theod. can express a simple question. It is difficult to see why Merx prefers ידעתי 'I know' (cf. sup.) to ידעת. Zophar wishes to show his knowledge. He does not ask himself what he knows. The clause stops at ידעת. The formula מני־עד is parallel to the 2nd hemistich. For the poetic form מני cf. 6: 16; 7: 6; 9: 3, etc. The word עד 'always' is generally used to imply future time; cf. the idiom לעד (19: 24). Here it implies past time; the expression מני־עד 'from the beginning' corresponds to מעולם. The formula is interposed between 'do you know this?' and 'namely that' of v. 4, but it bears on the observations made from v. 5 onwards. What is in question is a fact which has for all time been verifiable. Again, the 2nd hemistich, 'since man was placed on the earth', specifies that this fact has been unvarying since creation. The infinitive שׂים has as its object אָדָם and as its subject and indefinite term 'since one established man', i.e. 'since man was established'. In Gn 2: 8, God 'places' (וישׂם) man in the terrestrial Paradise. With the 2nd hemistich cf. Dt 4: 32, 'since the day when God created man on the earth', meaning: from the very origins of things.

5   For מקרוב, G πτῶμα ἐξαίσιον. Syr. 'from their belly' reads מקרב. For חנף, G παρανόμων, Aq. ὑποκριτοῦ, Vulg. hypocritae, Targ. דילטור, Syr. ܣܛܢܐ. G renders עדי־רגע by ἀπώλεια. In Vulg. ad instar puncti.

We have seen that the conjunction כי connected v. 5 with הזאת ידעת of v. 4 and that the temporal circumstances, expressed in the sequel of

6   Even though his stature rise to the heavens,
     And his head touch the clouds,
7   Like a ghost, he vanishes for ever,
     Those who used to see him, say: 'Where is he?'

v. 4, applied to the facts which the author is proposing to set forth and amplify. The theme has already been repeatedly expressed. The prosperity of the wicked lasts but an instant. It is merely a deceptive appearance (8: 13-18; 15: 29-35; 18: 5-21). On the word רִנָּה 'elation', used here in the construct state, cf. 3: 7. The class of the רְשָׁעִים is often stigmatised in the speeches of Job's friends (8: 22; 11: 20; 18: 5). The expression מִקָּרוֹב 'quite near' to symbolise a thing which is easily attained whether in space or time. The elation of the wicked is near, in the sense that it is a phenomenon which does not cover a long distance, its end is easily seen. In this way the poet evokes the brevity of the wicked man's exultation. On the word חֲנֵף cf. 8: 13. The formula עֲדֵי־רָגַע in the sense of the Latin *ad momentum*.

6 G αὐτοῦ τὰ δῶρα confuses שִׂיאוֹ with שַׁי 'gift'. The other versions connect שִׂיא with the root נשׂא: ἔπαρμα αὐτοῦ (Aq., Symm., Theod.), *superbia ejus* (Vulg.), ܣܘܪ̈ܒܐ 'his elevation' (Syr.), זוֹקְפֵיהּ 'his height' (Targ.). It is in error that Syro-hex. places the asterisk before εἰς οὐρανόν, which figures in Sah. For וְרֹאשׁוֹ, G ἡ δὲ θυσία αὐτοῦ: omission of ר and reading אשו (from אִשֶּׁה 'sacrifice'). The conjunction אִם in the sense of 'even if', 'supposing that' (9: 30). The parallelism between the two hemistichs shows that שִׂיאוֹ corresponds to רֹאשׁוֹ 'his head'. The image is that of the tree which proudly rears its head to the skies. Hence one cannot translate שִׂיאוֹ by 'his flight', as is proposed by Fried. Delitzsch

on the basis of Assyrian *še'u* 'to fly'. The versions, with the exception of G, have connected שִׂיא with נשׂא 'carry', 'raise'. In French *port* (from *porter*) is used with the implication of a majestic figure. The Hebrew שִׂיא will denote the 'stature', 'height', i.e. the part which rises erect and is crowned by the head. Hence we translate the 1st hemistich 'even though his stature rise to the heavens'. It is unnecessary to replace the unusual word שִׂיאוֹ by שְׂאֵתוֹ 'his elevation', which could not function as the subject of the masculine יעלה (contra Beer). Duhm would read שׂוֹאוֹ, in accordance with Ps 89: 10, where the term is used with reference to the rising of the waves. This is not the word we should expect. On the other hand, we believe that we have discovered a recurrence of שִׂיא 'his stature' in 15: 31 (cf. Comm.). The *hiph'il* of נגע with לְ before the complement to mean 'touch', 'reach' (Ps 88: 4b). We shall find לָעָב 'to the cloud' again in 38: 34.

7 G ὅταν γὰρ δοκῇ ἤδη κατεστηρίχθαι (marked by obelus in Jerome) seems to replace כגללו by כגדלו or בגדלו (Ball). Targ. היך רעיה 'like his excrement', Vulg. *quasi sterquilinium*, in accord with the sense of גֵּל or גֵּלָל 'excrement'. Syr. confuses כגללו with כעלעולה 'like a storm' (cf. 36: 33 עלעולה). For ראיו, G οἱ δὲ εἰδότες αὐτόν may come from οἱ δὲ ἰδόντες αὐτόν, which exists in G (א).

The expression כְּגֶלְלוֹ, compared with 1 K 14: 10, has been understood in its crude sense 'like his excrement' and rendered 'like his own dung' (Le Hir, Crampon, Segond), 'like the dung' (Loisy), 'like wretched

8   Like a dream he flies away and is found no more,
     He is put to flight like a nocturnal vision.
9   The eye which had observed him sees him no more,
     And the place where he was perceives him no longer.

10 After v. 19.

dung' (Renan). In order to soften somewhat this meaning, it has been proposed to see in גללו the dung heap of animals which is dried in Palestine so that it may be used as fuel for the baking of bread (cf. Ezk 4: 12, 15). This hypothesis of Wetzstein is adopted by Duhm, who translates 'like his dung fire'. But in this case what is the point of the suffix? Others have thought it well to change the text and to replace כגללו by כבדו 'his glory' (Cheyne), כגלגל 'like the chaff (of the grain)' (Graetz), כגדלו 'following his greatness' (Ehrlich). We ourselves think that the word גללו is derived from the Assyrian *gallû*, which originally meant an evil spirit, but which had acquired more particularly the meaning of 'ghost', as is attested by popular Greek tradition, which gave the name Γελλώ (variants Γιλλώ, Γελώ, Γιλού, Γυλού) derived from *gallû*, to the ghost which steals newborn babes. This *Gellô* was identified with *Lilith*, the ghoulish nocturnal spectre, and it was believed that the word Γελλώ came from the Hebrew; cf. Frank, *ZA*, **24**, pp. 161ff. and p. 334, on the equivalence *gallû*-Γελλώ and the characteristics of the werewolf presented by the Γελλώ. We think that our word *gellô* is precisely the Hebrew intermediary between *gallû* and Γελλώ. Thus the meaning of the 1st hemistich becomes perfectly clear: 'Like a ghost he vanishes for ever.' Cf. the use of לנצח in 14: 20. The expression ראיו 'those who saw him' recalls ראי 'he who saw me' in 7: 8. The interrogation איו exactly as in 14: 10. There is a striking resemblance between our passage and Ps 37: 35-6.

8 G ὥσπερ ἐνύπνιον ἐκπετασθέν and Vulg. *velut somnium avolans* have welded together the two members of the 1st hemistich, by rendering יעוף as a participle and omitting ו of ולא, to form a single clause. The *hoph'al* יֻדָּד has been treated as a *qal* by the versions. For ימצאהו, G οὐ μὴ εὑρεθῇ and Vulg. *non invenietur* interpret according to the sense. There is no reason to read יִמְצָא (contra Duhm).

Vv. 8-9 develop the idea contained in v. 7; cf. Is 29: 7, where we find as here the comparison with a dream, a vision of the night (כחלום חזיון לילה). Note the use of the plural יִמְצָאֻהוּ 'he is found', as we had יֶהְדְּפֻהוּ 'he is driven' in 18: 18. The *hoph'al* form of the verb נדד is supported by the use of the *hiph'il* in 18: 18. The correction to יָדַד (Hitzig, Budde, Duhm) is quite unconvincing, in spite of the versions, which have interpreted *ad sensum*.

9 V. 9, absent from Sah., marked with asterisk in Jerome and Syrohex., Cod. 248, did not exist in G. The present text comes from Theod. (cf. Syro-hex.). In the 2nd hemistich Targ. copies the MT, while Syr. translates by 'and they will visit his place no more'. Theod. ὁ τόπος αὐτοῦ and Vulg. *locus suus* have not hesitated to make of מקומו the subject of תשורנו.

Duhm argues from the lacuna of G that v. 9 should be suppressed, and claims that it is a paraphrase of v. 7b and a quotation of 7: 10. The arbitrary character of this proceeding is manifest from the fact that

11   His bones were replete with his youthful virility,
But it lies down in the dust with him!

Duhm will cut out v. 10, which existed in G, and will preserve vv. 11-12 which did not exist in G (cf. inf.). V. 9 is rightly placed after the allusion to the disappearance of the wicked man who vanishes 'like a dream'. The 2nd hemistich does indeed resemble 7: 10b but does not reproduce the text. It is a reminiscence rather than a citation. The verb שׁזף 'observe', 'notice' as in 28: 7. It recurs only in Ca 1: 6, where it means 'to tan', 'to scorch' by confusion with שׁדף (cf. דעך and זעך, Comm. on 17: 1). Literally, 'an eye has observed him and does not continue', i.e. 'the eye which had observed him sees him no more'; cf. the use of הוסיף in 34: 32; 38: 11; 40: 5. The 2nd hemistich is inspired by 7: 10b 'and the place where he was sees him no more'. It is clear that תְּשׁוּרֶנּוּ corresponds to יכירנו of 7: 10b. The subject is מְקוֹמוֹ, which is masculine, but which is found with אחת in the qerê of Jg 19: 13. The feminine verbs of the 1st hemistich have exercised a kind of attraction. It is unnecessary to seek in מקומו an accusative of place. The evidence of 7: 10b, the translation of Theod. and of Vulg. (probably also of Targ.), are so many guarantees that מקומו is the subject. The verb שׁור 'to perceive' as in 7: 8; 17: 15. As Duhm has rightly remarked, v. 10 breaks the sequence of ideas. Should it be removed, purely and simply? The resemblance of v. 10 to v. 19a is intentional; the word ירצו is chosen as a counterpart of רצץ in v. 19; the דלים, who figure in v. 19 as victims, become those to whom restitution is made in v. 10. We transfer v. 10 to a place after v. 19, of which it forms the logical sequel (cf. inf.).

10   After v. 19.

11   Of vv. 11-14 in G, Sah. has only v. 14a: καὶ οὐ μὴ δυνηθῇ βοηθῆσαι ἑαυτῷ. Now, this v. 14a is, in fact, a paraphrase of ולא יצזבנה in v. 13a (MT). The original text of G had thus kept only a single phrase of v. 13a. And it happens that Colb. attributes to Theod. vv. 11-13 and 14b of G. In Syro-hex. vv. 11, 12b, 13, 14b are marked with an asterisk and attributed to Theod. In Jerome the asterisk marks vv. 11-12. In Cod. 248, it is 11, 12, 13a which are preceded by the asterisk. The hesitations of the witnesses cannot prevail against the fact attested by Sah. and Colb. In any case, the presence in G of a part of v. 13a (i.e. G 14a) is a proof that the Hebrew text was not invented as an afterthought. The lacuna in G is accidental. For עלומו Theod. νεότητος αὐτοῦ, Symm. παραβάσεως, Vulg. vitiis adolescentiae ejus (in accord with 13: 26), Targ. חיליה 'of his strength' (Aram. עלם 'to be strong'), Syr. ܡܘܚܐ 'of marrow'.

The plural עֲלוּמִים is an abstract like נעורים 'youth' (13: 26). The word recurs in 33: 25; Ps 89: 46; Is 54: 4. The verb עלם basically means 'to be in a state of puberty, virile, with manly strength'. The abstract עלומים denotes puberty, then youth. In the light of the context, it is apparent that here it is really the idea of youthful virility which is expressed. In itself, עלומים never has the meaning of 'secret sins', postulated by Rosenmüller and Le Hir (cf. Symm. and Vulg.). The subject of תשכב is עֲלוּמָיו. When the plural conveys an abstraction, the verb can be in the 3rd person feminine singular (see Gesenius-Kautzsch, § 145k). Cf. Ps 103: 5, where נעוריכי 'your youth' is the subject of תתחדש Thus it is unnecessary to replace עלומו by עלומה, as Siegfried pro-

12   If evil is sweet in his mouth,
      If he hides it under his tongue,
13   If he keeps it and does not let it go,
      And if he holds it fast in the middle of his palate,
14   His food in his bowels is turned,
      It is poison of asps in his intestine.

poses. In 17:15-16 Job wonders whether his happiness and his hope will descend with him into the dust (עַל־עָפָר), i.e. into the grave or Sheol. Here Zophar declares that the youthful vigour of the wicked man will lie down with him in the dust; at the height of his youthful virility, he is struck down by death. This is the opposite fate to that of the righteous man who goes down to the grave in the ripeness of old age (5:26). The expression עַל־עָפָר שָׁכַב 'to lie down in the dust' recurs in 21:26a. In 7:21b we had לֶעָפָר אֶשְׁכָּב 'I lie down in the dust'.

12 On the text of G, cf. v. 11. Theod. and Vulg. agree in restricting to v. 12a the subordinate clause, which obliges them to render by futures the verbs of 12b and 13. Syr. twice translates רָעָה, the second time at the beginning of the 2nd hemistich. Targ. interprets יכחידנה by יכדבנה 'he causes it to lie'.

Vv. 12-13 form the protasis, vv. 14-15 the apodosis. The images contained in the description of the wicked man relishing the sweets of his sin well convey the idea of this gloomy pleasure. Evil is like a sweet which the guilty man lingeringly sucks, which he keeps under his tongue and on his palate until he has savoured its delights to the full. The organs of taste, i.e. the mouth, the tongue, the palate, are mentioned in turn. Evil is denoted by the feminine רעה (the only case in which it is met with in Job). The hiph'il of מתק has the meaning of

'to be sweet', 'to become sweet' in Sir 38:5; 40:30; 49:1. With our hemistich, 'if evil is sweet in his mouth' (בפיו), cf. Sir 49:1 'his name is sweet (ימתיק) to the palate (בחך) like honey'. In Assyrian, *matqu* 'sweet' is synonymous with *dišpu* (דבש) 'honey'. The *hiph'il* הכחיד here retains its etymological meaning of 'to hide' (cf. the *pi'el* in 6:10; 15:18). The wicked man hides evil 'under his tongue' in order the better to relish it; cf. Ca 4:11, 'honey and milk under your tongue'.

13 On the text of G, cf. v. 11. The negative οὐ of Theod. (absent from Colb. and Jerome) arises from a dittograph of the final letters of αὐτοῦ in v. 12. For וימנעה, Vulg. *et celabit*, less literal than καὶ συνάξει αὐτήν of Theod.

The expression יַחְמֹל עָלֶיהָ, literally 'he spares it', to mean 'he keeps it', shows the complacency with which the wicked man makes his pleasure last. The verb עזב 'let go', 'abandon' as in 10:1; 18:4. The wicked man keeps evil in his mouth, he does not loose it, he hesitates to swallow it so as to savour the pleasure of it as long as possible: 'and he holds it fast in the middle of his palate'. The palate, חֵךְ, is mentioned with the tongue as an organ of taste (6:30). Cf. Ca 2:3, 'and his fruit is sweet to my palate'.

14 On the text of G, cf. v. 11. Vulg. makes a single sentence of the two hemistichs: *panis ejus in utero illius vertetur in fel aspidum intrin-*

15   The wealth which he has swallowed, he vomits up,
      God casts it out of his belly;

16   It was poison of asps which he sucked,
      It is the tongue of a viper that kills him!

secus. For פתנים, Theod. ἀσπίδος, Vulg. *aspidum*, Targ. חורמנין 'vipers', Syr. ܠܘܬܐ 'dragon' (תנין).

Vv. 12-13 have described the wicked man voluptuously savouring evil things. Vv. 14-15 will show the effect of the food which eventually he has swallowed. 'His food in his bowels is turned': the verb הפך in the *niph'al* 'to turn' (19:19), to express the idea that food turns sour and unwholesome, just as we say that the wine or the milk has turned (cf. Comm. on 9:5). The result of this turning of the food is admirably depicted in the 2nd hemistich: 'It is poison of asps in his intestine'. The feminine מְרֹרָה denotes the gall bladder (Assyrian *martu*) or the liver (cf. v. 25), seats of bile and gall; root מרר 'to be bitter' (cf. *L'Emploi métaphorique*, p. 130). The ancients imagined that a poison was secreted by the gall bladder of serpents (Bochart, in *Hieroz.*, I, col. 24), whence the use of מררה in the sense of poison. The פֶּתֶן designates a poisonous serpent, distinct from the viper (v. 16). This is probably the asp (cf. Theod. and Vulg.). The expression בקרבו 'within him' means 'in his intestine'; parallelism between מֵעִים and קֶרֶב as in Is 16:11 (*L'Emploi métaphorique*, p. 112).

15 G πλοῦτος ἀδίκως συναγόμενος paraphrases חֵיל בלע. At the end of the hemistich, G(A) adds ἐκ κοιλίας αὐτοῦ (= מבטנו), which is found also in Sah. The reading ἐξ οἰκίας αὐτοῦ in the 2nd hemistich of G is a corruption of ἐκ κοιλίας αὐτοῦ. The word אל is rendered ἄγγελος in G, ἄγγελος θανάτου in G(A), to avoid the anthropomorphism. Syr. con-

nects מבטנו with the 1st hemistich and interprets חֵיל as 'food'.

The verse provides an explanation of the image of the preceding verses. The evil which the wicked man savoured and which turned to a poison in his bowels is in fact ill-gotten gain. The 1st hemistich, 'he has swallowed wealth and vomits it up', means 'the wealth which he has swallowed he vomits up again'; cf. v. 9a for the grammatical construction. The word חַיִל as in 5:5; 15:29.

The verb בלע preserves its literal meaning of 'swallow' (7:19). The *hiph'il* of ירש denotes the two contrary actions, 'to cause to possess' (cf. 13:26) and 'to dispossess', 'to expel'. It is God Himself who expels the wealth from the belly which had gluttonously devoured it. Cf. Jer. 51:44, 'and I will cause to come out of his mouth what he has swallowed'.

16 Sah. lacks the 1st hemistich, which, however, stood in G, whose reading θυμὸν δὲ δρακόντων θηλάσειεν (A θηλάσει) differs from that of Theod., Aq., and Symm. χολὴν ἀσπίδων μυζήσει (Colb., Olympiod.). For the word ראש, G θυμόν (meaning derived from that of 'head'), Vulg. *caput*, Targ. רישי 'the heads'; but Aq., Symm., Theod. χολήν are in agreement with Syr. ܡܪܬܐ, which rendered מררת in v. 14.

Budde would make of v. 16 a gloss on v. 14b. But the ambiguous ראש would not explain the simple term מְרֹרַת. The word ראש, homonym of ראֹש 'head', denotes both a poisonous plant and the poison of serpents; this double meaning is reflected in Dt 32:32, 33. The Aramaic רִישׁ, homonym of רֵישׁ 'head',

17 He will not see the streams of *fresh oil*,
    The torrents of honey and butter:
18 He gives back his *profits* and does not assimilate them,
    And *of* the fruits of his trading he has no enjoyment.

17 יִצְהָר; MT: נהרי.

18 יִגְעוֹ; MT: יגע. — בְּ" (Syr., variant); MT: "כ.

likewise possesses this double connotation (Targ. on Dt. 32: 32, 33).
Bochart had already shown that
κεφαλὴν ὄφεως of Sir 25: 15(22) arose
from a confusion of ראש 'poison'
with ראש 'head' (*Hieroz.*, I, col. 24).
Duhm bases himself on G δρακόντων
in order to change פתנים, which was
rendered ἀσπίδος in v. 14. He does
not see that the text which figures
in G at v. 14 is that of Theod. The
word אֶפְעָה 'viper' recurs only in
Is 30: 6; 59: 5. The meaning of the
verse is not doubtful. When the
godless man acquires the wealth of
others (v. 15), it is as though he
were sucking a poison. It is this
poison, symbolised by the 'tongue of
a viper', which kills him.

17 The versions are in agreement in making נהרי the complement of פלגות and in connecting it
with the 1st hemistich. G. renders
נהרי by νομάδων and נחלי by νομάς.
The expression אַל־יֵרֶא 'let him not
see!' is used to indicate a future; cf.
אַל־תִּירָא 'you will not be afraid' in
5: 22. The juxtaposition of נְהֲרֵי and
of נַחֲלֵי cannot be justified; it
destroys the balance between the
two hemistichs. The versions have
restored the normal proportion, but
have had to regard נהרי as an absolute state. It has been proposed to
erase נהרי or נחלי (Hupfeld, Merx,
etc.). But how explain the addition
of the one or the other since neither
word needs a gloss? An excellent
conjecture of Klostermann, quoted
by Beer (edition of Kittel) offers
the expected solution, namely to read

יִצְהָר 'oil', especially the oil which
flows from the press (cf. the verb
הַצְהִיר in 24: 11), instead of נהרי.
We shall have the פלגי שמן 'streams
of oil' in 29: 6. Instead of the ordinary פֶּלֶג the poet has used here
פְּלַגָּה from the Song of Deborah
(Jg 5: 15, 16). Note that in 29: 6 oil
is in parallelism with butter, which
figures in the 2nd hemistich. Honey
and butter here take the place of
the ordinary formula 'milk and
honey', to depict the wealth and
fertility of a country (Ex 3: 8, 17,
etc.). Among the Babylonians and the
Assyrians, one of the most valued
offerings was 'honey and butter' (*La
Relig. assyro-babylonienne*, p. 267).

18 The paraphrases of G have
produced three hemistichs. A reading משוא instead of משיב makes it
possible to recognise יגע in
εἰς κενὰ καὶ μάταια ἐκοπίασεν. Then
ולא יבלע כחיל becomes πλοῦτον (cf.
v. 15) ἐξ οὗ οὐ γεύσεται. Finally, a
second translation of כחיל brings
about the interpretation of the 2nd
hemistich: ὥσπερ στρίφνος ἀμάση-
τος, ἀκατάποτος. Instead of στρίφνος,
G(A) στρύχνον. Syro-hex. cites the
Greek word στρίφνος, but draws
attention to the variant στρύχνον. A
note in the margin of G(B) and Syro-
hex. explains the word στρίφνος. This
note is by Origen (*PG*, XVII, col.
74). Vulg. interprets the whole verse
in the sense of retribution: *luet
quae fecit omnia, nec tamen consum-
etur: juxta multitudinem adinventio-
num suarum, sic et sustinebit*. The
word יגע is rendered by 'trouble',

19   Because he has crushed *with violence* the poor,
      He has stolen a house instead of building it,

19   בְּעֹז; MT: עזב. — V. 19 after v. 19.

'toil' in Targ. and Syr., but Targ. sees in it 'the work of another'. Syr. reads בחיל instead of כחיל (cf. inf.). For יעלס, Targ. ידוץ 'he will rejoice' (reading עלז), Syr. ܢܬܐܠܡ 'he has profited' (reading הועיל).

V. 18 is conceived on the same lines as v. 15, where it is a question of giving back ill-gotten gains. The noun יְגַע is not found elsewhere. The root יגע 'to toil', 'to work' has produced יְגִיעַ 'work' (10: 3) and 'the result of work, its fruits' (cf. Comm. on 17: 5). In accordance with the parallelism, one should read יְגִעוֹ 'his profits, riches' (Budde, Graetz, Beer). The suffix has fallen out by haplography before וְלֹא. The clause begins by a participle and continues by an imperfect; cf. 12: 17, 19, 20, etc. The natural meaning of the 1st hemistich is thus 'he gives back his profits and does not assimilate them', the verb בלע of v. 15 being taken figuratively. The corrections of Duhm, who replaces מֵשִׁיב by מָשָׁךְ, יבלע by יבליג, and who suppresses כחיל, substitute for the thought of the author that of the commentator: 'He increases his gains and does not look happy.' כְּחֵיל תְּמוּרָתוֹ is interpreted as 'according to the measure of his profits' (Le Hir), or 'his restitutions will equal his wealth' (Renan). But the basic meaning of תְּמוּרָה is 'barter', 'trade' (28: 17). Since וְלֹא יַעֲלֹס corresponds to וְלֹא יִבְלָע, it is clear that חֵיל תְּמוּרתוֹ will be the complement of יְגִעוֹ, which represents the fruit of work. It is the result of trading that must be indicated by the second formula. Now, the word חַיִל 'strength', 'vigour' and 'wealth',

'riches' (cf. v. 15) denotes also the fruits which are the outward sign of the vigour and health of trees (Jl 2: 22). It is thus that כֹּחַ 'strength' and 'riches' (cf. 6: 22) is used to symbolise the produce of the earth (31: 39). Hence there is no rashness in translating חֵיל תְּמוּרתוֹ by 'the fruits of his trading'. Instead of כחיל, a certain number of MSS and even of editions (cf. Ginsburg) have read בְּחֵיל, which is confirmed by Syr. We have then the complement of וְלֹא יעלס, the copula having been placed within the hemistich (cf. 19: 20, 23). The verb עלס, of which the *niph'al* will be used in 39: 13, is a rare word. But the meaning is not doubtful, in the light of Pr 7: 18, where the *hithpa'el* means 'to enjoy mutually'. The Arabic *'alasa* denotes the enjoyment of food and drink. The root is related to עלז 'rejoice', 'be exultant' (cf. Targ.) and to עלץ, which has the same meaning. The sentence 'and he does not enjoy the fruits of his trading' offers a good parallel to the 1st hemistich.

19   G οἴκους interprets עזב according to בית of the 2nd hemistich. Targ. עסקא 'property' likewise regards עזב as a noun. Vulg. *confringens nudavit* joins the two verbs, while Syr. 'he has thought of abandoning' replaces רצץ by רצה (whence ܠܐܒܐ = התרצה). G(B) δυνατῶν, for דלים, is a corruption of ἀδυνάτων, preserved in G(A, C), Jerome (Bod. and Gall.), Sah., Syrohex., Eth., Arab. Baud. We find *validorum* in Jerome (Tur.). Syr. treats גזל as a noun 'of the robber'. G translates יבנהו by ἔστησεν.

V. 19 is subordinated to v. 10,

10   His sons will compensate the poor,
      And his own hands will restore his riches.

20   For his belly could never be appeased,

which gives the result of the violent actions performed by the evildoer. We have seen (cf. v. 9) that v. 10, in its present position, made a violent break between v. 9 and v. 11. On the other hand, it supplies the logical sequel to v. 19. We have the same construction as in 20-1: first the reason, then the ensuing fact. The juxtaposition of the verbs רצץ 'break', 'shatter' and עזב 'leave', 'abandon' has the effect of a progression in reverse: 'for he has crushed and abandoned the poor' (Le Hir), 'for he has illtreated the poor and has robbed them' (Renan, cf. Vulg.), 'because he has illtreated and neglected the poor' (Loisy). Attempts have been made to find a noun instead of עזב, some choosing עצב in the sense of 'reward painfully acquired', others deciding in favour of משב 'abode' or זרוע 'arm' (cf. Beer), or again of עֹזֶב, עֹזֶב, to which must then be given a meaning like 'hut', in the light of the Modern Hebrew מעזיבה, a sort of *pisé* structure (cf. Ehrlich). Ball reads ערף 'the neck'. But in accordance with Am 4:1 it seems in fact that דַּלִּים should be the direct complement of רצץ, which then acquires the meaning of 'crush' or 'grind down'. Hence we must see in עזב the fragment remaining from an indirect or circumstantial complement, which leads us to transfer the ב in such a way as to read בְּעֹז 'by force' or 'with force'. V. 19a will be translated 'because he has crushed the poor with violence'. The 2nd hemistich 'he has stolen a house and has not built it', means 'he has stolen a house instead of building it'. Cf. the construction of v. 15a.

10 The versions have confused יְרַצּוּ, from the verb רצה, with the

verb רצץ of v. 19. G ὀλέσαισαν is a substitute for ἔθλασαν (cf. ἔθλασεν for רצץ in v. 19), through θλασίαν which stands in G(A). Vulg. *egestate* and Syr. 'by poverty' regard דלים as an abstract. For אונו, G ὀδύναις, Vulg. *dolorem suum*, Targ. תקוף צעריה 'the force of his sorrow', Syr. ܒܢܝ̈ܗ 'in his progeny' (cf. the interpretation of אנו in Targ. of 18:12).

The choice of words in the 1st hemistich to form a counterpart of v. 19a in itself indicates the original position of v. 10. In 5:3-5 it is the sons of the fool who pay for their father's follies. The fortune which they possess is so much ill-gotten wealth. Similarly in our text: 'his sons will compensate the poor'. The verb רצה in post-Biblical Hebrew has the meaning of 'satisfy', 'give compensation'. In Lv 26:34, 41, 43, the meaning is that of 'atone for', 'expiate'. The *pi'el* takes as direct complement the person who is compensated. It is inappropriate to vocalise יָרַצּוּ (Fried. Delitzsch) in order to bring back the verb רצץ of v. 19. The parallelism with תְּשֵׁבְנָה 'will restore', 'will make restitution' proves that the expected meaning is that of רצה. The 2nd hemistich indicates a progression. Not only his sons but his own hands must make restitution. On אֹן 'strength' in the sense of riches, cf. חַיִל in v. 15 and the Comm. on 18:12.

20 V. 20b, absent from Sah., marked with asterisk in Jerome and Syro-hex., did not exist in G. The present text comes from Theod. (cf. Syro-hex.). G οὐκ ἔστιν αὐτοῦ (Α αὐτῷ) σωτηρία τοῖς (Α ἐν τοῖς) ὑπάρχουσιν (Α adds αὐτοῦ) omits כי of the opening and reads לא ישע לו for

It was impossible to escape his appetite,

לֹא יָדַע שְׁלוֹ (cf. Ps 3:3). G(A) has then οὐδὲ ἀνθήσει αὐτοῦ τὰ ἀγαθά, which translates v. 21b. In the original text of G, v. 21b formed the sequel to v. 20a, since the hemistichs 20b and 21a did not figure in the translation. Vulg. sums up the 1st hemistich as *nec est satiatus venter ejus* and paraphrases the 2nd as *et cum habuerit quae concupierat, possidere non poterit*. The word שְׁלוֹ is interpreted דִּיהֵי שְׁלִיו 'that he was quiet' in Targ., but ܪܘܝܐ 'his judgment' in Syr. For בַּחֲמוּדוֹ, Symm. σχὼν ἅ ἐπεθύμει (cf. Vulg.), Theod. ἐν ἐπιθυμίᾳ αὐτοῦ, Syr. ܘܒܪܓܝܓܬܗ 'and in his desires', Targ. בְּגוּשְׁמֵיהּ 'in his body'.

The verse opens with כִּי, in the same way as v. 19, which gave the reason for the punishment mentioned in v. 10 (to be placed after v. 19). It is in v. 21a that the formula עַל־כֵּן 'that is why' will introduce the punishment due to the misdeeds which are described in v. 20 and v. 21a. Let us notice, first of all, that v. 21a presents no ambiguity: 'no one escapes his feasting', i.e. that everybody is eaten and devoured by the evildoer who plays the part of a veritable ogre. Now, v. 20b has at the beginning בַּחֲמוּדוֹ, which corresponds to לְאָכְלוֹ of v. 21a. The passive participle of חמד 'covet', 'desire' can imply the object of greed (Ps 39:12), but also the subject, exactly like the Latin *appetitus* (Fried. Delitzsch). The latter sense is admirably suitable here: 'it was impossible to escape his appetite'. The preposition "בְּ is used with a verb of removal as in 4:21 (cf. Comm.). The *pi'el* of מלט is used exactly as in Am 2:15 with the complement נַפְשׁוֹ 'his soul', 'himself' understood (cf. Am 2:14) to mean 'escape from', 'flee from', etc. Cf.

the *pi'el* of פלט in 23:7. The subject is the impersonal 'one'. It now remains to explain the 1st hemistich. A certain number of moderns have corrected the text in accordance with G and have obtained a meaning quite different from that suggested by the MT. Thus Merx replaces בְּבִטְנוֹ and לֹא יָדַע שְׁלוֹ by לֹא יֵשַׁע לוֹ by בְּטוֹבִיו, whence: 'there is no salvation for him in his wealth'. This correction is slightly modified by Siegfried (בְּטוֹבוֹ 'in his happiness' instead of בְּטוֹבִיו) and by Beer (edition of Kittel) who reads לְטוֹבוֹ 'to his happiness'. Duhm vocalises שָׁלֵו instead of שְׁלוֹ and reads בְּמַטְמֹנוֹ instead of בְּבִטְנוֹ, after eliminating יָדַע, whence: 'he has no peace in his riches'. This radical correction is, like the preceding ones, justified by reference to the Septuagint. Ball returns to the hypothesis of Merx, but hesitates between בְּבֵיתוֹ 'in his house' and בְּאוֹנוֹ 'in his wealth' as words to be substituted for בְּבִטְנוֹ. In the face of all these conjectures, one wonders whether it is not possible to defend the text as it stands. Now, בְּבִטְנוֹ 'in his belly' is perfectly in line with בַּחֲמוּדוֹ 'from his appetite' and לְאָכְלוֹ 'from his feast' (v. 21). The expression לֹא יָדַע שְׁלוֹ reminds one of Is 59:8b, לֹא יָדַע שָׁלוֹם 'has not known peace'. It is clear that שְׁלוֹ, which takes the place of שָׁלוֹם in Is 59:8b, must be a noun, or rather the known adjective (16:12; 21:23) used substantively. The exact meaning of the root שְׁלוֹ (verb שָׁלָה) is 'to be quiet, calm' (3:26), i.e. without movement. Not to know tranquillity means to be restless, and when it is a question of the belly, to be always ravenous. We can speak normally of calming or appeasing hunger. It is the same type of image in the interpretation: 'his belly could never be appeased'.

21   No one escaped his gluttony,
      That is why his prosperity does not last!
22   At the height of his riches, he becomes distressed,
      All the blows of *misfortune* rain down upon him!

22 עָמָל (G, Vulg.); MT: עָמֵל.

21 V. 21a, absent from Sah., marked with asterisk in Jerome and Syro-hex., did not exist in G. The present text comes from Theod. (cf. Colb. and Syro-hex.). Syr. 'of his progeny' reads perhaps לאהלו instead of לאכלו. G ἀνθήσει interprets metaphorically the verb יחיל.

The 1st hemistich: 'no one escapes his gluttony', literally 'his eating', is parallel to v. 20a and v. 20b. The expression אֵין שָׂרִיד as in 18:19. To change לְאָכְלוֹ into לאהלו 'from his tent' (Michaelis, Grimme, following Syr.) is to anticipate v. 26c. The punishment of the wicked man appears only in the 2nd hemistich and is introduced by עַל־כֵּן 'that is why', which corresponds to כִּי 'because' of v. 20. The verb חיל has the meaning of 'to be firmly established', 'to endure' (Ps 10:5), whence חַיִל 'strength', 'wealth'. The meaning is simply 'it is for that reason that his happiness does not endure'. The instability of the prosperity of the wrongdoer is a well-worn theme (cf. v. 5). Duhm cuts out v. 21 as though it were a gloss. This verse is, however, the natural sequel of v. 20. We shall find טוב 'happiness', 'good' in Job's speech (21:16) on the prosperity of the wicked.

22 G ὅταν δὲ δοκῇ ἤδη πεπληρῶσθαι interprets שׁפקו in accordance with the Aram. ספק 'doubt', 'suppose'. Vulg. *cum satiatus fuerit, arctabitur, aestuabit* seems to render שׁפקו by *aestuabit*. In Targ. and Syr. שׁפקו is translated 'his measure'. G and Vulg. omit יד. For עמל, G

ἀνάγκη and Vulg. *dolor* vocalise עָמָל (cf. inf.), Syr. reads עול 'the evildoer'.

The writing במלאות suggests בְּמִלְאֹאת, but we ought to have the suffix. The *qerê* בִּמְלֹאת regards the *waw* as a *mater lectionis* and gives the correct reading. The word שֶׂפֶק, whence שִׂפְקוֹ, has the same meaning as שֶׂפֶק. 'abundance', 'wealth' (36:18). The root is ספק 'to be sufficient', 'to abound'. The 1st hemmistich expresses an antithesis similar to that of 18:12 (cf. Comm.) and of 15:21b. The verb צרר 'to be cramped, in straits' (18:7) is used as an impersonal with לְ" before the suffix, to connote the state of mind of a person who is in anxiety and distress (Gn 32:8; Jg 2:15; 10:9, etc.). Those who preserve עָמֵל 'unfortunate' (3:20) interpret יַד עָמֵל as 'the hand of the unfortunate one' who rises up to strike down the guilty man. But the verb בוא does not express the gesture of one who strikes; it suggests rather the advent of an evil, a scourge (3:24; 5:21). Even Ginsburg recognises that the vocalisation of עָמָל 'trouble', 'misfortune' (3:10; 4:8, etc.) of G and Vulg. is preferable to that of the MT. Let us note that Le Hir translates 'all the blows of misfortune', Renan 'all the blows of adversity'. The word יד 'hand' in the sense of 'blow', as in the Assyrian expression *qât ili* 'hand of the god' (cf. Comm. on 19:21), to characterise an evil sent by the deity. Note the use of תְּבוֹאֵנוּ, as we had יבואנו at the end of 15:21.

23   When he is occupied in filling his belly,
     (God) pours down upon him the fire of His wrath,
     And rains His *arrows* upon his flesh.

23   עָלֵימוֹ; MT: עָלְמָיו.

23 The 1st hemistich, absent from Sah., marked with asterisk in Syro-hex., did not exist in G. The present text is taken from Theod. (cf. Colb.). Vulg. translates *utinam impleatur venter ejus*, which necessitates *ut emittat . . . et pluat* for ישלח ...וימטר. Syr. علحم 'for the loss' reads לכלא instead of למלא. G νίψαι (which has become ῥίψαι in A) assigns to המטור 'to cause to rain' the meaning of 'wash'. Targ. בשלדיה 'in his corpse' connects לחומו with לחם 'meat', while Vulg. *bellum suum* and Syr. 'in his fight' connect with נלחם 'to fight'. G ὀδύνας seems to read בלהות (cf. 18:11) instead of בלחומו.

Duhm gets rid of the 1st hemistich, in which he sees a gloss on v. 22a. It is treating the literal sense too cavalierly to translate 'let him find the wherewithal to fill his belly!' (Le Hir), 'here is something to fill his belly' (Renan; cf. Segond and Crampon). The author wishes to show that punishments strike the godless man in the midst of his prosperity. The natural meaning of the 1st hemistich is simply 'when he is occupied in filling his belly', the jussive marking a clause which is subordinate to what follows, just as at the beginning of 22:28 (cf. Gesenius-Kautzsch, § 109h). The idiom היה ל'י 'to be in the process of' as in Gn 15:12. The poet has emphasised the voracity of the evildoer (vv. 20-21). The understood subject of the verbs ישלח and ימטר can only be God, since חרון אפו 'the fire of His wrath' always alludes to the divine anger. In Ps 11:6 it is Yahweh who 'rains down upon the wicked coals of fire (read פחמי instead of פחים,

following Symm. ἄνθρακας) and brimstone'. But it would be a serious mistake to substitute יהוה for יהי at the beginning (contra Wright, Budde), since יהוה is methodically excluded from the poetic book. In that case we should have to suppose that v. 23 is a gloss introduced later. Now, in vv. 24-5 the author describes for us the wicked man transfixed by the arrows of an archer. If we compare with 16:13, where God uses Job as a target, makes His shafts circle around him, pierces him pitilessly, we shall have no difficulty in recognising that God is the archer in question. Hence it is God who 'pours down upon him the fire of His wrath'. Cf. תשלח הרונך 'Thou dost unloose the fire of Thy wrath', in the Song of Moses (Ex 15:7). The 3rd hemistich is variously interpreted: 'it will rain upon him in the form of bread!' (Renan), 'let this rain become his bread!' (Le Hir), 'and He will sate him with a rain of shafts' (Segond). Most moderns consider בִּלְחוּמוֹ as meaning 'in his bread', 'for his bread'. None of the versions has understood the word thus. Now, Targ. translates בלחומו by 'in his corpse', which implies some sort of relation between לחום and the Arabic *laḥm*, *laḥam*, 'flesh', 'meat', with a plural form *luḥûm*. In Zeph 1:17 we find לְחֻמָם parallel to דמם 'their blood' and translated τὰς σάρκας αὐτῶν in G (cf. van Hoonacker, 'their corpses'). Hence we may retain the rare word בלחומו which we shall translate simply by 'on his flesh'. It is unnecessary to replace it by בלהות 'terrors' (Bickell, Loisy) or חבלים 'sorrows' (Merx),

24   If he flees before the armour of iron,
      Then it is the bow of brass which pierces him through,
25   And *a shaft* comes out of *his* back,
      A sword-flash comes out of his liver,
      On him terrors *fall*,

25 שֶׁלַח (G); MT: שלף. — מִגֵּוָה (G, Vulg., Targ.); MT: מִגֵּוָה. — Add יִפְּלוּ
before עליו.

following G, or again by פחם 'coal'
(Beer, following Ps 11:6). The
direct complement of ימטר is concealed in עָלֵימוֹ 'on him' (22:2). We
propose to read עָלְמָיו, plural of a
noun עֶלֶם, which would stand for
the Assyrian *ulmu* (just as we have
עֹל 'yoke', equivalent of *ullu*). This
word *ulmu* denotes a sharpened
weapon, in parallelism with the bow
in a text of Ashurbanipal (cf. Streck,
Assurbanipal, p. 261, n. 10). As a
divine weapon, its parallels are
šâru 'the wind' and *birqu* 'thunderbolt' in Ebeling, *Keilschrifttexte aus
Assur*, no. 30, l. 13). We shall have
precisely בָּרָק 'the thunderbolt' in
v. 25 and the brass bow in v. 24.
Since the meaning 'arrow' perfectly
suits *ulmu*, we have here עלמיו 'his
arrows'. The 3rd hemistich, 'and
rains His arrows upon his flesh',
quite naturally introduces the description which will follow. Note the
use of the jussive וְיַמְטֵר as we had
וְיִשְׁלַךְ in 15:33.

24 G καὶ οὐ μὴ σωθῇ, for יברח,
has not understood the relation
between the 1st and 2nd hemistichs.
Instead of מנשק ברזל, G ἐκ χειρὸς
σιδήρου, following 5:20. Vulg. paraphrases the 2nd hemistich: *et irruet
in arcum aereum*.

The word נֶשֶׁק keeps here its normal meaning of 'arm' or rather
'armour' (cf. 39:21). The two verbs
are both in the imperfect, but the
first indicates the hypothesis: 'if
he flees before the armour of iron'
(cf. Gesenius-Kautzsch, § 159c). The

active verb חלף in the sense of
'pierce', 'transfix' (Jg 5:26); cf.
Comm. on 9:11. The bow of brass
as in Ps 18:35. The poet attributes
to the bow the effect produced by
the arrow which it has released.
Parallelism between iron and brass
(40:18; 41:19). Duhm cuts out
v. 24, which does not seem to him
to suit the description(?).

25 The close עליו אמים, absent
from Sah., marked with asterisk in
Jerome and Syro-hex., did not exist
in G. The present text is derived
from Theod. (cf. Syro-hex.). G
διεξέλθοι δὲ διὰ σώματος αὐτοῦ βέλος
reads שָׁלַח (cf. Jl 2:28) instead of
שלף and vocalises מִגֵּוָה instead of
מִגֵּוָה. The vocalisation מִגֵּוָה is confirmed by Vulg. *de vagina sua* and
Targ. מתיקה 'from his sheath'. Syr.
replaces מגוה מגוה by גוה, translates
ܡ̈ܥܘܗܝ 'his bowels', which becomes
the subject of the verbs. G ἄστρα δέ
for וברק comes from ἀστραπή (Aq.
and Theod.); then ἐν διαίταις αὐτοῦ
reads מדרתו for מררתו. Note that
G περιπατήσαισαν, which translates
יהלך, belongs to the 2nd hemistich,
while Targ., Vulg., and Syr. are in
agreement with the MT in beginning
a 3rd hemistich with יהלך. The
words וברק ממררתו are interpreted
in Vulg. *et fulgurans in amaritudine
sua*. A verb is added in Syr.: 'and
the skin of his liver will be broken'.

Duhm cuts out the whole of the
beginning as far as יַהֲלֹךְ, a corollary
of his elimination of v. 24. He retains עליו אמים (which are precisely

26   Thick darkness [   ] *is reserved for him.*
      A fire which has not been kindled shall devour him,
      And shall consume whosoever survives in his tent.

26   Omit טמון and read לוֹ צָפוּן instead of לצפוניו (cf. G).

the words lacking in G) and he
changes יהלך into יהפכו 'turn'. By
joining יהלך to what precedes, we
obtain two perfectly balanced hemistichs: the verb יהלך corresponds to
יֵצֵא as in 41: 11a, 12a. Following the
versions, we find the vocalisation
מְגֵוָה indisputably preferable to
מִגְוָה, which is nowhere found. Since
the verb שלף has as its primary
sense 'to unsheath', the 1st hemistich is translated somewhat freely:
'the sword is unsheathed, and pierces
his body' (Le Hir), 'he tears the
shaft from his body' (Renan). What
is lacking in the MT is the parallel
word to בָּרָק. G supplies it in שָׁלַח
instead of שׁלף (cf. sup.). The copula
has remained attached to יצא in
order to give prominence to the
characteristic word (cf. 19: 20b,
23b and above v. 18). What is
denoted by שׁלח, from שׁלח 'to send'
(cf. the Latin *missile* from *missus*),
is some arrow-like weapon. The word
recurs in Neh 4: 11 and 2 Ch 23: 10.
On the homonym שֶׁלַח 'canal', cf.
33: 18. Hence the 1st hemistich
means 'and a shaft comes out of his
back'. The bow of brass of v. 24 has
shot the bolt which, piercing the
wicked one through and through,
comes out of his back. In parallelism
with שׁלח we have בָּרָק 'lightning
flash', 'thunderbolt', a term which
is used of the flash of the sword (Dt
32: 41) or the lance (Hab 3: 11) and
which corresponds to the Assyrian
birqu, a technical term denoting the
bolts and shafts with which the
hand of the storm god is armed.
The preposition מִן gives to the verb
הלך the sense of the Latin *ex-ire*.

On מְרֹרָה cf. v. 14. Cf. the description
of 16: 13, where מְרֵרָה denoted gall.
The form יַהֲלֹךְ as in 14: 20; 16: 6.
The words עָלָיו אֵמִים 'against him
terrors' begin a further description
which is part of the theme of 15: 20-
24: the misfortunes dreaded by the
wicked man. The plural אֵמִים (from
אֵמָה or אֵימָה, 9: 24; 13: 21) connotes
the terrors which overwhelm the
wretch, his fainting fits and gloomy
forebodings (Ps 55: 5; 88: 16). A
verb has disappeared by haplography between יהלך and עליו. This
verb, the subject of which is אֵמִים,
seems to us to be יִפְּלוּ (as in Gn 15:
12; Ex 15:16).

26   G πᾶν δὲ σκότος αὐτῷ ὑπομείναι
omits טמון and reads לוֹ צָפוּן instead
of לצפוניו (cf. inf). Aq. τοῖς ἐγκε-
κρυμμένοις αὐτοῦ and Targ. לטשׁיותיה
'for his secret' literally translate
לצפוניו, while Vulg. renders by *in
occultis ejus.* Syr. ܠܬܘܠܕܘܗܝ 'for
his progeny' is an interpretation
rather than a translation. For לא נפח,
G ἄκαυστον, but G (A) ἄσβεστον,
noted as a variant in the margin
of Syro-hex. 'which does not go
out'; cf. Jerome *inextinguibilis.* In
Targ. the fire is that of Gehenna.
The verb ירע is connected with רעע
by G κακῶσαι and Vulg. *affligetur*;
but Targ. ישׁרי 'he will camp' connects with רעה, 'graze', 'feed'. Syr.
ܢܐܒܫ 'will dry up' (?).

Literally the 1st hemistich would
run: 'all darkness is hidden for his
secret things.' Those who preserve
the MT agree in assigning to טָמוּן
'hidden' the meaning of 'reserved',

28   A flood will *sweep away* his house:
      Waters which flow in the day of divine anger!

27-28 Transpose v. 28 before v. 27.
28 יָגֹל (Targ.); MT: יִגֶל.

'destined for', but some see in 'his secret things' his hidden sins (cf. Knabenbauer), others, the treasures of the wicked (Le Hir, Dillmann, Renan, most moderns). Ehrlich considers that it is a reference to the members of the godless man's family whom he thinks to be in safety in their hiding places. The juxtaposition of טמון and לצפוניו arouses suspicion, since the verbs טמן and צפן express the same idea. Following G, טמון לו 'reserved for him' is suggested (Siegfried, Beer, Duhm, Budde). But it is the verb צפן which modifies the meaning of 'hide' to that of 'reserve' for some one (cf. Comm. on 15: 20 and 21: 19). The explanatory word, which does not exist in G, is טמון. We read לו צָפוּן instead of לצפוניו and thus recover the true text of G. The phrase כָּל־חֹשֶׁךְ 'all darkness', to convey the idea of all misfortunes (cf. Ec 5: 16), corresponds to כל־ יד עמל 'all the blows of adversity' of v. 22. The clause 'all darkness is reserved for him' prepares for the enumeration of the extraordinary ills which threaten the wicked. Add the relative אשר before the *pu'al* perfect of נפח 'fan flames', 'kindle' (41: 12). The punishment is the same as that of the company of Korah (Nu 16: 35; 26: 10), 'a fire which has not been kindled will devour him'. The verb אכל with אש as in 1: 16. The vocalisation תְּאָכְלֵהוּ is interesting if compared with תֶּרְצָחוּ of Ps 62: 4. We have here the remains of an old verbal form *qâtala* (cf. Perles, *Analekten*, Neue Folge, p. 69), which existed among the Canaanites and the Hebrews (*RB*, 1914, pp. 37ff.). Note that the feminine אש

does not influence the gender of נֶפַח, and that in consequence it may be regarded as the subject of יְרַע. Moreover, we have אש in the masculine in Ps 104: 4 and Jer 48: 45; cf. the double gender of מקום (v. 9). The jussive ירע, because it is a question of something inevitable (cf. 15: 33 and v. 23 above וימטר). The verb is רָעָה 'graze', 'browse', chosen as synonymous with אכל. It is to misunderstand the point of the description to change ירע שריד into יער שדד 'a bandit will arise', as Duhm proposes (following 15: 21). On the word שָׂרִיד cf. v. 21 and 18: 19, where we had 'and no survivor in the places where he stayed', the expression במגוריו corresponding to בְּאָהֳלוֹ 'in his tent' of our verse. The fire of heaven devours the wicked man and all those who dwell in his home. In 15: 34 'a fire devours the tents of corruption'. Complementary to the punishment by fire, we are to have punishment by water described in v. 28. Both vv. 27 and 28 begin with יגל, which suggests there has been an accidental transposition. It is quite obvious that vv. 27 and 29 form the conclusion of the speech. Hence we place v. 28 before v. 27.

27   After v. 28.

28   G ἑλκύσαι τὸν οἶκον αὐτοῦ ἀπωλεία εἰς τέλος connects נגרות with the 1st hemistich; cf. ἐν ἀπωλείᾳ for מגורת (Pr 10: 24), ἀπώλεια for מגור (Jer 49 = 30: 29). The end ἐπέλθοι αὐτῷ is inspired by מתקוממה לו of v. 27. For יגל, Vulg. *apertum erit* and Syr. ܐ ܓܠ 'are unveiled' connect with גלה, but

27   The heavens reveal his sin,
      And the earth rises up against him:

Targ. יטלטל 'will be tossed, moved
about' connects with גלל (as also
probably G ἐλκύσαι). The word יבול
is translated *germen* by Vulg. and
'wheat' by Targ. עבור. Following
the context, Syr. translates 'foundations'. The 2nd hemistich is paraphrased by Targ. 'his oil and his
wine will flow in the day of his anger'.
Vulg. *detrahetur* and Syr. אתישלא
'will be pulled, torn' regard נגרות as
a verb in a personal mode.

Attempts have been made to find in
יבול ביתו 'the produce of his house',
although יבול everywhere denotes
the fruits of the earth. Typical translations are: 'the abundance of his
storehouses is carried away' (Le Hir)
or 'the revenues of his house will be
scattered' (Renan), thus assigning
to גלה 'to deport' the sense of
remove or scatter; or else, in accordance with גלה, 'reveal', 'discover', 'unveil', 'the revenues of his
house will be disclosed' (Loisy). In
any event, the punishment is minimal after the ruin of the wicked man
himself and his family (v. 26). Now,
it is a question of what happens 'on
the day of His anger', i.e. when the
divine anger is revealed (cf. אפו 'His
wrath' in v. 23). In the light of Is
30: 27-8, this anger is manifested
above all by fire and flood. We have
seen punishment by fire in v. 26. We
now expect the mention of floods.
Now, the word יבול belongs to the
root יבל, from which stems the Akkadian *bubbulu* or *bibbulu* 'flood'.
On these words, cf. Meissner, *MDVG*,
10, p. 238. In the Code of Hammurabi,
we find the characteristic phrase
û lû bibbulum itbal 'whether it be
that a flood sweeps him away' (recto
XIII, 43f. and XIV, 5f.). It is a similar idea that we have here, and it is
enough to vocalise יָגֵל (from גלל)

with Targ., instead of יָגֵל, in order
to translate: 'a flood will sweep away
(literally, 'will roll') his house'. Cf.
the use of the *niph'al* of גלל in Am
5: 24, and note that גלל has as derivatives גַּלִּים 'waves', Akkadian *gillu*
'wave'. Note the resemblance of the
catastrophe to that which is described in Mt 7: 27. There remains to
be explained נִגְרוֹת, which seems to
be the *niph'al* participle feminine
plural of נגר. In 2 S 14: 14 we find
the phrase כַּמַּיִם הַנִּגָּרִים 'like the
running waters', and in La 3: 49
עֵינִי נִגְּרָה 'my eye has flowed'. This
meaning of the verb falls within the
framework of our interpretation of
v. 28. We regard the participle as a
real noun, similar to נֹזְלִים 'those
which flow' meaning 'springs' (Ex
15: 8; Is 44: 3, etc.). The word understood is probably תְּהוֹמוֹת, which is
very often used in the sense of
'waves'. The 2nd hemistich will mean
simply: 'waters which flow in the
day of his anger'. This furnishes an
explanation of the flood which has
been announced. There is thus no
need to modify נגרות, which has been
successively changed to נִכְרָת 'will
be exterminated' (Houbigant), וְנִגָּר
אתו 'and he has carried it away'
(Beer), מִגְעֶרֶת 'threat', 'curse'
(Duhm), וּגְרָפוֹ 'and he has swept it
away' (Ball).

27 Targ. interprets שמים as 'the
angels of the heights' and ארץ as
'the inhabitants of the earth'. Syr.
connects מתקוממה with נקם 'to be
avenged'.

This verse sums up the catastrophes which are stored up for the
impious man (22-6, 28). The whole
universe rises in condemnation of
him. Job has called as witnesses the

29   Such is the lot of the wicked which Elohim has appointed,
     And such the portion which he receives from God!

heavens and the earth (16: 18-19).
It is the heavens and the earth which
denounce the guilty man and assume the responsibility of punishing
him. 'The heavens reveal his sin and
the earth rises up against him.' The
verb התקומם 'rise up', 'stand erect',
'revolt' against some one; cf. the
participle in 27: 7. The earth is the
auxiliary of God, when it is a question of calling for vengeance (Gn
4: 10) or of punishing (Nu 16: 30-4).

28   After v. 26.

29   Symm. ἀντιλογίας regards רשע
as an abstract. G renders מאלהים by
παρὰ Κυρίου and מאל by παρὰ τοῦ
ἐπισκόπου. The translation of אמרו
by ὑπαρχόντων αὐτῷ (G) gives to
אמר the meaning of דבר 'thing'. One
cannot take this interpretation as
an authority for changing אמרו into
אונו, as Duhm would wish. On Targ.
מימריה cf. inf.
   The general conclusion is in the
style of Eliphaz (5: 27) and Bildad
(18: 21); cf. 8: 13a. The word אָדָם
renders the 1st hemistich rather
clumsy, but it recurs in 27: 13 which
is inspired by this verse. We find
again אָדָם רָשָׁע in Pr 11: 7. It is a
kind of compound word, the opposite
of 'good fellow'. The word חֵלֶק
'share' means fate (27: 13; 31: 2).
It has נַחֲלָה 'heritage' (ibid.) as a

parallel, meaning 'lot'. It is proposed
to interpret אָמְרוֹ 'his word' as meaning 'what is said about him', הָאָמוּר
עָלָיו (Rashi; cf. Dillmann, etc.).
It is a forced construction after the
construct state נַחֲלָת. The moderns
change אמרו into מורא 'rebellious'
(Beer), אונו 'his iniquity' (Duhm),
עָרִיץ 'tyrant' (Graetz, following
27: 13). We note that Targ. translates אמרו by מימריה and that
מימרי 'my word' means certainly 'my
person', in 7: 8; 19: 18; 27: 3 (cf.
Comm. on 1: 10), where the Hebrew
has simply בי 'in me'. Other examples are cited in the dictionaries of
Levy. The conclusion to be reached
from these facts is that Aramaic had
a usage similar to that of modern
Greek which says τοῦ λόγου μου for
'I' 'of me', τοῦ λόγου του 'he' 'of him'
etc., the word λόγος meaning the
person who is speaking, of whom
one is speaking, or to whom one is
speaking. It cannot be doubted that
we have here אָמְרוֹ 'his person',
meaning the wicked man of the 1st
hemistich. Thus all becomes clear:
'and such is the fate which his person receives from God'. The preposition מִן indicates the cause, here in
particular the author of what is
happening: the share of the wicked
man (which he receives) from God,
the fate of his person (which he
receives) from God.

1   Then Job spoke and said:
2   Listen carefully to my word,
     And may your consolations be limited to that!
3   Bear with me, and I in my turn will speak,
     And after I have spoken, you may mock.
4   Is it against a man that I raise my complaint?
     And in that case why should I not be impatient?

Chapter 21   Seventh speech of Job: see Introduction, p. xliv.

21: **2** For שִׁמְעוּ שָׁמוֹעַ, G ἀκού-σατε, ἀκούσατε, as in 13: 17, Vulg. *audite, quaeso*, Targ. 'hear and receive'. The 2nd hemistich, faithfully copied in Targ., is rendered ἵνα μὴ ᾖ μοι παρ' ὑμῶν αὕτη ἡ παρά-κλησις in G, *et agite poenitentiam* in Vulg., 'and there will be understanding in you' in Syr.

Job repeats verbally the 1st hemistich of 13: 17. The demonstrative זֹאת refers to the previous phrase; cf. 5: 27. The expression וּתְהִי זֹאת 'and may that be' corresponds to וּתְהִי of 13: 5. Cf. תְּהִי עוֹד in 6: 10. The meaning of the 2nd hemistich, 'and may that be your consolations', is not in doubt; and may your consolations be limited to that! Plural תַּנְחוּמוֹת as in 15: 11, where it was a question of the consolations of God. In 16: 2 Job began his speech by observing that his friends were 'harsh comforters'. It is robbing the text of its flavour to change וּתְהִי to וּבַל תְּהִי (Merx, Siegfried) in accordance with G.

3 G εἶτ' οὐ καταγελάσετέ μου confines וְאַחַר דְּבָרִי to εἶτα and introduces a negative (as in 2b). Vulg. *et post mea, si videbitur, verba, ridete*

gives a more elegant turn to the clause. With the exception of Targ., the versions render תַּלְעִיג by a plural, for the sake of harmony with the other verbs.

The verb נָשָׂא means 'endure', 'tolerate' (7: 21): 'Bear with me and I in my turn will speak.' Each in turn; cf. 33: 31 and 13: 13. 'And after I have spoken, you may mock', construction of the preposition אַחַר with the infinitive 'and after my speaking'; in 29: 22 we shall have אַחֲרֵי דְבָרִי 'after my words'. The *hiph'il* of לָעַג has the same sense as the *qal* in 9: 23; 11: 3; 22: 19. The transition from the 2nd person plural to the 2nd person singular is justified by the fact that Job first addresses all his friends, then turns to Zophar who was the last to speak. There is the same alternation in the opening of Job's speech in 16: 2-3.

4 G τί γάρ; in order to give more vivacity to the question. Vulg. stresses the meaning of the Hebrew: *numquid contra hominem disputatio mea est?* In Syr. the word אָנֹכִי is replaced by a colourless 'I will say', whence Siegfried gets הַאֹמַר (!). G sums up תִּקְצַר רוּחִי by θυμωθήσομαι. Vulg. subordinates the 2nd hemi-

5   Turn towards me and be appalled,
     And put your hands on your mouths,
6   For, when I think of it, I am terrified,
     And my flesh feels a shudder.
7   Why do the wicked continue to live,
     Grow old, and even increase in power?

stich to the preceding question: *ut merito non debeam contristari.*

The personal pronoun אָנֹכִי, placed first for emphasis, has the effect of strengthening the pronominal suffix of שִׂיחִי. Cf. אני ידי 'I, my hand', that is, 'my own hand' in Is 45: 12. Similar examples are given in Gesenius-Kautzsch, § 135f. הָאָנֹכִי recurs only in Nu 11: 12. According to 13: 3, it is clear that the 1st hemistich means: 'Is it against a man that I raise my complaint?' The preposition "לִ is used instead of אל found in 13: 3. The expression שִׂיחִי 'my complaint', on the lips of Job as in 7: 13; 9: 27; 10: 1; 23: 2. The elliptical וְאִם 'if it be so' forms the transition between the first and the second questions. The formula תִּקְצַר רוּחִי 'my breath is short', parallel to 'my nose is short' or 'my soul is short' (cf. Nu 21: 4; Jg 16:16, etc.), expresses the idea of impatience; cf. Comm. on 6: 11 and *L'Emploi métaphorique*, p. 81.

5   For הָשַׁמּוּ, Symm. ἄφθογγοι γίνεσθε, Targ. שְׁתוּקוּ 'be silent'. G renders עַל־פֶּה by ἐπὶ σιαγόνι (Syro-hex., Arab. Baud., Jerome *sub mento*), but G(A) ἐπὶ στόμα (Sah).

Job attracts attention by the phrase פְּנוּ־אֵלַי 'turn towards me', instead of פנו בי used in 6: 28. The *hiph'il* of שׁמם with the meaning of the *qal* (cf. הלעיג v. 3, הגיע 20: 6) in 17: 8 and of the *niph'al* (18: 20). 'And put your hands on your mouths', a gesture natural to one who wishes to keep silent; cf. 29: 9; 40: 4; Mic 7: 16 ישימו יד על־פה. Calmet notes that it was customary

to represent the god of silence, Harpocrates, with a finger on the mouth. Rosenmüller quotes Juvenal: *digito compesce labellum* (*Satires*, I, 160).

6   With the exception of Targ., the versions make פלצות the subject of אחז. G ὀδύναι translates פלצות as a feminine plural (cf. 20: 23c).

The conditional clause stops at זָכַרְתִּי. The 2nd hemistich is parallel to וְנִבְהַלְתִּי. The main clause is introduced by the *waw* as in 7: 4 (cf. Comm.). The verb זכר means 'remember' and 'recall one's memories', 'dream'. Eliphaz used the *niph'al* נבהל 'to be terrified' to depict the attitude of Job in the face of misfortune (4: 5). Job will have recourse to the same verb in 23:15. The subject of אָחַז is not פלצות 'trembling', 'shaking' (cf. Comm. on 9: 6) but בְּשָׂרִי 'my flesh'. Moreover, פלצות is feminine. Cf. אחזו שׂער 'they feel a shudder' (18: 20 and Comm.).

7   For עתקו, Vulg. *sublevati sunt.* G sums up the 2nd hemistich: πεπαλαίωνται δὲ καὶ ἐν πλούτῳ; Targ. נכסין and Vulg. *divitiis* agree with G to render חיל by 'riches'. Syr. 'heroes in strength' reads גבורי חיל instead of גברו חיל.

Job formulates in the clearest terms the problem which is the object of the discussion: 'Why do the wicked continue to live, grow old, and even increase in power?' There follows a description of the good fortune of the wicked, which is the very antithesis of the supposed misfortunes which Job's interlocutors, and especially Zophar (ch. 20), have

8   Their posterity are firmly established in their presence,
    And their offspring *abide* before their eyes.

9   Their houses are secure, without fear,

8   עֹמְדִים; MT: עמם.

depicted with such complacency and satisfaction. Far from being ephemeral (20: 5ff.), this prosperity grows old and increases with them. If the thesis of Job's friends were correct, the wicked man ought not even to be allowed to go on living: 'Why do the wicked continue to live?' They are not snatched away by a premature death, in the prime of their youth, as Zophar had claimed (20: 11); but 'they grow old'. The verb עתק 'to go forward', 'to move' (14: 18; 18: 4) in the sense of advance in age, grow old; cf. the Aramaic עתיק 'old' (cf. עַתִּיק in 1 Ch 4 :22), the Arabic 'ataqa 'to grow old', 'atîq 'old', 'ancient', etc. In 14: 18 Theod. renders יעתק by παλαιωθήσεται (cf. G here). The adverb גַּם 'also', 'even' expresses gradation. The verb גבר 'to grow' takes in the accusative the complement specifying the quality of which the growth is noted. We leave to חַיִל its general meaning of 'strength', 'power', rather than that of 'riches', 'wealth' (5: 5; 15: 29; 20: 15, 18), which would be less congruous with גבר. The questions asked by Job present a striking resemblance, in the ideas expressed, with those of Jer 12: 1-2 (Cf. Intro., pp. clviiff.).

8   G ὁ σπόρος αὐτῶν κατὰ ψυχήν (A adds αὐτῶν, Sah., Syro-hex.) omits נכון and reads לנפשם instead of לפניהם. The reading κατὰ τὴν ἐπιθυμίαν τῆς ἑαυτῶν καρδίας of Cod. 248 appears in Jerome *secundum desiderium animae* (obelus before *desiderium*) and Memph. The word עמם, not rendered in Syr., is translated *propinquorum turba* (vocalisation עָמָם) in Vulg.

The two hemistichs are not balanced. Further, עִמָּם 'with them' or 'near them' is tautological after לִפְנֵיהֶם 'before them'. Of modern exegetes, some cut out עמם (Bickell, Duhm), others לפניהם (Siegfried, Budde, Torczyner), supposed to be a dittograph of לעיניהם. But Ps 102: 29b, where we have וזרעם לפניך יכון 'and their posterity holds firm before Thee', proves that the 1st hemistich stops at לפניהם and that the 2nd begins at עמם. Ball showed a correct insight in finding in עמם a remnant of עֹמְדִים which is suggested by Is 66: 22, 'for as the new heavens and the new earth which I create, subsist (עמדים) before me (the word of Yahweh), so will your posterity and your name subsist'. It is unnecessary to transfer the copula. The word עמדים, parallel to נכון, has been given prominence (cf. 19: 20, 23; 20: 18). Job continues to affirm the opposite of the thesis of his friends who insisted on the sterility of the wicked man or the destruction of his posterity: Eliphaz (15: 33ff.), Bildad (18: 19), Zophar (20: 26). The words are deliberately chosen: parallelism between זֶרַע 'seed', 'posterity' and צֶאֱצָאִים 'shoots', as in 5: 25, where Eliphaz ascribes to the righteous man a numerous offspring. In v. 9 we shall have שָׁלוֹם with the same sense as in 5: 24. The audacity of Job's thesis will consist in the fact that he will apply to the impious man the very descriptions which have been given of the prosperity of the righteous.

9   For שׁלמוּ, G εὐθηνοῦσιν, Vulg. *securae sunt*, Syr. ܡܠܐܒ 'are in peace'.

And no rod of Eloah is upon them!
10   Their bull breeds without fail,
      Their heifer brings to birth without abortion.

G renders מפחד by φόβος δὲ οὐδαμοῦ.
Attempts have been made to
replace שָׁלוֹם by a verb: שָׁלוּ (Houbigant, Reiske, cf. Syr.), שָׁלְמוּ (Siegfried, Duhm), or by an adjective:
שְׁלֵוִים (Perles). But in 5: 24, a passage which inspires Job's speech (cf.
v. 8), we have the word שָׁלוֹם as
an attribute of אהלך 'your tent' (cf.
Comm.). We can therefore translate
'their houses are secure'. The idiom
מִפַּחַד 'without fear', in which the
מִן plays the part of the alpha privative in Greek (cf. 11: 15), merely
reinforces שָׁלוֹם. Cf. Pr 1: 33b, 'and
he will be at peace, without fear
(מפחד) of evil'. In 9: 34 Job pointed
out that there was no arbiter to
remove far from him the 'rod' of
God. This rod, instrument of divine
vengeance, does not strike the
wicked. With שֵׁבֶט אֱלוֹהַּ cf. יד אלוה in
19: 21b (Comm.). The verb is understood.

10   Targ. and Syr. retain the singular suffix of שׁוֹרוֹ and פרתו, while
G and Vulg. have recourse to plural
suffixes in order to secure harmony
with the context. G renders עבר
ולא יגעל by οὐκ ὠμοτόκησεν (omitting עבר ו' after שׁוֹרוֹ), Vulg. by
concepit et non abortivit. The interpretation of יגעל by 'to be abortive'
obliges G to translate שׁוֹרוֹ by ἡ
βοῦς αὐτῶν, while Vulg. bos eorum is
equivocal. Syr. reads יגעה 'lows'
instead of יגעל. G renders פרתו by
αὐτῶν ἐν γαστρὶ ἔχουσα. For תשכל,
G ἔσφαλεν reads תכשל.
Bochart writes a whole dissertation (Hieroz. I, cols. 291ff.) to
prove that שׁוֹרוֹ means 'his cow' and
that the terms עבר and געל mean
respectively 'to conceive' and 'to
lose semen'. But the contrast be-

tween שׁוֹרוֹ 'his bull' and פָּרָתוֹ 'his
heifer' is accentuated by the fact
that the verbs in the 1st hemistich
are masculine and those in the 2nd
feminine. The reference is to the
actions of the male and those of the
female. In Aramaic the verb עבר
in the pi'el has the meaning of 'to
conceive' and in the hithpa'el that
of 'to be pregnant'. But the Hebrew
pi'el has a causative meaning, 'introduce semen', i.e. 'fertilise', 'make
fecund'. Targ. well translates מבטין
impraegnans. Rashi adds the direct
complement את הנקבה 'the female'.
The hiph'il of געל is generally interpreted as meaning 'to arouse disgust', following the qal 'to be disgusted'. But the meaning of געל in
Aramaic is 'to sully' (cf. גאל in
3: 5). In the causative, it will mean
'to occasion an impurity', (and it is
very understandable how this idea
evolves into that of ejicere semen extra
vas naturale. The Hebraic tradition,
represented by Targ., Rashi, Qimchi, has decided in favour of a similar
sense: it does not emit the semen in
vain without its leading to pregnancy. The verb עִבַּר 'it fertilises'
is answered by תְּפַלֵּט 'it is delivered,
brings forth' in the 2nd hemistich.
The pi'el of פלט with the meaning
of 'to be delivered of' or 'to bear'
(cf. 23: 7b); cf. the pi'el of מלט in
20: 20. The meaning of deliverance
by bringing forth young is found
again in the pi'el of מלט (Is 34: 15;
cf. the hiph'il in Is 66: 7). We shall
see again the pi'el of פלט with the
sense of 'to bring forth' in 39: 3, as
corrected. The pi'el of שׁכל 'to be
barren' has not only the meaning of
'to make barren' but also that of 'to
miscarry', whether in speaking of
woman (Ex 23: 26) or of the female
beast (Gn 31: 38). The words שׁוֹר

11   They let their boys frolic like sheep,
      And their children delight in the dance.
12   They sing *to* the tambourine and the lyre,
      And they disport themselves to the sound of the pipe.

12 בְּתֹף (G, Vulg., Targ., Syr.); MT: כתף.

and פרה in the singular have attracted the singular suffix instead of the expected plural. Fecundity of animals is regarded as a divine blessing (Ps 144: 13). The accession of Ashurbanipal has as its consequence such fecundity: *bûlu šutêšur ina talitti* 'the cattle walk straight in giving birth' (Rassam Cylinder, I, 50).

11 G αἰώνια reads עולם for עוליהם. Double translation in Jerome. First, *et permanent sicut vetusta oves eorum* (following G), then *et mittunt sicut oves infantes eorum* (with asterisk), probably following a hexaplar reading. Symm. προβάλλονται and Vulg. *egrediuntur* vocalise יְשַׁלְּחוּ.

The *pi'el* of שלח has the meaning of 'release', 'allow to run' in reference to the feet of the ox and the ass in Is 32: 20. The 1st hemistich gives a very clear meaning: 'they let their young ones frolic like sheep'. The smaller animals, צאן (cf. 1: 3), is the term of comparison suggested by the ox and the cow of v. 10. Hence there is no reason to transfer v. 11 to follow v. 8 as is suggested by Merx, Siegfried, and Duhm. The עֲוִילִים are indeed the children who run about in the streets (cf. 19:18). In Zec 8: 5 the happiness of the city is symbolised by 'the lads and lasses playing in its squares'. With this v. 11 and the following compare the expressions of a correspondent of Ashurbanipal, to mark the blessings of the new reign: 'The old men dance, the children sing, the maidens exult with

joy', etc. (*La religion assyro-babylonienne*, pp. 172f.).

12 An accident to the text (permutation of consonants) has here resulted in כתף instead of בתף and (in v. 13) יבלו instead of יכלו. The best editions have restored בְּתֹף, which is confirmed by the versions. For בתף, Targ. בתפין, G ψαλτήριον (Jerome *psalterium*), Vulg. *tympanum*, Syr. ܦܠܓܐ (cf. inf.). G renders עוגב by ψαλμοῦ, but Jerome *organi* (with asterisk) follows a hexaplar reading: Aq. ὀργάνου (Vulg. *organi*).

Image of perfect happiness (cf. v. 11). The young people sing and play music in the public square (cf. Mt 11: 16-17). The verb נשא has the sense of נשא קול 'raise the voice', 'sing' (Is 42: 11). The word תף denotes the tambourine, Aramaic תֻּפָּא (cf. Targ.), Arabic *duff* (Sa'adia). The prototype is the Sumerian *dub* or *tup*, corresponding to the Assyrian *balaggu*, whence comes the Syriac ܦܠܓܐ (cf. above Syr.). The instrument which is coupled with the tambourine is generally the כִּנּוֹר, whence the Greek κινύρα, a sort of zither; cf. 1 S 10 :5; 2 S 6: 5, etc. Jewish tradition, represented by Targ., recognises in עוגב a kind of flute or pipe, אַבּוּבָא (Assyrian *imbûbu*, Arabic *ambûb*), which denotes both the reed and the flute. The tambourine is the percussion instrument, the guitar the stringed instrument, while the pipe completes the enumeration with the wind instrument.

13   They *end* their days in prosperity,
      And in peace they *go down* to Sheol.
14   Now they said to God: 'Go away from us!
      We do not wish to know Thy ways!
15   What is Shaddai that we should serve Him?
      And what profit should we gain by imploring Him?'

13   יְכַלּוּ (*qerê* and versions); *kethîb*: יבלו. — יֵחָתּוּ (Symm., Vulg., Targ.,
Syr.); MT: יֵחַתּוּ.

13 The *qerê* and the versions restore the correct reading יְכַלּוּ, which has been transformed into יבלו (*kethib*) as the result of a textual accident (cf. v. 12). G ἐν δὲ ἀναπαύσει preserves the etymological sense of רגע, which agrees with the context (cf. inf.). Instead of יֵחַתּוּ (from חתת), Symm. κατέρχονται, Vulg. *descendunt*, Targ. and Syr. נחתין correctly vocalise יֵחָתּוּ (from נחת).

In contrast with the premature death which Job's friends foresee for the wicked (15: 31; 20: 11), Job observes that they grow old like every one else (v. 7), and what is more, that they 'end their days in prosperity'. The *pi'el* of כלה is confirmed by 36: 11, which repeats our 1st hemistich. The adjective טוֹב connotes 'well being', 'prosperity' (2: 10; 7: 11). The expression בְּרֶגַע does not mean 'in an instant', as though it were a question of sudden death, but 'in peace'; 'in tranquillity' in accordance with the etymological sense of the root רגע 'to be at rest, in peace' (cf. G). In view of 17: 16 (cf. Comm.), it is clear that the verb used was נחת 'to go down', as has been well understood by Symm., Vulg., Targ., Syr., in agreement with which we vocalise יֵחָתּוּ, instead of יֵחַתּוּ 'they are terrified'. The 2nd hemistich: 'and in peace they go down to Sheol' furnishes an excellent parallel to the 1st: 'they end their days in prosperity'.

14 G replaces the plurals by singulars: λέγει, ἀπ' ἐμοῦ, βούλομαι. G(A) adds ὁ ἀσεβής as the subject of λέγει. ὁ ἀσεβής is found in Cod. 254 and in the margin of Syro-hex. Instead of *a me*, which translates ἀπ' ἐμοῦ in Jerome (Bod. and Gall.), we have *a nobis* (conformably with the MT) in Tur.

Eliphaz will reproduce the 1st hemistich (with הָאֹמְרִים instead of וַיֹּאמְרוּ) in 22: 17. There is the sharpest antithesis between the language of the wicked, who regard God as a troublesome preceptor, and that of the Psalmist: 'Yahweh, make me to know Thy ways, teach me Thy paths!' (Ps 25: 4). Instead of מִמֶּנּוּ, which is likely to be confused with the 3rd person singular masculine suffix, the Orientals read מִמֶּנּוּ. The ways of God are the works of God, whether inasmuch as He accomplishes them (40: 19) or inasmuch as He imposes them on His creatures, as here. The omission of לְ before the complement of חָפַצְנוּ (cf. 9: 3) lends greater vividness to the phrase. It is in full knowledge of the issues at stake that the wicked refuse to accept the divine precepts. We are here presented with a picture of vincible ignorance. In 18: 21 the unrighteous man is he who does not know God; in 8: 13 the godless is coupled with those who forget God.

15 V. 15, absent from Sah., marked with asterisk in Jerome,

16   Does not their happiness lie in their own hands?
      Is not the counsel of the wicked far from *Him*?

16 מִמֶּנּוּ (cf. G); MT: מֶנִּי.

Syro-hex., and Colb., did not exist in
G. The present text is derived from
Theod. (cf. Colb.) or from. Aq.
(cf. Syro-hex.). It may be that G
sought to avoid the blasphemies of
this verse, just as in v. 14 the use
of the singular had the effect of
diminishing the number of the
guilty. Syr. avoids all ambiguity by
repeating at the beginning 'and they
say' of v. 14.

An interrogative, followed by
כִּי, as in 3: 12b; 7: 17. Cf. Ex 5: 2,
where Pharaoh exclaims: "What
is Yahweh that I should hear
His voice?' In the latter text, the
relative אֲשֶׁר takes the place of כִּי,
just as in Latin *quod* may be a substitute for *ut*. In Pr 30: 9 Agur asks
God not to grant him too much
wealth, lest he be tempted to cry
out: 'Who is Yahweh?' The 2nd
hemistich shows the worthlessness
of the utilitarian morality recommended by Zophar and his associates. The wicked succeed as well
as the good and pious (Ec 9: 2).
Hence, what is the use of virtue, of
resort to God: 'and what profit
should we gain by imploring Him?'
Sometimes God reproaches the Israelites with saying: 'It is vain to
serve God and what profit is there in
observing His ordinances?' (Mal
3: 14). The verb פגע with בְּ" before
the complement means 'urge', 'implore' some one (cf. Jer 7: 16). In
22: 3 Eliphaz will express the antithesis of these remarks of the
wicked.

16 G ἐν χερσὶν γὰρ ἦν αὐτῶν τὰ
ἀγαθά may arise from an omission
of לֹא (Merx) or from an interpretation of הֵן לֹא in the sense of a
negative question (cf. inf.). The 2nd
hemistich ἔργα δὲ ἀσεβῶν οὐκ ἐφορᾷ

(A καθαρά) is a paraphrase of the
MT, but with מִמֶּנּוּ 'from him' instead of מֶנִּי 'from me'.

Siegfried gets rid of vv. 16-18 by
regarding them as an addition intended to correct Job's thesis. Budde
is content to eliminate v. 16, supposed to be a marginal correction.
Duhm proposes הֵן לֹא הֲלֹא for הֵן לֹא.
Even as it stands, the 1st hemistich
can fit with the context. The particle הֵן 'if' (4: 20; 12: 14-15; 13: 15;
19: 7) may have an interrogative
sense exactly like its synonym אִם
(6: 12; 19: 5). In 24: 25 and Jer
48: 27 we have אִם לֹא as an equivalent to הֲלֹא 'is not?' The meaning
of the 1st hemistich will be simply:
'Does not their happiness lie in their
own hands?' The wicked enjoy
happiness and prosperity as though
these things are their right and privilege; cf. the expression אֲשֶׁר בְּיָדוֹ in
12: 10. The word טוֹב was the very
term used by Zophar when he said
that the prosperity of the wicked
does not last (20: 21). The 2nd
hemistich is repeated in 22:18b,
where G ἀπ' αὐτοῦ read מִמֶּנּוּ as here;
this reading enables us to translate
correctly: 'the counsel of the wicked
is far from Him'. It is a question of
the assembly of the wicked on which
in 10: 3 God was said to smile. It is
held far from God, that is, far from
His watchfulness and His chastisement. Those who retain the MT are
compelled to see in this hemistich a
restrictive formula: 'Far from me be
the counsel of the impious!' (Le
Hir). But Job takes his part very
seriously, as is proved by the arguments which follow. He is noting
and recording facts which are in
flat contradiction of the accepted
theories. The wicked ask God to

17   How often is the lamp of the wicked extinguished,
     How often are they struck down by misfortune ?
     How often does He destroy evildoers in His wrath ?

remove Himself from them (v. 14),
they declare they do not need Him
(v. 15); the fact is that they have
their happiness under their own
control and have nothing in common
with a God who leaves them un-
disturbed to follow their own devices.
The 'counsel of the wicked' is mentioned in Ps 1:1. A further allusion
to this Psalm is found in v. 18.

17 For כמה, G οὐ μὴν δὲ ἀλλὰ
καί announces a refutation of what
precedes. Targ. כמה, Syr. ܟܡܐ,
Vulg. *quoties* are more faithful. Vulg.
translates אידם by *inundatio* (from
אד Gn 2:6). Syr. links חבלים with
the 2nd hemistich. For חבלים, G
ὠδῖνες, Vulg. *dolores*, but Targ.
עדבין 'lots'. Syr. transcribes the
singular ܚܒܠܐ. G ἔξουσιν αὐτοὺς
ἀπὸ ὀργῆς paraphrases יחלק באפו.
The interrogative כַּמָּה 'how
many?' (13:23), 'how long?' (7:19)
with the shade of meaning 'how
many times?', just as in Ps 78:40.
Job ironically questions the affirmation of Bildad (18:5-6): 'Yes, the
light of the wicked goes out, and
his flame of fire ceases to shine, the
light in his tent grows dim, and his
lamp is put out above him.' The
formula נר רשעים ידעך recurs in
Pr 13:9; 24:20. It is a commonplace. The happiness of the wicked,
symbolised by light, is changed into
misfortune, symbolised by darkness
(20:26). In 18:12 Bildad declared
that misfortune (איד as here) stands
beside the wicked. But how often
does this misfortune seize them?
The verb בוא has על before the
person to whom misfortune comes
(cf 2:11); the same meaning, with
the direct complement of the person,
is found in 15:21; 20:22. Ehrlich
considers the 3rd hemistich untrans-

latable. The word חַבָלִים is ambiguous. The meaning 'pains' is assigned to it (cf. G, Vulg.); but in this
case, it would be a question of the
pains of childbirth, for חֵבֶל (derived
from חבל 'conceive', 'give birth to')
is used only in this sense. Most interpreters see in חבלים the plural of
חֶבֶל 'rope', 'cord', used here with the
connotation of what is allotted to
each, after a field has been measured,
the 'lot' received by the heirs
(Targ.); cf. Ps 16:6. Then the translation is: 'He shares out lots in His
anger', that is: He fixes their fate
in His anger (cf. Le Hir), or He
metes out to them a portion of anger
(cf. Renan). But we expect a suffix
to designate those who are thus
harshly treated. Let us further note
the interpretation of חבלים by
'ropes' in the sense of 'traps' (Franz
Delitzsch, following 18:10). Everywhere we come up against grammatical difficulties. We ourselves propose to connect חבלים with the root
חבל 'to act badly' and 'to destroy',
'to ruin' (cf. Comm. on 17:1 and
34:31), which is reflected in the
Assyrian *ḫabâlu*. To this root belongs
the Assyrian *ḫabbilu*, of which the
generic sense is 'malevolent', 'producing evil'. The singular of חבלים
would be חֶבֶל, parallel to רָשָׁע. A
special characteristic of deity among
the Babylonians and Assyrians is
that they destroy the wicked. The
expression then used is *muḫalliq
raggi* 'who destroys the bad' or
muḫalliq limnûti 'who destroys the
wicked' (cf. dictionaries, s.v. ḫalaqu).
We recognise in יְחַלֵּק the same verb
as *ḫalâqu* in the *pi'el* (the form used
in the texts quoted above). The sense
of the 3rd hemistich is quite clear:
how often does He destroy the

18   And are they as straw before the wind,
      Like the chaff which a whirlwind has swept away?

19   Does Eloah store up his iniquity for his sons?
      Let Him punish the man himself, that he may learn!

wicked in His anger? This is a direct allusion to the affirmations of Bildad about the effects of divine wrath (20: 23, 28).

18 G renders לִפְנֵי by ὑπό, but G(A, C) πρό, quoted in the margin of Syro-hex.

The clause still depends on כַּמָּה 'how many times?' of v. 17. The affirmation challenged by Job's question is certainly that of Ps 1: 4, 'Not so are the wicked, but, on the contrary, they are as chaff (כַּמֹּץ) swept away by the wind (רוּחַ).' The comparison is amplified in two images: 'like straw before the wind, and like the chaff which a whirlwind has swept away!' The expression גְּנָבַתּוּ סוּפָה recurs in 27: 20, where it is a question of the punishment of the wicked. In 13: 25 Job likened his wretched life to a leaf whirled away (the verb נדף as in Ps 1: 4), to a dry wisp of straw (קַשׁ 'wisp of straw'). The verb גנב 'steal' is well chosen to depict the action of the squall of wind which suddenly sweeps away the straw (cf. 4: 12). Note that v. 16 alluded to the counsel of the wicked עצת רשעים, a phrase which also occurs in Ps 1.

19 The word אלוה, omitted in G, is restored in Jerome *Deus* (Bod., Tur.) and in the margin of Syro-hex. (according to Theod.). V. 19b, absent from Sah., marked with asterisk in Jerome, Syro-hex., Colb., did not exist in G. The present text derives from Theod. (cf. Syro-hex. and Colb.).

One cannot make G ἐκλίποι, at the beginning, a basis to justify the change from אֱלוֹהַ to אֵל־ (contra Ley, Duhm), for the translation ἐκλίποι is an attempt to render the verb יצפן after the dropping out of אלוה. Ancient commentators, among others Rashi, had perfectly well understood that the 1st hemistich conveys an objection which Job imagines to be voiced by his opponents in the argument: 'You say, Eloah stores up his misdeeds for his sons?' Such indeed is the argument to which Job's friends have recourse when with him they are compelled to recognise that the wicked man prospers in this world (5: 4; 20: 10). Moreover, it was a current notion that the sin of the fathers is inherited by the children (cf. 5: 4; Ex 20: 5; Dt 5: 9; Mt 27: 25). In our Commentary on 8: 4 we referred to the passage of Ezekiel which already makes a protest against this doctrine, until such time as the Saviour corrects on this point the prejudices of the Apostles (Jn 9: 1-3). The verb צפן 'to hide' used here with the connotation of of 'reserve', store up' (15: 20; 20: 26). The word אָוֶן denotes at the same time the wrong-doing and the punishment which infallibly flows from it (4: 8; 5: 6; 15: 35), just as the Akkadian *šêrtu* represents both punishment for sin and sin itself (*La religion assyro-babylonienne*, p. 235). The 2nd hemistich, which is further explained by v. 20, gives the reply to the objection: 'Let Him punish the man himself, that he may learn!' The *pi'el* of שלם has the meaning of restoring things to normal (8: 6), whence to 'reward' every man according to his works (v. 31; 34: 11) and, consequently, to carry out reprisals towards some one, to

20   Let his own eyes see his *calamity*,
     And let him drink of the wrath of Shaddai!
21   For what interest does he take in his house after his death,
     When the number of his months has been broken off?

20 פִּידוֹ (cf. versions); MT: כִידוֹ.

punish. The close: וְיֵדַע 'that he may know', i.e. that he may profit from the correction. Cf. 19: 29c.

20   For כִידוֹ, G τὴν ἑαυτοῦ σφαγήν, Vulg. *interfectionem suam*, Targ. תביריה 'his ruin', Syr. احربه 'his loss'. G ἀπὸ δὲ Κυρίου μὴ διασωθείη paraphrases the 2nd hemistich, in order to avoid the anthropomorphism.

V. 20 is the natural sequel to v. 19b. It is the guilty man himself who must be punished, his own eyes must see the chastisement. Cf. the phrase ועיני ראו 'and my eyes will see' in 19: 27. It is only in consequence of a series of subtle deductions that the meaning 'loss' is assigned to the *hapax* כִיד, following the Arabic *kaid*, the proper meaning of which is 'fraud', 'trickery' (cf. *Thesaurus* of Gesenius, s.v.). Rashi already felt that the word כיד was defective and read אִידוֹ 'his misfortune' (cf. אִידָם in v. 17). A reading פִּידוֹ seems to us to offer a better explanation of the error of audition which has given rise to כִידוֹ. The word פִּיד as in 12: 5; 15: 23 (cf. Comm.). Less probable are the readings כְּיָדוֹ 'like his hand', 'like his deed' (Hoffmann), כּוֹסוֹ 'his cup' (Ehrlich, in harmony with the 2nd hemistich), כִידוֹר 'the assault' (Wright, following 15: 24). The 2nd hemistich is suggested by the well-known image of the cup of divine fury which God pours out on the guilty (Is 51: 17; Jer 25: 15; Rev 16: 19). In 6: 4 the spirit of Job was said to drink the poison of the arrows shot by God. The anger of God is expressed simply by חֵמָה in 19: 29. The verb שתה with partitive מִן before its complement (Gn 9: 21; Ru 2: 9), as we say: drink *some* wine, *some* water.

21   V. 21, absent from Sah., marked with asterisk in Colb. and Jerome, did not exist in G. The present text is taken from Theod. (cf. Colb.). Syro-hex. attributes to Theod. only the words μετ' αὐτοῦ. For חצצו, Theod. διηρέθησαν, Aq. ἡμισεύθησαν (cf. Jerome *dimidiatus sit*, Vulg. *dimidietur*), Targ. אתפליגו 'are shared', 'are divided', Syr. 'are kept for his sons' (after v. 19a).

This verse shows clearly how vv. 19-20 were to be interpreted. It is not the sons of the guilty man but the latter himself who must be struck by the effects of divine justice. What does the wicked man care about the fate of his children? Once he is dead, he is no longer concerned about the situation in which his offspring find themselves: 'if his sons are honoured, he knows nothing of it. If they are despised, he does not perceive it' (14: 21). Literally the 1st hemistich runs: 'For what is his interest in his house after him?', meaning: 'For what interest does he take in his house after his death?' The word חֵפֶץ means 'wish', 'desire' (31: 16) and 'interest' (20: 3). The house implies the family. With אַחֲרָיו 'after him', to connote 'after his death', compare לורעו אחריו 'for his seed after him' of Gn 17: 19. In the Code of Hammurabi the formula *warki-ša* 'after her' (rev. XI, 81) means 'after her death', *warki abî-šu* 'after

22   Does man teach God knowledge?
     But it is He who judges the exalted ones!
23   One dies in his full maturity,
     When he is entirely happy and at ease,

his father' (rev. X, 19, 25) means 'after the death of his father'. The 2nd hemistich explains אחריו, the copula of the opening expressing temporal circumstance: 'when the number of his months has been broken off'. The phrase מִסְפַּר חֳדָשָׁיו as in 14: 5; cf. מספר שנים in 15: 20. The verb agrees with the plural noun which clarifies the collective; cf. ומספר ימיך רבים 'and the number of his days is considerable' (38: 21). The rare word חֲצָצוּ has been replaced by חֻרְצוּ in accordance with 14: 5 (Ewald, Graetz, etc.). But in that case the meaning would be: 'when the number of his months has been decreed' (cf. Comm. on 14: 5). The versions have seen a relation between חצץ and חצה 'divide', 'cut in half'. There exists in Assyrian a verb ḫaṣâṣu, ḫaṣṣuṣu (in the pi'el), the exact meaning of which is 'to break', especially reeds (cf. רצץ in Hebrew).

22 G πότερον οὐχὶ ὁ Κύριός ἐστιν ὁ διδάσκων σύνεσιν καὶ ἐπιστήμην reading הלא אל instead of הלאל, double translation of דעת. We shall again meet this text of G in 22: 2. Obelus before σύνεσιν in Syro-hex. Instead of ילמד, Syr. 'you teach', reads the 2nd person plural. For רמים, Targ. שמי מרומא 'the heavens on high'. G φόνους reads דמים. Syro-hex. cites in the margin the word σόφους, which replaces φόνους in G (A, C).

Gray and Torczyner would eliminate this v. 22 as alien to the context. But in fact it is altogether in the style of Job's present argument, for he is reproaching his friends with taking God's side (cf. 13: 7-10). They incorrigibly claim to instruct every one and even attempt to impose on God Himself the rigour of their doctrine. According to them, there must be an absolute correlation between moral and physical evil, between sin and death. But experience as it is invoked and described from v. 23 onwards proves that death strikes somewhat at random. Hence man must not attempt to teach God, and is all the more ill-advised to attempt it since God is the sovereign Judge, on whom everything depends. Man's part is to be silent and to note what happens, without constantly trying to discover explanations which conform to the human idea of justice. Thus the 1st hemistich will mean: 'Does man teach God knowledge?' The 2nd shows the absurdity of such a pretension: 'But it is He who judges the exalted ones!' We leave to the plural masculine participle רָמִים the vague character which it has in 2 S 22: 28 and Ps 78: 69. In fact, it is in all probability an allusion to the beings who dwell in the heights of the heavens (16: 19). Job's question reminds us of Is 40: 14, 'With whom has He consulted and who has instructed Him? And who has taught Him the way of judgment and knowledge, and has made Him to know the path of understanding?'

23 V. 23, absent from Sah., marked with asterisk in Colb. and Jerome, did not exist in G. The present text comes from Theod. (cf. Colb.), but has passed into Syro-hex. The verse is essential to the description, as is to be seen by the continuation וזה in v. 25, and the suffixes of עטיניו and עצמתיו in

24   When his *sides* are full of *fat*,
      And the marrow of his bones quite fresh!

24   עֲטִינָיו (cf. Syr.); MT: עטיניו. — חֵלֶב (G, Vulg., Syr.); MT: חָלָב.

v. 24. For בעצם תמו, Vulg. *robustus et sanus*, less literal than Theod. ἐν κράτει ἁπλοσύνης αὐτοῦ and Aq. ἐν ὀστεώσει ἁπλότητος αὐτοῦ. G(A) ἀφροσύνης, instead of ἁπλοσύνης, is cited in the margin of Syro-hex. The word כלו is omitted by Vulg. and Syr. The versions have assimilated שלאנן to שאנן; cf. Theod. εὐπαθῶν (Jer 30: 10), Vulg. *dives* (cf. *divitum* for שאנן in 12: 5), Targ. שדיך 'at ease', Syr. ܠܒܝܐ 'confident'.

Job is proposing to show that death strikes all human beings without discrimination, the happy (23-4) and the unhappy (25) alike, whatever their conduct may have been. Cf. 3: 17-19. The pronouns זֶה (23), וְזֶה (25), signify 'this one . . . that one', 'the one . . . the other' (1: 16, 17, 18). Note the use of עֶצֶם 'bone' to imply the inner essence of a thing, what constitutes its specific nature (*L'Emploi métaphorique*, p. 10). Hence בְּעֶצֶם תֻּמּוֹ 'in his full maturity'. The abstract תֹּם in the sense of physical perfection; in 4: 6 it was a question of moral perfection. With כֻּלּוֹ 'he wholly' cf. the use of כֻּלֹּה in 34: 13. The man in question is not imperfectly happy: 'he is wholly happy and at ease'. An alliterative influence has introduced שַׁלְאֲנָן instead of שַׁאֲנָן (12: 5), as has been recognised by the versions; cf. יתעלם (6: 16), נמרצו (6: 25), under the influence of the neighbouring word. It is שָׁלֵיו which has led to שלאנן. The writing שליו with a *mater lectionis*, as in Jer 49: 31; Sir 41: 1. The form שָׁלֵו is found in 16: 12; the verb in 3: 26. Note that in Sir 41: 1 it is also a question of death striking

the man who is at ease (אִישׁ שָׁלֵיו). It is contrasted with death striking the wretched one. Death is an evil for the former, a blessing for the latter.

24   The versions recognise in עטיניו the name of a part of the body: τὰ δὲ ἔγκατα αὐτοῦ (G), *viscera ejus* (Vulg.), ביזוי 'his breasts' (Targ.), ܟܣܝܘܗܝ 'his flanks' (Syr.). Targ. preserves חָלָב 'milk', but G στέατος, Vulg. *adipe*, Syr. ܚܠܒܐ vocalise חֵלֶב 'fat'. For מח עצמותיו, G μυελὸς δὲ αὐτοῦ (αὐτῶν in A, C, Sah., Jerome). Syr. and Vulg. make of עצמותיו the subject of ישקה.

The meaning accepted by modern critics for עֲטִינָיו is 'his pails' (cf. Dillmann, Budde, Duhm, Gray, etc.), following the Talmudic עטין which denotes the olive in the press, whence מעטן 'vat' of the press. Qimchi already refuted this interpretation (cf. Levy, *Neuhebr. und chald. Wörterbuch*, II, p. 635, s.v. עטין). The root עטן has the precise meaning of 'pressing the olives', and it is solely because of מלאו חלב 'are full of milk' that there has been postulated for עטין the meaning of 'pail' or 'breast' (cf. Targ.). Renan translated עטיניו by 'the pens of his flocks', following Ibn Ezra, Schultens, and Rosenmüller, who compare with the Arabic عطن, place where the camels rest near the drinking troughs. It may be seen that this derivation is no less subtle than the previous one. Now, it is obvious, in accordance with the exigencies of parallelism, that the vocalisation חֵלֶב 'fat' (G, Vulg., Syr.) is preferable to חָלָב 'milk'. In the description of the

25   And another dies with bitterness in his soul,
      Without having tasted of happiness;
26   Together they lie down in the dust,
      And the worms cover them!
27   Yes, I know your thoughts
      And the ideas which you imagine about me,

sated man (15: 27) we find that 'his face was hidden in fat, his loins had become big with fat'. Bochart has perfectly understood that עטיניו stemmed from עַטְמָיו 'his hips', in accordance with the Aramaic עטם, parallel to אטם and איטם in the sense of 'thigh', 'hip', 'side'. Thus we obtain: 'his hips are full of fat', parallel to 'the marrow of his bones is fresh'. The *hapax* מֹחַ 'marrow' (cf. מְמֻחִים 'full of marrow' in Is 25: 6) in Arabic *muḫḫ* 'marrow' and 'brain', in Assyrian *muḫḫu* 'skull' (Aramaic and Syriac מוחא, 'skull'). The *puʻal* of שׁקה to denote 'to be well watered, moist', hence 'to be fresh'. We have here an allusion to young, fresh marrow which has not yet been dried up by old age or death. In Pr 3: 8, good conduct is 'refreshing (שִׁקּוּי) for thy bones'.

25 Vulg. paraphrases the 2nd hemistich: *absque ullis opibus*. G οὐ φαγὼν οὐδὲν ἀγαθόν is more literal.

Death of the wretched unhappy man: 'and another dies with bitterness in his soul'. Literally: 'with a bitter soul'; cf. the מְרֵי נֶפֶשׁ 'those whose soul is bitter' (3: 20) and מַר נַפְשִׁי 'the bitterness of my soul' (7: 11; 10: 1). The perfect אָכַל in the 2nd hemistich is well chosen to convey the finality of past life: 'he has not tasted of happiness'. The preposition בְּ״ before the complement, with partitive implications; cf. the use of מִן (after שׁתה 'to drink') in v. 20. In Pr 9: 5, there is parallelism between שׁתה בְּ״ 'drink of . . .' and לחם בְּ״ 'eat of . . .'. After אָכַל usage has sometimes בְּ״ (Ex 12: 43-45), sometimes מִן (Gn 3: 3; Lev

7: 21). Note the feminine טוֹבָה 'happiness' (cf. Comm. on 17: 15) after טוֹב (v. 13) and טוּב (v. 16) in the same sense.

26 After ὁμοθυμαδὸν δέ, G(A) adds οἱ υἱοὶ αὐτοῦ, which is found in the margin of G (א).

At the beginning יַחַד 'together' with the connotation: 'in the same way' (3: 18). Compare with the 1st hemistich 17: 16b, 'shall we together descend into the dust?' The expression עַל־עָפָר יִשְׁכָּבוּ 'they lie down in the dust' recalls לֶעָפָר אֶשְׁכָּב (7: 21), עַל־עָפָר תִּשְׁכָּב (20: 11); cf. the verb שׁכב in 3: 13 and 14: 12. In Sheol or the tomb, worms are both the bed and the covering of the corpse (Is 14: 11). The 2nd hemistich is inspired by this image. The collective רִמָּה as in 17: 14.

27 G ὥστε οἶδα ὑμᾶς ὅτι τόλμῃ ἐπίκεισθέ μοι sums up the verse. The 2nd hemistich of Vulg. *et sententias contra me iniquas* closely follows Symm. καὶ τὰς ἐννοίας ὑμῶν τὰς ἀδίκους τὰς κατ' ἐμοῦ. For תחמסו, Targ. תחשלון 'you imagine', Syr. ܡܬܚܫܒܝܢ ܐܢܬܘܢ 'you meditate'.

The particle הֵן, not now in the sense of 'if' (v. 16), but with the value of 'behold, yes!' (הנה), in order to introduce a new theme (cf. 13: 1): 'yes, I know your thoughts!' As the verb חמס means 'to use violence' against some one (15: 33; cf. 16: 17; 19: 7), the 2nd hemistich has been interpreted as follows: 'your harsh imputations against me' (Le Hir), 'the opinions which wrong me in

28   You say to yourselves: 'Where is the house of the nobleman,
     And where is the tent in which the wicked dwelt?'

your minds' (Renan), 'your determination to crush me' (Loisy), etc.
A comparison with the Hebrew text
shows by what misplaced ingenuity
such translations are achieved. It is
clear that the 2nd hemistich is parallel to מַחְשְׁבוֹתֵיכֶם 'your thoughts'
and that the relative אֲשֶׁר is understood after מְזִמּוֹת. The word מזמות
(from the root זמם, cf. Comm. on
17: 11) generally means the plans
or manoeuvres which are hatched
against some one, though sometimes
it expresses simply the thoughts or
ideas which one has in the head
(Ps 10: 4). These ideas are made explicit in v. 28, 'namely that you say
to yourselves . . .', and they have
by no means the character of a
sinister plot being hatched against
Job. The verb חמס must be distinguished from חמס 'to use violence'
(cf. Thesaurus of Ben-Yehuda, III,
p. 1626), as has been realised by
Targ. and Syr. The meaning we expect is that of 'think', 'meditate',
'imagine'. Now, it happens that the
Syriac ܘܚܫܒ offers exactly this
meaning. With Jacob (ZATW, 1912)
we shall recognise in חמס a strengthening of המס (cf. הכר for חכר in
19: 3). The preposition עַל does not
mean 'against', but 'about', 'with
regard to'. The 2nd hemistich will
be translated quite simply: 'and the
ideas which you imagine about me'.
Hence it is unnecessary to change
תחמסו to תחפשׂו 'you meditate'
(Duhm), or to תחרשׁו 'you cultivate'
(Beer in the edition of Kittel).

28   Vv. 28-33, absent from Sah.,
marked with asterisk in Colb., Jerome, and Syro-hex. (with the exception of v. 32), did not exist in G.
The present text derives from Theod.
(cf. Colb. and Syro-hex.). Now,
neither v. 32 (Syro-hex.) nor v. 34

(G) are continuous with v. 27,
whereas vv. 28-33 form its natural
sequel. The lacuna of G is due to an
accident in the original text. The
word נדיב is translated ܙܪܝܩܐ 'the
righteous man' in Syr., but ἄρχοντος
(A ἀρχαῖος) in Theod., ארכונא
(ἄρχων) in Targ., principis in Vulg.
   The opening phrase, 'namely, you
say', shows quite clearly that Job
will be content to explain what his
interlocutors are thinking (v. 27).
The formula is the same as in the
previous speech of Job (19: 28), but
with a slightly different implication:
'but if you say' (19: 28). Ehrlich
proposes to cut out כִּי תֹאמְרוּ as being
'unpoetic'! He forgets to say what
his criterion of the 'poetic' is. The
direct speech from אַיֵּה makes necessary the introductory formula. The
question: 'Where is the house of the
nobleman?' implies the answer: it
has vanished! Cf. the use of אַיּוֹ
'where is he?' in 14: 10 and 20: 7,
אַיֵּה in 17: 15. Job's friends have
stressed the fact that the houses of
the wicked disappear without leaving
any trace behind them (8: 14-15;
15: 34; 18: 21, 20: 26, 28). The parallelism between נָדִיב 'nobleman'
(12: 21) and רְשָׁעִים 'the wicked'
suggests that נדיב is used in a pejorative sense. The author has in view
the man of rank who has risen by
extortion and violence (cf. Is 13: 2).
In 18: 21 we had the 'dwellings of
the unrighteous'; here, the dwellings
of the wicked are in apposition to
אֹהֶל, just as in the Assyrian expression, quoted by Fried. Delitzsch:
kultârê mûšabišunu 'the tents (which
are) their dwelling place', the tents
which they inhabit. Hence we translate: 'and where is the tent in which
the wicked dwelt?' It would be too

29   Have you not questioned those who travel the roads,
     And have you not understood their marks?

30   Namely, that in the day of calamity the wicked man is spared,
     In the day of wrath *he is merry*!

30   יַבְלִג; MT: יובלו.

easy a course to eliminate אהל as is done by Beer, Budde, Duhm, Ehrlich. Cf. אהל ביתי 'the tent, my house' in Ps 132:3. The 2nd hemistich recalls 8:22b, 'and the tent of the wicked will be no more'.

29 On the text of G, cf. v. 28. Theod. renders הלא שאלתם by ἐρωτήσατε. The 2nd hemistich is curiously paraphrased in Vulg. *et haec eadem illum intelligere cognoscetis.*

Job here counters the assertions of his friends by referring to the experience of travellers. In 15:17-19 Eliphaz appealed to the testimony of local tradition, or tradition which was not contaminated by foreign influences. Job widens the horizon: 'Have you not questioned those who travel the roads?' The form שְׁאֶלְתֶּם recurs in 1 S 12:13; 25:5. It is a softening of שְׁאַלְתֶּם, which comes from a form שָׁאַל, parallel to שָׁאֵל (Qimchi, quoted in Gesenius-Kautzsch, § 44d). The complement of שאל is in the accusative as in 12:7. The phrase עֹבְרֵי דָרֶךְ is classic idiom to denote those who travel the highroad (La 1:12; 2:15; Ps 80:13; 89:42; Pr 9:15). Here the allusion is almost to tramps or wandering labourers, who go from town to town, from village to village. Their custom was to write their names and their thoughts somewhere at the main cross-roads. The main roads of Sinai are dotted with these scribblings made by such passers of a day. 'And have you not understood their marks?', not 'irrefutable facts' (Renan) or 'what they have

taught us' (Le Hir), but rather the marks of their passage through. It is strange that modern critics try to find in אֹתָם 'their signs' abstract meanings, such as 'proofs', 'arguments', 'memories' (cf. Dillmann, Budde, Gray, Duhm, etc.). It is certainly the concrete 'mark', 'sign', 'character (in writing)' which the author intended, as is abundantly shown by the verb נכר, of which the pi'el, both here and in 34:19, has the same meaning as the hiph'il 'to recognise' in 2:12; 4:16; 7:10. Note that, in all these passages, the verb is accompanied by a negative.

30 On the text of G, cf. v. 28. For יחשך, Theod. κουφίζεται, Jerome and Vulg. *servatur.* Instead of עברות, Theod. ὀργῆς αὐτοῦ reads עברתו. For יובלו, Syr. ܡܬ̈ܝܒܠ, corruption of ܡܬ̈ܝܒܠ 'is led' (Merx).

The conjunction כי introduces the clause making explicit the testimony of travellers (cf. v. 28). The 1st hemistich is ambiguous. But if we translate 'that the wicked man is reserved for the day of calamity' (Le Hir), we are making Job say the opposite of what he is contending, namely that the wicked do not suffer a fate different from that of the righteous. Now, the expression לְיוֹם אֵיד can mean: 'in the day of calamity', just as we have ליום פקדה in the day of chastisement' (Is 10:3), לעתות בצרה 'in times of distress' (Ps 10:1); cf. לבקר 'in the morning' and לערב 'in the evening'. We translate the 1st hemistich: 'namely, that in the day of calamity the wicked man is spared'. The word אֵיד is used

31   Who denounces his conduct to his face,
      And who punishes him for what he has done?
32   And when to the grave he is carried,
      On a mound he keeps watch;

as in 18:12. The verb חשׁךְ 'to
restrain', 'to check' (7:11; 16:5-6)
also means 'to reserve' (38:23) and
'to spare' (33:18). It is the latter
sense which suits our passage. To
the formula ליום איד corresponds
לְיוֹם עֲבָרוֹת 'in the day of fury', i.e.
the day of divine wrath; cf. בְּיוֹם
אַפּוֹ 'in the day of divine anger' in
20:28. It is the *dies irae* of Zeph
1:15; Pr 11:4 (cf. Zeph 1:18;
Ezk 7:19.) The plural עברות as in
Ps 7:7. The structure of the verse
obliges us to see in יוּבָלוּ the parallel
word to יחשׁךְ. The difficulties
presented by the plural appear in the
translations: 'he is made to escape
punishment' (Renan), 'for the day
when vengeance must break out'
(Le Hir), etc. The changes from
יובלו to יֻצָּל 'he is saved' (Dillmann,
Graetz, Beer), יִפָּלֵט 'he escapes'
(Ball), give indeed a satisfactory
meaning, but one wonders how it is
that the MT can have lost the simple
and easy word in exchange for the
difficult יובלו. We ourselves see in
יובלו a wrong reading for יַבְלִג, from
the verb הבליג 'to be gay, cheerful,
lighthearted' (9:27; 10:20), which,
outside Job, appears only in Am.
5:9 and Ps 39:14. The wicked man
laughs at calamities because he is
sure that he will escape them. This
is precisely the opposite of the
theory of Eliphaz in 5:22.

31   On the text of G, cf. v. 28.
Syr. omits the suffix of דרכו. For
והוא עשה, Theod. καὶ ἃ αὐτὸς ἐποίησεν, Vulg. *quae fecit*.
   The 1st hemistich recalls 13:15b,
where we had דרכי 'my affairs' and
אל־פניו 'to His face'. There it was
a question of Job's discussing his

affairs before God. Here דַּרְכּוֹ means
'his conduct' (17:9) and עַל־פָּנָיו 'to
his face' shows that one is not afraid
of the person one is addressing; cf.
על־פניכם in 6:28. The verb הגיד
here assumes a more forceful meaning than that of 'reveal', 'announce'
(11:6; 15:18): 'who denounces his
conduct to his face?' No one dares
to protest against the way in which
the wicked man behaves. Cf. 9:12,
where Job, speaking of God, exclaims: 'If He plunders, who can
prevent Him? Who will say to Him:
What art Thou doing?'. דרכו 'his conduct' is balanced by וְהוּא עָשָׂה 'and
he has done', meaning, 'what he has
done' (cf. Theod. and Vulg.). Similar
phrases are found in 20:9, 15. Use
of ישׁלם־לו is as in 34:11, where
הוא־עשה is replaced by פעל אדם.
The *pi'el* of שׁלם has the sense of
'give back', 'requite', 'retaliate' (v.
19b). The law of retaliation *par pari
refertur* does not apply to the wicked
man.

32   On the text of G, cf. v. 28.
Syr. renders קברות by the singular.
Targ. and Syr. transcribe גדישׁ,
which is translated σωρῷ by Theod.
(it has become σωρῶν in B), θημω-
νίας by Aq., *congerie mortuorum* by
Vulg. The meaning of ישׁקוד is well
rendered by Theod. ἠγρύπνησεν, Vulg.
vigilabit, Targ. יעיר, less literally by
Syr. ܡܬܢܛܪ 'kept'.
   The wicked man is not disturbed
during his lifetime. He is no less well
treated than anybody else after his
death, when his body is carried to
the grave. Notice the emphasis of
והוא 'and he' repeated from v. 31b.
The plural קְבָרוֹת 'the tombs' (instead of קברים of 17:1) means the

33 Sweet to him are the clods of the torrent bed!
Behind him all move in procession,
And before him a numberless throng!

graveyard, the spot where there are many tombs. The expression לִקְבָרוֹת יוּבָל as we have לקבר אובל in 10: 19. The 2nd hemistich is an allusion to the statue of the dead man placed on his tomb. The word גָּדִישׁ, homonym of גדישׁ 'pile of sheaves' (5: 26), corresponds to the Arabic جدث (jadath, plural ajdâth) 'funeral mound', 'tomb'. The reference is to the tumulus which is erected on the spot where the deceased has been buried. A life-size bust or statue of the dead man was fitted, as is seen on Egyptian tombs or the tombs of Palmyra, etc. The effect was that the deceased seemed to be himself watching over his tomb. Note that it is specially a question of the nobleman (v. 28) and that, in consequence, the burial mound was more richly ornamented than was the case with the tombs of ordinary mortals. In 3: 14-15 Job has already drawn attention to these sumptuous mausolea. It is only weakening the text to change על into עליו 'a tumulus watches over him' (Grimme, Beer), or to replace ישקוד by the plural ישקדו 'watch is kept on the tumulus' (Merx, Duhm, Budde). Still less acceptable is the reading ישקוט 'he rests' (Graetz, Ehrlich), instead of the picturesque ישקוד. All the versions confirm the plain meaning of the MT.

33 On the text of G, cf. v. 28. For מתקו, Syr. ܚܠܐ 'swallowing', from מתק 'to suck' (24: 20). For רגבי נחל, Vulg. glareis Cocyti (allusion to the river of Hades). Theod. translates ימשׁוך by ἀπελεύσεται. The 1st hemistich is parallel to v. 32b. It is the clods which go to make up the גדישׁ 'tumulus'. The

verb מָתַק 'to be sweet'; cf. the hiph'il in 20: 12. The word רֶגֶב 'clod' of earth recurs only in 38: 38, where we have the plural רְגָבִים. A good parallel is furnished by ארגב 'mound', 'knoll', the existence of which in Hebrew is attested by the text of G ἐργάβ, ἀργάβ in 1 S 20: 19, 41 (cf. our Comm.). With the idea here expressed compare the Latin: sit ei terra levis! The last two hemistichs form a verse complete in itself describing the funeral procession of the wicked man. The deceased is carried to the graveyard, 'and behind him all move in procession, and before him a numberless throng'. It is misunderstanding the division of the lines to suppress v. 33c, as is done by Duhm, Ehrlich, Beer. There is a strict parallelism between 33b and 33c: לְפָנָיו corresponds to אֵין־מִסְפָּר אַחֲרָיו 'numberless' to כָּל־אָדָם 'every man', 'all'. No one is missing at the funeral ceremony; cf. the use of כל־אדם in 36: 25; 37: 7. The throng cannot be counted; cf. אין־מספר in 5: 9; 9: 10. The verb משׁך 'pull', 'draw out' (cf. 40: 25, and 28: 18) means also 'walk', 'move forward' (Jg 5: 14; 20: 37). Cf. the double meaning of the German verb ziehen. The interpretation of v. 33 b-c in the sense of a funeral procession is so perfectly clear that we feel it unnecessary to linger over the translations: 'and all men go the same way after him, just as numberless generations have preceded him' (Le Hir), 'he draws the whole world in his wake, and innumerable crowds have already gone before him' (Renan) — translations which are reflected in varying degrees in modern critical interpretations. The true meaning was

34   How then do you console me with such futile arguments!
      Of your replies nothing is left but deception!

recognised already by Berg (quoted, but not approved of, by Rosenmüller).

34 G τὸ δὲ ἐμὲ καταπαύσασθαι ἀφ' ὑμῶν οὐδέν interprets תשובתיכם as coming from the verb שבת and omits נשאר. Vulg. paraphrases the 2nd hemistich: *cum responsio vestra repugnare ostensa sit veritati*. Syr. ܩܘܕܡܝ 'before me' reads מעלי for מעל. Targ. renders מעל by שקר 'falsehood'.

Conclusion of Job's speech. He insinuated in v. 2 that the consolations of his friends were valueless and that their silence would be preferable. In 16: 2, he described them as 'miserable comforters'. After now refuting their arguments, he exclaims: 'How then do you console me with such futile arguments?'

The word הֶבֶל 'breath', 'what is vain, nothing, worthless', used adverbially (9: 29), marks the character of the consolations offered by his friends. Then we have: 'and your replies', *casus pendens*, to which is attached the clause: 'there remains deception'. From all the answers that have been given him Job retains only one impression: their talk is a gross delusion. The facts themselves contradict the thesis of his friends, and it has given him pleasure to expose these facts in their naked brutality. The true meaning of מַעַל, generally used with the verb מָעַל, is 'treachery', 'faithlessness', with regard to God or neighbour. Here the act of infidelity is concerned rather with the way of interpreting reality, their interpretation is disloyal to the facts; cf. 6: 15ff.

1   Then Eliphaz the Temanite spoke and said:
2   Is it to God that a man is useful?
     It is rather to himself that a wise man is useful!
3   Is it of any advantage to Shaddai that you should be righteous,
     And is it any gain to Him if you perfect your ways?

Chapters 22-31   Third cycle of speeches; see Introduction, pp. xlivff.
Chapter 22   Third speech of Eliphaz: see Introduction, pp. xlivf.

22: 2 G πότερον οὐχὶ ὁ Κύριός ἐστιν ὁ διδάσκων σύνεσιν καὶ ἐπιστήμην; reading הלא אל for הלאל and quotation of the text of G in 21: 22a (q.v.). Jerome adds (with asterisk) *et habitare facit super nos intelligentiam*, which comes from ὅτι κατασκηνώσει ἐφ᾽ ὑμᾶς (read as ἡμᾶς) σύνεσιν, reading of Aq. (according to Cod. 252) or of Theod. (according to the margin of Syro-hex.). The translation κατασκηνώσει (*habitare facit*) reads ישכן instead of יסכן (2°). A paraphrase of the 2nd hemistich explains the interpretation of Vulg. *numquid Deo potest comparari homo, etiam cum perfectae fuerit scientiae?* The word יסכן is translated by the verb אלף 'to teach' in Targ., which makes of כי יסכן an interpolated clause: 'and even if he teaches'. Syr. invents a meaning on the basis of a few words of the text: 'Do you, O man, in the presence of God assert that you equal Him in wisdom?'

The new speech of Eliphaz does not directly answer Job's arguments in ch. 21. The scandal caused by the prosperity of the godless does not exist for Eliphaz, since he regards this prosperity as apparent only. The ethics of Job's friends are essentially utilitarian. Virtue exists, and it must be rewarded; sin exists, and it must be punished. God commands man to be virtuous, but this is not for His own sake, but for the sake of man's own best interests: 'Is it to God that a man is useful? It is rather to himself that a wise man is useful!' The verb סכן 'to be useful, profitable' as in 15: 3. After the question, the conjunction כי can assume an adversative significance, 'but', 'on the contrary'; cf. 31: 18 and the *qerê* כי instead of the *kethîb* כי־אם in Jer 39: 12. The alternation of the prepositions ל׳׳ and על in לעפר and על־עפר (cf. Comm. on 21: 26), אל and על (cf. Comm. on 1: 11), ל׳׳ and אל (cf. Comm. on 21: 4), enables us to consider עלימו as answering to לאל. The form of the suffix in עלימו (cf. 27: 23) is supported by למו, instead of לו, in Is 44: 15; 53: 8. The משכיל is essentially the reasoning man (Pr 10: 5, 19; 14: 35, etc.); cf. שכל 'reason' (17: 4) and השכיל 'to understand' (34: 27). With the 2nd hemistich cf. Pr 9: 12. 'If you are wise, it is for yourself that you are wise.'

3 G τί γὰρ μέλει τῷ Κυρίῳ ἐὰν σὺ ἦσθα τοῖς ἔργοις ἄμεμπτος has passed from the first כי to the second. The sequel ἢ ὠφελία ὅτι ἁπλώσῃς (B in error ἀπώσῃς) τὴν ὁδόν σου,

326

4   Is it because of your piety that He corrects you,
     And goes to judgment with you?
5   Is it not rather because your wickedness is great,
     And because there is no limit to your sins?
6   The fact is that for no reason you took pledges from your
         brothers,
     And tore their garments from the naked.

absent from Sah., marked with asterisk in Jerome and Syro-hex., is derived from Theod. (cf. Colb.). Syr. has made the same mistake as G and connected מיראתך of v. 4 with v. 3. For the 2nd hemistich, Symm. ἐὰν ἄμωμος ἡ ὁδός σου (cf. Vulg. si immaculata fuerit via tua).

V. 3 is a development of v. 2a. God does not derive any benefit from the virtue of men. The word חֵפֶץ (21: 21), no longer simply the interest one takes in a thing, but the profit one derives from it. Parallelism with בֶּצַע 'gain'; cf. the expression מה־בצע 'What gain?' 'What profit?' (Gn 37: 26, etc.). The construction ה... ואם..., as in 8: 3; 11: 2. The verb צדק 'to be righteous' is thoroughly in the style of Eliphaz (4: 17; 15: 14). Similarly the formula 'that you perfect your ways'; cf. 'the perfection of your ways' in 4: 6, where we have parallelism with יִרְאָתֶךָ 'your piety', which occurs in v. 4.

4   Syr. connects מיראתך with v. 3. The versions interpret מיראתך in the sense of 'for fear of you', whence the paraphrase of G ἦ λόγον σου ποιούμενος (allusion to 9: 32-3), Jerome and Vulg. timens, Targ. המדדחל מנך.
     In the light of 4: 6 and 15: 4 (Eliphaz) it is clear that יִרְאָתֶךָ means 'your fear of God', 'your piety' (cf. v. 3). The natural meaning of the 1st hemistich is simply: 'Is it because of your piety that He corrects you?' The verb הוכיח as in 5: 17; 13: 10. The 2nd hemistich is inspired by

9: 32, where Job said that God was not a man like himself and that, in consequence, they could not go to law together. Eliphaz here supposes that God cites Job before a tribunal. Why? It is certainly not because of Job's piety, but because of the faults which will be enumerated in the verses that follow.

5   Jerome marks with obelus the verb est (G ἐστίν). Vulg. et non propter malitiam tuam plurimam has very well grasped the relation between v. 5 and v. 4; similarly Targ. הלא על 'is it not because . . .'.
     It is apparent that הֲלֹא 'is it not that' is the antithesis of ה 'is it that?' in v. 4. Eliphaz enquires with a touch of irony whether it is on account of his piety that Job has become the object of the chastisement that is being inflicted on him. The answer is evidently: No! Then it must be because Job is guilty. 'Is it not rather because your wickedness is great?' The word רָעָה (20: 12) comprises every aspect of wickedness. The idiom אֵין־קֵץ ל'' 'no end, no limit to . . .' as in Ec 4: 8, 16. Cf. הקץ ל'' in 16: 3. The use of מן implying causality in v. 4 enables the author to understand the conjunction כי after הֲלֹא. The two clauses depend on this understood conjunction.

6   Jerome introduces quia (with asterisk) in his text, probably following Aq. ὅτι, which takes the place of the colourless δέ used to render

7   You gave no water to the thirsty,
     And to the hungry you refused bread!
8   And the man of brute force got the land!
     And the favourite was settled in it!

כִּי in G. For אָחִיךָ tradition oscillates between אָחֶיךָ 'your brothers' and אָחִיךָ 'your brother' (cf. Ginsburg). The plural is supported by G, Vulg., Syr., while Targ. has the singular.

Eliphaz begins an enumeration of the faults which Job's afflictions compel one to postulate, in view of the teaching affirmed, namely that God does not chastise for virtue (v. 4) but for crimes (v. 5). In fact, Eliphaz presupposes that the problem is solved. The conjunction כִּי 'because' governs all the clauses which follow up to v. 10, where the phrase עַל־כֵּן 'that is why' will introduce the main clause. Cf. 20:20-1. The verb חבל means both 'to take as a pledge' (24:3, 9) and 'to take pledges' from some one. The adverb חִנָּם 'gratuitously' (1:9) and 'for no reason whatever', 'wrongly', 'unjustifiably' (2:3; 9:17). The 2nd hemistich explains the 1st. It was against the law to keep for more than one day a garment taken as a pledge (Ex 22:25-6). It was obligatory to return it before night so that the unfortunate person had the wherewithal to cover himself (ibid.). The verb הפשיט means strictly 'tear off', 'remove' some one's clothing (cf. 19:9), 'and you tore their garments from the naked'. The phrasing is ambiguous. Either it is a question of those who become naked because they are robbed of their garments (cf. Hos 2:5), or else of those whose rags already suggest nakedness. Rosenmüller quotes, in support of the latter sense, Seneca (*De benef.*, V, 13): *sic qui male vestitum et pannosum videt, nudum se vidisse dicit.* Clothing, food, and drink, such are the primary objects of justice and

charity (cf. Mt 25:42-3). V. 7 will make reference to food and drink.

7   G διψῶντας and πεινώντων regards עָיֵף and רָעֵב as collectives. But this translation cannot be used as authority for replacing the singulars by plurals (contra Merx).

The word מַיִם is thrown into prominence because the author has in view the most primary of all gifts, the cup of cold water given to the poor (Mt 10:42). The adjective עָיֵף 'tired', 'exhausted' is said especially of the thirsty (Is 29:8; Jer 31:25; Pr 25:25) and metaphorically of the ground which is not watered (Is 32:2; Ps 63:2; 143:6). Thus עָיֵף may be a substitute for צָמֵא (5:5) as a parallel word to רָעֵב 'hungry'. The *hiph'il* of שׁקה (not used in the *qal*) takes the place of the *hiph'il* of שׁתה 'to drink' (not used in the *hiph'il*); cf. the *pu'al* of שׁקה in 21:24. The verb מנע 'check', 'withhold' (20:13) in the sense of 'refuse' a thing (accusative) to some one (preposition מִן). The converse construction in 31:16. The faults to which Eliphaz draws attention are directly contrary to the precepts taught by the prophets: the duty of sharing one's bread with the hungry, and of covering with clothing those who are naked (Is 58:7; Ezk 18:7; cf. Mt 25:42-3).

8   G reverses the order of the two hemistichs. Jerome restores the order of the MT. The reading of G(B) ᾤκισας δὲ τοὺς ἐπὶ τῆς γῆς has dropped the word πτωχούς, which had a place in the original text, according to G (A, C, א), followed by Memph., Eth., Arab. Baud. It is the

9   You sent away widows empty-handed,
      And the arms of orphans *you crushed*!

9 תְּדַכֵּא (G, Vulg., Syr., Targ.); MT: יְדֻכָּא.

reading of G(B) which is adopted
by Sah., Jerome, Syro-hex., but
Syro-hex. quotes in the margin the
alternative reading. It would seem
that ᾤκισας comes from ישב בה of
the close, and that τοὺς πτωχοὺς
ἐπὶ τῆς γῆς rests on a reading ואיש דל
על־הארץ for the 1st hemistich.
There remains ונשׂוא פנים, which G
paraphrases as ἐθαύμασας δέ τινων
πρόσωπον. Vulg. *in fortitudine brachii
tui possidebas terram et potentissimus
obtinebas eam* applies to Job the
content of the verse. Syr. reads זורע
'sowing' instead of זרוע and interprets בה by 'of him'.

Despite the objections of Siegfried
and Peake, v. 8 may very well be
retained in its present context. Job
is said to have shown no pity on the
distressed (6-7), and he will further
be accused of dismissing without aid
the poor widows, and of crushing
the arms of the orphans (9). On the
other hand, he has submitted to the
will of the mighty man and favoured his creatures. Such is the natural meaning of v. 8: 'And the man
of brute force got the land. And the
favourite was settled in it!' The
phrase אִישׁ זְרוֹעַ 'the man of arm', 'the
man with force of fist' conveys the
image of the physically strong, for
it is in the arm that strength resides
(*L'Emploi métaphorique*, p. 140). As
a parallel term we have נְשׂוּא פָנִים
'raised of face', i.e. the favourite, the
one who has the right to raise his
eyes towards the master (op. cit.,
pp. 46f.). Our interpretation makes
it quite unnecessary to correct הארץ
to תרצה 'you used to favour', and
ישב בה to תיטיב or היטבתה 'you
treated well' (contra Ball). The Vulgate has well understood the meaning, but has attributed to Job him-

self the action that is being condemned, whereas Job was merely the
accomplice. Hence we cannot see in
אִישׁ זְרוֹעַ an allusion to Job himself
(contra Dillmann, Hontheim, etc.).
It is in v. 9 that the latter will once
more be directly attacked. The
word זרוע 'arm' constitutes the link
between v. 8 and v. 9, in which 'the
arms' of orphans will be mentioned.

9 Syr. replaces by the singular
the plurals זרעות יתמים. Instead of
יִדֻכָּא, G ἐκάκωσας, Vulg. *comminuis-
ti*, Targ. תשפף, Syr. ܡܚܡܟ have
read תְּדַכֵּא.

The widow and orphan have a
right to special protection (Ex 22:
21; Dt 24: 17; Is 1: 17, etc.). They
are generally coupled together, for
the orphan is usually the son of the
widow, his father being dead (24: 3;
31: 16-17). One of the objects of the
Code of Hammurabi is to secure
'equitable treatment for the orphan
and widow' (rev. XXIV, 61f.). The
pi'el of שׁלח with רֵיקָם 'empty', with
the meaning 'to dismiss empty-
handed' (Gn 31: 42; Dt 15: 13).
Those who retain יִדֻכָּא in the 2nd
hemistich are obliged to regard
זְרֹעוֹת as a complement of passive
construction (Gesenius-Kautzsch,
§ 121b). But the series of clauses in
the 2nd person (6-7) and also parallelism favour the reading תְּדַכֵּא,
which is attested by all the versions.
The *pi'el* of דכא in the sense of
'pound', 'grind', 'crush' (4: 19; 6: 9;
19: 2). 'To crush the arms of some
one' is to destroy all his strength (cf.
v. 8). In 38: 15 we shall see that the
'raised arm is broken'. Not only is
Job accused of having failed to help
widows in their need, but it is further

10   That is why around you there are snares,
      And sudden fear terrifies you;

11   *The light has become darkened*, you can no longer see,
      And a flood of waters drowns you!

11   אוֹר חָשַׁךְ (G); MT: אוֹר־חשׁך.

asserted that he has caused injury to
orphans. He has reserved all his
favours for the powerful (v. 8).

10 For סביבותיך, G ἐκύκλωσάν
σε, Syr. ܣܚܪܘܟ 'have surrounded
you', Vulg. *circumdatus es*. G renders
פחד by πόλεμος.

The main clause is introduced by
עַל־כֵן 'that is why', 'it is for that,
that . . .' after the subordinate
clauses governed by כי of v. 6. Cf. the
construction of 6: 3; 17: 4. Literally
סְבִיבוֹתֶיךָ 'around you', the feminine
plural of סביב fulfilling the function
of a preposition (cf. 29: 5). The
פַּחִים are the snares and nets which
Bildad dwelt on so complacently
(18: 8-10). After this description,
Bildad declared that terrors on all
sides seized the guilty one (18: 11).
The same idea is expressed in our
2nd hemistich: 'and sudden fear
terrifies you'. The verb בהל as in
4: 5 and 21: 6, where we had the
niph'al. The adverb פִּתְאֹם 'suddenly'
(5: 3; 9: 23), linked to פַּחַד 'fear'
(3: 25; 4: 14), plays the part of a
genitive determining the preceding
word. We find the same phrasing
פחד פתאם in Pr 3: 25, 'fear nothing
with sudden fear'.

11 Vulg. *et putabas te tenebras
non visurum* adds a verb in order to
preserve the MT. Similarly Targ. 'or
you will dwell in darkness and you
will not see'. Syr. ܐܡܬܝ 'from
whence?' reads אי instead of או.
G τὸ φῶς σοι σκότος (A, א εἰς σκότος)
ἀπέβη does not imply אוֹרְךָ חָשַׁךְ
(Merx, Bickell, etc.) but simply

אוֹר חָשַׁךְ, as can be seen from 18: 6,
where אוֹר חשׁך is translated τὸ φῶς
αὐτοῦ σκότος. As a result of its translation of the 1st hemistich, Vulg.
paraphrases the 2nd: *et impetu
aquarum inundantium non oppressum
iri*. For שׁפעת, reproduced in the
ܡܒܥ 'pouring out', 'flooding' of
Syr., we have סוגעת 'multitude' in
Targ. The translation of G κοιμη-
θέντα δὲ ὕδωρ σε ἐκάλυψεν probably
presupposes a variant וּשְׁכָבַת instead
of וְשִׁפְעַת. G has not grasped the true
meaning of שׁכבת 'pouring out'
(from the verb שׁכב 'lie', 'incline',
'pour out', cf. 38:37). It is not necessary to prefer the variant of G to
the Hebrew text which is supported
by 38: 34.

The MT 'or darkness, you do not
see' has been paraphrased in various
ways: 'in the heart of darkness with
no gleam of light' (Le Hir); 'surrounded by darkness which prevents
you from seeing' (Renan); 'do you
not then see this darkness ?' (Segond),
etc. The original reading אוֹר חָשַׁךְ is
not in doubt, following G and 18: 6.
We have quoted 18: 8-11 in connection with v. 10. The 1st hemistich,
'the light has become darkened, you
can no longer see', describes the
natural punishment which consists in
displacing the light of happiness by
the darkness of misery and misfortune (cf. 18: 5-6; 21: 17). The 2nd
hemistich clarifies the catastrophe
further by its reference to flood
(20: 28), 'and a flood of waters
drowns you!' The word שִׁפְעָה here
and in 38: 34 retains its etymological sense of 'flood' which later was
attenuated into that of 'great quantity' (cf. Targ. and Syr.). The *pi'el* of

12   Is not Eloah on high in the heavens?
     And behold the topmost stars, how high they are!
13   You have inferred from this: 'What does God know?
     Shrouded in the cloud, does He judge?

כסה is specially used to depict waters which 'cover', 'submerge' persons and things (Ex 14:28; 15:5, 10; Ps 78:53, etc.). The waters of the flood 'cover' (יכסו) the mountains (Gn 7:19-20). We shall find again the 2nd hemistich in 38:34, a fact which disallows the correction of שפעת into שכבת of G (contra Duhm).

12 G μὴ οὐχὶ ὁ τὰ ὑψηλὰ ναίων ἐφορᾷ (Jerome *nonne qui in excelso manet respicit*) omits אלוה (haplography after הלא) and connects וראה, read as יְרְאֶה, with the 1st hemistich. Next, τοὺς δὲ ὕβρει φερομένους ἐταπείνωσεν is a free interpretation, based on 40:11b (same beginning וראה). Vulg. *annon cogitas quod Deus excelsior caelo sit et super stellarum verticem sublimetur?* (cf. the beginning of v. 11), reading רם instead of רמו. Syr. reads הגביה instead of גבה, vocalises רָאֶה, and interprets רמו by the singular (cf. Vulg.): 'Yes, God has raised the heavens and has seen the rising of the chief of the stars.' Targ. is faithful to the MT and places בְּ before גבה according to the sense.

V. 12 links up with the words which will be attributed to Job in vv. 13 and 14. To suppress it, as Duhm suggests, is to abolish the transition between v. 11 and v. 13. The verse recalls Is 40:26-7, where the prophet says to the Israelites: 'Lift up your eyes on high and see: Who has created them? He who brings out their host by number and calls them all by a name, etc.', concluding: 'Why do you say, O Jacob, and why do you assert, O Israel: My way is hidden from Yahweh and my judgment takes place far from God?' The sequence of ideas is the same,

and Job's conclusion, if we are to believe his antagonist, will be the same as that of the Israelites, namely that God is too exalted, dwelling as He does behind the clouds, to concern Himself with the affairs of humanity. Hence we preserve the text, which will be translated simply: 'Is not Eloah on high in the heavens? And behold the topmost stars, how high they are!' The בְּ of place (cf. Targ.) is omitted before גֹּבַהּ, which becomes a sort of accusative of place (see Gesenius-Kautzsch, § 118g). Cf. the use of מרום in 'lift up your eyes on high' in Is 40:26-7. This parallel passage, where we have וּרְאוּ 'and see', proves that the imperative 'and behold' of the MT is preferable to the 'He sees' of G or the 'He has seen' of Syr. (cf. sup.). The presence of the *dagesh affectuosum* in רָמוּ has the effect of rendering the vowel emphatic (Gesenius-Kautzsch, § 20i). A twofold conclusion may be drawn from the fact that God dwells in the highest heavens: either He must *a fortiori* see the actions of men, or else He is relegated behind the clouds and does not see what is happening on the earth. It is this latter conclusion which Eliphaz imputes to Job and to the 'men of iniquity' (13-15).

13 Vv. 13-16, absent from Sah., marked with asterisk in Jerome and Syro-hex., did not exist in G. The present text is derived from Theod. (cf. Colb.). The translation ὁ ἰσχυρός for אל is in the style of Theod. The lacuna of G may be explained by the mistake of passing from ואמרת (v. 13) to האמרים (v. 17).

The copula of וְאָמַרְתָּ closely joins v. 13 to v. 12: 'and you have said

14   Veiled in clouds He does not see,
       And He walks on the circle of the heavens!'
15   Are you following the path of former times,
       Which was trodden by the men of iniquity,

(consequence drawn from evident facts): What does God know? Shrouded in the cloud, does He judge?' Eliphaz imputes to Job the language of the godless: 'and they say: How does God know and is there knowledge in the Most High?' (Ps 73: 11; cf. Ps 94: 7); 'and they say: Who sees us and knows us?' (Is 29: 15, cf. Ezk 8: 12). The word עֲרָפֶל (38: 9) denotes the thick cloud and darkness in which the God of Israel dwells at the moment of great theophanies (Ex 20: 21; Dt 4: 11; 2 S 22: 10; 1 K 8: 12, etc.). Eliphaz is attacking a whole school of thought by putting this doctrine into the mouth of Job. Albertus Magnus recognised here the principles later maintained by Averroes, while Calmet and Rosenmüller find a similar theory expressed by Lucretius (II. 646ff.):

Omnis enim per se divum natura necessest;
Immortali aevo summa cum pace fruatur,
Semota ab nostris rebus sejunctaque longe.

14   On the text of G, cf. v. 13. The reading ἀποκρυφῆς of G(B) is inferior to ἀποκρυφή (A, א, Syro-hex., Jerome *latibulum*). For ולא יראה, Theod. καὶ οὐχ ὁραθήσεται avoids the anthropomorphism (cf. Syr. 'and they do not see'). Vulg. adds a complement: *nec nostra considerat.* The word חוג is interpreted תקף רומא 'strength of the height' (of the heavens) in Targ.

The 1st hemistich, 'veiled in clouds He does not see', merely reinforces the idea expressed in v. 13b. Between God and the earth are interposed the clouds forming a thick opaque veil which, it is thought, the eye of the Judge cannot pierce. In 9: 24 Job alluded to the judges whose faces are veiled. The word סֵתֶר denotes the veil which covers the face (24: 15), and not the hiding place of Ps 18: 12; cf. the meaning of the verb סתר in 13: 24. Like גבה שמים in v. 12, the phrase הוג שָׁמַיִם 'circle of the heavens' is a kind of accusative of place. It was imagined that, at the moment of creation, God traced a circle (חוג) around the waters (26: 10; Pr 8: 27). This is the circle of the horizon which merges with our circle of the heavens and with the circle of the earth, mentioned in Is 40: 22. God is pictured as walking on the confines of the world, at the spot where the vault of the heavens rests on the earth and the waters. The verb יִתְהַלָּךְ stands at the end of the verse as in 18: 8.

15   On the text of G, cf. v. 13. For מתי־און, Theod. ἄνδρες δίκαιοι, corruption of ἄδικοι (cf. Symm.), preserved in Syro-hex. and Jerome *iniqui*. The reading δίκαιοι is quoted in the margin of Syro-hex. The words ולא־עת of v. 16 are connected by Syr. with the end of v. 15.

V. 16 will allude to the catastrophe of which the מְתֵי־אָוֶן 'men of iniquity' were victims. The phrase 'path of former times' recalls the נתיבות עולם 'ancient paths' (Jer 6: 16) and the שבילי עולם 'ways of old' (Jer 18: 15). In these two texts of Jeremiah it is a question simply of old paths trodden by the fathers of the generation to which the Pro-

16   Men who were carried off before the due time,
      When a river poured itself out over their foundations?

phet is addressing himself. Only the context makes clear whether the path is good or bad. The verb שָׁמַר 'keep', 'adhere to' in the sense of remaining on a certain path, following a given road. In 23:11 Job will say: דְּרָכוּ שָׁמַרְתִּי 'I have kept His way'. The same verb is used in Ps 18:22 when the Psalmist exclaims: 'for I have kept the ways of Yahweh'. Cf. Pr 2:20, 'so that you may walk in the way of good men and keep to (תִּשְׁמֹר) the paths of the righteous'. The word אֹרַח 'road' is used metaphorically, like its synonym דֶּרֶךְ (17:9; 21:31), to imply conduct. Now, in Gn 6:12 we see that 'all flesh had perverted its way on the earth' and in Gn 6:4 there is an allusion to the giants of former times (אֲשֶׁר מֵעוֹלָם). The 'path of former times' is certainly that of the men in the days of the Flood, as will be confirmed by v. 16. Hence it is going directly contrary to the essential meaning of the text to change עוֹלָם into עוֹלִים so as to produce, without any kind of support in the versions, 'the way of evil men' (Chajes, Torczyner, Ball). This correction would make of the 2nd hemistich 'that which was trodden by the men of iniquity', a simple explanation of עוֹלִים. But the verbs דַּרְכוּ and קֻמְּטוּ are in the perfect precisely because the conduct of the wicked and their punishment is a pattern that can be traced back to the remotest times, to the period of the Flood. The מְתֵי־אָוֶן 'men of iniquity', as we had מְתֵי־שָׁוְא 'men of deceit' (11:11); cf. the אַנְשֵׁי־אָוֶן 'men of iniquity' (34:36) and the אַנְשֵׁי־רֶשַׁע 'men of wickedness', parallel to פֹּעֲלֵי־אָוֶן 'evil-doers' in 34:8. The verb דָּרַךְ 'to tread under foot' (24:11) and 'to walk' (9:8), whence דֶּרֶךְ 'road', is chosen deliberately in

order to preserve for the metaphor the full force of its etymological meaning.

16   The transference of וְלֹא־עֵת to v. 15 obliges Syr. to make a complete paraphrase: 'and at the crossing of the river they were held back and they did not remember Him who had created their foundations'. On the text of G, cf. v. 13. Theod. ποταμὸς ἐπιρρέων οἱ θεμέλιοι αὐτῶν regards נָהָר יוּצַק as an attribute of יְסוֹדָם; but Symm. παρασύρει and Vulg. subvertit see in יוּצַק the verb, the subject of which is נָהָר and the complement יְסוֹדָם. On the other hand, Targ. makes of יְסוֹדָם the subject of יוּצַק and sees in נָהָר an accusative of place: 'at the bottom of the river'.

The verb קָמַט is Aramaic rather than Hebrew. It does not recur outside our passage and 16:8, where it had the meaning: 'seize', 'take possession of . . .'. The exact meaning of the root, in the light of the Syriac 'tie together', 'make a bundle of' and the Arabic 'swathe', is to fasten several things together and make a parcel of them to carry away with one. Hence quite naturally the pu'al will mean 'to be carried off', 'bundled away'. Such is the image conveying the idea of the collective punishment which overwhelms the guilty: 'men who were carried off before the due time'. The formula וְלֹא עֵת 'and it was not the time', used to express the idea of a premature death, is readily understood of itself, and it would be superfluous to replace by בְּלֹא עֵת found in some MSS and in Targ. In 15:32 we had בְּלֹא־יוֹמוֹ 'not in its day' (cf. Comm.). The most natural interpretation of the 2nd hemistich must preserve the order of the words, regarding יְסוֹדָם as an accusative of place (cf. vv. 12 and 14): 'A river

17   They said to God: 'Turn aside from us!
      And what will Shaddai do to *us*?'

18   Yet it was He who had filled their houses with prosperity;
      But the counsel of the wicked was far from *Him*.

17   לָנוּ (Syr.); MT: למו.

18   מִמֶּנּוּ (G; cf. Syr.); MT: למי.

poured itself out over their foundations.' The verb יצק has all the meanings of the Latin *fundere* 'shed', 'spill', 'pour out', 'melt' (cf. Comm. on 11:15). The special shade of meaning conveyed by the *pu'al* is 'to be poured out' in Lv 21:10 (oil) and in Ps 45:3 (grace). We have seen, in 4:19, that men had their foundation (יסודם as here) in the dust. The double meaning of עפר 'dust' and 'ground' (cf. 5:6) enables us to recognise here the earth itself in those foundations which were submerged by the pouring out of the waters of the Flood. The river is taken in the broadest sense to denote the 'mass of waters' which 'were on the earth' (Gn 7:6, 10) at the moment of the great catastrophe foreshadowed in the phrases of v. 15 (cf. Comm.). The interpretation of נָהָר as an accusative of result (Gesenius-Kautzsch, § 121d) produces as the meaning: 'their foundation was poured forth, flowed, in a river' (cf. Dillmann, Budde, etc.). But in that case one would have rather 'flowed like water' or 'like a river'. Note that Rashi did not hesitate to see in יסודם the complement of the verb (cf. Symm. and Vulg.).

17 The text of G begins again at v. 17, but the words לאל סור ממנו are omitted, while the 2nd hemistich is twice translated: Κύριος τί ποιήσει ἡμῖν; ἢ τί ἐπάξεται ἡμῖν ὁ Παντοκράτωρ; It can be seen that G read לָנוּ instead of למו (similarly Syr ܠܢ). Vulg. retains למו but paraphrases the 2nd hemistich: *et quasi*

nihil posset facere Omnipotens aestimabant eum.

Vv. 17-18 are cut out by a certain number of moderns (Budde, Beer, Duhm, Gray) on the ground that they form a gloss made up of reminiscences of 21:14-16. It is incontestable that the ideas and expressions are based on that passage. But Eliphaz repeats the very words of Job in order to show that those whose good fortune he has vaunted are the very ones who were victims of the catastrophe. By quoting 21:14a verbally and summing up in a single hemistich 21:15, Eliphaz echoes the typical remarks of the wicked: 'They who said to God: Turn aside from us! and what will Shaddai do to us?' With G and Syr., we adopt the reading לָנוּ instead of למו. Cf. עטיני instead of עטמי in in 21:24. It is quite obviously a question of the godless who wish to eliminate God. Job has been accused of the same attitude (vv. 12-14).

18 Instead of מני, G ἀπ' αὐτοῦ read מִמֶּנּוּ (cf. 21:16b), which Syr. has confused with מהם ܡܢܗܘܢ.

Instead of repeating 21:16a as a mere glossator might have done, Eliphaz declares that the prosperity which the wicked may have enjoyed flowed from God. Note the use of טוב 'good', with the implication of happiness, prosperity (21:13). The 2nd hemistich reproduces 21:16b, in order to emphasise the ingratitude of the wicked: 'but the counsel of the wicked was far from Him.' Read

19   The righteous see it and rejoice;
      And the innocent makes mock of them:
20   'Have not *their possessions* been destroyed?
      And has not a fire consumed their affluence?'

20   יָקָם (Theod.; cf. Vulg., Syr., Targ.); MT: קימנו.

מִמֶּנּוּ with G. The wicked, impiously unaware of blessings which flow from God, continue to live far from Him. In Ezk 11:15 there is an allusion to those who advise keeping aloof from Yahweh. It is the attitude of those who do not wish to know His ways (21:14). On one hand, they ask God to depart from them (v. 17); on the other, they do all they can to escape His action and influence.

19 G ἰδόντες does not necessarily presuppose ראו instead of יראו, which is supported by Targ. יחמון, Syr. ܣܘܢ, Vulg. *videbunt* (contra Duhm). G (B) omits αὐτούς (= למו), which has a place in G(A), Sah., Syro-hex. (with asterisk), Jerome *eos*.

Vv. 19-20 describe the effect produced on the righteous by the catastrophe in which the godless perish. Parallelism between צַדִּיקִים and נָקִי, as between ישרים and נקי (4:7; 17:8). The horizon of Eliphaz is widened. It is no longer merely at the historical moment of the Flood but every time when a similar disaster occurs that the righteous rejoice in what happens to the wicked. The imperfect יִרְאוּ, parallel to יִשְׂמְחוּ and to יִלְעַג, should be retained. The verb לעג as in 9:23; the *hiph'il* in 21:3. The conclusion יִלְעַג־לָמוֹ recurs in Ps 2:4, where it is God who mocks the rebels. The verse is drawn up on the pattern of certain passages of the Psalms, which depict the joy of the righteous in the face of the disasters which overtake the godless. Cf. Ps 52:8, which opens

with ויראו צדיקים 'and the righteous shall see it'; 69:33 'the humble see it and are glad'; 107:42 'upright men see it and are glad'; the same terms are used as here. The 2nd hemistich of Ps 107:42 was almost verbally repeated in 5:16b, which is also by Eliphaz.

20 V. 20, absent from Sah., marked with asterisk in Colb. and Jerome, did not exist in G. The present text is derived from Theod. (cf. Colb.). Syro-hex. has retained the asterisk only before the 2nd hemistich. For קימנו, Theod. ἡ ὑπόστασις αὐτῶν, Vulg. *erectio eorum*, Targ. מלמקום 'from rising', Syr. ܩܘܡܗܘܢ) 'of their hardness'. The versions are thus in agreement in reading the 3rd person plural suffix instead of the 1st person in קימנו.

V. 20 expresses the cry of joy which the righteous raise when they see that the godless perishes; cf. **18:** 21. There is the same movement of thought in Ps 52:8-9, which has already been quoted in connection with v. 19. The opening אִם־לֹא, just as הֲן־לֹא in 21:16, to express the negative question: is it that... not? Those who keep קִימָנוּ regard the *hapax* קים as a kind of abstract noun derived from קום and meaning 'hostility', but used with the connotation of a collective concrete noun: 'our adversaries' (Renan), 'our adversary' (Le Hir). In order to avoid the subtlety which such an interpretation requires, a certain number of moderns read נִכְחֲדוּ קָמֵינוּ. 'Have not our adversaries been cut off?'

21   Reconcile yourself with Him then, and make your peace,
      By this means your *yield* will be good!

21   תְּבוּאָתֶךָ (versions and some MSS); MT: תְּבוּאָתֶךָ.

(Olshausen, Siegfried, Duhm, Ball). But none of the versions has preserved any trace of קמינו, whereas they are unanimous in reading the 3rd person plural suffix. Now, Theod. ἡ ὑπόστασις αὐτῶν read יְקָמָם, as may be seen from Dt 11:6, where G renders היקום by τὴν ὑπόστασιν. Note further that in Gn 7:4, 23, the word היקום is a complement of the verb מחה 'blot out', 'destroy', 'annihilate', the *niph'al* of which has exactly the same meaning as the *niph'al* of כחד, which is used here (cf. 4:7; 15:28). We therefore read יְקָמָם, parallel to יִתְרָם of the 2nd hemistich. Michaelis had already suggested this correction, which has been accepted by Merx, Wright, Graetz, etc. The word יְקוּם, derived from קוּם, *sistere, subsistere*, means 'what exists', 'what has being and substance' (Gn 7:4; 23; Dt 11:6). Here the suffix makes the sense quite clear: 'what is theirs', 'their goods and possessions'. The 1st hemistich, 'have not their possessions been destroyed?', offers an excellent parallel to the 2nd, 'has not a fire consumed their affluence?' On יִתְרָם, cf. 4:21. Punishment by fire is generally coupled with punishment by water (20:26, 28). The verb אכל with אֵשׁ as subject (1:16; 15:34; 20:26). We have pointed out, on v. 19, that the horizon of Eliphaz was no longer limited to the precise catastrophe of v. 16, but extended to the sensational disasters as a whole by which the wicked were struck down and which the righteous applauded.

21   G γενοῦ δὴ σκληρός, ἐὰν ὑπομείνῃς reads עמו ושלם for אם תשלם and interprets in accordance with

9:4b (Ball). For הסכן, Vulg. *acquiesce*, Syr. ܠܐܬܘܣ 'compare thyself', Targ. אלף 'learn'. Syr. connects ושלם with the 2nd hemistich. Instead of תְּבוּאָתֶךָ, G ὁ καρπός σου, Vulg. *habebis fructus*, Targ. and Syr. עללתך 'your fruit', vocalise תְּבוּאָתֶךָ, a reading found in a few manuscripts of the Hebrew text (Ginsburg).

Faithful to his doctrine, Eliphaz prepares to finish his speech with a series of exhortations of an ethical kind, and bearing the stamp of the most materialistic utilitarianism; cf. 5:17-27. The verb סכן 'to be useful, profitable' (v. 2) means in the *hiph'il* 'to be accustomed to . . .' (Nu 22:30), or 'to have experience of . . .' (Ps 139:3). The presence of עם before the complement of the person introduces the shade of meaning 'to become familiar with some one once more', 'to be reconciled with him'. It has been proposed to see in וּשְׁלָם a clause dependent on הַסְכֶּן־נָא, the imperative being used to denote a sure consequence, whence the translation 'and you will be saved' (Renan), 'and you will have peace' (Segond). In that case the verb שלם would have its normal meaning: 'to be safe' (9:4). But we have seen in 2:9 (cf. Comm.) that the juxtaposition of the two imperatives implied a relation of succession rather than one of consequence. Now, the use of בָּהֶם 'by these things', 'by this means', at the beginning of the 2nd hemistich, requires an allusion to two distinct pieces of advice, the one expressed by הסכן, the other by שלם. Hence we must translate ושלם as 'and make peace' with him, the complement עמו referring both to הסכן and שלם. The verb becomes

22   Receive instruction from His mouth,
      And store up His words in your heart.
23   If you return to Shaddai and *humble yourself*,
      If you remove unrighteousness from your tent,

23   וְתֵעָנֶה (G); MT: תבנה.

a sort of denominative of שָׁלוֹם 'peace', without there being any need to replace it by the *hiph'il* וְהַשְׁלֵם, as Budde proposes. The masculine pronoun has a neuter sense in בהם 'by these things'; cf. עליהם 'because of these things' in Ezk 18:26; 33:19. Instead of seeking in תְּבוּאָתֶךָ a complex form, such as would combine both the imperfect תבא and the perfect באת (cf. Gesenius-Kautzsch, § 48d), it is more natural to find in it an incorrect vocalisation of תְּבוּאָתְךָ, which is attested by the versions and by a certain number of manuscripts. The word תְּבוּאָה denotes gain, profit, especially the increase or the yield of the land. It is a very prosaic expression and makes of virtue a matter of sheer bargaining. It is certainly appropriate to the outlook of Eliphaz.

22 G (A, א) ἔκλαβε, Jerome *accipe*, preserve the right translation of קח. It is in error that G (B) reads ἔκβαλε, which is also found in Sah., Syro-hex., Arab. Baud. For וְשִׂים, Syr. ܣܘܡܥ, reading וישם.

The verb לקח 'take', 'receive' instruction; cf. the use of the verb in 4:12 and the meaning of לֶקַח in 11:4 (Comm.). Cf. Pr 4:10, 'Listen, my son, and receive (וקח) my words.' It is from God's own mouth that true doctrine proceeds. Eliphaz is the man of revelations (4:12; 15:11), he likes to invoke divine teaching (5:17, 27). The word תּוֹרָה does not mean specifically the Law but the teaching which God imparts; cf. Is 1:10, where תורת אלהינו 'the teaching of our God' is

parallel to דבר־יהוה 'the word of Yahweh'. In Is 5:24 'the teaching of Yahweh of hosts' corresponds to 'the word of the Holy One of Israel'. The word of God descends from the ear that hears to the heart which is the seat of memory and understanding (*L'Emploi métaphorique*, p. 90). That is why Eliphaz adds: 'and store up His words in your heart'. Cf. Ps 119:11, 'I have hidden Thy word in my heart.'

23 G καὶ ταπεινώσῃς σεαυτόν reads וְתֵעָנֶה instead of תבנה (cf. inf.).

It is clear that the 2nd hemistich depends on the conjunction אִם; cf. 11:14, summed up here in a single clause. The verb תִּבָּנֶה is considered to be a main clause interpolated between two subordinate clauses. In that case what follows is anticipated, for we should have to translate: 'If you return to Shaddai, you will be rehabilitated', while the 2nd hemistich, 'if you put away unrighteousness from your tent', would not find its apodosis until the following verses. G has not invented the reading וְתֵעָנֶה, which is admirably adapted to the context: 'If you return to Shaddai and humble yourself.' This reading deviates less from the MT than וְתִכָּנַע (Merx, Siegfried) and has been generally adopted since Ewald. We lose the support of G if we replace תבנה by ותפנה 'and you turn yourself' (Reiske, Ball). The formula תָּשׁוּב עַד־שַׁדַּי recalls שׁוּב עַד־יהוה 'return to Yahweh', the idiom which conveys the thought of conversion (Dt 4:30; 30:2; Is 19:22, etc.). For the 2nd hemistich, cf. Comm. on 11:14.

24   Then *you will esteem* gold as though it were dust,
      And Ophir *as* the stone of the torrent beds;

24   וְשַׁתָּ לְעָפָר (Theod., Syr.); MT: וְשִׁית־עַל־עָפָר (*kethîb* of the Orientals:

יָשִׁית). — וּכְצוּר (Theod., Vulg., Syr., Targ.); MT: וּבְצוּר.

24 V. 24, absent from Sah., marked with asterisk in Colb., Jerome, and Syro-hex., did not exist in G. The present text is derived from Theod. (cf. Colb.). For וְשִׁית, Theod. θήσῃ and Syr. ܘܣܝܡ 'and you will gather', have read וְשַׁתָּ, while Vulg. *dabit* follows the *kethîb* of the Orientals, יָשִׁית. Targ. וְשׁוּי is in agreement with the MT. For בְצֻר, Vulg. *silicem*, Syr. ܟܣܦ 'silver', Targ. כְּרַךְ תַּקִּיף 'a strong place'. Theod. ἐν πέτρᾳ reads בְצוּר. Instead of וּבְצוּר, a certain number of MSS have וּכְצוּר, a reading followed by Theod. καὶ ὡς πέτρα, Vulg. *et pro silice*, Syr. 'and like the sand of the sea', Targ. וְהֵיךְ טִינָרָא 'and like the rock'. For אוֹפִיר, which has become Σωφείρ in Theod., we have χρυσίου πρωτείου in Symm. But Vulg. connects the word with נְחָלִים, whence *torrentes aureos*. The right interpretation 'gold of Ophir' in Syr. and Targ.

Vv. 24-5 form a whole. One cannot argue from the absence of v. 24 from G in justification of suppressing vv. 24-5 (Bickell, Duhm), for v. 25 does exist in G and v. 24 has not the marks of an addition. The rare word בֶּצֶר, the effect of assonance between בצר and צוּר, עָפָר and אוֹפִיר, are touches which belong to the poet rather than a glossator. Taking the MT as it stands, v. 24 has been translated in various ways: 'You will gather gold in the dust, and the ingots of Ophir among the stones of the torrents' (Le Hir); 'Cast the ingots of gold in the dust, the metals of Ophir amid the stones of the torrents' (Renan). This second trans-lation, which is the more literal, has been widely adopted (cf. *Bible du rabbinat français*, Segond, Crampon, etc.). It is supposed that the converted man throws away his gold, since the Almighty will take the place of riches in his life. The 1st hemistich can well be understood in this sense; but why bring in the stones of the torrents as the place where the treasures might be cast away? We note that the 2nd hemistich has been interpreted as the expression of a comparison by the ancient versions, which read וּכְצוּר instead of וּבְצוּר. Since the word צוּר is used, as in Ps 89: 44, for the construct state of צֻר 'pebble', the meaning of the 2nd hemistich will be simply: 'and Ophir as the stone of the torrents'. It is apparent that this is a well-chosen word to express an object of little value. Its parallel word is עָפָר 'dust'. Now, the verb שִׁית takes sometimes לְ'' sometimes כְּ'' before the complement which denotes that into which a thing is transformed, or to which it is likened (Gesenius-Buhl, s.v., no. 6). A slight correction, supported by Theod. and Syr., yields וְשַׁתָּ לְעָפָר instead of וְשִׁית־עַל־עָפָר. Hence: 'And you will count gold as the dust and Ophir as the stone of the torrent beds.' Gold has no further value. It is God who takes its place. The word בֶּצֶר recurs only in v. 25. For long it has been recognised that it meant 'gold', and it is also the meaning suggested by the parallelism with Ophir, which stands for the gold of Ophir. According to the *Thesaurus* of Gesenius, who adopts the opinion of Abu-l-walid, the word is supposed

25   For Shaddai Himself will be your ingots,
      And heaps of silver for you!

to derive from בצר 'to cut', and to
designate the vein-stones of gold or
silver as they are removed from the
mine. But it is more probable that
the root בצר corresponds to the
Arabic baṣara 'see', 'examine', and
that this root is at the basis of the
enigmatic מבצר as connected with
בחן 'who passes through the crucible' of Jer 6: 27. The exact meaning of בֶּצֶר would then be the gold
as it leaves the crucible; cf. the
Assyrian ṣarpu 'silver', from the
root צרף 'to pass through the crucible'. On Ophir, cf. 28: 16.

25 G βοηθὸς ἀπὸ ἐχθρῶν and Vulg.
contra hostes tuos treat בצריך as the
preposition "ב and צריך 'your adversaries'. Targ. translates by כרך
תוקפך 'your strong place' (cf. v. 24);
same etymology in Syr. 'for your
aid'. For the 2nd hemistich, G gives
the bold paraphrase: καθαρὸν δὲ
ἀποδώσει σε ὥσπερ ἀργύριον πεπυρω-
μένον. Vulg. interprets וכסף תועפות
as *et argentum coacervabitur*. For
תועפות, Syr. ܣܘܥܪܢܐ 'estimates',
probably from שׁעף. Targ. paraphrases: 'and more than money, sublime strength will be granted thee'.
The opening וְהָיָה, as in 8: 7. If
the converted believer can despise
money, it is because the Almighty
takes the place of all the treasures
in the world. Since the word בֶּצֶר
denotes the gold which leaves the
crucible (cf. v. 24), the plural will
denote ingots, as כספים denotes
silver coins (Gn 42: 25, 35) and
בדילים pieces of tin (Is 1: 25). The
2nd hemistich is parallel to בְּצָרֶיךָ,
the suffix of the latter being replaced by the dative לָךְ. It is evident
that כֶּסֶף תוֹעֲפוֹת corresponds to
בצרים. The construction recalls

כסף משנה 'money in double quantity'
meaning 'twice as much' (Gn 43: 12),
the word תועפות having to express
any quantity whatsoever. We find
תועפות in Ps 95: 4, where תועפות
הרים is contrasted with מחקרי ארץ
'the depths of the earth'. The
meaning 'peaks' is demanded by the
context here. On the other hand, in
Nu 23: 22; 24: 8 we find the תועפות
ראם which cannot be anything
else but 'the horns of the wild ox';
cf. these passages with Dt 33: 17.
The association of ideas between
the horns of the wild ox and the
peaks of mountains arises from the
fact that the horns are the upper,
projecting part of the animal (*L'Emploi métaphorique*, pp. 35ff.). It
thus becomes clear that the basic
meaning of תועפות is 'elevated projecting parts', etc. The etymology
suggested by Bochart and Rosenmüller, the root יעף stemming by
metathesis from יפע, Arabic يفع 'to
be elevated, steep', seems to us preferable to that which derives the
word from יעף 'to be fatigued', as
though the suggestion were that the
money has been acquired at the
cost of painful labour (*Thesaurus* of
Gesenius, I, p. 610). In our context,
the תועפות are the heaped-up piles
(*monticelli* 'little mountains') formed
by the accumulation of money. It
would be unwise to change this rare
and difficult word into עופרת 'lead'
(Wright), תועבות 'abominations'
(Voigt), in order to suggest that
money would be base and vile in the
eyes of the convert. To read תורתו
'His law' (Budde), or טוטפות 'phy-
lacteries' (Duhm), is surely to suppose that the copyist and the versions treat very cavalierly words
that are current in pious literature.
As for the attempt to reintroduce
here the Ophir of v. 24 by reading
ואופיר (Beer), it is treating the text

26 For then in Shaddai will be your delight,
And you will lift up your face towards Eloah.
27 You will call upon Him and He will hear you,
And you will acquit yourself of your vows.
28 When you decide on a matter, you will have good success,
And light will shine on your paths!

as though it were desperately corrupt, which is not the case.

26 Syr. omits the 1st hemistich. G avoids the anthropomorphism by paraphrasing the 2nd hemistich: ἀναβλέψας εἰς τὸν οὐρανὸν ἱλαρῶς.

While v. 23b summarised 11:14, v. 26 develops 11:15a where we have כִּי־אָז 'from that time' and תִּשָּׂא פָנֶיךָ 'you will lift up your face'. The 1st hemistich, with scarcely a change, is repeated in 27:10. The *hithpa'el* of עָנַג, to connote 'delight in', takes as its complement עַל־יהוה 'in Yahweh' in Is 58:14; Ps 37:4. Here, as in v. 23a, the author uses the classic formula and does not forget to substitute שַׁדַּי for יהוה. For the logic of vv. 23-6, cf. Is 58:13-14, where the movement of ideas is the same, the conjunction אִם laying down the conditions and the adverb אָז introducing the results, the first of which is precisely 'to delight in Yahweh'.

27 G paraphrases the 2nd hemistich: δώσει δέ σοι ἀποδοῦναι τὰς εὐχάς.

Eliphaz continues his homiletic speech by an exhortation to prayer: cf. 5:1, 8; 8:5-7; 11:13-15. The verb עָתַר in the *qal* (33:26) or the *hiph'il*, as here, with אֶל before the complement of the person, to connote *in-vocare*, 'call upon'. The 2nd hemistich is parallel to יִשְׁמָעֶךָ. The prayer is accompanied by a vow; the very fact of acquitting one's self of a

vow implies that the prayer has been granted. The accepted formula is שָׁלֵם 'complete' or 'consummate' one's vows. Cf. the same sequence of ideas: prayer that has been heard, and performance of vows, in Ps 22:25-6; 61:6-9; 65:2-3.

28 G ἀποκαταστήσει δέ σοι δίαιταν δικαιοσύνης comes from 8:6. It is in error that in Jerome the 2nd hemistich is marked with an asterisk. It is the 1st hemistich which has been replaced by 8:6.

'And you will decide a thing and it will succeed for you', i.e. when you decide on a thing, you will have good success. The two verbs are in the jussive and the first assumes a conditional meaning (Gesenius-Kautzsch, § 159d). Cf the use of the cohortative in 19:18b. The verb גָּזַר 'to cut', in the sense of 'to decide', *de-caedere*. This derivative meaning is fairly frequent in Biblical Aramaic. The word אֹמֶר 'word' here has the shade of meaning 'thing', 'matter', 'affair', exactly like דָּבָר. To denote that a matter is brought to a finish or a project fulfilled, recourse is had to the verb קוּם 'arise', 'stand', 'subsist' (Is 7:7; Pr 15:32). Light, the symbol of happiness, takes the place of the darkness to which Eliphaz made allusion in v. 11. The verb נָגַהּ 'to shine', with אוֹר as subject, as in 18:5. Light will irradiate the paths of Job. The unhappy man had complained of just the fact that God had plunged his paths in darkness (19:8). Cf. the promise of Zophar (11:17).

29   For *He* crushes [   ] pride
      And saves him who lowers his eyes;

29   הִשְׁפִּיל אֶת־ (cf. Vulg.); MT: הִשְׁפִּילוּ וַתֹּאמֶר.

29 Vv. 29-30, absent from Sah., marked by asterisk in Colb. and Syro-hex., did not exist in G. The present text is derived from Theod. (cf. Colb. and Syro-hex.). An incorrect copying of the signs in Jerome has the result that 28b and 29b are marked with asterisk, while 29a is marked by obelus. For כִּי־הִשְׁפִּילוּ, Theod. ὅτι ἐταπείνωσας σεαυτόν, Vulg. *qui enim humiliatus fuerit*, Targ. 'for the generation which is lowly', Syr. 'for him who is lowly'. Theod. remains faithful to the MT for the rest of the 1st hemistich, but we have in Vulg. *erit in gloria*, in Targ. 'will become lofty', Syr. 'he has said that he would rise'. Instead of עֵינַיִם, Targ. בְּסוּרְחָנָא 'in sin' reads עוֹן. The word יוֹשַׁע is vocalised יֹשַׁע by Vulg. *salvabitur* and Syr. ܢܦܪܩ, while Targ. תפרוק reads תּוֹשַׁע.

The 2nd hemistich is very clear: 'and He saves him who lowers his eyes'. The *hapax* שַׁח is derived from שָׁחַח 'abase', 'prostrate one's self', 'crouch' (9:13; 38:40). The שַׁח עֵינַיִם 'lowly as to the eyes' is the humble man who looks to the ground, by contrast with the גְּבַהּ עֵינַיִם 'lofty as to the eyes' (Ps 101:5), who is the proud. In accordance with doxological formulae, it is God who is the subject of יוֹשַׁע. We expect to find an antithesis in the 1st hemistich; but it does not appear in the present text. The plural הִשְׁפִּילוּ is regarded as dependent on דְּרָכֶיךָ 'your ways' of v. 28, and it is supposed that כִּי־הִשְׁפִּילוּ means 'when your ways lead downwards' (Rosenmüller, Dillmann). This is seeking a very curious meaning for the causa-

tive הִשְׁפִּיל 'to abase'. The word דרכיך has played its part in v. 28, where 'on your ways' was part of the classical image: light which irradiates pathways. To go back to this word and make of it the subject of a clause is to go quite contrary to the genius of the language. Such a phenomenon could only be understood if our v. 29 continued the description of v. 28b, and this is not the case. It is just as difficult to justify such translations as the following: 'to bowed heads Thou wilt cry: raise yourselves!' (Le Hir; cf. Crampon), 'humiliated, you will again gain the victory' (Renan), 'if humiliation comes, you will pray for your restoration' (Segond). One fact which is evident is that the verb הִשְׁפִּילוּ contains the counterpart to the closing יוֹשַׁע, and that we should read כִּי־הִשְׁפִּיל. We feel that the humiliation of the proud is foreshadowed in contrast to the salvation of the lowly; cf. 5:11, 'to exalt the lowly (שְׁפָלִים) on high and to raise the afflicted to safety (יֶשַׁע)'. Since the word גֵּוָה (32:17; Jer 13:17) is a contraction of גַּאֲוָה 'loftiness', 'pride', one is tempted to translate וַתֹּאמֶר גֵּוָה by 'and you will say: pride!' or again, 'and you will say: up!' But this interpretation is compatible neither with כִּי־הִשְׁפִּיל nor above all with the 2nd hemistich, which affirms a general proposition without reference to Job. Modern critics, almost unanimous in their reading הִשְׁפִּיל instead of הִשְׁפִּילוּ, are not agreed about the changing of וַתֹּאמֶר. Bickell and Loisy read אֶת־אָמִיר 'the peak', Budde אֱלוֹהַ 'God' (subject of הִשְׁפִּיל), Duhm simply אֹמֶר 'word', 'affair'. In the edition of

30   He delivers the innocent *man*
      And *you will escape* through the cleanness of your hands!

30   אִישׁ MT: אִי. — וְנִצַּלְתָּ; MT: ונמלט.

Kittel, Beer corrects וְתֹאמֶר גֵּוָה to
אֶת־רָם וְגֵאֶה 'the lofty and the proud'.
We think that the true solution consists in eliminating אמר, which is due
to a repetition of the word contained
in v. 28a, and in reading אֶת־ instead
of וֹת. Thus we obtain: 'For He
crushes pride' which is an excellent
parallel to 'and He saves him who
lowers his eyes'.

30   On the text of G, cf. v. 29.
The 1st hemistich is rendered ῥύσεται
ἀθῷον (Theod.), *salvabitur innocens*
(Vulg.); it is clear that such versions
ignore the אִי. The interpretation of
Syr. 'the innocent man will be delivered, wherever he be' connects אִי
with אֵי 'where'. Targ. takes a suggestion from the 2nd hemistich to
translate: 'He who is not pure will
be saved by purity.' For ונמלט,
Theod. καὶ διασώθητι. Instead of
כפיך, Vulg. *manuum suarum* and Syr.
ܐܝܕܘܗܝ 'his hands' read כַּפָּיו.

    This verse again is a *crux inter-
pretum*. Jewish tradition hesitates
about the meaning of אִי־נָקִי. On the
analogy of the proper name אִיכָבוֹד,
Rashi interprets in the sense of
אִין נָקִי 'not innocent', whence the
translations 'He will deliver the
guilty' (Le Hir), 'even the guilty
man will be saved' (Renan), etc.
Ibn-Ezra saw in אִי נָקִי 'the innocent
island' (!). Ibn Parchon proposes to
read נָקִי אֶת or אִישׁ נָקִי. If we take
אִי נָקִי as meaning the guilty, then
the verse will mean that the guilty
man is saved by the cleanness of
Job's hands. This idea is completely
out of accord with the context. When
the expression 'purity of hands',
בַּר יָדַיִם, is used (Ps 18: 21, 25;
2 S 22: 30), the reward always refers
to the one whose hands are clean.
It is certainly thus that the text is

understood by Vulg. and Syr., which
change 'your hands' to 'his hands'.
The interpretation of the 1st hemistich governs that of the second and
vice versa. Now, according to the
doctrine of Job's friends, it is the
innocent man and not the guilty who
is saved by God. If, with Ibn Parchon
(followed by Reiske and Dathe),
we read אִישׁ instead of אִי, we obtain
the general statement: 'He delivers
the innocent man.' The expression
אִישׁ נָקִי is confirmed by אָדָם רֶשַׁע
'the wicked man' of 20: 29. In the
light of what we know about the
theory of retribution, the complement 'by the cleanness of your hands'
must refer to the man who gains salvation, and not to some other represented by the subject of נִמְלָט. Note
that this *niph'al*, after the *pi'el* of the
1st hemistich, is tautological. Ginsburg suggested וְתִמָּלֵט, which suffers
from the same disadvantage. The
word concealed beneath ונמלט is
simply וְנִצַּלְתָּ 'and you will escape'
(*niph'al* of נצל). Thus we obtain:
'and you will escape by the cleanness
of your hands', a consequence of the
1st hemistich: 'He delivers the innocent man.' It is precisely the man
whose hands are clean (נקי) and
whose heart is pure (בר) who ascends
the hill of Yahweh in Ps 24: 4. We
may note among other corrections
the change of אִי to אֵל 'God' (Merx,
Grimme), which ought rather to
have appeared already in v. 29; the
reading יְמַלֵּא תַאֲוַת 'He fulfils the
desire' (Duhm), which is too far
removed from יְמַלֵּט אִי. The change of
כפיך to כפיו (Vulg. Syr.) has been
necessitated by the interpretation
given to נמלט. We have no need to
have recourse to this if we read
נִצַּלְתָּ (contra Duhm, Ball).

CHAPTER 23

1 Then Job spoke and said:
2 Today again my complaint is rebellious,
   My hand lies heavy on my groaning!

Chapters 23-24: 1-17,25   Eighth speech of Job; see Introduction, p. xlv.

23: 2 G καὶ δὴ οἶδα ὅτι ἐκ χειρός μου ἡ ἔλεγξίς ἐστιν replaces היום by ידעתי of v. 3 and reads מידי instead of מרי. Memph. 'with his hand' improves on the translation of G. The word מרי is connected with מרר 'to be bitter' by Vulg. *in amaritudine*, Targ. מריר, Syr. ܡܪܝܪ. G ἡ χεὶρ αὐτοῦ and Syr. ܐܝܕܗ read ידו instead of ידי. Targ. מחתי 'my blow' and Vulg. *manus plagae meae* interpret ידי in the sense of 'the hand which strikes me'.

The expression גַּם־הַיּוֹם 'today again' forms a good introduction to Job's speech. There is no need to suppose that an interval of a few days elapses between the new discussion and the previous one. What Job means is that in spite of his friends' arguments he will not be quiet. The substitution of ידעתי for היום and of מידי for מרי, following G, is a proof of the confidence which Bickell reposes in the Greek version. Loisy adopts these corrections and translates: 'Yes, I know it, my troubles are my own doing.' Job is thus supposed to fall completely into the trap set him by his friends, by confessing that he is himself the author of his own ills. Merx was more cautious, changing מידי to מידו 'with his hand' (following Memph.). But, even if Job attributes his misfortune to God, can one say that his lament also comes from God's hand? The same objection applies to the

change of מרי to משדי 'from Shaddai' timidly suggested by Beer in the Kittel edition. It would be better to read לשדי 'against Shaddai' (Ball), if this correction had the slightest support in the versions. The word מְרִי does not belong to the root מרר 'to be bitter' but to מרה 'to revolt'. The noun is used adjectivally as in Ezk 2: 8 and Pr 17: 11. Hence the meaning of the 1st hemistich will be simply: 'Today again my complaint is rebellious', i.e. I cannot repress it. The translation 'is bitter' (Driver-Gray) would imply מר or מריר instead of מרי (cf. Vulg., Targ., Syr.). But it is not easy to see how there should have been substituted for the easy term a word which would be more difficult to explain. Furthermore, the 2nd hemistich seems to confirm our interpretation of the 1st. The clause means literally 'my hand weighs on my groaning'. Job would like to suppress his groaning, but the hand which checks his sobs seems to weigh too heavily. We are getting astray from the literal sense if we assign to יָדִי 'my hand' the meaning of 'my sorrow', so as to interpret: 'my groans do not match my sorrow' (Le Hir, Crampon; cf. Renan). The preposition מִן and not עַל would be required if the author's intention had been to say that the suffering is heavier than the groaning. Still less probable is the change from ידי to ידו 'His hand' (following

343

3   Oh that I knew where I might find Him,
    That I might come to His dwelling!
4   I would draw up before Him a suit,
    And would fill my mouth with arguments;

G and Syr.), recommended by the moderns (Ewald, Merx, Dillmann, Duhm, etc.). In that case it would be the hand of God which weighs 'on the groaning' of Job. But the hand of God is heavy on a person but not on an experience of suffering. Duhm does not hesitate to do violence to the text, in order to give to 'on my groaning' the meaning of 'on myself who am groaning', as is apparent from his comment: 'on his groaning', 'on him, the one who groans'. The word אֲנָחָתִי retains its normal sense, as in 3: 24.

3 G τίς δ' ἄρα γνοίη ὅτι εὕροιμι αὐτόν fuses יתן and ידעתי, but Jerome *quid dabit* (Gall. adds *mihi*) *scire me et invenire eum* returns to the MT. The word ידעתי is omitted by Syr., which makes אבוא dependent on ואמצאהו 'Who then will bring it about that I might find means of gaining access to His dwelling?' For עד־תכונתו, G εἰς τέλος, but Jerome *usque ad solium ejus*: cf. Symm. ἕως τῆς ἕδρας αὐτοῦ and Vulg. *usque ad solium ejus*. In Targ. עד מדור בית מוקדשיה 'even to the place where His sanctuary lies'; in Syr. ܟܡܐ ܠܡܕܘܪܗ 'even to His dwelling place'.

The question מי־יתן 'who will grant?' governs the imperfect (6: 8; 13: 5; 14: 13), or the infinitive (11: 5), or the imperfect preceded by the copulative *waw* (19: 23). But the perfect ידע is often used with the meaning of the present (9: 2; 10: 13; cf. Gesenius-Kautzsch, § 106g), which enables us to make it directly dependent on מי־יתן. The expression ידעתי ואמצאהו co-ordinates two verbs, the second of which clarifies

the first: 'that I might know and that I might find Him', i.e. 'that I might know where to find Him'. Cf. Gn 47:6, וְאִם־יָדַעְתָּ וְיֶשׁ־בָּם 'and if you know that there are among them'. The verb אבוא also depends on מי־יתן; cf. 6: 8a. The word תְּכוּנָה is interpreted by Rashi as מכון כסאו 'the place of His throne' (cf. Targ., Symm., and Vulg., sup.). In Ezk 43: 11 the meaning of תכונה is 'arrangement', 'structure', while in Nah 2: 10 it alludes to a collection or a treasure. The verb כון has in fact in the *po'lel* and the *hiph'il* the meaning: 'prepare', 'arrange', 'set up', especially a seat (29: 7), a throne (Ps 9: 8; 103: 19), a sanctuary (Ex 15: 17). The abstract תכונה will mean the installation and, by extension, the residence (cf. Syr.), which, however, does not exclude the connotations accepted in Ezk and Nah. The idea common to these various passages is that of a special organisation or disposition, whether with reference to a building, or to precious objects, or to a dwelling place. To change תכונתו into מכונתו 'His place' (Ehrlich) is to change the uncommon word into something commonplace.

4 Syr. and Targ. faithfully copy the MT and render the Hebrew words by Aramaic ones. G(B) ἐμαυτοῦ is a corruption of ἐπ' αὐτοῦ (לפניו) preserved in G(A). Symm. ἔμπροσθεν αὐτοῦ is reflected in Jerome *coram eo* and the margin of Syro-hex. 'before Him'. For אמלא, G(B) ἐμπλῆσαι, G(A) ἐμπλήσει, but Syro-hex. ܐܡܠܐ and Jerome *impleam* return to the MT; cf. ἐμπλήσω of G (א^c·a).

The cohortatives of vv. 4-5 have

5　　I would know the words with which He would answer me,
　　　And I would understand what He would say to me!

6　　Is it by bringing to bear great might that He would dispute
　　　　with me?
　　　No! He would only have to *listen* to me!

6　וְיִשְׁמַע ; MT: יָשִׂם .

the meaning of conditionals, as in 16:4; 19:18. The verb עָרַךְ with מִשְׁפָּט as complement, in the sense of 'prepare', 'draw up' a lawsuit (13:18). The use of the *pi'el* of מלא with a double accusative: 'I would fill my mouth with arguments' (cf. 3:15; 22:18 for the construction). On the word תּוֹכָחוֹת cf. 5:17 and 13:6.

5　G(B) ἰάματα (Sah., Memph.) for מלים is a corruption of ῥήματα preserved in G (A, אᶜ·ᵃ), Syro-hex., and Jerome *causationes*. The relative is added before יַעֲנֵנִי by G, Vulg., Targ., while Syr. interprets מלים as though it were simply מה : 'I would know what He would answer me.'

Job wishes to hold a discussion with God. The friends are not wanted in this discussion (13:5-13). God will be able to declare His complaints and reply to the arguments of Job (13:22); 'I would know the words with which He would answer me!' The verb בִּין 'to understand' (13:1) is set in parallelism with יָדַע as in 15:9.

6　For the ה of the opening, G(B) καί, but G(A) καὶ εἰ, which is found again in the margin of Syro-hex., and is reflected in the *an* of Jerome. This interrogative is omitted by Syr. and interpreted by *nolo* in Vulg. The versions have added the direct complement of יָשִׂם , whence G εἶτα ἐν ἀπειλῇ μοι οὐ χρήσεται, Vulg. *nec magnitudinis suae mole me premat*, Syr. 'and if He does not impose fear on me', Targ. 'but no!

He will bring a suit against me'.

V. 6 is generally interpreted in the sense of Job's persuading himself that he will not have to fear too great a display of strength on the part of God. The 2nd hemistich is made antithetic to the 1st by understanding לִבּוֹ 'his heart' (which Duhm inserts into the text) after יָשִׂם , and such translations are given as: 'Would He oppose to me the weight of His greatness? No, rather He would grant me a propitious look!' (Le Hir); 'Would He cast the weight of His might into His argument with me? No, but He would grant me some attention' (*Bible du rabbinat français*). How can Job know that God will not try to intimidate him? Besides, as Ehrlich points out, the verb שִׂים with לֵב as complement, either explicit or implicit, would require "אֶל or עַל and not "בְּ before the person who is the object of the attention. Must we conclude with Ehrlich that the text of the 2nd hemistich is irremediably corrupt? A very slight correction, which we had hit upon, independently of Graetz, seems to us to solve all difficulties. It consists in reading וְיִשְׁמַע instead of יָשִׂם . The verb שמע with "בְּ before the complement often means 'to listen' (37:2). The particle אַךְ governs not only הוּא , but the whole clause; cf. 14:22. The 2nd hemistich will therefore mean: 'No! He would only have to listen to me!' Cf. Gn 27:13b. By this very fact, the discussion will not be arduous for God, who will be able to content Himself with remaining

7   *He would observe* the upright man who argues with Him,
       And I would be for ever delivered from my Judge.

7 יִשְׁמֹר:; MT: שָׁם.

passive. Then the opening interrogation bears essentially on בְּרָב־כֹּחַ,
an expression which recurs in Ps
33: 16 to mean 'with great might'.
Job invites his Judge to show Himself to him, and encourages Him to
initiate the proceedings. It will be
a trifling matter, since Job will go to
the trouble of furnishing all the
eloquence (v. 7), and God will only
have to listen. There is no need for
a display of strength for this purpose!
Job began by supposing that God
might answer him (v. 5). He now
corrects himself: God would not
even need to speak! The verb ריב
with עם before the person with
whom one argues (9: 3; 13: 19).

7 G ἀλήθεια γὰρ καὶ ἔλεγχος omits
שָׁם and reads ונכח instead of נוכח.
Vulg. *proponat aequitatem contra me*
connects שָׁם with the verb שׂוּם,
reads נֹכַח 'against' and עמי instead
of עמו. Targ. also reads עמי. Instead
of מִשְׁפָּטִי, G τὸ κρίμα μου and Vulg.
judicium meum vocalise מִשְׁפָּטְ. Syr.
paraphrases the whole verse: 'There,
in equity, I would come to judgment
with Him, and I would be justified
and would escape in the judgment.'
As it stands, the 1st hemistich
means 'there a righteous man discussing with Him'. The *niph'al* of
יכח (cf. the meanings of the *hiph'il*
in 5: 17) means 'to discuss' (Is 1: 18).
What is curious in the present text
is the presence of the present participle. Even Ben Yehuda (*Thesaurus*
s.v. יכח) postulates a verb used in a
personal mode. The translations do
the same: 'then the righteous man
would discuss with Him' (Le Hir);
'He would recognise that it is a
righteous man defending himself
against Him' (Renan). The *Bible du*

rabbinat français interprets נוֹכָח in
the sense of נֹכַח 'before', 'in the presence of', whence: 'it is a righteous
man who would then be found face
to face with Him'. The conditional
construction 'who would be found'
seems to be added to satisfy the
exigencies of the logic. Fried.
Delitzsch, followed by Hontheim,
reads שָׂם instead of שָׁם and וְנֹכַח
(cf. G) instead of נוכח, which yields
the meaning: 'He has set right and
justice with Him', a general affirmation which would be suited to a
doxology but far less to our context.
Beer tries to make use of this
change by substituting עמו for עִמָּדִי
'with me' (Vulg. Targ.). Torczyner
points out very truly that we should
require עִמָּדִי, for we find עמי only
in 10: 17, where the poet has desired
to avoid the repetition of עִמָּדִי,
which is used throughout the Book
of Job. Let us note first that 'a
righteous man discussing with Him'
may very well be understood as
referring to Job, who has just been
represented by the suffix of בִי (v. 6),
and who will again speak in the 1st
person in the 2nd hemistich. In
13: 16 Job has declared that a
godless man would not dare to
present himself before the tribunal
of God. This is not the situation
however in regard to the upright
man. The latter has nothing to
fear. We suppose that a *yod* has
fallen out, as a result of haplography,
after בִי of v. 6 and we restore
יִשְׁמֹר to take the place of שָׁם; cf.
או coming from אוֹר in 22: 11. God
'would observe the upright man
who argues with Him', a consequence of v. 6b. The 2nd hemistich
gives the final outcome of the law-

8   If I go to the east, He is not there,
       And to the west, I perceive Him not;
9   In the north *I have sought Him* and have not seen Him,
       I return to the south and again fail to find Him!

9   בְּקַשְׁתִּיו (Syr.); MT: בעשתו. — אֶעֱטֹף (Vulg., Syr.); MT: יעטף.

suit that has been initiated: 'and I would be for ever delivered from my Judge'. The *pi'el* of פלט, used without a direct complement (21: 10b), implies 'my soul', 'myself', and thus becomes a real reflexive verb 'to be delivered', 'to deliver one's self'; cf. the *pi'el* of מלט in 20: 20. The meaning offers no difficulty. Job wishes to be finished with his Judge and desires to have an encounter with Him once for all. Vain hope (vv. 8-9)! The change of vocalisation מִשְׁפָּטִי 'my judgment' (G, Vulg.) instead of מִשְׁפָטִי 'from my Judge' does not improve the text. It is only by pure hypothesis that to 'I would deliver my judgment' is assigned the meaning 'I would win my lawsuit' (contra Duhm).

8 The *kethîb* of the Orientals וְאֵינִי, instead of וְאֵינֶנּוּ, and also G καὶ οὐκ ἔτι εἰμί (Jerome *ultra non ero*) are dogmatic corrections designed to safeguard the doctrine of God's omnipresence. Syr. 'I do not know' interprets in the light of the context. Vulg. *non apparet* is a Latinism.

God eludes Job's search for Him. In whatever direction the latter looks, he cannot find his Judge. Vv. 8-9 mention the four points of the compass consistently with the orientation of the ancients. Before one (קֶדֶם) is the east; behind (אָחוֹר) the west; to the left (שְׂמֹאול) the north; to the right (יָמִין) the south. The Arabs still call the south *yamîn* and the north *šamâl*. The phrases are modelled exactly on the

pattern of those in 9: 11, where too we find the וְלֹא־אָבִין לוֹ of our 2nd hemistich. Must we conclude that vv. 8-9 are only 'empty and insignificant repetitions of 9: 11-12' (Duhm)? But it is no longer the same situation that is envisaged. In 9: 11-12 Job dwelt on the perfections of God which make Him inaccessible to the soundings of human knowledge. Here Job is the accused man seeking his Judge, to secure a hearing for his justification. To claim, with a certain number of modern critics (Budde, Siegfried, Volz, Gray, Ball), that vv. 8-9 separate v. 10 from v. 7 and have been interpolated, is to forget that the strophe corresponds to the desire expressed in v. 3, and that vv. 4-7 have merely given the reason for this desire. V. 10 will give the reason why God eludes such an encounter: 'for He knows', etc. There is some pedantry in the irony of Duhm: 'I go to the east, to the west — what does that mean? Will any man seek God in this fashion?' Form אֶהֱלֹךְ as in 16: 22.

9 V. 9, absent from Sah., marked with asterisk in Colb., Jerome, and (at least the 2nd hemistich) in Syro-hex., did not exist in G. The present text derives from Theod. (cf. Colb. and Syro-hex.). Targ. recognises the points of the compass in שמאול and ימין, translated צפונא 'north' and דרומא 'south', while the other versions render literally as the left and the right. Syr. ܒܥܝܬ 'I have sought' read בְּקַשְׁתִּי, which is preferable to בעשתו (cf. inf.). Similarly ܐܥܛܦ

10   For He knows *my* going and my *staying*,
      If He passes me through the crucible, I emerge as gold;

10   דַּרְכִּי וְעָמְדִי (Syr.); MT: דרך עמדי.

of Syr. and *si me vertam* of Vulg.
have read אעטף, which is preferable
to the יעטף of the MT (cf. inf.).

If בַּעֲשֹׁתוֹ of the MT is retained,
the translation becomes: 'If He turns
to the north' (Le Hir), 'If He exercises His power in the north' (Renan),
'if He is occupied in the north'
(Segond); literally, when He acts
in the north! But in that case the
style of vv. 8-9, where the verbs are
in the 1st person, is interrupted by
the prosaic 'when He acts'. A slight
modification, however, suggested by
Syr., secures the continuity of the
poetic style: בִּקַּשְׁתִּיו (instead of
בעשתו) 'I have sought Him'. Cf.
Ca 3:2, בקשתיו ולא מצאתיו 'I have
sought him and have not found
him'. The apocopated form אָחַז
(from חזה 'see') instead of a simple
imperfect; cf. יהי in 18:12. The verb
יַעֲטֹף would mean 'He covers Himself' as with a mantle (Ps 65:14;
73:6). The point would be that God
hides Himself in the south! The
Syriac ܥܛܦ means 'to return', and
this meaning derives from that of
'bend', 'bow', attested by the Arabic
عطف; cf. *declinare* in Latin. If we
read אֶעֱטֹף with Syr. and Vulg. we
obtain: 'I return to the south and
do not perceive Him.' The parallelism is excellent and the sentence
forms a fitting close to the preceding description.

10 For דרך עמדי, G ὁδόν μου
and Vulg. *viam meam*. But Syr.
דרכי ועמדי ܘܣܘܡܝ read
(cf. inf.). G transfers אצא to v. 11,
which causes the disappearance of
אחזה רגלי. Vulg. *quod per ignem
transit* changes אצא to יצא and completes the meaning.

V. 10 explains why God eludes the
searches of Job. The truth is that
God knows all things, and by that
very fact He knows that Job is not
guilty. Hence it is needless to initiate
a regular suit. עָמָדִי 'with me' is
generally regarded as a paraphrase
of the simple suffix, whence the
interpretation of דֶּרֶךְ עָמְדִי as 'my
way' (G, Vulg.), 'my paths' (Le
Hir), 'my conscience' (Renan), 'the
conduct that I adopt' (*Bible du
rabbinat français*). But our verse
strangely reminds us of the opening
of Ps 139: 'Yahweh, Thou hast
searched me and known me! Thou
knowest when I sit down and rise
up. Thou hast understood my
thought from afar, Thou hast measured my going and my resting, and
Thou hast known thoroughly all my
deeds' (vv. 1-3). In this Psalm the
expression כָּל־דְּרָכַי 'all my ways',
'all my deeds' is explained by a series
of antitheses: שבתי וקומי 'my sitting
down and my standing up', ארחי
ורבעי 'my walking and my resting',
literally 'my path and my lying
down'. And it is just such an antithesis which Syr. suggests in our
passage. We do not hesitate to read,
with Houbigant, דַּרְכִּי וְעָמְדִי, which
obviously means 'my going and my
staying'. The Hebrew text is thus
hardly changed at all, and the support of Syr. is of great value. The
word דֶּרֶךְ 'path', 'journey' here
assumes the meaning of 'walking',
just as אָרְחִי 'my path' in Ps 139:3
takes on the meaning of 'my going'.
As for עמדי, it is the infinitive of
עמד 'to stand', 'to remain standing',
'to stay' (14:2), the 1st person singular suffix being affixed as in
Jer 18:20. The word corresponds to
שבתי 'my sitting down' and to רבעי

11   My foot has held fast to His step,
      I have kept His way and have not turned aside;
12   I have not departed from the precept of His lips,
      And the words of His mouth have I hidden *in my bosom*.

12 בְּחֻקִּי (G, Vulg.); MT: מֵחֻקִּי.

'my lying down' of Ps 139. The clarification of עמדי frees us from the need to have recourse to the change to עבדו 'his servant' (contra Ehrlich), or to עמדתי '(the way in which) I go' (contra Budde). In the 2nd hemistich the verb בחן 'to pass through the crucible' (cf. Comm. on 7:18) leads to the comparison 'like gold'. The construction of the perfect with the imperfect marks the priority of one action in relation to another, even if the latter is present or future; cf. 7:20a; 21:31b.

11 G ἐξελεύσομαι δὲ ἐν ἐντάλμασιν αὐτοῦ brings in at this point אצא of v. 10, and drops אחזה רגלי. These latter words are restored in Jerome *tenuit pes meus* (with asterisk) and in the margin of Syro-hex., following Theod. (cf. Colb.) ἐκράτησεν ὁ πούς μου. Syr. transfers to v. 12 the phrase ולא־אט, to follow מחקו (instead of מחקי).

The form אַשֻׁרוֹ 'His step' as in Pr 14:15. We shall have אַשֻׁרִי 'my step' in 31:7. The verb אחז with ב" before the complement, to mean 'seize' (18:9) and 'hold fast to' (Ec 2:3; 7:18). The term דַּרְכּוֹ 'His way' means the way marked out by God. The verb שמר 'to keep', i.e. to follow a path faithfully, just as in 22:15. The *hiph'il* of נטה with the sense of 'deviate' (cf. Comm. on 9:8). The apocopated form אָט, as we had אָחֵז in v. 9. Cf. 31:7, where we find the words of our verse recurring. The continuity of the metaphor is noteworthy: God walks on a certain way, Job follows faithfully His steps, adhering to the

route marked out, and deviating neither to the right nor the left.

12 G ἀπὸ ἐνταλμάτων αὐτοῦ and Vulg. *a mandatis labiorum ejus* have vocalised מצות as a plural. The omission of שפתיו in G is due to a theological scruple, like the omission of פיו in ῥήματα αὐτοῦ. Duhm is inconsistent in deleting 'the lips' and leaving 'the mouth'.' G(A) adds ἵνα μὴ ἀποθάνω after the 1st hemistich. This reading arises perhaps from a ולא אמות instead of ולא אמיש. It figures in Syro-hex. Syr. read מחקו for מחקי and brought in here ולא־אט of v. 11. Instead of מחקי, G ἐν δὲ κόλπῳ μου and Vulg. *et in sinu meo* read בְּחֻקִּי, which is excellent (cf. inf.).

The words מִצְוַת שְׂפָתָיו 'the precept of His lips' denote the law which God commands men to obey. The equivalence between התורה 'the law' and המצוה 'the precept' (Ex 24:12; Jos 22:5; 2 K 17:34) enables us to retain the singular. Note that, in 22:22, we have parallelism between the singular תּוֹרָה and the plural אֲמָרָיו 'His words'. Thus it is not necessary to replace מִצְוַת by the plural מִצְוֹת, as is done by Merx and Siegfried (following G and Vulg.). The author is using a construction familiar to him by leaving within the body of the sentence the copula which should be placed first (4:6; 10:8; 14:7, 20, etc.). As a result, the words מצות שפתיו, separated from their immediate context, constitute a *casus pendens* and one can neglect the preposition מן by which they should be preceded. The sense is not in doubt: 'And I did not depart from

13   But He *has made His choice* and who is to prevent Him?
      What His soul has desired He will perform,

14   For He accomplishes *His* decree,
      And many such things lie in His thought!

13   בָּחַר; MT: באחד.

14   חָקוֹ (Vulg., Syr.); MT: חקי.

the precept of His lips.' The verb מוש or מיש 'to move' with the implication 'depart from'; cf. the use of סור in 2 S 22: 23b. It needs much good will to assign to מֵחֻקִּי the meaning 'religiously' (Le Hir) and to infer this meaning from a translation *ex lege mihi praestituta*. Some propose to take מחקי as meaning 'more than my own law', whence: 'I have made my own will subservient to the words of His mouth' (Segond, Crampon). But צָפַנְתִּי means 'I have hidden' or 'I have stored away'. These artificial interpretations indicate that the text is corrupt. The right reading is preserved in G and Vulg. (cf. sup.). If we read בְּחֻקִּי we obtain: 'I have hidden in my bosom the words of His mouth', as one hides a treasure. We have found בְּחֻקִּי in 19: 27. The formula בלבי צפנתי אמרתך 'in my heart I have hidden Thy word', from Ps 119: 11, removes all hesitation about the original text. Job alludes to the injunction of Eliphaz, who told him (22: 22): 'Receive instruction from His mouth, and store up His words in your heart!' For long he has practised this advice.

13 G εἰ δὲ καὶ αὐτὸς ἔκρινεν οὕτως paraphrases והוא באחד. Targ. ואין חוא יחידאי 'and if he is unique' and Vulg. *ipse enim solus est* regard the ב'' of באחד as a *bêth essentiae*, while Syr. merges the two members of the 1st hemistich to obtain the result: 'and what will *He* answer me to any single one of these things?' For ומי ישיבנו, Vulg. *et nemo avertere potest cogitationem ejus*. G renders ונפשו by ὃ γὰρ αὐτός. Syr. interprets

אותה as a 1st person sing. 'that I may please His soul'.

Those who maintain the reading בְּאֶחָד interpret וְהוּא באחד as 'and He is in one', i.e. fixed in a single purpose, or else 'and He is sole', following the implication of the *bêth essentiae* (cf. Targ. and Vulg.). Whence the translations: 'But He has decided and who can make Him revoke His decision?' (Renan); 'But He alone is master and who can stop Him?' (Le Hir). If now we compare with 9: 12a and 11: 10b, two hemistichs ending with ומי ישיבנו 'and who will prevent Him', we note that the first part of the sentence must include a hypothesis expressed by a verb. The solution, proposed both by Beer and Duhm, and accepted by most moderns, is suggested by Ps 132: 13, where the verb אִוָּה (used in our 2nd hemistich) has as a parallel בָּחַר. Read therefore בָּחַר instead of the inexplicable באחד. The verb בחר 'choose', 'prefer' (7: 15; 9: 14; 15: 5) is used with the implication of deciding in favour of one course rather than another. God acts from personal considerations and not in accordance with the logic to which Job's friends would restrict Him. The 2nd hemistich, 'and His soul has desired and He has performed it', i.e. what His soul has desired He will do. The formula נַפְשׁוֹ אִוְּתָה as in Mic 7: 1; Pr 21: 10. Note the use of נפש 'His soul' not only to mean 'Himself', but also because in the נֶפֶשׁ resides the strength of passion and desire.

14 The text of G for v. 14 is an initial translation of v. 15 (cf. v. 15).

15   That is why, because of Him, I am afraid;
       I ponder and I fear Him;
16   God has softened my heart,
       And Shaddai has made me afraid;

V. 14 was thus omitted in G. Instead of ישלים, Syr. اهلم has read אשלים. Vulg. *voluntatem suam* and Syr. ممحده 'His pact' have maintained the correct reading חֻקּוֹ (cf. inf.).

The 1st hemistich has been translated: 'and so He will accomplish what He has decreed concerning me' (Renan), or 'He will accomplish His designs with regard to me' (Segond). But חֻקִּי 'my decree' can hardly be said to mean the decree which concerns my life. In v. 13 Job stressed the point that God merely does as He pleases and fulfils His most capricious desires. The reading חֻקּוֹ, attested by Syr. and Vulg., yields a meaning which is in perfect harmony with the context: 'For He accomplishes His decree'. It is God who decides and who performs. Cf. the use of יַשְׁלִים in reference to God in Is 44: 26, 28. The closing line is a petulant sally. The words כָּהֵנָּה רַבּוֹת are equivalent to כאלה רבות of 16: 2. The expression עמו 'with Him' to mean 'in His thought' (10: 13; 27: 11). Duhm declares that the verse is not authentic or that it has been irretrievably corrupted. One cannot argue from G to suppress v. 14, which forms a natural sequel to v. 13 and a transition to v. 15. Job knows that his conduct, perfect as it is (10-12), does not influence God's attitude with regard to him. The changing of כִּי at the opening into כֵן 'thus' (Siegfried, Budde), or to לכֵן (Ley), is hardly suggested by the context itself.

15 Double translation of v. 15 in G. The first, constituting v. 14, is the earlier one. The second (v. 15), absent from Sah., marked with asterisk in Colb., Cod. 248, Jerome, and Syro-hex., is attributed to Theod. in Syro-hex., to Theod. and to Aq. in Colb. and Cod. 248. Both translations follow fairly closely the Hebrew text; but G renders ואפחד ממנו by ἐφρόντισα αὐτοῦ, less literal than καὶ πτοηθήσομαι ἐξ αὐτοῦ of Theod.

The opening עַל־כֵּן 'that is why' answers the argument of Eliphaz in 22: 10, where עַל־כֵּן was used to imply that Job's ills were the consequence of a series of crimes. It is not because of his sins that Job has been struck down. He is conscious of having walked in the right way (vv. 10-12). It is the pleasure of God which is the sole source of what is happening to him (vv. 13:14). There is a mystery here! And this mystery is frightening: 'That is why, because of Him, I am afraid; I ponder and I fear Him.' The *niph'al* of בהל, as in 4: 5; 21: 6. We shall have the *hiph'il* in v. 16. For the 2nd hemistich, 'I ponder and I fear Him', cf. 21:6a, 'for, when I think of it, I am afraid'. The verb התבונן 'reflect', 'ponder' (cf. Comm. on 11: 11).

16 Syr. ؤهسه 'and my head' reads וראשי instead of ושדי.

'And God has softened my heart', in consequence of the fear He arouses in me. The soft heart expresses lack of courage, fear (Dt 20: 3, 8; Is 7: 4, etc.); cf. *L'Emploi métaphorique*, p. 120. V. 16 merely emphasises v. 15, by drawing out the cause of the effects which have been described. The *hiph'il* of בהל (of which we had the *niph'al* in v. 15) has a similar meaning to the *pi'el* of

17   [   ] I have not been silent because of darkness,
     And because of the gloom which has veiled my face!

17   Omit כִּי.

22: 10. The subject of the *pi'el* of
בהל was פַּחַד 'fear' in 22: 10; we
had the verb פחד in v. 15.

17 G οὐ γὰρ ᾔδειν ὅτι ἐπελεύσεταί
μοι σκότος (A γνόφος) is a decided
deviation from the text. Merx, however, uses G in order to reconstitute
a sentence in which there remains
from the MT only כִּי־לֹא and חשֶׁךָ.
The word נצמתי is rendered ܐܶܬܬܰܟ݂ܺܝܬ
'I have been silent' in Syr. (cf. the
meaning of the Arabic ﺻﻤﺖ). Vulg.
nec faciem meam operuit caligo repeats
the negative in the 2nd hemistich.
For וּמִפְּנֵי G(B, א) πρὸ προσώπου δέ
μου (Jerome *et ante faciem meam*),
but G(B) πρόσωπον δέ μου (Sah.,
Eth., Arab. Baud.).
    V. 17 is a *crux interpretum*. From
the literal meaning: 'for I have not
been destroyed because of (or 'in
face of') darkness, and because of
my face (which) gloom has veiled',
such translations as the following
have been extracted: 'For it is not
calamity which amazes me, nor the
darkness with which my face is
veiled' (Le Hir; cf. Crampon); 'For
He has not taken me away before the
coming of the days of gloom, He has
not preserved me from darkness'
(Renan); 'For it is not darkness
which destroys me, it is not the gloom
with which I am overshadowed'
(Segond). The *Bible du rabbinat
français*, inspired by the exegesis of
Rashi, translates: 'Since, (on the
one hand) He has not destroyed me
by the darkness which overwhelms
me, and (on the other hand) He has
not willed to shelter me from this
thick darkness'. The general tendency is to oppose God to misfortune, as though Job's depression of
spirit were the effect of God's action
rather than of the calamity which

strikes him down (cf. Dillmann,
Ehrlich, etc.). Note that מִפְּנֵי־חשֶׁךָ
recurs in 37: 19 at the end of a negative sentence and means 'because of
darkness'. Now, we know that darkness symbolises misfortune. Job has
just said that it is because of God
that he is frightened (v. 15), that it
is God who has softened his heart
(v. 16). In 6: 17 the *niph'al* of צמת
had the meaning of 'dry up'. On the
plane of the mind and heart 'to
become dry' means to cease to speak,
to be silent, and it is the fact that in
Arabic and Aramaic (cf. Syr. above),
the root צמת means 'to be silent'.
If we admit that the opening כי is a
faulty dittograph of the preceding
ני, we shall be able to translate: 'I
have not been silent because of
darkness.' Misfortune has compelled
the sufferer to open his mouth and
to allow his bitter laments to be
heard. The meaning thus obtained
frees us from the need to change the
text as is done by most of the
moderns, who delete לֹא or כִּי־לֹא
(cf. Bickell, Budde, Beer, etc.), so
as to translate: 'I have been destroyed in consequence of darkness.'
Siegfried changes נִצְמַתִּי to נצפנתי
'I have hidden myself', while Fried.
Delitzsch postulates for נצמתי the
meaning 'I have fled'. The 2nd hemistich is easily understandable: 'and
because of my face which darkness
has veiled', a hypallage for 'because
of darkness which has veiled my
face'. This is an explanation, or
rather a development of מפני חשֶׁךָ
'because of darkness'. It is unnecessary to read וּפְנֵי instead of וּמִפְּנֵי,
for the reading of G(A) may arise
from haplography, the preposition
πρό having dropped out before
προσώπου (contra Bickell, Budde,
etc.).

CHAPTER 24

1   Why have times [   ] been hidden from Shaddai?
And why have those who know Him not seen His days?

1 Omit לֹא (G).

24: **1** G διὰ τί δὲ Κύριον ἔλαθον ὧραι did not have the לֹא of the 1st hemistich. The 2nd hemistich is lacking in G; but at the beginning of v. 2 G has ἀσεβεῖς δέ (A ἀσεβεῖς ἄνδρες), which comes from רְשָׁעִים and is necessary to the text (cf. inf.). G probably skipped from וִידְעֵי to רשעים. Later לֹא־חָזוּ יָמָיו was restored, whence Cod. 249 ἀσεβεῖς δὲ οὐκ εἶδον ἡμέρας αὐτοῦ, Jerome *impii autem nescierunt dies ejus* (with asterisk before *nescierunt*). Syro-hex. relegates to the margin the translation of οὐκ εἶδον ἡμέρας αὐτοῦ. The word מַדּוּעַ is omitted by Vulg. Instead of עִתִּים, Syr. reads עוֹלִים 'the wicked'. The *qerê* וְיֹדְעָיו is preferable to the *kethîb* וְיֹדְעוֹ or וְיֵדְעוּ, which is not consistent with the rest of the sentence. Targ. 'and those who know *me*' is due to a theological scruple.

The literal translation of the MT would be: 'Why have times not been hidden from Shaddai and (why is it that) those who know Him (*qerê*) do not see His days?' This text is no longer recognisable in Renan's interpretation: 'Why does not the Eternal so order times that His servants see the day of His righteousness?' Less arbitrary, but difficult to justify from a grammatical point of view, is the interpretation of Le Hir: 'Why, since all times are known to the Most High, is it that those who serve Him do not see His day?' (cf. Crampon). Consistently with

the meaning of צָפַן in 15: 20, 21: 19 (cf. Comm. on 15: 20), Dillmann and Budde would interpret נִצְפָּנוּ as 'are reserved'. There is the same idea in Segond's translation: 'Why does not the Almighty reserve times?' But it is the complement with לְ which gives to the verb נִצְפַּן 'to be hidden' the implication of 'to be reserved'. In Jer 16: 17 we find the use of the *niph'al* of צָפַן with מִן before the complement: וְלֹא־נִצְפַּן עֲוֹנָם מִנֶּגֶד עֵינָי 'and their fault is not hidden from before my eyes'. It is clear that נִצְפַּן מִן means 'to be hidden from'. Let us note that the 2nd hemistich, 'and why have those who know Him not seen His days?', offers a very satisfactory sense. Those who know God are the righteous, by contrast with those who do not know God (18: 21). Cf. Ps 36: 11, where 'those who know Thee' is in parallelism with 'the men of upright heart'. The righteous would like to 'see the days' (cf. Jn 8: 56) of the Almighty, i.e. the manifestation of His power on this earth, mainly by the punishment of the wicked and the recompense of the good (cf. vv. 2ff.). The change to יֹמוֹ 'His day' which Duhm postulates, in order to introduce an eschatological idea, has against it the parallelism with עִתִּים 'the times'. If the righteous do not witness the days of God, it is because God seems to be uninterested in what goes on on earth (v. 12). Times, that is to say, the great events which are unfurled in the course of ages,

353

2   *Wicked men* remove landmarks,
     They seize the flock and *its shepherd*,

3   They drive away the ass of the orphan,
     They take the widow's ox as a pledge,

2   Add רְשָׁעִים (G). — וְרֹעוֹ (G); MT: וַיִּרְעוּ.

seem to escape His attention. And it is this idea which was expressed by the 1st hemistich, which had not the negative לֹא, as is attested by the Septuagint: 'Why have times been hidden from Shaddai?' The negative has crept into the 1st hemistich from the 2nd. If we suppress it, there exists a perfect parallelism between the two propositions, for נִצְפְּנוּ 'have been hidden' corresponds to לֹא־חָזוּ 'they have not seen'. The sequel of the chapter shows how events seem to be outside the sphere of divine control. Duhm amuses himself by composing a tristich, adding לֹא after the first דִּין, עִמּוֹ after עִתִּים.

2   G ἀσεβεῖς δέ has preserved the subject which has disappeared from the MT, namely רְשָׁעִים (cf. G in 10:3; 11:20; 15:20, etc.). Vulg. *alii* adds a vague term which will recur in v. 5 and does not justify such a restoration as הֵמָּה (contra Budde). Syr. omits וַיִּרְעוּ. G σὺν ποιμένι reads וְרֹעוֹ, which is preferable to the MT (cf. inf.). The reading of G and that of the MT are combined in Jerome *gregem cum pastore rapientes paverunt*, with asterisk before *paverunt* (cf. Vulg. *et paverunt eos*).

The 1st hemistich is too short. It lacks the subject of the plural verbs. This subject was רְשָׁעִים, which we find in G (cf. Merx, Siegfried, Bickell, etc.). The verb יַשִּׂיגוּ represents יַסִּיגוּ (cf. נָשׂוֹג instead of נָסוֹג in 2 S 1:22), *hiph'il* of סוג, the exact meaning of which is to 'push back'

one's neighbours' boundaries, so as to increase one's own property. This is a type of wrongdoing which was strictly forbidden (Dt 19:14; 27:17; Hos 5:10; Pr 22:28; 23:10). Among the Babylonians and Assyrians, the displacement and removal of landmarks or boundaries is mentioned in a list of possible sins (*La religion assyro-babylonienne*, p. 228). As it stands, the 2nd hemistich means 'they have taken away a flock and have made to graze', from which is extracted the translation: 'they lead to pasture a flock which they have stolen'. But we should expect the pronominal suffix after וַיִּרְעוּ (cf. 20:19b). G σὺν ποιμένι had וְרֹעוֹ: 'they seize the flock and its shepherd' (Merx, Siegfried, Budde, etc.). This is an excellent reading, differing but slightly from that of the MT. The shepherd makes one whole with the flock (Jer 6:3; 51:23, etc.).

3   For חֲמוֹר, G ὑποζύγιον, Jerome *jumentum*, but the variant ὄνον, noted in Colb., is followed by Sah., Syro-hex, Eth., and Arab. Baud. The word ثوب 'garment' of the Arabic version is an erroneous copy of ثور 'ox', 'bull'; cf. Syr. ܬܘܪܐ as a translation of שׁוֹר.

V. 2 mentioned the theft of property and cattle. The fault becomes much more serious and abhorrent if the robber attacks defenceless creatures such as the widow and orphan, who have a right to special consideration (cf. Comm. on 22:9). The verb נהג is used to connote the action of driving before one flocks

9   They snatch the orphan from the breast,
       And they take as a pledge *the suckling* of the poor.
4   The needy turn aside from the road,
       All the poor of the land must needs hide themselves.

4-8 After v. 9.
9   וְעַל; MT: וְעַל.

which have been seized in a raid
(1 S 23: 5; 30: 2, 20). On the verb
חבל 'take as pledge' cf. Comm. on
22: 6 and Ex 22: 25. In Dt 24: 17 it
is forbidden to take as a pledge the
widow's garments. The description
of the wicked man's misdeeds is
continued in v. 9, which is out of
place in its present context. In fact,
from v. 4, we have the description
of the sufferings of those who belong
to the poorer classes (vv. 4-8).
Among these hardships is included
forced labour exacted for the profit
of the rich (v. 6). The wretched
condition of the workers is described
in vv. 7-8. Vv. 10-11 dwell on the
fact that their work profits others
and not themselves. V. 9, on the
contrary, shows how the wicked
recruit their labour force and thus
increase the number of the unfortunate. It forms a very natural
transition between vv. 2-3 and 4-8.

4-8 After v. 9.

9 Syr. 'booty' and Vulg. *de-
praedantes* connect שד with the
verb שדד 'to plunder'. But G ἀπὸ
μαστοῦ and Targ. מבזת have rightly
realised that we have here a variant
of the word שַׁד 'breast'. שֹׁד for שַׁד is
also found in Is 60: 16; 66: 11. Vulg.
et vulgum seems to read ועם instead
of ועל.
    V. 9 formed the sequel to v. 3 (cf.
Comm. on v. 3). The author shows
how the wicked, after usurping
property (v. 2) and stealing animals
(v. 3), even seize defenceless children,
to exploit them and reduce them to

a condition of slavery (4-8, 10-11).
Far from regarding this v. 9 as
a marginal variant or a gloss on
vv. 2-3 (Siegfried, Budde, Duhm,
etc.), we see in it a very interesting
progression in the unfolding of the
sequence of ideas. The verb גזל of v.
2 means properly to 'snatch away',
and it is this meaning which it retains here: 'they snatch the orphan
from the breast', after robbing the
widow and her children (v. 3). The
preposition עַל with the verb חבל
'take as a pledge' (v. 3) is inexplicable. An excellent conjecture of
Kamphausen, which had already
been foreshadowed by Michaelis,
consists in reading וְעַל instead of
וְעַל. The 2nd hemistich then becomes: 'and they take as a pledge
the suckling of the poor'. These are
the means of recruiting the army
of the unfortunate whose fate will
be described in the verses which
follow.

4 V. 4b, absent from Sah.,
marked with asterisk in Colb. and
Syro-hex., did not exist in G. The
present text comes from Theod. (cf.
Colb. and Syro-hex). Syr. makes of
אבינים the subject of יטו, which is
translated by a passive. In Vulg.
the 1st hemistich is rendered *sub-
verterunt pauperum viam*, which is
inspired by Symm. παρέτρεψαν γὰρ
πενήτων ὁδόν. G renders מדרך by
ἐξ ὁδοῦ δικαίας. Jerome places an
obelus before *justa*, which translates
δικαίας. The *kethîb* עֲנוֵי־ארץ is
followed by Theod. and Symm.

5   *Like* wild asses in the desert,
    They come forth seeking prey;
    Although they work until the evening,
    No bread for the children!

5 הַיךְ (G, Vulg., Syr.); MT: הן. — Transfer בפעלם to follow לטרף and
read עַד־עֶרֶב instead of ערבה. — לֹא; MT: לֹו.

πραεῖς γῆς, Vulg. *mansuetos terrae*,
Syr. 'the lowly of the earth'. But
Targ. מסכני ארעא 'the poor of the
earth' follows the *qerê* of the Orientals עֲנְוֵי־ארץ. Symm. ἀφανεῖς ἐποίησαν and Vulg. *oppresserunt* regard
חבאו as a *pi'el*, instead of a *pu'al*.

Those who are now to be described,
as distinct from the wicked of vv.
2-3, 9, are the victims who, from
their tenderest years, have fallen
into the hands of the exploiters. They
compose the mass of the אֶבְיֹנִים,
that is, the miserably poor who have
neither hearth nor home, and whose
work only goes to the profit of the
rich. If we recall the description of
the condition of the poor in the
Caractères of La Bruyère, we shall
recognise that Job is truly a pre-
cursor in this field. The verb יְשׁוּ is
generally regarded as a transitive
verb having the wicked as its subject.
It is supposed that the latter thrust
the poor out of the way. But parallelism suggests that we see in אביונים
the subject of the verb. We know
that the *hiph'il* of נטה has sometimes an intransitive meaning: 'to
turn aside from the way' (cf. Comm.
on 9: 8 and 23: 11). Hence we translate: 'the needy turn aside from the
road'. Cf. the use of the *qal* of נטה
with the complement מִדֶּרֶךְ in 31: 7.
There is no room for the poor on the
high roads. The *pu'al* of חבא, instead of the *niph'al*, is used to indicate that the poor hide themselves
out of necessity or by compulsion:
passive sense. One might hesitate
between the *kethib* עֲנְוֵי 'the lowly'
and the *qerê* עֲנִיֵּי 'the poor'. The
words עָנָו and עָנִי, which belong
to the same root, ענה 'to be abased',
have often been used interchangeably: cf. Gesenius-Buhl, s.v. עָנָו
no. 3. However, in 36: 6 we find the
word עֲנִיִּים 'the poor' opposed to
רָשָׁע 'the wicked'. The same contrast
is brought out in our passage. That
is why we decide in favour of the
qerê עֲנִיֵּי; cf. the word עָנִי in v. 9
(before v. 4).

5 The text of G ἀπέβησαν δὲ
ὥσπερ ὄνοι ἐν ἀγρῷ, ὑπὲρ ἐμοῦ ἐξελ-
θόντες τὴν ἑαυτῶν τάξιν seems at first
sight very different from the MT.
But we must take into account a
certain number of copyist's errors
which have crept into the Greek
version. Thus ὄνοι ἐν ἀγρῷ is for
ὄνοι ἄγριοι; cf. Jerome *asini feri* and
the translation of פֶּרֶא in 6: 5. The
words ὑπὲρ ἐμοῦ are for ἐπ' ἐρήμου,
which translated במדבר. Finally,
τὴν ἑαυτῶν τάξιν comes from τὴν
ἑαυτῶν πρᾶξιν (א) or τῇ ἑαυτῶν πράξει
(A), translation of בפעלם; cf. Sah.,
Syro-hex., Jerome *ad opus suum*. It
becomes clear that Duhm is very ill
advised in trying to extract from
ὑπὲρ ἐμοῦ a reading בעברי, supposed to come from בערבה. On the
other hand, ὥσπερ ὄνοι ἄγριοι presupposes הַיךְ, the equivalent of אֵיךְ
'like', instead of הן. This reading is
reflected in Vulg. *quasi* and Syr.
اٮ. The close of G, from ἡδύνθη,
absent from Sah., marked with asterisk in Colb., Jerome, Syro-hex.,

stems from Theod., the word ἠδύνθη corresponding to ערבה (rendered ἠδύς in Aq.). The words משחרי לטרף have thus been omitted in G. For ערבה, Vulg. *praeparant* reads perhaps ערכו. Syr. omits ערבה לו. Vulg. omits לו.

Even those who retain הֵן at the beginning translate as if the text had הֵיךְ or אֵיךְ: 'like the wild ass in the desert' (Le Hir); 'like wild asses in solitary places' (Renan). It is better to read הֵיךְ, which is attested by G, Vulg., and Syr. (cf. sup.). The wretched, driven from the high roads, hide in the desert (v. 4). They leave their dens at times and set out in search of food. Such is the thought expressed in our verse, as we catch a glimpse of it through the MT. But it is almost impossible to give a coherent meaning to the juxtaposed words. Le Hir tries to follow the Hebrew faithfully and concludes with the following translation: 'They come forth for their work, they seek avidly their prey; the desert supplies them with the means of maintaining their families.' Renan neglects בפעלם and translates: 'They (their victims) come out early in the morning to seek their food; the desert supplies them with bread for their children.' The interpretations of Crampon and Segond link up with those we have just quoted. Note that the last hemistich would mean literally: 'The desert is for them food for the young people.' Furthermore, יצאו בפעלם does not mean: 'They come forth for their work.' We should have at least לפעלם, as in Ps 104: 23. Houbigant already suggested a correction of the text, but he was too radical in suppressing משחרי לטרף and replacing בפעלם by לאכלם, then ערבה לו לחם by ערבו ללחם לו לחם. Merx supposes that words have dropped out of the text and that we are left with fragments only. There is no point in delaying over the fancies of Hoffmann, who reads פְּדָאִים

instead of פראים, עֲרֻבָּה 'earnest' 'pledge' instead of ערבה, etc. Budde replaces הן by הם 'them', suppresses בפעלם, connects ערבה with לטרף. It is supposed to be a question of seeking the booty which the desert offers, 'the prey of the desert'. Duhm does not claim to be able to restore the original text, but he substitutes בערבה for בפעלם, so as then to fabricate small detached sentences: 'Behold! wild asses in the desert, they come out into the steppe, they seek prey.' He then transfers to v. 6 the close, from לו, and does not hesitate to replace לַנְּעָרִים 'to the children' by a derivative of נער 'to shake' (38: 13). It is the unfortunate 'shaken ones' who lack bread! Ball reduces v. 5 to two hemistichs, by eliminating all that follows לטרף, and replacing בפעלם by כמו עירים 'like asses'. A spirit of arbitrariness seems to have presided over the various attempts to restore this unfortunate verse. Now, we note that a reading לא for לו, suggested by Budde and others, enables us to obtain as the last hemistich: 'no bread for the young people!' Again, if we read הֵיךְ at the beginning (cf. sup.), we have as the 1st hemistich: 'Like wild asses in the desert!' The picture the poet is going to give us is that of these wretches leaving their shelter in order to find some food. The word בפעלם has been attracted to a place after יצאו by a reminiscence of Ps 104:23a: יצא אדם לפעלו. In reality, it is משחרי לטרף which forms the sequel of יצאו 'they come forth seeking prey'. The *pi'el* of שחר as in 7: 21. Use of the construct state before the preposition ל" (18: 2; cf. Gesenius-Kautzsch, § 130a). There remains בפעלם ערבה which we read as בְּפָעֳלָם עַד־עֶרֶב, 'when they work until the evening', in the light of a comparison with Ps 104: 23b לעבדתו עדי־ערב 'to his work until the evening'. The parallelism between the nouns פֹּעַל

6   In the fields, *during the night*, they reap,
      And gather the grape harvest of the wicked!

7   Naked they spend the night, for want of clothing,
      And no coat protects them against the cold!

6   בַּלַּיְלָה; MT: בלילו.

and עֲבֹדָה in this passage of the Psalms enables us to give to the verb פָּעַל 'to do' the sense of 'to work'. It is understandable that עַד should have fallen out before עֶרֶב, the first two letters of which are the same as עד (by confusion of ר with ד). Thus v. 5 is composed of four hemistichs. The sequel will emphasise the disproportion between the labour of the poor and the reward. V. 5 speaks about work in the daytime. V. 6 will describe work at night.

6 G ἀγρὸν πρὸ ὥρας οὐκ αὐτῶν ὄντα ἐθέρισαν seems to have a double translation of בלילו, and in בלילו has been sought the origin of πρὸ ὥρας. But, following 15:32, πρὸ ὥρας should correspond to בלא יומו, which would not have yielded בלילו. It is more probable that πρὸ ὥρας has been added in the translation, as in 15:33. On the other hand, οὐκ αὐτῶν ὄντα certainly comes from בלילו, read as בלי לו; cf. Vulg. *agrum non suum* and Targ. חקלא מדלא דלהון. Syr. 'fodder which is not his' reads בליל בלי לו. G adds ἀδύνατοι as subject of the second clause and paraphrases ילקשׁ by ἀμισθὶ καὶ ἀσιτὶ ἠργάσαντο. Vulg. *et vineam ejus quem vi oppresserint* assigns to רשׁע a passive meaning, the victim of the wicked man. It is not clear to what בְּלִילוֹ 'his fodder' refers (cf. 6: 5). The reading בַּלַּיְלָה (35: 10), proposed by Houbigant, is rightly accepted by most moderns. Note the antithesis between work in the daytime (v. 5) and work at night. The object of the *qerê*

יִקְצוֹרוּ is avoidance of the *hiph'il* יַקְצִירוּ, which is a *hapax*. It is a fairly common custom in Palestine to reap the harvest during the nights of May or June. Likewise the grape harvest may be gathered at night: 'and they gather the grape harvest of the wicked!' We have רָשָׁע consistently in opposition to the poor (2-4). It is needless to change it to עָשִׁיר 'the rich' (contra Beer, Budde, etc.). The wicked man is he who has appropriated the goods of others (v. 2), essentially the man who is rich with ill-gotten gains. The verb לקשׁ is not found elsewhere; but the context shows clearly that the *pi'el* has a similar meaning to the *pi'el* of לקט 'to gather'. Here especially to reap the harvest. Note that, in vv. 10-11, the unfortunate will have to carry the sheaves which they have gathered for the profit of others and will press the grapes which they have plucked. We see no reason at all to find in this verse a description of the marauding in which these unfortunate folk are supposed to have indulged for the satisfaction of their hunger (contra Renan, Dillmann, Duhm, etc.). It is simply forced labour, and specifically night work following on work in the daytime (v. 5).

7 G γυμνοὺς πολλοὺς ἐκοίμισαν and Vulg. *nudos dimittunt homines* consider ילינו as a causative, hence ἀφείλαντο and *tollentes* in the 2nd hemistich. G ἀμφίασιν δὲ ψυχῆς αὐτῶν for כסות בקרה, is due to a faulty writing of ἐν ψύχει (בקרה). This

8   They are soaked by the mountain rain,
     And, for lack of shelter, they cling to the rock!
10   Naked they go, unclothed,
     And hungry they carry the sheaves;

9 After v. 3.

explanation of Merx is confirmed by Jerome *tegmen in frigore*.

Not only is it the case that these wretches have nothing to eat, but they have not either any means of protecting themselves from the cold. The adjective עָרוֹם 'naked' remains in the singular, because it describes the condition of the individual person; cf. שׁוֹלָל in 12: 17, 19. The verb לִין (17: 2; 19: 4) retains its etymological sense of 'to spend the night'. For מִבְּלִי 'for lack of' cf. 4: 11. We shall have וְאֵין כְּסוּת 'and no covering' in 26: 6, the word כסות preserving its basic sense of 'that which hides, veils'. Here it is that which protects from the cold, a blanket or garment, just as in 31: 19, where we have מבלי לבוש ואין כסות. The word קָרָה 'the cold' will recur in 37: 9. The resemblance between v. 7a and v. 10a is not a sufficient reason for eliminating v. 7 (contra Duhm). The idea is continued in v. 8.

8   The 1st hemistich, absent from Sah., marked with asterisk in Jerome and Syro-hex., did not exist in G. The present text stems from Theod. (cf. Colb. and Syro-hex.).

These unfortunates have not the wherewithal to clothe themselves (v. 7). That is why 'they are soaked by the mountain rain'. The word זֶרֶם is used of violent heavy showers of rain. The clouds rise from the plains and burst over the mountains. In Is 25: 4 Yahweh is a 'shelter from the storm', מַחְסֶה מִזֶּרֶם. It is this very word מַחְסֶה which is used in our 2nd hemistich. On the verb רטב

'to become wet, soaked', cf. 8: 16. Use of מִבְּלִי is as in v. 7. The *pi'el* of חבק means 'grasp', 'cling to'. We can picture the wretches caught by a terrible shower and clutching desperately the rocks because they have no hole or corner in which to take refuge. Cf. חבקו אשפתות 'they clutch the ash heaps' (La 4: 5).

9 After v. 3.

10   G ἐκοίμισαν is a reminiscence of v. 7. The other versions have read הלכו of the MT. G ἀδίκως for מבלי לבוש introduces an abstract idea; cf. ἐξ ὁδοῦ δικαίας (v. 4) and ὁδὸν δὲ δικαίων (v. 11). Syr. ܠܚܡܐ gives to עמד the meaning 'bread'.

V. 6 has shown the poor working in the harvest fields and vineyards for the profit of the wicked man. Vv. 7-8 have depicted their sad plight. Vv. 10-11 will emphasise the contrast between the exploited and the exploiter. It is a torture of Tantalus to have to carry sheaves when one suffers from hunger, or to have to crush the grape when one suffers from thirst. The rich man piles high his stocks in his granaries and fills his cellars, while his slave dies of hunger and thirst. V. 10a is based on v. 7a, but is not a mere repetition. The poor have not the means of clothing themselves for the night. Nor are they any better dressed during their working hours. The *pi'el* of הלך implies the repetition of the action denoted by the verb (30: 28). The 2nd hemistich, 'and hungry they carry the sheaves', suggests vividly the paradox in the

11   Between *two millstones* they press out the oil,
     They tread the wine presses while they are thirsty!

11   שׁוּרֹתָיִם; MT: שׁוּרֹתָם.

situation of the oppressor's victims.
The produce of the harvest (v. 6)
goes to benefit their taskmaster.

11 G ἐν στενοῖς ἀδίκως ἐνήδρευσαν
seems to read צרות for שׁורתם and
יצודו for יצהירו (cf. Beer). The word
στενοῖς has become σκοτινοῖς in
G(A), Cod. 248, Compl. The text
of Syr. is an amalgam of v. 10b and
v. 11, the words בֵּין שׁורתם being
translated twice over: 'in the house
of feasting' and 'at their meal' (cf.
Merx and Beer). Note that Syr.
connects שׁורתם with the Syriac
ܠܘܿܡܐ 'meal', 'banquet'. Vulg. *inter
acervos eorum meridiati sunt* connects
יצהירו with צהרים 'midday'; cf.
Syr. ܣܟܘܿܡ 'they lie down'. Targ.
משׁח יעצרון אשׁותהון ביני 'between
their walls they press out the oil'
connects שׁורתם with שׁוּר 'wall', and
יצהירו with יִצְהָר 'fresh oil' (20: 17).
The 2nd hemistich of G ὁδὸν δὲ
δικαίων οὐκ ᾔδεισαν does not translate
the Hebrew, but anticipates 13b.

The second hemistich offers no
difficulty: 'They tread the wine
presses while they are thirsty.' The
slaves make wine in the press but
are not allowed to taste it. Same
idea as in v. 10b. The word יֶקֶב
denotes specifically the vat in which
the grape is pressed. Cf. Is 16: 10b,
'no longer do they tread out the wine
in the presses' (ביקבים). The verb
דרך as in 9: 8; 22: 15. The *hapax*
יַצְהִירוּ is ambiguous, since it can be
connected as a verbal derivative
with צהרים 'midday', when 'they
take their siesta' (cf. Vulg. and Syr.),
or with יִצְהָר 'fresh oil' (20: 17),
whence 'they press out the oil' (cf.
Targ.). In the light of the general
context and of parallelism, it is this

second etymology which is correct.
There is no question of these unfortunate ones taking any rest: they
work night and day (5-6). They
have gathered in the corn and vin-
tage harvest (v. 6). They pile up the
sheaves (v. 10b) and they make the
wine (our 2nd hemistich). Another
labour is now imposed on them, and
it is this that is connoted by the
verb יצהירו. Cf. the *hiph'il* יַקְצִירוּ
in v. 6. The phrase בֵּין־שׁוּרֹתָם is
usually interpreted as 'between their
rows', i.e. between the rows of trees
which belong to the oppressors. This
meaning is derived from שׁוּרָה 'row'
(in the Talmud), and a comparison is
made with the Arabic *sûreh* 'row',
'line', 'sura of the Koran', etc. But
there is something odd about in-
stalling between lines of trees oil
presses which most often were
'simple basins cut out at different
levels on a rocky platform and
linked by pipes' (Vincent, *Canaan*,
pp. 77f.). Hence שׁוּרָה 'wall' has
been proposed, which would be the
same word as שָׁרוֹתֶיהָ 'his walls' in
Jer 5: 10. The meaning is supposed
to be the same as שׁוּר 'wall' (Gn 49:
22; 2 S 22: 30; Ps 18: 30). The slaves
would be making oil 'between their
walls' i.e. between the walls of their
masters, whence Renan's translation: 'in the store-rooms of their
despoilers'. The plural suffix, referring to persons who have not been
mentioned since v. 3 (the word
רשׁע is in the sing. in v. 6) has something irritating about it. Ibn Parchon
vocalised שׁוּרוֹתָיִם, which figures in a
manuscript of de Rossi. It is this
reading which seems to us the right
one, but on condition that we assign
to שׁוּרָה a meaning suitable to the

12   In the town, *the dying* groan,
      And the soul of the wounded cries out for help,
      But Eloah does not *hear* the *prayer*!

12   מֵתִים (Syr.); MT: מְתִים. — יִשְׁמַע תְּפִלָּה (cf. Syr.); MT: יָשִׂים תְּפִלָּה.

context. Now, the root שׁוּר has a meaning similar to תּוּר and דּוּר, *circuire*, *circumire*, and it is from this meaning that is derived the sense of 'wall' that is given to the word שׁוּר; cf. *Thesaurus* of Gesenius, II, p. 1383. Cf. the Arabic ḥêṭ or ḥâiṭ (plural ḥiṭân) 'wall' from the root حوط 'surround', 'protect', and Assyrian *dûru* 'wall' from the root דּוּר 'to turn'. Following this etymology we would suggest giving to שׁוּרָה the sense of 'millstone' (that which is round and turns), and so translating the 1st hemistich: 'between two millstones they press out the oil'. The press is sometimes made up of two big grinding stones, the upper pivoting upon the lower. Changes of the difficult word שׁוּרֹתָם into שִׁירֹתָם 'their songs' (Bickell) or שׁוֹרֹתָם 'their cows' (Hoffmann) are out of keeping with the context.

12 G οἱ ἐκ πόλεως καὶ οἴκων ἰδίων ἐξεβάλλοντο provides for Merx and Bickell the opportunity of re-translating the Greek into Hebrew, the former rendering ἐξεβάλλοντο by ינדחו, the latter (whom Duhm follows) by ינדו. Beer points out with truth that ἐξεβάλλοντο arises from the fact that G connects יִנְאָקוּ with קִיא 'to vomit' (cf. Jon 2:11). As for καὶ οἴκων ἰδίων, it is a translation of וּבָתִּים, which is a wrong reading of מְתִים. Symm. ἄνδρας στενάξαι ἐποίησαν for מְתִים יִנְאָקוּ influences Vulg. *fecerunt viros gemere*. Instead of the vocalisation מְתִים (Symm., Vulg., Targ.), Syr. ܡܝܬܐ vocalises מֵתִים. G νηπίων replaces חֲלָלִים by עֹלָלִים, which is accepted by Merx and Bickell. G αὐτὸς δὲ

διὰ τί τούτων ἐπισκοπὴν οὐ πεποίηται stops before תְּפִלָּה and assigns to יָשִׂים the meaning of 'attend', 'heed' (לִבּוּ understood). For תְּפִלָּה, Targ. חוּבָא 'fault'. Vulg. *et Deus inultum abire non patitur* is a bold paraphrase. Syr. 'and God does not accept their prayers' vocalises תְּפִלָּה (cf. inf.).

After showing what goes on in the fields, Job will show us that the situation is hardly more consoling in the towns. The 1st hemistich has been translated: 'from the heart of the towns, men groan' (Le Hir; cf. Crampon), retaining the Massoretic vocalisation. The hypothesis of Hitzig, 'from the town where men dwell' (following the πόλις ἄνδρων of Homer), eliminates the subject of יִנְאָקוּ. This subject is parallel to חֲלָלִים 'of the wounded' in the 2nd hemistich, a fact which suggests that we should read מֵתִים (with Syr.), the participle מֵת being understood in the sense of 'dying'. Fried. Delitzsch cites very appositely the passage from an Assyrian letter in which the correspondent writes: *mîtu anâku* 'I was dead'. The dying man is considered as already dead. The verb נאק, which recurs in Ezk 30:24, is parallel to נהק 'to bray' (6:5) and to the Assyrian *nâqu* (נוק), whence *tanûqatu* 'plaint', 'lamentation'. In Ezk 30:24 it is used with particular reference to the groans of the wounded חָלָל. It becomes apparent that there is no reason to share the assurance of Duhm, for whom the changes of יִנְאָקוּ to יָנְדוּ or יִנָּדְחוּ, and of חללים to עֹלָלִים, the whole in accord with G, do not even need justification.

14   The murderer rises at daybreak,
      He kills the poor and the needy. [   ]

13   After v. 16a,b.
14   V. 14c after v. 15.

The *pi'el* of שׁוע connotes the futile
cry, as in 19: 7. It is the soul which
cries, for it is localised in the blood
which cries out for vengeance (Gn
4: 10). The 3rd hemistich is interpreted, following the meaning of
תִּפְלָה in 1: 22, as if the verb שִׂים
implied לֵב or עַל־לֵב (cf. Dillmann)
Whence: 'And God pays no heed to
these crimes' (Le Hir); 'and God
takes no note of these indignities'
(Renan). The text of Ps 50: 23, cited
in favour of the construction of שִׂים
(meaning 'notice') with the accusative, should be used with caution.
Literally we ought to translate: 'and
Eloah does not charge with insanity'
(cf. 4: 18b). But we expect to find
mentioned those to whom God
should impute the evil, and these
are certainly not either the dying or
the wounded. We have seen that
Syr. read תְּפִלָּה, which is found
in two manuscripts of the Hebrew
text. The word יָשִׂים may come from a
corruption of יִשְׁמַע, just as in 23: 6b.
If we read יִשְׁמַע תְּפִלָּה (Graetz,
Budde, Steuernagel, Ehrlich) we
obtain a perfect meaning: 'and
Eloah does not hear the prayer'.
What is in view is the cries of the
wounded and dying. God remains
deaf to the appeal of the victim. To
transfer v. 12 to a place after v. 14b
(Budde) is to fail to appreciate the
force of the opening מֵעִיר 'from the
town', which is intended to mark a
contrast with vv. 2-11 where the
poet emphasised the misery of the
life of the countryside. Duhm, who
realised the desperate ingenuity involved in transforming into tristichs
(thanks to a certain number of
suppressions) vv. 1-11, retains on the
lips of Job only v. 25 of ch. 24. As

far as the resort to verses of three
hemistichs is concerned, this is not
the first time that we meet the phenomenon; cf. 3: 4, 5, 6, 9. The style
changes because the subject is no
longer the same. The crimes of the
townsmen succeed to those of the
country landowners. One cannot
deny that a certain amount of disorder prevails in the arrangement of
vv. 13-16. V. 13, which begins with
הֵמָּה, ought to allude to persons
already mentioned. It cannot here
be a question of the victims of v. 12,
but rather of the assassin, the robber,
the adulterer of vv. 14-16. The true
place of v. 13 is before לֹא־יָדְעוּ אוֹר,
completed by כִּי יַחְדָּו (cf. inf.) of
v. 16. Again, as Budde very properly
realised, v. 14c, in its original context, began v. 16. The following
is what we consider the most probable arrangement: 14a,b, 15, 14c,
16a,b, 13, 16c, 17.

13   After v. 16a,b.

14   Vv. 14c-18a, absent from
Sah., marked with asterisk in Colb.,
Jerome, and Syro-hex., did not exist
in G. The present text is derived
from Theod. (cf. Colb. and Syro-
hex.). Further, G γνοὺς δὲ αὐτῶν τὰ
ἔργα παρέδωκεν αὐτοὺς εἰς σκότος does
not render 14a-b. It forms a kind of
conclusion to v. 13, to show the
punishment which overtakes those
who fail to follow the path of justice
(following the translation which
G gives of v. 13; cf. inf.). Note that
γνοὺς δὲ αὐτῶν τὰ ἔργα is inspired by
34: 25a. In fact it is the passage
14-18a which was lacking to the
text of G.

V. 14 forms the sequel to v. 12,
which alluded to the cries of the

15 And the eye of the adulterer looks out for the twilight,
He says to himself: 'No eye can see me!'
And he covers his face with a veil.

14c And in the night *the robber prowls*,

14c יְהַלֶּךְ גַּנָּב; MT: יהי כגנב.

dying and the wounded. The author of such crimes is the murderer: 'He rises at daybreak, he kills the poor and the needy.' The expression לָאוֹר 'at the light', as we have לבקר 'in the morning' and לערב 'in the evening', to denote the break of day, the moment when the light emerges from the darkness. The objections of modern critics to לאור arise from the fact that v. 13 brings forward those who rebel against the light. Hence it is proposed to read לא אור 'no light, before the light' (Budde, Beer, Wright, etc.), or even לערב 'in the evening' (Duhm). But since we have transferred v. 13 to follow 16a-b (cf. Comm. on v. 12), there is no reason for us to change לאור. Note that the murderer 'rises'; he gets out of his bed, as soon as daylight appears, in order to perform his misdeeds. Duhm amuses himself by changing עָנִי וְאֶבְיוֹן, a phrase which seems to him colourless, into איבו וצרו 'his enemy and his adversary'! But the victims are the poor, those who have no protector to defend them. The murderer kills to kill, not to rob or avenge himself. He is the professional criminal. We had the parallelism between אביון and עני in v. 4. The 3rd hemistich is interpreted as meaning: 'and during the night he is like a thief', the jussive יהי having the sense of the simple imperfect (18:12a). The comparison is extremely weak. It would not have been so bad if at least it had been said that the murderer conceals himself 'like a thief'. But 'to be like a thief' does not amount to much where a murderer is concerned! Again, the classical list of criminals is the murderer, the thief, the adult-erer (Hos 4:2; Jer 7:9). In accordance with this classical enumeration of crimes (Hos 4:2; Jer 7:9), the robber has the right to a special mention by the side of the murderer and the adulterer. A very slight change, proposed by Merx, and admitted by most moderns, gives us יְהַלֶּךְ גַּנָּב instead of יהי כגנב. The *piʿel* of הלך 'walk', 'roam', 'prowl' as in v. 10. The meaning is clear: 'and in the night the robber prowls'. Thus understood v. 14c forms the first hemistich of a tristich which is continued in v. 16a-b, where we shall see the mode of action of the robber. He operates at night, but he has marked the houses during the day; cf. יוֹמָם in v. 16. Thus is explained the singular חָתַר which opens v. 16.

If we transfer v. 14c so that it forms the opening of v. 16, we have as the series of crimes: homicide, adultery, robbery. This is in fact the order of their mention in the decalogue of Ex 20:13, where forbidden actions are precisely murder (רצח), adultery (נאף), theft (גנב). We note that the murderer works 'at daybreak', the adulterer 'at twilight', the robber 'during the night'. They will be grouped together under the heading 'rebels against the light' in v. 13, which originally followed v. 16a-b.

15 On the text of G, cf. v. 14. Syro-hex. forgets the asterisk before v. 15a. Syr. reads תשורנו instead of תשרני, and translates 'will not see us'. At the close Targ. adds כלפי לעיל 'against Him who dwells on high', to suggest that the guilty man wishes to escape the eye of God. Syr. 'and he veils his face with darkness'

16   In the darkness he bores through houses
      Which he has marked during the daytime.

16   חָתַם (Syr.); MT: חתמו. — V. 16c at v. 17a.

separates סתר from its complement
פנים.

The second type of criminal is the
adulterer (cf. v. 14). 'And the eye
of the adulterer looks out for
the twilight'; the verb שׁמר means
'keep' and 'inspect', 'look out' (cf.
10:14 and 39:1), and the word
נֶשֶׁף 'twilight' (7:4). Darkness forms
a rampart for adultery: σκότος κύκλῳ
μου (Sir 23:25). The guilty man is
afraid of being seen, he reassures
himself by saying: 'No eye can see
me!' Cf. Sir 23:25, 'The man who
defiles his couch, saying in his soul:
who sees me?' At twilight, licentious
conduct begins. The prostitute places
herself on the watch בנשף 'from
twilight' (Pr 7:9). With לא־תשׁורני
עין 'the eye does not see me', cf.
7:8a, לא־תשׁורני עין ראי. The 3rd
hemistich, 'and he puts on a face-
veil', following the common expression הסתיר פנים 'to veil the face'
(13:24a). The word סֵתֶר = 'veil' (22:
14). These resemblances should be
noted as discountenancing those
who dispute the authenticity of the
whole passage.

16 On the text of G, cf. v. 14.
For יומם חתמו־למו, Theod. ἡμέρας
ἐσφράγισαν ἑαυτούς (Jerome *per diem
obsignaverunt semetipsos*), Symm. ὡς
ἐν σφραγῖδι κρύψουσιν ἑαυτούς. It is
apparent that these versions make
of למו a reflexive pronoun. Similarly
Vulg. *sicut in die condixerant sibi*,
but with a different meaning for
חתמו. Targ. and Syr. are agreed in
copying the MT, but Syr. has the
singular instead of the plural חתמו
(cf. inf.). Targ. adds בגנזיא 'in
hiding places'. Syr. adds דְּ before
לא־ידעו 'so that they may not know
the light'.

There is incompatibility between
חָתָר in the singular and חָתְמוּ in the
plural, as is apparent from the attempts at harmonisation in the
translations: 'Others pierce houses
in the darkness and hold themselves
in hiding during the daytime' (Le
Hir, etc.). The introduction of a
vague subject, such as 'others' or
simply 'they', 'one' (Dillmann, etc.),
is a subterfuge necessitated by an
unintelligible text. In reality it is
the subject of חתר which ought to
be found in the preceding passage.
Now, the verb חתר means 'pierce',
'bore through' a wall, make a breach
in it (Ezk 8:8; 12:5, 7, 12), and
'dig into' (Am 9:2). This is the
specific work of the burglar. On this
point there is a very instructive comparison between Ex 22:2, the Code
of Hammurabi, §§ 21ff., and the
Law of the Twelve Tables, VII, I,
in D. H. Müller, *Die Gesetze Hammu-
rabis*, p. 177. The thief does not enter
in by the door, but by other means
(Jn 10:1). The subject of חתר is
contained in v. 14c, which originally
stood before v. 16 and the tenor of
which was: וּבַלַּיְלָה יְהַלֵּךְ גַּנָּב 'and
in the night the robber prowls' (cf.
Comm. on v. 14). It is precisely the
robber whom we expect to be mentioned after the murderer and the
adulterer (ibid.). Note the correspondence between בַּלַּיְלָה and בַּחֹשֶׁךְ.
But does the robber work at ran-
dom? No, he has taken care to mark
during the daytime those houses
which are worthy of his exploits.
חָתְמוּ לָמוֹ is usually translated as
though למו were a reflexive pronoun (cf. the versions), and in v. 16b
is seen an allusion to the guilty who
hide themselves during the daytime.
But למו can equally well refer to

13   These are among them who rebel against the light:
      They have not known its ways
      And have not *returned* by its paths.

17   For together (16c) they have not known the light;
      The morning is as the darkness for them;

17   After v. 13 (below).
13   יָשֻׁבוּ (G, Vulg., Syr.); MT: יֵשְׁבוּ.
17   V. 16c after כי יחדו. — יָאִיר; MT: יכיר. — עָלֵימוֹ; MT: צלמות.

בתים (cf. לָמוֹ in 6: 19; 14: 21; 15: 28;
22: 19), the relative אֲשֶׁר being
understood. The *pi'el* of חתם will
not mean 'to seal' in the sense of to
shut in, but to mark with a seal, or
any other kind of mark, so as to
recognise a place. With Syr. we read
the singular חָתַם and translate:
'which he has marked during the day'.
The adverb יוֹמָם is opposed to בחשׁך
and to בלילה. Thus the tristich is
completed 14c, 16a-b. The words
לֹא־יָדְעוּ אוֹר do not form a hemistich. They were part of v. 17, where
כִּי יַחְדּוּ overloads the first sentence.

Budde proposes simply to transfer
יחדו to precede לֹא־יִדְעוּ. But it is
rather לֹא־יִדְעוּ אוֹר which must be
placed after כי יחדו. The conjunction כי 'for', 'because' depends on a
preceding clause. This is none other
than v. 13, which begins with הֵמָּה
'they', 'the latter', i.e. those who
have just been enumerated: the
murderer, the adulterer, the robber.
They are all enemies of the light
(cf. Comm. on v. 12 and v. 14).

17   After v. 13.

13   G ἐπὶ γῆς (A adds ἔτι) ὄντων
αὐτῶν seems to have read בְּמוֹ
רָאֵי אוֹר 'among those who see the
light' (the living), instead of בְּמֹרְדֵי
אוֹר. Others explain the text of G
by a reading בְּמַדֵּי, interpreted in
accordance with the Syriac ܡܕܪܐ
'clod of earth', or following the
Aramaic מְדוֹר 'habitation' (cf. Beer).
It is certain that Syr. ܟܡܕܥܝܢ has

read בְּמַדֵּי and connected it with
מְדוֹר. G καὶ οὐκ ἐπέγνωσαν ... οὐκ
ᾔδεισαν twice translates לֹא־הִכִּירוּ.
As in vv. 4 and 11, G ὁδὸν δικαιοσύνης
gives a moral sense to דרכיו. Instead
of יֵשְׁבוּ, G ἐπορεύθησαν, Vulg. *reversi
sunt*, and Syr. ܘܗܦܟܘ vocalise יָשֻׁבוּ,
which is preferable.

The natural place of v. 13, which
classes as belonging to one category
the criminals enumerated in vv.
14-16, is after v. 16b (cf. Comm. on
v. 12 and v. 16). The pronoun הֵמָּה
here as in 6: 7 and 32: 4, refers to
what precedes and not to what follows. With most moderns we vocalise
יָשֻׁבוּ (in accord with G, Vulg., and
Syr.), instead of יֵשְׁבוּ of the MT. One
returns by a path, one does not stay
in it. The verb מרד 'to rebel' takes
a preposition before the complement,
but the construct participle is fused
with the following word and eliminates the preposition. The criminals
dread the light of day, and do not
use the roads which it makes
luminous. The use of the words
דְּרָכָיו 'its ways', and נְתִיבֹתָיו 'its
paths', in speaking of the light,
recalls 38: 19-20, where it is a
question of the way which is flooded
with light and other ways which lead
to darkness. Let us not forget that
crimes are perpetrated at night
(14-16).

14-16   After v. 12.

17   On the text of G, cf. v. 14.
Vulg. translates כי יחדו בקר by *si*

When *its light shines*, terrors seize *upon them*!

18-24   Transfer these verses to stand between 27: 13 and 27: 14.

subito apparuerit aurora. Instead of בקר, Syr. ܟܐܒ 'they have sought' reads בקרו, which leads to יכירו, interpreted as 'they have found'. Symm. φωραθείς and Targ. אשתמודע regard הכיר as a passive. For בלהות the reading of Theod. is τάραχος in G(B) but ταραχάς in G (A, א^{c·a}), Syro-hex. The second part of the verse was omitted by Jerome as a result of homoeoteleuton (σκιὰ θανάτου and σκιᾶς θανάτου). Vulg. *et sic in tenebris quasi in luce ambulant* boldly para-phrases the 2nd hemistich in accord-ance with the meaning of the 1st.

V. 17 presents a certain number of anomalies. In the first place, the excessive length of the 1st hemi-stich, in which כי יחדו fulfils no function. Then the passage from the plural to the singular הכיר. Finally the repetition of צלמות. It will be difficult to discover a literal translation, except for בקר למו צלמות, in the usual interpretations: 'The morning is for them as the shadow of death: if they are recog-nised, what mortal alarms!' (Le Hir); 'for the morning is for them like the shadow of death; as soon as they see the day break, they ex-perience the terrors of death' (Re-nan). Still less shall we recognise the text in the following translation of the 2nd hemistich: 'for the ter-rors of the night are familiar to them' (Crampon). First we have to collect לא ידעו אור 'they know not the light', which remains over from v. 16, where the verse finished after למו and was followed by v. 13 (cf. Comm.). If we place לא ידעו אור of v. 16 after כי יחדו we obtain: 'for together they have not known the light'. It is a return to the idea ex-pounded in v. 13, namely that the criminals flee the light. The expres-sion יחדו as in 2: 11; 9: 32. The

words בֹּקֶר לָמוֹ צַלְמָוֶת constitute the 2nd hemistich: 'the morning is as the darkness for them'. When the light of dawn comes, the wicked regard it as darkness. In fact, their light is the night (38: 15). Their mentality is perverted: 'They change darkness into light and light into darkness' (Is 5: 20). The 3rd hemi-stich, which repeats צלמות and uses the singular הכיר instead of the plural, springs from a corruption of the text. Duhm changes the whole verse by reading בחרו for בקר, הליכות for בלהות, and by proposing a sort of synonym for the second צלמות: 'they have chosen for them-selves darkness, for they are famil-iar with murky ways.' And, since he has transfered כי יחדו to v. 16, he joins v. 18a to v. 17, so as to com-plete the tristich: 'he is rapid on the surface of the water'! All that is somewhat incoherent. We retain the characteristic word בַּלְהוֹת (18: 11, 14) and we read יָאִיר (41: 24) in-stead of יכיר, which is influenced by הכירו of v. 13. The subject of יאיר is בקר. The second צלמות probably comes from עָלֵימוֹ (6: 16; 21: 17).

Thus we obtain: 'When it shines, terrors seize upon them.' Terrors which are generally occasioned by darkness come upon the wicked during the daytime. Vv. 18-24 de-scribe the punishment and the death of the wicked. We shall see that v. 18 forms the natural sequel of 27: 13. The whole passage 18-24 has been torn away from its original context. We transfer it to a place between v. 13 and v. 14 of ch. 27: cf. Intro., pp. xlvi, xlixf. V. 25 forms the conclusion of this whole speech of Job.

18-24 After 27: 13.

25   If it is not so, who will convict me of lying,
      And reduce my words to nothing?

25 V. 25b, absent from Sah., marked with asterisk in Jerome and Syro-hex., did not exist in G. Our text comes from Theod. (cf. Cod. 137). Syr. ܘܦ ܣܐܠ 'his anger' vocalises אַפּוֹ instead of אֵפוֹ. Symm. παρὰ τῷ Θεῷ. Vulg. *ante Deum*, Syr. 'before God', vocalise לָאֵל? instead of לְאַל.

The word אֵפוֹ serves simply the purpose of strengthening the hypothesis. It is an enclitic as in 19: 6, 23. The resemblance between אִם־לֹא אֵפוֹ and 9: 24b is purely fortuitous, since there has been a transposition of הוּא and אֵפוֹ in 9: 24 (cf. Comm.). The phrase 'and if not' implies 'as I have said': and if it is not so! The *hiph'il* of כזב with declarative sense; cf. הרשׁיע (9: 20; 10: 2; 15: 6) and העקישׁ (9: 20). Hence: 'who will convict me of lying?' Job has already stressed his truthfulness (6: 28-30). Cf. the question of Our Lord: 'Which of you will convict me of sin?' (Jn 8: 46). Note the use of the jussive יָשֵׂם with the sense of a simple imperfect (13: 27; 15: 33, etc.). The phrase: שׂוֹם לָאַל 'reduce to nothing' corresponds exactly to נתן לאין of Is 40: 23. The particle אַל (11: 14b) is used as a real substantive in the place of לֹא. Siegfried replaces it by אִין; but the versions which have vocalised אַל (Symm., Syr., Vulg.) favour the consonants of the MT. Ehrlich reads: לָאֵל מִלָּתוֹ 'who will place his word with God?', which destroys the parallelism. To convict Job of lying would be to 'reduce to nothing' his speech.

CHAPTERS 25-6

25:1 Then Bildad the Shuhite spoke and said:
2   With Him are domination and terrible might;
     He establishes peace in His heights;
3   Can one number His armies?
     And against whom does not His *ambush* rise up?

Chapters 25, 26: 5-14. Third speech of Bildad: see Introduction, pp. xlviif.
3 אוֹרְבוֹ (G); MT: אורהו.

25:2 For הַמְשֵׁל, G τί γὰρ προοί-μιον reads הָמְשָׁל, while Syr. ܡܫܠܛ reads הַמְשֵׁל. G τὴν σύμπασαν gives to שָׁלוֹם a meaning derived from שָׁלֵם 'to be complete'. One of the Targums identifies with Michael and Gabriel the abstractions הַמשׁל ופחד.
The speech of Bildad includes a doxology which is reduced to a few verses. But the speech is thus truncated as the result of an accident to the text. In reality the speech does not stop at 25: 6; its natural sequel is found in 26: 5ff. Vv. 2-4 of ch. 26 have their sequel in 17: 2-12; cf. Intro., p. xlviii. Job has just been complaining of God's indifference towards the events of this world. Bildad does not offer a contrary theory. He contents himself with dwelling on the divine perfections in all their unfathomability. He uses the opportunity here presented to contrast the low degree of man with the greatness of God. Hence we must not expect a direct answer to the arguments of Job. And the latter will deride (26: 2-4) the purely spe-culative character of the reply. The word הַמְשֵׁל is a *hiph'il* infinitive used as a noun: what gives power or domination (cf. הַשְׁמֵד 'destruction' in Is 14: 23). Use of פַּחַד to express

the fear which God inspires: cf. 13: 11 (Comm.). The 1st hemistich is built on the same pattern as 12: 13a and 16a. Note the same use of עִמּוֹ 'with Him'. The verb עשׂה with שָׁלוֹם as complement to mean 'estab-lish peace'. God secures peace in His heights, i.e. in the heavens; cf. 16: 19 and 31: 2. We shall see also that the shades tremble before Him (26: 5). Neither heavenly beings nor those in Hell can revolt against Him. Moreover He has at His com-mand a whole host of warriors (v. 3). V. 2 is perfectly intelligible as it stands, and there is no need to change שָׁלוֹם into שִׁלּוּם 'retribution' (Schultens) or במרומיו into במרודיו 'on His rebels' (Wright).

3 G μὴ γὰρ τις ὑπολάβοι ὅτι is a paraphrase of הֲיֵשׁ. It is difficult to explain how G παρέλκυσις can arise from מספר, which is attested by the other versions. G ἔνεδρα παρ' αὐτοῦ reads אורבו 'His ambush' in-stead of אורהו. Symm. ἐπιτάγματα interprets אורהו 'His light' in a meta-phorical sense, which however does not prevent Siegfried from changing אורהו to תורתו 'His law'!
God is likened to a sovereign ruler commanding an army: 'Can one number His armies?' (literally: is

368

4   And how then should a man be just before God?
     How should he be pure, who is born of woman?

5   If even the moon does not *shine,*
     And if the stars are not pure in His eyes,

5   יָהֵל (versions); MT: יאהיל.

there a number to His bands?). Job has already spoken of the hosts which are enlisted in the service of God; cf. גדודיו in 19:12. The 2nd hemistich would mean: 'And on whom does His light not rise?' But then there is no longer any parallelism. The reading of G ἔνεδρα παρ' αὐτοῦ 'the ambushes laid by Him' implies אוֹרְבוֹ instead of אוֹרֵהוּ. In this case we have the present participle אוֹרֵב of the verb ארב 'to be in ambush, lying in wait' (31:9), used as a collective to denote the ambushed troops, as in Jg 16:9, 12. With Beer and Duhm, we propose to adopt this reading of G, which has the advantage of securing the parallelism: 'And against whom does not His ambush rise up?' No one can escape the vigilance of God's army. Ehrlich suggests replacing אורהו by אמרהו 'His word', which is much less suited to the context than the reading of G.

4 For עם־אל, Vulg. *comparatus Deo;* cf. *compositus Deo* in 9:2. G ἢ τίς ἂν ἀποκαθαρίσαι αὐτόν interprets יזכה as a *pi'el.* At the close, G(A) has an addition coming from 15:15 and 9:7. It is also found in Syro-hex., preceded by a diacritic sign.

Bildad here contrasts the imperfection of man with the divine majesty. He uses for his own purpose, though with a few modifications, the argument of Eliphaz in 4:17-19 and 15:14-16, strophes which inspire our vv. 4-6. He does not go to the trouble of inventing his own expressions. The 1st hemistich, 'and how should a man be just before God?', literally reproduces the phrasing of Job in 9:2b. The 2nd hemistich borrows all its language from 15:14.

5 G ἢ σελήνη συντάσσει connects עד with the verb יעד. The versions are agreed in explaining יאהיל by the verb הלל and in thus suggesting the true vocalisation יָהֵל (31:26), which has been distorted by the use of the *matres lectionis.*

The correspondence between הֵן and אַף (v. 6), attested by 4:18-19 and 15:15-16, disallows the replacing of הֵן עַד by הוֹעֵד (Wright, following G) or הַגֹּעֵר 'He who rebukes' (Perles). The preposition עַד before יָרֵחַ, in a negative sentence, means 'not even'; cf. לא נשאר עד אחד 'not even one man was left' (Jg 4:16). It is apparent that 'as far as to' then means 'even', 'including even'. Cf. Boileau: 'Everything finds readers, even (*jusqu'à*) d'Assoucy!' The ו of וְלֹא is expletive. The verb הלל 'to shine' (29:3; 31:26) and not אהל; vocalise יָהֵל (cf. sup.). Light is the symbol of purity. In Assyrian, the verb *elêlu* and the adjective *ellu* express the idea of light, purity, holiness. They belong to the root הלל. It is here the stars which serve as a term of comparison rather than the angels or the heavens (4:18; 15:15). The 2nd hemistich reproduces 15:15b with וכוכבים instead of ושמים.

6   How much less man, that maggot,
      And a son of man, that worm!
26:5 The Shades tremble beneath the earth,
      The waters and their inhabitants *become terrified*,

6 Continuation of v. 6 in 26: 5-14.
26: 5   Attach מִתָּחַת to the first hemistich and add יְחֹתּוּ before מַיִם

6 V. 6b, marked with asterisk and attributed to Theod. in Syrohex., exists in Sah. However, it is really a hexaplar reading, according to Cod. 255 (Beer). Targ. qualifies רמה by adding 'during his life', and תולעה by adding 'at his death'.

The parallel verses 4: 19 and 15: 16 emphasised respectively the frailty and the corruption of man. Bildad expresses this twofold idea by coupling an energetic epithet with the words אֱנוֹשׁ and בֶּן־אָדָם. Man is compared to the maggot רִמָּה (7: 5; 17: 14; 21: 26) and to the earthworm, תּוֹלֵעָה (from תלע 'to gnaw'). There is parallelism between רמה and תולעה in Is 14: 11, where the theme is the worms of the grave. Nothing could more vividly show the misery of man. The Psalmist said: 'I am a worm and no man' (Ps 22: 7). The formula בֶּן־אָדָם 'son of man' does not recur elsewhere in Job; we must read בין אדם in 16: 21 (cf. Comm.). The doxology of Bildad does not in reality stop here. After alluding to God who reigns on high (vv. 2-3) and, in parenthesis, indicating the powerlessness of man to justify himself before this sovereign Lord and Master, he will raise the veil which conceals Sheol. Even after death, man still trembles under the eye of God (26: 5-6). The passage 26: 2-4 is an introduction to 27: 2-12 and not to 26: 5-14, in which we find the sequel of Bildad's speech; cf. Intro., p. xlviii.

26: **1-4** After 26: 14.

26: **5** Vv. 5-11, absent from Sah.,

marked with asterisk in Jerome and Syro-hex., did not exist in G. The present text derives from Theod. (cf. Colb., and Syro-hex.). The ה of הרפאים is regarded as an interrogative in Aq., Symm., Theod. For רפאים, Aq. Ραφαείμ, Symm. θεομάχοι, Theod. γίγαντες (Jerome and Vulg. *gigantes*), Targ. גבריא, Syr. ܪܦܝܐ. Instead of μαιωθήσονται, which translates יחוללו in Theod., we have ματαιωθήσονται in G (א*); cf. Jerome *redigentur in nihilum*.

V. 5 continues 25: 6. After the heavens and the earth, come the infernal regions! The mention of Sheol in v. 6 abundantly shows that the Rephaim here represent the Shades, exactly as in Is 14: 9; Pr 9: 19. It is not a question of the giants, and it is impossible to find any sort of allusion to 'some legend like that of the *Asphaltite* lake, according to which giants in revolt against God were buried under the waters' (Renan). The verb יְחוֹלָלוּ, from חִיל 'to tremble' (cf. 13: 15), is in the *po'lal*, in order to show that the Shades cannot escape terror; cf. the use of the *pu'al* of חבא in 24: 4. It is unnecessary to replace it by the *hithpa'el* (Duhm), which would suggest the terror whose source lies in one's self (15: 20). Grimme proposes to read יָחֵלוּ לוֹ 'tremble before Him', but in that case we should have מפני or מלפני before the suffix (Driver). The 2nd hemistich should be translated 'beneath the waters and their inhabitants' (Renan), which is a strange indication for the dwelling place of the Shades. It has been proposed to replace וְשֹׁכְנֵיהֶם by

6   Sheol is naked before Him,
And Abaddon unveiled!

7   He stretches out the North over the void,
And poises the earth over nothingness.

מִשְׁכְּנֵיהֶם 'they whose habitations lie beneath the waters' (Merx, Bickell, Hontheim, etc.); but the suffix of the last word would then refer to the first word of the verse, which would be a somewhat forced construction. Furthermore the dwelling of the Shades will be mentioned in v. 6: it is Sheol or Abaddon. The 1st hemistich is too short. Again, as Ehrlich justly points out, the Hebrew phrase meaning 'under the waters' would be מִתַּחַת לַמִּים rather than מִתַּחַת מִים. If we read מִפַּחַת, attaching this word to the 1st hemistich (Ley, Ehrlich), we obtain: 'The Shades beneath the earth tremble.' The parallel verb to יְחוֹלָלוּ was יֵחַתּוּ (niph'al of חתת; cf. 39: 22), which has vanished by haplography after מִתַּחַת (Torczyner, cf. Beer). The 2nd hemistich offers an excellent parallel to the 1st: 'The waters and their inhabitants become terrified.' The inhabitants of the waters, i.e. of the sea (Gn 1: 10) are the sea monsters, all those strange beings who live in the waves (Ps 104: 25, 26). The heavens, the earth, Sheol, the waters — there is no place in which the terror aroused by the divine majesty does not prevail.

6 On the text of G, cf. v. 5. The word שְׁאוֹל is translated ὁ ᾅδης in Theod., *infernus* in Vulg., while Syr., Targ. retain the Hebrew name. For לַאֲבַדּוֹן, Targ. לְבֵית אֲבַדְנָא 'to the house of perdition', but Syr. simply الحربـ, Theod. τῇ ἀπωλείᾳ, Vulg. *perditioni*.
Note the parallelism between עָרוֹם and אֵין כְּסוּת, as in 24: 7, where the words preserved their basic meaning. Note the resemblance

between the 2nd hemistich and 31: 19b, where we have לָאֶבְיוֹן instead of לָאֲבַדּוֹן. God is everywhere, in Sheol as in the heavens (Ps 139: 8), and in consequence He sees all: 'Sheol is naked before Him.' Nothing, however, is more wrapped in darkness than the realm of the Shades, the very name of which is synonymous with darkness (17: 13), and where light itself resembles darkness (10: 21-2). Job has expressed the wish to be hidden in Sheol, in order to escape the glance of God (14: 13). Ridiculous desire! Not only is Sheol naked before God, but Abaddon too has no veil. On the word כְּסוּת, what hides, or covers, cf. 24:7. It is obvious that the word אֲבַדּוֹן, from the root אבד 'to perish', is an equivalent of שְׁאוֹל. We find 'Abaddon and death' (28: 22), 'Sheol and Abaddon' (Pr 27: 20). Parallelism between 'the grave' and 'Abaddon' in Ps 88: 12. The idea expressed in our verse is reflected in Pr 15: 11, 'Sheol and Abaddon are before Yahweh, how much more the hearts of the sons of men!'

7 On the text of G, cf. v. 5. For עַל־תֹּהוּ, Syr. مع ܣܘܚܕ 'of the desert'. The other versions are in agreement with the MT: Theod. ἐπ' οὐδέν, Targ. עַל לָמָא 'on nothing', Aq. ἐπὶ κενώματος, Vulg. *super vacuum*. For עַל־בְּלִימָה, well understood by the other versions, Targ. 'over the waters without anything supporting it'.
The participles refer to God, who is intimated by the suffix of נֶגְדּוֹ in v. 6; cf. 12: 17. The verb נטה means 'to stretch out', as in 9: 8 (cf.

8   He locks the waters in His clouds,
     And the cloud does not burst beneath them;
9   He covers the face of the *full moon*,
     Unfurling over it His cloud;

9 כְּסֶה; MT: כִּסֵּה. — פֵּרֵשׂ (Targ., Syr.; cf. Theod., Vulg.); MT: פַּרְשֵׁז.

Comm.). Job said that God 'alone stretches out the heavens' (9:8). Here 'God stretches out the North over the void'. Following the parallelism, some commentators seek in the phrase a designation of the earth, whose northern mountains, the least accessible, offer a refuge to deity (Is 14:13; Ezk 1:4; cf. Hirzel, Dillmann, Duhm, etc.). But the use of נטה in 9:8 and in Ps 104:2, as also in prophetic literature (Is 40:22; 42:5; 44:24, etc.; Jer 10:12; 51:15; Zec 12:1), where it is always a question of God 'stretching out the heavens', invites us to see in צָפוֹן a celestial region, namely the North, that part of the firmament around which the stars seem to be pivoted. God stretches it out over the תֹּהוּ, which is no longer simply the desert (6:18; 12:24), but 'the void', as in Gn 1:2, תֹהוּ וָבֹהוּ. First and foremost God must establish securely the stable part of the sky, since it serves as a pivot to the stars. In Is 40:17, 23 the word תֹהוּ has as its parallel אַיִן 'nothing'. Here it is בְּלִימָה, which does not recur elsewhere, but the meaning of which is immediately intelligible: בְּלִי מָה, οὔτι, *nullum* (*ne ullum*). Cf. the formation of בְּלִיַּעַל (34:18). God suspends the earth over the void. One can imagine its having a supporting base, but the latter would require still another, and so on *ad infinitum*. Calmet cites Ovid: *Terra pilae similis nullo fulcimine nixa* (*Fasti*, VI, 269).

8   On the text of G, cf. v. 5. Targ. מֵי מִטְרָא clarifies the point

that it is the rain waters that are being alluded to. The 2nd hemistich is paraphrased in Vulg. *ut non erumpant pariter deorsum*.

In Gn 1:6-7 it is the firmament which holds back the waters of the sky. Here it is the clouds compared to reservoirs of rainwater. The verb צָרַר (18:7; 20:22) in the transitive sense 'lock up', 'confine', 'shut in' as in a bag; cf. צְרוֹר in 14:17. Cf. Pr 30:4b, 'Who has wrapped up the waters in a garment?', verb צָרַר. The *niph'al* of בקע, in the sense of 'crack open', 'burst', is specially used to describe the reservoirs of heaven which burst open in Gn 7:11. It is also used of a wineskin which bursts (32:19, in the present state of the text). Now, the clouds are the 'wineskins of the sky' (38:37). They are solidly constructed, 'and the cloud does not burst beneath them', i.e. beneath their weight.

9   On the text of G, cf. v. 5. With the exception of Syr. ܠܡܣܬܪ, which connects כְּסֶה with כסה 'to cover', the versions see here כִּסֵּא 'throne', with or without the suffix: Theod. θρόνου, Vulg. *solii sui*, Targ. כּוּרְסְיָה. Syr. omits the suffix of עָנָנוֹ. Syr. ܦܪܣ and Targ. פרס connect פַּרְשֵׁז with פרשׂ (cf. inf.).

כְּסֶה is usually interpreted as a faulty writing of כִּסְאֹה (כִּסְאוֹ) 'His throne' (cf. Vulg. and Targ.): 'He veils the face of His throne' (Renan, Loisy, Crampon), or 'He firmly joins together the planks of His throne' (Le Hir). Duhm reaches much the same sense as Le Hir by reading

10   He has *described a circle* on the face of the waters,
      Up to the boundary between light and darkness.

10   חַק־חָג (Syr.); MT: חֹק־חָג.

פְּנֵי instead of פְּנֵי: 'He strengthens the pillars of His throne.' The throne of God would be the sky (Is 66:1), and the 2nd hemistich would refer to the clouded sky. But if the sky is the throne, it is not its face which is veiled by the cloud but its back or base. To change פְּנֵי to פְּנֵי (Duhm) is tantamount to postulating a plural פָּנִים instead of פְּנוֹת, which is the normal plural of פִּנָּה. The only instance in which פנים is found is Zec 14:10, in שער הפנים, which is a mistake for שער הפנה 'the gate of the corner' (Gray). Ibn Ezra recognised in כְּסֶה an erroneous vocalisation of כֶּסֶה 'full moon' of Ps 81:4, written כֵּסֶא in Pr 7:20. Older commentators like Houbigant, Reiske, and Berg did not hesitate to accept this solution. Beer, who adopted it in *Der Text des Buches Hiob*, does not even mention it in the Kittel edition, where he accepts the opinion of Duhm (cf. sup.). Now, the *pi'el* of אחז, which does not recur elsewhere, may have here the same meaning as the Assyrian *uḫḫuzu* 'to cover' an object with gold or silver. This meaning is attested, for the passive, by the *hoph'al* form (probably to be replaced by the *pu'al*) in 2 Ch 9:18, as is correctly pointed out by Perles (*Analekten*, II, p. 83 and p. 115). The 1st hemistich, 'He covers the face of the full moon', is clarified and elucidated by the 2nd, 'by unfurling over it His cloud'. The form פַּרְשֵׁז is a combination of פרש and פרז, the scribe not having made up his mind which of the two to adopt. In truth, it is פֵּרֵשׁ 'extending', 'unfurling' which was the original text; cf. Targ. and Syr. (sup.), confirmed by

Theod. ἐκπετάζων and Vulg. *expandit*.

10   On the text of G, cf. v. 5. Instead of חֹק־חָג, which is attested by Theod. πρόσταγμα ἐγύρωσεν and Vulg. *terminum circumdedit*, a variant חַק־חָג is supported by Syr. ܚܩ ܚܘܓܐ 'He has traced a circle' (cf. Targ. 'He has ordained that a firmament should be established', which implies חק as verb). Vulg. *usque dum finiantur* interprets עד־תכלית 'up to the completion'; cf. Syr. 'until it was completed'.

In Pr 8:27, which makes allusion to the work of creation, God is represented as tracing a circle on the face of the deep. The phrase used is בְּחֻקוֹ חוּג 'when He traced a circle'. There can hardly be any doubt that we should have here חַק־חָג 'He has traced a circle' (cf. Syr.), instead of חֹק־חָג 'He has prescribed a limit'. The verb חקק 'engrave', 'sketch out', 'trace'; cf. Comm. on 14:5 and 19:23. In 22:14 we had חוג שמים 'the circle of the heavens', to designate the horizon, which is also described by חוג הארץ 'the circle of the earth' (Is 40:22). Here, it is the circle which surrounds the 'face of the waters'. The earth was pictured as being encircled by an ocean, similar to the *apsû* of the Babylonians. There lay the *išid šamê* 'the foundation of the heavens', which coincided with the horizon. From this foundation of the heavens the sun emerged every morning, passing through the gate of the east (*Choix de textes*, p. 60, n. 9). Beyond lay the zone of darkness. The word תַּכְלִית 'completion', 'perfection' (11:7), and by that very fact connoting

11   The columns of the heavens are shaken,
     And are amazed at His threat;
12   By His strength He divided the sea,
     And by His understanding He smote Rahab;

the 'limit' of what may be reached (28:3), denotes in the present context the place at which the light ceases and darkness begins: 'limit of the light with the darkness', i.e. limit between light and darkness. It is the horizon which forms this limit.

11 On the text of G, cf. v. 5. Double reading in Theod. for the word ירופפו: G(B) ἐπετάσθησαν, (Syro-hex. and Memph.; cf. Beer) and G(A) ἐπεστάθησαν (Arab. Baud.). In Jerome we have *intremuerunt*, probably following Aq. διεκινήθησαν. For מגערתו, Syr. had حلاب 'by His rebuke' (cf. Ceriani and Syro-hex.), which has become in Walton مه حلاب.

The columns of the sky, as distinct from the columns of the earth (9:6), are the mountains which, on the horizon, support the arch of the heavens. Such was the way in which the Atlas mountain was envisaged in Greek mythology. The verb רפף does not recur elsewhere. The original meaning is easily inferred from Arabic رفّ 'to wink' and the Syriac ڧ 'to be moved'. The *po'lal* means 'to be shaken' (cf. Aq.): 'The columns of the heavens are shaken' (cf. 9:6). Note that in 9:6 the verb יתפלצון 'tremble' (speaking of the columns of the earth) is translated מתרפפין by Targ., which confirms perfectly the meaning of ירופפו in our passage. The verb תמה expresses in general the attitude of a person who is struck dumb by stupefaction. The mountains too are 'stupefied' under the effect of the divine threat. גַּעֲרָה is used to express Yahweh's threat to the elements in Ps 18:16

(cf. 2 S 22:16); 104:7; Is 50:2.

12 The text of G begins again at v. 12. For רגע, G κατέπαυσεν, Targ. גזר 'He has divided'. Syr. حجر reads גער (accepted by Siegfried). Vulg. *maria congregata sunt* is inspired by Gn 1:9. The *qerê* וּבִתְבוּנָתוֹ, instead of the mistaken *kethîb* ובתובנתו, is supported by all the versions. For מחץ, G(B) ἔστρωται (Jerome *vulneratus est*), G(A, C) ἔστρωσεν (Sah., Syro-hex.). The reading of G was ἔτρωσε (cf. Arab. Baud. ميت), which exists in a few MSS (cf. Beer), and which is attested indirectly by the *vulneratus est* of Jerome. The word רהב is translated τὸ κῆτος (G), ἀλαζονείαν (Symm.; cf. Vulg. *superbum*), גבריא 'the giants' (Targ.), حمّستا 'numerous' (Syr.).

God possesses 'wisdom and power, counsel and understanding' (12:13). According to Jer 10:12, it is 'by His strength' that He made the earth, and 'by His understanding' that He has stretched out the heavens. We find here precisely the same terms: בְּכֹחוֹ and בִתְבוּנָתוֹ. The verb רגע, here as in Is 51:15 and Jer 31:35, is akin to נגע and expresses the action of 'dividing', 'cleaving' the sea; cf. Comm. on 7:5. The change to גער (Siegfried, following Syr.) is contra-indicated, since we find רגע in Is 51:15; Jer 31:35. It is simply by conjecture that Gunkel changes רגע to גער in Jer 31:35 (*Schöpfung und Chaos*, p. 94). God divides the sea just as Marduk splits open the skull of Tiamat at the moment of creation (*Choix de textes*, pp. 55, 130). The sea is personified. It is identified

13   *His* breath has swept the heavens,
      His hand has pierced the fleeing serpent!

13   רוּחוֹ (Vulg.); MT: ברוחו.

with Rahab of the 2nd hemistich.
On Rahab, cf. Comm. on 3:8; 7:12.
In 9:13 the 'helpers of Rahab' were
prostrated beneath the feet of God.
The verb מחץ means 'to strike'
(5:18). From v. 7, we have been
having a cosmological description.
God creates the heaven and the
earth, confines the waters to the
clouds, traces a circle which the sea
cannot overstep, shakes, in His
fashion, the mountains, takes away
from the abyss any impulse to revolt.

13 G κλεῖθρα δὲ οὐρανοῦ δεδοίκασιν αὐτόν reads בריחי instead of
ברוחו and שָׁעָרָה instead of שפרה
(Dillmann). In accordance with the
meaning of שׁפר 'to be shining' and
'to be fair', Targ. paraphrases 'by
the breath of His mouth the face of
the heavens has become fair'. Vulg.
spiritus ejus ornavit coelos reads
רוחו and not ברוחו (cf. inf.). Syr.
renders שפרה by ܡܕܒܪ 'guiding',
which refers to God. G προστάγματι
avoids the anthropomorphism of
ידו. For חללה, G ἐθανάτωσεν and
Syr. ܩܛܠܐ 'has killed', from חלל
'pierce', 'fatally wound'; but Targ.
ברת 'has created' regards חללה as
the *po'lel* of חיל, with the meaning
of bring to birth (cf. 15:7), and it is
this sense which is at the basis of
Vulg. *et obstetricante manu ejus
eductus est coluber tortuosus*. The
נחש ברח is identified with Leviathan
in Targ.
    Literally translated the 1st hemi-
stich would run: 'by His breath the
sky is luminous' (i.e. light), where we
have an odd juxtaposition of two
nouns, of which one is in the masculine plural and the other in the
feminine singular. If we regard
שִׁפְרָה as a verb in the *pi'el* with the
dagesh omitted (cf. שָׁלְחָה in Ezk

17:7), it is not clear what its subject
can be in the text as it stands. Since
the 2nd hemistich begins with 'His
hand has pierced', it is obvious from
parallelism that רוחו ought to be the
parallel of יָדוֹ, and that the reading
ברוחו is due to a dittograph of the
final consonant of רהב (v. 12). Vulg.
has correctly read רוחו (cf. sup.).
Outside our passage, the root שׁפר
'to be sparkling, fair, pretty' appears
in Hebrew only in Ps 16:6, where
the verb שפרה means 'to please'.
The words שֶׁפֶר of Gn 49:21 and
שׁוֹפָר 'trumpet' represent the Assyrian *šapparu* 'ibex' (*L'Emploi métaphorique*, p. 35, n. 4), whilst שָׁפְרִיר
is the Assyrian *šipirru* 'sceptre'.
Now, in Arabic, the verb *safara* 'to
shine' means also 'to sweep' the
clouds away, *ut ventus nubes e coelo*
(Freytag, *Lexicon*, s.v.). We recognise this meaning in the *pi'el* of
שׁפר in our passage: 'His breath has
swept the skies clean.' God can
equally well bring the cloud (v. 9)
or drive it away. V. 13a is parallel
to v. 12a, while v. 13b is parallel to
v. 12b. It is unnecessary to search
for mythological implications in the
1st hemistich, as is done by Gunkel,
who bases himself on the text of G,
which arises from an incorrect reading of the Hebrew. Still less shall we
be tempted to translate: 'by His
spirit, His hand has stretched out
the heavens' (Daiches, in *Zeitschr.
für Assyriologie*, **25**, pp. 1 ff.,
on the basis of the Assyrian *šupar-
ruru* 'to stretch out' a net). The
balance of the verse is destroyed if
we make of ידו the subject of שפרה.
Concern to find reflected here elements in the Babylonian story of
creation inspires Lyon to translate:
'By the winds of the heavens He has
broken it', changing שפרה to שברה

14   If such are the outlines of His works,
How small is the whisper we hear of them!
And the thunder of His might, who shall understand it?

14   Continues in 26:1.

(*Journal of Bibl. Literature*, 1895, p. 592). But does one break with winds? The 2nd hemistich brings forward on to the scene the נָחָשׁ בָּרִחַ 'fleeing serpent' which, in the light of Is 27:1 is none other than Leviathan (cf. Targ.). On this monster of chaos, similar in nature to Rahab (v. 13) and Tannîn (7:12), cf. Comm. on 3:8 and 7:12. The analogy with v. 13b and with Is 51:9 (read המחצת instead of המחצבת, cf. Condamin) invites us to connect חֹלְלָה with חלל 'pierce', 'wound', used here in the *po'el* form: 'His hand has pierced the fleeing serpent.' This is an allusion to the struggle of God against the powers of chaos (3:8). Much less suitable to the context is the interpretation as the *po'lel* of חיל (cf. 15:7): 'His hand has brought to birth the fleeing serpent.' The subject would be ill chosen, and it would be necessary to paraphrase on the lines of Vulg. (cf. sup.).

14 V. 14a, absent from Sah., marked with asterisk in Syro-hex., did not exist in G. The present text is derived from a hexaplar author. The *qerê* דְּרָכָיו, supported by Vulg., Syr., Targ., is preferable to the *kethîb* דַּרְכּוֹ, adopted by the present text of G ὁδοῦ αὐτοῦ. On the other hand, it is the *kethîb* גְּבוּרָתוֹ, supported by all the versions, which is preferable to the *qerê* גְּבוּרֹתָיו. For ומה־שֵּמֶץ we have καὶ ἐπὶ ἰκμάδα in G (Jerome *et adhuc stillam*); cf. Vulg. *et cum vix parvam stillam*. Syr. interprets נשמע as a *niph'al*. The sentence begins with the conditional הֵן (25:14). The main

clauses are introduced by *waw*, as in 9:11a and 23:8a. With הֵן־אֵלֶּה cf. אַךְ־אֵלֶּה at the end of Bildad's speech (18:21). The קְצוֹת דְּרָכָיו are literally the 'ends of His ways', i.e. what is most distant from the point of departure; cf. קְצוֹת in 28:24. But, in the light of Pr 8:22, where the beginning of the divine words is called רֵאשִׁית דְּרָכּוֹ 'the beginning of His ways' (read דרכיו with G, Symm., and Vulg.), we see that the author's meaning here is the divine works of which human beings see only the edges, the outskirts, the apparent outlines. In 40:19 we shall have רֵאשִׁית דַּרְכֵי־אֵל 'the first of the works of God' (cf. Pr 8:22). The 2nd hemistich means: 'how small a whisper we hear of them!' The interrogative pronoun מָה is used in the exclamatory sense (6:25). The phrase שֵׁמֶץ דָּבָר is equivalent to קְצת דבר 'little'; cf. Comm. on 4:12. The complement בּוֹ refers to the understood relative אֲשֶׁר implied before נִשְׁמַע: How little is what we hear! The preposition "בְּ after the verb שׁמע even in the sense of 'hear' (15:8). The 3rd hemistich is an *a fortiori*: 'and the thunder of His might, who shall understand it?' The menaces of God to which allusion is made in v. 11 are manifested in thunder (Ps 104:7). We discern only a fractional part of the divine works; how then shall we understand the full scope of what is implied by the 'thunder of His might'? In 12:13 the גְּבוּרָה 'might', 'power' was part of the attributes of God. On the *hithpo'lel* of בין in the sense of 'understand' (Ps 107:43), cf. Comm. on 11:11.

26:1 Then Job spoke and said:
2   How you have helped the weak,
    And assisted the nerveless arm!
3   How you have counselled the ignorant,
    And abundantly shown your wisdom!

Chapters 26: 1-4, 27: 2-12   Ninth speech of Job: see Introduction, pp. xlviiif.

26: 1 Bildad's speech, which began at v. 2 of ch. 25, is separated from its sequel and conclusion by 26: 1-4, which form the preamble to Job's speech, whose sequel is to be found in ch. 27: 2ff. This is what necessitated in ch. 27 the introduction into the text of a new introductory formula: 'And Job continued his speech and he said.' In fact, our v. 1 introduces Job's reply to Bildad, and it will proceed from v. 4 of ch. 26 to v. 2 of ch. 27; cf. Intro., pp. xlviiif.

2 G and Vulg. have separated the verbs from their complements to stress the question. G further dissociates the elements of the two hemistichs with the following result: τίνι πρόσκεισαι ἢ τίνι μέλλεις βοηθεῖν; πότερον οὐχ ᾧ πολλὴ ἰσχὺς καὶ ᾧ βραχίων κραταιός ἐστιν; Vulg. remains more literal: cujus adjutor es? numquid imbecillis? et sustentas brachium ejus qui non est fortis? The words ללא and לא are rendered by the same expression לְ 'which has not' in Syr. In Targ. also we have דלא for לא, but ללא is interpreted by מדלית 'without'.

In vv. 2-4 we find again the alternation of the exclamatory מָה with the interrogative מִי, as at the end of Bildad's speech (26: 14). The vocalisation מֶה before a guttural (31: 2; cf. 7: 21). The words לֹא־כֹחַ and לֹא־עֹז play the part of real adjectives, the negative לֹא being equivalent to the alpha privative. Cf. the use of לֹא־דרך in 12: 24. A similar meaning is suitable for לֹא־חָכְמָה in v. 3. Cf. the use of the prefix 'non' in non-aggression, non-appearance, etc. The 1st hemistich means simply: 'How you have helped the weak!' Strength resides in the arm (cf. L'Emploi métaphorique, pp. 140f.). We have seen that אִישׁ זְרוֹעַ 'man of arm' denoted the strong (22: 8). The 2nd hemistich continues the irony: 'How you have assisted the nerveless arm!' The verb הוֹשִׁיעַ means both 'to save' (5: 15; 22: 29) and 'to help'. Parallelism here requires the latter meaning. Bildad contented himself with proclaiming a long doxology, the conclusion of which was that we cannot understand the work of God (26: 14). That was all he could find to relieve the distress of Job!

3 G and Vulg. interpret the 1st hemistich according to their translation of v. 2: τίνι συμβεβούλευσαι; cui dedisti consilium? For ללא, Syr. לְ, Targ. מדלית (cf. v. 2). G again

377

4   For whom have you uttered words,
     And whose spirit has flowed forth from you?

26: 5-14 After 25: 6.

separates the verb from the complement in the 2nd hemistich: τίνι
ἐπακολουθήσεις. But Vulg. *et prudentiam tuam ostendisti plurimam*
remains more literal.

The irony is continued in v. 3:
'How you have counselled the ignorant!' Job is at one and the same
time the weak, the man of nerveless
arm, the ignorant, literally the 'one
without wisdom'; cf. v. 2 for the
meaning of exclamatory מָה and of
לֹא חָכְמָה. Wisdom, חָכְמָה, is usually
coupled with counsel, עֵצָה (12:13).
He who is devoid of wisdom needs
to be advised. But where is the
counsel of Bildad? On the word
תֻּשִׁיָּה 'foresight', 'prudence', 'insight', cf. Comm. on 5: 12. In 12: 16
תשיה is classified among the divine
attributes, as is חכמה in 12: 13. The
verb הודיע, with an abstract term as
complement, to connote 'make
known', 'show forth' a certain
quality (32: 7). The complement
לָרֹב 'in a large quantity' (cf. רֹב
in 23: 6) is used ironically like the
preceding exclamations: 'How you
have abundantly shown your wisdom!' Changes such as that from
לרב to לָרָךְ 'to the little child'
(Reiske), or to לְבַעַר 'to a brutish
creature' (Graetz), postulated as a
result of too much concern for parallelism, have no sort of support in the
versions. In the light of the previous
sentences we should expect לְלֹא followed by an abstract term. There is no
compelling reason to change the text.

4 Vulg. *nonne eum qui fecit spi-
ramentum?* seems to have replaced
ממך by ממנו.
The verb הגיד, with a double accusative, as in 31: 37. Job now

adopts the interrogative style: 'For
whom have you uttered words?'
Duhm would interpret אֶת as a preposition: 'With whose help?' He claims
that the construction of הגיד with a
double accusative is exceptional and
that we must eliminate the suffix in
אגידנו of 31: 37. But the same construction is found in Ezk 43: 10,
where we have the accusative particle governing two complements.
The meaning of Job's question is not
doubtful. Bildad has been talking in
the air. Whom does he wish to teach?
Job knows as much as his friends
about these matters: 12: 3; 13: 2.
The 2nd hemistich runs literally:
'and whose spirit has flowed forth
from you?' Now, in 27: 3, which is
linked with our text by 27: 2, Job
declares: 'My whole spirit is still in
me.' It is not from Bildad that he
receives this spirit, which is not
only the principle of life (33: 4; cf.
Gn 2: 7) but also the principle of
wisdom (32: 8; cf. 20: 3). By the
tone of his speech, Bildad claims to
be announcing new truths, and imparting life and wisdom to those
who are devoid of these! The phrase
'to come forth', 'to flow forth' is
used, because it is through the mouth
and the words spoken that the spirit
of man reveals itself and communi-
cates itself to others. Cf. Mt 15: 15ff.,
where 'what comes out of the mouth'
manifests the secret thoughts of the
heart. In Assyrian *ṣit pî* 'what
comes out of the mouth' is the words.
Thus the 2nd hemistich strengthens
the 1st: the words of Bildad do not
engender the spirit of understanding
in anybody. The sequel to v. 4 is
found in 27: 2, where the speech of
is continued, while 26: 5 is the
sequel to Bildad's speech, 25: 1-6;
see Intro., pp. xlviiif.

27:2 By God who has set aside my right,
And by Shaddai who has embittered my soul!

3 So long as my spirit remains inviolate within me,
And the breath of Eloah is in my nostrils,

27:1 'And Job continued his speech and said'. An addition (cf. Comm.).

27:1 G ἔτι δὲ προσθεὶς Ἰὼβ εἶπεν τῷ προοιμίῳ will recur in 29:1. Hence we cannot follow Syro-hex., which puts an asterisk before ἔτι and attributes the text to Theod. without saying where this text ended. Sah. confirms G. For מֹשְׁלוֹ, Targ. and Syr. מתליה, Aq. τὴν παραβολὴν αὐτοῦ, Vulg. *parabolam suam* (cf. 29:1).

The addition of this v. 1 was necessitated by the accident to the text which has had the effect of separating 27:2 from 26:4. If we replace 26:5-14 in its natural context, i.e. after 25:6, the speech of Job continues at 27:2, and the introductory formula, borrowed from 29:1, where it is justified, is no longer needed here. For the explanation of this formula, cf. 29:1.

2 G(A, C) ὁ Κύριος instead of ὁ Θεός which translates אֵל in G(B), is followed by Sah., Syro-hex., Jerome *Dominus*, and Arab. Baud. The meaning of הסיר משפטי is softened by G ὃς οὕτω με κέκρικεν.

The interjection חַי־אֵל 'God is alive' announces an oath, like חי יהוה (1 S 14:39, 45) or חי האלהים (2 S 2:27). The meaning is clear: as truly as God is alive! We translate simply 'by God!' in accordance with the old formula of oaths. The relative אשר is understood after אל (cf. 3:3, etc.). The verb הסיר does not here mean 'to remove' (12:20, 24), but 'to set aside' (9:34) something that is inconvenient. Job has called on God to engage with him in a formal legal debate (23:3ff.) and God has eluded the challenge (23:8ff.).

Hence: 'by God who has set aside my right!' This expresssion will be severely condemned by Elihu (34:5). On מִשְׁפָּטִי 'my judgment', 'my right' (8:3), cf. 29:14. The very fact that God is unwilling to hear Job plunges the latter into bitterness. Job has already spoken about the bitterness of his soul (7:11; 10:1; cf. 3:20 and 21:25).

3 By haplography after ἐνούσης G has lost ἐν ἐμοί (= בי), which is found in G(A), Sah., Syro-hex., Jerome *in me*, Arab. Baud. Note the translation of בי by במימרי בי 'in my word, my person' in Targ. (cf. 1:10 and Comm. on 20:29). For באפי, G. τὸ περιόν μοι ἐν ῥινί. Syr. reduces the verse to a single sentence, by omitting נשמתי בי. Targ. פסק 'has ceased' interprets כל in accordance with the verb כלה.

The natural meaning of the 1st hemistich, supported by 2 S 1:9 (where we have the synonym נפשי instead of נִשְׁמָתִי) is simply 'as long as all my breath will be still in me'. God has brought great suffering on Job, but He has left him his life intact. And at the same time Job notes that he has still all his mind and spirit unharmed and that he has no need of the counsel of Bildad (26: 4b). The term נשמתי 'my spirit' is chosen, in preference to נפשי (2 S 1:9), because of its double meaning: spirit of life and spirit of wisdom (cf. Comm. on 26:4). The adverb עוֹד 'still' has been interpolated between כל and נשמתי. Attempts have been made to explain עוד as a real noun in order to translate: 'all the time

4   My lips shall not speak any falsehood,
       Nor my tongue utter a lie.

5   Far be it from me to admit that you are right;
       Until I die I will not renounce my integrity;

that my breath will be in me' (cf.
some ancient commentators cited
by Dillmann, and recently Budde,
Ehrlich). But then the כִּי of the
opening is no longer intelligible. The
'breath of God' is the principle of
life which flows from God (Gn 2: 7)
and which God takes back when it
pleases Him (34: 14). It is into a
man's nostril that God has breathed
it (Gn 2: 7; 7: 22; Is 2: 22). Note
the series נֶפֶשׁ 'soul' (v. 2), נְשָׁמָה
'spirit', רוּחַ 'breath'. After the nose
(v. 3) will come the lips and the
tongue (v. 4). These observations
would suffice to exclude the hypothesis of Duhm, who places v. 3
after v. 5. Budde remarks very justly
that v. 5 is sufficient to itself and has
no need of support.

4 G(A) τὸ στόμα μου, instead of
τὰ χείλη μου, which translates שְׂפָתַי
in G. Instead of וּלְשׁוֹנִי, G οὐδὲ ἡ
ψυχή μου.
       The conjunction אִם, after חִי־אֵל
(v. 2), as after חָלִילָה לִי (v. 5), gives
to the sentence a negative meaning;
cf. Gn 42: 15; 1 S 14: 45; 2 S 11: 11,
etc. This use of אִם is to be explained
by an implied imprecation: if I do
such a thing may I be treated like
the victim sacrificed at the moment
of the oath! Hence: I will by no
means do it! The imprecation is
made explicit in the formula: may
God do so and more also! Cf. our
commentary on 1 S 3: 17. Note the
parallelism between עַוְלָה 'falsehood'
and רְמִיָּה 'lie' as in 13: 7. For the
connection between עוֹלָה and the
lying word, cf. Comm. on 6: 29-30.
Here, as in 13: 7, עוֹלָה is a complement of the verb דִּבֵּר. The word

לָשׁוֹן is generally feminine. But in
Pr 26: 28 we find לִשּׁוֹן as the subject
of a verb in the masculine, which
enables us to preserve here יֶהְגֶּה.
The verb הגה means 'to murmur',
'to hum', in the sense of uttering
lies. Cf. Is 59: 3, where we have:
'your lips speak lies, your tongue
utters (תֶהְגֶּה) falsehood'. The same
parallelism between הגה and דבר
is found in Ps 37: 30.

5 Vulg. connects עַד־אֶגְוָע with the
2nd hemistich, which gives the right
caesura (cf. inf.). For תַּמְתִּי, Symm.
τῆς ἁπλότητός μου; cf. Aq. in 4: 6;
21: 23. The words אִם־אַצְדִּיק אֶתְכֶם
are omitted in Syr., while G neglects
מִמֶּנִּי at the end.
       Job once again insists on his inno-
cence. He cannot accept the thesis
of his friends: 'Far be it from me
to admit that you are right!' The
expression חָלִילָה לִי sit mihi in
profanum (cf. 34: 10), with the meaning absit a me (Vulg.), is followed by
the conjunction אִם before the statement which is rejected as sacrilegious
(1 S 24: 7; 2 S 20: 20). The hiph'il
of צדק 'to be right' (9: 15; 11: 2;
13: 18) is used to connote: 'admit to
be right'. Cf. the use of the pi'el in
33: 32. To connect עַד־אֶגְוָע with
the 1st hemistich, as is done by the
MT and the versions (with the exception of Vulg.), is to destroy the
balance of the verse. It is more probable that עַד־אֶגְוָע belongs to the
2nd hemistich and answers חָלִילָה לִי
of the opening. The formula אֶגְוָע
'I expire' is familiar with Job
(3: 11; 10: 18; 13: 19; 29: 18). The
verb הֵסִיר 'set aside', 'remove' (v. 2)
calls for the complement מִמֶּנִּי 'from

6   I have held fast to my righteousness and will not let it go,
      My heart is not *ashamed* of my days.

6   יֶחְפָּר‎; MT: יחרף‎.

me', which Bickell and Duhm delete,
following G. The context makes the
sense quite clear. Job will not renounce his integrity, as though it
did not belong to him. It is his own,
and he will claim it until death. Were
he to admit that his friends were
right, he would confess himself
guilty, and thus disown his integrity.
He will not do so. In 31:6, he will
again speak of his integrity: תֻּמָּתִי‎
as here. On תֻּמָּה‎ cf. Comm. on 2:3.

6 Vulg. *justificationem meam, quam
coepi tenere, non deseram* merges into
a single proposition the two elements
of the 1st hemistich. Syr. adds לי‎
after יחרף‎; cf. Vulg. *neque enim
reprehendit me.* G οὐ γὰρ σύνοιδα
ἐμαυτῷ ἄτοπα πράξας is a paraphrase
of the 2nd hemistich.

V. 6 develops the idea contained
in v. 5b. There is no reason to give
to החזיק‎ a different meaning from
that which it has in 2:3, 9 (contra
Duhm), where the construction is
the same as here. We have בְּצִדְקָתִי‎
because תמתי‎ (cf. 2:3, 9) has just
been used in v. 5. Similarly we have
had נשמתי‎ to avoid the repetition of
נפשי‎ in v. 3. The verb רפה‎ in the
hiph'il 'abandon', 'let go' (7:19).
With the 1st hemistich, cf. Ca 3:4,
אחזתיו ולא ארפנו‎ 'I have held him
and will not let him go.' The verb
חרף‎ means 'to outrage' (cf. חרפה‎
'outrage', 'shame', 16:10; 19:5). It
is by approximation that it is given
the meaning of 'condemn' (Le Hir)
or 'reproach' (Renan). Next, a partitive sense is assumed for מִיָּמָי‎ (cf.
Dillmann, etc.), or else a further
complement is understood, with the
result that not very exact translations are produced: 'My heart will

not condemn any of my days' (Le
Hir); 'My heart does not reproach
me with a single one of my days'
(Renan). Fried. Delitzsch relies on
the vocalisation יֶחֱרָף‎ (intransitive)
and on the Arabic خرف‎ 'to have one's
brain affected', 'to suffer delirium',
in order to translate: 'Never shall I
be of a different way of thinking my
life long!' But the context does not
in any way suggest an allusion to the
future. It is *hic et nunc* that Job
claims his innocence. Michaelis proposed to vocalise יֵחָרֵף‎ *niph'al* in the
sense of 'to be convinced' (?), while
Budde demands the *pi'el* יְחָרֵף‎ and
returns to the older interpretations:
'My conscience does not blame a
single one of my days.' It becomes
apparent that commentators do not
succeed in extracting an appropriate
meaning from the root חרף‎. Torczyner affirms that we should read
יחנף‎, following the expression חנפי
לב‎ (36:13): 'My heart does not play
the hypocrite with my whole life.'
We should expect a different formula
to reconcile מימי‎ 'with my days'
(the past) with יחנף‎ (the present).
Ehrlich, so as to make the two hemistichs materially symmetrical, replaces יחרף‎ by יֶרֶף‎ and מימי‎ by
מִתֻּמּוֹ‎: 'My heart does not waive its
claim to integrity.' This is attributing to the author a tiresome
repetition of the verb הרפה‎. The
best conjecture seems to us to be
that of Duhm, who reads simply
יֶחְפָּר‎ instead of יחרף‎. The verb
חפר‎ (6:20) 'to be confused', 'to
feel shame'. Thus we obtain: 'My
heart is not ashamed of my days',
i.e. of my life. Job proudly claims
as right all the actions of his past

7   May my enemy have the lot of the wicked,
     And my adversary that of the unrighteous man!
8   For what is the hope of the godless when he *prays*,
     When he *lifts up* his soul *to* Eloah?

8 יִפְגַּע ;MT: יבצע. — יִשָּׂא לֶאֱלוֹהַּ ;MT: ישל אלוה.

life. It is past deeds which constitute his 'righteousness'. He has no need to blush for them.

7 G paraphrases the whole verse, translating כרשע by ὥσπερ ἡ καταστροφὴ τῶν ἀσεβῶν and כעול by ὥσπερ ἡ ἀπώλεια τῶν παρανόμων (א ἀνόμων). Obelus in Syro-hex. before ἡ καταστροφή.

Some modern commentators would make this verse the beginning of Zophar's speech (cf. Bickell, Hoffmann, Duhm, Gray, Ball), retaining, for the speech of Job, only v. 12 (Duhm) or vv. 11-12 (Gray, Ball). We ourselves think that Zophar's speech begins only at v. 13 (Cf. Intro., pp. xlix f.). The essential is to attain a clear understanding of our v. 7. It is generally admitted, since Schnurrer (quoted by Rosenmüller), that Job here makes a frontal attack on his interlocutors and wishes for them the fate of the wicked man, for it is they and not he, who play the part of the guilty: 'He admits that God is severe towards the wicked; it is not he, however, but his false friends who are wicked' (Renan). This is not the meaning of the imprecation. Job has just said that he clings to his righteousness and will not let it go. Now, righteousness, צְדָקָה, is contrasted with wickedness, רֶשַׁע (35: 8), and the word רָשָׁע 'wickedness' has as a parallel עָוֶל 'unrighteousness' (34: 10). We meet here precisely that pair of words—the wicked man (רָשָׁע) and the unrighteous man (עַוָּל)—which were coupled in one of the previous speeches of Job

(16: 11). These observations permit us to connect v. 7 with v. 6. Job is a righteous man. Hence it is not he who should suffer the fate of the wicked man or the scoundrel. By an altogether oriental turn of speech, instead of saying: 'May I not suffer the fate of the wicked!' he says: 'May my enemy suffer the fate of the wicked!' To each one his due! The enemy of the righteous—that is he to whom the fate of the wicked is appropriate. The expression היה כ" 'to be as, like', is used with the connotation 'to suffer the fate of' (1 S 25: 26; 2 S 18: 32). The use of the participle מִתְקוֹמֵם (20: 27) in the sense of 'adversary'. Cf. Ps 59: 2, where we have parallelism between אֹיְבַי 'my enemies' and מִתְקוֹמְמַי 'my adversaries'.

8 For כי יבצע, G ὅτι ἐπέχει (Jerome *quid expectat*), Vulg. *si avare rapiat*, Syr. 'who possesses riches', Targ. 'if he amasses the treasure of lies', Aq., Theod. and Symm. ὅτι πλεονεκτεῖ. It is clear that the idea of ill-gotten gains is at the basis of these translations. G πεποιθὼς ἐπὶ Κύριον ἄρα σωθήσεται seems to read יציל instead of ישל. Targ. ינתר 'he causes to fall' and Vulg. *non liberet* connect ישל with נשל 'reject', 'make to fall'. Syr. ܐܘܥ 'he has raised' reads perhaps ישא (cf. inf.).

The verb יְבְצַע is capable of two interpretations. It is either related to בצע 'to make illicit gains' (cf. versions) or else to בצע 'to cut off' (cf. the *pi'el* in 6: 9). The latter sense is adopted by most moderns, who regard יבצע as intransitive: 'For what will be

9   Does God hear his cry,
      When calamity seizes him?

the hope of the impious man when he
is cut off?' (Le Hir). In order to
obtain a formal passive, it has been
proposed to replace יבצע by a
niph'al יִבָּצֵעַ (Oort), or by a pu'al
יְבֻצַּע (Budde). Some would find here
the pi'el of 6:9 and vocalise יְבַצֵּעַ
(Bickell). Cf. the translation of
Renan: 'What will be the hope of the
enemy in the day when God cuts
away...?' This interpretation of the
1st hemistich influences that of the
2nd: 'When God snatches away his
soul' (Le Hir), 'when God takes back
to Himself the thread of his life'
(Renan). The verb יֵשֶׁל is then related
to שלה 'to draw', 'to pull', which
does not occur elsewhere. Dillmann
proposes to read יֵשַׁל (from שלל 'to
remove'), which gives a similar
meaning, while Hoffmann reads יִשַּׁל
(from נשל; cf. Targ. above). Schnurrer saw in ישל a defective form of
ישאל, which made possible the translation: 'when God reclaims his soul'
(cf. Wellhausen, Budde, Duhm, etc.).
A comparison is then made with Lk
12:20 (cf. 1 K 3:11; 19:4; Jon
4:8), and the 2nd hemistich seems
to offer a good parallel to מי יבצע
'when he is cut off' (cf. Budde).
However, Duhm deletes כי יבצע,
which, he thinks, does not make
sense. Vv. 9-10 allude to the prayer
of the godless, not on his last day,
but in his moments of distress. The
author is not speaking of his death,
but of the inefficacy of his prayer.
Now, an excellent conjecture of
Perles, taken up by Torczyner, consists in reading יִשָּׂא לֶאֱלוֹהַּ (cf. Syr.)
instead of ישל אלוה. The change is
an insignificant one, but the meaning which results is admirably in
harmony with the context: 'when
he lifts up his soul to Eloah', i.e.
when he prays. The expression

נשא נפשו 'lift up one's soul' (Ps 25:1;
86:4; 143:8) is a definition of
prayer. Note that v. 10b is similar
to Ps 86:3b, while our 2nd hemistich uses the same terms as Ps
86:4b. Thus v. 9 becomes the quite
natural sequel of v. 8b. It is within
this order of ideas that we should
explain כִּי יִבְצָע of the 1st hemistich.
But בצע 'to make illicit gain' or בצע
'to cut off', 'to be cut off' cannot be
adapted to the context except by
great subtleties of interpretation.
A conjecture of Mandelkern (quoted
by Beer) seems to us to solve the
problem. That is to read יִפְגַּע (cf.
21:15) instead of יבצע. Then the
verse becomes: 'For what is the hope
of the godless man when he prays,
when he lifts up his soul to Eloah?'
We find here once again חָנֵף 'godless' (8:13). Now, in 13:16 Job
said: 'This, moreover, will be salvation for me, for no godless man
dare appear before Him!' If Job
belonged to the category of the
wicked, the unrighteous, the impious, he could not turn to God, as
his friends advise him to do. God
closes His ear to the appeals of the
wicked man (8-10), as Job knows
(11); if then his friends are unwilling
to agree that he is righteous, why
do they waste their time in exhorting
him (12)? Thus understood, the
passage 8-11 may very well remain
in the mouth of Job (contra Bernstein, Wellhausen, Duhm, etc.).

9 Syr. interprets the interrogative
ה as a negative. G(B) ὁ Θεός for אל
remains isolated, as in v. 2. The
other MSS have ὁ Κύριος (cf. v. 2).

If Job were not righteous, if he
formed part of the category alluded
to in v. 7, he would not be justified
in hoping in God and praying to
Him: 'Does God hear his cry, when

10   Is his delight in Shaddai?
Does he call upon Eloah at all times?

11   I teach you the ways of God,
What is in the mind of Shaddai I do not conceal;

calamity seizes him?' Job still accepts for the sake of argument the hypothesis postulated by his interlocutors, to whom he wishes to show their inconsistency. They treat him as a guilty man and at the same time encourage him to pray. But these two things are contradictory. The verb בוא with על before the complement which denotes the victim of misfortune (2:11). The word צָרָה as in 5:19.

10   G interprets the verse interrogatively: μὴ ἔχει τινὰ παρρησίαν ἔναντι αὐτοῦ; ἢ ὡς ἐπικαλεσαμένου αὐτοῦ εἰσακούσεται αὐτοῦ; The close εἰσακούσεται αὐτοῦ is inspired by v. 9a; ἢ τὴν δέησιν αὐτοῦ εἰσακούσεται ὁ Θεός; Syr. corrects the sense of the MT by adding: 'certainly God will hear him and will answer him' at the end of the verse.

The conjunction אם introduces the second question; cf. 6:12, 28. Job here repeats, in order to challenge them, the words of Eliphaz in 22:26a. And this again is a proof that the passage belongs to Job and not to some other of the speakers. After declaring that Job would find his delight in the Almighty, Eliphaz added: 'and you will lift up your face towards Eloah' (22:26b). That again is an impossibility, since the wicked man is by definition God's enemy. The exhortations of the friends mean nothing at all, so long as they do not admit Job's innocence, again affirmed in vv. 4-6. The 2nd hemistich, 'does he invoke Eloah at all times?', is confirmed by Ps 86:3, where we have אליך אקרא כל־היום. Note that the 2nd hemistich of v. 8 recalled Ps 86:4b. Duhm would change the text, with the help of G

and Syr. (whose tendentious character we have noted) by substituting אֱלֹוהַ בְּכָל־עֵת אלו היפגעה for 'will He welcome him?' Beer, using the same versions as a basis, proposes יעתר־לו 'will He grant his prayer?' instead of בכל־עת. On the other hand, it is to יִקְרָא that Ehrlich objects; he reads יקרב and adds אל before אלוה: 'does he approach God?' All these hypotheses might be justified if the text were desperately corrupt. But we see, on the contrary, that Ps 86:3 confirms the MT. Job refuses even to admit his first supposition, namely that the godless can ever pray to God. This is how his ideas are linked together. His friends constantly recommend him to have resort to God, but they refuse to recognise his innocence. Now, there is no point in the godless man's turning to God for help, since the Almighty will refuse to listen to him. And further, how suppose that this godless man is going to delight in the Almighty, as does the pious believer who prays all day? Hence Job's case is hopeless! If they refuse to believe in his righteousness (vv. 4-6), nothing is to be done (v. 12).

11   Syr. 'as for you, I deliver you up into the hand of God' fails to understand the meaning of the 1st hemistich. G τί ἐστιν ἐν χειρὶ Κυρίου paraphrases ביד־אל. Duhm takes advantage of this to replace אתכם by אשר, but he forgets that אתכם is translated in G by ἀναγγελῶ ὑμῖν. Targ. interprets יד as נבואת 'prophecy'. Syr. 'for your works are not hid from Him' seems to have repeated אתכם after אשר: 'what is with you', i.e. your works(?). Vulg. *docebo vos, per manum Dei, quae*

12   If you all have observed this,
      Why then do you do uselessly a vain thing?

Omnipotens habeat, nec abscondam
fuses the two hemistichs by making
of אשׁר עם־שׁדי the complement of
אורה.

Those who wish to remove v. 11
from Job are embarrassed by אֶתְכֶם,
which they propose to change to
אשׁר (Duhm; cf. sup.), or to אתך
מה־ (Beer, also following G). Now,
v. 11 forms a good introduction to
v. 12. Job's friends weary themselves
in vain (v. 12b), for Job understands
very well the ways and dealings of
God, and it is precisely in explaining
the divine attitude towards the
godless that he has shown the worthlessness of the exhortations with
which he is pursued: 'I teach you the
ways of God' (literally, the hand of
God). The hand is the instrument of
action (*L'Emploi métaphorique*, p.
144). Cf. Jer 16:21, 'I will make
them to know my hand and my
power.' The object of the teaching is
introduced by the preposition ב",
as in Pr 4:11; Ps 25:8. The idiom
'what is with Shaddai', to connote
what is in His mind and thought, is
well in conformity with Job's style
(10:13b; 23:14b).

12 For חזיתם, G (A) ἑοράκατε,
more literal than G (B, א, C) οἴδατε
(Sah., Syro-hex., Jerome *nostis*).
G κενὰ κενοῖς ἐπιβάλλετε, which renders הבל תהבלו, is understood as
καινὰ καινοῖς in Arab. Baud.

The principal clause is introduced
by *waw* (cf. 26:14). The words
אַתֶּם and כֻּלְּכֶם, which were in parallelism in 13:4, are now simply juxta-

posed: 'if you have observed it, all
of you!' The friends have observed
the same truth, namely that there is
no hope for the ungodly (8:13-15).
But, since they class Job among the
wicked and refuse to recognise his
righteousness, it is on their part a
sheer waste of time to attempt to
bring him back to the worship of
God. The expression הֶבֶל תֶּהְבָּלוּ
(etymological figure of speech)
means: 'you do in vain a vain thing'.
On the word הֶבֶל cf. 7:16. Job's
friends are talking in the air, their
speeches are irrelevant. Cf. 9:29,
where we have, as here, למה־זה הבל
'why shall I weary myself in vain?'
V. 12 recalls also 21:34, 'How then
do you console me with such futile
arguments! Of your answers nothing
is left but deception!' We have here
the sally by which Job closes his
speech. All that follows, from v. 13,
is a description of the ills which strike
the wicked man and his posterity. It
is one of the theses which have
been most vigorously opposed by
Job, in particular in ch. 21. V. 13
takes up the argument at the very
point where Zophar had left it in
20:29. Between this v. 13 and v. 14
the passage 24:18-24, completely
out of harmony on the lips of Job,
fits in admirably. The last speech
of Zophar, which has disappeared
from our present form of the text,
begins in reality at v. 13, continues
in 24:18-24, and concludes in
vv. 14-23 of our chapter; cf. Intro.,
pp. lf.

Then Zophar the Naamathite spoke and said:

27:13 This is the portion of the wicked man, *as decreed by* God,
And the lot which tyrants receive from Shaddai!

24:18 The one is a light thing on the surface of the waters,
Of the others the domain is accursed in the land,

Chapters 27:13, 24:18-24, 27:14-23. Third speech of Zophar: see Introduction, pp. xlixf.

27:13 Restore the introductory formula (20:1) before v. 13, and continue the speech by 24:18-24. — מֵאֵל (cf. G); MT: עִם־אֵל.

27:**13** The versions are in agreement with the MT as regards the alternation of the singular אָדָם רָשָׁע and the plural עָרִיצִים. Instead of עִם־אֵל, G παρὰ Κυρίου reads מֵאֵל (cf. inf.). For נַחֲלַת, G (B, C) κτῆμα (Syro-hex., Jerome *pars*), but G (A, אᶜˑᵃ) ὀργή (Sah.). G paraphrases יִקָּחוּ by ἐλεύσεται … ἐπ' αὐτούς.

Job's speech concludes with v. 12. V. 13 is a renewal of Zophar's speech, interrupted at v. 29 of ch. 20. This v. 29 is repeated almost verbatim, but the זֶה 'this', 'that' then referred to what preceded, whereas now it refers to what follows. The whole of ch. 20 amplified the theme of the punishment which overtakes the wicked. Zophar now returns to his thesis and develops it for the last time. This intention is announced in the introductory formula: 'This is the portion of the wicked man, as decreed by God, and this is the lot which tyrants receive from Shaddai!' In the light of 20:29, it is clear that the ע of עִם־אֵל is due to dittography and that we should read מֵאֵל with G. In 15:20 we had parallelism between רָשָׁע 'the wicked man' and עָרִיץ 'the tyrant'. Here, אָדָם רָשָׁע (20:29) and עָרִיצִים

'tyrants'. It is unnecessary to replace the plurals עָרִיצִים and יִקָּחוּ (which will be confirmed by 24:18) by singulars (contra Budde, Beer, Duhm). Note the construction which makes of עָרִיצִים the complement of נַחֲלַת and the subject of יִקָּחוּ. On the meaning of חֵלֶק 'portion' and of נַחֲלָה 'lot', cf. Comm. on 20:29. Thus Zophar announces the punishment decreed for the wicked and the tyrants. Now, v. 14 speaks only of 'his sons' and 'his shoots'. But in 24:18-24, a passage which has been mistakenly intercalated in Job's speech, we have the description of the misfortunes in store for the wicked man. V. 18, which opens this description, contains precisely a clause in the singular, קַל־הוּא, which refers to the wicked man, and two clauses in the plural referring to tyrants. Hence we restore 24:18-24 to its natural context by placing these verses between our v. 13 and the sequel which will allude to the posterity of the wicked. Cf. Intro., pp. xlviff.

14-23 After 24:24.

24:**18** G lacked v. 18a (cf. Comm.

No *wine-presser* turns *towards their* vineyard.

19   The drought and the heat carry away the snow waters,
Thus does Sheol *snatch away the sinner*;

24: 18   דֶּרֶךְ כַּרְמָם (cf. G); MT: דרך כרמים.

19   Transpose יגזלו to follow שלג and read יִגְזֹל וּשְׁאוֹל חוֹטֵא.

on 24: 14) up to בארץ. Syr. replaces הוא by the copula ו and omits לא יפנה. From בארץ, G translates: ἀναφανείη δὲ τὰ φυτὰ αὐτῶν ἐπὶ γῆς ξηρά, with vocalisation לֹא instead of לֹא, reading כַּרְמָם for כרמים (cf. inf.), translation of ציה (of v. 19) by ξηρά. Obelus in Syro-hex. before ἐπὶ γῆς. The word ציה is likewise connected with v. 18 by Aq., Symm., and Theod. (quoted in Syro-hex.).

To avoid the anomaly occasioned by the passage from the singular to the plural, it is generally proposed to replace קַל־הוּא by קַלּוּ (Budde, Beer, Grimme, etc.). But the idiom קַל־הוּא is thoroughly in agreement with the style of Job's friends, when they are speaking of the wicked man; cf. 8: 16a; 15: 22b, 23a. If we admit that v. 18 is not part of Job's speech, but belongs to the final speech of Zophar (which begins at 27: 13), the alternation of the singular and plural ceases to have anything odd about it. The 1st proposition refers to אָדָם רָשָׁע of 27: 13, the two others to עָרִיצִים. The 1st hemistich is elucidated by Hos 10: 7, where we find Samaria described as 'a twig on the face of the waters' (cf. van Hoonacker, in loc.). The adjective קַל has as its basic meaning: 'light'. The meaning 'rapid' is secondary (cf. the verb קָלַל in 7: 6; 9: 25). The wicked man is 'a light thing on the surface of the waters', he has no solidity; he floats or he is carried away by the current (cf. 20: 28). In the 2nd hemistich the verb תְּקַלַּל is chosen by reason of its assonance

with קַל. We have the *pu'al*, which is passive of the *pi'el* (cf. 3: 1): 'their domain is accursed in the land'. The wicked live in solitude and amid ruins (15: 28). The territory which they inhabit lies under a curse. Those who retain the 3rd hemistich as it stands interpret: 'they will not know the paths of the vineyards' (Le Hir), or 'never do they tread the path of the vineyards' (Renan). According to Le Hir, the sinner is denied access to his vineyards; according to Renan the wicked 'never lead the tranquil prosperous life of populations which have passed from the stage of the plundering nomad to that of settled agricultural tribes'. But we should have the plural at least, instead of יִפְנֶה, since it is now a question of 'their domain'. The reading of G כַּרְמָם 'their vineyard' instead of כְּרָמִים has the great advantage of furnishing the parallel word to חֶלְקָתָם 'their domain'. Bickell has quite correctly realised that the subject of יפנה is דרך, which he vocalises דֹּרֵךְ (cf. also Budde, Beer, etc.). The דֹּרֵךְ is he who treads the grapes in the vat; cf. the verb דרך in 24: 11. Cf. Is 63: 2; Am 9: 13. The verb פנה 'to turn towards' (6: 28; 21: 5) with accusative of direction: 'no wine presser turns towards their vineyard', for he will find no work there. It is a question of the vineyard of the wicked man. Zophar takes the opposite line to the affirmations of Job in 24: 6.

19   G, which has connected ציה with v. 18, replaces גַּם־חֹם by עמר יתום,

20 The womb which has *formed* him forgets him,
His name is no more mentioned.
Thus, like the tree, is unrighteousness broken down!

20 פְּתָקוֹ ;MT: מתקו. — שְׁמוֹ ;MT: רמה.

whence its translation: ἀγκαλίδα
γὰρ ὀρφανῶν ἥρπασαν. This is a combination of v. 9a with v. 10b. The
word שָׁאוֹל is omitted in G, the words
מִימֵי־שֶׁלֶג are transferred to v. 20,
with חטאו which is read חֶטְאוֹ (cf.
v. 20). Theod. καὶ γὰρ αὐτοί reads
גַם־הֶם instead of גַם־חֶם. Vulg. paraphrases the whole verse, reading
חֶטְאוֹ (with G): *ad nimium calorem
transeat ab aquis nivium et usque ad
inferos peccatum illius*. It is מִימֵי־שֶׁלֶג
which is regarded as the subject of
יגזלו in Syr. The word ישכחהו of
v. 20 is connected with v. 19 by
Targ.

The two hemistichs are dispropor-
tionate. Much good will is needed to
interpret שָׁאוֹל חָטָאוּ as 'thus Hell
swallows up the sinner' (Le Hir), or
'thus, as I know, the tomb devours
those who sin' (Renan). Ehrlich does
not attempt to interpret שָׁאוֹל
חטאו. Duhm throws these words
overboard, after sacrificing דרך
כרמים of v. 18. He recomposes a
fanciful tristich from vv. 18-19 thus
shortened. Voigt reads יחתו instead
of חטאו (cf. 21: 13b), but he regards
the words שָׁאוֹל יחתו as a gloss.
Grimme replaces מִימֵי שֶׁלֶג by מים
יִשְׁלֹךָ, the 2nd hemistich beginning
at יִשְׁלֹךָ, and he reads חָטָא 'the sinner' instead of חטאו. Budde contents
himself with removing מִימֵי and does
not hesitate to render שָׁאוֹל חטאו by
'Hell [carries off] those who have
sinned'. It is easy to restore the
balance between the 1st and 2nd
hemistichs. It is enough to transpose
מִימֵי־שֶׁלֶג and יגזלו. By linking the
ו of יגזלו with the word which follows
and vocalising חוֹטֵא (cf. Ball) instead of חטאו, we obtain for the

2nd hemistich יְגֹזֵל וּשְׁאוֹל חוֹטֵא, the
waw having been displaced to throw
into relief the verb יגזל, which is
understood in the 1st hemistich.
The word שָׁאוֹל leaves the verb in the
masculine (cf. 26: 6a). Bearing in
mind that גַם before חֶם plays the
part of a real copula (Ps 37: 25;
137: 1), we obtain as the meaning
of the verse: 'The drought and the
heat carry away the snow waters,
thus does Sheol snatch away the
sinner.' The verb גזל as in vv. 2 and 9.

20 G εἶτ' ἀνεμνήσθη αὐτοῦ ἡ
ἁμαρτία· ὥσπερ δὲ ὁμίχλη δρόσου
ἀφανὴς ἐγένετο: combination of חטאו,
vocalised חֶטְאוֹ (v. 19), with ישכחהו,
and of מִימֵי שלג (v. 19) with עוד
לֹא יזכר. The words רחם מתקו רמה
are omitted in G, for it is impossible
to find any traces of them in ἀπο-
δοθείη δὲ αὐτῷ ἃ ἔπραξεν, a transitional phrase, borrowed from 34: 11.
Vulg. assigns to רחם the meaning of
'mercy' and reads מָתְקוֹ: *obliviscatur
ejus misericordia*: *dulcedo illius vermes*. The word ישכחהו, connected
by Targ. with v. 19, is translated a
second time, in the paraphrase: 'The
cruel ones who have forgotten to be
merciful will be sweet to the worms.'
Syr. regards רחם as an equivalent of
מרחם 'from the mother's womb',
and translates מתקו רמה by 'the
worm is their sweetness' (cf. Vulg.).
Syr. adds 'the dead' as the subject of
יזכר, read as יזכרו. G συντριβείη δὲ
πᾶς ἄδικος ἴσα ξύλῳ ἀνιάτῳ reads עֻוָּל
for עולה (similarly Syr. ܠܐ), and
translates a first time רעה of v. 21.
Vulg. *quasi lignum infructuosum*
makes of עולה the complement of
עץ.

21   *He has harshly used* the barren childless woman,
      And has not been kind to the widow,

21   הָרַע (G, Targ.); MT: רעה.

The present distribution of the MT cuts the first part of the verse into three independent members. According as to whether we allow to מתק its ordinary meaning 'to be sweet' or postulate a meaning 'to suck' (following Syriac), we shall translate: 'The breast which carried them forgets them; they are the sweets of the worms; no one any longer remembers them' (Renan), or else: 'The maternal breast forgets them; the worms devour them; no memory of them remains' (Le Hir). But we notice immediately that לֹא־יִזָּכֵר and יִשָּׁכְחֵהוּ are in close parallelism, exactly as in Is 54:4. Again, in the light of Ps 83:5b (cf. Jer 11:19b), it seems indisputable that the subject of יזכר was שְׁמוֹ written שְׁמָה and later corrupted to רמה. This restitution of Gray, adopted by Ball, is preferable to the vocalisation רָמֹה 'his height' (Beer, Duhm, Budde), which would form a curious subject for יזכר. The 2nd hemistich, 'his name is no more mentioned', forms a good corollary to the descent of the sinner into Sheol. As subject of ישכחהו Beer proposes רְחֹב מְקֹמוֹ 'the square', 'the street', 'his place', that is, the street in which he lives (cf. Ru 4:10, שַׁעַר מקומו 'the gate of his native place'). The words רחם מתקו would be a substitute for רחב מקמו. The hypothesis of Beer is accepted by Budde and Duhm, though modified by Ball, who makes of מקמו 'the place where he was' the subject of ישכחהו and reads מחר 'tomorrow' instead of רחם: 'tomorrow his place will forget him'. But the word רְחֶם 'maternal womb' is characteristic. The seat at one and the same time of maternity, maternal love, and of

pity (cf. *L'Emploi métaphorique*, p. 134-5), it is essentially the organ which is incapable of forgetting: 'Does a mother forget her sucking child? Does she cease to have pity (מֵרַחֵם) on the fruit of her womb?' (Is 49:15). Hence we think it right to retain רחם. It is מְתָקוֹ which creates the difficulty. We propose to read פְּתָקוֹ, the verb פתק not used in Hebrew, corresponding to the Accadian *patâqu*: 'make', 'create', 'form'. The 1st hemistich would then mean: 'the womb which has formed him forgets him!' It is the climax of desertion to be forgotten by one's own mother. The conclusion is that 'like the tree, unrighteousness is broken down'. Cf. 19:10b, 'and He uproots my hope like the tree'. The *niph'al* of שבר as in 31:22; 38:15.

21 G omits לא תלד, which seems a pleonasm, and translates στεῖραν δὲ οὐκ εὖ ἐποίησεν. The words οὐκ εὖ ἐποίησεν are a second translation of רעה (already translated ἀνιάτῳ in v. 20) and read this time as הָרַע. Cf. Targ דמרע, which also reads הרע, but interprets by רעע 'to break'. Syr. 'the barren wicked woman' connects רעה with רעע 'to be wicked' (cf. G), but regards the word as an epithet of עקרה. Vulg. *pavit*, following רעה 'to graze'. For אלמנה, G(B, A) ἀγύναιον (Sah., Memph.), G (C, אc·a) γύναιον (Syro-hex., Jerome *mulieris*, Eth., Arab. Baud.). Syr. renders ייטיב by a plural.

On the basis of the omissions of G, Duhm invents a text in which all trace of the MT is lost. He combines רעה with the close of v. 20 and reads יעקר instead of עקרה: 'like

22   But *He who* by His power seizes the mighty,
       Rises up, and the other can no longer be sure of *his* life!

22   וּמָשַׁךְ ;MT: וּמָשַׁךְ. — בְּחַיָּיו (G, Targ., Vulg.); MT: בחיין.

a rotting tree he is uprooted'; then
he transfers עוֹלָה, read as עוּלָה 'her
suckling', to the end of v. 21 and
adds: לֹא רֵחַם 'he has not shown pity
to her sucking child' (the widow's).
Of course לֹא תֵלֵד disappears in the
process of this drastic revision. The
only correction which is irresistible
is that suggested independently
by Targ and G, namely הֵרַע instead
of רעה (cf. Budde, Beer). There is
excellent parallelism between הֵרַע
'he has used harshly' and יֵיטִיב לֹא
'he does not treat well'. The form
יֵיטִיב is a combination of the *hiph'il*
and *pi'el* of יטב; cf. יְיֵלִיל (Is 15: 2, 3;
16: 7) and יְיֵלִילוּ (Hos 7: 14), from
ילל 'to groan' (in the *hiph'il*). Other
examples in Gesenius-Kautzsch,
§ 70d. With עֲקָרָה לֹא תֵלֵד 'the barren
woman who does not bear', cf. עקרה
לֹא יָלָדָה of Is 54: 1. Those who
retain רֹעֶה connect it with רעה
'graze', 'browse' (20: 26); cf. Renan:
'these violent men who devour the
barren woman'. In this case one is
obliged to assign to 'graze' the meaning of 'plunder', 'ruin', etc., for the
complement expected would be
rather the goods possessed than
the person of the possessor. Parallelism strikingly favours הֵרַע. Thus
the verse assumes a quite general
meaning: 'He has harshly used the
barren childless woman, and has
not been kind to the widow.' The
barren woman who has no children
to defend her, and the widow who
has no longer any husband to help
her, are taken as types of weak
humanity having the right to
special consideration. The wicked
man or the tyrant recks not of it.
And it is for that reason that he
falls into the hands of God (v. 22).

22   G θυμῷ δὲ κατέστρεψεν ἀδυνάτους
suggests to Bickell אֹבְדִים instead
of אבירים (cf. Duhm, Beer). But
אֹבֵד is never rendered ἀδύνατος in G,
while אביר is translated δυνατός in
Jg 5: 22. Hence it is likely that
ἀδυνάτους is due to a corruption of
δυνατούς, which rendered אבירים.
Syr. takes מֹשֶׁד as a noun 'possession'
and makes of it the subject of יקום,
which is thus attached to the 1st
hemistich. A reading בחזיון instead
of בחיין supplies for Syr. as the 2nd
hemistich: 'and he will not believe
in the vision'. G κατὰ τῆς ἑαυτοῦ
ζωῆς (confirmed by Symm., cited in
Syro-hex.), Vulg. *vitae suae* and
Targ. בחיי read בְּחַיָּיו instead of
בחיין. It is the correct reading (cf.
inf.).

As is recognised even by the *Bible
du rabbinat français*, 'the end of this
chapter lacks clarity, and the sequence of the ideas leaves something
to be desired'. It is from v. 22 that
interpretations begin to diverge seriously, and we shall see how the
propositions, which follow each
other with such apparent incoh-
erence, may in fact be reconciled.
V. 21 brought back to the scene the
wicked man or the tyrant of 27: 13.
The 1st hemistich of v. 22 can only
refer to God, as is suggested by the
use of בְּכֹחוֹ 'by His power' (26:12;
36: 22). It is a question of the dealings of God with the אַבִּירִים, i.e. the
mighty; cf. אביר in 34: 20. Further,
v. 23b is almost identical with 34: 21,
where God is pictured as being in the
process of watching the actions of
man. Finally, v. 23a contains at the
opening the clause יִתֶּן־לוֹ 'He gives
to him', the subject referring to God
and the complement to the sinner.

23   He allowed him to take root in security,
      But His eyes were watching *his* ways.

23 דְּרָכָיו (Vulg.); MT: דרכיהם.

Modern exegetes have no difficulty in recognising that God intervenes here. Budde even proposes to add אֵל as the subject. But it is the verb מֹשֵׁךְ which causes divergences in the translations. From the normal meaning 'to draw' is inferred that of 'snatch' or that of 'lengthen', 'prolong'. Nor is there any agreement about the subject of יָקוּם, which may be either God or the evil man. Hence we have very different interpretations, of which the following are a few specimens: 'But God by His power dethrones the mighty; as soon as He rises they no longer count on their lives' (Le Hir); 'But God has none the less supported them by His power; they have risen up again when they had ceased to count on their lives' (Renan); 'He supported the exactions of the mighty. He could not be assured of a long life' (Loisy). In this latter translation, it is the wicked man who is the subject of מֹשֵׁךְ. Bickell and Duhm have also decided in favour of this sense, though they read אֹבְדִים instead of אבירים (cf. sup.). Duhm then sees himself compelled to replace יקום by יֻקַּם 'he is punished', and to extend his corrections into v. 23. We ourselves think that the verb מֹשֵׁךְ, here as in Ps 10: 9, has exactly the same sense as the Arabic *masaka* 'hold', 'seize', 'catch'. It is God who by His power catches the mighty. Just as in v. 23a the subject of יתן is God and the subject of יִשְׁעֵן the sinner, so here, the subject of יָקוּם is God, but the subject of יַאֲמִין is the sinner. If we vocalise מֹשֵׁךְ instead of מָשַׁךְ, we obtain a very coherent meaning: but

He who catches the mighty by His power, rises up, and the other can no longer be sure of his life. For the movement of the sentence cf. Ps 2: 4a, where the subject is 'He who dwells in the heavens'. The verb הַאֲמִין 'believe', 'trust in' 'rely on' (4: 18; 15: 15). Cf. Dt 28: 66: ולא תאמין בחייך 'and you will no longer be assured of your life'. With G, Targ., and Vulg. we read בְּחַיָּיו, confirmed by Dt 28: 66. In the midst of his wrongdoing, the wicked man is caught by the divine intervention. Punishment thus begins.

23 G μαλακισθεὶς μὴ ἐλπιζέτω ὑγιασθῆναι, ἀλλὰ πεσεῖται νόσῳ furnishes Bickell and Duhm with יַתֵּן instead of יתן and לֹא instead of לוֹ, but then each critic seeks varying equivalents of the text of G (cf. Budde). A simple comparison with 34: 21a shows the lack of consistency in the readings of G. Note that G μαλακίζεσθαι usually renders the verb חלה, never נתך. Syr. paraphrases ויתן לו לבטח by 'and he dwells in peace'. Targ. תיובתא לרחיץ 'return to trust' and Vulg. *locum poenitentiae* interpret לבטח in the sense of the respite granted the sinner to become converted, whence Vulg. *et ille abutitur eo in superbiam* for וישען. Instead of דרכיהם, Vulg. *in viis illius* reads דְּרָכָיו (cf. inf.). Syr. connects with v. 23 the רומו of v. 24.

Usually לָבֶטַח is regarded as an equivalent of להיות לבטח. God grants to the wicked man the feeling of being in safety, and in consequence he feels supported by God (cf. Dillmann). Hence the paraphrases: 'He grants them the security in which they are at ease' (Le Hir); 'God had

24   *He was exalted* a little, but is now no more,
     And *he* has collapsed like *the orach that one gathers*,
     And like a head of grain *he* has faded away.

24   כְּמַלּוּחַ יִקָּטְפוּן (cf. G); MT : — יְקַטְפוּן וְהֻמְּכוּ. (G); MT : וְהֻמַּךְ — רוּמוּ. MT : יָרוּם;
יָמַל; MT : יִמָּלוּ. — ככל יקפצון.
25   After 24:17.

given them security and confidence'
(Renan). But it should be noticed
that the verb יִתֵּן directly governs
וְיִשָּׁעֵן, exactly as in 19:23. In this
case the circumstantial complement
can stand before the *waw*; cf. 19:
23b, where בַּסֵּפֶר is placed before
וְיֻחָקוּ, although the sense is clearly:
'who will grant that they may be
engraved on brass?' We have the
same transposition of the complement in 19:20a, where לִנְצַח determines וַיֵּהֶלֶךְ (cf. Comm.). It follows
that לָבֶטַח determines וְיִשָּׁעֵן and
not יִתֶּן לוֹ. God 'allows him to take
root in security'. The *niph'al* of
שֵׁעַן as in 8:15; the expression לָבֶטַח
as in 11:18. The wicked man is at
ease, he has confidence in his happiness, he bases his life on his home and
family which he thinks stable and
permanent (8:15). But God is
watching him. Instead of דַּרְכֵיהֶם, the
plural suffix of which is influenced
by אַבִּירִים of v. 22, we read דְּרָכָיו
with Vulg.: 'but His eyes were
watching his ways'. Omission of the
verb as in 7:8b. The same idiom
stands in 34:21a, where it is a
question of the watch which God
keeps on human actions. Use of דֶּרֶךְ
in the plural in the sense of work,
action, way of behaving (cf. 21:31
and 26:14, Comm.).

24   G πολλοὺς γὰρ ἐκάκωσεν τὸ
ὕψωμα αὐτοῦ reads רוּמוֹ instead of
רוּמוּ and perhaps מְאֹד 'much' instead of מְעַט. Syr. ܐܢܘܢ ܐܠܐ 'and
they are no more' and Vulg. *et non
subsistent* harmonise וְאֵינֶנּוּ with the

context, while Targ. makes explicit
the noun contained in the suffix
וְלֵיתוֹי רַשִׁיעָא 'and the wicked is no
more'. G ἐμαράνθη δὲ ὥσπερ μολόχη
ἐν καύματι reads the singular instead
of the plural הֻמְּכוּ, and כְּמַלּוּחַ instead
of ככל. The reading of G (A) χλόη
(for μολόχη) is cited as a variant in
Olympiod. The other versions retain
the word כל 'all': *et humiliabuntur
sicut omnia et auferentur* (Vulg.),
'and they are abased like all things
that are cut down' (Targ.), 'and
all those who annoy perish' (Syr.).
It is clear that Syr. reads יקצפון
instead of יקפצון. G paraphrases the
3rd hemistich: ἢ ὥσπερ στάχυς ἀπὸ
καλάμης αὐτόματος ἀποπεσών. Syr.
'they wither and are crushed' translates יִמָּלוּ twice.

Many interpretations have been
suggested for this difficult verse.
The presence of וְאֵינֶנּוּ in the 1st
hemistich shows sufficiently plainly
that we have here the sequel to the
punishment of the wicked man and
that the verbs must be in the singular. If we regard the final *waw* of
יִמָּלוּ as a dittograph of the *waw*
which begins v. 25, we can read יָמַל
(14:2; 18:16) and then translate
the 3rd hemistich: 'and he fades
away like a head of grain'. Cf.
18:16b, 'and above, his branches
fade'. The comparative particle
כְּכָל suggests that we should seek
in the 2nd hemistich a clause parallel to the 3rd. However, from the
text as it stands an acceptable meaning can only with difficulty be
wrested, and it is by a series of in-

27:14 If his sons are many, it is for the sword,
    And his offspring have not bread in plenty.

genious devices that such translations as the following are obtained:
'They perish; they are mown down
like all men' (Le Hir); 'They fall, but
as all human beings fall' (Renan);
'Having fallen, he is buried like
any other man' (Loisy). The verb
מכך, which recurs only in Ps 106:43
(where the text is doubtful) and in
Ec 10:18, is an Aramaism (cf. Podechard on Ec 10:18). The basic
meaning is 'bend', 'collapse', and
this meaning is emphasised by the
use of the *hoph'al*. With G we read
the singular וְהֻמַּךְ 'and he has collapsed', which is the prelude to the
comparison. Instead of ככל 'like
all others', we expect the mention
of the plant parallel to the 'head of
grain' of the 3rd hemistich. G has not
invented ὥσπερ μολόχη, which is
equivalent to כְּמַלָּח. The similarity
of the name decided G to render
מַלָּח by μολόχη, which is the same
as μαλάχη 'mallow'. But in fact it is
the orach which is designated by
מַלּוּחַ (cf. 30:4). With Duhm, Beer,
Gray, Ball, we read כְּמַלָּח instead of
ככל. In 30:4 the word מלוח is the
complement of the verb קטף 'to
gather' (cf. 8:12). It is this verb
which is concealed in יקפצון 'they
are shut in' (cf. 5:16), which does
not yield a satisfactory sense. Siegfried reads יְקֻטְפוּן 'they are gathered',
Beer the singular יְקֻטַּף. Intermediate
between them is יְקֻטְפוּן. Note the use
of the plural to connote 'one' (4:19;
7:3; 15:28, etc.). The relative is
omitted as in 27:18b (above).
Hence we can translate the 2nd
hemistich: 'and he has collapsed
like the orach that one gathers'. The
plant that is plucked from the ground
bends and gives way on its stalk.
The 1st hemistich is conceived on the
model of 27:19b: He has opened

his eyes and he is no more! The
form רוֹמוּ is curious. It is explained
as deriving from רמם, supposed to
be parallel to רום (Gesenius-
Kautzsch, § 67m). But the plural
before ואיננו is unintelligible. The
reading: רוֹמוֹ 'his height' of G is
adopted by Bickell, Duhm, and
Beer: 'His height lasts a little and
then he is no more.' But it is clumsily inappropriate to bring in the
abstract 'his height' when it is a
question of the disappearance of the
wicked man. In fact, the latter is
compared to a plant which grows
for a time and then disappears (18:
16-17). All becomes clear if we read
יָרוּם for רוֹמוּ: 'He was exalted a
little, but is now no more.' The antithesis is the same as in the previous
speech of Zophar (20:6-7). V. 24
ends the description of the misfortunes in reserve for the wicked. It is
now their posterity who are going
to be hit (27:14ff.). Cf. Intro.,
pp. lf.

25 After 24:17.

27:**14** For בניו, G (B) οἱ υἱοὶ
αὐτῶν (Arab. Baud.), but G (A, א,
C) οἱ υἱοὶ αὐτοῦ (Sah., Jerome,
Syro-hex.). Targ. vocalises לָמוֹ instead of לְמוֹ, whence its paraphrase:
'because they slay with the sword'.
G ἐὰν δὲ καὶ ἀνδρωθῶσιν προσαιτή-
σουσιν is a very free translation, and
purely following the general sense
of the 2nd hemistich.

After the punishment of the
wicked man himself (24:18-24)
comes that of his family: 'If his
sons are many, it is for the sword,
and his offspring have not bread in
plenty.' The verb רבה has its normal sense of 'to be many' (cf. the
hiph'il in 9:17). In 39:4 it will have
the connotation of 'to increase'. The

15   Those who survive him are buried by death,
        And his widows weep not.

16   If he piles up silver like dust
        And heaps up garments like clay,

large number of children born to the wicked should not deceive. They are a prey for the sword. Note the use of the poetic לָמוֹ (29: 21; 38: 40; 40: 4), just as we have בְּמוֹ (cf. 9: 30, etc.) and כְּמוֹ (cf. 6: 15, etc.). The 2nd hemistich is a litotes. They are not filled to satiety with bread, i.e. they die of hunger. War and famine are the two great scourges (5: 20; Jer 14: 12; 15: 2). Job claimed that the progeny of the wicked are firmly rooted and lasting (21: 8). On the word צֶאֱצָאִים, cf. Comm. on 5: 25.

15 The 1st hemistich had been omitted by G(B). It is not found in Cod. 106 or in Eth. But it has a place in G(A, א, C), as in the derived versions, and it has been added in the margin of G(B). For שְׂרִידָיו, G(A) οἱ δὲ περίοντες αὐτῶν (Arab. Baud.; cf. v. 14), instead of αὐτοῦ of G (א, C), Sah., Jerome, Syro-hex. For וְאַלְמְנֹתָיו, G χῆρας δὲ αὐτῶν, Syr. 'and their widows'. G οὐθεὶς ἐλεήσει paraphrases תִבְכֶּינָה, regarded as a *niph'al*: 'will not be lamented'.

In fact, the wicked man should have neither posterity nor survivor (18: 19). If the whole family does not perish with him, it means but a deferment of their fate: 'those who survive him are buried by death'. After war and famine, the third scourge is the pestilence (Lv 26: 25-26; 2 S 24: 13; Jer 14: 12; 24: 10, etc.). It is pestilence which is personified by death, as in Jer 15: 2; 18: 21; 43: 11 (cf. the first-born of death, 18: 13). In Assyrian it is *mûtânu* (from *mûtu* 'death') which symbolises the pestilence, but in the El-Amarna letters we find the

Canaanism *mûtu* connoting 'pestilence' (*RB*, 1924, p. 16). The 1st hemistich makes very good sense if we suppose that the scourge personified undertakes to lay its victims in the tomb. Why force the sense as does Fried. Delitzsch, who connects במות with שְׂרִידָיו in order to translate: 'those who have escaped him only to find death'? Olshausen introduces a negative before יִקָּבֵרוּ, which obliges him to interpret בַּמָּוֶת as 'when they die'. The 2nd hemistich is found in its entirety in Ps 78: 64b, where it is a question of the widows in Israel. The widows of the dead man watch unmoved the succession of scourges which accompany or follow the death of their husband.

16 Syr. translates the verbs by plurals. Instead of מַלְבּוּשׁ, G χρυσίον, following Zec 9: 3b.

The 1st hemistich is a replica of Zec 9: 3b; but instead of placing gold in parallelism with silver, the author chooses the object 'garments' —one of the most appreciated of luxuries (2 K 7: 8; Zec 14: 14). The verb צבר 'to heap up' (Ps 39: 7), whether silver (here and Zec 14: 14) or gold (Sir 47: 18). Note the parallelism between כֶּעָפָר 'like dust' and כַּחֹמֶר 'like clay'; cf. 4: 19; 10: 9; 30: 19. The verb הכין 'put in order', 'prepare', 'arrange' (11: 13; 15: 35) in the sense of arranging in a pile, storing up provisions, 'massing' (Pr 6: 8; 30: 25). The 1st hemistich of v. 17 shows clearly that the allusion is to clothing, and not to gold, as is affirmed by the translation of G, made under the influence of Zec 9: 3.

17   He heaps them up, but a righteous man wears them,
      And it is an innocent man who inherits the silver!
18   He has built his house as a nest,
      And like a hut which a keeper has made.

17 G ταῦτα πάντα, instead of יכין, does not fit the context. Syr. again reads the plural for יכין (cf. v. 16) and omits נקי. G τὰ δὲ χρήματα αὐτοῦ translates וכסף.

V. 17a corresponds to 16b, while 17b corresponds to 16a—an example of inverted parallelism. The wicked man has hoarded money, but it will go to others; cf. Ps 39: 7b, 'He amasses riches and he knows not who shall gather them.' To the wicked man is opposed the righteous man צדיק or the innocent man נקי (cf. 17: 8-9 and 22: 18). The righteous man clothes himself with the garments of which the wicked have been stripped, and it is the innocent who inherit the wealth of the ungodly. This is indeed the doctrine of Job's friends. The goods of this world do not remain in the hands of the ungodly; they pass into those of the righteous. Cf. Pr 13: 22b, 'and the wealth of the sinner is reserved for the righteous', where there is a contrast between חוטא 'the sinner' (24: 19 above) and צדיק 'the righteous man'.

18 G ἀπέβη δὲ ὁ οἶκος αὐτοῦ ὥσπερ σῆτες καὶ ὥσπερ ἀράχνη omits the 2nd hemistich and twice translates כעש, the translation ὥσπερ ἀράχνη being based on a reading כעכביש, which is found also in Syr. ܐܝܟ ܓܘܓܝ 'like a spider's web' and Sa'adia 'like the spider' (cf. inf.). For ἀπέβη, cf. ἀποβήσεται in 8: 14b. The text of G has been completed by ἃ συνετήρησεν of Symm. (cf. Colb.) in Jerome *quae servavit* and Syro-hex. (with asterisk). G(A) adds ὁ πλοῦτος αὐτοῦ (following v. 19a) after ἀράχνη. The 2nd hemistich is interpreted *et*

sicut custos fecit umbraculum in Vulg. (transposition of סכה and נצר), 'and he has made his roof like a hut' in Syr.

The 1st hemistich is usually translated: 'he has built his house like the moth'; cf. עש in 4: 19; 13: 28. But can it be said of the moth that it builds for itself a house? Le Hir attenuates the expression by translating 'like the insect'. Following 8: 14, where there is mention of בית עכביש 'the spider's house', some moderns have decided in favour of a reading כעכביש 'like the spider', which seems confirmed by G and Syr. (Merx, Hitzig, Budde, etc.). But it should be pointed out that G has as a first translation ὥσπερ σῆτες, which corresponds to כעש, and that the reading כעכביש of G, Syr., and Sa'adia is based on a reminiscence of 8: 14. Translators have hesitated in face of כעש 'like the moth'. Again, in conformity with the 2nd hemistich, 'like a hut which a keeper has made', the object of the comparison must be the house, and not its builder. This fact lends all probability to the hypothesis already put forward by Schultens and taken up by Ehrlich, following which עש, homonym of עש 'moth', corresponds to the Arabic عشّ 'bird's nest in a tree'. Fried. Delitzsch also quotes the Assyrian *ašašu* 'nest'. The bird's nest is likened to a house in Ps 84: 4. Here we have the converse. Cf. Pr 27: 8, 'As a bird which flees from its nest, so is man who flees from his place.' The 1st hemistich will mean: 'He has built his house like a nest', with just as little stability of structure as the bird's nest. The other term of comparison

19   Rich, he goes to bed, but he *will do so no more*,
      He has opened his eyes, and it is for the last time!
20   Terrors strike him *in broad daylight*;
      At night, a whirlwind has carried him away;

19 יוֹסִף (G, Syr.); MT: יֶאֱסֹף.
20 יוֹמָם; MT: כְּמַיִם.

is the hut or booth, i.e. the fragile shelter erected by the keeper of a field as a place in which he can spend the night (Is 1: 8). It is the symbol of what is tottering (Is 24: 20). The relative is understood before עֹשֶׂה (cf. 24: 24).

19 V. 19b, absent from Sah., marked with asterisk in Jerome and Syro-hex., did not exist in G. The present text derives from Theod. (cf. Colb.). It is in error that Syro-hex. also attributes to Theod. the words καὶ οὐ προσθήσει, which are translated in Sah. and Jerome (without asterisk). For וְלֹא יֵאָסֵף, Vulg. *nihil secum auferet*, replacing the *niph'al* by the *qal*. G καὶ οὐ προσθήσει read יוֹסִיף, which is reflected in Syr. 'and he will never again rise'.

'Rich, he goes to bed'; cf. the use of עָרַם in 1: 21. The wicked man has massed treasures (v. 19). To what purpose? Those who retain the MT 'and he is not gathered' suppose that the meaning is deprivation of honourable burial (Rosenmüller, Le Hir, etc.), according to the idiom 'to be gathered to one's fathers'. But this does not provide a good parallel to וְאֵינֶנּוּ 'and he is no more' of the 2nd hemistich. Since Houbigant it has been recognised that יֵאָסֵף is a defective writing for יוֹסֵף or יוֹסִיף, just as we have תֻּסְפּוּן for תּוֹסְפוּן (Ex 5: 7) and וַיֹּסֶף for וַיּוֹסֶף in 1 S 18: 29. We find the same abuse of the *mater lectionis* in יָאֱהִיל for יְהֵל (25: 5). We find moreover יוֹסִיף in G and Syr. Note that Syr. adds the complement לָקוּם 'and he rises no more', which recalls Ps 41: 9, 'he who has lain down rises no more' (לֹא יוֹסִיף לָקוּם). Cf. 14: 12, 'and man will remain laid low and will rise no more', to describe the sleep of death. The expression וְלֹא יוֹסִיף connotes the idea that a certain action will never be repeated, that it has been done for the last time (20: 9; 34: 32; 40: 5). The image פָּקַח עֵינָיו 'to open one's eyes' contrasts with sleep (Pr 20: 13) or with death (2 K 4: 35). Here it is the last look of the dying man. The idiom וְאֵינֶנּוּ 'and he is no more' as in 24: 24a.

20 For בַּלָּהוֹת, G αἱ ὀδύναι, Vulg. *inopia*. G (א) renders סוּפָה by λαῖλαψ (21: 18), instead of γνόφος of G (A, B, C). Syr. connects with v. 20 the words יִשָּׂאֵהוּ קָדִים of v. 21.

The *hiph'il* of נָשַׂג as 41: 18, 'to strike'. The abstract subject denoted by a feminine plural allows the verb to be singular; cf. Gesenius-Kautzsch, § 145k. Cf. the use of the feminine sing. after בְּהֵמוֹת as subject in 12: 7a. The 1st hemistich is usually translated: 'terrors strike him like water', which is rather odd. Hence attempts have been made to intensify the image by interpreting כְּמַיִם as 'like a flood of waters' (Le Hir), or 'like a flood' (Renan), but this is extracting from the text more than it contains. The contrast to לַיְלָה in the 2nd hemistich suggests a replacement of כְּמַיִם by בַּיּוֹם (Merx), or יוֹמָם. (Wright, Budde, Ehrlich). In the light of 5: 14, 'in broad daylight they encounter darkness, and

21   The east wind sweeps him away and he is gone,
     And it drives him from his place.
22   Men hurl themselves at him without mercy,
     He tries to flee from the hand which strikes him;
23   They clap their hands at him in derision,
     And he is hissed away from wherever he is!

at the height of noon they grope as at night', the reading יוֹמָם seems to us plainly indicated. The end is copied from 21:18. God does not wait for the moment of death (v. 19) to punish the wicked; here and now the latter are victims of terrors by day and nightmares at night (15: 20-4; 18: 11-12, etc.).

21   Vv. 21-3, absent from Sah., marked with asterisk in Colb., Syrohex. (with the exception of 22b-23a), Jerome (with the exception of 22-3) did not exist in G. The present text derives from Theod. (cf. Colb. and Cod. 248). The absence of 22-3 could easily be explained by homoeoteleuton; cf. ממקמו at the end of v. 21 and v. 23. For קדים, Theod. καύσων, Vulg. *ventus urens*. The verb ילך is regarded as a *hiph'il* in Vulg. *et auferet*. For וישערהו, Vulg. *et velut turbo rapiet eum*.
  V. 21 amplifies the idea contained in v. 20b. 'The east wind sweeps him away and he is gone': קדים is chosen because of the harm it causes (cf. Comm. on 15: 2). The verb נשא 'to carry off' (13: 14; 30: 22). For וְיֵלַךְ 'and he is gone' cf. 7: 9; 14: 20; 19: 10). The verb שער, used in the *pi'el*, corresponds to סער (cf. ישיגו for יסיגו in 24: 2), whence סערה 'whirlwind', 'tempest' (38: 1; 40: 6). We have restored the *pu'al* of סער in 15: 30. The *qal* of שער in Ps 58: 10 and the *pi'el* of סער in Zec 7: 14 effectively express the action of sweeping away as the storm passes by. Here the etymological sense is still more in evidence, since it is the east wind which 'drives him from

his place'. The wicked man cannot remain rooted in one spot. He is condemned to wander through the world, as though driven onwards by some mysterious power. Thus was Cain after his crime (Gn 4: 12-15). Even if the wicked man wishes to settle down in one place, he is driven away by the crowd.

22   On the text of G, cf. v. 21.
  Vv. 22-3 describe the expulsion of the wicked man who is abandoned to public vengeance. It is clear that the subject of the verbs in v. 22a and v. 23 is the impersonal 'one'; use of the 3rd person singular (18: 6). The jussive וְיַשְׁלֵךְ with the sense of the imperfect (13: 27), just as in 15: 33b. They hurl any kind of weapon at the banished man. There is no need to express the complement of ישלך (cf. Nu 35: 20). The formula וְלֹא יַחְמֹל as in 16: 13 (cf. 6: 10). The unhappy man wishes to escape 'the hand' of the one who is hurling stones at him. The suffix in מִיָּדוֹ refers to the subject of ישלך. The verb ברח with מן before the object from which one flees (20: 24). The infinitive before the verb in the personal mode (13: 5, 10).

23   On the text of G, cf. v. 21. The suffix in עלימו is regarded as a plural in Targ. and Syr. but as a singular in Theod. ἐπ' αὐτοῦ and Vulg. *super eum*. G (א*) αὐτούς (instead of αὐτοῦ), which is found also in Syro-hex., Memph., Eth. We have *super eum* in Jerome (Bod., Tur.), *super eos* in Jerome (Gall.). For כפימו, Aq.

ταρσοὺς αὐτῶν, Targ. ידהון 'their hand', but Syr. 'his hand', Vulg. *manus suas*. The text of Theod. is χεῖρας αὐτῶν in G(B, א), χεῖρας αὐτοῦ in G(A, C), Jerome *manibus suis*, Syro-hex., Eth., Arab. Baud. For ממקמו, Vulg. *intuens locum ejus*.

The verbs are again in the singular and the meaning is not in doubt: they clap their hands, they hiss (cf. v. 22). Note the use of שׁפק instead of ספק, as we had שׁער for סער in v. 21. The verb ספק 'to beat' (34: 26) is accompanied by the complement כַּפַּיִם to denote 'clap hands', in sign of anger (Nu 24: 10), or of derision (La 2: 15). The object of scorn is preceded by the preposition על (La 2: 15). Here עָלֵימוֹ 'over him' as in 22: 2. The form כַּפֵּימוֹ 'his hands' is due to attraction by

עלימו. It is confirmed by פָּנֵימוֹ 'his face' (Ps 11: 7), and it is not necessary to replace it by כַּפָּיו 'his hands' or כַּפַּיִם 'both hands'. At the same time as they clap their hands, they hiss at the unhappy man. This again is a means of expressing scorn (Jer 49: 17; Zeph 2: 15). The person hissed at is preceded by the preposition על (Ezk 27: 36). In La 2: 15 the passers-by 'clap their hands at you, they hiss and wag their heads at the daughter of Jerusalem'. At the close, מִמְּקֹמוֹ 'from his place', i.e. from any place where he happens to be. The wicked are driven out wherever they are. Here Zophar's speech ends. Ch. 28 forms an independent whole; cf. Intro., pp. li and xcviif.

CHAPTER 28

1   Surely for silver there is a source,
      And for gold a place where it is refined,
2   Iron is extracted from the ground,
      And a hard stone becomes copper,

Chapter 28   Poem on Wisdom: see Introduction, pp. li and xcviif.

28: 1 G translates מוצא by τόπος ὅθεν γίνεται, Vulg. paraphrases: *venarum suarum principia*. For יזקו, G διηθεῖται (Jerome *purgatur*), the hexaplar authors χωνευθῇ (Vulg. *conflatur*). Syr. and Targ. retain the plural active voice.

V. 1 begins a couplet on the exploitation of metals. The כי of the opening is simply an introductory formula. 'I know', 'I note' is understood. Cf. Gn 18: 20, where כי has no further significance than 'surely'. The 1st hemistich is conceived on the lines of 14: 7a, 'For there is hope for the tree', answered by 14: 12, 'and man will remain laid low', just as v. 12 of our chapter answers v. 1. The word מוֹצָא 'issue', 'outlet' generally denotes the place from which waters spring, and it has this meaning in the inscription of the canal of Hezekiah (l. 5). It is also the point where the sun emerges on the horizon (Ps 75: 7); cf. the Canaanite *mûṣi šamši* 'the point where the sun rises', 'the east' in a letter of Arta-ḫepa of Jerusalem (Knudtzon, *El-Amarna*, no. 288, 6), and the Aramaic מוקא שמש 'point where the sun rises', 'the east' in the inscription of Panammu (l. 14; Lagrange, *ÉRS*, p. 495). In 1 K 10: 28 it connotes origin, provenance; here, the place of origin. The verb זקק connotes 'purify', 'cleanse', said at first of liquids

which are purified, then of the refining of metals (cf. Gesenius-Buhl, s.v.). This however is not the etymological meaning. The root זקק means 'to blow'; cf. the Assyrian *zaqâqu* (whence *zaqîqu* and *ziqziqqu*: 'the wind'), parallel to *zâqu* 'to blow' (speaking of the wind). From the meaning 'blow' derives that of 'inflate', 'distend', 'blow up', whence the Arabic *ziqq* (plural *ziqâq*) and the Aramaic זקא 'goatskin bottle', 'wineskin'. The Arabic *ziqq* is used especially of the bellows for the forge. Just as the Latin *conflare* 'blow', 'distend' has been used to denote 'refine' metals, so also the root זקק. It is only as the result of a very late derivation that it has come to express the cleansing of liquids (Is 25: 6). We shall find זקק again in 36: 27. Note the juxtaposition of the verb with the word it determines, with the relative omitted (cf. 24: 24; 27: 18). We know whence gold and silver come, but whence comes wisdom? This is the question which will be asked in v. 12, where we shall have the same expressions as in v. 1.

2 G γίνεται vaguely renders יקח. For אבן, G ἴσα λίθῳ, Syr. 'from stone'. Vulg. *et lapis solutus calore in aes vertitur* gives clearly the meaning of the 2nd hemistich.

After silver and gold, iron and

3   Man sets an end to darkness,
     And to the extremest limit he searches
     For the stone hidden in darkness and shade.

copper. The Hebrews had preserved
the memory of mines for the exploitation of metals which were
found in the peninsula of Sinai. The
mines of Punon, today Fenân, had
furnished the mineral necessary for
the making of the serpent of brass
(Nu 33: 42-3, compared with Nu
21: 4-10). The promised land is 'a
land whose stones are iron, and out
of whose hills you can dig copper'
(Dt 8: 9). The word עָפָר used with
the meaning of 'the soil', 'the
ground' (5: 6; 14: 8; 19: 25, etc.).
There is no reason to replace יְקַח
by יִקַּח (Duhm) or by יִקָּחוּ (Torczyner). The *hoph'al* of לקח serves as
a passive for the *qal* as in the el-
Amarna letters (*RB*, 1914, p. 58).
Following Dt 8: 9, which we have
just quoted, the 2nd hemistich means
simply: 'and a hard stone becomes
copper'. Passive participle יָצוּק
(from יצק 'to melt'), with the meaning
of 'hard'; cf. Comm. on 11: 15. The
word אֶבֶן, the plural of which is
אֲבָנִים, has been treated as masculine.
Corrections to יְצֻקּוּ 'they melt down,
or smelt' (Torczyner), יָצוּק 'one
melts down' (Hoffmann, Duhm,
Beer), יוּצַק 'is melted down' (Budde),
remove the picturesqueness from
the phrase. Some consider יצוק as
the 3rd person of a verb צוק, parallel
to יצק: 'they melt down stone into
copper' (cf. Dillmann). But it is
only in v. 3 that we shall have
active verbs with indeterminate
subject. With אבן יצוק cf. צור יצוק
in 29: 6 and יצוק כמו־אבן in
41: 16.

3   The passage contained between
ולכל of v. 3 and מעם־גר (inclusive)

of v. 4, absent from Sah., marked
with asterisk in Jerome and
Syro-hex., did not exist in G.
The present text derives from
Theod. (cf. Syro-hex.). Symm.
renders קץ by προθεσμίαν; cf. Vulg.
tempus.

This verse, like the one which follows, includes three hemistichs. It
describes the miner reaching the
deepest bowels of the earth. The subject of שָׂם is not made explicit. It is
implied by the הוּא of the 2nd hemistich. It is in fact the impersonal
'one' (27: 22-3). In 'Man sets an
end to darkness' note the use of
קֵץ as in 16: 3. Man dispels darkness
by penetrating to the bowels of the
earth and flooding these depths
with light. Duhm amuses himself by
fabricating a new text, inasmuch as
he reads בְּקֵשׁ for קץ שם, eliminates
ולכל, and replaces חוקר by חָקַר. All
these conjectures are determined
solely by the concern to reduce the
material to two hemistichs. In 26: 10
the word תַּכְלִית denoted the boundary where light ceases and darkness
begins (cf. Comm. on 11: 7). Here it
connotes the limit to which the
miner descends: 'and he searches to
the extremest limit', literally 'to
every limit'. On the verb חקר, cf.
Comm. on 5: 27. The end אֶבֶן אֹפֶל
וְצַלְמָוֶת 'the stone of darkness and
shade' introduces the complement
of חוקר. Cf. 10:21b 'the land of darkness and shade'. We have אפל
חשך and וצלמות instead of וצלמות
(3: 5; 10:21; Ps 107: 10, 14). This
stone of darkness and shadow represents those subterranean rocks which
are near to 'the land of darkness and
thick gloom', i.e. Sheol.

4   *A foreign people* has pierced *shafts*,
      Forgotten of human feet;
      They swing to and fro, they are poised far from men!

4   נְחָלִים עַם גֵּר (cf. Vulg., Syr.); MT: נחל מעם־גר.

4   On the text of G, cf. v. 3. Theod.
and Symm. διακοπή, Syr. ﻟﻮﻳﺨﺍ
'crack', 'fissure', 'break', vocalise
פֶּרֶץ instead of פָּרַץ. Syr. then
regards נחל as a verb: 'they have
inherited'. For מעם־גר, Theod.
ἀπὸ κονίας, Symm. and Aq. (in Syro-
hex.) ὅπου κονία, reading גֵּר 'lime'
(Is 27: 9) instead of גָּר (Field). Vulg.
a populo peregrinante and Syr. 'by
a proselyte people' have vocalised
מֵעַם instead of מֵעָם. Targ. sees in
גר a word derived from גרר or נגר
(20: 28) and translates: 'from a place
where canals branch out'. The text
of G begins again at the word
הנשכחים. The last two hemistichs are
fused in G: οἱ δὲ ἐπιλανθανόμενοι ὁδὸν
δικαίαν (A ὁδοὺς δικαιοσύνης, Jerome
viam justitiae) ἠσθένησαν ἐκ βροτῶν.
Interpretation of רגל in the moral
sense (cf. the translation of דרך in
24: 11, 13), translation of דלו from
דלל 'to be weak', omission of נעו.
This latter word is restored in Jerome
et commoti sunt (with asterisk) following Theod. ἐσαλεύθησαν. The
translation of Vulg. *eos quos oblitus
est pes egentis hominis et invios*
regards דלו מאנוש as the equivalent
of מאנוש דל. Syr. connects נעו with
v. 5. Targ. translates דלו by אזדקפו
'they have become exalted'.
    The divergences between the ver-
sions are sufficient evidence of the
difficulties of this verse, which
Calmet deems an enigma 'of which
it is almost impossible to find the
solution'. The first two hemistichs
are usually interpreted as follows:
'He has dug for himself a deep valley
far from passers-by, he has carved
out paths unknown to the feet of

the traveller' (Le Hir); 'He digs, far
away from the beaten track, tren-
ches unknown to the foot of living
man' (Renan); 'He digs, far away
from inhabited places, shafts unknown to the foot of the living'
(Crampon). Thus it becomes apparent that מֵעָם־גָּר 'from beside the
stranger (or the guest or the client)'
is rendered successively by 'far from
passers-by', 'far away from the
beaten track', 'far away from inhabited places'. Next we have the
plural הַנִּשְׁכָּחִים 'those who are forgotten', which becomes 'unknown
paths' or which is made into an
epithet for the singular נַחַל. Those
who regard the 2nd hemistich as
forming one whole with the 3rd
translate: 'They are there unknown
to passers-by, suspended and poised
far from human beings' (Loisy);
'His feet no longer serve to help him,
and he is suspended and poised far
from human beings' (Segond); 'Unknown to the foot of the passer-by,
he is suspended, swinging to and fro
far from men' (*Bible du rabbinat
français*). Then there is the statement 'those who are forgotten of the
foot', which is paraphrased more or
less successfully. Many corrections
have been proposed by modern
critics. Thus Bickell added אור
after גר, a conjecture accepted by
Budde, who then connects דַּלּוּ with
מִנִּי־רָגֶל: 'He digs a well, far from
him who dwells in light; forgotten
they are suspended with no footing,
they are poised far from men.' There
remains only מֵאֱנוֹשׁ נָעוּ for the 3rd
hemistich, and there is some difficulty in understanding 'forgotten,

5   Earth from which bread springs,
     And beneath which all is overturned as though by fire!

they are suspended without feet'!
Duhm recomposes a distich, following his usual procedure. He removes
מעם־גר, regarded as a variant of
מני־רגל (!), cuts out הנשכחים, regarded as a variant of אנושנעו (!),
which he replaces, moreover, by
במשכה 'with a rope'. It is unnecessary to discuss the arbitrary character
of these corrections. The change
from מעם־גר to מעפר (Merx) or
בעפר (Siegfried) rests on a faulty
understanding of the translations
ἀπὸ κονίας or ὅπου κονία (cf. sup.). On
the other hand, the vocalisation
עַם גֵּר 'a foreign people' (Giesebrecht,
Ehrlich) for עָם־גֵּר has a serious
support in Syr. and Vulg. This correction is happily completed by
Graetz, who attaches the first letter
of מעם to the preceding word. The
1st hemistich thus becomes, without
changing a single consonant, פָּרַץ
נְחָלִים עַם גֵּר 'a foreign people has
pierced shafts'. We have in נחלים
the noun to which will refer הנשכחים.
They are foreigners condemned by
the Egyptians to the heavy labour
of the mines. The verb פרץ 'make a
breach' (cf. פֶּרֶץ in 16: 14) and also
'perforate', 'pierce'. The word נַחַל
'valley', 'torrent' here designates the
shafts which the miners sink on the
mountain sides where the mineral is
found. Such are still to be seen in
the Wâdi Maghâra in Sinai. They are
truly 'forgotten of the foot' because
they seem inaccessible. Cf. Dt 31: 21,
where it is said that a song 'shall not
be *forgotten by the mouth* of his posterity'. The same idiom as here. The
two verbs דלל and נוע depict the
miner hanging to the rope which
holds him suspended in the void. The
first belongs to the same family as
the Arabic root *daldala* 'to wave' and
tadaldala 'to swing to and fro'

(speaking of a suspended object).
The second is used specially of the
branches of a tree 'swaying' in the
air (Jg 9: 9, 11, 13); cf. the *hiph'il*
'move', 'shake' in 16: 4. No spec-
tator watches these acrobatics: 'They
swing to and fro, they are poised far
from men!' The verbs are in the
plural since the subject is the collective עָם.

5 Vv. 5-9a, absent from Sah.,
marked with asterisk in Jerome
(also 9b) and Syro-hex., did not
exist in G. The present text is
derived from Theod. (cf. Colb.).
Syr. begins the verse by נעו of v. 4.
For תחתיה, Vulg. *in loco suo*. According to Targ. the 2nd hemistich implies 'Gehenna where the coldness of
snow is transformed into fire'. Vulg.
renders נהפך כמו־אש by *igni sub-
versa est*.
    Vv. 5-8 depict the earth in which
the miners work. First, there is the
contrast between what takes place
on the surface of the soil and what
goes on in the bowels of the earth:
'Earth from which bread springs,
and beneath which all is overturned
as though by fire!' The 1st hemistich
is confirmed by Ps 104: 14, 'He
who makes grass to grow for the
cattle and herbs for the use of man,
causing bread to come forth out of
the earth'. There is no reason to
change לָחֶם to להט 'flame' (Houbigant), or to יהלם 'jasper' (Torczyner). Bread can be said to come
from the earth since the grain grows
out of it. The 2nd hemistich shows
the underground being shaken up
by man's work. The verb נֶהְפָּךְ has
the sense of an impersonal passive:
'it is being overturned'; cf. הוּחַל
'it has been begun' in Gn 4: 26. On
the meanings of הפך in the *qal* and
niph'al cf. 9: 5. In 12: 15 it is the

6   A place whose stones are sapphire,
    And which contains dust of gold!
7   A path which no bird of prey knows,
    And no vulture's eye has perceived!

waters which overturn or overwhelm the earth (יהפכו). Here the agent seems to be fire. The idiom כְּמוֹ־אֵשׁ 'as though by fire' avoids inserting a preposition between the particle of comparison and the noun; cf. כמטר 'as after the rain' (omission of "ל) in 29: 23; כלילה 'as in the night' (omission of "ב) in 5: 14. It is apparent that it is unnecessary to change כמו to במו (Hirzel, Merx, Löhr). Ehrlich would vocalise אֵשׁ (with the *holem*) instead of אֵשׁ, so as to obtain an equivalent to the Aramaic אשׁיא 'foundations'. This would mean that the underground part becomes 'like the foundations' of a building!

6   On the text of G, cf. v. 5. Aq. and Symm. (quoted in Syro-hex.) read עֹפֶרֶת 'lead' instead of עֲפָרֹת 'dust'. Vulg. *et glebae illius aurum* models the 2nd hemistich on the 1st. Targ. sees here the garden of Eden', by contrast with the Gehenna of v. 3 (cf. sup.). Syr. paraphrases 'and a river of gold on its paths', connecting with v. 6 the word נתיב of v. 7.

Without its being necessary to replace the construct state מְקוֹם by the absolute מָקוֹם (Pareau), we may translate the 1st hemistich: 'a place whose stones are of sapphire'. The construct state plays the same part as it does when preceding a relative clause; cf. מְקוֹם in 18: 21b. Our translation is confirmed by Dt 8: 9, 'a land whose stones are of iron'. Less intelligible are 'its rocks are the place of sapphire' (Renan, Crampon), or 'he has drawn sapphire from its rocks' (Le Hir, not very literally). Sapphire will recur in v. 16 in parallelism with the gold of Ophir. The feminine suffix has been used (in אֲבָנֶיהָ) by reminiscence of ארץ in v. 5. Moreover we have had מָקוֹם in the feminine in 20: 9. It is complicating the text arbitrarily to refer לוֹ to סַפִּיר and see in the 2nd hemistich an allusion to sapphire mingled with gold (Umbreit, Hitzig, Duhm, Hontheim). If we compare with זהב להם of 3: 15a we realise that the sentence simply means: 'and which contains dust that is gold'.

7   On the text of G, cf. v. 5. The word עיט is rendered simply as 'bird' in Theod. πετεινόν, Vulg. *avis*, Targ. עיפא and Syr. ‏ܠܐܦܐ‎.

The word נָתִיב marks the beginning of a descriptive passage, exactly like ארץ in v. 5 and מקום in v. 6. Budde suppresses vv. 5-6, since he claims to find in the 'path' the shaft which man is described as sinking in v. 4. What the author wishes to impress on us is the utter inaccessibility of these mines of sapphire and gold, of these strata of earth overturned by man's labour. In an admirable hyperbole, he declares that the path which leads there is unknown to the birds of prey, that is, the eagle, the vulture, the kite, those birds whose flight is the most powerful and whose vision is the keenest. Duhm is shocked by the way in which the poet here expresses himself. He asks why the vulture should not know the path which leads to the mines. And he proposes to repeat v. 12 before v. 7, in which case it is wisdom whose path is unknown to the bird of prey. Thus we are confronted by a platitude worthy of

8　　Wild beasts have not trodden it,
　　　Nor has the leopard passed over it!
9　　On the silex man has laid his hand,
　　　Mountains he has overturned from their bases;
10　　Niles have been cut out through the rocks,
　　　And all that is precious, the eye has seen;

La Palisse. Duhm has already placed v. 12, which he makes into a refrain or *Leitmotiv*, at the beginning of the chapter. But our aesthetic sense is far more satisfied if v. 12 remains where it is, in its proper place. The poet is concerned to describe the superhuman efforts made by those who explore the earth for precious stones or rare metals. They penetrate to the very bowels of the earth and to the wildest and most desolate places. Their efforts are vain, they will not find wisdom there! Thus every thing prepares for the outburst of v. 12: 'But whence comes Wisdom? and where is the place of understanding?' In the 2nd hemistich we have the use of עֵין with שְׁזָפַתּוּ as in 20: 9a. The word אַיָּה 'vulture' stands also in 15: 23 (Comm.).

8　On the text of G, cf. v. 5. The hexaplar authors assign to שַׁחַץ its meaning of pride, whence, for בְּנֵי־שָׁחַץ, Theod. υἱοὶ ἀλαζόνων (Jerome *filii arrogantium*), Aq. υἱοὶ βαναυσίας, Symm. τέκνα σκανδάλου. But Syr. translates בְּנֵי־שַׁחַץ as 'the animals'; Targ. 'the sons of the lion' or 'men'. Vulg. *filii institorum* 'the sons of merchants' (?).

The בְּנֵי־שַׁחַץ 'sons of pride' recur only in 41: 26 where they denote carnivorous wild beasts; cf. *ferus*, *ferox* in Latin, *fier*, *féroce* in French. Just as in v. 7 we had at first the bird of prey, then the vulture, so here we have wild beasts, then the leopard. The *hiph'il* of דרך has the same sense as the *qal* in 22: 15. The wild beasts themselves dare not venture on the path where man risks his life to reach the mines. The verb עדה is an Aramaism; cf. עדא translating עבר in Targ. on Gn 15: 17; Jer 9: 9, etc. (Levy, *Chald. Wörterbuch*, II, p. 203). On the word שַׁחַל, cf. 4: 10; 10: 16.

9　The text of G resumes at v. 9b (cf. v. 5). For בַּחַלָּמִישׁ, Theod. ἐν ἀκροτόμῳ (Jerome *in durissimo lapide*), Vulg. *ad siliciem*, Syr. حماف لـهنس 'in the flint stones', Targ. בשמיר 'in diamond'.

V. 9 is conceived on the pattern of v. 3. The subject of the verb is 'man' or simply 'one'. The suffix of יָדוֹ refers to the understood subject. The stone חַלָּמִישׁ, the equivalent of the Assyrian *elmešu* and the Arabic *ḥalnabûs*, is the silex or flintstone (cf. Vulg. and Syr.). The verb שלח with יד as direct complement and בְּ before the person or object on which one lays one's hand (Gn 37: 22; 1 S 24: 7, 11, etc.). On הפך 'to overturn', 'to convulse', cf. v. 5. The phrase מִשֹּׁרֶשׁ 'by the root, the base' is very picturesque. Man strikes the mountain at its roots, at the point where it is firmly rooted in the ground; cf. שֹׁרֶשׁ in 13: 27. Man's action is like that of God who also 'overturns' the mountains (9: 5).

10　Vulg. *in petris* and Targ. בטינרין 'in the rocks' have well understood that the בְּ of בצורות was a preposition. The other versions have regarded בצורות as stemming from a root בצר. But while

11   Man has *explored the sources* of rivers,
     And what was hidden, he has brought forth into the light.

11   מַבְּכִי־־־חִפֵּשׂ (G, Vulg.); MT: מִבְּכִי־־־חִבֵּשׁ.

Theod. τὰ ὀχυρώματα and Syr. ܚܣܝܢܘܬܐ 'with force' relate the word to בצור 'strengthened', G δίνας, Aq. and Symm. ῥεῖθρα seem to see streams in בצורות, from the root בצר 'to cut' whence 'fissures', 'gorges', 'torrents'. Instead of δίνας (B, Sah., Syro-hex.), we have δεινάς in א, A, Arab. Baud., and θῖνας in C (cf. Jerome *ripas*). For עינו, G ὁ ὀφθαλμός μου (Sah., Syro-hex., Eth., Arab. Baud.), but G (A) ὁ ὀφθαλμὸς αὐτοῦ. We have *oculus meus* in Jerome (Bod., Gall.) and *oculus ejus* in Jerome (Tur.).

From an exaggerated concern for symmetry, Duhm would like the series 10a-11a, 10b-11b, while Hontheim proposes 10a-11a, 11b-10b. But vv. 10-11 are parallel the one to the other, 11a corresponding to 10a, and 11b to 10b. The 1st hemistich recalls Hab 3:9b, where we have: נהרות תבקע ארץ: 'Thou dost cleave the earth with rivers.' It is obvious that יְאָרִים 'Niles' is a poetic term for נהרות which will be used in v. 11; cf. נחלים in v. 4 (Comm.). The same use of יארים is found in Is 33:21. The meaning is clear: 'In the rocks man has dug Niles.' Cf. the use of the *qal* of בקע in Ps 74:15. The feminine plural צורות, instead of the masculine צורים, as we have נהרות side by side with נהרים. Torczyner suggests a vocalisation בְּצוּרֹות and proposes to translate: 'secrets' (from בצר 'to be inaccessible'). But it would be an unsuitable complement for בקע 'cleave', 'dig out'. Ehrlich proposes אורים 'lights' instead of יארים. But one does not cut out lights. The same commentator replaces כל־יקר 'every precious thing' by כְּלִי יָקָר, without taking into account the meaning of כלי, which

implies an object that is manufactured rather than what is found in the earth. With רָאֲתָה עֵינוֹ 'his eye has seen', cf. ראתה עיני of 13:1a (cf. 7:7; 29:11).

11 G βάθη δὲ ποταμῶν and Vulg. *profunda quoque pluviorum* have read מַבְּכֵי (from נבך) instead of מִבְּכֵי; cf. inf. The original verb was not חבש, but חִפֵּשׂ, as is proved by G ἀνεκάλυψεν, Vulg. *scrutatus est*, Aq. and Theod. ἐξερεύνησεν. With the exception of G ἑαυτοῦ δύναμιν, the versions vocalise תַּעֲלֻמָה (without the *mappiq*), which is found in a few editions of the MT (cf. Ginsburg).

As it stands in the MT, the 1st hemistich is somewhat difficult to interpret. It has been proposed to translate: 'He has bound the rivers (to prevent them) from weeping (or trickling)', and the oddity of the expression has been toned down by paraphrase: *fluminorum fletum cohibent* (Rosenmüller); 'he has checked the course of rivers' (Le Hir); 'he is able to stop the oozing of rivers' (Renan, Crampon). Now, the fact is that the text implied by G and Vulg. differs hardly at all from the MT and presents a perfect meaning. The vocalisation מַבְּכֵי, recognised already by Wetzstein, and the reading חִפֵּשׂ, which Houbigant already suggested, have been adopted by most moderns. The word מַבְּכֵי (construct plural) derives from the root נבך, which will recur in נבכי־ים 'the sources of the sea' (38:16). The root נבך corresponds to the Aramaic נבג 'to gush forth' and to the Arabic نبج 'to ooze forth'. The *pi'el* of חפש means 'search out', 'explore'

12   But whence *comes* Wisdom,
      And where is the place of understanding?
13   Man knows not the *way* which leads to it,
      And it is not to be found in the land of the living.

12   תֵּצֵא; MT: תִּמָּצֵא.
13   דַּרְכָּהּ (G); MT: ערכה.

(cf. חפר 3: 21). Man 'has explored the sources of the rivers', he has pierced to the subterranean strata of the earth whence the rivers rise. The 2nd hemistich corresponds to v. 10a. In penetrating to the depths of the earth, man 'brings forth to the light of day what lay hidden'. We read תַּעֲלָמָה (without the *mappiq*; cf. sup.), for the feminine suffix would not refer to any of the preceding words. We have had the plural of תעלמה in 11: 6. The word אוֹר plays the part of an accusative of place (instead of לְאוֹר); cf. 12: 22b 'and he makes what is shadowy come forth into the light'. Nothing that is hidden escapes man's eye. And yet he does not find Wisdom (v. 12)!

12 Syr. adds the 3rd pers. sing. masc. suffix to בינה.

V. 12, which will be repeated in a slightly modified form in v. 20, is the heart of the poem. Man's efforts enable him to reach the very bowels of the earth, and to extract thence the precious stones or metals which are hidden there. But Wisdom escapes him. Note that v. 12 is antithetic to v. 1, and marks the beginning of a new period. Wisdom and understanding, whose place of origin we are ignorant of, are set in opposition to silver and gold, whose sources we know all about. To the word מָקוֹם corresponded in v. 1 the word מוֹצָא. Now, the verb תִּמָּצֵא 'it is found' is hardly compatible with מֵאַיִן 'whence?', which requires a verb of movement. A very

slight correction enables us to read תֵּצֵא, corresponding to מוֹצָא (from יצא) of v. 1. Thus we shall have as the 1st hemistich: 'But whence comes Wisdom?', which dispenses us from the need to replace תמצא by תבוא of v. 20 (contra Bickell, Duhm). One Hebrew manuscript (Kenn. 157) has the reading תצא (cf. Gray). It may be that the reading תמצא is due to the influence of v. 13b. The parallelism between חָכְמָה 'Wisdom' and בִּינָה 'understanding' reappears in v. 20 and v. 28. The two words are normally coupled in the wisdom literature: Pr 1: 2; 4: 5, 7; 9: 10; 16: 16. Both חכמה and בינה are the object of knowledge (Pr 1: 2; 4: 1; cf. inf. 38: 4). The former expresses rather the wisdom that is handed down by way of tradition, the latter that which is acquired by discernment, insight, and judgment. Here the two words are regarded as synonymous: in vv. 13-19 they will hardly be distinguished at all, and the theme will be one single virtue, namely Wisdom. Cf. Bar 3: 15, in connection with φρόνησις and σύνεσις: τίς εὗρεν τὸν τόπον αὐτῆς καὶ τίς εἰσῆλθεν εἰς τοὺς θησαυροὺς αὐτῆς; Note that allusions to v. 13 occur in Bar 3: 20, 23, 31.

13 Instead of ערכה, G ὁδὸν αὐτῆς read דַּרְכָּהּ, which is the correct reading (cf. inf.). For בארץ החיים, G has simply ἐν ἀνθρώποις. 'The living' are qualified as 'the proud who sin during their lifetime' (Targ.). Vulg. *suaviter viventium* arises per-

14 The Abyss has said: 'It is not in me!'
And the Sea has said: 'It is not with me!'
15 Solid gold will not be taken in exchange for it,
And silver is not weighed to pay for it.

haps from a double reading of *viventium*. The sense is changed by Syr. 'and it is not found, *except* in the land of life'.

As it stands, the 1st hemistich is translated: 'man does not know the price of it'. But it is in vv. 15-19 that the theme will be the evaluation of Wisdom. What the author insists on here is the inaccessibility of Wisdom. After showing that man is able to penetrate to the places where silver, gold, and precious stones are hidden, he has emphasised that man knows the way which leads to these mysterious depths, even though the animals do not know it (vv. 7-8)! And it so happens that G supplies us with דַּרְכָּהּ 'its way', instead of עֶרְכָּהּ. Note that in Bar 3: 20, 23, 31 the author speaks successively of ὁδὸν ἐπιστήμης and ὁδὸν σοφίας. Now, it is indisputable that our 1st hemistich is reflected in these passages of Baruch; cf. ὁδὸν δὲ ἐπιστήμης οὐκ ἔγνωσαν (3: 20), ὁδὸν δὲ σοφίας οὐκ ἔγνωσαν (3: 23), οὐκ ἔστιν ὁ γινώσκων τὴν ὁδὸν αὐτῆς (3: 31). Houbigant did not hesitate to read דַּרְכָּהּ, and this is the reading accepted by most moderns. 'Its way', i.e. the way which leads to it; cf. the use of דֶּרֶךְ in Gn 3: 24. 'The land of the living' by contrast with the land of the dead, which is Sheol, the great land (*RB*, 1907, pp. 60f.). The same expression is found in Ps 52: 7; Is 38: 11; 53: 8.

14 Vv. 14-19, absent from Sah., marked with asterisk in Colb., Jerome, and Syro-hex., did not exist in G. The present text derives from Theod. (cf. Colb. and Syro-hex.). Targ. and Syr. transcribe the word תהום, which is translated ἄβυσσος (Theod.), *abyssus* (Vulg.).

The tone becomes loftier: nature now speaks in order to assert that it does not know where Wisdom is to be found. Successive personifications will bring forward on the scene the Abyss and the Sea (v. 14), then Abaddon and Death (v. 22). The personification of תהום makes it possible to assign to the word the masculine gender, although it is usually feminine (like the Babylonian *tiâmtu*, *tâmtu*). Parallelism between תְּהוֹם and יָם as in 38: 16. As regards תהום, which is the primordial abyss (Gn 1:.2) and the great reservoir of subterranean waters (Gn 7: 11; 49: 25), cf. Comm. on 3: 8; 7: 12; 9: 13. Man reaches even this sheet of water which lies underground (v. 11), but the Abyss declares that Wisdom is not to be found there. And the depths of the sea make the same reply to the exploration of the divers whose activities will be mentioned in v. 18.

15 On the text of G, cf. v. 14. Theod. δώσει reads יִתֵּן instead of יֻתַּן. For סגור, Theod. συνκλεισμόν; cf. Jerome *conclusum* (with obelus) and Aug. *inclusum*. In Syr., simply ܘܐܣܟ 'gold', but in Targ. דהב סנין 'purified gold', in Vulg. *aurum obrizum* (the word *obrizo* renders אופיר in Is 13: 12).

Budde rejects vv. 15-21, in order to weld v. 22 to v. 14. He cannot claim the support of G, whose lacuna extends from v. 14 (inclusive) to v. 19. Bickell suppressed in addition vv. 12-14. Duhm, usually so radical, protests against these deletions. The arguments of Budde can be reduced

16   It cannot be valued with the gold of Ophir,
      Nor with the precious carnelian, nor with the sapphire!

to the contention that v. 22 seems to be the logical sequel to v. 14. But it should be noticed that v. 20, just like v. 12, opens a new paragraph, which enables the poet to repeat an idea similar to the one which was his theme in the preceding paragraph. The word סְגוֹר, parallel to כֶּסֶף 'silver', is poetically used instead of זָהָב סָגוּר, which corresponds to the Assyrian *ḥurâṣu sagru* (read *sagru* and not *sakru*, in accordance with the form *sagiru*: Thureau-Dangin, *Huitième campagne de Sargon*, p. 58, n. 4). The meaning is 'solid gold', the words סגור and *sagru* being probably connected with סגר 'to shut'. The preposition תחת, connoting 'in the place of' (16:4), with the implication 'in exchange for'; cf. the use of בעד with the verb נתן in 2:4. The *niph'al* of שָׁקֵל, as in 6:2. The last word, מחירה 'its price' is an attribute of כסף; silver is not weighed (as) its price. In 1 K 21:2, כסף מחיר זה 'silver which is the price of it'. Cf. Pr. 3:14; 8:10; Wis 7:8-9. Not only is it impossible to find wisdom in the mines or in the sea, but it cannot be purchased in the markets.

16   On the text of G, cf. v. 14. The word כתם, which is certainly 'gold' for Theod. χρυσίῳ, Symm. χρυσίον, Syr. ܘܐܒܐ, is interpreted as פטלון = πέταλον 'leaf of metal' in Targ. For בכתם אופיר, Vulg. *tinctis Indiae coloribus*, which is an interpretation rather than a translation. The stone שהם is the onyx according to Theod. ἐν ὄνυχι, beryl according to Targ. בירולין and Syr. ܒܪܘܠܐ, the sardonyx according to Vulg. *lapidi sardonycho pretiosissimo*.
The *pu'al* of סלה, in the sense of 'to be valued', recurs only in v. 19,

but we find הַמְסֻלָּאִים 'those who are valued' in La 4:2. The Hebrew סלה corresponds to the Aramaic סלא, which probably derives from סַל 'basket' (Assyrian *sellu*, Aramaic סַלָּא, Arabic *salleh*). The basket was used as a means of measuring corn and grain. The words כֶּתֶם אוֹפִיר form a stereotyped phrase connoting 'the gold of Ophir' (Is 13:12; Ps 45:10). The comparison between כֶּתֶם טָהוֹר (v. 19) and זהב טהור (2 Ch 3:4), כתם טוב (La 4:1) and זהב טוב (2 Ch 3:5) certainly proves the equivalence between כֶּתֶם and זָהָב. We shall have כתם parallel to זהב in 31:24. The root of כתם is probably the Assyrian *katâmu* 'cover over', 'close'; cf. סגור in v. 15. The characteristic of the land of Ophir is its gold, so much so that the word אוֹפִיר of itself can mean the gold of Ophir (22:24). The land of Ophir has been localised in the Indies (cf. Vulg.), in Africa (Movers, etc.; cf. Gesenius-Buhl, s.v.), in Elam (Hüsing; cf. Gesenius-Buhl). But if we compare Gn 10:29 with Gn 2:11-12, we note that there exists an essential relation between Ophir and Havilah, which is also the country of gold and precious stones. Hence it is in Arabia that we have the best chance of discovering the location of Ophir, the name of which probably derives from the Arabic *wafara* 'to be abundant, plentiful'. Ancient texts concerning Arabia as a gold producing country have been collected by Bochart (*Phaleg et Canaan*, pp. 138ff.). The combined fleets of Solomon and Hiram departed from Elath in the Gulf of 'Aqaba, to reach, through the passage of the Red Sea, the southern coast of Arabia and bring back from thence the gold of

17   Neither gold nor glass can be compared to it,
      And a vase of fine gold is not the price of it.
18   Of corals and crystal no mention is even made;
      And the extraction of Wisdom is far more difficult than that
      of pearls.

Ophir (1 K 9: 26ff.; 10: 11). The stone שֹׁהַם is paired with fine gold in the enumeration of the products of Havilah (Gn 2: 12). The hypothesis of P. Haupt, who would see here a reference to electrum (*Oriental. Literatur-Zeitung*, 1913, col. 489), is contradicted by the various passages of Exodus (25: 7; 28: 9, 20, etc.), where the word שֹׁהַם occurs. In fact this stone is identical with the Assyrian *sâmtu, sându* (cf. תְּהוֹם and *tâmtu, tâmdu*), which very probably denotes here the carnelian (cf. Thureau-Dangin, *Huitième campagne de Sargon*, p. 52, n. 4, and Meissner, *Babylonien und Assyrien*, I, p. 351). Note that the stone *sâmtu*, purplish in hue, is usually mentioned along with a stone of blue colour, especially lapis-lazuli, *uknû*, for example in the *Descent of Ishtar*, rev. 1. 56. It is precisely sapphire, סַפִּיר, blue in colour, which here accompanies the שֹׁהַם. Sapphire was parallel with gold in v. 6.

17   On the text of G, cf. v. 14. For זְכוּכִית, Syr. זגוגית, Theod. ὕαλος, Vulg. *vitrum*. The versions render כְּלִי by the plural. Syr. mingles v. 18a with v. 17b. One of the Targums renders פז by אוברריזין; cf. *obrizum* of Vulg. v. 15.
      On the verb ערך cf. 13: 18. Here it is intransitive in sense, 'to be compared', as in Ps 89: 7 where יערך is parallel to ידמה 'is like'. The change from יערכנה to יערבנה (Hontheim) is contradicted by v. 19a. The word זְכוֹכִית does not recur elsewhere, but the meaning is not doubtful, in the light of the Aramaic

זגוגיתא and the Arabic *zajâjeh*. In the ancient world, glass had much more value than it has today. The negative לא governs the 2nd hemistich. On תְּמוּרָה 'exchange', 'commerce', cf. 20: 18. One might hesitate between the singular of the MT, כְּלִי, and the plural of the versions, כְּלִי. The word פז denotes pure gold. It surpasses זָהָב (Ps 19: 11), חָרוּץ (Pr 8: 19), כֶּתֶם (Ca 5: 11).

18   On the text of G, cf. v. 14. For ראמות Theod. μετέωρα, Symm. ὑψηλά, Vulg. *excelsa* (from the root רום), but Targ. סנדלכין (σανδαράκη), probably rubies (cf. Krauss, *Lehnwörter*, II, p. 400). The word גָּבִישׁ is transcribed γαβείς by Theod., whence Jerome *gabis* (which has become *gravis* in Tur.); it is connected with גבע גב by Symm. ὑπερηρμένα and Vulg. *eminentia*. According to Targ. בירולין (cf. v. 16), it is still a question of beryl. Theod. καὶ ἕλκυσον vocalises וּמְשֹׁךְ instead of וּמֶשֶׁךְ, while Symm. and Aq. γλυκὺ δέ seem to read ומתק. The word מפנינים is ill understood by Theod. ὑπὲρ τὰ ἐσώτατα (cf. Vulg. *de occultis*), Symm. ὑπὲρ πάντα τὰ περίβλεπτα, and Aq. παρὰ τὰ περίβλεπτα. There is nothing to be learned from Syr., which paraphrases v. 18, mingling it with v. 17b.
      The word רָאמוֹת recurs in Ezk 27: 16, where it denotes precious objects coming not from Aram, as the MT indicates, but from Edom (Cornill, following Aq., Symm., and G, which read אָדָם and not אֲרָם). In Pr 24: 7, where ראמות recurs, the text is doubtful. Jewish tradition is

19   The topaz of Ethiopia is not to be compared with it,
      With pure gold it cannot be valued!
20   Whence then comes Wisdom,
      And where is the place of understanding?
21   It has been hidden from the eyes of every living creature,
      And from the bird of the heavens has it been concealed!

quite firm in maintaining the sense 'corals' (*Thesaurus* of Gesenius, II, p. 1249). Saadia translates here by the Arabic *murjân* 'coral'. This meaning is very suitable, for we shall have the mention of pearls in the 2nd hemistich. Coral is abundant on the coasts of the Red Sea. It is understandable that the Edomites should have traded in it (Ezk 27: 16). The *hapax* גָּבִישׁ corresponds to אֶלְגָּבִישׁ 'hail' and denotes rock crystal; cf. the Greek κρύσταλλος 'hail', 'crystal'. In Assyrian there exists the stone *algameš*, which corresponds to אלגביש and means 'crystal' (cf. Scheil, *Rev. d'assyriologie*, **15**, p. 119). The *niph'al* of זכר is used impersonally: 'it is not mentioned'. The 2nd hemistich has been perfectly elucidated by Bochart (*Hieroz.*, II, cols. 68off.). The word מֶשֶׁךְ has the meaning 'extraction' (cf. the verb משך in Comm. on 21: 33). The פְּנִינִים are pearls. The Jews of today translate the proper name פְּנִנָּה as Perla. Moreover, it is מרגלין (*margarita*) which translates פנינים in Targ. The meaning is clear: the extraction of Wisdom is more costly than that of pearls. It involves greater difficulties, and hence the product has greater value.

19   On the text of G, cf. v. 14. For פטדת, Theod. τοπάζιον, Vulg. *topazius*, Syr. ﻣﺰﺟﻠﺒﺎﺗ (*margarita*), Targ. מרגלא ירקא 'green pearl'. Vulg. renders כתם by *tincturae* (cf. v. 16), Targ. by פיטלון (cf. v. 16). Syr. adds 'and nothing can be compared with it', which comes from Pr 8: 11.

The topaz of Ethiopia adds a new element to the description of vv. 16-18. This forbids us to see in v. 19a a mere gloss on v. 17a or in v. 19b a repetition of v. 16a (contra Duhm). The poet returns to his idea of v. 17, i.e. that nothing is comparable to Wisdom. He had mentioned gold and glass, he is now led to mention the topaz of Ethiopia because his horizon is now the Red Sea (v. 18). In the 2nd hemistich he will be careful to reverse the order of the words and to replace אופיר of v. 16 by טהור. It is as it were a summary of the whole passage, intended to bring in the refrain of v. 20. The word פִּטְדָה is always rendered by τοπάζιον in G. Its source in Ethiopia is confirmed by classical tradition, according to which topaz was gathered in an island of the Red Sea and exploited by the Troglodytes (*Thesaurus* of Gesenius, II, p. 1101). Pliny quotes the evidence of Juba, according to which there existed an island called Topazion in the Red Sea (*Hist. nat.*, XXXVII, 32; cf. VI, 34).

20   The text of G begins again at v. 20. The reading πόθεν εὑρέθη, for מאין תבוא, comes from v. 12. Sah. reverses the order of the two hemistichs.

V. 20 marks the beginning of a new section, v. 12 being simply repeated, with a slight modification: תָּבוֹא instead of תֵּצֵא (which has become later תִּמָּצֵא; cf. G).

21   Vv. 21b-22a, absent from Sah., marked with asterisk in Jerome (v.

22   Abaddon and Death have said:
     'With our ears, we have heard it talked of!'
23   Elohim has discerned the way to it,
     And it is He who has known where it was to be found,
24   When He looked to the ends of the earth,
     And saw all that lies under the heavens,

22b included) and Syro-hex., did not exist in G. The present text derives from Theod. (cf. Colb.). The *waw* of the opening is omitted in G, Syr., and Vulg. G πάντα ἄνθρωπον omits מֵעֵינִי, which is restored by Theod. ἐξ ὀφθαλμῶν, quoted in Syro-hex. and followed by Jerome *ab oculis omnis hominis*. G(A) adds the negative before ἐκρύβη, which translates נסתרה.

The *niph'al* of עלם, with מֵעֵינֵי before the person from whom the thing is hidden (Lv 4:13; Nu 5:13). Parallelism between נעלם and נסתר (Nu 5:13). The formula כָּל־חַי 'every living creature' is applied to the animals, as in 12:10. The animals of the earth are opposed to the birds of the heavens of the 2nd hemistich: cf. 12:7, where 'the birds of the heavens' are parallel to the beasts of burden. In 30:23 it will be all men who are denoted by כָּל־חַי (cf. Gn 3:20). V. 21 sums up in a verse the description of vv. 7-8.

22   On the text of G, for v. 22a, cf. v. 21. The word אבדון is rendered בית אבדנא (Targ.), اﺑﺪ (Syr.), ἡ ἀπώλεια (Theod.), *perditio* (Vulg.), exactly as in 26:6. Targ. interprets מות by מלאך מותא 'the angel of death'. For שָׁמְעָה, G αὐτῆς τὸ κλέος, Vulg. *famam ejus*.

Personification as in v. 14. On Abaddon, cf. 26:6. Instead of Sheol, it is now Death which is the parallel to Abaddon. The allusion is to the abode of the dead as in 30:23; 38:17. The phrase: בְּאָזְנֵינוּ שָׁמַעְנוּ 'we have heard with our ears' as in

Ps 44:2. The suffix of שִׁמְעָהּ refers to the object, not to the subject of the hearing (cf. דַּרְכָּהּ in v. 23): we have heard what is currently said of it, we have heard talk of it. The abode of the dead has, as it were, a vague suspicion of the mystery of Wisdom. The land of the living knew nothing of it (v. 13).

23   Syr. anticipates כי of v. 24 at the opening of v. 23.

Man has been shown to be ignorant of the way which leads to Wisdom (v. 13; cf. Comm.). God alone is able to know it. In the passage of Baruch, already quoted (cf. vv. 12-13), no one knows the path that leads to Wisdom except God: ἀλλὰ ὁ εἰδὼς τὰ πάντα γινώσκει αὐτήν, ἐξεῦρεν αὐτὴν τῇ συνέσει αὐτοῦ (Bar 3:32). There follows a description of the divine activity as here. Parallelism between הבין 'He has discerned' and יָדַע 'He has known', as in Mic 4:12. Wisdom was created at the origin of the world, and it is this which presided over the divine works (Pr 8:22-31). God knew it before anything else. It is thus that we understand the passage which follows: v. 24 forms the link between v. 23 and v. 25.

24   G renders לקצות־הארץ by τὴν ὑπ' οὐρανὸν πᾶσαν and תחת כל־השמים by τὰ ἐν τῇ γῇ πάντα. The word לעשות of v. 25 is connected by G with v. 24, whence πάντα ἃ (omitted by B) ἐποίησεν (Jerome *omnia quae fecit*).

כי is usually regarded as meaning 'for': God would know the sphere

25   To give to the wind a weight,
     And to gauge the waters with a measure,
26   When He imposed on the rain a limit,
     And made a way for the rumble of the thunder!

in which Wisdom abides, for He sees everything. But v. 23 means that God 'has known' the way which leads to Wisdom. V. 24 indicates the time when God took knowledge of this. It was when He was observing the ends of the earth with a view to organising the elements (vv. 25-6). It was then that He saw and examined Wisdom (v. 27). This interpretation agrees admirably with Pr 8: 22-31. Hence we translate: 'When He looked to the ends of the earth, And saw all that lies under the heavens.' The verb רָאָה 'to see' denotes the result of the action indicated by הִבִּיט 'to look at', 'to observe' (35: 5). Preposition לְ before the complement of הִבִּיט (Ps 74: 20; 104: 32). The קְצוֹת־הָאָרֶץ 'confines of the earth', as in Is 40: 28; 41:5, 9. The phrase תַּחַת כָּל־הַשָּׁמַיִם 'under the whole heavens' is conventional (37: 3; 41: 3). Naturally 'He sees under all the heavens' will mean: He sees all that lies under the heavens (cf. Vulg. *et omnia quae sub coelo sunt*). The earth and the heavens were founded 'by the wisdom' and 'by the understanding' of Yahweh (Pr 3: 19). There is nothing surprising about the fact that Wisdom, personified, appears to God at the moment of the divine creation of the world.

25   The word לַעֲשׂוֹת is assimilated to a perfect in G ἐποίησεν (in v. 24), to a present participle in Vulg. *qui fecit* and Syr. ܘܥܒܕ. G sums up the 2nd hemistich in two words ὕδατος μέτρα, whence Jerome *aquae mensuras*, which has become *atque mensuras* in Aug.
     V. 25 depends on v. 24, and there

is no reason to change לַעֲשׂוֹת into הָעֹשֶׂה (Duhm; cf. Vulg. and Syr.) or into בעשתו of v. 26 (Budde). God scans the farthest edges of the world in order to organise the creative process. It is at that moment that He discerns Wisdom (cf. v. 24). The 1st hemistich 'to give to the wind a weight' is admirable in expressive power. The wind is the lightest of things, and yet God determines for it a weight! The verb עשה 'to make', with לְ before the person on whose behalf one does something abstract (or to whom one gives something); cf. Gn 21: 6, 'God has made for me laughter', i.e. God has granted me laughter. The infinitive construction לעשות is extended, merging into a verb in the personal mode; cf. 5: 11. The same construction with the imperfect instead of the perfect in 29: 3; 38: 7. The basic meaning of תִּכֵּן is 'to estimate the measure' of a thing. What serves as a measuring instrument is preceded by בְּ, as here, in Is 40: 12. The connotation 'to gauge' fits in very well with our passage. According to the context, it is a question of the waters of the heavens brought by the winds, shed in the form of rain (v. 26) and accompanied by thunder (v. 26).

26   G ὅτε ἐποίησεν· οὕτως ἰδὼν ἠρίθμησεν retains only בעשתו of v. 26 and continues by v. 27a. What follows in G (viz. vv. 26b-27a) does not exist in Sah. and is marked by asterisk in Jerome (including 27b) and Syro-hex. This is the text of Theod. for vv. 26b-27a of the MT. Hence we have, in the present text of G, a double translation of v. 27a,

27   It was then that He saw it and appraised it,
      That He *discerned* it and even examined it closely! 28 [   ]

27 הֲבִינָהּ; MT: הֱכִינָהּ.

28 'And he said to man: Behold, the fear of Adonai is Wisdom, and to turn from evil is understanding.' An addition (see Comm.).

but no translation of למטר חק. Syr. הבם 'he has made' treats בעשׂתו as a perfect (cf. v. 25). Instead of חזיז, Syr. reads חזיון, whence its 'visions of the voices'. Vulg. translates לחזיז קלות by *procellis sonantibus*.

A new weather feature (cf. v. 24). In the light of 38:10 and Pr 8:29, it is clear that חק has here the sense of 'limit'; cf. Comm. on 14:5. The verb עשׂה takes here a meaning similar to that which it had in v. 25. The 2nd hemistich will be literally repeated in 38:25. The exact meaning of חֲזִיז קֹלוֹת is 'rumble of thunder', the plural of קֹול denoting the 'thunderclaps' (cf. the singular in 37:4), and the word חֲזִיז corresponding to the Arabic *hazîz* 'rumble' of thunder (*Thesaurus* of Ben-Yehuda, III, p. 1484). It is by extension that חזיז קלות will acquire the meaning of storm' (Sir 40:13). The plural חֲזִיזִים will first denote the rumblings of the thunder and then the storm (Zec 10:1; Sir 35:26). In modern Hebrew חזיז is used for the lightning and storm cloud.

27 On the text of G for v. 27a, cf. v. 26. Targ. adds: עם מלאכי שירותא 'with the angels at its command', after וַיִּסַפְּרָה.

The adverb of the opening, אז 'then', refers to vv. 24-6, which have described the creative activity of God. It is in the origins of things that God knew Wisdom: 'it was then that He saw it' (cf. Pr 8:22ff.). וַיְסַפְּרָה is considered to mean 'and He told of it', following the normal meaning of the *pi'el*. Whence the

translations: 'and He showed it' (Le Hir); 'and He proclaimed it' (Renan), etc. But the last verb חֲקָרָהּ 'He examined it' marks the climax of these intellectual operations. The gradation is not secured if God has already officially proclaimed the being of Wisdom. Now, the verb ספר can have in the *pi'el* the meaning of 'count', 'number' (38:37; Ps 22:18), exactly like the *qal* in 14:16. And in v. 25 the author has insisted precisely on the weight and the measure which God decreed for the elements. God sees Wisdom and He numbers it, He assesses its value. This explanation renders unnecessary the change from the *pi'el* to the *qal* which is proposed by Duhm, who postulates for the *qal* of ספר the meaning 'to examine'. The reading הֱכִינָהּ would mean 'He established it' or 'He prepared it', or again, 'He directed it'. But a variant, found in five manuscripts and several editions (cf. Ginsburg), offers הֲבִינָהּ 'He discerned it' (cf. v. 23), which is in perfect harmony with the other verbs. God sees Wisdom, He appraises it, He discerns it, He examines it closely. It forms the object of the divine contemplation. In Pr 8:30 Wisdom is in the presence of God; it plays in His presence. On the verb חקר cf. 5:27.

28 Syr. omits הן. For יראת אדני G ἡ θεοσέβεια.

The whole poem on Wisdom was intended to show that it is inaccessible to man and that God alone can discover it. Man succeeds in discovering metals and precious stones;

he reaches the most desolate spots and impracticable ways, penetrating even to the very bowels of the earth (1-11). But where is Wisdom to be found? Man does not know the way that leads to it, it does not exist on the earth at all (12-13), nor even in the depths of the sea (14). Can it be purchased with gold, silver, or jewels? No! Vv. 15-19 stress this point. Then the refrain is heard again: 'Whence then comes Wisdom, and where is the place of understanding?' (20). It eludes the vision of all living creatures (21), though the infernal abysses have a vague suspicion of its existence (22). It is God who knows it (23). He perceived it and contemplated it under all its aspects when He organised the world and imposed His law on the elements (24-7). Hence it is clearly metaphysical Wisdom, a personified being, as in Pr 8: 22-31, which forms the object of this sublime poem. V. 28, 'and He said to man: Behold, the fear of Adonai is Wisdom, and to turn from

evil is understanding', is added in order to draw a practical conclusion. The use of אֲדֹנָי, which does not once appear in the whole Book of Job, instead of אלהים of v. 23, the theological formulae 'to fear the Lord and depart from evil' (1: 1, 8; 2: 3; Pr 3: 7; 14: 16; 16: 16), the renewed use of חכמה and of בינה (12: 20), when the present description is concerned exclusively with הַחָכְמָה 'Wisdom' (בינה 'understanding' is introduced solely for the sake of parallelism)—these are all indications enabling us to recognise in v. 28 an addition intended to reduce to current ethics the speculative ideas of ch. 28. The prosaic character of the gloss is sufficiently evidenced by the introductory 'and He said to man' of which Budde would make a hemistich. Note that this author gets rid of the word אדני by reading יראתי 'my fear', while Torczyner supposes that the divine name was originally אֱלוֹהַ.

CHAPTER 29

1   And Job continued his speech and said,
2   Who will make me once more as I was in months now gone,
     In the days when Eloah made me secure?
3   What time He *caused* His lamp to shine over my head,
     And by His light I traversed the darkness!

Chapters 29-31   Tenth speech of Job: see Introduction, pp. lif.
3 בַּהֲלֹו (Targ.); MT: בְּהִלֹּו.

29: **1** G has the same formula as in 27: 1. Perhaps προοιμίῳ in both cases stems from παροιμίῳ, a translation of מָשָׁל (Drusius).

'And Job continued his speech and said', instead of the usual brief formula 'and Job spoke and said'. Ch. 28 was an interpolation in the discussion. Ch. 27 completed the speech of Zophar (cf. Comm. on 27: 13). Job no longer replies to his friends. The discussion is closed by the third speech of the third speaker. Job will now repeat the theme of all his speeches, and sum up his case in the following three points: his past happiness, his present sufferings, his righteousness always. Such is the problem which his friends have been unable to solve. Why, after enjoying a spell of supreme prosperity, has he fallen to the depths of wretchedness and infirmity, seeing that he has never failed in his duties? The exposition of Job is now fuller than in the previous speeches. Here is truly his מָשָׁל, that is, his supreme poetic utterance. That is why the formula of introduction is more solemn than was the case when the other parts of the debate were announced.

2 G ἔμπροσθεν ἡμερῶν reads ימי instead of כימי, and makes of this word the complement of קדם.

The whole of ch. 29 will be devoted to a description of the happiness of Job and the prestige he enjoyed before being struck down by his calamities. This vision of past felicity will be confronted by that of his present condition. The words ועתה 'and now' (30: 1, 9, 16) will mark the contrast. The memory of past happiness increases the sting of present ills. The opening cry is fraught with pathos: 'Who will make me once more such as I was in months now gone, In the days when Eloah made me secure?' The formula מִי יִתְּנֵנִי כ״, just as we have מי יתנך כ״ 'who will make you like a brother for me?' in Ca 8: 1. The preposition of time is understood after the particle כ״ 'as' (5: 14). The months and the days, just as we had the months and the nights in 7: 3. Note the use of קֶדֶם 'what lies before one', not now spatially (23: 8) but temporally. We often meet the formula ימי קדם 'past days'. The verb שמר 'safeguard', 'keep secure' (2: 6; 10: 12). The word ימי is in the construct state, because determined by the following preposition; cf. 18: 21b and 28: 6a.

3 The 1st hemistich is translated twice in Syr. Instead of בְּהִלֹּו, Targ. באנהרותיה read בַּהֲלֹו (*hiph'il*; cf. inf.).

415

4   Such as I was in the days of my autumn
     When Eloah *protected* my tent,

4   בְּסוֹךְ (G., Symm., Syr.); MT: בסוד.

The suffixes of נֵרוֹ and אוֹרוֹ refer to אֱלוֹהַ of v. 2b. The lamp and the light symbolise happiness (18:5-6; 21:17). Cf. Ps 36:10, 'by Thy light we see light', God being the source of this light which is the symbol of happiness. The Massoretic vocalisation regards הִלּוֹ (in בְּהִלּוֹ) as the infinitive *qal* of הלל (25:5; 31:26), with the suffix referring to the subject which follows. The construction may be grammatically justified, but then one is obliged to translate: 'when it shone, [namely] His lamp' (see Gesenius-Kautzsch, § 131n), which is a very clumsy turn of phrase. A slight change in the vocalisation yields בַּהֲלּוֹ, a contraction of בְּהַהֲלּוֹ (Beer, Duhm; cf. Olshausen, Budde), a reading supported by Targ. Thus we obtain the *hiph'il* infinitive (41:10), which offers perfect sense: 'When He caused His lamp to shine over my head'. Cf. Ps 18:29, 'for Thou, Thou dost cause my lamp to shine, O Yahweh'; *hiph'il* of אור, with נֵרִי 'my lamp' for complement. The lamp is 'above' the head; cf. 18:6. The 2nd hemistich with a verb in the finite personal form, as in 28:25b. The expression לְאוֹרוֹ 'in His light' with the verb הלך; cf. Is 60:3 'and nations will walk in thy light', וְהָלְכוּ גוֹיִם לְאוֹרֵךְ. The verb הלך with the accusative, to denote 'go through', 'traverse'; (cf. Dt 1:19; 2:7; 2 S 2:29).

4 It is difficult to see how G can have extracted ἐπιβρίθων (ἐπιτρίβων in א) ὁδούς (ὁδοῖς in A, C, אᶜ·ᵃ, Jerome *in viis*) from the words בִּימֵי חָרְפִּי. For חָרְפִּי, Theod. and Symm. νεότητός μου, Vulg. *adolescentiae meae*,

Targ. הריפותי, but Syr. ܣܥܡܬ 'of my shame' (from חרפה 'shame', 'disgrace'). Instead of בסוד, G ἐπισκοπὴν ἐποιεῖτο, Symm. περιέφρασσεν (cf. περιέφραξας for שֹׂכֶת in G, 1:10), Syr. ܣܟ ܘܗܘ 'He protected' have read בְּסוֹךְ (cf. inf.).

Literally: כַּאֲשֶׁר הָיִיתִי 'like him whom I have been'; cf. כַּאֲשֶׁר לֹא־הָיִיתִי in 10:19. The phrase depends on מִי־יִתְּנֵנִי of v. 2: 'Who will make me once more such as I was?' Job has spoken of the days and months that are now gone. They were the days of his autumn. The word חֹרֶף 'autumn' denotes maturity. Autumn is the season when the fruits are gathered because they are ripe. The root חרף is reflected in the Arabic *ḥarafa* 'to gather fruit', *ḥarâf* 'the season of gathering fruit', *ḥarîf* 'autumn'. It is unnecessary to bring in *ḥarûf* 'lamb' (Barth) in order to assign to חרפי the meaning of 'my youth'; it would rather be 'my childhood'. There is no reason to change the text in order to read פִּרְחִי 'my flower' (Volz, Budde), חֶלְמִי 'my health' (Ball, following the Aramaic). The 2nd hemistich should really be interpreted: 'in the familiarity of God upon my tent', whence are extracted: 'When God familiarly visited my tent' (Le Hir), 'when the friendship of God hovered over my tent' (Renan). On the word סוֹד cf. 15:8; 19:19. But the preposition עֲלֵי does not suit this context, and the phrase is oddly constructed. On the other hand, if we read בְּסוֹךְ with G, Symm., Syr., we obtain the verb סוך or סכך, parallel to שׂוּךְ or שׂכך (cf. 1:10; 3:23), in the sense of 'cover', 'protect'. The person or thing covered or protected may be pre-

5   When Shaddai was still with me,
     And my boys were *standing* around me,
6   When my very feet were bathed in butter,
     And the hard rock [   ] became rivers of oil!

5   Add עִמָּדִי at the end (cf. v. 6b, Comm.).
6   Omit עמדי, which comes from v. 5.

ceded by the preposition עַל after the verb סכך (Cf. Ex 33:22; 40:3; 1 K 8:7). The sense of the 2nd hemistich then becomes perfectly clear: 'When Eloah protected my tent'. The tent is a comprehensive term including place of residence and family (5:24; 8:22). In 31:31 Job will say: 'the people of my tent' to imply all those who live with him.

5 G ὅτε ἤμην ὑλώδης λίαν reads שׁדי מאד instead of שׁדי עמדי. Targ. avoids the anthropomorphism by prefixing מימר 'the word' before שׁדי (cf. 1:10, 11, etc.). Syr. renders נערי by 'my youth' and merges the two hemistichs into a single proposition.

The preposition ״ב to denote the time (as in vv. 3a, 4b, 6a, 7a) and the use of עמדי as in 28:14. The 2nd hemistich seems too short, and on the other hand v. 6b will be too long. The word עמדי, which is not needed in 6b, probably comes from עָמְדוּ (cf. v. 8b), which closed v. 5.

If so, we may compare with 21:8b, where עמם stands for עמדים (cf. Comm.) The 2nd hemistich, 'and my boys were standing around me', describes the family happiness which prevailed in the tent of Job. To change נְעָרַי into נְעָרַי 'my youth' (Hoffmann) is to confront ourselves with such a translation as 'when my youth was around me', which is not really intelligible. With סְבִיבוֹתַי cf. סביבותיך in 22:10a.

6 V. 6 has been omitted in Syr. For בְּחֵמָה, G βουτύρῳ, Vulg. *butyro*, Targ.

בלואי 'in butter'. G τὰ δὲ ὄρη μου ἐχέοντο γάλακτι paraphrases the 2nd hemistich. Vulg. *et petra fundebat mihi rivos olei* is more literal (the same sense is found in Targ.).

The word הֲלִיךְ is a *hapax*. The feminine הֲלִיכָה (6:19) denoted 'the thing which goes', i.e. 'the caravan', the masculine will mean: 'the thing which walks', 'the foot'; cf. the Assyrian 'what crushes' for the foot (*L'Emploi métaphorique*, p. 158). Comparing our text with 20:17, where rivers of fresh oil (cf. Comm.) stand in parallelism with torrents of honey and butter, it becomes apparent that חֵמָה stands for חֶמְאָה 'butter', as has been well understood by G, Vulg., Targ. 'When my feet were bathed in butter'—this implies a climax of wealth and prosperity. Asher dips his feet in oil (Dt 33:24), and one washes one's feet in the blood of one's enemies (Ps 58:11). The 2nd hemistich is of abnormal length, and it is not very clear how to interpret עִמָּדִי 'with me'. We should rather have expected לִי 'for me' (cf. Vulg., Le Hir, Renan, etc.). It is probable that עמדי is a survival of עָמְדוּ which concluded v. 5 (cf. Comm.). The word יָצוּק, which we have found qualifying אֶבֶן (28:2) and which denotes a characteristic of stone (41:16), must have the meaning 'hard', like cast iron (cf. Comm. on 11:15). It is here an epithet of צוּר 'rock'. Those who translate יָצוּק as 'flow' (from צוק, which would be the equivalent

7   When I went out by the gate which towers over the city,
     And on the square settled my seat,

8   The young men, on seeing me, would hide themselves,
     And the old men would get up and remain standing;

of יצק) cite 28: 2. But in this passage, as here, יָצוּק is the passive participle used adjectivally in the sense of 'hard'. Duhm eliminates צוּר, which is however confirmed by Dt 32: 12, where oil flows from the rock. He then reads יָצוּק עָמְדִי, which gives him: '*und mein Stehenbleiben Ölbäche ergoss*' ('and my standing still poured out rivers of oil'). This standing still which has the effect of pouring out rivers of oil is too bizarre for us to be able seriously to attribute it to our poet. We translate simply, after transferring עמדו (= עמדי) to its original context: 'and the hard rock became rivers of oil', same construction as in 28: 2b.

7 G ὄρθριος reads שַׁחַר instead of שַׁעַר. For שער עלי־קרת, Vulg. *ad portam civitatis*. The word קרת is read קראתי 'I have called' by Syr. Instead of אכין, G ἐτίθετο seems to read הֵכָן, while Vulg. *parabant* reads ייכינו. Syr. ܐܝܟ ܡܣܟܢܐ 'like a poor man' replaces אכין by כאביון (Rosenmüller).

The 1st hemistich, 'when I went out by the gate which towers over the city', is perfectly intelligible. There is no reason to suppress שַׁעַר, as Budde does, or to have recourse to שַׁחַר 'in the morning' as Ewald and Merx do (following G). The phrase יצא שער 'to go out by the gate' is good Hebrew idiom; cf. יצא פתח in 31: 34; יצא השדה 'to go out through the countryside' (Jer 6: 25); יצא את־העיר *egredi urbem* (Gn 44: 4; Ex 9: 29). The words עֲלֵי־קָרֶת 'over the city' determine the particular gate in question. It is the tall gate, the one

which towers high above the town. Note the use of קֶרֶת, a more ancient form than קִרְיָה (39: 7), to designate the city. The word exists in Phoenician inscriptions and in proper nouns like Carthage (*Qart-ḥadast*: 'new city'). Outside this passage of Job, קֶרֶת recurs only in Pr 8: 3; 9: 3, 14; 11: 2. Note שערים לפי־קרת 'the gates at the entrance of the city' (Pr 8: 3), which furnishes a confirmation of the MT in our text. It is by the gate of the town that is to be found the square, רְחוֹב, corresponding to the agora of the Greeks and the forum of the Romans. It is there that justice was administered (5: 4; 31: 21). The assembly of the people in Neh 8: 1-3 is held 'in the square which lies before the gate of the waters'. There sit the elders and the magistrates. Job takes his seat among them. The verb אָכִין, in a finite personal form, is in parallelism with the infinitive (v. 3; 28: 25). On הכין 'place', 'settle' a seat, cf. Comm. on 23: 3. Job will dwell on the prestige he enjoyed in the city.

8 G πάντες ἔστησαν is a free translation of קמו עמדו. The change from קמו to כֻּלָּם (Merx, in accord with G) is no happier than that from שער to שחר in v. 7. Syr. ܣܘܠܘܦܣܘܣ ܟܘ 'and they admired me' is an interpretation of עמדו 'they remained standing'.

The perfects which will follow (8-9, 10, 21) mark the customary attitude of those who found themselves in the presence of Job (cf. 1: 4). The young men, נְעָרִים, are contrasted with יְשִׁישִׁים, the old men. The former 'hide themselves' from

9 The princes restrained their words,
  And laid their hands on their mouths;
10 The voices of the chiefs became hushed,
  And their tongue cleaved to their palate.

motives of deference, they do not dare to appear before Job. The latter, who have a voice in affairs, get up and remain standing until Job invites them to sit down. The *niph'al* of חבא, as in 5:21. On the word יָשִׁישׁ, which is characteristic of the Book of Job, cf. 12:12. The verb עמד 'to remain standing' (v. 5, cf. Comm.) marks the result of the action expressed by קום 'to rise up'. The two verbs are juxtaposed in order to lend more vigour to the description.

9 G translates כף by δάκτυλον (cf. Vulg. *digitum*).

Not only the aged, but even the highest dignitaries showed their respect for the person of Job. First the princes, שָׂרִים as in 3:15. They restrain their words; cf. עצר במלין in 4:2 and עצר במים in 12:15. The image of the 2nd hemistich is expressive: 'and they laid their hands on their mouths', to prevent the words from being articulated. Cf. 21:5, 'and put your hands on your mouths', where we have יד instead of כַּף and עַל־פֶּה instead of לְפִיהֶם. Use of לְ ''/' is as in יד לפה 'hand on the mouth' in Pr 30:32. Same construction as here is found in Wis 8:12, χεῖρα ἐπιθήσουσιν ἐπὶ στόμα αὐτῶν. Rosenmüller cites the *Aeneid*: *conticuere omnes intentique ora tenebant.*

10 G οἱ δὲ ἀκούσαντες ἐμακάρισάν με is the translation of 11a. A second translation of 11a appears in G, but it comes from Theod. And, in fact, the present text of G at vv. 10b-11a is absent from Sah. and marked by asterisk in Syro-hex. It derives from Theod., according to Cod. 255 (cf. Beer). Hence the original text of G included G 10a and G 11b, which correspond to MT 11a and MT 11b. V. 10 was not translated in G. In order to explain נחבאו, Syr. adds the relative: 'the voices of the chiefs who were hidden', while Vulg. *vocem suam cohibebant duces* makes of נגידים the subject of נחבאו (similarly Targ.).

The נְגִידִים are the chiefs who are placed after the princes of v. 9; cf. נָגִיד in 31:37. The 1st hemistich has been subjected to several corrections, first because of the plural נֶחְבָּאוּ, and secondly because of the meaning of חבא. It has been proposed to read נֶחְבָּא (Ehrlich, Perles) and to see in the final *waw* a dittograph of the *waw* which follows. Or else, on the pretext that נחבאו is a reminiscence of v. 8, a change has been made to נאלם 'has become silent' (Siegfried, Budde) or to נכלא 'has been restrained' (Duhm). On the other hand, Hoffmann retains the plural and reads יחרשׁו 'are silent'. Merx suppressed נגידים נחבאו as being a doublet of נערים נחבאו (v. 8), while Hitzig eliminated the whole verse, following G. It should be noted that v. 10 is not a duplicate of v. 9. The idea is strengthened but not repeated. The plural נחבאו (due to attraction of the complement of קוֹל) is justified by similar cases (cf. Comm. on 22:12 and Gesenius-Kautzsch, § 146a). The *niph'al* of חבא does not mean merely 'to be hidden' (v. 8) but also 'to be veiled'; cf. חֶבְיוֹן 'veil' (from חבה parallel to חבא) in Hab. 3:4. We may translate without changing the text: 'The voices of the chiefs became hushed.'

21   They listened to me and *remained quietly attentive*,
      And they waited for my advice;
22   After I had spoken, they did not reply,

11-20 After 21-25.
21 Transpose וַיְדֹמּוּ and וְיִחֵלּוּ.

This explanation seems to us preferable to that of Chajes (quoted in
Gesenius-Buhl, s.v. חבא), who proposes to interpret in the light of the
Arabic خبا 'to become extinct', 'to
fade away', the Hebrew equivalent
of which is כבה and not חבא. The
2nd hemistich: 'and their tongue
cleaved to their palate' repeats a
current image, designed to express
either complete silence (Ps 137: 6;
Ezk 3: 26), or to depict the effect of
thirst (La 4: 4). The tongue and
palate as organs of speech appear in
6: 30.

Budde realised correctly that vv.
21-5, which are not adapted to their
present context, form the natural
sequel to v. 10. This passage continues the description of the attitude
of the great in the presence of Job:
they are silent and listen to him
(v. 21), they receive his words drop
by drop (v. 22), they stand open-
mouthed before him (v. 23), they
wait for his smile (v. 24). In short,
Job is their guide and leader (v. 25).
From v. 11 onwards the mind of the
hero returns to the thought of his
past happiness and the blessings
which were heaped upon him. Most
moderns have adopted the opinion
of Budde; cf. Duhm, Beer (edition of
Kittel), Hontheim, Torczyner, Volz,
etc.

11-20 After 21-5.

21 G (A, C) adds πρεσβύτεροι as
subject; cf. ܡܣܝܐ in the margin
of Syro-hex. Instead of יחלו, Symm.
ἐπήνουν reads יהללו (Beer, cf. Ps 88:
63). Tradition hesitates between
לְמוֹ עֲצָתִי in two words and
in one word (cf. Ginsburg, Baer, Beer

in Kittel's edition). The versions have
translated 'to my counsel': G ἐπὶ τῇ
ἐμῇ βουλῇ, Vulg. *ad consilium meum*,
Targ. למלכתי, Syr. ܠܡܠܟܬܗܘܢ.
This meaning agrees as well with
למו עצתי as with לְמוֹעֲצָתִי.

In their present context, vv. 21-5
have no subject for the plural verbs.
We have seen that G (A, C) added
πρεσβύτεροι. Sa'adia adds القوم 'the
people', Le Hir 'all', Renan 'those
present'. In reality, it is the princes
and the chiefs of vv. 9-10 who are
referred to. We have been told that
they did not dare to raise their voices
before Job. The description continues. The verb שמע with לְ before
the complement to connote 'listen to'
(cf. 15: 17). The vocalisation וְיִחֵלּוּ
is that of Ben-Asher, וְיִחֲלּוּ that of
Ben-Naphtali. We have the *dagesh
affectuosum* as in רָמוּ of 22: 12 (see
Gesenius-Kautzsch, § 20 i). The verb
is יחל 'to wait for'. Now, the complement למו עצתי or לְמוֹעֲצָתִי 'for my
counsel, my advice' is unintelligible
after יָדְמוּ 'they remained quiet' (from
דמם, 30: 27; 31: 34), while it forms
the natural sequel to וְיִחֵלּוּ, which
takes לְ before the thing awaited
(v. 23; 30: 26). If, with Wright, we
transpose וְיִחֵלּוּ and ידמו we obtain
a perfect meaning: 'They listened
to me and remained quietly attentive,
and they waited for my advice.' It
is unnecessary to take the correction
further by substituting יחלו for
וַיַּחְכּוּ, as Duhm proposes. The chiefs
are silent in order to allow Job to
speak, for his word has extraordinary
value for them (22-3).

22 Syr. ܠܐ ܟܒ 'they did not go

And my words fell upon them drop by drop!

23 They waited for me as men wait for the rain,
And they opened their mouths as for the spring showers;

24 If I smiled upon them, they hardly dared to believe it,
Nor was my smile lost on them!

astray' reads יֵשַׁגּוּ instead of יֵשְׁנוּ (Beer). G περιχαρεῖς δὲ ἐγίνοντο ὁπόταν αὐτοῖς ἐλάλουν paraphrases the 2nd hemistich and interprets תטף in the sense of 'to please', 'to be agreeable'; cf. Syr. ܚܣܡܬ 'was pleasing' and Targ. תשפר 'was agreeable'. Vulg. *stillabat* preserves the true meaning.

One might feel inclined to read דַּבְּרִי instead of דְּבָרִי, in accordance with אַחַר דַּבְּרִי of 21:3 (cf. Merx, Budde, Duhm, etc.). But all the versions have the noun. 'After my word', to mean 'after I had spoken', is easily understandable. Moreover, the verb שָׁנָה 'to do twice', 'to repeat' (cf. שְׁנַיִם 'two'), implies דָּבָר 'and they did not repeat' a word, they did not reply. The verb נטף 'to drip', 'to distil', is here taken intransitively as 'to fall drop by drop'; cf. נֹטְפֵי־מָיִם 'drops of water' in 36:27. The image is well chosen to show that Job had plenty of time to expound his ideas: 'and my words fell upon them drop by drop!'

23 G paraphrases the whole verse in order to obtain a new meaning: 'As a thirsty land waiting for the rain, so did they wait for my word.' Targ. adds אריסיא 'the gardeners' as the subject of פערו 'and like the gardeners who open their mouths'. For למלקוש, Vulg. *quasi ad imbrem serotinum*, Syr. ܐܝܟ ܘܠܓܫܡܐ 'as for the spring rain', Targ. למלקושא. The verb יחל 'to wait for' (v. 21a) retains here its normal vocalisation outside the pause. The preposition לְ is understood after the כְּ of כְּמָטָר; cf. v. 2 and 28:5. Hence: 'they waited for me as men wait for

the rain', which is a very expressive comparison, if we think of Edom or Palestine at the time when the protracted heat of summer makes the first showers of autumn most eagerly desired. The aim of the 2nd hemistich is to reinforce this image. At the end of winter, in March or April, the gardener impatiently awaits the final rains, the *pluvia serotina*, which must enable the young shoots to mature and to escape the effects of the drought which threatens. This rain is the מַלְקוֹשׁ, in contrast to the יוֹרֶה, which is the early rain, the one marking the opening of the winter season (Dt 11:14; Jer 5:24). It is essentially the beneficial rain (Jer 3:3; Hos 6:3; Jl 2:23) which is the object of earnest petition (Zec 10:1). The king's favour is like 'a cloud of מלקוש, i.e. the cloud which brings the spring rain (Pr 16:15). In this passage of Proverbs the king's favour has a parallel אור פנים 'the light of the face' which we shall find in v. 24b. On the expression פיהם פערו, cf. 16:10. Those to whom Job spoke remained agape, in face of the words which he let fall upon them drop by drop, as though it were some beneficent shower (v. 22).

24 Vv. 24b-25, absent from Sah. (reintegrated in Cod. D of Erman), marked with asterisk in Jerome, Syro-hex., Cod. 248, did not exist in G. The present text is derived from Theod. (cf. Syro-hex.). For לא יפילון, Theod. οὐκ ἀπέπιπτεν, Vulg. *non cadebat*, Syr. ܠܐ ܡܗܠܟܝܢ 'they did not walk', Targ. לא אסתכלון 'they did not look'.

25   I pointed out the way to them and I sat as chief,
      I was placed as a king among the troops;
      Where I led them, they were willing to go!

25 .כאשר אבלים ינחם — ‎MT: ‏בַּאֲשֶׁר אוֹבִילָם יַנְחוּ‎. — Vv. 11-20 after v. 25.

Following the parallelism, it is
clear that אֶשְׂחַק אֲלֵהֶם means 'I
smiled on them' and not 'I mocked
them', which would require the preposition עַל (30:1). To laugh at
some one or something is rendered
by שְׂחַק לְ‎'' (5:22; 39:7, 18, 22;
41:21). Note the asyndetic construction of two imperfects אשׂחק and
יַאֲמִינוּ, the former denoting hypothesis (20:24). Budde and Duhm
eliminate the לֹא before יאמינו,
Budde translating יאמינו by 'they
had confidence', Duhm vocalising
יֵאָמֵנוּ 'they were reassured' (*niph*al*).
But the verb האמין is regularly
used with the negative (4:18; 9:16;
15:15, 22, 31; 24:22; 39:24). In
accordance with 9:16, it is clear
that לֹא יאמינו means simply 'they
dared not believe'. The smile of Job
is for them something which is more
than they could have expected. The
phrase אוֹר פָּנִים 'light of the face'
symbolises cheerfulness, a smiling
face (Ps 89:16), and also kindness
(Ps 4:7; 44:4; Pr 16:15); cf.
L'Emploi métaphorique, pp. 54ff.
The *hiph*il* of נפל is easily understood when used with the complement אוֹר פני: they did not allow
'my smile' to be lost (literally 'to
fall'), they received my smile without letting its significance be lost on
them. We drop a thing which we do
not value (Nu 6:12); cf. *L'Emploi
métaphorique*, pp. 45f. One needs
to be very bold to change לֹא יפילון
into אבלים ינחם of v. 25c (Bickell,
Duhm, Budde), in order then to
eliminate this v. 25c. Nothing supports such a hypothesis. All the
versions have a verb with the negative (cf. sup.).

25 On the text of G, cf. v. 24.
Vulg. translates אבחר דרכם as *si
voluissem ire ad eos*. The word ראשׁ
is omitted by Syr., which links אשׁב
with the root שׁוּב. Targ. explains
'I sat as chief' by adding היך חתנא
'like a bridegroom'. For בגדוד,
Theod. ἐν μονοζώνοις (Jerome *cinc-
tus fortibus*), Vulg. *circumstante exer-
citu*. The 3rd hemistich is rendered
καθὼς ἀπάγει αὐτοὺς ὁδηγῶν by
Symm., which enables us to recover
the original text.

After the conference with the
princes, on the public square, we
now have the moment of departure
depicted. It is Job who takes the
lead and indicates the way to be
followed: 'I chose their way', i.e.
'I pointed out the way to them.' If
we interpret דַרְכָּם in the sense of
'the road which leads to their home'
(Vulg. *si voluissem ire ad eos*), we
shall translate: 'if I condescended
to visit them' (Le Hir), or 'when I
went to their home' (Renan). But
the phrases 'I sat as chief' and 'I was
placed as king among the troops'
suggest the idea of a solemn march,
led by Job. As regards the phrase
אֶשֵׁב רֹאשׁ 'I sat at the head', cf.
L'Emploi métaphorique, p. 27. The
word ראשׁ functions as an accusative
of place, equivalent to בְּרֹאשׁ. The
verb שׁכן in the sense of 'to be placed,
installed' (cf. 3:5). On גְּדוּד, 19:12;
25:3. The 3rd hemistich is interpreted as 'like him who consoles the
afflicted'; but in that case there is
no connection with the context.
Following Bickell, a few moderns
suppress it by transposing אבלים ינחם
to v. 24 and by supposing that
לֹא יפילון of this v. 24 is a corruption

11   The ear which heard these things congratulated me,
      And the eye which saw them bore witness to me,
12   For I delivered the poor man who cried,
      The orphan and him who had no helper;

of ינחם אבלים (Budde, Duhm, Beer). The text of Symm. (cf. sup.) has suggested to Herz a felicitous restoration of the original text: בַּאֲשֶׁר אוֹבִילֵם יֵנָחוּ 'where I led them they were willing to go' (*ZATW*, **20**, p. 163). This reading introduces only a slight change into the MT and offers a meaning in perfect harmony with the context. The happiness of Job and the esteem with which he is surrounded compel admiration all the more because he profits by it all to do good to those around him (vv. 11-17).

11 V. 11a, absent from Sah., marked with asterisk in Syro-hex., did not exist in G. The present text derives from Theod. (cf. v. 10). G μὲ ἐξέκλινεν reads תעיטני instead of תעידני (Beer, following 1 S 25:14).

Far from arousing envy, the prosperity of Job called forth blessings since it was coupled with beneficence. The opening כי governs both אֹזֶן שָׁמְעָה and עַיִן רָאֲתָה; the main clauses are introduced by the *waw* consecutive; numerous examples eare given in Gesenius-Kautzsch, § 111 h. Literally: 'As soon as the ear heard, it congratulated me', i.e. the ear which heard it congratulated me (cf. 30:11). Cf. 13:1 for the parallelism between the ear which hears and the eye which sees. The verb ראה with עין as subject (7:7; 28:10). The *pi'el* of אשר in the sense of 'declare happy', and 'congratulate' (Gn 30:13; Pr 31:28; Ca 6:9); cf. אשרי in 5:17. The *hiph'il* העיד with suffix, to mean: 'bear witness' with regard to some one, whether for ill (1 K 21:10, 13) or for good, as here; cf. καὶ πάντες ἐμαρτύρουν

αὐτῷ of Lk 4:22 (rendered וְכֻלָּם חֶעִידֻהוּ in the translation of Franz Delitzsch).

12 G ἐκ χειρὸς δυνάστου and Syr. ﻣﻦ ﺍﻭﻝﺟﺎ 'from oppression' have read מָשׁוֹעַ (cf. G in Ps 72:12). The copula of ולא is omitted in G, Syr., and Vulg. *et pupillum cui non esset adjutor*. G adds ἐβοήθησα at the end of the verse.

V. 12 begins the account of the reasons for which people bore witness to the goodness of Job's life (12-17). Contrary to the allegations of Eliphaz (22:6-9), Job made himself responsible for the defence of the poor and weak. There is a striking resemblance between our verse and Ps 72:12. Each word is found in the latter, whether verbatim or in the form of a synonym: אֶבְיוֹן for עֲנִי, יַצִּיל for אמלט, עֲנִי for יתום, and וְאֵין for ולא. This passage confirms the Massoretic vocalisation; but it should be noted that G and Syr. both read מָשׁוֹעַ (instead of מְשַׁוֵּעַ) in Ps 72:12. Those from whom Job rescues the weak do not appear until v. 17. Hence it seems preferable not to anticipate (by a reading מָשׁוֹעַ) and to retain מְשַׁוֵּעַ, a simple epithet of עֲנִי: 'for I delivered the poor man who cried'. The verb שוע, in the *pi'el*, 'cry aloud for help' (24:12). Parallelism between עֲנִי 'the poor' and יָתוֹם 'the orphan' (24:9). The conclusion וְלֹא־עֹזֵר לוֹ 'and he who has no helper', i.e. he whom no one offers to help. Cf. לא עזר למו in 30:13. The poor and the orphan are both alluded to in

13   The blessing of the wretched arose to me,
      And I made the widow's heart rejoice.

14   I put on righteousness and it clothed me,
      My just dealing was as a mantle and a tiara;

15   I was eyes to the blind,
      And feet was I to the lame;

this expression. It is unnecessary to cut out the *waw* (as do G, Syr., and Vulg.) in order to make of לא עזר לו an apposition to יתום.

13 V. 13a, absent from Sah., marked with asterisk in Jerome and Syro-hex., did not exist in G. The present text derives from Theod. and Aq. (cf. Syro-hex.). G στόμα δὲ χήρας με εὐλόγησεν boldly paraphrases the 2nd hemistich.

V. 13 is parallel to v. 12. The word עני corresponds to אֹבֵד, parallel to אביון in 31:19; while יתום corresponds to אַלְמָנָה. The use of עַל after the verb בוא slightly modified the meaning 'come' into the connotation 'ascend', 'rise up': 'the blessing of the wretched arose to me'. Cf. הביא על in 34:28. The participle of אבד 'to perish' (3:3; 4:9, 11, etc.) denotes one who is on the point of perishing as a result of misery (31:19; Pr 31:6; Sir 11:12). The *hiph'il* of רנן 'rejoice', 'sing' (38:7); cf. רְנָּה 'joy', 3:7; 20:5), to express the idea of rejoicing (Ps 65:9). Eliphaz had insinuated that Job did not show pity towards the widow and that he oppressed the orphans (22:9).

14 The rhythm is broken if we attach וילבשני to the 2nd hemistich, as is done by G, Vulg., and Syr. For וילבשני, Vulg. *et vestivi me*. G sums up כמעיל וצניף by ἴσα διπλοΐδι. The suffix of משפטי is omitted in G and Syr.

V. 14 links vv. 12-13 with vv. 15-17. It expresses the feeling of the righteousness which controlled the actions of Job and constituted him

the protector of the weak against the strong. The word צֶדֶק is used in its normal meaning 'righteousness', parallel to מִשְׁפָּט 'justice' (8:3). The two ideas are complementary: מִשְׁפָּט וּצְדָקָה 'justice and righteousness' (Jer 22:15; 23:5; 33:15). 'I had put on righteousness and it clothed me'; one puts on a quality, one is invested with it (8:22; 40:10). In Ps 132 we find in succession ילבשו־צדק 'let them be clothed with righteousness' (v. 9), אלביש ישע 'I will clothe with salvation' (v. 16), אלביש בשת 'I will clothe with shame' (v. 18). Righteousness, salvation, shame, are like a garment which clothes the individual, transforms him, adorns him, or mars him. The comparison is made more precise in the 2nd hemistich: 'My just dealing was a mantle and a tiara.' Cf. 19:9, 'He has robbed me of my glory and has removed the crown from my head' (cf. 31:36b). Despite the verdict of Duhm, we should retain the suffix of משפטי. Nothing would indicate the 1st person if this suffix were removed. The word מְעִיל connotes the mantle worn for parade (1:20; 2:12) and צָנִיף the royal tiara (Is 62:3) or tiara of the high priest (Zec 3:5). Similar images in Is 59:17, 'He put on righteousness as a breastplate, and on his head the helmet of salvation; he took vengeance as his tunic, and clothed himself with zeal as with a mantle' (Condamin's translation).

15 Targ. renders ענים by נהור עינין 'light of the eyes', which weakens the comparison. The words

16　I was a father to the needy,
　　And I investigated the cause of the stranger;
17　I broke the fangs of the wicked,
　　And made him drop his prey from his teeth.

עור and פסח are translated by plurals in G.

'I was eyes to the blind, And feet was I to the lame'—a veritable proverb which describes the effects flowing from Job's righteousness (v. 14). By applying the principles of this righteousness Job enlightens the judgment of him who was in error and extricates from his difficulties the man who was entangled in a lawsuit. With the 1st hemistich compare Nu 10: 31, 'and you will serve as eyes for us', a word of Moses to Hobab encouraging him to be the guide of the Hebrews through the desert. Hitzig cites Euripides: ὡς τυφλῷ ποδὶ ὀφθαλμὸς εἶ σύ (Phoenissae, 834-5). The words עִוֵּר 'blind' and פִּסֵּחַ 'lame' are often coupled (Lv 21: 18; Dt 15: 21; 2 S 5: 6, 8; Jer 21: 8).

16 For אֶחְקְרֵהוּ, Vulg. diligentissime investigabam.

The formula אָב אָנֹכִי 'I was a father' is both more expressive and more concise than וְהָיָה לְאָב 'and he will be for a father' (Is 22: 21), ἔσται εἰς πατέρα (1 Mac 2: 65). It is before the tribunal that the poor need a father to defend their cause. Here was a new opportunity for the exercise of Job's righteousness (v. 14). In the epilogue of his Code, Hammurabi asks that the oppressed should come and read his stele and should be able to say: 'Hammurabi is a lord who to his people is like a father who has produced offspring' (verso XXV, 20ff.). The word רִיב (13: 6) has here a juridical meaning of 'cause', 'suit' (cf. 31: 35). The defective writing of it suggests that we have here the construct state.

And, in fact, לֹא יָדַעְתִּי 'I have not known' forms the complement of רִב 'the cause of him whom I knew not'. Cf. מְקוֹם לֹא־יָדַע אֵל 'the place of him who knows not God' (18: 21). To translate as 'the cause which I did not know, I examined' would be too commonplace. What is extraordinary is the fact of taking an interest in the cause of a stranger. On the verb חָקַר cf. 5: 27.

17 The מְתַלְּעוֹת are the molars for G μύλας and Vulg. molas, the canines for Targ. and Syr. ניבי. For מִשְּׁנָיו, G ἐκ μέσου τῶν ὀδόντων αὐτῶν. Syrohex. places the obelus before ἐκ μέσου.

Job is engaged in a battle against iniquity: 'I broke the fangs of the wicked man.' On the meaning of עַוָּל, cf. Comm. on 16: 11. The evildoer is likened to a wild beast whose teeth are hit and broken (4: 10; Ps 3: 8). It is Job himself who by his righteousness prevents the wicked man from devouring the poor (cf. 5: 15) and removes his power of harming others. Cohortative form וָאֲשַׁבְּרָה, instead of the simple imperfect (1: 15, 17, 19). From the verb תָלַע 'to gnaw' (cf. תּוֹלֵעָה 'the gnawing worm', 25: 6) the pi'el participle מְתַלְּעוֹת 'the instruments for gnawing' is used as a parallel word to שִׁנַּיִם 'teeth' (Jl 1: 6; Pr 30: 14). We have by metathesis מַלְתְּעוֹת in Ps 58: 7. We may translate by the 'fangs', for מַתְלְעוֹת is especially applied to the teeth of wild beasts (Jl 1: 6; Ps 58: 7). The molars of man are 'the grinders' טֹחֲנוֹת (Ec 12: 3). The wicked sharpen their teeth and their fangs

18   And I said *to myself*: 'I shall die *in a ripe old age*,
      And my days will be as many as the sand;

18   עַמִּי זָקֵן (cf. G); MT: עִם־קִנִּי.

in order to devour the poor and
needy (Pr 30: 14). Job snatches
their victim from their grasp. The
verb הִשְׁלִיךְ 'throw', 'throw away'
(15: 33; 18: 7; 27: 22), in the sense
of 'cause to fall'. Since the villain is
likened to a ferocious wild beast, his
victim is spoken of as his prey טֶרֶף
(4: 11; 38: 39): 'and I dashed the
prey from his teeth'.

18 The words עַם־קִנִּי אָגְוַע are
twice translated in Syr.: 'I will save
the poor and will end as a reed'. The
first interpretation reads עַם עָנִי אוֹשִׁיעַ,
the second קָנֶה 'reed' instead of קִנִּי.
G ἡ ἡλικία μου γηράσει reads זָקֵן
instead of קִנִּי. For כַּחוֹל, Targ. הֵיךְ
חָלָא 'like the sand', Syr. 'like the
sand of the sea', but G ὥσπερ στέλεχος
φοίνικος, Vulg. *sicut palma* read
כְּנַחַל (Sir 50: 12 = 14). The rabbis
of the school of Nehardea vocalised
חוֹל, to distinguish from חוֹל 'sand'
(Qimchi).
   The words עַם־קִנִּי אֶגְוַע 'I shall die
with my nest' are interpreted to
mean death in the bosom of the
family: 'I shall die in the bosom of
my family' (Le Hir); 'I shall die in
my nest' (Renan). If need be, קִנִּי
'my nest' could mean 'my family';
but one would expect בְּקִנִּי 'in my
family' or בְּתוֹךְ קִנִּי 'in the midst of
my family' rather than עַם קִנִּי
'with my family'. It is attaching too
much credit to Syr. to reconstitute
a text עַם עָנִי אוֹשִׁיעַ 'The innocent
people will I rescue' (Wright) or to
replace קִנִּי by קָנֶה 'I shall die with
the reed' (Merx). What is expected
is a proposition expressing the idea
of longevity, in harmony with the
meaning of the 2nd hemistich. On the
basis of the translation of G, Sieg-

fried replaces אָגְוַע, which however
is very much in the style of Job
(3: 11; 10: 18; 13: 19; 27: 5), by
אֶזְקַן 'I shall grow old with my
family'; Cheyne (*Encyc. Biblica*, III,
col. 3765) reads בִּזְקָנַי 'in my old age'
instead of עַם־קִנִּי; Torczyner עַד זְקֹנִי
'until I am old'. Herz proposes to
see in קִנִּי the Egyptian word *qn*
'strength', which suggests to him a
subsequent change from כַּחוֹל to
בְּחַיִל 'in vigour' (*OLZ*, 1913, 345).
The difficulty is created by עַם־קִנִּי.
Now, with the help of the text of G,
we may read עַמִּי זָקֵן, the word עַמִּי
referring to וָאֹמַר and the word זָקֵן
referring to אָגְוַע. We have done
nothing more than displace the *yod*
and restore the *zayin* attested by G.
The verb אמר with עמי, just as we
have דבר with עמדי in the original
text of 9: 35 (cf. Comm.). The idiom
זָקֵן אָגְוַע 'I shall die old' is confirmed
by the use זקן with verbs meaning
'to die' (42: 17; Gn 25: 8; 35: 29).
The 2nd hemistich will clarify by
means of a comparison the length of
life which Job feels destined to
enjoy. The meaning seems to us to
admit of no doubt: 'and I shall
multiply days like the sand', my
days will be as numerous as the
grains of sand. The use of the *hiph'il*
of רבה with a complement in the
plural (9: 17; 34: 37; 40: 27) seems
to us decisive. The sand is the symbol expressive of great number, of
indefinite multiplicity, whether it
be a question of the sand of the sea
(Gn 32: 13; 41: 49, etc.) or of sand
without further qualification (Is
48: 19; Hab 1: 9). In Ps 139: 18
we have מֵחוֹל יִרְבּוּן 'they are more
numerous than the sand'. Notice the
use of the *hiph'il* of רבה 'to multiply,
make numerous' with כַּחוֹל 'like the

19   My root is accessible to the waters,
      And the dew lies all night on my branches;
20   My glory will always be fresh within me,
      And my bow ever new in my hand!'

sand', in Gn 22: 17. If we had had כנחל 'like a palm tree' (G, Vulg., in accordance with the sense of the Arabic *naḫl*) the expression used would have been אאריך ימים 'I shall prolong days' (Ehrlich, Torczyner). It is the idea of number contained in כחול which has brought about the use of אַרְבֶּה. An old Rabbinic tradition, which is already to be found in the Talmud (*Sanhedrin*, 108b), used to see in חול the phoenix, an animal whose fate it was not to die, and who was endowed with a new life every thousand years, because he had not eaten of the tree of the knowledge of good and evil (cf. Rashi). Moreover, the traditions of the ancient classical writers on the subject of the phoenix are well known. A few modern commentators have adopted the interpretation of the Jewish school and have translated כחול as 'like the phoenix' (Hitzig, Ewald, Budde, Duhm). But Bochart had already shown that the Rabbinic legend rests on the interpretation of כחול in the light of G ὥσπερ στέλεχος φοίνικος, and in view of the double sense of the Greek φοῖνιξ, both 'phoenix' and 'palm tree' (*Hieroz.*, II, 817ff.). In Ps 92: 13, the Hebrew כתמר (Vulg. *ut palma*) is rendered ὡς φοῖνιξ in G. The old Latin used by Tertullian (*De resurr. carnis*, XIII, in *PL*, II, col. 857) translates the Greek by *velut phoenix*. This interpretation is also reflected in the φυσιολόγος attributed to St Epiphanius (*PG*, XLIII, col. 528; Pitra, *Spicileg.*, III, 346). The presence of 'my nest' in the existing text of the 1st hemistich may have been responsible for suggesting the name of a bird as the meaning of חול, just as the roots and the branches

of v. 19 may have been responsible for the introduction of the palm tree (reading כנחל) of G and Vulg.

19 Vv. 19-20, absent from Sah., marked with asterisk in Jerome and Syro-hex. did not exist in G. The present text derives from Theod. (cf. Syro-hex.). Syr. connects טל with the Aramaic טלל (= צלל) whence 'in the shade'.

Continuation of the account of Job's illusions: 'My root is accessible to the waters, and the dew lies all night on my branches.' The comparison with the well-watered tree is quite natural (8: 16-17; 14: 7-9; 18: 16). Opposition between root and branches, קָצִיר (14: 9), as in 18: 16. The righteous man is like the tree which grows alongside the stream and the leaves of which do not wither (Ps 1: 3). It is during the night that the dew becomes deposited on the leaves. That is why recourse is had to the verb לין 'to spend the night' (17: 2; 19: 4).

20 On the text of G, cf. v. 19. The word חדש was translated καινή in Theod. A reading κενή (B, א, A) has been followed by Syro-hex. and Memph.

Nothing at all authorises the substitution of כִּדוֹנִי 'my javelin' (Hoffmann, Beer in Kittel's edition) for כְּבוֹדִי 'my glory'. Parallelism must not not be pushed to extremes. The bow is a symbol, but glory is a quality specified by עִמָּדִי 'my glory will always be fresh within me'. The adjective חָדָשׁ 'new' is used to denote what keeps its original freshness, or what is constantly being renewed

(La 3: 23). The expression עמדי 'in me' (6: 4; 23: 10); cf. the preposition עָם in 10: 13; 23: 14; 27: 11.

Events have belied the hopes of Job: 'He has stripped me of my glory' (19: 9). The bow is the emblem of force (Gn 49: 24). To break the bow of some one is to reduce him to a state of utter weakness (Jer 49: 35; Hos 1: 5). The bow of Job must remain ever new and pre-serve all its power: 'and my bow is renewed in my hand'. The *hiph'il* of חלף as in 14: 7. After this return of thought to his former happiness and the illusions he cherished, Job falls back to contemplate the sad reality of the present: 'and now ...' (30: 1).

21-5   After v. 10.

CHAPTER 30

1   And now they mock me,
      Those who are younger than I,
      Whose fathers I disdained too much
      To set them with the dogs of my flock!

30: 1 The phrase ועתה...לימים is twice translated in G νυνὶ δὲ κατεγέλασάν μου. ἐλάχιστοι νῦν νουθετοῦσίν με ἐν μέρει. The second translation begins at νῦν, and the word ἐλάχιστοι must be connected with what precedes (A, C, Sah., Jerome *nunc autem derident me infimi*) and not with what follows (B, Syro-hex.). It is possible that ἐν μέρει is a corruption of ἡμέραις, which might have translated לימים (Beer). Jerome *nunc monent me minores tempore* replaces ἐν μέρει by a subject which may stem from Symm. (in Syro-hex.) οἱ νεώτεροί μου τοῖς χρόνοις; cf. Vulg. *juniores tempore*. G ὧν ἐξουδένουν τοὺς πατέρας αὐτῶν did not exist in the original text; this phrase is marked by asterisk in Syro-hex. and is not represented in Sah. It is found in Jerome *quorum spernebam parentes*. The translation of G for אשר...צאני has simply omitted אבותם: οὓς οὐχ ἡγησάμην ἀξίους (A + εἶναι) κυνῶν τῶν ἐμῶν νομάδων. This text was omitted in Jerome (Tur., Bod.) and has been restored in Jerome (Gall.). Syr. renders לשית by ܣܠܐ ܚܫܒܬ ܐܢܘܢ 'and I have not counted them'.

This verse is composed of two lines, each containing two hemistichs. Duhm declares that vv. 2-8 belong to another poem and that v. 1 is merely an artificial transition from the preceding chapter to vv. 2-8. But the opening וְעַתָּה 'and now' which points to the contrast between Job's present misery and his former happiness will recur like a refrain in vv. 9 and 16. Besides, Job has emphasised the deference and respect with which both young and old treated him (29: 8). He now notes the difference of attitude. The verb שׂחק, with על before the complement, to denote 'laugh at', 'mock' (Ps 52: 8; La 1: 7), is more forceful than שׂחק ל'' (5: 22). It marks a deliberate contrast with אשׂחק אלהם 'I smiled on them' of 29: 24. The subject of שָׂחֲקוּ עָלַי is constituted by the 2nd hemistich: 'smaller than I in days', i.e. 'those who are younger than myself'. This expression has excellent support in 32: 6 צעיר אני לימים 'I am small in regard to days', in opposition to ואתם ישׁישׁים 'and you are old'. It is a pure whim to cut out מִמֶּנִּי לְיָמִים (Merx, Wright, Siegfried, Budde), or to replace צְעִירִים by צֹעֲרִים 'shepherds' (Bickell, following Zec 13: 7), or לימים by לְאָמִּים 'the populace' (Hoffmann). Cf. 19: 18, 'Even youngsters have shown scorn for me.' The mention of their fathers in the second line shows clearly that it is a question of children mocking Job, like the urchins pursuing Elisha (2 K 2: 23-4). Not only is it that those who mock Job should show him respect because they are younger than he, but furthermore they are of low extraction. And it is on this point that the poet will dwell

429

2   Even the strength of their hands, what good would it have
     been to me?

     Men whose *vigour* had *wholly* perished

2   עֲנָמוֹ :MT ;עלימו. — כָּלָה :MT ;כלח.

up to v. 9. Their fathers were merely
wretched fellows: 'whose fathers I
disdained too much to set them
with the dogs of my flock'. The verb
מאס 'to despise', as in 9:21; 10:3;
19:18. The dogs are the keepers of
the flock (Is 56:10-11).

2 Vv. 2-4a are absent from Sah.
There is an asterisk before 2-3 in
Cod. 248, before 2 in Syro-hex.,
before 2b-3a in Jerome. Now, we
shall see that in v. 4 G has summarised vv. 3-4. Hence a new translation
has been added for vv. 2-4a. This
translation is attributed to Theod.
by Syro-hex., but only as far as v. 2
is concerned. It seems, however,
that vv. 3-4a of G must also belong
to Theod. There is the same concern
for literalism as in v. 2. The versions
are in agreement with the MT as
regards the reading למה לי, which
Vulg. paraphrases *mihi erat pro
nihilo*. For כלח, Theod. συντέλεια
and Aq. παντελές are thinking of the
root כלה; Symm. πᾶν τὸ πρὸς ζωήν
(Jerome *omnis vita*) seems to read
כל לחי. Cf. Vulg. *et vita ipsa puta-
bantur indigni*. The interpretation of
Targ. by כוך 'tomb' is influenced by
5:26. Syr. ܟܠܗ ܚܡܣܠ 'all strength'
reads כל־חיל.

V. 2 will stress the physical degen-
eracy of the fathers mentioned at
the end of v. 1. Job has just said
that he would not have been willing
to put them with the dogs of his
flock. Even had they had strength,
they would not have been of any
help to him; how much more so if
they are weak creatures! The expression למָה לי *ad quid mihi*? shows
how little Job thinks of the services

they might have been able to render
him: 'Even the strength of their
hands, what good would it have
been to me?' Cf. the use of למה לי
in Gn 25:32; 27:46. The changes
of כָּמַה לוֹ to למה לי 'had become
faint, languishing' (Duhm), or רָפָה
לוֹ 'had become relaxed' (Ball),
deprive the passage of its personal
note. The 2nd hemistich is a *crux
interpretum*. Those who assign to
כֶּלַח (5:26) the meaning 'maturity,'
'mature age' translate more or less
literally: 'they did not live to a
mature age' (Le Hir), 'incapable of
reaching maturity' (Renan; cf.
Crampon). These are all attempts
to paraphrase the Hebrew text
which Dillmann seeks to copy in a
German version: '*für sie ist volle
Reife verloren*'. It would appear at
first sight that עָלֵימוֹ אָבֶד could not
be translated: 'for them has perished,
has been lost'. It will be noticed that
עלימו is rendered *für sie* by Dillmann,
an ihnen by Budde, *ihnen* by Duhm,
within them by Gray, *with them* by
Ball, whereas the literal translation
should be: 'upon them' 'over them'
or 'against them'. The difficulty
presented by עלימו remains entire
if we give to כלח its normal meaning
of 'old age' (cf. Comm. on 5:26). It
is only conjecturally that Segond
translates: 'they are incapable of
reaching old age'. The changes from
כלח to כל־חיל 'all vigour' (Beer,
following Syr.), or to כל־לח 'all
freshness' (Hontheim, Budde), fail
to get rid of the anomaly עלימו אבד.
Ehrlich proposes to vocalise עָלֵמוֹ
אָבֶד כֹּחַ, which he translates: '*da der
jüngste unter ihnen bereits kraftlos*

3   Through dearth and dismal famine!
They would gnaw *the roots* of the wasteland,
Their mother was a devastated and desolate region;

3   Add עִקְּרֵי. — אִמָּם; MT: אמשׁ.

ist'. But the repetition of כח from the 1st hemistich and the translation of עלמו 'their sucking child' by 'the youngest of them' hardly favour this correction. Without deviating too much from the text as we have it, we read עֻזָּמוֹ 'their vigour' (Ps 89: 18) instead of עלימו and כָּלֹה (cf. Olshausen) instead of כלח. The word עֹז is used of physical strength (26: 2; 41: 14). The 2nd hemistich, 'their vigour had wholly perished', will be explained by the 1st hemistich of v. 3. Hunger and privations had reduced to nothing the physical powers of these unfortunates who are compelled to roam the countryside in order to look for the roots of wild plants and find nourishment from them. In truth Job had no temptation to employ them in his service.

3 On the text of G, cf. v. 2. Vv. 3-4 are omitted in Syr. and Arab. The meaning 'barren' for גלמוד (15: 34) is adopted by Theod. ἄγονος, Vulg. *steriles*, Targ. דלא ולד. For עֹרְקִים, Targ. ערקין, Vulg. *qui rodebant*, but Theod. οἱ φεύγοντες. Then Theod. very literally: ἄνυδρον ἐχθὲς συνοχὴν καὶ ταλαιπωρίαν. Targ. plays on the word אמשׁ, by translating: 'dark as eventide'. Vulg. renders אמשׁ שׁואה ומשׁאה by *squallentes calamitate et miseria*.

The 1st hemistich, 'through dearth and dismal famine', connects with v. 2. The instrumental ב" explains why 'their vigour had wholly perished'. The word חֶסֶר 'lack of' (Pr 10: 21) and 'scarcity', 'dearth' (Pr 28: 22). The Aramaic כָּפָן as in 5: 22. On גַּלְמוּד 'barren', 'dismal',

cf. 3: 7; 15: 34. The word is perfectly clear as an epithet qualifying כפן, and we see no reason to change it to גֻּלָּמוּ 'are coiled up' or 'are crumpled up' (Hitzig, Duhm, Budde, etc.). The verb גלם in 2 K 2: 8 means 'to roll up' a cloak. The participle הָעֹרְקִים begins a verse (cf. v. 4 הקטפים), the 1st hemistich of which is evidently too short. Furthermore, the word אֶמֶשׁ 'yesterday' hardly suits the context, as it is easy to see from some generally accepted translations: 'they browsed in the desert place, *a soil long since* arid and desolate' (Le Hir, Crampon) 'reduced to browsing in desert places, *the age-old earth* of emptiness and silence' (Renan); 'they flee into barren places, *long since* abandoned and deserted' (Segond). Let us observe the double sense of ערק 'to gnaw' and 'to flee': in Aramaic, ערק 'to flee' (with the meaning 'gnaw' in the *pa'el* in Syriac), in Arabic عرق 'to gnaw' and 'to depart'. Since what is in question is a band of hungry men seeking plants in which to feed themselves (v. 4), the meaning 'to gnaw' seems the more likely. What is lacking in the 1st hemistich is the complement of הערקים, which cannot be צִיָּה 'the drought' (24: 19) or 'the steppe' (for ארץ ציה cf. Is 35: 1; Jer 50: 12). Duhm proposed יָרָק, the disappearance of which after הערקים is easily to be explained; but 'the verdure of the steppe' is not a thing that one gnaws at. Ball's restoration עִקְּרֵי 'the roots' (Aramaic עקרא, Syriac حمڌ, Arabic عقّار) seems to

4   They plucked the orach from the bush
        And the root of the broom was their bread!

us the more likely to be right. The
Aramaic word has been chosen (a
word which translates שֹׁרֶשׁ 'root' in
Targ. of 19: 28; 28: 9; 29: 19; 30: 4),
in order to avoid the repetition of
שֹׁרֶשׁ of v. 4. Cf. the use of כפן after
רעב 'famine' in 5: 20: 22. The
resemblance between עקרי and
ערקים has caused haplography. The
words שׁוֹאָה וּמְשֹׁאָה form a parono-
masia. They recur as a pair in 38: 27;
Zeph 1: 15; Sir 51: 10. The root
שׁאה means 'to be devastated' (Is
6: 11), and the figure of speech is
sufficiently well preserved if we
translate שׁוֹאָה וּמְשֹׁאָה by 'devastation and desolation' (cf. Driver-
Gray). In 38:27, the phrase is parallel to צִיָּה (read מְצִיָּה instead of מצא;
cf. Comm.), exactly as here. Just as
ציה implies ארץ 'the earth' (understood), so also שׁוֹאָה וּמְשֹׁאָה. Hence
we need not replace אמשׁ by אֵם
'mother' (Hoffmann, Ehrlich) or by
ארץ 'earth' (Olshausen), since שׁוֹאָה
וּמְשֹׁאָה means 'land of devastation and
desolation' in 38: 27. On the other
hand, we have seen that אמשׁ
'yesterday' cannot be understood
in the context, for we cannot legiti-
mately assign to it the meaning of
'long since' postulated by the translators: the etymological sense of
אמשׁ is 'the previous evening' (Assyrian amšat for an mušat 'in the
evening', 'yesterday'). Duhm proposes יְמַשְּׁשׁוּ 'they grope', which
properly demands the idea of darkness (5: 14; 12: 25). The comparison
with v. 4b strikingly favours the
reading אִמָּם 'their mother' (in the
sense of 'their nurse') proposed by
Klostermann and accepted by
Budde.

4   G οἱ περικυκλοῦντες (for περι-
κλῶντες = הקטפים; cf. Codd. 161,
248, 253, Compl. and Syro-hex.,
Beer) ἅλιμα ἐπὶ ἠχοῦντι does not
exist in Sah. and is marked with
asterisk in Jerome. It is the reading
of Theod. (cf. v. 2). The translation
ἐπὶ ἠχοῦντι connects שׁיח with the
verb שׁיח 'speak', 'groan', 'sing' (cf.
v. 7). Then οἵτινες ἅλιμα ἦν αὐτῶν
τὰ σῖτα is a summary of v. 4, the
word ἅλιμα representing מלוח, the
words αὐτῶν τὰ σῖτα representing
לחמם. The phrase ἄτιμοι δὲ καὶ
πεφαυλισμένοι, ἐνδεεῖς παντὸς ἀγαθοῦ
is an anticipation of v. 8a (Beer).
Finally, οἱ καὶ ῥίζας ξύλων ἐμασῶντο
ὑπὸ λιμοῦ μεγάλου, omitted in G(B)
but in G (א, A), Sah., Syro-hex.,
Jerome, is the result of a combination of v. 4b and v. 3a. The word
מלוח is translated ἅλιμα in G and
Theod. (similarly in Aq., according
to Syro-hex.). The 1st hemistich is
rendered by Symm. ἀποκνίζοντες
φλοιοὺς φυτῶν, whence Jerome qui
rodebant cortices arborum (with asterisk); cf. Vulg. et mandebant herbas
et arborum cortices. The words מלוח
עלי-שׂיח are interpreted הובי חולף
עסבי מיכלא 'thorns instead of edible
plants' in Targ. For רתמים, G ξύλων
(cf. sup.), Symm. ξύλων ἀγρίων; these
are vague translations. Vulg. interprets by juniperorum (cf. 1 K 19: 5).
Targ. merely replaces the Hebrew
by the Aramaic רתימין (cf. 1 K
19: 5); Aq. and Theod. transcribe
ῥαθαμίν (cited in Syro-hex.). We
have seen (v. 2) that v. 3 was lacking in Syr. and Arab.

        The verse is parallel to the pre-
ceding one, which begins with הערקים
of v. 3 (cf. Comm.). The verb קטף
'to pluck' as in 8: 12 and 24: 24
(corrected). We have seen that the
word מָלוּחַ had disappeared from
24: 24 but that it existed in the
original text as attested by G. In a
learned dissertation (Hieroz., III,
chap. 16, pp. 874ff.) Bochart has

5   From human society they were banished,
        Men howled in pursuit of them as in chasing a thief,
6   So that they dwelt beside torrents,
        In the holes of the earth and the rocks;

conclusively proved that the plant מלוח from the root מלח 'to be salted' did indeed correspond to the orach, that saline plant which the Greeks called ἅλιμα (cf. G here and in 24: 24; Aq. and Theod. here), a word derived from ἅλς 'salt' and reflected in the Latin *halimus, alimus*. The word שִׂיחַ, used in the plural in v. 7, is simply the bush, as in Gn 2: 5; 21: 15. It is unnecessary to postulate here the meaning of the Arabic *šiḥ* 'absinth' (contra Wetzstein, Hitzig, etc.). The phrase עֲלֵי־שִׂיחַ is to be explained by the fact that the orach is found 'on a bush'. According to Tristram, this plant grows in veritable thickets around the Dead Sea (Cf. *Dict. de la Bible*, I, pp. 1032ff.). The translation of Saadia, 'leaves of a tree' for עלי־שיח is a vague interpretation and does not authorise the change to ועלי שיח 'leaves of a bush' proposed by Hontheim. The word רֹתֶם occurs in 1 K 19: 4, 5 and denotes the shrub under which the prophet Elijah lies down in his journey to Sinai. The allusion is evidently to the *ratam* of the Arabs. All travellers who have crossed the peninsula of Sinai have heard the Bedouin denote by the term *retem* a sort of gorse which is browsed on constantly by the camels. In the light of Ps 120: 4, where we find גחלי רתמים 'glowing coals of the *retems*', some authors would change לַחְמָם to לְחַמָם 'that they may be warm' or to לְחַמֵּם 'to warm them' (cf. Budde). But to warm one's self with broom wood would not be specially painful. It is the normal habit of the Arabs. On the other hand, the context is quite favourable to the obvious interpretation of the

Massoretic text: 'and the root of the broom was their bread'. These outlaws have no other nourishment but what was supplied by the grasses and roots of the steppe.

5 G ἐπανέστησάν μοι κλέπται continues its summary (cf. vv. 2-4). Vulg. *de convallibus* reads מִן־גֵּי instead of מִן־גֵּו. Syr. omits יריעו and connects בערוץ נחלים of v. 6 to v. 5. The whole verse is paraphrased by Vulg., which sees here the sequel to the description of vv. 4-5; *qui de convallibus ista rapientes, cum singula reperissent, ad ea cum clamore currebant.*

Use of the *pu'al* of גרש with מן before the complement, as in Ex 12: 39. The word גֵּו does not denote the back, as in 20: 25, but corresponds to the Phoenician גו 'corporation', 'community' (Lidzbarski, *Handbuch*, p. 249), and to the Syriac ܓܘܐ 'society', 'community'. It is unnecessary to change to גוי 'nation', as is proposed by Böttcher, Merx, etc. 'They were banished from human society' expresses well the condition of life of these creatures who were reduced to living in the desert. When they appear, they awaken terror. The whole village rises up against them: 'Men howled in pursuit of them as in chasing a thief.' The *hiph'il* of רוע denotes the collective outcry aroused by the feeling of indignation (as here) or by enthusiasm (38: 7). The preposition על introduces the object on which the cries are concentrated. It is omitted after the *kaph* of comparison (cf. 28: 5b; 31: 2, 23).

6 ὧν οἱ οἶκοι αὐτῶν ἦσαν τρῶγλαι πετρῶν again summarises (cf. 2-5).

7   Among bushes they brayed,
     They were crouched in a heap under the thistles.

Syr. begins at לשכן (cf. v. 5) and separates as two distinct complements
the words חורי עפר. Vulg. renders
בערוץ by *in desertis* and וכפים
vel super glaveam. For בערוץ נחלים,
Targ. בתקוף פצידי נחליא 'in the
firm part of torrent beds'.

Expelled from society, these
wretched men take refuge in shelters
such as nature provides. Cf. 24: 8.
Attempts have been made to connect
ערוץ with the root ערץ 'to make
afraid' (13: 25) or 'to dread' (31: 34),
so as to interpret ערוץ נחלים by
'wild valleys' (Renan), 'dreadful
valleys' (Segond, Crampon). In fact,
what is in question here is a word
equivalent to the Arabic عرض ('*arḍ*),
plur. عروض, which denotes the pre-
cipitous side of a mountain or valley.
Michaelis had already discerned this
meaning which has since been
proposed by Wetzstein and Barth.
It is unnecessary to replace ערוץ
by חרוץ 'the hollow' (Ehrlich) or by
חריצי 'the crevices' (Grimme). The
preposition of לשכן denotes the
result of the expulsion described in
v. 5: 'with the result that they
dwelt'. The verb שכן 'to dwell' may
govern the accusative (15: 28), which
explains the omission of the preposition ב" in the 2nd hemistich. Note
the use of עפר in the sense of
'ground', 'soil' (cf. Comm. on 5: 6).
'The holes of the ground' are the
natural caves in which men (1 S
14: 11) or animals (Nah 2: 13)
take refuge. The Aramaic כֵּפִים
'rocks' recurs in Jer 4: 29. The word
exists in Assyrian *kâpu ša šade* 'the
rock of the mountains' (Delitzsch,
AHW, p. 346).

7 V. 7a, absent from Sah., marked
with asterisk in Jerome and Syro-
hex., did not exist in G. Our present
text derives from Theod. (cf. Cod.

137). Theod. εὐήχων, for שיחים, is
not due to a distortion of συήχων as
a transcription for שיחים (Merx), but
to an interpretation in accordance
with the root שיח 'speak', 'groan',
'sing' (cf. v. 4). Vulg. ascribes a
connotation of joy to ינהקו, whence
the 1st hemistich *qui inter hujuscemodi laetabantur*, which brings
about *delicias computabant* for יספחו.
Syr. omits ינהקו and transfers
יספחו to v. 8. For חרול, G φρύγανα
ἄγρια, Vulg. *sentibus*, Targ. היגי
'thorns' (Syr. ﬂﬁ). The verb
יספחו is rendered διῃτῶντο (G),
מתחברין   'associating   together'
(Targ.), ﹸﹺﹶﹴﹷﹲ 'are overthrown'
(Syr. in v. 8).

The word שיח as in v. 4. The verb
נהק 'to bray' as in 6: 5, to suggest the
hoarse cries called forth by hunger.
The word חָרוּל recurs in Zeph 2: 9,
where, despite the corrupt state of
the text (cf. van Hoonacker), one
can recognise the reference to a
plant which grows in ruined cities.
In Pr 24: 31 the חָרֻל grows on the
field of the idle man, as also the
קמשונים. The plural קמשונים derives
from קמוש, parallel to חוֹח 'thorn'
(31: 40) in Is 34: 13; Hos 9: 6. It
is clear that חרול denotes a thorny
plant which grows of itself in fallow
ground. Jewish tradition has pronounced in favour of the meaning
'nettles', and Rashi writes the
French word *ortie* in his commentary.
We ourselves, however, think that
the author alludes to the thistle,
which reaches extraordinary proportions in desolate ground and on
the site of ruins in Palestine. In any
event, we must distinguish חרול
from the Syriac ﬂﬁﹶﹴ, which corresponds to the Assyrian *ḫallûru* and
the Arabic *ḫullar* 'chick-pea'. The
verb ספח in the *niph'al* means 'join'

8   Sons of base men and sons even of nameless men,
     They were *cut off* out of the land!
9   And now I have become their song,
     And an object of derision to them.

8   נִכְרָתוּ; MT: נכאו.

(Is 14:1), in the *hithpaʻel* 'unite', 'join one's self' (1 S 26:19). The *puʻal* brings out very well the passivity of these wretches: 'they were huddled' against each other. It is unnecessary to weaken the expression by reading the *niphʻal* as is proposed by Budde, followed by a few other commentators. Ball would push parallelism further by changing יספחו to יצריחו 'they cry' or to יספדו 'they lament'. But one cannot demand absolute parallelism, and it is better to retain the new feature which is added to the description.

8   G ἀφρόνων υἱοὶ καὶ ἀτίμων ὄνομα first translates בלי־שם by ἀτίμων (cf. ἄτιμοι δὲ καὶ πεφαυλισμένοι in v. 4) and adds a second interpretation of שם. The word ὄνομα is connected with the 2nd hemistich by Sah. and Jerome *nomen et honor extinctus a terra*. G καὶ κλέος ἐσβεσμέ-νον ἀπὸ γῆς again repeats שם (translated κλέος) in the 2nd hemistich and interprets נכאו as if we had נכבא (for נכבה). Vulg. renders בלי־שם by *ignobilium* and paraphrases the 2nd hemistich *et in terra penitus non parentes*. Targ. interprets בלי־שם by הדיוטין (ἰδιῶται) 'men of the people'. Syr., which has connected with v. 8 יספחו of v. 7, vocalises שָׁם instead of שֵׁם and places this word at the beginning of the 2nd hemistich.

V. 8 brings back to the scene the contemporaries of Job. Vv. 1-7 have emphasised the abject condition of their parents. These people of low origin are 'sons of base men and sons even of nameless men!' The adverb גַּם marks the descending gradation. The father is not only a נָבָל, that is, a branded creature, vile and abject (cf. Comm. on 2:10), but also a בְּלִי־שֵׁם, a nameless one. Fried. Delitzsch very rightly compares with בני בלי־שם the Assyrian expression *apil lâ mamman* 'son of a nobody'. נְכָאוּ is usually regarded as an Aramaic form, corresponding to the root נכה. 'to strike'. But the expression: 'they were struck from the ground' does not make sense. The same objection applies to the change to נדכאו 'they were crushed' (Beer) or to נחבאו 'they hid' (Joüon in Gesenius-Buhl, s.v. נכא). The true solution is supplied by Torczyner, who reads נִכְרָתוּ 'they were cut off'.

The meaning is excellent: they were cut off from the land, they were accounted as nothing. After eliminating the picturesque description of vv. 2-8, Duhm sees himself faced by ועתה of v. 9, which would have to follow immediately on ועתה of v. 1. He does not hesitate the throw overboard v. 1 and to begin the chapter at v. 9!

9   G renders נגינתם literally κιθάρα ... αὐτῶν, but Vulg. *eorum canticum* and Targ. זמרהון 'their song' effectively express the idea. Syr. ܢܣܝܗ 'their care'. For למלה, G θρύλημα 'gossip', 'subject of talk', and Targ. לשותא 'for conversation' are nearer to the MT than Vulg. *in proverbium* and Syr. ܠܬܡܗܐ 'an object of amazement'.

Repetition of וְעַתָּה from v. 1 (cf. v. 16). The word נְגִינָה denotes the

10   They have held me in abhorrence, they have remained aloof
         from me,
      And they have not spared to spit in my face!
11   He who has untied his rope now handles me roughly,
      As also he who *has* cast off the bit from *his* face!

11   מִפָּנָיו שִׁלַּח ;MT: מפני שלחו.

stringed instrument used for the accompaniment of the Psalms. In modern Hebrew it serves to designate music in general. This meaning is already found in the Assyrian *nigûtu, ningûtu*, which belongs to the same root as נגינה. In Ps 69: 13 the plural נגינות denotes drinking songs. Our passage recalls La 3: 14, 'I have been a laughing stock for all my people, their song (נגינתם) the whole day long.' The expression היה לְמִלָּה 'to be for words' is similar to היה למשל 'to be the subject of a proverb' (cf. Comm. on 17: 6); the meaning is to be the theme of satirical conversations. Since the word 'fable' comes from *fabula* and, in the last analysis, from *fari* 'to talk', we may translate: 'I have become their fable', i.e. their laughing-stock.

10 G interprets רחקו מני by ἀπο-στάντες μακράν. Vulg. translates the 2nd hemistich elegantly: *et faciem meam conspuere non verentur.*

The 1st hemistich expresses the idea that misfortune causes others to remain aloof from the victim (cf. 19: 13-19). The *pi'el* of תעב to mean 'to hold in abhorrence', as in 9: 31; 19: 19. Note the use of מֶנִּי in pause (21: 16). The verb חשׂך as in 7: 11 and the noun רק as in 7: 19. With the 2nd hemistich cf. 17: 6, 'I am he in whose face they spit', and Is 50: 6b, 'I have not turned away my face from shame and spitting.'

11 Vv. 11-13 (as far as נתיבתי inclusive), absent from Sah., marked

with asterisk in Syro-hex., did not exist in G. Our present text derives from Theod. (cf. Codd. 137, 255 and Syro-hex.). The *kêthib* יִתְרוֹ, followed by G and Vulg., is preferable to the *qerê* יִתְרִי, followed by Targ. and Syr. The word יֶתֶר is interpreted as 'quiver' by G φαρέ-τραν αὐτοῦ and Vulg. *pharetram enim suam.* Syr. כאוֿב 'behind me' or 'after me' paraphrases in accordance with יֶתֶר 'what remains'. The verbs פתח ויענני are regarded as plurals in Syr. For שׁלחו, we have the singular in Vulg. *posuit.* Double tradition for Theod., either ἐξαπέστειλεν (followed by Syro-hex.) or ἐξαπέστειλαν (followed by Jerome *miserunt*). For מפני Vulg. *in os meum*; cf. Syr. כפפמב 'in my mouth'.

Siegfried deletes v. 11 as unintelligible. The difficulty of the text is fairly obvious if we compare the various translations: 'They loosen their rein and subject me to their insults, and they put a bit in my mouth' (Le Hir); 'They cast off all restraint, they insult me; in my presence they throw away the bit and bridle' (Renan; cf. Segond and Crampon); 'They seek only the means of vexing me and they have cast off all respect for me' (Loisy). Let us note first of all that the 1st hemistich is built up on exactly the same pattern as 29: 11, where the clause beginning with כִּי is followed by the main clause which is introduced by the *waw* conversive. The verb פתח, in the *pi'el*, means 'untie', 'undo' a rope (38: 31) or

12   On the right hand *witnesses* spring up,
      They have drawn my feet *into the net*,
      And have cast up roads against me. [   ]

12   Transfer עֵדִים (instead of אֵידָם at the end) to follow יָקוּמוּ, and בַּפַּח
(instead of פִרחַח) to precede רַגלִי.

bonds (12:18; 39:5). It is clear
that יִתְרוֹ (*kethîb*, G, Vulg.) denotes
'his rope', in accordance with the
meaning of יֶתֶר in Jg 16:7-9. The
pi'el of ענה 'to be humble' (cf.
22:23, Comm.) retains its normal
sense of 'oppress' or 'illtreat' (37:23).
'As soon as he has untied his rope, he
handles me roughly', i.e. (comparing
with 29:11), he who has untied his
rope handles me roughly. It is an
allusion to him whom Job had kept
tied up like a domestic animal.
Freed now from all restraint, he
illtreats his former master. Such
seems to us to be the natural
meaning, and it will help us to
understand the 2nd hemistich. Let
us note that, in 39:5, we have
parallelism between the *pi'el* of
פתח and the *pi'el* of שׁלח. This
simple fact suggests to us the reading שִׁלַּח (Vulg.; cf. Theod.) instead
of שְׁלחוּ. If the final letter of שׁלחו
is placed after מפני, we obtain מִפָּנָיו,
which allows the translation: 'and
he has cast off the bit from his face',
the word רֶסֶן 'the bit' (Is 30:28)
being parallel to יתרו 'his rope' and
the verb שִׁלַּח corresponding to
פתח. The presence of מִן before the
complement gives to the *pi'el* of
שׁלח 'drop', let loose', 'send away',
etc., the implication of 'throw right
away'. It is clear that, the 2nd
hemistich being parallel to כי־יתרו
פתח, the only principal clause is
ויענני. This interpretation seems to
us more natural than that which
makes of God the subject of פתח
'for God has loosened the string of
my (bow)' (Cappel, Dillmann,

Ehrlich, Driver-Gray, following the
qerê), which then obliges one to
translate the 2nd hemistich: 'they
have dropped the bit in my presence'
(Dillmann). Thus we should pass
from God to the people around Job,
and there would be no close link
between the image of the opening
and that of the close of the verse.
Duhm, following Bickell, replaces
רסן by דגלי, which would have
become רגלי in v. 12. God would not
be content with loosening the string
of the bow but He would also cause
the banner carried before Job to
fall! According to Budde, all the
verbs should be made plural and we
should read יתרם 'their rope' (cf.
Ball). The meaning comes to much
the same thing as that which we have
obtained by simply transposing a
letter.

12   On the text of G, cf. v. 11. The
word פרחח, omitted in Syr., is connected with פרח 'grow', 'flourish' by
Aq. βλαστῶντος and Theod. βλαστοῦ.
Vulg. sees here a metaphor *orientis
calamitatis* (which has become *cala-
mitates*) *meae*. Targ. interprets by
בניהון 'their sons'. For רגלי, Theod.
πόδα αὐτῶν. Syr. omits אידם, which
Vulg. *quasi fluctibus* connects with
אֵד (cf. 36:27).

    Like the preceding one, this verse
is a *crux interpretum*. Here again we
propose to cite the main translations
in order to show how commentators
attempt to deduce a meaning from
the text as it stands: *Consurgentes
ad dextram meam pulli meos impellunt
pedes, aggerantque contra me perni-
ciosas vias suas* (Rosenmüller); 'On
my right an insolent band arises,

13   They have destroyed my path with a view to ruining me,
      They *rise up*, no one *checks* them;

13   יַעֲלוּ‎; MT: יעילו‎.‏ — עֹצֵר‎; MT: עֹזֵר‎.‏

they make my feet to stumble; they have carved out a way to me in order to ruin me' (Le Hir); 'Wretches arise on my right hand; they try to make my feet totter, they make smooth their murderous ways in order to attack me' (Renan; cf. Crampon); 'These wretches arise on my right, and push my feet, they make ways against me in order to bring about my downfall' (Segond); 'A band of men rises up on my right, and they kick me, they make ready their sinister paths to reach me' (Loisy). It is clear that the *hapax* פִּרְחָה‎ (also written פְּרְחָה‎) is rendered in turn by *pulli*, 'an insolent troop', 'wretches', 'a band'. Etymologically the word is connected with פרח‎, whence אֶפְרֹחַ‎ 'brood', 'hatch', 'chicks' (39: 30); cf. Targ. 'their sons'. Ehrlich proposes to see in יָמִין‎ the Aramaic plural of יוֹם‎ and to assign to 'days' the meaning of advanced in age: '*Gegen das Alter erhebt sich die junge Brut*.' But there is something strange about this brood which rises up and then, according to the same commentator, kicks and cuffs. Budde changes עַל־יְמִין‎ to עָלַי‎ 'against me' (cf. Hontheim) and (following Merx, Wright, Duhm, etc.) deletes רַגְלַי‎ שִׁלֵּחוּ‎. We have seen that Bickell and Duhm transferred רַגְלַי‎, read as דַּגְלֵי‎, to v. 11. It is in fact difficult to explain 'they loosen my feet' or 'they throw my feet'. Hence are suggested רַגְלֵיהֶם‎ (Ewald) or רַגְלִימוֹ‎ (Hontheim): 'they hurl their feet (at me)'. Everywhere we are faced by difficulties. Now, we note that the 2nd hemistich is overloaded by אֵידָם‎ 'their misfortune' (cf. אֵיד‎ in 18: 12; 21: 17, 30). The sense is

complete after אָרְחוֹת‎: 'and they have cast up roads against me'. Cf. 19: 12, וַיָּסֹלּוּ עָלַי דַרְכָּם‎ 'and they cast up their road against me'. Further, we know that the accuser stands on the right of the accused (Ps 109: 6; Zec 3: 1). In 16: 8 Job complained of one who 'rose up' as witness against him. Comparing these expressions, we propose to read עֵדִים‎ instead of אֵידָם‎ and to transfer the word to the end of the 1st hemistich. The unintelligible פִּרְחָה‎ is due to a distortion of בַּפַּח‎ which was part of the 2nd hemistich. In this way we obtain a 1st hemistich עַל־יָמִין יָקוּמוּ עֵדִים‎ 'on my right witnesses rise up'; a 2nd בַּפַּח רַגְלִי‎ יִשְׁלְחוּ‎ 'they have cast my feet into the net'. The 3rd hemistich begins a new image, in which Job's enemies are compared to attacking troops. The sequence of ideas is the same as in 19: 6-12. On the word פַּח‎ cf. 18: 9; 22: 10. The use of the *pi'el* of שלח‎ (cf. v. 11) with בפח‎ is analogous to the use of the *pu'al* with בְּרֶשֶׁת‎ in 18: 8.

13   On the text of G, cf. v. 11. The words ἐξετρίβησαν τρίβοι μου, which correspond to נתסו נתיבתי‎, belong to Theod. Then G ἐξέδυσαν γάρ μου τὴν στολήν seems to have read מְעִילִי‎ instead of יַעִילוּ‎. The phrase לְהֹוָתִי‎ is twice translated in Syr., first with the sense of 'gratuitously', next 'about what has happened to me'. For יַעִילוּ‎, Syr. ܚܕܝ 'they have rejoiced' (= יָגִילוּ‎ Beer). Vulg. paraphrases לְהֹוָתִי יַעִילוּ‎ by *insidiati sunt mihi* and omits to translate לָמוֹ‎. It is at v. 14 that we shall find the text of G for לֹא עֹזֵר לָמוֹ‎.

14　As by a wide breach, they come on,
　　They have rolled themselves under the ruins.

The division of the verse is abnormal. If we connect לְהַיָּתִי with the preceding words, we obtain an excellent meaning: 'They have destroyed my path with a view to ruining me.' The verb נתס is a *hapax*, equivalent to נתץ of 19:10. To destroy some one's path is to deprive him of the means of escape. That is why there is added לְהַיָּתִי 'for my misfortune' or 'for my ruin'; on הַיָּה or הַוָּה, cf. Comm. on 6:2. Job compares himself to a besieged city (cf. 19:12). The enemies have banked up their roads in order to reach him (v. 12c). They leave him no escape. Those who maintain לְהַיָּתִי יְעִילוּ 'they help towards my downfall' are embarrassed by לֹא עֹזֵר לָמוֹ, which becomes 'may they themselves be deprived of all aid!' (Le Hir), or 'who would wish to lend them help?' (Renan). Since it is a question of people who are attacking, it is an obvious suggestion to read יַעֲלוּ 'they go up' (Bickell) instead of יעילו. The end of the verse is influenced by 29:12b. A very slight correction, proposed by Dillmann and accepted by several moderns, restores עֹצֵר instead of עֹזֵר. The construction remains the same as in 29:12b, 'no one stops them'. The verb עצר 'check', 'stop' (4:2; 12:15; 29:9) is used with לי'' before the complement of person as in 2 K 4:24. There is no need for us to have recourse to the improbable hypotheses of Duhm, who replaces להית יעילו by יהרסו מעגלי 'they destroy my tracks' and לא עזר למו by אלי עטרו רמיו 'his archers surround me' (following G in v. 14, q.v.).

replaces לא עזר למו of v. 13. It is difficult to see to what distortion or interpretation of the text this translation is due; but one cannot find in it the traces of an original reading אלי עטרו רמי 'his archers surround me' (contra Duhm), which corresponds neither to G nor to the MT. Further, G, which seems to read כחפץ instead of כפרץ, paraphrases the whole of v. 14: κέχρηταί μοι ὡς βούλεται· ἐν ὀδύναις πέφυρμαι. Cf. Vulg. *et ad meas miserias devoluti sunt*, for the 2nd hemistich. Vulg. *quasi rupto muro et aperta janua* separates פרץ from its epithet רחב. Targ. גללי ימא 'waves of the sea' confuses רחב with רהב (9:13; 26:12). For שאה, Syr. ܟܠܐܠ 'tempest', Targ. רגושא 'crash'.

The poet continues to amplify his metaphor. The assailants arrive 'as if by a wide breach'. The preposition is omitted after כ'' (cf. v. 5). The word פֶּרֶץ 'breach' as in 16:14; the adjective רָחָב 'wide' as in 11:9. On the verb אתה, cf. 3:25. The form יֶאֱתָיוּ as in 16:22. The text is perfectly intelligible, given the terms of the description, and it is unnecessary to replace רחב by רהב (contra Perles, *Analekten*, Neue Folge, p. 38), in order to translate 'like the overflowing of the waves', in agreement with Targ. The word שֹׁאָה 'devastation' (cf. v. 3) here denotes the ruins heaped up in consequence of the breaking down of the wall. The phrase 'they roll themselves under the ruins' is very expressive. The *hithpalpel* of גלל is used with the meaning of the *hithpo'el* in 2 S 20:12. We do not see why the word תחת should assume here the meaning of 'like' (34:26), to yield the result: 'like a torrent' (contra Hitzig).

14　G βέλεσιν αὐτοῦ κατηκόντισέν με

15   Terrors have turned to attack me,
      Like the wind they drive away my nobleness,
      And as a cloud my salvation has passed away!

16   And now my soul is poured out upon me,
      Days of affliction seize me;

---

15 Syr. reads הפכו instead of ההפך and רדפו instead of תרדף. Vulg. *redactus sum in nihilum* connects בלהות with the root בלה 'to be annihilated'. G ᾤχετο vocalises תְּרָדֵף instead of תִּרְדֹּף. For נדבתי, G μοῦ ἡ ἐλπίς, Vulg. *desiderium meum*, Targ. רבנותי 'my mastery'. Syr. ܐܘܪܚܬܝ 'my ways' reads נתיבתי. The translation of עברה, omitted in G, is restored in Jerome *transiit* (with asterisk) and in the margin of Syro-hex., following Aq. and Theod. παρῆλθεν.

The verb הָהֻפַּךְ, at the beginning of the sentence, remains in the masculine singular, although the subject is feminine plural of things (Gesenius-Kautzsch, § 145o). The passive is regarded as a kind of impersonal. The sense of the *hoph'al* 'to be turned' corresponds to that of the *niph'al* in 19:19, and the required translation is simply: 'terrors have turned against me'. Cf. the personified terrors in 18:11, 14; 27:20. In the light of 18:11b it is clear that בַּלָהוֹת is the subject of תִרְדֹּף, just as this word is the subject of תשיגהו in 27:20. Hence there is no reason to replace the *qal* by a *niph'al* (Budde, Hontheim) or to read תֻּנֶּדֵף 'is carried away' (Duhm, following 13:25). The terrors are compared with the wind which sweeps everything away in front of it: 'like the wind they drive away my nobleness'. The verb רדף does not mean only 'to pursue' (19:22, 28) but also 'to drive away' (Lv 26:36). The word נְדִיבָה, feminine of נָדִיב 'noble' (12:21; 21:28), is used as an abstract noun, 'nobleness of mind'.

The plural נְדִיבוֹת, in Is 32:8, denotes the noble deeds of the נָדִיב in contrast to 'baseness' נְבָלָה, which is the characteristic of the נָבָל (cf. v. 8). In Ps 51:14 we have parallelism between שׂשׂון ישׁעך 'the joy of Thy salvation' and רוח נדיבה 'the spirit of nobleness'. And it is precisely יִשְׁעָתִי 'my salvation' which is here the parallel to נדבתי. Hence it would be unwise to change נדיבתי to טובתי 'my happiness' (Duhm) or to תקותי 'my hope' (Volz); cf. ישׁועה in 13:16. The cloud is the symbol of what passes away for ever (7:9). The verb עבר, as when it is a question of waters which pass away (6:15; 11:16).

16 V. 16a, absent from Sah., marked with asterisk in Jerome and Syro-hex., did not exist in G. The present text derives from Theod. (cf. Cod. 248 and Syro-hex.). Syr. omits עלי and translates עני by ܡܘܟܟܝ 'my humiliation'.

Job returns to his sorrow. The opening וְעַתָּה as in vv. 1 and 9. The word עָלַי 'upon me' indicates the object of the lament (10:1). It is confirmed by Ps 42:5, 'and I poured out (ואשׁפכה) my soul upon me (עלי).' Thus it is quite arbitrarily that Duhm suppresses it. The *hithpa'el* of שׁפך 'pour', 'shed' (12:21; 16:13), as in La 2:12; 4:1. The soul is poured out when it melts under the blows of affliction (1 S 1:15; Ps 42:5). The יְמֵי־עֹנִי 'days of affliction' recur in La 1:7. One wonders why Duhm replaces ימי by אֵמֵי 'terrors'. The reappearance of

17   At night my bones are pierced [   ]
     And my veins find no sleep.
18   With great force He *grips* my clothing,
     And He clasps me like the collar of my tunic.

17   נִקָּרים ;נֻקַּר; MT: נקר מעלי.
18   יִתְפֹּשׂ (cf. G); MT: יתחפש.

ימי־עני v. 27 confirms the phrase
rather than makes it suspect. In
36:8 we shall find חבלי־עני 'cords
of affliction' used to depict painful
bonds. The verb אחז is used with
direct complement to express a
sorrow which 'seizes' (Is 21:3).

17   The versions have recognised in
לילה a temporal qualification 'during
the night'. G does not translate
מעלי. Vulg. *doloribus* reads perhaps
עמלי. For ערקי, Vulg. *qui me come-
dunt*, Targ. דמעסן יתי 'those who
oppress me'; G τὰ δὲ νεῦρά μου and
Syr. ܒܣܪܝ 'my body' are nearer
to the true sense. Syr. places ברב־כח
of v. 18 at the end of v. 17.

It is during the night that suffering becomes most intense (7:3,
13-14). The text of the first hemistich is ambiguous. It is possible to
make of לַילה the subject of נִקַּר, in
which case it is night personified
which pierces the bones of the sufferer (cf. Dillmann, Renan, etc.).
Otherwise it is עֲצָמַי, regarded as a
neuter plural, which is the subject of
נקר. The verb is then in the *niph'al*.
But in any event one is embarrassed
by מֵעָלַי 'over me', which Duhm
simply deletes. We ourselves propose to see in עלי a repetition of the
עלי of v. 16 and to connect the מ with
the preceding word. Hence we read
נִקָּרִים, which terminates the 1st
hemistich: 'at night my bones are
pierced'. Use of לילה as in 27:20b.
The parallel word to עצמי is עֹרְקִי,
which is usually interpreted to mean
'the things which gnaw me' (cf.
ערק in v. 3 and Vulg. *qui me come-

dunt*). Whence 'the ill which gnaws
me' (Le Hir, Crampon), 'the ills
which gnaw me' (Renan), 'the
sorrow which gnaws me' (Segond).
But G saw in ערקי 'my nerves' and
Syr. 'my body' (cf. sup.). Jewish
tradition, attested by Ibn Ezra,
Qimchi, Rashi, recognises in ערקי a
word similar to the Arabic عرق,
plural عروق which Sa'adia transcribes ערוק. The normal meaning
of the Arabic 'urûq is 'veins'. The
2nd hemistich will thus be translated: 'and my veins do not sleep'.
The ancients did not distinguish
between the arteries and the veins.
What the sick man is describing is
the acceleration of the pulsations as
a result of his fever. The word שכב
is chosen purposely, because it is a
question of the night time which is
devoted to sleep.

18   V. 18b, absent from Sah.,
marked with asterisk in Jerome and
Syro-hex., did not exist in G. The
present text derives from Theod.
(cf. Syro-hex.). Vulg. *in multitudine
eorum* is an allusion to the *doloribus*
of v. 17. For יתחפש, Vulg. *consumitur*,
Targ. יתבלש 'is sought for' (more
literal). G ἐπελάβετο does not read
יתחפש but יתפש (cf. inf.). Syr.,
which has connected ברב־כח with
v. 17, paraphrases very freely: 'I
have clad myself in my coat and
have girded my tunic about me.'
For כפי, Theod. ὥσπερ τὸ περιστό-
μιον, Vulg. *quasi capitio*, Targ. אגב
'by means of'.

The literal translation of the 1st
hemistich should be: 'With great
force my garment is disguised.' The

19   He has cast me into the mire,
And I have come to resemble dust and ashes!

20   I cry out unto Thee and Thou dost not answer me,
I stand up and Thou *payest no* heed to me.

20   וְלֹא תִתְבֹּנֶן (cf. Vulg.); MT: ותתבנן.

phrase בְּרָב־כֹּחַ as in 23:6; the *hithpa'el* of חפשׂ 'search out', 'examine' (cf. Comm. on 28:11) assumes the meaning of 'make one's self sought', 'disguise one's self' (1 S 28:8; 1 K 20:38, etc.). The difficulty of giving an acceptable interpretation is sufficiently apparent from the paraphrases to which commentators have been obliged to have recourse: 'As a result of his violence, my mantle of honour has become changed into a garment of mourning' (Le Hir); 'Sorrow has made me unrecognisable' (Renan); 'Through the violence of my illness, my clothes are losing their shape' (Segond; cf. Crampon). A first fact to be noted is that ברב־כח refers to God, who will be addressed directly in v. 20. The idiom is characteristic; cf. 23:6; 63:1. But it cannot remain suspended in the void, and the verb must have as its subject God understood, which is impossible if we leave יתחפשׂ as it stands. Hence it is not amending the text to replace לבושׁי by בשׂרי 'my flesh' (Budde), in order to obtain: 'By the almighty power of God, my flesh is disguised'! Duhm substitutes כחשׁ for כח and יתחבא for יתחפשׂ. In that case it is the garment which shrinks as a result of his extreme thinness! The idea is much too far-fetched. The true solution was that of Houbigant, who, following G, read יִתְפֹּשׂ instead of יתחפשׂ: 'With great force He (God) holds my garment.' The verb תפשׂ used to denote the action of seizing a mantle (1 K 11:30). God catches the adversary by his clothing and, like a vigorous wrestler, seizes him by the

neck: 'like the collar of my tunic He clasps me'. Literally יאזרני means 'He girdles me' (38:3; 40:7). The word פֶּה 'mouth' means the opening through which the head is passed (Ex 28:32, etc.); cf. *L'Emploi métaphorique*, p. 85.

19 G interprets הרני לחמר by ἥγηται (which has become ἥγησαι in B, אָ) δέ με ἴσα πηλῷ; cf. Vulg. *comparatus sum luto* and Targ. אשׁוו יתי לטינא 'they have likened me to mud'. Syr. translates הרני by ܘܫܕܘܢܝ 'they have cast me'. G paraphrases אתמשׁל by μοῦ ἡ μερίς.

The subject of הֹרָנִי is God, understood, as in v. 18, and it is not necessary to add אֶל before לַחֹמֶר, as do Budde, Duhm, etc. The *hiph'il* of ירה 'to throw' has the sense of the *qal* (cf. 28:8a). The meaning does not appear to us to be in doubt: 'He has thrown me into the mire.' Cf. 9:31, 'Then Thou dost plunge me into mire and filth.' The changes from הרני to הורדני 'He has caused me to go down' (Duhm) or הורתני 'Thou hast cast me' (Volz) have no other object but to lengthen the 1st hemistich. We must be satisfied with its brevity. The verb משׁל appears only here in the *hithpa'el*. Note the construction with כ״ to mean 'to be like'; cf. the *niph'al* with כ״ in Ps 49:13, 21. On the idiom עָפָר וָאֵפֶר 'dust and ashes', cf. Comm. on 2:8. Parallelism between חֹמֶר 'mire' and עָפָר 'dust' is found in 27:16, between חמר 'clay' and אפר 'ashes' in 13:12.

20 V. 20b, absent from Sah.,

21   Thou hast become cruel towards me,
      With all the vigour of Thy hand Thou dost persecute me.
22   Thou dost bear me away on the wind and makest me to ride
         on it,
      And a storm drenches me with water.

marked with asterisk in Jerome and Syro-hex., did not exist in G. The present text derives from Theod. (cf. Syro-hex.). Theod. ἔστησαν δὲ καὶ κατενόησάν με replaces עמדתי and תתבנן by 3rd person plurals. Syr. ܡܩܡ reads עָמַדְתָּ instead of עמדתי. Vulg. *et non respicis me* restores the negative before תתבנן.

'I cry out unto Thee and Thou dost not answer me.' Cf. 19:7, both for the thought and the expressions used. The 2nd hemistich is interpreted: 'I hold myself in Thy presence and Thou dost look on me with coldness' (Le Hir); 'I stand upright and Thou dost look at me with indifference' (Crampon); 'I stand up and Thou dost pierce me with Thy glance' (Segond). But the verb התבונן, with ״ב before its complement, means simply 'pay heed', 'give attention' (Sir 3:22; 9:5). In accordance with parallelism it is evident that the negative existed in the original text, as has been well understood by Vulg. We must restore וְלֹא תִּתְבֹּנֵן 'and Thou payest no heed to me'. In order to maintain ותתבנן, Merx, Budde, and others replace עמדתי by עָמַדְתָּ, 'Thou dost stand', of Syr. But they are then obliged to assign to תתבנן a pejorative sense which is not natural. Duhm takes the correction further by reading מהתבנן 'Thou hast ceased to pay attention to me' (see the use of עמד מן in Gn 29:35). In fact, עמדתי 'I stand up' expresses the attitude of prayer (Jer 15:1) and answers אשוע, while ולא תתבנן בי corresponds to ולא תענני.

21   G(B) ἐπέβησαν and G(A) ἀπέ-

βησαν stem from ἐπέβης, preserved in G (א) and supported by Sah., Syro-hex., Jerome *aggressus es*. A reading לך instead of לי furnishes Syr. with: 'and Thou hast made of me Thy adversary'. G μὲ ἐμαστίγωσας reads תשטטני (cf. שׁוֹט 'lash') instead of תשטמני.

On the *niph'al* of הפך, cf. Comm. on 9:5. Same construction as in 41:20b. Cf. Is 63:10: וַיֵּהָפֵךְ לָהֶם לְאוֹיֵב 'and He has become an enemy for them'. The word אכזר 'cruel' as in La 4:3, where we have also לאכזר. The locution עֹצֶם יָד 'vigour of the hand' recurs in Dt 8:17. Here בעצם ידך corresponds to ברב־כח in v. 18. The verb תִּשְׂטְמֵנִי 'Thou dost persecute me' is supported by 16:9. There is no cogent reason to prefer with Merx the reading of G.

22   G ἔταξας δέ με ἐν ὀδύναις does not translate the 1st hemistich. It is an interpretation of the 2nd, with בְּשֹׁאָה instead of תשוה (cf. v. 14, where שאה is rendered ὀδύναις). Then καὶ ἀπέρριψάς με ἀπὸ σωτηρίας, marked with asterisk in Jerome and Syro-hex., is a new translation of the 2nd hemistich, borrowed from Theod. (cf. Syro-hex.). Note that this translation has passed into Sah. For ותמגגני, Vulg. *elisisti me*, Targ. ותמסני 'and Thou dost make me to melt', Syr. ܘܡܡܝܬܬܢܝ 'and Thou hast mortified me'. The *qerê* תֻּשִׁיָּה (instead of the *kethîb* תֻּשְׁוֶּה) is followed by Theod. ἀπὸ σωτηρίας, Vulg. *valide*. It is difficult to see to what corresponds Targ. בתשיותא or בתשייתא (cf. Levy, *Chald. Wörter-*

23   I know that Thou art leading me to Death,
      To the meeting place of every living creature!

buch, II, p. 564). Syr. interprets תשוה by a verb ܣܐܘܣܐܘ 'and Thou hast weakened me'.

God makes sport of the sufferer. After casting him into the mire (v. 19), He bears him off through the air: 'Thou dost bear me away on the wind and makest me to ride on it.' The verb נשא as in 27: 21. Cf. Ps 18: 10, where God 'rides on a cherub and flies, and soars on the wings of the wind'. The 2nd hemistich notes the result of this trip. Whether we adopt the *qerê* תְּשֻׁיָּה or the *kethib* תְּשֻׁוָּה, the word must be the subject of תְּמֹגְגֵנִי. The basic meaning of the root מוג is 'undulate', 'billow'; cf. the Arabic *mawj* 'wave', 'billow'. The *po'lel* form of מוג is used in Ps 65: 11 to express the idea 'cause to become fluid', 'liquefy', the clods of earth under the pouring down of the rain. The *qerê* תְּשֻׁיָּה 'foresight' (5: 12), 'prudence' (12: 16; 26: 3), 'understanding' (11: 6), is unintelligible as the subject of תמגגני 'makes me fluid', 'melts me'. Hence Duhm, who adopts תשיה, is obliged to read מתשיה (cf. Theod.) and to interpret the 2nd hemistich: 'and Thou dost dissolve me without support'. This means assigning to תשיה a meaning which it nowhere has in the Bible. Furthermore, it is not clear what connection there is between dissolution and lack of support. On the other hand, the *kethib* תְּשֻׁוָּה is but a variant of תְּשֻׁאָה, used in the plural with the meaning of 'shouts' (36: 29; 39: 7; Is 22: 2; Zec 4: 7). The word belongs to the same root as שׁוֹאָה or שָׁאָה, which means not only 'devastation', 'ruins' (vv. 3, 14), but also 'storm' (Ezk 38: 9; Pr 1: 27). This latter sense is perfectly suitable to our passage, and is suggested by 36: 29 (cf.

Comm.). Job is in the act of riding through the air, like a cloud swept by the wind (Is 60: 8). Suddenly the cloud bursts: 'and a storm dissolves me in water'. The picturesque phrasing is removed if we replace תשוה by תְּשַׁדֵּנִי 'Thou dost destroy me' (Merx; cf. Syr.). Siegfried suggests מתשועה (cf. Theod.), which is attended by the same disadvantages as מתשיה of Duhm (cf. sup.).

23 G θάνατός με ἐκτρίψει makes of מות the subject of תשיבני. Syr. reads: ממות 'I know that Thou wilt bring me back from death to the house of reunion for all the living.' Targ. interprets בית by בית קבורתא 'burial place'. Vulg. separates מועד from בית: *ubi constituta est domus omni viventi*. G paraphrases the 2nd hemistich: οἰκία γὰρ παντὶ θνητῷ γῆ.

Job does not cherish any illusions about the fate awaiting him: 'I know that Thou art leading me to death.' Cf. 1: 21, 'Naked I came out of my mother's womb and naked I shall return', i.e. I shall return to the bosom of the earth (cf. Comm.). The conjunction כי has been placed before ידעתי, but it ought to follow this verb. Its function is not to join v. 23 and v. 22 but to introduce the clause announced by ידעתי 'I know'. The word מָוֶת is an accusative of place (29: 25, the word רֹאשׁ). Death is here the same as Sheol; cf. Comm. on 28: 12. It is there that all the living gather (3: 17ff.). For the ideas about Sheol, cf. Comm. on 7: 9. Note the phrase בֵּית מוֹעֵד 'house of reunion', 'meeting place', just as we have הר מועד 'mountain of meeting' (Is 14: 13) and אהל מועד 'tent of meeting'. On the formula: כָּל־חַי 'every living creature', cf. 28: 21.

24   Yet *I* did not strike the *poor man* with my hand,
      If in his distress *he cried out for my help*!

24 בְעָנִי ;MT: בעי. — אֶשְׁלַח (G); MT: ישלח. — לִי יְשַׁוֵּעַ (cf. G); MT: לְהֶן שׁוּעַ.

24 G εἰ γὰρ ὄφελον δυναίμην ἐμαυτὸν χειρώσασθαι vocalises לֹא instead of לֹא, reads בִּי instead of בעי, and אֶשְׁלַח instead of ישלח. Syro-hex. places an asterisk before χειρώσασθαι and gives the various translations of בעי, which Field retranslates into Greek: ἐν ἰσχύι (Symm.), εἰκῇ (Theod.), εἰς τὸ ἐκπορθῆσαι or ἐξαναλῶσαι (Aq.). Vulg. puts the verb in the 2nd person singular and interprets בעי by *ad consumptionem eorum*. For בעי, Syr. حلك 'against me' (cf. G), Targ. ברתחא 'with anger'. G ἢ δεηθείς (A δεηθῆναι, Jerome *rogare*) γε ἑτέρου καὶ ποιήσει μοι τοῦτο seems to read לי כן יעשה instead of לְהֶן שׁוּעַ and continues its interpretation of the 1st hemistich. Vulg. harmonises with its translation of בעי by *ad consumptionem eorum* in that it renders the 2nd hemistich *et si corruerint, ipse salvabis*. Cf. the paraphrase of Syr. 'and when I cry to Him, He will save me'. Targ. renders לְהֶן שׁוּעַ by יקבל צלותהון 'He welcomes their prayers'.

The *Bible du rabbinat français* admits that 'this verse is far from clear in the original' and translates: 'But does not one stretch out one's hand when one sinks? Does one not cry out for help when one succumbs to misfortune?' The word בְּעִי is interpreted 'when one sinks, collapses', because עִי is regarded as a singular of עִיִּים 'ruins'. Cf. Le Hir: 'Oh that there at leas this hand might no longer be stretched out over a heap of ruins, that in his downfall man might find his salvation!' Renan boldly deviates from the text: 'Vain prayer...! he stretches out his hand; what is the use of protesting against his blows?' Here

בעי is connected with the root בעה 'to pray' in Aramaic. Knabenbauer returns to an old interpretation of Cappel (already refuted by Rosenmüller) which consists in postulating for עי the meaning of 'tumulus': *non in tumulum mittet manum*. The closing words לְהֶן שׁוּעַ are hardly less unintelligible than בעי. A conjecture of Dillmann, which has found considerable favour with modern commentators, consists in reading טֹבֵעַ 'he who is drowning' instead of בעי (cf. Bickell, Budde, Duhm, Gray). The correction is then completed by changing לְהֶן שׁוּעַ to לֹא יְשַׁוֵּעַ (Bickell), which affords as the meaning of the verse: 'Does not he who is drowning stretch out his hand? In his distress does he not cry out?' But בְּפִידוֹ 'in his misfortune' (15:23; 21:20) looks then like a bit of padding after the description of the drowning man who stretches out his hand for some one to save him. In his study of the text and in the edition of Kittel, Beer enumerates the many hypotheses which have attempted to provide a meaning adapted to the context. Now, v. 25 alludes to the compassion which Job practised towards the needy, the latter being rendered by אֶבְיוֹן. The parallel word to אביון is usually עָנִי (cf. 24:4, 14). As has been recognised by Wright, Voigt, Beer, it is this word which is concealed in בעי, which should in fact be read as בְעָנִי. By a mistake the *nun* has been transferred to the form לְהֶן, which is inexplicable. Following G, we may read אֶשְׁלַח instead of ישלח. Thus the 1st hemistich becomes: 'However, I did not

25   Did I not weep with him for whom life was harsh?
        Was not my soul grieved for the needy?

26   It was happiness that I hoped for but it was misfortune which
        came,
        I expected light and darkness came!

strike the poor man with my hand!' The 2nd hemistich will explain in what circumstances. Since the *nun* of לֹהֶן comes from בֵעָנִי (cf. sup.), we are left simply with לֹה. In the light of G, it seems indeed that the original text had לִי. The ה of לֹה springs from a combination of two *yods*, the one at the end of לִי and the other at the beginning of יְשַׁוֵּעַ (which later became שׁוע). Hence we read לִי יְשַׁוֵּעַ, and we obtain: 'if in his distress he cried out for my help'. Job did not treat brutally the poor man who implored his aid. This forms an excellent prelude to v. 25.

25 For לְקֹשֶׁה־יוֹם (reproduced in Targ.), G ἐπὶ παντὶ ἀδυνάτῳ, Vulg. *super eo qui afflictus erat*. The two words are clumsily separated by Syr., which translates יוֹם as 'during the day'. For לָאֶבְיוֹן, G ἄνδρα ἐν ἀνάγκαις (A ἀνάγκη).

But Job not only refrained from brutally repulsing the poor man in his troubles. He treated him on the contrary with compassion and shared sympathetically in his misery. Beside עָנִי 'poor' and אֶבְיוֹן 'needy' we find קְשֶׁה־יוֹם 'harsh of day' (cf. קָשֶׁה in Comm. on 9: 4), he whose days are hard, and for whom life is harsh. The same description, with a slightly different meaning, is found in the original text of 1 S 1: 15 (following G). The clause introduced by אִם־לֹא is interrogative as in 17: 2. The verb עגם is a *hapax*, the meaning of which is similar to אגם 'to be sad' (cf. אֲגְמֵי־נֶפֶשׁ in Is 19: 10). The Assyrian *agâmu* means 'to be vexed, irritated'; the noun *têgimtu* 'anger'

(Thureau-Dangin, *Huitième campagne de Sargon*, p. 21, n. 5) presupposes a root עגם, which is what we find here. In order to bring this v. 25 into harmony with his interpretation of v. 24, Duhm changes בְּכִיתִי to בְּכִית 'tear', נַפְשִׁי to נַפְשׁוּ, אֶבְיוֹן to אָבַד. There is not the slightest support in the versions for such changes. Albertus Magnus rightly compares with this verse Ro 12: 15-16 and 1 P 3: 8.

26 G ἐγὼ δὲ ἐπέχων ἀγαθοῖς translates כִּי טוֹב קִוִּיתִי, but the sequel ἰδοὺ συνήντησάν μοι μᾶλλον ἡμέραι κακῶν derives from v. 27b. It has been thought that G corresponded to v. 26 and omitted v. 27, which was later restored on the basis of Theod. (cf. v. 27).

The subordinate clause is introduced by כִּי, the main clause by *waw* consecutive; cf. the construction of 19: 18b. Antithesis between what one hopes for and what happens (Is 5: 7b; Jer 8: 15). The illusions of Job have been described in 29: 18-20. The *pi'el* of קוה with its complement in the accusative (7: 2). Note the contrast between טוֹב 'happiness' and רָע 'evil', 'misfortune' (2: 10) as also between אוֹר 'light' and אֹפֶל 'darkness'; light is the symbol of happiness, darkness that of misfortune (cf. Comm. on 22: 11). The verb בוא is used to mark the onset of trouble: 3: 26; 4: 5; 5: 21, etc.). The cohortative אֲיַחֲלָה is used as a simple imperfect (cf. 1: 15ff.). The good conduct of Job (vv. 24-5) authorised him to expect a better fate!

27   My bowels seethe continually with agitation,
     And I am confronted with days of affliction!
28   I have walked about all tanned when there was no sunshine,
     I have risen in the assembly and cried out;

27 G has in v. 26 the translation of v. 27b. Hence vv. 26b-27a were lacking in its text. The gap was filled by the introduction of the text of Theod. as v. 27. That is why v. 27 is absent from Sah. and marked with asterisk in Jerome and Syrohex. (which attributes it to Theod.). For רתחו, Syr. simply ܘܐܬܒܣ 'have been troubled'. Targ. connects דמו with דָּם 'blood', whence 'there is no appearance of blood in them'. Syr. adds the 1st person singular suffix to עני.

The bowels מֵעִים (20:14) are the seat of painful emotions (cf. *L'Emploi métaphorique*, p. 135). The verb רתח is used in the *pi'el* (Ezk 24:5) and in the *hiph'il* (inf. 41:23) in the sense of 'cause to boil'. Here the *pu'al*: 'my bowels have been in a state of ebullition, have seethed'. Cf. La 1:20, מֵעַי חֳמַרְמָרוּ 'my bowels have been in ferment' (cf. La 2:11). The phrase וְלֹא־דָמּוּ 'and they have not remained calm' (cf. דמם in 29:21; 31:34) is used to express the idea that the bowels bubble without ceasing. The *pi'el* of קדם conveys the idea 'come to meet one' (cf. 3:12). The 'days of affliction' as in v. 16. The 2nd hemistich gives the reason for what is described in the 1st. It is because each day which confronts Job is a day of sorrow that his bowels are constantly writhing in pain. One wonders why Duhm wishes to eliminate this v. 27, which continues the description of the ills announced by v. 26.

28 The word קדר, well translated אוכם 'black' in Targ., is interpreted metaphorically by G στένων, Vulg. *maerens*. The two meanings merge in Syr. ܐܘܟܡܐܝܬ 'with blackness' or 'with sadness'. Targ. renders בלא חמה by מדלית שמשא 'without sunshine', but Vulg. *sine furore* and Syr. ܘܠܐ ܚܡܬܐ 'without anger' vocalise חֵמָה. Similarly G, whose reading ἄνευ θυμοῦ (Compl.) has become ἄνευ φιμοῦ; cf. Symm. ἀθυμῶν.

The meaning of the 1st hemistich is simply: 'I have walked about all tanned when there was no sunshine.' The word קֹדֵר, participle of קדר 'to be dark, swarthy in hue', strictly speaking means 'tanned', 'bronzed' and it is only derivatively that it will assume the meaning of 'sad', 'afflicted' (5:11) or 'covered' (6:16). Doubtless in Ps 38:7 the phrase קֹדֵר הִלָּכְתִּי means 'I have walked about afflicted', but in our text the deliberate antithesis with בְּלֹא חַמָּה demands that we should retain the literal meaning of קדר. In fact, חַמָּה 'heat' is poetically used to denote the sun (Is 24:23; 30:26; Ca 6:10), and it is the sun which blackens the skin (Ca 1:6). The meaning is very clear. German exegetes are not satisfied with it and correct חמה to חמדה 'desire' (Beer), חדוה 'joy' (Voigt), נחמה 'consolation' (Duhm, Budde), all with the object of avoiding the literal meaning of קדר. Thus they exclude the fine antithesis of the poet. Use of the *pi'el* of הלך as 24:10. For בלא, cf. 8:11. The complement בַּקָּהָל refers to קַמְתִּי; cf. Ps 24:3b. The imperfect אֲשַׁוֵּעַ has modal significance and thus can be juxtaposed to a perfect (Gesenius-Kautzsch, § 102c); cf. 32:22. Duhm considers that this hemistich is 'quite stupid'. However,

29   I have been a brother for jackals,
     And a companion for ostriches!

30   My skin has become black on me,
     And my bones have been burnt by fever.

one can very well imagine such a personage as Job suddenly getting up to cry aloud with pain. Duhm thinks that he is being more knowing than the author by reading בקהל שׁוֹעֵל 'I stand amid foxes (or jackals)'. But the word קָהָל denotes a congregation, or a church, not a gathering of animals. Beer proposes בקולי or בקול instead of בקהל. In this case Job would be said to cry aloud with his own voice. How could he do otherwise?

29 For לתנים, Targ. לירורין (which has later become לירודין) and Syr. ܠܟܠܒܐ 'to wild dogs and jackals', more correct than G σειρήνων and Vulg. *draconum*. For לבנות יענה, G στρουθῶν, Vulg. *struthionum*, but Theod. θυγατέρων στρουθῶν, which has passed into Jerome *filiarum struthionum* and into Syro-hex. (with asterisk).

'I have been a brother for jackals, and a companion for ostriches', because of the groans and shrieks which are typical of the animals with which Job associates himself (v. 28b). The verse is modelled exactly like 29: 15-16a. Cf. 17: 14, where Job says to the grave: 'thou art my father' and to the worms: 'you are my mother and sister'. The תַּנִּים are the jackals which run across the desert, the symbolic name of which being מקום תנים 'place of jackals' (Ps 44: 20), or מעון תנים 'abode of jackals' (Jer 9: 10, etc.). The plaintive cry of these animals has caused them to be nicknamed, by onomatopoeia, *wâwî* among the Arabs, אִיִּים (in the plural) among the Hebrews. The ostrich too is an animal which utters a mournful

cry (cf. Comm. on 39: 13), whence the name of רְנָנִים (ibid.). Its ordinary name in the Bible is בַּת הַיַּעֲנָה (plural בְּנוֹת יַעֲנָה), the meaning of which is probably 'daughter of the desert' (in accordance with the Arabic *wa'neh*; cf. Gesenius-Buhl, s.v. יענה). The words תנים and בנות יענה are in parallelism in Mic 1: 8b, the tenor of which echoes our verse: 'I will make a lamentation like the jackals and a groaning like the ostriches.' In La 4: 3 (*qerê*) the תנים have as parallel יְעֵנִים, masculine plural of a word יָעֵן, fabricated on the pattern of יענה.

30 G renders מעלי by μεγάλως. The word חרה is omitted in G. The reading συνεφρύγη of Theod. (cf. Syro-hex.) has passed into G(A), Syro-hex. (with asterisk) and Jerome *frixa sunt* (with asterisk). For שׁחר, Syr. ܡܣܘܕ 'rugged', wrinkled'. For מני־חרב, Syr. ܐܝܟ ܕܒܚܘܡܐ 'as by the heat'.

'My skin has become black on me'; cf. v. 28a. The **verb** שׁחַר 'to become black' is a *hapax*, but we have שָׁחֹר 'black' (Lv 13: 31, 37; Zec 6: 2, 6), שְׁחוֹר 'soot' (La 4: 8). The swarthiness of the skin is designated by שְׁחוֹרָה אֲנִי 'I am black' (Ca 1: 5), אֲנִי שְׁחַרְחֹרֶת 'I am become swarthy' (Ca 1: 6). The locks of hair are black (שְׁחֹרוֹת) 'like the raven' (Ca 5: 11). It is unnecessary to assign to מֵעָלָי a subtle meaning 'and falls into tatters' (Renan, Crampon). The sense of מֵעָלַי is quite simply 'on me', literally 'above me'; cf. the use of מֵעַל in Dt 8: 4 and 29: 4. The versions do not support the chan_e of

31 My lyre has been used for lamentation,
And my pipe to accompany the voice of weepers!

מעלי into מחלי 'by illness' which is
proposed by Ball. Note the use of
עֶצֶם 'bone' in the singular (2:5) to
denote the frame as a whole, all the
bones. The verb חרר 'to be burnt'
is used in the *niph'al* in Ezk 24:10
to suggest the material combustion
of bones, and in Ps 102:4 in a metaphorical sense: 'my bones are burned
like a fire of live coals'. The word חֹרֶב
'heat' denotes the inner fire kindled
by the fever from which Job suffers.
Budde has no more justification for
deleting this verse than he had for
deleting v. 27. Why should we not
allow Job to allude to his physical
sufferings?

31 G εἰς πάθος comes from εἰς
πένθος, which has been preserved
in G(A). It is εἰς πένθος which translated לאבל in Aq., Symm., Theod.
(cf. Field, following Syro-hex.). For
לקול בכים, G εἰς κλαυθμὸν ἐμοί. The
word ἐμοί is omitted by Jerome *in
fletum* and by Syro-hex.

The verb היה 'to be', with ל״
before its complement, to connote
'serve the purpose of' (Gn 1:14ff.;
17:7; 28:21, etc.). It was the phrase
used in Nu 10:31, which we cited
in connection with 29:15. The words
כִּנּוֹר and עוּגָב as in 21:12. The noun
אֵבֶל 'mourning' (cf. the verb in
14:22) denotes the funeral lament
(Mic 1:8). In La 5:15 it is contrasted with מחולנו: 'our dance has
been changed into lamentation'. The
parallel locution is קוֹל בֹּכִים 'voice
of the weepers', very fitting to the
context after the mention of funereal
lamentation.

CHAPTER 31

1   I had concluded a covenant with my eyes,
    And refused to pay any attention to a virgin!

2   What then is the portion which Eloah from on high sends,
    And what is the lot decreed by Shaddai from the heights?

31: **1**   Vv. 1-4, absent from Sah., marked with asterisk in Cod. 248, Syro-hex., and Jerome (except v. 4), did not exist in G. The present text derives from Theod. (cf. Syro-hex.). For ומה, Aq. καὶ τί and Targ. ומה, but Theod. καὶ οὐ, Symm. καὶ οὐδ', Vulg. *ut ne*, Syr. וְלָא have recognised in מה a negative meaning.

Job continues to defend his conduct (29: 14-17). He has been scrupulous to the point of not allowing his eyes to rest on a virgin, for it is the eyes which control the heart (v. 7) and through them that lust penetrates the soul (Mt 5: 28). Job has subjected himself to a veritable law: 'I have concluded a covenant with my eyes.' The phrase כרת ברית, literally 'to cut a covenant' (cf. the Greek ὅρκια τέμνειν) is to be explained by the fact that a victim was cut into two and one passed between the two halves (Gn 15: 10; Jer 34: 18). The use of the preposition "ל before the indirect complement does not imply that it is a question of a command given by a superior to an inferior (Gray), since it is found also before יהוה in 2 Ch 29: 10. In fact authors use sometimes עם (40: 28) or את 'with', sometimes "ל 'with regard to' before the person with whom one binds one's self by a pact of alliance. Duhm would change וּמָה אֶתְבּנָן to מהתבונן, the preposition מן denoting abstention. But ומה, confirmed by all the versions, is perfectly understandable if

we assign to מה the negative meaning (cf. sup.) which we have met in 16: 6 (cf. Comm.). Furthermore, we find ומה as an equivalent to the Latin *ne* in Ca 8: 4 and Pr 20: 24. The verb התבונן with על before the complement to connote 'pay attention to'. Cf. Sir 9: 5, בבתולה אל תתבונן 'Pay no heed to a virgin!' (preposition "ב as above, 30: 20). The Son of Sirach gives the reason for the prohibition: 'lest you should be compelled to pay fines because of her'. Job does not inquire what the consequence of such action would be. He declares merely that he has avoided even the occasion of sinning. Hence he might be justified in expecting a better fate than the one which has been meted out to him (vv. 2-4).

2   On the text of G, cf. v. 1. Theod. καὶ ἔτι comes from καὶ τί (cf. Aq. in v. 1). Targ. renders חלק by חולק טב 'good portion'. Vulg. adds *in me* in the 2nd hemistich: *quam enim partem haberet in me Deus desuper?*

Vocalisation מֶה on account of the following guttural (26: 2). The words חֵלֶק and נַחֲלָה as in 20: 29 and 27: 13, but with subjective instead of objective complement. There it was a question of the part and lot reserved by God for the wicked man; here it is the part and lot which God grants. The expression מִמָּעַל is juxtaposed to אֱלוֹהַ as in 3: 4 (cf. below, v. 28b). It has as parallel

3   Should it not be misfortune for the unjust,
     And tribulation for the evil-doers?

4   Does He not see my ways,
     And does He not count all my steps?

מִמְּרוֹמִים 'from the heights', i.e. from the height of the heavens (16: 19; 25: 2). The question which Job asks is elucidated by v. 3. God ought to award misfortune to the wicked man as his due heritage. In point of fact, however, it turns out that it is the most scrupulous of righteous men who is the victim. V. 4 will ask a new question: might it be the case that God does not see the deeds of His servant? Such is the logical sequence of ideas in vv. 1-4. Job has the right to count on happiness and well-being, since he is righteous (v. 1) and misfortune is what the wicked man deserves and should be allotted (vv. 2-3). But it is the contrary which takes place (30: 26). Hence it is that God shows Himself to be indifferent to human affairs (v. 4).

3   On the text of G, cf. v. 1. The word נכר is translated by Syr. (in accordance with etymology) ܢܘܟܪܝܘܬ 'estrangement', Theod. ἀπαλλοτρίωσις, Vulg. alienatio. But Targ. תבירה 'ruin', 'misfortune' gives clearly the correct sense.

It is arbitrary to try to lengthen the 1st hemistich by adding נָכוֹן 'prepared' (Ley, Duhm), which in effect changes the meaning. V. 3 gives the answer to v. 2. Job seems to be agreeing with current ethics as expounded by his interlocutors, according to whom misfortune (אֵיד as here) dogs the footsteps of the wicked (18: 12). But he has often affirmed that experience contradicts this theory, and, when he has spoken of misfortune, אֵיד, it has been to say that it spared the wicked and guilty

man (21: 17, 30). On the word עַוָּל, cf. Comm. on 16: 11. The form qatl, נֵכֶר, has the same meaning as the form qutl, נֹכֶר, used in Ob 12 with the sense of 'tribulation'. The root נכר means not only 'to be alien' but also 'to be hostile' (Assyrian nakâru), 'to be harsh, hateful' (Arabic nakura) The expression פֹּעֲלֵי אָוֶן 'doers of iniquity' (34: 8, 22) is part of the vocabulary of the Psalms. Cf. Pr 10: 29; 21: 15, מחתה לפעלי און 'terror for the evil doers'.

4   On the text of G, cf. v. 1. The asterisk has been forgotten by Jerome before this v. 4. Instead of the plural דְּרָכַי, Theod. reads the singular ὁδόν μου.

God then should reserve misfortune for the guilty (v. 3). Now, it turns out that it is precisely the righteous man who is victimised. It follows then that God seems to take no account of the good deeds of Job. The plural דְּרָכַי 'my ways', i.e. 'my good works', 'my conduct', is thoroughly in accord with the style of the Book of Job (4: 6; 13: 15; 22: 3). The pronoun הוּא is placed for emphasis after the interrogative הֲלֹא and before the verb; cf. הֲלֹא אַתָּ (1: 10) and הֲלֹא־הֵם (8: 10). The 2nd hemistich is inspired by 14: 16, which was also spoken by Job. The metaphor of ways and footsteps is continued by the use of the verb הלך 'to walk' and of רַגְלִי 'my foot', in v. 5. This is a proof that one cannot argue on the basis of the lacuna in G to eliminate vv. 1-4, as is suggested by Hatch, Bickell and a few others, who are refuted by Budde.

5   Have I walked with falsehood,
     And has my foot hastened towards deceit?
6   Let Him weigh me in the scales of justice,
     And let Eloah know my integrity!
7   If my step deviated from the way,
     And my heart followed the sight of my eyes,
     And if any stain sullied my hands,

5 The text of G begins again at v. 5. G γελοιαστῶν replaces the abstract שָׁוְא by a concrete.

We regard the particle אִם of the opening as interrogative (6:12; 19:5), which enables us to establish a nexus between vv. 5-6, instead of making v. 6 a kind of parenthesis and seeing in v. 5 a clause parallel to v. 7. Note that vv. 2-4 are likewise cast in the form of questions. Hence: 'Have I walked with falsehood?' The verb הלך is used with עם before the person whom one accompanies (34:8). In the light of 34:8, one might be inclined to read אַנְשֵׁי שָׁוְא 'men of falsehood' (Ley) or מְתֵי שָׁוְא (Bickell, Grimme), instead of the abstract. שָׁוְא. But the parallelism with מִרְמָה 'deceit' favours the MT. The phrase 'walk with falsehood' is perfectly understandable; it means taking falsehood as one's companion, and the guide of one's steps, i.e. one's deeds. On the word שָׁוְא, cf. 7:3; 11:11. The form וַתַּחַשׁ stems from חוש 'hasten' (20:2), conjugated by analogy with the ל"ה verbs (Gesenius-Kautzsch, § 72ff). Note the use of the preposition על with the same meaning as אל 'towards' (cf. 1:8, 11). The images of the road, steps, walking, the feet, will be continued in v. 7.

6 G ἕσταμαι γάρ avoids the anthropomorphism of יִשְׁקְלֵנִי 'let Him weigh me!' For תֻמָּתִי, Vulg. simplicitatem meam (cf. 1:1).

'Let Him weigh me in the scales of justice!', the verb שקל in the metaphorical sense as in 6:2, where we likewise have מֹאזְנָיִם 'the two scales of the balance', for 'the balance'. The מֹאזְנֵי־צֶדֶק 'balance of justice', i.e. 'a just, true, balance' (Lv 19:36; Ezk 45:10), by antithesis with מֹאזְנֵי מִרְמָה 'balance of deceit', 'false balance' (Pr 11:1; 20:23). Among the Egyptians, the heart of the dead man was placed on one scale of the balance, and truth, represented by the image of the goddess Mat, was placed on the other (cf. Où en est l'histoire des religions? I, p. 123). It was then that the negative confession took place. Job begins by asking God to assess justly his conduct as a whole. He will then enter into a real and detailed negative confession. The word תֻמָּתִי 'my perfection', 'my integrity' as in 27:5, where Job vindicates his conduct as a whole. In the prose narrative (2:3, 9) Job clings unshakeably to his 'perfection', תמתו.

7 After ἐκ τῆς ὁδοῦ (מִנִּי הַדֶּרֶךְ), G(A) adds αὐτοῦ (Sah.). For עֵינַי, G simply τῷ ὀφθαλμῷ, but G(A) adds μοῦ (Sah., Syro-hex.). At the end, the word מְאוּם stands for מוּם; it is one of the 48 words which have a superfluous 'aleph (Ochla veochla, no. 103; cf. Baer). The kethîb of the Orientals implies מְאוּמָה 'something', which is reflected in Syr. ܡܕܡ and is at the basis of G δώρων. Vulg. macula certainly reads מוּם, while Targ. מדעם חבולא 'something evil' combines the meanings of מְאוּמָה and מוּם.

The metaphors of vv. 4-5 are con-

8   Then let me sow and another eat,
       And let my shoots be uprooted!

9   If my heart has been seduced by a woman,
       And I have lurked at my neighbour's door,

tinued in v. 7. With the 1st hemistich, 'if my step deviated from the way', cf. 23: 11, 'My foot has held fast to His step, I have kept His way and have not turned aside'; same use of the words אָשֻׁר and דֶּרֶךְ as also of the verb נטה. 'The way' is the way which God has marked out and shown to men as the right way (Dt 9: 12, 16). In Is 30: 11, the rebels cry out to the prophets: 'Depart from the path, turn aside from the way!' The eyes supply the heart with the nourishment for lust (cf. v. 1). The heart must not be in tow to the eyes: 'if my heart has followed the sight of my eyes'. The verb הלך with לב as subject and אחר before the complement (Ezk 20: 16). The 3rd hemistich has merely a fortuitous resemblance to Dt 13: 18, 'let nothing that is forbidden cleave to your hand', where the word מאומה 'something' is clarified by the context. Here it is indeed a question of מום 'stain', 'blemish' (11: 15), and it is probably as a result of a reminiscence of Dt 13: 18 that the *kethîb* of the Orientals has vocalised מְאוּמָה. Bickell and Duhm delete this 3rd hemistich, whilst Volz attacks the 2nd. After the mention of the foot, the eyes, the heart, one is not surprised to find the hands figuring as a principle of action. It is usually to the hands that is assigned the stain occasioned by sin (11: 14; 16: 17) or the purity which righteousness confers (22: 30).

8   Syr. has misunderstood this v. 8 and has made it a contrast to v. 7: 'On the contrary, if I sowed, then I ate, and if I planted, then I grew great, and amassed wealth', i.e. I did not profit by the work of others,

but by my own. G ἄριζος δὲ γενοίμην ἐπὶ γῆς seems to read ארצה for צאצאי and אשרש for ישרשו.

The cohortative אֶזְרְעָה expresses desire and is continued by a jussive: 'then let me sow and another eat'. Cf. the antitheses of 27: 17 and 5: 5, where we have יאכל as here. It is the sower who ought to eat the produce of his land, and the one who plants who should profit by his work, for 'they do not plant that another might eat' (Is 65: 22, ואחר יאכל as here). The punishment would consist in seeing another reap what one has sown one's self: 'Thou shalt sow and thou shalt not reap' (Mic 6: 15). The word צֶאֱצָאַי 'my shoots' (5: 25; 21: 8; 27: 14) is here taken in its literal sense, to connote plants which shoot up out of the ground (Is 34: 1; 42: 5). The *pu'al* of שרש in the sense of 'to be uprooted': cf. the meaning of the *pi'el* in Ps 52: 7.

9   G γυναικὶ ἀνδρὸς ἑτέρου joins רעי to אשה, which enables it to interpret על־פתח by ἐπὶ θύραις αὐτῆς.

After speaking of sins in general, Job now goes into detail. First adultery (24: 15), for the woman in question is the neighbour's wife, as is to be seen from the 2nd hemistich: 'If my heart has been seduced by a woman', literally, 'on a woman', i.e. 'on account of a woman'. The heart follows the vision of the eyes (v. 7), that is why Job has forbidden himself to look even at a maiden (v. 1), all the more, at a married woman. The verb פתה 'to seduce' and 'to be seduced' (v. 27), whence פֹּתֶה 'fool', 'madman' (5: 2). In v. 27, it is still the heart that is seduced. A characteristic of the adulterer is that

10   Then let my wife turn the millstone for another,
       And let others bend down upon her!   11 [   ]

11 'For that is a shameless deed and a criminal fault'. Gloss (cf. Comm.).

he lurks in wait for dusk (24:15) and stands guard to seize the chance of the husband's absence (Pr 7:19). The word רֵעַ denotes the neighbour, as in the Decalogue (Ex 20:17; Dt 5:18). The verb ארב 'lie in wait', 'watch'; cf. Comm. on 25:3.

10 As in the case of v. 8, Syr. interprets in the sense of an opposition to v. 9: 'On the contrary, my wife turned the millstone for another and she baked bread in another place.' G ἀρέσαι is a corruption of ἀλέσαι, which translated תטחן. Targ. interprets the 1st hemistich in an obscene sense: 'then let my wife lie with another!' Cf. Vulg. *scortum alterius sit uxor mea*! G τὰ δὲ νήπιά μου ταπεινωθείη vocalises עוּלַי instead of ועליה and leaves aside אחרין (cf. v. 11).

Job demands the law of retaliation. The wife will become a servant, and by that very fact, the concubine of another. The function of the slave, either male or female, is to grind the wheat for daily bread (Ex 11:5; Is 47:2). A rabbinical interpretation, followed by Targ. and Vulg., assigns to טחן 'to grind' the meaning of 'to have intercourse with some one.' This interpretation is cited by St Jerome in connection with Jg 16:21 (cf. Lagrange, in loc.). It has influenced the translation of Vulg. in La 5:13b where the word טְחוֹן occurs: *adolescentibus impudice abusi sunt*. It is clear that the 1st hemistich should retain its normal meaning, which is confirmed by Ex 11:5; Is 47:2. As is shown by the 2nd hemistich, Job would not have had recourse to a periphrasis. The verb כרע means 'bend', 'crouch' (4:4;; 39:3). The

word אַחֲרִין has the termination of the Aramaic plural (cf. 4:2).

11 G θυμὸς γὰρ ὀργῆς ἀκατάσχετος, τὸ μιᾶναι ἀνδρὸς γυναῖκα. Ball puts forward several hypotheses with regard to the Hebrew origin of this text which in no way agrees with the MT. Bickell and Beer had already tried to find traces of it in the Hebrew. If we take into account the fact that אחרין of v. 10 is not rendered in G, we can envisage θυμὸς γὰρ ὀργῆς as arising from כי חרון, the word חרון replacing אחרין. The epithet ἀκατάσχετος 'which cannot be contained' translates perhaps ואין פליטה 'and no way out', which might be a corruption of ועון פלילי. As for τὸ μιᾶναι ἀνδρὸς γυναῖκα, it is not a translation, but rather an explanation of זמה, following Nu 5:13ff. The *qerê* rightly transposes the pronouns היא and הוא. The reading עָוֹן פְּלִילִים combines עָוֹן פלילים and עָוֹן פְּלִילִי (v. 28). Vulg. *iniquitas maxima* and Targ. סורחן פריש 'extraordinary sin' are found again in v. 28 as a translation of עון פלילי. Syr. reads עין 'eye' instead of עון.

V. 11 does not form a verse properly speaking. It cannot be improved with the help of G (cf. sup.), and it is quite arbitrary to add חַטָא 'sin' or דָּבָר 'thing' (Ley) before זִמָּה. Equally arbitrary is the addition וְסָרָה 'and a falling off, betrayal' after זמה (Duhm, who would support this supposition by G ἀκατάσχετος!). The phrase כִּי־הִיא זִמָּה (*qerê*) 'for this is a shameless deed' recalls זמה היא 'this is a shameless offence' (Lv 18:17; 20:14). It is a reflection of a general kind which does not

12   For it is a fire which devours even unto Abaddon,
      And all my harvest would it *consume*!
13   If I disregarded the right of my manservant
      And of my maidservant, when they disputed with me,

12   תְּשָׂרֵף; MT תשרש.

belong to Job. It is in v. 12 that
Job, by means of a forceful image,
will describe the nature of the sin
from which he defends himself.
The expression עֲוֹן פְּלִילִים would
mean: 'a fault that must be submitted to the judges'; cf. פְּלִילִים
'judges' in Ex 21:22. It is probable,
as the vocalisation suggests, that
we should read עָוֹן פְּלִילִי (cf. Targ.
and Vulg.), as in v. 28, which gives
a very natural meaning: a criminal
fault, coming under the jurisdiction
of the courts (*criminalis* from *cri-
men*). The statement: 'and it is a
criminal misdeed' reinforces the first
gloss: 'for this is a lewd action'.

12 G renders עַד־אֲבַדּוֹן by ἐπὶ
πάντων τῶν μερῶν (Jerome *in omnibus membris*). It is a periphrasis of
'even unto Abaddon, to the very
bottom'. For אבדון, Targ. and Syr.
אבדנא, Vulg. *perditionem* (cf. 26:6;
28:22). Instead of תבואתי, G οὗ δ'ἂν
ἐπέλθῃ reads תָּבוֹא.

V. 12 explains Job's horror at the
sin of adultery. We have seen that
Abaddon was a synonym of Sheol
(26:6; 28:22) and that Sheol was
situated under the earth (7:9).
Abaddon or Sheol well expresses the
idea of ultimate depths (11:8). With
the 1st hemistich, cf. Dt. 32:22a,
'For a fire has been kindled by my
wrath and it burns even to the
nether Sheol.' The 2nd hemistich
should be translated: 'and it uproots all my produce', the *pi'el* of
שרש having the sense of 'uproot'; cf.
the *pu'al* in v. 8. But it is not the
work of fire to uproot. If we compare
with Is 47:14, we shall not hesitate

to read תְּשָׂרֵף (Duhm) instead of
תשרש, the ב"י before כל being ex-
plainable by the partitive meaning
(21:25). In the light of Dt 32:22b,
where the fire kindled by God
'devours the earth and its fruits', it
is clear that תְּבוּאָתִי does not mean
merely 'my revenues, incomings'
(22:21) but specifically 'the revenue
of my land', 'my produce, yield'.
This is one of the most frequent
connotations of תְּבוּאָה. One cannot
avoid comparing with Pr 6:27-9,
where adultery is likened to a fire
and burning thistles.

13   The 2nd hemistich is omitted in
Jerome (Tur.).
Job has not violated the claims
of justice in his relations with his
neighbour (v. 9). He was careful
to fulfil its demands also in his own
household. In 19:15-16 he described the attitude of his manservant and maidservants after he
had been visited by calamity. And
yet he had not swerved from justice
in his dealings with them. By the
exigencies of the rhythm, the *athnaḥ*
should be placed under עַבְדִּי. The
verb מאס 'to despise' with an abstract complement (5:17; 9:21).
Note the use of משפט in the sense
of 'the right' (8:3; 29:14). In בְּרִבָם
we may see either the infinitive of
ריב 'dispute', 'contest a point'
(9:3; 10:2, etc.) or the noun רִיב
(29:16; cf. inf. v. 35). The meaning
remains the same; when they disputed with me. The rights of slaves
were reduced to a minimum in
Hebrew law (Ex 21:1-11). Job

14   What shall I do when God arises,
      And when He inspects, what shall I answer Him?

15   Was it not He who made me who made him in the womb also,
      And was it not He alone who formed us in the womb?

admits that the slave has the right to argue with or press a claim against his master.

14 Syr. introduces v. 14 by the phrase: 'but I have said'. G ἐὰν ἔτασίν μου ποιῆται and Vulg. *cum surrexerit ad judicandum* clarify the meaning of יָקוּם.

The opening וּמָה, as in v. 2, welds together the two parts of the argument. The verb קוּם is well chosen to convey the idea that God rises up to judge humanity (Ps 76: 10). Cf. the use of the same verb in 16: 8; 19: 25; 30: 11. The verb פקד 'visit', 'inspect' (5: 24; 7: 18) is just the one that is normally used to suggest the trial which God imposes on mankind, and the sanctions which follow this process (35: 15). The *hiph'il* of שׁוב with the sense of 'reply' (13: 22). Duhm proposes to place v. 14 before v. 18 in order to obtain two strophes of four hemistichs: 16-17 and 14-18. But v. 15 is connected with vv. 13-14, just as v. 12 is joined to vv. 9-10, in order to give the reasons which have guided the conduct of Job.

15 G avoids anthropomorphism by a paraphrase of the 1st hemistich: πότερον οὐχ ὡς καὶ ἐγὼ ἐγενόμην ἐν γαστρί, καὶ ἐκεῖνοι γεγόνασιν; The participle and the perfect of עשׂה are reversed in the word order of Vulg. *fecit me qui et illum operatus est.* G again translates ויכננו by γεγόναμεν δέ. Vulg. *et formavit me in vulva unus* makes of אֶחָד the subject of יכננו (read as יְכֹנְנוּ), while the other versions regard it as an epithet of רחם.

V. 15 explains why Job respected the rights of his subordinates. The clause is introduced by הֲלֹא (vv. 3-4), which replaces the כי of v. 12. We have here an allusion to the formation of the foetus in the maternal womb. Cf. 10: 8ff. and see Comm. on 10: 10. The slave and his master are equal as regards the mode of their conception and birth as they are also in death (3: 17-19). The reason is that they are made by one and the same Creator. Note the use of בֶּטֶן 'belly' to denote the maternal womb (3: 10; 10: 19; 15: 35). The verb עשׂה is used as in 10: 8-9. The Massoretic vocalisation is right in placing the article before רֶחֶם, which enables us to see in אֶחָד not an epithet of רחם but the subject of יכננו: 'Is it not He alone who has shaped us in the womb?' The slave and the master are not fashioned in one and the same womb, but by the same Creator. God alone can form the embryo and guide its development to completion (cf. Comm. on 10: 10). The verb used is the *po'lel* of כון, with the omission of a *nun* to avoid having three times in succession the same letter: יְכֹנְנֵנוּ becomes יְכֹנֵנוּ. (Gesenius-Kautzsch, § 72cc). The *po'lel* of כון has the meaning of 'dispose', 'prepare', exactly like the *hiph'il* in 15: 35, where the subject is בטנם 'their belly' (cf. Comm.). Hence it is a question of arranging the parts of the foetus so as to compound out of it a whole, i.e. to organise and shape the structure of the human body. Cf. Dt 32: 6, הוא עשׂך ויכננך 'it is He who has made you and fashioned you'; Ps 119: 73, ידיך עשׂוני ויכוננוני 'Thy hands have made me and fashioned me'. The progression between 'make' (עשׂה) and 'fashion'

16   Did I refuse to the poor what they desired,
     And did I allow the widow's eyes to languish?
17   Did I eat my morsel of bread alone,
     While the orphan had none?
18   On the contrary, from my childhood *I brought up the one* like
        a father,
     And from my mother's womb I guided the other!

18   אֲגַדְּלֶנּוּ; MT: גדלני.

(כונן) is found in our verse as also in these texts.

16 G χρείαν ἥν ποτ' εἶχον paraphrases חפץ. For אכלה, Vulg. *expectare feci*.

After the works of justice, those of mercy. We regard אם of the opening as interrogative (v. 5): 'Did I refuse to the poor what they desired?' The construction of מנע with the accusative of the person who is refused, and the preposition מן before the thing that is refused (Nu 24: 11, Ec 2: 10). We have seen the converse construction in 22: 7. Job now refutes the allegations of Eliphaz in 22: 7-9. The word חֵפֶץ 'wish' is used to denote the object of desire, what one wishes (cf. Pr 3: 15). The דַּלִּים denotes the 'poor', 'weak', 'underprivileged' (20: 10, 19), types of which category are the widow and the orphan (22: 9; 24: 3). The *pi'el* of כלה means 'make languishing' or 'allow to languish' the eyes of some one (Lv 26: 16; cf. the *qal* in 11: 20; 17: 5).

17 The words ἐξ αὐτοῦ, a translation of ממנה, omitted in G (B, A) and Sah., are marked with asterisk in Cod. 255, Syro-hex., and Jerome. They have been restored in G (C, א c·a), Memph.

The verbs are still dependent on the interrogative אם of v. 16. The oriental must not eat alone: a meal is truly a *coena*, a communal action. In To 4: 16 we find ἐκ τοῦ ἄρτου σου δίδου πεινῶντι, which is inspired by Is 58: 7. The word פַּת, with or without לֶחֶם as determining word, denotes the morsel of bread: the root פתת 'to break' (Lv 2: 6). The verb אכל has the partitive מן before the complement (cf. Gn 2: 16, 17, etc.).

18   V. 18, absent from Sah., marked with asterisk in Jerome and Syro-hex., did not exist in G. The present text derives from Theod. (cf. Colb. and Syro-hex.). Theod. ἐξέτρεφον and ὡδήγησα omits the suffixes of גדלני and אנחנה. Vulg. *crevit mecum miseratio* and Syr. ܐܚܫܘܒ ܪܚܡܬ 'sorrows have brought me up' vocalise כְּאָב instead of כְּאָב, which obliges Vulg. to render אנחנה by *egressa est mecum*, while Syr. ܐܢܫܬܐ 'groans' will connect אנחנה with the root אנח. Targ. דברני בניחותא 'he has led me into peace' derives אנחנה from the verb נוח.

V. 18 forms the conclusion of vv. 16-17, just as v. 15 concluded vv. 13-14 and v. 12 vv. 9-10. This arrangement is sufficient to exclude the hypothesis of Duhm, who destroys the whole symmetry by placing v. 14 before v. 18, so as to make God the subject of the verbs, which become גִּדְּלַנִי 'He has trained me' and נָחַנִי 'He has guided me' (these corrections had been already proposed by Merx). Let us note in the first place that מִנְּעוּרַי 'from my

19   If I saw a wretch without clothing,
      And a poor man without a coat,
20   Did not his loins bless me,
      And was he not warmed by the fleece of my lambs?

youth' (cf. 13: 26) and מִבֶּטֶן אִמִּי 'from my mother's womb' (cf. 1: 12) are peculiar to Job and cannot be changed to מנעוריו 'from his youth' and מבטן אמו 'from his mother's womb' (contra Hoffmann). The verse alludes to actions which Job was in the habit of performing from his earliest years. The expression כְּאָב 'like a father', in the 1st hemistich, shows that the orphan of v. 17 is the object of one of these actions, while אַנְחֶנָּה 'I guided her' in the 2nd hemistich indicates as the object of the second action the widow mentioned in v. 16. Job has already boasted of his kindness to the widow and orphan in 29: 12-13. A slight change, suggested by parallelism, restores to the verse its natural meaning: a reading אֲגַדְּלֶנּוּ (cf. 7: 17) instead of גדלני. It is thus that the verse is read by Graetz, Grimme, Budde. The *pi'el* of גדל, in the sense of 'to make grow up', 'to rear', is the very word used for the action of bringing up children (Is 1: 2; 23: 4, etc.). The widow has no need to be brought up. It is enough to guide her steps through life. This is connoted by the *hiph'il* of נחה (38: 32). The conjunction כִּי answers the interrogation of vv. 16-17, just as in 22: 2. In order to avoid all ambiguity we have tried to clarify the suffixes: the one (the orphan) and the other (the widow). We note that without venturing to change the text Le Hir discovered its true meaning: 'No, from my childhood, like a father have I reared him; while from my mother's womb, I have guided the steps of the widow.' There is hyperbole in Job's apology when he implies that

he has not waited for the age of discretion to render services which are expected from a full-grown man.

19 G renders אוֹבֵד מִבְּלִי לְבוּשׁ by γυμνὸν ἀπολλύμενον and וְאֵין כְּסוּת by καὶ οὐκ ἠμφίασα αὐτόν. The word לָאֶבְיוֹן will be rendered ἀδύνατοι δὲ in v. 20. Jerome *non habentem velamen* (with asterisk) stems from a reading cited in the margin of Syrohex. with the mention 'not in Origen's copy'.

'If I saw a wretch without clothing'; cf. 29: 13, where the word אֹבֵד 'perishing of want' is associated with יתום 'orphan' and אלמנה 'widow', which in our context have been mentioned in vv. 16-18. Parallelism between מִבְּלִי לְבוּשׁ and אֵין כְּסוּת as in 24: 7. The style changes in the 2nd hemistich, the proposition literally repeating 26: 6b with לָאֶבְיוֹן instead of לָאֲבַדּוֹן. Compare, for the sequence of ideas between 17-18 and 19-20, the precepts of Is 58: 7 and To 4: 16, already cited in connection with v. 17. It is apparent that charity includes the sharing of bread with the needy and of clothing with him who is naked. Same series of obligations in Ezk 18: 7. Cf. Mt 25: 35-6; 37-8. The word כְּסוּת 'what hides, covers' in the sense of a coat (24: 7).

20 G ἀδύνατοι δὲ comes from לָאֶבְיוֹן, which is not translated in v. 19, while the close οἱ ὦμοι αὐτῶν is an interpretation of חֲלָצוֹ. Syr. confuses the verb בֵּרְכוּנִי with the noun בִּרְכִּי 'my knees'.

The expression אִם־לֹא has interrogative sense (cf. v. 31). By the

21   If I have shaken my hand to threaten an orphan,
      Because I knew that I was supported in the gate,
22   Then let my shoulder fall from its nape of neck,
      And my arm become detached from its humerus!

use of an admirable figure of speech the part of the body which benefits from the gift is personified. In 29: 13 Job said that the blessing of the needy rose up towards him. On the word חֲלָצַיִם 'lumbar region', 'loins', which will recur in 38: 3; 40: 7, cf. *L'Emploi métaphorique*, pp. 131f. The word גֵּז, from גזז 'cut off', 'shear' (1: 20), denotes the fleece (Latin *tunsio* from *tundere*); cf. Dt. 18: 4 גֵּז צֹאנְךָ 'the fleece of thy flock', the word צֹאן meaning especially the smaller cattle, like sheep and goats (1: 3). The *hithpaʻel* of חמם does not appear elsewhere.

21   For עַל־יָתוֹם, G simply ὀρφανῷ, but the preposition ἐπ' is restored in Syro-hex. (with asterisk) and in Jerome *super*. Similarly Syro-hex. and Jerome place the suffix (preceded by asterisk) after χεῖρα, which translates יָדִי in G. The 2nd hemistich is paraphrased *etiam cum viderem me in porta superiorem* in Vulg. The text of G πεποιθὼς ὅτι πολλή μοι βοήθεια περίεστιν comes perhaps from a reading תִּשָּׁאֵר instead of בשער (Ball). Syr. regards עזרתי as a verb: 'I have helped him'.

The *hiphʻil* of נוף has the meaning of 'to shake' the hand against some one in minatory fashion (Is 11: 15; 19: 16; Zec. 2: 13): 'if I have shaken my hand to threaten an orphan'. The change from עַל־יָתוֹם to עֲלֵי־תָם 'against a perfect man' (Graetz, Duhm, Budde) is not more felicitous here than in 6: 27. Note that, in 29: 12, the orphan is in the company of the wretched one, אֹבֵד (v. 19), and of 'him whom none

help' (cf. 2nd hemistich). Job has refrained from abusing his importance in the city, and the support which the judges were accustomed to give him. The 2nd hemistich would be, translated literally: 'when I saw my support in the gate', i.e. when I saw that I was supported by the tribunal. The idiom: בַּשַּׁעַר 'in the gate' to connote the place where justice is administered (5: 4). Job has already alluded to the primary part which he played in the assemblies of the forum (29: 7). It is before the tribunal that the unfortunate run the risk of being crushed by the powerful (5: 4).

22   For מִקְנֶה, G (B, א) ἀπὸ τοῦ ἀγκῶνος (Syro-hex.), but G (A, C) adds μοῦ (Sah., Jerome). Vulg. renders מִקְנֶה by *cum suis ossibus*.

The imprecation of v. 22 is governed by the hypothesis of v. 21; same relation as in 7-8 and 9-10. The *raphê* on the final ה of שִׁכְמָה and of קָנֶה indicates the elimination of the *mappiq* which ought to be in the consonant of the 3rd person feminine singular suffix (Gesenius-Kautzsch, § 91e). On the distinction between שְׁכֶם 'nape of the neck' and כָּתֵף 'shoulder', cf. *L'Emploi métaphorique*, p. 93. The form אֶזְרוֹעַ for זְרוֹעַ recurs only in Jer 32: 21. In Aramaic we meet דרע and אדרע. The word קָנֶה 'reed' (40: 21) denotes sometimes the beam of the balance (Is 46: 6). If the arms are stretched out, it becomes apparent that the humerus corresponds to the beam of the balance, while the hand corresponds to the scale (*L'Emploi métaphorique*, p. 150). Hence קָנֶה

23   For the fear of *God came upon ne,*
     And I could not stand before the divine majesty!

24   Have I made of gold the ground of my confidence,
     And have I said to pure gold: 'My security!'

23   אֶל יָאתָא לִי (cf. G, Vulg., Syr.) ; MT : אֵלִי אֵיד אֵל.

will be used for the humerus: 'and
may my arm be detached from its
humerus!' The *niph'al* of שבר
recurs, with זרוע 'arm' as its subject,
in 38: 15b (cf. 24: 20). The presence
of the complement preceded by
מן shows that what the author has
particularly in mind is a fall occasioned by rupture. That is why we
translate תִּשָּׁבֵר by 'become detached'.

The law of retaliation operates with
regard to culpability. The arm has
been guilty (v. 21), thus it is the arm
that must be punished. Similarly,
in vv. 8 and 10, the nature of the
punishment depended on the nature
of the fault.

23   Vv. 23b-24a, absent from Sah.,
marked with asterisk in Jerome and
Syro-hex., did not exist in G. The
present text derives from Theod.
(cf. Syro-hex.). Syr. twice translates
v. 23a. For פַּחַד אֵלִי, G φόβος Κυρίου
(Κυρίου omitted in B), that is, פַּחַד אֵל
Vulg. *semper enim quasi tumentes
super me fluctus timui Deum* transposes אֵל and אֵלִי, then interprets
אֵיד in the sense of אֵד (cf. 30: 12).
The reading פַּחַד אֵל, presupposed
by G and Vulg., is confirmed by
Syr. 'the fear of God'. Instead of
אֵיד אֵל, G συνέσχεν με and Syr. (2°)
ܐܚܕ ܠܝ read יָאתָא לִי (cf. inf.).
Theod. interprets מִשְּׂאֵתוֹ by ἀπὸ τοῦ
λήμματος αὐτοῦ, Targ. by מן מספייה
'because of His fear'. Syr. paraphrases the 2nd hemistich: 'and
because of fear I was not able to rise'.
Vulg. assigns to שְׂאֵתוֹ the sense of
'support him', 'lift him', whence:
et pondus ejus ferre non potui.

As it stands, the 1st hemistich
ought to be translated: 'for a terror
for me was the misfortune (which
came) from God', from which are
derived: 'for I have always feared
the vengeance of God' (Le Hir) or
'always, in fact, have I feared the
blows which God strikes' (Renan).
But in 13: 11 we had parallelism
between שְׂאֵתוֹ. 'His majesty' and
פַּחְדּוֹ 'His fear', which makes almost
irresistible here the reading פַּחַד אֵל
'the fear of God' (G, Vulg., Syr.) instead of פַּחַד אֵלִי. The final *yod* of
אֵלִי belonged to the following word.
If we juxtapose the letters, we get
יָאידְאֵל, which is a corruption of
יָאתָא לִי (Duhm, Budde, Hontheim,
Beer) attested by G and Syr. The
verb אתא recurs in Dt 33: 21 and
Is 21: 12. It corresponds to אתה
(3: 25; 16: 22; 30: 14), but retains
its Aramaic formation. Its meaning
is the same as the Hebrew בוא
(Comm. on 3: 25). It will be noticed
that the word פחד is the subject of
ויאתיני in 3: 25. The verb יכל means
not only 'to be able' but also 'to
hold out', 'to resist' (Gn 30: 8; 32:
26, 29, etc.). V. 23 serves as an introduction to vv. 24-5. It is the fear
of God and not the love of wealth
which guides the conduct of Job.
We see no reason to transfer this
verse to a position after v. 14
(Bickell) or after v. 28 (Duhm).

24   On the text of G, cf. v. 23. The
reading of Theod. εἰς χοῦν μου,
preserved as the text of G, is a corruption of ἰσχύν μου (Compl., Ald.);
cf. Jerome and Vulg. *robur meum.*

25   Did I rejoice because my fortune was great,
      And because my hand had gained much?
26   Is it that, when I saw the sun shining
      And the moon advancing in splendour,

The 2nd hemistich is twice translated in Syr. For לכתם, Theod. λίθῳ πολυτελεῖ, Vulg. *obrizo*, Targ. לפטלון (Greek πέταλον, cf. 28: 16, 19), Syr. (1°) חלא מאפא לחאֿ 'on the precious stone', (2°) חלא מבֿחֿ 'on pure gold'.

Again the interrogative אִם (vv. 5, 16, 20). The verb שִׂים with a double accusative, to connote that one makes of one thing something else. Cf. the use of שִׂים in Ps 40: 5, 'he who has made Yahweh his trust'. Parallelism between כֶּסֶל 'confidence' and מִבְטָח 'security' recurs in 8: 14. On כֶּתֶם, cf. 28: 16, 19. Although the word is synonymous with זָהָב 'gold', it is preferred to denote the idea of fine or pure gold (ibid.). To vary the style, Job introduces direct speech in the 2nd hemistich (cf. 17: 14). The Psalms condemn him who puts his trust in riches rather than in God: 'This is the man who makes not God his refuge and who trusts in the abundance of his riches' (Ps 52: 9); 'those who trust in their wealth and boast of the abundance of their riches, not one of them is able to ransom his brother, nor to give to God the price of his own ransom' (Ps 49: 7-8). Cf. also Pr 11: 28, 'He who trusts in his riches will fall, while the just flourish like the leaves.'

25   G translates וכי by εἰ δὲ καί, just like the אם of the opening, which has the effect of distorting the sense of the 2nd hemistich, regarded as parallel to the 1st instead of being merely parallel to כי־רב חילי. For כביר, G ἀναριθμήτοις, Vulg. *plurima*, Targ. בסוגעא 'in quantity', Syr. סגֿי 'much'.

The verse is parallel to v. 24 and the opening אם is interrogative. It is not clear why Hitzig would suppress this v. 25. The verb שמח with כי before the clause which expresses the object of joy; the same construction as in 3: 22. With כִּי־רַב חֵילִי cf. כי־רב זרעך in 5: 25. On חַיִל 'fortune', cf. 5: 5; 15: 29, 20: 15. The object of confidence was precisely חֵילָם 'their fortune', parallel to רב־עשרם 'abundance of their riches' in Ps 49: 7, which we quoted in connection with v. 24. The 2nd hemistich forms a clause parallel to כי־רב חילי. The word כַּבִּיר 'great' (8: 2; 15: 10) means also 'much' (Is 16: 14). Same phenomenon is found for רבב and its derivatives: 'to be many' and 'to be great'. The hand is the organ which receives money and holds wealth (*L'Emploi métaphorique*, pp. 147f). The verb מצא 'meet', 'find', with יָד as subject, to connote 'gain' something. In other contexts, the expression implies that the hand 'finds' what it needs, that a thing is found under one's hand (1 S 20: 7; 25: 8, etc.). It is not in wealth that Job has placed his hopes and his delight. He has in fact put into practice the advice of Eliphaz: 'For Shaddai Himself will be your ingots and heaps of silver for you' (22: 25).

26   G renders אם־אראה by ἢ οὐχ ὁρῶμεν. For אור, Syr. נוהֿסֿוֿ 'light', but G ἥλιον, Vulg. *solem*, Targ. אסתהר (ἀστήρ). After τὸν ἐπιφαύσκοντα, which translates כי יהל, G ἐκλείποντα derives from הלך of the 2nd hemistich. Then σελήνην δὲ φθίνουσαν renders וירח יקר, the word יקר being perhaps read as ירק 'pale'

27   My heart was secretly allured,
      And my hand kissed my mouth?

(Ball). Finally, οὐ γὰρ ἐπ’ αὐτοῖς
ἐστιν (Jerome *non enim in ipsis est*)
seems to be an explanatory gloss
which has crept into the text. For
יקר, Vulg. *clare*, Targ. זיותן 'brilliant'.
Syr. translates הלך in v. 27 and interprets יקר by ܣܟܒ (which has
become ܣܟܝ in Walton's Polyglot)
'dear', which is the epithet used
of the moon when it is at the
full.

The clauses of v. 27 are introduced
by the *waw* conversive, which co-
ordinates them with v. 26. In such a
case, the interrogative can very well
govern strictly the verbs of v. 27
while the verbs of v. 26 form subordinates. The syntax is the same
as in Is 5:4, 'Why have I waited
for it to bring forth grapes and it has
brought forth wild grapes?', that is,
why, when I was expecting it to
bring forth grapes, has it in fact
brought forth wild grapes? Similarly
in Nu 32:6, 'Will your brothers
come to fight and you will remain
here?', i.e. while your brothers
come to fight, will you remain here?
For other examples, cf. Gesenius-
Kautzsch, § 150m. The word אוֹר
'light', as a result of parallelism,
denotes the sun (37:21; Hab 3:4).
Cf. חַמָּה in 30:28. The verb יָהֵל as
in 25:5 where it was written יאהיל
with the *matres lectionis* (cf. Comm.)
and was applied to the moon, יָרֵחַ,
which we find here in our 2nd hemistich. The writer places before the
verb הלך an adjective which characterises the state or the attitude
of the one who walks; cf. 24:10;
30:28. The word יָקָר 'dear', precious' (28:10, 16) is especially used,
like the Assyrian *aqartu*, in speaking
of precious stones. Whence the
meaning 'splendid', which is most
appropriate to the moon proceeding
majestically through the sky.

27 V. 27a, absent from Sah.,
marked with asterisk in Jerome and
Syro-hex, did not exist in G. The
present text derives from Theod.
(cf. Syro-hex.). Syr. puts at the
beginning הלך of v. 26. For יפת,
Theod. ἠπατήθη, Symm. ἐπλατύνθη,
Vulg. *laetatum est*, Syr. ܐܠܬܦܝ 'has
been enticed', but Targ. שרגג 'has
enticed'. G εἰ δὲ χεῖρά μου ἐπιθεὶς
ἐπὶ στόματί μου ἐφίλησα paraphrases
the 2nd hemistich. Similarly Vulg. *et
osculatus sum manum meam ore meo*.

A comparison with Dt 11:16,
'take care that your heart be not
enticed', where we have the *qal* יִפְתֶּה,
proves that the verb פתה can have,
in the *qal*, the meaning of being enticed (cf. the participle in 5:2) and
that it is not necessary to replace the
וַיִּפְתְּ by the *niph'al* of v. 9, as is
proposed by Beer. The testimony
of Targ. favours the Massoretic
vocalisation, and the other versions
have translated according to the
sense. The idiom בַּסֵּתֶר 'in secret'
(13:10), to express the stealthy
character which marks idolatrous
cults. The 2nd hemistich: 'and my
hand kissed my mouth' although
the kiss is the action of the mouth,
and not of the hand. It is the hand
which, in the gesture of adoration
(*adorare* from *ad os*) is placed on the
mouth. Among the Assyrians and
Babylonians, the ideogram conveying the conception of prayer represents the hand on the mouth (*La
religion assyro-babylonienne*, pp.
247f.) and thus makes clear the
original form of adoration (ibid.). It
is unnecessary to dwell on the cult
of the sun and the moon in Egypt,
in Chaldaea, in Assyria, among the
Arabs and the other Semites (cf.
Lagrange, *ÉRS*, pp. 45off.). It was
in particular since the time of Manasseh that astral religions had pene-

28   That again would have been a criminal fault,
     Since I should have denied the God who reigns on high!
29   Did I rejoice in the misfortune which overtook my enemy,
     And did I exult because evil had struck him?
30   I did not even allow my palate to sin,
     By asking for his life with a curse!

trated the land of Judah (2 K 21 : 3ff.).
In Dt 4 : 19 the people of Israel are
warned against the worship of the
sun, moon, and stars. Cf. Jer 8 : 1-2;
2 K 23 : 5.

28 For עֲוֹן פְּלִילִי, G ἀνομία ἡ
μεγίστη, Vulg. *iniquitas maxima,*
Targ. סוּרחָן פָּרִישׁ (cf. v. 11). Syr.
connects עֲוֹן with עֵין 'eye' and
translates: 'he too has seen my acts
of deceit'. G interprets אֶל מִמַּעַל by
Κυρίου τοῦ ὑψίστου; cf. Vulg. *Deum
altissimum.* Syr. omits מִמַּעַל.
V. 28 emphasises vv. 26-7 by
giving the reason for Job's avoidance of the cult of the stars. The
1st hemistich, anticipated in v. 11,
is here quite in place. Legal penalties
against the cult of the stars are
decreed in Dt 17:2-7. They explain
עֲוֹן פְּלִילִי *culpa criminalis* (cf. Comm.
on v. 11). The structure of the verse
is the same as in 13: 16, where the
1st hemistich begins by גַּם־הוּא and
the 2nd by the explanatory כִּי. We
translate by the conditional tense
since the fault stigmatised by Job is
purely hypothetical (cf. v. 12). The
pi'el of כחשׁ in the sense of 'deny'
(8: 18) with לְ instead of בְּ before
the complement. To deny or abjure
God is one of the most monstrous of
crimes (Jos 24: 27; Is 59: 13; Jer
5: 12). The word מִמַּעַל 'from on
high' (cf. v. 2 and 3: 4) ends by
becoming an epithet for God. The
author uses the expression because
the cult of the stars is in fact the
substitution of the creatures 'from
on high' (Ex 20: 4; Is 45: 8) for their
Creator.

29 For מַשְׂנְאִי, G (B, ℵ, C) ἐχθρῶν
μου (Sah.), but G(A) ἐχθροῦ μου
(Jerome and Syro-hex.). Then G
καὶ εἶπεν ἡ καρδία μου Εὖγε (A and C
add εὖγε) is an interpretation *quoad
sensum* of the 2nd hemistich (following Ps 35: 25).
The אִם is interrogative (vv. 5, 16,
20, 24, 25, 26). Note the resemblance
to v. 25, where we have אִם־אֶשְׂמַח
at the beginning and the verb מָצָא
in the 2nd hemistich. Outside Job
(12: 5; 30: 24; cf. 15: 23; 21: 20) the
word פִּיד 'misfortune' recurs only
in Pr 24: 22. 'Did I rejoice when
misfortune overtook my enemy?'
Job was a stranger to what the Ger-
mans call *Schadenfreude,* the delight
that is felt when misfortune strikes
one's enemy. He practises the counsel
of Pr 24: 17, 'Rejoice not at the fall
of your enemy, and let not your
heart exult when he stumbles!' In
Ex 23: 4-5 Israel is exhorted to help
the enemy in his difficulties. The
Psalmist complains because his adversaries rejoice over his fall (Ps
35: 15, 19-21). The *pi'el* participle of
שׂנא 'to hate' is normally used to
denote one who professes hatred,
in Latin *osor*; cf. the *qal* participle in
8: 22. The *hithpa'el* of עוּר in the
sense of 'exult' (cf. Comm. on 17: 8).
The verb מָצָא with רַע 'evil' as subject, as in Gn 44: 34, to imply the evil
which meets some one, the misfortune which overtakes him. Cf. 5: 18,
where רַע is the subject of נָגַע 'to
strike', and 30: 26, where it is the
subject of בוֹא 'to come', 'to happen'.

30 G deviates completely from the
MT: ἀκοῦσαι ἄρα τὸ οὖς μου τὴν κατά-

31   Have they not said, the people of my tent,
      'Who can be found who has not been satisfied with his meat?'

ραν μου, θρυληθείην δὲ ἄρα ὑπὸ λαοῦ μου κακούμενος. It looks as if G is reconstituting a text with fragments of the Hebrew: בְּאָלָה gives rise to τὴν κατάραν μου, לִשְׁאָל is read as לִמְשָׁל (whence θρυληθείην), רַע of v. 29 becomes κακούμενος, while אֹהֶלִי of v. 31 becomes ὑπὸ λαοῦ μου. Syr. 'and my soul has not required one of these things' reads בְּאֵלֶּה instead of בְּאָלָה and נַפְשִׁי instead of נַפְשׁוּ. Targ. and Vulg. are faithful to the MT.

The interrogative clauses of v. 29 imply a negative answer. That is why the speech is continued in a negative sentence. The palate, an organ of speech like the tongue, is responsible for sins in words (6: 30). The verb נתן with לְ before the infinitive means 'allow to' (Gn 20: 6; 31: 7, etc.). In 9: 18 the preposition was omitted (cf. Comm.). The 2nd hemistich explains the 1st. The לְ before the verb שְׁאַל lends to the infinitive the implication of a real gerundive. The phrase שְׁאַל נֶפֶשׁ 'demand the soul of some one' implies that the curse is aimed at bringing about his death (1 K 19: 4; Jon 4: 8). Imprecation is commonly practised among orientals. Its object is often to compass the death of some one. Solomon is congratulated for not having demanded the soul of his enemy (1 K 3: 11).

31   G renders אִם־לֹא by εἰ δὲ καὶ πολλάκις and reads אָמַהֹתִי, αἱ θεράπαιναί μου, instead of מְתֵי, the complement אֹהֲלִי having been transferred to v. 30 (q.v.). The omission of לֹא in the 2nd hemistich brings about the translations: τίς ἂν δῴη ἡμῖν τῶν σαρκῶν αὐτοῦ πλησθῆναι (G) and quis det de carnibus ejus ut saturemur (Vulg.). Syr. reads וְלֹא.

The opening אִם לֹא is interrogative (v. 20). With מְתֵי אָהֳלִי 'the men of

my tent' to suggest those who live with Job, cf. מְתֵי סוֹדִי 'the men of my confidence' to mean 'my confidants' in 19: 19. The people of the tent are opposed to גֵּר 'the alien' and אֹרַח 'the passer-by' of v. 32. The former are the members of the tribe or family (cf. 8: 22). The Arabic اهل, which corresponds to אֹהֶל, designates family and kin. The 2nd hemistich has been variously interpreted. Critics have thought they should see in בְּשָׂרוֹ 'his flesh' Job's own flesh, in accordance with 19: 22b, which resembles our text. Hence the following paraphrase has been suggested: 'May it please heaven that no enemy be sated with his flesh!' (cf. Hitzig). Ehrlich sees in 'his flesh' that of the enemy mentioned in v. 29: 'May it please heaven that we be never satiated with his flesh!', i.e. that we never have too much of it. This would indicate a contrast between the conduct of Job (v. 29) and the demands for vengeance which he would be accustomed to hear from his kinsmen. According to Jacob (ZATW, 1912, p. 287), we ought to interpret מבשרו 'of his flesh' in a figurative way: 'of his kin': is there any one among his kinsmen who is not sated? We ought certainly to note that v. 31 is closely joined to v. 32 by the following progression of ideas: family, alien, passer-by. All have had occasion to be gratified by the benefits which Job had conferred on them. To those who had no place of refuge (v. 32) he offered the hospitality of his tent. To those who already enjoy the protection of his tent he offers food. The peak of generosity is to kill sheep in honour of the guests. It thus becomes apparent that בשרו means 'his meat' that which he offers to his friends. The word נִשְׂבָּע

32   No stranger spent the night without shelter,
      But I opened my doors *to the passer-by*.
38   If my land has cried out against me,
      And my furrows have wept with it,

32 לָאֹרַח (G, Aq., Vulg., Targ.); MT: לָאֹרַח.
33-37 After 38-40.
34 הֲמֹון; MT: הָמֹון.

is the *niph'al* participle forming the
complement of מִי יִתֵּן (cf. v. 35)
and מבשׂרו is the complement of
נשׂבע (19: 22). We might imitate
the Hebrew with the help of Latin:
quis det de carne ejus non satiatum?

32 Aq. translates גר by προσήλυτος.
Instead of לָאֹרַח 'on the road',
G παντὶ ἐλθόντι, Aq. ὁδοιπόρῳ, Vulg.
viatori, Targ. לְאַכְסַנְיָא (ξένος) have
certainly read לָאֹרַח (cf. inf.).
G ἀνέῳκτο and Vulg. *patuit* replace
אפתח by יִפְתַּח.

The question of v. 31 is continued
by a negative sentence (cf. 29-30).
It is not only that the people in the
immediate entourage of Job have
profited by his liberality, but strangers themselves have had cause to
be gratified by it: 'No stranger
spent the night without shelter.'
The גֵּר is the stranger or alien who
seeks refuge (19: 14-15). The verb
לין 'spend the night' in its literal
sense (cf. 17: 2; 19: 4). The parallelism between גֵּר and אֹרַח in Jer
14: 8 is sufficient to justify the
reading לָאֹרַח of the versions, instead of לָאֹרַח 'on the road', which
is here meaningless. The אֹרַח is the
passer-by (2 S 12: 4; Jer 14: 8; Sir
42: 3). It is also the guest who stays
one night; cf. מְלֹון ארחים 'shelter
for passers-by' (Jer 9: 1), the place
where they pass the night (מְלֹון
from לין). The law of hospitality
requires that one should retain the
traveller under one's roof, as soon as
night time arrives (Gn 19: 2; Jg

19: 15-16; Lk 24: 29). We insert at
this point vv. 38-40, which were
forgotten by the copyist and added
to the end of the chapter. Vv. 33-4
form the prelude to vv. 35-7, which
terminate the speeches of Job.

33-7 After 38-40a, b (cf. Intro.,
p. liii).

38 G and Syr. omit the suffix of
אדמתי. For ויחד, Vulg. renders excellently *et cum ipsa*.
    The natural link between v. 38
and v. 39 does not allow us to
accept the hypothesis of Duhm,
according to whom the complaints
of the land are aroused by the
failure to observe the year of release
(Dt 15), or the practice of forbidden
methods of sowing (Lv 19: 19). The
land protests because it has been
acquired by usurpation: *res clamat
domino!* The verb זעק 'to cry out'
(cf. the *hiph'il* in 35: 9) with עָלַי
'against me'; cf. 16: 10 'they open
their mouth against me'. The land
is personified. Earth has a mouth in
which it swallows innocent blood
that has been shed (Gn 4: 11) or the
guilty (Nu 16: 30). It cries as does
innocent blood (Gn 4: 10). It protests against him who has usurped
it. The 2nd hemistich forms a logical
sequel to the image conjured up in
the 1st. The adverb יַחַד 'likewise',
'also', i.e. 'with it' (3: 18; 6: 2;
21: 26; cf. Vulg. above). The word
תֶּלֶם 'furrow' will recur in 39: 10.
The form יִבְכָּיֻן in pause, as in Is
33: 7, where the verb is parallel to
צעקו (here תזעק).

39   Because I had eaten its fruits without paying
      And had caused the death of its owner,

40ab Then instead of wheat may thorns shoot up,
      And instead of barley foul-smelling weeds!

39 Vulg. well renders כחה by *fructus ejus*. G μόνος after ἔφαγον translates again יחד of v. 38. Syr. סבוֹאֵ֥ 'sad' certainly arises from the corruption of a word in which was contained סבֵּ֥ 'master' and which translated בעליה; cf. Targ. מרהא. G is in agreement with Targ. in rendering בעליה by a singular κυρίου τῆς γῆς. For הפחתי, G ἐλύπησα, Vulg. *afflixi*, Syr. וֹסַאܠ 'I have afflicted'. Targ. preserves the verb.

The use of the perfect marks the subordinate relation of v. 39 to v. 38. The conjunction אִם assumes the meaning of כִּי (7:13; 14:5). The word כֹּחָה 'its strength' exactly as in Gn 4:12, to denote what the strength of the earth produces, crops or fruit; cf. Comm. on 20:18. Moreover, we have חַיִל, synonymous with כֹּחַ, in parallelism with פְּרִי 'fruit' in Jl 2:22. To eat the produce of the soil without due payment is to profit from what belongs to others (20:15, 19). As in the case of אֲדֹנִים, the plural בְּעָלִים is sometimes regarded as a plural of majesty (Ex 21:29; Is 1:3). Thus has it been interpreted by G and Targ. (cf. sup.). Hence we may translate בְּעָלֶיהָ by 'its master', 'its owner'. What in fact is in question is the portion of land occupied by Job (v. 38) and, by hypothesis, the property of another. The verb נפח has the meaning 'breathe in' and 'breathe out', 'expire' (cf. Comm. on 11:20). In Mal 1:13 the *hiph'il* means 'blow' (cf. van Hoonacker, in loc.). With נֶפֶשׁ as the complement, the normal meaning would be 'to

cause him to breathe out his soul'. Thus the expression מפח־נפש means the action of giving up the ghost in 11:20. The various locutions in which נפש figured with the verb נפח or its derivatives were later weakened to mean no more than to be oppressed by sadness or stifled by pain. Whence, for the *hiph'il*, the meaning of 'sadden' some one. The versions have decided in favour of this latter meaning (cf. sup.). Targ. imitates the Hebrew, but we should note that the Aramaic favours the meaning 'to afflict' for the *hiph'il* of נפח and 'affliction' for the noun מפח; cf. Comm. on 11:20. In the light of Jer 15:9, where נָפְחָה נַפְשָׁהּ means 'she breathes out her soul', to depict the mother on the point of dying of grief, it seems that we may adopt for the 2nd hemistich the literal sense: 'and I have caused the soul of his master to be breathed out', while recognising at the same time that it is not necessarily a question of death, but rather of the distress or grief caused to the owner by an unjust act.

40a, b. Because of the parallelism, the versions have assigned to באשה the meaning of thorn: βάτος (G), *spina* (Vulg.), הזמי (Targ.), סבֵּ֥ל (Syr.). Symm. is less precise: ἀτελεσφόρητα 'which do not grow to maturity'.

The imprecation is aimed at the thing which has been the instrument of sin (cf. v. 10 and v. 22). The cultivated land will become like the land which is unsown and desolate, and which naturally produces thorns and brambles (Gn 3:18). Wheat (חִטָּה) and barley (שְׂעֹרָה) are the most appreciated of products. They

33 Have I like the common herd concealed my trangressions,
    Hiding my faults in my bosom,

34 Because I dreaded the *din of* the capital
    And the scorn of families terrified me,
    And so remained quiet and did not go out of doors?

34 הֲמוֹן‎; MT: הָמוֹן‎.

are coupled together in Dt 8:8 and
Jl 1:11. The use of תַּחַת as in 16:4.
The verb יצא 'shoot up' out of the
soil, speaking of plants which germinate and spring up (5:6; 14:2).
The *hapax* בָּאְשָׁה (from the root באש
'to have a foul smell') denotes a
fetid weed which grows in uncultivated soil. This is annual mercury,
called dead nettle or malodorous
nettle. The strophe consisting of
38-40a, b, terminates the apology
of Job. He will now show that he has
lived in broad daylight (33-4) and
that he has nothing to fear from an
examination of his conduct (35-7).
Far from having to hide away, he
can walk with his head erect. It is
here that vv. 33-7 are most naturally to be placed (cf. Intro., p. liii).

33 G sums up v. 33 thus: εἰ δὲ καὶ
ἁμαρτὼν ἀκουσίως ἔκρυψα τὴν ἁμαρτίαν μου. Targ. renders כאדם by
'like Adam', while Vulg. *quasi homo*
and Syr. اسِ اِنِسً interpret by 'like
a man'.

The אם of the opening is interrogative and the verb is in the perfect,
as in vv. 5, 24, 31. The *pi'el* of כסה,
to connote 'hide', 'dissimulate' a
fault; cf. Ps 32:5, where the complement of לֹא־כִסִּיתִי 'I have not
dissimulated' is עֲוֹנִי 'my fault' of our
2nd hemistich, and Pr 28:13, where
מכסה 'concealing' has as its complement פְּשָׁעָיו 'his transgressions'. As
regards the parallelism between
פְּשָׁעַי 'my transgressions' and עֲוֹנִי
'my fault', cf. Comm. on 10:6.
The phrase כְּאָדָם may mean 'like
Adam' (cf. Targ.) or 'like a man'

(in the manner of men); cf. Vulg.
and Syr. V. 33 is explained by v. 34,
where it is clear that the thought
is that of avoiding embarrassment
and confusion before others. Now,
it was from God that Adam hid his
fault, and one is bound to admit
that in the mouth of Job the phrase
'like Adam' seems too Jewish in
tone. We find כאדם in Hos 6:7
and Ps 82:7. The explanation of
van Hoonacker (commenting on
Hosea) fits both these passages:
like a man, i.e. 'vulgarly', without
going any further than the commonest human level. We can retain this
meaning for our text. Thus we avoid
such corrections as that to באדם
'in the midst of men' (Duhm) or
that to מאדם 'from men' (Graetz,
Perles). It is a spontaneous impulse,
a kind of common instinct, to seek
to hide one's faults from others. The
2nd hemistich is modelled on v. 30b,
the phrase לְטָמוֹן playing the part
of a gerund: 'my hiding'. The *hapax*
חֹב (from חבב 'to love') corresponds
to the Aramaic חוּבָּא (same root),
which translates the Hebrew חֵק
or חֵיק 'bosom', 'lap' (19:27); cf.
Levy, *Chald. Wörterbuch*, I, pp. 232f.
The nomads are accustomed to hide
in their breasts, for lack of pockets,
the objects which they carry about
with them. In order to avoid a tristich for v. 34, Duhm cuts out v. 33b
and replaces it by v. 34a. But the
parallelism between עוני and פשעי
is a good proof of the common
origin of the two hemistichs of v. 33.

34 G οὐ γὰρ διετράπην πολυοχλίαν
πλήθους corresponds to the 1st hemi-

35   Would that some one would listen to me!
      Behold! here is my signature! Let Shaddai answer me!
      As for the indictment which my adversary has drawn up,

stich, but distorts the meaning of כי.
Then τοῦ μὴ ἐξαγορεῦσαι ἐνώπιον
αὐτῶν is inspired by Ps 32:5, the
resemblance of which to v. 33 we
have already noted. Thus the text
of G fails to reflect v. 34b. Finally,
the 3rd hemistich is rendered εἰ δὲ
καὶ εἴασα ἀδύνατον ἐξελθεῖν θύραν μου
κόλπῳ κενῷ, which implies ואביון
instead of ואדם (cf. v. 20 of G) and
אצא instead of אֵצֵא, the words
κόλπῳ κενῷ explaining the meaning
thus obtained. Vulg. assigns to כי
the meaning of *si*, whence its translation of the 3rd hemistich: *et non
magis tacui, nec egressus sum ostium.*
Syr. vocalises אצא (like G) and
וְאָדָם instead of וְאָדָם: 'If I have
trodden under foot the strength of
many! On the contrary, many of the
families have shattered me and I
have turned no one out of doors!'
To complete its homily, Syr. adds:
'and I have not thought of the words
of the lips; the exhortations of God
have mortified me'. Targ. interprets
אערוץ by אתגבר 'I strengthened
myself', and המון רבה by רכפת גיותניא
'the multitude of the proud'.
    V. 34 gives the reason why Job
might have sought to conceal his
faults. On the verb ערץ, cf. Comm.
on 13:25. The word הָמוֹן is masculine and cannot be coupled with the
feminine רַבָּה. Albrecht proposes to
read רָב (*ZATW*, 1895, p. 318),
which furnished as text: 'a great
multitude' (2 Ch 13:8). Chajes
vocalises הֲמוֹן, construct state (cf.
Gesenius-Buhl, s.v.). This slight
modification permits us to translate
'the din of the capital', a phrase
confirmed by המון קריה 'noise of the
city' (39:7) and המון עיר 'noise of
the town' (Is 32:14). Ehrlich treats
רבה as an adverb, 'greatly', as in

Ps 78:15; 89:8. But then the clause
becomes over-emphatic: 'because I
greatly dreaded the crowd'. The
2nd hemistich explains the 1st. If
Job fears to appear in public it is
because he does not wish to expose
himself to scorn and contempt:
'and the scorn of families terrified
me'. The word בוז as in 12:5, 21.
The *hiph'il* of חתת with the sense of
the *pi'el* in 7:14 (cf. Jer 1:17). The
3rd hemistich shows the result of
shame: 'and I remained quiet and did
not go out of doors'. On the verb
דמם, cf. 29:21; 30:27. The verb
יצא with direct complement פֶּתַח
'door', instead of שַׁעַר of 29:7, because here it is a question of the
door of the house (v. 9) and not of
the gate of the town. Thus Job did
not fear to go out of his house, and
to appear in public. He had nothing
to hide. And now he demands the
greatest publicity for his conduct.
His final impulse will be to appeal
to the tribunal of God. He wishes
judgment to be given in the broad
light of day (vv. 35-7). Thus we
may discern the link between vv.
33-4 and the close of the chapter.

35   The 1st hemistich, absent from
Sah., marked with asterisk in Jerome
and Syro-hex., did not exist in G.
The present text derives from Theod.
(cf. Syro-hex.). It is by error that
the 2nd hemistich also has the
asterisk in Colb. and Jerome. It
exists in Sah., and is not marked
with asterisk in Syro-hex. The first
לי is omitted in Theod. and Syr. G
interprets the 2nd hemistich by
χεῖρα δὲ Κυρίου εἰ μὴ ἐδεδοίκειν
(Jerome *manum Domini si non
timui*). Targ. רגוגי 'my desire' and
Vulg. *desiderium meum* read תאותי
instead of תוי, while Syr. ܠܐܘܗ ܝ

'if it were' reads the Aramaic איתוי (Beer). G paraphrases the 3rd hemistich: συγγραφὴν δὲ ἦν εἶχον κατά τινος, and joins it to v. 36. Vulg. *et librum scribat ipse qui judicat* renders כתב by a subjunctive, as does also Syr. ܢܘܟܬܒ. The words איש ריבי are inverted in Syr. 'the judgments of man'.

The 1st hemistich is constructed on the pattern of v. 31b, the participle being the complement of מִי־יִתֶּן. The verb שמע has לְ before its complement (cf. 15: 17). The desire expressed by Job recalls 19: 23-4, where the solemn affirmations of vv. 25-7 were preceded by a similar wish. Job is conscious of now completing the statement of his case: 'Here is my signature! Let Shaddai answer me!' He has consistently wished to debate his case with God alone (13: 3). He has put forward the alternatives: 'Then call and I will answer, or else I will speak and Thou shalt reply!' (13: 22-3). In 23: 3 he sought to find God in order to expound his arguments in the divine presence (23: 4-7). But up to now God has remained silent (29: 20). Job has continued to speak alone and has said all that he has to say: 'Here is my signature!' It is now God's turn to speak: 'Let Shaddai answer me!' The תָּו is a sign with which God marks the forehead of those who are to be spared (Ezk 9: 4, 6; Rev. 7: 1ff.). Whence the verb in the *hiph'il* הִתְוִית 'thou shalt mark with a *taw*' in Ezk 9: 4. This sign is none other than the last letter of the alphabet having the sign of a cross. As in our days, the illiterate were accustomed to make the mark of a cross beneath a document in token of their signature. That is why we may translate תָּוִי by 'my signature'. It goes without saying that the expression is to be understood in the most general sense, and does not class Job as one of the illiterate. The sentence stops at v. 35b, after which we have a new idea, beginning at וְסֵפֶר and continuing in v. 36 (cf. G). Job has appended his signature to his apologia. But he is faced by his accuser (16: 7ff.). The סֵפֶר 'letter', 'document', 'book' sometimes denotes a legal document, such as the *libellum repudii*, the act of divorce (Dt 24: 1, 3; Is 50: 1) or the deed of purchase (Jer 32: 11-12, 14, 16). Here it is a question of the indictment drawn up by the hostile party. It is the formal charge. Job is not asking his adversary to write it down. That has already been done, and one cannot give to the perfect כָּתַב the meaning of the optative, 'may he write', as is done by Renan, Le Hir, etc. The relative אֲשֶׁר is understood before the verb. He who has written the indictment is אִישׁ רִיבִי 'my man in the case' or 'the man of my case' (cf. רב in 29: 16). Sometimes אִישׁ רִיב is taken as objective genitive: he with whom one wrangles (Jg 12: 2; Jer 15: 10). But here it is the opposing party, the man who draws up the formal indictment. There can be no doubt about the meaning of the 2nd hemistich: 'and the indictment which my adversary has drawn up'. Budde has no difficulty in showing the futility of the corrections which have been proposed for so clear a text. Graetz wished to read ובספר instead of וספר and to vocalise כָּתַב: 'and (who will give me) some one to write down my case?' This is involving one's self once more in the disadvantage occasioned by the translation of כתב as an optative (cf. sup.), Still more fantastic is the reading of Grimme (vocalisation כָּתֵב and substitution of יְיַשְׁרֵנִי for אִישׁ רִיבִי): here is a written document, may it justify me! Ley cuts out רִיבִי, which is the thematic word, and in which he sees

36 Shall I not wear it on my shoulder,
    Shall I not bind it as crowns about my head?

37 My steps in life will I recount unto him,
    Like a chief will I present myself before him!

only a gloss on סֵפֶר! Hence we leave the text intact, seeing that it presents no special difficulties, and look for the thought of the author rather than that of modern commentators who insist on correcting the text. Job is so completely convinced of his right that he knows in advance the futility of charges which might be drawn up against him. On the contrary, he will use the accusing document as an ornament and brandish it as a trophy (v. 36). We leave to 'my opposing party' its most general sense, for we do not know whether he means God or friends. It is the adversary as a general conception, a type, the שָׂטָן of Ps 109: 6.

36 G again summarises v. 36: ἐπ' ὤμοις ἂν περιθέμενος στέφανον ἀνεγίνωσκον. Vulg. renders אִם־לֹא by *ut* and עֲטָרוֹת by *quasi coronam*.

At the beginning אִם־לֹא interrogative (vv. 20, 31). The word שְׁכֶם 'nape of neck' (v. 22) means essentially the part of the body on which a burden is carried, and thus becomes synonymous with כָּתֵף 'shoulder' (*L'Emploi métaphorique*, pp. 93f.). To carry a thing on one's shoulder is to render it conspicuous, as in Is 22: 22 where 'the key of the house of David' is placed by God 'on the shoulder' (עַל־שִׁכְמוֹ) of His servant Eliakim. The 2nd hemistich makes clear that it is a question of something honourable. Far from blushing at the accusatory document, Job will roll it up to make of it crowns of glory for his head. The verb עָנַד recurs only in Pr 6: 21, where it refers to the teachings of parents: 'bind them constantly about your heart, tie them to your neck'. The sense of עָנַד, parallel to קָשַׁר, is not in any doubt. By a metathesis of consonants in the root, we get the word מַעֲדַנּוֹת 'bonds', 'ties' in 38: 31.

Note that in 19: 9 Job had complained that God had stripped him of his glory, removing the crown from his head. The word used for crown was עֲטָרֶת, the plural of which, עֲטָרוֹת, we have here. It is apparent that our 1st hemistich describes indeed an act of personal glorification. According to Hoffmann and Ehrlich, the suffixes refer not to סֵפֶר of v. 35, but to שְׁמַע, the meaning being that Job would be ready to place on his shoulders, like a darling child (Ehrlich), any one who would agree to listen to him. Such an interpretation might, if need be, suit the 1st hemistich. But how is it compatible with the image contained in the 2nd? Without disputing the fact that persons might be compared to a crown (Pr 12: 4; 17: 6), it must be admitted that they are not woven together to form crowns. The metaphor is one thing, and the material description implying that the object can lend itself to such a figure of speech is another. Now, the document, in the form of a roll, is perfectly appropriate to the image used by Job.

37 G καὶ εἰ μὴ ῥήξας αὐτὴν ἀπέδωκα, οὐθὲν λαβὼν παρὰ χρεοφιλέτου seems to have transformed מִסְפַּר צְעָדַי into כְּמוֹ נָגִיד and אִם לֹא פְּרַצְתִּי into כְּמוֹ נָשֶׁה 'like a creditor' (whence the paraphrase παρὰ χρεοφιλέτου = χρεωφιλέτου 'on the part of a debtor'). Vulg. *et quasi principi* makes of נָגִיד a complement of אֲקָרְבֶנּוּ.

40c   (The words of Job are ended.)

The verbal suffixes of v. 36 referred to the indictment of the adversary. Those of v. 37 refer to the adversary himself, the אִישׁ רִיבִי of v. 35. The verb הִגִּיד has a double accusative; cf. Comm. on 26: 4. In 14: 16 Job accepted the hypothesis that God was counting his steps. Above (v. 4) he has inquired whether God did not see his ways and count all his steps. The number of the steps is a way of conveying the idea of the sum total of a man's actions. The metaphor is thoroughly in harmony with the genius of Hebrew; cf. vv. 4-5, 7. Job does not fear to present himself before any one whomsoever (vv. 33-4). He is proud even of what his adversary might have invented by way of accusation (vv. 35-6). That is why he adds: 'like a chief will I present myself before him!' Not in the attitude of a guilty man but his head erect like an innocent one. The *pi'el* of קרב assumes a meaning similar to the *pi'el* of קדם in 30: 27 (with the personal suffix). It is impossible to translate 'I would present it', referring to the indictment, for it is surely evident that the suffix corresponds to that of אֲגִידֶנּוּ. The intransitive meaning for the *pi'el* of קרב is, moreover, attested by Ezk 36: 8, where קֵרְבוּ means 'draw near to', 'are on the point of . . .'. It is here that we must place the note 'The words of Job are ended' which is at present at the end of v. 40. Cf. the similar notes to Ps 72: 20 and Jer 51: 64. G transfers καὶ ἐπαύσατο Ἰὼβ ῥήμασιν to the beginning of ch. 32.

38-40a,b   After v. 32.

CHAPTER 32

1 And these three men ceased to answer Job because he was righteous in *their* eyes.

2 Then was kindled the anger of Elihu, the son of Barachel, the Buzite, of the family of Ram. Against Job was his anger kindled because the latter justified himself before Elohim,

Chapters 32-37 Speeches of Elihu: see Introduction, pp. livff. and xcviiiff.
1 בְּעֵינֵיהֶם (G, Symm., Syr.); MT: בעיניו.

32:1 Instead of שלשת האנשים האלה, G οἱ τρεῖς φίλοι αὐτοῦ in agreement with 2:11. Syr. paraphrases מענות by 'who sought to condemn him'. Instead of בעיניו, G ἐναντίον αὐτῶν, Symm. ἐπ' αὐτῶν, Syr. ܟܒܥܝܢܝܗܘܢ have read בְּעֵינֵיהֶם (cf. inf.).

'And these three men ceased to answer Job' presents a change of style which should be noted. Up to now, it was a question of the three friends (cf. G): 2:11ff. They now become personages almost foreign to the rest of the prose narrative. They are the three interlocutors in a debate. Note that in Ezk 14:14, 16, 18, the formula שלשת האנשים האלה 'these three men' is used to designate the three righteous persons: Noah, Job, Daniel. Note the construction of שבת with מִן and the infinitive (Jer 31:36; Hos 7:4). The end of the verse 'because he was righteous in his own eyes' does not give the reason for the silence which now descends on the three men who have argued with Job. The latter has unceasingly pleaded his innocence, and we know that he has consistently considered himself to be righteous. His friends have been unyielding up to the moment when Job, raising the tone of the debate, made his formal apology, his negative confession, without concerning himself with those who were engaged in discussion with him (31). He ended by appealing to the deity (31:35-7). The friends have now no reason to intervene. Their silence is interpreted as a recognition of the rectitude of Job, and this in itself implies too a condemnation of the God who can crush an innocent man (v. 3). This is what the reading of the original text was; it bore בְּעֵינֵיהֶם 'in their eyes' (G, Symm., Syr.); cf. Geiger, *Urschrift*, pp. 332f. If the discussion is closed, it is because Job 'is righteous in their eyes'. Elihu will not be able to tolerate this surrender.

2 For ויחר אף, Vulg. *et iratus indignatusque est*, then *iratus est autem* for חרה אפו of v. 2, *indignatus est* for חרה אפו of v. 3. G renders הבוזי by βουζείτης, which has become Σωβίτης in Sah. (as in v. 6), Ζωβίτης in Aristeas (Eusebius, *Praep. evang.* IX, 25). For the proper noun רם G(B, א) 'Ράμ, G(A 'Ραμά (Sah.) 'Ραμάν), G(C) 'Αράμ (Eth.); cf. Symm. Συρίας. We have ܪܡ in Syr. (cf. Syro-hex. ܪܡ. Targ. sees in רם substitute for אברהם 'Abraham'. After רם, G adds τῆς Αὐσείτιδος χώρας (1:1), marked with obelus in

472

3   And against his three friends his anger was kindled because
     they had not found any reply and thus had condemned *Elohim*.

3   הָאֱלֹהִים; MT: אִיּוֹב (scribal correction).

Jerome and Syro-hex. For מאלהים, Targ. מן אלהא, Syr. ܠܒ ܡ ܐܠܗܐ 'better than God', G ἐναντίον Κυρίου, Vulg. *coram Deo*.

The expression חרה אף, to connote that anger is aroused (cf. 19: 11), recurs three times in vv. 2-3. First in the most general sense, then analysing the object of the anger: Job (v. 2) and 'his three friends' (v. 3). The new speaker is called אֱלִיהוּא, also written אֱלִיהוּ (v. 4 and 35: 1). It is the name of the grandfather of Elkanah (1 S 1: 1), of a brother of David (1 Ch 27: 18), of a warrior of Manasseh (1 Ch 12: 21), of a Levite (1 Ch 26: 7). The substitution of אֱלִיאָב (1 Ch 6: 12) or of אֱלִיאֵל (1 Ch 6: 19) for אליהוא, as the name of the grandfather of Elkanah, proves that הוּא 'he' replaces a divine name in אֱלִיהוּא 'he is my God.' Cf. the name of the ancient king of Assyria *Ilu-šu-ma* 'he is God'. Elihu's father is בְּרַכְאֵל 'God has blessed', a name which reminds us of בֶּרֶכְיָה and בֶּרֶכְיָהוּ 'Yah, Yahu has blessed'—names which recur several times in the onomasticon of the Old Testament (cf. Βαραχίου in Mt 23: 35). On the name of Buz, cf. Intro. p. xxiii. The expression מִמִּשְׁפַּחַת 'of the family of . . .' as in Ru 2: 1, 3. The proper noun רָם is not an abbreviation of אֲרָם (Symm. Συρίας is due to a corruption of 'Ράμ into 'Αράμ; cf. sup.) It is the name of a person who is found among the descendants of Judah (Ru 4: 19; 1 Ch 2: 9-10, 25, 27). A new sentence begins at בְּאִיּוֹב and its pendant will be v. 3. Elihu is angry with Job 'because he justified himself before Elohim'. The *pi'el* of צדק with the

reflexive pronoun represented by 'his soul' as in Jer 3: 11. The connotation 'justify' will be assigned to the *pi'el* in 33: 32 (cf. the *hiph'il* in 27: 5). Of course in this context it is a question of justifying one's self by one's arguments as an accused person would do before his judge. Note the use of מֵאֱלֹהִים, as we have מֵאֱלוֹהַּ in 4: 17 and מֵאֵל in 35: 2, to connote 'in the presence of God', and not 'more than God' (cf. Comm. on 4: 17). In Jer 3: 11, which is quoted to justify the translation 'more than God', the parallel established is that between Israel and Judah. They are both in the position of the accused. Here we have the accused and the Judge. The relation of the two terms is no longer the same.

3   For רֵעָיו, G(B, C) φίλων, but G (אe·a, A) adds αὐτοῦ (Sah., Syro-hex.). Vulg. interprets מַעֲנֶה by *responsionem rationabilem*. The complement אֶת־אִיּוֹב is placed before וַיַּרְשִׁיעוּ by G and Syr., which occasions the introduction of the 3rd person singular suffix after וַיַּרְשִׁיעוּ. G καὶ ἔθεντο αὐτὸν εἶναι ἀσεβῆ translates the MT, supported by Targ., Syr., Vulg. A reading εὐσεβῆ has crept into G (אe·c, A*) and is noted in the margin of Syro-hex.

The opening: 'and against his three friends his anger was kindled' is complementary to 'against Job his anger was kindled' of v. 2. In the latter text, the cause of the anger was denoted by the preposition עַל followed by the infinitive (cf. 10: 7, where we have the same type of phrase with a slightly different meaning). Here the cause of the anger is introduced by עַל אֲשֶׁר 'for this reason', 'because' (2 S 3: 30). It

4   Now Elihu had waited, while *they were speaking* to Job, for they were older than he in days.

4 בְּדַבְּרָם; MT: בדברים.

is 'because they had not found any reply' that the anger of Elihu blazes forth. V. 5 will stress that 'there was no reply in the mouth of the three men'. The end of the verse is ambiguous, for one might translate 'and they had not condemned Job', making the negative apply to the consecutive verb (cf. 3: 10b) or 'and they had condemned Job', although they had found no adequate reply to his arguments. The latter interpretation has against it v. 1, in which the three men, far from condemning Job, are reduced to silence because they find that he is righteous (cf. Comm.). The former seems to consider the fact of their finding no adequate reply the equivalent of their not condemning him. But we should expect a less energetic verb: they no longer knew what to say, they remained quiet, etc. (cf. vv. 15-16). It has been proposed to correct וַיַּרְשִׁיעוּ to וִיצַדִּיקוּ 'and they justified Job' (Geiger, Buhl), following the reading εὐσεβῆ, which replaces ἀσεβῆ in some witnesses of G. But this tradition is very weak and has against it G(B, C), Syro-hex. (in the text), Jerome *impium*. It is clear that εὐσεβῆ is due to a correction of ἀσεβῆ. The corrector saw that there was a contradiction between καὶ ἔθεντο αὐτὸν εἶναι ἀσεβῆ, which translated וירשיעו, and ἦν γὰρ δίκαιος ἐναντίον αὐτῶν of v. 1. The Massoretic tradition regards the word אִיּוֹב as a 'correction of scribes', *tiqqun sopherîm*, intended to avoid the contact of the divine name הָאֱלֹהִים with the verb וירשיעו 'and they condemned'. We have met a similar phenomenon in 7: 20. At other times it was the pejorative verb that was changed (1: 5, 11; 2: 5, 9).

Hence we should not hesitate to see in אִיּוֹב an euphemism for הָאֱלֹהִים. It is God whom the three friends of Job condemn by their silence. By ceasing to make any reply to the unhappy man, they seem to admit that Job has been struck by calamity, in spite of his innocence, and this runs counter to the ineradicable prejudice that divine justice is manifested on this earth. Ehrlich points out quite rightly that, had it been a question of condemning Job, we should have had אֹתוֹ (in harmony with רֵעָיו) and not אֶת־אִיּוֹב. On the *hiph'il* of רשע in the sense of 'condemn', cf. 9: 20; 10: 2; 15: 6.

4 V. 4b, (from כִּי) absent from Sah., marked with asterisk in Cod. 248, Syro-hex., and Jerome (Bod.), did not exist in G. The present text derives from Theod. (cf. Syro-hex.). G δοῦναι ἀπόκρισιν Ἰώβ interprets אֶת־אִיּוֹב בדברים in the light of vv. 3 and 5, without its being necessary to presuppose לְהָשִׁיב (Duhm) after חכה. Vulg. *expectavit Job loquentem* is another attempt to assign a meaning to the MT. Symm. ἔπληξεν reads הִכָּה, Syr. ⲥⲃⲙⲁⲩ ⲟⲟⲁ 'he corrected' reads הֹכַח instead of חִכָּה (cf. Beer).

The MT 'and Elihu had waited for Job in words because they were older than he in days' yields with difficulty an acceptable meaning. Le Hir inverts the clauses: 'as they were older than he, he waited until Job had spoken'. Renan solves the problem by a free paraphrase: 'Now Elihu had not so far been able to reply because they were older than he.' According to v. 5, in which Elihu once again notes the silence on the part of the interlocutors of

5   And Elihu perceived that there was no further reply in the
     mouth of the three men, and his anger was kindled.
6   And Elihu, son of Barachel, the Buzite, spoke and said:
     I am tender in years,
     And you are aged,
     That is why I was afraid and feared
     To manifest to you my knowledge.

Job, it is apparent that the new speaker has waited for the close of the previous discussions. As he will say himself (vv. 6f.), he has not dared to speak while the older men were still speaking. Wright has well understood that we should vocalise בְּדַבְּרָם instead of בִּדְבָרִים. It is not essential to place אֶת־אִיּוֹב after בדברם, since חִכָּה governs the whole of the end of the sentence. The verb חכה in the *pi'el*, as in 3:21. The complement לְיָמִים 'in days' (v. 6 and 30:1) makes it clear that it is a question of men old in years rather than in wisdom; cf. v. 7.

5 V. 5, absent from Sah., marked with asterisk in Syro-hex., did not exist in G. The present text derives from Theod. (cf. Syro-hex.). Only the end of the verse καὶ ἐθυμώθη ὀργῇ αὐτοῦ is marked with asterisk in Colb. (and is attributed to Theod.) and Jerome (Tur.). Vulg. omits אֱלִיהוּא and renders וַיִּחַר אַפּוֹ by *iratus est vehementer* (cf. v. 2).

V. 5 summarises the introduction to the speeches of Elihu. If this preamble seems prolix, it resembles in this way the style of Elihu in the whole ch. 32. One cannot use this prolixity of style as a justification for the elimination of vv. 2-5, as is done by Hoffmann and Budde. The laboured emphasis of the author is deliberate. It explains, in advance, both the length and the warmth of the speeches of this new character. He is moved to speak by anger—an anger which has been accumulating

during a long wait. It finally bursts forth when the young man, whose patience is exhausted, perceives 'that there is no reply in the mouth of the three men'. The words כִּי אֵין מַעֲנֶה 'because there is no reply' recur in Mic 3:7.

6 Syr. adds ܡܢܟܘܢ 'more than you' after לימים. For זחלתי, G ἡσύχασα, Vulg. *demisso capite*, Syr. ܘܕܚܠܬ.

The introductory formula repeats the indications relative to Elihu (4:1; 8:1; 11:1, etc.); cf. v. 2. V. 6 contains two verses each of which consists of two hemistichs. Opposition between אֲנִי and אַתֶּם in relation to age as expressed by לְיָמִים 'in days' (v. 4). Cf. the locution: 'smaller than I in days', to connote 'younger than I' in 30:1. On the word יָשִׁישׁ 'old', characteristic of the Book of Job, cf. 12:12. The second verse is linked to the first by עַל־כֵּן 'that is why' (9:22). The verb זָחַלְתִּי does not come from זחל 'to crawl' (12:8), but from the old Aramaic זחל (inscription of Zakir, I. 13), which later became דחל 'to be afraid' (Dn 5:19; 6:27). It has been well understood thus by Syr. Cf. the alteration of זעך (17:1) and דעך (18:5, 6; 21:17). The second verb וָאִירָא 'and I feared' constitutes the link between זחלתי and the 2nd hemistich. The *pi'el* of חוה 'explain', 'manifest' (15:17; cf. אַחַוְתִּי 'my explanation' in 13:17) will recur in vv. 10, 17 and in 36:2. It is con-

7   I said to myself: 'Age will speak,
       And length of years will make wisdom known!'
8   But it is an inspiration in man,
       And a spirit from Shaddai which makes wise;
9   It is not the aged who are wise,
       Nor old men who understand what is right.

structed with a double accusative; cf. הַגִּיד in 31:37. The word דֵּעַ 'what one knows',' 'knowledge' is peculiar to Elihu (vv. 10, 17; 36:3; 37:16).

7 G places the negation οὐχ... οὐκ in both hemistichs (Sah., Jerome *non ... neque*, Eth.). But it is omitted in G(A, C) and marked by obelus in Syro-hex. For יָמִים, G ὁ χρόνος, Vulg. *aetas prolixior*. G renders וְרֹב שָׁנִים by ἐν πολλοῖς δὲ ἔτεσιν and translates the *hiph'il* יֹדִיעוּ as a *qal* οἴδασιν.

The verb אָמַרְתִּי, to denote private personal thoughts (7:13; 9:22). Note the use of the plural יָמִים 'days' in the sense of many days, age, in parallelism with רֹב שָׁנִים 'great number of years'. The latter formula is clearly differentiated from מִסְפַּר שָׁנִים 'number of years' in 15:20. The *hiph'il* of יָדַע is simply 'make known' (10:2; 13:23). In 12:12 Job declared that 'among old men is found wisdom and in great age there is understanding'. There, as here, it was a question of חָכְמָה.

8 For רוּחַ־הִיא, Symm. πνεῦμα θεοῦ, Targ. רוּחַ נְבוּאָתָא 'spirit of prophecy'. Vulg. renders אָכֵן by *sed ut video*. The suffix of תְּבִינֵם is omitted in Vulg. *dat intelligentiam*. Similarly in G ἔστιν ἡ διδάσκουσα (A adds μέ, א* adds σέ). The suffix αὐτούς is restored, in accordance with Aq. and Theod., in Syro-hex. (with asterisk) and in Jerome *eos* (without asterisk).

By an excessive concern for paral-

lelism, attempts have been made to change הִיא into יהוה (Dathe) or into אֵל in agreement with Symm. (Houbigant, Bickell, Budde, etc.). But it should be noted that in 27:3 'all my spirit' (נִשְׁמָתִי) corresponds to the 'breath of Eloah' (רוּחַ אֱלוֹהַ) which is in man's nostrils, according to Gn 2:7. The breath in man is the principle of both life and wisdom, for it emanates directly from the Creator: cf. Comm. on 12:9-10 and on 26:4. The construction רוּחַ־הִיא with relative understood is similar to that of אֵשׁ הִיא in 31:12. Note the parallelism between רוּחַ and נְשָׁמָה (4:9; 27:3; 33:4; 34:14). With the use of בֶּאֱנוֹשׁ 'in man' after רוּחַ־הִיא cf. נִשְׁמָתִי בִי 'my spirit in me' in 27:3. נִשְׁמַת שַׁדַּי will recur in 33:4; cf. נִשְׁמַת אֱלוֹהַ (4:9); נִשְׁמַת־אֵל (37:10); רוּחַ אֱלוֹהַ (27:3); רוּחַ־אֵל (33:4). The plural suffix of תְּבִינֵם because of the collective אֱנוֹשׁ. The *hiph'il* of בִּין preserves its causative connotation 'to make understand', 'to render intelligent' (6:24).

9 G πολυχρόνιοι and Vulg. *longaevi* well interpret רַבִּים and do not imply any other text than MT. Syr. ܗܘ ܩܕܡܘܗܝ 'great number of days' reads רֹב יָמִים following v. 7b.

The word רַבִּים, parallel to זְקֵנִים, denotes those who are great by reason of age; cf. צָעִיר in v. 6 and 30:1. The presence of רַב שָׁנִים 'great number of years' in v. 7 prevents any ambiguity. In Gn 25:23

10   That is why I have said: 'Listen to me!
      I too will manifest my knowledge.'
11   Well now, I have waited for your words,
      I listened keenly to your arguments;
      While you were searching for words,

we have the antithesis between רַב 'great' and צָעִיר 'small', to connote the elder and the younger: רב יעבד צעיר 'the elder will serve the younger.' In Arabic *kebîr* 'great' is used with the meaning of 'aged', 'elder'. Because the versions have well understood the meaning, one cannot suppose justified the change from רבים to רַבֵּי יָמִים (Ley) or to שָׂבִים 'old' (Beer, Budde). Duhm proposes רֹב יָמִים (cf. Syr.). But the parallelism with the concrete זקנים is not in favour of this correction. The verb חכם 'to be wise' is part of the vocabulary of Proverbs. It has as parallel יָבִינוּ מִשְׁפָּט 'understand what is right', the word משפט 'judgment' connoting 'what is just, right' (8: 3; 34: 12). Job claimed that among old men wisdom (חכמה) was to be found, and that in great age was intelligence (תבונה); cf. 12: 12. Eliphaz too appealed to the experience of those who were more aged than Job's father (15: 10). The youthful Elihu despises old age, for he notes that his elders have not been able to refute Job in argument. Duhm would place vv. 15-17 here, which obliges him to delete v. 10, with the exception of the word לָכֵן, which he puts at the head of v. 15. But v. 10 is very well connected with v. 9, and the locution לָכֵן אָמַרְתִּי has good support in עַל־כֵּן אמרתי of 9: 22. The repetition of v. 10b as the 2nd hemistich of v. 17 only accentuates the presumption of Elihu.

10 G ἀκούσατέ μου, Vulg. *audite me*, Syr. ܐܘܨܒܟܘ read the plural instead of the singular שִׁמְעָה. But Targ. קבל מני 'hearken thou to me' is in agreement with the MT.

The opening לָכֵן 'that is why' closely joins v. 10 to v. 9. In 20: 2 this idiom referred to what followed. Note the use of אָמַרְתִּי as in v. 7. The energetic imperative שִׁמְעָה will recur in 34: 16. In spite of the versions, which harmonise the expression with the rest of the passage, we retain the singular (cf. 33: 1, 31, 33). The verb שמע is used with לְ before the complement (15: 17). Compare שְׁמַע־לִי in 33: 31, 33. The 2nd hemistich will be repeated in v. 17. The *pi'el* of חוה as in v. 6, with the complement דֵּעִי. The movement of thought is the same as in 15: 17, where Eliphaz uses as here the verb חָוָה and the imperative שְׁמַע־לִי 'I will explain to you, listen to me!' The presumption of Elihu reveals itself in the use of אַף־אָנִי 'I too' (cf. v. 17).

11 Jerome borrows from Symm. the text of vv. 11-17, preceded by asterisk (cf. Field). Syro-hex. will cite in the margin (with asterisk) the translation of Symm. for vv. 13b-17. The text of G is one of the most interesting as regards the affiliation of the versions. G(B) has simply ἐνωτίζεσθέ μου τὰ ῥήματα ὑμῶν ἀκουόντων, ἄχρι οὗ ἐτάσητε λόγους. But G (א ᶜ·ᵃ, A, C) have ἐρῶ γάρ before ὑμῶν. These words figure in Sah. and Eth., they are merely noted in the margin of Syro-hex. The end ἄχρι οὗ ἐτάσητε λόγους, like the whole of v. 12, is absent from Sah., marked with asterisk in Colb., Cod. 248, and Syro-hex.

12   On you I was concentrating my attention!
      And lo, none of you criticises Job,
      Or refutes his assertions!

This passage stems from Theod. (cf. Syro-hex.). G (A) has a long addition before ἄχρι: ἰδοὺ ἤκουσα τοὺς λόγους ὑμῶν ἐνωτισάμην μέχρι συνέσεως ὑμῶν. The λόγους of the end (cf. sup.) becomes τοὺς λόγους ὑμῶν in G(A). We note first that v. 11c and v. 12 of the MT did not exist in G and that the present text is taken from Theod. Next, the reading of G(B) and of Syro-hex. (in the text) is an interpretation of v. 11a-b, though with the omission of הן הוחלתי of the opening, and a paraphrase of עד־תבונתיכם as ὑμῶν ἀκουόντων. Thus it is clear that ἐνωτίζεσθέ μου τὰ ῥήματα reflects לדברי האזינו (cf. 34: 2), which is a corruption of לדבריכם אזין. The words ἐρῶ γάρ have been added to complete the verse. The long addition of G (A) is a new translation of v. 11a-b. It brings the text back into line with the MT. Vulg. renders v. 11b-c by *audivi prudentiam vestram, donec disceptaremini sermonibus*. For לדבריכם, Syr. 'to you and your words'. Instead of תבונתיכם, Syr. 'until you ceased' seems to read תכליתכם 'until your completion' (cf. Beer).

Elihu returns to his point of departure: 'Well now, I have waited for your words.' הוחלתי will recur in v. 16. In the speeches of Job and his friends, it is the *pi'el* and not the *hiph'il* of יחל which was used (6: 11; 14: 14; 29: 21, 23; 30: 26). The complement is introduced by ל'' (29: 21, 23; 30: 26). The form אזין for אאזין. (Gesenius-Kautzsch, § 68i) as, probably, תזינו in 18: 2 (cf. Comm.). The same phenomenon is seen in מלפנו for מאלפנו (35: 11). The correction of אזין עד to אבין על עד (Ehrlich) is not necessary. We find the preposition עַד before the com-

plement of האזין in Nu 23: 18. It adds an implication to the meaning. The meaning now is not merely lending an ear to a spoken word, but listening intently to something which one finds it difficult to catch. Cf. the use of עד 'as far as' in 11: 7. The word תְּבוּנָה 'intelligence', 'understanding' (12: 12, 13; 26: 12) is used in the plural to denote 'reasons', 'arguments' which are aimed at persuading (cf. Ps 49: 4). A new verse begins at עַד־תַּחְקְרוּן. The 2nd hemistich will be formed by the first words of v. 12 as far as וְהִנֵּה, which is the beginning of a verse. The conjunction עד before an imperfect can have the meaning of 'while' (Ps 141: 10). This meaning suits our passage perfectly: 'while you were searching for words'. The verb חקר retains here its basic meaning 'to seek out', whence 'scrutinise' (5: 27; 13: 9), 'explore', 'investigate' (28: 3), 'study' (29: 16). While Job's friends were trying to find the appropriate words for use in the discussion, Elihu was listening attentively: 'I was concentrating my attention on you!' (v. 12a). The main clause after a temporal subordinate clause can be introduced by the *waw* (Gesenius-Kautzsch, § 11200). Same use of עד (in עָדֵיכֶם) as in עַד־תְּבוּנֹתֵיכֶם of v. 11, to express the difficulty. The verb התבונן will again be followed by עד before its complement in 38: 18.

12 The text of G comes from Theod., that of Jerome is borrowed from Symm. (cf. v. 11). For וְעָדֵיכֶם, Syr. ܘܣܗܕܘܬܟܘܢ reads וְעֵדֵיכֶם 'and your testimonies'.

We have linked the opening with v. 11, which has thus given us a

13   Do not therefore say: 'We have found wisdom,
     It is God who *instructs us*, not a man!'

13 יַלְּפֶנּוּ; MT: ידפנו.

complete verse: 'while you were searching for words, I was concentrating my attention on you'. The change from 'on you' to 'on your testimonies' (Syr.) which is recommended by Michaelis and some others does not seem to us warranted. Elihu waits in vain for the words and arguments of Job's friends (v. 11). He has not to verify their testimony but to bear witness to their defeat. He is obliged to listen with extreme attention to see whether they will eventually discover the words which they are seeking. This is the exact meaning of עָדֵיכֶם אֶתְבּוֹנָן (cf. Comm. on v. 11). The following verse gives the result of this close observation: 'and lo, none of you criticises Job, or refutes his assertions'. Note the construction of אֵין with the participle and its complement (2:13b; 10:7b). According to Driver, לְאִיּוֹב refers to אֵין 'there is no one to correct Job' (cf. Jer 50:32; Ps 142:5, etc.). But it should be noted that, in 10:7b, we have as here the complement before the participle: ואין מידך מציל 'and none delivers from thy hand'. Hence we may regard לאיוב as the complement of מוֹכִיחַ, which gives a better parallel to עוֹנֶה אֲמָרָיו. At the close, מִכֶּם depends on אֵין of the 1st hemistich. The same construction is found in La 1:2. The verb הוֹכִיחַ with the meaning of 'criticise' (cf. Comm. on 5:17) taking לְ'' before the person criticised (Pr 9:7; 15:12; 19:25). With עונה אמריו 'answering his assertions', cf. 33:13b, where the verb ענה has as its complement כל דבריו 'to all his words'. The name of Job was never mentioned in the speeches of his friends. Elihu

does not hesitate to introduce it into his verses (v. 12; 33:1, 31; 34:5, 7, 35, 36; 35:16; 37:14).

13 G Κυρίῳ προσθέμενοι reads יספנו instead of ידפנו. The end לֹא־אִישׁ is connected by G with v. 14 (q.v.). Syr. treats פֶן as a simple relative. On the text of Jerome, cf. v. 11. Syro-hex. cites in the margin the translation of Symm. for vv. 13b-17.

As it stands, v. 13 can only with difficulty be attached to what precedes or follows. It has been attempted to see in it a sort of preamble to v. 14. It is supposed that Job's friends are tempted to bow to his wisdom or to sympathise with his misfortune: 'And do not say: this man is wisdom personified; God alone, and not man, can overcome him' (Renan); 'And do not say: he has found (reading מצא following Bickell) wisdom, God can overcome him and not man' (Loisy); 'And do not say however: in him we have found wisdom; it is God who can confound him, and not man' (Segond); 'Do not say: we have found wisdom, it is God who strikes him and not man' (Le Hir, Crampon). The idea which all these translations have in common is to interpret 'we have found wisdom' as though it implied that his friends had met in Job a wisdom which silenced them and obliged them to recognise, in the case submitted to them, a supernatural intervention. But it should be noted that מָצָאנוּ חָכְמָה 'we have found wisdom' is to be explained by vv. 7 and 9, in which Elihu declares that, contrary to his expectation, old men do not possess wisdom. Their silence before Job

14   Hence *I* shall not marshal my words in order *as they did*,
      And it is not with your words that I shall reply to him!

14 אֶעֱרֹךְ (Syr.); MT: ערך. — כְּאֵלֶּה (G); MT: אֵלִי.

proves that they have not acquired it as one acquires a possession; cf. the use of מצא in 31: 25. This is indeed the meaning of מצא חכמה 'to find wisdom' in the Book of Proverbs (3: 13; 8: 17, 35). The conjunction פֶּן, which has the sense of the Greek μή and the Latin *ne*, not only marks the negative imperative (Is 36: 18) but closely joins the clause to the preceding one. Cf. the use of פֶּן־תֹּאמַר 'do not then say' after אַל־תֹּאמַר 'say not' in Sir 15: 11-12. We may translate the 1st hemistich: 'Do not therefore say: we have found wisdom!' This claim, which might well have been justifiably voiced by old men (v. 7), is no longer appropriate after the defeat they have suffered. The 2nd hemistich will be parallel to the first part of the direct speech; cf. vv. 7 and 10. It is only by means of ingenious subtleties that to נדף 'drive away', 'carry off' (by the action of the wind) is assigned the meaning of 'succeed in doing something', 'overcome', 'confound' or of 'strike' (cf. sup.). One manuscript has replaced יִדְּפֶנּוּ by יִרְדְּפֶנּוּ 'persecutes him' (reading adopted by Graetz), another has read יֶהְדְּפֶנּוּ 'repels him'. But what link is there between the 2nd hemistich (even when thus modified) and 'we have found wisdom'? We feel that a very slight change is necessary, that of reading יְלִפֵּנוּ instead of ידפנו. We have here the *pi'el* of אלף with disappearance of the א, exactly as in מַלְּפֵנוּ of 35: 11 (cf. sup., v. 11). On the verb אָלֵף, cf. 15: 5. The meaning of the 2nd hemistich will then be: 'it is God who instructs us, not a man'. If the friends had found

wisdom, it would be because God had revealed it to them, for it is inaccessible to mortals (28: 12-22) and it is God alone who knows its secrets (28: 23-7). The interlocutors of Job prove by their silence that they do not surpass the common level of mortal beings. The link between v. 13 and v. 14 is now clear. Elihu will be careful not to use the same arguments as the others, since the latter have not found wisdom. He will surrender himself to the breath of inspiration (vv. 18-19), for it is by that means that he will hear the voice of God (v. 8).

14   G omits the 2nd hemistich and places at the beginning of v. 14 לֹא־אִישׁ (read as לְאִישׁ) of v. 13: ἀνθρώπῳ δὲ ἐπετρέψατε λαλῆσαι τοιαῦτα ῥήματα. In accordance with 16: 2, where τοιαῦτα πολλά translates כְּאֵלֶּה רַבּוֹת, it seems that G read כְּאֵלֶּה (cf. inf.) instead of אֵלִי (Bickell, Gray). Vulg. renders the 1st hemistich by *nihil locutus est mihi*. On the text of Jerome, cf. v. 11. The translation of Symm. is cited in the margin of Syro-hex. The 1st hemistich is translated: 'I shall not speak against words' in Syr., which read אֶעֱרֹךְ אֵלִי instead of ערך אלי (cf. inf.).

The MT is easily translated: 'and he has not drawn up words against me and by your words I shall not answer him.' On the meaning of ערך cf. 13: 18. But the connection between the two hemistichs is not at all apparent. Elihu is declaring that he will not use the words of Job's friends in order to make a reply to Job. This is in truth the gist of his speech. If he used the same

15 They became dismayed, they ceased to reply,
    Words failed them.

arguments he would run the risk of incurring the same defeat. But why should he say that Job has not addressed words to him, seeing that he has not been taking part in the discussion and intervenes at this point only because the situation is desperate? Now, a first fact to be noted is that the reading אֶעֱרָךְ, supported by Syr., furnishes the parallel word to אֲשִׁיבֶנּוּ; cf. 23:4, where 'I would institute (אערכה) a case before him' has as a parallel 'and I would fill my mouth with recriminations'. A haplography has given rise to לא ערך instead of לא אערך (cf. Reiske, Beer). Next it is proposed to read אליו (in two manuscripts) so that one might translate: 'and I will not put words in order against him' (cf. Beer). But Gray very truly points out that מלין corresponds to בְּאִמְרֵיכֶם (antithetic parallelism (and that G read: כְּאֵלֶּה מלין (cf. sup.), which gives the exact counterpart to באמריכם. A further haplography explains the passage from אערך כאלה to ערך אלי. Thanks to Syr. and G, we can reconstitute the original text: 'hence I shall not marshal my words in order as they did, and it is not with your words that I shall reply to him!' On the expression כאלה, cf. 12:3; 16:2. At the end of the verse אשיבנו as in 31:14. Elihu does not wish to expose himself to having to remain silent in the face of Job (v. 12). The first set of speakers have not been able to find the wisdom which would have enabled them to make an effective reply (v. 13). It is necessary to strike out a new path. Vv. 15-16 will emphasise the silence of Job's friends as a preparation for v. 17, in which Elihu will declare once again that he proposes to make a reply. The arrogance and presump-

tion of Elihu become apparent in these oratorical precautions by which he seeks to arouse attention to what he will say only after much devious talk.

15 Vv. 15-16, absent from Sah., marked with asterisk in Cod. 248, Colb., Syro-hex., did not exist in G. The text, as it now stands, is derived from Theod. (cf. Syro-hex.). On the text of Jerome, cf. v. 11. Syro-hex. cites in the margin the reading of Symm. for vv. 15-16 (cf. v. 13). Syr. attaches to v. 15 והוחלתי of v. 16. For העתיקו, Theod. ἐπαλαίωσαν; cf. 9:5 and 21:7.

Elihu continues his reflections. To an imaginary audience, he depicts the friends of Job, standing agape and dumbfounded: 'They became dismayed, they ceased to reply, words failed them.' The verb חתת 'to be terrified' is used here to connote the consternation which results from fear. The verb העתיק, in the hiph'il but with the sense of the qal (20:6b; 21:3b), to mean 'to go beyond' (Gn 12:8; 26:22). Words pass beyond Job's friends, they no longer come to their minds, words fail them. Strictly one might interpret: 'they have allowed words to pass far beyond them', they have allowed them to escape. But if so, it would be a question of a voluntary action; cf. the use of העתיק in 9:5. Budde approves the omission of vv. 15-16 by G. But it should be pointed out that G omits v. 14b also. Now, v. 14a ends with מלין, v. 15 with מלים. An error of homoeoteleuton explains the disappearance of 14b-15. Instead of vv. 16-17, G has only a meagre summary to which will be affixed a new introduction to the speeches of Elihu, on the lines of 34:1 (cf. Comm. on v. 17). Duhm transfers vv. 15-17 to a place after

16   And I have waited! But since they do not speak,
      Since they have ceased and have replied no more,
17   I too will reply for my part,
      I too will manifest my knowledge!

v. 9, and this obliges him to cut out v. 10 (cf. sup.). But v. 9 alludes to old age as deprived of wisdom, and not specially to the friends of Job, whose attitude is described in vv. 15-16. Elihu has just observed (v. 12) that no one is capable of making any reply to the words of Job. That is because the speakers find nothing further to say (v. 15). They leave the field free for the young man (vv. 16-17).

16 On the text of G, cf. v. 15. On the text of Jerome, cf. v. 11. The translation of Symm. is quoted in the margin of Syro-hex. (cf. v. 13). Theod. ἐλάλησα is perhaps meant for ἐλάλησαν (Compl.) = ידברו.

כִּי cannot be interpreted in the sense of 'until', which would have been rendered by כד or עד־כי, as Dillmann justly remarks. Hence the meaning is not: 'I have waited until they speak no more.' On the other hand, to render by means of an interrogative, 'and must I wait? Since they have ceased to speak', etc., is to modify arbitrarily the meaning of the perfect וְהוֹחַלְתִּי, which has been already used in v. 11 to connote 'I have waited'. In reality, והוחלתי 'and I have waited . . .' forms an independent clause, the purpose of which is to show that Elihu has practised patience. From כִי, the clauses give the reason for the intervention of Elihu which is thrown into relief by v. 17. It is 'since they do not speak, since they have ceased and have replied no more' that 'I too will reply, for my part, I too will manifest my knowledge' (v. 17). Thus is to be understood the repetition לֹא־עָנוּ עוֹד, which Budde finds unendurable. It is not necessary

to change וחוחלתי into וְהַחִלּוֹתִי 'and I have begun' (Ehrlich), or into וְהוֹאַלְתִּי 'and I have decided' (Torczyner). Elihu has no need to say that he is beginning or is now deciding to speak. This we already know. The point which he is anxious to emphasise is the long wait which has been imposed on him by the useless speeches of Job's friends. This wait only ceases when the latter find that no further reply is in their power.

17 G ὑπολαβὼν δὲ Ἐλιοῦς λέγει· πάλιν λαλήσω (v. 18). Fragments of the MT are apparent in πάλιν λαλήσω, which corresponds to עוֹד of the end of v. 16 and to אענה of the beginning of v. 17 (Beer). Thus, then, G has retained only the last word of vv. 14b-16 (cf. Comm on v. 15), and has replaced by the ordinary formula of introduction (34: 1; 35: 1) the whole of the part that is missing. G (C) omits this formula of introduction. On the text of Jerome, cf. v. 11. Syro-hex. cites in the margin the translation of Symm. (cf. v. 13). Following the text of Symm., Jerome has *homini vero permisistis loqui talia verba* which translates v. 14 of G. It is apparent that the translation of Symm. has been added as an afterthought to complete the reduced text of G. The word חלקי is rendered ܡܠܬܐ 'my word' in Syr.

The *hiph'il* אַעֲנֶה with the same sense as the *qal* (cf. v. 15b). Repetition of אַף־אָנִי 'even I', 'I too' (cf. v. 10b), to emphasise the very personal character of Elihu's intervention. Then חֶלְקִי 'my part', as one says in Greek τὸ σὸν μέρος (with κατά understood) 'for thy part'. It is a kind of apposition to the personal

18 For I am full of words,
    My inner inspiration constrains me:
19 Behold, my inner being is like wine which has no outlet,
    Like a wine which *bursts* new wineskins!

19 יְבַקַּע (Vulg.); MT: יִבָּקֵעַ.

pronoun אֲנִי. The change from חֶלְקִי to לִקְחִי 'my doctrine' (11:4), recommended by Graetz and Ehrlich, has against it the use of the verb עָנָה. One would expect a verb similar to חוה of the 2nd hemistich; for example, הִגִּיד or הוֹדִיעַ. One manifests, makes known, a doctrine, one does not answer it. The 2nd hemistich reproduces v. 10b.

18 For הֱצִיקַתְנִי, G ὀλέκει γάρ με, Vulg. *et coarctat me*, Targ. עֲקַתְנִי (= MT), but Symm. συγκαίει με reads הִשִּׁיקַתְנִי (from נשק, *hiph'il*: 'to light' 'to kindle', 'to inflame') and Syr. (ܐܬܦܫܛܬ) 'has spread' reads הִסִּיכַתְנִי (from נסך, *hiph'il*, 'to spread').

The changes from כִּי to אָנֹכִי (Beer) or כִּי אֲנִי (Duhm) have no other purpose than to lengthen the 1st hemistich. Likewise the addition of פִּי 'my mouth' after כִּי (Ley). The versions offer nothing more than the MT. Elihu has just declared that he proposes to make a reply. He is not in the situation of Job's friends whom words fail (v. 15): 'for I am full of words'. Defective form מָלֵתִי, as we have יָצַתִי (for יָצְאָתִי) in 1:21. In 15:2, Eliphaz asked whether the wise man fills his belly with east wind, the belly being, like the heart, the seat of wisdom (*L'Emploi métaphorique*, p. 134). It is in the belly, i.e. in the inner man, that is to be found the spirit which prompts intelligent answers (v. 8). 'The breath of my belly' is thus in truth 'my inner inspiration'. The *hiph'il* of צוק has the general meaning of 'constrain', 'urge', 'press'. In Jg

14:17; 16:16 it is to wear some one down by repeated entreaties (cf. Lagrange, in loc.). The meaning of such words as 'press', 'urge' is faithful to the basic image and also reflects the required implication: 'My inner inspiration constrains me'. Elihu can no longer resist the spirit which urges and constrains him. The comparison in v. 19 will show how violent is this pressure.

19 G ὥσπερ ἀσκὸς γλεύκους ζέων (A γέμων) anticipates כָּאֹבוֹת of the 2nd hemistich. For יין, Symm. οἶνος νέος; cf. Targ. חֲמַר חֲדַת. Vulg. translates by *mustum*; cf. G γλεύκους (Jerome *musto*). Syr. (ܡܨܚ) 'afflicted' reads perhaps עֳנִי 'sorrow' instead of יין. For לֹא יִפָּתֵחַ, G δεδεμένος, Symm. ἀδιάπνευστος; cf. Vulg. *absque spiraculo*. G ἢ ὥσπερ φυσητὴρ χαλκέως reads חֲרָשִׁים instead of חֲדָשִׁים. Syr. vocalises אֹבוֹת instead of אֹבוֹת and connects חֲדָשִׁים to חֹדֶשׁ, whence 'like the fruit in its month'. Vulg. renders אֹבוֹת by *lagunculas*; cf. Targ. לְגִינִין. Instead of the *niph'al* יִבָּקֵעַ, Vulg. *disrumpit* reads the *pi'el* of יְבַקַּע, an excellent reading (cf. inf.).

The word בִּטְנִי 'my belly', 'my inside' of v. 18 leads to this comparison. The literal translation of the 1st hemistich would run: 'my belly is like a wine which is not opened', i.e. which is sealed to the point of being able to find no outlet, no means of escape. Cf. the *niph'al* of פתח with the negative in 12:14. The inner spirit of Elihu constrains him (v. 18) in the same way as wine

20   I will speak in order that I may be relieved,
      I will open my lips and will reply!
21   I will not side with any one,
      Nor will I confer a title on any one,

sealed in a wineskin ferments and
seeks a means of escape. In the 2nd
hemistich, it is this very word אֹבוֹת
'skins' which is used. It is the only
case in the Bible where אוֹב, plural
אֹבוֹת, has its physical meaning of
'skin bottle'. Elsewhere it denotes a
ghost, a necromancer, necromancy:
cf. our Comm. on 1 S 28: 3, 7. An
attempt has been made to interpret
חֲדָשִׁים by 'new wine' and to see in
אבות חדשים skins full of new wine.
Then to יִבָּקַע ·is assigned as subject
the feminine בטני, or else יבקע is
changed to תבקע (Duhm). The artificiality of this interpretation is
sufficiently apparent from Gray's
translation: 'like skins (filled with)
new wine, it is ready to burst'. Nor
can we give אבות as a subject to
יבקע so as to translate: 'like brand-
new vessels ready to burst' (Le Hir)
or 'like a new wineskin which cracks'
(Renan). What should be noticed
above all is that the comparison is
concerned with the wine fermenting
in a sealed vessel. The belly, i.e.
the inner self of Elihu, is in the same
state of fermentation. If the comparison bore also on the recipient,
we should have the singular, 'like a
wineskin' and the feminine תבקע.
In fact, we may regard חדשים as a
simple epithet of אבות, which is a
masculine plural of feminine form;
cf. the singular אוֹב in the masculine
in Lv 20: 27. Thus we have new
wineskins which are to contain
new wine (Mt 9: 17). The strength
of the wine is measured precisely by
its action of the skins which contain
it (ibid.). Wine which has no outlet
will burst new skins, just as the inner
inspiration of Elihu insists on finding
expression at all costs. With Vulg.
we vocalise יִבָּקֵעַ (the subject of

which will be the masculine יין of
the 1st hemistich) and we make of
אבות חדשים the complement of this
transitive verb. The ''כ of comparison before אבות implies יין of the
1st hemistich. Hence the clause
'which bursts new wineskins' becomes parallel to 'which has no
outlet'. On the meaning of בקע cf.
Comm. on 26: 8.

20 For שׂפתי, G τὰ χείλη (Syro-
hex., Jerome), G(A) adds μου (Sah.,
Memph.) The end of the verse
ואענה is omitted in G. But ἀποκριθῶ,
following Theod. (cf. Colb.), is
restored in G (א ͨ·ͨ), Syro-hex. (with
asterisk), Jerome *respondebo*.
   The cohortative אֲדַבְּרָה 'I will
speak' as in 7: 11; 9: 35; 10: 1. The
copulative *waw* before the imperfects
יָרְוַח and אֶעֱנֶה introduces subordinate clauses and assumes the meaning of the Latin *ut*: 'I will speak in
order that I may be relieved.' The
impersonal ירוח ל'' 'it is a relief
for ...' just as in 1 S 16: 23. Cf. the
mode of expression ינוח לי 'it would
be rest for me' in 3: 13b. Note the
parallelism between 'speak' and
'open the lips' (11: 5).

21 G interprets the Hebraism 'to
lift up one's face' in the sense of feel
shame before some one, or show
deference to some one: ἄνθρωπον
γὰρ οὐ μὴ αἰσχυνθῶ. But Jerome
neque enim erubescam faciem viri is
close to the MT: Vulg. *et Deum
homini non aequabo* vocalises אֵל
instead of אֶל in the 2nd hemistich.
For אכנה, G ἐντραπῶ, cf. Syr. ܐܒܗܬ
'I shall be ashamed'.
   The formula אַל־נָא usually denotes a negative wish addressed to

22   For I do not know how to give titles of distinction,
      If I did so, my Maker would carry me off in a flash!

someone else: Gn 13:8; 18:3; 2 S 13:25. Here simply a solemn negative, as is shown by the use of לֹא in the 2nd hemistich. On the expression נשֹא פנים, cf. 13:8. The exact meaning of the *pi'el* of כנה is to give a mark of distinction, a title (Is 44:5; 45:4; Sir 36:7; 44:23; 47:6). This meaning perfectly suits our verse and the following one. It is unnecessary to change it to the meaning 'flatter', as is generally done. Elihu will not take any one's side and will not use pompous titles. He has observed that he is on the same footing as others.

22 G θαυμάσαι πρόσωπον (B πρόσωπα) for אכנה is a reminiscence of אשֹא פני of v. 21. Syr. ܐܟܢܐ remains faithful to its translation of אכנה in v. 21. Vulg. *nescio enim quamdiu subsistam* connects אכנה with the verb כון. Targ. adds אפין 'face' as the complement of ישֹאני. Instead of עשֹני, G καὶ ἐμὲ σῆτες ἔδονται reads עָשִׁים (from עָש, cf. 4:19; 27:18).

Syr. ܚܝܠܝ 'my force' following the Aramaic עושֹנא 'force'.

Note the juxtaposition of two personal verbs, the second dependent on the first (6:28; 10:16; 19:3), 'for I do not know how to give titles of distinction'. Elihu will remain faithful to his habits. He has a weighty reason for so doing. This reason is that his Creator would not suffer him to do otherwise: 'in a flash my Maker would carry me off!' The expression: כִּמְעַט 'like a little', 'yet a little' means sometimes 'very nearly' at other times 'in little or no time' (Ps 2:12; 81:15; Pr 5:14). The verb נשֹא 'to carry off' like the wind (27:21). Cf. 30:22a. The participle עשֹני *factor meus* (Vulg.) as in 31:15; cf. 33:4, 6. One might imagine that Elihu is now about to enter on his subject. But vv. 1-7 of ch. 33 are still an exordium addressed more particularly to Job. It has pleased the author to depict the new speaker as interminably prosy.

CHAPTER 33

1   Be good enough, then, O Job, to hear my words,
     And lend an ear to all my speeches:
2   See now, I have opened my mouth,
     My tongue has spoken in my palate!
3   My heart *will repeat words imbued with knowledge,*
     My lips will speak clearly.

3   אַמְרֵי דָעַת ‎;MT: ‎אמרי ודעת‎. — ‎יֹשֶׁר ‎:MT ‎;יָשַׁר‎.

33: 1   G omits כל before דברי.
Elihu now addresses Job directly
(cf. 32: 10), and he has no hesitation
in mentioning his name in his verses
(cf. 32: 12). Note the construction
of וְאוּלָם with the imperative followed by נָא, as in 1: 11; 12: 7, 'Be
good enough, then, O Job, to hear
my words;' also the use of the
cohortative הַאֲזִינָה (cf. שמעה in
32: 10) with the accusative (37: 14).
In 34: 2 we find the same phrases
applied to Job's friends: שמעו···מלי
and האזינו. Parallelism between שמע
and האזין (cf. 34: 16).

2   Vulg. renders דברה by *loquatur*.
For בחכי, Syr. ܟܦܘܡܝ 'in my
mouth'. G omits בחכי, which is
restored in five MSS as also ἐν τῷ
λάρυγγί μου in Jerome *in gutture meo*
(with asterisk) and in Syro-hex.
(with asterisk). The restoration
comes from Theod. (cf. Syro-hex.).
It does not exist in Sah.
On the formula הִנֵּה־נָא cf. 13: 18,
where it is followed as here by a verb
in the perfect. It will recur in 40: 15,
16. The verb פתח with 'my mouth',
instead of 'my lips' (32: 20) as
complement; cf. 3: 1. The tongue
and the palate are the organs of
speech (6: 30; 31: 30). Here we have

in turn the mouth, the tongue, the
palate. It is not clear why Bickell
would suppress this verse as being
'too prosaic even for Elihu'! From
the very beginning of Elihu's speech
we have been meeting such phrases
whose banality was intended by the
author. We are dealing with a man
who talks for the sake of talking,
and who with much bustle announces that he is about to declare extraordinary things which we are still
waiting to hear. V. 3 will be no less
empty than v. 2. Ehrlich would give
body to Elihu's style, and he
replaces בְחָכִּי by בְחָבִּי 'in my
breast' (31: 33) which he makes
the direct complement of דִּבְּרָה:
'my tongue expresses my inner
thought'. Neither the versions, nor
the parallelism, nor the general
meaning authorise this change.

3   G καθαρά μου ἡ καρδία ῥήμασιν
(A ἐν ῥήμασιν) reads יָשָׁר instead of
יֹשֶׁר. Aq. and Theod. render ישר by
εὐθεῖα, Symm. by ἀπλῆ; cf. Vulg.
simplici corde meo sermones mei. Syr.
'the words of my mouth are true and
the speech of my lips is well chosen'
reads יָשָׁר, replaces לבי אמרי by
אמרי פי and omits דעת. G καθαρά
νοήσει reads מלל instead of מללו.

486

5   If you can, answer me,
       Prepare yourself and stand in front of me!

4   After v. 6.

Targ. follows the MT, rendering
ברור by בריר. Vulg. *et sententiam
puram labia mea loquentur* makes of
ברור the epithet of דעת.

There is disproportion between
the 1st and the 2nd hemistichs. The
literal translation of the MT would
be: 'My words are the uprightness
of my heart and my lips have
spoken knowledge in purity.' This
is paraphrased in various ways:
'My words will spring from an upright heart and my lips will say
nothing except what is certain' (Le
Hir); 'My words express the uprightness of my heart and my lips will say
frankly what I think' (Renan); 'It
is in the uprightness of my heart
that I propose to speak, it is the
pure truth that my lips will express'
(Segond). In Crampon's Bible we
find a combination of the translation
of Le Hir (1st hemistich) with that
of Segond (2nd hemistich). In order
to restore the equilibrium between
the two hemistichs, Grimme and
Steuernagel suppress דעת (cf. Syr.).
Nevertheless, 'my words are the
uprightness of my heart' remains a
strange turn of expression. A slight
change, proposed by Wright and
Duhm, accepted by Beer, Gray, and
Ball, consists in reading אִמְרֵי דָעַת
'words of knowledge' instead of
אִמְרֵי וְדַעַת; vocalisation דָּעַת because of the *athnaḥ*. We find
אמרי־דעת in Pr 19: 27, אמרי בינה
'words of understanding' in Pr 1: 2,
אמרי יֹשֶׁר 'words of uprightness' in
6: 25 (above). The 2nd hemistich
is very clear: 'my lips will speak
clearly'. In Zeph 3: 9 the word
בָּרוּר 'pure' (cf. בַּר in 11: 4) is an
epithet of שָׂפָה 'lip'. What is in
question is lips that are unstained
by impurity (cf. van Hoonacker).

The original meaning 'sparkling',
'clean', 'clear' (cf. Comm. on 11: 4)
is preserved in our passage, where
ברור is used adverbially. On the
verb מִלֵּל cf. 8: 2. 'My heart' of the
1st hemistich becomes the parallel
term to 'my lips'. The verb corresponding to מלל is concealed by
יֹשֶׁר. Duhm proposes to read יָשָׁק
'overflows' (Jl 2: 24), Beer רָחַשׁ 'has
been stirred', 'has uttered (?)' of
Ps 45: 2. But we note that there is
a verb שׁוּר having the meaning of
'repeat', 'say over again', which we
shall find again in vv. 14 and 27. It
is this verb which seems to us to
explain Hos 14: 9, אני עניתי ואשורנו
'I have answered and I will repeat
it!' If we vocalise יָשֻׁר instead of
יֹשֶׁר we obtain: 'My heart will
repeat words of knowledge', which
is an excellent parallel to 'and my
lips will speak clearly'. It is very
apparent that v. 4 separates v. 3
from its natural sequel, which is
v. 5. Budde, Duhm, and Beer delete
v. 4 as a gloss based on v. 6 and
32: 8. But if we place v. 4 after v. 6
it becomes clear that v. 6 finds a
natural continuation in v. 4 (cf.
Comm.). We do not hesitate to make
this slight transposition, and we
shall have occasion to observe that
v. 4 is not a mere variant of 32: 8, as
Budde and Duhm claim.

4   After v. 6.

5   After הֲשִׁיבֵנִי, G adds πρὸς ταῦτα,
while Syr. adds ܦܬܓܡܐ 'a word'.
Vulg. interprets the 2nd hemistich
as if ערכה were a noun used adverbially: *et adversus faciem meam
conspice*. At the close, G adds καὶ

6   Behold now, I am like you in relation to God,
     I too have been moulded of clay;

ἐγὼ κατὰ σέ, which translates הן אני
כפיך of v. 6.

'If you can, answer me', imperative הֲשִׁיבֵנִי as in 13: 22. We then
have two energetic imperatives:
עֶרְכָה and הִתְיַצָּבָה (v. 1; 32: 10).
The 2nd hemistich is to be interpreted in the light of 41: 2, where we
have: וּמִי הוּא לְפָנַי יִתְיַצָּב 'and who
can stand before him?'. It is clear
that here לְפָנַי refers to התיצבה
'stand in front of me'. The verb ערך
will not here mean 'set in order'
arguments, words (13: 18; 23: 4;
32: 14) but rather 'get in battle
array' (6: 4) and, since a single
personage is in question, 'get ready'
for the struggle. Cf. the images of
38: 3; 40: 7. Elihu is beginning a
regular tournament. He will show
that Job and he are equally matched;
they are two creatures moulded of
the same clay and animated by the
same breath of life (6: 4). In this
contest Job will not be able to plead
the superiority of his opponent and
the terrors he arouses in him (v. 7).

6 G ἐκ πηλοῦ διήρτισαι σὺ ὡς καὶ
ἐγώ· ἐκ τοῦ αὐτοῦ διηρτίσμεθα (Jerome,
Syro-hex.). The word πηλοῦ is
repeated at the end in G (A, א c·a),
Sah. The opening הן־אני כפיך has
been translated by G in v. 5. We
have here a double translation of
מחמר···אני. The doublet becomes
still more apparent from the repetition of πηλοῦ at the end of the verse.
It may be seen that G has omitted
the word לאל. Vulg. renders לאל by
fecit Deus, while Symm. οὐκ εἰμὶ
Θεός reads לא אל.

Job will be confronted by an
opponent who is a man like himself.
No longer will he be able to exclaim:
'for He is not a man like myself that
I might answer Him, that we might
go to law together!' (9: 32). The
assurance of Elihu must comfort
him: 'Behold now, I am like you in
relation to God, I too have been
moulded of clay.' The phrase כְּפִיךָ
'like your mouth' means 'like you';
the same use of kî pî is found in
Assyrian (L'Emploi métaphorique,
p. 85). It is natural to understand
לָאֵל 'for God' in the ordinary sense:
'from God's angle', 'as far as God is
concerned'. Elihu and Job are both
of them creatures as against the
Creator. In 10: 9 Job had declared
that God had made him 'as with
clay' (cf. Comm. on 4: 19). Elihu has
no different an origin: 'I too have
been moulded of clay.' The verb
קרץ, here used in the pu'al, has as
its basic sense 'pinch', 'grip'. It
denotes the action of pursing the
lips (Pr 16: 30) and of winking the
eyes (Pr 6: 3; 10: 10; Ps 35: 19).
In Assyrian the verb qarâṣu, in the
qal or the iphte'al, denotes the action
of the potter who grips and fashions
the clay between his fingers (Choix
de Textes, p. 138, ll. 5ff. and p. 188, l.
34). It is precisely this verb qarâṣu
with the complement ṭiṭṭa, ṭîṭa (טיט)
'mud', 'clay' which is used to describe the formation of man by the
divine potter whose material is clay
(ibid., and cf. Muss-Arnolt, Handwörterbuch, p. 933). The meaning 'to
bite', which has also become attached to qarâṣu, arises from the
idea of gripping with the teeth. Thus
we have the explanation of qirṣu 'a
pinch' and of qarṣu 'a morsel', the
former coming from qarâṣu 'to
pinch', the latter from qarâṣu 'to
bite' (morsel comes from the Latin
morsellus, derived from morsus). The
idiom qarṣa akâlu 'to eat a morsel' of
some one, to mean 'to calumniate',
has passed into Aramaic and New
Hebrew (cf. Comm. on 19: 22). For
the final גַּם־אָנִי, instead of אַף־אָנִי

4   The breath of God has made me,
      And the spirit of Shaddai has quickened me;

7   Thus then no terror of me will scare you,
      And my *hand* will not *lie heavy* on you!

8   You have done nothing but talk in my ears,
      And I have heard the sound of the words:

7 וְכַפִּי (G); MT: וְאִכְפִּי. — תִּכְבַּד; MT: יִכְבַּד.

(32: 10, 17), cf. 7: 11; 13: 2. After
the formation of the body it is quite
natural to find that of the soul (v. 4).

7 After v. 4 (below).

4 For עִשְׂתַנִי, Syr. احـنـلـ 'has
awakened me' (reading עֹרַרְתַּנִי).
Targ. renders נשׁמת by מֵימַר 'word'.
G ἡ διδάσκουσά με reads תְּחֻוֵּנִי (from
חוה) instead of תְּחַיֵּנִי.
     For the position of this v. 4, cf.
Comm. on v. 3. In 10: 8-11 the
development of the foetus included
two aspects: the organisation of the
human body and the inbreathing
into it of life. Similarly in Gn 2: 7
God first moulds the body and then
imparts to it the breath of life. If
Elihu resembles Job by his corporeal
origins (v. 6), he does not differ
from him by his spiritual origins:
'The breath of God has made me and
the spirit of Shaddai has quickened
me.' The divine workmanship consists in transforming man into a
living being by imparting to him
the divine breath of life; cf. Comm.
on 32: 8, where we have parallelism
between רוּחַ and נִשְׁמַת שַׁדַּי.

5-6 After v. 3.

7 For וְאַכְפִּי, G οὐδὲ ἡ χείρ μου
reads וְכַפִּי (cf. inf.), Vulg. *et eloquen-
tia mea* separates וְאַךְ פִּי. Targ.
translates by וְטוּנִי 'and my burden',
Syr. by סּوبـفـﻮ 'and my care'.
     Elihu is making ironic allusion to
the reflections of Job in 9: 34 and
13: 21. Job begged that the terror
of God should not scare him. Elihu

repeats the same terms: 'Thus the
terror of me will not scare you.' The
interjection הִנֵּה 'thus then' introduces the logical conclusion to the
preceding verses. Since Job is now
face to face with a man like himself, he need no longer be afraid.
אַכְפִּי has been interpreted as 'my
burden' (cf. Targ.) in the light of
the verb אכף 'press on', 'grip tightly' (Pr 16: 26; Sir 46: 5). Le Hir
and Renan translate 'the weight of
my majesty'. In Syriac the root אכף
means 'to give one's careful attention to' and 'to compel', 'to oblige'.
The exact meaning of אכפי should
be 'my pressure', 'my demand'. In
13: 21 parallelism brought into line
with each other 'remove Thy hand
from upon me' and 'may Thy terror
not crush me'. In 9: 34 we had
'who would take his rod from over
me' corresponding to 'so that His
terror should not make me afraid'.
Terror is aroused by the hand, armed
with the rod, raised to smite. As
most moderns (since Olshausen)
have recognised, the reading of
G וְכַפִּי 'and my hand' gives the
original text. Because of the gender
of כַּף, we must read at the end
תִּכְבַּד; G βαρεῖα ἔσται. Cf. 23: 2b,
'my hand lies heavy on my groaning'
where ידי is the subject of כבדה and
where the preposition על introduces
the complement. Elihu is not like
God whose 'hand lies heavy' on
human beings (1 S 5: 6, 11; Ps 32: 4).

8 V. 8a, absent from Sah., marked
with asterisk in Colb., Jerome, Syro-
hex., did not exist in G. The present

9   'I am pure, without transgression,
      I am clean, there is no fault in me!
10   But see, He finds *pretexts* against me,
      He regards me as His enemy,

10 תּוֹאֲנוֹת (Syr.); MT: תנואות.

text is derived from Theod. (cf. Colb. and Syro-hex.) and corresponds to that of Aq. (cf. Syro-hex.). For מלין, G ῥημάτων, but G (A, א) adds σοῦ (Sah., Jerome, Syro-hex.); cf. Vulg. *verborum tuorum*, Syr. ܡܠܝܟ.

The expression: אַף אָמַרְתָּ 'only you have said' to connote 'you have merely said', foreshadows the direct speech which will be placed in Job's mouth (vv. 9-11). The verb אמר with the complement באזני פ '' 'to speak in the ears' (Jg 17:2; Is 49: 20). Cf. the use of באזני with שמע in 28:22. The 2nd hemistich stresses the fact that Job's words have been grasped by Elihu: 'and I have heard the sound of the words'. The verb שמע with קול as the direct complement (3:18, 4:16). The change from מִלִּין to מִלֶּיךָ 'your words', in accordance with the versions (cf. sup.), is not essential. The MT is supported by G (B, C) and Targ.

9 G διότι λέγεις comes from אך אמרת, which had not been translated in v. 8 (cf. sup.). Syr. ܕܐܡܪܬ. 'since you have said', in order to introduce the direct speech. G(A) adds τοῖς ἔργοις after οὐχ ἥμαρτον (instead of ἁμαρτῶν) which translates בלי פשע. For חף, G ἄμεμπτος, Vulg. *immaculatus*, Targ. שזיג 'washed'. Syr. twice translates the second clause (from חף) and renders חף first by ܘܟܝ 'just' and then by ܢܛܝܪ 'preserved'.

The *athnaḥ* should be placed under פשע, which ends the 1st hemistich. The parallelism is strict: חַף אָנֹכִי corresponds to זַךְ אָנִי, then וְלֹא עָוֺן לִי

corresponds to בְּלִי פֶשַׁע. The *hapax* חף replaces בַּר, parallel to זַךְ in 11:4. The versions were not mistaken as to the meaning. The root of חף is חפף, which, in New Hebrew, means 'to wash' the head and which is paralleled by חוף 'to wash' in Syriac, *ḥâpu* 'to clean' in Assyrian. Hence the adjective will mean 'clean' in the moral sense. The quality is made clear by the denial of the contrary fault; cf. Ca 4:7, 'You are all fair, my love, and there is no blemish in you.' On פשע and עון, cf. Comm. on 10:6. בלי־פשע will recur in 34:6. Elihu cites the thesis of Job in general terms. In vv. 10-11 he will give verbal quotations.

10 For תנואות, G μέμψιν, Vulg. *querelas*, Targ. תרעומתא 'complaints', Syr. ܥܠܠܬܐ 'pretexts'. The word לו, omitted in G, is reflected in Sah. and Jerome *sibi* (with asterisk). It is translated in the margin of Syro-hex. and attributed to the 'three' (Aq., Theod., and Symm.).

The first word הֵן connects v. 10 with v. 9, announcing an observed fact such as occasions surprise, just like והנה 'and behold now' in Is 5:7. Job declares that he is without fault and in spite of that God, who is the understood subject, treats him as an enemy! The word תְּנוּאוֹת belongs to the root נוא, the basic meaning of which, as in Arabic and Assyrian, is 'to oppose'. The other implications assumed by the *hiph'il*, e.g. 'disown', 'turn aside', 'thwart' are derived from this original sense, which re-

11   He puts my feet in the stocks,
      And watches all my steps!'
12   Now, in that, you are not right: such is my answer to you!
      For Eloah is greater than man.

appears in the noun תְּנוּאָה of Nu 14: 34, 'and you will know my opposition'. Hence we find the free translations: 'yet God finds in me reasons for anger' (Le Hir); 'God seeks, in His hostility to me, motives for hatred' (Renan). But literally we should have to say that God finds oppositions against Job, a statement which is not easily to be explained. Rashi already had recognised that תנואות was to be read as תֹּאֲנוֹת, which he interpreted by עֲלִילוֹת 'pretexts', thus agreeing with the translation of Syr. (cf. sup.). He rightly quoted Jg 14: 4, where we see that Yahweh seeks 'a pretext' (תֹּאֲנָה) against the Philistines. The meaning of the 1st hemistich is therefore: 'but see, He finds pretexts against me'. The 2nd hemistich repeats verbally the terms of 13: 24b, where Job said to God: 'Why dost Thou regard me as an enemy to Thyself?' Cf. again 19: 11b, 'and He regards me as His adversary'. V. 11 will quote 13: 27. Elihu selects those words which, in his opinion, are the most characteristic expressions of Job's feelings.

11   For בסד, G ἐν ξύλῳ (cf. Comm. on 13: 27), but G(A) ἐν κυκλώματι (cf. ibid.). Vulg. and Syr. are faithful to their translation of בסד in 13: 27; Targ. בשיע 'in cement' (cf. ibid.). G renders רגלי by the singular τὸν πόδα μου as in 13: 27; but Vulg. *pedes meos*, and no longer *pedem meum* as in 13: 27.

Elihu now cites the first two hemistichs of 13: 27. He omits 13: 25-6 in order to dwell on those expressions which seem to him the most reprehensible. For commentary, cf. 13: 27. Duhm, following Bickell, deletes

v. 11, which seems to him a quotation added by a reader. One wonders why this reader has not rather chosen 13: 25 or 13: 26, which continue the quotation made in v. 10!

12   G πῶς γὰρ λέγεις Δίκαιός εἰμι καὶ οὐκ ἐπακήκοέν μου; αἰώνιος γάρ ἐστιν ὁ ἐπάνω βροτῶν. The words πῶς γὰρ λέγεις come from הֵךְ זֹאת instead of הֵן זאת. Then G reads צדקתי ולא אֶעֱנֶה instead of לֹא־צדקת אענך. The words ὁ ἐπάνω βροτῶν paraphrase ירבה...מאנוש, and αἰώνιός ἐστιν comes from עולם, a corruption of אלוה מ...· The other versions are in agreement with the MT.

The opening הֵן־זֹאת recalls הנה־זאת of Eliphaz in 5: 27. The pronoun זאת makes clear the object of the verb צָדַקְתָּ and plays the part of an accusative, just as in Ezk 20: 27. The verb צדק 'to be just' and 'to be right'; cf. Comm. on 9: 15. The text of G is directly inspired by 9: 15a and cannot take precedence of the MT and the other versions. Those who wish to substitute the Greek version for the MT are obliged to replace the verb צדק by צעק (Bickell, Duhm). The text which Duhm finally accepts is: הנה אם אצעק לא ענה 'behold, if I cry, He does not answer', which reflects 19: 7. One wonders why the Massoretes and the Septuagint have both set aside this almost verbal quotation. But it should not be forgotten that Bickell and Duhm have deleted v. 11. They need to complete the words of Job and to delay somewhat the reply of Elihu. Duhm does not hesitate to correct the 2nd hemistich also on the basis of G, though at the same time modifying the

13   Why have you made it a grievance against Him,
      That He does not answer all man's words?

reading implied by G. He replaces
ירבה by מעלים, which is supposed
to have been corrupted to מעולם,
whence the αἰώνιος of G. The meaning would be that 'Eloah hides Himself from man', an allusion to the
words of Job in 9: 11-12. If a desperately corrupt text were in question, we could admire the sagacity
of the critic. But the reading of G
can be explained on different lines
(cf. sup.), and it does but render obscure a perfectly clear text. The verb
רבה, like רבב, means 'to be many'
and 'to be great'. The meaning of
the 2nd hemistich is simply: 'since
Eloah is greater than man'. This
clause is connected with what follows,
the parenthetic 'I will answer you'
completing the first clause. For the
contrast between אֱלוֹהַ and אֱנוֹשׁ, cf.
4: 17a. God is greater than man, He
need not argue with an inferior. Cf.
the formula familiar among the
Arabs and forming part of the
Muslim prayer: allah akbar: 'God is
greater!'

13   G adds at the beginning λέγεις
δέ (cf. vv. 9 and 12). Then διὰ τί
τῆς δίκης μου οὐκ ἐπακήκοεν πᾶν
ῥῆμα; G(B) adds μοῦ before πᾶν, but
Sah., Jerome, and Syro-hex. are in
agreement with G (א, A, C) in omitting this second μοῦ. Hence one cannot argue on the basis of G for the
reading of דברי 'my words' (Bickell,
Duhm) instead of דבריו. It is
apparent that G replaces ריבות by
ריבתי and omits אליו and כי. It is
a proof of the liberty of treatment
in which the Greek version indulges
in this passage (cf. v. 12). Under the
influence of אענך of v. 12, Vulg.
renders the 2nd hemistich by quod
non ad omnia verba responderit
tibi.

The sequence of ideas seems to us

to be very clear. Elihu observes, and
Job agrees with him, that God is
greater than man (v. 12). Why then
complain if God does not reply to
all the words that man adresses to
Him? And Job has in fact declared
that, if man wishes to dispute with
God, God answers him not once in
a thousand times (9: 2-3). The
allusion is transparent, and it proves
that כָּל־דְּבָרָיו 'all his words' refers
to אֱנוֹשׁ of v. 12. It is difficult to see
why Budde thinks 'inevitable' the
change from דבריו to דבריך 'your
words', recommended by Hitzig and
others. It is for want of having
grasped the relation between vv.
12-13 and 9: 2-3 that this correction,
which is not supported by the versions, has been proposed. The text
of the Vulg. does not presuppose
דבריך, for if it did we should have
ad omnia verba tua and not responderit tibi which is influenced by v. 12
(cf. sup.). We have seen above that
G had not the first person suffix in
its original text (contra Bickell,
Duhm). The following is the reasoning of Elihu: since God is greater
than man, why have you made it a
cause of grievance that He does not
reply to all man's words? The verb
ריב (cf. Comm. on 9: 3) with אל
before the indirect complement to
mean 'complain', 'nurse a grievance'
(Jg 21: 22; Jer 2: 29; 12: 1). The
form ריבוֹתָ is interesting as a survival of a perfect similar to the permansive Assyrian qatlâta (RB, 1913,
p. 391, n. 3); cf. בִּינֹתִי in Dn 9: 2.
The 2nd hemistich introduces the
object of the accusation. The verb
ענה with the accusative to connote
'reply to' words as in 32: 12b. V.
14 will show that God is not accustomed to reply to all words. He
speaks once and that must suffice.

14   The fact is that God speaks once,
      And He does not repeat His word.

15   In a dream, a vision of the night,
      When men are plunged in heavy sleep,
      And they sleep upon their beds,

---

14 G ἐν γὰρ τῷ ἅπαξ λαλήσαι ὁ Κύριος, ἐν δὲ τῷ δευτέρῳ omits ישורנה, which is restored (with asterisk) in Jerome *non consideravit* (Tur. *consideravit*) *illud*. Following שׁוּר 'look', 'perceive' (7:8), Targ. renders לא ישורנה by לא אצטריך למסכיה 'He has no need to consider it'. But Vulg. *idipsum non repetit* and Syr. ܥܠ ܡܟܟܟܟ 'not repeating' have well understood the meaning of the verb שׁוּר in this passage (cf. inf.).

Job has no reason to be astonished if God at times seems deaf to the appeals of man (v. 13). For He does not deal with man on equal terms. He does not enter into discussion as two opponents would do before a tribunal. His word is decisive and commanding, it is uttered once for all: 'The fact is that God speaks once, and He does not repeat His word!' Cf. 40:5, where we have parallelism between אַחַת 'once' and שְׁתַּיִם 'twice'.

In this passage the verbs that correspond to דברתי 'I have spoken' are לא אשנה 'I will not repeat' (cf. Comm.) and לא אוסיף 'I will not begin again'. We expect here a similar verb. It has been proposed, on the basis of Syr. and Vulg., to change יְשׁוּרֶנָּה to ישנה 'he repeats' (Houbigant, Michaelis, etc.). But we have met in v. 3 (cf. Comm.), and we shall meet again in v. 27, the verb שׁוּר with the sense of 'repeat', 'say once more'. This meaning is admirably suited here, and we recognise it in the translations of Vulg. and Syr. We have no need to change the text and to read ישנה (cf. sup.), ישיבה 'He retracts it' (Duhm), ישמענה 'one hears it' (Graetz). Those who try to preserve the sense

of שׁוּר 'see', 'look' (Targ., cf. 7:8) translate: 'if God deigns to speak once, the second time one sees Him no more' (Le Hir), or again 'God speaks, however, sometimes in one way, sometimes in another, and man pays no heed to it' (Segond, cf. Crampon). The difficulties presented by these interpretations have led Siegfried and Budde to read תשׁורנה 'you perceive it'. The objection still remains the same, namely that the word of God is addressed to the sense of hearing, not to that of sight. And why change the subject of ישׁורנה, which, in the light of 40:5, is certainly the same as that of ידבר? Everything confirms the interpretation of ישׁורנה as 'He repeats it'. The homonymity of the roots שׁוּר 'to look' and שׁוּר 'to repeat' is not more strange than that of אמר 'to see' (Assyrian *amâru*) and אמר 'to say'. The verses which follow will show how God speaks to man.

15 Syr. begins by 'and by the lips He does not teach', which is a new translation of v. 14b with the reading בשׂפתים instead of בשׁתים (Beer). G ἢ ἐν μελέτῃ seems to read הגיון instead of חזיון. For תרדמה, Vulg. *sopor*, Syr. ܐܠܐ 'sleep', but G δεινὸς φόβος, Targ. שׁינתא עמקתא 'deep sleep'. By a mistake of homoeoteleuton, Sah. omits the 3rd hemistich and v. 16a, which ends with ἀνθρώπων (cf. ἀνθρώπους at the end of v. 15b).

Elihu is inspired by the account of the dream of Eliphaz (4:12ff.) and quotes 4:13 almost verbally. But while for Eliphaz the dream was only the occasion of a divine manifestation, it here becomes the very

16   Then He makes a revelation to men,
      And by *apparitions* He *terrifies them.*

16 וּבְמֹרָאִים (cf. G); MT: ובמסרם. — יְחִתָּם (G, Aq., Symm.); MT: יַחְתֹּם.

instrument of revelation: 'in a dream, a vision of the night'. The formula חֶזְיוֹן לַיְלָה is in apposition to חֲלוֹם. Cf. Is 29: 7, כַּחֲלוֹם חֲזוֹן לַיְלָה 'like a dream, a vision of the night'. There is parallelism between חלום and חזיון לילה in 20: 8 and between חלמות and חזיונות in 7: 14. God reveals Himself in a dream, בחלום (Gn 20: 3, 6; 31: 11, 24; Nu 12: 6; 1 K 3: 5). In Jl 3: 1 dreams are linked with prophecies and visions. The 2nd hemistich, which cites 4: 13b verbally, is deleted by a certain number of critics (Bickell, Budde, Duhm, etc.). It is supposed to be a gloss added under the influence of 4: 13. But is not this supposed gloss very much to the point for Elihu, who, taking 4: 13 as his inspiration, has thus completed his quotation? Note that תַּרְדֵּמָה denotes a mysterious deep sleep very suitable as the organ of revelation (Comm. on 4: 13). The abstract תְּנוּמָה from נום 'to sleep' is the parallel word to שֵׁנָה 'sleep', in Ps 132: 4; Pr 6: 4. Similarly the plural תנומות corresponds to שנות (Pr 6: 10; 24: 33). The literal translation of the 3rd hemistich would run: 'in sleeps on a bed'. It is intended as a description of the state into which men are plunged when wrapped in a mysterious torpor. Then (v. 16), that is, during such a slumber, the revelation takes place.

16 במסרם, G ἐν εἴδεσιν φόβου τοιούτοις. The characteristic word of G is not φόβου (cf. δεινὸς φόβος in v. 15), but εἴδεσιν. It is the Hebrew וּבְמֹרָאִים and not וּבְמוֹרָאִים (Duhm) which lies at the basis of G (cf. inf.).

The other versions have read וּבְמֹסָרָם; cf. Aq. καὶ ἐν παιδείᾳ αὐτῶν, Vulg. *et erudiens eos,* Targ. and Syr. ובמרדותהון 'and in their correction' (root רדה). The word יַחְתֹּם is vocalised יְחִתָּם by G αὐτοὺς ἐξεφόβησεν, Aq. πλήξει αὐτούς, Syr. 'He humiliates them' (cf. inf.).

The idiom גלה אזן 'to uncover the ear' corresponds to the Assyrian *uznâ puttû* 'to open the ears', and connotes 'to announce', 'to inform' (*L'Emploi métaphorique*, p. 89). It is met with in the Bible to denote simply the idea of conveying news to some one (1 S 20: 2, 12, 13; 20: 8, 17; Ru 4: 4), but also, when God is the subject, to suggest a special revelation (1 S 9: 15; 2 S 7: 27); cf. 36: 10, 15. The 2nd hemistich is remarkable for the number of interpretations to which it lends itself. If we retain the Massoretic vocalisation, we should have to translate: 'and with their bond He seals' or else: 'and He seals their bond', the word מוֹסֵר coming from the root אסר (cf. 39: 5). Since it is difficult to understand what might be the meaning of 'sealing the bond' of people who are asleep, it has in general been decided to favour the vocalisation וּבְמֹסָרָם, which is attested by Aq., Vulg., Syr., and Targ. (cf. sup.). Whence the translations: 'and marks with a seal the warnings He gives them' (Le Hir), 'and seals there (in the ear) His warnings' (Renan, Crampon). The text becomes clearer if we vocalise יְחִתָּם (G, Aq., Syr.), the *hiph'il* of חתת (31: 34) with suffix. This would then give us: 'and by their punishment He terrifies them'. But Dill-

17   To turn man away from *pride*,
      He hides from man *His action*.

17   מִגֵּוָה מַעֲשֵׂהוּ ; MT: מעשה וגוה.

mann points out quite rightly that the object of punishment is not to terrify. It is rather a means of converting (v. 17). Graetz proposes למוסרם 'for their punishment', i.e. 'in order to correct them' (cf. 36: 10). But it is in v. 17 that the aim pursued by God in revealing His will to men will be indicated. What is expected in the 2nd hemistich is an action performed by God using some means shown by the preposition בּ″. Following the interpretation of G, we read וּבְמַרְאִים, which is preferable to Duhm's וּבמוראים (cf. sup.). The word מַרְאָה 'appearance' (4: 16) also denotes 'vision', 'apparition' (Ezk 8: 4; 11: 24; Dn 8: 16, etc.). We translate: 'and by apparitions He terrifies them', which furnishes an excellent parallel to 7: 14, 'then Thou dost scare me with dreams, and by visions dost Thou terrify me'.

17   For מעשה, G ἀπὸ ἀδικίας; G(A) adds αὐτοῦ (Sah.). The translation of G does not presuppose מפשע (Houbigant), מעשק (Graetz), מעולה (Bickell, Duhm). It is an interpretation of מעשה bad 'action', as is proved by Targ. עובדא בישא. Vulg. *ab his quae facit* and Syr. ܡܢ ܚܒ̈ܠܘܗܝ 'from his works' have read מַעֲשֵׂהוּ; cf. G(A), Sah. The preposition מן has been added by the versions before מעשה, on account of the verb הסיר. The original text had simply מַעֲשֵׂהוּ (cf. inf.). G τὸ δὲ σῶμα αὐτοῦ ἀπὸ πτώματος ἐρρύσατο seems to read וְגֵוָה instead of וְגֵוָה and מִשְׁבֵּר instead of מגבר. Syr. ܘܦܓܪܗ 'and his body' also reads וְגֵוָה. Vulg. *et liberet eum de superbia* paraphrases the MT.

It is impossible to justify grammatically the current translations: 'to turn him aside from his evil deeds and to cure him of his pride' (Renan), 'to withdraw man from his works and to cleanse him of his pride' (Le Hir), 'so as to turn man away from evil and to save him from pride' (Segond), 'so as to turn man away from his evil deeds and to withdraw him from pride' (Crampon). Such interpretations imply the preposition מן before מַעֲשֶׂה, as do also the versions. They assign to יְכַסֶּה 'He hides' or 'He veils' (9: 24; 15: 27; 16: 18, etc.) a meaning which is not appropriate to it, such as 'cure', 'cleanse', 'save', 'draw back'. Bickell in his first edition translated back into Hebrew the Greek text, a process which compelled him to substitute מעולה (cf. Duhm) for מעשה and to read as the 2nd hemistich: וְגֵוָה מִשְׁבֵּר יַפְצֶה, whence Loisy: 'to turn him away from sin and to save his body from destruction'. In his second edition Bickell gives up his 2nd hemistich and merely changes יכסה into יְכַסֵּחַ (Reiske, Budde, Duhm). The verb כסה is found in the passive participle of the *qal* only in Is 33: 12; Ps 80: 17. The meaning appropriate to it is 'to cut', and the translation suggested is: 'and to cut pride away from man'. On the word גֵּוָה cf. 22: 29. Ehrlich reaches quite a different meaning, since he replaces להסתיר מאדם by מאדם להסיר and interprets גוה by 'His greatness': hiding His action from man and not disclosing to man His greatness. We have seen that the word מעשה was at the basis of the translation of G and that there was no reason to replace it by a word meaning ini-

18   He saves his soul from the Pit,
      And his life from passing through the Canal.

quity, transgression, etc. Further-more, the idiom מִגֶּבֶר יְכַסֶּה 'He hides from man' is excellent Hebrew, and we shall not lightly abandon it. Now, we find in Gn 18: 17 the following question: 'shall I hide from Abraham what I propose to do?' It is the *pi'el* of כסה with מן before Abraham which is used to connote 'hide from'. The direct complement is אשר אני עשה 'what I do'. If we suppose that, in our verse, the word גוה originally stood before מעשה, we obtain מַעֲשֵׂהוּ מגבר יכסה 'He hides from man His action', and we note that מעשהו is supported by Vulg. and Syr. The resemblance to Gn 18: 17 becomes striking. The 1st hemistich explains why God hides His action from man, namely in order that the latter may not grow proud: 'to avert man from pride'. The original text had מִגֵּוָה, but the מ has fallen out by haplography after אדם. The simple transference of the word גוה has given us the key to this *crux interpretum*. For the construction of הסיר, cf. 27: 5.

18 For שחת, Targ. שוחתא, G θανάτου, Vulg. *corruptione*, Syr. ܣܚܠܐ 'perdition'. G summarises the 2nd hemistich as: καὶ μὴ πεσεῖν αὐτὸν ἐν πολέμῳ. The interpretation ἐν πολέμῳ rests on the meaning 'arrow' for שֶׁלַח (cf. inf.). Cf. Targ. בשלחא, Vulg. *in gladium*. The phrase מעבר בשלח is simply rendered by ܡܢ ܐܒܕܢ 'from ruin' in Syr.

The beneficent action of God, described in vv. 15-17, has as its result the salvation of man: 'He preserves his soul from the pit.' On the verb חשך, cf. Comm. on 21: 30. The word שַׁחַת 'pit', grave', as in 17: 14. Parallelism between נֶפֶשׁ 'soul' and חַיָּה 'living being', 'vital essence' (vv.

20, 22, 28; 36: 14). The phrase נֶפֶשׁ חַיָּה 'living soul' (Gn 1: 20) has been split up into its two elements. It is not really possible to say in English 'his living one' with the sense of 'his soul'. Hence we resign ourselves to translating חַיָּתוֹ by 'his life'. עבר בשלח is interpreted as 'pass (away) by the sword' (cf. Vulg.), or more precisely, 'pass (away) by the arrow' (cf. Targ.). The word שֶׁלַח has in fact the meaning of 'shaft', 'arrow' (cf. Comm. on 20: 25). But a violent death is not here in question, any more than it is in 36: 12, where the expression 'pass through the *šelaḥ*' recurs. This expression is here parallel to 'the Pit' and in 36: 12 to the idea 'to expire'. In both cases to change to בִּשְׁאֹלָה 'in Sheol' (Duhm) is too easy a simplification. Now, in v. 28 we find, in a context precisely similar to that of our v. 18, the formula מעבר בשחת 'to pass through the Pit' which corresponds to מעבר בשלח. It follows that שֶׁלַח is a synonym of שַׁחַת. It so happens that there exists a word שֶׁלַח connoting 'conduit', 'canal', 'channel', which we recognise in Jl 2: 8, 'fall through the channel' (verb נפל with בעד as in 2 K 1: 2, 'fall through the lattice'). The same word is used, in the plural, of the waters which irrigate the garden of the spouse in Ca 4: 12, where it is a metaphor. The proper noun שֶׁלַח (Is 8: 6), Σιλωάμ (connected with the root שלח 'to send' in Jn 9: 7 ἀπεσταλμένος) denotes the channel of Siloah and is merely a diminutive of שֶׁלַח; cf. ברכת השלח 'pool of Shelah' in Neh 3: 15, where Vulg. interprets by *piscina Siloe* (cf. κολυμβήθραν τοῦ Σιλωάμ in Jn 9: 7). Finally, the Assyrian *šiliḫtu*,

19   He *corrects him* by pain upon his bed,
     And by a continual shaking of his bones;

19   וְהוֹכַח אֹתוֹ (cf. G, Vulg., Syr., and v. 20); MT: וְהוּכַח.

related to 'the river', also denotes a
channel or canal. These facts incline
us to interpret עבר בשלח by 'pass
through the Canal'. We see here
an allusion to the vertical canal,
analogous to the well of souls, which
allows the spirit of the departed to
pass into Sheol beneath the earth.
To pass through the waters of the
Canal would mean to descend into
the underworld after passing through
the Pit (v. 28), i.e. the grave. The
image is derived from the feature of
Phoenician tombs, where descent
is by a vertical channel.

19 V. 19b, absent from Sah.,
marked with asterisk in Colb. and
Syro-hex., did not exist in G. The
present text comes from Theod.
(cf. Syro-hex.). G πάλιν δὲ ἤλεγξεν
αὐτόν, Vulg. *increpat quoque*, Syr.
ܣܘܟܚܗ 'and he covers' read וְהוֹכַח
instead of וְהוּכַח, whence the suppression of the suffix of מִשְׁכָּבוֹ in
G ἐπὶ κοίτης and Vulg. *in lectulo*. The
Westerns have the *kethîb* וְרִיב, but
the Orientals וְרוֹב (*qerê* of the
Westerns and Orientals). It is ורוב
which is reflected in Theod. καὶ
πλῆθος, Vulg. *et omnia*, Targ. וסוגעי,
Syr. ܘܣܘܓܐܐ. For אתן, Theod.
ἐνάρκησεν, Vulg. *marcescere facit*; but
Targ. תקיפין 'strong' and Syr. ܢܕܫ
'strengthens' preserve the normal
meaning of אֵיתָן (12: 19).
One might hesitate between the
reading of the MT וְהוּכַח 'and he
is chastened' and that of the versions (with the exception of Targ.)
וְהוֹכַח 'and He chastens (him)'. To
introduce the new hypothesis, Duhm
proposes גַּם יֻכַּח 'also he is chastened',
following G πάλιν δέ. But the trans-

lation of G adds what is expected.
Beer and Budde read אוֹ יוֹכְחֶנּוּ 'or
else He chastens him', which is half
suggested by the versions. In our
opinion, the text read וְהוֹכַח followed by the suffix אֹתוֹ the remains
of which are found in וזהמתו (cf.
inf.) of v. 20. On the meaning of
הוֹכַח, cf. Comm. on 5: 17. God had
used dreams and apparitions to
terrify man and prevent him from
taking his faults to extremes. Now
it is pain and sorrow—and this
applies specially to Job—which is
to be the instrument of divine pity.
What is in question is physical pain,
an illness which keeps man 'on his
bed'; cf. עֲלֵי מִשְׁכָּב in v. 15. The
qerê וְרוֹב is influenced by 4: 14. The
versions which have decided in
favour of this reading (cf. sup.)
change the meaning of אתן (Theod.,
Vulg.) or translate: 'and the multitude of his bones are strong' (Targ.),
'and he strengthens the multitude
of his bones' (Syr.). In order to
reconcile such interpretations with
the context, it is proposed to translate: 'when the totality of his bones
is still strong' (Ewald, Dillmann).
But the use of the *waw* at the
beginning of this hemistich suggests that the allusion is to an early
symptom of the illness. Duhm, who
adopts the *qerê*, changes אתן very
arbitrarily into אָסֵר 'crippled'. He
quotes the Septuagint, which is
missing here (cf. sup.), and doubtless
alludes to Theod. ἐνάρκησεν 'has
become benumbed'. But Theod. is
probably interpreting אתן as an
equivalent of אישׁן, derived from
ישׁן 'to sleep'. Those who adopt the
kethîb וְרִיב find here the root רִיב
'dispute', 'contest', etc., and see
in it 'a striking image of the de-

20   His life turns away in disgust [   ] from bread,
      And his soul from appetising food;

20 וְזִהֲמָה; MT: וזהמתו (cf. v. 19).

struction of the equilibrium of forces which are struggling among themselves' (Le Hir). But this striking image yields only paraphrases: 'and his bones are violently agitated' (Le Hir); 'by the continual tearing of his bones' (Renan); 'when an unending strife comes upon him shaking his bones' (Segond). Note that אֵתָן, which is meant for אֵיתָן, certainly has here its basic meaning of 'perpetual', 'unremitting' (cf. Comm. on 12:19), and that this meaning is perfectly suitable to a description of a diseased state of the body. Now, there exists in Assyrian a word *rîbu* which denotes the phenomenon of earthquakes, and which belongs to a hollow root *râbu* 'to be agitated', 'to be shaken', 'to quiver'; cf. Streck, *Babyloniaca,* **2**, pp. 209ff. This is indeed the meaning we expect when the allusion is to a preliminary symptom of the fever whose other effects will be described in the verses which follow. The 2nd hemistich specifies the type of pain of which the sufferer is a victim: 'and a continual trembling of his bones'. It becomes clear that it is not necessary to change ריב or רוב into רָקָב 'rotting state' as is proposed by Beer.

20 V. 20b, absent from Sah., marked with asterisk in Jerome and Syro-hex., did not exist in G. The present text is taken from Theod. (cf. Syro-hex.). Syr. places before v. 20 a first translation of v. 21a. G πᾶν δὲ βρωτὸν σίτου οὐ μὴ δύνηται προσδέξασθαι and Vulg. *abominabilis ei fit in vita sua panis* paraphrase the 1st hemistich. Syr. renders וזהמתו by ܠܐ ܣܒܥ 'he is not sated'. Targ. adds 'and in consequence of the

disgust which overcomes him', before מרחיקא נפשיה 'his soul rejects', in order to give a full meaning to וזהמתו נפשו. Theod. ἐπιθυμήσει and Syr. ܪܓ 'desires' make of תאוה a verbal form of אוה 'to desire'. Vulg. translates מאכל תאוה by *cibus ante desiderabilis.*

After the shiverings symptomatic of fever comes loss of appetite. For the parallelism between נֶפֶשׁ and חַיָּה, cf. v. 18. The verb זהם is not found elsewhere in the Bible, but it is probable that the original text of 6:7 had זִהֲמָה (cf. Comm.). The root זהם means etymologically to be fat, then to be dirty (Latin *crassus* has both senses), as is to be seen from the Arabic *zahima*. In Aramaic it is the meaning 'dirty', 'sordid', 'filthy' which has prevailed. From this meaning is derived that of 'smelling foul'; cf. Syriac ܪܗܡ 'fetid', ܪܗܡܘܬܐ 'bad smell'. The idea of disgust or repulsion is naturally linked with meanings of that kind. Hence, for the *pi'el*, here and in 6:7, 'to feel repulsion', 'to be disgusted'. Cf. the use of the *pi'el* of תעב in 9:31; 19:19; 30:10. The presence of the suffix in זהמתו is strange, for the direct object is לחם and there is no reason to anticipate it by translating 'and it has been disgusted by it, by bread'. In the light of 6:7 and Ps 107:18, where we have כל־אכל תתעב נפשם 'their soul is horrified by all food', it seems to us evident that the text had זִהֲמָה and that the final תו comes from אֹתוֹ, which was the complement of וְהוֹכַח in v. 19. We translate חיתו by 'his life', as in v. 18, for lack of an exact equivalent to 'his living one', synonymous with 'his soul': 'and

21   His wasted flesh disappears from view,
      And his bones are emaciated, they can no longer be seen,

his life is disgusted with bread'. We may retain for לֶחֶם its normal meaning of bread, so as not to anticipate the 2nd hemistich, where it is a question of dainty appetising foods which tempt. Cf. לֶחֶם חֲמֻדוֹת 'food of desire' in Dn 10: 3.

21 The 1st hemistich is rendered ἕως ἂν σαπῶσιν αὐτοῦ αἱ σάρκες (G), tabescet caro ejus (Vulg.). The first translation of Syr. (before v. 20) and the second (here) connect ראי with the verb ירא 'to fear'. By the first translation of Syr. the verb יכל is interpreted as coming from כלה, by the second it is confused with אכל. G καὶ ἀποδείξη τὰ ὀστᾶ αὐτοῦ κενά probably renders the kethîb וּשְׁפִי by ἀποδείξη and assigns to לא ראו 'are not seen' the meaning of no longer existing (κενά). Vulg. et ossa quae tecta fuerant nudabuntur reads the qerê וְשֻׁפּוּ and interprets לא ראו by quae tecta fuerant. Under the influence of v. 19b, Syr. renders וּשְׁפִי עצמתיו by ܘܣܓܝ̈ܐܢ ܓܪ̈ܡܘܗܝ 'and the multitude of his bones'. For לא ראו, Syr. 'he does not see'. Targ. וּשְׁפִין 'are crushed' reads the qerê וְשֻׁפּוּ.

   Note the use of the jussive יְכַל with the sense of the imperfect (13: 27; 15: 33; 18: 9, 12, etc.). The word רֳאִי (1 S 16: 2; Nah 3: 6) or רֶאִי (Gn 16: 13) denotes sight or vision: an abstract noun derived from ראה 'to see'. The meaning of the 1st hemistich is not in doubt: 'His flesh disappears from view'. The context shows clearly that this is in consequence of the leanness due to a sick man's diet (v. 20). Hence it is unnecessary to change מֵרֳאִי to מֵרֳזִי 'as a result of thinness' (Duhm). The word רֹזִי is doubtful in Is 24: 16 (cf. Condamin); מְרֹזוֹן would be

preferable (Budde), but is not necessary. We stand by the text as it is. Following the kethîb שְׁפִי, whose normal meaning is 'bare hill', and pressing the meaning of the root שפה (Aramaic שׁפא) 'to be smooth, polished', critics assign to שְׁפִי עצמתיו 'the polish of his bones' a translation adapted to the context: 'his denuded bones disappear' (Renan); 'and his emaciated limbs are scarce visible any more' (Le Hir). It is apparent how subtle such an interpretation is and how difficult it is to make 'the polish of his bones' fit with לא רָאוּ 'are not seen'. The qerê וְשֻׁפּוּ, supported by Vulg. and Targ., enables us to see here a pu'al form (just as in the case of רָאוּ) of the verb שְׁפָה. This verb exists in the niph'al in the phrase הַר־נִשְׁפָּה 'bare mountain' of Is 13: 2. The noun שְׁפִי (cf. the kethîb) denotes the 'glabrous' hill, the hill that is denuded of vegetation (Is 41: 18; 49: 9, etc.). The meaning 'polish' 'sharpen' which שפה has in Modern Hebrew clearly corresponds to these images. In Aramaic the verb שׁפא, שְׁפִי, means 'crush', 'pound', and is thus akin to שׁוּף, שׁפף (cf. Comm. on 9: 17); but it also has the meaning of 'polish', which is found again in the Syriac ܫܦ. Usually critics compare the Arabic سفى, the basic meaning of which is 'to raise the dust' and, in the 4th form 'to grow thin', whence the noun سفا 'dust', 'leanness'.

But there is a verb شَفَّ 'to be thin, transparent', and 'to have become emaciated' or 'to render emaciated'. It is rather in such a verb that we would see the root corresponding to שפה ('ע''ע) instead of (ע''י). In fact the general meaning 'polish', 'sharpen' results in 'to make slender,

22　His soul draws nigh to the Pit,
　　And his life to the *abode of the dead*.
23　If there stand beside him an Angel,
　　One interpreter among a thousand,
　　To reveal to man his duty

22　לְמִקוֹם מֵתִים ;MT: לממתים.
23　Transfer v. 26c to the end of this verse (cf. Comm.).

thin' and, in speaking of the body, 'to make emaciated'. This last meaning agrees very well with the tenor of our passage: 'and his bones are emaciated'. It is the equivalent of יכל בשרו of the 1st hemistich, while לא ראו corresponds to מראי. This explanation seems to us to be preferable to that of Yahuda (*JQR*, **15**, pp. 712f.), who takes شفّ in the sense of 'to be transparent,' so as to translate: 'his bones which were not seen become visible'. In reality the root conveys the idea of transparency, resulting from thinness, and not that of visibility. The bones have become so lean that they 'are no longer seen, no longer apparent'. Let us leave to Budde the bad taste of correcting ראו to נאוו 'they are not beautiful'(!). It is difficult to see why Duhm eliminates לא ראו.

22 For לשחת, G εἰς θάνατον, Vulg. *corruptioni*, Syr. ܠܣܚܠܐ, Targ. לשוחתא; cf. v. 18. The word ממתים is literally translated *mortiferis* in Vulg., while G interprets by ᾅδη 'Hades'. We have simply the sense of 'death' in Syr. ܡܘܬܐ and Targ. מיתותא.

The illness whose symptoms have been described has now reached its final stages. Logically it must lead to the grave: 'and his soul draws nigh to the Pit'. The word שחת as in v. 18 and v. 28. There is parallelism between נפשו and חיתו (vv. 18 and 28). The word which corresponds to שחת is מְמִתִים, plural participle *hiph'il* of מות. Critics have

wished to see here an equivalent of the Assyrian *mušmîtûti* 'those who kill', a category of infernal demons. But there is no need for the intervention of these exterminators, since the sick man will die quite naturally, and nothing suggests that these demons have their abode in the beyond. Hoffmann and Perles read למו מתים 'their soul draws near to the dead'. Budde adopts this reading. What however is expected is a word parallel to 'the Pit', i.e. the grave or Sheol. For this reason the Greek translation interpreted by Hades (cf. sup.). The present text seems to us to have resulted from haplography. There stood in the text לְמִקוֹם מֵתִים, and the eye of the scribe passed from the first *mêm* to the second, whence לממתים. 'The place of the dead' designated either the grave or Sheol; cf. 30: 23b. It forms an excellent parallel to שחת.

23 The text of G, here as in v. 24, is clearly longer than that of the MT. We have, first, ἐὰν ὦσιν χίλιοι ἄγγελοι θανατηφόροι, εἷς αὐτῶν οὐ μὴ τρώσῃ αὐτόν. In Cod. 23 we find οὐκ ἀποκρίνονται αὐτῷ after θανατη-φόροι; cf. Jerome *non respondebit ei* (with asterisk). Note that θανατη-φόροι comes from ממתים of v. 22, where Vulg. translates by *mortiferis*. The words οὐ μὴ τρώσῃ αὐτόν, which will recur in 41: 19, seem to us a paraphrase of מליץ, connected with מלץ 'to be soft, sweet' (cf. Comm. on 6: 25). Then ἐὰν νοήσῃ τῇ καρδίᾳ ἐπιστραφῆναι πρὸς Κύριον, marked with obelus in Syro-hex., oddly

26c *And restore to man his righteousness,*
24   And if he has pity on him and says:

24 פְּדָהוּ (cf. Targ., Syr.); MT: פדעהו. — Add נַפְשׁוֹ at the end (cf. Comm.).

combines v. 22b and v. 23a of ch. 22. Finally, ἀναγγείλη δὲ ἀνθρώπῳ τὴν ἑαυτοῦ μέμψιν, τὴν δὲ ἄνοιαν αὐτοῦ δείξη comes from a double translation of להגיד···ישרו. The second translation, from τὴν δέ, is marked by obelus in Jerome and Syro-hex. The word ישרו has been connected with יסר 'criticise', 'reproach', 'correct': first the reproach, τὴν ἑαυτοῦ μέμψιν, then what motivates it, τὴν δὲ ἄνοιαν αὐτοῦ. G treats the MT very freely (cf. vv. 5-6, 12-13). Vulg. renders מליץ by *loquens*. The 1st hemistich is paraphrased in Targ. 'if there is virtue in him, an angel prepares to intervene, an advocate (פרקליטא, παράκλητος) from among a thousand accusers (קטיגוריא, κατήγορος)'. Syr. translates מליץ by ܘܦܡܥ ܠܗ 'who hears him'. Vulg. interprets the 2nd hemistich as *ut annuntiet hominis aequitatem.*

We left the sick man on the brink of the grave (v. 22). It is then that divine intervention takes place. Between man and God is found an intermediary whose function is to protect man and to shield him from divine anger; such a one is Michael in Dn 12:1. The 1st hemistich stops at מַלְאָךְ: 'if there stand beside him an angel!' Use of עָלָיו is as in 1 K 22:19. The translation 'for him' agrees less well with יֵשׁ. What is needed is a verb of intercession as in 42:8. The change from אִם to אָז 'then' (Duhm, following v. 16) is unnecessary. Vv. 23-4 show in what conditions the happy event indicated by v. 25 takes place. Budde departs from his usual attitude of reserve by suppressing מלאך and אחד מני־אלף. Siegfried deleted אֶחָד מני־אלף. But the formula מֵלִיץ אֶחָד מִנִּי־אֶלֶף is confirmed by Ec

7:28, where we have אדם אחד מאלף 'one man in a thousand' (cf. Sir 6:5). The exact meaning of the word מֵלִיץ is 'interpreter', as may be clearly seen from Gn 42:23, where the word is translated ἑρμηνευτής (G), *interpres* (Vulg.), מתורגמן 'dragoman' (Targ.). The angel serves as an interpreter between God and man and performs the function of the Prophets, who are called מליציך 'Thy interpreters' in Is 43:27. The revelation takes place through their mediation (Gn 31:11; 1 K 13:18; 2 K 1:15, etc.). The sequel 'to reveal to man his duty' explains the function of the interpreter. The word יֹשֶׁר 'uprightness' (6:25) here denotes what makes man יָשָׁר 'upright', i.e. 'duty'. Cf. the use of משפט in 32:9. A parallel member is missing. Now, we have in v. 26c a hemistich which ends with לֶאֱנוֹשׁ צִדְקָתוֹ, corresponding exactly to לאדם ישרו, while וַיָּשֶׁב continues לְהַגִּיד. The clause introduced by ל with a following infinitive is continued by the imperfect with the *waw* consecutive, just as in Ps 50:16. A similar construction is found in 38:7. The word צִדְקָה has the same meaning as in 27:6. The angel reveals to man his duty and thus enables him to regain his uprightness. The transference of v. 26c, which introduces parallelism between ישרו and צדקתו, frees us from the need to change ישרו into מוסרו 'his punishment'. This correction of Duhm has but slender support in τὴν ἑαυτοῦ μέμψιν of G, whose translation is very free.

24 As in the case of v. 23, G again deviates seriously from the MT. The

'Exempt him from going down into the Pit,
I have found the ransom of his soul!'

opening ἀνθέξεται τοῦ μὴ πεσεῖν εἰς θάνατον omits the words ויחננו ויאמר and paraphrases פדעהו מרדת שחת; cf. θάνατον for שחת in v. 22. The sequel ἀνανεώσει δὲ αὐτοῦ τὸ σῶμα ὥσπερ ἀλοιφὴν ἐπὶ τοίχου (Jerome *et renovabit corpus suum sicut litura in pariete*, with obelus before *corpus ... pariete*) combines the end of v. 24 with the 1st hemistich of v. 25; the words ἀνανεώσει δὲ αὐτοῦ τὸ σῶμα correspond to בשרו מנער, while ὥσπερ ἀλοιφὴν ἐπὶ τοίχου interprets כֹּפֶר in accordance with Gn 6:14, where Aq. translates ἀλοιφήσεις ἀλοιφῇ. Finally, τὰ δὲ ὀστᾶ αὐτοῦ ἐμπλήσει μυελοῦ reads ישביע מח עצמיו instead of ישוב לימי עלומיו of v. 25. It is misunderstanding the character of G to try to retranslate it into Hebrew, in vv. 23-4, as is done by Duhm, who adds that it is not easy to discern 'whether the tetrastich is original or whether it is not simply a marginal quotation'. Syr. and Targ. are agreed in rendering פדע by the verb פרק 'to deliver' and כפר by פורקנא 'redemption', 'ransom'. Vulg. renders פדעהו by *libera eum* and כפר by *in quo ei propitier*. For שחת, the same translations as in vv. 18 and 22.

The clause 'and if he has pity on him and says' forms a sort of parenthesis in the poetry, exactly like ישר···ויאמר of v. 27. The thread is taken up again from the direct speech. The meaning of the whole passage is missed if we introduce אל 'God' after וַיְחָנֶּנּוּ, as do Steuernagel and Budde, to convey the notion that it is God who speaks the words which follow. It is rather the angel, the mediator between man and God, who intercedes for the dying man and begs mercy for him (cf. v. 23), after bringing him into a penitent state of mind (ibid.). Instead of פְּדָעֵהוּ, which contains a *hapax* פדע, a few manuscripts have read פְּרָעֵהוּ, accepted by Wright, Beer, Graetz, etc. The meaning would then be: 'leave him' or 'avoid him' (cf. Pr 4:15) and not 'deliver him', as the context requires. Budde interprets: '*mach ihn frei!*' but he deletes מֶרֶדֶת שַׁחַת. Now, in v. 28 we shall have the verb פדה used in a very similar context. There Targ. and Syr. render פדה by the verb פרק which they have used here (cf. sup.). The original text had פְּדָהוּ, and the letter ע is merely a *mater lectionis* (it is still by ע that the Jews reproduce the vowel *e*, *é*, *è*, in their transcriptions of foreign names). Hence with Hirzel, Ewald, Dillmann, and others, we read פְּדָהוּ 'exempt him'. Cf. Ps 49:8, where the verb פדה is in parallelism with נתן כפר 'to give a ransom'. The verb פדה 'redeem' also means 'to free', 'to deliver' (5:20; 6:23) whether from a present evil or from one to come, whence the connotation 'exempt' (cf. v. 28). For the word שחת after ירד, cf. the construction of 17:16a. In Ps 30:10 we have ברדתי אל־שחת 'in my descent into the Pit'. In v. 28 it will be a question of 'going down into the Pit'; cf. vv. 18 and 22. The 2nd hemistich is too short. Everything leads us to believe that originally it included כֹּפֶר נַפְשׁוֹ 'the ransom of his soul' (Bickell, Beer, Budde), as in Ex 30:12 (cf. Pr 13:8), and that נפשו dropped out before רטפש (v. 25), which finished with the same consonants (same case in v. 22). The word כֹּפֶר, which will recur in 36:18, is used in a symbolical sense; it is the redemption, the ransom, which the angel offers to God to save man who is in danger of death (Ex 21:30). One might say that suffering and ocnversion (vv.

25   His flesh *becomes fresh* with youth,
     He returns to the days of his early manhood,
26   He invokes Eloah and He delights in him,
     And he sees His face with joy [   ],

25   יְרְטַב; MT: רטפש.
26   V. 26c after v. 23.

19-23) constitute the price of the ransom.

25 For רטפש, G ἀπαλυνεῖ, Vulg. *consumpta est*, Targ. אתקליש 'grows thin', Syr. ܢܫܬܚܠܦ 'changes'. The variant אתחליש of Targ. would mean rather 'grows weak'. G renders מנער by ὥσπερ νηπίου; cf. Syr. 'as in his childhood' and Targ. 'more than youth'. Vulg. *a suppliciis* connects with נער 'to shake' (38:13). The 2nd hemistich is paraphrased in G ἀποκαταστήσει δὲ αὐτὸν ἀνδρωθέντα ἐν ἀνθρώποις.

The consequence of the intervention of the mediator is that the sick man is restored to health. The 2nd hemistich is clear: 'he returns to the days of his early manhood'. On the abstract עֲלָמִים, cf. 20:11. Hence the idea of the author is a rejuvenation of the man who was on the point of dying. The *hapax* רטפש has been compared to the Syriac ܪܛܦܫܐ (metathesis), the meaning of which is 'lean meat' (cf. Targ.). But רטפש represents the verb whose complement is מנער. We should have to translate: 'his flesh has grown thin through youth', which is not in harmony with the context. Most moderns have accepted the suggestion of Altschüller (*ZATW*, 6, p. 212), who corrects רטפש to טָפַשׁ 'has grown fat', the ר being a dittograph of the last letter of כפר. For the sake of greater symmetry, יִטְפַּשׁ has been proposed (Siegfried, Budde, Duhm, Beer, etc.). The verb טפש is used in Ps 119:70 with the meaning of 'to be closed,

blocked' (derived from the connotation 'to be fat'), and depicts the heart which is inaccessible to divine instruction. Here it is interpreted in the sense of 'to swell' from the effect of a renewal of youth. But the literal meaning would be 'to grow fat' with youth, and it is difficult to see in what sense youth can be said to fatten. The same objection applies to the assimilation of רטפש to the Assyrian *ritpašu* 'is dilated' (Perles), and furthermore the word would be transcribed רתפש. In 21:24 the freshness of youth was thus described: 'and the marrow of his bones is very fresh'. The verb used was יְשֻׁקֶה, a *pu'al* of שקה 'to water'. One may therefore wonder, with the ancient Jewish commentators, whether רטפש does not conceal a form of רָטֹב 'to be well watered, moist, fresh' (8:16; 24:8). Torczyner rightly sees in רטפש a transformation of רטב under the influence of בשרו. We read יְרְטַב (cf. 24:8), which allows us to translate: 'his flesh becomes fresh with youth', youth conveying the idea of youthful vigour and sap, exactly like עלומים in 20:11. The parallelism is excellent, and the image in harmony with the style of Hebrew poetry. Youth is a renovation, a growing fresh, whereas old age dries up.

26 For וירצהו, G καὶ δεκτὰ αὐτῷ ἔσται, Vulg. *placabilis ei erit*. Syr. doubly translates: 'and He will hear him and will delight in him'. G renders וירא פניו by εἰσελεύσεται δὲ προσώπῳ ἱλαρῷ. Syr. considers ירא as a *niph'al* 'and he will appear

27   He tells of his experience to men, saying:
       'I had sinned and had falsified the right,
       But I have not been punished for it:

before Him'. For צדקתו, Targ. כצדקתיה 'according to his righteousness'.

The sick man is restored to grace and favour. He can now address God with full confidence: 'He invokes Eloah, and He delights in him.' On the verb עתר, cf. 22:27, where we have 'you will call to Him and He will answer you'. The verb רצה 'to delight in', 'to be favourable to' (cf. Comm. on 14:6). The sequel of 22:27 'and you will acquit yourself of your vows' proves that the subject of יָרָא is the same as that of יֶעְתַּר (contra Budde). It is not the *hiph'il* but the *qal* which is used: 'and He sees his face with delight'. The word תְּרוּעָה 'delight', 'pleasure', as in 8:21, does not denote temple music (contra Duhm). It is simply the expression of the joy which succeeds to sadness. The idiom 'to see the face of God' implies the idea of coming before God as a servant comes into the presence of his master, or as a subject presents himself to his sovereign (*L'Emploi métaphorique*, pp. 48f.). What follows, 'and He restores to man his righteousness', does not fit the context. We should have simply 'and He restores to him his righteousness' if the hemistich alluded to the conversion and healing of the sick man. Hence Duhm proposes to change וישב to ויספר 'and he tells, narrates', or to ויבשר 'and he proclaims', so as to make v. 26c the parallel member to the 1st hemistich of v. 27. Fried. Delitzsch and Ehrlich arrive at the same result by postulating for השיב the meaning of 'report', 'narrate'. But the parallelism between לאנוש and על־אנשים is rather disturbing. Again, we have seen that v. 26c, taken in its natural meaning, forms a parallel hemistich to v. 23c (cf. Comm.).

In reality, v. 27a is, like v. 24a, an introduction to the direct speech. It does not require a parallel member.

27 G εἶτα τότε ἀπομέμψεται ἄνθρωπος αὐτὸς ἑαυτῷ λέγων connects ישר with the root יסר (cf. v. 23) and probably reads עליו אנוש instead of על אנשים. By a transposition of העויתי (confused with מה עשיתי) and of חטאתי, and in consequence of reading ואשר instead of וישר, G then translates: οἷα συνετέλουν; καὶ οὐκ ἄξια ἤτασέν με ὧν ἥμαρτον. The rhythm completely disappears from this translation. Syro-hex. marks with obelus αὐτὸς ἑαυτῷ λέγων οἷα συνετέλουν. Vulg. *respiciet homines* connects ישר with שור 'look', 'see' (cf. Targ. in v. 14). Targ. יתריץ 'he is upright' and Syr. ܘܐܡܪ ... ܠܡܚ 'he says what is right' interpret by the root ישר 'to be right, upright'. For וישר העויתי, Vulg. *et vere deliqui*; cf. Syr. ܘܫܪܝܪܐܝܬ 'and truly'. The last hemistich is rendered: *et ut eram dignus non recepi* (Vulg.) 'and I have not been profitable to myself' (Syr.). Targ. follows the MT closely by translating שוה as הוא שוי 'has been equal'.

Since Schultens, it has generally been agreed to see in יָשֹׁר a mistaken writing of יָשִׁר 'he sings' (from שִׁיר), whence 'then he sings before men' (Le Hir), 'he goes away singing among men' (Renan). But it is strange that no version gives evidence for so easy a reading. Torczyner reads ישרם 'and their uprightness', parallel to צִדְקָתוֹ. But we have seen that v. 26c was not to be coupled with v. 27a. Ehrlich would read ישיב and assign to it the meaning of 'narrate' which he has already postulated for ישב in v. 26c. This however produces tautology.

28   He has exempted my soul from passing through the Canal.
     And my life sees the light!'
29   Behold, such are the things which God does
     Twice and thrice in His dealings with man,

The form יָשֹׁר is a jussive, used with the sense of the imperfect (cf. v. 21), of the verb שׁוּר 'to repeat' (cf. vv. 3 and 14). The converted man repeats to men the marvels which God has wrought on his behalf. What he says is introduced by וַיֹּאמֶר 'and he says'. Elihu puts in the mouth of his fictitious character Job's exclamation in 7: 20, 'I have sinned'. The *hiph'il* of עוה with the meaning 'to cause to deviate' (cf. Comm. on 8: 3). The adjective יָשָׁר is used substantively to express 'what is right', synonymous with מִשְׁפָּט and צדק in 8: 3. The natural meaning of the last hemistich is well expressed in a note by Le Hir: *non aequatum est mihi*. But this author translates in the text: 'and God has not in my case wrought His works'. This is to anticipate v. 28. Budde goes further by adding אֵל between וּ and לֹא, which obliges him to vocalise שָׁוָה or to read הִשְׁוָה 'and God has not done the like to me'. One cannot invoke the support of G to add at the end כְּחַטָּאתִי 'according to my sin' (Bickell) or כַּעֲוֹנִי 'according to my fault' (Duhm). The best course is to retain the construction of the MT, the verb שׁוה conveying an impersonal meaning similar to the Latin expression: *par pari refertur*. Hence we may translate: 'it has not been requited to me', or 'I have not been punished', since it is a question of a sin which normally would call for reprisals. The sinner has not been treated according to his deeds. It is God who has had pity on him, and, at the last moment, has saved him (v. 28).

Syro-hex., did not exist in G. The present text derives from Theod. (cf. Colb. and Syro-hex.). But we shall see that v. 30 of G represents, in reality, v. 28 of the MT. It is vv. 29-30 which have disappeared from G (cf. v. 30). The *kethîb* נפשי is followed by Theod. and Syr., the *qerê* נפשו by Targ. and Vulg. The same applies to the *kethîb* חיתי and the *qerê* חיתו, if we note that Vulg. translates simply by *vivens*. For שחת, Theod. διαφθοράν, Vulg. *interitum*, Targ. שוחתא, Syr. ܫܚܠ (cf. vv. 18, 22, 24). Targ. interprets באור by בנהורא מעליא 'the light from on high'.

God is of course the subject of the verbs. The angel has been only a mediator (cf. vv. 18 and 24). In the light of what follows in the story, the *kethîb* נַפְשִׁי and חַיְתִי is certainly preferable to the *qerê* נַפְשׁוֹ and חַיְתוֹ. It is still the converted man who is speaking. The verb פדה as in v. 24 (cf. Comm.). Parallelism between נֶפֶשׁ 'soul' and חַיָּה 'living essence' (vv. 18, 20, 22). The phrase 'to pass through the Pit' takes the place of 'pass through the Canal' cf. v. 18 and 36: 12. The verb ראה with בְּ before the direct complement (3: 9; 20: 17). The light is the light of the living in contrast to death (Ps 56: 14). On the relation between light and life, cf. Comm. on 3: 20. The abortive are those who have not seen the light (3: 16). In Assyrian the expression *nûra amâru* 'to see the light' represents the state of the living. The dead do not 'see the light' (*Choix de Textes*, p. 213, l. 35, and p. 327, l. 9).

28   Vv. 28-9, absent from Sah., marked with asterisk in Jerome and

29   On the text of G, cf. v. 28. The dual פַּעֲמָיִם is regarded as a plural by

30   To bring back his soul from the Pit,
        That he may be illuminated with the light of the living!

Theod. ὁδοὺς τρεῖς, Vulg. *tribus vici-bus*, Syr. ܠܬܠܬ ܙܒܢ 'three times'. Symm. δὶς τρίς and Targ. תרי זמנין ותלת 'two times and three' are faithful to the MT. For עם־גבר, Symm. πρὸς ἕκαστον; cf. Vulg. *per singulos*.

Vv. 29-30 form the conclusion of the thesis of Elihu on the subject of God's dealings with mankind. This mysterious divine operation is not subject to discussion (vv. 12-14): it is a unilateral action, terminating in the salvation of man, who does not perceive it until afterwards. With the opening הֶן־כָּל־אֵלֶּה cf. הן־זאת in v. 12 and הן־כל in 13:1. The formula 'two times, three times' is not an allusion to v. 14, where 'God speaks once and does not repeat what He says'. It is an expression of progression and marks the uninterrupted course of an action; cf. Comm. on 5:19. We find the same formula in Sir 13:7. The preposition עם 'with' marks the goal towards which the action denoted by the verb tends; cf. עמדי in 10:12.

30 G ἀλλ' ἐρύσατο τὴν ψυχήν μου ἐκ θανάτου ἵνα ἡ ζωή μου ἐν φωτὶ αἰνῇ αὐτόν. We have ψυχή instead of ζωή in A. G does not translate v. 30, but rather v. 28, which, as we have seen, had been introduced on the basis of Theod. In fact, it is vv. 29-30 which have disappeared from G, in consequence of the resemblance between v. 28 and v. 30. It is clear that G read the *kethîb* and not the *qerê* in v. 28. Syr. renders להשיב by a participle (cf. inf.). As a result of its translation of גבר in v. 29, Vulg. renders נפשו by *animas eorum*. For שחת, Vulg. *corruptione*, Targ. שוחא, Syr. ܫܚܠ (cf. v. 28). Instead of לאור, Vulg. *illuminet* and Targ. לאנהרא read the *hiph'il* לאיר, Syr. ܠܡܚܙܐ 'in order to see' (following v. 28).

V. 30 is constructed on the lines of vv. 17 and 23c. There is no reason to change להשיב to השיב or משיב (contra Beer). The evidence of Syr. is weak. This version regards the infinitive preceded by ל'' as a kind of gerundive. In v. 23 Syr. had already rendered להגיד by an imperfect. The aim pursued by God is the salvation of the guilty man and not his death: 'I have no pleasure in the death of the wicked but that the wicked may turn from his way and live' (Ezk 33:11). The 1st hemistich is thus perfectly comprehensible: 'to bring back his soul from the Pit'. The sufferer was on the brink of the grave (v. 22). God rescues him from that situation. The 2nd hemistich expresses a consequence of his return to life: 'that he may be illuminated with the light of the living'. The *niph'al* of אור (written לאור for להאור) marks the passive of the *hiph'il*, since the *qal* is intransitive and has no passive (Gesenius-Kautzsch, § 51f). As is shown by the use of באור החיים in Ps 56:14, the light of the living is a circumstantial complement which denotes what illuminates man who lives on this earth. To change the *niph'al* לאור into the *hiph'il* לאיר (Wright), or into להאיר בו 'to make to shine upon him' (Duhm), is to make this light the consequence of special action of the part of God. The change to לראות 'in order to see' (Budde, Ehrlich, following Syr.) would merely harmonise with v. 28b. Reiske proposed בארץ 'on the earth' instead of באור: cf. Ps 27:33, 'the land of the living'. Ehrlich adds בארץ after לראות אור so as to achieve a closer approximation to the text of the Psalms: 'to see

31   Be attentive, O Job, listen to me,
       Be silent and I will speak;

32   If you have words to speak, answer me,
       Speak on, for I wish to justify you;

33   If not, do thou listen to me,
       Be silent, and I will teach you wisdom.

the blessing of Yahweh in the land of the living'. All these hypotheses deal very cavalierly with a conception which in itself is perfectly clear, namely that to be illuminated by the light of the living is simply to be alive; cf. Comm. on v. 28; 3: 20; 18: 18.

31 Vv. 31b-33, absent from Sah., marked with asterisk in Jerome (with the exception of 31b) and Syro-hex., did not exist in G. The present text is taken from Theod. (cf. Colb.). We have seen that v. 30 of G translated v. 28 and that vv. 29-30 of the MT were absent from G. Of the passage vv. 29-33, there is therefore only v. 31a which is translated in G. The lacuna is filled in G(A), Cod. 23, and in the margin of Syro-hex. by an addition after v. 30 of G (i.e. MT 28). This addition includes first 34: 1-2 together with τὸ καλόν (for τὶ καλόν) of 34: 4, followed by ὅτι εἴρηκεν Ἰώβ of 34: 5. Then we find the translation of Theod. for 33: 29 (in G, cf. sup.) and 33: 30 (not in G). G renders הקשׁב by ἐνωτίζου. For ואנכי אדבר, Vulg. *dum ego loquor.*

Recall to attention: 'Be attentive, Job, listen to me!' Cf. v. 1 and 32: 10. Verb קשׁב in the *hiph'il*, in parallelism with שׁמע, as in 13: 6. Elihu does not vary his style much; cf. שׁמעה־לי in 32: 10. Attention requires the silence of the audience; cf. 13: 5-6. The end of the verse וְאָנֹכִי אֲדַבֵּר as in 21: 3a.

32 On the text of G, cf. v. 31. Syr. adds 'to you' after ישׁ; cf. Vulg.

si autem habes quod loquaris. The imperative דבר is omitted in Syr. For צדק, Theod. δικαιωθῆναί σε; cf. Vulg. *te apparere justum.*

Elihu changes his mind. He has ordered Job to be silent, but perhaps the latter after all has something to say: 'if there are any words', 'in your mouth' or 'in your mind' understood (cf. Syr.). Cf. the formula אם־בינה in 34: 16. The beginning אם־יֵשׁ as in v. 23. Note the use of הֲשִׁיבֵנִי 'answer me' as in v. 5, after the conditional clause. The 2nd hemistich is ironical: 'speak on, for I wish to justify you!' It is precisely because the friends of Job have seemed by their eventual silence to justify him that Elihu has entered on the scene (32: 1-5). In v. 12 he made clear in what way Job was not right. The verb חפץ is followed by the infinitive without the preposition ל" (13: 3; 21: 14). The *pi'el* of צדק in the sense of 'declare to be right'; cf. the *qal* in v. 12 and the *hiph'il* in 27: 5.

33 On the text of G, cf. v. 31. The word σοφίαν, which translates חכמה in Theod., is omitted by G (B) but is found in the other manuscripts, as also in Syro-hex. and Jerome.

Another alternative. It is the one in favour of which Elihu will decide: 'if not!' Note the opposition of אם־אַיִן to אם־יֵשׁ of v. 32, and the use of אַיִן as in 3: 9. Elihu is not at all afraid of repeating himself, and it would be unkind of us to rob him of v. 33, which is deleted by Budde. V. 32 introduced a note of qualification. But this qualification is set aside by the exclamation 'if not!', which allows him to repeat his injunctions שְׁמַע־לִי and הַחֲרֵשׁ of v. 31.

Unlike old men who do not know wisdom (32: 7, 13), the young Elihu proposes to teach wisdom. He has already declared that he would show forth his knowledge (32: 10, 17); now it is wisdom in general which he intends to expound and treat. That is why, in 34: 2, he will invoke the sages.

CHAPTER 34

1   Then Elihu spoke and said:

2   Hear, O wise men, my words,
      And you, O learned men, lend ear to me,

3   For the ear discerns words,
      As the palate tastes food;

4   Let us examine for ourselves what is just,
      Let us know between ourselves what is good.

34: 1 New speech of Elihu: cf. 32: 6; 35: 1.

the learned man, the erudite, the initiated person.

2 G ἀκούσατέ μου shortens שִׁמְעוּ מִלַּי.... We have τὰ ῥήματά μου in Cod. 249, *verba mea* in Jerome, 'my words' (with asterisk before the translation of ῥήματα) in Syro-hex. The word לִי of the end is omitted in G. The sentence ends with τὸ καλόν in G (A, C), Sah., Memph. This is a translation of מה־טוב of v. 4; cf. the text of G (A) in 33: 30-1. A mistake of homoeoteleuton (הַאֲזִינוּ in v. 2 and בִינוּ in v. 4) has caused the disappearance of vv. 3-4 (from לִי of v. 2) in the text of G; cf. v. 3.

Elihu addresses to the whole audience the same invitation as to Job in 33: 1; cf. v. 16. He calls the speakers in the debate 'wise men' and 'learned men' by irony. They claimed, indeed, to possess wisdom and knowledge. Well, it is wisdom which Elihu proposes to teach. Parallelism between חֲכָמִים 'the wise' and יֹדְעִים 'those who know', 'the learned', as in Ec 9: 11. The verb ידע, without complement, denotes 'know', 'possess knowledge' (8: 9), whence the use of the present participle as a noun. The Assyrian *mûdû* (from *idû* 'to know', ידע) denotes

3 Vv. 3-4, absent from Sah., marked with asterisk in Jerome and Syro-hex., did not exist in G. The present text derives from Theod. (cf. Colb. and Syro-hex.). The lacuna of G, which begins at לִי of v. 2, is explained by an error of homoeoteleuton (cf. v. 2). In G(A) and Cod. 23, the word οὖς, which translates אֹזֶן, has become νοῦς. For יִטְעַם, Vulg. *gustu dijudicat.*

Elihu repeats the proverb spoken by Job in 12: 11, but he begins with the conjunction כִּי, so as to base himself on the general recognition of the fact, and he changes the 2nd hemistich slightly. It is unnecessary to harmonise by changing לֶאֱכֹל to לוֹ אֹכֶל (Budde). The infinitive אֱכֹל is used substantively like the Assyrian *akâlu* 'to eat', and 'what one eats'. Cf. the use of *manger* in French. The preposition לְ before the direct complement is an Aramaism (cf. 5: 2, 7).

4 On the text of G, cf. v. 3. For נֵדְעָה, Vulg. *videamus* and for מה־טוב *quid sit melius.*

509

5   Since Job has said: 'I am righteous,
     But God has set aside my right,
6   Concerning my right, *He* speaks falsely,
     My *wound* is incurable, although I am innocent!'

6 יְכַזֵּב (G); MT: אכזב. — מֶחָצִי; MT: חצי.

The function of the ear is to discriminate what is best in the words which it hears. According to the parallelism, מִשְׁפָּט corresponds to מַה־טּוֹב *quid bonum*. The meaning 'what is just' (32: 9) is thus perfectly suitable. The verb בחר is not used in its basic sense of 'to choose' but in that of 'to examine', which, in Aramaic, it has in common with בחן; cf. Syr. in 7: 18. Essentially, the roots בחן and בחר develop a common idea: to test by the crucible, to examine carefully, finally to choose what is deemed good (cf. Comm. on 7: 18). Thus the 1st hemistich means: 'Let us examine for ourselves what is just', the complement לָנוּ suggesting that each auditor must profit from his own investigation. Cf. the use of לך 'for you' in 5: 27. The 2nd hemistich already expresses the result of the inquiry: 'Let us know between ourselves what is good.' The phrase בֵּינֵינוּ, which limits the circle of investigators, will recur in v. 37. The interrogative מָה plays the part of a relative in the indirect question; cf. 23: 5. We find מה־טּוֹב in Mic 6: 8. Thus Job is to undergo a veritable examination which will be conducted by Elihu.

5 Following 33: 8, Syr. renders אמר by 'you have said'. Then Syr. reads צדקת instead of צדקתי and retranslates the 1st hemistich, whence its composite rendering: 'You have said, Job, and you were innocent when you said: I have been justified.' At the end Syr. reads עלי 'against me', which comes from

על of the opening of v. 6 (cf. v. 6). For הסיר Vulg. *subvertit*.

Elihu returns to the technique he used in 33: 8-11, which is that of incriminating Job through his words. The verb: צָדַקְתִּי 'I am righteous' sums up 33: 9. Job uttered the verb צדקתי 'I am righteous', but as a hypothesis only, in 9: 15; 10: 15 (cf. 9: 20). In 27: 2 he exclaimed: 'by God who has set aside my right'. This time Elihu quotes verbatim.

6 Vv. 6b-7, absent from Sah., marked with asterisk in Jerome and Syro-hex., did not exist in G. The present text derives from Theod. (cf. Syro-hex.). Syr., which has transferred על (read עלי) to v. 5, renders v. 6 as: 'Who is the man who has perished without sin?' (reading אֱנוֹשׁ instead of אָנוּשׁ, omission of משׁפטי אכזב). For אכזב, G ἐψεύσατο (cf. inf.). The verb is treated as a noun in Aq., Symm., and Theod. ψεῦσμα (cf. Vulg. *mendacium est*). Targ. makes of אָנוּשׁ, read as אֱנוֹשׁ (cf. Syr.), the complement of אכזב and interprets אנושׁ חצי by 'the man who shoots arrows'.

The efforts of ancient commentators to preserve אָכַזֵּב are mentioned by Rosenmüller, who eventually decides in favour of the meaning *mendax appareo*! This is the interpretation which prevails in the translations of Le Hir 'in spite of my innocence, I am considered a liar', Renan 'when I protest that I am righteous, I am thought to be a liar' (cf. Loisy, Crampon), Segond 'I am right and I am adjudged a liar'. But the *pi'el*

7   What man is as Job,
     Who drinks derision like water,
8   Who goes about in company with evildoers,
     And walks with men of wickedness?

of כזב has always the meaning 'to lie' (6:28). The reading of G ἐψεύσατο implies a form יְכַזֵּב 'he lies'. The 3rd person has been changed to the 1st in order to avoid the odium of such an insinuation; cf. Comm. on 32:3. The natural meaning of the 1st hemistich will therefore be: 'concerning my right, He lies'. The 1st hemistich thus continues v. 5b, where God was accused of setting aside the right of Job. The change of אֲכַזֵּב to אֶכָּזֵב 'I am deceived' (Duhm) would be acceptable if G did not afford a solution which permits us to understand why the text has been changed. Ehrlich proposes אִכָּאֵב 'I suffer' and translates עַל־מִשְׁפָּטִי by 'against my right'. But the preposition על creates ambiguity, for it should express rather the cause or the object of the suffering; cf. 14:22. Job has never claimed to suffer because of his righteousness, but in spite of it. Note that all the versions have the root כזב and differ only as regards the form used. The usual interpretation is חִצִּי 'my arrow' in the sense of the wound occasioned by the arrow which is in me (6:4). This is far too subtle, and it is better, with Duhm, to read מַחֲצִי 'my wound' (Is 30:26). The end of the בְּלִי־פָשַׁע 'without transgression' (33:9) forms a kind of apposition to the suffix of מחצי: 'My wound is incurable, although I am innocent.' We render בלי־פשע by 'innocent', the word בלי playing the part of the alpha privative; cf. לא־חכמה, לא־עז, לא־כח in 26:2-3.

7   On the text of G, cf. v. 6.
     The 2nd hemistich quotes almost verbatim 15:16b, where Eliphaz

said of man in general that he drinks injustice like water. Elihu applies the image to Job, but replaces עולה 'wickedness' by לַעַג 'mockery', 'derision'; cf. the verb לעג 'to mock' in 9:23; 11:3; 22:19. It is a question of that mockery whose target is religious or moral truths, a sort of sceptical irony whose chief representatives are called לֵצִים 'mockers' (Ps 1:1; Pr 1:22, etc.). The relative is understood after the comparative term 'like Job'; cf. 7:2.

8   We have seen that vv. 6b-7, in the Greek text, derived from Theod. At the beginning of v. 8 we find οὐχ ἁμαρτὼν οὐδὲ ἀσεβήσας, which is a remnant of the translation of v. 6b in G. In fact, οὐχ ἁμαρτών corresponds to בלי־פשע as in 33:9, and οὐδὲ ἀσεβήσας comes from a second reading with רשע instead of פשע (cf. G ἀσεβεῖν for the verb רשע in 10:2, 7, 15). Syro-hex. marks with obelus this translation of G, while Colb. points out that the words are not in the Hebrew. For וארח לחברה, G ἢ ὁδοῦ κοινωνήσας, Vulg. qui graditur, Syr. 'and he is an associate and companion'. Instead of ἀσεβῶν, which renders אנשי־רשע in G, Jerome viris impiis (with asterisk before viris); cf. Syro-hex.

The perfect with the waw shows the sequel to v. 7b. The verb ארח 'to pass by' (31:32) and 'to go about', whence אֹרַח 'route' (iter, itum). The word חֶבְרָה is a hapax representing the nomen unitatis of חֶבֶר 'company', 'society' (cf. חַבָּרִים in 40:30). Cf. נהרה (3:4) and עננה (3:5). The phrase ארח לחברה 'to go

9   For he has said: 'It is no profit to man,
     To make Elohim his delight.'
10   But, men of heart, listen to me,
     Far from God be wickedness,
     And from Shaddai unrighteousness!

in company with' or, as we say, 'to go about with' naturally requires the preposition עִם 'with'. The פֹּעֲלֵי־אָוֶן 'evildoers' will recur in v. 22. Elihu borrows the word from Job (31: 3). The infinitive construct, preceded by ל״, may continue a clause whose verb is personal and finite. This construction is especially used in the style proper to late books of the OT (Gesenius-Kautzsch, § 114p). The אַנְשֵׁי־רֶשַׁע 'men of wickedness' are contrasted with the אַנְשֵׁי־לֵבָב 'men of heart' of v. 10. The word אַנְשֵׁי replaces מְתֵי of similar expressions used by Job and his friends (11: 11; 19: 19; 22: 15; 31: 31). Elihu here makes use of, and strengthens, the insinuations of Eliphaz in 22: 15-17. He abandons the interrogative note and does not fear to affirm. The phrase הלך עם as in 31: 5.

9 For כִּי־אָמַר, G μὴ γὰρ εἴπῃς; cf. Syr. ܘܐܡܪܬ 'since you have said'. The various meanings of סכן appear in the translations of לֹא יִסְכָּן: οὐκ ἔσται ἐπισκοπή (G), οὐχὶ σωθήσεται (Symm.), ܠܐ ܪ̈ܓ 'he is not pure' (Syr.), non placebit (Vulg.); but Theod. οὐ κινδυνεύσει. Double translation of v. 9 in Targ., where לֹא יִסְכָּן is rendered first by לֹא יָאלֵף 'he does not progress', then by לֹא יִסְתְּכַן 'he is not in danger' (cf. Theod.). G renders the 2nd hemistich by καὶ ἐπισκοπὴ αὐτῷ παρὰ Κυρίου. Vulg. etiam si cucurrerit cum eo connects רְצֹתוֹ with the verb רוּץ; cf. Targ. (2°) במרהטיה 'in his course'.

Elihu condemns in their entirety the allegations made by Job on the subject of the prosperity of the wicked (21: 7-13) and the misfortunes of the righteous (9: 22-4). If there is no reward for good, nor punishment for evil, the consequence is then that 'it is no profit to man to make Elohim his delight'. The verb סכן 'to be useful or profitable' and 'derive benefit' (15: 3; 22: 2, 21). The verb רצה 'to delight in' (33: 26) with the preposition עִם before the object of delight (Ps 50: 18). The contradiction between Job's innocence and the treatment of which he is the victim (vv. 5-6) is explained in the theory which Elihu attributes to him, namely that virtue is useless. There is no reason to delete this v. 9, as Budde claims there is (he suppresses also v. 10a). We cannot argue on the basis of the meaning of סכן, for it is very understandable that the meaning 'to be useful' develops into that of 'to be useful to one's self', 'to derive benefit'.

10 For אַנְשֵׁי לֵבָב (literally translated in Syr. 'men of heart' and Vulg. viri cordati), G συνετοὶ καρδίας, Targ. אַנְשֵׁי חכימי 'wise men'. G interprets חלילה as if it were חָלִילָה לִּי (27: 5), whence: μή μοι εἴη ἔναντι Κυρίου. But Symm. ἀπείη τοῦ Θεοῦ ἀνομία is reflected in Jerome absit a Domino impietas! For עָוֶל, G ταράξαι τὸ δίκαιον (Jerome turbare quod justum est). Syr. adds ܘܢܥܒܕ 'that He should do' before רֶשַׁע and עָוֶל.

In v. 2 Elihu invited the 'wise' and the 'learned' to lend an ear to his words. Here the address is to 'men of heart', that is, intelligent men, for the heart is the seat of intelligence (L'Emploi métaphorique, pp. 122f.). The 'men of heart' will recur in v. 34. Cf. the epithet 'wise of heart' in 9: 4. Elihu addresses the

11   For the work of man, He requites it to him,
      And according to man's conduct, so He treats him!

friends of Job in the same terms as he had addressed Job himself (32: 10). Here לָכֵן marks a contrast with what precedes and corresponds to the Arabic *lâkinna, lâkin* (cf. v. 25). Elihu certainly abuses the device of recalling his audience to attention; but this is no reason for deleting such phrases (contra Budde). Duhm recomposes a whole verse with the help of v. 2. But the verse begins at חָלִלָה. Note the defective writing of חָלִלָה, as in Gn 18: 25. The construction חלילה לִ״ (27: 5) with מִן before the banished object is altogether normal. Doubtless the infinitive is more frequently used after מִן, but the abstract nouns רֶשַׁע 'wickedness' and עָוֶל 'unrighteousness' are real verbal nouns: wickedness = to do evil; unrighteousness = to commit unrighteous deeds (cf. Syr.). We see no need to vocalise רשע as an infinitive (Budde, Duhm), or to prolong the final member of the phrase, by reading מפעל עול 'to do unrighteousness' (Budde) or by replacing ושדי by ולשדי (Bickell, Duhm). The brevity of the 2nd hemistich is explained by the fact that the parallelism concerns only the words לָאֵל מֵרֶשַׁע. Note that עָוֶל corresponds to רֶשַׁע, just as the concrete עַוָּל was complementary to רֶשַׁע in 27: 7.

11 V. 11b, absent from Sah., marked with asterisk in Cod. 248 and Jerome, did not exist in G. The asterisk is omitted in Syro-hex. The text of Jerome *et juxta viam suam unusquisque reperiet*, for v. 11b, follows Symm. καὶ κατὰ τὴν ὁδὸν αὐτοῦ ἑκάστῳ συμβήσεται rather than Theod. (now in G) καὶ ἐν τρίβῳ ἀνδρὸς

εὑρήσει αὐτόν. The reading ἐν τρίβῳ presupposes בארח in place of כארח. For פעל of the beginning, G καθὰ ποιεῖ and Syr. 'according to the works' are influenced by the 2nd hemistich.

God does not act unjustly. He renders to every man according to his works. This is the thesis which was amplified by Bildad in ch. 8. The meaning of the 1st hemistich is very clear in the light of 21: 31 (where we have as here יְשַׁלֶּם־לוֹ): 'for the work of man, He requites it to him'. The phrase פֹּעַל אָדָם 'the work of man' takes the place of הוּא־עשׂה 'he has done' of 21: 31. Cf. Ru 2: 12, 'May Yahweh recompense to you your work!' In Jer 25: 14; 50: 29, we find the same expressions, but with the כ״ of comparison before פעל: to reward according to the work, to treat some one according to his actions. It is not necessary to add this כ״ before פעל, as is proposed by Reiske, Graetz, and Beer, following G and Syr., which are influenced by the 2nd hemistich and the current idiom. Driver quotes in favour of the MT Pr 12: 14b, 'and the action of man's hands He requites' (verb הֵשִׁיב instead of שָׁלֵם). This doctrine of retribution according to works recurs in similar terms in Ps 62: 13; Pr 24: 12; Sir 16: 15 (14). Cf. Ro 2: 6 and Mt 16: 27. Elihu expounds accepted ideas on ethics. The 2nd hemistich is to be interpreted according to the meaning in Sir 16: 15 (14) where we have: וכל־אדם כמעשיו ימצא 'and every man according to his works finds . . .', the phrase כְּאֹרַח אִישׁ 'according to man's conduct' corresponding to כמעשיו. For the use of אֹרַח 'path', 'way', in the sense of 'conduct' cf.

12   No, in truth, God does not work evil,
      And Shaddai does not pervert the right!
13   Who has entrusted to Him *His* earth,
      And who has given Him charge of the whole world?

13   אַרְצָה ;MT: אָרְצָה.

דֶּרֶךְ in 17:9; 21:31, etc., and the metaphors of 31:4-7. Literally the 2nd hemistich would run: 'and following the conduct of man, He makes him to find'. Cf. the meaning of מצא in 31:25.

12 G assigns to אַף־אָמְנָם an interrogative sense which involves the suppression of the negatives: οἴη δὲ τὸν Κύριον ἄτοπα ποιήσειν; ἢ ὁ παντοκράτωρ ταράξει κρίσιν (A τὸ δίκαιον), + ὃς ἐποίησεν τὴν γῆν; (from v. 13; cf. inf.). The verb ירשיע is interpreted in the sense of 'to do evil' by G (cf. sup.), and Syr. ܚܒܪ ܠܗ. Vulg. *condemnabit* (+ *frustra*) and Targ. יחיב retain the normal meaning of the *hiph'il* 'to condemn'.

Elihu returns to his idea of v. 10, namely that evil and injustice are incompatible with God. The formula אַף־אָמְנָם as in 19:4. Here אַף retains its full value of affirmation or categorical denial. Hence the translation will be: 'not truly'. The *hiph'il* of רשע with the sense of the *qal*, 'to do evil', as in Ps 106:6; Dn 9:5; 12:10. The same use of the *hiph'il* for the verbs נגע and לעג recurs in 20:6; 21:3. The 2nd hemistich repeats 8:3a almost verbatim (cf. Comm.). The word מִשְׁפָּט as in vv. 5-6.

13 G paraphrases the 1st hemistich: ὃς ἐποίησεν τὴν γῆν, linked with v. 12. Then τίς δέ ἐστιν ὁ ποιῶν τὴν ὑπ' οὐρανὸν, καὶ τὰ ἐνόντα πάντα; is inspired by Ps 24:1. Vulg. *quem constituit alium super terram*? seems to interpret עליו as meaning 'other

than He'. Instead of כָּלָה, Vulg. *quem fabricatus est* vocalises כָּלָה. Syr. omits עליו and interprets שָׂם by ܥܒܕ 'has made'. Targ. understands the verb 'to make' before ארצה: 'Who has enjoined Him to make the earth?'

God derives His authority from Himself alone: 'Who has entrusted to Him His earth?' The form אַרְצָה recurs in 37:12, where it has replaced אַרְצָה 'His earth', as may be clearly seen if we compare 37:12 with Pr 8:31. Hence we read אַרְצָה (for אַרְצוֹ which figures in one manuscript). The verb פקד with על before the name of the person corresponds to the Assyrian expression *paqâdu ana* 'entrust to': cf. Ezr 1:2 and 2 Ch 36:23. Instead of having then the infinitive preceded by ל' 'to entrust to some one the accomplishment of a thing', as in the two passages quoted, we may have the accusative of the thing, as in Nu 4:27, 'and you will entrust to their charge all that they have to carry'. It is the turn of phrase we have here and in 36:23. The original meaning of פקד is 'visit', 'inspect' (7:18; 31:14), from which derives the sense of giving orders, imposing on (36:23), or submitting to the charge of some one, entrusting to him (here). The complement עליו is understood after שָׂם, which then means 'to impose' on some one (v. 23) or 'to entrust' him with something (here). Cf. the expression שִׂים עַל 'impose on' (Ex 5:8; 22:24). The question 'And who has given

14   If He *takes back* to Himself [   ] his breath
      And withdraws from him his spirit,
15   Then all flesh perishes together,
      And man returns to dust.
16   If you have understanding, listen to this,

14   יָשִׂיב (*kethîb* of the Orientals, G, Syr.); MT: יָשִׂים. — Omit לבו.

Him charge of the whole world?' forms an excellent parallel to the 1st hemistich. The parallelism is spoilt if we change שׂם to שָׁמַר 'and who has kept?' (Budde) or if we introduce here לבו of v. 14: 'and who pays heed?' (Duhm). The presence of לבו in v. 14 is to be explained in a different way (cf. inf.).

14 G εἰ γὰρ βούλοιτο συνέχειν, καὶ τὸ πνεῦμα παρ' αὐτῷ κατασχεῖν omits רוחו and paraphrases the 1st hemistich. The verb συνέχειν comes from יָשִׂיב, *kethîb* of the Orientals in place of the *qerê* יָשִׂים. Vulg. *direxerit* and Targ. יָשׂוּי have decided in favour of יָשִׂים, but Syr. ‎ܡܬܗܦܟ‎ 'taking back' is in favour of the *kethîb*.

In its present state, the verse is obviously overloaded, for the 2nd hemistich contains the synonyms רוחו and נִשְׁמָתוֹ as complements of יֶאֱסֹף. Let us note in the first place that if we make a division after רוחו we obtain as the 2nd hemistich 'and if He withdraws from him his spirit', which at once recalls Ps 104: 29, 'Thou dost withdraw their breath and they die' (verb אסף as here, verb גוע as in v. 15). In the 1st hemistich, we then have רוחו parallel to נשמתו (4: 9; 27: 3; 32: 8; 33: 4) and יָשִׂים אֵלָיו answering to אליו יאסף. The *kethîb* of the Orientals, supported by G and Syr., suggests our reading יָשִׂיב which gives (leaving aside לבו):

'if He takes back to Himself his breath', the breath which God has imparted to man (cf. Comm. on 32: 8) and which, after death,

'returns to God' (verb שׁוב, Ec 12: 7). The disturbing factor is לבו, which overloads the verse and was introduced after the transformation of יָשׂיב into יָשׂים to explain the meaning of the verb שׂים. It is far too subtle to assign God Himself as a complement to the expression יָשׂים לבו 'he places his heart', i.e. 'he pays attention', and to translate: '*Gesetzt Gott denkt nur an sich selbst*' (Dillmann), 'if He considered only Himself' (Renan). Since Houbigant, who had certainly recognised the true text, most exegetes have adopted the *kethîb* of the Orientals and drop לבו, which then has no function. This is one of these cases where the correction is almost irresistible.

15 For עַל־עָפָר Vulg. *in cinerem*, Syr. ‎ܠܥܦܪܗ‎ 'to his dust'. At the end, G adds ὅθεν καὶ ἐπλάσθη, marked by obelus in Jerome and Syro-hex. This is a gloss following Gn 3: 19.

The verb גוע is a characteristic word of the vocabulary of the Book of Job (3: 11; 10: 18; 13: 19; 14: 10, etc.). The idiom כָּל־בָּשָׂר 'all flesh', just as we had כל־חי 'every living creature' (12: 10; 28: 21), to imply all animals or all human beings (Gn 6: 12f., 17; 7: 15, etc.). Vv. 14-15 express the same idea as Ps 104: 29. The adverb יַחַד 'together' to denote 'at one and the same time'. When man dies, he returns to dust; cf. Comm. on 10: 9.

16 For זאת, Vulg. *quod dicitur*. At

Lend an ear to the sound of my words!

17 Do you really think that one who hates justice would govern,
    And will you condemn the supremely righteous One?

the close, G simply ῥημάτων instead of מלי 'my words'.

The opening 'and if there is understanding' recalls 'if there are words' of 33:32. The versions have rendered as if the text read: 'and if you have understanding'; this arises from the needs of the translation, and it is not necessary to change בִּינָה to בִּינֹת, as Beer and Budde suggest, following Houbigant. The verse brings further recall to attention (cf. 33:31) to open up a new paragraph. Note the emphatic שְׁמָעָה as in 32:10. The verb הַאֲזִין is parallel to שְׁמַע; cf. v. 2 and 33:1. With קוֹל מִלַּי 'the sound of my words', cf. קול מלין in 33:8. Elihu does not much vary his formulae.

17 G ἴδε σύ (Jerome videto) is the result of a double iotacism. The original text had εἰ δὲ σοί, which remains in G(A), Sah., and Syrohex. It is a paraphrase of הַאַף. We then have τὸν μισοῦντα ἄνομα καὶ τὸν ὀλλύντα τοὺς πονηροὺς, ὄντα αἰώνιον δίκαιον. The words ὄντα αἰώνιον δίκαιον correspond to צדיק כביר, the word תרשיע being linked with v. 18 (cf. inf.). It seems that τὸν μισοῦντα ἄνομα are the result of a theological correction, the aim of which was to avoid applying to God the qualification 'hating justice', while καὶ τὸν ὀλλύντα τοὺς πονηροὺς breaks up יחבוש ואם into יחבל שואים(?). Vulg. interprets יחבוש by sanari potest and regards כביר as an adverb: in tantum condemnas. Targ. renders יחבוש by יסתמר 'is kept' and replaces תרשיע by the 3rd person (יחיב 'he condemns'). Aq. and Symm. translate יחבוש by ἐπιδήσει. Syr. 'he who hates judgment is not innocent, and if he is innocent he is not condemned justly' interprets

חבש in the sense of 'to be bound' by a condemnation, gives to כביר the meaning of 'unjustly', and reads ירשיע instead of תרשיע (cf. Targ.).

The question הַאַף 'Is it truly the case?' brings forward an inadmissible hypothesis (40:8; Gn 18:23; Am 2:11). If Job were right, i.e. if God were not just (cf. v. 12), how could He govern the world? Cf. Gn 18:25, 'Shall not He who judges the whole earth do right?' The phrase שׂנֵא מִשְׁפָּט 'to hate the right', as we have 'to hate understanding' (Pr 1:22), 'to hate the good' (Mic 3:2). The meaning of משפט as in v. 5. The verb חבש 'tie', 'bind' (5:18), has been interpreted as a passive by Vulg., Targ., and Syr. We expect here the meaning of 'to govern', 'to reign', or some similar meaning. Now, in Is 3:7, we find the expression לֹא־אֶהְיֶה חֹבֵשׁ 'I am not one who binds (or dresses a wound)' to mean: I am not a chief. It has been thought that the image used alluded to the function of a doctor assumed by the king. We ourselves think, however, the root חבש here and in Is 3:7 means strictly speaking 'to bind on the yoke' and that from it comes the Assyrian abšânu (generally read as apšânu) 'yoke'. The חֹבֵשׁ is he who subdues peoples. Thus the 1st hemistich is elucidated: 'Is it really the case that He who hates right would govern?' The answer is evident. Hence God who governs all things cannot be described as the enemy of justice. On the contrary, He is the supremely just One. On the word כַּבִּיר cf. 8:2. The speeches of Job tend to condemn Him who is just above all others, as also did the silence of his friends (32:3). V. 18 will show the sovereign power of the Judge of the universe.

18 *He who* says to a king: Worthless man!
    And to nobles: You wicked one!
19 He who does not side with princes,
    Nor discriminate between a rich man and a poor man,
    Since they are all the work of His hands:

18 הָאֹמֵר (G, Vulg., Syr.); MT: הַאֲמֹר.

18 V. 18b, absent from Sah.,
marked with asterisk in Jerome and
Cod. 248, did not exist in G. The
present text is taken from Theod.
The opening of G ἀσεβὴς ὁ λέγων
connects תרשיע (read רשע) of v. 17
with v. 18 and vocalises הָאֹמֵר. This
vocalisation is reflected in Vulg. *qui
dicit* and Syr. וֶאֹמַר. For בליעל, G
παρανομεῖς, Vulg. *apostata*, Targ.
רשיעא 'wicked man', Syr. כֹּמאל 'impious man'. By repeating מלך in the
2nd hemistich, Syr. arrives at the
meaning 'king of chiefs', 'king of
princes' (!). Vulg. *qui vocat duces
impios* eliminates the direct speech.
Instead of הַאֲמֹר 'does one say?',
the reading הָאֹמֵר 'he who says'
(G, Vulg., Syr.) is preferred even by
Le Hir, Renan, Ginsburg. V. 18,
parallel to v. 19, which begins with
the relative אֲשֶׁר, forms an apposition
to God 'the supremely righteous
One' of v. 17: 'He who says to a
king: Worthless man! and to nobles:
You wicked ones!' The word בְּלִיַּעַל
is compounded (like בלימה of 26: 7)
by means of the negative בלי 'without'. The second element is יעל,
whence הועיל (15: 3; 21: 15) 'to be
of use', 'to be profitable'. The root
יעל means therefore 'to be advantageous', 'to have value': the בליעל
is the good-for-nothing, worthless
man! In 21: 28, the נדיב 'nobleman'
was paralleled by רשעים 'the wicked'.
We shall not be surprised to learn
that God can say to noblemen: you
wicked one! There is only one king,
but many noblemen on whom God
pours scorn (12: 21). The epithet

remains however in the singular, on
account of the parallelism. It is
addressed to each of the nobles.

19 G ὃς οὐκ ἐπαισχυνθῇ (A αἰσχυνθῇ)
πρόσωπον ἐντίμου is a first translation of v. 19a; cf. G in 32: 21. Then
οὐδὲ οἶδεν τιμὴν θέσθαι ἁδροῖς (A
ἀνδρῶν) paraphrases v. 19b by reading גדול instead of דל. Finally,
θαυμασθῆναι πρόσωπα αὐτῶν does not
correspond to v. 19c but offers a
second translation of v. 19a; cf. G
in 13: 10. Hence v. 19c is not rendered in G. Instead of translating
נכר שוע לפני, Syr. repeats נשא פני
of the 1st hemistich. Vulg. paraphrases לפני־דל by *cum disceptaret
contra pauperem*. The verb נכר is
interpreted as a *niph'al* in Targ.
אשתמודע 'is recognised'.
God is no respecter of persons.
The formula נשא פני is typical of
Elihu's style (32: 21). On the meaning, cf. 13: 8. After the king and
noblemen, we have the mention of
princes שָׂרִים (3: 15; 29: 9), 'He who
does not side with princes'. The
locution אֲשֶׁר לֹא־נָשָׂא, parallel to
הָאֹמֵר 'He who says' of v. 18, makes
use of the perfect of habit. On the
pi'el of נכר cf. 21: 29. The change to
הכיר (Duhm) is not justified. The
word שׁוֹעַ, parallel to נדיב 'nobleman'
(Is 32: 5), is the one which G interprets by δυνάστης in 29: 12. In the
light of the Arabic root وسع 'to be
free, at ease' (in the 2nd form, 'to
enrich'), the basic meaning of שׁוֹעַ
is 'rich', 'opulent'. Thus the word
is opposed to דָּל 'weak', 'poor'

20   In a moment they die *and pass away*;
      In the middle of the night a people are swept with tumult;
      And effortlessly He deposes a potentate.

20   Transfer ויעברו to precede וחצות.

(20: 10, 19; 31: 16). The idiom לִפְנֵי
'ahead', 'before' specifies that God
does not give recognition to a rich
man rather than a poor man. He
does not make any distinction
between the two. The reason why
all are on the same footing is that
they are all the work of His hands.
Cf. the reasons adduced by Job
in 31: 15 and those put forward by
Elihu in 33: 6. The expression
מַעֲשֵׂה יָדָיו is used as in 14: 15.

20 It is impossible to adjust to the
MT the text of G: κενὰ δὲ αὐτοῖς
ἀποβήσεται τὸ κεκραγέναι καὶ δεῖσθαι
ἀνδρός (C αὐτοῖς). Perhaps we have
here the paraphrase of an interpretation beginning at וחצות and breaking up יגעשׁ עם into יגע שׁועם 'and
their cry strikes the middle of the
night', i.e. their cry has no effect(?).
The sequel ἐχρήσαντο γὰρ παρανόμως
paraphrases יעברו, and the end
ἐκκλινομένων ἀδυνάτων reads יסורו
for יסיר and אובד for אביר, omitting
לא ביד. Syr. omits the word עם and
translates ויסירו as if the text read
ויכירו 'and they recognise'. Targ.
applies to the people of Sodom the
phrase: 'they die suddenly' and
sees an allusion to the Egyptians
in 'the people'.
    This verse has caused much em-
barrassment to modern commentators, who have wished to change
the text. Budde replaces עם by
שׁועים (v. 19), but hesitates between
יסיר 'he sets aside', יוסר 'he is set
aside', יסורו 'they go away' (which
would require אבירים). Duhm reads
מעם, and interprets יגעשׁו מעם by
'they are driven forth from the
people'. Ehrlich replaces עם by
שׁרים and אביר by אבירים; he reads

ויסרו (cf. sup.) instead of ויסירו.
Torczyner substitutes ינע שׁועם 'he
expels the rich' (cf. v. 19) for יגעשׁ
עם and reads יסיר for יסירו. Ball, in
accordance with 9: 26, replaces יגעשׁ
עם by יגועו עם־עשׁ 'they die like
a moth' and אביר by אבירים. In
reality the anomaly begins at the
1st hemistich, where we have a
statement 'in a moment they die'
(cf. רגע in 20: 5), followed by 'and
in the middle of the night' which, in
the light of Ex 11: 4 and Ps 119: 62,
connects with what follows rather
than with what precedes. Thus it
has been understood by the *Bible
du rabbinat français*: 'In the twink-
ling of an eye, they die, and in the
middle of the night, the people are
shaken and disappear; the powerful are cut off and no hand [rises].'
But if וְחֲצות begins the 2nd clause
there is a complete lack of balance
between the first two hemistichs.
Everything becomes clear if we suppose that וְיָעֲבֹרוּ has been accidentally transposed. If we replace it in
position after יָמֻתוּ, we obtain as
1st hemistich: 'In an instant they
die and pass away', which recalls:
'Thou dost attack him and for ever
he departs', an allusion to the death
of man in 14: 20. The 2nd hemistich
is then: 'and in the middle of the
night a people are shaken with
tumult'. The plural יְגֹעֲשׁוּ is used
because of the collective עם. The
puʿal of געשׁ assumes a meaning
similar to the *hithpoʿel* in Jer 46: 8,
'to be agitated' (speaking of the
waves). The author refers to the
tumult of a people in the throes of
revolution. The sequel then becomes
quite natural: 'and effortlessly He

21   For His eyes watch the ways of man,
     And He sees all his steps:
22   There is no darkness and no depth of shade,
     In which evildoers can hide from Him.
25   But He knows their deeds,
     He overthrows *them* in the night and they are crushed!

23-24. After v. 25.
25   וַהֲפָכָם (Syr.); MT: והפך.

deposes a potentate'. The verb
הסיר 'set aside', 'remove' has the
same connotation in 1 K 15: 13, to
remove from power, from the throne,
i.e. 'to depose'. The word אַבִּיר
'mighty one, 'potentate', as in
24: 22. The phrase לֹא בְיָד 'not by
the hand', i.e. without having to
use force. Cf. לֹא־בְדַעַת 'without
knowledge' and לֹא בְהַשְׂכִּיל 'without reason' in v. 35. Elihu is stressing
the vicissitudes of social life. For
God, there is no distinction between
king, noblemen, princes, rich and
poor (vv. 18-19). They are all alike
subject to death (v. 20a), and those
in high places may become the
victims of a popular rising (v. 20, bc).
Cf. the ideas expressed in vv. 24-6.

21 G αὐτὸς γὰρ ὁρατής ἐστιν avoids
the anthropomorphism of עיניו. The
2nd hemistich is paraphrased λέλη-
θεν δὲ αὐτὸν οὐδὲν ὧν πράσσουσιν. Syr.
'all the ways' anticipates כל of the
2nd hemistich before דרכי.
    God is the sovereign Lord and
all-seeing Judge: 'for His eyes are
on the ways of man', an almost
word for word quotation from 24:
23b. The 2nd hemistich is inspired by
the words of Job in 31: 4, 37 (cf.
14: 16). Cf. Sir 23: 19 (28), where
the eyes of the Lord watch 'all the
ways of men'.

22 G οὐδὲ ἔσται τόπος τοῦ κρυβῆναι
τοὺς ποιοῦντας τὰ ἄνομα sums up v.
22. After *neque erit locus*, Jerome
adds *et non est umbra mortis* (with
asterisk), which comes from Aq. and

Theod. (quoted in the margin of
Syro-hex. and in Colb.). It is the
translation of ואין צלמות.
    Note the association of חֹשֶׁךְ
'darkness' and צַלְמוּת 'shade' as in
3: 5; 10: 21; 12: 22 (cf. Ps 107: 10,
14). The *niph'al* of סתר (3: 23)
means 'to hide there', i.e. that they
may hide there. The פֹּעֲלֵי אָוֶן 'evildoers' as in v. 8; 31: 3. The idea
that darkness cannot conceal man
from the eyes of God is well brought
out in Ps 139: 11-12. Cf. also Jer
23: 24; Am 9: 2-3; Sir 23: 19(28);
Mt 6: 4; 10: 26. V. 23 is not an immediate sequel to v. 22, but draws
the conclusion from the argument
of the whole passage (17-22). Now,
v. 25, which begins with לָכֵן 'but'
(cf. Comm.), expresses exactly the
idea which naturally flows from
v. 22, namely that 'God knows their
works', those of evildoers, and that
He punishes them in the night.
This v. 25, which has no link with
its present context, as is pointed
out by those who seek to eliminate it
(cf. Budde, Duhm), forms the logical
conclusion to v. 22. That is why we
place it here.

23-4 After v. 25.

25 V. 25b, absent from Sah.,
marked with asterisk in Jerome and
Syro-hex., did not exist in G. The
present text is derived from Theod.
It is by error that v. 25a is also
marked with asterisk in Colb. and
Jerome. For לכן יכיר, G has

23   For He does not appoint for man a *time*,
      That he might go before God for judgment;

23 **מוֹעֵד**; MT: **עוּד**.

simply ὁ γνωρίζων. Syr. interprets
יכיר מעבדיהם by 'He knows them
in the light of their works'. The 2nd
hemistich is rendered καὶ στρέψει
νύκτα καὶ ταπεινωθήσεται (A, C
ταπεινωθήσονται) in Theod., *et idcirco
inducet noctem et conterentur* in Vulg.
The word **וידכאו** is connected by
Syr. with v. 26. Instead of **הפך**, Syr.
reads **הפכם** 'and He overthrew them
at night'.

The phrase **לָכֵן** cannot here mean
'that is why' (20: 2; 32: 10; 37: 24).
Bickell proposes to change it to
כֵּן 'thus' or **כִּי** 'for'. But in v. 10 and
in 42: 3 it seems indeed that **לכן**
corresponds to the Arabic *lâkin* or
lâkinna 'but'. The hapax **מַעֲבָּד** is
an Aramaism (from **עבד** 'do',
'work') instead of the Hebrew
מַעֲשֶׂה 'deed', 'action'. If we translate
the 1st hemistich as 'but He knows
their deeds', we have the natural
sequel to v. 22, where we have seen
that the evildoers could not escape
the all-seeing eye of God. Hence
there is no need for us to regard
v. 25 as a gloss on vv. 21-2 (Budde,
who deletes also vv. 26-8 and v.
29c) or to see in the words **לָכֵן**
לַיְלָה··· a variant of v. 20 (Duhm,
who connects **וְיִדַּכָּאוּ** with v. 26).
In reality, **לילה** of the 2nd hemistich
is complementary to the darkness
and shadows of v. 22 and indicates
the time of the punishment which
the evildoers cannot escape; cf.
27: 20. With Syr., we read **וְהֲפָכָם**
'and He overthrows them' (cf. **הפכם**
in 9: 5). The verb **הפך** 'overthrow', 'overturn' with a personal
object (Pr 12: 7). The meaning of
the 2nd hemistich is clear: 'and He
overthrows them in the night and
they are crushed'. For the form

וְיִדַּכָּאוּ in pause cf. **וְיִדַּכָּאוּ** in 5: 4.

23 V. 23a, absent from Sah.,
marked with asterisk in Jerome and
Syro-hex., did not exist in G. The
present text is derived from Theod.
(cf. Syro-hex.), but Jerome *quia non
in homine positum est* derives
from Symm. οὐ γὰρ ἐπ' ἀνθρώπῳ
κεῖται ἔτι. Vulg. paraphrases the 1st
hemistich: *neque enim ultra in hominis potestate est*. The verb **ישׂים** is
treated as a passive 'has been placed'
in Syr. (cf. Symm.). G ὁ γὰρ Κύριος
πάντας ἐφορᾷ does not translate the
2nd hemistich but sums up v. 21.

God is the sovereign Lord (17-20)
and nothing escapes him (21-2).
Now, Job had said: 'He is not a man
like myself that I might answer
Him, that we might go to law together' (9: 32). It is not only that the
two adversaries have not to present
themselves before the same bar of
judgment, but God has no need to
summon man since He finds him
wherever he seeks refuge. Those who
preserve **עוּד** translate: 'God does
not look at man twice' (Le Hir), or
'God has no need to look at man
twice' (Renan, cf. Crampon). But
the verb **שׂים** with **על** before the name
of a person means 'to impose a
charge or obligation on some one
(cf. v. 13; Ex 5: 8; 22: 24). The
change from **עוּד** to **מוֹעֵד** (the *mem*
having fallen out by haplography
after **ישׂים**), proposed both by Reiske
and Wright, has been rightly accepted by most moderns. In Ex
9: 5 we find precisely **וישׂם יהוה מועד**
'and Yahweh fixed a time'; cf. **מועד**
in 30: 23. The 1st hemistich therefore
means: 'for He does not appoint
for man a time'. Such an appoint-
ment would imply presenting one's
self, on the day fixed, before God

24 He shatters the great without inquiry,
    And sets up others in their place;
26 As wicked men, He smites them,
    In the place *where* there are spectators,

25 After v. 22.
26-27 Transfer אשר of v. 27 to precede ראים of v. 26.

(whence the use of אֶל־אֵל 'unto God' and not אֶת־אֵל 'with God' as postulated by Ehrlich), in order to be judged. But God does not need to use the formalities of legal procedure, He acts by sovereign authority (vv. 24ff.). Note the use of לַהֲלֹךְ, as we had להסתר in v. 22. The idiom הלך במשפט 'to go for judgment' as we have בוא במשפט 'to come to judgment' (9: 32; 22: 4) and הביא במשפט 'to bring to judgment' (14: 3).

24 G ὁ καταλαμβάνων ἀνεξιχνίαστα links with 9: 10a (where אין־חקר was translated ἀνεξιχνίαστα), which leads to an exact quotation of 9: 10b ἔνδοξά τε καὶ ἐξαίσια, ὧν οὐκ ἔστιν ἀριθμός instead of our 2nd hemistich. Vulg. *conteret multos et innumerabiles* interprets חקר in the sense of 'number', while Syr. renders לא־חקר by ولا صمى 'without end'. Targ. sees in כבירים the waves of the sea which swell in the midst of the waters (following Is 17: 12). Syr. reads אחד instead of אחרים, whence احسى 'together'.

God has no need to adopt the procedure of judgment: 'He shatters the great without inquiry.' The Aramaic verb רעע 'to shatter' (Is 24: 19; Ps 2: 9) instead of the Hebrew רצץ (20: 19). The word כַּבִּיר (v. 17) is used substantively; cf. אבּיר in v. 20. The phrase לֹא־חֵקֶר 'no inquiry, investigation' to mean 'without inquiry'; cf. ולא־חקר in 36: 26; אין־חקר in 5: 9; 9: 10. The meaning of חֵקֶר 'search', 'investigation' (cf. 5: 9),

here specifically 'inquiry'; cf. the use of the verb חקר to connote 'to study a case' in 29: 16. Of course God replaces those whom He has deposed: 'and He sets up others in their place'. The *hiph'il* of עמד signifies 'to cause to stand', 'to raise up', 'to constitute' (1 K 12: 32; 2 Ch 19: 5, etc.).

25 After v. 22.

26 It is in error that Colb. and Jerome mark with asterisk vv. 26-7, which in fact exist in Sah. and are not marked with asterisk in Syrohex. The text of Theod. does not begin before v. 28. We have seen that v. 25b came from Theod., but here G ἔσβεσεν δὲ ἀσεβεῖς contains a fragment of the original translation, for ἔσβεσεν δὲ translates וידעך, which arises from וידכא (v. 25). It becomes apparent that the word תחת is omitted in G. For the 2nd hemistich G ὁρατοὶ δὲ ἐναντίον αὐτοῦ Sah.), but G(A) καὶ ὁρατοὶ ἐγένοντο ἐναντίον τῶν ἐχθρῶν (cf. ἐναντίον ἐχθροὶ αὐτοῦ in Codd. 249, 252). Following Jerome *et gloriosos coram inimicis suis* and Syro-hex. 'and glorified before his enemies' (with obelus before 'enemies'), the original reading was doubtless ὁρατοὶ δὲ ἐναντίον ἐχθρῶν αὐτοῦ. We recognise ראים in ὁρατοί and ἐχθρῶν in מקום, connected with קום 'to rise up against', 'to be hostile' (Dt 33: 11; Ps 18: 40). Vulg. *quasi impios percussit eos in loco videntium* grasp very well the meaning of the verse, as does also 1st Targ., although 2nd Targ. gives a free interpretation. Syr. places first וידכא of v. 25 (cf. G), reads רשעם 'their wickedness' in-

27   Because they have turned aside from following Him,
      And have not understood all His ways,
28   By causing to rise up towards Him the cry of the weak,

stead of רשעים, and connects ראים with ירא 'to fear', whence 'and they are humiliated beneath the iniquity of their works in the place of fear'.

There is a lack of balance between the two hemistichs. Various attempts have been made to connect סְפָקָם with the 2nd hemistich, and to extend the first. We do not propose to linger over the hypothesis of Bickell, which is however accepted by Budde, and which consists in introducing חמתו 'His fury' as the subject of תחת, which is vocalised תָּחַת 'His fury shatters (or terrifies) the wicked'. God is the subject of the verbs, and it is not at all clear why recourse should have been had to 'His fury' solely in v. 26a. If the versions afforded the slightest support, we might if need be admit such a change of style. Such however is not the case. Duhm and Beer place at the head of v. 26 וידכאו of v. 25 (cf. G and Syr.), whilst Duhm replaces רשעים by רסיסים (Am 6:11) 'and they are crushed beneath ruins'; Beer vocalises רִשְׁעָם (after Houbigant; cf. Syr.) 'and they are crushed beneath their wickedness'. But וידכאו marks the result of the action expressed by והפך לילה of v. 25. If it is removed from v. 25, we are then obliged to suppress לכן...לילה (Duhm, Beer), and we have seen that v. 25 was to be integrally maintained and made the sequel of v. 22. The word תחת 'under' also means 'in the place of' (v. 24) and, derivatively, 'in guise of', 'like': cf. Sir 30:25, 'good like (תחת) delicacies'. The verb ספק 'to beat', especially to clap hands (27:23) or beat with the hands (Jer 31:19; Ezk 21:17) will here have the special connotation of 'slap', 'smite' as a sign of scorn. Instead of

changing ראים into רפאים 'in the place of the Shades' (Reiske, Wright, Ball) or into רעים 'like evil men' (Ehrlich), we prefer to keep the present text and to restore to the hemistich normal proportions by placing the relative אֲשֶׁר, which overloads the beginning of v. 27, between בַּמְקוֹם and ראים. The construction is exactly the same as in Hos 2:1; Ezk 21:35 (omission of the adverb שָׁם after אשר marking the relative of place). V. 26: 'As wicked men, He smites them, in the place where there are spectators' shows vividly the contempt which God entertains for the eminent persons of v. 24 (cf. vv. 18-20). The perfect ספק, as we had נשא in v. 19.

27   For אשר על־כן, Vulg. qui quasi de industria, G simply ὅτι 'because' (cf. Targ. and Syr.). G paraphrases מאחריו by ἐκ νόμου θεοῦ and renders וכל־דרכיו by δικαιώματα δὲ αὐτοῦ.

The relative אֲשֶׁר, which overloads the 1st hemistich, belonged originally to v. 26 (cf. Comm.). The formula עַל־כֵּן, like לָכֵן in 20:2, belongs to what follows, not to what precedes, for it introduces the cause of the punishments which have just been related. The sense is 'because', and it is the same sense which seems demanded in Ps 45:3. The verb סור with מאחרי before the complement of person, to denote the opposite of הלך אחרי 'to go after' God or the Baals (1 S 12:20; 2 K 18:6, etc.). The ways of God are His precepts or His teachings (21:14). On the verb השכיל 'to understand', cf. 22:2.

28   V. 28-33, absent from Sah., marked with asterisk in Jerome,

So that He hears the cry of the poor.

29   If He rests, who can *stir* Him?
     And if He hides His face, who shall perceive Him?

29 יַרְעֹשׁ; MT: ירשע. — יָחַז; MT: יחד.

Syro-hex., and Colb. (with the exception of v. 32), did not exist in G.
The present text is derived from
Theod. (cf. Syro-hex.). The repetition
of צעקת is confirmed by κραυγήν...
καὶ κραυγήν of Theod.

V. 28 shows one of the ways in
which these sinners have turned
aside from following God. The idiom
לְהָבִיא has the sense of a gerund
(31: 30). The verb הביא, with על
before the complement of person
(Gn 18: 19). The preposition is deliberately chosen because what is in
question is a prayer which rises up
to God; cf. the use of בוא with על in
29: 13. The verb שמע requires צעקה
as in 27: 9, and there is no reason to
replace צעקת by a synonym as
Duhm proposes to do in order to
avoid the repetition of the same word.
Note the parallelism between עניים
'the poor' and דל 'the weak', 'the
needy' (cf. v. 19). The copula at
the beginning of the 2nd hemistich
brings the clause under the government of the preposition "ל, which
becomes a conjunction.

29 On the text of G, cf. v. 28. For
והוא ישקט, Theod. καὶ αὐτὸς ἡσυχίαν
παρέξει, Symm. αὐτοῦ δὲ ἠρεμίαν
διδόντος (cf. Vulg. *ipso enim conce-
dente pacem*). Syr. translates ישקט
and ישורנו by ܡܚܒ 'send away',
'release'. Targ. interprets פנים by
שכינתא 'dwelling', 'hypostasis' of
God, in order to avoid anthropomorphism.

Elihu returns to his thought of
God's absolute independence (vv.
13ff.). The construction of the first
two hemistichs offers no difficulty.

The succession of imperfects or jussives to express hypothesis and its
realisation is fairly common; cf.
Gesenius-Kautzsch, § 159c, d. The
2nd hemistich is conceived exactly
like 22: 28a. Let us begin by explaining this 2nd hemistich, which
will throw light upon the 1st. It is
still a question of God: 'And if He
hides His face, who will perceive
Him?' The phrase הסתיר פנים has
been applied to God by Job himself
(13: 24). On the verb שׁוּר, cf. 7: 8.
The antithesis is thus firmly marked,
the second clause indicating something which becomes impossible if
the hypothesis is realised. Let us
now examine the hypothesis announced by the 1st hemistich. The
hiph'il of שקט 'to be at rest', 'to be
calm, quiet' (3: 26) sometimes means
'to soothe' (Pr 15: 18) or 'give rest'
(Ps 94: 13), sometimes 'to take rest',
'to rest' (Is 57: 20; Jer 49: 23). It
is in the latter sense that we shall
meet השקיט in 37: 17. Hence we may
translate וְהוּא יַשְׁקֵט by 'and if He
rests', which implies a cessation of
movement, just as 'and if He hides
His face' implies disappearance.
What is expected is the action rendered impossible by the given hypothesis. Now, 'and who will condemn?'
has no logical nexus with 'and if He
rests'. It is only by a stretch of ingenuity that one can translate: 'who
can find occasion to criticise when
God forgives?' (Renan), or 'and if
He grants them peace, who shall
oppress them?' (Le Hir). The verb
which is contrasted with השקיט is
not הרשיע, but rather הרעיש 'stir
up,' 'shake' (Is 14: 16; Ezk 31: 16)
or 'make to leap' (Job 39: 20).

Now *He watches* nations and persons,

30 So that no one [   ] of those who ensnare the people should
reign.

30 Transfer חנף to follow אמר of v. 31.

Already R. Samuel BƏn-Nissim recognised the equivalence of ירשע and
ירעש in our verse (*RÉJ*, **21**, p. 126).
With Hitzig and some moderns we
therefore read יָרְעָשׁ. The suffix has
been omitted, as after פָּנִים, no ambiguity being possible in view of
יְשׁוּרֶנּוּ 'If He rests, who can stir
Him?' God is sovereign Lord of His
own actions, He moves only according to His eternal will, just as
He reveals Himself only when He
chooses. Cf. the antitheses of 9: 12
and 11: 10. The 3rd hemistich seems
in the present arrangement to overload the text, whether we translate
'over nations and over private individuals' (Renan), 'whether it be
that He acts thus for a people or for
all men in general' (Le Hir), 'whether
it be a nation or a man whom He
treats thus' (Crampon). In reality
the 3rd hemistich is the first part
of the verse which continues with
v. 30. The verb is concealed in the
word יָחַד. Schnurrer proposed to
connect it with the Arabic *ḥadda* 'to
be provoked'. But it is a question
of forestalling evil rather than under-
going its effects, and the same objection applies to the change from
יחד to יחרה 'He becomes angry'
(Grimme). Duhm reads יער 'He
watches', Beer יפקד 'He takes care'.
The best solution is that of Ehrlich,
who recognises in יחד a corruption
of יָחֱז (an apocopated form of יחזה
'He sees'); cf. 23: 9. The verb חזה
with על before the object of the
vision has the same meaning as
ראה על 'look upon', 'watch over'
(cf. the formula of v. 21) in Ex
1: 16; 5: 21. God watches over the

nation and the individual, so as to
prevent the latter from unjustly
oppressing the former (v. 30).

30 On the text of G, cf. v. 28. Syr.
'so that there does not reign' follows
the vocalisation of the MT, while
Theod. βασιλευών, Vulg. *qui regnare
facit*, and Targ. ממני מלכא 'setting
up as king' vocalise מַמְלִיךְ. For חנף,
Theod. ὑποκριτήν, Vulg. *hypocritam*,
Targ. דילטור (cf. 8: 13; 13: 16, etc.).
For ממקשי עם, Theod. ἀπὸ δυσκολίας
λαοῦ, Vulg. *propter peccata populi*,
Targ. 'because of snares in the
people', Syr. 'and a sinner against
the people'.

It is impossible to compose a
whole verse with v. 30, and it is
only by means of ingenious paraphrases that exegetes obtain: 'over-
throwing the throne of the godless
man, and destroying the nets with
which he ensnared his people' (Le
Hir), 'to make to cease the reign of
the godless man and to prevent him
from becoming the scourge of his
people' (Renan). Note that אָדָם
corresponds to אדם of v. 29c, just
as עָם is complementary to גּוֹי. The
word חָנֵף overloads the text and
comes from v. 31, where it is the
subject of אמר (cf. Comm.). Thus
we obtain the hemistich parallel to
v. 29c: 'so that no one of those who
ensnare the people should reign'. The
pregnant construction מִמְּלֹךְ *ut non
regnet*, as we have מֵרְאֹת *ita ut non
videat* (Gn 27: 1), to show that a
certain action is excluded as a result
of an action expressed in the previous clause (Gesenius-Kautzsch,

31   If *a godless man says to Eloah*: '*I have been led astray,*
      I will *no longer* do evil;

31   Read אֵלֹהַ אָמַר (MT: אל האמר) and then add חנף from v. 30. — נִשֵּׂאתִי;
MT: נשאתי. — עוֹד after אחבל אֶחְבֹּל.

§ 119y). The word אדם has the same meaning as אִישׁ, before the partitive מִן (Gn 23: 6; 39: 11). The מֹקְשֵׁי עָם are 'the snares of the people'; cf. מוֹקְשִׁים in 40: 24. The metaphor alludes to those who ensnare others in their nets; cf. Ex 10: 7; Jg 2: 3; 1 S 18: 21. The change from מקשׁי to מעקשׁ 'perverting' (Houbigant) removes an essentially Biblical image.

31   On the text of G, cf. v. 28. For האמר (interpreted: אפשר דאתאמר 'can it be said?' in Targ.), Theod. ὁ λέγων vocalises הָאֹמֵר (cf. v. 18). Syr. omits אל by haplography, which then gives אֵלֹהַ אמר 'since God has said' (cf. inf.). Symm. ῥῆσιν ἀνέλαβον and Vulg. *locutus sum* combine in a single formula האמר and נשאתי. For לא אחבל (transcribed in Targ.), Theod. οὐκ ἐνεχυράσω, Symm. οὐχ ἕξω ἀκωλύτως, Vulg. *te quoque non prohibebo*. Syr. 'I do not destroy those who do not sin' places the words בלעדי אחזה (reading יחטא instead of אחזה) of v. 32 at the end of v. 31.

V. 31 and v. 32a are a *crux interpretum*. הָאֹמֵר is usually interpreted as a question (cf. Targ.), whence 'for has he ever said to God: I have borne the penalty of my crime; I shall not fall into it again?' (Le Hir); 'Has this impious man said to God: I have been punished, I shall not sin again?' (Renan). But the interrogative construction appears in v. 33. Vv. 31-2, compared with 33: 23-8, express the feelings of the repentant sinner. V. 32b is quite specific in this way: 'If I have committed an in-

justice, I will not do so again!' V. 31a introduces the hypothesis of conversion. A wrong division has given rise to the present text; but the original text, a trace of which has remained in Syr., had אֵלֹהַ אָמַר and not אל האמר. The subject of אמר is חָנֵף, which has erroneously been transferred to v. 30 (cf. Comm.). If we compare with כי אמרתי 'if I say' of 7: 13, we shall not hesitate to render the 1st part of v. 31 as: 'if a godless man says to Eloah'. This is a formula of introduction similar to those which introduce the direct speech in 33: 24, 27. The word נִשֵּׂאתִי corresponds to חטאתי of 33: 27. It is difficult to obtain an appropriate meaning with נשא 'bear', 'endure', 'tolerate', for it would require a direct complement which has in fact been arbitrarily added in the translations (cf. Le Hir and Renan, sup.). The reading נִשֵּׂאתִי 'I have been led astray' (Is 19: 13) is preferable to נִשֵּׂאתִי 'I have exalted myself' (Duhm) or to הִתְנַשֵּׂאתִי 'I have revolted' (Beer), for the fact of having been beguiled suggests a certain extenuation and justifies the restriction of 'if I have committed injustice' in v. 32 (cf. Torczyner). The parallelism between the end of v. 31 and v. 32b emphasises the value of the addition of עוֹד (lost by haplography) after אֶחְבֹּל; the repetition of the final letters of אחבל has given rise to בלעדי of v. 32 (cf. Comm.). The verb חבל 'to act wrongly' (cf. Comm. on 21: 17), as in Neh 1: 7. The close will therefore be translated: 'I will no longer do evil.'

32   *Until* I see, do Thou instruct me,
     If I have committed injustice, I will do so no more!'

33   Is it your opinion that He will requite the wrong?
     Since you have despised . . . .
     Since it is you who are summing up and not I,
     Say then what you know!

32   עֲדֵי; MT: בלעדי.

32 On the text of G, cf. v. 28. Theod. ἄνευ ἐμαυτοῦ ὄψομαι reads בְּלְעָדַי. Syr. connects בלעדי אחזה with v. 31 and לא אסיף with v. 33. Vulg. *si erravi* seems to read אחטא (cf. Syr. in v. 31) instead of אחזה. For פעלתי, Vulg. *locutus sum*.

The 2nd hemistich offers no difficulty: 'If I have committed injustice, I will do so no more.' The abstract עָוֶל, instead of עולה, as in v. 10. The formula לא אסיף 'I will not do again' (40:5); cf. 20:9; 27:19). The 1st hemistich would mean literally: 'Without my seeing, do Thou instruct me!', and it is from pure necessity that to בִּלְעֲדַי אֶחֱזֶה is assigned such meanings as 'what I cannot see' (Renan), 'what I do not know' (Le Hir, Crampon), 'what I do not see' (Segond), or even *si quid inscius admisi* (Rosenmüller). The consonants בל of בלעדי arise from אחבל of v. 31. The text in v. 31 read עוד אחבל, and v. 32 began with עֲדֵי (poetic for עַד). A dittograph of בל and a haplograph of בלעדי עוד עדי have given rise to בלעדי. Hence we translate the 1st hemistich: 'Until I see, do Thou instruct me!' This explanation frees us from the necessity of changing the text by reading אם חטאתי 'if I have sinned' (Beer, following Vulg.). The evidence of Vulg. and Syr. in favour of a verb חטא 'to sin' is counterbalanced by that of Theod. and Targ. in favour of חזה. The change from אחזה to אחזר 'I become converted' (Torczyner, in the light of the mean-ing of חזר in the Talmud) has the disadvantage of making the verse begin with אחזר, which gives us a 1st hemistich that is too short.

33 On the text of G, cf. v. 28. For מאסת, Vulg. *displicuit tibi*, Syr. 'as regards your sin'. Vulg. renders תבחר by *coepisti loqui*. It seems that Targ. תתרעי 'you are agreed' reads a *niph'al* instead of a *qal* תבחר.

Yet another *crux interpretum*. Let us note that a complete verse is intact from כִּי־אַתָּה: 'Since it is you who are summing up and not I, say then what you know.' The verb בחר 'examine' (v. 4) and consequently 'judge', 'discriminate', for 'choose' (cf. Comm. on v. 4 and on 7:18). For the interrogative מָה in the indirect question as in v. 4 and 23:5, cf. מה־ידעת in 15:9. Thus Elihu is inviting Job to formulate an assessment on a given case. The question is posed by the 1st hemistich: 'Is it your opinion that He will requite the wrong?' The use of the conjunction עם in 10:13 and 27:11, to suggest what is in the mind of some one, what he thinks, permits us to assign to מֵעִמְּךָ 'from with you' the meaning of 'according to you', 'in your opinion'. The *pi'el* of שלם means 'to requite', 'to repay an equivalent' (v. 11; 21:19, 31). The feminine suffix plays the part of a neuter pronoun referring to what precedes; cf. ישׁרנּה in 33:14. It is an allusion to what should be the cause of reprisals, namely the sin that has been committed (21:19).

34   Men of heart will say to me,
      As would any wise man listening to me:
35   'Job does not speak with knowledge,
      And his words are not uttered according to reason!'
36   *But* Job will be examined to the very end,
      With regard to replies that are *worthy* of men of iniquity;

36   אֲבָל (G, Syr.); MT: אבי. — כְּאַנְשֵׁי (G); MT: באנשי.

Elihu asks Job for his opinion as to what God will do when the sinner becomes converted. He has already expressed his own opinion (33: 23-30). His theory has not convinced Job, and we think that this is what was contained in a hemistich of which only the first words remain: 'since you have despised . . .'. This no doubt was followed by 'my teaching', 'my doctrine'. The implication is that Job has rejected the words of Elihu in their totality in order to preserve his liberty of judgment: 'since it is you who are summing up, and not I!' It seems to us impossible to combine into one single phrase כִּי־אַתָּה and כִּי־מָאַסְתָּ תְבָחָר so as to translate: 'It is for you to choose what you repudiate, what pleases you, and not I' (Le Hir), or again 'because it is you who are expressing your disdain or manifesting your preferences, you and not I' (*Bible du rabbinat français*). A simple comparison with the text is sufficient to show by what subterfuges such an interpretation is reached. And how shall we find the Hebrew words reflected in the paraphrase of Renan: 'Will God take your advice about punishing such a man? Will He say to you: Be thou judge in my place?'

34   The text of G begins again at v. 34. G διὸ συνετοὶ καρδίας is inspired by v. 10a. For אנשי לבב (literally translated in Syr.), Vulg. *viri intelligentes* (instead of *cordati* of v. 10), Targ. 'men wise of heart'. G replaces the first לי by ταῦτα and the second

לי by μοῦ τὸ ῥῆμα, which has become 'my words' in Sah. and Syro-hex. (with obelus before 'words').

Elihu considers that he has won the debate since Job does not reply. It is only in order to triumph over his opponent that he will continue his exposition. As in v. 10, he appeals to men of heart, i.e. to men of understanding (cf. Comm. on v. 10), and he quotes their approbation (v. 36). The 2nd hemistich merely makes explicit אַנְשֵׁי לֵבָב. The expression שֹׁמֵעַ לִי 'listening to me' as in 31: 35.

35   The versions translate very literally, but Vulg. exaggerates when it renders לֹא־בְדַעַת by *stulte*.
   Verdict of the wise: 'Job does not speak with knowledge!' Elihu has boasted of uttering 'words of knowledge' (33: 3; cf. Comm.), while Eliphaz has insinuated that Job replied only with 'a windy knowledge' (15: 2). Parallelism between דֵּעָה 'knowledge' and הַשְׂכִּיל 'reason' recurs in Jer. 3: 15. Note the vocalisation of the *hiph'il* infinitive here and in Jer 3: 15. This infinitive is taken substantively (cf. Pr 1: 3; 21: 16). On the verb הִשְׂכִּיל cf. v. 27.

36   Targ. צבינא 'desire' (i.e. I desire) connects אבי with the root אבה 'will', whereas Vulg. interprets אבי by *pater mi*! G οὐ μὴν δὲ ἀλλὰ reads אֲבָל, confirmed by Syr. ܐܠܦܝܢ 'certainly' (cf. inf.). G μάθε seems to read בין instead of יבחן. Then μὴ δῷς ἔτι ἀνταπόκρισιν reads אל־תשיב instead of על־תשבת, whereas

37   For he adds to his sin:
      In our midst he *casts doubt upon his* transgression
      And he multiplies his words against God!

37 פְּשָׁעוֹ; MT: פשע. — יַסְפִּיק; MT: יספוק.

Vulg. *ne desinas ab homine iniqui-tatis* reads אל־תשבת and regards the verb as belonging to the root שבת. Syr. וin reads ואל סוס and חשבת. Instead of באנש, G ὥσπερ οἱ ἄφρονες reads כָּאֲנָשֵׁי.

We cannot render אָבִי by 'my father', which would be addressed to no one in particular. On the other hand, the examples cited in favour of an interjection אבי, namely 1 S 24: 12 and 2 K 5: 13, can be explained very well by the translation 'my father'. Wetzstein would assign to אבי the meaning of 'I pray' by postulating a verb corresponding to the Arabic *baya* which is used in the Hauran to connote 'to enter as a suppliant', to implore'; *bît* 'I have implored', *binâ* 'we have implored', etc. But this verb, which is peculiar to the dialect of the Hauran, repre-sents only a local usage, and has no support in other Semitic languages. We cannot have recourse to it in order to explain a Hebrew *hapax*. Some have attempted to derive אבי from אבה 'will' (cf. Targ.), so that אבי would mean 'my desire is that . . .'. Nowhere is this derivative substantive met with. Hoffmann compared with אבוי (Pr. 23: 29), which is an interjection parallel to אוי 'ah!' 'alas!' and the meaning of which is not appropriate here. Still less may we see in אבי a *hiph'il* of בוא to mean 'I introduce' arguments by means of which Job will be examined (Schultens); we should then have to add a connecting idea between אבי and יַבְחֵן. If we note that G and Syr. translate אֲבָל, which has the meaning of 'in truth' (Syr.) and 'but', 'however' (G), we

shall not hesitate to read אֲבָל (which is preferable to אֻלָם of Bickell, Siegfried, and to אָכֵן of Michaelis) instead of אבי. The restrictive adverb concerns the fact that Job has already been condemned by the wise (vv. 34-5). In spite of that, Elihu proposes to pursue his investigation: 'But Job will be examined to the very end.' On the verb בחן, cf. 7: 18. The idiom עַד־נֶצַח *usque in aeternum* (Ps 49: 20) indicates that the in-quiry will be carried out 'to the very end'. The object of this inquiry is the answers of Job; cf. תְּשֻׁבֹת in 21: 34. If we keep the preposition בְּ" before אֲנָשֵׁי, we are obliged to suppose that it is a question of answers which are habitually given 'among men of iniquity'. The expression would be too forceful. With G we can read כָּאֲנָשֵׁי (a reading which is found in three manuscripts). It is a question of replies which are 'like' those made by men of iniquity. The אַנְשֵׁי אָוֶן are contrasted with אנשי לבב of vv. 10, 34. Cf. the מתי און of 22: 15 and the פעלי און of v. 22.

37 G changes the meaning com-pletely by substituting the 1st person plural for the 3rd person singular ἵνα μὴ προσθῶμεν ἐφ' ἁμαρ-τίας ἡμῶν, whence πολλὰ λαλούντων ῥήματα for וירב אמריו. Instead of ἁμαρτίας, G (א, A, C) ἁμαρτίαις (Syro-hex., Jerome *peccata nostra*). The word פשע is regarded by G as the subject of יספוק: ἀνομία δὲ ἐφ' ἡμῖν λογισθήσεται. It becomes apparent that יספוק is treated as a passive; cf. Vulg. *constringatur* and Syr. ܡܣܦܩ.

'sought for'. Syr. makes פשע the subject of יספוק also. Vulg. paraphrases the 1st hemistich *et tunc ad judicium provocet sermonibus suis Deum*. Instead of וירב, Syr. סומבס seems to read ויקרב.

The usual translation is 'for he adds to his sin a transgression', and this translation seems to have support in Is 30:1, 'to add sin on sin'. But in this case we are embarrassed by בֵּינֵינוּ יִסְפּוֹק, which Duhm simply deletes. If כפים 'hands' (27:23) is understood, critics translate בינינו יספוק by 'he claps his hands among us', whence the paraphrases: 'he mocks in the midst of us' (Le Hir), 'he openly mocks at us' (Renan). In any case, the hemistich is too short, and it is no improvement to read פנינו יספוק 'he smites our face' (Ehrlich). Budde restores it to the required proportions by adding כפיו 'his hands' after יספוק. But we should expect 'clap hands *against* us' rather than 'clap hands *among* us' (cf. 27:23). Note that the mean-

ing of the 1st hemistich is complete after חַטָּאתוֹ 'for he adds to his sin'. Cf. the constructions of Dt 4:2; 13:1; Pr 30:6. G and Syr. have connected פשע to the 2nd hemistich. Now, the verb ספק has, in Aramaic, the meaning 'to doubt' and in the causative construction 'to cast doubt on'. The way in which Job aggravates his sin is by being unwilling to recognise it or confess it. The aim of a considerable part of the argument has been to wrest such a confession from him. Elihu has also reproached Job with his assertions of his innocence (33:8ff.; 34:5ff.). Hence we propose to read פִּשְׁעוֹ instead of פשע and to vocalise יַסְפִּיק instead of יִסְפּוֹק. The 2nd hemistich brings out the chief grievance entertained against Job. The other grievance consists in his complainings against God: 'and he multiplies his words against God'. With וְיֶרֶב compare וְתֶרֶב in 10:17. Note the apocopated imperfect (cf. 33:21).

1 Then Elihu spoke and said:
2 Did you consider this to be wise,
  Did you think: it is my justification in the sight of God?
3 When you say: 'What does it matter to Thee?
  What *do I to Thee if I sin?*'

3 אֶפְעַל אִם חָטָאתִי (cf. G); MT: אעיל מחטאתי.

35: **1** V. 1 is omitted in G (C). Vulg. *igitur Eliu haec rursum locutus est* instead of *pronuntians itaque Eliu etiam haec locutus est* in 34: 1.

2 It is in error that Jerome marks vv. 2-3 with asterisk. G τί τοῦτο ἡγήσω ἐν κρίσει; translates as if the text read מה־זאת and not הזאת. The function of אמרת is well understood by Vulg. *ut diceres* and Syr. וֹאמרܝܬ. G paraphrases σὺ τίς εἶ ὅτι εἶπας. Syro-hex. places the obelus before σὺ τίς εἶ. Instead of צדקי, G Δίκαιός εἰμι, Vulg. *justior sum*, Syr. וֹܙ ܕܟܝܬ 'I am righteous', Targ. דכיית 'I am pure' interpret in the light of 4: 17; 9: 2; 25: 4.

Elihu once more addresses Job, whom he mentioned at the end of ch. 34 as having to undergo a new examination (vv. 35-7). The opening הֲזֹאת recalls הֲן־זאת of 33: 12, but the demonstrative is linked with what follows: 'Did you consider this to be wise?' The verb חשב with ל׳ before the complement to mean 'consider as' (13: 24; 19: 15; 33: 10). Note the use of מִשְׁפָּט in the sense of 'what is right, wise' (32: 9; 34: 4). The explanation of the word זאת does not begin until v. 3. The 2nd hemistich is parallel to the 1st, the perfect אָמַרְתָ corresponding to חָשַׁבְתָ.

We see no reason to replace the noun צִדְקִי by the verb צִדַקְתִי, as is done by the versions in accord with the use of this verb with מִן in 4: 17 (cf. 9: 2; 25: 4) and 32: 2. The phrase צִדְקִי מֵאֵל means 'my justification before God'. Elihu no longer criticises Job for having wished to justify himself (32: 12; 33: 8-12). What he means here is that Job has a false idea of what might justify him. In fact, the demonstrative זאת is the complement of אמרת as of חשבת: 'Did you think (say within yourself): this is my justification before God?' The words כִי־תאמר of v. 3 will explain the false notion of Job.

3 G(B) omits v. 3. By an error of homoeoteleuton (מה···מה) we have simply ἢ ἐρεῖς τί ποιήσω ἁμαρτών in G (A, C, אᶜ·ᵃ), Compl., Sah., Memph. The text is completed by τί κατευθύνει σοι (after ἐρεῖς) in Cod. 249, the margin of Syro-hex., and Jerome *quid prodest tibi*. Note that τί ποιήσω ἁμαρτών preserves the original text of the 2nd hemistich (cf. inf.). For מה־יסכן לך, Symm. ὅτι οὐδὲν συμβαλεῖταί σοι, Vulg. *non tibi placet quod rectum est*. Syr. reads תסכן instead of יסכן.

V. 2 is explained by כִי־תאמַר 'when you say'. As they stand, the

530

4   I will answer you with words,
     And your friends with you!

5   Look at the heavens and see;
     Consider the clouds; they are higher than you!

words of Job should be translated: 'What interest is there for Thee? How do I profit from my sin?' The construction of סכן is as in 22:2; the verb הועיל is parallel to סכן in 15:3. This meaning is strange. How can Job ask himself what profit he derives from his sin, he who has always asserted his innocence? It does not help to replace לָךְ by לִי in the 1st hemistich (Duhm), for the translation recommended for the 2nd hemistich, 'In what way am I bettered without sin?' (Duhm), remains as contrary to the literal sense as the translations of Le Hir: 'What have I more than if I had sinned?', or Renan: 'In what way am I better treated than if I had sinned?' Furthermore, Job never made such remarks. By comparing v. 6 with 7:20, Ehrlich has discovered the original text of the 2nd hemistich: מָה אֶפְעַל אִם חָטָאתִי 'What do I if I sin?' This correction has good confirmation in G: τί ποιήσω ἁμαρτών. The remark alluded to is that of Job in 7:20, 'If I sin, what do I to Thee, O Thou Watcher of men?' The complement לָךְ is not now expressed after אפעל, precisely because it is explicit in the 1st hemistich. Note that the proposed change is very slight. The juxtaposition of אם and חטאתי has given rise to מחטאתי, while the presence of the verb סכן in the first clause has occasioned אעיל instead of אפעל. The true meaning of מַה־יִּסְכָּן־לָךְ will be 'what does it matter to Thee?', derived from: 'What concern is there for Thee?' Of course it is to God that Job is addressing his question (7:20). Elihu will reply that doubtless man cannot afflict God through his sin, and in this he

will seem to agree thoroughly with Job (vv. 4-7); but there is one's neighbour (v. 8). It is the neighbour who suffers from the wrongdoing of man (vv. 8-9).

4   Vulg. *itaque ego respondebo sermonibus tuis* transfers the suffix of אֲשִׁיבֶךָ. G καὶ τοῖς τρισὶν φίλοις σου, for וְאֶת־רֵעֶיךָ, recalls the Prologue.

Budde thinks it strange that the speech is also addressed to the friends of Job. But Elihu is talking to the onlookers (34:2-4, 10-15, 34:7). He is now making up for the long silence which he maintained in the presence of the other speakers (32:6ff.). Note the construction of הֵשִׁיב 'to answer' with the personal suffix (33:5, 32) and the accusative מִלִּין which replaces דָּבָר 'word' (Gn 37:14; Nu 22:8, etc.).

5   Syr. renders ראה and שׁור by a single verb. For שְׁחָקִים, Vulg. *aethera*.

Elihu is directly inspired by Eliphaz: 'Is not Eloah on high in the heavens? And behold the topmost stars, how high they are!' (22:12). After the stars Eliphaz mentions the clouds (22:13). Here the clouds are parallel to the heavens. In 38:37 they will be described as 'the water-skins of the skies'. The verb שׁור 'to perceive', in the sense of 'to consider', because of the parallelism with הַבֵּט which indicates the primary action resulting in vision (28:24). The verb גבה with מן before the complement denotes 'to be higher than' (cf. 11:8a). God is above the sky and the clouds (22:14). The action of man cannot attain unto Him or affect Him (6-7). It affects only man (8).

6   If you sin, what effect do you produce in Him,
      And if your transgressions are many, what do you do to Him?

7   If you are righteous, what do you give to Him,
      Or what does He receive from your hand?

8   It is a man like yourself whom your wickedness affects,
      And a son of man whom your righteousness influences. . . .

9   Through excess of oppression they cry out,
      Under the arm of the mighty they cry for help!

6 G omits the complements בו and לו. For ורבו פשעיך, G εἰ δὲ καὶ πολλὰ ἠνόμησας.

'If you sin, what effect do you produce in Him?' Elihu seems to be adopting the theory of Job (v. 3; 7: 20). God is not affected by sin. He is above the world and escapes the action of man (v. 5). But man's wrongdoing has consequences as far as other people are concerned (v. 8). And Job has noted precisely this (24). Hence the necessity of divine intervention. The concern for variation of style prompts בו instead of לו in the 1st hemistich and sets in parallelism the synonyms פעל and עשה. The conjunction אם is understood before רבו פשעיך. The perfect is used in the subordinate clauses because the actions are completed in the past in relation to their effects.

7 Vv. 7b-10a, absent from Sah., marked with asterisk in Jerome, Syro-hex., Colb., did not exist in G. The present text comes from Theod. (cf. Colb. and Syro-hex.).

Once more Elihu bases himself on the speech of Eliphaz (22: 2-3). Just as sin cannot affect God harmfully, so human righteousness does not profit the Almighty: 'If you are righteous, what do you give to Him?' The verb לקח means 'to receive' (22: 22; 27: 13), 'or what does He receive from your hand?' The 2nd hemistich is parallel to 'what do you give to Him?'

8 On the text of G, cf. v. 7. Follow-

ing 22: 3, Syr. interprets the expressions איש כמוך and בן־אדם by 'yourself'. Targ. sees the wicked man in איש and the innocent man in בן־אדם. Vulg. makes the thought more explicit by adding *nocebit* to the 1st hemistich, and *adjuvabit* to the 2nd.

Elihu concludes by continuing the alternative expressed in vv. 6-7. It is man and not God who is affected by the evil or goodness of man. The expression 'a man like yourself' proves that it is a question of the neighbour, not of Job himself. Cf. 33: 6, where Elihu said: 'Behold, I am as you are in regard to God!' Wickedness, רשע, is parallel to unrighteousness or iniquity (34: 8, 10). Its antithetic term is righteousness, צדקה, which expresses the condition of the righteous man (27: 6). The formula בן־אדם 'son of man' is synonymous with איש, as with אנוש (25: 6). V. 8 forms a link between vv. 5-7 and v. 9. The being who suffers from man's evil and the one who profits by his righteousness can be none other than a man like himself. Hence the cries of the victims and their appeals for justice.

9 On the text of G, cf. v. 7. For עשוקים, Theod. συκοφαντούμενοι, Syr. ܠܘܥܬܐ 'oppression'; but Symm. συκοφαντιῶν (Jerome *calumniantium*), Vulg. *calumniatorum*, Targ. טלומין 'oppressors' vocalise עשׁקים. For מזרוע, Symm. διὰ

10   But *they* have not said: 'Where is Eloah who has made *us*,
      He who causes songs to be heard in the night,

10   אָמְרוּ (Syr.); MT: אמר. — עָשֵׂנוּ (Syr.); MT: עשׂי.

βίαν, Vulg. *propter vim brachii*; cf. Targ. מתקוף אדרע 'by the strength of the arm'.

It is not necessary to change the vocalisation עֲשׁוּקִים, since we find the same abstract plural in Am 3:9; Ec 4:1. The use of מֵרוֹב before an abstract denotes excess of evil (La 1:3), 'Through excess of oppression they cry out'. The *hiph'il* of זעק with the sense of the *qal*; cf. Comm. on 34:12. The same use of הזעיק is found in Jon 3:7. The *qal* will recur in v. 12. The רַבִּים whose arm oppresses the weak are no longer the *majores natu* of 32:9 but the great and exalted in general, such as the כבירים of 34:24ff. The special characteristic of the latter is that they cause the poor to cry out (34:28). It is unnecessary to replace רבים by רעים 'the wicked' or by כבירים (contra Beer), since רב means both 'numerous' and 'great'. The arm is the instrument of violence (22:8). Job has emphasised the plight of the unfortunate who lament without being heard (24:12). Elihu notes the same thing. But he will suggest an explanation.

10   The text of G is resumed at v. 10b. Syr. reads אָמְרוּ and עָשֵׂנוּ, which are preferable to the MT (cf. inf.). Targ. interprets זמרות as the songs of the angels before God. G φυλακάς reads אַשְׁמֻרוֹת, while Syr. ܡܚܫܒܬܐ 'thought' seems to confuse זמרות with מזמות.

The aim of vv. 10-11 is to explain why the cry of the distressed (v. 9) is not heard (v. 12). It is because their cries are not addressed to God. We might, if need be, retain the singular 'and he has not said', 'he

who cries' being implied. In that case, we should have to keep עֹשָׂי. 'He who has made me', 'my Creator', the plural of the participle being regarded as a plural of majesty. But we have already had the participle of עשׂה with the 1st person singular suffix where עֹשֵׂנִי (31:15; 32:22) was used. Now, in v. 11 in מלפנו the suffix used is that of the 1st person plural. If we consider that the word expected, namely עָשֵׂנוּ 'who has made *us*', in apposition to יהוה in Ps 105:6, may have lost its last syllable by haplography before נתן, we shall give preference to the reading of Syr. 'who has made us', by reading עָשֵׂנוּ instead of עשׂי (Budde, Oort, etc.). The transformation of עשׂנו into עשׂי has had as its consequence the reading אָמַר instead of אָמְרוּ (Syr.), as demanded by the context. We restore this reading which permits us to translate: 'and they have not said: where is Eloah who has made us?' The first thought of the unhappy ones should have been to turn towards God their Creator. He, in fact, reminds men of His presence by the voices of nature: 'He who causes songs to be heard in the night.' The use of the verb נתן 'to give' with קול as the complement to mean 'to give voice' and especially 'to thunder' (cf. קול 'thunder', plural קֹלוֹת, 28:26) allows us to retain the complement זְמִרֹות 'songs'. What is being alluded to is storms in the night. The crash of thunder is thought of as the songs of God. It is by this means that He makes Himself heard to men. Such is the literal interpretation, which is preferable to the symbolical one: 'who inspires songs of joy in the

11   He who instructs us by the beasts of the earth,
     And by the birds of the heavens makes us wise?'
12   Consequently they cry—but without His answering—
     Because of the pride of the wicked!

midst of calamity' (Le Hir). Bickell replaces זמרות by שמרות 'guards', following G (cf. Ball, אשמרות). But it would rather be a question of 'watches' in the night which do not require a special intervention of God. Ehrlich proposes מארות 'lights', following Gn 1:17. But the lights in question are the sun and the moon. Here we are only concerned with the night. Wright reads מזרות 'constellations'. But can we say that God places constellations 'in the night'? We should surely have had 'in the heavens'. Hence we leave the text intact.

11 G ὁ διορίζων με, for מלפנו, harmonises with ὁ ποιήσας με of v. 10. The word יחכמנו, not translated in G, is restored σοφίζει ἡμᾶς in Cod. 23 and Cod. 253. This translation is quoted in the margin of Syro-hex. and attributed to Aq., while Jerome has *sapientiorem me facit* in the text. God reminds man of His reality, not merely by the voice of the thunder (v. 10), but also by that of the beasts and birds. In 12:7 Job declared that the beasts and the birds of the heavens knew as much as his friends. Elihu is alluding to this passage. The form מַלְּפֵנוּ is due to a contraction of מְאַלְּפֵנוּ; cf. וַתְּאַזְּרֵנִי (2 S 22:40) for וַתְּאַזְּרֵנִי (Ps 18:40), etc. (Gesenius-Kautzsch, § 68k). The *pi'el* of אלף, as in 15:5; 33:33 and 32:13 (cf. Comm.) is peculiar to the Book of Job. The בהמות ארץ 'beasts of the earth' are contrasted with the birds of the heavens (12:7). The verb חכם 'to be wise' (32:9) assumes, in the *pi'el*, the causative meaning 'to make wise' (Ps 105:22; 119:98). Commentators generally see in the pre-

position מן the mark of comparison. It is supposed that God has made man better informed than the beasts of the earth, and wiser than the birds of the heavens! Such an observation is surely too commonplace. It is precisely his understanding which makes man superior to the animals. Since the point at issue is the fact that God discloses Himself to men, is it not more natural to see in v. 11 the sequel to v. 10b, where it was said that God manifested Himself through His thunder? But He has no need to have recourse to this extraordinary and striking means of self-disclosure. Even the quadrupeds and the birds teach us about Him (12:7). The preposition מן denotes the instrument (4:9; 7:14, etc.). God instructs us 'by the beasts of the earth', He makes us wise 'by the birds of the heavens'.

12 V. 12a, absent from Sah., marked with asterisk in Jerome and Syro-hex., did not exist in G. The present text is derived from Theod. (cf. Syro-hex.). Syr. adds 'to them' after יענה. The adverb שָׁם connects v. 12 with what precedes. As in the case of the Greek ἐκεῖ and the Latin *ibi*, the connotation of time 'then' may be attributed to שם 'there'; cf. Ps 14:5; Ec 3:17 (cf. Podechard). To this idea is added the implication of consequence in Ps 66:6, where the adverb means 'consequently'. Such is the meaning which is suitable here. It is because they have not had resort to God that these men in distress are not heard. Hence Job should not be surprised that the oppressed utter cries which are vain (24:12). The verb צעק instead of

13   It is a pure waste of words: God does not hear,
      And Shaddai does not perceive it!

14   How much less when you say that you do not perceive Him,
      That a case is before Him and you are waiting for Him,

the *hiph'il* of זעק (v. 9), in order to vary the style. In the light of Is 19: 20, where we have יצעקו…מפני לחצים 'they cry … because of the oppressors', it is clear that the 2nd hemistich determines יִצְעֲקוּ, whilst וְלֹא יַעֲנֶה is a kind of parenthesis. It is 'because of the pride of the wicked' that the unhappy ones utter cries of distress (34: 28). The formula מִפְּנֵי replaces מִן of v. 9.

13   G ἄτοπα γάρ reads כִּי־שׁוא instead of אַך־שׁוא. Syr. composes a new clause by connecting אַך־שׁוא with 12b. By negligence, G renders לֹא־יִשְׁמַע by οὐ βούλεται … ἰδεῖν and omits the second לֹא: αὐτὸς γὰρ ὁ Παντοκράτωρ ὁρατής ἐστιν. Vulg. makes the following negative govern the word שׁוא *non ergo frustra audiet Deus*. To make explicit the suffix of ישׁורנה Vulg. produces *causas singulorum intuebitur*.

אַך־שָׁוא is usually regarded as the complement of the verb יִשְׁמַע and as implied in the suffix of יְשׁוּרֶנָּה. Hence the translations: 'It is iniquity alone that God does not hear, the Almighty does not look upon it' (Le Hir), or 'God, in fact, does not listen to frivolity, the Almighty does not cast a glance at it' (Renan). Since the word שׁוא is masculine, a few authors propose to replace ישׁורנה by יְשׁוּרֻּו (Duhm, Oort, Budde, etc.), while Bickell added שפת 'lip' before שׁוא (a pure hypothesis). Ehrlich supposes that שׁוא plays the part of a predicate in relation to the rest of the verse, which is supposed to express the thesis of Job. This obliges him to understand as implied 'that you say': '*Es führt zu nichts, dass du sagst,*

Gott höre nicht', etc. It should be noted however that 'God does not hear' corresponds to 'and He does not reply' of v. 12 and has as its parallel 'and Shaddai does not perceive it' of the 2nd hemistich. The 3rd person feminine suffix has the meaning of a neuter pronoun, just as in 33: 14; 34: 33. It sums up the previous verses: in vain do they cry out and complain, God does not perceive it! Hence we have two negative clauses: God does not hear, Shaddai does not see. It is for that reason that He does not reply (v. 12). By that very fact, the cries of the sufferers are vain, and this is what is expressed, in our opinion, by אַך־שׁוא 'it is nought but vanity' (cf. שׁוא in Commentary on 7: 3), which is equivalent to an English idiom like 'a pure waste of time'. The formula refers to the cries previously mentioned. Cf. the expression אַך־רִיק 'it is only in vain' (to connote likewise 'a pure waste of words'), referring to what follows, in Ps 73: 13.

14   G τῶν συντελούντων τὰ ἄνομα καὶ σώσει με does not correspond to the 1st hemistich, which may have disappeared through homoeoteleuton (ישׁורנה v. 13 and תשׁורנו). We do not know whence G has derived the words which it juxtaposes to v. 13. Vulg. *non considerat* and Targ. לא יסכנה 'He does not see it' read ישׁורנו instead of תשׁורנו. The versions regard דין as an imperative which G κριθῆτι and Vulg. *judicare* render by the passive. For ותחולל לו, G εἰ δύνασαι αἰνέσαι αὐτὸν ὡς ἔστιν (reading תהלל instead of תחולל). Syr. ܘܡܦܝܣ 'and begs' connects תחולל with the *pi'el* of חלה. This verse is the logical sequel to

15   And further, when you say that His anger does not punish
       anything,
       And that He does not really know *transgression*!

15 בְּפֶשַׁע (Theod., Symm., Vulg.); MT: בפש.

v. 13. If the unhappy are not heard
by God, it is because in their distress
they have not turned towards Him.
How much more likely is it that Job
will not be heard, he who treats
God with insolence, and utters, with
regard to Him, unbecoming words
(vv. 14-15), as empty of meaning as
they are numerous (16). The opening
אַף־כִּי 'how much less', as in
9:14; 25:6. Job has asserted that
he could not see God (23:8f.). We
have next: 'a case is before Him and
you await Him', an unmistakable
allusion to those passages in which
Job declares that he has drawn up
the details of the case and is awaiting
the Judge (13:18ff.; 31:35ff.), or
in which he cries out against violence
and asserts that justice is not done
him (19:7). Note the use of דִּין
instead of מִשְׁפָּט, which is the standard term in the speeches of Job and
his friends. With דִּין לְפָנָיו cf. 23:4a,
'I would draw up a case before
Him'. The form תְּחוֹלֵל belongs to a
verb חִיל which is the equivalent of
יחל 'to await'; cf. the *hithpoʿlel* in
Ps 37:7. Following this passage,
Perles proposes to replace דִּין by
דֹם: 'Be silent before Him and wait
for Him!' But this meaning is not
appropriate to the context. Elihu is
examining one by one the arguments of Job; he has no need to
impose silence on him, since Job
has not taken up the challenge
which was made to him in 33:32-3.
Nor do we see the need to postulate
for דִּין a meaning similar to the
Arabic *dâna* 'to stoop', 'to submit'
and to translate: 'Be submissive
towards Him!' (Jacob, *ZATW*,
1912, p. 287). Elihu is not concerned to make exhortations. He
mentions Job's remarks in order to
contradict them.

15 Vv. 15-16, absent from Sah.,
marked with asterisk in Jerome and
Syro-hex., did not exist in G. The
present text is derived from Theod.
(cf. Syro-hex.). The negative אֵין
is regarded as an equivalent of לֹא
by Syr. and Vulg., while Targ.
translates כִּי אִין 'because as if He
were not'. Theod. ἐπισκεπτόμενος and
Symm. ἐπιλογιζόμενος seem to read
פָּקַד, which involves the vocalisation
אַיִן instead of אֵין. The word ידע is
rendered *ulciscitur* in Vulg. A confusion of ידע with ירע and of בפש with
נפש gives rise to 'and He does not
harm the soul' of Syr. Instead of
בפש, Theod. παράπτωμά τι (παρα-
πτώματι in Compl., cf. Syro-hex.),
Symm. παραπτώματα (Jerome *delic-
ta*), Vulg. *scelus* have read בְּפֶשַׁע,
the correct reading (cf. inf.).

The opening וְעַתָּה 'and now' introduces a new complaint of Elihu.
We may render by 'and further'. The
verb תֹּאמַר of v. 14 is understood
after כִּי: 'and further, when you say
that . . .'. Elihu is attacking ch. 21,
where Job emphasised at length the
impunity of the wicked and their
prosperity. God does not punish
them (21:14-21). This is what is
suggested by the words: 'His anger
punishes nothing.' In spite of the
fashion for vocalising אֵין פָּקַד (following Theod. and Symm.), we
prefer to adhere to the MT. The
word אַיִן is the complement of פקד
'visit', 'inspect', 'punish' (cf. Comm.
on 31:14). The verbs are in the
perfect tense, but the action they

16   Yes, Job opens his mouth to no purpose,
      It is from lack of knowledge that he multiplies words!

denote is prolonged into the present, whence the translation by the present often required by the perfect ידע (9: 2; 10: 13, etc.). The preposition ‏ב‎״ before the complement of ידע to connote the knowledge one has of a thing (Ps 31: 8). The *hapax* פּשׁ is usually connected with פּשׁשׁ, supposed to be parallel to פּושׁ 'frolic', 'leap', whence the meaning 'petulance', 'arrogance' is somehow extracted for פּשׁ. Otherwise critics resort to פּושׁ 'abound', 'multiply', and translate פּשׁ by 'abundance'. Houbigant already had recognised that בפשׁ was a corruption of בְּפֶשַׁע (Theod., Symm., Vulg.), which yields excellent sense: 'and He knows nothing of a transgression'. The verb ידע with מאד as in Ps 139: 14.

16   On the text of G, cf. v. 15. Instead of יכבר, Symm. βαρεῖς ἐποιήσατο and Theod. βαρύνει read יכבד.

The sequel of the speech addressed to Job will be found in 36: 2ff. But Elihu declared that he would also reply to the friends (v. 4). It is to them that he now turns in a sort of parenthesis, to draw their attention to the fact that the assertions of Job are vain and uninformed by knowledge. In making remarks such as those which he has just recalled, 'Job opens his mouth to no purpose, it is from lack of knowledge that he multiplies words!' Cf. the way in which Elihu condemns the assertions of Job in 34: 7. Note the use of הֶבֶל in an adverbial sense (9: 29; 21: 34). The verb פצה, in antithesis to פתח (33: 2), is applied to beings without reason (cf. Ehrlich on Gn 4: 11). The phrase בִּבְלִי־דָעַת 'through lack of knowledge' recurs in 36: 12. We shall have בלי־דעת 'without knowledge' determining מִלִּין in 38: 2. The *hiph'il* of כבר means 'to multiply' as in 16: 4 (cf. Comm.). This verb, which recurs only in 36: 31, replaces הרבה of the speeches of Job.

CHAPTER 36

1   Elihu continued and said:

2   Be patient with me a little and I will instruct you,
     For I have yet words to speak on behalf of Eloah!

3   I will give wide scope to my knowledge,
     And I will justify my Maker;

36: 2 G ἐν ἐμοί for לאלוה is a theological correction. Vulg. *habeo quod pro Deo loquar* well conveys the meaning.

Elihu renews his direct address to Job. The 1st hemistich is composed of Aramaic words which, according to Rashi, would be translated into Hebrew as הוחל לי מעט ואגידך. The *pi'el* of כתר corresponds to the Aramaic *pa'el* in the sense of 'to wait'. The word זְעֵיר, a diminutive meaning 'a little', is found in Is 28: 10, 13. Elihu has a predilection for the *pi'el* of הוה (32: 6, 10, 17). It is clear, in the light of v. 3b, that לֶאֱלוֹהַּ means 'for Eloah', 'on behalf of, in favour of, Eloah'. Cf. the use of לאל and of לו in 13: 7. It is unnecessary to add לי (Duhm) after עוד. We have here the same ellipsis as in 33: 32a, 33a. It is quite arbitrary to replace לאלוה by לאליהוא, 'to Elihu' (contra Hoffmann).

3 For למרחוק, G μακράν, Symm. διὰ μακροῦ, Vulg. *a principio*. Targ. and Syr. (cf. Vulg.) do not take into account the ל". A wrong vocalisation of ולפעלי furnishes G with ἔργοις δέ μου. The word אמנם of v. 4 (translated ἐπ' ἀληθείας) is connected by G with v. 3.

The use of לְמֵרָחוֹק 'into the distance' in 39: 29 proves that the expression here denotes the term of the movement and not its point of departure, as is suggested by the translation of Le Hir: 'I will renew my theme from a higher point of view', or that of Renan: 'I will derive my principles from afar.' The correct meaning harmonises very well with the verb נשא 'to carry'. To carry one's knowledge into the distance is to make it resound to the ends of the earth. Cf. the use of למרחוק in Ezr 3: 13 and 2 Ch 26: 15. Elihu is fond of using דֵּעִי 'my knowledge' (32: 6, 10, 17). There is no reason to substitute רֹעִי (Hoffmann), which would mean 'my shepherd'. What would be the meaning of 'I will carry my shepherd into the distance'? The expression אֶתֵּן־צֶדֶק means 'I will justify', the noun צֶדֶק assuming the same shade of meaning as the verb צדק in 27: 5; 33: 12, 32. Ehrlich claims that פָּעֳלִי must denote the abstract פֹּעַל with suffix, and that we ought to translate by 'my action'. But the meaning is more intelligible if we adhere to the ordinary interpretation which sees in פעלי the present participle of פעל with suffix: and Him who has made me I will show to be right. Ehrlich objects that God as Creator is never represented by the participle of פעל. But this is to forget that פעל is introduced here as a simple synonym of עשה (cf. 35: 6) and that פעלי is equivalent to עֹשֵׂנִי 'He who has made me' found in 31: 15; 32: 22 (cf. Comm. on 35: 10).

538

4   For in truth my words are no lie,
     It is one perfect in knowledge who is beside you!
5   Yes, God is great *in might*,
     And He does not despise the *pure* in heart.

5 Transfer כח to precede ולא. — בַּר (Syr.); MT: כביר (second).

4 G begins v. 4 at לֹא־שֶׁקֶר (cf. v. 3) and translates לֹא־שֶׁקֶר מִלַּי simply as καὶ οὐκ ἄδικα ῥήματα. A repetition of לא before תמים involves ἀδίκως συνίεις for תמים דעות, while עמך will be transferred to v. 5. We cannot make G an authority for correcting the MT here, as is proposed by E. G. King (*Journ. of Theol. Studies*, **15**, p. 80). Syr. omits לא before שֶׁקֶר, which results in a meaning contrary to what is expected. Its reading דעתי 'my knowledge', instead of דעות, is not an improvement (contra Houbigant). Theod. ἄμωμοι vocalises תַּמִּים. Vulg. et *perfecta scientia probabitur tibi* sees in תמים an epithet of דעות.

The opening כִּי־אָמְנָם 'for in truth' connects v. 4 with vv. 2-3. It is because he is no liar that Elihu has the right to plead on God's behalf. The expression תְּמִים דֵּעוֹת corresponds to תמים דעים of 37: 16. We have the plural of the feminine דֵּעָה instead of the masculine דֵּע (v. 3). The plural of דֵּעָה denotes Knowledge, with a capital letter! Note עִמָּךְ as in 35: 4. We must not diminish anything of Elihu's pretension. It is indeed he who claims to be 'perfect in knowledge'!

5 Vv. 5b-9, absent from Sah., marked with asterisk in Jerome and Syro-hex., did not exist in G. The present text is derived from Theod. (cf. Syro-hex. and Colb.). G γίγνωσκε δὲ ὅτι paraphrases עמך of v. 4. Then ὁ Κύριος οὐ μὴ ἀποποιήσηται τὸν ἄκακον comes directly from 8: 20, where the Hebrew text greatly resembles our 1st hemistich. Targ. adds צדיקא 'the righteous' as the complement of ימאס and, separating לב from כח, translates 'great in might' and 'wise of heart' (cf. 9: 4a). Syr. 'he who is pure like milk' reads בר instead of the second כביר and כחלב for כח לב. Vulg. makes the first כביר the complement of ימאס and summarises: *Deus potentes non abjicit, cum ipse sit potens.*

As it stands, this verse is very strange. First we have 'Yes, God is great', then 'and He does not despise' (without complement), finally a resumption of כַּבִּיר 'great by force of heart'. If we compare with 8: 20 we see that לֹא יִמְאַס requires a complement which will be the counterpart of the wicked man, רָשָׁע, mentioned in v. 6. A correction of Nichols (quoted by Budde) resolves all difficulties. If we transfer כֹּחַ so that it precedes וְלֹא, we obtain first of all 'Yes, God is great in might', the phrase כַּבִּיר כֹּחַ reminding us of אמיץ כח 'robust in might' (9: 4) and of שַׂגִּיא־כֹחַ 'great in might' (37: 23). Next we shall read בַּר (cf. Syr.) instead of the second כביר, which yields the expression בַּר לֵב 'pure of heart' (Ps 24: 4; 73: 1; Mt 5: 8). God 'does not despise him who is pure in heart', as we had 'God despises not the perfect' in 8: 20. The might of God does not prevent Him from taking into account the conduct of man. On the one hand, 'He does not despise the pure in heart' is a litotes for the idea that He takes the greatest care of him. On the other

6   He does not allow the wicked to live,
     But gives justice to the poor;

7   He does not take away the *right* of the righteous.
     He has placed kings on the throne,
     And has seated them there for ever! But they have exalted
        themselves,

7 דִּינוֹ (cf. G in v. 17); MT: עֵינָיו. — וְשָׁת MT: וְאֵת.

hand, 'He does not allow the wicked to live' (v. 6) is a litotes for 'He slays the wicked'. Duhm drastically emends v. 5 by eliminating כביר ולא and כח, and then reading כבד instead of the second כביר: 'Yes, God rejects the perverse of heart.' The solution which we have adopted preserves the integrity of the verse and supplies the transition between v. 5a and v. 6a.

6 On the text of G, cf. v. 5. For יחיה, Vulg. *salvat*.

The 1st hemistich, 'He does not allow the wicked to live', is the counterpart to v. 5b, 'and He does not despise the pure in heart' (cf. Comm.). It is also an answer to Job's question: 'Why do the wicked continue to live?' (21: 7). It is precisely ch. 21 which was specially aimed at by Elihu (cf. Comm. on 35: 15). The victims of the wicked are the poor (34: 28; 35: 12). God owes it to Himself to do them justice.

7 On the text of G, cf. v. 5. Targ. ועם and Theod. καὶ μετά interpret אֵת in the prepositional sense. For לנצח, Theod. εἰς νῖκος. Syr. places לנצח after ויגבהו.

The 1st hemistich corresponds to v. 6b. The verb גרע 'to pull down', whence 'to curtail', 'to suppress' (15: 4), and 'to take for one's self' (15: 8), is difficult to understand with the complement עֵינָיו 'his eyes'. It is only by approximation that it is translated: 'He does not withdraw His eyes from the righteous' (Le Hir), or 'He does not avert His glance from the righteous' (Renan). Now,

v. 7a is translated by G in v. 17 under the form οὐχ ὑστερήσει δὲ ἀπὸ δικαίων κρίμα, which suggests the reading דִּינוֹ instead of עֵינָיו (Bickell, Budde, Beer). In this way we obtain excellent sense: 'He does not take from the righteous man his right.' The parallelism with v. 6b is perfect. Hence it is unnecessary to have recourse to a deeper modification of the text, such as replacing מצדיק עֵינָיו by צדק מעני 'He does not rob the lowly of justice', which is proposed by Duhm. Another couplet begins at וְאֶת־מְלָכִים. It is no longer a question of the righteous or the wicked but of the great ones of the earth. Elihu proposes to show how God deals with them (cf. 34: 18-20, 24-8). The opening וְאֵת is strange, whether we regard אֵת as the accusative particle, 'and kings on the throne', or whether we see in it the preposition 'with': 'and with kings on the throne'. A verb is lacking. We do not improve the text by reading וְאִם (Duhm): 'and if there are kings on the throne'. In that case we should have to suppress the copula of וַיּשִׁיבֵם. The solution of the difficulty is furnished by Perles (*Analekten*, II, p. 41), who reads וְשָׁת 'and He has placed' instead of וְאֵת. There is the same confusion of שׁ and א in Gn 1: 26, where בְּכָל־הָאָרץ stands for בְּכָל־הַשָּׁרֶץ, and in Pr 28: 18, where בְּאַחַת stands for בְּשַׁחַת. The expression 'and He has placed kings on the throne' is confirmed by Ps 132: 11, אָשִׁית לְכִסֵּא: 'I will set on a throne.' The sequel is natural: 'and He has seated them for ever,

8   And *behold them* now bound with fetters,
     They are tied with the cords of affliction!
9   Then He reveals to them their work
     And their transgressions, namely that they were becoming
        proud;
10   And He has made to them a revelation, by way of warning,
     And commands them to return from iniquity.

8   וְהִנָּם; MT: וְאִם.

and they have exalted themselves'. The double meaning of גבה 'to be high' (35:5) and 'to be proud' enables us to grasp the sequence of ideas. The kings grow proud of their exalted position (v. 9), and this brings about their punishment. God then intervenes and their conversion ensues (cf. 33:14-30).

8   On the text of G, cf. v. 5. Targ. adds 'the wicked', as the object of these punishments. Syr. separates חבלי from its complement עני, which is interpreted as meaning לעני 'to poverty'.

As a result of their pride, the kings are reduced to captivity. V. 8 is intended to mark the succession of events, in relation to v. 7. The conjunction אִם would introduce a hypothesis, which in fact does not belong here. It is in vv. 11-12 that the alternatives will be set forth. We should expect, moreover, a verb in the finite personal mode rather than אֲסוּרִים. That is why Budde would read אסרם 'He has bound them', which no longer agrees with the niph'al יִלָּכְדוּן. We propose simply וְהִנָּם instead of וְאִם: 'and behold them now bound with fetters, they are tied with the cords of affliction!' The word זִקִּים (for זנקים) belongs to the same word group as the Assyrian *sanâqu* 'tie', 'bind', and denotes especially the fetters which bind the feet of prisoners (cf. 13:27; 33:11). The verb לכד 'to catch' (in a snare, in cords) and 'to bind'; cf.

the parallelism between מלכדת and חבל in 18:10. The חַבְלֵי־עֹנִי are the 'cords of affliction', those which cause pain; cf. יְמֵי־עֹנִי 'days of affliction' (30:16), אֲסִירֵי־עֹנִי 'prisoners of affliction' (those who suffer, Ps 107:10), בְּנֵי־עֹנִי 'sons of affliction' (Pr 31:5). The theme of Elihu about imprisoned kings is probably inspired by the story of Manasseh (2 Ch 33:10-13): elevation to the throne, pride, punishment, conversion. In 12:18 Job recognised that God 'has loosened the bond of kings and has bound a girdle around their loins'.

9   On the text of G, cf. v. 5. The versions read the plural 'their actions', instead of the singular פָּעֳלָם 'their action'. For כִּי יִתְגַּבָּרוּ, literally reproduced in Targ. and Syr., we have ὅτι ἰσχύσουσιν in Theod., *quia violenti fuerunt* in Vulg.

Elihu repeats the terms of 33:23b. No longer is it an intermediary, but God Himself who 'reveals to them their action', i.e. who makes known to them in what way they have erred. The 2nd hemistich clarifies the issue. First it is a question of an evil conduct: 'and their transgressions'. The evil of this conduct springs from pride: 'namely that they were becoming proud'. The plural of פֶּשַׁע as in 35:6. The *hithpa'el* of גבר 'to be defiant' (15:25) and 'to show one's self insolent, proud'.

10   The text of G is resumed only for v. 10a. Vv. 10b-11, absent from Sah., marked with asterisk in Jer-

11   If they hearken and serve Him,
     They finish their days in happiness,
     And their years in delights.

12   And if they do not hearken, they pass through the Canal,
     And die from lack of knowledge!

ome and Syro-hex., did not exist in G. The present text is derived from Theod. (cf. Syro-hex. and Colb.). G ἀλλὰ τοῦ δικαίου εἰσακούσεται confuses למוסר with למישר. Targ. paraphrases און 'their evil works which are like nothingness'.

Here it is 33:16 which Elihu recalls by employing the expression וַיִּגֶל אָזְנָם 'and He has made to them a revelation' (cf. Comm. on 33:16). The aim of this revelation is to warn the sinner and correct him. Hence לַמּוּסָר מוסר 'by way of warning': on cf. 5:17. The verb אמר has the same meaning as the Arabic 'amara 'order', 'enjoin' (9:7). God bids them 'return from iniquity'. The verb שׁוּב means 'to return' from evil unto God (22:23).

11   On the text of G, cf. v. 10. For ויעבדו, Vulg. et observaverint. About 70 MSS have יְכַלּוּ instead of יְכַלּוּ. The versions have read יכלו, with the exception of Symm. παλαιώσουσιν, which reads יבלו. For בנעימים, Symm. μετ' εὐδοξίας (cf. Vulg. in gloria).

Elihu summarises the thesis of Eliphaz with regard to the connection between return to God and happiness (22:23-30). In his exposition of ch. 33 he envisaged conversion above all as a means of avoiding death (33:14ff.). Here the result is more positive. Elihu sets out the two alternatives, by opposing אִם and וְאָם־לֹא, just as we found אִם־יֵשׁ and אָם־אִין in 33:32-3. The same procedure occurs in Is 1:19-20. First alternative: 'if they hearken and serve Him'. The verb עבד implies

the complement, God. Cf. the use of יראה 'fear' for the fear of God (4:6). The reading יְכַלּוּ is preferable to יבלו, in the light of 21:13, where the original text had יכלו (cf. Comm.). We have here the same formula: 'they end their days in happiness'. Elihu adds 'and their years in delights', which it would be ungracious to cut out, as does Duhm from fear of having three hemistichs. Plural of נָעִים 'pleasant' in the sense of 'pleasant things', 'delights'. We have in turn נעימים and נעימות 'delights' in Ps 16:6, 11.

12   The present text of G, in v. 12, is a combination of vv. 12-13, which will necessitate another translation of v. 13 (cf. inf.). With Beer, one might recognise traces of חנפי־לב …לא ישׁעו in ἀσεβεῖς δὲ οὐ διασώζει (ישׁוע) connected with (ישׁע), of בבלי דעת in παρὰ τὸ μὴ βούλεσθαι εἰδέναι αὐτοὺς τὸν Κύριον, ואם־לא ישׁמעו in καὶ διότι νουθετούμενοι ἀνήκοοι ἦσαν. For בשׁלח, Vulg. per gladium, Targ. בזיני קרבא 'by the weapons of combat', Syr. ܚܒܠܐ 'in perdition' (cf. 33:18). Vulg. renders בבלי דעת by in stultitia.

The other alternative: 'and if they do not hearken'. Then it is death, without mincing matters: 'they pass through the Canal'. On this expression, cf. 33:18, 28. The change to בשׁאלה which Duhm proposes is no more convincing here than in 33:18. The verb גוע as in 34:15. The phrase: בִּבְלִי דָעַת 'from lack of knowledge' (35:16) gives the reason for their dying.

13   As for the hypocrites at heart, who *nourish* spite,
      Who do not cry out when He has fettered them,
14   Their soul dies in youth,
      And their life ends in adolescence!

13   יִשְׁמְרוּ; MT: ישׂימו.

13 V. 13, absent from Sah., marked with asterisk in Jerome and Syrohex., did not exist in G. The present text is derived from Theod. (cf. Syrohex.). We have seen that traces of the original translation of G are reflected in v. 12. Vulg. *simulatores et callidi* twice translates חנפי־לב. Syr. connects אף with the 2nd hemistich, and twice translates ישׁועו: 'and they will not cry out, they will cry with anger'. Vulg. interprets אף by *iram Dei*. After ישׁועו, Targ. adds רחמיה 'His mercy'.

We have seen (cf. 8:13) that חנף meant profane, apostate, unbelieving, but also hypocritical. It is the latter sense which is here suggested by the complement לֵ. The חנפי־לב are 'the hypocrites in heart', those defined by Our Lord in the words: 'within you are full of hypocrisy and iniquity' (Mt 23:28). Owing to the vagueness of meaning of the verb שׂים, the translation of יָשִׂימוּ אַף presents difficulties. Rosenmüller interprets by *iram accumulant* and quotes Ro 2:5, θησαυρίζεις σεαυτῷ ὀργήν. But the verb שׂים does not mean 'to pile up'. Le Hir, who cites this opinion in a note, translates by: 'they become angry'. But it is difficult to derive the latter meaning from that of 'to place anger'. Hence it has been supposed that 'in their heart' (Dillmann, Duhm, etc.) should be understood; cf. Renan 'the ungodly conceive vexation in their heart'. Heathe and Michaelis vocalise יַשִּׂמוּ (from נשם) 'they stir up', which does not accord with the 2nd hemistich: 'they do not cry out when He has fettered them'.

It is apparent that what the author has in mind is a hypocritical attitude. They do not manifest their feelings when they are lashed by the blows of the divine punishment which has been mentioned in v. 8. If we read יִשְׁמְרוּ instead of ישׂימו we obtain the expected meaning: 'as for the hypocrites at heart, they nourish spite'. The verb שׁמר is used with a complement connoting anger, to convey the idea of one who nurses anger in his heart (Am 1:11; cf. Jer 3:5). This slight correction seems to us preferable to יאשׁמו 'they render themselves guilty' (Torczyner), which necessitates the transference of יסיפו to the 2nd hemistich. The reading 'they increase' (Graetz) is too considerable a change and has but slender support in Syr. Use of the *pi'el* of שׁוע as in 35:9.

14 Vulg. renders בנער by *in tempestate*. For בקדשׁים, G τιτρωσκομένη (obelus in Colb.) ὑπὸ ἀγγέλων. Hence G reads בקדושׁים (cf. 15:15). Vulg. *inter effeminatos* and Targ. היך מרי זנו 'like male prostitutes' recognise here the קדשׁים of Dt 23:18, etc. Syr. ܟܡܒܢܐ 'by hunger' (?).

The parallelism between חַיָּה and נֶפֶשׁ is typical of the style of Elihu (33:18, 20, 22, 28) and argues against the elimination of vv. 13-14 (contra Budde). The jussive form תָּמֹת is poetic, and takes the place of the imperfect (cf. 33:21). It is unnecessary to seek for נֹעַר a special meaning such as 'shock' (Schultens). The expression בַּנֹּעַר 'in youth' (13:26; 33:25) denotes

15 He saves the poor man by his very poverty,
    And by wretchedness He discloses Himself to them,
16 And similarly He will remove you from the jaws of trouble;
    Instead of it, you will enjoy unrestricted abundance,
    And [   ] your table will be filled with fatness.

16 Omit נחת.

premature death. The parallelism of בַּקְּדֵשִׁים with בנער invites us to see in the plural an abstract term similar to נְעוּרִים 'youth', 'adolescence' (31 : 18), זְקֻנִים 'old age' (Gn 21 : 2, 7, etc.), בְּחוּרִים 'adolescence' (Nu 11 : 28, etc.), עֲלוּמִים 'youth' (Job 20 : 11; 33 : 25). Now, the קָדֵשׁ is the male sacred prostitute, hired for purposes of debauchery, like the קְדֵשָׁה 'female prostitute' (Dt 23 : 18, etc.); cf. Vulg. and Targ. The infamous part incumbent on him presupposes quite a youthful age. The abstract קְדֵשִׁים connotes this age which borders on adolescence; it is the age of the youthful prostitutes. We prefer this explanation to that of Renan and Duhm, who consider that the mode of life of the sacred prostitute predisposed him to early death. The latter interpretation would suggest כקדשים 'like the male sacred prostitutes' (cf. Le Hir, Crampon, Segond), rather than בקדשים which is supported by the parallelism with בנער.

15 G ἀνθ' ὧν ἔθλιψαν ἀσθενῆ καὶ ἀδύνατον seems to read ילחצו (in accordance with בלחץ of the 2nd hemistich) instead of יחלץ, and בן־עני instead of בעניו. Then κρίμα δὲ πραέων ἐκθήσει translates v. 6b, where we had the text of Theod. In accordance with the meaning of יחלץ, Vulg. renders בעניו by de angustia sua. For אזבם, Vulg. aurem ejus, by harmonisation. Syr. replaces the pi'el יחלץ by a niph'al and אזנם by ארחם 'their way'.

V. 15 serves as a preamble to a new couplet. Elihu now proposes to apply to Job his theory that suffering is intended as means of redemption. The pi'el of חלץ is found frequently in the Psalms with the meaning of 'to save'. It is God who 'saves the poor man by his poverty itself'. Note the use of the instrumental "ב as in 33 : 15, 19. Salvation is accompanied by a revelation: 'and through wretchedness He has disclosed Himself to them', literally 'He opens their ear'. The same expression stands in v. 10 (cf. 33 : 16). The collective sense of the word עני permits us to retain the plural suffix in אָזְנָם. Note the play of words involved in יְחַלֵּץ and לַחַץ.

16 V. 16, absent from Sah., marked with asterisk in Jerome and Syrohex., did not exist in G. The present text is derived from Theod. (cf. Syrohex.). We have seen that v. 15b of G corresponded to v. 6b of the MT. The sequel will be v. 17 of G, which corresponds to v. 7a of the MT (cf. inf.). The reading προσεπιηπάτησέν σε of Theod. is a corruption of προσέτι ἠπάτησέν σε (אc.a). For מפי־צר, Theod. ἐκ στόματος ἐχθροῦ. Vulg. joins רחב to the 1st hemistich: igitur salvabit te de ore angusto latissime. The word רחב is regarded as a verb 'He has expanded' in Targ. The negative לא is omitted by Syr. 'and expansion instead of restriction'. Theod. interprets רחב in the sense of רהב (26 : 12), whence ἄβυσσος, κατάχυσις ὑποκάτω αὐτῆς. Vulg. renders לא־מוצק תחתיה by et non habente fundamentum subter se. The word נחת is con-

17   And you will judge [   ] the judgment of the wicked,
      And *your hands* will seize justice:

17   Omit מלא. — Add יָדֶיךָ at the end.

nected with נחת 'to descend' (instead of נוח) by Theod. καὶ κατέβη
τράπεζά σου πλήρης πιότητος. Vulg.
makes of נחת a noun: *requies autem
mensae tuae erit plena pinguedine.*

A glance at the versions suffices
to show the number of interpretations of which this verse has been
the object. Ehrlich refuses to translate the passage 16-19, which seems
to him unintelligible. Each commentator proposes a new correction.
Sometimes הֲסִיתְךָ is changed to
הסירך 'He withdraws you' (Hirzel,
Hitzig), or to הסיעך 'He snatches
you' (Beer). Or again תַּחְתֶּיהָ is
changed to תחתיך 'under you'
(Bickell), or to החתך 'frightens you'
(Duhm). Then it is וְנַחַת which, together with רַחַב, is transferred by
Duhm so as to precede מִפִּי, and
changed into ונתח 'and a morsel of
meat' by Voigt. We cannot examine
one by one each of these hypotheses
which in general have remained
without influence. The opening וְאַף
'and also' introduces the application
to Job of the general truth announced in v. 15. The verb הֲסִיתְ
corresponds to יחלץ of v. 15. We
have seen (2:3) that the *hiph'il* of
סות meant 'to stir up' against some
one. In v. 18, it will mean 'to lead
astray'. As has been recognised by
Fried. Delitzsch, in the light of the
derivative Assyrian *šitu, šittu* 'other',
the basic idea of the root סות is 'to
be other, different', whence the causative 'make different', 'change',
'lead astray', and consequently
'change the dispositions', 'excite'
against some one. When the indirect
complement is preceded by מן, the
causative 'to make other' will be
used in the sense of depriving some

one of what belonged to him or was
thought to belong to him. Hence in
2 Ch 18:31 we find the formula
ויסיתם אלהים ממנו 'and God took
them away from him'. This shade of
meaning is appropriate to our text:
'and similarly He will remove you
from the jaws of trouble'. The word
צָר denotes anguish, misery, which,
like a wild beast, opens its mouth
to devour its prey. Cf. 15:24, where
'distress and anguish' overshadow
the wicked. The words רַחַב 'breadth'
'space' (38:18) and מוּצָק 'restriction', 'cramping anguish' (from צוק,
Is 8:23) are antithetical. We had
וּמְצוּקָה 'and anguish' strengthening
צָר 'distress' in 15:24. If we compare
with Ps 4:2, 'in distress (בצר)
Thou hast brought me into a large
room' (הרחבת לי), we guess that the
2nd hemistich will express the idea
of abundance succeeding wretchedness. That is why we leave תחתיה,
the feminine suffix denoting the
state of distress and fulfilling the
function of a neuter: 'instead of that'
(cf. 35:13). It is difficult to find for
נַחַת a meaning which fits the context, whether we connect this word
with נוח 'to rest', or whether we
derive it from נחת 'to descend'. Perhaps we have here simply the
remains of a dittograph of תחת (in
תחתיה). If we eliminate this intrusive word, we obtain an excellent
meaning for the 3rd hemistich: 'and
your table will be filled with fatness'.
Cf. the end of Bildad's speech
(8:21-2).

17 G οὐχ ὑστερήσει δὲ ἀπὸ δικαίων
κρίμα is a translation of v. 7a, which
followed v. 6b, the translation of
which we have had in v. 15. V. 16

18   [   ] *Take care* lest a generous gift cause you to err,

18   Omit כִי. — חֵמָה; MT: חֵמָה.

has been intercalated, following
Theod., between v. 6b (=15) and
v. 7a (=17). Vulg. *causa tua quasi
impii judicata est* paraphrases the
first three words. The word דִין is
joined to the 1st hemistich in Syr.:
'and he judges the wicked with plenitude of judgment'. For יתמכו, Vulg.
recipies, Targ. סעדין 'helping', Syr.
ܢܣܬܡܟܘܢ 'they are taken'.

This verse again is an enigma.
Critics translate the 1st hemistich
after a fashion, by assigning to the
verb מלא an active sense: 'but if you
fill up the measure of the impious'
(Le Hir, Crampon); 'you had filled
up the measure of the crimes of the
wicked man' (Renan); 'but if you
defend your cause like an impious
man' (Segond); 'and you behave
like a wicked man' (Loisy), etc. The
plural יִתְמֹכוּ is embarrassing and is
not explained by translations such
as 'you will have to bear the sentence and the penalty for it' (Le
Hir), or 'you have suffered the
sentence and the penalty for it'
(Loisy). As in the case of v. 16, the
corrections that have been proposed
have usually been unsuccessful.
Grimme read רְשָׁעִים רָאָת instead
of רשע מלאת, which yields 'you
will see the judgment of the wicked'.
But it is as judge, and not as witness, that the favourite of God will
figure in the verses which follow.
Duhm suppresses the second דִין,
reads מִשְׁפָּטוֹ, replaces יתמכו by
תמכך, whence 'and his judgment
has seized you' for the 2nd hemistich.
Houbigant merely replaced יתמכו
by יתמהו: 'judgment and sentence
make him perfect'. Reiske split up
יתמכו into כונת יתום: 'you will
award judgment for the orphan'.
We will be excused from setting out
the other hypotheses which arise with

each commentary. Let us notice first
that מלא is a repetition of the same
word which is found in v. 16. If we
delete it we obtain, connecting the
second דִין with the 1st hemistich:
וְדִין רָשָׁע תָּדִין 'and the judgment of
the wicked you will judge'. Cf. the
expression דִין דִין 'to judge judgment,
(Assyrian *dîna dânu*) in Jer 5:28;
22:16; 30:13. What is lacking now
is the subject of יתמכו. The verb
תמך 'seize', 'hold' corresponds to
the Assyrian *tamâhu* used in the
expression *itmuhû qâtâ-ia* 'my hands
have seized'. Now, in Dt 32:41, we
find the formula במשפט ידי ותאחז
'and my hand will seize judgment'.
We propose to add יָדֶיךָ 'your hands',
one element of which remains in the
כִי of v. 18, where the conjunction is
superfluous. The 2nd hemistich will
mean simply: 'and your hands will
seize justice', which is parallel to
'you will judge the judgment of
the wicked'. Adversity does not
merely lead to happiness (v. 16), it
permits a man to resume his former
rank in the magistracy. Job was a
judge in his country (29:11-17).
Vv. 18-19 are counsels which Elihu
adds to forewarn against abuses
which might creep in during the
exercise of this office.

18 The versions give to חֵמָה its
normal meaning of 'anger'. G seems
to fuse 17a and 18a to reach the
result: θυμὸς δὲ ἐπ᾽ ἀσεβεῖς ἔσται.
Instead of ἔσται, G(A) ἥξει (Sah.).
Then G δι᾽ ἀσέβειαν δώρων ὧν ἐδέχοντο
ἐπ᾽ ἀδικίαις paraphrases בשפק ורב
כפר. The end אל־יטך, translated as μή
σε ἐκκλινάτω, is connected with v. 19.
Vulg. *non te ergo superet ira, ut aliquem opprimas* derives שפק from
ספק 'to strike'. Targ. במסת מזלא
'by the abundance of wealth' derives

And lest a large reward make you turn aside!
19-20 [   ]

19-20 'Can one compare your crying out to Him in distress with all the energies of might? Do not long for the night, in order that peoples may go up to their place.' This text is foreign to our context, and its elements do not belong together.

from שׁפק 'to be rich'. Syr. transfers אל־יטך to v. 19 (cf. G) and totally changes the sense of the text (cf. Beer).

This verse again is difficult to interpret. Let us notice first that the 2nd hemistich, 'lest a large reward makes you turn aside', suggests that we shall find here the continued expression of the idea in v. 17, namely that Job becomes happy once more and resumes his office of judge. Elihu then exhorts him not to allow himself to be corrupted. The word כּפֶר 'ransom' (33: 24) implies the bribery intended to blind the eyes of justice (1 S 12: 3). The *hiph-'il* of נטה (23: 11; 24: 4), has the causative meaning 'to make to deviate' (cf. the *qal* in 31: 7). It is clear that the complement of the 2nd hemistich is פֶּן־יְסִיתְךָ בְשָׂפֶק 'do not be led astray by generosity'. The *hiph'il* of סות in its normal sense of 'lead astray' (cf. Comm. on v. 16). The 3rd person sing. to connote 'one' (17: 6; 27: 22, 23). Parallelism invites us to connect here the *hapax* שֶׁפֶק (in pause שָׁפֶק) from the verb שׁפק or ספק 'to be sufficient', 'to abound'; cf. שֶׂפֶק in 20: 22. The meaning 'munificence', 'generosity' is preferable to 'punishment', which Dillmann postulates from ספק 'to strike' (cf. Vulg.) in order to translate: '*denn Hitze darf dich nicht reizen bei der Züchtigung*'(!). There remains to be explained כִּי־חֵמָה of the opening. If we assign to חֵמָה the meaning of 'anger', we shall seek in vain for a translation appropriate to the context. It is only by

desperate shifts of ingenuity that commentators produce such translations as: 'for His anger is imminent; fear lest He reject you with violence, and lest your magnificent offerings are unable to save you' (Le Hir), or 'do not hope to turn away the divine anger by a gift, and do not be led astray by your confidence that a large ransom will enable you to escape' (Renan). We have seen in כִּי a fragment of יְדִיךְ (cf. v. 17). Fried. Delitzsch (on 19: 29) has well recognised that חֵמָה belongs to the same word-group as the Arabic حمى 'defend', 'protect', 'keep safe', and thus has the same meaning as the Hebrew שׁמר in הִשָּׁמֶר 'keep yourself from' 'take care not to' (v. 21). It should also be noted that, even in the *qal*, שׁמר may mean 'take care not to' (Jos 6: 18). Hence we vocalise חַמֵּה and translate: 'take care lest a generous gift lead you astray', which has as a parallel member: 'and lest a large reward make you turn aside'. It is a warning to the judge.

19 The end of G καὶ πάντας τοὺς κραταιοῦντας ἰσχύν, absent from Sah., marked with asterisk in Syro-hex., is derived from Theod. (cf. Colb. and Syro-hex.). The opening μή σε ἐκκλινάτω translates אל־יטך of v. 18. Then ἑκὼν ὁ νοῦς δεήσεως ἐν ἀνάγκῃ ὄντων ἀδυνάτων seems to make the negative לא belong to the 2nd hemistich, for δεήσεως ἐν ἀνάγκῃ translates only שׁוע בצר. How has היערך produced ἑκὼν ὁ νοῦς? Vulg. *depone magnitudinem tuam absque tribulatione* treats היערך as an imperative and connects שׁוֹעַ with the same root as שׁוֹעַ of 34: 19. For the 2nd hemistich, Vulg. *et omnes robustos fortitudine* (cf. Theod.). 1st Targ. omits לֹא בצר and, interpreting מאמצי through the verb מצא, translates the 2nd hemistich: 'and do all those who are powerful find strength?' 2nd Targ. restores לֹא בצר and translates the 2nd hemistich 'and do all those who are robust in might attain to vigour?' Syr. 'He is strong against you in order to save you, so that no misery comes to you from those who are powerful in might': the word שׁוֹעַ is connected with ישׁע, the formula לֹא בצר is joined to the 2nd hemistich, and וכל is replaced by מכל.

The variety of the interpretations given by the versions is an indication of the difficulty of the text. Note that the word שׁוֹעַ may be derived from שׁוֹעַ 'to cry' or from שׁוֹעַ (= ושׁע; cf. 34: 19) 'to be rich' (cf. Vulg.), or from ישׁע 'to save' (cf. Syr.). Further, we may read בְּצָר as two words 'in distress' or as one word בֶּצֶר 'gold' (22: 24). We shall not be surprised by the many translations that are current: 'Will He have regard to your riches, which are of no importance to Him? Will He respect all the resources of your power?' (Le Hir; cf. Crampon); 'Do you think that He will take account of your riches? Gold and all the treasures in the world are nothing to Him' (Renan); 'Can He take your cries for gold and riches?' (Loisy); 'Would your cries be sufficient to deliver you from distress, nay, even all the strength that you might unfold?' (Segond). The *Bible du rabbinat français* notes that 'the text of verses 17-22 is full of obscurity' and that it is 'impossible to give a satisfactory translation of them'. However, it proposes to interpret our v. 19 as follows: 'Can God value your imploring cries to such an extent as to spare you suffering and

hard efforts?' Hypotheses designed to correct the text are not lacking. Bickell vocalises יערך as a *niph'al* and reads לֹא בְצָר לְכֹל (for וְכֹל), whence: 'Will your cry come before Him (who is) inaccessible to all the energies of might?' Duhm also reads לוֹ instead of לֹא, but replaces שׁוֹעֲךָ by שִׂיחֲךָ: 'Will your lament in distress and all the efforts of strength rise up against Him?' Ehrlich declares that the Hebrew of these new phrases is enough to make one's hair stand on end. Grimme reads הַאָרֵךְ for היערך and בֶּצַע for בצר: 'prolong your cry, no gain!' But how is this to be reconciled with the 2nd hemistich? We notice that the reading לוֹ for לֹא allows us to translate שׁוֹעֲךָ לוֹ בְצָר by 'your cry towards Him in distress'. The word שׁוֹעַ, which is not found elsewhere (cf. Comm. on 30: 24), is the masculine of שַׁוְעָה 'cry', 'appeal', from the verb שׁוֹעַ 'to cry out for help'. It is in distress that the Psalmist cries out to God (Ps 18: 7; 66: 14; 81: 8, etc.). This prayer is opposed by 'all the energies of might' of the 2nd hemistich. Now, the verb ערך means 'to put in a line' and 'to place in parallelism' with the object of comparing (cf. Comm. on 13: 18 and on 28: 17, 19). No comparison can be established between the cry of the faithful believer to his God and the total energies of sheer might. God alone is 'robust in strength', אמיץ כח (9: 4, 19). To cry out unto Him is to petition the help of a power that is greater than all human might. 'Can one make a comparison between your cry unto Him, in distress, and all the energies of sheer might?' The answer is negative. Prayer is the greatest force in the world. Such is the meaning which, with all reserve, we would suggest for this enigmatic verse, which, like v. 20, ought to belong to some other context.

21   Take care not to turn to iniquity,

21   בָּחַרְתָּ (Syr.); MT: בָּחַרְתָּ.

20 V. 20, absent from Sah., marked with asterisk in Syro-hex. and Jerome (except the 1st hemistich), did not exist in G. The present text is derived from Theod. (cf. Colb. and Syro-hex.). For אַל־תִּשְׁאַף, Theod. μὴ ἐξελκύσῃς, Jerome *noli extrahere* (Aug., Gall.), which has become *noli extollere* in Bod. and Tur. The text of Syr. 'and of oppression (וֹסֶמ) in the night' belongs to the same type of interpretation as Targ. לָא תִדחוק 'do not be hasty' for אַל־תִּשְׁאַף. Another Targ. interprets the 1st hemistich: 'Do not commit adultery with the wife of your neighbour at night.' Syr. twice translates עַמִּים תַּחְתָּם: 'and He stirs up peoples to take your place and nations to replace you yourself'. For תַּחְתָּם, Theod. ἀντ' αὐτῶν, Vulg. *pro eis*, Symm. ἐπὶ τόπους αὐτῶν (cf. Targ. בְּאַתְרֵיהוֹן).

Gray declares that v. 20 is perhaps the least intelligible of this whole passage. We must quote the chief translations of modern critics: 'Do not be like those who impatiently wait for the night to send their brigands out to plunder' (Le Hir); 'So do not long for that night when whole peoples are annihilated on the spot' (Renan); 'Do not sigh for the coming of the night which removes peoples from their place' (Segond); 'Do not invoke with your prayers the night which surrounds peoples all of a sudden' (Loisy). Jewish exegesis has believed that the text alludes to those famous nights when the catastrophes took place of which Amraphel, the Egyptians, and Sennacherib were victims (cf. Rashi). What should be noted is that each hemistich provides an acceptable meaning. The use of שָׁאַף in 7: 2 allows us to translate v. 20a: 'Do not sigh after the coming of the night.' A comparison with 34: 24b

obliges us to translate v. 20b: 'that peoples may go up to their place'. It is clear that this 2nd hemistich alludes to some event in which one people displaces another in revolution. It probably forms the conclusion of a description similar to that of 34: 17-20. Thus then we have here two propositions which are intelligible separately, but whose connection eludes us. The second is clearly alien to this context, but the first, 'Do not sigh after the coming of the night', may possibly have belonged to the series of counsels which Elihu is giving. Night is the time when crimes are committed (24: 14, etc.); we must not long for its coming like those who have a horror of the light (24: 17). In any case, we do not know the sequel to this v. 20a. Since, on the other hand, v. 21 connects perfectly with v. 18, we are justified in concluding that v. 20, as also v. 19, has been mistakenly introduced here. The two truncated texts have been artificially combined, and that is why it is impossible to give to them a coherent interpretation. It is better to admit one's ignorance than to reconstitute arbitrarily a sentence like that of Duhm: 'May folly not deceive you, to make you exalt yourself with him who thinks himself wise!' The author of this metamorphosis says that he is not deviating too much from the consonants of the received text. But תִּשְׁאַף הַלַּיְלָה has become תִּשְׁאַךְ הֲלַלַת and עַמִּים תַּחְתָּם has become עַם מִתְחַכֵּם. Ball gives free rein to his fancy and, as a result of unexpected changes, makes the text say: 'Do not prolong the night in drinking wine until day dawns in its place' (!) One might go far on these lines.

21 Vv. 21b-22a, absent from Sah.,

It is because of that that you *have been* tried by affliction.
22   Yes, God is sublime in strength:
Who is a master like Him?
23   Who has imposed on Him His way?
And who has said to Him: 'Thou hast done wrong?'

marked with asterisk in Jerome and Syro-hex., did not exist in G. The present text is derived from Theod. (cf. Syro-hex.). Syr. interprets בחרת by the *'ethpe'el* 'you have been tried'. For מעני, Vulg. *post miseriam*.

V. 21 is parallel to v. 18. Vv. 19-20 (cf. Comm.) are alien to the context. To the word חֲמֵה 'take care' of v. 18 (cf. Comm.) there now corresponds הִשָּׁמֶר 'beware lest'. The *niph'al* of שמר with the negative אַל before the verb which denotes what is forbidden, as in Ex 10:28 (cf. Jg 13:4). Generally it is פֶּן which is used, but we had it in v. 18 after חמה. The verb פנה 'turn', 'turn one's self', in a certain direction (cf. 24:18). The 2nd hemistich presents an anomaly, עַל־זֶה as the complement of בָּחַרְתָּ 'for you have preferred this (iniquity) to affliction'. We never find עַל before the direct object of the verb בחר 'choose', 'prefer'. Budde, followed by a few other critics, replaces עַל־זֶה by עֹולָה: 'for you have chosen injustice rather than affliction'. But the 1st hemistich warns against resorting to injustice, while the 2nd, if thus understood, would imply that the fault has in fact been committed. Now, the expression עַל־זֶה means 'because of this' or 'because of that' (La 5:17). It forms quite a natural transition between the two hemistichs: 'for because of that'. As has been felt by Syr., the verb בחר is used here in its Aramaic sense of 'examine', 'test', the root בחר being equivalent to בחן (cf. 7:18; 34:4). With Dathe and Wright we shall vocalise בָּחַרְתָּ (*pu'al*), following Syr.,

and shall thus obtain a perfect meaning for the 2nd hemistich: 'it is because of that that you have been tried by affliction'. It is because one turns towards iniquity that one later undergoes the trial. The word עֹנִי as in v. 8 and v. 15. The preposition מן can be used after a passive to denote the cause of the action suffered (cf. Gn 9:11; 2 S 7:29, etc.); cf. Gesenius-Kautzsch, § 121f.

22   On the text of G for v. 22a, cf. v. 21. Syr. omits the suffix of כחו. Vulg. paraphrases the 2nd hemistich: *et nullus ei similis in legislatoribus*. G δυνάστης reads מרא instead of מורה.

Recurrence of הֶן־אֵל (v. 5), which we shall meet again in v. 26. The *hiph'il* of שגב 'to be very high' (5:11) is used in the sense of the *qal* (32:15; 34:12; 35:9). Usually recourse is had to the *niph'al* of the same verb to suggest the unique grandeur of God (Is 2:11, 17; Ps 148:33). But it is taking too far a concern for accepted usage to replace ישגיב by נשגב (contra Ehrlich). Beer reads יִשְׂגֵּי (from שגא 'to be great, high') and regards ב as a dittograph. Such a correction is superfluous, since the MT offers a perfect meaning. For בְּכֹחוֹ as applied to God, cf. 24:22; 26:12. The rôle assigned to God by Elihu (33:14ff.; 35:11; 36:9ff.) makes it unnecessary to change מֹורֶה 'teacher', 'master' into מָרֵא 'lord' (G). Ehrlich proposes מֹורָא 'object of fear'. No version shows any trace of this reading.

23   G omits עליו and renders דרכו

24   Remember to magnify His work,
     Of which men have sung!
25   Every man beholds it,
     Every man sees it from afar.

by αὐτοῦ τὰ ἔργα, which will translate פעלו in v. 24. Syr. reads עלי־ instead of עליו. Vulg. *quis poterit scrutari vias ejus?* seems likewise to read עלי־. G ἔπραξεν replaces פעלת by the 3rd person.

The 1st hemistich repeats 34:13a almost word for word. The complement דַּרְכּוֹ 'His way, dealings' (21:31) changes the sense of פקד עלי 'entrust to' into that of 'impose on' (cf. Comm. on 34:13). Hence: 'Who has imposed on Him His way?' God receives commands from no one. He escapes all control. Cf. 9:12b, 'Who shall say to Him: What dost Thou?' The verb פעל with עַוְלָה as the complement; we had עול פעלתי 'I have committed injustice' in 34:32. Cf. the idiom פעל און 'to commit iniquity' (34:22).

24   Vv. 24b-25a, absent from Sah., marked with asterisk in Jerome and Syro-hex., did not exist in G. The present text is derived from Theod. (cf. Colb. and Syro-hex.). It is in v. 25b that we shall find the text of G for v. 24b. G (A) inserts οὖν Ἰώβ after μνήσθητι of the opening. For פעלו, G αὐτοῦ τὰ ἔργα (cf. v. 23). Vulg. *ignores* reads תשגיא instead of תשגיא. For שררו, Theod. ἦρξαν (from שרר). The other versions rightly connect with שיר 'to sing'; cf. Vulg. *de quo cecinerunt viri*. The כל of v. 25 is connected with אנשים by Syr. 'all men'. Targ. adds צדיקין 'just' as the epithet of אנשים.

The expression זְכֹר כִּי 'remember that', as in 7:7. The *hiph'il* of שגא (12:23) to denote 'increase' and 'magnify'. On the verb שגא, שגה cf. 8:11. Note the use of פעלו 'His work', parallel to דרכו 'His

way' of v. 23a and also an echo of the verb פעל of v. 23b. The 2nd hemistich, 'which men have sung of', is an allusion to poets and Psalmists who have taken as the theme of their songs the wonderful works of God. The *po'lel* of שיר 'to sing' (Zeph 2:14; 2 Ch 29:28) is used above all in the participle מְשׁוֹרֵר 'singer', '*cantor*'.

25   On the text of G for v. 25a, cf. v. 24. Then G ὅσοι τιτρωσκόμενοί εἰσιν βροτοί is a translation of v. 24b, the word שררו being merged with אשר and אנשים being read a first time as אֲנָשִׁים (Beer). Syr. has translated כל in v. 24. The word אנוש is omitted in Syr. It is rendered ἕκαστος by Symm. (cf. Vulg. *unusquisque*).

'Every man beholds it', i.e. the work of God (v. 24). The verb חזה with ב'' before the direct object, as we had ראה ב'' (33:28), to express that one sees with some pleasure, that one gazes at or contemplates (Is 47:13). The plural חָזוּ because of the collective. We had the singular with כָּל־אָדָם in 21:33. Parallelism between אֱנוֹשׁ and אדם (cf. 33:23c-26c), hence the needlessness of repeating כל before אנוש. The *hiph'il* of נבט as in 35:5. מֵרָחוֹק is used not to connote 'from the most distant days', as Ehrlich would have it, but simply 'from afar' (2:12; 36:3). One can only contemplate from afar off the work of God, to such an extent does this work transcend human powers of observation. The allusion is chiefly to phenomena in the heavens (vv. 27ff.), which are beyond human understanding (35:5).

26 Yes, God is great and we do not know how great,
The number of His years is unsearchable.

27 He draws upwards the drops of water,
He volatilises the rain into mist,

27 יָזֹק; MT: יזקו.

26 Vv. 26-7, absent from Sah., marked with asterisk in Jerome and Syro-hex., did not exist in G. The present text is derived from Theod. (cf. Syro-hex.). Syr. ܝܕܝܥܐ 'known' vocalises נוֹדַע instead of נֵדָע. For ולא נדע, Symm. ὑπὲρ τὴν γνῶσιν ἡμῶν; cf. Vulg. *vincens scientiam nostram.*

The opening הֶן־אֵל (vv. 5, 22) is an excellent indication of authenticity (contra Budde, Duhm, Beer). There is no reason whatever to delete v. 26, which introduces the passages on the wonderful works of God in nature: 'Yes, God is great and we do not know how great.' The adjective שַׂגִּיא 'great' (from שׂגא; cf. v. 24) recurs only in 37: 23. It is an Aramaic word much used throughout the Book of Daniel. The phrase וְלֹא נֵדָע 'and we do not know' implies as complement what has just been spoken of: and we do not know how great God is! We find the same turn of phrase in 8: 9 and 37: 5. The 2nd hemistich, 'the number of His years and no investigation', offers yet another instance where the copula is out of place, and shifted from its normal position at the beginning of the clause; cf. 4: 6; 20: 18; 23: 12. The meaning is clear: 'and the number of His years is unfathomable' (cf. לֹא־חֵקֶר 'without investigation' in 34: 24 and אֵין חֵקֶר 'unfathomable' in 5: 9; 9: 10). God has no age. His work is therefore not limited by time.

27 On the text of G, cf. v. 26. Theod. interprets כי יגרע by ἀριθμηταὶ δὲ αὐτῷ. For יגרע, Vulg. *aufert,*

Targ. ימנע 'prevents'. In agreement with its interpretation of אד in 30: 12, Vulg. paraphrases the 2nd hemistich: *et effundit imbres ad instar gurgitum.* For לאדו, Theod. εἰς νεφέλην, Targ. לענניה 'to its clouds'. Syr. reads לבדו and puts נטפי before מטר; then, by a series of approximations, concludes with the following meaning: 'if He counts the pillars of the heavens (שמים instead of מים) and if He imagines the drops of rain in His solitude'.

The first phenomenon on which Elihu will insist is that rain which orientals appreciate as one of the very greatest of divine favours. Its coming is fraught with mystery, and counts as a special blessing. The phenomenon of the condensation of water in the clouds and its subsequent fall to the ground is described in vv. 27-8. The conjunction כִּי at the beginning of the verse is intended to introduce the proofs of the greatness of God (v. 26a). First, God 'draws upwards drops of water'. The verb גרע in the *piʻel* has a frequentative meaning. We have seen, in v. 7, that גרע meant in turn 'to shave off', hence 'to cut off', and 'to draw to one's self', 'to attract' (15: 8). This latter meaning is quite suitable here, and there is no need to connect it with the Arabic جرع 'to drink in gulps', 'to absorb', as is proposed by Perles and Jacob (*OLZ*, 1914, col. 179), following Rosenmüller. It is not a question of God's absorbing the water but of His causing it to rise into the air in the form of vapour. Duhm changes נִטְפֵי־מָיִם into נְטָפִים מָיָם 'drops of the sea' (cf. Hontheim, Beer, Gray,

28   Which clouds will pour down
      And distil on the multitude;

etc.). But the absolute state 'drops' is a grave difficulty. One says drops of water, oil, etc. The correction would be better if מָיִם were simply added after מים: 'for He attracts drops of water from the sea'. But then the hemistich would be too long. The 2nd hemistich is paraphrased: 'which liquefy in the form of rain and give rise to its mists' (Renan); 'which fall again in rains under their weight' (Le Hir; cf. Crampon); 'He reduces them to mist and forms the rain' (Segond). The difficulty lies first in the plural form יָזֹקּוּ, which should have drops of water as its subject. How is it possible to translate literally? 'They dissolve (refine) the rain for its mist' makes no sense, even if we postulate for יזק the meaning of 'filter'. According to parallelism, it would seem that God remains the subject of the verb. With some moderns we read יָזֹק instead of יזקו. Now, it is clear that לְאֵדוֹ here denotes the term of the action expressed by זקק. The word אֵד means 'mist', 'fog'. In the light of Gn 2:6 this is what makes up for the absence of rain in the watering of the land. The verb זקק (28:1) strictly means 'blow', whence the derivative implications: *conflare*, melt, cleanse. In this context we would prefer to assign to it the meaning of 'volatilise', which easily connects with that of 'blow', 'reduce to vapour'. Thus the 2nd hemistich would mean: 'He volatilises the rain into mist'. Fog is formed by the drops of water which God has drawn upwards. These drops of water hang suspended in the form of vapoury mist or steam. It is in v. 28 that the phenomenon of condensation will be described. Duhm reads מאדו instead of לאדו and thus anticipates the description

of v. 28. Houbigant proposed לנאדו 'for his waterskin', 'in his waterskin or bottle'. We should then have to attribute to זקק the meaning 'enclose', 'seal up', and we should expect rather בנאדו.

28   The opening of G ῥυήσονται παλαιώματα, absent from Sah., marked with asterisk in Jerome and Syrohex., is derived from Theod. (cf. Syro-hex.). Then ἐσκίαζεν δὲ νέφη ἐπὶ ἀμυθήτῳ βροτῷ is a translation of v. 28, but with יצלו instead of יזלו and omission of ירעפו. The whole passage called v. 28a and 28b in the edition of Swete (from ὥραν ἔθετο to ἀπὸ σώματος), a passage absent from Memph. and marked with obelus in Colb., Jerome, and Syro-hex., is merely an interpretation of 36:33 and 37:1. Hence G omitted vv. 29-32 (cf. v. 29). Vulg. translates very freely: *qui de nubibus fluunt, quae praetexunt cuncta desuper*. The verb יזלו retains the meaning of נזל 'descend' in Syr. 'which the heavens cause to descend at the right time'. Further, Syr. transfers שְׁחָקִים to the 2nd hemistich: 'and the clouds drip down on men'. It seems that ירעפו, read as ירעו (from רוע), has been placed before רב in Syr. 'and they rejoice greatly'. Targ. reads ירפא instead of ירעפו: 'the clouds of Him who heals because of the prayer of the great man'(!).

After evaporation, condensation. The relative אֲשֶׁר refers to מָטָר 'the rain' of v. 27. The basic meaning of נזל is 'to descend' (cf. Arabic and Syriac), as may still be seen in Jer 9:17, where there is parallelism between נזל and ירד. In Hebrew, the meaning 'descend' has been reserved for ירד, while נזל has come to mean 'to flow': the water flows down from its source towards the valley and the torrent. In Is 45:8 and Jer

31   It is by them that He *feeds* the peoples,
     That He gives food in abundance.

29   *Who* can understand too the unfurlings of the clouds,
     The rumblings of His pavilion?

29-30   After v. 31.
31   יָזוּן; MT: ידין.
29   מִי (Syr.); MT: אם.

9:17 נזל is used as a transitive verb in the sense of 'make to flow', 'pour down'. It is thus that the verb is used here with a direct object. The reference is to the rain 'which the clouds will pour down'. In Is 45:8 the verb נזל, used transitively, has as its parallel the *hiph'il* of רעף, of which the *qal* (Pr 3:20) means 'distil', 'stream from'. This the clouds 'distil', shed the rain drop by drop 'on a numerous man', i.e. on the multitude. The rain is intended for humanity, which, without it, could not wrest its sustenance from the soil (Gn 2:5). V. 31 explains precisely how בָּם 'by them', i.e. by the clouds, God provides food for His creatures. This v. 31, which, in its present context, does not fit in with the rest of the description, formed originally the sequel to v. 28 (Budde, Hontheim, etc.).

29-30   After v. 31.

31   On the text of G, cf. v. 29 (inf.). The expression למכביר is interpreted 'in quantity' by Targ. לסוגעא and Syr. ܠܣܘܓܐܐ (cf. Symm. τροφὴν παμπόλλην), but Aq. τῷ παμπληθύοντι (cf. Jerome *plurimis* and Vulg. *multis mortalibus*), Theod. τῷ ἰσχύοντι (א, A, Syro-hex.), which has become τῷ ἀκούοντι in G (B).

The opening 'for by them' directly connects v. 31 with v. 28, the suffix of בָּם referring to שְׁחָקִים. In its present context, v. 31 interrupts a description of the storm which has nothing whatever to do with the beneficent rain which has been the subject of v. 28. The 2nd hemistich, 'He gives food in abundance', is immediately understandable. It is thanks to the rain and the clouds that man can till the soil (cf. v. 28). The expression לְמַכְבִּיר replaces לָרֹב 'in abundance', 'in quantity' of 26:3. The participle of הכביר 'to multiply' (35:16) is treated as an abstract noun. The 1st hemistich, 'for by them He judges the peoples', is not parallel to the 2nd. The phrase יָדִין עַמִּים is a reminiscence of Ps 7:9; 96:10. Houbigant had already noted that ידין was meant for יָזוּן (Aramaic, and Modern Hebrew) 'He feeds'. The meaning is excellent: 'for by them He feeds the peoples, He gives food in abundance'.

29   Vv. 29-33, absent from Sah., marked with asterisk in Jerome and Syro-hex., did not exist in G. The present text is derived from Theod. (cf. Syro-hex.). Syr. ܘܡܢܘ 'and who?' reads מִי instead of אם (cf. inf.). For מפרשי־עב, Theod. ἀπεκτάσεις νεφέλης, Symm. ἐκτεῖναι νεφέλην (cf. Vulg. *si voluerit extendere nubes*), Targ. פרישתא דעיבא 'the extensions of the cloud'. Syr. ܣܦܩ 'and has extended' resolves מפרשי into מי פרש The word תשאות is interpreted as רכפת ענניה 'the mass of its clouds' in Targ., ܡܢ ܣܓܝܐ 'of the multitude' in Syr. But Theod. ἰσότητα σκηνῆς αὐτοῦ, Symm. ἐξ ἴσης ὡς σκηνήν, Vulg. *quasi tentorium suum* connect תשאות with the root שוה (33:27).

30   Behold He has unrolled His *mist*,
        And has veiled the depths of the sea;

30   אֵדוֹ (Theod.); MT: אורו.
31   After v. 28.

The reading אַף מִי, instead of אַף
אִם, has been preserved by Syr. It
removes the conjunction אִם, which,
if we adhere to the MT, we are
obliged to regard as an interrogation:
'does one understand too?' More
natural is the exclamation: 'who
will understand too?' We might also
be somewhat tempted to replace
מִפְרְשֵׂי by מִפְלְשֵׂי (Ehrlich), following 37: 6, where we have מִפְלְשֵׂי־עָב
'the balancings of the clouds'. But
the phrase פרש ענן למסך 'He has
stretched out clouds as a curtain'
(Ps 105: 39) invites us to retain
here מִפְרְשֵׂי־עָב 'the unfurlings of
the clouds'; cf. פרש 'to stretch out',
'to unfurl' in 26: 9 (cf. Comm.).
Torczyner would see in מפרש the
Arabic *mifrâš* 'carpet', 'covering',
which obliges him to read מפרשו
'His carpet', to connect עב with the
2nd hemistich, and to read יָכִין 'prepares' (Graetz), instead of יָבִין.
Again he modifies תְּשֻׁאוֹת of the 2nd
hemistich into תשוית, in which he
seeks the Aramaic תשויתא 'carpet'.
But it should be noticed that סֻכָּתוֹ
'His pavilion' (27: 18) is the parallel
word to עָב 'cloud', for the cloud is
the 'pavilion' of God (Ps 18: 12). The
word תְּשֻׁאוֹת recurs in 39: 7, where
it denotes the cries of the leader. The
singular exists in the form תְּשֻׁאָה
(*kethîb*) in 30: 22 and denotes the
storm. Here we have 'rumblings'
of the cloud, the crash and roar of
the thunder.

30   On the text of G, cf. v. 29. For
אורו, Theod. ἤδώ (margin of Syro-
hex.) which nas become ἡ ῷδή in
G (B): reading אֵדוֹ instead of אורו
(cf. inf.). Targ. מטרא 'the rain' does
not imply any other reading than
אורו (cf. v. 32 and 37: 15).

The 2nd hemistich is very clear:
'and He has veiled the depths of the
sea'. The שָׁרְשֵׁי הַיָּם 'roots of the sea'
as we had 'the root' of the mountains (28: 9), 'the roots' of the feet
(13: 27), to denote the point at
which something is buried in the
soil, the lowest point. We cannot at
all see the advantage of changing
שרשי הים to ראשי הרים 'the heads of
the mountains' (contra Duhm,
Budde, Beer, Ehrlich, etc.). The 1st
hemistich is more difficult to interpret. As it stands in the MT, it is
translated: 'He stretches out around
Him His light' (Le Hir); 'At times
He covers Himself with His lightnings as with a curtain' (Renan).
There is implied here an antithesis
between the light which plays in
the clouds and the darkness which
covers the seas. But the reading אֵדוֹ
of Theod. (cf. v. 27), instead of אורו
(which is influenced by v. 32), supplies a much clearer meaning: 'Behold, He has unrolled over it His
mists.' The suffix of עָלָיו anticipates
הים 'the sea'. It is because God un-
folds His mist over the sea that the
depths of the abyss become veiled.
It is an allusion to the dense fog
which frequently lies over the sea.
It would be quite arbitrary to change
כִּסָּה (15: 27; 23: 17) to כסאו 'His
throne' (contra Marshall, quoted
by Gray).

31   After v. 28.

32   With both hands He has *lifted up* the lightning,
     And has commanded it to hit a mark.

32   נָסָה (= נָשָׂא); MT: כסה.

32 On the text of G, cf. v. 29. For על־כפים, Jerome and Vulg. *in manibus*. Targ. interprets the 1st hemistich 'because of the rapine wrought by hands, He witholds the rain': אור rendered by מטרא (cf. v. 30). Then, by contrast, Targ. interprets the 2nd hemistich: 'and He commands it (the rain) to come down in response to one who prays': במפגיע translated according to the meaning of פגע in 21: 15. Syr. connects יצו with יצא 'to go out'. For במפגיע, Theod. ἐν ἀπαντῶντι (Jerome *in contrarium*), Symm. ὥστε ἀπαντῆσαι (cf. Vulg. *ut rursus adveniat*), Syr. 'that they should come to meet him' (verb ܦ‍ܓ‍ܥ = פגע).

V. 32 is the natural sequel to v. 30, which describes the darkness occasioned by the clouds. Rosenmüller declared that v. 32 is *obscurissimus locus in quo explicando vix duos interpretes consentientes reperias*. But it seems clear, in accordance with the trend of the description, that here we have an allusion to the storm heralded by the piling up of the clouds. Now, in 37: 3, 11 the word אור has clearly the meaning of 'lightning flash'. The difficulty lies in the use of כסה 'hide', 'conceal' (v. 30) with על־כַּפַּיִם 'on two palms'. It is evading this difficulty to translate: 'The lightning flashes in His hands' (Le Hir), 'His hands are clad with sparkling facets' (Renan), 'He takes the light in His hands' (Segond). On the other hand, one cannot quite see what would be the meaning of '*Die Hände hüllt er in seinem Strahl*' (Budde). The text is transformed by Duhm, who at this point brings in the idea of a sling as if it were a question of hail. In that case we should have to rewrite the

1st hemistich as: על־כף יפלס האור 'On a sling He balances the thunderbolt', and read וַיְקַלְּעֵהוּ 'and He hurls it' instead of ויצו עליה. We ourselves think that it is the verb כסה which proceeds from a corruption of the text. The original verb was נָשָׂא, which has become, by an aural error, נָסָה (cf. 4: 2), then כסה. If we compare with Ps 91: 12, where we have precisely על־כפים with the verb נשא 'they will bear you up in both hands', we can translate the 1st hemistich: 'with both hands He has lifted up the lightning'. The image is that of God brandishing the lightning flash and ready to fling it in a given direction. Since Olshausen, most moderns change מַפְגִּיעַ to מִפְגָּע 'target' (7: 20), so as to translate the 2nd hemistich: 'He orders it to move against a target.' But this turn of phrase is difficult to understand in a literal sense. In point of fact, the preposition ב" should introduce the content of the command. In v. 31 we have met the *hiph'il* participle מכביר in the abstract sense 'abundance', 'profusion'. We also find מַשְׁחִית in the sense of 'destruction', 'ruin'. It would seem that sometimes the *hiph'il* participle represents an older infinitive, similar to the Arabic *maṣdar* of the *maqtil* form. It may be interpreted thus here. The causative of פגע in the sense of 'hitting' what is aimed at; cf. מפגע in 7: 20. The word אור has been regarded as a feminine (Jer 13: 16). Note that the Assyrian *urru* (אור) is always feminine. It is unnecessary to replace עָלֶיהָ by עליו in conformity with the normal gender of אור in the Bible.

33   The flock has warned its *shepherd*,
      The flock *which sniffs* the coming *storm*.

33   עַל־עוֹלָה ‎:MT ;עַלְעוֹלָה — .אַף ‎:MT ;שָׁאַף — .רֵעוֹ ‎:MT ;רֹעוֹ.

33 On the text of G, cf. v. 29. The original translation of G is found in v. 28a (Swete): ὥραν ἔθετο κτήνεσιν, οἴδασιν δὲ κοίτης τάξιν. It is clear that G placed רעו, read as ידעו, after מקנה, which is connected with the 1st hemistich. The other versions all translate רעו as 'his friend'. The 2nd hemistich is rendered Κύριος κτῆσις καὶ περὶ ἀδικίας in Theod. It seems that Κύριος is due to a first reading of the abbreviation κς springing from κτῆσις. Jerome deviates from Theod. and connects עולה with עלה 'to ascend': *contra eum qui ascendre nititur* (cf. Vulg. *et ad eam possit ascendere*). Targ. has no less than three translations of v. 33. All of them connect מקנה with קנא 'to be zealous, provoked', whereas the other versions are faithful to the sense of 'possession': Theod. κτῆσις, Aq. κτήσεις, Vulg. *possessio ejus*, Syr. ܣܘܒܠܬ. The word אף is interpreted as 'anger' in Symm. ζῆλον and Targ רוגזא. For עַל־עוֹלָה, Aq. ἐπὶ παρανομίαις (cf. Theod. above), Syr. ܠܥܘܠܐ 'to the impious'. Targ. connects עולה with עלה 'to ascend' (cf. Jerome and Vulg. above).

No less ambiguous than the preceding verse, v. 33 had already been the object of twenty-eight interpretations in the time of Schultens. We have seen that the versions were in disagreement as to the meaning of מִקְנֶה, of אַף, and of עוֹלָה. Let us add that רֵעוֹ 'his companion' can also mean 'his will' (from רעה), 'his roar, crash' (from רוע). We shall not therefore be surprised to find the most divergent translations: *annuntiat tempestatem ejus fragor praesagitque pecus vel ascensuram* (Rosenmüller); 'His thunder declares Him to every creature when He

goes forth to battle' (Le Hir, who connects מקנה with the 1st hemistich); 'the noise of His march declares Him, the terror of the flocks reveals His drawing nigh' (Renan; cf. Crampon); 'He announces Himself with a roaring; the flocks have a presentiment of His approach' (Segond); 'His thunder announces Him when His jealous fury pursues iniquity' (Loisy, who reads מקנא; cf. Targ.). Not very literal is the interpretation of the *Bible du rabbinat français*: 'He reveals His presence by thunder, instrument of divine wrath against the proud.' It is clear that the general tendency is to interpret in the sense of a coming storm. The presence of מִקְנֶה 'flock' (1:3) favours this interpretation, for the ancients had noted that animals were aware of the approach of storms: *aut bucula coelum Suspiciens patulis captavit naribus auras* (*Georgics*, I, 375ff.). Now, it has been noticed quite rightly that the inexplicable עַל־עוֹלָה 'against one who ascends', if changed to עַל־עַוְלָה 'against unrighteousness' (Aq., Theod.) or to עַל־עַוָּל 'against the wicked' (Syr.), is only the division of an Aramaic word עַלְעוֹלָה, feminine of עלעולא 'storm' (cf. Syr. in 20:7; 30:14; Targ. in 38:1; 40:6). Thus we obtain the characteristic and expected word (Reifmann, Graetz, Perles, etc.). But we cannot retain between מקנה 'flock' and עלעולה 'storm' the particle אף 'also', 'even'. Still less can we regard אף as meaning 'nostril' or 'anger'. Following the description in Virgil which we have quoted above, we propose to read שָׁאַף 'sniffing', 'smelling' (cf. 5:5). The

2nd hemistich becomes: 'the flock which sniffs the storm'. This is the subject of יַגִּיד of the beginning. The indirect object is עָלָיו (neuter suffix) 'about it', 'with regard to it'; the direct object is רעו, which we vocalise as רֹעוֹ 'its shepherd'. Thus, by the simple change of אַף to שֶׁאָף,

we obtain a coherent meaning for v. 33: 'the flock warns its shepherd, the flock which sniffs the storm'. This indeed reminds us of the heifer of Virgil which sucks in the winds and hence is able to declare the approach of a storm.

CHAPTER 37

1   That again is why my heart throbs,
       And leaps out of its place!
2   Listen then to the thunder of His voice,
       And the groaning which comes from His mouth.

37: 1 Vv. 1-5a, 6b, 7a, absent from Sah., marked with asterisk in Jerome, Colb., Syro-hex. (except v. 1b), did not exist in G. The present text is derived from Theod. (cf. Syro-hex.). The original text of 37: 1 in G, like v. 28b (Swete), follows 36: 28a (which corresponds to 36: 33 of the MT). It runs thus: ἐπὶ τούτοις πᾶσιν οὐκ ἐξίσταταί σου ἡ διάνοια, οὐδὲ διαλλάσσεταί σου ἡ καρδιά ἀπὸ σώματος. It is clear that G read לבך instead of לבי. Syr. reads לבו 'his heart'.

As against Bickell and Duhm, who wish to change אף into הלא and לבי into לבך (following G in 36: 28b), Budde notes quite rightly that Job will not be addressed until v. 14. In reality אף 'so too' forms the link between 36: 33, where the animals' presentiment of the storm was spoken of, and 37: 1, where Elihu himself feels struck by the same terror. Note the use of זאת exactly as in 33: 12. The preposition ל denotes the cause: 'for that reason'. The verb חרד means 'quiver', 'tremble'; cf. the hiph'il in 11: 19. יתר is generally connected with נתר, the hiph'il of which means 'to untie' (6: 9) and the qal of which would mean 'to become loose, untied'. But the Assyrian verb tarâru 'to tremble' is specifically used to depict the spasmodic movements of the heart (Boissier, Rev. d'Assyriologie, **8**, p. 37). The complement ממקומו 'from its place' (14: 18;

18: 4) shows that the suggestion is that the heart 'leaps out of' the breast.

2 On the text of G, cf. v. 1. For שמעו שמוע, Theod. ἄκουε ἀκοήν (but Jerome *audite sonitum*), Aq. ἤκουσα ἀκοήν. Theod. clarifies the suffix of קלו: θυμοῦ Κυρίου (but Jerome *et voces ejus*). Syr. places ברגז after קלו and interprets הגה by ܘܐܠܝ 'judgment'.

Elihu draws the attention of his hearers to the roar of the thunder. The opening שִׁמְעוּ שָׁמוֹעַ 'listen then!' as in 13: 17; 21: 2. The ב before the complement makes clear the meaning of 'listen' (15: 8). The abstract רֹגֶז 'agitation', 'anger' (3: 17, 26; 14: 1) means also the crash of the thunder, as is attested by the 8th form of the Arabic *rajaza*, the basic meaning of which is 'thunder', 'cause a crashing noise'. Because of the 2nd hemistich, we must keep for קֹלוֹ 'His voice' its proper meaning, while recognising that the voice of God is the thunder (28: 26). The rare word הֶגֶה means 'murmur', 'groaning sound' (Ezk 2: 10; Ps 90: 9): cf. הגה 'murmur', 'utter sounds' (27: 4). With מִפִּיו יֵצֵא compare 15: 13a, 'and you let words proceed from your mouth'. The noise of the thunder is the sound which comes from the mouth of God. In 35: 10 it was the song which resounds in the night.

3   Under the whole heavens He hurls His lightning,
     And it reaches to the borders of the earth.

4   Behind Him roars a voice,
     He thunders with His exalted voice,
     And does not withhold *the lightnings*,
     When His voice is heard.

4 יעקבם ;יְעַקֵּב בְּרָקִים :MT יעקבם.

3 On the text of G, cf. v.1. For
ישרהו, Theod. ἀρχὴ αὐτοῦ (from
שרר 'command'), Aq. ἐφοδεύσεις
αὐτοῦ and Vulg. *ipse considerat*
(from שור), Targ. תריצותיה 'His
rectitude' (from ישר), Syr. ܢܫܒܚܘܢܝܗܝ
'they praise Him' (from שיר),
Jerome *circuit* (following Symm.).
For כנפות, Theod. πτερύγων, but
Jerome *finibus* (following Symm.
ἄκρων).
The expression תַּחַת־כָּל־הַשָּׁמַיִם
'under all the heavens' as in 28:24;
41:3. The parallel phrase was
לקצות־הארץ 'to the ends of the
earth' in 28:24. Here we have
עַל־כַּנְפוֹת הָאָרֶץ 'to the extremities
of the earth'. The plural of כָּנָף
'wing' denotes the borders, the
fringes, of a garment or a carpet.
The earth was likened to a carpet
which was shaken in the morning by
its 'wings' (38:13). The four 'wings'
of the earth are the cardinal points,
the four corners of the world (Is
11:12; Ezk 7:2). It is unnecessary
to change יִשְׁרֵהוּ to יְשׁוּרֵהוּ 'they
perceive it' (cf. Vulg. and Aq.), as
is proposed by Ehrlich. The verb
שרה corresponds to the Aramaic שרא,
to the Syriac ܫܪܐ 'untie', 'loosen',
'release'. The suffix of ישרהו anticipates אֹרוֹ 'His lightning' (36:32);
cf. the construction of 36:30. Hence
we may translate: 'Under the whole
heavens He hurls His lightning, And
it reaches to the borders of the
earth.'

4 On the text of G, cf. v.1. Syr.

omits יִשְׁאַג קוֹל. For יעקבם, which is
faithfully copied by Syr., we have
יעכבנון. 'He withholds them' in Targ.,
ἀνταλλάξει αὐτούς in Theod. Note
that Symm. καὶ οὐκ ἄν ἐξιχνιασθήσε-
ται (for ולא יעקבם) is followed by
Jerome *et non poterit investigari* (cf.
Vulg. *et non investigabitur*).
After the lightning, the thunder:
'behind Him roars a voice'. The word
קוֹל as in v. 2. The verb שאג 'to roar',
whence שְׁאָגָה (3:24; 4:10), to
suggest the roaring of God in the
thunder (Jer 25:30; Am 1:2). The
reading קֹלוֹ 'His voice' (Duhm,
Budde) has no support in the versions. The 2nd hemistich explains
what is this voice which roars: 'He
thunders with His exalted voice',
literally, with his voice of elevation.
The word גָּאוֹן 'elevation' (40:10)
and 'pride' (35:12; 38:11). The
hiph'il of רעם (cf. the substantive in
26:14) to mean 'to thunder', with
the complement בְּקוֹל as in 40:9.
Note the poetic use of the jussive
instead of the imperfect (33:21;
36:14). The end of the verse is
translated: 'but none can follow its
traces, despite this reverberating
voice' (Le Hir); 'when man hears
His voice, the shaft has already gone
from His hand' (Renan); 'when
man hears His voice, the lightning
has already gone' (Crampon); 'He
no longer withholds the lightning,
as soon as His voice is heard'
(Segond). More literal, the *Bible du
rabbinat français* renders וְלֹא יְעַקְּבֵם
by 'He no longer holds them back',

5   God by His voice *works* marvels,
     He achieves great things beyond our knowledge,
6   When to the snow He says: Fall on the earth! [   ]

5   יַעֲמֹל ;‎ MT: ירעם.

6   Omit וגשם מטר. — עֹזוּ ;‎ MT: עֻזּוֹ.

noting that the plural suffix represents the flashes of lightning. The *pi'el* of עקב has the meaning of 'hold back' by the heel (עָקֵב, 18:9), as we see from the explanation given of the name of יַעֲקֹב in Gn 25:26. In Aramaic, it is the *pi'el* of עכב which has assumed the meaning of 'hold back', 'check' (cf. Targ.). It is apparent that it is a reference to God no longer withholding the manifestations of the storm, but it is not clear to what the plural suffix of יעקבם should refer. An excellent solution is suggested by Budde, who reads יַעֲקֹב בְּרָקִים. It is very understandable that the resemblance of the letters has occasioned the haplography. The 3rd hemistich will mean simply: 'and He does not withhold the lightnings'. Duhm combines יעקבם with כי to obtain יעקב מפיו, then he replaces גאונו by גרוני, which results in odd phrases: 'He does not restrain His throat, from His mouth His voice is heard.' This is too many anthropomorphisms for the characterisation of thunder. We have already had מפיו in v. 2. In reality, the end of the verse 'when His voice is heard' forms a 4th hemistich. When the thunder has begun to rumble, lightnings are incessant.

5   The text of G reappears at v. 5b: ἐποίησεν γὰρ μεγάλα ἃ οὐκ ἤδειμεν. נפלאות, Theod. θαυμάσια, but Jerome and Vulg. *mirabiliter* (probably following Symm.). The word נפלאות is regarded by Syr. as a complement of עשה. Targ. paraphrases נפלאות by 'the marvels which He must do'.
     The 2nd hemistich, 'doing great things which we do not know', is inspired by 5:9 and 9:10. The formula וְלֹא נֵדַע 'and we do not know' implies the complement 'these things' (8:9; 36:26). The parallel word to גְדֹלוֹת is נִפְלָאוֹת 'marvels' as in 5:9; 9:10. But the rest of the 1st hemistich, 'God thunders by His voice', does not suit either the context or the passages quoted. The word אֵל 'God' is part of the original text; cf. the נפלאות אל 'wonders of God' in v. 14. Again, בְּקֹלוֹ 'by His voice' is compatible not only with what precedes but also with what follows. It is the word of God which will be mentioned in v. 6. For the verb corresponding to עשֹה 'doing' has been substituted יַרְעֵם under the influence of v. 4b. We read יַעֲמֹל 'He works, performs' (which may have given rise to ירעם after the falling out of the ל before אל). The verb עמל has its normal meaning of 'do', 'perform', as in Arabic and Aramaic. Note the parallelism between the imperfect and the participle (12:17, 19). Thus we obtain: 'God by His voice works marvels, He achieves great things beyond our knowledge.' Duhm proposes to change ירעם to יראנו 'He shows us', but the complement 'by His voice' has then to be suppressed. The parallelism with עשֹה does not favour this conjecture. Budde proposes to put עשֹה at the beginning of the verse, and then to place after it נפלאות ואין חקר. This is to follow 5:9 and 9:10 too closely, without taking into account sufficiently the text before us.

6   V. 6a is preserved in G, but v.

And to torrential rains: *Be strong*!

7   *On* every man He puts a seal,
    That all *men* might know His work.

7 בְּעַד (cf. 9:7); MT: בְּיַד. — אֲנָשִׁים; MT: אַנְשֵׁי.

6b is from Theod. (cf. v. 1). Jerome *nubi* is a corruption of *nivi* (= G χιόνι). The word הוא is connected with היה 'to be' (Aramaic הוא) by Targ. and Syr. הוי, G γίνου, but Vulg. *ut descendat* links it with הוה 'to fall'. The 2nd hemistich is literally translated by Theod. But Vulg. has simply *et hiemis pluviis et imbri fortitudinis suae*. The two kinds of rain, that of the spring and that of the winter, are detailed in Targ. The 2nd hemistich is shortened in Syr. and coupled to v. 7: 'and the rain, the abundant spring rain, He has sealed in the hand of all men'.

The opening, 'When to the snow He says', introduces the account of the marvels produced by the voice of God. The imperative הֱוֵא is clearly differentiated from הֱוֵה 'be' (Gn 27:29). The verb does not correspond to the Aramaic הוא (for הוה, היה 'to be'), but to the Arabic هوى 'to fall from above'; cf. the substantive הַוָּה, הַיָּה (6:2). The word אֶרֶץ plays the part of an accusative of direction; cf. 5:11. The versions, while connecting הוא with הוה 'to be' (with the exception of the Vulg.), favour the reading of the MT. It is unnecessary to change הוא to רוא (Graetz, Perles), רוה (Siegfried), הרא (Torczyner), from the root רוה, רוא 'to water'. Ehrlich proposes רד 'descend', and in so doing only replaces the rare word by the common one. The 2nd hemistich is redundant. It has long been noticed that וְגֶשֶׁם מָטָר is repeated, and that in consequence the original text had simply וגשם מטרות עזו. In Zec 10:1 we have the expression מטר גשם 'torrential rain'. It is clear that

גשם מטרות 'shower of rains' is a kind of compound word which could equally well be rendered by 'rains of shower'. Instead of עֻזּוֹ 'its force', 'its vigour' we expect a verb parallel to הוא. With Hoffmann we vocalise עֹזּוּ 'be strong'. Cf. the use of the verb עזז in connection with the fountains of the deep in Pr 8:28. Less attractive is the correction of Duhm, who reads וגשם ומטר תעזו 'and to the shower and the rain: you will be strong!'

7 V. 7b is preserved in G, but v. 7a is from Theod. (cf. v. 1). Syr. joins v. 7a to v. 6b. For כל־אנשי, Syr. ܠܟܠܗܘܢ 'to the world'. G renders מעשהו by τὴν ἑαυτοῦ ἀσθένειαν, which necessitates πᾶς ἄνθρωπος as a translation of כל־אנשי.

Effects of the inclement weather mentioned in v. 6. The usual interpretation of the 1st hemistich is: 'He puts a seal on the hand of every man.' The meaning would be that God prevents human work by sending snow and rain. But the hand of man can continue to work in all weathers. What the author rather suggests, in the light of v. 8, is that man cannot leave his home when the weather is bad. Now, we find in 9:7, ובעד כוכבים יחתם 'and He puts a seal on the stars', to mean that God prevents the stars from emerging on the horizon. With Graetz, Beer, Duhm, Ehrlich, and others, we read בְּעַד instead of בְּיַד: 'on every man He puts a seal', He holds the whole world under seal. The phrase כָּל־אָדָם as in 36:25 (cf. 21:33). The parallel is כָּל־אַנְשֵׁי, the construct state of which is in-

8 And the beasts return to their dens,
   And in their lairs they remain.
9 From the south comes a whirlwind,
   And from the north biting cold;

explicable. The final ם has fallen out
by haplography before מֶעֲשֵׂהוּ. Read
אֲנָשִׁים (Olshausen, etc.). For the
last word מעשהו 'His action', cf. our
restoration of 33:17. Ehrlich would
read מעטהו 'his littleness', 'his
insignificance', following G τὴν ἑαυτοῦ ἀσθένειαν. But מעט does not
tally with the idea of weakness. It
seems that G explains מעשהו 'His
action' pejoratively.

8 For במו־ארב, G ὑπὸ σκέπην
(Jerome sub protectione). G renders
the 2nd hemistich by ἡσύχασαν δὲ
ἐπὶ κοίτης (Jerome et quieverunt in
cubili); cf. Syr. ﬞﬞﬞﬞﬞ 'on its
litter'.
   Not only man but also the beasts
are shut in as a result of rain and
snow: 'and the beasts return to their
dens'. Here חַיָּה denotes living creatures in general, the animal world;
cf. 5:23; 39:15; 40:20. Note the
poetic form בְּמוֹ (9:30; 16:4, 5;
19:16). The word אֶרֶב (from ארב,
25:3; 31:9) denotes an ambush
(38:40) and, here, the place where
the beast lies concealed, the lair.
The plural of מְעֹנָה 'abode' often
designates the lairs of wild beasts
(38:40; Nah 2:13; Ps 104:22;
Ca 4:8).

9 It is in error that Colb. attributes
to Theod. the 2nd hemistich of G.
For מן־החדר, G ἐκ ταμείων (Jerome
de promptuariis), Vulg. ab interior-
ibus, Syr. ﬞﬞﬞ 'from the chamber', Targ. מן אדרון עילא 'from the
lofty chamber'. G interprets סופה
by ὀδύναι, but Jerome tempestas
(cf. Theod. and Symm. καταιγίς, Aq.
συσσεισμός, Vulg. tempestas). For

ממזרים, Aq. and Theod. transcribe
Μαζορίμ or Μαζούρ (cf. Syro-hex.),
while G translates ἀπὸ δὲ ἀκρωτηρίων
(Jerome et de promontoriis), Vulg.
et ab Arcturo, Targ. מכות מזרים
'from the window of the north', Syr.
ﬞﬞﬞﬞﬞ 'from showers'.
   The poet passes to a new subject.
After the snow and the rain, the
wind and the hoar frost. The expression הַחֶדֶר 'the chamber' recalls
the chambers of the south (9:9). It
is a poetic description for that area
where are piled up the south winds
(cf. Comm. on 9:9). Duhm is being
more explicit than the poet when he
adds תימן 'south' after חדר without
article. The word סוּפָה 'whirlwind',
'hurricane', 'tempest', as in 21:18;
27:20. It is from the south that this
hurricane comes (Is 21:1). Following the parallelism, it is clear that
מְזָרִים must mean a point of the
horizon whence comes the cold
(קָרָה; cf. 24:7). Etymologically,
מזרים is the pi'el participle of זרה
'shed abroad', 'scatter', 'disperse'
(cf. 18:15). In the Koran the winds
of the north which scatter the rain
are called الذاريات 'the scattering' or
'the dispersing' (Sura 51, 1). And
in fact Qimchi defines the מזרים as
'the winds which blow and disperse',
רוחות נושבים ומזרים (Thesaurus of
Gesenius, I, p. 430). It is clear that
the Jewish grammarian has not
hesitated to treat רוחות 'winds' as
a masculine, in view of the double
gender of the word רוח (cf. 1:19;
4:15). This is an answer to Duhm,
who claims that if מזרים denoted
winds we ought to have the feminine.
The Babylonians and the Assyrians
described the four points of the compass by the names of winds. Hence

10   By the breath of God ice *is* produced,
      And the stretch of the waters becomes a solid mass.

11   At times the cloud hurls a *thunderbolt*,
      The stormcloud scatters its lightning

10 יֻתַּן (Symm., Syr., Targ.); MT: יִתֶּן.

11 בָּרָק; MT: ברי. — עָנָן; MT: עֲנַן.

it is quite likely that מזרים represents the winds of the north. The change to מזוים 'granaries' (Voigt, Budde, etc.) would be rather tempting if the Hebrew מזוים of Ps 144: 13 (מְזָוֵינוּ) were not in dispute. It is conjecturally that Hoffmann sees in מזרים, which he translates 'the Winnowers', the name of a constellation, the feminine of which would be מזרות, 'the Mazzaroth' of 38: 32. The vocalisation clearly distinguishes מְזָרִים, which comes from זרה, and מַזָּרוֹת, which comes from נזר (cf. 38: 32). The word קָרָה as in 24: 7.

10 V. 10a, absent from Sah., marked with asterisk in Colb., Cod. 248, and Jerome, did not exist in G. The present text is derived from Theod. Instead of יִתֶּן (Theod. δώσει), Symm. δοθήσεται (Jerome *dabitur*), Syr. ܐܬܝܗܒ, Targ. יתיהב have vocalised יֻתַּן, which is preferable (cf. inf.). G οἰακίζει δὲ τὸ ὕδωρ ὡς ἐὰν βούληται passes from מים to בתחבולתו of v. 12. Vv. 11-12a have thus been omitted in G (cf. inf.). For במוצק, Targ. באתכותא 'as a spreading out', Syr. ܡܣܚܐ 'He causes to fall'. Vulg. paraphrases the whole verse: *flante Deo concrescit gelu, et rursum latissimae funduntur aquae.*

After the cold, the ice. With מִנִּשְׁמַת־אֵל 'by the breath of God', cf. מנשמת אלוה (4: 9) and נשמת שדי (32: 8). The *qal* יִתֵּן 'He gives' does not agree with 'by the breath of God', nor above all with בְּמוּצָק 'in

a solid' of the close. The *pu'al* יֻתַּן, supported by Symm., Syr., and Targ., is from every point of view preferable: 'by the breath of God ice is produced'. Mandelkern and Ehrlich would change יִתֶּן into יֻתַּךְ 'is melted'. But in that case the 2nd hemistich is no longer understandable. In fact, we have seen (on 11: 15) that the passive participles יָצוּק and מוּצָק meant 'hard', 'solid', a meaning derived from 'melted down' (cf. Buxtorf, *Lexicon*, s.v. יצק solidum, *solidum, ut id quod e metallis fusum est*). The verb יתן is understood before במוצק. The natural meaning of the 2nd hemistich is therefore: 'and the stretch of waters (is formed) into a solid, solidifies'. Thaw would have been attributed to the heat (6: 16-17). Cf. the use of למוצק in 38: 38.

11 Vv. 11-12a (as far as ἐντείληται αὐτοῖς inclusive), absent from Sah., marked with asterisk in Jerome and Syro-hex., did not exist in G. The present text is derived from Theod. (cf. Colb. and Syro-hex.). G ταῦτα συντέτακται παρ' αὐτοῦ ἐπὶ τῆς γῆς merely summarises the Hebrew from כל־אשר. Note that בתחבולתו has been translated by G in v. 10. The tendency of G is to shorten these difficult passages. The word ברי is connected with ברר 'to be pure' by Targ. ברירותא 'purity' and Theod. ἐκλεκτόν, with בר 'wheat' by Jerome and Vulg. *frumentum*, with פרי 'fruit' by Symm. καρπῷ. Syr. renders אף־ברי by ܣܝܡܬܠܐ 'and weakly' (?). For יטריח, Theod. καταπλάσσει

12 And the latter, wheeling in circles,
   Revolves according to His designs,
   So that they perform all His commands,
   On the face of *His* terrestrial world,

12 Add יִתְהַלֵּךְ after מתהפך. — אַרְצָה (Syr.); MT: אָרְצָה.

(A καταπλήσσει), Aq. ἐνοχλήσει or παρενοχλήσει (Field, following Syrohex.), Vulg. *desiderat*, Targ. מטרח, Syr. ܡܬܡܬܚܐ 'extended'.

The *hapax* בְּרִי has been very variously explained. An attempt has been made to see in it a compound word consisting of the preposition בְּ" and of רִי", supposed to mean 'humidity' (from the root רוה 'moisten', 'water', etc.). Whence the translations: 'He loads the clouds with vapours' (Le Hir); 'He loads the clouds with moist vapours' (Renan); cf. Crampon, Segond, *Bible du rabbinat français*, etc. In the light of a Jewish translation quoted by Rashi, we should see in ברי or אַף־בְּרִי the proper name of the angel set in charge of the clouds and rain. Formerly I had thought it right to identify ברי with Βορέας, known among the Cassites under the form *Buriaš* (*The Journal of the Palestine Oriental Society*, **2**, pp. 66f.). But this foreign word suddenly making its appearance among the Hebrews as the name of a wind now seems to me a scarcely admissible idea. Duhm would replace ברי by ברד: 'He loads the clouds with hail'; but then the parallelism with the 2nd hemistich becomes very precarious. The right solution seems to us to have been found by Beer (followed by Hontheim, Budde, etc.). It consists in reading בָּרָק 'thunderbolt' (cf. v. 4) instead of ברי. The *hapax* יַטְרִיחַ does not necessarily belong to the root טרח 'load', 'tire', 'fatigue', whence טֹרַח 'load', 'burden'. It can be linked with the Arabic طرح 'fling', 'hurl'. The particle אַף

of the opening has no other purpose than to introduce a new phenomenon, that of the storm. The word אוֹרוֹ at the close of the 2nd hemistich has already been used in v. 3 to mean 'His lightning'. It is complementary to ברק 'thunderbolt'. To the word עָב corresponds ענן, which we may easily vocalise עָנָן as an absolute, a vocalisation which is in fact found in a few ancient editions (cf. Beer). The 2nd hemistich, 'the stormcloud scatters its lightning', is thus in perfect parallelism with the 1st. The *hiphʻil* of פוץ retains here its essential meaning 'scatter', 'dissipate', whereas in 18:11 it assumed the connotation of 'drive away'.

12 On the text of G, cf. v. 11. Up to לפעלם inclusive, it is the text of Theod. which has been taken into G. From כל אשר G is satisfied to summarise: ταῦτα συντέτακται παρ' αὐτοῦ ἐπὶ τῆς γῆς. The pronoun הוא is taken as referring to God by Theod. καὶ αὐτός, Targ. and Syr. והוא. But Aq. καὶ αὐτή (Jerome *et ipsa*) and Vulg. *quae* refer it to the stormcloud. For מסבות, Theod. κυκλώματα, Aq. μεταστροφαῖς, but Symm. κυκληδόν (Jerome and Vulg. *per circuitum*). The *kethîb* בְּתַחְבּוּלָתוֹ is followed by Symm. ἐν τῇ κυβερνήσει αὐτοῦ (cf. Vulg. *voluntas gubernantis*), the *qerê* בְּתַחְבּוּלָתָיו is followed by Aq. ἐν οἰακώσεσιν (cf. the translation of G in v. 10), Syr. ܡܚܫܒܬܐ 'thoughts'. Theod. transcribes ἐν Θεεβουλαθώθ. Combined with εἰς ἔργα αὐτῶν, which translates לפעלם, this transcription has given rise to ἐν τοῖς κατωτάτω θεὶς ἔργα αὐτῶν (Olympiod., Colb., some MSS;

13   Whether it be for punishment that *He accomplishes His will*,

13   אִם־לְאַרְצוֹ ;MT: יַמְלֵא רְצוֹנוֹ.

cf. Field). For ארצה, Syr. ؤاجبه 'His earth' reads אַרְצֹה (cf. inf.). A double targum paraphrases this verse so as to make it mean the help which God gives to the works of man.

The presence of מִתְהַפֵּךְ 'wheeling' (cf. Comm. on 9:5) excludes any hesitation about the attribution of וְהוּא 'and this'. It is here a question of the lightning, the thunderbolt, mentioned in v. 11, for מתהפכת is the epithet which qualifies the flaming sword placed at the gates of the Garden of Eden (Gn 3:24), and we know that the thunderbolt is a weapon (20:25; cf. Comm.). It has long been noted that לְפָעֳלָם belongs not to the first but to the second part of the verse. The complement of the verb is כֹּל אֲשֶׁר יְצַוֵּם, with which it forms one whole. Hence we must place the *athnaḥ* beneath בתחבולתו (cf. Rosenmüller, Le Hir, Renan, etc.). Thus it becomes apparent that the second part of the verse contains two hemistichs which are clearly recognisable as such. But something is lacking in the first part. Now, we can form a complete hemistich by joining מתהפך to וְהוּא מְסִבּוֹת: 'and the latter, wheeling in circles'. The feminine plural מסבות is used adverbially, just as סביבות 'surroundings' plays the part of a preposition, 'around' (22:10; 29:5). The word מֵסַב properly means 'round', 'circle' (from סבב 'turn', 'surround'). The masculine plural will mean 'surroundings', 'environment' (2 K 23:5), but the feminine plural retains a more abstract meaning. There remains only the word בתחבולתו for the 2nd hemistich, and we have not got the verb of which the pronoun הוא is the subject. It is probable that this verb was יִתְהַלָּךְ, which Budde puts

before מתהפך, but which it would be better to put after, since מסבות forms a whole with מתהפך (cf. Ley, Duhm, Hontheim). It is easy to understand how יתהלך has fallen out by haplography after מתהפך. The word תַּחְבּוּלָה is used only in the Book of Proverbs and always in the plural, which fact suggests that here we should adopt the *qerê* בְּתַחְבּוּלֹתָיו. The root is חבל 'to bind' in the sense of 'to combine'. The תחבולות are the 'combinations', 'designs', 'plans', etc. (Pr 1:5; 11:14; 12:5; 20:18; 24:6). Of course it is a question of the plans of God, who has been mentioned in v. 10 and to whom referred the suffix of אורו 'His lightning' in v. 11. The poet proposes to show that the natural phenomena are only the executors of the divine plan. It is in this sense that the verse should be understood: 'so that they perform all His commands on the face of His terrestrial world'. The plural suffixes of פָּעֳלָם and יְצַוֵּם have seemed strange to some moderns, who have suggested the reading לִפְעֹל מִכֹּל and then יְצַוֵּהוּ (Graetz, Beer, Budde). In that case one must regard מן of מכל as the partitive מן: 'to do of whatever He bids them'. But this preposition, which is readily understandable with verbs meaning 'eat', 'drink', 'taste', etc. is much less congruous with the verb 'to do'. The poet has in view the thunderbolt and the lightning of v. 11 or natural phenomena in general. For the last word the vocalisation אַרְצֹה (cf. 34:13) is irresistible in the light of Pr 8:31. It is 'on the face of His terrestrial world' that natural phenomena execute the will of God.

13 V. 13, absent from Sah., marked with asterisk in Jerome and Syro-

Whether it be for mercy that He brings it to pass.

14 Lend an ear to this, O Job,
Pause and observe the wonders of God!

15 Do you know how God commands them
And how His stormcloud makes lightning to flash forth?

hex., did not exist in G. The present text is derived from Theod. (cf. Syro-hex.). Targ. again paraphrases v. 13, in which it recognises three different kinds of rain: on the sea and the desert, on the trees of the mountains and hills, on the fields and the vineyards. For לשבט, Theod. εἰς παιδείαν, Syr. ܠܪܘܪܒܢܐ 'to the princes', Symm. εἰς φυλήν (cf. Jerome *in tribu* and Vulg. *in una tribu*). Instead of לחסד, Syr. reads לחסיד. Vulg. *sive in quocumque loco misericordiae suae* interprets לחסד in accordance with its translation of the 1st hemistich: *sive in una tribu, sive in terra sua*.

The antithesis lies between אם־לְשֵׁבֶט and אם־לְחֶסֶד. The will of God is realised whether it be for punishment or mercy. The word שֵׁבֶט 'rod' (9: 34; 21: 9) denotes the correction inflicted by means of the rod, the scourge (*flagellum*) or punishment in general (cf. La 3: 1). The phrase אם־לְאַרְצוֹ 'whether for his country' is embarrassing, since it is not in harmony with the abstractions 'whether it be for punishment ... whether for mercy'. Some exegetes are satisfied to eliminate אם before ארצו (cf. Dillmann, Budde), whence such translations as: 'whether it be that He wishes to punish His creatures' (Renan); 'it is as it were a rod with which He smites His earth' (Segond). Hoffmann replaces לארצו by לרצו 'by favour', whilst Hitzig reads אם לא רצו 'if they are not content'. Duhm proposes ולמארה 'and for a curse'. What we expect after לשבט is the parallel expression to יַמְצִאֵהוּ of the close. One may recognise in אם

לארצו the result of a wrong division of יְמַלֵּא רְצוֹנוֹ 'He accomplishes His will'. At the end, the *hiph'il* of מצא can have the sense of the *qal*: 'attain', 'reach', etc. (11: 7; 31: 29). Cf. the use of the *hiph'il* in 32: 15; 34: 12; 35: 9; 36: 22. The meaning of the verse is quite clear and simply continues the sense of v. 12. God uses His natural forces as an instrument sometimes for punishment, sometimes for mercy. It is thanks to them that He executes His will.

14 Syr. replaces עמד by שמע 'hear'. For והתבונן, G(B) νουθετούμενος, but G (א, A, C) νουθετοῦ (Sah., Syro-hex., Jerome *et commonere*).

Elihu had first addressed himself to all his listeners (v. 2). He now returns to Job: 'Lend an ear to this, O Job.' Cf. 33: 1. The demonstrative זאת is an allusion to the ironical questions which are to follow (34: 17). The verb עמד 'stand', 'stop', in the sense of 'remain quiet' (32: 16). The *hithpo'lel* of בין with the accusative (Is 43: 18; 52: 15) to express 'observe'; cf. 11: 11; 23: 15. The 'wonders of God' were announced in v. 5.

15 For התדע, G οἴδαμεν, but G(A) οἴδας (cf. Symm. ἄρα γνώσῃ). Then G ὅτι ὁ Θεὸς ἔθετο ἔργα αὐτοῦ reads פעליו instead of עליהם. Targ. adds גזירתא 'decree' as the complement of שׁום. Vulg. *quando praeceperit Deus pluviis* reads perhaps לגשם instead of עליהם (Houbigant). G paraphrases the 2nd hemistich: φῶς ποιήσας ἐκ σκότους. Targ. interprets אור עננו by ענני מטריה 'His clouds of rains', as if we had ענן אורו of v. 11 (cf. 36: 30).

16　Do you know anything of the balancings of the clouds,
　　Miracles of One who is perfect in knowledge?

The questions חֲתֵדַע 'do you know?' (vv. 15-16) are ironical. We shall find them again, with the verb in the perfect, in 38: 33; 39: 1. The complement of ידע is introduced by the preposition בְּ״ (35: 15). The verb שׂים with עַל before the complement in the sense of imposing a charge or assigning a function (34: 23; cf. Comm. on 38: 10). The suffix of עֲלֵיהֶם refers to natural phenomena in general (cf. v. 12). Man does not know exactly how God imposes His will on nature: 'Do you know how Eloah commands them?' The infinitive clause is continued by a clause whose verb is in the perfect (5: 11; 28: 25); cf. Gesenius-Kautzsch, § 114r). The hiph'il of יפע usually has the meaning 'gleam', 'shine' (3: 4; 10: 3, 22). But if we compare with v. 11, it becomes clear that עֲנָנוֹ is the subject of הוֹפִיעַ and that אוֹר is the complement. Hence we must keep for הוֹפִיעַ a causative sense. As a result of the command of God, 'His stormcloud makes lightning to flash forth'. The word אוֹר as in vv. 3 and 11. We do not see at all the necessity to prefer for the 1st hemistich the text of G, as is done by some moderns who replace עליהם by פעליו (cf. Bickell, Duhm). The complement 'His deeds', 'His actions' does not fit with שׂים 'place', 'dispose'. When שׂים has the meaning of 'do', it is never in a general sense, but in recognised idioms (Gesenius-Buhl, s.v. שׂים, 6). To say that one does not know how God performs His actions is far too banal an idea and is unconnected with a context whose meaning is very precise.

16 G ἐπίσταται, for התדע, is a corruption of ἐπίστασαι, which is found in G(A). We have scis in

Jerome (Tur.) but scit in Jerome (Bod., Gall.). For מפלשׂי, G διάκρισιν (from פרש), Vulg. semitas (from פלס 'to make smooth a road'), Syr. ܡܐܦܩܐ 'exit', Targ. מבשקרני 'the investigations'. G ἐξαίσια δὲ πτώματα πονηρῶν reads רעים instead of דעים and translates מפלאות twice, interpreting the second time by the root נפל 'to fall'. Vulg. renders מפלאות by magnas (which becomes an epithet of semitas) and תמים דעים by et perfectas scientias (cf. perfecta scientia for דעות תמים in 36: 4). Syr. makes of תמים דעים a qualification of מפלאות, while Targ. makes of it a genitive: 'the marvels of Him who is perfect in knowledge'.

The preposition עַל cannot introduce the direct complement of תֵּדַע, but simply the name of the thing which is the subject of discussion or talk. We have the same use of על with חזה 'to see' (Is 1: 1), שמע 'to hear' (Gn 41: 15). The proper meaning of על is therefore 'with regard to', 'concerning' and the verb ידע implies its direct object 'something'. The expression מִפְלְשֵׂי־עָב, and not now מפלשי-עב (36: 29), is supported by alliteration with מִפְלָאוֹת. And conversely מפלאות, and not נפלאות (v. 14). If we replace מפלשׂי by מפרשׂי (Budde) or מפלאות by נפלאות (Siegfried, Budde), we are getting rid of these variations in style. The meaning of the hapax מִפְלָשׂ is inferred from the root פלשׂ, which is equivalent to פלס 'equalise', 'smooth', 'balance', whence פֶּלֶס 'balance' (Is 40: 12; Pr 16: 11; Sir 42: 4). The word מפלאות is again a hapax, but the meaning is not in doubt in the light of the root פלא and the synonym נפלאות. The expression תְּמִים דֵּעִים 'perfect in

17   You, whose garments are hot,
      When the earth rests because of the south wind,
18   Will you, with Him, spread forth clouds,
      Solid as a mirror of molten metal?

knowledge' which now takes the place of תמים דעות, a pretentious epithet of Elihu in 36:4, is a periphrasis for God. The miracles of the 'one who is perfect in knowledge' are equivalent to נפלאות אל 'the wonders of God', of v. 14. It is cutting up the phrase too much to treat תמים דעים as an ironic vocative: 'O Thou perfect in knowledge' (contra Ehrlich). All the audacity of Duhm is needed to recompose, supposedly on the basis of G, a second hemistich on the pattern: מפיל תהום מרעם 'making an abyss fall as a result of the thunder'(!). Likewise on the basis of G, Beer timidly proposes (ed. Kittel): פתאם מפלות רעים 'suddenly the wicked fall' (!).

17 The end מדרום did not exist in G. We find ἀπὸ νότου in G (א c.a), Compl., Ald., but these words are absent from Sah. and marked with asterisk in Jerome, Syro-hex., Colb. They come from Theod., like v. 18 (cf. inf.). G and Syr. omit אשר, which Vulg. paraphrases by nonne. For בהשקט, Vulg. cum perflata fuerit, in accordance with the context. Syr. ليرل 'it has gone' is a corruption of للقل 'it rests' which translated בהשקט (Baumann).

It is impossible to interpret אשׁר as 'why?' (Renan) or as 'whence comes it that?' (Le Hir). This way of making v. 17 dependent on התדע 'do you know?' of v. 16 forces the meaning of the relative אשׁר. In reality, the 1st hemistich means simply: 'You, whose garments are hot.' The adjective חָם 'hot' recurs only in Jos 9:12. The hiph'il of שקט is used with the sense of the qal 'to rest', exactly as in 34:29. The word

דָּרוֹם 'south' denotes the south wind, the Notos or the Auster which brings overpowering heat (Lk 12:55). All becomes drowsy under the influence of the warm wind. This is the time when 'the earth rests because of the south wind'. What is most desired then is some clouds which would intercept the rays of the sun and refresh the atmosphere. Thus the ironical allusion in v. 18 becomes perfectly intelligible: 'Will you, with Him, spread forth clouds?' There is no reason at all, as can clearly be seen, to place v. 18 after v. 20 (Duhm) or after 38:3 (Ehrlich).

18 V. 18, absent from Sah., marked with asterisk in Jerome and Syrohex., did not exist in G. The present text is derived from Theod. (cf. Syro-hex.). Nor had G מדרום of v. 17. Symm. ἐξ ὕψους, at the beginning, comes from ממרום (for מדרום) of v. 17. For לשחקים, Theod. εἰς παλαιώματα (cf. 36:28). Symm. εἰς αἰθέρα (cf. Vulg. in 35:5), Aq. εἰς τροπάς, Jerome and Vulg. coelos, Syr. ܠܪܩܝܥܐ 'firmament'. For כראי, Theod. and Aq. ὡς ὅρασις, Symm. ὀφθῆναι (Jerome ad videndum), Vulg. quasi aere, Targ. כאספקלריא (quasi speculare). Syr. 'that they may be supported together' seems to read כאחד instead of כראי.

We have seen, in v. 17, the logical link that exists between the sensation of heat and the desire for the coming of clouds. The interrogative is implied before תַּרְקִיעַ. The movement is the same as in vv. 15-16. The hiph'il of רקע 'spread out', 'thin', 'flatten', is a well-chosen word to depict the clouds extended in the sky like a firmament (רָקִיעַ). The preposition לְ" before the accusative as in 5:2,

19   Tell *me* what we shall say to Him.
      We shall cease to argue, on account of the darkness!
20   Is He told, when I speak?
      When a man has spoken, is He informed?

19   הוֹדִיעֵנִי (*kethîb* of the Orientals, G, Syr.): MT: הוֹדִיעֵנוּ.

7; 12:23; 34:3. The word רְאִי
(from ראה 'to see') recurs in Sir
12:11, with the meaning of 'mirror'.
Cf. מַרְאָה 'mirror' in Ex 38:8. The
mirrors of the ancients were of molten metal (Ex 38:8; cf. Lesêtre,
article 'Miroir' in the *Dictionnaire
de la Bible*, IV, col. 1123ff.). Note
that מוּצָק properly means 'molten'
and, by derivation, 'hard', 'firm',
'solid' (v. 10; cf. 11:15).

19 G adds διὰ τί at the beginning
and paraphrases the 2nd hemistich:
καὶ παυσώμεθα πολλὰ λέγοντες. Vulg.
paraphrases also: *nos quippe in-
volvimur tenebris*. Instead of הודיענו,
the *kethîb* of the Orientals has
הוֹדִיעֵנִי (10:2; 13:23; 38:3; 40:7;
42:4); cf. G δίδαξόν με and Syr.
אוֹדַעַיני. The reading נסתאל 'we
hide' of Syr., for נערך, is probably
an error for נסתאלוי (cf. Targ. נסדר).
The reading הוֹדִיעֵנוּ 'make us to
know' harmonises with נאמר and
נערך. It is less good than הוֹדִיעֵנִי
'make me to know', which is supported by G, Syr., and the passages
quoted above. Elihu continues his
ironical comments: 'Tell me what
we shall say to Him.' If Job is the
collaborator or the confidant of
God (vv. 15-18), it is for him to
disclose the secrets of wisdom. Note
the use of מָה as in 23:5; 34:4. The
verb ערך in the sense of putting
together words, drawing up arguments (13:18; 32:14). The complement is understood (Ps 5:4). The
phrase מִפְּנֵי־חֹשֶׁךְ 'on account of
the darkness' is supported by 23:17.

We cannot replace חֹשֶׁךְ, which is a
symbol of ignorance (Ec 2:13-14; cf.
Podechard), by חֹשֶׂךְ which Perles
postulates, from the root חשׂך. This
word would mean 'lack of words'.
But to cease to speak for 'lack of
words' is a remark worthy of La
Palisse.

20 G μὴ βίβλος ἢ γραμματεύς μοι
παρέστηκεν, ἵνα ἄνθρωπον ἑστηκὼς
κατασιωπήσω; is the result of a series
of transformations of the Hebrew:
double translation of היספר, read
as סֵפֶר 'book' and סֹפֵר 'scribe', a
reading לי instead of לו, omission
of כי אדבר, substitution of עמד for
אמר and of אבלע for יבלע. For
היספר, Vulg. *quis narrabit?* Syr.
reads ואספר instead of היספר. For
יבלע, Vulg. *devorabitur*, Syr. נתבלע
'will be devoured', but Targ. קטרג
'he will accuse'. A second Greek
translation of the 2nd hemistich,
ἐὰν εἴπῃ ἀνὴρ καταποθήσεται, is noted
in Colb. and added in Cod. 249.
Elihu continues in the tone of v.
19. It is for Job to show him how to
speak to God, for his own vocabulary
is too poor for this purpose: 'Is He
told, when I speak?' The *pu'al* of
ספר to mean 'to be recounted' (cf.
the *pi'el* in 12:8; 15:17). The 3rd
person in the passive as in Latin
fertur, *narratur*, etc. (Gn 4:26;
הוּחַל 'it was begun', 'one began').
The conjunctions אִם and כִּי interchange their normal meanings in the
2nd hemistich, since אִם־אָמַר אִישׁ
is the counterpart of כִּי־אֲדַבֵּר.
Hence 'when a man has spoken'

21   And now the light could no more be seen,
      It was darkened by the clouds,
      But a wind has passed and has swept them away.

corresponds to 'when I speak', and in consequence כִּי יְבֻלַּע must have a meaning similar to הֲיְסֻפַּר־לוֹ 'is He told?' Jacob has quite rightly noted (*ZATW*, 1912, p. 287) that there existed, alongside בלע 'to swallow up' (Arabic بلع) another root בלע (Arabic بلغ) which, in the 2nd form, means 'to make known', 'to inform'. The passive of the 2nd form (i.e. of the *pi'el*) will mean 'to be informed', so that our 2nd hemistich, which has so much puzzled exegetes, will be translated simply: 'When a man has spoken, is He informed?' Elihu is only a man and his words have no particular value. He is going to withdraw from the discussion. The motives to which he appeals apply equally to Job. We are freed from the need to look for explanations based on בלע 'swallow up', 'destroy', explanations which result in such translations as the following: *aut fabitur homo? Sane absorberetur* (Rosenmüller); 'whoever tried it, would be destroyed' (Le Hir); 'will a man ask to be destroyed?' (Loisy); 'has ever a man desired his ruin?' (Renan; cf. Segond, Crampon, etc.). Duhm rewrites a 1st hemistich following the pattern of 40: 2, יְסוֹר instead of יספר and ידבר instead of אדבר: 'is there a censor for him when he speaks?' But לוֹ 'for him' does not very well fit in with יסור 'a censor'. Note that in such cases יבלע is assigned the meaning of 'to be confounded', with the meaning of the root בלל! Ehrlich would connect יספר with the Arabic *safara* 'drive away', 'dissipate', 'sweep away' the cloud. But we have already noted that this root became שפר in Hebrew (26: 13). It is not to the cloud but to God that the suffix of לוֹ refers.

21 G πᾶσιν δ' οὐχ ὁρατὸν τὸ φῶς paraphrases the 1st hemistich. Targ. renders אור by מטרא 'rain' (cf. v. 15). The 2nd hemistich is twice translated in G. The first interpretation, τηλαυγές ἐστιν ἐν τοῖς παλαιώμασιν, absent from Sah., comes from Theod. (cf. the translation of שחקים in v. 18 and 36: 28), but it has passed into Syro-hex. and Jerome *quod refulget in nubibus*. The second translation ὥσπερ τὸ παρ' αὐτοῦ ἐπὶ νεφῶν is that of G. It is lacking in Jerome, which has, in its place, *et spiritus transiet et mundabit eas*. This is the translation of Aq. (noted in the margin of Syro-hex.) for the 3rd hemistich, which is omitted in G. The 2nd hemistich is paraphrased *subito aer cogetur in nubes* in Vulg. For בשחקים, Syr. 'in the firmament of the heavens' (cf. v. 18).

Elihu returns to his description of natural phenomena. In v. 18 he inquired ironically if it was possible for man to stretch forth clouds in order to intercept the rays of the sun. He now supposes that the clouds have piled up in the sky: 'And now the light could no more be seen, it was darkened by the clouds.' It is a question of the light of the sun (31: 26). We had לֹא רָאוּ אוֹר in 3: 16. Here the plural has the sense of the indefinite pronoun 'one' (cf. 4: 19; 6: 2; 7: 3, etc.). It is unnecessary to change ראו to רָאִנוּ 'we see' (contra Budde). Duhm puts the 2nd hemistich after יאתה of v. 22. This transposition is suggested by a wrong interpretation of בָּהִיר in the sense of 'brilliant', 'luminous' (Aramaic בהר 'to shine', Arabic بهر 'to be luminous'). Fried. Delitzsch has recognised for בהיר the meaning 'dark', 'darkened', suggested by the Syriac ܟܡܝܪ 'dark', ܟܡܝܪܘܬܐ

22   From the north stream rays of gold;
      Around Eloah lies a crushing glory;
23   As for Shaddai, we cannot attain to Him!
      He is great in power and judgment,
      He is the *Lord* of righteousness and oppresses not;

23 וְרֹב; MT: וָרֹב.

'gloomy', ܟܡܘܢ 'twilight'. The light is intercepted by the clouds (v. 18). God then brings forth another phenomenon: 'and a wind has passed and has swept them away'. Cf. the use of the verb עבר in 30:15. The *pi'el* of טהר 'to be pure' (4:17) to denote 'purify', 'cleanse', 'sweep away'. V. 22a finishes the description. After the sky has been swept clear, the gold of the sun's rays can shine forth once more.

22 For זהב, G νέφη χρυσαυγοῦντα. Syr. regards נורא as synonymous with נהר, whence its translation 'and the light of God'. Syr. then passes on to שגיא of v. 23. G confuses אלוה with אלה: ἐπὶ τούτοις μεγάλη ἡ δόξα καὶ τιμὴ Παντοκράτορος. It is apparent that שדי of v. 23 is connected by G with v. 22. Targ. and Vulg. are agreed in seeing in נורא an epithet of הוד.

The doxology which is to terminate the chapter begins at the 2nd hemistich, the parallel of which is v. 23a: parallelism between אֱלוֹהַּ and שַׁדָּי. The 1st hemistich, 'from the north stream rays of gold', describes the state of the sky when the golden rays of the sun border the clouds which are being dispersed by the wind (v. 21). There is no reason to change זהב into זֹהַר 'light', as is done by most moderns, following Graetz. The verb אתה 'come', 'arrive' as in 3:25; 16:22; 30:14. After dwelling on the mysteries of the world of nature, Elihu concludes by declaring that *a fortiori* we can-

not reach the majesty of God. By poetic licence the epithet נוֹרָא has been placed before the noun הוֹד. It is taking purism too far to put back נורא after הוד, as does Budde. It would be far better to read, with Houbigant, נִרְאָה 'has been seen' instead of נורא. The word הוֹד, which is well known from the formula הוד והדר 'glory and honour' (40:10), here denotes the external 'glory' which surrounds God who is present in the clouds. We meet it again in 39:20.

23 We have seen that G connected שׁדי with v. 22 and that Syr. omitted the beginning up to שגיא. G καὶ οὐχ εὑρίσκομεν ἄλλον ὅμοιον τῇ ἰσχύι αὐτοῦ doubtless reads שֵׁנִי instead of שגיא. Vulg. *digne eum invenire non possumus* interprets שׁדי as from די 'sufficiency', etc. G ὁ τὰ δίκαια κρίνων, οὐκ οἴει ἐπακούειν αὐτόν; omits ומשפט, connects רב with the root ריב, and יענה with ענה 'to answer'. Vulg. omits רב and renders ולא יענה by *et enarrari non potest*. The complement ומשפט is linked with שׂגיא־כה in Syr. and Vulg. (cf. inf.). Syr. connects יענה with ענה 'to answer' (cf. G). V. 23 is doubly paraphrased in Targ.

Around God is shed a mysterious emanation of glory (v. 23) which conceals Him from mortal sight. Such is the meaning which is most suitable to the sentence: 'As for Shaddai, we cannot attain to Him.' The verb מצא 'find', 'reach' as in 23:3 (cf. 11:7). The complement is

24   That is why men fear Him;
     He does not even look upon all the wise of heart!

given prominence and again referred
to in the suffix of the verb: *casus
pendens* (cf. 29:16b). According
to the normal rhythm, it is clear that
וּמִשְׁפָּט forms one hemistich with
שַׂגִּיא־כֹחַ (change the position of the
athnaḥ): 'great in power and justice'.
It is thus that the verse is divided in
Vulg. *magnus fortitudine et judicio*
and in Syr. The Aramaic שׂגיא has
the sense of כביר or גדול 'great'
(36:26). We have found כביר כח
'great in power' in 36:5 (cf. Comm.).
To power is added וּמִשׁפט 'judgment', 'justice', as in Mic 3:8
מלאתי כח ‥‥ומשפט 'I am filled with
power . . . and judgment.' The
similarity of meaning between שׂגיא,
כביר and רב suggests the vocalisation רַב instead of רֹב and inclines us
to see in רַב־צְדָקָה 'a master of
justice' a parallel expression to
'great in power and judgment'. We
have had the same phenomenon in
11:2, where רֹב has been substituted
for רַב. The *piʿel* of עָנָה has the
meaning of 'to ill-treat' or 'to oppress'
(cf. 30:11). It is used here without
complement because it is a question
of a divine attribute, of God 'who
oppresses not'. If we left the text
as it is, we should have to translate:
'He does not oppress the greatness
of justice', which would not be a very
remarkable eulogy. Perles proposes
רִב 'suit' instead of רֹב, but a 'suit

of justice', for 'a just suit' is rather
strange and is with difficulty reconcilable with the meaning of יְעַנֶּה.

24 G φοβηθήσονται αὐτὸν...φοβηθή-
σονται δὲ αὐτόν repeats יראוהו (instead of יראה of the 2nd hemistich)
and omits the negative לֹא. Syr. is
in agreement with G. 1st Targ.
לא ידחל 'he does not fear' connects
יראה with ירא 'to fear'. Vulg. *et non
audebunt contemplari omnes qui sibi
videntur esse sapientes* is an interpretation rather than a translation.

The opening, 'that is why men
fear Him', offers no difficulty. Note
the use of לָכֵן as in 32:10. God is the
supremely just Being. Fear is the
sentiment which men must experience in His presence. The parallel
word to אֲנָשִׁים is 'all the wise of
heart'. The use of חכם לבב (9:4)
and of אנשי לבב (34:10) does not
permit us to assign to כל־חכמי־לב
a pejorative connotation, such as
those 'who claim to be wise' (*Bible
du rabbinat français*; cf. Vulg.). God,
being supreme justice, has no need
to take account of all human wisdom,
even though that wisdom might be
real. Unite 'all the wise of heart',
God does not even notice them! He
is surrounded by so formidable a
glory that one cannot attain unto
Him (v. 23), or attract His attention (vv. 19-20).

CHAPTER 38

1   And Yahweh answered Job from the heart of the tempest,
      and said:
2   Who is this who darkens Providence
      By words devoid of insight?

Chapters 38-41 Speeches of Yahweh: see Introduction, pp. lviiiff. and lxxxvff.

38: 1 G adds to the opening μετὰ δὲ τὸ παύσασθαι 'Ελιοῦν τῆς λέξεως. Syro-hex. marks with obelus ܡܢ which renders ὁ Κύριος (= יהוה). The *kethîb* joins מנהסערה into a single word, but the *qerê* separates into the normal מן הסערה. G translates מן הסערה by διὰ λαίλαπος καὶ νεφῶν. Targ. and Syr. render הסערה by עלעולא (cf. 36: 33), but Targ. adds דצערא 'of sorrow'.

It is to Job that Yahweh addresses Himself. Same formula as in 40: 1, but with the addition of מִן הַסְּעָרָה 'from the heart of the tempest'. On the word סערה, cf. 27: 21. The tempest, like storm in general, is the seat of theophanies; cf. the coming of God in the storm (שׂערה and סערות) Nah 1: 3; Zec 9: 14; the coming of the stormy wind from which will emerge the mysterious figures of Ezk 1: 4; the tempestuous phenomena which surround Yahweh in Ps 50: 3 (the verb used is שׂער). In the light of 40: 3 and 42: 1, it is clear that the dialogue here introduced is between Yahweh and Job. No account is taken of the speeches of Elihu. The apostrophe of v. 2 is aimed at Job, as appears from the apologies which he stammers out in 40: 4-5 and 42: 2ff. If it is maintained, as is done by some authors (among others Budde), that the expression 'from the heart of

the tempest' is an allusion to the phenomena described by Elihu in 36: 29-37: 4, we must conclude that this expression has been added subsequently in order to join ch. 38 to ch. 37. In fact, the storm described by Elihu is not introduced in order to prepare the way for a theophany, but as one of the extraordinary phenomena which manifest the power of God. It is mingled with other manifestations, and above all it does not end the description, which would be necessary if it were intended to form a transition between the speeches of Elihu and those of Yahweh. Hence one cannot make too much of the 'tempest'. It simply provides the framework within which the word of Yahweh rings out.

2 G ὁ κρύπτων με βουλήν makes explicit a complement of the person, but does not imply any text other than the MT (contra Bickell, who reads עצתי); cf. 42: 3. Similarly the end ἐμὲ δὲ οἴεται κρύπτειν is a free interpretation of דעת following the 1st hemistich (cf. 42: 3), and does not suggest a special text. The phrase is marked with obelus in Jerome and Syro-hex. For במלין בלי, G συνέχων δὲ ῥήματα ἐν καρδίᾳ, reading בלב instead of בלי. The word συνέχων is expletive (7: 11;

3   Gird up your loins then like a man;
     I will question you and you will inform me!
4   Where were you when I laid the foundations of the earth?
     Tell me that, if you know the truth.

10:1; 34:14). Vulg. translates broadly: *quis est iste involvens sententias sermonibus imperitis?* For מחשיך, Targ. כמחשיך *quasi obscurans*. Syr. ܘܡܣܟ̈ܠܐ 'who thinks' reads perhaps מחשב.

According to the answers made by Job in 40:4-5 and 42:2-6, it is evident that the question 'who is this who?' alludes to Job himself and not to Elihu, as has sometimes been claimed. It is to Job that the whole of the direct speech is addressed, from v. 3. With מִי זֶה cf. מִי הוּא of 4:7; 13:19; 17:3. 'Counsel' is part of the attributes of God, just like wisdom, power, and understanding (12:13). This divine counsel is none other than the Providence by which He foresees all and provides for all in the light of that vision. This Providence is a light which the words of man can only darken. The verb חשך, whence חֹשֶׁךְ 'darkness', is used in the *hiph'il*, with the meaning of 'darken' (Am 5:8; 8:9). In 42:3 we shall have מעלים 'hiding', which is more prosaic than מַחְשִׁיד. The phrase בְּלִי־דַעַת 'without knowledge' is an epithet of מִלִּין, the word בלי playing the part of an alpha privative (cf. 24:10; 33:9). Cf. the allegation of Elihu in 35:16, 'it is from lack of knowledge that he multiplies words'.

3   Targ. גֻּבְרָא and Syr. ܓܒܪܐ read גִּבּוֹר instead of גֶּבֶר (G ἀνήρ, Vulg. *vir*). For והודיעני, G σὺ δέ μοι ἀποκρίθητι and Vulg. *et responde mihi* give to the *hiph'il* of ידע a meaning appropriate to the context.

The verse will be repeated in 40:7, with omission of the expletive *waw*

which begins the 2nd hemistich and which is not rendered in Syr., Vulg. The verb אזר means 'to gird' or 'to tighten' (30:18) in the expression 'to gird up the loins' in order to prepare one's self for fight or for a hard task; cf. Jer 1:17, where we have מָתְנֶיךָ instead of חֲלָצַיִם; Lk 12:35, 37. Cf. Is 11:5, 'and righteousness will be the girdle of his hips (מתנים) and faithfulness the girdle of his loins (חלציו)'. The loins are the part of the body which the combatant must tense preparatory to his struggle. If they are relaxed, it spells defeat (Is 45:1); cf. *L'Emploi métaphorique*, pp. 131f. As the word גֶּבֶר 'a male', 'a man', corresponds to the Greek ἀνήρ, to the Latin *vir*, it is not necessary to replace it by גִּבּוֹר 'strong man', 'warrior' (Targ. Syr.), as Hoffmann, Beer, and Budde suggest. Even the word אִישׁ 'a man' has sometimes the connotation 'virile', 'strong' (1 K 2:2). The verb שָׁאַל 'ask' in the sense of 'question', 'interrogate' with the accusative of the person (12:7; 21:29). The imperative הוֹדִיעֵנִי 'make me to know' has been used by Job himself in addressing God (10:2; 13:23) and by Elihu in addressing Job (37:19). Invariably there was a complement indicating the object of the question. Here the *hiph'il* is used absolutely in the sense of 'instruct', 'inform'. The context obliges us to render the imperative by a future tense expressing command.

4   G ἀπάγγειλον δέ μοι, Vulg. *indica mihi*, Syr. ܚܘܢܝ 'show me' add the personal complement of הגד. For אִם־יָדַעְתָּ בִינָה, Vulg. *si habes intelligentiam*.

5   Who fixed its measurements—if you know that—
      Or who stretched a measuring line upon it?
6   On what were its bases sunk,
      Or who laid its corner-stone?

Yahweh reduces the problem to a question of origins. In order to understand the things that happen in the world and to apprehend the divine 'counsel' (v. 2), it would be necessary to have been present at the origin of things. Before everything else, God 'founds' the earth and the heavens: Is 48:13; Zec 12:1; Pr 3:19; Ps 24:2; 78:69, etc. Where was Job at the dawn of creation? Cf. 15:7, 'Are you the first man to have been born and were you brought forth before the hills?' It is then that Job might have been able to apprehend Wisdom (חָכְמָה) or Understanding (בִּינָה), for it was at that moment that these two attributes of God were principally active (15:8; 28:27; Pr 3:19). The verb הגיד means 'declare', 'inform', 'show' as the counterpart of שָׁאל 'ask'; cf. 12:7. The expression ידע בינה 'to know understanding' makes of בינה the object on which understanding is exercised, i.e. truth; cf. Is 29:24; Pr 4:1; 2 Ch 2:12. We have יודעי בינה לעתים 'those who know the truth as to the times' in 1 Ch 12:33, instead of the simple phrase יודעי העתים 'those who know the times' (Est 1:13).

5   The word קו is literally translated by G σπαρτίον and Syr. ܚܘܛܐ 'thread'. The idea of measure appears in Vulg. *lineam*, Aq. κανόνα, Symm. σχοινίον μέτρου. Targ. too freely translates מתקולתא 'balance'.

The earth is likened to a building. Mention of the laying of the foundations has been made in v. 4. It is now a question of deciding the proportions of it and creating a harmonious whole: 'who has fixed its measurements?' The *hapax* מְמַדֶּיהָ

'its measurements' comes from a word מֵמַד (cf. מֵסַב from סבב) derived from מדד 'to measure' and corresponding to the Akkadian *namandu* (for *mamandu, mamaddu*), which means 'measure'. There is no reason to change it to מוסדיה 'its foundations' (contra Mandelkern, Joüon). Equally pointless is the correction of Ehrlich, who replaces שָׂם by שֵׁם 'name' and proposes to explain ממדיה as a *pi'el* participle of מדה (= מדד) so as to translate: 'What is the name of him who measured it?' The parenthetic כִּי תֵדַע means 'if you know it' as at the end of Pr 30:4 (cf. 7:13 for the meaning of כי). On the verb נטה cf. 9:8. The expression 'to stretch a line upon...' exactly as in Zec 1:16, suggests the preliminaries of construction. The same expression will also mean to level (as with a line), to raze a building (La 2:8).

6   For אדניה, G οἱ κρίκοι (A στύλοι) αὐτῆς, Vulg. *bases illius*, Targ. סמכיהא 'its bases', 'its pedestals', Syr. ܣܘܦܝܗ̇ 'its ends'. G πεπήγασιν and Targ. טמיען 'sunk' render הטבעו more faithfully than Vulg. *solidatae sunt* and Syr. ܐܚܕܬ 'hold'. For אבן פנתה, G λίθον γωνιαῖον ἐπ' αὐτῆς.

The earth rests on pillars (9:6). The pillars have pedestals or bases: 'On what were its bases sunk?' One can go on thus *ad infinitum*. In 26:7 'God suspends the earth over the void'. The word אֶדֶן denotes the pedestal, base, plinth of a pillar, column, etc. (Ex 26:19ff., etc.; Ca 5:15). The *hoph'al* of טבע as in Pr 8:25, 'before the mountains were sunk (rooted in the ground)'. The

7   When the morning stars sang in chorus,
     And all the sons of Elohim shouted in acclamation.
8   *Who* shut in, with double doors, the sea,
     What time it burst forth, issuing from the womb?

8   מִי סָךְ (Vulg.); MT: וַיָּסֶךְ.

exact meaning would be conveyed by 'to be plunged in, dug in' (Jer 38: 22). The preposition עַל instead of בְּ (Jer 38: 22) to suggest that the pedestals must be placed 'on' something. Contrasted with the foundations which are sunk deep in the earth is the 'corner-stone' which crowns the edifice and which is also called 'head of the corner' (Ps 118: 22). In Jer 51: 26 a careful distinction is made between 'the stone for the corner' and the 'stone for the foundations'. The verb ירה 'to throw' in the sense of 'laying' the first or the last stone. In Assyrian *nadû* 'to throw' is used with *uššê* 'foundations' as its complement to connote *fundamenta jacere*. The meaning of the verb has been broadened with the result that to ירה has been assigned a vaguer connotation, for example in Gn 31: 51, where it is a question of 'erecting' a mound.

7   Syr. כַּד and G ὅτε ἐγενήθησαν (A ἐγενήθη) have perhaps read בְּרֹא instead of בְּרָן. For בְּנֵי אֱלֹהִים, G ἄγγελοί μου, Targ. כָּתֵי מַלְאֲכַיָּא 'angelic hosts', Syr. כַּד פֿלאכֿ־ל 'sons of angels'; cf. 1: 6.

It is to the sound of fanfares and trumpets that a new building is opened (Zec 4: 7; Ezr 3: 10). Since man has not yet been created, it is the stars which witness the creation of the earth and 'sing in chorus'. The verb רָנַן 'extol', 'sing', whence רְנָנָה (3: 7; 20: 5). The adverb יַחַד 'together' to indicate the unison of voices: 'as a choir', 'in chorus'. The stars of the morning, as we had the

stars of dawn (3: 9) are placed in parallel with the 'sons of God', which are the angels (cf. 1: 6). Cf. Ps 148: 2-3, where the angels, the sun, the moon, and 'all the stars of light' are in turn invited to re-echo the praise of God. The infinitive construction is continued by an imperfect with the *waw* consecutive (cf. 33: 23-26c). The verb הֵרִיעַ means 'to shout in acclamation' (30: 5). Parallelism between רָנַן and הֵרִיעַ recurs in Is 44: 23 and Zeph 3: 14.

8   Instead of וַיָּסֶךְ (Syr., Targ.), read as וָאֶסֹךְ by G ἔφραξα, the original text is reflected in Vulg. *quis conclusit*? (cf. inf.). By haplography, Syr. reads דַּלְתֵי יָם 'the gates of the sea' instead of בִדְלָתַיִם יָם. Vulg. renders מֵרֶחֶם by *quasi de vulva*. At the close, Syr. translates בְּשׂוּמוֹ (instead of בְּשׂוּמִי of v. 9).

A new description begins. After the creation of the earth, that of the sea. The opening וַיָּסֶךְ seems to make of the sentence a direct sequel to v. 7b: 'and he has shut in'. But the subject is not made explicit. We should at least need 'and I have shut in', as the Septuagint has understood. If we compare v. 4a and vv. 5-7, we note that v. 8b and vv. 9-11 are the adverbial clauses dependent on a main interrogative clause whose verb was in the perfect (cf. v. 5). Instead of וַיָּסֶךְ we read מִי סָךְ (cf. Vulg.) with Merx, Wright, etc. On the verb סוּךְ or שׂוּךְ, cf. 1: 10 and 3: 23. We have the same construction as in Hos 2: 8. The dual of דֶּלֶת is meant to suggest the two leaves of the door locked

9   When I made a stormcloud its garment,
     And a thick dark cloud its swaddling band.
10   When I *imposed* on it my bounds,
     I *shattered* bolt and doors,

10   Transpose וָאֶשְׁבֹּר and וָאָשִׂים.

together by the bolt (v. 10). Hence we may translate the 1st hemistich: 'Who shut in, with double doors, the sea?' The sea is thought of as bursting out of the soil. The verb גיח 'spring forth', 'burst forth' (40: 23), whence גִּיחוֹן, the name of a spring (1 K 1: 33, etc.) and a river (Gn 2: 13). The proposition מֵרֶחֶם יֵצֵא 'it issues forth from the womb' is juxtaposed to the infinitive phrase to mark the concomitance of the two actions. What is in question is the womb of the earth; cf. 1: 21. The sea is likened to a new-born child (v. 9) who must be controlled.

9   Syr. ܥܒܕ 'he has made' adds a verb to replace בְּשׂוּמִי which is transferred to v. 8. G ὀμίχλη δὲ αὐτὴν ἐσπαργάνωσα (Jerome *et nebula obvolvi illud*) paraphrases the 2nd hemistich. Similarly Vulg. *et caligine illud quasi pannis infantiae obvolverem* (cf. *quasi de vulva* in v. 8).

The child needs to be swaddled. The comparison of v. 8b is here extended: 'when I made a stormcloud its garment, and a thick dark cloud its swaddling band'. Same construction as in v. 8b (cf. v. 7a). Alongside the general term לְבוּשׁ 'clothing' (24: 7, 10, etc.), the author here takes care to use the more precise term חֲתֻלָּה 'swaddling band'. The meaning of this *hapax* is not in doubt, in the light of the *puʿal* and the *hophʿal* of חתל, which mean 'to be swaddled' in Ezk 16: 4. A substantive חִתּוּל 'bandage' figures in Ezk 30: 21. The root חתל and its derivatives

have persisted in post-Biblical Hebrew with the same meanings; cf. *Thesaurus* of Ben-Yehuda, IV, pp. 1824f. and p. 1818. The swaddling band of the new-born babe is the dark stormcloud, עֲרָפֶל (22: 13b).

10   Syr. renders by ܥܒܕ 'and he made' the words וָאֶשְׁבֹּר and וָאָשִׂים. G ἐθέμην δὲ αὐτῇ ὅρια and Vulg. *circumdedi illud terminis meis* interpret rightly in accordance with the expected meaning. Syr. ܩܝܡܐ 'pact' omits the suffix of חֻקִּי (cf. G). Targ. explains the 2nd hemistich: 'and I have placed shores like bolts and doors'.

V. 9 described a circumstance parallel to v. 8b. Here we have the real sequel to the passage of description begun in v. 8. The sea has been depicted as a new-born babe issuing from the maternal womb and covered with swaddling bands. It is going to become an adult being capable of receiving commands (v. 11) and of becoming subject to a law. If the 2nd hemistich, 'and I placed a bolt and doors', offers no difficulty, it is almost impossible to interpret the 1st, 'and I broke on it (or 'against it') my boundary'. Nothing in fact justifies us in assigning to שבר the meaning 'to trace', 'to mark out' postulated by Perles (cf. Gesenius-Buhl, s.v. שבר). The word חֹק 'decree' (23: 4) 'limit' (14: 5, 13; 28: 26) can hardly be reconciled with שבר 'to break'. It seems clear that 'my limit' indicates the check which God imposes on the waters of the sea which are to be stayed at a particular point of the shore (v. 11). Modern critics correct

11   And I said: 'To this point shall you come and no farther,
      Here the pride of your waves will be *destroyed*.'

11   יִשְׁתַּבֵּר גָּאוֹן ;MT: יָשִׁית בגאון.

אֶשְׁבֹּר to אָשִׁית 'I placed' (Merx, Wright), אֶשְׁכֹּר (for אסכר) 'I closed' (Hoffmann), אֶשְׁטֹר 'I inscribed' (Beer), אֶשְׁמֹר 'I kept' (Ehrlich). Duhm adopts a hypothesis formulated by Dillmann and proposes חֻקּוֹ 'its limit' instead of חֻקִּי. But the difficulty presented by שׁבר remains. We ourselves believe that there has simply been a transposition of וָאָשִׂים and וָאֶשְׁבֹּר. If we restore ואשׂים to its original position, we obtain as the 1st hemistich: 'I imposed on it my bounds': the verb שׂים with עַל (34: 23; 37: 15). The word of God, as will be made explicit in v. 11, suffices to contain the sea. Hence there is no more need of the doors mentioned in v. 8. Thus is explained the 2nd hemistich (after the transposition of ואשׁבר): 'and I shattered bolt and doors!' Notice the use of שׁבר with the complement בריח in Am 1: 5; Jer 51: 30; La 2: 9, and the Assyrian idiom *sikkura ašabbir* 'I will break the bolt', parallel to *amaḫḫaṣ daltum* 'I will burst open the door' (*Choix de textes*, pp. 328-329, l. 17).

11 The versions have been embarrassed by ישית בגאון of the 2nd hemistich. G ἀλλ' ἐν σεαυτῇ συντρι-βήσεταί σου τὰ κύματα and Vulg. *et hic confringes tumentes fluctus tuos* seem indeed to have been thinking of the verb שׁבר (cf. inf.). G ἐν σεαυτῇ may spring from בגוך, instead of בגאון. Targ. תְּשַׁוֵּי 'you will place' and Syr. 'you will remain' are in agreement with Vulg. in reading a verb in the 2nd person singular.
    The word of God will be the sole bridle to the angry, unleashed waves:

'And I said: To this point shall you come and no farther!' The opening וַיֹּאמֶר, introducing a quotation, is not included in the prosody. It is a sort of insertion (33: 24, 27). It should not, however, be suppressed (contra Bickell). Still less should we cut out תָּבוֹא, which is essential on account of וְלֹא תֹסִיף (contra Duhm). The expression ולא תסיף 'and you will not continue' as in 20: 9; 40: 5. The orthography וּפֹא is meant for וּפֹה; cf. אֵפוֹא (9: 24) alongside אֵיפֹה (4: 7; 38: 4) and אֵפוֹ (17: 15; 19: 6, 23; 24: 25). It is misunderstanding the translation of G to imagine וּבְכֹה 'and this way' (Beer); cf. sup. Besides, בכה would mean 'thus' (1 K 22: 20). The end should be translated: 'and He will put to the pride of your waves', which is odd. A complement is supplied to יָשִׁית, namely the word חֹק of v. 10, and a comparison is made with 14: 13. But the complement is too distant to be understood here. Furthermore, it is חֻקִּי 'my boundary', and not simply חֹק, in v. 10. The indirect object ought to be introduced by ל", as in 14: 13. And what is the subject of יָשִׁית? The translation *et hic ponatur terminus contra elationem fluctuum tuorum* (Rosenmüller) cannot really be extracted from the Hebrew. Two excellent corrections have been suggested. One, that of Ewald, is based on G and Vulg. (indirectly) and consists in reading יִשָּׁבֵר (instead of ישית ב"): 'and here the pride of your waves will be broken'. Cf. the use of גאון as a complement of שׁבר in Lv 26: 19. The other correction, which we owe to Bickell, replaces

12   Have you ever, since your life began, commanded the morning,
      And made the dawn to know its place?
13   That it might seize the corners of the earth,
      And that the wicked might be shaken from off it.

ישית ב'' by יִשְׁבֹּת 'and here the pride
of your waves will cease'. Cf. the use
of גאון as complement of the *hiph'il*
of שבת in Is 13: 11; Ezk 7: 24. Gray
proposes יִשָּׁבֵת, following Ezk 30: 18;
33: 28, where גאון is the subject of
the *niph'al* of שבת. We think that
a letter has dropped out after ב,
namely ר, which resembles ב in
ancient writing. Hence we read
יִשְׁתַּבֵּר (for ישית ב''), *hithpa'el* of
שבר with metathesis (cf. יִשְׁתַּמֵּר
from שמר). We do not change the
order of the consonants, whereas
the readings ישבר and ישבת eliminate or transpose the *taw*.

12 G ἢ ἐπὶ σοῦ does not imply
הַמֵּמֶּך instead of הַמֵּמִיך (contra
Bickell, Beer). It is a Hellenism:
'have you, in your time?' (Gray).
Vulg. interprets הַמֵּמִיך by *numquid
post ortum tuum*, while 2nd Targ.
paraphrases: 'were you in existence
in the days of Genesis?' G συντέταχα
φέγγος (C φθέγγος) πρωινόν reads
צִוִּיתִי instead of צִוִּית. The *qerê*
יָדַעְתָּ הַשַּׁחַר gives the original reading which later became ידעתה שחר
(*kethîb*). G ἑωσφόρος δὲ ἴδεν τὴν
ἑαυτοῦ τάξιν reads יָדְעָה in the *qal*,
instead of יָדַעְתָּ. Syr. 'do you know
what is the place of the dawn?' (cf.
2nd Targ.) also reads the *qal* instead
of the *pi'el*.

Vv. 12-15 propose to depict the
emergence of the day, not merely
at the dawn of creation, but at each
successive dawn. The idiom מִיָּמֶיךָ
'from your days' is a good Hebrew
expression to signify 'never in your
life' (1 S 25: 28; 1 K 1: 6): 'Have
you, since your life began, commanded the morning?' The morning, like

the dawn, is personified. Both receive orders and docilely follow the
instructions given them. The dawn
has eyelids (3: 9; 41: 10). It is
capable of knowing the position
allocated to it, but it is God alone
who can instruct it: 'Have you made
the dawn to know its place?' The
pi'el of ידע with a double accusative.
It seems indeed that in Ps 104:19b
we should read יַדַּע (with Aq. and
Symm.): 'He makes the sun to
know its setting.' In Ec 1: 5, the
sun longs to reach 'its place',
מְקוֹמוֹ as here. At the moment
decreed by God, not only the stars,
but also the meteors have their place
marked out in the heavens.

13 Vulg. continues the interrogation of v. 12, rendering לאחז by
et tenuisti concutiens and וינערו by
et excussisti. 2nd Targ. specifies that
it is an allusion to the land of Israel.
For וינערו, G ἐκτινάξαι.

It is evident that לֶאֱחֹז 'in order
to seize' continues v. 12b and
denotes the action that is to be accomplished by the dawn. God
informs it of its place 'that it might
seize the corners of the earth'. The
earth is imagined as a carpet whose
'wings' (כַּנְפוֹת; cf. G πτερύγων) are
the four corners (cf. Comm. on
37: 3). On this carpet the wicked
indulge in their evil courses during
the night (24: 13-17). The dawn
arrives and in an instant seizes the
four corners of the carpet and shakes
it. In English the verb 'to shake'
can have as its complement the
object that is shaken (shake a
carpet) or the thing of which one
rids the object by shaking the latter
(to shake off the dust). It is with

14   It becomes like sealed clay,
     And it is *dyed* like a garment.

14   וְתִצָּבַע; MT: ויתיצבו.

the latter implication that the Hebrew verb is used here. The wicked are like the dust on the carpet which is the earth, they are shaken off it. Hence the *niph'al*, with, as subject, the things that are cast away by a shaking. The indirect complement will be the object itself which is thus cleaned. In Jg 16: 20 the *niph'al* of נער is used without complement: 'to shake one's self'. In Is 52: 2 the *hithpa'el* has as its complement מעפר 'from the dust'; this time it is a question of shaking the object to free it *from* dust. The letter ע is left suspended in רְשָׁעִים here and in v. 15. Two other cases of suspended letters are the ע of מיער (Ps 80: 14) and the נ of מנשה (Jg 18: 30). These letters have been added subsequently and have not found a place in the body of the word. It would indeed be a pity to delete v. 13b which is so vividly expressive. No serious reason is given by Hoffmann or by Duhm. The latter amuses himself by seeing in vv. 12-15 the fusion of two tetrastichs, one of which would include 12, 13a, 14a and would be original, the other having been later added in the margin (13b, 14b, 15). There is not the slightest shadow of proof offered for this fantasy. It will be seen from the commentary that the hemistichs are perfectly well joined to each other.

14 G reads חיתם for חותם, whence its 1st hemistich: ἢ σὺ λαβὼν γῆν πηλὸν ἔπλασας ζῶον. Instead of γῆν, G(C) γῆς (Sah., Jerome *terrae*). Syr. 'their bodies' seems to read גותם (Baumann). The two Targums render חמר חותם by טינא חותמא; Vulg. *lutum signaculum*. It is difficult to see how G has been able to derive

from the MT its 2nd hemistich: καὶ λαλητὸν αὐτὸν ἔθου ἐπὶ γῆς. The 1st Targ. renders לבוש by כסו זהים 'dirty garment', the 2nd by כסו סריק 'empty garment'.

Jewish exegesis has seen in this verse a reference to death and resurrection, the 1st hemistich suggesting the earthy colour of the corpse and the 2nd the aspect it assumes when it rises to life again with its same clothes (cf. Rashi and the anonymous commentary edited by Wright and Hirsch). It is difficult to extract this interpretation from the literal meaning of the Hebrew. By far the commonest explanation is that which regards the 1st hemistich as depicting the awakening of nature in the first rays of dawn, the objects then assuming their distinct contours, like clay under the seal. The 2nd hemistich would thus represent the adornment of the earth in the light of day. With this interpretation in view, recourse is had to subtle paraphrases: 'To give to the earth a shape, as with clay under the seal, to deck it with light as a garment' (Le Hir); 'When it appears, the world is transformed like sealed earth; the universe discloses itself clad in a rich vesture' (Renan). It is clear that the subject of תִּתְהַפֵּךְ is 'the earth' of v. 13. The particle כְּ before the substantive gives to the verb 'to turn' the meaning of 'become like' (cf. the *niph'al* of הפך in 30: 21). Cf. the use of שׁוּב before כ״ in וישב בשרו כבשר 'and his flesh became again like the flesh . . . .' (2 K 5: 14); similarly for סבב 'to turn' in יסוב כל־הארץ כערבה 'the whole land will become as a plain' (Zec 14: 10). Hence the 1st hemistich should be translated: 'it becomes like sealed clay'. Now, sealed clay was a technical term in

15   Then from the wicked their light is withheld,
      And the raised arm is broken.
16   Have you reached the springs of the sea,
      And have you walked in the deeps of the abyss,

the ancient world the meaning of which was very precise. Targ. has translated טינא חותמא, showing clearly the equivalence of טִין, in Hebrew טִיט (for ṭînt), and of חֹמֶר. In Arabic ṭîn maḥtûm 'terra sigillata' denotes the lozenges of Lemnos clay which were used in ancient medicine. The following passage of Pliny gives the reasons for this description: *Palman enim Lemniae* (to the clay of Lemnos) *dabant, minio proxima haec est, multum antiquis celebrata, cum insula in qua nascitur. Nec nisi signata venumdabatur: unde et sphragidem appellavere* (Nat. hist., XXXV, 14, 1 in ed. of Littré). Hence we may identify the 'clay of seal' or the 'sealed clay' of our verse with the ṭîn maḥtûm of the Arabs, the σφραγίς of the Greeks, the *lemnia* of Pliny. One of its characteristics was its red colour which made it resemble *minium*. The pink hues of the earth at sunrise justify the comparison: the earth becomes like sealed clay! It goes without saying that 'like a garment' in the 2nd hemistich should be applied to a similar comparison. The plural וְיִתְיַצְּבוּ 'they stand forth' can only with difficulty stand beside 'like a garment'. Ehrlich and Beer (ed. Kittel) have recognised that the distorted verb of the MT was צבע 'to dye'. The falling out of the final ע (cf. the suspended ע in vv. 13 and 15) has transformed וְתִצָּבַע into ויתיצבו. Our interpretation of the 1st hemistich is confirmed by this correction which enables one to translate: 'and it is dyed like a garment'. The allusion is to the colouring which the dawn lends to objects. In order the more easily to delete v. 14b, Duhm accepts the correction of Hoffmann,

who reads לָבֹשׁ 'with shame' instead of לִבוּשׁ 'garment'! But v. 14b joins quite naturally to 14a. No more than in the case of v. 13 can we find any trace of the juxtaposition of incongruous elements.

15 For וימנע, G ἀφεῖλας δέ (cf. ἔπλασας in v. 14). G renders אורם by τὸ φῶς. For תשבר, G συνέτριψας, Aq. and Symm. συντρίψεις.

Vv. 13-14 have described the effect of dawn on the earth. Here now is the suggestion of its effect on human beings, an effect foreshadowed in v. 13b. The wicked regard the darkness as their light; for them night is day (cf. Comm. on 24:17). Hence when the light of dawn appears, it is as if the light of the wicked vanished: 'and from the wicked their light is withheld'. Construction of מנע in the *niph'al* as in Jl 1:13. Cf. the *qal* in 22:7; 31:16. The 2nd hemistich 'and the raised arm is broken' recalls 31:22, where the *niph'al* תִּשָּׁבֵר has as its subject וְאֶזְרֹעִי 'and my arm'. The arm upraised instead of the hand (Ex 14:8; Nu 15:30; 33:3); the hand and the arm are the seat of strength and violence (*L'Emploi métaphorique*, pp. 139f.).

16 For נבכי־ים, G πηγὴν θαλάσσης, Vulg. *profunda maris* (cf. Syr. 'the depths of the sea'), Targ. מערבלי סגור ימא 'the swirling eddies of the bounds of the sea'. For חקר תהום, G ἴχνεσιν ἀβύσσου, Vulg. *novissimis abyssi*. Syr. and Targ. transcribe תהום by תהומא. Targ. renders חקר by פשפוש 'exploration' (etymological sense), Syr. by ܩܠܬܐ 'foundations'.

17   Have the gates of Death been revealed to you,
      And have you seen the gates of the Shadow?
18   Have you considered the vast stretches of the earth?
      Say so, if you know its entire extent!

A new series of ironical questions. It is not only the origins of things (earth, sea, daylight) which elude human beings. They cannot penetrate to the depths of the abysses (16-17) or the confines of the world (18-20). The sequence of ideas is very logical, and one wonders why Duhm upsets the whole passage by placing 19-20 before 16:17. The *hapax* נִבְכֵי means the 'sources' (cf. G), as we have seen in connection with מַבְּכֵי (28:11). The sources of the sea are the depths from whence the water gushes forth incessantly to fill that immense reservoir. Cf. 'the roots of the sea' in 36:30. The word חֵקֶר denotes the object to discover the nature of which research is made; the nature of a thing, its basis and root (cf. Comm. on 11:7). There is parallelism between יָם 'the sea' and תְּהוֹם 'the abyss' (28:14). תהום will recur in v. 30. The *hithpa'el* of הלך has ב' before the name of a place where one walks (1:7; 2:2), instead of the accusative (22:14b).

17   G adds φόβῳ (marked by obelus in Syro-hex.) after σοί (= לְךָ). For ושערי צלמות, Vulg. *et ostia tenebrosa*, Targ. 'and the gates of the shadow of death in Gehenna'. G πυλωροὶ δὲ ᾅδου ἰδόντες σε ἔπτηξαν; reads שֹׁעֲרֵי instead of שַׁעֲרֵי and regards תראה as a causative of ירא.

At the bottom of the abyss is found the entrance to the kingdom of the dead, which is essentially 'infernal' in the etymological sense of the word (cf. Comm. on 7:9). After the reply of the sea and the abyss in 28:14, we had that of Abaddon and Death (28:22). The gates of Death

give entrance to Sheol. They are mentioned in Ps 9:14; 107:18. The שערי שאול 'gates of Sheol' recur in Is 38:10; cf. the πύλας ᾅδου in Wis 16:13. The realm of the Shades is a city enclosed by gates well known to the Babylonians (*RB*, 1907, pp. 65ff.). The *niph'al* of גלה in the sense of 'to be shown, revealed'; cf. the *pi'el* in 12:22; 20:27. To the gates of Death correspond the 'gates of the Shadow', the word צלמות denoting especially the shade of the Underworld (10:21f.). The difference in the complement permits us to keep the two שַׁעֲרֵי, for we have here compound words שערי מות and שערי צלמות. The 2nd hemistich merely dwells on the idea expressed in the 1st. The gates are shown, the visitor sees them. Hence it is not necessary to vocalise שֹׁעֲרֵי 'the gatekeepers' (following G) as Duhm proposes. The phrase 'to see the gatekeepers' seems too insipid. If it is a question of human persons, one accosts them and speaks to them. Note that Vulg., Syr., and Targ. have not hesitated to retain 'the gates' and that G has modified the meaning of the final verb in order to animate somewhat 'the gatekeepers'. The same repetition and before the same verb תֵּרָאֶה recurs in v. 22b.

18   Syr. puts at the beginning of v. 18 the word תראה (not translated in v. 17) and does not translate התבוננת. G and Vulg. do not render עד. For ארץ, G τῆς ὑπ' οὐρανόν (cf. 1:7), Targ. 'land of the Garden of Eden'. Syr. transforms the verse completely by putting כלה of the close in the place of עד and trans-

19   In what avenue dwells the light,
     And darkness, what is its place?

20   That you may lead them to their sphere,
     And perceive the pathways to their home?

21   You know it, for you were already born,
     And the number of your days is considerable!

ferring הגד אם־ידעת to the beginning of v. 19. For הגד, G ἀνάγγειλον δή μοι, Vulg. *indica mihi*, Syr. ܚܘܐ; cf. v. 4. G πόση τίς ἐστιν vaguely paraphrases אם ידעת כלה.

Extent, as well as depth (v. 17), escapes the investigation of man: 'Have you considered the vast stretches of the earth?' The verb התבונן 'give heed to', 'reflect upon', with עד before the complement (32:12), to mark the difficulty of the task. The substantive רחב 'breadth', 'expanse' (36:16), in the plural 'stretches'. The 2nd hemistich reproduces v. 4b, with כלה instead of בינה. In Ps 139:4 we have the last two words יָדַעְתָּ כֻלָּה 'you know it wholly', which confirms our text remarkably and argues against a change from כלה to מלה 'word' (Graetz), גבלה 'its frontier' (Budde), כמה 'how much' (Duhm, following the paraphrase of G). Cf. also 34:13b. Hence we translate simply: 'Say so, if you know its entire extent.' As in v. 4, Job is invited to show forth his knowledge. If he has traversed the whole earth, he must know in what secret recess the light and darkness are concealed and whence in turn they come to manifest themselves to the world (vv. 19-20).

19 G paraphrases אי־זה הדרך by ποίᾳ δὲ γῇ; cf. Vulg. *in qua via lux habitet?* Syr. begins by הגד אם־ידעת of v. 18.

The interrogative אי־זה as in 28:12, 20 (cf. 2:2). The phrase אי־זה הדרך followed by a verb in

personal mode means: 'by what way?' (1 K 13:12; 2 K 3:8). We shall meet it again in v. 24. We can understand very well: 'in what avenue dwells the light?', i.e. in what direction, by what way? The 2nd hemistich evokes 28:12b, 20b. חשך is given prominence by its position, and is contrasted with אור at the end of the parallel member.

20 Syr. repeats at the beginning 'if you know' (18-19) and leaves untranslated תבין, תקחנו. G εἰ ἀγάγοις με reads תקחני. Vulg. *ut ducas unumquodque ad terminos suos* makes explicit the suffix of תקחנו.

The singular suffixes represent at the same time אור and חשך, and this fact obliges us to translate them by plurals. The verb לקח 'to take' with אל before the name of the place, means 'lead', 'carry to' (Est 2:8, 16). We find the same meaning with אל before the name of a person (2 K 2:20). Most moderns have accepted the correction of Hoffmann, who replaces תָּבִין by תְּבִיאֵנּוּ (defective writing תבין) so as to translate as 'you introduce it' (*hiph'il* of בוא). But the versions all have the verb בין. Now, in 28:23 we have אלהים הבין דרכה 'Elohim has discerned the way of it', and it so happens that v. 19 has asked the question: 'in what avenue dwells the light?' V. 20b replies ironically: 'that you may discern the pathways to their home'.

21 For ידעת, G οἶδα, instead of οἶδας which is found in א, Syro-hex., Jerome *scis*. An inversion of

22   Have you penetrated to the reservoirs of the snow,
     And have you seen the reservoirs of the hail,
23   Which I have stored up for times of trouble,
     For the days of battle and war?
24   In what path are the *mists* dispersed,
     And is the east wind scattered over the earth?

24   אֵד (cf. G); MT: אוֹר.

the words כִּי־אָז furnishes Vulg.
with *sciebas tunc quod nasciturus
esse*? Targ. and Syr. treat ידעת as
an interrogative.

The irony becomes still more
evident: 'You know it, for you were
already born and the number of
your days is considerable!' Already
at that time, that is to say, in the
first days, the time when the course
of the world was ordered (4-11).
This is the complement to 'where
were you?' of v. 4. Cf. the ironical
question of Eliphaz (15: 7): 'Were
you the first man born and were
you brought forth before the hills?'
The plural רַבִּים by attraction (cf.
Comm. on 31: 21).

22 Syr. interprets תראה by an
impersonal construction 'are visible
to you'. Targ. sees here an allusion
to the snow which must torment the
wicked in Gehenna and to the hail
which was hurled at Pharaoh and
the Egyptians (in v. 23).

Duhm would replace the second
אוֹצְרוֹת by אוֹצְרֵי 'treasurers'. But
what would the 'treasurers of the
hail' mean exactly? A comparison
with v. 17b proves that we must
keep the repetition of the word (G,
Vulg., Syr.). The opening הֲבָאתָ as
in v. 16, the end תִּרְאֶה as in v. 17.
The word אוֹצָר designates what is
carefully stored and the place where
it is kept. It means both the treasure
and the treasury, the provisions and
the granary, the wine-cellar. Here,
as in Ps 33: 7, where God encloses
the deeps (תהומות) in אצרות, it is

a question of 'reservoirs' where the
snow and the hail are stored up for
God's disposal and used in the great
crises of history (v. 23). Even the
wind is held in reservoirs, and it is
God who brings it forth at the same
time as the rain (Ps 135: 7).

23 For אשר חשכתי, G ἀπόκειται
δέ σοι, Syr. ܘܐܝܠܝܢ 'which are
reserved'. On the interpretation of
Targ., cf. v. 22. The word צָר is
rendered by ἐχθρῶν (G), *hostis*
(Vulg.), ܐܘܠܨܢܐ 'necessity' (Syr.).

On the verb חשׂך 'spare', 'reserve',
cf. 21: 30. With לְעֶת־צָר 'for the
time of woe', cf. עתות בצרה 'time
in trouble' (Ps 9: 9; 10: 1) and especially the current idiom עֵת צָרָה
'time of distress or anguish'. The
masculine צָר as in 15: 24; 36: 16, 19.
Violent natural phenomena, such
as storms, rain, hail, are weapons in
the hand of God (Is 30: 30; Sir
39: 29-31). Hail especially is an
instrument of divine vengeance,
whether against the Egyptians (Ex
9: 22-6) or against malefactors in
general (Is 28: 17). Hailstones are
a mark of divine intervention in the
battle against the Amorite kings
(Jos 10: 11). Hail is an element
in the theophanies (Is 30: 30-1;
Ps 18: 13-14). The expression קְרָב
וּמִלְחָמָה as in Assyrian *qablu û
tâhazu* 'battle and war'.

24 G πόθεν δὲ ἐκπορεύεται summarises אי־זה הדרך יחלק. For אוֹר, G
πάχνη, which renders כְּפֹר in v. 29.

25   Who has cleft a channel for the torrential rains,
      And a way for the rumble of the thunder,

The word קדים, correctly rendered by Targ. רוח קדומא 'east wind', is interpreted as νότος (G), *aestus* (Vulg.), simply ܘܣܘ 'wind' (Syr.). For ארץ, G τὴν ὑπ' οὐρανόν; cf. v. 18.

The 1st hemistich is strongly reminiscent of v. 19a. The only difference lies in the verb יְחֻלָּ., used here instead of יֹשְׁכן. The meaning of the text as it stands is: 'In what path is light distributed?' But light was the theme in v. 19. The atmospheric phenomena which follow are the east wind, rainstorms, thunder, which are not naturally coupled with light. Since Ewald, a certain number of authors have replaced אוֹר by רוּח 'wind', parallel to קָדים (15:2; cf. Merx, Wright, Budde, etc.). But it is not easy to see how רוּח should have been transformed into אוֹר. In the light of G πάχνη, Siegfried reads כְּפֹר 'hoar frost', which however would be an anticipation of v. 29. Beer proposes קִיטוֹר. in the sense of 'mist', 'fog' (Ps 119:83). Closer to the text, and in our opinion more probable, is the reading אֵד 'mist' (36:27), proposed by Hoffmann and accepted by Bickell, Duhm, and Hontheim. We have met אורו for אֵדוֹ (cf. Theod.) in 36:30. The Greek πάχνη which translates קיטור 'mist', 'fog' in Ps 119:83 may have been chosen to render אֵד. The *niph'al* of חלק 'to be divided' with the connotation of 'to be dispersed' when it is a question of something which cannot be cut into pieces. After the fog comes the east wind, which brings dryness and drought (cf. Comm. on 15:2). No one can track the path followed by the wind (Ec 11:5). The *hiph'il* of פוץ (37:11) is to be taken in the intransitive sense: 'to be shed,

scattered' (Ex 5:12). Purely arbitrary is the change from קדים to קָרים 'cold waters' postulated by Duhm.

25 Syr. omits the 1st hemistich. For לשטף, G ὑετῷ λάβρῳ, Vulg. *vehementissimo imbri*, Targ. (1st and 3rd) לשטפא, Targ. (2nd) לשטפא דתהומא 'for the inundation of the abyss'. For תעלה, G ῥύσιν, Vulg. *cursum*, Aq. and Theod. ὑδραγωγόν, Targ. (1st) קובתא 'reservoir', (2nd) חריצי מיא 'ditches of waters', (3rd) מרזבא דמיא 'gutter of waters' (cf. Comm. on 6:17). For לחזיז קלות, G κυδοιμῶν (but Jerome *vocibus tempestatis*; cf. Symm. εἰς ψόφον βροντῆς, Aq. εἰς κτύπον φωνῶν), Vulg. *sonantis tonitrui*. The three Targums interpret חזיז קלות as referring to the clouds which pour out rain to the accompaniment of thunder. Syr. reads חזיז וקלות.

The 2nd hemistich reproduces 28:26b verbatim. The parallel word to חֲזִיז קֹלות 'rumble of the thunder' was מָטָר 'rain' in 28:26. Here we have שֶׁטֶף (from שטף 'to flood' 14:19) to denote inundation, but also the rainstorms whose lashing rain carries everything with it; cf. גֶּשֶׁם שֶׁטֶף 'torrential rain' in Ezk 13:11, 13; 38:22. The meaning of תְּעָלָה (Arabic تلعة 'stream') is 'gutter', whether it is a small artificial ditch (1 K 18:32, 35, 38) or a true aqueduct (2 K 18:17; 20:20). In Ps 65:10 the rain is described as פֶּלֶג אֱלֹהִים 'stream of God'. The word פלג 'stream', 'brook' (cf. 20:17; 29:6) comes from the root פלג 'divide', 'cut up' (Gn 10:25), the *pi'el* of which is used here in the sense of 'cutting out' a channel.

26   To cause it to rain on a land uninhabited by men,
     On a desert place where there are no human beings,
27   To water the devastated and desolate land,
     And to make grass spring up *from the steppe*?
28   Has the rain a father?
     Or who has begotten the drops of dew?

27   מֹצִיָה; MT: מצא.

26 Vv. 26-7, absent from Sah., marked with asterisk in Jerome, Syrohex., Colb., Cod. 248, did not exist in G. The present text is derived from Theod. For לֹא־אָדָם בּוֹ, Vulg. *ubi nullus mortalium commoratur*.

The desert is uninhabited and uninhabitable. And yet it rains there. How are we to understand this anomaly? Man himself certainly would not think of bestowing rain on lands that are barren and uncultivated. Once more, we are faced by a mystery and marvel of nature. The opening with לְ, here and in v. 27, as we had לְאֵחֹז in v. 13. The *hiph'il* of מטר was used figuratively in 20:23. Here we have the literal meaning. With אֶרֶץ לֹא־אִישׁ 'a land without man' cf. the English expression 'no man's land'. Here לֹא־אִישׁ has a meaning similar to לֹא־דֶרֶךְ in 'trackless desert' of 12:24. On the other hand, in Is 31:8 לֹא־אִישׁ 'no man' is a periphrasis for God. The description of the desert 'where there is no man' is much more concise than in Jer 2:6. The relative אֲשֶׁר is implied and understood after מִדְבָּר; cf. 3:3a.

27 On the text of G, cf. v. 26. For שֹׁאָה וּמְשֹׁאָה, Theod. ἄβατον καὶ ἀοίκητον, Vulg. *inviam et desolatam*, Targ. רגושא ואתרגושתא 'noise and tumult', but Syr. ܟܠ ܚܒ̈ܝ 'all bushes'. For מֹצָא דֶשֶׁא, literally rendered by Theod., Syr., Targ., we have *herbas virentes* in Vulg.

Continuation of the description begun in v. 26; to לְהַמְטִיר correspond לְהַצְמִיחַ and לְהַשְׂבִּיעַ. The *hiph'il* of שׂבע 'satisfy', 'sate' (9:8), with the shade of meaning 'water', 'irrigate', following the meaning of the *qal* in Pr 30:16, 'the land is not irrigated (שׂבעה) with water'. On שֹׁאָה וּמְשֹׁאָה 'devastation and desolation', description of the desert, cf. 30:3. Following the use of מוֹצָא in 28:1, we should have to translate the 2nd hemistich: 'to make to blossom the place where grass grows'. But מֹצָא דֶשֶׁא 'place where grass springs up' is no longer a periphrasis for the desert. It then becomes a question of the countryside in general. It has been proposed to read צָמֵא instead of מֹצָא, the word צָמֵא 'thirsty' (v. 5) having a possible connotation 'the ground of thirst', that is to say, the desert (Is 44:3); cf. Wright, Budde, Duhm, Driver, etc. The meaning thus becomes: 'and to make grass grow in the desert place'. A comparison with 30:3, where the word צִיָּה 'steppe' has as its parallel שֹׁאָה וּמְשֹׁאָה, inclines us to prefer the reading of Beer, מֹצִיָה instead of מֹצָא.

28 G τίς ἐστιν ὑετοῦ πατήρ and Vulg. *quis est pluviae pater* translate less literally than Symm., Aq., Targ., Syr., which adhere strictly to the formula 'is there to...?' For אֶגְלֵי, G βώλους, Vulg. *stillas*, Targ. רסיסי 'drops', Syr. ܢܦ̈ܠܬܐ 'drops'. Syr.

29   From whose womb has the ice emerged?
        And the hoar frost of the heavens, who has given it birth?
30   The waters are frozen hard as stone,
        And the face of the deep becomes a solid mass!

transfers טל to the beginning of v. 29.

In order to conform to the demands of their strophic system, Bickell and Duhm cut out this verse which is so simple and expressive. Beer also wonders, in the edition of Kittel, if this v. 28 is not simply a variant of v. 29. But v. 29 alludes to the mother, v. 28 to the father. Note the distinction between the *hiph'il* הוֹלִיד 'to beget' (v. 28) and the *qal* יָלַד 'to give birth (to a child)' (v. 29). The two verses are inseparable. It is quite arbitrary to eliminate either. The 1st hemistich should be translated: 'Has the rain a father?' Cf. the construction of 28: 1a. The *hapax* אֶגְלֵי is interpreted by 'drops' in the versions, with the exception of G, which translated by 'clods'. But the dew is deposited not in the shape of clods of earth, but rather in drops. By confusion with אגני, it has been proposed to see in אֶגְלֵי טַל 'pools of dew'. But this meaning would hardly be suitable for the complement of הוֹלִיד 'has begotten'.

29 For כְּפֹר, G πάχνην (cf. v. 24a), Syr. ممصم} 'azure'. G renders שמים by ἐν οὐρανῷ, Vulg. by *de coelo*.

After the father (v. 28), the mother. The phrase 'comes forth out of the belly', as in 1: 21; 3: 11. The belly is the maternal womb (ibid.). The word קֶרַח has sometimes the meaning of 'hail' (Ps 147: 17). Here, because of v. 30, it retains its normal meaning of 'ice' (6: 16; 37: 10). The word כְּפֹר denotes the hoar frost, which was regarded as congealed dew (Ex 16: 14). The hoar frost like the snow is sent from the heavens by God Himself (Ps 147: 16). Manna is compared to it (Ex 16: 14), salt is compared to it (Sir 43: 19). V. 30 will show the effects produced by the frost.

30 G ἣ καταβαίνει ὥσπερ ὕδωρ ῥέον; deviates from the literal meaning of the 1st hemistich. Vulg. *in similitudinem lapidis aquae durantur* is more faithful. For יתחבאו, Syr. ممحصم 'becoming hard' (cf. Vulg.), Targ. קרישין ומטמרין 'frozen and congealed'. For וּפְנֵי תְהוֹם, G πρόσωπον δὲ ἀσεβοῦς. The word ἀσεβοῦς is a corruption of ἀβύσσου (Compl.) which translated תהום in v. 16. For יתלכדו, G (B) τίς ἔπτηξεν, but G (א, A) τίς ἔτηξεν, which is reflected in Syro-hex. and Jerome *tabefecit*. For יתלכדו, Vulg. *constringitur*, Syr. ᵃ}ᵃᵇ 'taking', Targ. מן קורא מתאחדין 'seized by the cold'.

'The waters are frozen hard as stone', becoming ice. Hitzig has very rightly realised that the *hithpa'el* יִתְחַבָּאוּ does not belong to חבא 'to hide', but to another root חבא 'to congeal', 'to coagulate', coming from חמא, whence חֶמְאָה 'butter'. The passage from חמא to חבא is attested by the transformation of חמאה to חאותא (Syriac ᵃᵗᵒᵈ 'butter'). It is unnecessary to change יתחכאו to יתחבאו 'stop' (Berg), or יתחברו 'join' (Ehrlich). If we invert יתחבאו and יתלכדו (Merx, Budde, etc.), we obtain a quite good meaning. However, the comparison 'like stone' is more intelligible with 'become frozen' than with 'become gripped'. Moreover, it is impossible to say that the face of the deep 'is hidden' as a result of the freezing. The face of the deep is opposed to

31   Will you tie the bands of the Pleiades,
      Or loose the cords of Orion?

32   Will you bring out the Corona in its due time?
      And the Bear, with its little ones, will you guide?

its depths (v. 16); cf. עַל־פְּנֵי תְהוֹם in Gn 1: 2. The hithpaʻel of לכד 'to take', with the connotation 'to become set' so as to form a solid mass. Cf. the use of prendre (= take) in French: 'la rivière a pris' (= the river has become frozen) or 'le lait prend' (= the milk curdles). In 41: 9b the same יִתְלַכָּדוּ will refer to the scales of the crocodile which become locked together so as to be inseparable. Our verse recalls 37: 10 where the frost solidifies the sheet of waters.

31 The word מַעֲדַנּוֹת is rendered δεσμόν (G), μόρια (Symm.), micantes stellas (Vulg.), שִׁירֵי 'chains' (Targ.), ܚܘܦ̈ܬܐ 'by the face' (Syr. following פְּנֵי of v. 30). For כִּימָה, which is transcribed ܟܐܡܐ (Syr.), כִּימְתָא (Targ.), we have the translation Πλειάδος in G and Symm., Pleiadas in Vulg. The words מֹשְׁכוֹת כְּסִיל are rendered φραγμὸν Ὠρίωνος (G), gyrum Arcturi (Vulg.), ܐܘܪܚܐ ܕܓܢܒܪܐ 'way of the giant' (Syr.), אֶשְׁלֵי דְגַנְדִּין נַפְלָא 'the cords which pull the giant' (Targ.). Instead of תִּפְתַּח, Syr. ܣܪܚܬ 'you have seen'.

We now pass on to the constellations. The verb קָשַׁר 'bind', 'tie', 'knot' (40: 29) is used in the piʻel because of the parallelism with the piʻel of פתח 'untie', 'unbind', 'loosen' a cord (12: 18; 30: 11). The hapax מַעֲדַנּוֹת 'bonds', 'bands' is due to a metathesis of the consonants in עֲנֹד 'tie' (31: 36). The word מַעֲדַנֹּת of 1 S 15: 32 belongs to the root מעד 'reel', 'stagger', and is to be vocalised מְעַדְנִית (cf. our Comm.). On כִּימָה 'Pleiades' and כְּסִיל 'Orion', cf. Comm. on 9: 9. The Pleiades form a cluster of stars which need to be

firmly bound together: 'Will you tie the bands of the Pleiades?' The word מֹשְׁכוֹת 'cords' is again a hapax the meaning of which is not in doubt in the light of the root מֹשֵׁךְ 'pull', 'lengthen'. We have seen (9: 9) that the constellation of Orion was identified with Nimrod. It is a sort of chained Prometheus: 'or will you untie the cords of Orion?'

32 V. 32, absent from Sah., marked with asterisk in Jerome and Syrohex., did not exist in G. The present text is derived from Theod. (cf. Syro-hex.). For מַזָּרוֹת Theod. μαζουρώθ, Vulg. luciferum, Targ. שְׁטָרֵי מָזְלַיָּא 'constellations', Syr. ܚܫܠܐ 'chariot'. The 2nd hemistich is translated καὶ Ἕσπερον ἐπὶ κόμης αὐτοῦ ἄξεις αὐτά; by Theod. The words ἐπὶ κόμης come from ἐπὶ οἰκοδομῆς (Aq. in Syro-hex.; cf. Jerome super aedificationem), the word בְּנָיה being connected with בנה 'to build'. For עַיִשׁ, which has become ܚܒܘܠܐ in Syr., we have Vesperum in Vulg. (cf. Ἕσπερον of Theod.), זַגְתָא 'the Hen' in Targ. The verb תנחם is translated consurgere facis (Vulg.), 'you rise up opposite' (Syr.).

'Will you bring out the Corona in its due time?' The hiphʻil of יצא, as in Is 40: 26, to denote the controlling action which makes the stars appear on the horizon. In the light of the description as a whole, it is clear that מַזָּרוֹת denotes a single planet or star. Hence we cannot identify מזרות with מַזָּלוֹת, which designates sometimes the signs of the zodiac, sometimes the planets, in Jewish tradition. It is true that Theod. here renders מזרות by Μαζουρώθ, which in 2 K 23: 5 is the word used

33   Do you know the laws of the heavens?
Do you fulfil on earth what is written there?

by G to translate מַזָּלוֹת. But it should be noted that מַזָּרִים, which is totally different from מַזָּרוֹת, is rendered Μαζουρ by Aq. in 37:9. The Greek translators have been embarrassed by the words מַזָּלוֹת, מַזָּרוֹת, מַזָּרִים, whence the use of proper names which tended to identify these astronomical data. It is equally by an approximation that Targ. has rendered מַזָּרוֹת by שִׁטְרֵי מַזָּלַיָּא 'constellations', as if it were a question of מַזָּלוֹת. The use of בְּעִתּוֹ 'in its time' obliges us to see in מַזָּרוֹת a plural of majesty, like בְּהֵמוֹת (40:15). If we proposed to translate in a distributive sense, 'each one in its time', we should need at least בְּעִתָּהּ, the feminine suffix. Syr. and Vulg. have rightly realised that what is being referred to is a unity and not something collective (cf. sup.). It remains to discover what is alluded to by the constellation called מַזָּרוֹת. The root נזר has furnished נֶזֶר 'diadem', 'crown'. The substantive מַזָּרָה (for manzarah), in the plural מַזָּרוֹת, will denote the 'Crown' par excellence (Michaelis): the Corona Borealis, a very fine constellation which it is not surprising to see linked with the Great Bear. It is not very likely that the original text contained any other word but מַזָּרוֹת, which is supported by the versions. Ball however would change to מסרו (Assyrian mašrû) or to מזרוק (Arabic mizrâq 'lance') or even to תמוז Tammuz(!). As regards עָשׁ (9:9), here עַיִשׁ, as the name of the Great Bear, and 'its sons', 'its little ones', to designate the Little Bear, cf. Comm. on 9:9. The preposition עַל is used here in the sense of in addition, together with; cf. אֵם עַל־בָּנִים 'the mother with the sons' (Gn 32:12) and עַל־הַדָּם 'with

the blood' (Lv 19:26; 1 S 14:32). The Bear with its little ones is put at the beginning, whence the use of the pronominal suffix in תַּנְחֵם 'will you guide them?' The hiph'il of נחה as in 31:18. The reading תְּנַחֵם 'will you console?' (Merx, Hitzig, etc.) has the parallelism against it. It is difficult to see what astro-mythological legend would be alluded to by the idea of consolation offered to the Bear for the loss of its little ones.

33 For חֻקּוֹת, G τροπάς. The 2nd hemistich becomes ἢ τὰ ὑπ' οὐρανὸν ὁμοθυμαδὸν γινόμενα in G. It seems that τὰ ὑπ' οὐρανόν corresponds to בָּאָרֶץ (cf. vv. 18, 24). For מִשְׁטָרוֹ, Vulg. rationem ejus, Syr. ܢܡܘܣܗ 'law' (which also translates חֻקּוֹת), Targ. שִׁטְרֵי גִלְגְּלֵיהּ 'the paths of its revolutions'.

Duhm proposes to vocalise יָדַעְתָּ and to translate: 'Do you teach the heavens their laws?' But, as Budde rightly objects, this would result in a different construction: suffix after חֻקּוֹת (cf. v. 12b). Hence we must keep the very simple text: 'Do you know the laws of the heavens?' Cf. the openings הֲיָדַעְתָּ (39:1) and הֲתֵדַע (37:15, 16). The חֻקּוֹת שָׁמַיִם 'laws of the heavens' are the work of God (Jer 33:25). The suffix of מִשְׁטָרוֹ refers to שָׁמַיִם in spite of the difference of number (Gesenius-Kautzsch § 145m). The hapax מִשְׁטָר, by comparison with שֹׁטֵר 'functionary', is usually given the meaning of 'function', 'power', whence: 'Do you regulate their influences on the earth?' (Le Hir; cf. Renan, etc.); 'Do you control its power over the earth?' (Segond). But etymologically the words שֹׁטֵר and מִשְׁטָר can be linked with the Assyrian šaṭâru

34 Will you raise your voice to the clouds,
   That a flood of waters may submerge you?
35 Will you send forth lightnings and will they go?
   And will they say to you: here we are?
36 Who has imparted wisdom to the ibis,
   Or who has endowed the cock with understanding?

'to write'. The meaning of 'function', 'power' would therefore fit only very indirectly משטר. Fried. Delitzsch sees in משטרו an equivalent of šiṭir šamâmi 'writing of the sky', a periphrasis by which the Assyrians designated the stars. He is then obliged to paraphrase the 2nd hemistich: *'oder richtest du her sein Sternenzelt auf der Erde?'* In fact the substantive משטר is equivalent to maṣṭaru and malṭaru (with change from š to l before the dental), which means in Akkadian 'inscription' and 'writing', 'what is written'. We consider the suffix as objective. The meaning of the 2nd hemistich is clear: 'Do you fulfil on earth what is written there?' The verb שים with the meaning of 'do', 'realise', with the accusative and ב" (Jer 43:19; Ps 68:43, etc.).

34 G paraphrases the 1st hemistich καλέσεις δὲ νέφος φωνῇ. For שפעת־מים Aq., Symm., Theod. ὁρμὴ ὑδάτων, Vulg. *impetus aquarum*, Targ. רכפת מיא 'mass of waters', Syr. ܘܣܓܝ 'quantity of waters'. Instead of תכסך 'will cover you', Syr. reads תכסה 'will you cover?', which obliges it to put ב" before שפעת G καὶ τρόμῳ ὕδατος λάβρῳ ὑπακούσεται seems indeed to have had the variant תַּעֲנֶךָ in place of תכסך.

In the light of v. 35, it is a question of commanding the elements. The clouds are not subject to the commands of men. It is God whom they obey. It would be in vain for man to ask them for rain. With the 1st hemistich cf. 20:6. The 2nd hemistich echoes 22:11b. No

more than in the case of the latter text are we compelled to choose the variant of G (contra Duhm).

35 For הנגו, G τί ἐστιν; but Symm. πάρεσμεν, Vulg. *adsumus*.

The *pi'el* of שלח in the sense of 'unleash', 'release' (12:15; 20:23): 'Will you send forth lightnings and will they go?' The lightnings are the servants of God, whose will they accomplish (36:32; 37:11-13). With the 1st hemistich cf. Bar 3:33, ὁ ἀποστέλλων τὸ φῶς καὶ πορεύεται. The formula הנגו 'here we are' is that of servants (1 S 3:4-6, etc.). The 2nd hemistich is applied to the stars in Bar 3:35, ἐκάλεσεν αὐτούς, καὶ εἶπον Πάρεσμεν.

36 G seems to have connected טחות with טוה 'spin', whence the paraphrase of the whole verse: τίς δὲ ἔδωκεν γυναιξὶν ὑφάσματος σοφίαν ἢ ποικιλτικὴν ἐπιστήμην. Vulg. is closer to the text: *quis posuit in visceribus hominis sapientiam? vel quis dedit gallo intelligentiam?* For בטחות, Syr. ܟܣܝܐ 'secretly', Targ. בכלין 'in the reins'. Syr. reads שכוי לבינה, whence ܣܘܟܐ ܠܚܟܡܬܐ 'the view to intelligence'. 1st Targ. renders לשכוי by ללבא 'to the heart', but 2nd translates לתרנגול ברא 'to the wild cock' (cf. Vulg. *gallo*) and adds 'to praise its Lord'.

The exegesis of this verse has a whole history attached to it, especially as regards the 2nd hemistich. The words נָתַן לַשֶּׂכְוִי בִינָה have in fact been incorporated in the Jewish morning prayer, one of the benedictions of which runs thus: 'Blessed be Thou, Adonai, our God, king of the world, who hast given to the *sekwî* understanding to distinguish day from night.' The meaning of שֶׂכְוִי in this liturgical text is 'cock'.

It is in this sense that the text of our verse is interpreted by Vulg. and one of the Targums (cf. sup.). This meaning is not known to G or Syr. The word שכוי does not appear elsewhere, so that it is impossible to deduce its meaning from the Bible itself. According to R. Levy, in the Jerusalem Talmud (*Berakoth*, IX, 2) it was in Rome that the cock was called שכוי. But R. Simeon-ben-Laqish in the Babylonian Talmud (*Rosh-hashanah*, 26a) asserts that it was in the territory of Gennesaret that the cock was called שכוי. Rashi thinks that this interpretation belongs to the 'language of the wise' (commenting on our passage). Rashi mentions the interpretation of שכוי by לב 'heart'. This is that of 1st Targum, and it is accepted by Qimchi and Ibn Ezra. Sa'adia interprets by the Arabic مزخرف 'frivolous'(?). In short, two traditions conflict as regards the interpretation of שכוי: either 'cock' or 'heart'. The translation 'cock' is supported by the usage of Gennesaret and Rome, according to the Talmud; the translation as 'heart' is based on etymology. In fact שכוי is linked to the root שכה, Aramaic סכי, סכא, the basic meaning of which is 'look at', 'examine' (cf. Syr. ܣܟܐ 'sight'). From this root are derived שְׂכִיּוֹת 'sights'(?) of Is 2:16 and מַשְׂכִּית 'image', 'imagination'. As is observed by König (*Wörterbuch*, p. 463b), the derivative שכוי would have as its proper meaning 'speculation', 'reflection' and, by extension, 'heart' as the organ of speculation (cf. 1st Targ.). Let us note that the traditional translation, 'or who has given to the cock intelligence?', is better adapted to the context than the other version:

'or who has given to the heart understanding?' In fact the author is referring not to psychological phenomena but to physical phenomena. The cock heralds the sunrise and is not unconnected with the rain (cf. inf.). It can be mentioned along with the lightnings and storm-clouds, which are likewise endowed with a certain degree of intelligence (vv. 34-5, 37-9). The essential point is to discover whether parallelism favours this interpretation. It is in fact noteworthy that the 1st hemistich corresponds word by word with the 2nd: 'who has put?' = 'who has given?'; 'wisdom' = 'understanding'; לַשֶּׂכְוִי = בַּטֻּחוֹת. On the basis of Ps 51:8, it has been proposed to assign to בטחות the meaning of 'in the inward parts' or 'in the reins' (cf. Vulg. and Targ.), and it cannot be denied that טָחוֹת has been regarded by the versions as denoting something hidden (cf. the translations of G, Vulg., and Syr. in Ps. 51:8). Targ. renders בטחות by 'in the reins' not only here but also in Ps 51:8. But the meaning of Ps 51:8 remains very doubtful in view of this interpretation which is based on a very subtle etymology: טָחוֹת from טוח 'coat', 'overlay'. Modern critics have not been able to accept this derivation. An attempt has been made to connect with the Arabic طاح 'wander' so as to translate טחות by 'meteors' (Schultens, who attributes to שכוי the meaning 'phenomenon'), or with طخاء 'black cloud' (Hirzel, Hitzig, Dillmann, etc.). All this creates new difficulties if we compare with the 2nd hemistich. If שכוי is the cock, could we not find in טחות the name of an animal which would also be remarkable for its understanding? Hoffmann has recognised in טחות the name of an Egyptian god, Thot, the famous Hermes Trismegistos, and has sought in שכוי the Coptic

37   Who can number the clouds by wisdom,
     And who can tilt the water-skins of heaven,

σουχι, the name of the planet Mercury. The equivalence of טחות with Thot, which is written in Egyptian *dhwtj*, in Coptic θοουτ, seems to us excellent. And it is interesting to note that Grimme thinks he finds the mention of the god Thot, written precisely טחות, in the inscriptions of Sinai (*Sinai*, p. 73). Even if the readings of Grimme are debatable, the mere fact that this erudite Semitic scholar transcribes Thot as טחות furnishes indirect proof of the soundness of the hypothesis of Hoffmann. But we shall be careful not to identify טחות, Thot, with the Egyptian god or with Hermes Trismegistos. It is simply a question of the bird of Thot, namely the ibis, found so often on the trees bordering the Nile. Like the cock, the ibis had a special reputation for wisdom. The vogue of Thot-Hermes as the god of wisdom and writing makes it unnecessary to adduce lengthy proofs. The special characteristic of the ibis was to announce an imminent rising of the waters of the Nile. Furthermore, the cock is not only the herald of morning, the chantecleer of nature, but also popular traditions, which are still current in Palestine, bring this creature into close connection with the imminence of rain (Jaussen, 'Le Coq et la pluie', *RB*, 1924, pp. 574ff.). The rising of the Nile, the rain from heaven, these are two phenomena which fit well together in the description with which we are concerned. The birds which announce the coming of these phenomena give proof of great wisdom and understanding. Their place is clearly indicated in this context. That is why we abandon the interpretation usually accepted, which sees here a reference to the organs of thought or imagination, to revive the

early tradition which recognised an allusion to the cock in שכוי.

37 Vulg. paraphrases the 1st hemistich: *quis enarrabit coelorum rationem*? For שחקים, well rendered by G νέφη and Syr. ܚܒܐ 'clouds', 1st Targ. שבעתי שמיא 'the seven heavens', 2nd Targ. כוכבי שמיא 'the stars of the heavens'. The phrase נבלי שמים, rendered simply by G as οὐρανόν, is translated ὄργανα οὐρανοῦ by Theod. (cf. Jerome *organa coeli* with asterisk before *organa*), *concentum coeli* by Vulg. 1st Targ. translates by כילול שמיא 'the measures of the sky'. 2nd Targ. well understands the metaphor: 'the clouds which resemble the waterskins (זיקיא) of heaven'. Syr. very arbitrarily ܚܡܣܘܝܐ ܥܡܘܕܐ 'pillars of the sky'. For ישכיב, G εἰς γῆν ἔκλινεν, Vulg. *dormire faciet*, Syr. ܐܩܝܡ 'will erect', 1st Targ. ישרי 'lays', 2nd Targ. ישכיב, which equals the MT.

The complement בְּחָכְמָה 'by wisdom' implies an intellectual activity and perfectly suits the *pi'el* of ספר in the sense of 'count', 'number' (28:27). Hence it is unnecessary to change יְסַפֵּר to ישבר 'He breaks' (Wright, Strahan), יסב (*hiph'il* of סבב) 'He makes to turn' or יפרש 'He extends' (Duhm), ישפר (*pi'el* of שפר in 26:13) 'He makes to shine', 'He illuminates' (Döderlein, Dathe). Ehrlich postulates for the *pi'el* of ספר a sense similar to the 2nd form of سفر 'chase away', 'disperse' clouds. We have recognised this Arabic verb in שפרה of 26:13 and we have no need to find it again here, since the natural meaning of ספר is very well adapted to the context. It is a question of counting the clouds rightly, for they are waterskins whose contents should only

38   When the dust hardens into a mass,
        And the clods agglomerate?
39   Do you hunt a prey for the lioness,
        And do you satisfy the appetite of the young lions,

be poured out with deliberate purpose. The word שְׁחָקִים calls for the complementary term שׁמים as in 35: 5. The נִבְלֵי שָׁמַיִם are the 'water-skins of heaven'; cf. נבלי מרום 'water-skins of the height', with the same meaning in Sir 43: 8. The cloud forms a solid container which holds the water (26: 8). To empty a water-skin it must be tilted. The verb שכב 'to lie down' will connote in the *hiph'il* 'to cause to lie', 'to make slope', 'to tilt' (cf. G).

38 The 1st hemistich is interpreted κέχυται δὲ ὥσπερ γῆ κονία (G), *quando fundebatur pulvis in terra* (Vulg.), 'who has scattered dust on the earth?' (Syr.). These three versions are agreed in giving to מוצק the meaning 'earth'. Targ. כד אשתאס עפרא לשתאסה 'when the soil was made as a foundation'. For the 2nd hemistich, G κεκόλληκα (A κεκόλληκεν) δὲ αὐτὸν ὥσπερ λίθῳ κύβον (A κύβον λίθοις, followed by Syro-hex. and Jerome *lapidibus cubum*); Syr. 'and who has made solid the rocks?'

The opening בְּצֶקֶת denotes a circumstance concomitant with that expressed in v. 37 (cf. vv. 7, 8b, 9). The word מוּצָק 'molten', 'hard', 'solid' (cf. 11: 15; 37: 10) marks the term of the action expressed by the word יצק. The verb יצק is used intransitively 'to flow', 'to be spilt' in 1 K 22: 35. Here it assumes a meaning appropriate to its complement למוצק, namely, 'to harden'. We ought literally to translate 'when the dust hardens into a solid thing' or 'when the dust hardens into a mass'. The effect of the rain is to agglomerate the dust into a compact mass. The 2nd hemistich expresses a similar idea: 'and when the clods agglomerate'. Note the finite verb following the infinitive (vv. 7, 13). The word רְגָבִים as in 21: 33. The *pu'al* of דבק will recur in 41: 9, with the meaning of 'to be stuck, welded together'. Duhm does not notice the contradiction which exists between his translation of the 1st hemistich, '*wenn das Erdreich zerfliesst zu einem Guss*' and of the 2nd, '*und die Schollen zusammenkleben*'.

39 Syr. 'who gives?' (cf. v. 38). For ללביא, G λέουσιν. The word חית is interpreted as 'soul' by G ψυχάς, Vulg. *animam*, Syr. ܢܦܫܐ, but Targ. paraphrases the 2nd hemistich: 'and will you provide for the subsistence of the lionesses?' For כפירים, Vulg. *catulorum ejus*, G δρακόντων (cf. 4: 11).

On the words לָבִיא and כְּפִירִים cf. 4: 10, 11. The verb צוד as in 10: 16. The prey is denoted by the characteristic word טֶרֶף (4: 11; 29: 17), 'Do you hunt a prey for the lioness?' Questions in the 2nd person are resumed (vv. 31-5). We pass now to the animal kingdom. Alongside its normal meaning 'what lives', 'soul' (33: 18, 20, 22, 28; 36: 14), the word חַיָּה can also mean 'appetite'; cf. the Arabic *nafs* in the expression *mâ li nafs lil'akl* 'I have not any taste for eating' and the phrase בעל נפש 'gluttonous' (Pr 23: 2). With the turn of phrase used cf. Pr 6: 30, לְמַלֵּא נפשׁו כי ירעב 'to satisfy his appetite when he is hungry'. It is the lioness which must provide for her young when they are hungry (4: 11).

40   When they are crouched in their dens,
      When they lie in wait in the thicket?
41   Who prepares for the raven its nourishment,
      When its little ones cry out to God,
      And stagger for lack of food?

40 Syr. continues its procedure of harmonisation: 'Who has multiplied the animals in the desert?' (cf. vv. 38-9): resumption of חית of v. 39 and vague translation of במעונות. The 1st hemistich is interpreted δεδοίκασιν γὰρ ἐν κοίταις αὐτῶν (G; cf. 37:8), *quando cubant in antris* (Vulg.). Targ. retains the verb שחח and renders במעונות by במדורתא 'in the dwelling places'. For בסכה למו־ארב, G ἐν ὕλαις ἐνεδρεύοντες. Vulg. summarises the 2nd hemistich: *et in specubus insidiantur*.

Instead of ב" with the infinitive (v. 38), we have כי with the imperfect in a slightly different sense from that of v. 20, where כי meant 'in order that'. The verb שחח with its basic meaning: 'to crouch' (cf. 9:13; 22:29). We have met מְעוֹנוֹת and אֶרֶב in 37:8. But here אֶרֶב keeps its etymological sense of 'ambush' (cf. the verb ארב in 25:3 Comm. and 31:9). The preposition לְמוֹ as in 27:14; 29:21. The word סֻכָּה 'booth' (27:18; 36:29) denotes the thicket; cf. סֹךְ in Jer 25:38; Ps 10:9. The description of Ps 10:8-9 refers to the wicked man, who is being likened to a wild beast, expressions similar to those of this v. 40.

41 G, which added a suffix to מעונות of v. 40, renders צידו simply by βοράν. For אל־אל, G πρὸς Κύριον. The words לבלי־אכל, well rendered by Vulg. *eo quod non habeant cibos*, Targ. מדלית מיכלא 'lack of food', Syr. ܡܢ ܚܠܦ ܡܐܟܘܠܬܐ 'absence of food', are paraphrased as τὰ σῖτα ζητοῦντες in G.

The raven is introduced here, as a carnivorous creature, just like the lion: 'Who prepares for the raven its nourishment?' The verb הכין means 'to prepare' (15:35). We must not confuse צידו 'its fodder' (from ציד) with צידו 'its prey' and 'its game' (from צוד v. 39). The raven feeds on dead flesh, and not on game which has been hunted. In Ps 147:9 it is said of God that 'He gives to the beasts their food, and to the young ravens when they cry'. To בני־ערב in this passage corresponds ילָדָו 'its young' (cf. ילדיהן in 39:3). The *pi'el* of שוע has אל before the person to whom one cries out in supplication (30:20). Apart from the meaning 'wander', the verb תעה also offers us that of 'stagger' (12:25; cf. Comm.), which is very suitable here. The effects of hunger are akin to those of drunkenness. The expression לִבְלִי as in Is 5:14, where לבלי־חק means 'without limit'. Cf. the use of אכל for the fodder of birds of prey in 9:26; 39:29. The presence of the raven between the lion and other quadrupeds (39:1ff.) has seemed suspect to some commentators. Hence it has been proposed to change the vocalisation of לָעֹרֵב and to read לָעֶרֶב 'in the evening', so as to make the description of v. 41 refer to the lion (cf. Wright, Duhm, Beer). But it is difficult to apply the suffixes of the words צידו and ילָדָו to the word לָבִיא of v. 39. In fact, v. 40 comprises in a single subject the lioness and the young lions. Hence we should have to go back to v. 39a to find the animal presupposed by the singular suffix. Furthermore, the young lions have been designated by their name (v. 39b). They would recur as 'her young'. Note especially that the opening מִי יָכִין introduces a new fact (vv. 36, 37). Beer proposes יִפְעוּ 'they cry' (Is 42:14), instead of יתעו. But this verb would dupli-

cate יְשַׁוְּעוּ. It has left no trace in the versions and would cause ambiguity before לבלי, which would seem to indicate the aim of the appeals. The change of the plural יתעו to a singular יתעה (Bickell, Budde) is unnecessary. It is probable that a hemistich parallel to v. 41a is lacking.

CHAPTER 39

1   Are you acquainted [   ] with the way in which the antelopes
     of the rock bring forth,
     Do you observe the calving of the hinds?
2   Do you count the months that they must fulfil,
     And do you know the time when they bring forth?

1 Omit עֵת.

39: 1 The 1st hemistich, absent from Sah., marked with asterisk in Jerome and Syro-hex., did not exist in G. The present text is derived from Theod. (cf. Syro-hex.). This translation of Theod. is placed after v. 3a in G(A). For יַעֲלֵי, reproduced in Targ., we have τραγελάφων (Theod.), *ibicum* (Vulg.), ܘ‍ܝ‍ܥ‍ܠ‍ܐ 'the female ibexes' (Syr.). Vulg. renders חֹלֵל אֵילוֹת by *vel paturientes cervas*. G interprets חֹלֵל by ὠδῖνας.

The interrogative ה also governs תִּשְׁמֹר, תִּסְפֹּר and יָדַעְתָּ (v. 2). The opening הֲיָדַעְתָּ 'are you acquainted with?' as in 38: 33; cf. הֲתֵדַע (37: 15, 16). As it stands, the 1st hemistich would be translated: 'Do you know the time when the antelopes of the rock bring forth?' This line is long and anticipates v. 2b: 'and do you know the time of their bringing forth?' It has for long been noted that עֵת is due to an accidental repetition of the final letters of הֲיָדַעְתָּ (Bickell, Hontheim, Steuernagel). If we delete it, there remains: 'Are you acquainted with the bringing forth of the antelopes of the rock?' This very simple change is preferable to that proposed by Grimme, which consists in suppressing לֶדֶת and in interpreting עֵת as referring to the time when the male animal is in rut. Still more arbitrary

is the hypothesis of Duhm, who reads הֲיָדַעְתָּ עַשְׁתָּרֹת 'Have you taught sexual desire (to the ibex)?', the word עשתרות being understood in the very problematic sense attributed to it in Dt 7: 13; 28: 4, 18, 51! Beer deviates completely from the text by suggesting תַּאֲנַת 'amorous desire' (of animals) in the place of עֵת לֶדֶת (cf. ed. Kittel). The formula יַעֲלֵי־סָלַע recalls צוּר הַיְעֵלִים 'rock of the ibex' of 1 S 24: 3. In Ps 104: 18 we find 'the mountains which are high for the ibexes (לַיְעֵלִים), the rocks (סְלָעִים) which are a refuge for the badgers (לַשְׁפַנִּים)'. The יָעֵל is the ibex, the chamois, and also the antelope. Here it is a question of the female, which is why we adopt the translation 'antelope'. In Arabic the word وَعِل (= יעל) designates the chamois and the antelope. There is the strictest parallelism between לֶדֶת 'to bring forth' and חֹלֵל (*po'lel* of חִיל; cf. 15: 7) 'give birth to' (Is 51: 2), as between יַעֲלֵי 'antelopes' and אַיָּלוֹת 'hinds', between הֲיָדַעְתָּ 'do you know?' and תשׁמר 'do you observe?' (24: 15).

2 G renders ירחים תמלאנה by μῆνας αὐτῶν πλήρεις τοκετοῦ, but πλήρεις is omitted in Sah., Syro-hex.,

597

3   They crouch, they *drop* their offspring,
    They bring forth what they have carried;

3   תְּפַלֵּטְנָה; MT: תפלחנה.

Jerome *menses partus earum*. Then G ὠδῖνας δὲ αὐτῶν ἔλυσας translates v. 3b, thus omitting v. 2b and v. 3a. The word תמלאנה, omitted in Syr., is rendered *conceptus earum* in Vulg., more literally דשלמן 'that they accomplish' in Targ.

The 1st hemistich speaks of the months of pregnancy, the second of the date of bringing forth. The verb ספר 'to count', in the *qal* (14: 16; 31: 4), instead of the *pi'el* 'to estimate' (28: 27; 38: 37). The relative is understood after יְרָחִים. The *pi'el* of מלא in the sense of 'fulfil' a period of time (Gn 29: 27, 28); cf. ἐπλήσθη and ἐπλήσθησαν (Lk 1: 57; 2: 6). Of course we must retain the *qal* of ידע (cf. v. 1) and not replace it by a *pi'el* as Duhm would. The question refers to knowledge.

3   We have seen that v. 3b was translated by G in v. 2. The present text of G both at vv. 3b and 4 comes from Theod. (cf. Syro-hex.). The passage is lacking in Sah. and is marked with asterisk in Jerome and Syro-hex. As for v. 3a of G, ἐξέθρεψας δὲ αὐτῶν τὰ παιδία ἔξω φόβου; it is the translation of v. 4a of the MT (cf. v. 4). Vulg. paraphrases the whole verse: *incurvantur ad foetum et pariunt et rugitus emittunt*. Theod. renders the 2nd hemistich: ὠδῖνας δὲ αὐτῶν ἐξαποστελεῖς; Targ. similarly interprets חבליהם by צעריהון 'their pains'. Syr. summarises vv. 3-4: 'and when they kneel down and bring forth, and when their young are reared and weaned'. The *pi'el* of פלח means: 'cleave' 'plough', 'pierce' (cf. 16: 13). We cannot assign to it as a complement יַלְדֵיהֶן 'their young' (cf. ילדו in 38: 41). Duhm gets rid of ילדיהן.

Olshausen proposed to replace תְּפַלַּחְנָה by תְּפַלֵּטְנָה 'they drop (young)' (21: 10). This slight correction saves the sense. It seems to us preferable to the transposition of ילדיהן and חבליהם, which is suggested by Houbigant and accepted by Wright, Ehrlich, etc. We shall in fact see that חֶבְלֵיהֶם is the natural complement of תְּשַׁלַּחְנָה. The verb כרע 'to crouch' is used of the woman in travail (1 S 4: 19). The 1st hemistich is very natural: 'they crouch, they drop their offspring'. On the meaning of the *pi'el* of פלט, cf. 21: 10. Parallelism is strictly observed as in v. 1. To the verb תפלחנה corresponds תשלחנה, the *pi'el* of שלח meaning 'to let go', 'to cast off' (12: 15; 20: 23; 30: 11, 12; 38: 35) what is embarrassing. In the light of the Arabic حبل 'to conceive', whence حبل 'foetus', 'fruit', and in accordance with the meaning of the *pi'el* of חבל 'to conceive' (in Ps 7: 15 and Ca 8: 5), it is clear that חבליהם (from חֶבֶל) here denotes the result of conception, 'what they have carried'. Ehrlich, who makes חבליהם the complement of תפלחנה in consequence of the transposition referred to above, proposes to translate: 'they break their umbilical cords', interpreting חבליהם by חֶבֶל 'cord'. The *pi'el* of פלח does not mean 'to break' a thread, a cord, but to 'cleave' an object. It would have been very badly chosen for the supposed action. Note the masculine suffix in חבליהם (1: 14, 42: 15), instead of the feminine in ילדיהן. We shall have בניהם in v. 4. No ambiguity is possible.

4   Their young become robust, they grow up in the desert place,
     They go off, and return no more to them.
5   Who gave the onager its freedom,
     And who unloosed the bonds of the wild ass,
6   To which I have apportioned the steppe for a home,
     And the salt land for a dwelling place?

4   On the text of G, and of Syr., cf.
v. 3. V. 4a is translated by G at v. 3a.
Instead of יחלמו, G ἐξέθρεψας δέ
seems to have read תלחם. As for
ἔξω φόβου, it is probably a paraphrase of יראה בבר ירבו בבר read as
'fear outside'. For יחלמו, Theod.
ἀπορρήξουσιν, Vulg. *separantur*, Targ.
מתחילן 'strengthen themselves'. For
בבר, Theod. ἐν γενήματι, Vulg. *ad
pastum*, Targ. בעבורא 'thanks to
the corn', but Symm. ἐν ἀγριότητι.

The verb חלם has the meaning of
'become strong' in post-Biblical
Hebrew. The *hiph'il* means 'to
restore strength to some one':
ותחלימני 'and Thou dost restore my
strength' (Is 38: 16). In Syriac the
root חלם has developed in the sense
of 'to be in good health'. König well
explains the development of this
root: to gain strength, become
pubescent, have dreams (*Wörterbuch*, pp. 110f.). It is the latter meaning which has triumphed in Hebrew.
The change from יַחְלִמוּ to יִגְמְלוּ 'are
weaned' (Beer, following Is 18: 5)
has but slender support in Syr.,
which summarises vv. 3-4 (cf. v. 3).
The verb יִרְבּוּ 'they grow up' (cf.
רבה in 33: 12) and not 'they are
numerous', as in the similar passage
27: 14. Symm. has correctly understood that בַר (in pause בָּר) corresponds to the Arabic بَرّ, whence بَرا
'outside' بَرِيّة 'desert'; cf. Syr. ܟܢܐ
'field', 'countryside', ܟܢ 'the open',
etc. Cf. חוץ 'outside', 'out of doors'
and 'countryside', חוצות 'fields'
(5: 10; 18: 17). So soon as their
growth is complete, the fawns leave

their mothers: 'they go off, and
return no more to them'. The verb
יצא 'to go out' and 'to leave' (v. 21).
The suffix לָמוֹ is not a dative
reflexive, but represents the mothers
which the author has been speaking
of from v. 1: masculine plural instead of the feminine, as in חבליהם
(v. 3) and בניהם.

5   For מסרות ערוד, G has simply
δεσμοὺς αὐτοῦ, Vulg. *vincula ejus*,
Syr. ܢܝܪ ܕܝܠܗ 'of him the yoke'. It
is clear that these versions have not
translated ערוד, which is the synonym of פרא in the 1st hemistich.
    Parallelism between פֶּרֶא, the
Hebrew name of the onager, and the
hapax עָרוֹד which is its Aramaic
name: cf. 16: 19; 40: 18. The phrase
שִׁלַּח חָפְשִׁי 'to send away free' is the
classic idiom for the connotation 'to
set at liberty' a slave (Dt 15: 12, 13,
18, etc.). By a bold turn of thought
the poet supposes that the onager
is merely a domestic ass which has
been released from servitude. In
order to do this, it was necessary to
remove its bonds: 'and who un-
loosed the bonds of the wild ass?'
The verb פִּתַּח as in 30: 11. In 12: 18,
the complement of פתח was מוֹסֵר
'bond' (cf. Comm.), derived from
אסר 'to bind'; we have here the
feminine plural מֹסְרוֹת (construct
state; cf. מוֹסְרוֹת in the absolute
state, Jer 5: 5; 27: 2).

6   V. 6b, absent from Sah., marked
with asterisk in Colb., Jerome,
Syro-hex., did not exist in G. The

7   He mocks at the tumult of the city,
     He hears not the shouts of the driver,
8   He scours the mountains, his pasturage,
     And goes in search of all green plants.
9   Is the buffalo willing to serve you?

present text is derived from Theod. (cf. Syro-hex.). Vulg. interprets the 1st hemistich by *cui dedi in solitudine domum*. Instead of שַׂמְתִּי, Syr. حكב reads שָׂם 'he who has placed'. Theod. renders עֲרָבָה by the n. pr. Ἀραβά. For מְלֵחָה, Theod. ἁλμυρίδα (Jerome *salsuginem*), Vulg. *in terra salsuginis*, Syr. حالوٹ مكسل 'in the salted place', Targ. אַרְעָא צַדְיָא 'desert land'.

The wild freedom which the onager enjoys enables it to avoid towns and dwell in desert places. In 24: 5 the unhappy ones wandered 'like onagers in the desert'. The word chosen for 'desert' was the ordinary word מִדְבָּר. Here we have first עֲרָבָה 'steppe', then מְלֵחָה 'salted' (Ps 107: 34). Esarhaddon describes Arabia as a 'soil of salt' (*RB*, 1911, pp. 104, 208). In Jer. 17: 6 we have the series מִדְבָּר, עֲרָבָה and finally אֶרֶץ מְלֵחָה 'salted land'. In order to transform a place into a barren desert, the soil was sown with salt (Jg 9: 45).

7 For תְּשֻׁאוֹת נֹגֵשׂ, G μέμψιν δὲ φορολόγου, Vulg. *clamorem exactoris*, Targ. אִתְרַגּוּשְׁתָּא דַרְדִי 'the uproar of the driver'. Syr. paraphrases the 2nd hemistich: 'and he has no fear of the voices of chiefs'.

The verb שָׂחַק with לְ״ 'mock', 'laugh at' (5: 22). With הֲמוֹן קִרְיָה 'tumult of the city', cf. הֲמוֹן עִיר 'tumult of the town' in Is 32: 14 and הֲמוֹן רַבָּה 'the noise of the capital' (31: 34, cf. Comm.). The onager prefers the joys of liberty to the bustle of the town. And above all, 'he hears not the shouts of the driver' The word תְּשֻׁאוֹת as in 36: 29 (cf.

Comm.). The 2nd hemistich is inspired by 3: 18, but the term נֹגֵשׂ, which in that text denoted the inspector, the supervisor of forced labour, here denotes expressly the 'driver' of animals, as in Is 9: 3, where the 'rod of the driver' is coupled with the yoke and the crossbar (or collar); cf. Condamin.

8 V. 8, absent from Sah., marked with asterisk in Jerome and Syrohex., did not exist in G. The present text is derived from Theod. (cf. Syrohex.). For יָתוּר, Theod. κατασκέψεται, Vulg. *circumspicit*, Targ. יָאֵל 'he explores'; but Syr. سحمم)ل. 'and in quantity' seems to read יֶתֶר. Instead of יִדְרוֹשׁ, Syr.)ل.ه 'he tramples' has read יָדֹשׁ.

Following the pattern of v. 7, it seems indeed that יָתוּר is the verb corresponding to יִדְרוֹשׁ of the close. It is thus that the word has been understood by Theod., Vulg., Targ. The vocalisation יָתוּר, instead of יָתוּר, is an oddity, like that of יְהוֹא, instead of יְהֵוא, in Ec 11: 3. The word מִרְעֵהוּ 'his pasturage' is a kind of apposition to הָרִים 'he scours the mountains, his pasturage'. The preposition אַחַר before the complement of דרשׁ 'to search for' (10: 6) shows the beast following a certain track with the greatest care. The *hapax* יָרוֹק, instead of יָרָק 'verdure', 'vegetables', belongs to the same word group as the Assyrian *aruqtu* (feminine of *arqu* 'green', 'vegetable') and *urqu* 'kitchen-garden'.

9 The word רִים, Targ. רִימְנָא, Syr.

Will he spend the night at your crib?

10 Will you bind [   ] *a* rope about *his neck*?
Will he harrow the *furrows* behind you?

10 Omit רים. — בַּעֲנָקוֹ עֲבֹת; MT: בתלם עבתו. — תְּלָמִים (cf. G); TM: עמקים (transpose עמק and תלם).

רֵאם, is interpreted μονόκερως (G), ρινόκερως (Aq.), *rhinoceros* (Vulg.).

Another type of wild animal is introduced, the רֵים or רְאֵם, which corresponds to the Assyrian *rêmu*, the ideogram of which is composed of the sign 'ox' and the sign 'mountain', to denote the wild ox, the buffalo. Again the irony brings out the contrast between the wild beast and the domestic animal: 'Is the buffalo willing to serve you?' The verb אבה is almost always used with a negative. Our passage affords an exception to the rule, as do also Is 1: 19; Sir 6: 33. The verb לין or לון preserves its etymological sense of 'spending the night' (cf. 29: 19). It is at night that the oxen return from the fields to the stable. The word אֵבוּס 'manger', 'crib' recurs only in Is 1: 3; Pr 14: 4. The Assyrian *abûsu*, feminine *abusatu*, has the same meaning.

10 There is a gap in the MS of Sah., from 39: 10 to 40: 13 (= G 8). The text of G δήσεις δὲ ἐν ἱμᾶσι ζυγὸν αὐτοῦ, ἢ ἑλκύσει σου αὔλακας ἐν πεδίῳ; may be reconstructed in the following way: התקשר בעבתו אם־ ישדד תלמיך בעמק. It is apparent that G omits the words רים and אחריך. The phrase בעבתו has become ἐν ἱμᾶσι ζυγὸν αὐτοῦ; cf. Is 5: 18, where כעבות is translated ὡς ζυγοῦ ἱμάντι. The word תלם has passed into the 2nd hemistich; cf. σοῦ αὔλακας (cf. 31: 38). Vulg. translates רים by *rhinocerota* (cf. v. 9) and interprets בתלם עבתו by *ad arandum loro tuo* (עבתך). Targ. renders עבתו by באשליה 'by its rope'. The 2nd hemistich is literally translated by

Symm. ἢ ὁμαλίσει κοιλάδας ἀκολουθῶν σοι. Vulg. interprets אם־ישדד עמקים by *aut confringet glebas vallium*. The word עמקים is rendered by גלמתא 'depressions', 'small elevations', in Targ. Paraphrase of the whole verse in Syr.: 'Will you bind a yoke to the neck of the buffalo, or will you take a team of oxen into a rough place?'

The 1st hemistich is overloaded by the presence of רים, which comes from a repetition of v. 9 (cf. G). If we delete the word רים, there remains: 'Will you bind to a furrow its rope?', which is rather strange. The preposition בְּ" before the complement of קשר denotes the object which one binds with rope or thread, etc. (Jos 2: 18, 21). One does not bind a furrow with rope. Budde reads תקשרהו and בעבתו 'Do you bind him to the furrow by his rope?' He supposes that the expression is intended to mean to compel the buffalo to follow the track of the furrow, an interpretation that is rather too subtle. According to Duhm, we should read בעבות תלמו 'by his furrow rope (rope of furrow)', which is a very odd expression. Ehrlich considers the 1st hemistich unintelligible. Beer, following G, suggests a transposition of תלם and עמק, so as to obtain תְּלָמִים instead of עמקים and בַּעֲנָקוֹ 'to the nape of his neck' (cf. Aramaic עֻנקָא, Assyrian *unqu*) instead of בתלם. Now, in Sir 38: 26, G ἐκδοῦναι αὔλακας corresponds to the Hebrew לשדד בתלמים (cf. Peters). This expression remarkably confirms the hypothesis of Beer, who finds יְשַׂדֵּד תְּלָמִים in the 2nd hemistich; cf. G ἢ ἑλκύσει σου αὔλακας. Naturally the suffix of

11   Will you trust him because his strength is great,
      And will you commit to him your labour?

12   Do you rely on him to return,
      And bring back your grain *to* your threshing floor?

12   וְגׇרְנְךָ; MT: לְגׇרְנֶךָ.

עֲבֹתוֹ, transferred to בַּעֲנָקוֹ, will be suppressed. The 1st hemistich: הֲתִקְשָׁר בַּעֲנָקוֹ עֲבֹת 'Will you bind a rope about his neck?' naturally leads to the 2nd: 'Will he harrow the furrows behind you?' With הֲתִקְשָׁר cf. תִּקְשׁׄר in 38:31. The verb שׂדד in the *pi'el* means 'to harrow' (Is 28:24; Hos 10:11; Sir 38:26), rather than 'plough'. The etymological sense of the root שׂדד is 'to pull' (Assyrian *šadâdu*). The *pi'el* expresses repetition of the action: to make a series of pulls (*tractus* from *trahere*) on a field (cf. König, *Wörterbuch*, p. 459, s.v.). The poet pictures the driver pulling behind him the ox which is attached to the harrow.

11 For יְגִיעֶךָ, G τὰ ἔργα σου, Vulg. *labores tuos*.

The wild animal cannot be made use of as though he were a domestic animal. Doubtless he has enormous strength, but man cannot trust his untamed character: 'Will you trust him because his strength is great?' The 2nd hemistich, 'and will you commit to him your labour?', effectively conveys the state of mind of the farmer who can trust his ox and leave it to perform automatically the daily work. The word יְגִיעַ in its meaning of 'toil', 'hard labour' (Gn 31:42; cf. v. 16).

12 The translation of בוֹ, omitted in G, is found in αὐτῷ of G(A), *ei* (Jerome). It is quoted in the margin of Syro-hex., according to 'all' the hexaplar witnesses. The *qerê* יָשִׁיב is at the basis of the versions:

ἀποδώσει (G), *reddat* (Vulg.), יתיב (Targ.). Syr. translates by ܘܢܕܟܐ 'to cleanse' (?) and reverses the order of זרעך and גרנך.

The *hiph'il* הֶאֱמִין, followed by a proposition beginning with כִּי, to connote 'believe' (9:16) or 'rely on', 'expect' (15:22) that something will happen. The complement בוֹ 'in him' designates the person in whom one trusts (4:18) and from whom one expects something. Hence the translation will be: 'Do you rely on him to return?' It is in fact clear that the *kethîb*, יָשׁוּב, which enables us to divide the verse into two hemistichs, is preferable to the *qerê* יָשִׁיב, which presupposes, as do also the Massoretic vocalisation and the versions, that the 1st hemistich included זַרְעֶךָ 'that he will bring back your grain'. In this case we should have one hemistich excessively long and another too short. Note that the 2nd hemistich וְגׇרְנְךָ יֶאֱסֹף would in fact mean 'and that he will garner your threshing floor' or, if we regard גרנך as a locative, 'and that he will garner in your threshing floor'. In 34:14 we have parallelism between השיב and אסף (cf. Comm.). The verb אסף means 'collect', 'gather', and also 'bring back', 'take back' (cf. 34:14). A slight change consists in reading לְגׇרְנְךָ instead of וְגׇרְנֶךָ. The meaning is clear: 'and (do you hope) that he will bring back your grain to your threshing floor?' The buffalo does not come back to the stable, he does not return to the farm pulling a cart loaded with grain.

13   The wing of the ostrich is gay,
     She possesses a gracious plumage and pinions!

13   אַם; MT: אִם.

13 Vv. 13-18, marked with asterisk in Jerome, Syro-hex. (with the
exception of v. 13a), Colb. (with the
exception of v. 13), did not exist in
G. The present text is derived from
Theod. (cf. Syro-hex.). The presence
of νεέλασα in G(A, א) constitutes a
proof that v. 13a (in spite of the fact
that Syro-hex. has forgotten the
asterisk) also belongs to Theod.
It seems indeed that Theod. has
endeavoured to preserve the Hebrew
words of v. 13 in the following
translation: πτέρυξ τερπομένων (+
νεέλασα, A, א^{e.c}), ἐὰν συλλάβη ἀσιδὰ
καὶ νεσσά. The word τερπομένων
corresponds to רננים translated in
accordance with etymology (cf.
inf.). Then we have νεέλασα = נעלסה,
ἀσιδά = חסידה, καὶ νεσσά = ונצה.
The words ἐὰν συλλάβη correspond
therefore to אם־אברה, the noun
being regarded as a verb. It is
necessary to collate the other translations: πτερύγιον αἰνούντων συνανα-
πλέκεται...ἐρωδιοῦ καὶ ἱέρακος (Aq.,
whose translation for אם־אברה is
missing), πτέρον ἀγλαϊσμοῦ περιφύεται,
εἰ ἐναγκαλίσεται ὁ κύκνος πτίλους
αὐτοῦ (Symm.), *penna struthionis
similis est pennis herodii et accipitris*
(Vulg.). Targ. renders רננים נעלסה
by 'the wild cock which praises
(משבחא) and glorifies (ומקלסא)'.
For חסידה ונצה, Targ. חוריתא
ונוציתא 'stork and vulture'(?). Syr.
translates רננים by ܡܒܚ 'which
praise' (cf. Targ.) and paraphrases
the rest of the verse: 'it rises up and
flies and comes and makes a nest'(?).
   This verse is a *crux interpretum*.
The Septuagint probably faltered in
face of the difficulties of the text,
with the result that the whole of
the passage relative to the ostrich
(13-18) was suppressed. That it is
a question of the ostrich, the de-

scription contained in vv. 14-18
leaves no doubt. But the juxtaposition of the words in v. 13 makes
possible so many combinations that
Schultens already counted as many
as twenty different interpretations
which we cannot review here. Let
us quote the most recent versions:
'The wing of the ostrich ceaselessly
flaps, but is it a pious wing, or even
a wing?' (Renan); 'And the ostrich
with its noisy wings!... It has
neither the tenderness nor the flight
of a bird' (Le Hir); 'The wing of
the ostrich is gaily spread out; one
would suppose it were the wing and
the plumage of the stork' (Segond);
'The wing of the ostrich flaps gaily;
but its wing is not gracious, neither
is its plumage' (Loisy); 'The ostrich
flaps its wings gaily; if only its
wings and its feathers were tenderly
faithful!' (*Bible du rabbinat français*).
The word רְנָנִים is a *hapax*, the root
of which is רנן 'to be jubilant', 'to
sing' (38: 7), whence the translations of Theod., Aq., Symm.,
Syr. While Targ. mistakes the animal
designated as 'the singers' (cf. sup.),
Vulg. does not hesitate to translate
by *struthio* 'ostrich'. As is pointed
out by Bochart (*Hieroz.*, II, cols.
238ff.), the Arabs give the description 'song' to the cry of the female
ostrich and in this way differentiate
it from the shrill clamours of the
male. Sa'adia translated literally as
صرنين 'the singers'. The verb נֶעֱלָסָה
is the *niph'al* of עלס which we have
met in 20: 18, with the meaning of
'enjoy' (cf. Comm.); the root is
connected with עלז and עלץ. The
niph'al will mean 'to be gay, merry'.
The 1st hemistich means: 'The wing
of the ostrich is gay' (cf. v. 18). The
difficulties of the 2nd hemistich

14   When she leaves her eggs on the ground,
      And warms them on the soil,

spring from the ambiguous words חֲסִידָה and נֹצֶה. The former is the feminine adjective 'pious', 'gracious' or else the name of a bird, namely the stork (Targ.), *avis pia* (cf. Lv 11:19; Dt 14:18, etc.). Symm. identifies it with the swan, Aq. and Vulg. with the heron (cf. sup.). In these interpretations, it is natural that נֹצָה also becomes a bird's name, and it is thus that, by assimilation to נֵץ, we find the word נצה translated as 'sparrow-hawk' in Aq. and Vulg. (cf. sup.). But one fact seems to us to dominate everything else. To the word אֶבְרָה 'feather' (Ps 68:14) corresponds נֹצָה 'pinions' as may be clearly seen from Ezk 17:3, where the description of the eagle comprises in turn הַכְּנָפַיִם 'the two wings', הָאֵבֶר 'the plumage', הַנּוֹצָה 'the pinions'. In Assyrian likewise the word *kappu* 'wing' (כנף) is associated with *abru* 'feather' (אבר, אברה), and *nâṣu* 'pinions' (נוצה); cf. Holma, *Die Namen der Körperteile*, p. 140 and p. 145. The vogue of ostrich feathers inclines us to see in חֲסִידָה an epithet of אֶבְרָה 'gracious plumage'. The inexplicable אִם is due to an error in vocalisation. The word was אֵם 'mother', used as a feminine in the sense of the Arabic *abû* 'father', with the connotation that what is referred to 'possesses' a certain object or quality, etc. Everything then becomes perfectly clear: 'The wing of the ostrich is gay, she possesses a gracious plumage and pinions!' This is intended as an introductory observation to bring before us the picture of a rare bird (cf. 40:15). The subsequent verses emphasise the contrasts which are found in the behaviour of this bird, the ostrich. Van Hoonacker

already proposed the vocalisation אֵם 'mother', though he changed all the words of the 2nd hemistich to yield the translations: 'a mother who has utterly lost all tenderness' (*RB*, 1913, pp. 420ff.). Ehrlich, who also reads אֵם, rejects חסידה interpreted as 'ostrich' (!) to the end of the verse, deletes ונצה, and replaces אברה by אכזריה 'cruel' (!). Hoffmann proposed חסרה instead of חסידה and placed אברה after חסרה, while retaining the vocalisation אִם: 'Does she lack feathers and pinions?' We will be excused from continuing the enumeration of the various hypotheses. Let us merely insist on the fact that we have not changed a single consonant of the text.

14 On the text of G, cf. v. 13. For ביציה, Syr. ܒܢܬܐ 'her daughters'. Vulg. *tu forsitan in pulvere calefacies ea* vocalises תְּחֹמֵם instead of תְּחַמֵּם; cf. Syr. ܡܚܡܡܐ ܠܗܘܢ 'warming them'.

The ancients had noticed that the ostrich abandons her eggs on the ground, and takes no care to place them in a nest. Texts have been collected by Bochart (*Hieroz.*, II, cols. 250ff.). This is how Buffon expresses himself on the matter: 'In the torrid zone, ostriches are content to place their eggs on a mass of sand which they have roughly piled up with their feet, and where the heat of the sun in itself makes them hatch out.' The phrase לָאָרֶץ 'on the earth' (2:13; 15:29; 16:13) has as a parallel עַל־עָפָר 'on the soil' (19:25; 41:25). By reason of euphony, the masculine plural suffix after תְּחַמֵּם 'it warms (them)' has been omitted. There is no reason whatever to read תַּנִּחֵם 'she deposits

15   She forgets that a foot might crush them,
     And that a wild beast might trample them:
16   She is harsh towards her young as though they were not hers,
     She is unconcerned about the uselessness of all her labour!
17   This is because Eloah has deprived her of wisdom,
     And has not imparted to her understanding!

them' (from נוח), as is proposed by Beer, who neglects the evidence of the versions. We have had the *hithpa'el* of חמם in 31: 20. Vv. 14-15 are a sort of preamble to v. 16. By its behaviour the ostrich seems to set little store by its progeny.

15   On the text of G, cf. v. 13. Theod. renders ותשכח by καὶ ἐπελάθοντο, but G(A) preserves ἐπελάθετο. Syr. translates the 1st hemistich: 'and she forgets that she has bird's feet', probably as a result of interpreting זור in the sense of 'to fly' (Baumann).

The verb שכח 'to forget' in the sense of 'not to think of' (9: 27). The meaning of זור is 'to squeeze' (Jg 6: 38) and 'to crush' (Is 59: 5). The singular suffixes in תְּזוּרֶהָ and תְּדוּשֶׁהָ take the place of ביציה 'her eggs'; cf. 6: 20 (Gesenius-Kautzsch, § 135p). The expression חַיַּת הַשָּׂדֶה 'wild beast' as in 5: 23; 40: 20. The verb דושׁ in its basic sense of 'to trample'.

16   On the text of G, cf. v. 13. For הקשיח, Theod. ἀπεσκλήρυνεν, Vulg. *duratur*, but Targ. שחנא 'she hatches', Syr. هوهم۸ 'she multiplies'. Targ. and Syr. interpret ללא־לה by 'which are not hers', but Theod. ὥστε μὴ ἑαυτήν and Vulg. *quasi non sint sui* are more literal. For יגיעה, Theod. ἐκοπίασεν, Syr. עמ۸ 'she has tired herself', Vulg. *laboravit*. For בלי־פחד, Vulg. *nullo timore cogente*.

The *hiph'il* of קשׁח recurs in Is 63: 17 with the sense of 'to harden' the

heart. The object is here 'her sons' or 'her young' (v. 4), marking the term of the action performed by the subject: she treats her young harshly, she is cruel towards them. The use of feminine suffixes dispels all ambiguity, which enables us to keep the masculine form הִקְשִׁחַ. The expression לְלֹא־לָהּ, the meaning of which is not doubtful (cf. Theod., Vulg.), implies the verb חשׁב 'esteem', 'consider' (13: 24; 19: 15): counting them as not her own. The phrase לָרִיק יְגִיעָהּ recalls Is 49: 4, לריק יגעתי 'I have laboured in vain'. In Is 65:23 the formula 'they will not labour in vain' is followed by ולא ילדו לבהלה 'and they will not bring forth for ruin'. Here the labour is again an allusion to giving birth or laying eggs. The בְּלִי־פַחַד 'without fear', 'without concern', is a compound noun like בלי־שם (30: 8), בלי־דעת (38: 2).

17   On the text of G, cf. v. 13. Syr. ۸مه۸ 'has multiplied' reads השגה instead of הִשָּׁהּ. For בבינה, Theod. ἐν τῇ συνέσει and Targ. בביונתא, but Symm. simply σύνεσιν, Jerome *intellectum*, Vulg. *intelligentiam*, Syr. همحلا.

Reason for the behaviour of the ostrich: her proverbial stupidity. It is God who is the author of wisdom and understanding (38: 36). He has not imparted this gift to the ostrich: 'It is because Eloah has deprived her of wisdom and has not imparted to her understanding.' The *hiph'il* of נשׁה, literally 'to make forget', i.e.

18   But as soon as she rears herself up,
      She laughs at the horse and his rider!

19   Do you give to the horse his vigour?
      Do you clothe his neck with a mane?

to deprive of a quality which ought to be there. The verb חלק 'to endow with', 'to impart' something to some one, with the partitive ב" before the complement denoting what one imparts. Cf. the use of ב" in 7: 13; 21: 25.

18 On the text of G, cf. v. 13. For במרום תמריא, Theod. ἐν ὕψει ὑψώσει, Vulg. *in altum alas erigit*, Targ. במרומא טיסא 'upwards she flies'. Syr. 'she rears herself erect like the palm tree' connects תמריא with תָּמָר 'palm tree'.

The poet proposes to finish by a feature which, in contrast with the preceding description, conjures up the great speed of the ostrich. This animal, so heartless and stupid, has the gift of rapidity in flight. The idiom כָּעֵת 'like the time' to connote 'as soon as the time is at hand', 'as soon as'. We have כְּעֵת מוּתָהּ 'at the moment of her death' in 1 S 4: 20. The phrase בַּמָּרוֹם 'in the height', 'on high' (Hab 2: 9); cf. למרום in 5: 11. It is unnecessary to change to במרוץ 'in her running' (Hitzig, Duhm), still less to בא מרים '(at the moment when) the archers arrive' (! Wright, Budde). The complement במרום refers to תָּמְרִיא. The verb מרא comes from a root cognate with מרה 'to be rebellious'; cf. מרד 'to revolt'. Revolt implies a rising up. We propose to recognise in מרא the meaning of 'rising up' physically. The *hiph'il* assumes a meaning similar to the *qal* (20: 6; 21: 3, etc.). The 1st hemistich will therefore be 'as soon as she rears herself up'. We are thus freed from the necessity of having recourse to the reading תמהר 'she hastens' (Hontheim) or תאמיר 'she

rises' (from אמיר 'top', Graetz). The verb שׂחק with ל" (cf. v. 7). The last words לסוס ולרכבו 'at the horse and his rider' recall סוס ורכבו 'the horse and his rider' of the Song of Moses (Ex 15: 1). They form a natural transition between the ostrich and the horse, סוס, of v. 19.

19 The text of G begins again with this verse. For רעמה, G φόβον, Symm. κλαγγήν, Theod. χρεμετισμόν (Jerome and Vulg. *hinnitum*), Targ. תוקפא 'strength', Syr. ‏‎ 'weapon'.

Here begins the classic description of the horse. The opening is marked by a question (cf. 9-12): 'do you give to the horse his vigour?' The word גְּבוּרָה designates both physical strength and moral strength (12: 13; 26: 14). The 2nd hemistich contains a difficult word, the *hapax* רַעְמָה, which is usually connected with רעם 'to thunder' (37: 4, 5), to produce the meaning 'shout' (Symm.) or 'neighing' (Theod., Jerome, Vulg.). But it is difficult to translate in this sense, for it can hardly be said that the neck is clothed with neighing, still less with thunder (contra Le Hir). The meaning 'weapon', postulated by Syr., stems from the fact that the thunderbolt is regarded as a weapon (20: 25); but then it is a question of lightning. It is likely that Targ. has been guided simply by parallelism in its translation by 'strength'. There remains G φόβον 'fear', which goes back to the original meaning of the root רעם (parallel to רעש, רעל, רעד), namely *commoveri*, *tremere*. This meaning has persisted in Ezk 27: 35, where רעמו פנים (following the parallelism) simply means 'the high dignitaries tremble'. What has confused com-

20   Do you make him leap like the locust?
      His proud neighing strikes terror!

21   *He* paws in the valley and exults mightily,
      He goes forth to meet the weapons of war,

21   יַחְפּוֹר (G, Vulg., Syr.); MT: יחפרו.

mentators in this passage of Ezekiel is that they have kept for פנים the meaning 'faces' whereas it quite clearly denotes 'personages', 'high officials' (*L'Emploi métaphorique*, p. 60), in parallelism with 'their kings'. In 1 S 1:6, the *hiph'il* of רעם means 'to make tremble' with anger. The shaking caused in the heavens by the phenomenon of thunder has made it possible to use the same root רעם for the connotation 'to thunder'. The substantive רַעַם means 'thunder' (26:14). The feminine רַעְמָה can mean the thing which quivers and shakes. Here the allusion is to the 'mane' which streams in the wind. Cf. the Greek φόβη 'mane' alongside φόβος 'fear', the two words stemming from φέβομαι 'to be afraid', 'to tremble'. Hence we may retain the meaning proposed by Gesenius (*Thesaurus*, II, p. 1297) and which has been abandoned in the dictionary of Gesenius-Buhl. Bochart already, by a different line of reasoning, proposed to translate רעמה as 'mane' (what is lifted up, following the sense of רעם in Syriac); cf. *Hieroz.*, I, col. 119. The horse's mane is truly the clothing of its neck, just as the head of hair is the cloak or veil of woman (1 Co 11:15). It is too lightly getting rid of the difficulty created by רעמה to read simply עצמה 'might' (Hontheim) or רקמה 'motley' in the sense of 'mane' (Duhm).

20 G περιέθηκας δὲ αὐτῷ πανοπλίαν does not translate v. 20a but paraphrases v. 19b, assigning to רעמה a meaning similar of that of Syr. V.

20a is therefore omitted by G. The 2nd hemistich is literally translated by Vulg. *gloria narium ejus terror*. G δόξαν δὲ στηθέων αὐτοῦ τόλμη is adapted to v. 19b (retranslated as v. 20a). Targ. renders נחרו by לשלושתא דנחיריה 'the mucus of his nostrils'. Syr. 'do you terrify him with fear?' completely changes the meaning of the 2nd hemistich.

In Jl 2:4 it is the locust which is compared to the horse (cf. Rev. 9:7). The root רעש 'to quiver', 'to shake' (34:29) recurs in v. 24 to denote the impatient quivering of the war-horse. The comparison with a locust makes it clear that the meaning is 'to jump', 'to leap': do you make him leap like the locust? The word נַחֲרוֹ presupposes a *hapax* נַחַר with the same meaning as נַחֲרָה 'neighing' (Jer 8:16), from the root נחר 'to breathe', 'to blow' (Jer 6:29) especially 'to snort', whence נחירים 'nostrils' (41:12). The idiom הוֹד נַחֲרוֹ 'the glory of his neighing' (cf. הוֹד in 37:22; 40:10) should be compared with הוֹד קוֹלוֹ 'glory of his voice' (Is 30:30) to connote 'his glorious voice'. The use of the noun אֵימָה 'terror' as an attribute is more expressive than would be a simple adjective אַיְמָה 'terrible' (contra Bickell, Duhm). The interpretation of Budde, who regards אימה as a parallel word to הוֹד 'glory, terror, is his neighing', is not in conformity with the grammatical construction.

21 G ἀνορύσσων, Vulg. *fodit*, Syr. ܣܦܒ have correctly read יַחְפּוֹר instead of יחפרו. Vulg. paraphrases

22   He laughs at fear and is not dismayed;
      He does not recoil from the sword.

23   On him the quiver rattles,
      The flash of the lance and javelin.

the 1st part of the verse: *terram ungula fodit, exultat audacter*. For בכח, Syr. ܒܚܝܠ 'in the valley', on account of the parallelism with בעמק. G connects בכח with the 2nd hemistich: ἐκπορεύεται δὲ εἰς πεδίον ἐν ἰσχύι. It is apparent that G retranslates בעמק, which figures already in ἐν πεδίῳ of the 1st hemistich. The words לקראת־נשק will be translated by G in v. 22. Syr. interprets the 2nd hemistich very broadly: 'and he sets off on his course with armour'.

It is clear that יַחְפְּרוּ is a defective writing of יַחְפּוֹר which is preserved in G, Vulg., Syr. The verb חפר 'to dig' (3:21) is here used to connote the action of the horse which 'paws' the ground. In Arabic the horse's hoof can be called *ḥâfir* 'that which digs'. It is in the valley that the horse's impatience is manifested, for it is there that armies are drawn up in battle array (Jg 7:1, 8, 12; Is 28:21, etc.). The verb שִׂישׂ 'to exult' as in 3:22. The complement בְּכֹחַ 'with strength' conveys the idea of the horse's exultation reaching its maximum pitch of intensity on account of the prospect of the fight. It is not necessary to link בכח to the 2nd hemistich (G, Budde, Duhm, etc.). The 1st hemistich includes two short clauses which balance each other, exactly as in v. 22a. The verb יצא 'go out' is especially used to denote the action of setting forth to war or of marching to the fight (1 S 8:20; Is 42:13, etc.) At the close, נֶשֶׁק 'armour', 'weapons' (20:24).

22 G συναντῶν βασιλεῖ καταγελᾷ represents the end of v. 21 (cf. sup.)

combined with ישׂחק. It was βέλει (A, אᵉ·ᶜ), a translation of נשק of v. 21, and not βασιλεῖ which stood in the original text. The words לפחד ולא יחת have been omitted by G, which, after καταγελᾷ, translates the 2nd hemistich literally. Vulg. summarises v. 22: *contemnit pavorem, nec cedit gladio*. For פחד, Syr. ܚܦܪܐ 'pit', reading פחת.

The verb שׂחק with ל" as in v. 18. The horse 'laughs at fear'. Cf. 5:22, where שׂחק, with ל" before the complement, means to 'mock at' a scourge. One laughs at something which one does not fear or which is unknown to one. The horse does not know fear 'and he is not dismayed'. The verb חתת (32:15), in the *niph'al* as in 26:5 (cf. Comm.). Notice the antithesis between שׁוּב מִפְּנֵי 'return from before' and יֵצֵא לִקְרַאת 'go out to meet' (v. 21.). The general term נשק 'armour', 'weapons' is here answered by the more specific term חֶרֶב 'sword'. We had the formula מִפְּנֵי חֶרֶב in 19:29. The reckless bravery of the horse and its keenness for combat have become proverbial. Cf. the description given by Buffon: 'As intrepid as his master, the horse sees danger and confronts it; he adapts himself to the clash of arms, he likes it and seeks it and is inspired with the same ardour.'

23 G ἐπ' αὐτῷ γαυριᾷ τόξον καὶ μάχαιρα connects תרנה with רנן and summarises the 2nd hemistich in καὶ μάχαιρα. G(A) adds ὀξυσθενής (translation of להב) before μάχαιρα. Jerome has as the 2nd hemistich: *lanceae hastaeque tremore* (with asterisk), stemming from Theod. (ac-

24   In his excitement and impatience he swallows the ground,
      He can no longer stand still when the trumpet sounds.

cording to the quotation in the margin of Syro-hex.). For תרגה, Vulg. *sonabit*, Targ. תשדי 'is hurled', Syr. מאהבדלא 'praised'. For אשפה, Targ. זינא 'the weapon', which is too vague. Vulg. *vibrabit hasta et clypeus* regards להב as a verb. Targ. interprets להב by שננא חרבא 'the sharp sword'. For כידון, Targ. רומחא (which translates חנית in Syr.) 'lance', Syr. נרכא 'lance'.

As has been understood by G, Vulg., Syr., the verb רנה, which is not met with elsewhere, represents a root parallel to רנן 'to sing' (38:7), with the implication 'resound', 'rattle'. It is a question of arrows which rattle against each other in the quiver. They are called בני אשפה 'sons of the quiver' in La 3:13. The word אשפה corresponds to the Akkadian *išpatu* 'quiver'. Note the series of arms: armour in general (v. 21), the sword (v. 22), here the quiver, the lance, and the javelin. The association חנית וכידון 'lance and javelin' as in 1 S 17:45. The glitter of the metal is depicted by להב 'flame'; cf. Nah 3:3, where we have להב חרב 'the flame of the sword' alongside ברק חנית 'the flash of the lance'. In Jg 3:22 the flame connotes specially the blade, the flashing part of the sword. Cf. 'the flame (להט with the same meaning as להב) of the wheeling sword', which is placed by God on the way of approach to the Tree of Life (Gn 3:24).

24 G καὶ ὀργῇ ἀφανιεῖ τὴν γῆν omits ברעש. Vulg. *fervens et fremens sorbet terram* retains all the force of the MT, while Symm. ὡς καταπίνων softens it down. Targ. יעבד גומתא 'he makes a hole' and Syr. יוסא כלא 'he runs upon' likewise diminish the force of יגמא. Targ. reproduces word

for word the 2nd hemistich, but Syr. 'and he has no fear of the sound of the trumpet' returns to the idea expressed in v. 22. G καὶ οὐ μὴ πιστεύσῃ and Vulg. *nec reputat* assign to the verb האמין the meaning of 'believe' (cf. 29:24).

The roots רעש 'to be shaken' (v. 20; 34:29) and רגז 'to be agitated, excited' (12:6) are associated in Is 14:16; Ps 77:19. The substantives רעש (41:21) and רגז (3:17, 26, etc.) suggest the condition of the horse at the moment when the fight begins. It is this condition which provokes the manifestations then described. Hence one may translate בְּרַעַשׁ וְרֹגֶז by 'with excitement and impatience'. With a great wealth of erudition, Bochart shows how the expression יְגַמֶּא־אָרֶץ 'he swallows the ground' is characteristic of the genius of Arabic poets, who generally use the verb *iltaham* 'swallow in a single draught' to depict the mare devouring space: *iltaham al-faras al-arḍ* 'the mare has swallowed the earth' (*Hieroz.*, I, cols. 143ff.). In Gn 24:17 the *hiph'il* of גמא means 'to make swallow', 'to give drink to'. In Aramaic the cognate verb is גמע, which will be used to translate עלע 'to swallow' in v. 30. The phrase לֹא יַאֲמִין is capable of two interpretations. Either: 'he does not believe' (29:24), i.e. 'he does not dare to believe' in his happiness, in the prospect of the fight proclaimed by the sound of the trumpet (cf. G and Vulg.). In that case we should have to translate: and he cannot believe that it is the sound of the trumpet! But, in the light of v. 25a, it is more natural to admit that כִּי··· introduces simply an adverbial clause of time 'when there is sound of trumpet', i.e. when the trumpet sounds. Now, the verb אמן can be

25   At the sound of the trumpet, he says: 'Aha!'
      And from afar he sniffs the smell of battle,
      The thunder of the captains and the cries of war!

26   Is it by your understanding that the hawk is clad with
          feathers,
      That it spreads its wings southwards?

taken in its etymological sense which is 'to be firm', 'to stand still' (cf. the *niph'al* in Is 22: 23, 25), whence the derived meaning: 'to be faithful, true' (in the *niph'al*), 'to have confidence', 'to believe' (in the *hiph'il*). The meaning of the *hiph'il* will be similar to that of the *qal* (cf. v. 18). The meaning thus obtained is: 'and he can no longer stand still when the trumpet sounds', which recalls so vividly the lines of Virgil (*Georgics*, III, 83f.): *tum si qua sonum procul arma dedere, stare loco nescit.*

25 G σάλπιγγος δὲ σημαινούσης and Vulg. *ubi audierit buccinam* interpret בְּדֵי שֹׁפָר in accordance with the end of v. 24. Syr. has simply حمل 'at the noise'. The 3rd hemistich is rendered σὺν ἅλματι καὶ κραυγῇ by G, which seems to read עַם instead of רַעַם. Vulg. translates וּתְרוּעָה by *et ululatum exercitus* (antithesis of *exhortationem ducum*), Syr. by ܚܘܝܠܐ 'by his neighing'.

The word דַי 'a sufficiency of . . .' is expletive after בְּ, just as in בְּדֵי־רִיק 'in vain' and בְּדֵי־אֵשׁ 'in fire' of Jer 51: 58. Thus then בְּדֵי שֹׁפָר means simply 'at the trumpet', i.e. at the sound of the trumpet. The horse is treated as human, he speaks and says: 'Aha!' The interjection הֶאָח is a shout of joy (Is 44: 16; Ezk 25: 3; 26: 2, etc.). Even before he is on the field of battle, the steed sniffs the smell of the fray: 'and from afar he sniffs the smell of battle!' We would say rather, in more modern terms, that he smells the powder. The *hiph'il* of רוח in the

sense of 'smell', 'sniff'; cf. רִיחַ 'smell' (14: 9). The 3rd hemistich explains and amplifies the word מִלְחָמָה 'battle'. On the one hand, 'the thunder of the captains', the word רַעַם 'thunder' (26: 14) denoting the bursts of shouting by the generals giving their orders. Compare conversely קוֹל 'voice' to connote 'thunder'. The word תְּרוּעָה is well chosen to signify the shouts of war (Jer 4: 19; 49: 2; Am 1: 14). We have in Am 2: 2 both קוֹל שׁוֹפָר 'sound of the trumpet' and תרועה 'battle cry'.

26 For יֵאֵבֶר, G ἔστηκεν, Syr. ܩܐܡ 'has been' seem to read the *niph'al* of עבד. Vulg. *plumescit* and Targ. יתאבר are faithful to the MT. G paraphrases the 2nd hemistich: ἀναπετάσας τὰς πτέρυγας ἀκίνητος, καθορῶν τὰ πρὸς νότον; Jerome marks with asterisk *respiciens ad austrum*.

The opening question marks the beginning of a new description (cf. v. 19): 'Is it by your understanding?' Cf. מבינתי in 20: 3. The verb אבר does not appear elsewhere. The *hiph'il* makes it a denominative of אֶבְרָה, אֵבֶר 'feathers', 'pinions' (cf. v. 13). The meaning is not doubtful: to grow feathers, become clad with plumage. The bird designated by the name of נֵץ (cf. Comm. on v. 13) is certainly the hawk, as is abundantly shown by Bochart (*Hieroz.*, II, cols. 266ff.). It figures among the unclean beasts in Lv 11: 16; Dt 14: 15. The 2nd hemistich, 'it spreads its wings southwards', alludes to some species of migratory hawks. There

27   Is it at your command that the eagle soars,
      And builds his nest aloft?
28   He dwells on a rock and spends the night there,
      On the crag of a rock and a fastness,

is no reason at all to translate:
'against the wind of the south'
(contra Duhm); if so, we should
have rather עַל־תֵּימָן; cf. Jer 48:40
(אֶל for עַל); 49:22. The description
begins with the hawk and continues
with the eagle (v. 27). The author's
theme is the bird of prey whose
characteristics are as well illustrated
by the eagle as by the hawk.

27 For יַגְבִּיהַ, G ὑψοῦται, Vulg.
elevabitur, Targ. יִתְגְּבַּה and Syr.
ܢܬܥܠܐ 'rises up'. G renders the
2nd hemistich: γὺψ δὲ ἐπὶ νοσσιᾶς
αὐτοῦ. Vulg. explains very well
יָרִים by *in arduis ponet*. Syr. places
at the end of v. 27 the word סֶלַע of
v. 28.
      The question הֲמִבִּינָתְךָ 'is it by
your understanding?' is balanced by
אִם־עַל־פִּיךָ 'is it at your command?'
Note the use of פֶּה 'mouth' to connote what proceeds from the mouth,
the word or command; cf. עַל־פִּי
פַרְעֹה 'on the order of Pharaoh'
(Gn 45:21), עַל־פִּי יְהוָה 'at the
command of Yahweh' (Ex 17:1,
etc.) (*L'emploi métaphorique*, pp.
84f.). The *hiph'il* of גבה implies the
complement עוּף: 'raise its flight'
(5:7). Duhm, following Bickell,
deletes יַגְבִּיהַ נֶשֶׁר, supposed to be a
quotation from Jer 49:16. But in
the latter passage we have 'if you,
like the eagle, make your nest on
high', which expresses rather the
idea contained in our 2nd hemistich.
In order to save his strophic scheme,
Duhm sees himself obliged to eliminate further כִּי (a dittograph!) and
סֶלַע יִשְׁכֹּן of v. 28, which is said to
have sprung from Jer 49:16 like
יַגְבִּיהַ נֶשֶׁר. But Jer 49:16 has a
rather different text שֹׁכְנִי בְחַגְוֵי
הַסֶּלַע 'those who dwell in the clefts

of the rock'. Bochart cites Aristotle
and Pliny as witnesses of the idea of
the ancients that the eagle builds its
eyrie at an almost inaccessible height
(*Hieroz.*, II, col. 173). Steuernagel
and Budde lengthen the 2nd hemistich by changing יָרִים to יָכִין בֶּהָרִים
'he establishes amid the mountains'.
But the place where the eagle situates its nest will be given in v. 28.
In fact, the poet has added כִּי 'that'
which is expletive after the interrogative (cf. הֲכִי 'is it that?' in 6:22),
in order to give more body to the
2nd hemistich, which may be translated quite simply: 'and that he
builds his nest aloft?' In Assyrian an
inaccessible fortress is qualified by
the phrase *kîma qinni našri ašarid
iṣṣurê* 'like the nest of the eagle, the
first of birds' (Prism of Sennacherib,
III, 68-9).

28 V. 28b, marked with asterisk
in Jerome and Syro-hex., did not
exist in G. The present text is derived from Theod. (cf. Syro-hex.). The
word סֶלַע of the opening is omitted
in G, which renders v. 28a by καθ-
εσθεὶς αὐλίζεται. Syr. translates by
ܒܟܐܦܐ 'on the rock' linked to
v. 27. Vulg. *et in praeruptis silicibus
commoratur* transfers וְיִתְלֹנָן to the
2nd hemistich. Symm. ἠρεμῶν seems
to read יִשְׁמֹן instead of יִשְׁכֹּן.
      It is on the jutting peak of the
rock that the eagle likes to take
refuge: 'he dwells on a rock and
spends the night there'. The verb
שָׁכַן 'to dwell' with the accusative
(15:28). The *hithpa'el* of לוּן or
לִין 'to spend the night' (31:32), as
in Ps 91:1. We have יִתְלֹנָן as a
parallel to יָשִׂים קִנּוֹ 'he places his
nest' (cf. v. 27b) in Sir 14:26. The
2nd hemistich makes vividly precise

29   From thence he spies out a prey,
       His eyes pierce to the farthest distance!

30   And his young *lick up* the blood,
       Wherever there are dead bodies, there he is!

30 יְלָעוּ (cf. Syr.); MT: יעלעו.

the spot chosen by the king of birds: 'on the crag of a rock and a fastness'. The 'tooth of rock' (cf. 1 S 14: 4). as in 'la Dent du Midi', indicates a very sharp peak (*L'Emploi métaphorique*, p. 88). The מְצוּדָה is the natural fortress formed by certain mountain crests (1 S 22: 4f.; 24: 23). Such is the observatory whence the eagle spies out his prey.

29 V. 29b, marked with asterisk in Jerome and Syro-hex., did not exist in G. The present text is derived from Theod. (cf. Syro-hex.). Syr. places וּמצודה, which is translated ܘܣܡ ܨܝܕܗ 'and by his hunting' (reading וּמְצֵידָה), at the beginning of v. 29 and summarises v. 29a by ܡܣܬܡܟ 'he supports himself'. G renders משם by ἐκεῖσε ὤν.

The verb חפר 'to seek' by digging, (3: 21; cf. above v. 21) or again by spying out, as here: 'to watch keenly'. Use of אֹכֶל 'fodder' as in 38: 41. The phrase לְמֵרָחוק figured, in a moral sense, in 36: 3. On the other hand, we had הביט 'to look', together with מרחוק 'from afar', in 36: 25. Quotations testifying to the keenness of the eagle's vision would be endless. Bochart recalls the description of Apuleius: *cum igitur eo sese aquila extulit ... inde cuncta despiciens ... circumtuetur et quaerit quorsus potissimum in praedam superne sese ruat* (*Florida*, 2; ed. Teubner, p. 2).

30 The *hapax* יעלעו is translated φύρονται (G), ἐστομισμένοι (Aq.), καταρροφῶσιν (Symm.), *lambent* (Vulg.), גמען 'swallow' (Targ.; cf· גמא in v. 24), ܠܚܣ 'lap up' (Syr.). For חללים, Symm. σάρκες τετρωμένων, Syr. ܡܩܛܠܐ ܕܩܛܠܐ 'a slaying of slain'. G παραχρῆμα εὑρίσκονται for שם הוא replaces the singular by a plural. Vulg. *statim adest* agrees with G as to the meaning of the idiom, but preserves the singular.

The word אֶפְרֹחַ, in the plural, denotes the young that have just been hatched out (Dt 22: 6; Ps 84: 4). The root is probably פרח 'shoot forth', 'bud' (14: 9). The writing יְעַלְעוּ presupposes a verb עלע which does not exist. On the other hand, there does exist a verb לעע (Syr. ܠܥ; cf. sup.) with the meaning 'lap up', 'lick up' (Ob 16; Sir 31: 17); cf. Comm. on 6: 3. The Arabic ولع has exactly the same shade of meaning. The Syriac version uses precisely the verb ܠܥ to render the Hebrew לקק 'to lap' (Jg 7: 5-7). In 1 K 21: 19 and 22: 38 the verb לקק has as its complement אֶת־דָּם. It is used with reference to the dogs which 'lap up' the blood of Naboth and Jezebel. These facts sufficiently demonstrate the thesis that the extraordinary יעלעו is a distortion of יְלָעוּ 'they lap up', the superfluous ע being perhaps a *mater lectionis*. The reading יְלַעְלֵעוּ, which has been generally accepted since Gesenius, seems to us less probable then יְלָעוּ which, as an Aramaic form, corresponds to יְלֹקוּ of 1 K 21: 19; 22: 28. The young of the eagle feed on blood: σαρκῶν δὲ ἥδεται βορᾷ καὶ πίνει αἷμα, καὶ τὰ νεόττια ἐκτρέφει τοῖς αὐτοῖς (Aelianus, *De nat. anim.*, X, 14). With the 2nd hemistich, cf. Gn 21: 17, בַּאֲשֶׁר הוּא שָׁם *in quo hic ibi*, to connote 'there where he is'. Here first of all וּבַאֲשֶׁר חֲלָלִים 'there where there are dead bodies', then שָׁם הוּא 'he is there!' The word חָלָל, which properly designates one who is fatally wounded (cf. 24: 12), literally 'the pierced one' eventually comes to be applied to any one who dies of a violent death, and to the corpse that is exposed without decent burial (Dt 21: 1, 2, 3, 6, etc.). With the 2nd hemistich, cf. Mt 24: 28: ὅπου ἐὰν ᾖ τὸ πτῶμα ἐκει συναχθήσονται οἱ ἀετοί and Lk 17: 37: ὅπου τὸ σῶμα, ἐκεῖ καὶ οἱ ἀετοὶ ἐπισυναχθήσονται.

CHAPTER 40

1   And Yahweh addressed Job and said:

2   Will *he who* argues with Shaddai *yield*?

        Will he who criticises Eloah answer that?

---

2   רָב (Symm., Vulg., Targ.); MT: רֹב. — יָסוֹר (Theod., Vulg.); MT: יִסּוֹר.

40: 1   Vv. 1-2a, marked with asterisk in Syro-hex., did not exist in G. The present text is derived from Theod. (cf. Syro-hex.). It has been claimed that this v. 1 should be suppressed so as to make of v. 2 the natural sequel to 39: 30. But in that case we should have to eliminate also v. 2a, of which, however, G has preserved traces in v. 4 (cf. inf.). After the descriptions which fill up ch. 38-9, the author feels the need to bring back Yahweh on to the scene, so as to pose the final question. It is this question which Job answers in vv. 4-5. The introductory formula is reduced to the simplest terms, for it has as a counterpart that which leads to the reply of Job in v. 3. When the author wishes to preface a long speech, he adds the indication 'from the heart of the storm' (v. 6; 38: 1). Theod. renders יהוה by Κύριος ὁ Θεός but Jerome has simply *Dominus*, as also has Syro-hex. مذيٰ.

2   On the text of G for v. 2a, cf. v. 1. Theod. μὴ κρίσιν μετὰ ἱκανοῦ ἐκκλινεῖ; vocalises הָרֹב and יָסוֹר. Vulg. *numquid qui contendit cum Deo tam facile conquiescit?* and Targ. אפשר דנצי עם שדי יתרדי 'will he who argues with Shaddai stand corrected?' vocalise הָרֹב and יָסוֹר (Vulg.), יִנָּסֵר (Targ.). Symm. ἆρα ὁ δικαζόμενος πρὸς τὸν ἱκανὸν περιγενήσεται; vocalises הָרֹב and reads

יִנָּתֵר instead of יסר. יָסַר. Syr. ﺳﺤﺐﺳ ﺍﻧﺴ ﻓﻠﻜﻤﻮﺳ ﻭﻟﺪﺍﻫ 'many are the counsels of God' connects רב with רבב and reads סודי instead of יסור. Vulg. paraphrases the 2nd hemistich: *utique qui arguit Deum debet respondere ei.*

The 1st hemistich is usually interpreted as if רֹב were the infinitive of ריב; cf. הָרֹב in Jg 11: 25. In this case commentators assign to the *hapax* יָסוֹר (from the root יסר 5: 17) the meaning 'censor': form *qittôl* (Comm in 16: 7). Whence the translations: 'Will this censor of the Most High continue to contend with Him?' (Le Hir); 'Can the censor of the Almighty stand against Him?' (Renan). Literally: 'Is a censor (capable of) disputing with the Almighty?' One is surprised to find this infinitive absolute רֹב thus used instead of a verb in the finite personal mode, the more so as the normal infinitive would be רִיב or רֹב; cf. 9: 3. The versions have correctly realised that the subject is in reality the word רב and the verb יסור. If we vocalise רָב (with Symm., Vulg., and Targ.) we obtain the present participle of ריב (Is 45: 9). The phrase רָב עִם־שַׁדָּי 'he who argues with Shaddai' is the exact counterpart of מוֹכִיחַ אֱלוֹהַּ 'he who criticises Eloah'; cf. הוֹכִיחַ in 6: 25.

3   And Job answered Yahweh and said:
4   If I have been thoughtless, what shall I answer Thee?
     I will lay my hand on my mouth:
5   I have spoken once and will not *repeat* it,
     Twice, and I will not begin again!

5   אֶשְׁנֶה; MT: אענה.

We shall then vocalise יָסוּר (with Theod. and Vulg.). The verb סור without complement to connote 'yield' and 'cease' (Am 6:7; Is 11:13). The 1st hemistich will be translated: 'Will he who argues with Shaddai yield?' The 2nd hemistich presents the contrary hypothesis: 'Will he who criticises Eloah answer that?' The feminine suffix with the sense of the neuter 'that' (Gesenius-Kautzsch, § 135p). The corrections of Fried. Delitzsch (הַרְבֵּה for הרב and יַסֵּר for יסור), which yield for the 1st hemistich the meaning: 'Shaddai would have still much to teach' conflict with the requirements of parallelism.

3   V. 3 is modelled on v. 1. It introduces the short intervening remark of Job (4-5) which is like a moment's rest in the long speech of Yahweh. At v. 6 recurs the solemn formula of 38:1.

4   V. 4 of G (39:34) is redundant. Colb. indicates that the words τί ἔτι ἐγὼ ἀποκρίνομαι (marked with obelus) are not found in the Hebrew. Syro-hex. marks with obelus the passage τί ἔτι... πρὸς ταῦτα; Jerome τί ἔτι... ἀκούων τοιαῦτα. Jerome has the best division, for the text corresponding to the Hebrew begins at οὐθὲν ὤν, which is the equivalent of הן קלתי. What precedes comes from v. 2, the 1st part of which has disappeared from G, the present text being derived from Theod. (cf. vv. 1-2). One recognises יסור מוכיח אלוה of v. 2 in νουθετούμενος καὶ ἐλέγχων Κύριον. The words τί ἔτι

ἐγὼ κρίνομαι seem to be a paraphrase of הריב עם־שדי (for הרב עם־שדי of v. 2). Finally, ἀκούων τοιαῦτα is due to some kind of distortion of יענגה. For הן קלתי, Symm. ἰδοὺ κούφως ἐποίησα, Vulg. *qui leviter locutus sum*, Targ. הא אזדלזלית 'behold I have become weak', Syr. ܟܙܝ ܠܝ 'I have diminished'.

'If I have been thoughtless, what shall I answer Thee?', the same turn of phrase as in 7:20a, where the conjunction was understood. The verb קלל in its basic sense of 'to be light', from which is derived that of 'to be swift' (7:6; 9:25). The *hiph'il* of שוב with the suffix implying 'to answer' some one (13:22; 33:5). The image of the 2nd hemistich as in 21:5; 29:9. Use of the poetic לְמוֹ (27:14; 29:21; 38:40). Job promises to keep silence; he will make no further reply (v. 5).

5   G omits ולא אענה, which is necessary to the verse if not to the sense. Vulg. interprets ולא אענה by *quod utinam non dixissem*.

The 1st hemistich, 'I have spoken once and will not answer', has something abnormal about it. In accordance with the parallelism we should expect rather: 'and I will not repeat'. Cf. 33:14, 'God speaks once and He does not repeat His word.' Instead of אענה one should read אֶשְׁנֶה, with Hitzig and most critics. This slight correction yields the expected meaning; cf. the verb שנה in 27:14. The use of וּשְׁתַּיִם 'and twice' as a sequel to to אַחַת is exactly as in 33: 14, where בשתים corresponds to באחת.

6   And Yahweh answered Job, from the heart of the tempest,
         and said:

7   Gird up your loins then like a man,
         I will question you and you shall instruct me.

8   Will you in truth annul my judgment,
         Will you condemn me that you yourself might be justified?

9   Have you an arm like God's,
         And do you thunder with a voice like His?

10   Deck yourself then with pride and greatness of soul,

The end ולא אוסיף 'and I will not begin again' as we have ולא תוסיף (20:9; 38:11), ולא יוסיף (27:19; cf. Comm), לא אוסיף (34:32).

6 G renders ויען by ἔτι δὲ ὑπολαβών. For מן הסערה (sic; cf. 38:1), G ἐκ τοῦ νέφους, Targ. and Syr. same translations as in 38:1; similarly Vulg. *de turbine*.

Repetition of the solemn formula which introduces Yahweh's long speech (38:1). We shall have later (v. 7) the repetition of 38:3 which brings Job on to the scene. Cf. the repetition of 20:29 in 27:13 (cf. Comm.).

7 G adds to the beginning μή, ἀλλά. For גֶּבֶר, Targ. גַּבְרָא and Syr. ܐܢܫܐ (cf. 38:3).

We feel no difficulty in retaining as an introduction this verse which repeats 38:3. A new series of questions now begins (vv. 8ff.). The author prefaces them with the formula: 'I will question you and you shall instruct me', which is quite a natural preamble.

8 G translates האף תפר by μὴ ἀποποιοῦ. Symm. renders תפר by the rare word παρακυρώσεις 'you will annul' (cf. Vulg. *irritum facies*). Syr. simply ܠܝ 'to me' instead of משפטי. In order to avoid the odious implication of תרשיעני G has recourse to a long periphrasis: οἴει δέ με ἄλλως σοι κεχρηματικέναι ἢ ἵνα ἀναφανῇς δίκαιος;

The opening האף as in 34:17, 'is it that truly?' Then the *hiph'il* of פרר with the meaning of 'break', used figuratively to connote 'suppress', 'annul' (5:12; 15:4). In French there is a similar metaphor in 'casser un jugement'. There is no appeal against the judgment of God. Man cannot elude it: 'Will you in truth annul my judgment?' The *hiph'il* of רשע in its normal meaning of 'condemn' (9:20; 15:6; 32:3; etc.). God ironically asks if Job will presume to condemn Him in order to stand forth as justified himself; the verb צדק as in 9:15 (cf. Comm.).

9 G renders כאל by κατὰ τοῦ Κυρίου, כמהו by κατ' αὐτοῦ.

In order to annul God's judgment it would be necessary to wield power equal to His own. Power is seated in the arm (22:8-9; 35:9; 38:15): 'Have you an arm like God's?' Note כָּאֵל 'like God' to connote 'like (that of) God', and כָּמֹהוּ 'like Him' to connote 'like (that of) Him'; cf. Ca 5:12, 'his eyes are like (those of) doves'; Is 63:2, 'and thy garments like (those of) one who treads in the wine-press'. Thunder is a manifestation of the power of God (37:2-5): 'And do you thunder with a voice like His?' Cf. ירעם בקול גאונו 'He thunders with His exalted voice' (37:4).

10 Vulg. translates by verbs גבה (*in sublime erigere*) and הוד (*esto*

Clothe yourself with glory and honour!

11 Pour forth the overflowings of your wrath,
    Look upon every proud creature and humble him!

12 Look upon every *haughty being*, abase him!
    And crush the wicked where they stand!

12 גָּבַהּ; MT: גאה.

gloriosus). The word ὕψος renders גאון in G, גבה in Theod.

The irony continues: 'Deck yourself then with pride and greatness of soul!' The verb עדה 'to adorn one's self', as in Ezk 16: 11. The construction עֲדֵה־נָא recalls אזר־נא of v. 7. The word גָּאוֹן 'elevation', 'pride' was used to qualify the divine thunder in 37: 4. As for גֹּבַהּ 'height', 'elevation', (22: 12), it strengthens גאון and produces an effect of alliteration, exactly as in הוד והדר 'glory and honour' (Ps 21: 6; 96: 6, 111: 3). The irony of the 2nd hemistich is all the more pointed because in Ps 104: 1 the Psalmist says to God: 'Thou art clothed with glory and honour.' Exactly the same words. The verb לבש has abstract nouns as complements (8: 22; 29: 14).

11 G ἀπόστειλον δὲ ἀγγέλους ὀργῇ (A ἐν ὀργῇ σου), πᾶν δὲ ὑβριστὴν ταπείνωσον seems to read עברות (interpreted according to the sense of עבדים in 4: 18) instead of עברות, and omits the suffix of אפך and also וראה. Vulg. *disperge superbos in furore tuo* regards עברות as concrete. Targ. renders עברות אפך by רוגתא דנחיריך 'the fury of your nostrils'; cf. Syr. ܘܝܣܐ ܣܝ 'the fierceness of your anger'.

The *hiph'il* of פוץ retains its normal meaning of 'scatter', 'pour out' (cf. 37: 11; 38: 24). The word עֶבְרוֹת 'furies' (21: 30) is completed by אַפֶּךָ 'of your wrath'. In order to avoid the anomaly of 'furies of your wrath' we may assign to עברות its etymological sense of 'overflowings' (root עבר 'exceed', 'overflow'). A comparison with 22: 12b, where we have the same movement as here, proves that וּרְאֵה belongs to the original text and cannot be deleted, as Bickell proposes on the basis of G. To God alone it belongs to humble what is exalted, and to raise what is lowly (5: 11; 1 S 2: 7; Is 13: 11; 25: 11). The adjective גֵּאֶה (from גאה 'to be exalted, proud', 8: 11), as in Is 2: 12.

12 G reduces v. 12a: ὑπερήφανον δὲ σβέσον. Vulg. *respice cunctos superbos et confunde eos* renders גאה by the word which translated עברות in v. 11. Syr. has fused vv. 11b and 12a into a single hemistich. G σῆψον δὲ ἀσεβεῖς παραχρῆμα connects הדך to דכך; cf. Jerome and Vulg. *contere*; Targ. דעדק 'pulverise'. Aq. ἐπίρριψον and Syr. ܐܪܡܐ 'throw' read הדף. For תחתם, rendered παραχρῆμα in G, we have *in loco suo* in Vulg., באתריהון 'in their places' in Targ., ܟܐܦܘܣܠ 'in their place' in Syr.

The 1st hemistich seems to be a repetition of v. 11b. It should be noted, however, that we have הַכְנִיעֵהוּ 'abase him' instead of הַשְׁפִּילֵהוּ. Further, the translation of G suggests a word synonymous with גֵּאֶה, very probably גֹּבַהּ (Duhm) which differs by a single consonant only. We have the succession גֵּאֶה

13   Hide them together in the ground,
      Imprison their persons in the dungeon,

14   And I myself will praise you,
      Because your right hand has saved you!

15   Behold now Behemoth [   ] before you!

15   Omit אֲשֶׁר־עָשִׂיתִי.

and גֵּבָה, just as we had the substantives גָּאוֹן and גֹּבַה in v. 10. The *hapax* הָדַךְ is changed to הדף 'push!' by Graetz and Duhm (cf. Aq., Syr.). But the verb הדד has been preserved in post-Biblical Hebrew with the meaning of 'crush' (*Thesaurus* of Ben-Yehuda, II, 1043); cf. דכא (4: 19), דוך, דכך, דכה. In Arabic the root هدك means 'knock down', 'overturn'. It is therefore unnecessary to vocalise הָדֵךְ (Hoffmann) so as to find the *hiph'il* of דכך (G, Vulg., Targ.). The Massoretes have preserved a root הדד which they had no reason to invent. The end תַּחְתָּם 'under them' also means 'in their place' (34: 24; 36: 20), and especially 'on the spot' (cf. G παραχρῆμα). Cf. the use of תחת with a suffix to denote the place where some one stands, 'on the spot' (Ex 16: 29; Jos 6: 5; Jg 7: 21; 1 S 14: 9; 2 S 2: 23). Hence: 'and crush the wicked where they stand!' The irony continues.

13   The text of Sah. resumes with this verse (cf. 39: 10). For חבוש בטמון, G ἀτιμίας ἔμπλησον, Vulg. *demerge in foveam.* Syr. translates בטמון by ܒܥܦܪܐ 'in the dust', because of בעפר in the 1st hemistich. The 1st hemistich, 'hide them together in the ground', reminds one of Is 2: 10, 'enter into the rock and hide in the ground' (הטמן בעפר). Use of בעפר to mean not 'in the dust' but rather 'in the ground', 'under the ground' (14: 8); cf.

טמון בארץ 'hidden in the ground' in 18: 10. Cf. Mt 25: 25, ἔκρυψα... ἐν τῇ γῇ. The verb חבש 'to bind' (5: 18; 34: 17) here assumes the same meaning as the Arabic حبس 'to imprison' (*habs* 'prison', 'dungeon'). The participle טָמוּן 'hidden' (3: 16; 18: 10) in the sense of 'hiding place' and 'dungeon'. It is unnecessary to replace בטמון by בדמן 'in the dunghill', as Ehrlich would. The word פְּנֵיהֶם 'their faces' merely replaces the suffix of טמנם. It is a metaphor for 'their persons' or 'they themselves' (*L'Emploi métaphorique*, pp. 59f.); Greek πρόσωπον, Latin *persona.*

14   For v. 14a, G has simply ὁμολογήσω, Vulg. *et ego confitebor.*
      The irony continues. If Job can take up the challenges of God (vv. 8-13), then God will recognise his power (v. 9). Such is the implication of וְגַם־אֲנִי 'and even I myself...'; cf. גַּם־אָנִי in 7: 11; 13: 2. The phrase אוֹדֶךָ 'I will praise you' is deliberately chosen, for it is frequently found on the lips of the Psalmist when he addresses God (Ps 18: 50; 30: 13; 35: 18; 43: 4, etc.). Thus the rôles would be reversed. In Hebrew it is said that some one is saved by his own right hand when no one else intervenes to effect his salvation. Sometimes it is the right hand which saves, as here (Ps 98: 1), sometimes the hand (Jg 7: 2; 1 S 25: 26), sometimes the arm (Is 59: 16; 63: 5).

15   Vulg. *Behemoth* and Syr. ܒܗܡܘܬ

Like the ox, he eats grass!
16 See how his strength lies in his loins,
    And his vigour in the muscles of his belly!

have correctly understood that בהמות represents one special kind of animal. G θηρία, Aq. and Theod. κτήνη, Targ. בעיריא 'brute beasts' have translated the plural of בהמה. G has not got אשׁר עשׂיתי, of which the translation ἃ ἐποίησεν has been added subsequently in Cod. 249, and is found in the margin of Syro-hex. (following Aq. and Theod.), as also in Jerome *quam feci*.

Job no longer answers the challenge flung at him by God. The description of the wonders of the animal kingdom will be continued with the picture of those two monsters familiar to the ancient Egyptians, the hippopotamus and the crocodile. Let us note especially that on the stellar ceiling of the Ramesseum the hippopotamus carries the crocodile along its spine (cf. Maspero, *Hist. ancienne*, I, p. 92, Fig.). In his description of the animals of Egypt Herodotus gives in succession one of the crocodile (II, 68-70) and one of the hippopotamus (II, 71). Similarly, Pliny (*Hist. nat.*, VIII, 37-9 or 25-6). There is nothing to add to the masterly dissertations of Bochart to prove that Behemoth, described in vv. 15-24, is indeed the hippopotamus, while Leviathan, the portrait of which begins at v. 25 and is continued in the whole of ch. 41, is in truth the crocodile (*Hieroz.*, II, cols. 753-69 and 769-96). These are the characteristic animals of the Nile. There has been postulated for בְּהֵמוֹת an Egyptian word which is supposed to mean 'ox of the waters' (cf. Italian *bomarino*). Such a word does not exist. The form is nothing more than the plural of בְּהֵמָה (12:7), and it makes of בהמות a designation of majesty, the brute beast *par excellence*. Yahweh introduces the animal by the phrase הִנֵּה־נָא 'behold now!' (13:18; 33:2). The relative clause אֲשֶׁר־עָשִׂיתִי 'which I have made' did not exist in the text followed by G. It seems like an echo of Ps 104:26, where Leviathan is accompanied by the qualifying זֶה־יָצַרְתָּ 'which Thou hast formed'. The intention was to show that even the most extraordinary creatures are the work of God. With a certain number of modern critics we may delete this relative clause which unduly lengthens the 1st hemistich. There remains then עִמָּךְ 'with you' in the sense of 'beside you', 'before you' (17:3; 36:4). Cf. והנה עמך 'and behold here with you' in 1 K 2:8. The remarkable fact is that the hippopotamus, despite its extraordinary strength, is satisfied to feed on a vegetable diet: 'he eats grass like the ox!' The resemblance between the hippopotamus and the ox, which caused the former to be named 'the marine ox' (*bomarino* in Italian), had much struck the ancients (Herodotus, II, 71). Pliny observes that it feeds on crops and has the same kind of hoof as the ox: *depascitur segetes . . . ungulis binis quales bobus* (*Hist. nat.*, VIII, 39). The word חָצִיר as in 8:12.

16 Syr. summarises v. 16: 'and his strength in his secret'. Targ. at this point brings forward Leviathan, which should not appear before v. 25. The suffixes of מתניו and אונו, omitted in G, are restored in G(A), Sah., Jerome (with asterisk) and in the margin of Syro-hex. For בשׁרירי בטנו, G ἐπʼ ὀμφαλοῦ γαστρός, Vulg. *in umbilico ventris ejus*, Targ. כפרת דכרסיה 'in the navel of his belly'.

Contrast between the strength of the hippopotamus and his vege-

17   He stiffens his tail like a cedar tree,
       The sinews of his thighs are knotted,

18   His bones are tubes of bronze,
       His limbs are like bars of iron!

table diet. Repetition of הנה־נא of v. 16, to arouse attention: 'see then . . . !' Physical vigour is seated in the loins (Nah 2 : 2; cf. *L'Emploi métaphorique*, p. 131). The word אוֹן 'vigour' (18 : 7) forms the pendant to כֹּחַ. In spite of G, Targ., Vulg., we cannot assign to the plural שְׁרִירֵי the meaning of 'navel'. The author would have written the singular; cf. שָׁרֵּךְ 'your navel cord' (Ezk 16 : 4), and שָׁרְרֵךְ 'your navel' (Ca 7 : 3). The Aramaic שרר has the meaning of 'to be firm, hard', which is reflected in the Hebrew שְׁרִירוּת 'hardness', 'hardening'. The concrete plural שְׁרִירֵי, which is a *hapax*, denotes the hard resistant parts, the muscles of the belly.

17 For יחפץ, G ἔστησεν, Vulg. *stringit*, Syr. ܪܡܣܒ 'he makes erect' (Arab. يرفع 'he lifts up'), but Targ. כפף 'he bends'. G renders ארז by κυπάρισσον, which is less literal than κέδρος of the other Greek versions (cited in Colb.). G renders the 2nd hemistich by τὰ δὲ νεῦρα αὐτοῦ συμπέπλεκται. It is apparent that פחד is omitted in this translation. G(A) adds ὥσπερ σχοινία 'like cables' before συμπέπλεκται. For פְּחָדָו, Targ. פחדוי 'his testicles', Vulg. *testiculorum ejus*. We find likewise ܦܣܣܘܡ̈ܘ (Syr.), افخاذه (Arab. and Saʿadia), but in Syriac and Arabic the connotation is 'his thighs' (cf. inf.). For ישרגו, Vulg. *perplexi sunt* (cf. G), Targ. משבשין 'are entwined with each other', while Syr. ܪܡܣܒ 'become erect' translates much like the יחפץ of the opening.

Apart from חפץ 'to will', there exists another verb whose imperfect is יַחְפֹּץ and which means 'to make taut, stiffen' (cf. Comm. on 9 : 3). Ibn Ezra continues the translation of G, Syr., Arab., when it interprets יחפץ as יעמיד 'he makes erect'. The shade of meaning 'stiffen' (cf. Vulg. *stringit*) is more appropriate to the description of the tail of the hippopotamus, which is short and hard. It may be that the root חפץ meant at first 'to make taut, stiffen', and then 'to will', tension of the nerves and muscles suggesting tension of the will. In parallelism with 'his tail' we have פְּחָדָו, translated 'his thighs' (Syr., Arab., Saʿadia) or 'his testicles' (Targ., Vulg.). It should be noted that Syriac and Arabic assign to the word, derived from the root פחד, the meaning 'thigh', whereas the Aramaic of Targ. assigns to it the meaning 'testicle'. We can understand how the meaning 'thigh', by euphemism, has been modified into that of 'testicle' (cf. the meanings attributed to 'feet' and 'knee': *L'Emploi métaphorique*, p. 108), whereas the reverse process is not so easily understandable. We shall therefore translate: 'the sinews of his thighs are knotted'. The verb שרג recurs only in La 1 : 14, where we have the *hithpaʿel* with the meaning 'knotted together'. Cf. 10 : 11, 'and Thou hast woven me of bones and sinews'. We shall find the mention of bones in v. 18.

18 G translates v. 18a freely: αἱ πλευραὶ αὐτοῦ πλευραὶ χάλκειαι. For גרמיו, G ἡ δὲ ῥάχις αὐτοῦ, Vulg. *cartilago ipsius*. G renders כמתיל ברזל by σίδηρος χυτός. For כמתיל, Symm. ὡς συμβλήματα, Vulg. *quasi laminae*,

19 He is the first of God's works,
    He who was *created a tyrant to his companions*.

19 הֶעָשׂוּ נֹגֵשׂ חֲבֵרוֹ (cf. G for הֶעָשׂוּ); MT: הָעֹשׂוֹ יִגַּשׁ חַרְבּוֹ.

Targ. הֵיךְ מְטַלְנָא. Syr. does not translate מֵטִיל.

After the sinews (v. 17), the bones; cf. 10: 11. The poet contents himself with choosing as a parallel to עֲצָמָיו 'his bones' the synonymous Aramaic word גַּרְמָיו; the same method is used in 16: 19; 39: 5. The word אָפִיק 'bed' of a torrent (6: 15) and 'stream' came eventually to designate the channel through which the water drains, whether a canal, or, as here, a pipe or tube. In 41: 7 it will be a row (cf. Comm.). אפיק of 12: 21 belonged to another root. 'His bones are tubes of bronze', bronze being the stock image for solidity (6: 22; 20: 24; 41: 19). Parallelism between bronze and iron (20: 24; 41: 19). The meaning of the *hapax* מְטִיל is decided by the Arabic *maṭala* 'flatten', 'laminate', 'render ductile', whence *maṭṭâl* 'plate-metal worker'. The result of the operation is מטיל 'bar' of forged iron.

19 For דַּרְכֵי־אֵל, G πλάσματος Κυρίου. Then G renders הֶעָשׂוּ by a passive πεποιημένον (contra Vulg., Targ., Syr., which follow the MT). The end ἐνκαταπαίζεσθαι ὑπὸ τῶν ἀγγέλων αὐτοῦ ceases to have any connection with the text. It recurs in 41: 25. It is a reminiscence of Ps 104: 26. For יגש חרבו, Syr. וְנְדַּחֵם מְזַּל 'who makes war'.

'He is the first of God's works'; cf. the use of רֵאשִׁית in 8: 7. On דַּרְכֵי־אֵל 'the works of God', cf. 26: 14. In Pr 8: 22, Wisdom is created by Yahweh as 'the first of His works', רֵאשִׁית דַּרְכּוֹ (vocalise דְּרָכָו with G, Symm., Vulg.; and cf. above 26: 14). Those who keep the 2nd hemistich as it stands translate: 'but His Creator

guides his sword' (Le Hir): 'His creator has given him his sword' (Renan). The *Bible du rabbinat français*, which risks a literal translation, 'He who has made him has given him pleasure with a sword', adds: 'In the opinion of most exegetes, *these obscure words, which are diversely interpreted*, refer to the sharp teeth of the beast which are of an excessive length.' In spite of the quotations of Bochart (*Hieroz.*, II, cols. 76off.), it seems to us difficult to see in חַרְבּוֹ 'his sword' an allusion to the teeth of the hippopotamus. The term could be understood only if it were a question of a weapon of 'defence' similar to those of the elephant or the wild boar. Further, the *hiph'il* of נגש, which means 'to bring, offer gifts', would require an indirect complement. Besides, הָעֹשׂוֹ 'He who has made it' would be doubly determined by the article and the suffix. One should have עֹשׂוֹ; cf. עֹשֵׂנִי (31: 15; 32: 22) and עֹשֵׂהוּ (4: 17). On the other hand, G reads here הֶעָשׂוּ 'he who is made', just as in 41: 25, where, as here, the reference is to an extraordinary beast. A very slight change, suggested by Giesebrecht and Duhm, permits us then to read נֹגֵשׂ חֲבֵרוֹ 'the tyrant of his companions'. The word נֹגֵשׂ (3: 18; 39: 7) in the sense of 'tyrant' (Is 14: 2, 4). The companions are the other animals mentioned in v. 20. The meaning obtained is very much to be preferred to the prosaic 'he who is made of great stature', obtained by Ehrlich through the change of יגש חרבו to גֵּשָׁה רַבָּה. Let us note further the interpretation of Hoffmann and of Gunkel, who connect

20   For the mountains bring him a tribute,
      As do all the wild beasts which play there.
21   Under the lotus plants he lies,
      In a covert of reeds and swamp,

חרבו with חרב 'to be parched', 'to be waste' (cf. 3:14, Comm.), so as to translate: 'he who is made to draw near to his land' (Hoffmann), 'he who is made to dominate the desert' (Gunkel). But the hippopotamus is an amphibious creature whose life is spent in marshes and alongside rivers; it is not an animal of the desert.

20 G deviates considerably from the MT: ἐπελθὼν δὲ ἐπ' ὄρος ἀκρότομον ἐποίησεν χαρμονὴν τετράποσιν ἐν τῷ Ταρτάρῳ, reading כי יבוא ל/ instead of כי בול/, ישאו־לו instead of ישאו־לו וכל (homoeoteleuton), interpretation of שם in the light of 3:17-19, and omission of ישחקו. Vulg. *huic montes herbas ferunt* interprets בול by יבול; cf. Targ. עלל 'harvest'. Syr. ﻮﺳﻤﻬﻟ ﻞﻟﻋ 'and many mountains' reads כול instead of בול. The words ישחקו־שם are omitted in Syr.

Generally the *hapax* בֻּל is interpreted as an equivalent of יְבוּל 'produce of the soil': 'in fact, the mountain grass suffices for his food' (Le Hir, not very literal); 'the mountains bring him his nourishment' (Renan). But it is thus apparent that the meaning of בול or יבול is changed to that of 'food', 'fodder'. More in conformity with the etymology is the interpretation of the *Bible du rabbinat français*: 'the mountains produce fodder for him'. But what becomes of the initial כִּי? Duhm justified it by reading ישא לו 'he exacts for himself' as does a tyrant (cf. v. 19). For those who keep the text intact it is clear that הָרִים is the subject of ישאו just as in Ps 72:3, where we have ישאו הרים.

This fact conflicts with the hypothesis of Ball, otherwise very attractive, which consists in recognising in the *hapax* בול the Assyrian *bûlu* 'cattle', 'herd' and in regarding בֻּל הָרִים as the parallel to כָּל־חַיַּת הַשָּׂדֶה. On this hypothesis it is difficult to explain the initial כי, which is omitted by Ball. We ourselves think that the formula בול...נשא corresponds to the Assyrian *našû bilta* 'to bring tribute', the words בול and *biltu* belonging to the same root יבל and ובל. The 1st hemistich will mean 'for the mountains bring a tribute'. This affords the explanation of v. 19b, which represents the hippopotamus as the tyrant lording it over his companions (cf. Comm.). The mountains are brought in here because they are the habitat of the wild beasts, which are denoted by the collective כל־חית השדה (5:23; 39:15). We understand the relative to be implied before יְשַׂחֲקוּ, and we thus obtain: 'and all the wild beasts which play there'. Cf. Ps 104:26b, 'Leviathan which Thou hast formed to play there'. Same use of the *pi'el* of שחק (cf. v. 29). Hence the mountains and their inhabitants bring their tribute to the tyrant. Our interpretation frees us from the need to have recourse to changing הרים to יארים 'Niles', 'canals' (Wright) or to נהרים 'rivers' (Siegfried). It permits us to retain שָׁם, which Duhm would transfer to v. 21 by the division ישחק : ושם.

21 G renders צאלים by means of a vague phrase, παντοδαπὰ δένδρα, while Vulg. *umbra*, Targ. and Syr. טלליא, connect with צלל. G παρὰ πάπυρον καὶ κάλαμον καὶ βούτομον (A

22 The *shades of the* lotus cover him,
   The willows of the torrent encircle him.

23 If the river swells violently, he is not disturbed,
   He remains calm, even if Jordan dashes up to his mouth.

22 צְלָלֵי before צאלים ; MT: צללו after צאלים.

inverts πάπ. and κάλ.) replaces סתר
by a first translation of קנה (cf. Is
19:6). Vulg. *et in locis humentibus*
bases itself on 8:11 for the translation of בצה. Syr. ܐܒ reads רבצה
instead of ובצה.

After describing the hippopotamus the poet proposes to depict its
dwelling place on the banks of the
river. The 1st hemistich is very picturesque: 'Under the lotus plants he
lies.' The word צֶאֱלִים, which recurs
only in v. 22 and the singular form
of which is unknown to us, corresponds to the Arabic ضال and to the
Syriac ܨܐܠܐ 'lotus plant'. The poet
then conveys the salient features
of the landscape where the amphibious creature delights to disport
himself: 'in a covert of reeds and
swamp'. The word בִּצָּה as in 8:11.

22 G renders צאלים by δένδρα μεγάλα (cf. 21). Vulg. *umbrae* and Targ.
טלליא connect with צלל (cf. v. 21).
Syr. fuses צאלים צללו in ܒܛܠܠ
'the shadows'. For צללו יסבהו, G
simply σὺν ῥαδάμνοις; cf. Symm. σὺν
ταῖς παραφυάσιν for צללו (?). G καὶ
κλῶνες ἀγροῦ, for ערבי-נחל, is a
corruption of κ. κ. ἄγνου, which
is preserved by G (A, א^c·a), Compl.,
Syro-hex.

Parallelism between two verbs
which have the same sounds יְסֻכֻּהוּ
'cover him', יְסָבֻּהוּ 'surround him'.
On סכך (= שׂכך), cf. Comm. on
1:10. It is difficult to interpret the
1st hemistich: 'The lotus plants
shelter him, *his* shadow'; it is only
by way of approximation that
critics translate: 'The lotus plants

cover him with *their* shadow' (Le
Hir, Renan, etc.). It is doing violence
to the grammar to regard צְלָלוֹ as
in apposition to the subject and to
translate: '*Lotusbäume als sein
Schatten decken es*', which Dillmann
explains by '*Lotusbäume machen sein
Schattendach*' (!). Duhm goes wildly
astray by reading וסך נעצוצים 'and
a thicket of bushes' instead of
יסכהו צאלים. We suggest a transposition of צללו, reading צְלָלֵי (Jer
6:4) before צאלים. The meaning
becomes perfectly clear: 'The shadows of the lotus plants cover him'.
The tree known by its plural form
עֲרָבִים, construct עַרְבֵי, found in Lv
23:40; Is 15:7; 44:4; Ps 137:2, is
certainly the willow, which is very
frequently found on the banks of
the lower Euphrates (cf. Ps 137:2),
as I was able to observe during my
journey of 1923 to Mesopotamia.

The Arabic غرب also designates the
willow, and it is very likely that the
Assyrian *urbatu* (= ערבה) again
designates the same tree (Holma,
Beitr. zum assyr. Lexikon, p. 89).
With the עַרְבֵי-נַחַל 'willows of the
torrent' cf. נחל הערבים 'torrent of
the willows' in Is 15:7.

23 Vv. 23-24b, absent from Sah.,
marked with asterisk in Jerome and
Syro-hex., did not exist in G. The
present text is derived from Theod.
(cf. Syro-hex.). G paraphrases v.
23a: ἐὰν γένηται πλήμμυρα, οὐ μὴ
αἰσθηθῇ. Vulg. *ecce, absorbebit fluvium
et non mirabitur* regards נהר as a
complement of יעשק.

The verb עשק, the normal mean-

24   *Who* will catch him by his eyes,
      Who will pierce his nose with *thorns*?

24   Add מִי־הוּא at the beginning. — בְּקַמּוֹשִׁים; MT: במוקשים.

ing of which is 'oppress', 'illtreat', has seemed irreconcilable with the context, whence the changes to יִשְׁקַע 'sinks' (Gunkel, Budde, following Am 9: 5), יִשְׁפַּע 'overflows' (Beer), יָשֹׁק 'gushes forth' (Duhm). But the Assyrian *ešqu*, which is synonymous with *dannu* 'strong', seems to us to belong to a root עשק 'to be strong', whence is derived the meaning of עשק in Hebrew: 'force', 'do violence to', 'oppress' (cf. *vis, violentia*, etc.). Hence we propose to translate: 'if the river swells violently, he is not disturbed'. The verb חפז denotes the emotion of fear (Dt 20: 3) and the panic flight caused by this emotion (cf. the *qerê* of 2 K 7: 15). The conjunction הֵן of the 1st hemistich has a counterpart in the conjunction כִּי meaning 'if' (cf. 38: 4, 5, 18). Hence the verb יִבְטַח must be translated separately: 'he remains calm' (11: 18), which is parallel to 'he is not disturbed'. The Jordan is chosen as an example of a river, so as to have a parallel to נהר; cf. the use of יְאֹרִים 'Niles' to connote channels in 28: 10. There is no reason whatever to suppress it (contra Budde). The verb גיח was applied to the sea gushing out from the womb in 38: 8. Here the river leaves its beds and floods the spot where the monster is lying. The water rises 'up to his mouth'. Those who have seen the buffaloes (Arabic *jâwâmiz*) on the edges of Lake Huleh sunk in the water as far as the neck and letting only the tip of their muzzle show above the water line will understand the scene to which our 2nd hemistich alludes. Since Bickell and Wright, a certain number of moderns transfer אֶל־פִּיהוּ to v. 24 in order to shorten the verse.

Gunkel then retains only אל, read as אֵל 'God', which he makes the subject of יקחנו. A mythological interpretation of the whole passage is alone responsible for this hypothesis which dismisses פיהו too lightly. Duhm on the other hand eliminates אל and retains פיהו, read as מי־הוא and made the subject of יקחנו. We conclude by a similar solution, in retaining אל־פיהו in v. 23 and supposing that מי־הוא has disappeared from v. 24 by haplography (cf. inf.). Let us further note that Grimme, who transfers אל־פיהו to v. 24, is obliged to change בעיניו to בעלו 'his master' so as to have a subject for יקחנו.

24   On the text of G, cf. v. 23. Theod. renders בעיניו by the sing. ἐν τῷ ὀφθαλμῷ αὐτοῦ. For יקחנו, Vulg. *quasi hamo capiet eum*. Syr. ܟܬܢܘܗܝ 'in his clouds' reads בעניו instead of בעיניו. The word אף is omitted in Syr., which interprets ינקב by ܢܣܬܠ 'will be taken'. For אף, Vulg. *nares ejus*, Targ. נחיריה which translates אפו in v. 26. We have ῥῖνα in Theod., but G(A) adds αὐτοῦ (Syro-hex.).

The 1st hemistich: 'by his eyes he takes him' is obviously incomplete. It is only out of concern to save the text that critics make such translations as: 'nevertheless men catch him face to face' (Le Hir); 'do men try to attack him face to face?' (Renan). Still bolder is the interpretation of the *Bible du rabbinat français*: 'Can one seize him when his eyes are open?', with the added note: בעיניו 'obscure expression'. A first improvement which is convincing is that of restoring at the beginning מִי־הוּא (13: 19; 17: 3) which has fallen out by haplography after

25   Will you fish Leviathan with a hook?
And with a cord will you bind his tongue?

26   Will you put a reed in his nose,
And with a hook will you pierce his jaw?

פיהו of v. 23 (Budde, Hontheim, etc.). Ehrlich, who accepts this restoration, claims that בְּעֵינָיו refers to the eyes of the hunter and that the interrogative clause 'who with his eyes will take him?' means: who can ensnare him by gazing at him? But, taking into account the passage as a whole (cf. vv. 25-7), where the parts of the body are those of the animal described, it would rather seem that בעיניו 'by his eyes' refers to the eyes of the hippopotamus. The turn of thought is the same as in Ezk 8: 3. Hence we shall translate: 'Who will catch him by his eyes?' We find here an allusion to a technique mentioned by Herodotus which consists in stuffing the eyes of the animal with clay: πρῶτον ἁπάντων ὁ θηριευτὴς πηλῷ κατ' ὧν ἔπλασε αὐτοῦ τοὺς ὀφθαλμούς (II, 70). It is unnecessary to change בעיניו to בשניו 'by his teeth' as Reiske proposed. The 2nd hemistich is similar to v. 26b. The form יְנָקֶב־ instead of יָקֹב־ is determined by the pause (Gesenius-Kautzsch, § 66f.). We should expect, at the end, אַפּוֹ 'his nose', as in v. 26a. But any ambiguity is impossible since we have twice already in the 1st hemistich the 3rd person masculine singular suffix. The word בְּמוֹקְשִׁים 'with traps' (cf. 34: 30) creates a special difficulty, for one does not pierce the nose of an animal with snares or traps. An excellent conjecture of Ehrlich is בְּקִמּוֹשִׁים 'with thorns' (cf. Comm. on 30: 7). The 2nd hemistich then becomes: 'Who will pierce his nose with thorns?' Cf. the use of בחוח in v. 26. It is easy to understand the whole irony of this passage. The hippopotamus has nothing in common with those animals which man captures and holds by the simple device of a barb stuck into the nose. The description of the crocodile will begin with that feature which concludes the description of the hippopotamus.

25 The word לויתן, simply transcribed in Aq., Symm., Vulg., Targ., is translated by δράκοντα in G and by ܠܘܝܬܢ 'dragon' in Syr. (cf. 3: 8). Then G περιθήσεις δὲ φορβεὰν περὶ ῥῖνα αὐτοῦ; is the translation of v. 26a (cf. inf.). V. 25b was therefore absent from G. For תשקיע, Theod. (in v. 26) δήσεις, Aq. συνδήσεις (cf. Syro-hex.), Vulg. *ligabis*.

After the hippopotamus, the crocodile, another curiosity of the Nile (cf. Comm. on v. 15). It is called Leviathan, from the name of a monstrous dragon connected with Egypt (cf. 3: 8). An interrogative is understood before תִּמְשֹׁךְ. We have seen that v. 24 was also interrogative. The verb משׁך has quite clearly the meaning of 'extracting' from the water, i.e. 'fishing'; cf. מֶשֶׁךְ 'extraction' (28: 8). The word חַכָּה denotes the hook (Is 19: 8; Hab 1: 15). Once the animal is captured, he is held, it is supposed, by the tongue: 'and with a cord will you bind his tongue?' The verb השׁקיע has been recognised by Michaelis as belonging to the root שׁקע which, in the Samaritan text of Lv 8: 13, translates חבשׁ 'bind', 'tie'. That is how in fact the verb has been understood by Aq., Theod., Vulg.

26 V. 26a, absent from Sah., marked with asterisk in Jerome and Syro-hex., did not exist in G. The present text is derived from Theod.

27 Will he multiply his prayers to you,
   Will he speak to you tender words?
28 Will he make a pact with you?
   Will you take him as your servant for ever?

In point of fact, this v. 26a was rendered by G as v. 25b of the MT, which was not translated by G. For אגמן, G φορβεάν (in v. 25b), Theod. κρίκον, Vulg. *circulum*, Targ. אונקלא (= ἀγκύλος), Syr. ܦ ܠܓܡܐ 'bridle'. For חוח, G ψελίῳ, Theod. χαλινῷ, Vulg. *armilla*, Targ. סלוא 'thorn', Syr. ܚܘܓܗ 'his dance' (reading חול).

The crocodile has been captured and bound. He is going to be treated as a captive. Once the animal has been secured by the tongue, it is easy to pierce the nose and the jaw. One should remember the treatment inflicted on prisoners by the Assyrian kings, a good illustration of which is given in the *Dictionnaire de la Bible*, I, col. 637, Fig. 158. Ashurbanipal expresses himself in these terms: 'With the sharp knife which my hand held, I pierced his jaw; I caused a rope to be passed through his chin', (*RB*, 1911, p. 361). The word אַגְמוֹן denotes a reed or bulrush (Is 9: 13; 19: 15; 58: 5). The meaning of the 1st hemistich is perfectly clear: 'Will you put a reed in his nose?' The reed takes the place of the rope. Bochart with fine appositeness cites Pliny (*Hist. nat.*, XIX, 9): *junco Graecos ad funes usos nomine credamus quo herbam eam appellant* (cf. *Hieroz.*, II, cols. 771f.). The Greek σχοῖνος means both reed and rope. The 2nd hemistich recalls v. 24b. The word חוֹח indicates in the first place the thorn or the brier (31: 40), then, by derivation, the hook with which a prisoner is secured (2 Ch 33: 11). It is by confusion with חָח 'ring', 'bracelet' that G translates ψελίῳ and Vulg. *armilla*. Since it is a question of an instrument with which the jaws are pierced, it is

clear that we must retain חוח in its meaning of 'hook'. Hence: 'and with a hook will you pierce his jaw?'

27 G λαλήσει δέ σοι δεήσει (read δεήσεις with A) confounds in a single word ירבה and ידבר. The word תחנונים was rendered by δεήσεις ἱκετηρίας (cf. A), whence come δεήσει, ἱκετηρία. According to Syrohex., Symm. read רבות instead of רכות.

The *hiph'il* of רבה in the sense of 'multiply' (9: 17; 34: 37): 'Will he multiply his prayers to you?' The abstract תַּחֲנוּן, derived from חנן of which the *hithpa'el* has the meaning of 'beseech' (8: 5; 11: 15), corresponds to the Assyrian *tênînu* 'prayer', 'supplication'. The 2nd hemistich, 'will he speak to you tender words?', is in the highest degree ironic. There may be here an allusion to the tears of the crocodile. The feminine plural of רַךְ (cf. רכך in 23: 16) 'soft', 'tender' suggests sweet honeyed words, by contrast with קָשׁוֹת which denotes harsh words (Gn 42: 7, 30).

28 For לעבד עולם, G δοῦλον αἰώνιον, Vulg. *servum sempiternum*, Targ. לעבד פלח לעלם 'as a servant to toil for you for ever', Syr. ܥܒܕܐ ܠܥܠܡ 'servant for ever'.

In 39: 9ff. it was a question of the domestication of the buffalo. Still less probable is that of the crocodile! 'Will he make a pact with you?', which is the same type of expression as in 31: 1. Cf. the pact with the stones and the wild beasts (5: 23). The verb תִּקָּחֶנּוּ, as we had יקחנו in v. 24. The phrase לקח ל'' corresponds exactly to the English 'to take for'; cf. 2 K 4: 1 'to take for servants',

29   Will you sport with him as with the sparrow,
     And will you tie him up for your little girls?

30   Will partners bargain about him,
     And offer him for sale among traders?

לקח ...לעבדים עבד עולם. The idiom עבד עולם
'servant of eternity' to connote the
idea of a servant for life, one who has
finally renounced liberty (Dt 15: 17;
1 S 27: 12).

29 G ὥσπερ στρουθίον παιδίῳ adds
before לנערותיך a word such as
כיענים (cf. La 4: 3), which comes
from כנענים of v. 30. For לנערותיך,
Vulg. *ancillis tuis*, Syr. 'for the days
of your adolescence' (reading
לנערותך).

The ironic comments continue:
'Will you sport with him as with
the sparrow?' The *pi'el* of שחק as in
v. 20 and Ps 104: 26. The preposition is understood before the כ״
marking comparison (5: 14, etc.).
Bochart recalls Catullus, *Passer
deliciae meae puellae, Quicum ludere
...*, and Plautus, *aut coturnices
dantur, quicum lusitent* (cf. *Hieroz.*,
II, col. 772). Everywhere and always
sparrows, doves, and other birds
have served for the amusement of
children. Whence the 2nd hemistich:
'and will you tie him up for your
little girls?' The verb קשר as in
38: 31; 39: 10.

30 G ἐνοιτοῦνται δὲ ἐν αὐτῷ derives
יכרו from כרה 'to feast'; cf. Targ.
יעבדון ... שירותא 'will they have a
banquet?' Vulg. *concident eum* seems
to connect יכרו with כרת, while
Syr. נתכמשון 'gather together' interprets in the light of the context. For
חברים, G ἔθνη, Targ. חכימיא 'the
wise'; but Vulg. *amici* and Syr.
חברוהי 'associates' translate more
faithfully. The word כנענים is rendered by a proper name in Aq.
Χαναναίων, but by a common noun
in Symm. μεταβόλων, Vulg. *negotia-
tores*, Targ. תגריא 'the traders',

Syr. סגיאין 'many'. G μεριτεύονται
δὲ αὐτὸν Φοινίκων ἔθνη (A, C, γένη)
read בני כנענים (cf. inf.).

The verb כרה, which means 'to
buy' before the accusative (Dt 2: 6,
Hos 3: 2), assumes the connotation, 'bargain' when the complement
is preceded by the preposition על
(6: 27). The substantive חֵבֶּר is a
hapax of which the meaning is
'associate' (cf. Syr.), from חבר
'join together', 'associate', whence
חֶבְרָה 'association', 'company (34:
8). It is from this root that is derived
ḫabiru 'confederate' (*RB*, 1924, pp.
14f.), which is similar to חָבֵר 'companion'. Here it is a question of the
men joined together for the purpose
of fishing in common; cf. Lk 5: 10,
ὁμοίως δὲ καὶ Ἰάκωβον καὶ Ἰωάννην
υἱοὺς Ζεβεδαίου, οἳ ἦσαν κοινωνοὶ τῷ
Σίμωνι. The associates must first of
all estimate the value of their catch:
'Will partners bargain about him?'
Then they have to sell their merchandise: 'Will they offer him for
sale among traders?' It is supposed
that traders pass by, as in the story
of Joseph sold by his brothers (Gn
37: 25). They are called 'Canaanites',
a tribal term which finally came to
denote traders, merchants, those
who engage in commerce (Is 23: 8;
Zec 14: 21; Pr 31: 24). The verb
חצה 'to cut in half', 'to divide', in
the sense of 'sell' the dead body of
an animal (Ex 21: 35). Those between whom the sharing up takes
place are preceded by בין 'between'
(Nu 31: 27). Gunkel proposes to read
בְּנֵי so as to translate: 'Do the sons
of the Canaanites share it up?' This
correction seems to be supported by
G. But we ought to have the article
before כְּנַעֲנִים, as in בני היונים 'the

31 Will you stab his skin all over with darts?
    And his head with the fishing harpoon?

32 If you lay your hand on him,
    Think of the fight, you will not do it again!

sons of the Ionians' of Jl 4:6. Besides, the word כנענים has here lost
its character as an ethnic designation
to become no more than a simple
appellative for 'traders'. It is not the
sons of the traders but the traders
themselves who come to make their
purchases. Finally, the poet makes
a clear distinction between those
who are associated for the purpose
of fishing and those to whom they
sell their catch. The former bargain
and sell, the latter merely take
delivery of the goods sold to them.
In the light of the fact that in Is
23:8 the parallel word to כנעניה
'her merchants' is סחריה 'her traders', one cannot maintain, as Beer
would, that חברים is a mistake for
סחרים. We must retain the uncommon term and not substitute
for it the banal one, much less
expressive.

31 The end of G, καὶ ἐν πλοίοις ἁλι-
έων κεφαλὴν αὐτοῦ, absent from Sah.,
marked with asterisk in Jerome, is
derived from Theod. The remainder,
πᾶν δὲ πλωτὸν συνελθὸν οὐ μὴ ἐνέγ-
κωσιν (A ἐνέγκῃ) βύρσαν μίαν οὐρᾶς
αὐτοῦ, is a paraphrase which implies
a reading שְׂכִיּוֹת (= πλοίων in Is
2:16, Ball). It is impossible to say
whence is derived οὐρᾶς αὐτοῦ which
follows βύρσαν μίαν (= עורו). For
בשׂכות, Vulg. sagenas (שבכות), Targ.
במטללתא 'of a pavilion' (בסכות),
Syr. ܟܡܣܪ 'flesh' (בשרות). The
words בצלצל דגים are rendered
gurgustium piscium (Vulg.), בגונא
דנוניא 'in the breeding place of fishes'
(Targ.). By confusing ܢܘܢ 'fish' with
ܢܘܪܐ 'fire', Syr. reaches the translation 'shadow of fire'.
    The words שְׂכּוֹת and צִלְצַל are

hapax legomena. The former, with
which should be compared שִׂכִּים
'thorns' (Nu 33:55), belongs to the
root שׂכך, which is connected with
שׂוֹך (1:10), and with the Arabic
šawkeh 'thorn'. In Assyrian the verb
šakâku means 'to be sharp, pointed',
whence šikkatu 'sharp point' (Christian, OLZ, 1920, col. 55). The שׂכות
are most probably the darts which
are flung at an animal to kill it from
a distance: 'Will you stab his skin
all over with darts?' The pi'el of מלא
in the sense of 'fill', and, derivatively,
'riddle', 'fill with holes'. The parallelism of עורו 'his skin' with רֹאשׁ
'his head' invites us to see in בְּצִלְצַל
דָגִים the expression corresponding
to בשׂכות. Hence the reference will
be to a weapon with which more
especially the head of the animal
may be attacked. In the light of
Egyptian drawings, the allusion is
to the harpoon which was used in
hunting the hippopotamus and the
crocodile (Dictionnaire de la Bible,
I, Figs. 472-3, cols. 1552ff.; II, Fig.
408, col. 1126). This weapon can
be flung from a distance — an action
which makes it vibrate and resound,
whence the name צְלָצַל, derived
from צלצל 'vibrate', 'sound', 'ring',
Arabic ṣalṣala, Hebrew צְלָל; cf.
צְלָצַל 'whirring insect', 'cricket',
צְלְצְלִים 'cymbals'. The complement
דָגִים makes it clear that the reference is to the fishing harpoon, which
is used when fishing in a boat on the
Nile, as in the scenes mentioned
above.

32 After πόλεμον, which translates
מלחמה, G adds τὸν γινόμενον ἐν
σώματι αὐτοῦ, which constitutes an

explanation. Syr. regards זכר as a substantive, whence its translation 'and do not continue the mention of the fight!' The end καὶ μηκέτι γινέσθω, which translates אל־תוסף in G(A, C, א^{c.a}, Sah., Syro-hex., Jerome *et amplius non fiat*), has disappeared from G(B). Vulg. interprets אל־תוסף by *nec ultra addas loqui*.

'Lay your hand on him!', a hypothetical imperative; cf. Gesenius-Kautzsch, § 110f. The main verbs are also in the imperative: think of the fight, do not do it twice! The sequence of ideas is very clear: if you lay hands on him, think of the struggle that will ensue, you will not do it twice! Cf. Pr 20: 13b, 'open your eyes, be filled with bread' to mean: if you open your eyes, you will be filled with bread. Usually the copulative *waw* precedes the imper-

ative of the main clause: 'Do this and live', i.e. if you do this, you will live (Gn 42: 18). The verb זכר in the sense of 'think' 'recollect' (21: 6). The vocalisation תּוֹסַף in pause, instead of תּוֹסֵף (Dt 13: 1), by analogy with verbs of 3rd guttural (cf. Gesenius-Kautzsch, § 69v). Cf. חָרְחַק in 13: 21. The description continues in ch. 41. But 41: 1 is not the logical sequel to our verse. The 3rd person suffix of תַחְלָתוֹ and the verb יטל imply some other character than the one to whom the direct speech is being addressed. In our opinion, there has been an accidental shift of verses. If we place 41: 1 after 41: 2, everything becomes quite natural again, and there is no further need to have resort to the ingenious devices of commentators (cf. inf.).

CHAPTER 41

2   *Is he not* cruel, as soon as awakened?
     And who can stand and face *him*?

1-2   Transfer v. 1 to follow v. 2.
2   הֲלֹא ; MT : לֹא. — לְפָנָיו (Targ.); MT : לְפָנִי.

41 : 1   After v. 2.

2 G οὐδὲ δέδοικας ὅτι ἡτοίμασταί μοι (A σοι) seems to read יערכני instead of יעירנו. Vulg. *non quasi crudelis suscitabo eum* reads אעירנו; cf. Aq. and Theod. ἐξεγείρω αὐτόν. For לֹא־אכזר, Targ. לא אכזראה, Aq. and Theod. οὐδὲ μὴ ἀσπλαγχνήσω. Syr. translates the 1st hemistich: 'he does not go away when he is awakened', reading אך זר for אכזר. The *kethib* יְעִירֶנּוּ is supported by Targ. יעירניה. The reading יְעוּרֶנּוּ is a *qerê* of the Orientals. Instead of לפני, Targ. קדמוי and some MSS have לפניו.

For the reasons mentioned in 40: 32, we begin ch. 41 with v. 2, of which the sequel is v. 1. We should note at once that the reading יְעִירֶנּוּ is preferable to יְעוּרֶנּוּ, which gives a suffix to the intransitive verb עור 'to awaken'. In 3: 8, where the meaning was precisely 'to waken Leviathan', we had the *pol'el* which is replaced here by the *hiph'il* יְעִירֶנּוּ. Further, the 3rd person singular suffix has as its consequence that in the 2nd hemistich the reading should be לְפָנָיו (cf. Targ.) instead of לְפָנִי 'before me'. For the 2nd hemistich we thus obtain the natural meaning: 'and who can stand and face him?' The phrase התיצב לפני as in Dt 9: 2; Jos 1: 5. To אכזר is generally

assigned the meaning 'bold', 'rash', so as to translate the 1st hemistich: 'no one is bold enough to attack him' (Le Hir); 'and if no man is found sufficiently bold to provoke him' (Renan); 'no one is bold enough to irritate him' (Segond). But אכזר means 'cruel' (30: 21; La 4: 3) or 'harmful' (Dt 32: 33), and not 'bold', 'rash'. Furthermore, as Ehrlich very truly points out, the Hebrew construction would require לְ before the infinitive, or the copulative *waw* before the imperfect, and not כִּי. Various corrections have been proposed. Without dwelling upon those of Gunkel and Cheyne (quoted by Driver-Gray), which, in order to give the text a mythological bearing, introduce an angel (מלאך for לא אכ), let us mention לא יזכר 'he does not recollect' (Beer), לא אזכיר 'I do not mention' (Ehrlich), which are hardly compatible with the sequel: 'that he wakens him'. Giesebrecht proposes to read אברך instead of אכזר כי 'I do not congratulate the man who wakens him', which is highly dubious. The true solution is afforded by transferring to the beginning the interrogative ה of הגם (cf. Comm. on v. 1). Thus we obtain: הֲלֹא אכזר 'is he not cruel?' (Grimme, Gray). But instead of interpreting כי in the sense of the Latin *ut*, which necessitates the translation: 'is he not (too) fierce for one to stir him up?' (Gray), we ourselves recognise in כי a conjunction of time: 'Is he not cruel,

1   See now, his expectation is disappointed: [   ]
    He is knocked down by the mere sight of him!

3   Who has confronted *him* and *has* remained safe?
    No one under the whole heavens!

1   Omit ה of הגם (cf. v. 2).
3   הַקְדִּימוֹ; MT: הקדימני. — וַיִּשְׁלָם (G); MT: ואשלם. — לֹא; MT: לִי.

as soon as one wakens him?', the implication being that it is better to leave the crocodile in his torpor. We find here the natural sequel to 40: 32, where the poet advises not to touch the animal. It is rather reminiscent of our proverb: Let sleeping dogs lie.

1 G(B) has lost the 1st hemistich οὐχ ἑόρακας αὐτόν, which exists in the other MSS and in the derived versions. The sequel οὐδὲ ἐπὶ τοῖς λεγομένοις τεθαύμακας; reads אמריו instead of מראיו. It is difficult to see how G has been able to extract from the Hebrew text its interpretation, which has resort to the 2nd person singular for the sake of harmonising with 40: 32. Vulg. renders נכזבה *frustrabitur eum* and אל־מראיו by *videntibus cunctis*. Syr. deviates completely from the MT by its interpretation: 'See, your foot is delivered, and God will also take away his bitterness', which implies a reading אֵל instead of אֶל and an interpretation of מראיו by the root מרר 'to be bitter'. Note that Symm. ὁ Θεός also reads אֵל. Targ. follows the MT faithfully.

Modern critics are agreed in replacing the 3rd person by the 2nd: תוחלתך 'your expectation' (Gunkel, Cheyne, Budde, Steuernagel, etc.) and תֻּטָּל 'you are overthrown' (Steuernagel, Budde). Some, in order to introduce a mythological note, change יטל to יָטִיל, which takes as its object אֵל (Gunkel) or אֵלִים (Cheyne), in agreement with Symm.

and Syr., and as its subject מָרְאוֹ 'his terror': his terror overthrows even a god (or gods)! The only correction which is unavoidable is the elimination of the ה of הגם, and we have seen that this ה was in place at the beginning of v. 2, where the original text had הֲלֹא. The translation of v. 1 will be quite simply: 'See now, his expectation is disappointed; he is knocked down by the mere sight of him!' If we put this v. 1 after v. 2, we understand at once that what is in question is the man who has been so bold as to confront the crocodile (v. 2b). His expectation is disappointed; he hoped to escape the danger, but at the mere sight of the crocodile he falls flat. The form מַרְאָיו instead of מַרְאֵהוּ 'his sight' (4: 16), singular and not plural (Gesenius-Kautzsch, § 93ss). The verb טול (in Arabic 'to be long, lengthened') is used in the *hiph'il* with the sense of 'stretch lengthwise on the ground', whence 'knock over', 'throw', etc. The *hoph'al* here, as in Ps 37: 24, has of course the connotation of 'to be thrown down' or 'to fall down flat, all one's length'.

2 Before v. 1.

3 G καὶ ὑπομενεῖ reads וַיִּשְׁלָם instead of ואשלם (cf. inf.). For תחת כל־שמים, G εἰ πᾶσα ἡ ὑπ' οὐρανόν (cf. 28: 24). Targ. adds בעובדי בראשית 'in the works of the beginning' as an explanation of הקדימני. The natural sense of the MT is well rendered by Vulg. *quis*

4   I will not keep silence about his limbs,
       And *I* will tell of *his incomparable* might.

4   וְאֲדַבֶּר גְּבוּרָתוֹ אֵין־עֲרֶךְ ;MT: ערכו וחין גבורות ודבר־.

ante dedit mihi, ut reddam ei? omnia quae sub coelo sunt, mea sunt.

As it stands, this verse seems to refer to God. In particular, the 2nd hemistich 'all that exists under the heavens is mine!' seems to be an allusion to the sovereign dominion of God over the creatures. As for the 1st hemistich, it is interpreted as implying the complete independence of God with regard to His creation (cf. Vulg.): 'Who has forestalled me in a favour in such a way as to make me indebted to him?' (Le Hir); 'To whom am I obliged that I should have to acquit myself towards him?' (Renan). But G had וישלם, i.e. י instead of א.

Now, it happens that if we exchange the א of אשלם with the י of לי, we obtain for the close of the 2nd hemistich לא־הוא 'that man does not exist' (Jer 5:12). The phrase תַּחַת כָּל־הַשָּׁמַיִם as in 28:24; 37:3, to suggest the entire world. Just as we had לפני instead of לפניו in v. 2, so we have הקדימו instead of הקדימני (Gunkel, Cheyne, Beer). The meaning of the 3rd verse is perfectly in harmony with the rest of this description: 'Who has confronted him and has remained safe? No one under the whole heavens!' The *hiph'il* of קדם with a meaning similar to the *pi'el* in 3:12; 30:27: to go before, encounter, confront. We should compare 9:4b, 'who has resisted him and remained safe?' The same verb וישלם. With the final לא הוא cf. לא־אחד (similar meaning) in 14:4.

4 V. 4, absent from Sah., marked with asterisk in Colb., Jerome, Syro-hex., did not exist in G. The present text is derived from Theod.

(cf. Syro-hex.). The *qerê* of the Orientals לו, instead of לא, has no kind of support in the versions and contradicts the expected sense. Vulg. renders the 1st hemistich by *non parcam ei*: cf. Aq. περὶ αὐτοῦ and Theod. δι' αὐτόν for בדיו. Targ. כדבוביה 'his falsehoods' connects בדיו with בדא, while Syr. ܣܘܟܡܗ 'his strength' seems to read בידו. Vulg. paraphrases the 2nd hemistich: *et verbis potentibus et ad deprecandum compositis.* It is apparent that חין is linked to the root חנן. Similarly in Theod. καὶ λόγον δυνάμεως ἐλεήσει τὸν ἴσον αὐτοῦ, Aq. καὶ δωρήσεται τάξει αὐτοῦ (for וחין ערכו), Targ. ובעותא דעלייה 'and the supplication which is on him'. Symm. (quoted in Syro-hex.) 'yet a very powerful word will not oppose me' reads perhaps אין instead of חין (cf. inf.). Syr. does not translate וחין ערכו and renders דבר גבורות by 'the sinews of his strength'(?).

The word בַּדָּיו 'his limbs' is seriously supported by 18:13. The translation 'I will not keep silence about his limbs' presents no difficulty. On the *hiph'il* of חרש cf. 11:3. There is no reason to change to יחדש, as does Duhm, to translate: 'he will not renew his boastings' (בדיו interpreted in accord with בדיך of 11:3, q.v.). Graetz is no less arbitrary in replacing בדיו by מדיו 'his measures'. The 2nd hemistich is less easy to interpret. It is generally considered that the *hapax* חין comes from חנן (cf. the translations above), and to it is assigned a meaning similar to that of חֵן 'grace'. The word דְּבַר is regarded as an expletive 'a word of . . .', i.e. 'as regards', and the plural גְּבוּרוֹת

5   Who has lifted up the front of his garment?
     Who can penetrate to the lining of his *cuirass*?
6   Who has opened the doors of his *mouth*?
     Around his teeth, terror reigns!

5   סְרִינוֹ (G); MT: רסנו.
6   פִּיו (Syr.); MT: פניו.

becomes a plural of majesty. The meaning would then be: '(I will not be silent) as regards the strength and grace of its structure.' Some prefer to assign to עֶרְכּוֹ 'its organisation' the meaning 'its armour' (cf. Renan). But the prosaic דבר, followed by the plural גבורות, which usually denotes something exalted, is rather redundant. Houbigant had recovered the original text by means of a very slight correction: וַאֲדַבֵּר גְּבוּרָתוֹ 'and I will tell of his vigour' (cf. גבורה in 39: 19). The *waw* of וחין is thus connected with the preceding word. Instead of חין ערכו, we do not hesitate to read, following a suggestion of Ehrlich, אֵין עֶרֶךְ 'without comparison', 'incomparable'; cf. אֵין חֵקֶר 'unfathomable' (5: 9; 9: 10; 36: 26). On the meaning 'comparison' attributed to עֶרֶךְ, cf. the verb ערך in 28: 17, 19. The 2nd hemistich, 'and I will tell of his incomparable strength', affords the most natural parallel to the 1st, 'I will not keep silence about his limbs.' The slight corrections which we have adopted free us from the necessity of changing חין to חיל 'vigour' (Houbigant) or to הון 'the practical aspect' of his equipment (Duhm, who sees in the verse a description of the hunter).

5   For בכפל רסנו, G εἰς δὲ πτύξιν θώρακος (reading סְרִינוֹ), Symm. εἰς ὑποδίπλωσιν φολίδος αὐτοῦ, Vulg. *in medium oris ejus*, Targ. בכפלא פרומבייה 'in the double part of his halter'. Syr. reads בנפל instead of

ܒܟܦܠ, whence ܡܐ ܕܢܦܠ ܡܨܝܕܬܐ, 'When the net falls'. The words מי יבוא are transferred by Syr. to v. 6.

The *pi'el* of גלה to connote 'uncover' (12: 22; 20: 27) and 'to lift up' a veil, a garment (Is 22: 8; 47: 2; Nah 3: 5), 'who has lifted up the front of his garment?' Note the use of פנים 'face' to denote the front part, the face of the garment as opposed to the back (Is 25: 7); cf. *L'Emploi métaphorique*, pp. 64f. Quite naturally the word כֶּפֶל, which means 'double', always used elsewhere in the dual (11: 6), will designate the inside part, the lining. If we preserve the MT, we must wonder what can be the meaning of 'the lining of his bit'; cf. רֶסֶן in 30: 11. It is only very freely that critics translate 'the double row of his rack' (Renan, cf. Loisy, Crampon), or, more freely still, 'his mouth defended by a double bridle' (Le Hir), 'between his jaws' (Segond). G read סְרִינוֹ 'his cuirass', 'his coat of mail'; סִרְיֹן exists alongside שִׁרְיוֹן, as the Assyrian *siriâm* is found alongside the Babylonian *širiâm* (cf. Jer 46: 4; 51: 3). The excellent reading of G, which is accepted by Wright, Budde, Duhm, etc., removes the difficulty raised by רסנו. After asking 'Who has lifted up the front of his garment?', the poet goes on to ask: 'Who can penetrate to the inside of his cuirass?' The crocodile's skin is a veritable coat of mail (cf. v. 7).

6   Syr., which connects מי יבוא of

7   His *back* is made of rows of bucklers,
     Made firm by a sharp *rock-like* seal:

7 גֵּוָה (G, Aq., Vulg.); MT: גַּאֲוָה. — סָגַר אֹתָם; MT: סְגוּר. — צָר (G); MT: צַר.

v. 5 to v. 6, transfers אֵימָה to the beginning of v. 7. For פָּנָיו, Syr. ܦܘܡܗ 'his mouth' = פִּיו (v. 11), an excellent reading.

It is difficult to see what can be the meaning of 'the doors of his face' in reference to the crocodile. The phrases פִּתְחֵי פִיךָ 'the doors of thy mouth' (Mic 7: 5) and דַּל־שְׂפָתַי 'the door of my lips' (Ps 141: 3) prove clearly that one should read פִּיו with Syr. Thus we have: 'Who has opened the doors of his mouth?' The *pi'el* of פתח retains the meaning of the *qal* in 31: 32. The doors of the mouth are the jaws which bristle with rows of teeth. 'Around his teeth, terror reigns', cf. the use of אֵימָה in 39: 20. The preposition סְבִיבוֹת as in 22: 10; 29: 5.

7 Syr. brings in here אֵימָה from v. 6, which gives 'the fear which is in the torrent', then 'his mouth is pressed tight and bound and sealed'. Targ. is alone in interpreting גַּאֲוָה in the sense of 'elevation'. The versions have read גַּאֲוָה or גֵּוָה 'his back': τὰ ἔγκατα αὐτοῦ (G), τὸ σῶμα αὐτοῦ (Aq.), *corpus illius* (Vulg.); confusion of גֵּו 'back' with גְּוָה 'body' in Aq. and Vulg. For אֲפִיקֵי מָגִנִּים, G ἀσπίδες χάλκειαι, Aq. ὑπερεκχύσεις θυρεῶν, Vulg. *quasi scuta fusilia*. The interpretation of Targ. 'the heights of the reservoirs are shields for him' is an attempt to extract a meaning from גַּאֲוָה 'elevation'. Targ. afterwards remains very close to the MT. The 2nd hemistich is translated σύνδεσμος αὐτοῦ ὥσπερ σμιρίτης λίθος (G), ἀποκλείστου σφραγὶς στενή (Aq.), and paraphrased *compactum squamis se prementibus* (Vulg.). The translation of Renan, 'superb

are the lines formed by his scales' (cf. Crampon), shows how very awkward it is to retain גַּאֲוָה 'elevation', 'magnificence'. Houbigant, Bochart, and most moderns vocalise גֵּוָה 'his back' (with G, Aq., Vulg.). The אֲפִיקֵי מָגִנִּים designate the 'rows of bucklers' which are the scales of the crocodile. The word אָפִיק denotes the bed of a torrent (6: 15), a stream of water, a tube (41: 7), the well-marked-out watercourse, or gutter, trench, and finally a row of objects. Cf. our expression 'a river of diamonds'. The scales of the crocodile are envisaged as little round bucklers; cf. the bulging bucklers of 15: 26. The word סָגוּר does not refer to the back, as is clear from the rest of the description (v. 8a), but must describe the component parts of the back, the bucklers. Following G σύνδεσμος αὐτοῦ, it is proposed to read סְגֹרוֹ and to translate by 'his chest' (Bickell, Duhm, following Hos 13: 8). But, in the first place, the meaning of 'chest', 'breast' for סְגוֹר is most doubtful. Secondly, it seems that what is being described is still the scales of the back, as is shown by v. 8. We ourselves think that a word has fallen out by an error of homoeoteleuton and that the text actually read סָגַר אֹתָם. The relative אֲשֶׁר is understood. One might translate חוֹתָם צָר by 'a narrow seal' with the connotation of a seal which grips tightly. But G σμιρίτης λίθος suggests the vocalisation צֹר 'stone', 'flint' (22: 24). Cf. the 'knives of flint' in Jos 5: 2-3. The back of the crocodile is composed of rows of bucklers which 'have been made firm by a seal of stone'. The verb סָגַר 'close',

8   They are so closely knit the one to the other,
     That no breath of air can penetrate between them;
9   They cleave fast together, each one to the next,
     They clasp each other, and cannot be separated.
10   *His* sneezing makes the light sparkle,
     And his eyes are like the eyelids of the dawn!

10   עֲטִישָׁתוֹ (G, Aq., Vulg., Targ.); MT: עטישתיו.

in the sense of 'fix', 'prevent from moving'; French *fermer* is derived from *firmare* 'to render fixed', 'to make firm'.

8 V. 8a, absent from Sah., marked with asterisk in Colb., Jerome, Syro-hex., did not exist in G. The present text is derived from Theod. (cf. Colb. and Syro-hex.). It is in error that Jerome marks v. 8b also with asterisk. Targ. adds ניבו 'its canine teeth' as the subject of יגשׁ.

V. 8 continues the description of the crocodile's hide. The little bucklers 'are closely knit the one to the other', as in the manoeuvre of the Roman soldiers known as the *testudo*. 'tortoise'. The 2nd hemistich, 'no breath of air can penetrate between them', is admirable in expressive power. One must really be entirely lacking in any sense of oriental poetry to insist on replacing רוח by רֶוַח 'hole', as is done by Hontheim, Beer, Budde! The word רוח is generally feminine, but is found also in the masculine; cf. 1: 19; 4: 15. The hyperbole had already surprised Aq. and Symm., who rendered רוח by διάστημα.

9 V. 9, absent from Sah., marked with asterisk in Jerome and Syro-hex., did not exist in G. The present text is derived from Theod. (cf. Syro-hex.). It is in error that Colb. attributes only v. 9b to Theod. The literalism of Theod. is recognisable in ἀνὴρ τῷ ἀδελφῷ αὐτοῦ for

אישׁ־באחיהו. Vulg. renders the 2nd hemistich: *et tenentes se nequaquam separabuntur*.

There is no reason at all to suppress this verse, which is an inconvenience to the strophic system of Bickell and Duhm. If these authors claim the support of G, they ought also to delete v. 8a, which they take care not to do. The similarity of meaning between this verse and the preceding one may have occasioned the same words in the Greek translation, whence the error of homoeoteleuton. Note the idiom 'man with his brother' even in speaking of inanimate things, just as we have אשה אל־אחתה 'woman with her sister', in regard to the tapestries of the tabernacle in Ex 26: 3. Cf. also Gn 15: 10. We may interpret by 'each one to the next'. The verb יְדֻבָּקוּ in the plural, because it has as subject מגנים, while אישׁ is distributive. The *pu'al* of דבק as in 38: 38; the *hithpa'el* of לכד as in 38: 30; the *hithpa'el* of פרד as in 4: 11. All these verbs preserve here their original meaning.

10 Instead of the plural עטישתיו, G ἐν πταρμῷ αὐτοῦ, Aq. πταρμὸς αὐτοῦ, Vulg. *sternutatio ejus*, Targ. זרירוי have the singular עֲטִישָׁתוֹ, which is the correct reading (cf. inf.). For תהל אור, Aq. φέγγος πυρός; cf. Vulg. *splendor ignis*. Syr. 'his orbits are full of fire' interprets the 1st hemistich in the light of the 2nd. G renders כעפעפי־שׁחר by εἶδος ἑωσ-

11   Out of his mouth, flames proceed,
         Sparks of fire shoot forth;
12   Smoke streams from his nostrils,
         As from a heated and *boiling* pot:

12   אַגֵּם (Vulg., Syr.); MT: אגמון.

φόρου. Syr. translates כעפעפי by
اسو ربكمس 'like rays'.

The expression תָּהֶל אוֹר 'makes
the light to sparkle', confirmed by
29:3 (cf. Comm.) and especially
by Is 13:10, requires a feminine
singular subject, which is no other
than עֲטִישָׁתוֹ 'his sneezing'; we should
read thus, with G, Aq., Vulg., Targ.
The sneezing of the crocodile is produced by the action of the sun, as
had been observed by the ancients.
Bochart quotes Strabo: ἡλιάζονται
κεχηνότες (XVII, i, 39) and Aelian:
ἐπὶ τὴν ὄχθην προελθὼν κατὰ τῆς
ἀκτῖνος κέχηνεν (*De nat. animal.*,
III, 11). When the animal sneezes,
the tiny drops which he causes to
spurt out from the water glint in the
sun, and it is in this way that 'his
sneezing makes the light to sparkle'.
The *hapax* עֲטִישָׁה belongs to the root
עטש, which is onomatopoeic, and
which is found in post-Biblical
Hebrew and the Aramaic עֲטַשׁ, as
also in the Arabic عطس 'to sneeze'.
The eyelids of the dawn have been
mentioned in 3:9. Bochart cites
appositely a passage from Horapollo
(*Hieroglyphica*, I, § 68; ed. Conrad
Leemans, p. 61): ἀνατολὴν δὲ λέγοντες,
δύο ὀφθαλμοὺς κροκοδείλου ζωγρα-
φοῦσι· ἐπειδήπερ παντὸς σώματος ζώου
οἱ ὀφθαλμοὶ ἐκ τοῦ βυθοῦ ἀναφαίνονται.

11   G renders לפידים by λαμπάδες
καιόμεναι. Syr. twice translates כידודי
אש and regards ''כ as a particle of
comparison. For כידודי אש, G
ἐσχάραι πυρός, but 'the other' Greek
interpreters have δαλοὶ πυρός, Targ.
גוצין דנור 'sparks of fire'. Vulg.

paraphrases the 2nd hemistich: *sicut
tedae ignis accensae.*

The same effect is depicted as in
v. 10. Around the mouth of the crocodile there shoot sprays of water
which in the dazzling brilliance of
the sunshine seem to be so many
flaming torches: 'out of his mouth,
flames proceed'. The word אֵשׁ 'of
fire' is understood after לפידים (cf.
Gn 15:17; Zec 12:6; Dn 10:6),
for the word is used later in the
verse. With the form יְהֲלֹכוּ compare
אֲהֲלֹךְ (14:20; 16:6; 20:25); יַהֲלֹךְ
(16:22; 23:8). Jewish tradition has
not varied with regard to the meaning of כִּידֹודֵי אֵשׁ 'sparks of fire'. The
hapax כִּידֹוד is a form analogous to
נִיחֹוחַ 'what is soothing, pleasant,
of sweet savour', a word which
derives from נוח. The root of כידוד
is known from the Arabic كيد 'to
make a spark shoot forth from the
stone' (Barth). Notice that נִיצֹוץ
'spark', by which Qimchi translates
כידוד, is formed in the same way,
but stems from the root נצץ; ע''ע
parallel to ע''ע or ע''י. The *hithpa'el*
of מלט 'escape' assumes the meaning of 'escape' in speaking of inanimate things.

12   G interprets the 2nd hemistich
very freely: καμίνου καιομένης πυρὶ
ἀνθράκων. Syr. reads כדור for כדוד,
whence 'like the heat of a boiling
pot'. For ואגמון, Vulg. *atque ferventis*,
Targ. דעבד כיפא 'which foams'.
The *hapax* נְחִיר 'nostril' from the
root נחר (39:20) corresponds to
the Assyrian *naḥiru* and to the Ara-

13   His breath kindles coals,
      And a flame darts from his mouth!

14   Strength resides in his neck,
      And terror leaps before him.

maic נְחִירָא; cf. the Arabic *minḥar* 'nostril', 'nose'. Note the relation between יהלכו of v. 11 and יצא of v. 12, as in 20: 25 (cf. Comm.). The word עָשָׁן 'smoke' is used in the sense of vapour. The word דּוּד denotes the pot that is placed over the fire (1 S 2: 14), the cauldron. The phrase כָּדוּד 'as *from* a cauldron'; cf. כצפור 'as *with* the sparrow' (40: 29). The participle of נפח 'fan', 'kindle' with the meaning of 'heated' (cf. the *puʿal* in 20: 26), as in סיר נפוח 'boiling pot' (Jer 1: 13), כור נפוח 'heated oven' (Sir 43: 4). Instead of אגמון, which would mean 'rush' or 'cord' (40: 26), the text had simply אֲגַם (cf. Vulg., Syr.) 'boiling', the final *nun* arising from an anticipation of נפשו. The verb אגם is cognate with the Arabic اَجَمَ 'to be hot, boiling' and the Assyrian *agâmu* 'to be boiling with anger'.

13   For נפשו, which is preserved in Syr. and Targ., G has the abstract ἡ ψυχὴ αὐτοῦ, but Vulg. renders excellently by *halitus ejus*. By haplography before φλὸξ δέ, G has lost φλέξει, which translated תלהט; cf. Symm. and Theod. quoted in the margin of Syro-hex. The restoration has been made in Jerome *accendet*.
     The word נֶפֶשׁ retains its etymological sense 'breath', 'breathing'. The line 'his breath kindles coals' is very understandable after 'his sneezing makes the light sparkle' of v. 10. If a few Greek MSS have read ὡς ἄνθρακες, it was in order to complete the clause after the disappearance of φλέξει which translated תְּלַהֵט (cf. sup.). One cannot use this isolated reading as an authority for the change to כגחלים which is suggested

by Siegfried, Budde, Duhm. It would be needlessly weakening the Hebrew. To assert that גֶּחָלִים cannot form a complement to תלהט because the word denotes burning coals, would be in effect to forbid also the expression גחלי־אֵשׁ 'coals of fire' of Lv 16: 12; Ps 18: 9, etc. Do we not normally say 'light the fire?' With the close, 'and a flame darts from his mouth', cf. v. 11a and note the alternation of the verbs הלך and יצא (cf. v. 12a). One thinks of the passage of *Phèdre* where Racine describes the sea monster which

Se roule et leur présente une gueule
      enflammée
Qui les couvre de feu, de sang et de
      fumée.

14   Targ. and Syr. have preserved תדוץ, while G τρέχει and Vulg. *praecedit* have read תרוץ. For דאבה, maintained in Targ. דאבונא, G has vaguely ἀπωλία, Aq. ἐκλιμία (cf. Vulg. *egestas*), Syr. ܝܐܣܠܐ 'fear'.
     'Strength resides in his neck': the verb לין as in 17: 2. The neck, like the nape, is the seat of physical strength (15: 26). The phrase לְפָנָיו 'before him', with the verb דוץ (a *hapax* corresponding to the Syriac ܝܣܐ 'jump', 'dance', 'leap'), evokes in our minds the picture of David dancing before the ark (2 S 6: 14-16). We retain the rare and picturesque expression. The change from תָּדוּץ to תרוץ 'runs' (Houbigant, Nöldeke, Beer, etc., following G and Vulg.) would imply that the crocodile also runs, whereas he remains in the river or near to it. Houbigant and Beer, still following G, propose אבדן instead of דְּאָבָה. But אבדן

15   The flaps of his flesh form a solid mass,
      If pressed, it yields not;

denotes a specific spot (26: 6; 28: 22) and not a terror-bringing scourge. The *hapax* דְּאָבָה belongs to the root דאב 'languish', 'pine'. The phrase דַּאֲבוֹן נֶפֶשׁ 'languor of soul' is used to connote the idea of dejection or despair (Dt 28: 65). The word דאבה conveys the idea of that which causes dismay, robs the soul of all strength, namely the terror which the crocodile strikes into man's heart.

15 V. 15b, absent from Sah., marked with asterisk in Cod. 248, Jerome, and Syro-hex., did not exist in G. The present text is derived from Theod. (cf. Syro-hex.). For מַפְּלֵי, G σάρκες Vulg. *membra*, Targ. שֶׁלְדִי 'the bones'. Syr. transfers בַּל־יִמּוֹט to v. 16 and vaguely translates what remains of v. 15: 'his flesh is fine and fat and well supported'. For יָצוּק עָלָיו, Theod. καταχέει ἐπ' αὐτόν, Symm. περικεχυμέναι αὐτῷ (cf. Jerome *circumfusae ei*), Targ. יתיסד עֲלֵי 'is founded on him'. Vulg. interprets the 2nd hemistich in a very original way: *mittet contra eum fulmina et ad locum alium non ferentur*.

The word מַפָּל, derived from נפל 'to fall', recurs in Am 8: 6, where מַפַּל בָּר means 'the residue of the wheat', *what falls* to the ground when the grain is threshed. In the body of an animal, it implies the part which falls away, and in accordance with the use of מַפָּל עוֹר 'the folds of the skin' in post-Biblical Hebrew, it connotes the flaps, or dewlaps. The verb דָּבַק 'to cleave together', 'to stick fast' (29: 10; 31: 7), is used without complement to denote the intransitive 'to be compact', 'to form a solid mass of flesh'; it is a question of a compact whole the parts of which are firmly knit each to other. It is unnecessary to postul-

ate the *puʿal*, which would mean that some one has welded the parts together (contra Duhm). Grimme would read כפלי instead of מפלי; but, in the light of v. 5, this would mean the 'linings' or the 'folds' of the flesh. This is not the subject which we expect for דבקו. It is difficult to refer מפלי to יָצוּק עָלָיו בשרו, as is apparent from the free translations: 'fixed on him' (Renan); 'like molten brass' (Le Hir); 'molten on him' (Segond), etc. The difficulty is evaded by Bickell and Beer, who delete v. 15b, as also the whole part between the first and second יצוק of v. 16, although G omitted only v. 15b. Examining the text closely, it seems that יצוק עליו must lead up to בַּל־יִמּוֹט 'it moves not', which has as its subject the masculine בְּשָׂרוֹ. The use of מוט with the poetic negative בַּל is frequent in the Psalms (10: 6; 16: 8; 21: 8; 30: 7, etc.; cf. Driver-Gray). Now, the word יצוק may be merely a homonym of the two יצוק of v. 16. We ourselves recognise in it the 3rd person singular of the imperfect of צוק, of which the *hiph'il*, with its object in the accusative, means 'to press' (in a moral, figurative sense); cf. 32: 18; Jg 14: 17; 16: 16. The *qal*, followed by על, will mean 'to press' (in a physical sense), and we can translate יצוק עליו by 'one presses on it', i.e. on the flesh, the singular denoting something impersonal, as in 27: 22-3. Note that the root צוק has as its basic meaning 'to be tight, squeezed together', of which we have here the transitive connotation. The 2nd hemistich is now very clear: 'if pressed, it yields not!' The flesh remains immovable and resistant. This is indeed what we should expect of the flesh of the crocodile.

16   His heart is hard as stone,
      Hard indeed like the lower millstone!

17   The *billows* are afraid of his majesty;
      The *waves of the sea* draw back.

17 גַּלִּים ;MT: אֵלִים. — מִשְׁבְּרֵי יָם ;MT: משברים.

16 The versions vary the translations of יָצוּק: πέπηγεν... ἕστηκεν (G), *indurabitur* ... *stringetur* (Vulg.), מתיסד 'firmly settled' ... אתיך 'molten', 'firm' (Targ.), نصصر 'molten', 'solid' ... محنزۃ 'firmly fixed' (Syr.). For פֶּלַח תַּחְתִּית, well rendered in Targ., we have ὥσπερ ἄκμων ἀνήλατος (G), *quasi malleatoris incus* (Vulg.), احز وحنصمل 'like marble' (Syr.).

Duhm, who would eliminate everything between עָלָיו of v. 15 and כְּפָלַח of v. 16 (cf. Bickell and Beer on v. 15), makes a joke in bad taste when he says that the author cannot have seen the heart of the animal and that to attribute to the heart the hardness of stone is sheer nonsense! The heart is the seat of vitality and strength. When it is 'hard as stone', the implication is that the courage and spirit is unshakeable. Ezekiel distinguishes between the heart of stone and the heart of flesh (11:19; 36:26). On the word יָצוּק 'hard', 'solid' cf. Comm. on 11:15 and the phrase אֶבֶן יָצוּק 'hard stone' in 28:2. The 2nd hemistich strengthens the 1st: 'hard indeed like the lower millstone!' The lower millstone פֶּלַח תַּחְתִּית is contrasted with the פֶּלַח רֶכֶב 'upper millstone' (Jg 9:53; 2 S 11:21), that is, the millstone of the runner or rider. It is the lower millstone which becomes most quickly worn, since it supports the weight of the other as well as the rotatory movement.

17 G paraphrases the whole verse: στραφέντος δὲ αὐτοῦ φόβος θηρίοις τετράποσιν ἐπὶ γῆς ἀλλομένοις. Vulg. *cum sublatus fuerit* renders מַשֵּׂתוֹ as a clause with the verb in the infinitive (cf. G.), but Targ. ממספייה 'from fear of him' and Syr. مں ܕܚܠܬܐ 'by fear of him' see a noun in שֵׂת (cf. inf.). For אֵלִים, Vulg. *angeli*, Aq. and Symm. ἰσχυροί, Targ. and Syr. תקיפין 'the mighty'. Vulg. *et territi purgabuntur* summarises the 2nd hemistich. Syr. regards משברים as a single word: ومحنزۃ 'those who are firm'. Targ. paraphrases יתחאו by ידון עליהון 'he gives judgment against them'.

The opening מִשֵּׂתוֹ is for מִשְּׂאֵתוֹ 'of his majesty' (31:23b); cf. שְׂאֵתוֹ in 13:11. The verb גור with מִן before what causes the fear (cf. 19:29). The word אֵלִים can denote אֵילִים 'the chiefs', written defectively as in Ezk 32:21. The translation would be: 'the chiefs are afraid of his majesty'. In that case we are obliged to interpret שְׁבָרִים 'the breaches' (Ps 60:4) in the sense of 'cracks' in the heart. But we should have a complement such as רוּחַ 'spirit', 'courage'; cf. Is 65:14; Pr 15:4. Already Döderlein, Dathe, Reiske, quoted by Beer, split up משברים ים into משבר ים, or more precisely מִשְׁבְּרֵי יָם (Buhl; cf. Ps 93:4) 'the waves of the sea'. And at once the correction is irresistible: אֵלִים changed to גַּלִּים 'billows' (38:11), suggested by Mandelkern, Beer, Budde, Ehrlich. The parallelism is excellent: 'the billows are afraid of his majesty, the waves of the sea draw back'. The *hithpa'el* of

18   The sword of one who touches him gives way,
      As does the spear, the arrow, and the dart;
19   He regards iron as straw,
      Bronze as rotten wood;

חטא 'to fail' (cf. 5:24) has the meaning of 'to retire'; cf. חסר 'to fail' and 'to retire', in speaking of the waters (Gn 8:3, 5). There is the same idea in the line of Racine (cf. v. 13):

Le flot qui l'apporta recule
épouvanté!

Other corrections, less satisfactory, have been proposed. Thus Giesebrecht, who retains the word אֵלִים, changes משברים to גבורים משניו 'the valiant are dismayed in face of his teeth'. Duhm proposes משמרים guards'. The changes of יתחבאו to יתחבאו 'hide' (Gunkel) or to יֵחַתּוּ 'are terrified' (Joüon, Beer) are unnecessary once one has understood the meaning of יתחטאו.

18   V. 18b, absent from Sah., marked with asterisk in Colb., Cod. 248, Jerome, did not exist in G. The present text is derived from Theod. G paraphrases v. 18a: ἐὰν συναντή-σωσιν αὐτῷ λόγχαι, οὐδὲν μὴ ποιήσωσιν. Vulg. omits מסע and fuses the two hemistichs into a single sentence: *cum apprehenderit eum gladius, sub-sistere non poterit neque hasta, neque thorax*. Note that Theod. reduces v. 18b to δόρυ καὶ θώρακα, while Symm. translates οὐδὲ λόγχης ἆρσις καὶ θώρακος, whence Jerome *hastae ele-vatio et thoracis*. The word שריה is translated שרינא 'cuirass' in Targ. (cf. Theod., Symm., Jerome, Vulg.). For מסע, Targ. 'the sling which hurls stones'. Syr. renders משיגהו by ܬܪܥܐ 'door', which translated דלתי in v. 6. The 2nd hemistich is interpreted 'he can endure the spears of the chiefs' in Syr.

The versions have given very

diverse renderings of the *casus pendens* מַשִּׂיגֵהוּ 'he who touches him'. Their interpretation cannot support a more banal reading תשיגהו, postulated by Beer. In reality, we have here the complement of the nouns which are to be enumerated: of him who touches him, the sword gives way! The *hiph'il* of נשׂג as in 27:20. The changes to ממגניו 'because of his bucklers' (Budde), משׂיאו 'because of his height' (Duhm), are no happier than משׁגה 'leading astray' (!) of Bickell. The verb קום in the sense of 'hold firm' as in 8:15; 15:29. Instead of the negative לא, used in the latter texts, we have here בְּלִי with the imperfect, a very uncommon construction (Is 32:10; Hos 8:7). In Hos 9:16 we have not the *kethîb* בלי but the *qerê* בַּל. We have found בַּל before the imperfect in v. 15. The 2nd hemistich simply reinforces the 1st by enumerating the other weapons which are used in hunting. First the spear (39:23). Then the *hapax* מַסָּע which is derived from נסע, Arabic نسغ 'to throw', but in which we incline to recognise rather the Arabic *minza'* 'arrow hurled to a distance', from the root نزع, which corresponds precisely to the Hebrew נסע 'to pull up', 'to set off', etc. Similarly it is by Arabic that is to be explained the *hapax* שִׁרְיָה (confused with שריון by the versions) an equivalent of *sirweh*, 'little arrow'. It is unnecessary to change to שדיה, as Hoffmann would, following the Syriac ܫܕܝܐ 'javelin'.

19   Syr. explains רקבון by 'in which rot falls'.

The various kinds of weapon

20   The son of the bow cannot put him to flight,
      Slingstones become for him as stubble;

21   The shaft *seems to him* a mere straw,
      And he laughs at the vibration of the javelin!

21   נֶחְשַׁב לוֹ ;MT: נחשבו.

which can be used in close combat are summed up by the iron and bronze, which are placed in parallelism as in 20: 24; 40: 18. The first term of comparison is straw, which flies away in the slightest breath of wind and has no weight (21: 18). The phrase חָשׁב ל״ 'regard as' (v. 24; 13: 24; 19: 15; 33: 10; 35: 2): he regards iron as straw, bronze as rotten wood. The *hapax* רִקָּבוֹן 'rot' belongs to the root רקב; cf. 13: 28; 19: 20 (Comm.).

20 Syr. reads מן instead of בן. For לֹא־יַבְרִיחֻנּוּ, G οὐ μὴ τρώσῃ αὐτόν, which already figures in 33: 23 (cf. Comm.). The phrase בֶּן־קֶשֶׁת 'son of the bow' is rendered by 'the bowman' in Symm. ἀνὴρ τοξότης and Vulg. *vir sagittarius*, but G τόξον χάλκειον (Jerome *sagitta aerea*) and Targ. גִּרָא קַשְׁתָּא 'arrow of the bow' recognise here the weapon and not the one who uses it. G paraphrases the 2nd hemistich ἥγηται μὲν πετροβόλον χόρτον. Jerome translates πετροβόλον by *balistam*.

In Arabic poetry arrows are called *binât al-kanâ'in* 'daughters of the quivers'; cf. La 3: 13 בְּנֵי אַשְׁפָּתוֹ 'sons of his quiver', to connote arrows. 'The son of the bow' has the same meaning as the son of the quiver, for the arrow is first contained in the quiver and then shot from the bow. After mentioning the instruments used in fighting at close quarters (v. 19), the poet makes reference to the weapons which strike from a distance: arrows and slingstones. The word קַשׁ, chosen because of קֶשֶׁת, is properly the stubble (13: 25). The *niph'al* of הפך with ל״ means

'to turn into', 'to become as' (30: 21; cf. the *hithpa'el* in 38: 14). The stones of the sling become for him nothing more than a bit of stubble. The comparison implies the height of contempt.

21 V. 21a, absent from Sah., marked with asterisk in Colb., did not exist in G. The present text is derived from Theod. Vv. 21a, 22, 23, 24a, are not translated in Syr., nor consequently in Arab. For תּוֹתָח, Theod. σφυρά, Vulg. *malleum*, Targ. נַרְגִּיא 'clubs'. The words לְרַעַשׁ כִּידוֹן are translated σεισμοῦ πυρφόρου (G), σειομένου θυρεοῦ (Symm.), *vibrantem hastam* (Vulg.), לרגוש רומחא 'at the noise of the lance' (Targ.). Syr. simply ܐܠ ܣܪܦ 'of the lance'.

To avoid the repetition of קַשׁ of v. 20, Beer proposes כְּקָנֶה 'like a reed' and claims to see in this the reading of G ὡς καλάμη. But, in the first place, it would be the text of Theod., since G does not preserve v. 21a (cf. sup.). Then the word καλάμη 'stubble', and not 'reed', never translates קָנֶה (= κάλαμος), whilst it does very frequently render קַשׁ (Ex 5: 12; 15: 7; Ps 83: 14, etc.). Instead of the plural נֶחְשָׁבוּ, which is difficult to explain, Houbigant had already read נֶחְשַׁב לוֹ, which is accepted by most moderns. The *niph'al* of חָשׁב with כ״ before the term of comparison (18: 3) and ל״ before the person who compares (Is 40: 17), used in the sense of the Latin *videri alicui*. The subject is the *hapax* תּוֹתָח, in which Barth has recognised the Assyrian *tartahu*, the

22   Under him are points of a potsherd,
      Like a threshing-sledge he leaves his mark on the mire.
23   He makes the deep to boil like a cauldron,
      He transforms the sea into an unguent-pot;

basic meaning of which is 'arrow', 'shaft' (Jensen, *ZDMG*, 1913, pp. 506f.): a shaft seems to him a mere straw. The expression שְׂחֹק לִי 'to laugh at' as in the description of the onager (39: 7), of the ostrich (39: 18), of the horse (39: 22). Note that we had רַעַשׁ 'agitation', excitement' in 39: 24 and כִּידוֹן 'javelin' in 39: 23. The shade of meaning implied by רעשׁ in this context is 'vibration', 'whirr'.

22   On the text of Syr. and Arab., cf. v. 21. G ἡ στρωμνὴ αὐτοῦ ὀβελίσκοι ὀξεῖς connects חרשׁ with חרשׂ; likewise Symm. and Theod. σιδήρια τέκτονος. Vulg. *radii solis* identifies חרשׁ and חרס of 9: 7. The paraphrase of G for v. 22b arises from an interpretation of חָרוּץ in the sense of gold. Cf. Vulg. *et sternet sibi aurum quasi lutum*. Similarly Targ. דהבא סנינא 'purified gold' for חרוץ.
      The opening is completely changed by Duhm, who reads הֵחַת instead of תחתיו and חָרָשׁ instead of חרשׂ, to translate: 'He breaks the sharp tools of the blacksmith.' But it is difficult to see what the blacksmith has to do with this context. Further, Bochart already quoted a passage of Aelian (*De nat. animal.*, X, 24), in which the description of the back and the tail of the crocodile ends with these words: λεπίσι μὲν γάρ τε καὶ φολίσι πέφρακται, καὶ ὡς ἂν εἴποι τις ὥπλισται, καὶ ἐοίκασιν ὀστράκοις καρτεροῖς. This is very similar to our 1st hemistich: 'under him are points of a potsherd'. Note that חָרָשׂ is rendered ὀστράκων by Aq. The *hapax* חַדּוּדֵי stems from the root חדד 'to be sharp, pointed'. The

points of the postherd (cf. חֶרֶשׁ in 2: 8) convey the image of the rough prickly surface of the crocodile's skin. The mark they leave on the ground conjures up the picture of the traces left by the threshing-sledge for threshing corn. This instrument is equipped, on its inner surface, with pieces of flint and basalt, the purpose of which is to crush the grains of wheat. The exact word which designates the threshing-sledge is מוֹרַג (2 S 24: 22), of which the characteristic epithet חָרוּץ 'cutting' (Is 41: 15) is used poetically with the meaning of the substantive (Is 28: 27; Am 1: 3). The verb רפד in the *pi'el* 'to stretch out' a couch (17: 13) is here used in the *qal* to mean 'lay on the ground', 'imprint on the soil'. The belly of the crocodile leaves on the mud the same kind of marks as would be left by a threshing-sledge. The image is very clear. One does not see why Duhm suppresses it, replacing the rare word ירפד by דרבן, reading חריץ instead of חרוץ and עליו instead of עלי, to conclude with a meaning which is completely alien to the context: 'a spur, a pick, against him is as mud' (!).

23   On the text of Syr. and Arab., cf. v. 21. For מצולה, G τὴν ἄβυσσον, Targ. מצולתא. Vulg. *profundum mare* joins ים to the 1st hemistich, which occasions the paraphrase *et ponet quasi cum unguenta bulliunt* for the two words ישים כמרקחה; cf. Symm. ὡς ἀναβρασσομένην ἄρτυσιν. The word מרקחה is translated ἐξάλιπτρον (G), מתכלא 'stove' (Targ.).
      V. 22 shows the marks left on the ground by the body of the crocodile.

24   Behind him he leaves a glistening wake:
     One would suppose the abyss to be a hoary head.
25   On earth there is not his like,
     He who was created intrepid!

Here now is the description of the traces he leaves on the face of the waters: he makes the deep to boil and bubble like a seething cauldron! The verb רתח, which we have met in the *pu'al* in 30: 27. The word סיר denotes the utensil placed over the fire for cooking food. It is almost synonymous with דוד of v. 12 (cf. Comm.). The meaning of מְצוּלָה or מְצוֹלָה is 'gulf' (Ps 69: 3, 16; 107: 24), and by extension, the bottom of the sea (Jon 2: 4). The word מֶרְקָחָה denotes both perfume (Ezk 24: 10) and unguent-pot. The sea reeks with sweet perfumes like a censer (cf. v. 12).

24 The text of Syr. and Arab. resumes with v. 24b (cf. v. 21). The clause ἐλογίσατο ἄβυσσον εἰς περίπατον, absent from Sah., marked with asterisk in Colb., Jerome, Syro-hex., did not exist in G. The present text is derived from Theod. It is a second translation of v. 24b, or rather of the words נתיב יחשב תהום. G τὸν δὲ τάρταρον τῆς ἀβύσσου ὥσπερ αἰχμάλωτον already translated the 2nd hemistich by connecting שׂיבה with the root שׁבה. It is thus v. 24a which was lacking in G. The addition following Theod. fails of its purpose. Vulg. *lucebit* and Targ. ינהר 'sparkles' assign to יאיר the meaning of the *qal*. For לשׂיבה, Syr. ܐܝܟ ܝܒܫܐ 'like dry ground' reads ליבשׁה.
     We leave to the *hiph'il* of אור its causative sense which is the most natural: 'Behind him he leaves (he lights) a glistening wake.' In the wake of the crocodile flashes a luminous line; the white foam glistens in the sun or the moonlight. For both idea and expression, cf. v. 10a. The

verb יַחְשׁב is impersonal: 'one thinks' (cf. v. 15b). The construction חשׁב לי׳ as in v. 19. On תְּהוֹם cf. 28: 14. The word שִׂיבָה 'hoary head', 'grey hairs' (*canities*) suggests the phosphorescent surface of the foaming water. The literal translation, 'one counts the abyss as a hoary head', furnishes the basis of our translation. Bochart mentions the Homeric expressions πολιὴ ἅλς, πολιὴ θάλασσα. He also compares the line of Catullus, in the epithalamium of Peleus (v. 13):

Tortaque remigio spumis incanuit
unda.

These examples and others which are met with in classical texts confirm the splendid Hebrew image of our verse. There is no need to change יחשב to חשׁך and שׁיבה to שׂביב, as does Duhm, who then proceeds to transfer אַחֲרָיו to the beginning of v. 24b and חשׁך to v. 24a: 'He makes a pathway to shine in the darkness, behind him the deep becomes flames of fire.' Gunkel based himself on G in transforming אחרית יאור אחריו יאיר to and reading לְשִׁבְיָה at the close: 'The depths of the river form his pathway, he regards the abyss as booty.' It is sufficient to compare these hypotheses in order to appreciate the high value of the Massoretic text, which is both very clear and very poetical.

25 G πεποιημένον ἐνκαταπαίζεσθαι ὑπὸ τῶν ἀγγέλων μου deviates from v. 25b. This text is already found in 40: 19b. Reminiscence of Ps 104: 26. Vulg. paraphrases משׁלו: *potestas*

26   He gazes at every haughty creature,
     He is king over all wild beasts!

quae comparetur ei. This implies a
fusion of the two meanings of מָשָׁל
'domination' (Symm. ἐξουσία αὐτοῦ,
Targ. שׁוּלטָנֵיהּ) and 'likeness' (G
ὅμοιον αὐτῷ). Syr. reads אונו instead
of אין, whence 'his might patrols
the earth'. For לבלי־חת, Vulg. *ut
nullum timeret*, Targ. דלא יתבר 'that
he should not be afraid'. Syr. 'he who
has brought to ruin everything
exalted that he has seen' reads הֶעָשֶׂה
instead of העשׂו, omits חת, and combines v. 25b with v. 26a.

One might hesitate between the
abstract מָשְׁלוֹ (from מָשָׁל) 'his
likeness' and the concrete expression
מָשְׁלוֹ 'his like' (Merx, etc.). The
meaning is not doubtful: 'there
is not his like on the earth'. The
phrase עַל־עָפָר as in 19: 25; 39: 14.
The participle הֶעָשׂוּ 'he who was
created' as in 40: 19 (cf. Comm.).
The preposition לְ before בְּלִי־חָת
is expletive as in לבלי אכל 'without
food' (38: 41) and לבלי חק 'without
limit' (Is 5: 14). The 2nd hemistich
means: 'he who was created intrepid', literally 'fearless'; cf. בלי
playing the part of the alpha privative in 30: 8; 33: 9; 38: 2. The word
חַת 'fear', 'terror' (Gn 9: 2) is equivalent to the Assyrian *ḫattu*: cf. חֲתַת
in 6: 21. Nothing can justify the

changes of לבלי־חת to לבעל תחת
'like a lord of hell' (!, Gunkel), or
to לבעל חַיּת 'like a lord of the animals' (Giesebrecht, Beer), or again
to לבעל תחתיות 'like a lord of the
infernal regions' (Cheyne, *JQR*, 1897,
p. 579). There is no need to anticipate v. 26.

26   G τῶν ἐν τοῖς ὕδασιν, Targ. בני
כוורי 'the little fishes', Syr. ܐܢܫܐ
'the reptiles', have read שֶׁרֶץ instead
of שׁחץ.

Most moderns have adopted a
conjecture of Gunkel, who reads אֹתוֹ
instead of אֵת and יִירָא instead of
יראה, so as to render the 1st hemistich: 'every haughty creature fears
him'. But the MT is strongly supported by 40: 11b, 12a, where the
verb ראה in the sense of 'look at'
has in turn as objects כָּל־גֵּאֶה 'every
proud being' and כָּל־גָּבֹהַּ (cf.
Comm.) 'every haughty being'.
Hence we translate simply: 'he
gazes at every haughty creature'. The
crocodile is afraid of no one, he
lowers his glance before no one
whomsoever. The reason for this
assurance is given in the 2nd hemistich, which at the same time brings
the whole description to an end: 'he
is king over all wild beasts'. On
בני־שׁחץ, cf. 28: 8.

CHAPTER 42

1   And Job answered Yahweh and said:

2   I know that Thou canst do all things,
    And that no plan is unrealisable with Thee;

3   [ ] But I have declared—and I did not understand—
    Marvels beyond my scope—and I did not realise it!

3 Omit 'who is this who hides counsel [by words] without knowledge?', which comes from 38: 2.

42: 1 The same formula as in 40: 3. The passage 2-6 is parallel to 40: 4-5. The natural sequel to 41: 26 would be 42: 7. But the poet wished to bring on to the scene for the last time the hero of his story. Just as 40: 3-5 formed the conclusion of the first speeches of Yahweh, so 42: 1-6 concludes the last speeches. The prose Epilogue does not take these interludes into account. It has in view only the long descriptions which are truly the characteristic part of the final section of the poetic book.

2 The *kethîb* seems to have יָדַעְתָּ, but the *qerê* agrees with the versions in reading יָדַעְתִּי; cf. Ps 140: 13. Instead of מזמה, G οὐθέν reads מְאוּמָה (cf. inf.).

Job recognises that God is Disposer supreme and that His power is limitless: 'I know that Thou cast do all things.' This is tantamount to a confession of the futility of discussions concerning divine intervention in human affairs (38: 2). A certain number of moderns wish to change מְזִמָּה to מאומה in accord with G (Hoffmann, Graetz, Beer). But, in Gn 11: 6 לֹא־יִבָּצֵר מֵהֶם 'will not be impossible to them' has as subject כֹּל אֲשֶׁר יָזְמוּ לַעֲשׂוֹת

'whatever they think of doing'. Here the word מְזִמָּה 'idea', 'purpose', 'plan' (21: 27) takes the place of the clause which serves as subject in Gn 11: 6. Hence we propose to translate: 'and that no plan is unrealisable with Thee'. God can accomplish whatever He wills. He eludes the control of human thought and wisdom.

3 G goes back to its translation of 38: 2 in order to complete the text. Instead of ὁ κρύπτων με βουλήν (38: 2), G reads ὁ κρύπτων σε βουλήν, an adaptation to the context. Likewise καὶ σὲ οἴεται κρύπτειν, instead of ἐμὲ δὲ οἴεται κρύπτειν (38: 2). For συνέχων δὲ ῥήματα ἐν καρδίᾳ (38: 2), G φειδόμενος δὲ ῥημάτων. It is clear that במלין of 38: 2 has disappeared after עצה. Syr. restores حڢٮڷ, while Targ. and Vulg. adhere to the MT. G translates very freely from לכן: τίς δὲ ἀναγγελεῖ μοι ἃ οὐκ ᾔδειν, μεγάλα καὶ θαυμαστὰ ἃ οὐκ ἠπιστάμην; Vulg. *ideo insipienter locutus sum* recalls ἐλάλησα ἀνοήτως of Symm. translating הגדתי ולא אבין. Syr. ܝܣܒܐܠ 'Thou hast taught me' reads הגדתני. Vulg. paraphrases from נפלאות: *et quae ultra modum excederent scientiam meam*. The words ולא אדע are placed before נפלאות in Syr.

4   [   ]   5   I had heard of Thee by hearsay,
        But now my eye has seen Thee.
6   That is why I sink down and repent,
        On dust and ashes!

4 Omit 'Listen then, and I myself will speak, I will question you and you shall instruct me', which is a combination of 33:31 and 38:3b.

It is clear that מי...דעת is a variant of 38:2, the word מַעֲלִים explaining מחשיך and the complement במלין having fallen out by haplography before בלי. It is from לכן that the reflections of Job are continued. The meaning of לָכֵן is simply 'but', as in 34:25. The complement of הִגַּדְתִּי is נִפְלָאוֹת, the same construction as in 31:37. There is a parenthesis וְלֹא אָבִין 'and I did not understand', which has as a parallel וְלֹא אֵדַע 'and I did not know': cf. 14:21; 15:9. The closing ולא אדע is likewise suggested by נפלאות 'marvels' (37:5b). A confession of ignorance is appropriate when man is faced by divine mysteries (5:9; 9:10; 36:26). The complement מִמֶּנִּי 'more than I' implies 'beyond the scope of my understanding', the preposition מִן expressing the opposite meaning to עִם of 15:9 (cf. Comm.).

4 G again adapts material to the context (cf. v. 3) by interposing Κύριε between נא and ואנכי.
    The 2nd hemistich reproduces materially 40:7b and comes from 38:3b, a continuation of the doublet which we had at the beginning of v. 3 (= 38:2). As for the 1st hemistich, it borrows its elements from 33:31 (cf. 33:1). It expresses the tone of God speaking to Job and not that of Job speaking to God.

5 G adds τὸ πρότερον at the end of the 1st hemistich, by contrast with νυνὶ δέ (ועתה) of the 2nd.

The idiom לְשֵׁמַע אֹזֶן *ad auditum auris* is found in Ps 18:45 and Sir 43:24. The meaning here is: 'by hearsay'. Audition is opposed to vision; cf. 28:22b in antithesis to 28:21. The phrase שְׁמַעְתִּיךָ does not mean 'I have heard Thee' but 'I have heard about Thee'. Cf. שְׁמַעֲנוּהָ 'we have heard about it' in Ps 132:6. The 2nd hemistich stresses the difference between knowing by hearsay and knowing as a result of immediate apprehension and vision. Job has witnessed the realisation of the hope formulated in 19:27, 'Him whom I myself shall see and whom my very eyes shall behold, He and none other'. The verb ראה with עין as subject (13:1; 28:10; 29:11, etc.). Note above all the parallelism between the eye which sees and the ear which hears (13:11; 29:11).

6 Targ. adds the complement עתרי 'my wealth' to אמאס. G ἐφαύλισα ἐμαυτὸν καὶ ἐτάκην offers a double translation of אמאס, which is rendered κατέγνων ἐμαυτοῦ (Symm.), *ipse me reprehendo* (Vulg.), ܐܫܬܩܠ 'I am silent' (Syr.). G interprets the 2nd hemistich: ἥγημαι δὲ ἐγὼ ἐμαυτὸν γῆν καὶ σποδόν. Targ. gives a figurative meaning to 'dust and ashes': I console myself with regard to my sons who are but dust and ashes.
    The adverb עַל־כֵּן 'that is why' and not now לכן, which had the meaning 'but' in v. 3. The verb מאס is the one which we have recognised in 7:5, 16 with the meaning of 'melt away', 'sink down' (root מאס parallel to מסס); cf. Comm. on 7:5.

This self-humiliation springs from an act of repentance: 'I mortify myself and repent'. The final expression 'on dust and ashes' is characteristic on the lips of Job. We know that the hero is seated on the *mazbaleh*, that mixture of dust and ash which is piled up at the entrance of villages; cf. Comm. on 2:8. The only accusation which Job can level against himself is that of having discussed things which escape man's understanding (v. 3). God who can do all things (v. 2) has not disdained to disclose Himself (v. 5) in order to put an end to barren disputes by the description of the marvels which He has lavishly scattered throughout the universe. It is this description which has formed the substance of the preceding speeches. Hence the author neglects to allude to this last intervention of Job. The Epilogue in prose will begin with the words: 'and it came to pass after Yahweh had addressed these words to Job'.

EPILOGUE (42:7-17)

7 And after Yahweh had spoken these words to Job, Yahweh said to Eliphaz the Temanite: 'My anger is kindled against you and against your two friends because you have not spoken the truth concerning me as has my servant Job.

8 And now take seven calves and seven rams, go to my servant Job and you will offer up a burnt offering for yourselves. And Job my servant will intercede for you: *then* I will have regard to him by not inflicting on you any disgrace for not having spoken about me the truth as has my servant Job.'

Chapter 42: 7-17   Prose Epilogue: see Introduction, pp. xxxi ff., lxiii ff., lxxii ff.

8   כִּי־אָז; MT: כי אם־.

42: 7   G renders את־הדברים האלה by πάντα τὰ ῥήματα ταῦτα (A omits ταῦτα), אלי by ἐνώπιόν μου, נכונה by ἀληθὲς οὐδέν (obelus before οὐδέν in Syro-hex.). To avoid anthropomorphism, G renders חרה...רעיך by ἥμαρτες σὺ καὶ οἱ φίλοι σου. For אלי, Vulg. *coram me* and Syr. ܩܘܕܡܝ 'before me' (cf. G).

Observe the use of אַחַר in the sense of 'after that'; אֲשֶׁר is understood (cf. Jer 41: 16). In 21: 3, we had אחר with the infinitive of דבר to express the same meaning. In Assyrian the preposition *arki* 'behind', 'after' is frequently used as a conjunction. The first speaker was Eliphaz. It is he who is mentioned by name. The verb חרה with אַף as subject, as in 32: 2, 3, 5. The complement אֵלַי does not mean 'to me' but 'concerning me'; use of אֶל instead of עַל after the verb דבר, to connote 'speak on the subject of', just as in Jer 40: 16b. On the interchange of אל and על, cf. Comm. on 1: 11. The feminine נְכוֹנָה 'the right

thing', 'the truth' recurs in Ps 5: 10 'for there is no truth in their mouth'. Cf. the Assyrian *kettu*, feminine of *kênu* (derived from כון), to connote 'justice' and 'truth'. The expression 'my servant Job' recalls the Prologue (1: 8; 2: 3). It will recur with emphasis in v. 8. Job has spoken without understanding (v. 3). His friends have affirmed things that are false, they have not spoken the truth. That is why God is angry with them. Job, who has remained 'the servant' of Yahweh, will be used as an intermediary to effect reconciliation (vv. 8-9).

8   G omits לכם, which is restored in Jerome *vobis* (with asterisk) and in the margin of Syro-hex. (after Symm. and Theod., with asterisk). In Sah. too we find the translation of לכם. For העליתם, G ποιήσει and Syr. ܢܣܩ 'he will sacrifice' anticipate: it is the prayer which will be reserved to Job as his part. G renders כי אם...נבלה by εἰ μὴ γὰρ δι' αὐτόν, ἀπώλεσα ἂν ὑμᾶς. The text has been brought back into line with the MT by the addition (before εἰ μὴ γὰρ

648

9   So they went, Eliphaz the Temanite and Bildad the Shuhite
    and Zophar the Naʿamathite, and they did as Yahweh had
    said and Yahweh had regard to Job.
10 Then Yahweh rehabilitated the position of Job, because he

of a whole clause, absent from Sah.,
marked with asterisk in Syro-hex.,
borrowed from Theod. ὅτι εἰ μὴ
πρόσωπον αὐτοῦ λήμψομαι. G omits
אלי, which is restored in Jerome
ad me (with asterisk) and in the
margin of Syro-hex. (following Aq.
and Theod.).

The opening וְעַתָּה as in v. 5. The
verb לקח with the *dativus ethicus*
(2: 8). The Prologue also mentions
burnt offerings, and the terms used
are the same (1: 5). The victims will
be seven calves and seven rams.
Compare the sacrifice offered by
Balak and Balaam: a calf and a ram
on each altar, the altars being seven
in number (Nu 23: 1ff.). Seven
calves and seven rams must be
offered on each of the seven days of
the Passover (Ezk 45: 23). The presence of Job is indispensable; likewise
the presence of Samuel was necessary
for the sacrifice offered by Saul
(1 S 13: 8ff.). The preposition בְּעַד
'for', 'in favour of' as in 6: 22. The
verb התפלל 'to pray' with על before
the person on whose behalf one
prays (2 Ch 30: 18). The preposition
is usually בעד (cf. v. 10), but this
has just been used. The author is
concerned to vary his style. Job
is to play the part of intercessor like
Abraham (Gn 20: 7), Moses (Nu
21: 7; Dt 9: 20), Samuel (1 S 7: 5;
12: 19, 23), Jeremiah (Jer 37: 3).
The conjunctions כִּי and אִם duplicate each other. Duhm proposes את
instead of אִם; some remove כי,
others אם (cf. Budde). We ourselves
read כִּי־אָז which simply means
'then', 'from that moment', 'in that
case' (11: 15; 22: 26), 'then I will
have regard to him'. On the expression נשא פנים cf. 13: 8. The con-

struction with לְבִלְתִּי is exactly the
same as in Gn 19: 21, 'I will have
regard to you ... by not over-
throwing the city of which you
speak.' The substantive נְבָלָה normally designates something abominable, disgraceful (cf. נבל in 2: 10;
30: 8), and the idiom עשה נבלה
means 'to commit folly' (Gn 34: 7;
Dt 22: 21; Jos 7: 15, etc.). This
formula usually has the complement
בישראל 'in Israel'. But here עִמָּכֶם
'with you' introduces the person who
is the object of the action; cf. עשה
חסד עם 'bestow a favour on some
one'. Hence it is a question of an
action on the part of God, and we
cannot keep the meaning of 'something foul, abominable'. Now, etymologically נבל means 'to be dis-
graced, stigmatised' (cf. Comm. on
2: 10), which enables us to assign to
נבלה here the sense of 'disgrace'.
We may therefore translate: 'so as
not to inflict on you some disgrace'.
The end is the same as in v. 7.

9   G avoids recognising three kings
in the three friends of Job, as in
2: 11. For נעמתי, G ὁ Μειναῖος as
everywhere. After ἐποίησαν (ויעשו),
G(A) adds ἑαυτοῖς. Targ. interprets
the two יהוה by מימר דיי 'word of
Yahweh' (cf. 1: 10 and Comm. on
20: 29). G καὶ ἔλυσεν τὴν ἁμαρτίαν
αὐτοῖς διὰ Ἰώβ interprets וישא...איוב
in accordance with v. 8.

There is no mention of Elihu. The
three friends do as Yahweh has bid-
den them do. The end as in v. 8. Out
of negligence the copula has been
omitted before צפר.

10 The Massoretes have hesitated
between the reading שָׁבִית (*kethib*)

interceded for his friends, and Yahweh doubled all that had belonged to him.

11   Hence they came to him, all his brothers and all his sisters and all his acquaintances of yore, and they ate bread with him in his house. They pitied him and consoled him for all the misfortune which had been sent upon him by Yahweh and they gave him each one a piece of money and a ring of gold.

and שְׁבוּת (qerê); cf. Jer 49: 39; Ezk 16: 53; 39: 25, etc. The expression שָׁב אֶת־שְׁבִית is rendered ηὔξησεν (G), ἐπέστρεψε τὴν ἀποστροφήν (Symm. in Field, following Syro-hex.), ἐπεστράφη πρὸς μετάνοιαν (Theod. ibid.); cf. Vulg. conversus est ad poenitentiam. The word שְׁבִית is interpreted by ܫܒܝܬܐ 'captivity' (Syr.), גּוֹלַת 'exile' (Targ.). For יהוה, Targ. מֵימַר דיי both times (cf. v. 9). G περὶ τῶν φίλων (A, C add αὐτοῦ) and Vulg. pro amicis suis are in agreement with Targ. and Syr. 'for his companions' in reading רֵעָיו instead of רֵעֵהוּ. Then G adds ἀφῆκεν αὐτοῖς τὴν ἁμαρτίαν (cf. v. 9). G διπλᾶ ... εἰς διπλασιασμόν is a redundant translation of לְמִשְׁנֶה.

The idiom composed of the verb שׁוּב or הֵשִׁיב and the complement שְׁבִית, שְׁבוּת has been variously explained. Sometimes שְׁבוּת or שְׁבִית is connected with the root שׁוּב (cf. Symm., Theod., Vulg.) and to שׁוּב שׁבוּת is assigned the meaning of 'bring about a return' of things, cause a revolution, or something of that sort: cf. König, Hebr. und aram. Wörterbuch p. 478. Without denying that שְׁבוּת or שְׁבִית may, if need be, be linked with the root שׁוּב (cf. Condamin, on Jer 29: 14), it must nevertheless be admitted that the vocalisation שְׁבוּת שְׁבִית, which disregards the radical waw, is not favourable to this etymology. Ehrlich proposes to see in שְׁבִית, שְׁבוּת a passive participle of שָׁבַת 'to cease' (on Dt 30: 3). The phrase would then mean: 'to restore what has ceased to exist'. But in that case it is difficult to understand the complement of the person: 'what has ceased to exist of Job'(?). The most likely hypothesis is that שְׁבוּת and שְׁבִית are abstract nouns coming from שׁבה 'to lead into captivity'. It is in this way that the phrase is understood by Targ. and Syr. (cf. sup.). Note that בַּשְּׁבִית in Nu 21: 29 has as its equivalent in the Samaritan text בַּשְּׁבִי 'in captivity'. By alliteration, שׁוּב (or הֵשִׁיב) has been joined to שְׁבוּת or שְׁבִית, to connote 'to bring back what has been taken away (with special reference to the captives of Israel)'. The expression then became proverbial and came to be used in the sense of: to restore matters, to put things once more on a firm footing. The versions harmonise by reading רֵעָיו 'his companions' instead of רֵעֵהוּ 'his neighbour' (31: 9). The formula אֵת כָּל־אֲשֶׁר לִ׳׳ as in the Prologue (1: 10, 12). V. 12 will furnish the explanation of the 'twofold' increase.

11 G adds ἤκουσαν δέ and πάντα τὰ συμβεβηκότα αὐτῷ in accordance with 2: 11. The addition πάντα ... αὐτῷ is marked by obelus in Syrohex. For וַיֹּאכְלוּ...בְּבֵיתוֹ, G φαγόντες δὲ καὶ πιόντες παρ᾽ αὐτῷ. But Jerome et cum bibissent et comedissent apud eum is followed by panem in domo ejus (= MT), which is found (with asterisk) in the margin of Syro-hex. Obelus before καὶ πιόντες in Syro-hex. For וַיָּנִדוּ לוֹ, Vulg. et moverunt super eum caput. G renders וַיְנַחֲמוּ

12   And Yahweh blessed the new state of Job more than his
     former one: and he had fourteen thousand sheep, and six
     thousand camels, a thousand yoke of oxen, and a thousand
     she-asses.

13   He had also fourteen sons and three daughters.

אתו by καὶ ἐθαύμασαν. G neglects הרעה, but Jerome *in omnibus malis*. For קשׂיטה, translated by 'lamb' in G, Targ., Syr., Vulg., we have the correct interpretation in Symm. νόμισμα. G deviates from the MT by rendering ואישׁ···אחד as καὶ τετρά-δραχμον χρυσοῦν ἄσημον (B χρυσοῦ καὶ ἀσήμου), but Jerome *et vir inaurem auream unam* (= MT). For נזם Targ. and Syr. קדשׁא 'nose-ring', 'ear-ring', Symm. ἐπίρρινον, Theod. ἐνώτιον (cf. Jerome and Vulg. *inaurem*).

The text is here inspired by 2: 11, and it is this fact which has occasioned the modifications introduced by G. Use of ידע as in 19: 13. The expression לְפָנִים 'of old time', 'of yore' is ironical. The well-known lines of Ovid should be compared:

Donec eris felix multos numerabis amicos,
Tempora si fuerint nubila solus eris.

The friends, like the kinsfolk, had faded out during the period of Job's misfortunes. They reappear with the return of prosperity. 'To eat bread with some one' means to share a meal with him (cf. Gn 43: 32, etc.). To correct this very Hebraic idiom, claiming the support of G (Beer in the ed. of Kittel), would imply that one regards the language of the translator as superior to that of the original. The formulae וַיָּנֻדוּ לוֹ וַיְנַחֲמוּ אֹתוֹ as in 2: 11. Note also כָּל־הָרָעָה 'all the misfortune' (2: 11). They bring gifts in accordance with the established oriental custom. The קְשִׂיטָה is a unit of value characteristic of the patriarchal age (Gn

33: 19; Jos 24: 32). The versions (with the exception of Symm.) have preferred the meaning 'lamb' which is still supported by some rabbis (Levy, *Neuhebr. und chald. Wörterbuch*, IV, p. 396). R. Akiba and Qimchi give formal sanction to the meaning 'piece of money', while Ibn Ezra translates by כבשׂה קטנה 'little sheep'. It seems that the lamb was chosen as a basis for uniformity in exchange. A weight of gold or silver, corresponding to the prices of the lamb, was called the *qesiṭah*. Among the ancient Romans the index of wealth was possession of cattle. On the oldest coins was pictured an ox, a sheep, a pig, whence the close connection of ideas as between *pecus* and *pecunia*. It is a similar phenomenon which we meet in the use of קשׂיטה 'lamb' to designate a specific amount of money. The נֶזֶם, a ring which the elegant ladies of Syria and Egypt passed through their nose (Gn 24: 47; Is 3: 21), was one of the most highly valued of gifts (Gn 24: 22).

12 Targ. again interprets יהוה by מימר דיי (cf. 9-10). For ויהי לו, G ἦν δὲ τὰ κτήνη αὐτοῦ. The same prolixity in the translation of אתונות by ὄνοι θήλειαι νομάδες (cf. 1: 3).

Antithesis between אַחֲרִית and רֵאשִׁית exactly as in 8: 7. A comparison with 1: 3 shows the literal fulfilment of the concluding statement of v. 10.

13 Targ. renders שׁבענה by ארבסר 'fourteen', the other versions by 'seven'.

The existence of a dual form in *ân*, attested among the Babylonians,

14   To the one he gave the name of Turtle-dove, to the second that
      of Cinnamon, and to the third that of Horn-of-Paint.

15   In the whole land were not found any women so fair as the
      daughters of Job. And their father endowed them with a
      portion of the heritage along with their brothers.

16   After that, Job lived on for a hundred and forty years and
      he saw his sons and his sons' sons, a span of four generations.

the Aramaeans, the Canaanites, and the Arabs (*RB*, 1914, pp. 354f.), enables us to recognise in שִׁבְעָנָה the dual of שֶׁבַע 'seven' to which has been added the feminine ending of cardinal numbers before a masculine plural. Hence it is really a question of fourteen sons (cf. Targ.). The number given in 1:2 has simply been doubled. For the oriental, it is the sons who count. Daughters are not an index of wealth and status, hence their number is not doubled. Note that, in 1 Ch 25:5, the king's seer, Heman, also had fourteen sons and three daughters.

14 Targ., Syr., Aq., and Symm. are satisfied to transcribe, more or less exactly, the names of the three daughters. But G and Vulg. translate. Thus יְמִימָה, connected with יָמִים 'days', becomes Ἡμέραν (G), *Diem* (Jerome and Vulg.); קְצִיעָה becomes Κασίαν (G), *Cassiam* (Jerome and Vulg.); קֶרֶן הַפּוּךְ is rendered Ἀμαλθαίας κέρας (G, Jerome *Cornu Amaltheae*), *Cornu stibii* (Vulg.).

The proper noun יְמִימָה is the Arabic *yamâmeh*, feminine of *yamâm* 'ringdove', 'turtle-dove'. The nomads like to give their daughters the names of gracious beasts or birds. They choose also names of plants or precious stones. The קְצִיעָה is an aromatic plant, mentioned along with myrrh and aloes in Ps 45:9. The versions are agreed in recognising in it the cassia, κασία, *cassia*. It is a question here of the aromatic cassia,

which is still called cinnamon or canella. The Hebrew פּוּךְ 'cosmetic paint' corresponds to the Greek φῦκος just as קְצִיעָה corresponds to κασία, קִנָּמוֹן to κιννάμωνον, etc. Cosmetic paint, like oil and unguents, was accustomed to be kept in a horn (1 S 16:1, 13; 1 K 1:39); cf. the use of the horn as a vessel in which to keep anointing oil among the Babylonians (*Choix de textes*, p. 257, ll. 188ff.).

15 G omits the suffixes of אֲבִיהֶם and אֲחִיהֶם. They are restored in Sah., Syro-hex., and Memph., but not in Jerome.

The impersonal construction נִמְצָא 'there was found' permits the verb to remain in the singular despite the plural subject; cf. Gesenius-Kautzsch, § 121a. Grammars give series of examples of the use of the masculine plural suffix instead of the feminine. Hence we may leave as they are לָהֶם, אֲבִיהֶם, and אֲחִיהֶם (cf. 1:14; 39:3). It is interesting that the daughters were admitted to share in the heritage even while their brothers were alive. According to Nu 27:8, they were allowed to inherit only if there were no male descendants.

16 G interprets זֹאת by τὴν πληγήν. Instead of 140, G counts 170 years, but Jerome *centum quadraginta* = MT. Then G adds τὰ δὲ πάντα ἔτη ἔζησεν διακόσια τεσσαράκοντα ὀκτώ (B omits ὀκτώ, which is found in Sah., Jerome, Syro-hex., but not in Eth.). The addition of G is marked by

17   Then Job died, old and full with days.

obelus in Colb., Jerome, Syro-hex. The end (from וירא), absent from Sah., marked with asterisk in Colb., Jerome, and Syro-hex., did not exist in G. The present text is derived from Theod. (cf. Syro-hex.).

The divergence between the numbers given in the MT and in G may arise from their being written in figures. Joseph, who lived 110 years, saw his grandchildren only to the third generation (Gn 50: 23). To see one's sons' sons is the supreme benediction (Ps 128: 6), it is the crown of old age (Pr 17: 6).

17 V. 17, absent from Sah., marked with asterisk in Syro-hex., did not exist in G. The present text is derived from Theod. (cf. v. 16). But G then has a long addition which begins with γέγραπται δὲ αὐτὸν πάλιν ἀναστήσεσθαι μεθ' ὧν ὁ Κύριος ἀνίστησιν and continues by a text which claims to be a translation 'of the Syriac book': οὗτος ἑρμηνεύεται ἐκ τῆς Συριακῆς βίβλου. These complements of G are found of course in Sah., Jerome, Syro-hex., Eth. and are marked by obelus in Jerome and Syro-hex. Moreover, Arab. has the passage coming from 'the Syriac book'. On these additions, cf. Intro., pp. xixf.

The formulae are the traditional ones (Gn 25: 8; 35: 29; 1 Ch 29: 28).

ANALYSIS OF THE INTRODUCTION

INDEX OF SUBJECTS